Oxford Colour German Dictionary Plus

Oxford Colour German Dictionary Plus

Revised second edition

GERMAN–ENGLISH
ENGLISH–GERMAN

DEUTSCH–ENGLISCH
ENGLISCH–DEUTSCH

OXFORD
UNIVERSITY PRESS

OXFORD
UNIVERSITY PRESS

Great Clarendon Street, Oxford OX2 6DP

Oxford University Press is a department of the University of Oxford. It furthers the University's objective of excellence in research, scholarship, and education by publishing worldwide in

Oxford New York

Auckland Bangkok Buenos Aires Cape Town Chennai Dar es Salaam Delhi Hong Kong Istanbul Karachi Kolkata Kuala Lumpur Madrid Melbourne Mexico City Mumbai Nairobi São Paulo Shanghai Taipei Tokyo Toronto

Second edition published 2001
Revised second edition published 2004

British Library Cataloguing in Publication Data

Data available

Library of Congress Cataloging in Publication Data

Data available

ISBN 0-19-860901-9
ISBN 0-19-860899-3 (US edition)

10 9 8 7 6 5 4 3 2

Typeset by Morton
Word Processing Ltd
Printed in China

Contents

Preface

The *Oxford Colour German Dictionary Plus* is a dictionary designed primarily for students of German. Its clear presentation and use of colour headwords make it easily accessible. It contains completely new sections, not found in the *Oxford Colour German Dictionary*, on German life and culture, letter-writing, and German grammar, making it even more useful for students up to intermediate level.

List of contributors

Revised Second Edition

Editor:

Gunhild Prowe

Second Edition

Editors:

Roswitha Morris
Robin Sawers

Supplementary Material:

Robin Sawers
Neil and Roswitha Morris
Valerie Grundy
Eva Vennebusch

Data Capture:

Susan Wilkin
Anne McConnell
Anna Cotgreave

Proof-reading:

Andrew Hodgson

First Edition

Editors:

Gunhild Prowe
Jill Schneider

Introduction

The text of this dictionary reflects recent changes to the spelling of German ratified in July 1996. The symbol * has been introduced to refer from the old spelling to the new, preferred one:

> **As*** *nt* **-ses, -se** *s.* **Ass**
> **dasein*** *vi sep (sein)* **da sein**, *s.* **da**
> **Schiffahrt*** *f s.* **Schifffahrt**

Where both the old and new forms are valid, an equals sign = is used to refer to the preferred form:

> **aufwändig** *a* = **aufwendig**
> **Tunfisch** *m* = **Thunfisch**

When such forms follow each other alphabetically, they are given with commas, with the preferred form in first place:

> **Panther, Panter** *m* **-s, -**
> panther

In phrases, *od* (oder) is used:

> ...**deine(r,s)** *poss pron* yours;
> **die D∼en** *od* **d∼en** *pl* your family *sg*

On the English–German side, only the preferred German form is given.

- A swung dash ∼ represents the headword or that part of the headword preceding a vertical bar |. The initial letter of a German headword is given to show whether or not it is a capital.
- The vertical bar | follows the part of the headword which is not repeated in compounds or derivatives.
- Square brackets [ ] are used for optional material.
- Angled brackets ‹ › are used after a verb translation to indicate the object; before a verb translation to indicate the subject; before an adjective to indicate a typical noun which it qualifies.

- Round brackets ( ) are used for field or style labels (see list on pages xxiii–xxv), and for explanatory matter.
- A box □ indicates a new part of speech within an entry.
- *od* (oder) and *or* denote that words or portions of a phrase are synonymous. An oblique stroke / is used where there is a difference in usage or meaning.
- ≈ is used where no exact equivalent exists in the other language.
- A dagger † indicates that a German verb is irregular and that the parts can be found in the verb table on pages 601–606. Compound verbs are not listed there as they follow the pattern of the basic verb.
- The stressed vowel is marked in a German headword by _ (long) or . (short). A phonetic transcription is only given for words which do not follow the normal rules of pronunciation. These rules can be found on page xi.
- German headword nouns are followed by the gender and, with the exception of compound nouns, by the genitive and plural. These are only given at compound nouns if they present some difficulty. Otherwise the user should refer to the final element.
- Nouns that decline like adjectives are entered as follows: **-e(r)** *m/f*, **-e(s)** *nt*.
- Adjectives which have no undeclined form are entered in the feminine form with the masculine and neuter in brackets **-e(r,s)**.
- The reflexive pronoun **sich** is accusative unless marked (*dat*).

Proprietary terms

This dictionary includes some words which are, or are asserted to be, proprietary names or trademarks. Their inclusion does not imply that they have acquired for legal purposes a non-proprietary or general significance, nor is any other judgement implied concerning their legal status. In cases where the editor has some evidence that a word is used as a proprietary name or trademark this is indicated by the letter (P), but no judgement concerning the legal status of such words is made or implied thereby.

Phonetic symbols used for German words

a	Hand	hant	ŋ	lang	laŋ
a:	Bahn	ba:n	o	Moral	mo'ra:l
ɐ	Ober	'o:bɐ	o:	Boot	bo:t
ɐ̯	Uhr	u:ɐ̯	o̯	loyal	lo̯a'ja:l
ã	Conférencier	kõferã'si̯e:	õ	Konkurs	kõ'kʊrs
ã:	Abonnement	abɔnə'mã:	õ:	Ballon	ba'lõ:
a͜i	weit	va͜it	ɔ	Post	pɔst
a͜u	Haut	ha͜ut	ø	Ökonom	øko'no:m
b	Ball	bal	ø:	Öl	ø:l
ç	Ich	ɪç	œ	göttlich	'gœtlıç
d	dann	dan	ɔ͜y	heute	'hɔ͜ytə
d͜ʒ	Gin	d͜ʒɪn	p	Pakt	pakt
e	Metall	me'tal	r	Rast	rast
e:	Beet	be:t	s	Hast	hast
ɛ	mästen	'mɛstən	ʃ	Schal	ʃa:l
ɛ:	wählen	'vɛ:lən	t	Tal	ta:l
ɛ̃	Cousin	ku'zɛ̃:	t͜s	Zahl	t͜sa:l
ə	Nase	'na:zə	t͜ʃ	Couch	ka͜ut͜ʃ
f	Faß	fas	u	Kupon	ku'põ:
g	Gast	gast	u:	Hut	hu:t
h	haben	'ha:bən	u̯	aktuell	ak'tu̯ɛl
i	Rivale	ri'va:lə	ʊ	Pult	pʊlt
i:	viel	fi:l	v	was	vas
i̯	Aktion	ak't͜si̯o:n	x	Bach	bax
ɪ	Birke	'bɪrkə	y	Physik	fy'zi:k
j	ja	ja:	y:	Rübe	'ry:bə
k	kalt	kalt	y̆	Nuance	'ny̆ã:sə
l	Last	last	ʏ	Fülle	'fʏlə
m	Mast	mast	z	Nase	'na:zə
n	Naht	na:t	ʒ	Regime	re'ʒi:m

ʔ Glottal stop, e.g. Koordination / koʔɔrdina't͜si̯o:n /.

: length sign after a vowel, e.g. Chrom / kro:m /.

' Stress mark before stressed syllable, e.g. Balkon / bal'kõ:/.

Guide to German pronunciation

Consonants

Produced as in English with the following exceptions:

b	as	p	*at the end of a word or syllable*
d	as	t	*at the end of a word or syllable*
g	as	k	*at the end of a word or syllable*
ch	as in Scottish loch		*after a, o, u, au*
	like an exaggerated h as in huge		*after i, e, ä, ö, ü, eu, ei*
-chs	as	x	(as in box)
-ig	as	-ich / ɪç /	*when a suffix*
j	as	y	(as in yes)
ps			the p is pronounced
pn			the p is pronounced
qu	as	k + v	
s	as	z	(as in zero) *at the beginning of a word*
	as	s	(as in bus) *at the end of a word or syllable, before a consonant, or when doubled*
sch	as	sh	
sp	as	shp	*at the beginning of a word*
st	as	sht	*at the beginning of a word*
v	as	f	(as in for)
	as	v	(as in very) *within a word*
w	as	v	(as in very)
z	as	ts	

Vowels

Approximately as follows:

a	short	as	u	(as in but)
	long	as	a	(as in car)
e	short	as	e	(as in pen)
	long	as	a	(as in paper)
i	short	as	i	(as in bit)
	long	as	ee	(as in queen)
o	short	as	o	(as in hot)
	long	as	o	(as in pope)
u	short	as	oo	(as in foot)
	long	as	oo	(as in boot)

Vowels are always short before a double consonant, and long when followed by an h or when double

ie	is pronounced	ee	(as in keep)

Diphthongs

au	as	ow	(as in how)
ei ai	as	y	(as in my)
eu äu	as	oy	(as in boy)

Pronunciation of the alphabet

English/Englisch		*German/Deutsch*
eɪ	a	a:
bi:	b	be:
si:	c	t͜se:
di:	d	de:
i:	e	e:
ef	f	ɛf
dʒi:	g	ge:
eɪtʃ	h	ha:
aɪ	i	i:
dʒeɪ	j	jɔt
keɪ	k	ka:
el	l	ɛl
em	m	ɛm
en	n	ɛn
əʊ	o	o:
pi:	p	pe:
kju:	q	ku:
a:(r)	r	ɛr
es	s	ɛs
ti:	t	te:
ju:	u	u:
vi:	v	fa͜u
'dʌblju:	w	ve:
eks	x	ɪks
waɪ	y	'ʏpsilɔn
zed	z	t͜sɛt
eɪ umlaut	ä	ɛ:
əʊ umlaut	ö	ø:
ju: umlaut	ü	y:
es'zed	ß	ɛs't͜sɛt

Glossary of grammatical terms

Abbreviation A shortened form of a word or phrase: **etc.** = **usw.**

Accusative The case of a direct object; some German prepositions take the accusative

Active In the active form the subject of the verb performs the action: **he asked** = **er hat gefragt**

Adjective A word describing a noun: **a *red* pencil** = **ein *roter* Stift**

Adverb A word that describes or changes the meaning of a verb, an adjective, or another adverb: **she sings *beautifully*** = **sie singt *schön***

Article The definite article, **the** = **der/die/das**, and indefinite article, **a/an** = **ein/eine/ein**, used in front of a noun

Attributive An adjective or noun is attributive when it is used directly before a noun: **the *black* dog** = **der *schwarze* Hund**; ***farewell* speech** = **Abschiedsrede**

Auxiliary verb One of the verbs – as German **haben, sein, werden** – used to form the perfect or future tense. **I will help** = **ich *werde* helfen**

Cardinal number A whole number representing a quantity: **one/two/three** = **eins/zwei/drei**

Case The form of a noun, pronoun, adjective, or article that shows the part it plays in a sentence; there are four cases in German – nominative, accusative, genitive, and dative

Clause A self-contained section of a sentence that contains a subject and a verb

Collective noun A noun that is singular in form but refers to a group of individual persons or things, e.g. **royalty, grain**

Collocate A word that regularly occurs with another; in German, **Buch** is a typical collocate of the verb **lesen**

Comparative The form of an adjective or adverb that makes it "more": **smaller** = **kleiner**, **more clearly** = **klarer**

Compound adjective An adjective formed from two or more separate words: **selbstbewusst (selbst + bewusst)** = **self-confident**

Compound noun A noun formed from two or more separate words: **der Flughafen (Flug+ Hafen)** = **airport**

Compound verb A verb formed by adding a prefix to a simple verb; in German, some compound verbs are separable **(an|fangen)**, and some are inseparable **(verlassen)**

Conditional tense A tense of a verb that expresses what would happen if something else occurred: **he would go** = **er würde gehen**

Conjugation Variation of the form of a verb to show tense, person, mood, etc.

Conjunction A word used to join clauses together: **and** = **und, because** = **weil**

Dative The case of an indirect object; many German prepositions take the dative

Declension The form of a noun, pronoun, or adjective that corresponds to a particular case, number, or gender; some German nouns decline like adjectives, e.g. **Beamte, Taube**

Definite article: the = **der/die/das**

Demonstrative pronoun A pronoun indicating the person or thing referred to; ***this* is my bicycle** = ***das* ist mein Fahrrad**

Direct object The noun or pronoun directly affected by the verb: **he caught *the ball*** = **er fing *den Ball***

Direct speech A speaker's actual words or the use of these in writing

Ending Letters added to the stem of verbs, as well as to nouns and adjectives, according to tense, case, etc.

Feminine One of the three noun genders in German: **die Frau** = **the woman**

Future tense The tense of a verb that refers to something that will happen in the future: **I will go** = **ich werde gehen**

Gender One of the three groups of nouns in German: masculine, feminine, or neuter

Genitive The case that shows possession; some prepositions in German take the genitive

Imperative A form of a verb that expresses a command: **go away!** = **geh weg!**

Imperfect tense The tense of a verb that refers to an uncompleted or a habitual action in the past: **I went there every Friday** = **ich ging jeden Freitag dorthin**

Impersonal verb A verb in English used only with **'it'**, and in German only with **'es'**: **it is raining** = **es regnet**

Indeclinable adjective An adjective that has no inflected forms, as German **klasse, Moskauer**

Indefinite article: a/an = **ein/eine/ein**

Indefinite pronoun A pronoun that does not identify a specific person or object: **one** = **man, something** = **etwas**

Indicative form The form of a verb used when making a statement of fact or asking questions of fact: **he is just coming** = **er kommt gleich**

Indirect object The noun or pronoun indirectly affected by the verb, at which the direct object is aimed: **I gave *him* the book** = **ich gab *ihm* das Buch**

Indirect speech A report of what someone has said which does not reproduce the exact words

Infinitive The basic part of a verb: **to play** = **spielen**

Inflect To change the ending

or form of a word to show its tense or its grammatical relation to other words: **gehe** and **gehst** are inflected forms of the verb **gehen**

Inseparable verb A verb with a prefix that can never be separated from it: **verstehen, ich verstehe**

Interjection A sound, word, or remark expressing a strong feeling such as anger, fear, or joy: **oh!** = **ach!**

Interrogative pronoun A pronoun that asks a question: **who?** = **wer?**

Intransitive verb A verb that does not have a direct object: **he died suddenly** = **er ist plötzlich gestorben**

Irregular verb A verb that does not follow one of the set patterns and has its own individual forms

Masculine One of the three noun genders in German: **der Mann** = **the man**, **der Stuhl** = **the chair**

Modal verb A verb that is used with another verb (not a model) to express permission, obligation, possibility, etc., as German **können, sollen**, English **might, should**

Negative expressing refusal or denial; **there aren't any** = **es gibt keine**

Neuter One of the three noun genders in German: **das Buch** = **the book, das Kind** = **the child**

Nominative The case of the subject of a sentence; in sentences with **sein** and **werden** the noun after the verb is in the nominative: **that is my car** = **das ist mein Auto**

Noun A word that names a person or a thing

Number The state of being either singular or plural

Object The word or words naming the person or thing acted upon by a verb or preposition, as '**Buch**' in **er las das Buch** or '**ihm**' in **ich traue ihm**

Ordinal number A number that shows a person's or thing's position in a series: **the *twenty-first* century** = **das *einundzwanzigste* Jahrhundert, the *second* door on the left** = **die *zweite* Tür links**

Part of speech A grammatical term for the function of a word; noun, verb, adjective, etc., are parts of speech.

Passive In the passive form the subject of the verb experiences the action rather than performs it: **he was asked** = **er wurde gefragt**

Past participle The part of a verb used to form past tenses: **she had *gone*, er hat *gelogen***

Perfect tense The tense of a verb that refers to a completed action in the past or an action that started in the past and is still going on: **I have already eaten** = **ich habe schon gegessen; I have been reading all day** = **ich habe den ganzen Tag gelesen**

Person Any of the three groups of personal pronouns

and forms taken by verbs; the **first person** (e.g. **I/ich**) refers to the person(s) speaking, the **second person** (e.g. **you/du**) refers to the person(s) spoken to; the **third person** (e.g. **he/er**) refers to the persons spoken about

Personal pronoun A pronoun that refers to a person or thing: **he/she/it** = **er/sie/es**

Phrasal verb A verb in English combined with a preposition or an adverb to have a particular meaning: **run away** = **weglaufen**

Phrase A self-contained section of a sentence that does not contain a full verb

Pluperfect tense The tense of a verb that refers to something that happened before a particular point in the past: **als ich ankam, *war* er schon *losgefahren*** = **when I arrived, he *had* already *left***

Plural Of nouns etc., referring to more than one: **the trees** = **die Bäume**

Possessive adjective An adjective that shows possession, belonging to someone or something; **my** = **mein/meine/mein**

Possessive pronoun A pronoun that shows possession, belonging to someone or something: **mine** = **meiner/meine/meins**

Predicate The part of a sentence that says something about the **subject**, e.g. **went home** in **John went home**

Predicative An adjective is predicative when it comes after a verb such as **be** or **become** in English, or after **sein** or **werden** in German: **she is beautiful** = **sie ist schön**

Prefix A letter or group of letters added to the beginning of a word to change its meaning; in German, the prefix can move from separable verbs (**an|fangen**), but stays fixed to inseparable verbs (**verlassen**)

Preposition A word that stands in front of a noun or pronoun, relating it to the rest of the sentence; in German prepositions are always followed by a particular case, usually either the accusative or dative, but occasionally the genitive: **with** = **mit (+ dative)**, **for** = **für (+ accusative)**, **because of** = **wegen (+ genitive)**

Present participle The part of a verb that in English ends in **-ing**, and in German adds **-d** to the infinitive: **asking** = **fragend**

Present tense The tense of a verb that refers to something happening now: **I make** = **ich mache**

Pronoun A word that stands instead of a noun: **he** = **er**, **she** = **sie**, **mine** = **meiner/meine/meins**

Proper noun A name of a person, place, institution, etc., in English written with a capital letter at the start; **Germany**, the **Atlantic**, **Karl**, **Europa** are all proper nouns

Reflexive pronoun A pronoun that goes with a

reflexive verb: in German **mich, dich, sich, uns, euch, sich**

Reflexive verb A verb whose object is the same as its subject; in German, it is used with a reflexive pronoun: **du sollst dich waschen** = **you should wash yourself**

Regular verb A verb that follows a set pattern in its different forms

Relative pronoun A pronoun that introduces a subordinate clause, relating to a person or thing mentioned in the main clause: **the man *who* visited us** = **der Mann, *der* uns besucht hat**

Reported Speech Another name for **Indirect speech**

Sentence A sequence of words, with a subject and a verb, that can stand on their own to make a statement, ask a question, or give a command

Separable verb A verb with a prefix that can be separated from it in some tenses: **anfangen**, **anzufangen**, **angefangen**, but **ich fange an**, **du fingst an**

Singular Of nouns etc., referring to just one: **the tree** = **der Baum**

Stem The part of a verb to which endings are added; **fahr-** is the stem of **fahren**

Subject In a clause or sentence, the noun or pronoun that causes the action of the verb: ***he* caught the ball** = ***er* fing den Ball**

Subjunctive A verb form that is used to express doubt or unlikelihood: **if I were to tell you that ...** = **wenn ich dir sagen würde, dass ...**

Subordinate clause A clause which adds information to the main clause of a sentence but cannot be used as a sentence by itself

Suffix A letter or group of letters joined to the end of a word to make another word, as **–heit** in **Schönheit**

Superlative The form of an adjective or adverb that makes it "most": **the *smallest* house** = **das *kleinste* Haus**, **most clearly** = **am klarsten**

Tense The form of a verb that tells when the action takes place: present, future, imperfect, perfect, pluperfect

Transitive verb A verb that is used with a direct object: **she read the book** = **sie las das Buch**

Verb A word or group of words that describes an action: **the children *are playing*** = **die Kinder *spielen***

Abbreviations/Abkürzungen

adjective	*a*	Adjektiv
abbreviation	*abbr*	Abkürzung
accusative	*acc*	Akkusativ
Administration	*Admin*	Administration
adverb	*adv*	Adverb
American	*Amer*	amerikanisch
Anatomy	*Anat*	Anatomie
Archaeology	*Archaeol*	Archäologie
Architecture	*Archit*	Architektur
Astronomy	*Astr*	Astronomie
attributive	*attrib*	attributiv
Austrian	*Aust*	österreichisch
Motor vehicles	*Auto*	Automobil
Aviation	*Aviat*	Luftfahrt
Biology	*Biol*	Biologie
Botany	*Bot*	Botanik
Chemistry	*Chem*	Chemie
collective	*coll*	Kollektivum
Commerce	*Comm*	Handel
conjunction	*conj*	Konjunktion
Cookery	*Culin*	Kochkunst
dative	*dat*	Dativ
definite article	*def art*	bestimmter Artikel
demonstrative	*dem*	Demonstrativ-
dialect	*dial*	Dialekt
Electricity	*Electr*	Elektrizität
something	*etw*	etwas
feminine	*f*	Femininum
figurative	*fig*	figurativ
genitive	*gen*	Genitiv
Geography	*Geog*	Geographie
Geology	*Geol*	Geologie
Geometry	*Geom*	Geometrie
Grammar	*Gram*	Grammatik
Horticulture	*Hort*	Gartenbau
impersonal	*impers*	unpersönlich
indefinite article	*indef art*	unbestimmter Artikel
indefinite pronoun	*indef pron*	unbestimmtes Pronomen
infinitive	*inf*	Infinitiv

inseparable	*insep*	untrennbar
interjection	*int*	Interjektion
invariable	*inv*	unveränderlich
irregular	*irreg*	unregelmäßig
someone	*jd*	jemand
someone	*jdm*	jemandem
someone	*jdn*	jemanden
someone's	*jds*	jemandes
Journalism	*Journ*	Journalismus
Law	*Jur*	Jura
Language	*Lang*	Sprache
literary	*liter*	dichterisch
masculine	*m*	Maskulinum
Mathematics	*Math*	Mathematik
Medicine	*Med*	Medizin
Meteorology	*Meteorol*	Meteorologie
Military	*Mil*	Militär
Mineralogy	*Miner*	Mineralogie
Music	*Mus*	Musik
noun	*n*	Substantiv
Nautical	*Naut*	nautisch
North German	*N Ger*	Norddeutsch
nominative	*nom*	Nominativ
neuter	*nt*	Neutrum
or	*od*	oder
Proprietary term	*P*	Warenzeichen
pejorative	*pej*	abwertend
Photography	*Phot*	Fotografie
Physics	*Phys*	Physik
plural	*pl*	Plural
Politics	*Pol*	Politik
possessive	*poss*	Possessiv-
past participle	*pp*	zweites Partizip
predicative	*pred*	prädikativ
prefix	*pref*	Präfix
preposition	*prep*	Präposition
present	*pres*	Präsens
present participle	*pres p*	erstes Partizip
pronoun	*pron*	Pronomen
Psychology	*Psych*	Psychologie
past tense	*pt*	Präteritum
Railway	*Rail*	Eisenbahn
reflexive	*refl*	reflexiv
regular	*reg*	regelmäßig
relative	*rel*	Relativ-
Religion	*Relig*	Religion

see	*s.*	siehe
School	*Sch*	Schule
separable	*sep*	trennbar
singular	*sg*	Singular
South German	*S Ger*	Süddeutsch
someone	*s.o.*	jemand
something	*sth*	etwas
Technical	*Techn*	Technik
Telephone	*Teleph*	Telefon
Textiles	*Tex*	Textilien
Theatre	*Theat*	Theater
Television	*TV*	Fernsehen
Typography	*Typ*	Typographie
University	*Univ*	Universität
auxiliary verb	*v aux*	Hilfsverb
intransitive verb	*vi*	intransitives Verb
reflexive verb	*vr*	reflexives Verb
transitive verb	*vt*	transitives Verb
vulgar	*vulg*	vulgär
Zoology	*Zool*	Zoologie
familiar	[!]	familiär
slang	⊠	Slang
old spelling	*	alte Schreibung

German–English Dictionary

Aal *m* **-[e]s, -e** eel
Aas *nt* **-es** carrion; ⊠ swine
ab *prep* (+ *dat*) from ● *adv* off; (*weg*) away; (*auf Fahrplan*) departs; **ab und zu** now and then; **auf und ab** up and down
abändern *vt sep* alter; (*abwandeln*) modify
Abbau *m* dismantling; (*Kohlen-*) mining. **a~en** *vt sep* dismantle; mine <*Kohle*>
abbeißen† *vt sep* bite off
abbeizen *vt sep* strip
abberufen† *vt sep* recall
abbestellen *vt sep* cancel; **jdn a~** put s.o. off
abbiegen† *vi sep* (*sein*) turn off; **[nach] links a~** turn left
Abbildung *f* **-, -en** illustration
abblättern *vi sep* (*sein*) flake off
abblend|en *vt/i sep* (*haben*) **[die Scheinwerfer] a~en** dip one's headlights. **A~licht** *nt* dipped headlights *pl*
abbrechen† *v sep* ● *vt* break off; (*abreißen*) demolish; (*Computer*) cancel ● *vi* (*sein/haben*) break off
abbrennen† *v sep* ● *vt* burn off; (*niederbrennen*) burn down ● *vi* (*sein*) burn down
abbringen† *vt sep* dissuade (**von** from)
Abbruch *m* demolition; (*Beenden*) breaking off
abbuchen *vt sep* debit
abbürsten *vt sep* brush down; (*entfernen*) brush off
abdanken *vi sep* (*haben*) resign; <*Herrscher:*> abdicate
abdecken *vt sep* uncover; (*abnehmen*) take off; (*zudecken*) cover; **den Tisch a~** clear the table
abdichten *vt sep* seal
abdrehen *vt sep* turn off
Abdruck *m* (*pl* **¨e**) impression. **a~en** *vt sep* print
abdrücken *vt/i sep* (*haben*) fire; **sich a~** leave an impression
Abend *m* **-s, -e** evening; **am A~** in the evening; **heute A~** this evening, tonight; **gestern A~** yesterday evening, last night. **A~brot** *nt* supper. **A~essen** *nt* dinner; (*einfacher*) supper. **A~mahl** *nt* (*Relig*) [Holy] Communion. **a~s** *adv* in the evening
Abenteuer *nt* **-s,-** adventure; (*Liebes-*) affair. **a~lich** *a* fantastic
aber *conj* but; **oder a~** or else ● *adv* (*wirklich*) really
Aber|glaube *m* superstition. **a~gläubisch** *a* superstitious
abfahr|en† *v sep* ● *vi* (*sein*) leave; <*Auto:*> drive off ● *vt* take away; (*entlangfahren*) drive along; use <*Fahrkarte*>; **abgefahrene Reifen** worn tyres. **A~t** *f* departure; (*Talfahrt*) descent; (*Piste*) run; (*Ausfahrt*) exit
Abfall *m* refuse, rubbish; (*auf der Straße*) litter; (*Industrie-*) waste
abfallen† *vi sep* (*sein*) drop, fall; (*übrig bleiben*) be left (**für** for); (*sich neigen*) slope away. **a~d** *a* sloping
Abfallhaufen *m* rubbish-dump
abfällig *a* disparaging
abfangen† *vt sep* intercept
abfärben *vi sep* (*haben*) <*Farbe:*> run; <*Stoff:*> not be colour-fast
abfassen *vt sep* draft
abfertigen *vt sep* attend to; (*zollamtlich*) clear; **jdn kurz a~** [!] give s.o. short shrift
abfeuern *vt sep* fire

abfind|en† *vt sep* pay off; (*entschädigen*) compensate; **sich a~en mit** come to terms with. **A~ung** *f* **-, -en** compensation

abfliegen† *vi sep* (*sein*) fly off; (*Aviat*) take off

abfließen† *vi sep* (*sein*) drain *or* run away

Abflug *m* (*Aviat*) departure

Abfluss *m* drainage; (*Öffnung*) drain. **A~rohr** *nt* drain-pipe

abfragen *vt sep* **jdn** *od* **jdm Vokabeln a~** test s.o. on vocabulary

Abfuhr *f* **-** removal; (*fig*) rebuff

abführ|en *vt sep* take *or* lead away. **A~mittel** *nt* laxative

abfüllen *vt sep* **auf** *od* **in Flaschen a~** bottle

Abgase *ntpl* exhaust fumes

abgeben† *vt sep* hand in; (*abliefern*) deliver; (*verkaufen*) sell; (*zur Aufbewahrung*) leave; (*Fußball*) pass; (*ausströmen*) give off; (*abfeuern*) fire; (*verlauten lassen*) give; cast <*Stimme*>; **jdm etw a~** give s.o. a share of sth

abgehen† *v sep* ● *vi* (*sein*) leave; (*Theat*) exit; (*sich lösen*) come off; (*abgezogen werden*) be deducted ● *vt* walk along

abgehetzt *a* harassed. **abgelegen** *a* remote. **abgeneigt** *a* **etw** (*dat*) **nicht abgeneigt sein** not be averse to sth. **abgenutzt** *a* worn. **Abgeordnete(r)** *m/f* deputy; (*Pol*) Member of Parliament. **abgepackt** *a* pre-packed

abgeschieden *a* secluded

abgeschlossen *a* (*fig*) complete; <*Wohnung*> self-contained. **abgesehen** *prep* apart (from **von**). **abgespannt** *a* exhausted. **abgestanden** *a* stale. **abgestorben** *a* dead; <*Glied*> numb. **abgetragen** *a* worn. **abgewetzt** *a* threadbare

abgewinnen† *vt sep* win (**jdm** from s.o.); **etw** (*dat*) **Geschmack a~** get a taste for sth

abgewöhnen *vt sep* **jdm/sich das Rauchen a~** cure s.o. of/ give up smoking

abgießen† *vt sep* pour off; drain <*Gemüse*>

Abgott *m* idol

abgöttisch *adv* **a~ lieben** idolize

abgrenz|en *vt sep* divide off; (*fig*) define. **A~ung** *f* **-** demarcation

Abgrund *m* abyss; (*fig*) depths *pl*

abgucken *vt sep* [!] copy

Abguss *m* cast

abhacken *vt sep* chop off

abhaken *vt sep* tick off

abhalten† *vt sep* keep off; (*hindern*) keep, prevent (**von** from); (*veranstalten*) hold

abhanden *adv* **a~ kommen** get lost

Abhandlung *f* treatise

Abhang *m* slope

abhängen[1] *vt sep* (*reg*) take down; (*abkuppeln*) uncouple

abhäng|en[2]† *vi sep* (*haben*) depend (**von** on). **a~ig** *a* dependent (**von** on). **A~igkeit** *f* **-** dependence

abhärten *vt sep* toughen up

abheben† *v sep* ● *vt* take off; (*vom Konto*) withdraw; **sich a~** stand out (**gegen** against) ● *vi* (*haben*) (*Cards*) cut [the cards]; (*Aviat*) take off; <*Rakete:*> lift off

abheften *vt sep* file

Abhilfe *f* remedy

abholen *vt sep* collect

abhör|en *vt sep* listen to; (*überwachen*) tap; **jdn** *od* **jdm Vokabeln a~en** test s.o. on vocabulary. **A~gerät** *nt* bugging device

Abitur *nt* **-s** ≈ A levels *pl*

abkaufen *vt sep* buy (*dat* from)

abklingen† *vi sep* (*sein*) die away; (*nachlassen*) subside

abkochen *vt sep* boil

A

abkommen† *vi sep (sein)* **a~ von** stray from; *(aufgeben)* give up. **A~** *nt* **-s,-** agreement
Abkömmling *m* **-s, -e** descendant
abkratzen *vt sep* scrape off
abkühlen *vt/i sep (sein)* cool; **sich a~** cool [down]
Abkunft *f* **-** origin
abkuppeln *vt sep* uncouple
abkürz|en *vt sep* shorten; abbreviate <*Wort*>. **A~ung** *f* short cut; *(Wort)* abbreviation
abladen† *vt sep* unload
Ablage *f* shelf; *(für Akten)* tray
ablager|n *vt sep* deposit. **A~ung** *f* **-, -en** deposit
ablassen† *vt sep* drain [off]; let off <*Dampf*>
Ablauf *m* drain; *(Verlauf)* course; *(Ende)* end; *(einer Frist)* expiry. **a~en**† *v sep* ● *vi (sein)* run *or* drain off; *(verlaufen)* go off; *(enden)* expire; <*Zeit:*> run out; <*Uhrwerk:*> run down ● *vt* walk along; *(absuchen)* scour (**nach** for)
ableg|en *v sep* ● *vt* put down; discard <*Karte*>; *(abheften)* file; *(ausziehen)* take off; sit, take <*Prüfung*>; **abgelegte Kleidung** cast-offs *pl* ● *vi (haben)* take off one's coat; *(Naut)* cast off. **A~er** *m* **-s,-** *(Bot)* cutting; *(Schössling)* shoot
ablehn|en *vt sep* refuse; *(missbilligen)* reject. **A~ung** *f* **-, -en** refusal; rejection
ableit|en *vt sep* divert; **sich a~en** be derived (**von/aus** from). **A~ung** *f* derivation; *(Wort)* derivative
ablenk|en *vt sep* deflect; divert <*Aufmerksamkeit*>. **A~ung** *f* **-, -en** distraction
ablesen† *vt sep* read
ablicht|en *vt sep* photocopy. **A~ung** *f* photocopy
abliefern *vt sep* deliver
ablös|en *vt sep* detach; *(abwechseln)* relieve; **sich a~en** come off; *(sich abwechseln)* take turns. **A~ung** *f* relief
abmach|en *vt sep* remove; *(ausmachen)* arrange; *(vereinbaren)* agree. **A~ung** *f* **-, -en** agreement
abmager|n *vi sep (sein)* lose weight. **A~ungskur** *f* slimming diet
abmelden *vt sep* cancel; **sich a~** *(im Hotel)* check out; *(Computer)* log off
abmessen† *vt sep* measure
abmühen (sich) *vr sep* struggle
Abnäher *m* **-s,-** dart
abnehm|en† *v sep* ● *vt* take off, remove; pick up <*Hörer*>; **jdm etw a~en** take/*(kaufen)* buy sth from s.o. ● *vi (haben)* decrease; *(nachlassen)* decline; <*Person:*> lose weight; <*Mond:*> wane. **A~er** *m* **-s,-** buyer
Abneigung *f* dislike (**gegen** of)
abnorm *a* abnormal
abnutz|en *vt sep* wear out. **A~ung** *f* **-** wear [and tear]
Abon|nement /abɔnəˈmã:/ *nt* **-s, -s** subscription. **A~nent** *m* **-en, -en** subscriber. **a~nieren** *vt* take out a subscription to
abpassen *vt sep* wait for; **gut a~** time well
abraten† *vi sep (haben)* **jdm von etw a~** advise s.o. against sth
abräumen *vt/i (haben)* clear away
abrechn|en *v sep* ● *vt* deduct ● *vi (haben)* settle up. **A~ung** *f* settlement; *(Rechnung)* account
Abreise *f* departure. **a~n** *vi sep (sein)* leave
abreißen† *v sep* ● *vt* tear off; *(demolieren)* pull down ● *vi (sein)* come off
abrichten *vt sep* train
Abriss *m* demolition; *(Übersicht)* summary

abrufen† *vt sep* call away; (*Computer*) retrieve
abrunden *vt sep* round off
abrüst|en *vi sep* (*haben*) disarm. **A∼ung** *f* disarmament
abrutschen *vi sep* (*sein*) slip
Absage *f* **-, -n** cancellation; (*Ablehnung*) refusal. **a∼n** *v sep* ● *vt* cancel ● *vi* (*haben*) **[jdm] a∼n** cancel an appointment [with s.o.]; (*auf Einladung*) refuse [s.o.'s invitation]
Absatz *m* heel; (*Abschnitt*) paragraph; (*Verkauf*) sale
abschaffen *vt sep* abolish; get rid of <*Auto, Hund*>
abschalten *vt/i sep* (*haben*) switch off
Abscheu *m* **-** revulsion
abscheulich *a* revolting
abschicken *vt sep* send off
Abschied *m* **-[e]s, -e** farewell; (*Trennung*) parting; **A∼ nehmen** say goodbye (**von** to)
abschießen† *vt sep* shoot down; (*abfeuern*) fire; launch <*Rakete*>
abschirmen *vt sep* shield
abschlagen† *vt sep* knock off; (*verweigern*) refuse
Abschlepp|dienst *m* breakdown service. **a∼en** *vt sep* tow away. **A∼seil** *nt* tow-rope
abschließen† *v sep* ● *vt* lock; (*beenden, abmachen*) conclude; make <*Wette*>; balance <*Bücher*> ● *vi* (*haben*) lock up; (*enden*) end. **a∼d** *adv* in conclusion
Abschluss *m* conclusion. **A∼zeugnis** *nt* diploma
abschmecken *vt sep* season
abschmieren *vt sep* lubricate
abschneiden† *v sep* ● *vt* cut off ● *vi* (*haben*) **gut/schlecht a∼** do well/badly
Abschnitt *m* section; (*Stadium*) stage; (*Absatz*) paragraph
abschöpfen *vt sep* skim off
abschrauben *vt sep* unscrew
abschreck|en *vt sep* deter; (*Culin*) put in cold water <*Ei*>. **a∼end** *a* repulsive. **A∼ungsmittel** *nt* deterrent
abschreib|en† *v sep* ● *vt* copy; (*Comm & fig*) write off ● *vi* (*haben*) copy. **A∼ung** *f* (*Comm*) depreciation
Abschrift *f* copy
Abschuss *m* shooting down; (*Abfeuern*) firing; (*Raketen-*) launch
abschüssig *a* sloping; (*steil*) steep
abschwellen† *vi sep* (*sein*) go down
abseh|bar *a* **in a∼barer Zeit** in the foreseeable future. **a∼en**† *vt/i sep* (*haben*) copy; (*voraussehen*) foresee; **a∼en von** disregard; (*aufgeben*) refrain from
abseits *adv* apart; (*Sport*) offside ● *prep* (+ *gen*) away from. **A∼** *nt* **-** (*Sport*) offside
absend|en† *vt sep* send off. **A∼er** *m* sender
absetzen *v sep* ● *vt* put *or* set down; (*ablagern*) deposit; (*abnehmen*) take off; (*abbrechen*) stop; (*entlassen*) dismiss; (*verkaufen*) sell; (*abziehen*) deduct ● *vi* (*haben*) pause
Absicht *f* **-, -en** intention; **mit A∼** intentionally, on purpose
absichtlich *a* intentional
absitzen† *v sep* ● *vi* (*sein*) dismount ● *vt* [!] serve <*Strafe*>
absolut *a* absolute
absolvieren *vt* complete; (*bestehen*) pass
absonder|n *vt sep* separate; (*ausscheiden*) secrete. **A∼ung** *f* **-, -en** secretion
absorbieren *vt* absorb
abspeisen *vt sep* fob off (**mit** with)
absperr|en *vt sep* cordon off; (*abstellen*) turn off; (*SGer*) lock. **A∼ung** *f* **-, -en** barrier

A

abspielen *vt sep* play; (*Fußball*) pass; **sich a~** take place
Absprache *f* agreement
absprechen† *vt sep* arrange; **sich a~** agree
abspringen† *vi sep* (*sein*) jump off; (*mit Fallschirm*) parachute; (*abgehen*) come off
Absprung *m* jump
abspülen *vt sep* rinse
abstamm|en *vi sep* (*haben*) be descended (**von** from). **A~ung** *f* - descent
Abstand *m* distance; (*zeitlich*) interval; **A~ halten** keep one's distance
abstatten *vt sep* **jdm einen Besuch a~** pay s.o. a visit
Abstecher *m* **-s,-** detour
abstehen† *vi sep* (*haben*) stick out
absteigen† *vi sep* (*sein*) dismount; (*niedersteigen*) descend; (*Fußball*) be relegated
abstell|en *vt sep* put down; (*lagern*) store; (*parken*) park; (*abschalten*) turn off. **A~gleis** *nt* siding. **A~raum** *m* box-room
absterben† *vi sep* (*sein*) die; (*gefühllos werden*) go numb
Abstieg *m* **-[e]s, -e** descent; (*Fußball*) relegation
abstimm|en *v sep* ● *vi* (*haben*) vote (**über** + *acc* on) ● *vt* coordinate (**auf** + *acc* with). **A~ung** *f* vote
Abstinenzler *m* **-s, -** teetotaller
abstoßen† *vt sep* knock off; (*verkaufen*) sell; (*fig: ekeln*) repel. **a~d** *a* repulsive
abstreiten† *vt sep* deny
Abstrich *m* (*Med*) smear
abstufen *vt sep* grade
Absturz *m* fall; (*Aviat*) crash
abstürzen *vi sep* (*sein*) fall; (*Aviat*) crash
absuchen *vt sep* search
absurd *a* absurd
Abszess *m* **-es, -e** abscess
Abt *m* **-[e]s,⸚e** abbot
abtasten *vt sep* feel; (*Techn*) scan
abtauen *vt/i sep* (*sein*) thaw; (*entfrosten*) defrost
Abtei *f* **-, -en** abbey
Abteil *nt* compartment
Abteilung *f* **-, -en** section; (*Admin, Comm*) department
abtragen† *vt sep* clear; (*einebnen*) level; (*abnutzen*) wear out
abträglich *a* detrimental (*dat* to)
abtreib|en† *vt sep* (*Naut*) drive off course; **ein Kind a~en lassen** have an abortion. **A~ung** *f* **-, -en** abortion
abtrennen *vt sep* detach; (*abteilen*) divide off
Abtreter *m* **-s,-** doormat
abtrocknen *vt/i sep* (*haben*) dry; **sich a~** dry oneself
abtropfen *vi sep* (*sein*) drain
abtun† *vt sep* (*fig*) dismiss
abwägen† *vt sep* (*fig*) weigh
abwandeln *vt sep* modify
abwarten *v sep* ● *vt* wait for ● *vi* (*haben*) wait [and see]
abwärts *adv* down[wards]
Abwasch *m* **-[e]s** washing-up; (*Geschirr*) dirty dishes *pl.* **a~en**† *v sep* ● *vt* wash; wash up <*Geschirr*>; (*entfernen*) wash off ● *vi* (*haben*) wash up. **A~lappen** *m* dishcloth
Abwasser *nt* **-s,⸚** sewage. **A~kanal** *m* sewer
abwechseln *vi/r sep* (*haben*) **[sich] a~** alternate; <*Personen:*> take turns. **a~d** *a* alternate
Abwechslung *f* **-, -en** change; **zur A~** for a change
abwegig *a* absurd
Abwehr *f* **-** defence; (*Widerstand*) resistance; (*Pol*) counter-espionage. **a~en** *vt sep* ward off. **A~system** *nt* immune system
abweich|en† *vi sep* (*sein*) deviate/(*von Regel*) depart (**von** from); (*sich unterscheiden*) differ (**von** from). **a~end** *a* divergent;

(*verschieden*) different. **A~ung** *f* **-, -en** deviation

abweis|en† *vt sep* turn down; turn away <*Person*>. **a~end** *a* unfriendly. **A~ung** *f* rejection

abwenden† *vt sep* turn away; (*verhindern*) avert

abwerfen† *vt sep* throw off; throw <*Reiter*>; (*Aviat*) drop; (*Kartenspiel*) discard; shed <*Haut, Blätter*>; yield <*Gewinn*>

abwert|en *vt sep* devalue. **A~ung** *f* **-, -en** devaluation

Abwesenheit *f* **-** absence; absent-mindedness

abwickeln *vt sep* unwind; (*erledigen*) settle

abwischen *vt sep* wipe

abzahlen *vt sep* pay off

abzählen *vt sep* count

Abzahlung *f* instalment

Abzeichen *nt* badge

abzeichnen *vt sep* copy

Abzieh|bild *nt* transfer. **a~en**† *v sep* ● *vt* pull off; take off <*Laken*>; strip <*Bett*>; (*häuten*) skin; (*Phot*) print; run off <*Kopien*>; (*zurückziehen*) withdraw; (*abrechnen*) deduct ● *vi* (*sein*) go away, <*Rauch:*> escape

Abzug *m* withdrawal; (*Abrechnung*) deduction; (*Phot*) print (*Korrektur-*) proof; (*am Gewehr*) trigger; (*A~söffnung*) vent; **A~̈e** *pl* deductions

abzüglich *prep* (+ *gen*) less

Abzugshaube *f* [cooker] hood

abzweig|en *v sep* ● *vi* (*sein*) branch off ● *vt* divert. **A~ung** *f* **-, -en** junction; (*Gabelung*) fork

ach *int* oh; **a~ je!** oh dear! **a~ so** I see

Achse *f* **-, -n** axis; (*Rad-*) axle

Achsel *f* **-, -n** shoulder. **A~höhle** *f* armpit. **A~zucken** *nt* **-s** shrug

acht *inv a*, **A~** *f* **-, -en** eight

Acht *f* **A~ geben** be careful; **A~ geben auf** (+ *acc*) look after; **außer A~ lassen** disregard; **sich in A~ nehmen** be careful

acht|e(r,s) *a* eighth. **a~eckig** *a* octagonal. **A~el** *nt* **-s,-** eighth.

achten *vt* respect ● *vi* (*haben*) **a~ auf** (+ *acc*) pay attention to; (*aufpassen*) look after

Achterbahn *f* roller-coaster

achtlos *a* careless

achtsam *a* careful

Achtung *f* **-** respect (**vor** + *dat* for); **A~!** look out!

acht|zehn *inv a* eighteen. **a~zehnte(r,s)** *a* eighteenth. **a~zig** *a inv* eighty. **a~zigste(r,s)** *a* eightieth

Acker *m* **-s,̈-** field. **A~bau** *m* agriculture. **A~land** *nt* arable land

addieren *vt/i* (*haben*) add

Addition /-'tsi̯o:n/ *f* **-, -en** addition

ade *int* goodbye

Adel *m* **-s** nobility

Ader *f* **-, -n** vein

Adjektiv *nt* **-s, -e** adjective

Adler *m* **-s,-** eagle

adlig *a* noble. **A~e(r)** *m* nobleman

Administration /-'tsi̯o:n/ *f* **-** administration

Admiral *m* **-s,̈-e** admiral

adop|tieren *vt* adopt. **A~tion** /-'tsi̯o:n/ *f* **-, -en** adoption. **A~tiveltern** *pl* adoptive parents. **A~tivkind** *nt* adopted child

Adrenalin *nt* **-s** adrenalin

Adres|se *f* **-, -n** address. **a~sieren** *vt* address

Adria *f* **-** Adriatic

Adverb *nt* **-s, -ien** /-i̯ən/ adverb

Affäre *f* **-, -n** affair

Affe *m* **-n, -n** monkey; (*Menschen-*) ape

affektiert *a* affected

affig *a* affected; (*eitel*) vain

Afrika *nt* **-s** Africa

Afrikan|er(in) *m* **-s,-** (*f* **-, -nen**) African. **a~isch** *a* African

After *m* **-s,-** anus

A

Agen|t(in) *m* **-en, -en** (*f* **-, -nen**) agent. **A~tur** *f* **-, -en** agency
Aggres|sion *f* **-, -en** aggression. **a~siv** *a* aggressive
Agnostiker *m* **-s,-** agnostic
Ägypt|en /ɛ'gʏptən/ *nt* **-s** Egypt. **Ä~er(in)** *m* **-s,-** (*f* **-, -nen**) Egyptian. **ä~isch** *a* Egyptian
ähneln *vi* (*haben*) (+ *dat*) resemble; **sich ä~** be alike
ahnen *vt* have a presentiment of; (*vermuten*) suspect
Ahnen *mpl* ancestors. **A~forschung** *f* genealogy
ähnlich *a* similar; **jdm ä~ sehen** resemble s.o. **Ä~keit** *f* **-, -en** similarity; resemblance
Ahnung *f* **-, -en** premonition; (*Vermutung*) idea, hunch
Ähre *f* **-, -n** ear [of corn]
Aids /e:ts/ *nt* **-** Aids
Airbag /'ɛ:ɐ̯bɛk/ *m* **-s, -s** (*Auto*) air bag
Akademie *f* **-, -n** academy
Akadem|iker(in) *m* **-s,-** (*f* **-, -nen**) university graduate. **a~isch** *a* academic
akklimatisieren (sich) *vr* become acclimatized
Akkord *m* **-[e]s, -e** (*Mus*) chord. **A~arbeit** *f* piece-work
Akkordeon *nt* **-s, -s** accordion
Akkumulator *m* **-s, -en** /-'to:rən/ (*Electr*) accumulator
Akkusativ *m* **-s, -e** accusative. **A~objekt** *nt* direct object
Akrobat|(in) *m* **-en, -en** (*f* **-, -nen**) acrobat. **a~isch** *a* acrobatic
Akt *m* **-[e]s, -e** act; (*Kunst*) nude
Akte *f* **-, -n** file; **A~n** documents. **A~ntasche** *f* briefcase
Aktie /'aktsi̯ə/ *f* **-, -n** (*Comm*) share. **A~ngesellschaft** *f* joint-stock company
Aktion /ak'tsi̯o:n/ *f* **-, -en** action. **A~är** *m* **-s, -e** shareholder
aktiv *a* active
aktuell *a* topical; (*gegenwärtig*) current

Akupunktur *f* **-** acupuncture
Akustik *f* **-** acoustics *pl*
akut *a* acute
Akzent *m* **-[e]s, -e** accent
akzept|abel *a* acceptable. **a~ieren** *vt* accept
Alarm *m* **-s** alarm; (*Mil*) alert. **a~ieren** *vt* alert; (*beunruhigen*) alarm
Albdruck *m* nightmare
albern *a* silly ● *vi* (*haben*) play the fool
Albtraum *m* nightmare
Album *nt* **-s, -ben** album
Algebra *f* **-** algebra
Algen *fpl* algae
Algerien /-i̯ən/ *nt* **-s** Algeria
Alibi *nt* **-s, -s** alibi
Alkohol *m* **-s** alcohol. **a~frei** *a* non-alcoholic
Alkohol|iker(in) *m* **-s,-** (*f* **-, -nen**) alcoholic. **a~isch** *a* alcoholic
all *inv pron* **all das/mein Geld** all the/my money; **all dies** all this
All *nt* **-s** universe
alle *pred a* finished
all|e(r,s) *pron* all; (*jeder*) every; **a~es** everything, all; (*alle Leute*) everyone; **a~e** *pl* all; **a~es Geld** all the money; **a~e beide** both [of them/us]; **a~e Tage** every day; **a~e drei Jahre** every three years; **ohne a~en Grund** without any reason; **vor a~em** above all; **a~es in a~em** all in all; **a~es aussteigen!** all change!
Allee *f* **-, -n** avenue
allein *adv* alone; (*nur*) only; **a~ stehend** single; **a~ der Gedanke** the mere thought; **von a~[e]** of its/<*Person*> one's own accord; (*automatisch*) automatically ● *conj* but. **A~erziehende(r)** *m/f* single parent. **a~ig** *a* sole. **A~stehende** *pl* single people
allemal *adv* every time; (*gewiss*) certainly
allenfalls *adv* at most; (*eventuell*) possibly

aller|beste(r,s) *a* very best; **am a~besten** best of all. **a~dings** *adv* indeed; (*zwar*) admittedly. **a~erste(r,s)** *a* very first
Allergie *f* **-, -n** allergy
allergisch *a* allergic (**gegen** to)
Aller|heiligen *nt* **-s** All Saints Day. **a~höchstens** *adv* at the very most. **a~lei** *inv a* all sorts of ● *pron* all sorts of things. **a~letzte(r,s)** *a* very last. **a~liebste(r,s)** *a* favourite ● *adv* **am a~liebsten** for preference; **am a~liebsten haben** like best of all. **a~meiste(r,s)** *a* most ● *adv* **am a~meisten** most of all. **A~seelen** *nt* **-s** All Souls Day. **a~wenigste(r,s)** *a* very least ● *adv* **am a~wenigsten** least of all
allgemein *a* general, *adv* -ly; **im A~en (a~en)** in general. **A~heit** *f* **-** community; (*Öffentlichkeit*) general public
Allianz *f* **-, -en** alliance
Alligator *m* **-s, -en** /-'to:rən/ alligator
alliiert *a* allied; **die A~en** *pl* the Allies
all|jährlich *a* annual. **a~mählich** *a* gradual
Alltag *m* working day; **der A~** (*fig*) everyday life
alltäglich *a* daily; (*gewöhnlich*) everyday; <*Mensch*> ordinary
alltags *adv* on weekdays
allzu *adv* [far] too; **a~ oft** all too often; **a~ vorsichtig** over-cautious
Alm *f* **-, -en** alpine pasture
Almosen *ntpl* alms
Alpdruck *m* = **Albdruck**
Alpen *pl* Alps
Alphabet *nt* **-[e]s, -e** alphabet. **a~isch** *a* alphabetical, *adv* -ly
Alptraum *m* = **Albtraum**
als *conj* as; (*zeitlich*) when; (*mit Komparativ*) than; **nichts als** nothing but; **als ob** as if *or* though
also *adv & conj* so; **a~ gut** all right then; **na a~!** there you are!
alt *a* old; (*gebraucht*) second-hand; (*ehemalig*) former; **alt werden** grow old
Alt *m* **-s** (*Mus*) contralto
Altar *m* **-s,¨-e** altar
Alt|e(r) *m/f* old man/woman; **die A~en** old people. **A~eisen** *nt* scrap iron. **A~enheim** *nt* old people's home
Alter *nt* **-s,-** age; (*Bejahrtheit*) old age; **im A~ von** at the age of
älter *a* older; **mein ä~er Bruder** my elder brother
altern *vi* (*sein*) age
Alternative *f* **-, -n** alternative
Alters|grenze *f* age limit. **A~heim** *nt* old people's home. **A~rente** *f* old-age pension. **a~schwach** *a* old and infirm
Alter|tum *nt* **-s,¨-er** antiquity. **a~tümlich** *a* old; (*altmodisch*) old-fashioned
altklug *a* precocious
alt|modisch *a* old-fashioned. **A~papier** *nt* waste paper. **A~warenhändler** *m* second-hand dealer
Alufolie *f* [aluminium] foil
Aluminium *nt* **-s** aluminium, (*Amer*) aluminum
am *prep* = **an dem; am Montag** on Monday; **am Morgen** in the morning; **am besten** [the] best
Amateur /-'tø:ɐ̯/ *m* **-s, -e** amateur
Ambition /-'t̮si̯o:n/ *f* **-, -en** ambition
Amboss *m* **-es, -e** anvil
ambulan|t *a* out-patient ... ● *adv* **a~t behandeln** treat as an out-patient. **A~z** *f* **-, -en** out-patients' department
Ameise *f* **-, -n** ant
amen *int*, **A~** *nt* **-s** amen
Amerika *nt* **-s** America
Amerikan|er(in) *m* **-s,-** (*f* **-, -nen**) American. **a~isch** *a* American
Ammoniak *nt* **-s** ammonia

A

Amnestie *f* **-, -n** amnesty
amoralisch *a* amoral
Ampel *f* **-, -n** traffic lights *pl*
Amphitheater *nt* amphitheatre
Amput|ation /-'tsi̯o:n/ *f* **-, -en** amputation. **a~ieren** *vt* amputate
Amsel *f* **-, -n** blackbird
Amt *nt* **-[e]s,¨-er** office; (*Aufgabe*) task; (*Teleph*) exchange. **a~lich** *a* official. **A~szeichen** *nt* dialling tone
Amulett *nt* **-[e]s, -e** [lucky] charm
amüs|ant *a* amusing. **a~ieren** *vt* amuse; **sich a~ieren** be amused (**über** + *acc* at); (*sich vergnügen*) enjoy oneself

---

an

● *preposition (+ dative)*

! Note that **an** plus **dem** can become **am**

····➤ (*räumlich*) on; (*Gebäude, Ort*) at. **an der Wand** on the wall. **Frankfurt an der Oder** Frankfurt on [the] Oder. **an der Ecke** at the corner. **am Bahnhof** at the station. **an ... vorbei** past

····➤ (*zeitlich*) on. **am Montag** on Monday. **an jedem Sonntag** every Sunday. **am 24. Mai** on May 24th

····➤ (*sonstige Verwendungen*) **arm/reich an Vitaminen** low/rich in vitamins. **jdn an etw erkennen** recognize s.o. by sth. **an etw leiden** suffer from sth. **an einer Krankheit sterben** die of a disease. **an [und für] sich** actually

● *preposition (+ accusative)*

! Note that **an** plus **das** can become **ans**

····➤ to. **schicke es an deinen Bruder** send it to your brother. **er ging ans Fenster** he went to the window

····➤ (*auf, gegen*) on. **etw an die Wand hängen** to hang sth on the wall. **lehne es an den Baum** lean it on *or* against the tree

····➤ (*sonstige Verwendungen*) **an etw/jdn glauben** believe in sth/ s.o. **an etw denken** think of sth. **sich an etw erinnern** remember sth

● *adverb*

····➤ (*auf Fahrplan*) **Köln an: 9.15** arriving Cologne 09.15

····➤ (*angeschaltet*) on. **die Waschmaschine/der Fernseher/das Licht/das Gas ist an** the washing machine/television/light/gas is on

····➤ (*ungefähr*) around; about. **an [die] 20 000 DM** around *or* about 20,000 DM

····➤ (*in die Zukunft*) **von heute an** from today (onwards)

---

analog *a* analogous; (*Computer*) analog. **A~ie** *f* **-, -n** analogy
Analphabet *m* **-en, -en** illiterate person. **A~entum** *nt* **-s** illiteracy
Analy|se *f* **-, -n** analysis. **a~sieren** *vt* analyse. **A~tiker** *m* **-s,-** analyst. **a~tisch** *a* analytical
Anämie *f* **-** anaemia
Ananas *f* **-, -[se]** pineapple
Anatomie *f* **-** anatomy
Anbau *m* cultivation; (*Gebäude*) extension. **a~en** *vt sep* build on, (*anpflanzen*) cultivate, grow
anbei *adv* enclosed
anbeißen† *v sep* ● *vt* take a bite of ● *vi* (*haben*) <*Fisch:*> bite
anbeten *vt sep* worship
Anbetracht *m* **in A~** (+ *gen*) in view of
anbieten† *vt sep* offer; **sich a~** offer (**zu** to)
anbinden† *vt sep* tie up
Anblick *m* sight. **a~en** *vt sep* look at
anbrechen† *v sep* ● *vt* start on; break into <*Vorräte*> ● *vi* (*sein*) begin; <*Tag:*> break; <*Nacht:*> fall
anbrennen† *v sep* ● *vt* light ● *vi* (*sein*) burn

anbringen† *vt sep* bring [along]; (*befestigen*) fix

Anbruch *m* (*fig*) dawn; **bei A~ des Tages/der Nacht** at daybreak/nightfall

Andacht *f* **-, -en** reverence; (*Gottesdienst*) prayers *pl*

andächtig *a* reverent; (*fig*) rapt

andauern *vi sep* (*haben*) last; (*anhalten*) continue. **a~d** *a* persistent; (*ständig*) constant

Andenken *nt* **-s,-** memory; (*Souvenir*) souvenir

ander|e(r,s) *a* other; (*verschieden*) different; (*nächste*) next; **ein a~er, eine a~e** another ● *pron* **der a~e/die a~en** the other/others; **ein a~er** another [one]; (*Person*) someone else; **kein a~er** no one else; **einer nach dem a~en** one after the other; **alles a~e/nichts a~es** everything/nothing else; **unter a~em** among other things. **a~enfalls** *adv* otherwise. **a~erseits** *adv* on the other hand. **a~mal** *adv* **ein a~mal** another time

ändern *vt* alter; (*wechseln*) change; **sich ä~** change

andernfalls *adv* otherwise

anders *pred a* different; **a~ werden** change ● *adv* differently; <*riechen, schmecken*> different; (*sonst*) else; **jemand a~** someone else

anderseits *adv* on the other hand

andersherum *adv* the other way round

anderthalb *inv a* one and a half; **a~ Stunden** an hour and a half

Änderung *f* **-, -en** alteration; (*Wechsel*) change

andeut|en *vt sep* indicate; (*anspielen*) hint at. **A~ung** *f* **-, -en** indication; hint

Andrang *m* rush (**nach** for); (*Gedränge*) crush

androhen *vt sep* **jdm etw a~** threaten s.o. with sth

aneignen *vt sep* **sich** (*dat*) **a~** appropriate; (*lernen*) learn

aneinander *adv & pref* together; <*denken*> of one another; **a~ vorbei** past one another; **a~ geraten** quarrel

Anekdote *f* **-, -n** anecdote

anerkannt *a* acknowledged

anerkenn|en† *vt sep* acknowledge, recognize; (*würdigen*) appreciate. **a~end** *a* approving. **A~ung** *f* **-** acknowledgement, recognition; appreciation

anfahren† *v sep* ● *vt* deliver; (*streifen*) hit ● *vi* (*sein*) start

Anfall *m* fit, attack. **a~en**† *v sep* ● *vt* attack ● *vi* (*sein*) arise; <*Zinsen:*> accrue

anfällig *a* susceptible (**für** to); (*zart*) delicate

Anfang *m* **-s,⸚e** beginning, start; **zu** *od* **am A~** at the beginning; (*anfangs*) at first. **a~en**† *vt/i sep* (*haben*) begin, start; (*tun*) do

Anfänger(in) *m* **-s,-** (*f* **-, -nen**) beginner

anfangs *adv* at first. **A~buchstabe** *m* initial letter. **A~gehalt** *nt* starting salary

anfassen *vt sep* touch; (*behandeln*) treat; tackle <*Arbeit*>; **sich a~** hold hands

anfechten† *vt sep* contest

anfertigen *vt sep* make

anfeuchten *vt sep* moisten

anflehen *vt sep* implore, beg

Anflug *m* (*Avia*) approach

anforder|n *vt sep* demand; (*Comm*) order. **A~ung** *f* demand

Anfrage *f* enquiry. **a~n** *vi sep* (*haben*) enquire, ask

anfreunden (sich) *vr sep* make friends (**mit** with)

anfügen *vt sep* add

anfühlen *vt sep* feel; **sich weich a~** feel soft

anführ|en *vt sep* lead; (*zitieren*) quote; (*angeben*) give. **A~er** *m*

leader. **A~ungszeichen** *ntpl* quotation marks
Angabe *f* statement; (*Anweisung*) instruction; (*Tennis*) service; **nähere A~n** particulars
angeb|en † *v sep* ● *vt* state; give <*Namen, Grund*>; (*anzeigen*) indicate; set <*Tempo*> ● *vi* (*haben*) (*Tennis*) serve; (! *protzen*) show off. **A~er(in)** *m* **-s,-** (*f* **-, -nen**) ! show-off. **A~erei** *f* **-** ! showing-off
angeblich *a* alleged
angeboren *a* innate; (*Med*) congenital
Angebot *nt* offer; (*Auswahl*) range; **A~ und Nachfrage** supply and demand
angebracht *a* appropriate
angeheiratet *a* <*Onkel, Tante*> by marriage
angeheitert *a* ! tipsy
angehen † *v sep* ● *vi* (*sein*) begin, start; <*Licht, Radio:*> come on; (*anwachsen*) take root; **a~ gegen** fight ● *vt* attack; tackle <*Arbeit*>; (*bitten*) ask (**um** for); (*betreffen*) concern
angehör|en *vi sep* (*haben*) (+ *dat*) belong to. **A~ige(r)** *m/f* relative
Angeklagte(r) *m/f* accused
Angel *f* **-, -n** fishing-rod; (*Tür-*) hinge
Angelegenheit *f* matter
Angel|haken *m* fish-hook. **a~n** *vi* (*haben*) fish (**nach** for); **a~n gehen** go fishing ● *vt* (*fangen*) catch. **A~rute** *f* fishing-rod
angelsächsisch *a* Anglo-Saxon
angemessen *a* commensurate (*dat* with); (*passend*) appropriate
angenehm *a* pleasant; (*bei Vorstellung*) **a~!** delighted to meet you!
angeregt *a* animated
angesehen *a* respected; <*Firma*> reputable
angesichts *prep* (+ *gen*) in view of
angespannt *a* intent; <*Lage*> tense
Angestellte(r) *m/f* employee
angewandt *a* applied
angewiesen *a* dependent (**auf** + *acc* on); **auf sich selbst a~** on one's own
angewöhnen *vt sep* **jdm etw a~** get s.o. used to sth; **sich** (*dat*) **etw a~** get into the habit of doing sth
Angewohnheit *f* habit
Angina *f* **-** tonsillitis
angleichen † *vt sep* adjust (*dat* to)
anglikanisch *a* Anglican
Anglistik *f* **-** English [language and literature]
Angorakatze *f* Persian cat
angreif|en † *vt sep* attack; tackle <*Arbeit*>; (*schädigen*) damage. **A~er** *m* **-s,-** attacker; (*Pol*) aggressor
angrenzen *vi sep* (*haben*) adjoin (**an etw** *acc* sth). **a~d** *a* adjoining
Angriff *m* attack; **in A~ nehmen** tackle. **a~slustig** *a* aggressive
Angst *f* **-,¨e** fear; (*Psych*) anxiety; (*Sorge*) worry (**um** about); **A~ haben** be afraid (**vor** + *dat* of); (*sich sorgen*) be worried (**um** about); **jdm A~ machen** frighten s.o.
ängstigen *vt* frighten; (*Sorge machen*) worry; **sich ä~** be frightened; be worried (**um** about)
ängstlich *a* nervous; (*scheu*) timid; (*verängstigt*) frightened, scared; (*besorgt*) anxious
angucken *vt sep* ! look at
angurten (sich) *vr sep* fasten one's seat-belt
anhaben † *vt sep* have on; **er/es kann mir nichts a~** (*fig*) he/it cannot hurt me
anhalt|en † *v sep* ● *vt* stop; hold <*Atem*>; **jdn zur Arbeit a~en** urge s.o. to work ● *vi* (*haben*) stop; (*andauern*) continue. **a~end** *a* persistent. **A~er(in)** *m* **-s,-** (*f* **-,**

-nen) hitchhiker; **per A~er fahren** hitchhike. **A~spunkt** *m* clue

anhand *prep* (+ *gen*) with the aid of

Anhang *m* appendix

anhängen[1] *vt sep* (*reg*) hang up; (*befestigen*) attach

anhäng|en[2]† *vi* (*haben*) be a follower of. **A~er** *m* **-s,-** follower; (*Auto*) trailer; (*Schild*) [tie-on] label; (*Schmuck*) pendant. **A~erin** *f* **-, -nen** follower. **a~lich** *a* affectionate

anhäufen *vt sep* pile up

Anhieb *m* **auf A~** straight away

Anhöhe *f* hill

anhören *vt sep* listen to; **sich gut a~** sound good

animieren *vt* encourage (**zu** to)

Anis *m* **-es** aniseed

Anker *m* **-s,-** anchor; **vor A~ gehen** drop anchor. **a~n** *vi* (*haben*) anchor; (*liegen*) be anchored

anketten *vt sep* chain up

Anklage *f* accusation; (*Jur*) charge; (*Ankläger*) prosecution. **A~bank** *f* dock. **a~n** *vt sep* accuse (*gen* of); (*Jur*) charge (*gen* with)

Ankläger *m* accuser; (*Jur*) prosecutor

anklammern *vt sep* clip on; **sich a~** cling (**an** + *acc* to)

ankleben *v sep* ● *vt* stick on ● *vi* (*sein*) stick (**an** + *dat* to)

anklicken *vt sep* click on

anklopfen *vi sep* (*haben*) knock

anknipsen *vt sep* [!] switch on

ankommen† *vi sep* (*sein*) arrive; (*sich nähern*) approach; **gut a~** arrive safely; (*fig*) go down well (**bei** with); **nicht a~ gegen** (*fig*) be no match for; **a~ auf** (+ *acc*) depend on; **das kommt darauf an** it [all] depends

ankreuzen *vt sep* mark with a cross

ankündig|en *vt sep* announce. **A~ung** *f* announcement

Ankunft *f* **-** arrival

ankurbeln *vt sep* (*fig*) boost

anlächeln *vt sep* smile at

anlachen *vt sep* smile at

Anlage *f* **-, -n** installation; (*Industrie-*) plant; (*Komplex*) complex; (*Geld-*) investment; (*Plan*) layout; (*Beilage*) enclosure; (*Veranlagung*) aptitude; (*Neigung*) predisposition; **[öffentliche] A~n** [public] gardens; **als A~** enclosed

Anlass *m* **-es,¨e** reason; (*Gelegenheit*) occasion; **A~ geben zu** give cause for

anlass|en† *vt sep* (*Auto*) start; [!] leave on <*Licht*>; keep on <*Mantel*>. **A~er** *m* **-s,-** starter

anlässlich *prep* (+ *gen*) on the occasion of

Anlauf *m* (*Sport*) run-up; (*fig*) attempt. **a~en**† *v sep* ● *vi* (*sein*) start; (*beschlagen*) mist up; <*Metall:*> tarnish; **rot a~en** blush

anlegen *v sep* ● *vt* put (**an** + *acc* against); put on <*Kleidung, Verband*>; lay back <*Ohren*>; aim <*Gewehr*>; (*investieren*) invest; (*ausgeben*) spend (**für** on); draw up <*Liste*>; **es darauf a~** (*fig*) aim (**zu** to) ● *vi* (*haben*) <*Schiff:*> moor; **a~ auf** (+ *acc*) aim at

anlehnen *vt sep* lean (**an** + *acc* against); **sich a~** lean (**an** + *acc* on)

Anleihe *f* **-, -n** loan

anleit|en *vt sep* instruct. **A~ung** *f* instructions *pl*

anlernen *vt sep* train

Anliegen *nt* **-s,-** request; (*Wunsch*) desire

anlieg|en† *vi sep* (*haben*) **[eng] a~en** fit closely; **[eng] a~end** close-fitting. **A~er** *mpl* residents; **'A~er frei'** 'access for residents only'

anlügen† *vt sep* lie to

anmachen *vt sep* [!] fix; (*anschalten*) turn on; dress <*Salat*>
anmalen *vt sep* paint
Anmarsch *m* (*Mil*) approach
anmeld|en *vt sep* announce; (*Admin*) register; **sich a∼en** say that one is coming; (*Admin*) register; (*Sch*) enrol; (*im Hotel*) check in; (*beim Arzt*) make an appointment; (*Computer*) log on. **A∼ung** *f* announcement; (*Admin*) registration; (*Sch*) enrolment
anmerk|en *vt sep* mark; **sich** (*dat*) **etw a∼en lassen** show sth. **A∼ung** *f* **-, -en** note
Anmut *f* **-** grace; (*Charme*) charm
anmutig *a* graceful
annähen *vt sep* sew on
annäher|nd *a* approximate. **A∼ungsversuche** *mpl* advances
Annahme *f* **-, -n** acceptance; (*Adoption*) adoption; (*Vermutung*) assumption
annehm|bar *a* acceptable. **a∼en**† *vt sep* accept; (*adoptieren*) adopt; acquire <*Gewohnheit*>; (*sich zulegen, vermuten*) assume; **angenommen, dass** assuming that. **A∼lichkeiten** *fpl* comforts
Anno *adv* **A∼ 1920** in the year 1920
Annon|ce /a'nõ:sə/ *f* **-, -n** advertisement. **a∼cieren** /-'si:-/ *vt/i* (*haben*) advertise
annullieren *vt* annul; cancel
Anomalie *f* **-, -n** anomaly
anonym *a* anonymous
Anorak *m* **-s, -s** anorak
anordn|en *vt sep* arrange; (*befehlen*) order. **A∼ung** *f* arrangement; order
anorganisch *a* inorganic
anormal *a* abnormal
anpass|en *vt sep* try on; (*angleichen*) adapt (*dat* to); **sich a∼** adapt (*dat* to). **A∼ung** *f* **-** adaptation. **a∼ungsfähig** *a* adaptable. **A∼ungsfähigkeit** *f* adaptability
Anpfiff *m* (*Sport*) kick-off
Anprall *m* **-[e]s** impact. **a∼en** *vi sep* (*sein*) strike (**an etw** *acc* sth)
anpreisen† *vt sep* commend
Anprob|e *f* fitting. **a∼ieren** *vt sep* try on
anrechnen *vt sep* count (**als** as); (*berechnen*) charge for; (*verrechnen*) allow <*Summe*>
Anrecht *nt* right (**auf** + *acc* to)
Anrede *f* [form of] address. **a∼n** *vt sep* address; speak to
anreg|en *vt sep* stimulate; (*ermuntern*) encourage (**zu** to); (*vorschlagen*) suggest. **a∼end** *a* stimulating. **A∼ung** *f* stimulation; (*Vorschlag*) suggestion
Anreise *f* journey; (*Ankunft*) arrival. **a∼n** *vi sep* (*sein*) arrive
Anreiz *m* incentive
Anrichte *f* **-, -n** sideboard. **a∼n** *vt sep* (*Culin*) prepare; (*garnieren*) garnish (**mit** with); (*verursachen*) cause
anrüchig *a* disreputable
Anruf *m* call. **A∼beantworter** *m* **-s,-** answering machine. **a∼en**† *v sep* ● *vt* call to; (*bitten*) call on (**um** for); (*Teleph*) ring ● *vi* (*haben*) ring (**bei jdm** s.o.)
anrühren *vt sep* touch; (*verrühren*) mix
ans *prep* = **an das**
Ansage *f* announcement. **a∼n** *vt sep* announce
ansamm|eln *vt sep* collect; (*anhäufen*) accumulate; **sich a∼eln** collect; (*sich häufen*) accumulate; <*Leute:*> gather. **A∼lung** *f* collection; (*Menschen-*) crowd
ansässig *a* resident
Ansatz *m* beginning; (*Versuch*) attempt
anschaffen *vt sep* [**sich** *dat*] **etw a∼** acquire/(*kaufen*) buy sth
anschalten *vt sep* switch on

ạnschau|en *vt sep* look at. **a~lich** *a* vivid, *adv* -ly. **A~ung** *f* **-, -en** (*fig*) view

Ạnschein *m* appearance. **a~end** *adv* apparently

ạnschirren *vt sep* harness

Ạnschlag *m* notice; (*Vor-*) estimate; (*Überfall*) attack (**auf** + *acc* on); (*Mus*) touch; (*Techn*) stop. **a~en**† *v sep* ● *vt* put up <*Aushang*>; strike <*Note, Taste*>; cast on <*Masche*>; (*beschädigen*) chip ● *vi* (*haben*) strike/(*stoßen*) knock (**an** + *acc* against); (*wirken*) be effective ● *vi* (*sein*) knock (**an** + *acc* against)

ạnschließen† *v sep* ● *vt* connect (**an** + *acc* to); (*zufügen*) add; **sich a~ an** (+ *acc*) (*anstoßen*) adjoin; (*folgen*) follow; (*sich anfreunden*) become friendly with; **sich jdm a~** join s.o. ● *vi* (*haben*) **a~ an** (+ *acc*) adjoin; (*folgen*) follow. **a~d** *a* adjoining; (*zeitlich*) following ● *adv* afterwards

Ạnschluss *m* connection; (*Kontakt*) contact; **A~ finden** make friends; **im A~ an** (+ *acc*) after

ạnschmiegsam *a* affectionate

ạnschmieren *vt sep* smear

ạnschnallen *vt sep* strap on; **sich a~** fasten one's seat-belt

ạnschneiden† *vt sep* cut into; broach <*Thema*>

ạnschreiben† *vt sep* write (**an** + *acc* on); (*Comm*) put on s.o.'s account; (*sich wenden*) write to

Ạnschrift *f* address

ạnschuldig|en *vt sep* accuse. **A~ung** *f* **-, -en** accusation

ạnschwellen† *vi sep* (*sein*) swell

ạnsehen† *vt sep* look at; (*einschätzen*) regard (**als** as); [**sich** *dat*] **etw a~** look at sth; (*TV*) watch sth. **A~** *nt* **-s** respect; (*Ruf*) reputation

ạnsehnlich *a* considerable

ạnsetzen *v sep* ● *vt* join (**an** + *acc* to); (*veranschlagen*) estimate ● *vi* (*haben*) (*anbrennen*) burn; **zum Sprung a~** get ready to jump

Ạnsicht *f* view; **meiner A~ nach** in my view; **zur A~** (*Comm*) on approval. **A~s[post]karte** *f* picture postcard. **A~ssache** *f* matter of opinion

ạnsiedeln (sich) *vr sep* settle

ansọnsten *adv* apart from that

ạnspannen *vt sep* hitch up; (*anstrengen*) strain; tense <*Muskel*>

Ạnspielung *f* **-, -en** allusion; hint

Ạnspitzer *m* **-s,-** pencil-sharpener

Ạnsprache *f* address

ạnsprechen† *v sep* ● *vt* speak to; (*fig*) appeal to ● *vi* (*haben*) respond (**auf** + *acc* to)

ạnspringen† *v sep* ● *vt* jump at ● *vi* (*sein*) (*Auto*) start

Ạnspruch *m* claim/(*Recht*) right (**auf** + *acc* to); **A~ haben** be entitled (**auf** + *acc* to); **in A~ nehmen** make use of; (*erfordern*) demand; take up <*Zeit*>; occupy <*Person*>; **hohe A~̈e stellen** be very demanding. **a~slos** *a* undemanding. **a~svoll** *a* demanding; (*kritisch*) discriminating; (*vornehm*) up-market

ạnstacheln *vt sep* (*fig*) spur on

Ạnstalt *f* **-, -en** institution

Ạnstand *m* decency; (*Benehmen*) [good] manners *pl*

ạnständig *a* decent; (*ehrbar*) respectable; (*richtig*) proper

ạnstandslos *adv* without any trouble

ạnstarren *vt sep* stare at

anstạtt *conj & prep* (+ *gen*) instead of

ạnsteck|en *v sep* ● *vt* pin (**an** + *acc* to/on); put on <*Ring*>; (*anzünden*) light; (*in Brand stecken*) set fire to; (*Med*) infect; **sich a~en** catch an infection (**bei**

from) ● *vi* (*haben*) be infectious. **a~end** *a* infectious. **A~ung** *f* **-, -en** infection

anstehen† *vi sep* (*haben*) queue

anstelle *prep* (+ *gen*) instead of

anstell|en *vt sep* put, stand (**an** + *acc* against); (*einstellen*) employ; (*anschalten*) turn on; (*tun*) do; **sich a~en** queue [up]. **A~ung** *f* employment; (*Stelle*) job

Anstieg *m* **-[e]s, -e** climb; (*fig*) rise

anstiften *vt sep* cause; (*anzetteln*) instigate

Anstoß *m* (*Anregung*) impetus; (*Stoß*) knock; (*Fußball*) kick-off; **A~ erregen** give offence (**an** + *dat* at). **a~en†** *v sep* ● *vt* knock; (*mit dem Ellbogen*) nudge ● *vi* (*sein*) knock (**an** + *acc* against) ● *vi* (*haben*) adjoin (**an etw** *acc* sth); **a~en auf** (+ *acc*) drink to; **mit der Zunge a~en** lisp

anstößig *a* offensive

anstrahlen *vt sep* floodlight

anstreichen† *vt sep* paint; (*anmerken*) mark

anstreng|en *vt sep* strain; (*ermüden*) tire; **sich a~en** exert oneself; (*sich bemühen*) make an effort (**zu** to). **a~end** *a* strenuous; (*ermüdend*) tiring. **A~ung** *f* **-, -en** strain; (*Mühe*) effort

Anstrich *m* coat [of paint]

Ansturm *m* rush; (*Mil*) assault

Ansuchen *nt* **-s,-** request

Antarktis *f* **-** Antarctic

Anteil *m* share; **A~ nehmen** take an interest (**an** + *dat* in). **A~nahme** *f* **-** interest (**an** + *dat* in); (*Mitgefühl*) sympathy

Antenne *f* **-, -n** aerial

Anthologie *f* **-, -n** anthology

Anthrax *m* **-** anthrax

Anthropologie *f* **-** anthropology

Anti|alkoholiker *m* teetotaller. **A~biotikum** *nt* **-s, -ka** antibiotic

antik *a* antique. **A~e** *f* **-** [classical] antiquity

Antikörper *m* antibody

Antilope *f* **-, -n** antelope

Antiquariat *nt* **-[e]s, -e** antiquarian bookshop

Antiquitäten *fpl* antiques. **A~händler** *m* antique dealer

Antrag *m* **-[e]s,¨-e** proposal; (*Pol*) motion; (*Gesuch*) application. **A~steller** *m* **-s,-** applicant

antreffen† *vt sep* find

antreten† *v sep* ● *vt* start; take up <*Amt*> ● *vi* (*sein*) line up

Antrieb *m* urge; (*Techn*) drive; **aus eigenem A~** of one's own accord

Antritt *m* start; **bei A~ eines Amtes** when taking office

antun† *vt sep* **jdm etw a~** do sth to s.o.; **sich** (*dat*) **etwas a~** take one's own life

Antwort *f* **-, -en** answer, reply (**auf** + *acc* to). **a~en** *vt/i* (*haben*) answer (**jdm** s.o.)

anvertrauen *vt sep* entrust/ (*mitteilen*) confide (**jdm** to s.o.)

Anwalt *m* **-[e]s,¨-e, Anwältin** *f* **-, -nen** lawyer; (*vor Gericht*) counsel

Anwandlung *f* **-, -en** fit (**von** of)

Anwärter(in) *m(f)* candidate

anweis|en† *vt sep* assign (*dat* to); (*beauftragen*) instruct. **A~ung** *f* instruction; (*Geld-*) money order

anwend|en *vt sep* apply (**auf** + *acc* to); (*gebrauchen*) use. **A~ung** *f* application; use

anwerben† *vt sep* recruit

Anwesen *nt* **-s,-** property

anwesen|d *a* present (**bei** at); **die A~den** those present. **A~heit** *f* **-** presence

anwidern *vt sep* disgust

Anwohner *mpl* residents

Anzahl *f* number

anzahl|en *vt sep* pay a deposit on. **A~ung** *f* deposit

anzapfen *vt sep* tap

Anzeichen *nt* sign

Anzeige *f* **-, -n** announcement; (*Inserat*) advertisement; **A~ erstatten gegen jdn** report s.o. to the police. **a~n** *vt sep* announce; (*inserieren*) advertise; (*melden*) report [to the police]; (*angeben*) indicate

anzieh|en† *vt sep* ● *vt* attract; (*festziehen*) tighten; put on <*Kleider, Bremse*>; (*ankleiden*) dress; **sich a~en** get dressed. **a~end** *a* attractive. **A~ungskraft** *f* attraction; (*Phys*) gravity

Anzug *m* suit

anzüglich *a* suggestive

anzünden *vt sep* light; (*in Brand stecken*) set fire to

anzweifeln *vt sep* question

apart *a* striking

Apathie *f* - apathy

apathisch *a* apathetic

Aperitif *m* **-s, -s** aperitif

Apfel *m* **-s,̈** apple

Apfelsine *f* **-, -n** orange

Apostel *m* **-s,-** apostle

Apostroph *m* **-s, -e** apostrophe

Apothek|e *f* **-, -n** pharmacy. **A~er(in)** *m* **-s,-** (*f* **-, -nen**) pharmacist, [dispensing] chemist

Apparat *m* **-[e]s, -e** device; (*Phot*) camera; (*Radio, TV*) set; (*Teleph*) telephone; **am A~!** speaking!

Appell *m* **-s, -e** appeal; (*Mil*) roll-call. **a~ieren** *vi* (*haben*) appeal (**an** + *acc* to)

Appetit *m* **-s** appetite; **guten A~!** enjoy your meal! **a~lich** *a* appetizing

Applaus *m* **-es** applause

Aprikose *f* **-, -n** apricot

April *m* **-[s]** April

Aquarell *nt* **-s, -e** water-colour

Aquarium *nt* **-s, -ien** aquarium

Äquator *m* **-s** equator

Ära *f* - era

Araber(in) *m* **-s,-** (*f* **-, -nen**) Arab

arabisch *a* Arab; (*Geog*) Arabian; <*Ziffer*> Arabic

Arbeit *f* **-, -en** work; (*Anstellung*) employment, job; (*Aufgabe*) task; (*Sch*) [written] test; (*Abhandlung*) treatise; (*Qualität*) workmanship; **sich an die A~ machen** set to work; **sich** (*dat*) **viel A~ machen** go to a lot of trouble. **a~en** *v sep* ● *vi* (*haben*) work (**an** + *dat* on) ● *vt* make. **A~er(in)** *m* **-s,-** (*f* **-, -nen**) worker; (*Land-, Hilfs-*) labourer. **A~erklasse** *f* working class

Arbeit|geber *m* **-s,-** employer. **A~nehmer** *m* **-s,-** employee

Arbeits|amt *nt* employment exchange. **A~erlaubnis, A~genehmigung** *f* work permit. **A~kraft** *f* worker. **a~los** *a* unemployed; **~los sein** be out of work. **A~lose(r)** *m/f* unemployed person; **die A~losen** the unemployed *pl*. **A~losenunterstützung** *f* unemployment benefit. **A~losigkeit** *f* - unemployment

arbeitsparend *a* labour-saving

Arbeitsplatz *m* job

Archäo|loge *m* **-n, -n** archaeologist. **A~logie** *f* - archaeology

Arche *f* - **die A~ Noah** Noah's Ark

Architek|t(in) *m* **-en, -en** (*f* **-, -nen**) architect. **a~tonisch** *a* architectural. **A~tur** *f* - architecture

Archiv *nt* **-s, -e** archives *pl*

Arena *f* **-, -nen** arena

arg *a* bad; (*groß*) terrible

Argentin|ien /-iən/ *nt* **-s** Argentina. **a~isch** *a* Argentinian

Ärger *m* **-s** annoyance; (*Unannehmlichkeit*) trouble. **ä~lich** *a* annoyed; (*leidig*) annoying; **ä~lich sein** be annoyed. **ä~n** *vt* annoy; (*necken*) tease; **sich ä~n** get annoyed (**über jdn/etw** with s.o./ about sth). **Ä~nis** *nt* **-ses, -se** annoyance; **öffentliches Ä~nis** public nuisance

Arglist *f* - malice

arglos *a* unsuspecting

Argument *nt* **-[e]s, -e** argument. **a~ieren** *vi* (*haben*) argue (**dass** that)
Arie /ˈa:ri̯ə/ *f* **-, -n** aria
Aristo|krat *m* **-en, -en** aristocrat. **A~kratie** *f* **-** aristocracy. **a~kratisch** *a* aristocratic
Arkt|is *f* **-** Arctic. **a~isch** *a* Arctic
arm *a* poor
Arm *m* **-[e]s, -e** arm; **jdn auf den Arm nehmen** [!] pull s.o.'s leg
Armaturenbrett *nt* instrument panel; (*Auto*) dashboard
Armband *nt* (*pl* **-bänder**) bracelet; (*Uhr-*) watch-strap. **A~uhr** *f* wrist-watch
Arm|e(r) *m*/*f* poor man/woman; **die A~en** the poor *pl*
Armee *f* **-, -n** army
Ärmel *m* **-s,-** sleeve. **Ä~kanal** *m* [English] Channel. **ä~los** *a* sleeveless
Arm|lehne *f* arm. **A~leuchter** *m* candelabra
ärmlich *a* poor; (*elend*) miserable
armselig *a* miserable
Armut *f* **-** poverty
Arran|gement /arãʒəˈmã:/ *nt* **-s, -s** arrangement. **a~gieren** /-ˈʒi:rən/ *vt* arrange
arrogant *a* arrogant
Arsch *m* **-[e]s,¨-e** (*vulg*) arse
Arsen *nt* **-s** arsenic
Art *f* **-, -en** manner; (*Weise*) way; (*Natur*) nature; (*Sorte*) kind; (*Biol*) species; **auf diese Art** in this way
Arterie /-i̯ə/ *f* **-, -n** artery
Arthritis *f* **-** arthritis
artig *a* well-behaved
Artikel *m* **-s,-** article
Artillerie *f* **-** artillery
Artischocke *f* **-, -n** artichoke
Arznei *f* **-, -en** medicine
Arzt *m* **-[e]s,¨-e** doctor
Ärzt|in *f* **-, -nen** [woman] doctor. **ä~lich** *a* medical
As* *nt* **-ses, -se** *s.* **Ass**
Asbest *m* **-[e]s** asbestos
Asche *f* **-** ash. **A~nbecher** *m* ashtray. **A~rmittwoch** *m* Ash Wednesday
Asiat|(in) *m* **-en, -en** (*f* **-, -nen**) Asian. **a~isch** *a* Asian
Asien /ˈa:zi̯ən/ *nt* **-s** Asia
asozial *a* antisocial
Aspekt *m* **-[e]s, -e** aspect
Asphalt *m* **-[e]s** asphalt. **a~ieren** *vt* asphalt
Ass *nt* **-es, -e** ace
Assistent(in) *m* **-en, -en** (*f* **-, -nen**) assistant
Ast *m* **-[e]s,¨-e** branch
ästhetisch *a* aesthetic
Asth|ma *nt* **-s** asthma. **a~matisch** *a* asthmatic
Astro|loge *m* **-n, -n** astrologer. **A~logie** *f* **-** astrology. **A~naut** *m* **-en, -en** astronaut. **A~nomie** *f* **-** astronomy
Asyl *nt* **-s, -e** home; (*Pol*) asylum. **A~ant** *m* **-en, -en** asylum-seeker
Atelier /-ˈli̯e:/ *nt* **-s, -s** studio
Atem *m* **-s** breath. **a~los** *a* breathless. **A~zug** *m* breath
Atheist *m* **-en, -en** atheist
Äther *m* **-s** ether
Äthiopien /-i̯ən/ *nt* **-s** Ethiopia
Athlet|(in) *m* **-en, -en** (*f* **-, -nen**) athlete. **a~isch** *a* athletic
Atlant|ik *m* **-s** Atlantic. **a~isch** *a* Atlantic; **der A~ische Ozean** the Atlantic Ocean
Atlas *m* **-lasses, -lanten** atlas
atmen *vt/i* (*haben*) breathe
Atmosphäre *f* **-, -n** atmosphere
Atmung *f* **-** breathing
Atom *nt* **-s, -e** atom. **A~bombe** *f* atom bomb. **A~krieg** *m* nuclear war
Atten|tat *nt* **-[e]s, -e** assassination attempt. **A~täter** *m* assassin
Attest *nt* **-[e]s, -e** certificate
Attrak|tion /-ˈtsi̯o:n/ *f* **-, -en** attraction. **a~tiv** *a* attractive
Attribut *nt* **-[e]s, -e** attribute

ätzen *vt* corrode; (*Med*) cauterize; (*Kunst*) etch. **ä~d** *a* corrosive; <*Spott*> caustic

au *int* ouch; **au fein!** oh good!

Aubergine /obɛr'ʒi:nə/ *f* **-, -n** aubergine

auch *adv & conj* also, too; (*außerdem*) what's more; (*selbst*) even; **a~ wenn** even if; **sie weiß es a~ nicht** she doesn't know either; **wer/wie/was a~ immer** whoever/however/whatever

Audienz *f* **-, -en** audience

audiovisuell *a* audio-visual

Auditorium *nt* **-s, -ien** (*Univ*) lecture hall

auf

● *preposition (+ dative)*

····➤ (*nicht unter*) on. **auf dem Tisch** on the table. **auf Deck** on deck. **auf der Erde** on earth. **auf der Welt** in the world. **auf der Straße** in the street

····➤ (*bei Institution, Veranstaltung usw.*) at; (*bei Gebäude, Zimmer*) in. **auf der Schule/Uni** at school/university. **auf einer Party/Hochzeit** at a party/wedding. **Geld auf der Bank haben** have money in the bank. **sie ist auf ihrem Zimmer** she's in her room. **auf Urlaub** on holiday

● *preposition (+ accusative)*

····➤ (*nicht unter*) on[to]. **er legte das Buch auf den Tisch** he laid the book on the table. **auf eine Mauer steigen** climb onto a wall. **auf die Straße gehen** go [out] into the street

····➤ (*bei Institution, Veranstaltung usw.*) to. **auf eine Party/die Toilette gehen** go to a party/the toilet. **auf die Schule/Uni gehen** go to school/university. **auf Urlaub schicken** send on holiday

····➤ (*bei Entfernung*) **auf 10 km [Entfernung] zu sehen/hören** visible/audible for [a distance of] 10 km

····➤ (*zeitlich*) (*wie lange*) for; (*bis*) until; (*wann*) on. **auf Jahre [hinaus]** for years [to come]. **auf ein paar Tage** for a few days. **etw auf nächsten Mittwoch verschieben** postpone sth until next Wednesday. **das fällt auf einen Montag** it falls on a Monday

····➤ (*Art und Weise*) in. **auf diese [Art und] Weise** in this way. **auf Deutsch/Englisch** in German/English

····➤ (*aufgrund*) **auf Wunsch** on request. **auf meine Bitte** on *or* at my request. **auf Befehl** on command

····➤ (*Proportion*) to. **ein Teelöffel auf einen Liter Wasser** one teaspoon to one litre of water. **auf die Sekunde/den Millimeter [genau]** [precise] to the nearest second/millimetre

····➤ (*Toast*) to. **auf deine Gesundheit!** your health!

● *adverb*

····➤ (*aufgerichtet, aufgestanden*) up. **auf!** (*steh auf!*) up you get! **auf und ab** (*hin und her*) up and down

····➤ (*aufsetzen*) **Helm/Hut/Brille auf!** helmet/hat/glasses on!

····➤ (*geöffnet, offen*) open. **Fenster/Mund auf!** open the window/your mouth!

aufatmen *vi sep* (*haben*) heave a sigh of relief

aufbahren *vt sep* lay out

Aufbau *m* construction; (*Struktur*) structure. **a~en** *v sep* ● *vt* construct, build; (*errichten*) erect; (*schaffen*) build up; (*arrangieren*) arrange; **sich a~en** (*fig*) be based (**auf** + *dat* on) ● *vi* (*haben*) be based (**auf** + *dat* on)

aufbauschen *vt sep* puff out; (*fig*) exaggerate

aufbekommen† *vt sep* get open; (*Sch*) be given [as homework]

aufbessern *vt sep* improve; (*erhöhen*) increase

aufbewahr|en *vt sep* keep; (*lagern*) store. **A~ung** *f* - safe keeping; storage; (*Gepäck-*) left-luggage office

aufblas|bar *a* inflatable. **a~en**† *vt sep* inflate

aufbleiben† *vi sep* (*sein*) stay open; <*Person:*> stay up

aufblenden *vt/i sep* (*haben*) (*Auto*) switch to full beam

aufblühen *vi sep* (*sein*) flower

aufbocken *vt sep* jack up

aufbrauchen *vt sep* use up

aufbrechen† *v sep* ●*vt* break open ●*vi* (*sein*) <*Knospe:*> open; (*sich aufmachen*) set out, start

aufbringen† *vt sep* raise <*Geld*>; find <*Kraft*>

Aufbruch *m* start, departure

aufbrühen *vt sep* make <*Tee*>

aufbürden *vt sep* **jdm etw a~** (*fig*) burden s.o. with sth

aufdecken *vt sep* (*auflegen*) put on; (*abdecken*) uncover; (*fig*) expose

aufdrehen *vt sep* turn on

aufdringlich *a* persistent

aufeinander *adv* one on top of the other; <*schießen*> at each other; <*warten*> for each other; **a~ folgend** successive; <*Tage*> consecutive.

Aufenthalt *m* stay; **10 Minuten A~ haben** <*Zug:*> stop for 10 minutes. **A~serlaubnis, A~sgenehmigung** *f* residence permit. **A~sraum** *m* recreation room; (*im Hotel*) lounge

Auferstehung *f* - resurrection

aufessen† *vt sep* eat up

auffahr|en† *vi sep* (*sein*) drive up; (*aufprallen*) crash, run (**auf** + *acc* into). **A~t** *f* drive; (*Autobahn-*) access road, slip road; (*Bergfahrt*) ascent

auffallen† *vi sep* (*sein*) be conspicuous; **unangenehm a~** make a bad impression

auffällig *a* conspicuous

auffangen† *vt sep* catch; pick up

auffass|en *vt sep* understand; (*deuten*) take. **A~ung** *f* understanding; (*Ansicht*) view

aufforder|n *vt sep* ask; (*einladen*) invite. **A~ung** *f* request; invitation

auffrischen *v sep* ●*vt* freshen up; revive <*Erinnerung*>; **seine Englischkenntnisse a~** brush up one's English

aufführ|en *vt sep* perform; (*angeben*) list; **sich a~en** behave. **A~ung** *f* performance

auffüllen *vt sep* fill up

Aufgabe *f* task; (*Rechen-*) problem; (*Verzicht*) giving up; **A~n** (*Sch*) homework *sg*

Aufgang *m* way up; (*Treppe*) stairs *pl*; (*Astr*) rise

aufgeben† *v sep* ●*vt* give up; post <*Brief*>; send <*Telegramm*>; place <*Bestellung*>; register <*Gepäck*>; put in the paper <*Annonce*>; **jdm eine Aufgabe a~** set s.o. a task; **jdm Suppe a~** serve s.o. with soup ●*vi* (*haben*) give up

Aufgebot *nt* contingent (**an** + *dat* of); (*Relig*) banns *pl*

aufgedunsen *a* bloated

aufgehen† *vi sep* (*sein*) open; (*sich lösen*) come undone; <*Teig, Sonne:*> rise; <*Saat:*> come up; (*Math*) come out exactly; **in Flammen a~** go up in flames

aufgelegt *a* **gut/schlecht a~ sein** be in a good/bad mood

aufgeregt *a* excited; (*erregt*) agitated

aufgeschlossen *a* (*fig*) openminded

aufgeweckt *a* (*fig*) bright

aufgießen† *vt sep* pour on; (*aufbrühen*) make <*Tee*>

aufgreifen† *vt sep* pick up; take up <*Vorschlag, Thema*>

aufgrụnd *prep* (+ *gen*) on the strength of

Aufguss *m* infusion

aufhaben† *v sep* ● *vt* have on; **den Mund a~** have one's mouth open; **viel a~** (*Sch*) have a lot of homework ● *vi* (*haben*) be open

aufhalten† *vt sep* hold up; (*anhalten*) stop; (*abhalten*) keep; (*offenhalten*) hold open; hold out <*Hand*>; **sich a~** stay; (*sich befassen*) spend one's time (**mit** on)

aufhäng|en *vt/i sep* (*haben*) hang up; (*henken*) hang; **sich a~en** hang oneself. **A~er** *m* **-s,-** loop

aufheben† *vt sep* pick up; (*hochheben*) raise; (*aufbewahren*) keep; (*beenden*) end; (*rückgängig machen*) lift; (*abschaffen*) abolish; (*Jur*) quash <*Urteil*>; repeal <*Gesetz*>; (*ausgleichen*) cancel out; **gut aufgehoben sein** be well looked after

aufheitern *vt sep* cheer up; **sich a~** <*Wetter:*> brighten up

aufhellen *vt sep* lighten; **sich a~** <*Himmel:*> brighten

aufhetzen *vt sep* incite

aufholen *v sep* ● *vt* make up ● *vi* (*haben*) catch up; (*zeitlich*) make up time

aufhören *vi sep* (*haben*) stop

aufklappen *vt/i sep* (*sein*) open

aufklär|en *vt sep* solve; **jdn a~en** enlighten s.o.; **sich a~en** be solved; <*Wetter:*> clear up. **A~ung** *f* solution; enlightenment; (*Mil*) reconnaissance; **sexuelle A~ung** sex education

aufkleb|en *vt sep* stick on. **A~er** *m* **-s,-** sticker

aufknöpfen *vt sep* unbutton

aufkochen *v sep* ● *vt* bring to the boil ● *vi* (*sein*) come to the boil

aufkommen† *vi sep* (*sein*) start; <*Wind:*> spring up; <*Mode:*> come in

aufkrempeln *vt sep* roll up

aufladen† *vt sep* load; (*Electr*) charge

Auflage *f* impression; (*Ausgabe*) edition; (*Zeitungs-*) circulation

auflassen† *vt sep* leave open; leave on <*Hut*>

Auflauf *m* crowd; (*Culin*) ≈ soufflé

auflegen *v sep* ● *vt* apply (**auf** + *acc* to); put down <*Hörer*>; **neu a~** reprint ● *vi* (*haben*) ring off

auflehn|en (sich) *vr sep* (*fig*) rebel. **A~ung** *f* **-** rebellion

auflesen† *vt sep* pick up

aufleuchten *vi sep* (*haben*) light up

auflös|en *vt sep* dissolve; close <*Konto*>; **sich a~en** dissolve; <*Nebel:*> clear. **A~ung** *f* dissolution; (*Lösung*) solution

aufmach|en *v sep* ● *vt* open; (*lösen*) undo; **sich a~en** set out (**nach** for) ● *vi* (*haben*) open; **jdm a~en** open the door to s.o. **A~ung** *f* **-, -en** get-up

aufmerksam *a* attentive; **a~ werden auf** (+ *acc*) notice; **jdn a~ machen auf** (+ *acc*) draw s.o.'s attention to. **A~keit** *f* **-, -en** attention; (*Höflichkeit*) courtesy

aufmuntern *vt sep* cheer up

Aufnahme *f* **-, -n** acceptance; (*Empfang*) reception; (*in Klub, Krankenhaus*) admission; (*Einbeziehung*) inclusion; (*Beginn*) start; (*Foto*) photograph; (*Film-*) shot; (*Mus*) recording; (*Band-*) tape recording. **a~fähig** *a* receptive. **A~prüfung** *f* entrance examination

aufnehmen† *vt sep* pick up; (*absorbieren*) absorb; take <*Nahrung, Foto*>; (*fassen*) hold; (*annehmen*) accept; (*leihen*) borrow; (*empfangen*) receive; (*in*

Klub, Krankenhaus) admit; (*beherbergen, geistig erfassen*) take in; (*einbeziehen*) include; (*beginnen*) take up; (*niederschreiben*) take down; (*filmen*) film, shoot; (*Mus*) record; **auf Band a~** tape[-record]

aufopfer|n *vt sep* sacrifice; **sich a~n** sacrifice oneself. **A~ung** *f* self-sacrifice

aufpassen *vi sep* (*haben*) pay attention; (*sich vorsehen*) take care; **a~ auf** (+ *acc*) look after

Aufprall *m* **-[e]s** impact. **a~en** *vi sep* (*sein*) **a~en auf** (+ *acc*) hit

aufpumpen *vt sep* pump up, inflate

aufputsch|en *vt sep* incite. **A~mittel** *nt* stimulant

aufquellen† *vi sep* (*sein*) swell

aufraffen *vt sep* pick up; **sich a~** pick oneself up; (*fig*) pull oneself together

aufragen *vi sep* (*sein*) rise [up]

aufräumen *vt/i sep* (*haben*) tidy up; (*wegräumen*) put away

aufrecht *a & adv* upright. **a~erhalten**† *vt sep* (*fig*) maintain

aufreg|en *vt* excite; (*beunruhigen*) upset; (*ärgern*) annoy; **sich a~en** get excited; (*sich erregen*) get worked up. **a~end** *a* exciting. **A~ung** *f* excitement

aufreiben† *vt sep* chafe; (*fig*) wear down. **a~d** *a* trying

aufreißen† *v sep* ● *vt* tear open; dig up <*Straße*>; open wide <*Augen, Mund*> ● *vi* (*sein*) split open

aufrichtig *a* sincere. **A~keit** *f* - sincerity

aufrollen *vt sep* roll up; (*entrollen*) unroll

aufrücken *vi sep* (*sein*) move up; (*fig*) be promoted

Aufruf *m* appeal (**an** + *dat* to). **a~en**† *vt sep* call out <*Namen*>; **jdn a~en** call s.o.'s name

Aufruhr *m* **-s, -e** turmoil; (*Empörung*) revolt

aufrühr|en *vt sep* stir up. **A~er** *m* **-s,-** rebel. **a~erisch** *a* inflammatory; (*rebellisch*) rebellious

aufrunden *vt sep* round up

aufrüsten *vi sep* (*haben*) arm

aufsagen *vt sep* recite

aufsässig *a* rebellious

Aufsatz *m* top; (*Sch*) essay

aufsaugen† *vt sep* soak up

aufschauen *vi sep* (*haben*) look up (**zu** at/(*fig*) to)

aufschichten *vt sep* stack up

aufschieben† *vt sep* slide open; (*verschieben*) put off, postpone

Aufschlag *m* impact; (*Tennis*) service; (*Hosen-*) turn-up; (*Ärmel-*) upturned cuff; (*Revers*) lapel; (*Comm*) surcharge. **a~en**† *v sep* ● *vt* open; crack <*Ei*>; (*hochschlagen*) turn up; (*errichten*) put up; (*erhöhen*) increase; cast on <*Masche*>; **sich** (*dat*) **das Knie a~en** cut [open] one's knee ● *vi* (*haben*) hit (**auf etw** *acc/dat* sth); (*Tennis*) serve; (*teurer werden*) go up

aufschließen† *v sep* ● *vt* unlock ● *vi* (*haben*) unlock the door

aufschlussreich *a* revealing; (*lehrreich*) informative

aufschneiden† *v sep* ● *vt* cut open; (*in Scheiben*) slice ● *vi* (*haben*) [!] exaggerate

Aufschnitt *m* sliced sausage, cold meat [and cheese]

aufschrauben *vt sep* screw on; (*abschrauben*) unscrew

Aufschrei *m* [sudden] cry

aufschreiben† *vt sep* write down; **jdn a~** <*Polizist*:> book s.o.

Aufschrift *f* inscription; (*Etikett*) label

Aufschub *m* delay; (*Frist*) grace

aufschürfen *vt sep* **sich** (*dat*) **das Knie a~** graze one's knee

aufschwingen† **(sich)** *vr sep* find the energy (**zu** for)
Aufschwung *m (fig)* upturn
aufsehen† *vi sep (haben)* look up (**zu** at/(*fig*) to). **A~** *nt* **-s** **A~ erregen** cause a sensation; **A~ erregend** sensational
Aufseher(in) *m* **-s,-** (*f* **-, -nen**) supervisor; (*Gefängnis-*) warder
aufsetzen *vt sep* put on; (*verfassen*) draw up; (*entwerfen*) draft; **sich a~** sit up
Aufsicht *f* supervision; (*Person*) supervisor. **A~srat** *m* board of directors
aufsperren *vt sep* open wide
aufspielen *v sep* ●*vi (haben)* play ●*vr* **sich a~** show off
aufspießen *vt sep* spear
aufspringen† *vi sep (sein)* jump up; (*aufprallen*) bounce; (*sich öffnen*) burst open
aufspüren *vt sep* track down
aufstacheln *vt sep* incite
Aufstand *m* uprising, rebellion
aufständisch *a* rebellious
aufstehen† *vi sep (sein)* get up; (*offen sein*) be open; (*fig*) rise up
aufsteigen† *vi sep (sein)* get on; <*Reiter:*> mount; <*Bergsteiger:*> climb up; (*hochsteigen*) rise [up]; (*fig: befördert werden*) rise (**zu** to); (*Sport*) be promoted
aufstell|en *vt sep* put up; (*Culin*) put on; (*postieren*) post; (*in einer Reihe*) line up; (*nominieren*) nominate; (*Sport*) select <*Mannschaft*>; make out <*Liste*>; lay down <*Regel*>; make <*Behauptung*>; set up <*Rekord*>. **A~ung** *f* nomination; (*Liste*) list
Aufstieg *m* **-[e]s, -e** ascent; (*fig*) rise; (*Sport*) promotion
Aufstoßen *nt* **-s** burping
aufstrebend *a (fig)* ambitious
Aufstrich *m* [sandwich] spread
aufstützen *vt sep* rest (**auf** + *acc* on); **sich a~** lean (**auf** + *acc* on)
Auftakt *m (fig)* start
auftauchen *vi sep (sein)* emerge; (*fig*) turn up; <*Frage:*> crop up
auftauen *vt/i sep (sein)* thaw
aufteil|en *vt sep* divide [up]. **A~ung** *f* division
auftischen *vt sep* serve [up]
Auftrag *m* **-[e]s,¨e** task; (*Kunst*) commission; (*Comm*) order; **im A~** (+ *gen*) on behalf of. **a~en**† *vt sep* apply; (*servieren*) serve; (*abtragen*) wear out; **jdm a~en** instruct s.o. (**zu** to). **A~ geber** *m* **-s,-** client
auftrennen *vt sep* unpick, undo
auftreten† *vi sep (sein)* tread; (*sich benehmen*) behave, act; (*Theat*) appear; (*die Bühne betreten*) enter; (*vorkommen*) occur
Auftrieb *m* buoyancy; (*fig*) boost
Auftritt *m (Theat)* appearance; (*auf die Bühne*) entrance; (*Szene*) scene
aufwachen *vi sep (sein)* wake up
aufwachsen† *vi sep (sein)* grow up
Aufwand *m* **-[e]s** expenditure; (*Luxus*) extravagance; (*Mühe*) trouble; **A~ treiben** be extravagant
aufwändig *a* = **aufwendig**
aufwärmen *vt sep* heat up; (*fig*) rake up; **sich a~** warm oneself; (*Sport*) warm up
Aufwartefrau *f* cleaner
aufwärts *adv* upwards; (*bergauf*) uphill; **es geht a~ mit jdm/etw** s.o./sth is improving
Aufwartung *f* **-** cleaner
aufwecken *vt sep* wake up
aufweichen *v sep* ●*vt* soften ●*vi (sein)* become soft
aufweisen† *vt sep* have, show
aufwend|en† *vt sep* spend; **Mühe a~en** take pains. **a~ig** *a* lavish; (*teuer*) expensive
aufwert|en *vt sep* revalue. **A~ung** *f* revaluation

aufwickeln *vt sep* roll up; (*auswickeln*) unwrap
Aufwiegler *m* **-s,-** agitator
aufwisch|en *vt sep* wipe up; wash <*Fußboden*>. **A~lappen** *m* floorcloth
aufwühlen *vt sep* churn up
aufzähl|en *vt sep* enumerate, list. **A~ung** *f* list
aufzeichn|en *vt sep* record; (*zeichnen*) draw. **A~ung** *f* recording; **A~ungen** notes
aufziehen† *v sep* ● *vt* pull up; hoist <*Segel*>; (*öffnen*) open; draw <*Vorhang*>; (*großziehen*) bring up; rear <*Tier*>; mount <*Bild*>; thread <*Perlen*>; wind up <*Uhr*>; ([I] *necken*) tease ● *vi* (*sein*) approach
Aufzug *m* hoist; (*Fahrstuhl*) lift, (*Amer*) elevator; (*Prozession*) procession; (*Theat*) act
Augapfel *m* eyeball
Auge *nt* **-s, -n** eye; (*Punkt*) spot; **vier A~n werfen** throw a four; **gute A~n** good eyesight; **unter vier A~n** in private; **im A~ behalten** keep in sight; (*fig*) bear in mind
Augenblick *m* moment; **A~!** just a moment! **a~lich** *a* immediate; (*derzeitig*) present ● *adv* immediately; (*derzeit*) at present
Augen|braue *f* eyebrow. **A~höhle** *f* eye socket. **A~licht** *nt* sight. **A~lid** *nt* eyelid
August *m* **-[s]** August
Auktion /-'tsio:n/ *f* **-, -en** auction
Aula *f* **-, -len** (*Sch*) [assembly] hall
Au-pair-Mädchen /o'pɛ:r-/ *nt* aupair
aus *prep* (+ *dat*) out of; (*von*) from; (*bestehend*) [made] of; **aus Angst** from or out of fear; **aus Spaß** for fun ● *adv* out; <*Licht, Radio*> off; **aus sein auf** (+ *acc*) be after; **aus und ein** in and out; **von sich aus** of one's own accord; **von mir aus** as far as I'm concerned
ausarbeiten *vt sep* work out
ausarten *vi sep* (*sein*) degenerate (**in** + *acc* into)
ausatmen *vt/i sep* (*haben*) breathe out
ausbauen *vt sep* remove; (*vergrößern*) extend; (*fig*) expand
ausbedingen† *vt sep* **sich** (*dat*) **a~** insist on; (*zur Bedingung machen*) stipulate
ausbesser|n *vt sep* mend, repair. **A~ung** *f* repair
ausbeulen *vt sep* remove the dents from; (*dehnen*) make baggy
ausbild|en *vt sep* train; (*formen*) form; (*entwickeln*) develop; **sich a~en** train (**als/zu** as); (*entstehen*) develop. **A~ung** *f* training; (*Sch*) education
ausbitten† *vt sep* **sich** (*dat*) **a~** ask for; (*verlangen*) insist on
ausblasen† *vt sep* blow out
ausbleiben† *vi sep* (*sein*) fail to appear/ <*Erfolg:*> materialize; (*nicht heimkommen*) stay out
Ausblick *m* view
ausbrech|en† *vi sep* (*sein*) break out; <*Vulkan:*> erupt; (*fliehen*) escape; **in Tränen a~en** burst into tears. **A~er** *m* runaway
ausbreit|en *vt sep* spread [out]. **A~ung** *f* spread
Ausbruch *m* outbreak; (*Vulkan-*) eruption; (*Wut-*) outburst; (*Flucht*) escape, break-out
ausbrüten *vt sep* hatch
Ausdauer *f* perseverance; (*körperlich*) stamina. **a~nd** *a* persevering; (*unermüdlich*) untiring
ausdehnen *vt sep* stretch; (*fig*) extend; **sich a~** stretch; (*Phys & fig*) expand; (*dauern*) last
ausdenken† *vt sep* **sich** (*dat*) **a~** think up; (*sich vorstellen*) imagine
Ausdruck *m* expression; (*Fach-*) term; (*Computer*) printout. **a~en** *vt sep* print

ausdrücken *vt sep* squeeze out; squeeze <*Zitrone*>; stub out <*Zigarette*>; (*äußern*) express
ausdrucks|los *a* expressionless. **a~voll** *a* expressive
auseinander *adv* apart; (*entzwei*) in pieces; **a~ falten** unfold; **a~ gehen** part; <*Linien, Meinungen:*> diverge; <*Ehe:*> break up; **a~ halten** tell apart; **a~ nehmen** take apart *or* to pieces; **a~ setzen** explain (**jdm** to s.o.); **sich a~ setzen** sit apart; (*sich aussprechen*) have it out (**mit jdm** with s.o.); come to grips (**mit einem Problem** with a problem). **A~setzung** *f* **-, -en** discussion; (*Streit*) argument
auserlesen *a* select, choice
Ausfahrt *f* drive; (*Autobahn-, Garagen-*) exit
Ausfall *m* failure; (*Absage*) cancellation; (*Comm*) loss. **a~en**† *vi sep* (*sein*) fall out; (*versagen*) fail; (*abgesagt werden*) be cancelled; **gut/schlecht a~en** turn out to be good/poor
ausfallend, ausfällig *a* abusive
ausfertig|en *vt sep* make out. **A~ung** *f* **-, -en in doppelter A~ung** in duplicate
ausfindig *a* **a~ machen** find
Ausflug *m* excursion, outing
Ausflügler *m* **-s,-** [day-]tripper
Ausfluss *m* outlet; (*Abfluss*) drain; (*Med*) discharge
ausfragen *vt sep* question
Ausfuhr *f* **-, -en** (*Comm*) export
ausführ|en *vt sep* take out; (*Comm*) export; (*erklären*) explain. **a~lich** *a* detailed ●*adv* in detail. **A~ung** *f* execution; (*Comm*) version; (*äußere*) finish; (*Qualität*) workmanship; (*Erklärung*) explanation
Ausgabe *f* issue; (*Buch-*) edition; (*Comm*) version
Ausgang *m* way out, exit; (*Flugsteig*) gate; (*Ende*) end; (*Ergebnis*) outcome. **A~spunkt** *m* starting-point. **A~ssperre** *f* curfew
ausgeben† *vt sep* hand out; issue <*Fahrkarten*>; spend <*Geld*>; **sich a~ als** pretend to be
ausgebildet *a* trained
ausgebucht *a* fully booked; <*Vorstellung*> sold out
ausgefallen *a* unusual
ausgefranst *a* frayed
ausgeglichen *a* [well-]balanced
ausgeh|en† *vi sep* (*sein*) go out; <*Haare:*> fall out; <*Vorräte, Geld:*> run out; (*verblassen*) fade; **gut/schlecht a~en** end well/badly; **davon a~en, dass** assume that. **A~verbot** *nt* curfew
ausgelassen *a* high-spirited
ausgemacht *a* agreed
ausgenommen *conj* except; **a~ wenn** unless
ausgeprägt *a* marked
ausgeschlossen *pred a* out of the question
ausgeschnitten *a* low-cut
ausgesprochen *a* marked ●*adv* decidedly
ausgestorben *a* extinct; **[wie] a~** <*Straße:*> deserted
Ausgestoßene(r) *m/f* outcast
ausgezeichnet *a* excellent
ausgiebig *a* extensive; (*ausgedehnt*) long; **a~ Gebrauch machen von** make full use of
ausgießen† *vt sep* pour out
Ausgleich *m* **-[e]s** balance; (*Entschädigung*) compensation. **a~en**† *v sep* ●*vt* balance; even out <*Höhe*>; (*wettmachen*) compensate for; **sich a~en** balance out ●*vi* (*haben*) (*Sport*) equalize. **A~streffer** *m* equalizer
ausgrab|en† *vt sep* dig up; (*Archaeol*) excavate. **A~ung** *f* **-, -en** excavation
Ausguss *m* [kitchen] sink
aushaben† *vt sep* have finished <*Buch*>

aushalten† *vt sep* bear, stand; hold <*Note*>; (*Unterhalt zahlen für*) keep; **nicht auszuhalten, nicht zum A~** unbearable

aushändigen *vt sep* hand over

aushängen[1] *vt sep* (*reg*) display; take off its hinges <*Tür*>

aushäng|en[2]† *vi sep* (*haben*) be displayed. **A~eschild** *nt* sign

ausheben† *vt sep* excavate

aushecken *vt sep* (*fig*) hatch

aushelfen† *vi sep* (*haben*) help out (**jdm** s.o.)

Aushilf|e *f* [temporary] assistant; **zur A~e** to help out. **A~skraft** *f* temporary worker. **a~sweise** *adv* temporarily

aushöhlen *vt sep* hollow out

auskennen† **(sich)** *vr sep* know one's way around; **sich mit/in etw** (*dat*) **a~** know all about sth

auskommen† *vi sep* (*sein*) manage (**mit/ohne** with/without); (*sich vertragen*) get on (**gut** well)

auskugeln *vt sep* **sich** (*dat*) **den Arm a~** dislocate one's shoulder

auskühlen *vt/i sep* (*sein*) cool

auskundschaften *vt sep* spy out

Auskunft *f* **-,¨-e** information; (*A~sstelle*) information desk/ (*Büro*) bureau; (*Teleph*) enquiries *pl*; **eine A~** a piece of information

auslachen *vt sep* laugh at

Auslage *f* [window] display; **A~n** expenses

Ausland *nt* **im/ins A~** abroad

Ausländ|er(in) *m* **-s,-** (*f* **-, -nen**) foreigner. **a~isch** *a* foreign

Auslandsgespräch *nt* international call

auslass|en† *vt sep* let out; let down <*Saum*>; (*weglassen*) leave out; (*versäumen*) miss; (*Culin*) melt; (*fig*) vent <*Ärger*> (**an** + *dat* on). **A~ungszeichen** *nt* apostrophe

Auslauf *m* run. **a~en**† *vi sep* (*sein*) run out; <*Farbe:*> run; (*Naut*) put to sea; <*Modell:*> be discontinued

ausleeren *vt sep* empty [out]

ausleg|en *vt sep* lay out; display <*Waren*>; (*auskleiden*) line (**mit** with); (*bezahlen*) pay; (*deuten*) interpret. **A~ung** *f* **-, -en** interpretation

ausleihen† *vt sep* lend; **sich** (*dat*) **a~** borrow

Auslese *f* **-** selection; (*fig*) pick; (*Elite*) elite

ausliefer|n *vt sep* hand over; (*Jur*) extradite. **A~ung** *f* handing over; (*Jur*) extradition; (*Comm*) distribution

ausloggen *vi sep* log off *or* out

auslosen *vt sep* draw lots for

auslös|en *vt sep* set off, trigger; (*fig*) cause; arouse <*Begeisterung*>; (*einlösen*) redeem; pay a ransom for <*Gefangene*>. **A~er** *m* **-s,-** trigger; (*Phot*) shutter release

Auslosung *f* draw

auslüften *vt/i sep* (*haben*) air

ausmachen *vt sep* put out; (*abschalten*) turn off; (*abmachen*) arrange; (*erkennen*) make out; (*betragen*) amount to; (*wichtig sein*) matter

Ausmaß *nt* extent; **A~e** dimensions

Ausnahm|e *f* **-, -n** exception. **A~ezustand** *m* state of emergency. **a~slos** *adv* without exception. **a~sweise** *adv* as an exception

ausnehmen† *vt sep* take out; gut <*Fisch*>; **sich gut a~** look good. **a~d** *adv* exceptionally

ausnutz|en, ausnütz|en *vt sep* exploit. **A~ung** *f* exploitation

auspacken *vt sep* unpack; (*auswickeln*) unwrap

ausplaudern *vt sep* let out, blab

ausprobieren *vt sep* try out

Auspuff *m* **-s** exhaust [system]. **A~gase** *ntpl* exhaust fumes. **A~rohr** *nt* exhaust pipe

auspusten *vt sep* blow out

ausradieren *vt sep* rub out

ausrauben *vt sep* rob

ausräuchern *vt sep* smoke out; fumigate <*Zimmer*>

ausräumen *vt sep* clear out

ausrechnen *vt sep* work out

Ausrede *f* excuse. **a~n** *v sep* ● *vi* (*haben*) finish speaking ● *vt* **jdm etw a~n** talk s.o. out of sth

ausreichen *vi sep* (*haben*) be enough. **a~d** *a* adequate

Ausreise *f* departure. **a~n** *vi sep* (*sein*) leave the country. **A~visum** *nt* exit visa

ausreißen† *v sep* ● *vt* pull *or* tear out ● *vi* (*sein*) [!] run away

ausrenken *vt sep* dislocate

ausrichten *vt sep* align; (*bestellen*) deliver; (*erreichen*) achieve; **jdm a~** tell s.o. (**dass** that); **ich soll Ihnen Grüße von X a~** X sends [you] his regards

ausrotten *vt sep* exterminate; (*fig*) eradicate

Ausruf *m* exclamation. **a~en**† *vt sep* exclaim; call out <*Namen*>; (*verkünden*) proclaim; **jdn a~en lassen** have s.o. paged. **A~ezeichen** *nt* exclamation mark

ausruhen *vt/i sep* (*haben*) rest; **sich a~** have a rest

ausrüst|en *vt sep* equip. **A~ung** *f* equipment; (*Mil*) kit

ausrutschen *vi sep* (*sein*) slip

Aussage *f* **-, -n** statement; (*Jur*) testimony, evidence; (*Gram*) predicate. **a~n** *vt/i sep* (*haben*) state; (*Jur*) give evidence, testify

ausschalten *vt sep* switch off

Ausschank *m* sale of alcoholic drinks; (*Bar*) bar

Ausschau *f* **- A~ halten nach** look out for

ausscheiden† *vi sep* (*sein*) leave; (*Sport*) drop out; (*nicht in Frage kommen*) be excluded

ausschenken *vt sep* pour out

ausscheren *vi sep* (*sein*) (*Auto*) pull out

ausschildern *vt sep* signpost

ausschimpfen *vt sep* tell off

ausschlafen† *vi/r sep* (*haben*) **[sich] a~** get enough sleep; (*morgens*) sleep late

Ausschlag *m* (*Med*) rash; **den A~ geben** (*fig*) tip the balance. **a~gebend** *a* decisive

ausschließ|en† *vt sep* lock out; (*fig*) exclude; (*entfernen*) expel. **a~lich** *a* exclusive

ausschlüpfen *vi sep* (*sein*) hatch

Ausschluss *m* exclusion; expulsion; **unter A~ der Öffentlichkeit** in camera

ausschneiden† *vt sep* cut out

Ausschnitt *m* excerpt, extract; (*Zeitungs-*) cutting; (*Hals-*) neckline

ausschöpfen *vt sep* ladle out; (*Naut*) bail out; exhaust <*Möglichkeiten*>

ausschreiben† *vt sep* write out; (*ausstellen*) make out; (*bekanntgeben*) announce; put out to tender <*Auftrag*>

Ausschreitungen *fpl* riots; (*Exzesse*) excesses

Ausschuss *m* committee; (*Comm*) rejects *pl*

ausschütten *vt sep* tip out; (*verschütten*) spill; (*leeren*) empty

aussehen† *vi sep* (*haben*) look; **wie sieht er/es aus?** what does he/it look like? **A~** *nt* **-s** appearance

außen *adv* [on the] outside; **nach a~** outwards. **A~bordmotor** *m* outboard motor. **A~handel** *m* foreign trade. **A~minister** *m* Foreign Minister. **A~politik** *f* foreign policy. **A~seite** *f* outside. **A~seiter** *m* **-s,-** outsider; (*fig*) misfit. **A~stände** *mpl* outstanding debts

außer *prep* (+ *dat*) except [for], apart from; (*außerhalb*) out of; **a~ sich** (*fig*) beside oneself ● *conj* except; **a~ wenn** unless. **a~dem** *adv* in addition, as well ● *conj* moreover

äußer|e(r,s) *a* external; <*Teil, Schicht*> outer. **Ä~e(s)** *nt* exterior; (*Aussehen*) appearance

außer|ehelich *a* extramarital. **a~gewöhnlich** *a* exceptional. **a~halb** *prep* (+ *gen*) outside ● *adv* **a~halb wohnen** live outside town

äußer|lich *a* external; (*fig*) outward. **ä~n** *vt* express; **sich ä~n** comment; (*sich zeigen*) manifest itself

außerordentlich *a* extraordinary

äußerst *adv* extremely

äußerste|(r,s) *a* outermost; (*weiteste*) furthest; (*höchste*) utmost, extreme; (*letzte*) last; (*schlimmste*) worst. **Ä~(s)** *nt* **das Ä~** the limit; (*Schlimmste*) the worst; **sein Ä~s tun** do one's utmost; **aufs Ä~** extremely

Äußerung *f* **-, -en** comment; (*Bemerkung*) remark

aussetzen *v sep* ● *vt* expose (*dat* to); abandon <*Kind*>; launch <*Boot*>; offer <*Belohnung*>; **etwas auszusetzen haben an** (+ *dat*) find fault with ● *vi* (*haben*) stop; <*Motor:*> cut out

Aussicht *f* **-, -en** view/(*fig*) prospect (**auf** + *acc* of); **weitere A~en** (*Meteorol*) further outlook *sg*. **a~slos** *a* hopeless

ausspannen *v sep* ● *vt* spread out; unhitch <*Pferd*> ● *vi* (*haben*) rest

aussperren *vt sep* lock out

ausspielen *v sep* ● *vt* play <*Karte*>; (*fig*) play off (**gegen** against) ● *vi* (*haben*) (*Kartenspiel*) lead

Aussprache *f* pronunciation; (*Gespräch*) talk

aussprechen† *vt sep* pronounce; (*äußern*) express; **sich a~** talk; come out (**für**/**gegen** in favour of/against)

Ausspruch *m* saying

ausspucken *v sep* ● *vt* spit out ● *vi* (*haben*) spit

ausspülen *vt sep* rinse out

ausstatt|en *vt sep* equip. **A~ung** *f* **-, -en** equipment; (*Innen-*) furnishings *pl*; (*Theat*) scenery and costumes *pl*

ausstehen† *v sep* ● *vt* suffer; **Angst a~** be frightened; **ich kann sie nicht a~** I can't stand her ● *vi* (*haben*) be outstanding

aussteigen† *vi sep* (*sein*) get out; (*aus Bus, Zug*) get off; **alles a~!** all change!

ausstell|en *vt sep* exhibit; (*Comm*) display; (*ausfertigen*) make out; issue <*Pass*>. **A~ung** *f* exhibition; (*Comm*) display

aussterben† *vi sep* (*sein*) die out; (*Biol*) become extinct

Aussteuer *f* trousseau

Ausstieg *m* **-[e]s, -e** exit

ausstopfen *vt sep* stuff

ausstoßen† *vt sep* emit; utter <*Fluch*>; heave <*Seufzer*>; (*ausschließen*) expel

ausstrahl|en *vt/i sep* (*sein*) radiate, emit; (*Radio, TV*) broadcast. **A~ung** *f* radiation

ausstrecken *vt sep* stretch out; put out <*Hand*>

ausstreichen† *vt sep* cross out

ausströmen *v sep* ● *vi* (*sein*) pour out; (*entweichen*) escape ● *vt* emit; (*ausstrahlen*) radiate

aussuchen *vt sep* pick, choose

Austausch *m* exchange. **a~bar** *a* interchangeable. **a~en** *vt sep* exchange; (*auswechseln*) replace

austeilen *vt sep* distribute

Auster *f* **-, -n** oyster

austragen† *vt sep* deliver; hold <*Wettkampf*>; play <*Spiel*>

Austral|ien /-i̯ən/ *nt* **-s** Australia. **A~ier(in)** *m* **-s,-** (*f* **-, -nen**) Australian. **a~isch** *a* Australian

austreiben† *vt sep* drive out; (*Relig*) exorcize

austreten† *v sep* ● *vt* stamp out; (*abnutzen*) wear down ● *vi* (*sein*) come out; (*ausscheiden*) leave (**aus etw** sth); **[mal] a~** [!] go to the loo

austrinken† *vt/i sep* (*haben*) drink up; (*leeren*) drain

Austritt *m* resignation

austrocknen *vt/i sep* (*sein*) dry out

ausüben *vt sep* practise; carry on <*Handwerk*>; exercise <*Recht*>; exert <*Druck, Einfluss*>

Ausverkauf *m* [clearance] sale. **a~t** *a* sold out

Auswahl *f* choice, selection; (*Comm*) range; (*Sport*) team

auswählen *vt sep* choose, select

Auswander|er *m* emigrant. **a~n** *vi sep* (*sein*) emigrate. **A~ung** *f* emigration

auswärt|ig *a* non-local; (*ausländisch*) foreign. **a~s** *adv* outwards; (*Sport*) away. **A~sspiel** *nt* away game

auswaschen† *vt sep* wash out

auswechseln *vt sep* change; (*ersetzen*) replace; (*Sport*) substitute

Ausweg *m* (*fig*) way out

ausweichen† *vi sep* (*sein*) get out of the way; **jdm/etw a~en** avoid/ (*sich entziehen*) evade s.o./sth

Ausweis *m* **-es, -e** pass; (*Mitglieds-, Studenten-*) card. **a~en**† *vt sep* deport; **sich a~en** prove one's identity. **A~papiere** *ntpl* identification papers. **A~ung** *f* deportation

auswendig *adv* by heart

auswerten *vt sep* evaluate

auswickeln *vt sep* unwrap

auswirk|en (sich) *vr sep* have an effect (**auf** + *acc* on). **A~ung** *f* effect; (*Folge*) consequence

auswringen *vt sep* wring out

auszahlen *vt sep* pay out; (*entlohnen*) pay off; (*abfinden*) buy out; **sich a~** (*fig*) pay off

auszählen *vt sep* count; (*Boxen*) count out

Auszahlung *f* payment

auszeichn|en *vt sep* (*Comm*) price; (*ehren*) honour; (*mit einem Preis*) award a prize to; (*Mil*) decorate; **sich a~en** distinguish oneself. **A~ung** *f* honour; (*Preis*) award; (*Mil*) decoration; (*Sch*) distinction

ausziehen† *v sep* ● *vt* pull out; (*auskleiden*) undress; take off <*Mantel, Schuhe*> ● *vi* (*sein*) move out; (*sich aufmachen*) set out

Auszug *m* departure; (*Umzug*) move; (*Ausschnitt*) extract; (*Bank-*) statement

Auto *nt* **-s, -s** car; **A~ fahren** drive; (*mitfahren*) go in the car. **A~bahn** *f* motorway

Autobiographie *f* autobiography

Auto|bus *m* bus. **A~fahrer(in)** *m*(*f*) driver, motorist. **A~fahrt** *f* drive

Autogramm *nt* **-s, -e** autograph

Automat *m* **-en, -en** automatic device; (*Münz-*) slot-machine; (*Verkaufs-*) vending-machine; (*Fahrkarten-*) machine; (*Techn*) robot. **A~ik** *f* **-** automatic mechanism; (*Auto*) automatic transmission

automatisch *a* automatic

Autonummer *f* registration number

Autopsie *f* **-, -n** autopsy

Autor *m* **-s, -en** /-'to:rən/ author

Auto|reisezug *m* Motorail. **A~rennen** *nt* motor race

Autorin *f* **-, -nen** author[ess]

Autori|sation /-'tsi̯o:n/ *f* - authorization. **A~tät** *f* -, -en authority
Auto|schlosser *m* motor mechanic. **A~skooter** /-sku:tɐ/ *m* -s,- dodgem. **A~stopp** *m* -s **per A~stopp fahren** hitch-hike. **A~verleih** *m* car hire [firm]. **A~waschanlage** *f* car wash
autsch *int* ouch
Axt *f* -,¨-e axe

Bb

B, b /be:/ *nt* - (*Mus*) B flat
Baby /'be:bi/ *nt* -s, -s baby. **B~ausstattung** *f* layette. **B~sitter** /-sɪtɐ/ *m* -s,- babysitter
Bach *m* -[e]s,¨-e stream
Backbord *nt* -[e]s port [side]
Backe *f* -, -n cheek
backen *vt/i*† (*haben*) bake; (*braten*) fry
Backenzahn *m* molar
Bäcker *m* -s,- baker. **B~ei** *f* -, -en, **B~laden** *m* baker's shop
Back|obst *nt* dried fruit. **B~ofen** *m* oven. **B~pfeife** *f* [!] slap in the face. **B~pflaume** *f* prune. **B~pulver** *nt* baking-powder. **B~stein** *m* brick
Bad *nt* -[e]s,¨-er bath; (*Zimmer*) bathroom; (*Schwimm-*) pool; (*Ort*) spa
Bade|anstalt *f* swimming baths *pl*. **B~anzug** *m* swim-suit. **B~hose** *f* swimming trunks *pl*. **B~kappe** *f* bathing-cap. **B~mantel** *m* bathrobe. **b~n** *vi* (*haben*) have a bath; (*im Meer*) bathe ● *vt* bath; (*waschen*) bathe. **B~ort** *m* seaside resort. **B~wanne** *f* bath. **B~zimmer** *nt* bathroom
Bagger *m* -s,- excavator; (*Nass-*) dredger. **B~see** *m* flooded gravel-pit
Bahn *f* -, -en path; (*Astr*) orbit; (*Sport*) track; (*einzelne*) lane; (*Rodel-*) run; (*Stoff-*) width; (*Eisen-*) railway; (*Zug*) train; (*Straßen-*) tram. **b~brechend** *a* (*fig*) pioneering. **B~hof** *m* [railway] station. **B~steig** *m* -[e]s, -e platform. **B~übergang** *m* level crossing
Bahre *f* -, -n stretcher
Baiser /bɛ'ze:/ *nt* -s, -s meringue
Bake *f* -, -n (*Naut, Aviat*) beacon
Bakterien /-i̯ən/ *fpl* bacteria
Balanc|e /ba'lã:sə/ *f* - balance. **b~ieren** *vt/i* (*haben/sein*) balance
bald *adv* soon; (*fast*) almost
Baldachin /-xi:n/ *m* -s, -e canopy
bald|ig *a* early; <*Besserung*> speedy. **b~möglichst** *adv* as soon as possible
Balg *nt & m* -[e]s,¨-er [!] brat
Balkan *m* -s Balkans *pl*
Balken *m* -s,- beam
Balkon /bal'kõ:/ *m* -s, -s balcony; (*Theat*) circle
Ball[1] *m* -[e]s,¨-e ball
Ball[2] *m* -[e]s,¨-e (*Tanz*) ball
Ballade *f* -, -n ballad
Ballast *m* -[e]s ballast. **B~stoffe** *mpl* roughage *sg*
Ballen *m* -s,- bale; (*Anat*) ball of the hand/(*Fuß-*) foot; (*Med*) bunion
Ballerina *f* -, -nen ballerina
Ballett *nt* -s, -e ballet
Ballon /ba'lõ:/ *m* -s, -s balloon
Balsam *m* -s balm
Balt|ikum *nt* -s Baltic States *pl*. **b~isch** *a* Baltic
Bambus *m* -ses, -se bamboo
banal *a* banal
Banane *f* -, -n banana
Banause *m* -n, -n philistine

Band¹ *nt* **-[e]s,¨-er** ribbon; (*Naht-, Ton-, Ziel-*) tape; **am laufenden B~** [!] non-stop
Band² *m* **-[e]s,¨-e** volume
Band³ *nt* **-[e]s, -e** (*fig*) bond
Band⁴ /bɛnt/ *f* **-, -s** [jazz] band
Bandag|e /ban'da:ʒə/ *f* **-, -n** bandage. **b~ieren** *vt* bandage
Bande *f* **-, -n** gang
bändigen *vt* control, restrain; (*zähmen*) tame
Bandit *m* **-en, -en** bandit
Band|maß *nt* tape-measure. **B~scheibe** *f* (*Anat*) disc. **B~wurm** *m* tapeworm
Bang|e *f* **B~e haben** be afraid; **jdm B~e machen** frighten s.o. **b~en** *vi* (*haben*) fear (**um** for)
Banjo *nt* **-s, -s** banjo
Bank¹ *f* **-,¨-e** bench
Bank² *f* **-, -en** (*Comm*) bank. **B~einzug** *m* direct debit
Bankett *nt* **-s, -e** banquet
Bankier /baŋ'kie:/ *m* **-s, -s** banker
Bankkonto *nt* bank account
Bankrott *m* **-s, -s** bankruptcy. **b~** *a* bankrupt
Bankwesen *nt* banking
Bann *m* **-[e]s, -e** (*fig*) spell. **b~en** *vt* exorcize; (*abwenden*) avert; **[wie] gebannt** spellbound
Banner *nt* **-s,-** banner
bar *a* (*rein*) sheer; <*Gold*> pure; **b~es Geld** cash; **[in] bar bezahlen** pay cash
Bar *f* **-, -s** bar
Bär *m* **-en, -en** bear
Baracke *f* **-, -n** (*Mil*) hut
Barb|ar *m* **-en, -en** barbarian. **b~arisch** *a* barbaric
bar|fuß *adv* barefoot. **B~geld** *nt* cash
barmherzig *a* merciful
barock *a* baroque. **B~** *nt & m* **-[s]** baroque
Barometer *nt* **-s,-** barometer
Baron *m* **-s, -e** baron. **B~in** *f* **-, -nen** baroness
Barren *m* **-s,-** (*Gold-*) bar, ingot; (*Sport*) parallel bars *pl.* **B~gold** *nt* gold bullion
Barriere *f* **-, -n** barrier
Barrikade *f* **-, -n** barricade
barsch *a* gruff
Barsch *m* **-[e]s, -e** (*Zool*) perch
Bart *m* **-[e]s,¨-e** beard; (*der Katze*) whiskers *pl*
bärtig *a* bearded
Barzahlung *f* cash payment
Basar *m* **-s, -e** bazaar
Base¹ *f* **-, -n** [female] cousin
Base² *f* **-, -n** (*Chem*) alkali, base
Basel *nt* **-s** Basle
basieren *vi* (*haben*) be based (**auf** + *dat* on)
Basilikum *nt* **-s** basil
Basis *f* **-,Basen** base; (*fig*) basis
basisch *a* (*Chem*) alkaline
Bask|enmütze *f* beret. **b~isch** *a* Basque
Bass *m* **-es,¨-e** bass
Bassin /ba'sɛ̃:/ *nt* **-s, -s** pond; (*Brunnen-*) basin; (*Schwimm-*) pool
Bassist *m* **-en, -en** bass player; (*Sänger*) bass
Bast *m* **-[e]s** raffia
basteln *vt* make ● *vi* (*haben*) do handicrafts
Batterie *f* **-, -n** battery
Bau¹ *m* **-[e]s, -e** burrow; (*Fuchs-*) earth
Bau² *m* **-[e]s, -ten** construction; (*Gebäude*) building; (*Auf-*) structure; (*Körper-*) build; (*B~stelle*) building site. **B~arbeiten** *fpl* building work *sg*; (*Straßen-*) road-works
Bauch *m* **-[e]s, Bäuche** abdomen, belly; (*Magen*) stomach; (*Bauchung*) bulge. **b~ig** *a* bulbous. **B~nabel** *m* navel. **B~redner** *m* ventriloquist. **B~schmerzen** *mpl* stomach-ache *sg*. **B~speicheldrüse** *f* pancreas
bauen *vt* build; (*konstruieren*) construct ● *vi* (*haben*) build (**an**

etw *dat* sth); **b~ auf** (+ *acc*) (*fig*) rely on
Bauer[1] *m* **-s, -n** farmer; (*Schach*) pawn
Bauer[2] *nt* **-s,-** [bird]cage
bäuerlich *a* rustic
Bauern|haus *nt* farmhouse. **B~hof** *m* farm
bau|fällig *a* dilapidated. **B~genehmigung** *f* planning permission. **B~gerüst** *nt* scaffolding. **B~jahr** *nt* year of construction. **B~kunst** *f* architecture. **b~lich** *a* structural
Baum *m* **-[e]s, Bäume** tree
baumeln *vi* (*haben*) dangle
bäumen (sich) *vr* rear [up]
Baum|schule *f* [tree] nursery. **B~wolle** *f* cotton
Bausch *m* **-[e]s, Bäusche** wad; **in B~ und Bogen** (*fig*) wholesale. **b~en** *vt* puff out
Bau|sparkasse *f* building society. **B~stein** *m* building brick. **B~stelle** *f* building site; (*Straßen-*) roadworks *pl*. **B~unternehmer** *m* building contractor
Bayer|(in) *m* **-s, -n** (*f* **-, -nen**) Bavarian. **B~n** *nt* **-s** Bavaria
bay[e]risch *a* Bavarian
Bazillus *m* **-, -len** bacillus
beabsichtig|en *vt* intend. **b~t** *a* intended; intentional
beacht|en *vt* take notice of; (*einhalten*) observe; (*folgen*) follow; **nicht b~en** ignore. **b~lich** *a* considerable. **B~ung** *f* **-** observance; **etw** (*dat*) **keine B~ung schenken** take no notice of sth
Beamte(r) *m*, **Beamtin** *f* **-, -nen** official; (*Staats-*) civil servant; (*Schalter-*) clerk
beanspruchen *vt* claim; (*erfordern*) demand
beanstand|en *vt* find fault with; (*Comm*) make a complaint about. **B~ung** *f* **-, -en** complaint
beantragen *vt* apply for
beantworten *vt* answer
bearbeiten *vt* work; (*weiter-*) process; (*behandeln*) treat (**mit** with); (*Admin*) deal with; (*redigieren*) edit; (*Theat*) adapt; (*Mus*) arrange
Beatmungsgerät *nt* ventilator
beaufsichtig|en *vt* supervise. **B~ung** *f* **-** supervision
beauftragen *vt* instruct; commission <*Künstler*>
bebauen *vt* build on; (*bestellen*) cultivate
beben *vi* (*haben*) tremble
Becher *m* **-s,-** beaker; (*Henkel-*) mug; (*Joghurt-, Sahne-*) carton
Becken *nt* **-s,-** basin; pool; (*Mus*) cymbals *pl*; (*Anat*) pelvis
bedacht *a* careful; **darauf b~** anxious (**zu** to)
bedächtig *a* careful; slow
bedanken (sich) *vr* thank (**bei jdm** s.o.)
Bedarf *m* **-s** need/(*Comm*) demand (**an** + *dat* for); **bei B~** if required. **B~shaltestelle** *f* request stop
bedauer|lich *a* regrettable. **b~licherweise** *adv* unfortunately. **b~n** *vt* regret; (*bemitleiden*) feel sorry for; **bedaure!** sorry! **b~nswert** *a* pitiful; (*bedauerlich*) regrettable
bedeckt *a* covered; <*Himmel*> overcast
bedenken† *vt* consider; (*überlegen*) think over. **B~** *pl* misgivings; **ohne B~** without hesitation
bedenklich *a* doubtful; (*verdächtig*) dubious; (*ernst*) serious
bedeut|en *vi* (*haben*) mean. **b~end** *a* important; (*beträchtlich*) considerable. **B~ung** *f* **-, -en** meaning; (*Wichtigkeit*) importance. **b~ungslos** *a* meaningless; (*unwichtig*)

unimportant. **b~ungsvoll** *a* significant; (*vielsagend*) meaningful

bedien|en *vt* serve; (*betätigen*) operate; **sich [selbst] b~en** help oneself. **B~ung** *f* **-, -en** service; (*Betätigung*) operation; (*Kellner*) waiter; (*Kellnerin*) *f* waitress. **B~ungsgeld** *nt* service charge

Bedingung *f* **-, -en** condition; **B~en** conditions; (*Comm*) terms. **b~slos** *a* unconditional

bedroh|en *vt* threaten. **b~lich** *a* threatening. **B~ung** *f* threat

bedrücken *vt* depress

bedruckt *a* printed

bedürf|en† *vi* (*haben*) (+ *gen*) need. **B~nis** *nt* **-ses, -se** need

Beefsteak /'bi:fste:k/ *nt* **-s, -s** steak; **deutsches B~** hamburger

beeilen (sich) *vr* hurry; hasten (**zu** to)

beeindrucken *vt* impress

beeinflussen *vt* influence

beeinträchtigen *vt* mar; (*schädigen*) impair

beengen *vt* restrict

beerdig|en *vt* bury. **B~ung** *f* **-, -en** funeral

Beere *f* **-, -n** berry

Beet *nt* **-[e]s, -e** (*Hort*) bed

Beete *f* **-, -n rote B~** beetroot

befähig|en *vt* enable; (*qualifizieren*) qualify. **B~ung** *f* **-** qualification; (*Fähigkeit*) ability

befahrbar *a* passable

befallen† *vt* attack; <*Angst:*> seize

befangen *a* shy; (*gehemmt*) self-conscious; (*Jur*) biased. **B~heit** *f* **-** shyness; self-consciousness; bias

befassen (sich) *vr* concern oneself/(*behandeln*) deal (**mit** with)

Befehl *m* **-[e]s, -e** order; (*Leitung*) command (**über** + *acc* of). **b~en**† *vt* **jdm etw b~en** order s.o. to do sth ● *vi* (*haben*) give the orders. **B~sform** *f* (*Gram*) imperative. **B~shaber** *m* **-s,-** commander

befestigen *vt* fasten (**an** + *dat* to); (*Mil*) fortify

befeuchten *vt* moisten

befinden† **(sich)** *vr* be. **B~** *nt* **-s** [state of] health

beflecken *vt* stain

befolgen *vt* follow

beförder|n *vt* transport; (*im Rang*) promote. **B~ung** *f* **-, -en** transport; promotion

befragen *vt* question

befrei|en *vt* free; (*räumen*) clear (**von** of); (*freistellen*) exempt (**von** from); **sich b~en** free oneself. **B~er** *m* **-s,-** liberator. **B~ung** *f* **-** liberation; exemption

befreunden (sich) *vr* make friends; **befreundet sein** be friends

befriedig|en *vt* satisfy. **b~end** *a* satisfying; (*zufrieden stellend*) satisfactory. **B~ung** *f* **-** satisfaction

befrucht|en *vt* fertilize. **B~ung** *f* **-** fertilization; **künstliche B~ung** artificial insemination

Befugnis *f* **-, -se** authority

Befund *m* result

befürcht|en *vt* fear. **B~ung** *f* **-, -en** fear

befürworten *vt* support

begab|t *a* gifted. **B~ung** *f* **-, -en** gift, talent

begeben† **(sich)** *vr* go; **sich in Gefahr b~** expose oneself to danger

begegn|en *vi* (*sein*) **jdm/etw b~en** meet s.o./sth. **B~ung** *f* **-, -en** meeting

begehr|en *vt* desire. **b~t** *a* sought-after

begeister|n *vt* **jdn b~n** arouse s.o.'s enthusiasm. **b~t** *a* enthusiastic; (*eifrig*) keen. **B~ung** *f* **-** enthusiasm

Begierde *f* **-, -n** desire

Beginn *m* **-s** beginning. **b~en**† *vt/i* (*haben*) start, begin

beglaubigen *vt* authenticate
begleichen† *vt* settle
begleit|en *vt* accompany. **B~er** *m* **-s, -** companion; (*Mus*) accompanist. **B~ung** *f* **-, -en** company; (*Mus*) accompaniment
beglück|en *vt* make happy. **b~wünschen** *vt* congratulate (**zu** on)
begnadig|en *vt* (*Jur*) pardon. **B~ung** *f* **-, -en** (*Jur*) pardon
begraben† *vt* bury
Begräbnis *n* **-ses, -se** burial; (*Feier*) funeral
begreif|en† *vt* understand; **nicht zu b~en** incomprehensible. **b~lich** *a* understandable
begrenz|en *vt* form the boundary of; (*beschränken*) restrict. **b~t** *a* limited. **B~ung** *f* **-, -en** restriction; (*Grenze*) boundary
Begriff *m* **-[e]s, -e** concept; (*Ausdruck*) term; (*Vorstellung*) idea
begründ|en *vt* give one's reason for. **b~et** *a* justified. **B~ung** *f* **-, -en** reason
begrüß|en *vt* greet; (*billigen*) welcome. **b~enswert** *a* welcome. **B~ung** *f* **-** greeting; welcome
begünstigen *vt* favour
begütert *a* wealthy
behaart *a* hairy
behäbig *a* portly
behag|en *vi* (*haben*) please (**jdm** s.o.). **B~en** *nt* **-s** contentment; (*Genuss*) enjoyment. **b~lich** *a* comfortable. **B~lichkeit** *f* **-** comfort
behalten† *vt* keep; (*sich merken*) remember
Behälter *m* **-s,-** container
behand|eln *vt* treat; (*sich befassen*) deal with. **B~lung** *f* treatment
beharr|en *vi* (*haben*) persist (**auf** + *dat* in). **b~lich** *a* persistent
behaupt|en *vt* maintain; (*vorgeben*) claim; (*sagen*) say; (*bewahren*) retain; **sich b~en** hold one's own. **B~ung** *f* **-, -en** assertion; claim; (*Äußerung*) statement
beheben† *vt* remedy
behelf|en† **(sich)** *vr* make do (**mit** with). **b~smäßig** *a* make-shift ● *adv* provisionally
beherbergen *vt* put up
beherrsch|en *vt* rule over; (*dominieren*) dominate; (*meistern, zügeln*) control; (*können*) know. **b~t** *a* self-controlled. **B~ung** *f* **-** control
beherzigen *vt* heed
behilflich *a* **jdm b~ sein** help s.o.
behinder|n *vt* hinder; (*blockieren*) obstruct. **b~t** *a* handicapped; (*schwer*) disabled. **B~te(r)** *m/f* handicapped/disabled person. **B~ung** *f* **-, -en** obstruction; (*Med*) handicap; disability
Behörde *f* **-, -n** [public] authority
behüte|n *vt* protect. **b~t** *a* sheltered
behutsam *a* careful; (*zart*) gentle

bei
● *preposition (+ dative)*
! Note that **bei** plus **dem** can become **beim**
····➤ (*nahe*) near; (*dicht an, neben*) by; (*als Begleitung*) with. **wer steht da bei ihm?** who is standing there next to *or* with him? **etw bei sich haben** have sth with *or* on one. **bleiben Sie beim Gepäck/bei den Kindern** stay with the luggage/the children. **war heute ein Brief für mich bei der Post?** was there a letter for me in the post today?
····➤ (*an*) by. **jdn bei der Hand nehmen** take s.o. by the hand
····➤ (*in der Wohnung von*) at ...'s home *or* house/flat. **bei mir [zu Hause]** at my home *or* ! place. **bei seinen Eltern leben** live with one's parents. **wir sind bei Ulrike**

eingeladen we have been invited to Ulrike's. **bei Schmidt** at the Schmidts'; (*Geschäft*) at Schmidts'; (*auf Briefen*) c/o Schmidt. **bei jdm/einer Firma arbeiten** work for s.o./a firm. **bei uns tut man das nicht** we don't do that where I come from.

····➤ (*gegenwärtig*) at; (*verwickelt*) in. **bei einer Hochzeit/einem Empfang** at a wedding/reception. **bei einem Unfall** in an accident

····➤ (*im Falle von*) in the case of, with; (*bei Wetter*) in. **wie bei den Römern** as with the Romans. **bei Nebel** in fog, if there is fog. **bei dieser Hitze** in this heat

····➤ (*angesichts*) with; (*trotz*) in spite of. **bei deinen guten Augen** with your good eyesight. **bei all seinen Bemühungen** in spite of *or* despite all his efforts

····➤ (*Zeitpunkt*) at, on. **bei diesen Worten errötete er** he blushed at this *or* on hearing this. **bei seiner Ankunft** on his arrival. **bei Tag/Nacht** by day/night.

····➤ (*Gleichzeitigkeit, mit Verbalsubstantiv*) **beim ...en** while *or* when ...ing. **beim Spazierengehen im Walde** while walking in the woods. **beim Überqueren der Straße** when crossing the road. **sie war beim Lesen** she was reading. **wir waren beim Frühstück** we were having breakfast

beibehalten† *vt sep* keep

beibringen† *vt sep* **jdm etw b~** teach s.o. sth; (*mitteilen*) break sth to s.o.; (*zufügen*) inflict sth on s.o.

Beicht|e *f* **-, -n** confession. **b~en** *vt/i* (*haben*) confess. **B~stuhl** *m* confessional

beide *a & pron* both; **b~s** both; **dreißig b~** (*Tennis*) thirty all.

b~rseitig *a* mutual. **b~rseits** *adv & prep* (+ *gen*) on both sides (of)

beieinander *adv* together

Beifahrer(in) *m(f)* [front-seat] passenger; (*Motorrad*) pillion passenger

Beifall *m* **-[e]s** applause; (*Billigung*) approval; **B~ klatschen** applaud

beifügen *vt sep* add; (*beilegen*) enclose

beige /bɛ:ʒ/ *inv a* beige

beigeben† *vt sep* add

Beihilfe *f* financial aid; (*Studien-*) grant; (*Jur*) aiding and abetting

Beil *nt* **-[e]s, -e** hatchet, axe

Beilage *f* supplement; (*Gemüse*) vegetable

beiläufig *a* casual

beilegen *vt sep* enclose; (*schlichten*) settle

Beileid *nt* condolences *pl*. **B~sbrief** *m* letter of condolence

beiliegend *a* enclosed

beim *prep* = **bei dem; b~ Militär** in the army; **b~ Frühstück** at breakfast

beimessen† *vt sep* (*fig*) attach (*dat* to)

Bein *nt* **-[e]s, -e** leg; **jdm ein B~ stellen** trip s.o. up

beinah[e] *adv* nearly, almost

Beiname *m* epithet

beipflichten *vi sep* (*haben*) agree (*dat* with)

Beirat *m* advisory committee

beisammen *adv* together; **b~ sein** be together

Beisein *nt* presence

beiseite *adv* aside; (*abseits*) apart; **b~ legen** put aside; (*sparen*) put by

beisetz|en *vt sep* bury. **B~ung** *f* **-, -en** funeral

Beispiel *nt* example; **zum B~** for example. **b~sweise** *adv* for example

beißen† *vt/i* (*haben*) bite; (*brennen*) sting; **sich b~** <*Farben:*> clash

Bei|stand *m* **-[e]s** help. **b~stehen**† *vi sep* (*haben*) **jdm b~stehen** help s.o.

beistimmen *vi sep* (*haben*) agree

Beistrich *m* comma

Beitrag *m* **-[e]s,¨e** contribution; (*Mitglieds-*) subscription; (*Versicherungs-*) premium; (*Zeitungs-*) article. **b~en**† *vt/i sep* (*haben*) contribute

bei|treten† *vi sep* (*sein*) (+ *dat*) join. **B~tritt** *m* joining

Beize *f* **-, -n** (*Holz-*) stain

beizeiten *adv* in good time

beizen *vt* stain <*Holz*>

bejahen *vt* answer in the affirmative; (*billigen*) approve of

bejahrt *a* aged, old

bekämpf|en *vt* fight. **B~ung** *f* fight (*gen* against)

bekannt *a* well-known; (*vertraut*) familiar; **jdn b~ machen** introduce s.o.; **etw b~ machen** *od* **geben** announce sth; **b~ werden** become known. **B~e(r)** *m/f* acquaintance; (*Freund*) friend. **B~gabe** *f* announcement. **b~lich** *adv* as is well known. **B~machung** *f* **-, -en** announcement; (*Anschlag*) notice. **B~schaft** *f* **-** acquaintance; (*Leute*) acquaintances *pl*; (*Freunde*) friends *pl*

bekehr|en *vt* convert. **B~ung** *f* **-, -en** conversion

bekenn|en† *vt* confess, profess <*Glauben*>; **sich [für] schuldig b~en** admit one's guilt. **B~tnis** *nt* **-ses, -se** confession; (*Konfession*) denomination

beklag|en *vt* lament; (*bedauern*) deplore; **sich b~en** complain. **b~enswert** *a* unfortunate. **B~te(r)** *m/f* (*Jur*) defendant

bekleid|en *vt* hold <*Amt*>. **B~ung** *f* clothing

Beklemmung *f* **-, -en** feeling of oppression

bekommen† *vt* get; have <*Baby*>; catch <*Erkältung*> ● *vi* (*sein*) **jdm gut b~** do s.o. good; <*Essen:*> agree with s.o.

beköstig|en *vt* feed. **B~ung** *f* **-** board; (*Essen*) food

bekräftigen *vt* reaffirm

bekreuzigen (sich) *vr* cross oneself

bekümmert *a* troubled; (*besorgt*) worried

bekunden *vt* show

Belag *m* **-[e]s,¨e** coating; (*Fußboden-*) covering; (*Brot-*) topping; (*Zahn-*) tartar; (*Brems-*) lining

belager|n *vt* besiege. **B~ung** *f* **-, -en** siege

Belang *m* **von B~** of importance; **B~e** *pl* interests. **b~los** *a* irrelevant; (*unwichtig*) trivial

belassen† *vt* leave; **es dabei b~** leave it at that

belasten *vt* load; (*fig*) burden; (*beanspruchen*) put a strain on; (*Comm*) debit; (*Jur*) incriminate

belästigen *vt* bother; (*bedrängen*) pester; (*unsittlich*) molest

Belastung *f* **-, -en** load; (*fig*) strain; (*Comm*) debit. **B~smaterial** *nt* incriminating evidence. **B~szeuge** *m* prosecution witness

belaufen† **(sich)** *vr* amount (**auf** + *acc* to)

belauschen *vt* eavesdrop on

beleb|en *vt* (*fig*) revive; (*lebhaft machen*) enliven. **b~t** *a* lively; <*Straße*> busy

Beleg *m* **-[e]s, -e** evidence; (*Beispiel*) instance (**für** of); (*Quittung*) receipt. **b~en** *vt* cover/(*garnieren*) garnish (**mit** with); (*besetzen*) reserve; (*Univ*) enrol for; (*nachweisen*) provide evidence for; **den ersten Platz b~en** (*Sport*) take first place.

B

B~schaft *f* **-, -en** work-force. **b~t** *a* occupied; <*Zunge*> coated; <*Stimme*> husky; **b~te Brote** open sandwiches

belehren *vt* instruct

beleidig|en *vt* offend; (*absichtlich*) insult. **B~ung** *f* **-, -en** insult

belesen *a* well-read

beleucht|en *vt* light; (*anleuchten*) illuminate. **B~ung** *f* **-, -en** illumination

Belg|ien /-i̯ən/ *nt* **-s** Belgium. **B~ier(in)** *m* **-s,-** (*f* **-, -nen**) Belgian. **b~isch** *a* Belgian

belicht|en *vt* (*Phot*) expose. **B~ung** *f* **-** exposure

Belieb|en *nt* **-s nach B~en** [just] as one likes. **b~ig** *a* **eine b~ige Zahl** any number you like ●*adv* **b~ig oft** as often as one likes. **b~t** *a* popular

bellen *vi* (*haben*) bark

belohn|en *vt* reward. **B~ung** *f* **-, -en** reward

belustig|en *vt* amuse. **B~ung** *f* **-, -en** amusement

bemalen *vt* paint

bemängeln *vt* criticize

bemannt *a* manned

bemerk|bar *a* **sich b~bar machen** attract attention. **b~en** *vt* notice; (*äußern*) remark. **b~ enswert** *a* remarkable. **B~ung** *f* **-, -en** remark

bemitleiden *vt* pity

bemüh|en *vt* trouble; **sich b~en** try (**zu** to; **um etw** to get sth); (*sich kümmern*) attend (**um** to); **b~t sein** endeavour (**zu** to). **B~ung** *f* **-, -en** effort

benachbart *a* neighbouring

benachrichtig|en *vt* inform; (*amtlich*) notify. **B~ung** *f* **-, -en** notification

benachteiligen *vt* discriminate against; (*ungerecht sein*) treat unfairly

benehmen† **(sich)** *vr* behave. **B~** *nt* **-s** behaviour

beneiden *vt* envy (**um etw** sth)

Bengel *m* **-s,-** boy; (*Rüpel*) lout

benötigen *vt* need

benutz|en, (*SGer*) **benütz|en** *vt* use; take <*Bahn*> **B~ung** *f* use

Benzin *nt* **-s** petrol

beobacht|en *vt* observe. **B~er** *m* **-s,-** observer. **B~ung** *f* **-, -en** observation

bequem *a* comfortable; (*mühelos*) easy; (*faul*) lazy. **b~en (sich)** *vr* deign (**zu** to). **B~lichkeit** *f* **-, -en** comfort; (*Faulheit*) laziness

berat|en† *vt* advise; (*überlegen*) discuss; **sich b~en** confer ●*vi* (*haben*) discuss (**über etw** *acc* sth); (*beratschlagen*) confer. **B~er(in)** *m* **-s,-**, (*f* **-, -nen**) adviser. **B~ung** *f* **-, -en** guidance; (*Rat*) advice; (*Besprechung*) discussion; (*Med, Jur*) consultation

berechn|en *vt* calculate; (*anrechnen*) charge for; (*abfordern*) charge. **B~ung** *f* calculation

berechtig|en *vt* entitle; (*befugen*) authorize; (*fig*) justify. **b~t** *a* justified, justifiable. **B~ung** *f* **-, -en** authorization; (*Recht*) right; (*Rechtmäßigkeit*) justification

bered|en *vt* talk about; **sich b~en** talk. **B~samkeit** *f* **-** eloquence

beredt *a* eloquent

Bereich *m* **-[e]s, -e** area; (*fig*) realm; (*Fach-*) field

bereichern *vi* enrich

bereit *a* ready. **b~en** *vt* prepare; (*verursachen*) cause; give <*Überraschung*>. **b~halten**† *vt sep* have/(*ständig*) keep ready. **b~legen** *vt sep* put out [ready]. **b~machen** *vt sep* get ready. **b~s** *adv* already

Bereitschaft *f* **-, -en** readiness; (*Einheit*) squad. **B~sdienst** *m* **B~sdienst haben** (*Mil*) be on stand-by; <*Arzt:*> be on call. **B~spolizei** *f* riot police

bereit|stehen† *vi sep (haben)* be ready. **b~stellen** *vt sep* put out ready; (*verfügbar machen*) make available. **B~ung** *f* **-** preparation. **b~willig** *a* willing

bereuen *vt* regret

Berg *m* **-[e]s, -e** mountain; (*Anhöhe*) hill; **in den B~en** in the mountains. **b~ab** *adv* downhill. **B~arbeiter** *m* miner. **b~auf** *adv* uphill. **B~bau** *m* **-[e]s** mining

bergen† *vt* recover; (*Naut*) salvage; (*retten*) rescue

Berg|führer *m* mountain guide. **b~ig** *a* mountainous. **B~kette** *f* mountain range. **B~mann** *m* (*pl* **-leute**) miner. **B~steiger(in)** *m* **-s,-** (*f* **-, -nen**) mountaineer, climber

Bergung *f* **-** recovery; (*Naut*) salvage; (*Rettung*) rescue

Berg|wacht *f* mountain rescue service. **B~werk** *nt* mine

Bericht *m* **-[e]s, -e** report; (*Reise-*) account. **b~en** *vt/i (haben)* report; (*erzählen*) tell (**von** of). **B~erstatter(in)** *m* **-s,-** (*f* **-, -nen**) reporter

berichtigen *vt* correct

beriesel|n *vt* irrigate. **B~ungsanlage** *f* sprinkler system

Berlin *nt* **-s** Berlin. **B~er** *m* **-s,-** Berliner

Bernhardiner *m* **-s,-** St Bernard

Bernstein *m* amber

berüchtigt *a* notorious

berücksichtig|en *vt* take into consideration. **B~ung** *f* **-** consideration

Beruf *m* profession; (*Tätigkeit*) occupation; (*Handwerk*) trade. **b~en**† *vt* appoint; **sich b~en** refer (**auf** + *acc* to); (*vorgeben*) plead (**auf etw** *acc* sth); ● *a* competent; **b~en sein** be destined (**zu** to). **b~lich** *a* professional; <*Ausbildung*> vocational ● *adv* professionally; **b~lich tätig sein** work, have a job. **B~sberatung** *f* vocational guidance. **b~smäßig** *adv* professionally. **B~sschule** *f* vocational school. **B~ssoldat** *m* regular soldier. **b~stätig** *a* working; **b~stätig sein** work, have a job. **B~stätige(r)** *m/f* working man/woman. **B~ung** *f* **-, -en** appointment; (*Bestimmung*) vocation; (*Jur*) appeal; **B~ung einlegen** appeal. **B~ungsgericht** *nt* appeal court

beruhen *vi (haben)* be based (**auf** + *dat* on)

beruhig|en *vt* calm [down]; (*zuversichtlich machen*) reassure. **b~end** *a* calming; (*tröstend*) reassuring; (*Med*) sedative. **B~ung** *f* **-** calming; reassurance; (*Med*) sedation. **B~ungsmittel** *nt* sedative; (*bei Psychosen*) tranquillizer

berühmt *a* famous. **B~heit** *f* **-, -en** fame; (*Person*) celebrity

berühr|en *vt* touch; (*erwähnen*) touch on. **B~ung** *f* **-, -en** touch; (*Kontakt*) contact

besänftigen *vt* soothe

Besatz *m* **-es,¨-e** trimming

Besatzung *f* **-, -en** crew; (*Mil*) occupying force

beschädig|en *vt* damage. **B~ung** *f* **-, -en** damage

beschaffen *vt* obtain, get ● *a* **so b~ sein, dass** be such that. **B~heit** *f* **-** consistency

beschäftig|en *vt* occupy; <*Arbeitgeber:*> employ; **sich b~en** occupy oneself. **b~t** *a* busy; (*angestellt*) employed (**bei** at). **B~ung** *f* **-, -en** occupation; (*Anstellung*) employment

beschämt *a* ashamed; (*verlegen*) embarrassed

beschatten *vt* shade; (*überwachen*) shadow

Bescheid *m* **-[e]s** information; **jdm B~ sagen** *od* **geben** let s.o. know; **B~ wissen** know

bescheiden *a* modest. **B~heit** *f* **-** modesty

bescheinen† *vt* shine on; **von der Sonne beschienen** sunlit

bescheinig|en *vt* certify. **B~ung** *f* **-, -en** [written] confirmation; (*Schein*) certificate

beschenken *vt* give a present/ presents to

Bescherung *f* **-, -en** distribution of Christmas presents

beschildern *vt* signpost

beschimpf|en *vt* abuse, swear at. **B~ung** *f* **-, -en** abuse

beschirmen *vt* protect

Beschlag *m* **in B~ nehmen** monopolize. **b~en**† *vt* shoe ● *vi* (*sein*) steam *or* mist up ● *a* steamed *or* misted up. **B~nahme** *f* **-, -n** confiscation; (*Jur*) seizure. **b~nahmen** *vt* confiscate; (*Jur*) seize

beschleunig|en *vt* hasten; (*schneller machen*) speed up <*Schritt*> ● *vi* (*haben*) accelerate. **B~ung** *f* **-** acceleration

beschließen† *vt* decide; (*beenden*) end ● *vi* (*haben*) decide (**über** + *acc* about)

Beschluss *m* decision

beschmutzen *vt* make dirty

beschneid|en† *vt* trim; (*Hort*) prune; (*Relig*) circumcise. **B~ung** *f* **-** circumcision

beschnüffeln *vt* sniff at

beschönigen *vt* (*fig*) gloss over

beschränken *vt* limit, restrict; **sich b~ auf** (+ *acc*) confine oneself to

beschrankt *a* <*Bahnübergang*> with barrier[s]

beschränk|t *a* limited; (*geistig*) dull-witted. **B~ung** *f* **-, -en** limitation, restriction

beschreib|en† *vt* describe. **B~ung** *f* **-, -en** description

beschuldig|en *vt* accuse. **B~ung** *f* **-, -en** accusation

beschummeln *vt* [!] cheat

Beschuss *m* (*Mil*) fire; (*Artillerie-*) shelling

beschütz|en *vt* protect. **B~er** *m* **-s,-** protector

Beschwer|de *f* **-, -n** complaint; **B~den** (*Med*) trouble *sg*. **b~en** *vt* weight down; **sich b~en** complain. **b~lich** *a* difficult

beschwindeln *vt* cheat (**um** out of); (*belügen*) lie to

beschwipst *a* [!] tipsy

beseitig|en *vt* remove. **B~ung** *f* **-** removal

Besen *m* **-s,-** broom

besessen *a* obsessed (**von** by)

besetz|en *vt* occupy; fill <*Posten*>; (*Theat*) cast <*Rolle*>; (*verzieren*) trim (**mit** with). **b~t** *a* occupied; <*Toilette, Leitung*> engaged; <*Zug, Bus*> full up; **der Platz ist b~t** this seat is taken. **B~tzeichen** *nt* engaged tone. **B~ung** *f* **-, -en** occupation; (*Theat*) cast

besichtig|en *vt* look round <*Stadt*>; (*prüfen*) inspect; (*besuchen*) visit. **B~ung** *f* **-, -en** visit; (*Prüfung*) inspection; (*Stadt-*) sightseeing

besiedelt *a* **dünn/dicht b~** sparsely/densely populated

besiegen *vt* defeat

besinn|en† **(sich)** *vr* think, reflect; (*sich erinnern*) remember (**auf jdn/etw** s.o./sth). **B~ung** *f* **-** reflection; (*Bewusstsein*) consciousness; **bei/ohne B~ung** conscious/unconscious. **b~ungslos** *a* unconscious

Besitz *m* possession; (*Eigentum, Land-*) property; (*Gut*) estate. **b~en**† *vt* own, possess; (*haben*) have. **B~er(in)** *m* **-s,-** (*f* **-, -nen**) owner; (*Comm*) proprietor

besoffen *a* [✖] drunken; **b~ sein** be drunk

besonder|e(r,s) *a* special; (*bestimmt*) particular; (*gesondert*) separate. **b~s** *adv* [e]specially, particularly; (*gesondert*) separately

besonnen *a* calm

besorg|en *vt* get; (*kaufen*) buy; (*erledigen*) attend to; (*versorgen*) look after. **b~t** *a* worried/ (*bedacht*) concerned (**um** about). **B~ung** *f* **-, -en** errand; **B~ungen machen** do shopping

bespitzeln *vt* spy on

besprech|en† *vt* discuss; (*rezensieren*) review. **B~ung** *f* **-, -en** discussion; review; (*Konferenz*) meeting

besser *a & adv* better. **b~n** *vt* improve; **sich b~n** get better. **B~ung** *f* **-** improvement; **gute B~ung!** get well soon!

Bestand *m* **-[e]s,¨e** existence; (*Vorrat*) stock (**an** + *dat* of)

beständig *a* constant; <*Wetter*> settled; **b~ gegen** resistant to

Bestand|saufnahme *f* stocktaking. **B~teil** *m* part

bestätig|en *vt* confirm; acknowledge <*Empfang*>; **sich b~en** prove to be true. **B~ung** *f* **-, -en** confirmation

bestatt|en *vt* bury. **B~ung** *f* **-, -en** funeral

Bestäubung *f* **-** pollination

bestaunen *vt* gaze at in amazement; (*bewundern*) admire

best|e(r,s) *a* best; **b~en Dank!** many thanks! **B~e(r,s)** *m/f/nt* best; **sein B~es tun** do one's best

bestech|en† *vt* bribe; (*bezaubern*) captivate. **b~end** *a* captivating. **b~lich** *a* corruptible. **B~ung** *f* **-** bribery. **B~ungsgeld** *nt* bribe

Besteck *nt* **-[e]s, -e** [set of] knife, fork and spoon; (*coll*) cutlery

bestehen† *vi* (*haben*) exist; (*fortdauern*) last; (*bei Prüfung*) pass; **~ aus** consist/(*gemacht sein*) be made of; **~ auf** (+ *dat*) insist on ● *vt* pass <*Prüfung*>

besteig|en† *vt* climb; (*aufsteigen*) mount; ascend <*Thron*>. **B~ung** *f* ascent

bestell|en *vt* order; (*vor-*) book; (*ernennen*) appoint; (*bebauen*) cultivate; (*ausrichten*) tell; **zu sich b~en** send for; **b~t sein** have an appointment; **kann ich etwas b~en?** can I take a message? **B~schein** *m* order form. **B~ung** *f* order; (*Botschaft*) message; (*Bebauung*) cultivation

besteuer|n *vt* tax. **B~ung** *f* **-** taxation

Bestie /ˈbɛsti̯ə/ *f* **-, -n** beast

bestimm|en *vt* fix; (*entscheiden*) decide; (*vorsehen*) intend; (*ernennen*) appoint; (*ermitteln*) determine; (*definieren*) define; (*Gram*) qualify ● *vi* (*haben*) be in charge (**über** + *acc* of). **b~t** *a* definite; (*gewiss*) certain; (*fest*) firm,. **B~ung** *f* fixing; (*Vorschrift*) regulation; (*Ermittlung*) determination; (*Definition*) definition; (*Zweck*) purpose; (*Schicksal*) destiny. **B~ungsort** *m* destination

Bestleistung *f* (*Sport*) record

bestraf|en *vt* punish. **B~ung** *f* **-, -en** punishment

Bestrahlung *f* radiotherapy

Bestreb|en *nt* **-s** endeavour; (*Absicht*) aim. **B~ung** *f* **-, -en** effort

bestreiten† *vt* dispute; (*leugnen*) deny; (*bezahlen*) pay for

bestürz|t *a* dismayed, (*erschüttert*) stunned. **B~ung** *f* **-** dismay, consternation

Bestzeit *f* (*Sport*) record [time]

Besuch *m* **-[e]s, -e** visit; (*kurz*) call; (*Schul-*) attendance; (*Gast*) visitor; (*Gäste*) visitors *pl*; **B~ haben** have a visitor/visitors; **bei jdm zu** *od* **auf B~ sein** be staying with s.o. **b~en** *vt* visit; (*kurz*) call on; (*teilnehmen*) attend; go to <*Schule, Ausstellung*>. **B~er(in)** *m* **-s,-** (*f* **-, -nen**) visitor; caller. **B~szeit** *f* visiting hours *pl*

betagt *a* aged, old

betätig|en *vt* operate; **sich b~en** work (**als** as). **B~ung** *f* **-, -en** operation; (*Tätigkeit*) activity

betäub|en *vt* stun; <*Lärm:*> deafen; (*Med*) anaesthetize; (*lindern*) ease; deaden <*Schmerz*>; **wie b~t** dazed. **B~ung** *f* **-** daze; (*Med*) anaesthesia. **B~ungsmittel** *nt* anaesthetic

Bete *f* **-, -n Rote B~** beetroot

beteilig|en *vt* give a share to; **sich b~en** take part (**an** + *dat* in); (*beitragen*) contribute (**an** + *dat* to). **b~t** *a* **b~t sein** take part/(*an Unfall*) be involved/(*Comm*) have a share (**an** + *dat* in); **alle B~ten** all those involved. **B~ung** *f* **-, -en** participation; involvement; (*Anteil*) share

beten *vi* (*haben*) pray

Beton /be'tɔŋ/ *m* **-s** concrete

betonen *vt* stressed, emphasize

beton|t *a* stressed; (*fig*) pointed. **B~ung** *f* **-, -en** stress

Betracht *m* **in B~ ziehen** consider; **außer B~ lassen** disregard; **nicht in B~ kommen** be out of the question. **b~en** *vt* look at; (*fig*) regard (**als** as)

beträchtlich *a* considerable

Betrachtung *f* **-, -en** contemplation; (*Überlegung*) reflection

Betrag *m* **-[e]s,¨e** amount. **b~en**† *vt* amount to; **sich b~en** behave. **B~en** *nt* **-s** behaviour; (*Sch*) conduct

betreff|en† *vt* affect; (*angehen*) concern. **b~end** *a* relevant. **b~s** *prep* (+ *gen*) concerning

betreiben† *vt* (*leiten*) run; (*ausüben*) carry on

betreten† *vt* step on; (*eintreten*) enter; '**B~ verboten**' 'no entry'; (*bei Rasen*) 'keep off [the grass]'

betreu|en *vt* look after. **B~er(in)** *m* **-s,-** (*f* **-, -nen**) helper; (*Kranken-*) nurse. **B~ung** *f* **-** care

Betrieb *m* business; (*Firma*) firm; (*Treiben*) activity; (*Verkehr*) traffic; **außer B~** not in use; (*defekt*) out of order

Betriebs|anleitung, B~anweisung *f* operating instructions *pl*. **B~ferien** *pl* firm's holiday. **B~leitung** *f* management. **B~rat** *m* works committee. **B~störung** *f* breakdown

betrinken† **(sich)** *vr* get drunk

betroffen *a* disconcerted; **b~ sein** be affected (**von** by)

betrüb|en *vt* sadden. **b~t** *a* sad

Betrug *m* **-[e]s** deception; (*Jur*) fraud

betrüg|en† *vt* cheat, swindle; (*Jur*) defraud; (*in der Ehe*) be unfaithful to. **B~er(in)** *m* **-s,-** (*f* **-, -nen**) swindler. **B~erei** *f* **-, -en** fraud

betrunken *a* drunken; **b~ sein** be drunk. **B~e(r)** *m* drunk

Bett *nt* **-[e]s, -en** bed. **B~couch** *f* sofa-bed. **B~decke** *f* blanket; (*Tages-*) bedspread

Bettel|ei *f* **-** begging. **b~n** *vi* (*haben*) beg

Bettler(in) *m* **-s,-** (*f* **-, -nen**) beggar

Bettpfanne *f* bedpan

Betttuch (Bettuch) *nt* sheet

Bett|wäsche *f* bed linen. **B~zeug** *nt* bedding

betupfen *vt* dab (**mit** with)

beug|en *vt* bend; (*Gram*) decline; conjugate <*Verb*>; **sich b~en** bend; (*lehnen*) lean; (*sich fügen*) submit (*dat* to). **B~ung** *f* **-, -en** (*Gram*) declension; conjugation

Beule *f* **-, -n** bump; (*Delle*) dent

beunruhig|en *vt* worry; **sich b~en** worry. **B~ung** *f* **-** worry

beurlauben *vt* give leave to
beurteil|en *vt* judge. **B~ung** *f* **-, -en** judgement; (*Ansicht*) opinion
Beute *f* **-** booty, haul; (*Jagd-*) bag; (*eines Raubtiers*) prey
Beutel *m* **-s,-** bag; (*Tabak- & Zool*) pouch. **B~tier** *nt* marsupial
Bevölkerung *f* **-, -en** population
bevollmächtigen *vt* authorize
bevor *conj* before; **b~ nicht** until
bevormunden *vt* treat like a child
bevorstehen† *vi sep* (*haben*) approach; (*unmittelbar*) be imminent. **b~d** *a* approaching, forthcoming; **unmittelbar b~d** imminent
bevorzug|en *vt* prefer, (*begünstigen*) favour. **b~t** *a* privileged; <*Behandlung*> preferential
bewachen *vt* guard
Bewachung *f* **-** guard; **unter B~** under guard
bewaffn|en *vt* arm. **b~et** *a* armed. **B~ung** *f* **-** armament; (*Waffen*) arms *pl*
bewahren *vt* protect (**vor** + *dat* from); (*behalten*) keep; **die Ruhe b~** keep calm
bewähren (sich) *vr* prove one's/<*Ding:*> its worth; (*erfolgreich sein*) prove a success
bewähr|t *a* reliable; (*erprobt*) proven. **B~ung** *f* **-** (*Jur*) probation. **B~ungsfrist** *f* [period of] probation. **B~ungsprobe** *f* (*fig*) test
bewältigen *vt* cope with; (*überwinden*) overcome
bewässer|n *vt* irrigate. **B~ung** *f* **-** irrigation
bewegen[1] *vt* (*reg*) move; **sich b~** move, (*körperlich*) take exercise
bewegen[2]**†** *vt* **jdn dazu b~, etw zu tun** induce s.o. to do sth
Beweg|grund *m* motive. **b~lich** *a* movable, mobile; (*wendig*) agile. **B~lichkeit** *f* **-** mobility; agility. **B~ung** *f* **-, -en** movement; (*Phys*) motion; (*Rührung*) emotion; (*Gruppe*) movement; **körperliche B~ung** physical exercise. **b~ungslos** *a* motionless
Beweis *m* **-es, -e** proof; (*Zeichen*) token; **B~e** evidence *sg*. **b~en†** *vt* prove; (*zeigen*) show; **sich b~en** prove oneself/<*Ding:*> itself. **B~material** *nt* evidence
bewerb|en† (sich) *vr* apply (**um** for; **bei** to). **B~er(in)** *m* **-s,-** (*f* **-, -nen**) applicant. **B~ung** *f* **-, -en** application
bewerten *vt* value; (*einschätzen*) rate; (*Sch*) mark, grade
bewilligen *vt* grant
bewirken *vt* cause; (*herbeiführen*) bring about
bewirt|en *vt* entertain. **B~ung** *f* **-** hospitality
bewohn|bar *a* habitable. **b~en** *vt* inhabit, live in. **B~er(in)** *m* **-s,-** (*f* **-, -nen**) resident, occupant; (*Einwohner*) inhabitant
bewölk|en (sich) *vr* cloud over; **b~t** cloudy. **B~ung** *f* **-** clouds *pl*
bewunder|n *vt* admire. **b~nswert** *a* admirable. **B~ung** *f* **-** admiration
bewusst *a* conscious (*gen* of); (*absichtlich*) deliberate. **b~los** *a* unconscious. **B~losigkeit** *f* **-** unconsciousness; **B~sein** *nt* **-s** consciousness; (*Gewissheit*) awareness; **bei B~sein** conscious
bezahl|en *vt/i* (*haben*) pay; pay for <*Ware, Essen*>. **B~ung** *f* **-** payment; (*Lohn*) pay. **B~fernsehen** *nt* pay television; pay TV
bezaubern *vt* enchant
bezeichn|en *vt* mark; (*bedeuten*) denote; (*beschreiben, nennen*) describe (**als** as). **b~end** *a* typical. **B~ung** *f* marking; (*Beschreibung*) description (**als** as); (*Ausdruck*) term; (*Name*) name
bezeugen *vt* testify to

bezichtigen *vt* accuse (*gen* of)
bezieh|en† *vt* cover; (*einziehen*) move into; (*beschaffen*) obtain; (*erhalten*) get; (*in Verbindung bringen*) relate (**auf** + *acc* to); **sich b~en** (*bewölken*) cloud over; **sich b~en auf** (+ *acc*) refer to; **das Bett frisch b~en** put clean sheets on the bed. **B~ung** *f* **-, -en** relation; (*Verhältnis*) relationship; (*Bezug*) respect; **B~ungen haben** have connections. **b~ungsweise** *adv* respectively; (*vielmehr*) or rather
Bezirk *m* **-[e]s, -e** district
Bezug *m* cover; (*Kissen-*) case; (*Beschaffung*) obtaining; (*Kauf*) purchase; (*Zusammenhang*) reference; **B~e** *pl* earnings; **B~ nehmen** refer (**auf** + *acc* to); **in B~ auf** (+ *acc*) regarding
bezüglich *prep* (+ *gen*) regarding ● *a* relating (**auf** + *acc* to)
bezwecken *vt* (*fig*) aim at
bezweifeln *vt* doubt
BH /be:'ha:/ *m* **-[s], -[s]** bra
Bibel *f* **-, -n** Bible
Biber *m* **-s,-** beaver
Biblio|thek *f* **-, -en** library. **B~thekar(in)** *m* **-s,-** (*f* **-, -nen**) librarian
biblisch *a* biblical
bieg|en† *vt* bend; **sich b~en** bend ● *vi* (*sein*) curve (**nach** to); **um die Ecke b~en** turn the corner. **b~sam** *a* flexible, supple. **B~ung** *f* **-, -en** bend
Biene *f* **-, -n** bee. **B~nstock** *m* beehive. **B~nwabe** *f* honey-comb
Bier *nt* **-s, -e** beer. **B~deckel** *m* beer-mat. **B~krug** *m* beer-mug
bieten† *vt* offer; (*bei Auktion*) bid
Bifokalbrille *f* bifocals *pl*
Bigamie *f* **-** bigamy
Bikini *m* **-s, -s** bikini
Bilanz *f* **-, -en** balance sheet; (*fig*) result; **die B~ ziehen** (*fig*) draw conclusions (**aus** from)
Bild *nt* **-[e]s, -er** picture; (*Theat*) scene
bilden *vt* form; (*sein*) be; (*erziehen*) educate
Bild|erbuch *nt* picture-book. **B~fläche** *f* screen. **B~hauer** *m* **-s,-** sculptor. **b~lich** *a* pictorial; (*figurativ*) figurative. **B~nis** *nt* **-ses, -se** portrait. **B~schirm** *m* (*TV*) screen. **B~schirmgerät** *nt* visual display unit, VDU. **b~schön** *a* very beautiful. **B~telefon** *nt* videophone
Bildung *f* **-** formation; (*Erziehung*) education; (*Kultur*) culture
Billard /'bɪljart/ *nt* **-s** billiards *sg*. **B~tisch** *m* billiard table
Billett /bɪl'jɛt/ *nt* **-[e]s, -e** & **-s** ticket
Billiarde *f* **-, -n** thousand million million
billig *a* cheap; (*dürftig*) poor; **recht und b~** right and proper. **b~en** *vt* approve. **B~ung** *f* **-** approval
Billion /bɪlio:n/ *f* **-, -en** million million, billion
Bimsstein *m* pumice stone
Binde *f* **-, -n** band; (*Verband*) bandage; (*Damen-*) sanitary towel. **B~hautentzündung** *f* conjunctivitis. **b~n**† *vt* tie (**an** + *acc* to); make <*Strauß*>; bind <*Buch*>; (*fesseln*) tie up; (*Culin*) thicken; **sich b~n** commit oneself. **B~strich** *m* hyphen. **B~wort** *nt* (*pl* **-wörter**) (*Gram*) conjunction
Bind|faden *m* string. **B~ung** *f* **-, -en** (*fig*) tie; (*Beziehung*) relationship; (*Verpflichtung*) commitment; (*Ski-*) binding; (*Tex*) weave
binnen *prep* (+ *dat*) within. **B~handel** *m* home trade
Bio- *pref* organic
Bio|chemie *f* biochemistry. **b~dynamisch** *m* organic. **B~graphie, B~grafie** *f* **-, -n** biography
Bio|hof *m* organic farm. **B~laden** *m* health-food store

Biolog|e *m* **-n, -n** biologist. **B~ie** *f* **-** biology. **b~isch** *a* biological; **b~ischer Anbau** organic farming; **b~isch angebaut** organically grown

Bioterrorismus *m* bioterrorism

Birke *f* **-, -n** birch [tree]

Birm|a *nt* **-s** Burma. **b~anisch** *a* Burmese

Birn|baum *m* pear-tree. **B~e** *f* **-, -n** pear; (*Electr*) bulb

bis *prep* (+ *acc*) as far as, [up] to; (*zeitlich*) until, till; (*spätestens*) by; **bis zu** up to; **bis auf** (+ *acc*) (*einschließlich*) [down] to; (*ausgenommen*) except [for]; **drei bis vier Minuten** three to four minutes; **bis morgen!** see you tomorrow! ● *conj* until

Bischof *m* **-s,⸚e** bishop

bisher *adv* so far, up to now

Biskuit|rolle /bɪs'kvi:t-/ *f* Swiss roll. **B~teig** *m* sponge mixture

Biss *m* **-es, -e** bite

bisschen *inv pron* **ein b~** a bit, a little; **kein b~** not a bit

Biss|en *m* **-s,-** bite, mouthful. **b~ig** *a* vicious; (*fig*) caustic

bisweilen *adv* from time to time

bitt|e *adv* please; (*nach Klopfen*) come in; (*als Antwort auf 'danke'*) don't mention it, you're welcome; **wie b~e?** pardon? **B~e** *f* **-, -n** request/(*dringend*) plea (**um** for). **b~en**† *vt/i* (*haben*) ask/ (*dringend*) beg (**um** for); (*einladen*) invite, ask

bitter *a* bitter. **B~keit** *f* **-** bitterness. **b~lich** *adv* bitterly

Bittschrift *f* petition

bizarr *a* bizarre

bläh|en *vt* swell; <*Vorhang, Segel:*> billow ● *vi* (*haben*) cause flatulence. **B~ungen** *fpl* flatulence *sg*, 🄸 wind *sg*

Blamage /bla'ma:ʒə/ *f* **-, -n** humiliation; (*Schande*) disgrace

blamieren *vt* disgrace; **sich b~** disgrace oneself; (*sich lächerlich machen*) make a fool of oneself

blanchieren /blã'ʃi:rən/ *vt* (*Culin*) blanch

blank *a* shiny. **B~oscheck** *m* blank cheque

Blase *f* **-, -n** bubble; (*Med*) blister; (*Anat*) bladder. **b~n**† *vt/i* (*haben*) blow; play <*Flöte*>. **B~nentzündung** *f* cystitis

Blas|instrument *nt* wind instrument. **B~kapelle** *f* brass band

blass *a* pale; (*schwach*) faint

Blässe *f* **-** pallor

Blatt *nt* **-[e]s,⸚er** (*Bot*) leaf; (*Papier*) sheet; (*Zeitung*) paper

Blattlaus *f* greenfly

blau *a*, **B~** *nt* **-s,-** blue; **b~er Fleck** bruise; **b~es Auge** black eye; **b~ sein** 🄸 be tight; **Fahrt ins B~e** mystery tour. **B~beere** *f* bilberry. **B~licht** *nt* blue flashing light

Blech *nt* **-[e]s, -e** sheet metal; (*Weiß-*) tin; (*Platte*) metal sheet; (*Back-*) baking sheet; (*Mus*) brass; (🄸 *Unsinn*) rubbish. **B~schaden** *m* (*Auto*) damage to the bodywork

Blei *nt* **-[e]s** lead

Bleibe *f* **-** place to stay. **b~n**† *vi* (*sein*) remain, stay; (*übrig-*) be left; **ruhig b~n** keep calm; **bei etw b~n** (*fig*) stick to sth; **b~n Sie am Apparat** hold the line; **etw b~n lassen** not to do sth. **b~nd** *a* permanent; (*anhaltend*) lasting

bleich *a* pale. **b~en**† *vi* (*sein*) bleach; (*ver-*) fade ● *vt* (*reg*) bleach. **B~mittel** *nt* bleach

blei|ern *a* leaden. **b~frei** *a* unleaded. **B~stift** *m* pencil. **B~stiftabsatz** *m* stiletto heel. **B~stiftspitzer** *m* **-s,-** pencil sharpener

Blende *f* **-, -n** shade, shield; (*Sonnen-*) [sun] visor; (*Phot*)

diaphragm; (*Öffnung*) aperture; (*an Kleid*) facing. **b~n** *vt* dazzle, blind

Blick *m* **-[e]s, -e** look; (*kurz*) glance; (*Aussicht*) view; **auf den ersten B~** at first sight. **b~en** *vi* (*haben*) look/(*kurz*) glance (**auf** + *acc* at). **B~punkt** *m* (*fig*) point of view

blind *a* blind; (*trübe*) dull; **b~er Alarm** false alarm; **b~er Passagier** stowaway. **B~darm** *m* appendix. **B~darmentzündung** *f* appendicitis. **B~e(r)** *m/f* blind man/woman; **die B~en** the blind *pl.* **B~enhund** *m* guidedog. **B~enschrift** *f* braille. **B~gänger** *m* **-s,-** (*Mil*) dud. **B~heit** *f* **-** blindness

blink|en *vi* (*haben*) flash; (*funkeln*) gleam; (*Auto*) indicate. **B~er** *m* **-s,-** (*Auto*) indicator. **B~licht** *nt* flashing light

blinzeln *vi* (*haben*) blink

Blitz *m* **-es, -e** [flash of] lightning; (*Phot*) flash. **B~ableiter** *m* lightning-conductor. **b~artig** *a* lightning ... ● *adv* like lightning. **b~en** *vi* (*haben*) flash; (*funkeln*) sparkle; **es hat geblitzt** there was a flash of lightning. **B~licht** *nt* (*Phot*) flash. **b~sauber** *a* spick and span. **b~schnell** *a* lightning ... ● *adv* like lightning

Block *m* **-[e]s,¨-e** block ● **-[e]s, -s** & **¨-e** pad; (*Häuser-*) block

Blockade *f* **-, -n** blockade

Blockflöte *f* recorder

blockieren *vt* block; (*Mil*) blockade

Blockschrift *f* block letters *pl*

blöd[e] *a* feeble-minded; (*dumm*) stupid

Blödsinn *m* **-[e]s** idiocy; (*Unsinn*) nonsense

blöken *vi* (*haben*) bleat

blond *a* fair-haired; <*Haar*> fair

bloß *a* bare; (*alleinig*) mere ● *adv* only, just

bloß|legen *vt sep* uncover. **b~stellen** *vt sep* compromise

Bluff *m* **-s, -s** bluff. **b~en** *vt/i* (*haben*) bluff

blühen *vi* (*haben*) flower; (*fig*) flourish. **b~d** *a* flowering; (*fig*) flourishing, thriving

Blume *f* **-, -n** flower; (*vom Wein*) bouquet. **B~nbeet** *nt* flower-bed. **B~ngeschäft** *nt* flower-shop, florist's. **B~nkohl** *m* cauliflower. **B~nmuster** *nt* floral design. **B~nstrauß** *m* bunch of flowers. **B~ntopf** *m* flowerpot; (*Pflanze*) pot plant. **B~nzwiebel** *f* bulb

blumig *a* (*fig*) flowery

Bluse *f* **-, -n** blouse

Blut *nt* **-[e]s** blood. **b~arm** *a* anaemic. **B~bahn** *f* blood-stream. **B~bild** *nt* blood count. **B~druck** *m* blood pressure. **b~dürstig** *a* bloodthirsty

Blüte *f* **-, -n** flower, bloom; (*vom Baum*) blossom; (*B~zeit*) flowering period; (*Baum-*) blossom time; (*Höhepunkt*) peak, prime

Blut|egel *m* **-s,-** leech. **b~en** *vi* (*haben*) bleed

Blüten|blatt *nt* petal. **B~staub** *m* pollen

Blut|er *m* **-s,-** haemophiliac. **B~erguss** *m* bruise. **B~gefäß** *nt* blood-vessel. **B~gruppe** *f* blood group. **b~ig** *a* bloody. **B~körperchen** *nt* **-s,-** corpuscle. **B~probe** *f* blood test. **b~rünstig** *a* (*fig*) bloody, gory. **B~schande** *f* incest. **B~spender** *m* blood donor. **B~sturz** *m* haemorrhage. **B~transfusion, B~übertragung** *f* blood transfusion. **B~ung** *f* **-, -en** bleeding; (*Med*) haemorrhage; (*Regel-*) period. **b~unterlaufen** *a* bruised; <*Auge*> bloodshot. **B~vergiftung** *f* blood-poisoning. **B~wurst** *f* black pudding

Bö *f* **-, -en** gust; (*Regen-*) squall

Bob *m* **-s, -s** bob[-sleigh]

Bock *m* **-[e]s,¨e** buck; (*Ziege*) billy goat; (*Schaf*) ram; (*Gestell*) support. **b~ig** *a* [!] stubborn. **B~springen** *nt* leap-frog
Boden *m* **-s,¨** ground; (*Erde*) soil; (*Fuß-*) floor; (*Grundfläche*) bottom; (*Dach-*) loft, attic. **B~satz** *m* sediment. **B~schätze** *mpl* mineral deposits. **B~see (der)** Lake Constance
Bogen *m* **-s,-** *&* **¨** curve; (*Geom*) arc; (*beim Skilauf*) turn; (*Archit*) arch; (*Waffe, Geigen-*) bow; (*Papier*) sheet; **einen großen B~ um jdn/etw machen** [!] give s.o./sth a wide berth. **B~schießen** *nt* archery
Bohle *f* **-, -n** [thick] plank
Böhm|en *nt* **-s** Bohemia. **b~isch** *a* Bohemian
Bohne *f* **-, -n** bean; **grüne B~n** French beans
bohner|n *vt* polish. **B~wachs** *nt* floor-polish
bohr|en *vt/i* (*haben*) drill (**nach** for); drive <*Tunnel*>; sink <*Brunnen*>; <*Insekt:*> bore. **B~er** *m* **-s,-** drill. **B~insel** *f* [offshore] drilling rig. **B~turm** *m* derrick
Boje *f* **-, -n** buoy
Bolzen *m* **-s,-** bolt; (*Stift*) pin
bombardieren *vt* bomb; (*fig*) bombard (**mit** with)
Bombe *f* **-, -n** bomb. **B~nangriff** *m* bombing raid. **B~nerfolg** *m* huge success
Bon /bɔŋ/ *m* **-s, -s** voucher; (*Kassen-*) receipt
Bonbon /bɔŋˈbɔŋ/ *m & nt* **-s, -s** sweet
Bonus *m* **-[sses], -[sse]** bonus
Boot *nt* **-[e]s, -e** boat. **B~ssteg** *m* landing-stage
Bord[1] *nt* **-[e]s, -e** shelf
Bord[2] *m* (*Naut*) **an B~** aboard, on board; **über B~** overboard. **B~buch** *nt* log[-book]
Bordell *nt* **-s, -e** brothel
Bordkarte *f* boarding-pass
borgen *vt* borrow; **jdm etw b~** lend s.o. sth
Börse *f* **-, -n** purse; (*Comm*) stock exchange. **B~nmakler** *m* stockbroker
Borst|e *f* **-, -n** bristle. **b~ig** *a* bristly
Borte *f* **-, -n** braid
Böschung *f* **-, -en** embankment
böse *a* wicked, evil; (*unartig*) naughty; (*schlimm*) bad; (*zornig*) cross; **jdm** *od* **auf jdn b~ sein** be cross with s.o.
bos|haft *a* malicious, spiteful. **B~heit** *f* **-, -en** malice; spite; (*Handlung*) spiteful act/ (*Bemerkung*) remark
böswillig *a* malicious
Botani|k *f* **-** botany. **B~ker(in)** *m* **-s,-** (*f* **-, -nen**) botanist
Bot|e *m* **-n, -n** messenger. **B~engang** *m* errand. **B~schaft** *f* **-, -en** message; (*Pol*) embassy. **B~schafter** *m* **-s,-** ambassador
Bouillon /bʊlˈjɔŋ/ *f* **-, -s** clear soup. **B~würfel** *m* stock cube
Bowle /ˈbo:lə/ *f* **-, -n** punch
Box *f* **-, -en** box; (*Pferde-*) loose box; (*Lautsprecher-*) speaker; (*Autorennen*) pit
box|en *vi* (*haben*) box ● *vt* punch. **B~en** *nt* **-s** boxing. **B~er** *m* **-s,-** boxer
brachliegen† *vi sep* (*haben*) lie fallow
Branche /ˈbrã:ʃə/ *f* **-, -n** [line of] business. **B~nverzeichnis** *nt* (*Teleph*) classified directory
Brand *m* **-[e]s,¨e** fire; (*Med*) gangrene; (*Bot*) blight; **in B~ geraten** catch fire; **in B~ setzen** *od* **stecken** set on fire. **B~bombe** *f* incendiary bomb
Brand|stifter *m* arsonist. **B~stiftung** *f* arson
Brandung *f* **-** surf
Brand|wunde *f* burn. **B~zeichen** *nt* brand
Branntwein *m* spirit; (*coll*) spirits *pl*. **B~brennerei** *f* distillery

B

bras|ilianisch *a* Brazilian. **B~ilien** /-iən/ *nt* **-s** Brazil

Brat|apfel *m* baked apple. **b~en**† *vt/i* (*haben*) roast; (*in der Pfanne*) fry. **B~en** *m* **-s,-** roast; (*B~stück*) joint. **b~fertig** *a* oven-ready. **B~hähnchen** *nt* roasting chicken. **B~kartoffeln** *fpl* fried potatoes. **B~pfanne** *f* frying-pan

Bratsche *f* **-, -n** (*Mus*) viola

Bratspieß *m* spit

Brauch *m* **-[e]s,Bräuche** custom. **b~bar** *a* usable; (*nützlich*) useful. **b~en** *vt* need; (*ge-, verbrauchen*) use; take <*Zeit*>; **er b~t es nur zu sagen** he only has to say

Braue *f* **-, -n** eyebrow

brau|en *vt* brew. **B~er** *m* **-s,-** brewer. **B~erei** *f* **-, -en** brewery

braun *a*, **B~** *nt* **-s,-** brown; **b~ werden** <*Person:*> get a tan; **b~ [gebrannt] sein** be [sun-]tanned

Bräune *f* **-** [sun-]tan. **b~n** *vt/i* (*haben*) brown; (*in der Sonne*) tan

Braunschweig *nt* **-s** Brunswick

Brause *f* **-, -n** (*Dusche*) shower; (*an Gießkanne*) rose; (*B~limonade*) fizzy drink

Braut *f* **-,¨e** bride; (*Verlobte*) fiancée

Bräutigam *m* **-s, -e** bridegroom; (*Verlobter*) fiancé

Brautkleid *nt* wedding dress

Brautpaar *nt* bridal couple; (*Verlobte*) engaged couple

brav *a* good; (*redlich*) honest ● *adv* dutifully; (*redlich*) honestly

bravo *int* bravo!

BRD *abbr* (**Bundesrepublik Deutschland**) FRG

Brech|eisen *nt* jemmy; (*B~stange*) crowbar. **b~en**† *vt* break; (*Phys*) refract <*Licht*>; (*erbrechen*) vomit; **sich b~en** <*Wellen:*> break; <*Licht:*> be refracted; **sich** (*dat*) **den Arm b~en** break one's arm ● *vi* (*sein*) break ● *vi* (*haben*) vomit, be sick. **B~reiz** *m* nausea. **B~stange** *f* crowbar

Brei *m* **-[e]s, -e** paste; (*Culin*) purée; (*Hafer-*) porridge

breit *a* wide; <*Schultern, Grinsen*> broad. **B~e** *f* **-, -n** width; breadth; (*Geog*) latitude. **b~en** *vt* spread (**über** + *acc* over). **B~engrad** *m* [degree of] latitude. **B~enkreis** *m* parallel

Bremse[1] *f* **-, -n** horsefly

Bremse[2] *f* **-, -n** brake. **b~n** *vt* slow down; (*fig*) restrain ● *vi* (*haben*) brake

Bremslicht *nt* brake-light

brenn|bar *a* combustible; **leicht b~bar** highly [in]flammable. **b~en**† *vi* (*haben*) burn; <*Licht:*> be on; <*Zigarette:*> be alight; (*weh tun*) smart, sting ● *vt* burn; (*rösten*) roast; (*im Brennofen*) fire; (*destillieren*) distil. **b~end** *a* burning; (*angezündet*) lighted; (*fig*) fervent **B~erei** *f* **-, -en** distillery

Brennessel* *f s.* **Brennnessel**

Brenn|holz *nt* firewood. **B~ofen** *m* kiln. **B~nessel** *f* stinging nettle. **B~punkt** *m* (*Phys*) focus. **B~spiritus** *m* methylated spirits. **B~stoff** *m* fuel

Bretagne /bre'tanjə/ **(die) -** Brittany

Brett *nt* **-[e]s, -er** board; (*im Regal*) shelf; **schwarzes B~** notice board. **B~spiel** *nt* board game

Brezel *f* **-, -n** pretzel

Bridge /brɪtʃ/ *nt* **-** (*Spiel*) bridge

Brief *m* **-[e]s, -e** letter. **B~beschwerer** *m* **-s,-** paperweight. **B~freund(in)** *m(f)* pen-friend. **B~kasten** *m* letter-box. **B~kopf** *m* letter-head. **b~lich** *a & adv* by letter. **B~marke** *f* [postage] stamp. **B~öffner** *m* paper-knife. **B~papier** *nt* notepaper. **B~tasche** *f* wallet. **B~träger** *m* postman. **B~umschlag** *m*

envelope. **B~wahl** *f* postal vote. **B~wechsel** *m* correspondence
Brikett *nt* **-s, -s** briquette
Brillant *m* **-en, -en** [cut] diamond
Brille *f* **-, -n** glasses *pl*, spectacles *pl*; (*Schutz-*) goggles *pl*; (*Klosett-*) toilet seat
bringen† *vt* bring; (*fort-*) take; (*ein-*) yield; (*veröffentlichen*) publish; (*im Radio*) broadcast; show <*Film*>; **ins Bett b~** put to bed; **jdn nach Hause b~** take/(*begleiten*) see s.o. home; **um etw b~** deprive of sth; **jdn dazu b~, etw zu tun** get s.o. to do sth; **es weit b~** (*fig*) go far
Brise *f* **-, -n** breeze
Brit|e *m* **-n, -n, B~in** *f* **-, -nen** Briton. **b~isch** *a* British
Bröck|chen *nt* **-s,-** (*Culin*) crouton. **b~elig** *a* crumbly; <*Gestein*> friable. **b~eln** *vt/i* (*haben/sein*) crumble
Brocken *m* **-s,-** chunk; (*Erde, Kohle*) lump
Brokat *m* **-[e]s, -e** brocade
Brokkoli *pl* broccoli *sg*
Brombeere *f* blackberry
Bronchitis *f* **-** bronchitis
Bronze /ˈbrõ:sə/ *f* **-, -n** bronze
Brosch|e *f* **-, -n** brooch. **b~iert** *a* paperback. **B~üre** *f* **-, -n** brochure; (*Heft*) booklet
Brösel *mpl* (*Culin*) breadcrumbs
Brot *n* **-[e]s, -e** bread; **ein B~** a loaf [of bread]; (*Scheibe*) a slice of bread
Brötchen *n* **-s,-** [bread] roll
Brotkrümel *m* breadcrumb
Bruch *m* **-[e]s,⸚e** break; (*Brechen*) breaking; (*Rohr-*) burst; (*Med*) fracture; (*Eingeweide-*) rupture, hernia; (*Math*) fraction; (*fig*) breach; (*in Beziehung*) break-up
brüchig *a* brittle
Bruch|landung *f* crash-landing. **B~rechnung** *f* fractions *pl*. **B~stück** *nt* fragment. **B~teil** *m* fraction
Brücke *f* **-, -n** bridge; (*Teppich*) rug
Bruder *m* **-s,⸚** brother
brüderlich *a* brotherly, fraternal
Brügge *nt* **-s** Bruges
Brüh|e *f* **-, -n** broth, stock. **B~würfel** *m* stock cube
brüllen *vt/i* (*haben*) roar
brumm|eln *vt/i* (*haben*) mumble. **b~en** *vi* (*haben*) <*Insekt:*> buzz; <*Bär:*> growl; <*Motor:*> hum; (*murren*) grumble **B~er** *m* **-s,-** 🄸 bluebottle. **b~ig** *a* 🄸 grumpy
brünett *a* dark-haired
Brunnen *m* **-s,-** well; (*Spring-*) fountain; (*Heil-*) spa water
brüsk *a* brusque
Brüssel *nt* **-s** Brussels
Brust *f* **-,⸚e** chest; (*weibliche, Culin: B~stück*) breast. **B~bein** *nt* breastbone
brüsten (sich) *vr* boast
Brustschwimmen *nt* breaststroke
Brüstung *f* **-, -en** parapet
Brustwarze *f* nipple
Brut *f* **-, -en** incubation
brutal *a* brutal
brüten *vi* (*haben*) sit (*on eggs*); (*fig*) ponder (**über** + *dat* over)
Brutkasten *m* (*Med*) incubator
brutto *adv*, **B~-** *pref* gross
BSE *f* **-** BSE
Bub *m* **-en, -en** (*SGer*) boy. **B~e** *m* **-n, -n** (*Karte*) jack, knave
Buch *nt* **-[e]s,⸚er** book; **B~ führen** keep a record (**über** + *acc* of); **die B~̈er führen** keep the accounts
Buche *f* **-, -n** beech
buchen *vt* book; (*Comm*) enter
Bücher|ei *f* **-, -en** library. **B~regal** *nt* bookcase, bookshelves *pl*. **B~schrank** *m* bookcase
Buchfink *m* chaffinch
Buch|führung *f* bookkeeping. **B~halter(in)** *m* **-s,-** (*f* **-, -nen**) bookkeeper, accountant. **B~haltung** *f* bookkeeping, accountancy; (*Abteilung*)

accounts department. **B~handlung** *f* bookshop

Büchse *f* **-, -n** box; (*Konserven-*) tin, can

Buch|stabe *m* **-n, -n** letter. **b~stabieren** *vt* spell [out]. **b~stäblich** *adv* literally

Bucht *f* **-, -en** (*Geog*) bay

Buchung *f* **-, -en** booking, reservation; (*Comm*) entry

Buckel *m* **-s,-** hump; (*Beule*) bump; (*Hügel*) hillock

bücken (sich) *vr* bend down

bucklig *a* hunchbacked

Bückling *m* **-s, -e** smoked herring

Buddhis|mus *m* **-** Buddhism. **B~t(in)** *m* **-en, -en** (*f* **-, -nen**) Buddhist. **b~tisch** *a* Buddhist

Bude *f* **-, -n** hut; (*Kiosk*) kiosk; (*Markt-*) stall; (! *Zimmer*) room

Budget /bʏˈdʒeː/ *nt* **-s, -s** budget

Büfett *nt* **-[e]s, -e** sideboard; (*Theke*) bar; **kaltes B~** cold buffet

Büffel *m* **-s,-** buffalo

Bügel *m* **-s,-** frame; (*Kleider-*) coathanger; (*Steig-*) stirrup; (*Brillen-*) sidepiece. **B~brett** *nt* ironing-board. **B~eisen** *nt* iron. **B~falte** *f* crease. **b~frei** *a* non-iron. **b~n** *vt/i* (*haben*) iron

Bühne *f* **-, -n** stage. **B~nbild** *nt* set. **B~neingang** *m* stage door

Buhrufe *mpl* boos

Bukett *nt* **-[e]s, -e** bouquet

Bulgarien /-i̯ən/ *nt* **-s** Bulgaria

Bull|auge *nt* (*Naut*) porthole. **B~dogge** *f* bulldog. **B~dozer** /-doːzɐ/ *m* **-s,-** bulldozer. **B~e** *m* **-n, -n** bull; (✖ *Polizist*) cop

Bumme|l *m* **-s,-** ! stroll. **B~lei** *f* **-** ! dawdling

bummel|ig *a* ! slow; (*nachlässig*) careless. **b~n** *vi* (*sein*) ! stroll ● *vi* (*haben*) ! dawdle. **B~streik** *m* go-slow. **B~zug** *m* ! slow train

Bums *m* **-es, -e** ! bump, thump

Bund[1] *nt* **-[e]s, -e** bunch

Bund[2] *m* **-[e]s,⸚e** association; (*Bündnis*) alliance; (*Pol*) federation; (*Rock-, Hosen-*) waistband; **der B~** the Federal Government

Bündel *nt* **-s,-** bundle. **b~n** *vt* bundle [up]

Bundes|- *pref* Federal. **B~genosse** *m* ally. **B~kanzler** *m* Federal Chancellor. **B~land** *nt* [federal] state; (*Aust*) province. **B~liga** *f* German national league. **B~rat** *m* Upper House of Parliament. **B~regierung** *f* Federal Government. **B~republik** *f* **die B~republik Deutschland** the Federal Republic of Germany. **B~tag** *m* Lower House of Parliament. **B~wehr** *f* [Federal German] Army

bünd|ig *a & adv* **kurz und b~ig** short and to the point. **B~nis** *nt* **-sses, -sse** alliance

Bunker *m* **-s,-** bunker; (*Luftschutz-*) shelter

bunt *a* coloured; (*farbenfroh*) colourful; (*grell*) gaudy; (*gemischt*) varied; (*wirr*) confused; **b~e Platte** assorted cold meats. **B~stift** *m* crayon

Bürde *f* **-, -n** (*fig*) burden

Burg *f* **-, -en** castle

Bürge *m* **-n, -n** guarantor. **b~n** *vi* (*haben*) **b~n für** vouch for; (*fig*) guarantee

Bürger|(in) *m* **-s,-** (*f* **-, -nen**) citizen. **B~krieg** *m* civil war. **b~lich** *a* civil; <*Pflicht*> civic; (*mittelständisch*) middle-class. **B~liche(r)** *m/f* commoner. **B~meister** *m* mayor. **B~rechte** *npl* civil rights. **B~steig** *m* **-[e]s, -e** pavement

Bürgschaft *f* **-, -en** surety

Burgunder *m* **-s,-** (*Wein*) Burgundy

Büro *nt* **-s, -s** office. **B~angestellte(r)** *m/f* office-worker. **B~klammer** *f* paper-clip.

B~kratie *f* **-, -n** bureaucracy. **b~kratisch** *a* bureaucratic
Bursche *m* **-n, -n** lad, youth
Bürste *f* **-, -n** brush. **b~n** *vt* brush. **B~nschnitt** *m* crew cut
Bus *m* **-ses, -se** bus; (*Reise-*) coach
Busch *m* **-[e]s,¨-e** bush
Büschel *nt* **-s,-** tuft
buschig *a* bushy
Busen *m* **-s,-** bosom
Buße *f* **-, -n** penance; (*Jur*) fine
Bußgeld *nt* (*Jur*) fine
Büste *f* **-, -n** bust; (*Schneider-*) dummy. **B~nhalter** *m* **-s,-** bra
Butter *f* **-** butter. **B~blume** *f* buttercup. **B~brot** *nt* slice of bread and butter. **B~milch** *f* buttermilk. **b~n** *vt* butter
b.w. *abbr* (**bitte wenden**) P.T.O.

Cc

Café /ka'fe:/ *nt* **-s, -s** café
Camcorder /'kamkɔrdɐ/ *m* **-s, -** camcorder
camp|en /'kɛmpən/ *vi* (*haben*) go camping. **C~ing** *nt* **-s** camping. **C~ingplatz** *m* campsite
Caravan /'ka[:]ravan/ *m* **-s, -s** (*Auto*) caravan; (*Kombi*) estate car
CD /tse:'de:/ *f* **-, -s** compact disc, CD. **CD-ROM** /tse:de:'rɔm/ *f* **-,-(s)** CD-ROM
Cell|ist(in) /tʃɛ'lɪst(ɪn)/ *m* **-en, -en** (*f* **-, -nen**) cellist. **C~o** /'tʃɛlo/ *nt* **-, -los** & **-li** cello
Celsius /'tsɛlziʊs/ *inv* Celsius, centigrade
Cent /tsent/ *m* **-[s], -[s]** cent
Champagner /ʃam'panjɐ/ *m* **-s** champagne
Champignon /'ʃampɪnjɔŋ/ *m* **-s, -s** [field] mushroom
Chance /'ʃã:s[ə]/ *f* **-, -n** chance
Chaos /'ka:ɔs/ *nt* **-** chaos
Charakter /ka'raktɐ/ *m* **-s, -e** /-'te:rə/ character. **c~isieren** *vt* characterize. **c~istisch** *a* characteristic (**für** of)
charm|ant /ʃar'mant/ *a* charming. **C~e** /ʃarm/ *m* **-s** charm
Charter|flug /'tʃ-, 'ʃartɐ-/ *m* charter flight. **c~n** *vt* charter
Chassis /ʃa'si:/ *nt* **-,-** /-'si:[s], -'si:s/ chassis
Chauffeur /ʃɔ'fø:ɐ/ *m* **-s, -e** chauffeur; (*Taxi-*) driver
Chauvinist /ʃovi'nɪst/ *m* **-en, -en** chauvinist
Chef /ʃɛf/ *m* **-s, -s** head; [!] boss
Chemie /çe'mi:/ *f* **-** chemistry
Chem|iker(in) /'çe:-/ *m* **-s,-** (*f* **-, -nen**) chemist. **c~isch** *a* chemical; **c~ische Reinigung** dry-cleaning; (*Geschäft*) dry-cleaner's
Chicorée /'ʃɪkore:/ *m* **-s** chicory
Chiffre /'ʃɪfɐ, 'ʃɪfrə/ *f* **-, -n** cipher
Chile /'çi:le/ *nt* **-s** Chile
Chin|a /'çi:na/ *nt* **-s** China. **C~ese** *m* **-n, -n, C~esin** *f* **-, -nen** Chinese. **c~esisch** *a* Chinese. **C~esisch** *nt* **-[s]** (*Lang*) Chinese
Chip /tʃɪp/ *m* **-s, -s** [micro]chip. **C~s** *pl* crisps
Chirurg /çi'rʊrk/ *m* **-en, -en** surgeon. **C~ie** /-'gi:/ *f* **-** surgery
Chlor /klo:ɐ/ *nt* **-s** chlorine
Choke /tʃo:k/ *m* **-s, -s** (*Auto*) choke
Cholera /'ko:lera/ *f* **-** cholera
cholerisch /ko'le:rɪʃ/ *a* irascible
Cholesterin /ço-, kolɛste'ri:n/ *nt* **-s** cholesterol
Chor /ko:ɐ/ *m* **-[e]s,¨-e** choir
Choreographie, Choreografie /koreogra'fi:/ *f* **-, -n** choreography
Christ /krɪst/ *m* **-en, -en** Christian. **C~baum** *m* Christmas tree.

C

C~entum *nt* **-s** Christianity **c~lich** *a* Christian
Christus/'krɪstʊs/ *m* **-ti** Christ
Chrom /kro:m/ *nt* **-s** chromium
Chromosom /kromo'zo:m/ *nt* **-s, -en** chromosome
Chronik /'kro:nɪk/ *f* **-, -en** chronicle
chronisch /'kro:nɪʃ/ *a* chronic
Chrysantheme /krʏzan'te:mə/ *f* **-, -n** chrysanthemum
Clique /'klɪkə/ *f* **-, -n** clique
Clown /klaun/ *m* **-s, -s** clown
Club /klʊp/ *m* **-s, -s** club
Cocktail /'kɔkte:l/ *m* **-s, -s** cocktail
Code /'ko:t/ *m* **-s, -s** code
Comic-Heft /'kɔmɪk-/ *nt* comic
Computer /kɔm'pju:tɐ/ *m* **-s,-** computer. **c~isieren** *vt* computerize. **C~spiel** *nt* computer game
Conférencier /kõferã'sie:/ *m* **-s,-** compère
Cord /kɔrt/ *m* **-s, C~samt** *m* corduroy
Couch /kautʃ/ *f* **-, -es** settee
Cousin /ku'zɛ̃:/ *m* **-s, -s** [male] cousin. **C~e** /-'zi:nə/ *f* **-, -n** [female] cousin
Creme /kre:m/ *f* **-s, -s** cream; (*Speise*) cream dessert
Curry /'kari, 'kœri/ *nt & m* **-s** curry powder ● *nt* **-s, -s** (*Gericht*) curry
Cursor /'kø:ɐsə/ *m* **-s, -** cursor
Cyberspace /'saibəspe:s/ *m* **-** cyberspace

Dd

da *adv* there; (*hier*) here; (*zeitlich*) then; (*in dem Fall*) in that case; **von da an** from then on; **da sein** be there/(*hier*) here; (*existieren*) exist; **wieder da sein** be back ● *conj* as, since
dabei (*emphatic*: **dabei**) *adv* nearby; (*daran*) with it; (*eingeschlossen*) included; (*hinsichtlich*) about it; (*währenddem*) during this; (*gleichzeitig*) at the same time; (*doch*) and yet; **dicht d~** close by; **d~ sein** be present; (*mitmachen*) be involved; **d~ sein, etw zu tun** be just doing sth
Dach *nt* **-[e]s,¨er** roof. **D~boden** *m* loft. **D~luke** *f* skylight. **D~rinne** *f* gutter
Dachs *m* **-es, -e** badger
Dachsparren *m* **-s,-** rafter
Dackel *m* **-s,-** dachshund
dadurch (*emphatic:* **dadurch**) *adv* through it/them; (*Ursache*) by it; (*deshalb*) because of that; **d~, dass** because
dafür (*emphatic:* **dafür**) *adv* for it/them; (*anstatt*) instead; (*als Ausgleich*) but [on the other hand]; **d~, dass** considering that; **ich kann nichts dafür** it's not my fault
dagegen (*emphatic:* **dagegen**) *adv* against it/them; (*Mittel, Tausch*) for it; (*verglichen damit*) by comparison; (*jedoch*) however; **hast du was d~?** do you mind?
daheim *adv* at home
daher (*emphatic:* **daher**) *adv* from there; (*deshalb*) for that reason; **das kommt d~, weil** that's because ● *conj* that is why
dahin (*emphatic:* **dahin**) *adv* there; **bis d~** up to there; (*bis dann*) until/(*Zukunft*) by then; **jdn d~bringen, dass er etw tut** get s.o. to do sth
dahinten *adv* back there
dahinter (*emphatic:* **dahinter**) *adv* behind it/them; **d~ kommen** (*fig*) get to the bottom of it
Dahlie /-iə/ *f* **-, -n** dahlia

dalassen† *vt sep* leave there
daliegen† *vi sep* (*haben*) lie there
damalig *a* at that time; **der d~e Minister** the then minister
damals *adv* at that time
Damast *m* **-es, -e** damask
Dame *f* **-, -n** lady; (*Karte, Schach*) queen; (*D~spiel*) draughts *sg*. **d~nhaft** *a* ladylike
damit (*emphatic:* **damit**) *adv* with it/them; (*dadurch*) by it; **hör auf d~!** stop it! ● *conj* so that
Damm *m* **-[e]s,¨-e** dam
dämmer|ig *a* dim. **D~licht** *nt* twilight. **d~n** *vi* <*haben*> <*Morgen:*> dawn; **es d~t** it is getting light/(*abends*) dark. **D~ung** *f* dawn; (*Abend-*) dusk
Dämon *m* **-s, -en** /-ˈmoːnən/ demon
Dampf *m* **-es,¨-e** steam, (*Chem*) vapour. **d~en** *vi* (*haben*) steam
dämpfen *vt* (*Culin*) steam; (*fig*) muffle <*Ton*>; lower <*Stimme*>
Dampf|er *m* **-s,-** steamer. **D~kochtopf** *m* pressure-cooker. **D~maschine** *f* steam engine. **D~walze** *f* steamroller
danach (*emphatic:* **danach**) *adv* after it/them; <*suchen*> for it/ them; <*riechen*> of it; (*später*) afterwards; (*entsprechend*) accordingly; **es sieht d~ aus** it looks like it
Däne *m* **-n, -n** Dane
daneben (*emphatic:* **daneben**) *adv* beside it/them; (*außerdem*) in addition; (*verglichen damit*) by comparison
Dän|emark *nt* **-s** Denmark. **D~in** *f* **-, -nen** Dane. **d~isch** *a* Danish
Dank *m* **-es** thanks *pl*; **vielen D~!** thank you very much! **d~** *prep* (+ *dat or gen*) thanks to. **d~bar** *a* grateful; (*erleichtert*) thankful; (*lohnend*) rewarding. **D~barkeit** *f* **-** gratitude. **d~e** *adv* **d~e [schön** *od* **sehr]!** thank you [very much]! **d~en** *vi* (*haben*) thank (**jdm** s.o.); (*ablehnen*) decline; **nichts zu d~en!** don't mention it!
dann *adv* then; **selbst d~, wenn** even if
daran (*emphatic:* **daran**) *adv* on it/them; at it/them; <*denken*> of it; **nahe d~** on the point (**etw zu tun** of doing sth). **d~setzen** *vt sep* **alles d~setzen** do one's utmost (**zu** to)
darauf (*emphatic:* **darauf**) *adv* on it/them; <*warten*> for it; <*antworten*> to it; (*danach*) after that; (*d~hin*) as a result. **d~hin** *adv* as a result
daraus (*emphatic:* **daraus**) *adv* out of *or* from it/them; **er macht sich nichts d~** he doesn't care for it
darlegen *vt sep* expound; (*erklären*) explain
Darlehen *nt* **-s,-** loan
Darm *m* **-[e]s,¨-e** intestine
darstell|en *vt sep* represent; (*bildlich*) portray; (*Theat*) interpret; (*spielen*) play; (*schildern*) describe. **D~er** *m* **-s,-** actor. **D~erin** *f* **-, -nen** actress. **D~ung** *f* representation; interpretation; description
darüber (*emphatic:* **darüber**) *adv* over it/them; (*höher*) above it/ them; <*sprechen, lachen, sich freuen*> about it; (*mehr*) more; **d~ hinaus** beyond [it]; (*dazu*) on top of that
darum (*emphatic:* **darum**) *adv* round it/them; <*bitten, kämpfen*> for it; (*deshalb*) that is why; **d~, weil** because
darunter (*emphatic:* **darunter**) *adv* under it/them; (*tiefer*) below it/ them; (*weniger*) less, (*dazwischen*) among them
das *def art & pron s.* **der**
dasein* *vi sep* (*sein*) **da sein**, *s.* **da**. **D~** *nt* **-s** existence
dass *conj* that
dasselbe *pron s.* **derselbe**

Daten|sichtgerät *nt* visual display unit, VDU. **D~verarbeitung** *f* data processing
datieren *vt/i* (*haben*) date
Dativ *m* **-s, -e** dative. **D~objekt** *nt* indirect object
Dattel *f* **-, -n** date
Datum *nt* **s, -ten** date; **Daten** dates; (*Angaben*) data
Dauer *f* **-** duration, length; (*Jur*) term; **auf die D~** in the long run. **D~auftrag** *m* standing order. **d~haft** *a* lasting, enduring; (*fest*) durable. **D~karte** *f* season ticket. **d~n** *vi* (*haben*) last; **lange d~n** take a long time. **d~nd** *a* lasting; (*ständig*) constant. **D~welle** *f* perm
Daumen *m* **-s,-** thumb; **jdm den D~ drücken** *od* **halten** keep one's fingers crossed for s.o.
Daunen *fpl* down *sg*. **D~decke** *f* [down-filled] duvet
davon (*emphatic:* **davon**) *adv* from it/them; (*dadurch*) by it; (*damit*) with it/them; (*darüber*) about it; (*Menge*) of it/them; **das kommt d~!** it serves you right! **d~kommen**† *vi sep* (*sein*) escape (**mit dem Leben** with one's life). **d~laufen**† *vi sep* (*sein*) run away. **d~machen (sich)** *vr sep* [!] make off. **d~tragen**† *vt sep* carry off; (*erleiden*) suffer; (*gewinnen*) win
davor (*emphatic:* **davor**) *adv* in front of it/them; <*sich fürchten*> of it; (*zeitlich*) before it/them
dazu (*emphatic:* **dazu**) *adv* to it/ them; (*damit*) with it/them; (*dafür*) for it; **noch d~** in addition to that; **jdn d~ bringen, etw zu tun** get s.o. to do sth; **ich kam nicht d~** I didn't get round to [doing] it. **d~kommen**† *vi sep* (*sein*) arrive [on the scene]; (*hinzukommen*) be added. **d~rechnen** *vt sep* add to it/them
dazwischen (*emphatic:* **dazwischen**) *adv* between them; in between; (*darunter*) among them. **d~kommen**† *vi sep* (*sein*) (*fig*) crop up; **wenn nichts d~kommt** if all goes well
Debat|te *f* **-, -n** debate; **zur D~te stehen** be at issue. **d~tieren** *vt/i* (*haben*) debate
Debüt /de'by:/ *nt* **-s, -s** début
Deck *nt* **-[e]s, -s** (*Naut*) deck; **an D~** on deck. **D~bett** *nt* duvet
Decke *f* **-, -n** cover; (*Tisch-*) table-cloth; (*Bett-*) blanket; (*Reise-*) rug; (*Zimmer-*) ceiling; **unter einer D~stecken** [!] be in league
Deckel *m* **-s,-** lid; (*Flaschen-*) top; (*Buch-*) cover
decken *vt* cover; tile <*Dach*>; lay <*Tisch*>; (*schützen*) shield; (*Sport*) mark; meet <*Bedarf*>; **jdn d~** (*fig*) cover up for s.o.; **sich d~** (*fig*) cover oneself (**gegen** against); (*übereinstimmen*) coincide
Deckname *m* pseudonym
Deckung *f* **-** (*Mil*) cover; (*Sport*) defence; (*Mann-*) marking; (*Boxen*) guard; (*Sicherheit*) security; **in D~ gehen** take cover
defin|ieren *vt* define. **D~ition** /-'tsio:n/ *f* **-, -en** definition
Defizit *nt* **-s, -e** deficit
deformiert *a* deformed
deftig *a* [!] <*Mahlzeit*> hearty; <*Witz*> coarse
Degen *m* **-s,-** sword; (*Fecht-*) épée
degeneriert *a* (*fig*) degenerate
degradieren *vt* (*Mil*) demote; (*fig*) degrade
dehn|bar *a* elastic. **d~en** *vt* stretch; lengthen <*Vokal*>; **sich d~en** stretch
Deich *m* **-[e]s, -e** dike
dein *poss pron* your. **d~e(r,s)** *poss pron* yours; **die D~en** *od* **d~en** *pl* your family *sg*. **d~erseits** *adv* for your part.

d~etwegen *adv* for your sake; (*wegen dir*) because of you, on your account. **d~etwillen** *adv* **um d~etwillen** for your sake. **d~ige** *poss pron* **der/die/das d~ige** yours. **d~s** *poss pron* yours
Dekan *m* **-s, -e** dean
Deklin|ation /-'tsio:n/ *f* **-, -en** declension. **d~ieren** *vt* decline
Dekolleté, Dekolletee /dekɔl'te:/ *nt* **-s, -s** low neckline
Dekor *m & nt* **-s** decoration. **D~ateur** /-'tø:ɐ/ *m* **-s, -e** interior decorator; (*Schaufenster-*) window-dresser. **D~ation** /-'tsio:n/ *f* **-, -en** decoration; (*Schaufenster-*) window-dressing; (*Auslage*) display. **d~ativ** *a* decorative. **d~ieren** *vt* decorate; dress <*Schaufenster*>
Deleg|ation /-'tsio:n/ *f* **-, -en** delegation. **D~ierte(r)** *m/f* delegate
delikat *a* delicate; (*lecker*) delicious; (*taktvoll*) tactful. **D~essengeschäft** *nt* delicatessen
Delikt *nt* **-[e]s, -e** offence
Delinquent *m* **-en, -en** offender
Delle *f* **-, -n** dent
Delphin *m* **-s, -e** dolphin
Delta *nt* **-s, -s** delta
dem *def art & pron s.* **der**
dementieren *vt* deny
dem|entsprechend *a* corresponding; (*passend*) appropriate ● *adv* accordingly; (*passend*) appropriately. **d~nächst** *adv* soon; (*in Kürze*) shortly
Demokrat *m* **-en, -en** democrat. **D~ie** *f* **-, -n** democracy. **d~isch** *a* democratic
demolieren *vt* wreck
Demonstr|ant *m* **-en, -en** demonstrator. **D~ation** /-'tsio:n/ *f* **-, -en** demonstration. **d~ieren** *vt/i* (*haben*) demonstrate
demontieren *vt* dismantle
Demoskopie *f* **-** opinion research
Demut *f* **-** humility
den *def art & pron s.* **der**. **d~en** *pron s.* **der**
denk|bar *a* conceivable. **d~en**† *vt/i* (*haben*) think (**an** + *acc* of); (*sich erinnern*) remember (**an etw** *acc* sth); **das kann ich mir d~en** I can imagine [that]; **ich d~e nicht daran** I have no intention of doing it. **D~mal** *nt* memorial; (*Monument*) monument. **d~würdig** *a* memorable
denn *conj* for; **besser/mehr d~ je** better/more than ever ● *adv* **wie/wo d~?** but how/where? **warum d~ nicht?** why ever not? **es sei d~ [, dass]** unless
dennoch *adv* nevertheless
Denunz|iant *m* **-en, -en** informer. **d~ieren** *vt* denounce
Deodorant *nt* **-s, -s** deodorant
deplaciert, deplatziert /-'tsi:ɐt/ *a* (*fig*) out of place
Deponie *f* **-, -n** dump. **d~ren** *vt* deposit
deportieren *vt* deport
Depot /de'po:/ *nt* **-s, -s** depot; (*Lager*) warehouse; (*Bank-*) safe deposit
Depression *f* **-, -en** depression
deprimieren *vt* depress

der, die, das, *pl* **die**
● *definite article*
(*acc* **den, die, das,** *pl* **die**; *gen* **des, der, des,** *pl* **der**; *dat* **dem, der, dem,** *pl* **den**)
····➤ the. **der Mensch** the person; (*als abstrakter Begriff*) man. **die Natur** nature. **das Leben** life. **das Lesen/Tanzen** reading/dancing. **sich** (*dat*) **das Gesicht/die Hände waschen** wash one's face/hands. **3 Euro das Pfund** 3 euros a pound
● *pronoun*
(*acc* **den, die, das,** *pl* **die**; *gen* **dessen, deren, dessen,** *pl*

D

deren; *dat* **dem, der, dem**, *pl* **denen**)

● *demonstrative pronoun*

····➤ that; (*pl*) those

····➤ (*attributiv*) **der Mann war es** it was 'that man

····➤ (*substantivisch*) he, she, it; (*pl*) they. **der war es** it was 'him. **die da** (*person*) that woman/girl; (*thing*) that one

● *relative pronoun*

····➤ (*Person*) who. **der Mann, der/dessen Sohn hier arbeitet** the man who/whose son works here. **die Frau, mit der ich Tennis spiele** the woman with whom I play tennis, the woman I play tennis with. **das Mädchen, das ich gestern sah** the girl I saw yesterday

····➤ (*Ding*) which, that. **ich sah ein Buch, das mich interessierte** I saw a book that interested me. **die CD, die ich mir anhöre** the CD I am listening to. **das Auto, mit dem wir nach Deutschland fahren** the car we are going to Germany in *or* in which we are going to Germany

derb *a* tough; (*kräftig*) strong; (*grob*) coarse; (*unsanft*) rough

deren *pron s.* **der**

dergleichen *inv a* such ● *pron* such a thing/such things

der-/die-/dasselbe, *pl* **dieselben** *pron* the same; **ein- und dasselbe** one and the same thing

derzeit *adv* at present

des *def art s.* **der**

Desert|eur /-'tø:ɐ̯/ *m* **-s, -e** deserter. **d~ieren** *vi* (*sein/haben*) desert

desgleichen *adv* likewise ● *pron* the like

deshalb *adv* for this reason; (*also*) therefore

Designer(in) /di'zainɐ, -nərɪn/ *m* **-s,-** (*f*, **-, -nen**) designer

Desin|fektion /dɛsʔɪnfɛk'tsi̯o:n/ *f* disinfecting. **D~fektionsmittel** *nt* disinfectant. **d~fizieren** *vt* disinfect

dessen *pron s.* **der**

Destill|ation /-'tsi̯o:n/ *f* **-** distillation. **d~ieren** *vt* distil

desto *adv* **je mehr d~ besser** the more the better

deswegen *adv* = **deshalb**

Detektiv *m* **-s, -e** detective

Deton|ation /-'tsi̯o:n/ *f* **-, -en** explosion. **d~ieren** *vi* (*sein*) explode

deut|en *vt* interpret; predict <*Zukunft*> ● *vi* (*haben*) point (**auf** + *acc* at/(*fig*) to). **d~lich** *a* clear; (*eindeutig*) plain

deutsch *a* German. **D~** *nt* **-[s]** (*Lang*) German; **auf D~** in German. **D~e(r)** *m/f* German. **D~land** *nt* **-s** Germany

Deutung *f* **-, -en** interpretation

Devise *f* **-, -n** motto. **D~n** *pl* foreign currency *or* exchange *sg*

Dezember *m* **-s,-** December

dezent *a* unobtrusive; (*diskret*) discreet

Dezernat *nt* **-[e]s, -e** department

Dezimalzahl *f* decimal

d.h. *abbr* (*das heißt*) i.e.

Dia *nt* **-s, -s** (*Phot*) slide

Diabet|es *m* **-** diabetes. **D~iker** *m* **-s,-** diabetic

Diadem *nt* **-s, -e** tiara

Diagnose *f* **-, -n** diagnosis

diagonal *a* diagonal. **D~e** *f* **-, -n** diagonal

Diagramm *nt* **-s, -e** diagram; (*Kurven-*) graph

Diakon *m* **-s, -e** deacon

Dialekt *m* **-[e]s, -e** dialect

Dialog *m* **-[e]s, -e** dialogue

Diamant *m* **-en, -en** diamond

Diapositiv *nt* **-s, -e** (*Phot*) slide

Diaprojektor *m* slide projector

Diät *f* **-, -en** (*Med*) diet; **D~ leben** be on a diet

dich *pron* (*acc of* **du**) you; (*refl*) yourself

dicht *a* dense; (*dick*) thick; (*undurchlässig*) airtight; (*wasser-*) watertight ● *adv* densely; (*nahe*) close (**bei** to). **D∼e** density. **d∼en**[1] *vt* make watertight

dicht|en[2] *vi* (*haben*) write poetry. ● *vt* write. **D∼er(in)** *m* **-s,-** (*f* **-, -en**) poet. **d∼erisch** *a* poetic. **D∼ung**[1] *f* **-, -en** poetry; (*Gedicht*) poem

Dichtung[2] *f* **-, -en** seal; (*Ring*) washer; (*Auto*) gasket

dick *a* thick; (*beleibt*) fat; (*geschwollen*) swollen; (*fam; eng*) close; **d∼ machen** be fattening. **d∼flüssig** *a* thick; (*Phys*) viscous. **D∼kopf** *m* [!] stubborn person; **einen D∼kopf haben** be stubborn

die *def art & pron s.* **der**

Dieb|(in) *m* **-[e]s, -e** (*f* **-, -nen**) thief. **d∼isch** *a* thieving; <*Freude*> malicious. **D∼stahl** *m* **-[e]s,¨-e** theft

Diele *f* **-, -n** floorboard; (*Flur*) hall

dien|en *vi* (*haben*) serve. **D∼er** *m* **-s,-** servant; (*Verbeugung*) bow. **D∼erin** *f* **-, -nen** maid, servant

Dienst *m* **-[e]s, -e** service; (*Arbeit*) work; (*Amtsausübung*) duty; **außer D∼** off duty; (*pensioniert*) retired; **D∼ haben** work; <*Soldat, Arzt:*> be on duty

Dienstag *m* Tuesday. **d∼s** *adv* on Tuesdays

Dienst|bote *m* servant. **d∼frei** *a* **d∼freier Tag** day off; **d∼frei haben** have time off; <*Soldat, Arzt:*> be off duty. **D∼grad** *m* rank. **D∼leistung** *f* service. **d∼lich** *a* official ● *adv* **d∼lich verreist** away on business. **D∼mädchen** *nt* maid. **D∼reise** *f* business trip. **D∼stelle** *f* office. **D∼stunden** *fpl* office hours

dies *inv pron* this. **d∼bezüglich** *a* relevant ● *adv* regarding this matter. **d∼e(r,s)** *pron* this; (*pl*) these; (*substantivisch*) this [one]; (*pl*) these; **d∼e Nacht** tonight; (*letzte*) last night

dieselbe *pron s.* **derselbe**

Dieselkraftstoff *m* diesel [oil]

diesmal *adv* this time

Dietrich *m* **-s, -e** skeleton key

Differential* /-ˈtsi̯aːl/ *nt* **-s, -e** *s.* **Differenzial**

Differenz *f* **-, -en** difference. **D∼ial** *nt* **-s, -e** differential. **d∼ieren** *vt/i* (*haben*) differentiate (**zwischen** + *dat* between)

digital *a* digital

Digital- *pref* digital. **D∼kamera** *f* digital camera. **D∼uhr** *f* digital clock/watch

Dikt|at *nt* **-[e]s, -e** dictation. **D∼ator** *m* **-s, -en** /-ˈtoːrən/ dictator. **D∼atur** *f* **-, -en** dictatorship. **d∼ieren** *vt/i* (*haben*) dictate

Dill *m* **-s** dill

Dimension *f* **-, -en** dimension

Ding *nt* **-[e]s, -e** & [!] **-er** thing; **guter D∼e sein** be cheerful; **vor allen D∼en** above all

Dinosaurier /-i̯ɐ/ *m* **-s,-** dinosaur

Diözese *f* **-, -n** diocese

Diphtherie *f* **-** diphtheria

Diplom *nt* **-s, -e** diploma; (*Univ*) degree

Diplomat *m* **-en, -en** diplomat

dir *pron* (*dat of* **du**) [to] you; (*refl*) yourself; **ein Freund von dir** a friend of yours

direkt *a* direct ● *adv* directly; (*wirklich*) really. **D∼ion** /-ˈtsi̯oːn/ *f* **-** management; (*Vorstand*) board of directors. **D∼or** *m* **-s, -en** /-ˈtoːrən/, **D∼orin** *f* **-, -nen** director; (*Bank-, Theater-*) manager; (*Sch*) head; (*Gefängnis*) governor. **D∼übertragung** *f* live transmission

Dirig|ent *m* **-en, -en** (*Mus*) conductor. **d∼ieren** *vt* direct; (*Mus*) conduct

Dirndl *nt* **-s,-** dirndl [dress]
Diskette *f* **-, -n** floppy disc
Disko *f* **-, -s** [!] disco. **D~thek** *f* **-, -en** discothèque
diskret *a* discreet
Diskus *m* **-, -se** & **Disken** discus
Disku|ssion *f* **-, -en** discussion. **d~tieren** *vt/i* (*haben*) discuss
disponieren *vi* (*haben*) make arrangements; **d~ [können] über** (+ *acc*) have at one's disposal
Disqualifi|kation /-'tsi̯o:n/ *f* disqualification. **d~zieren** *vt* disqualify
Dissertation /-'tsi̯o:n/ *f* **-, -en** dissertation
Dissident *m* **-en, -en** dissident
Distanz *f* **-, -en** distance. **d~ieren (sich)** *vr* dissociate oneself (**von** from). **d~iert** *a* aloof
Distel *f* **-, -n** thistle
Disziplin *f* **-, -en** discipline. **d~arisch** *a* disciplinary. **d~iert** *a* disciplined
dito *adv* ditto
diverse *attrib a pl* various
Divid|ende *f* **-, -en** dividend. **d~ieren** *vt* divide (**durch** by)
Division *f* **-, -en** division
DJH *abbr* (**Deutsche Jugendherberge**) [German] youth hostel
DM *abbr* (**Deutsche Mark**) DM
doch *conj & adv* but; (*dennoch*) yet; (*trotzdem*) after all; **wenn d~ ...!** if only ...! **nicht d~!** don't!
Docht *m* **-[e]s, -e** wick
Dock *nt* **-s, -s** dock. **d~en** *vt/i* (*haben*) dock
Dogge *f* **-, -n** Great Dane
Dogm|a *nt* **-s, -men** dogma. **d~atisch** *a* dogmatic
Doktor *m* **-s, -en** /-'to:rən/ doctor. **D~arbeit** *f* [doctoral] thesis
Dokument *nt* **-[e]s, -e** document. **D~arbericht** *m* documentary. **D~arfilm** *m* documentary film
Dolch *m* **-[e]s, -e** dagger
Dollar *m* **-s,-** dollar
dolmetsch|en *vt/i* (*haben*) interpret. **D~er(in)** *m* **-s,-** (*f* **-, -nen**) interpreter
Dom *m* **-[e]s, -e** cathedral
Domino *nt* **-s, -s** dominoes *sg*. **D~stein** *m* domino
Dompfaff *m* **-en, -en** bullfinch
Donau *f* **-** Danube
Donner *m* **-s** thunder. **d~n** *vi* (*haben*) thunder
Donnerstag *m* Thursday. **d~s** *adv* on Thursdays
doof *a* [!] stupid
Doppel *nt* **-s,-** duplicate; (*Tennis*) doubles *pl*. **D~bett** *nt* double bed. **D~decker** *m* **-s,-** doubledecker [bus]. **d~deutig** *a* ambiguous. **D~gänger** *m* **-s,-** double. **D~kinn** *nt* double chin. **d~klicken** *vi* (*haben*) double-click (**auf** + *acc* on). **D~name** *m* double-barrelled name. **D~punkt** *m* (*Gram*) colon. **D~stecker** *m* two-way adaptor. **d~t** *a* double; <*Boden*> false; **die d~te Menge** twice the amount ● *adv* doubly; (*zweimal*) twice; **d~t so viel** twice as much. **D~zimmer** *nt* double room
Dorf *nt* **-[e]s,⸚er** village. **D~bewohner** *m* villager
dörflich *a* rural
Dorn *m* **-[e]s, -en** thorn. **d~ig** *a* thorny
Dorsch *m* **-[e]s, -e** cod
dort *adv* there. **d~ig** *a* local
Dose *f* **-, -n** tin, can
dösen *vi* (*haben*) doze
Dosen|milch *f* evaporated milk. **D~öffner** *m* tin *or* can opener
dosieren *vt* measure out
Dosis *f* **-, Dosen** dose
Dot-com-Firma *f* dot-com (company)
Dotter *m & nt* **-s,-** [egg] yolk
Dozent(in) *m* **-en, -en** (*f* **-, -nen**) (*Univ*) lecturer
Dr. *abbr* (**Doktor**) Dr

Drache *m* **-n, -n** dragon. **D~n** *m* **-s,-** kite. **D~nfliegen** *nt* hang-gliding

Draht *m* **-[e]s,⸚e** wire; **auf D~** [!] on the ball. **D~seilbahn** *f* cable railway

Dram|a *nt* **-s, -men** drama. **D~atik** *f* **-** drama. **D~atiker** *m* **-s,-** dramatist. **d~atisch** *a* dramatic

dran *adv* [!] = **daran; gut/schlecht d~ sein** be well off/in a bad way; **ich bin d~** it's my turn

Drang *m* **-[e]s** urge; (*Druck*) pressure

drängeln *vt/i* (*haben*) push; (*bedrängen*) pester. **d~en** *vt* push; (*bedrängen*) urge; **sich d~en** crowd (**um** round) ● *vi* (*haben*) push; (*eilen*) be urgent; **d~en auf** (+ *acc*) press for

dran|halten† **(sich)** *vr sep* hurry. **d~kommen**† *vi sep* (*sein*) have one's turn

drauf *adv* [!] = **darauf; d~ und dran sein** be on the point (**etw zu tun** of doing sth). **D~gänger** *m* **-s,-** daredevil

draußen *adv* outside; (*im Freien*) out of doors

drechseln *vt* (*Techn*) turn

Dreck *m* **-s** dirt; (*Morast*) mud

Dreh *m* **-s** [!] knack; **den D~ heraushaben** have got the hang of it. **D~bank** *f* lathe. **D~bleistift** *m* propelling pencil. **D~buch** *nt* screenplay, script. **d~en** *vt* turn; (*im Kreis*) rotate; (*verschlingen*) twist; roll <*Zigarette*>; shoot <*Film*>; **lauter/leiser d~en** turn up/down; **sich d~en** turn; (*im Kreis*) rotate; (*schnell*) spin; <*Wind*:> change; **sich d~en um** revolve around; (*sich handeln*) be about ● *vi* (*haben*) turn; <*Wind*:> change; **an etw** (*dat*) **d~en** turn sth. **D~stuhl** *m* swivel chair. **D~tür** *f* revolving door. **D~ung** *f* **-, -en** turn; (*im Kreis*) rotation. **D~zahl** *f* number of revolutions

drei *inv a*, **D~** *f* **-, -en** three; (*Sch*) ≈ pass. **D~eck** *nt* **-[e]s, -e** triangle. **d~eckig** *a* triangular. **d~erlei** *inv* a three kinds of ● *pron* three things. **d~fach** *a* triple. **d~mal** *adv* three times. **D~rad** *nt* tricycle

dreißig *inv a* thirty. **d~ste(r,s)** *a* thirtieth

dreiviertel* *inv a* **drei viertel**, *s.* **viertel**. **D~stunde** *f* three-quarters of an hour

dreizehn *inv a* thirteen **d~te(r,s)** *a* thirteenth

dreschen† *vt* thresh

dress|ieren *vt* train. **D~ur** *f* **-** training

dribbeln *vi* (*haben*) dribble

Drill *m* **-[e]s** (*Mil*) drill. **d~en** *vt* drill

Drillinge *mpl* triplets

dringlich *a* urgent

Drink *m* **-[s], -s** [alcoholic] drink

drinnen *adv* inside

dritt *adv* **zu d~** in threes; **wir waren zu d~** there were three of us. **d~e(r,s)** *a* third; **ein D~er** a third person. **d~el** *inv a* third. **D~el** *nt* **-s,-** third. **d~ens** *adv* thirdly. **d~rangig** *a* third-rate

Drog|e *f* **-, -n** drug. **D~enabhängige(r)** *m/f* drug addict. **D~erie** *f* **-, -n** chemist's shop. **D~ist** *m* **-en, -en** chemist

drohen *vi* (*haben*) threaten (**jdm** s.o.)

dröhnen *vi* (*haben*) resound; (*tönen*) boom

Drohung *f* **-, -en** threat

drollig *a* funny; (*seltsam*) odd

Drops *m* **-,-** [fruit] drop

Drossel *f* **-, -n** thrush

drosseln *vt* (*Techn*) throttle; (*fig*) cut back

drüben *adv* over there

Druck[1] *m* **-[e]s,⸚e** pressure; **unter D~ setzen** (*fig*) pressurize

Druck^{2} *m* **-[e]s, -e** printing; (*Schrift, Reproduktion*) print. **D~buchstabe** *m* block letter
drucken *vt* print
drücken *vt/i* (*haben*) press; (*aus-*) squeeze; <*Schuh:*> pinch; (*umarmen*) hug; **Preise d~** force down prices; (*an Tür*) **d~** push; **sich d~** [!] make oneself scarce; **sich d~ vor** (+ *dat*) [!] shirk. **d~d** *a* heavy; (*schwül*) oppressive
Drucker *m* **-s,-** printer
Druckerei *f* **-, -en** printing works
Druck|fehler *m* misprint. **D~knopf** *m* press-stud. **D~luft** *f* compressed air. **D~sache** *f* printed matter. **D~schrift** *f* type; (*Veröffentlichung*) publication; **in D~schrift** in block letters *pl*
Druckstelle *f* bruise
Drüse *f* **-, -n** (*Anat*) gland
Dschungel *m* **-s,-** jungle
du *pron* (*familiar address*) you; **auf Du und Du** on familiar terms
Dübel *m* **-s,-** plug
Dudelsack *m* bagpipes *pl*
Duell *nt* **-s, -e** duel
Duett *nt* **-s, -e** [vocal] duet
Duft *m* **-[e]s,¨e** fragrance, scent; (*Aroma*) aroma. **d~en** *vi* (*haben*) smell (**nach** of)
dulden *vt* tolerate; (*erleiden*) suffer ● *vi* (*haben*) suffer
dumm *a* stupid; (*unklug*) foolish; ([!] *lästig*) awkward; **wie d~!**. **d~erweise** *adv* stupidly; (*leider*) unfortunately. **D~heit** *f* **-, -en** stupidity; (*Torheit*) foolishness; (*Handlung*) folly. **D~kopf** *m* [!] fool.
dumpf *a* dull
Düne *f* **-, -n** dune
Dung *m* **-s** manure
Düng|emittel *nt* fertilizer. **d~en** *vt* fertilize. **D~er** *m* **-s,-** fertilizer
dunk|el *a* dark; (*vage*) vague; (*fragwürdig*) shady; **d~les Bier** brown ale; **im D~eln** in the dark
Dunkel|heit *f* **-** darkness. **D~kammer** *f* dark-room. **d~n** *vi* (*haben*) get dark
dünn *a* thin; <*Buch*> slim; (*spärlich*) sparse; (*schwach*) weak
Dunst *m* **-es,¨e** mist, haze; (*Dampf*) vapour
dünsten *vt* steam
dunstig *a* misty, hazy
Duo *nt* **-s, -s** [instrumental] duet
Duplikat *nt* **-[e]s, -e** duplicate
Dur *nt* **-** (*Mus*) major [key]
durch *prep* (+ *acc*) through; (*mittels*) by; **[geteilt] d~** (*Math*) divided by ● *adv* **die Nacht d~** throughout the night; **d~ und d~ nass** wet through
durchaus *adv* absolutely; **d~ nicht** by no means
durchblättern *vt sep* leaf through
durchblicken *vi sep* (*haben*) look through; **d~ lassen** (*fig*) hint at
Durchblutung *f* circulation
durchbohren *vt insep* pierce
durchbrechen^{1}† *vt/i sep* (*haben*) break [in two]
durchbrechen^{2}† *vt insep* break through; break <*Schallmauer*>
durchbrennen† *vi sep* (*sein*) burn through; <*Sicherung:*> blow
Durchbruch *m* breakthrough
durchdrehen *v sep* ● *vt* mince ● *vi* (*haben/sein*) [!] go crazy
durchdringen† *vi sep* (*sein*) penetrate; (*sich durchsetzen*) get one's way. **d~d** *a* penetrating; <*Schrei*> piercing
durcheinander *adv* in a muddle; <*Person*> confused; **d~ bringen** muddle [up]; confuse <*Person*>; **d~ geraten** get mixed up; **d~ reden** all talk at once. **D~** *nt* **-s** muddle
durchfahren *vi sep* (*sein*) drive through; <*Zug:*> go through
Durchfahrt *f* journey/drive through; **auf der D~** passing through; **'D~ verboten'** 'no thoroughfare'

Durchfall *m* diarrhoea. **d∼en**† *vi sep* (*sein*) fall through; (! *versagen*) flop; (*bei Prüfung*) fail

Durchfuhr *f* - (*Comm*) transit

durchführ|bar *a* feasible. **d∼en** *vt sep* carry out

Durchgang *m* passage; (*Sport*) round; **'D∼ verboten'** 'no entry' . **D∼sverkehr** *m* through traffic

durchgeben† *vt sep* pass through; (*übermitteln*) transmit; (*Radio, TV*) broadcast

durchgebraten *a* **gut d∼** well done

durchgehen† *vi sep* (*sein*) go through; (*davonlaufen*) run away; <*Pferd:*> bolt; **jdm etw d∼ lassen** let s.o. get away with sth. **d∼d** *a* continuous; **d∼d geöffnet** open all day; **d∼der Zug** through train

durchgreifen† *vi sep* (*haben*) reach through; (*vorgehen*) take drastic action. **d∼d** *a* drastic

durchhalte|n† *v sep* (*fig*) ● *vi* (*haben*) hold out ● *vt* keep up. **D∼vermögen** *nt* stamina

durchkommen† *vi sep* (*sein*) come through; (*gelangen, am Telefon*) get through

durchlassen† *vt sep* let through

durchlässig *a* permeable; (*undicht*) leaky

Durchlauferhitzer *m* **-s,-** geyser

durchlesen† *vt sep* read through

durchleuchten *vt insep* X-ray

durchlöchert *a* riddled with holes

durchmachen *vt sep* go through; (*erleiden*) undergo

Durchmesser *m* **-s,-** diameter

durchnässt *a* wet through

durchnehmen† *vt sep* (*Sch*) do

durchnummeriert *a* numbered consecutively

durchpausen *vt sep* trace

durchqueren *vt insep* cross

Durchreiche *f* **-, -n** hatch

Durchreise *f* journey through; **auf der D∼** passing through. **d∼n** *vi sep* (*sein*) pass through

durchreißen† *vt/i sep* (*sein*) tear

Durchsage *f* **-, -n** announcement. **d∼n** *vt sep* announce

Durchschlag *m* carbon copy; (*Culin*) colander. **d∼en**† *v sep* ● *vt* (*Culin*) rub through a sieve; **sich d∼en** (*fig*) struggle through ● *vi* (*sein*) <*Sicherung:*> blow

durchschlagend *a* (*fig*) effective; <*Erfolg*> resounding

durchschneiden† *vt sep* cut

Durchschnitt *m* average; **im D∼** on average. **d∼lich** *a* average ● *adv* on average. **D∼s-** *pref* average

Durchschrift *f* carbon copy

durchsehen† *v sep* ● *vi* (*haben*) see through ● *vt* look through

durchseihen *vt sep* strain

durchsetzen *vt sep* force through; **sich d∼** assert oneself; <*Mode:*> catch on

Durchsicht *f* check

durchsichtig *a* transparent

durchsickern *vi sep* (*sein*) seep through; <*Neuigkeit:*> leak out

durchstehen† *vt sep* (*fig*) come through

durchstreichen† *vt sep* cross out

durchsuch|en *vt insep* search. **D∼ung** *f* **-, -en** search

durchwachsen *a* <*Speck*> streaky; (! *gemischt*) mixed

durchwählen *vi sep* (*haben*) (*Teleph*) dial direct

durchweg *adv* without exception

durchwühlen *vt insep* rummage through; ransack <*Haus*>

Durchzug *m* through draught

dürfen†

● *transitive & auxiliary verb*

····➤ (*Erlaubnis haben zu*) be allowed; may, can. **etw [tun] dürfen** be allowed to do sth. **darf ich das tun?** may *or* can I do

D

that? **nein, das darfst du nicht** no you may not *or* cannot [do that]. **er sagte mir, ich dürfte sofort gehen** he told me I could go at once. **hier darf man nicht rauchen** smoking is prohibited here. **sie darf/durfte es nicht sehen** she must not/was not allowed to see it.

····➤ (*in Höflichkeitsformeln*) may. **darf ich rauchen?** may I smoke? **darf/dürfte ich um diesen Tanz bitten?** may/might I have the pleasure of this dance?

····➤ **dürfte** (*sollte*) should, ought. **jetzt dürften sie dort angekommen sein** they should *or* ought to be there by now. **das dürfte nicht allzu schwer sein** that should not be too difficult. **ich hätte es nicht tun/sagen dürfen** I ought not to have done/said it

● *intransitive verb*

····➤ (*irgendwohin gehen dürfen*) be allowed to go; may go; can go. **darf ich nach Hause?** may *or* can I go home? **sie durfte nicht ins Theater** she was not allowed to go the theatre

dürftig *a* poor; <*Mahlzeit*> scanty

dürr *a* dry; <*Boden*> arid; (*mager*) skinny. **D~e** *f* **-, -n** drought

Durst *m* **-[e]s** thirst; **D~ haben** be thirsty. **d~ig** *a* thirsty

Dusche *f* **-, -n** shower. **d~n** *vi/r* (*haben*) **[sich] d~n** have a shower

Düse *f* **-, -n** nozzle. **D~nflugzeug** *nt* jet

Dutzend *nt* **-s, -e** dozen

duzen *vt* **jdn d~** call s.o. 'du'

DVD *f* **-, -s** DVD

Dynam|ik *f* **-** dynamics *sg*; (*fig*) dynamism. **d~isch** *a* dynamic; <*Rente*> index-linked

Dynamit *nt* **-es** dynamite

Dynamo *m* **-s, -s** dynamo

Dynastie *f* **-, -n** dynasty

D-Zug /'de:-/ *m* express [train]

Ee

Ebbe *f* **-, -n** low tide

eben *a* level; (*glatt*) smooth; **zu e~er Erde** on the ground floor ● *adv* just; (*genau*) exactly; **e~ noch** only just; (*gerade vorhin*) just now; **das ist es e~!** that's just it! **E~bild** *nt* image

Ebene *f* **-, -n** (*Geog*) plain; (*Geom*) plane; (*fig: Niveau*) level

eben|falls *adv* also; **danke, e~falls** thank you, [the] same to you. **E~holz** *nt* ebony. **e~so** *adv* just the same; (*ebenso sehr*) just as much; **e~so gut** just as good; *adv* just as well; **e~so sehr** just as much; **e~so viel** just as much/many; **e~so wenig** just as little/few; (*noch*) no more

Eber *m* **-s,-** boar

ebnen *vt* level; (*fig*) smooth

Echo *nt* **-s, -s** echo

echt *a* genuine, real; authentic ● *adv* [!] really; typically. **E~heit** *f* **-** authenticity

Eck|ball *m* (*Sport*) corner. **E~e** *f* **-, -n** corner; **um die E~e bringen** [!] bump off. **e~ig** *a* angular; <*Klammern*> square; (*unbeholfen*) awkward. **E~zahn** *m* canine tooth

Ecu, ECU /e'ky:/ *m* **-[s], -[s]** ecu

edel *a* noble; (*wertvoll*) precious; (*fein*) fine. **e~mütig** *a* magnanimous. **E~stahl** *m* stainless steel. **E~stein** *m* precious stone

Efeu *m* **-s** ivy

Effekt *m* **-[e]s, -e** effect. **E~en** *pl* securities. **e~iv** *a* actual, *adv* -ly; (*wirksam*) effective

EG *f* **-** *abbr* (**Europäische Gemeinschaft**) EC

egal *a* **das ist mir e~** [!] it's all the same to me ● *adv* **e~ wie/wo** no matter how/where

Egge *f* **-, -n** harrow

Ego|ismus *m* **-** selfishness. **E~ist(in)** *m* **-en, -en** (*f* **-, -nen**) egoist. **e~istisch** *a* selfish

eh *adv* (*Aust, fam*) anyway

ehe *conj* before; **ehe nicht** until

Ehe *f* **-, -n** marriage. **E~bett** *nt* double bed. **E~bruch** *m* adultery. **E~frau** *f* wife. **e~lich** *a* marital; <*Recht*> conjugal; <*Kind*> legitimate

ehemalig *a* former. **e~s** *adv* formerly

Ehe|mann *m* (*pl* **-männer**) husband. **E~paar** *nt* married couple

eher *adv* earlier, sooner; (*lieber, vielmehr*) rather; (*mehr*) more

Ehering *m* wedding ring

Ehr|e *f* **-, -n** honour. **e~en** *vt* honour. **e~enamtlich** *a* honorary ● *adv* in an honorary capacity. **E~engast** *m* guest of honour. **e~enhaft** *a* honourable. **E~ensache** *f* point of honour. **E~enwort** *nt* word of honour. **e~erbietig** *a* deferential. **E~furcht** *f* reverence; (*Scheu*) awe. **e~fürchtig** *a* reverent. **E~gefühl** *nt* sense of honour. **E~geiz** *m* ambition. **e~geizig** *a* ambitious. **e~lich** *a* honest; **e~lich gesagt** to be honest. **E~lichkeit** *f* **-** honesty. **e~los** *a* dishonourable. **e-würdig** *a* venerable, (*als Anrede*) Reverend

Ei *nt* **-[e]s, -er** egg

Eibe *f* **-, -n** yew

Eiche *f* **-, -n** oak. **E~l** *f* **-, -n** acorn

eichen *vt* standardize

Eichhörnchen *nt* **-s,-** squirrel

Eid *m* **-[e]s, -e** oath

Eidechse *f* **-, -n** lizard

eidlich *a* sworn ● *adv* on oath

Eidotter *m & nt* egg yolk

Eier|becher *m* egg-cup. **E~kuchen** *m* pancake; (*Omelett*) omelette. **E~schale** *f* eggshell. **E~schnee** *m* beaten egg-white. **E~stock** *m* ovary

Eifer *m* **-s** eagerness. **E~sucht** *f* jealousy. **e~süchtig** *a* jealous

eifrig *a* eager

Eigelb *nt* **-[e]s, -e** [egg] yolk

eigen *a* own; (*typisch*) characteristic (*dat* of); (*seltsam*) odd; (*genau*) particular. **E~art** *f* peculiarity. **e~artig** *a* peculiar. **e~händig** *a* personal; <*Unterschrift*> own. **E~heit** *f* **-, -en** peculiarity. **E~name** *m* proper name. **e~nützig** *a* selfish. **e~s** *adv* specially. **E~schaft** *f* **-, -en** quality; (*Phys*) property; (*Merkmal*) characteristic; (*Funktion*) capacity. **E~schaftswort** *nt* (*pl* **-wörter**) adjective. **E~sinn** *m* obstinacy. **e~sinnig** *a* obstinate

eigentlich *a* actual, real; (*wahr*) true ● *adv* actually, really; (*streng genommen*) strictly speaking

Eigen|tor *nt* own goal. **E~tum** *nt* **-s** property. **E~tümer(in)** *m* **-s,-** (*f* **-, -nen**) owner. **E~tumswohnung** *f* freehold flat. **e~willig** *a* self-willed; <*Stil*> highly individual

eignen (sich) *vr* be suitable

Eil|brief *m* express letter. **E~e** *f* **-** hurry; **E~e haben** be in a hurry; <*Sache:*> be urgent. **e~en** *vi* (*sein*) hurry ● (*haben*) (*drängen*) be urgent. **e~ig** *a* hurried; (*dringend*) urgent; **es e~ig haben** be in a hurry. **E~zug** *m* semi-fast train

Eimer *m* **-s,-** bucket; (*Abfall-*) bin

ein

● *indefinite article*

····➤ a, (*vor Vokal*) an. **ein Kleid/Apfel/Hotel/Mensch** a dress/an apple/a[n] hotel/a human being.

so ein such a. **was für ein ...** (*Frage*) what kind of a ...? (*Ausruf*) what a ...!

● *adjective*

····➤ (*Ziffer*) one. **eine Minute** one minute. **wir haben nur eine Stunde** we only have an/(*betont*) one hour. **eines Tages/Abends** one day/evening

····➤ (*derselbe*) the same. **einer Meinung sein** be of the same opinion. **mit jdm in einem Zimmer schlafen** sleep in the same room as s.o.

einander *pron* one another

Einäscherung *f* **-, -en** cremation

einatmen *vt/i sep* (*haben*) inhale, breathe in

Einbahnstraße *f* one-way street

einbalsamieren *vt sep* embalm

Einband *m* binding

Einbau *m* installation; (*Montage*) fitting. **e~en** *vt sep* install; (*montieren*) fit. **E~küche** *f* fitted kitchen

einbegriffen *pred a* included

Einberufung *f* call-up

Einbettzimmer *nt* single room

einbeulen *vt sep* dent

einbeziehen† *vt sep* **[mit] e~** include; (*berücksichtigen*) take into account

einbiegen† *vi sep* (*sein*) turn

einbild|en *vt sep* **sich** (*dat*) **etw e~en** imagine sth; **sich** (*dat*) **viel e~en** be conceited. **E~ung** *f* imagination; (*Dünkel*) conceit. **E~ungskraft** *f* imagination

einblenden *vt sep* fade in

Einblick *m* insight

einbrech|en† *vi sep* (*haben/sein*) break in; **bei uns ist eingebrochen worden** we have been burgled. **E~er** *m* burglar

einbringen† *vt sep* get in; bring in <*Geld*>

Einbruch *m* burglary; **bei E~ der Nacht** at nightfall

einbürger|n *vt sep* naturalize. **E~ung** *f* **-** naturalization

einchecken /-tʃɛkən/ *vt/i sep* (*haben*) check in

eindecken (sich) *vr sep* stock up

eindeutig *a* unambiguous; (*deutlich*) clear

eindicken *vt sep* (*Culin*) thicken

eindringen† *vi sep* (*sein*) **e~en in** (+ *acc*) penetrate into; (*mit Gewalt*) force one's/<*Wasser:*> its way into; (*Mil*) invade

Eindruck *m* impression

eindrücken *vt sep* crush

eindrucksvoll *a* impressive

ein|e(r,s) *pron* one; (*jemand*) someone; (*man*) one, you

einebnen *vt sep* level

eineiig *a* <*Zwillinge*> identical

eineinhalb *inv a* one and a half; **e~ Stunden** an hour and a half

Einelternfamilie *f* one-parent family

einengen *vt sep* restrict

Einer *m* **-s,-** (*Math*) unit. **e~** *pron s.* **eine(r,s)**. **e~lei** *inv a* ● *attrib a* one kind of; (*eintönig, einheitlich*) the same ● *pred a* [!] immaterial; **es ist mir e~lei** it's all the same to me. **e~seits** *adv* on the one hand

einfach *a* simple; <*Essen*> plain; <*Faden, Fahrt*> single; **e~er Soldat** private. **E~heit** *f* **-** simplicity

einfädeln *vt sep* thread; (*fig; arrangieren*) arrange

einfahr|en† *v sep* ● *vi* (*sein*) arrive; <*Zug:*> pull in ● *vt* (*Auto*) run in. **E~t** *f* arrival; (*Eingang*) entrance, way in; (*Auffahrt*) drive; (*Autobahn-*) access road; **keine E~t** no entry

Einfall *m* idea; (*Mil*) invasion. **e~en**† *vi sep* (*sein*) collapse; (*eindringen*) invade; **jdm e~en** occur to s.o.; **was fällt ihm ein!** what does he think he is doing!

Einfalt *f* **-** naïvety

einfarbig *a* of one colour; <*Stoff, Kleid*> plain

einfass|en *vt sep* edge; set <*Edelstein*>. **E~ung** *f* border, edging

einfetten *vt sep* grease

Einfluss *m* influence. **e~reich** *a* influential

einförmig *a* monotonous. **E~keit** *f* - monotony

einfrieren† *vt/i sep* (*sein*) freeze

einfügen *vt sep* insert; (*einschieben*) interpolate; **sich e~** fit in

einfühlsam *a* sensitive

Einfuhr *f* **-, -en** import

einführ|en *vt sep* introduce; (*einstecken*) insert; (*einweisen*) initiate; (*Comm*) import. **e~end** *a* introductory. **E~ung** *f* introduction; (*Einweisung*) initiation

Eingabe *f* petition; (*Computer*) input

Eingang *m* entrance, way in; (*Ankunft*) arrival

eingebaut *a* built-in; <*Schrank*> fitted

eingeben† *vt sep* hand in; (*Computer*) feed in

eingebildet *a* imaginary; (*überheblich*) conceited

Eingeborene(r) *m/f* native

eingehen† *v sep* ● *vi* (*sein*) come in; (*ankommen*) arrive; (*einlaufen*) shrink; (*sterben*) die; <*Zeitung, Firma:*> fold; **auf etw** (*acc*) **e~** go into sth; (*annehmen*) agree to sth ● *vt* enter into; contract <*Ehe*>; make <*Wette*>; take <*Risiko*>

eingemacht *a* (*Culin*) bottled

eingenommen *pred a* (*fig*) taken (**von** with); prejudiced (**gegen** against)

eingeschneit *a* snowbound

eingeschrieben *a* registered

Einge|ständnis *nt* admission. **e~stehen†** *vt sep* admit

eingetragen *a* registered

Eingeweide *pl* bowels, entrails

eingewöhnen (sich) *vr sep* settle in

eingießen† *vt sep* pour in; (*einschenken*) pour

eingleisig *a* single-track

einglieder|n *vt sep* integrate. **E~ung** *f* integration

eingravieren *vt sep* engrave

eingreifen† *vi sep* (*haben*) intervene. **E~** *nt* **-s** intervention

Eingriff *m* intervention; (*Med*) operation

einhaken *vt/r sep* **jdn e~** *od* **sich bei jdm e~** take s.o.'s arm

einhalten† *v sep* ● *vt* keep; (*befolgen*) observe ● *vi* (*haben*) stop

einhändigen *vt sep* hand in

einhängen *vt sep* hang; put down <*Hörer*>

einheimisch *a* local; (*eines Landes*) native; (*Comm*) homeproduced. **E~e(r)** *m/f* local native

Einheit *f* **-, -en** unity; (*Maß-, Mil*) unit. **e~lich** *a* uniform. **E~spreis** *m* standard price; (*Fahrpreis*) flat fare

einholen *vt sep* catch up with; (*aufholen*) make up for; (*erbitten*) seek; (*einkaufen*) buy

einhüllen *vt sep* wrap

einhundert *inv a* one hundred

einig *a* united; **[sich** (*dat*)**] e~ sein** be in agreement

einig|e(r,s) *pron* some; (*ziemlich viel*) quite a lot of; (*substantivisch*) **e~e** *pl* some; (*mehrere*) several; (*ziemlich viele*) quite a lot; **e~es** *sg* some things; **vor e~er Zeit** some time ago

einigen *vt* unite; unify <*Land*>; **sich e~** come to an agreement

einigermaßen *adv* to some extent; (*ziemlich*) fairly; (*ziemlich gut*) fairly well

Einigkeit *f* **-** unity; (*Übereinstimmung*) agreement

einjährig *a* one-year-old; **e~e Pflanze** annual

einkalkulieren *vt sep* take into account

einkassieren *vt sep* collect

Einkauf *m* purchase; (*Einkaufen*) shopping; **Einkäufe machen** do some shopping. **e~en** *vt sep* buy; **e~en gehen** go shopping. **E~swagen** *m* shopping trolley

einklammern *vt sep* bracket

Einklang *m* harmony; **in E~ stehen** be in accord (**mit** with)

einkleben *vt sep* stick in

einkleiden *vt sep* fit out

einklemmen *vt sep* clamp

einkochen *v sep* ● *vi* (*sein*) boil down ● *vt* preserve, bottle

Einkommen *nt* **-s** income. **E~[s]steuer** *f* income tax

Einkünfte *pl* income *sg*; (*Einnahmen*) revenue *sg*

einlad|en† *vt sep* load; (*auffordern*) invite; (*bezahlen für*) treat. **E~ung** *f* invitation

Einlage *f* enclosure; (*Schuh-*) arch support; (*Programm-*) interlude; (*Comm*) investment; (*Bank-*) deposit; **Suppe mit E~** soup with noodles/dumplings

Ein|lass *m* **-es** admittance. **e~lassen**† *vt sep* let in; run <*Bad, Wasser*>; **sich auf etw** (*acc*) **e~lassen** get involved in sth

einleben (sich) *vr sep* settle in

Einlege|arbeit *f* inlaid work. **e~n** *vt sep* put in; lay in <*Vorrat*>; lodge <*Protest*>; (*einfügen*) insert; (*Auto*) engage <*Gang*>; (*Culin*) pickle; (*marinieren*) marinade; **eine Pause e~n** have a break. **E~sohle** *f* insole

einleit|en *vt sep* initiate; (*eröffnen*) begin. **E~ung** *f* introduction

einleuchten *vi sep* (*haben*) be clear (*dat* to). **e~d** *a* convincing

einliefer|n *vt sep* take (**ins Krankenhaus** to hospital). **E~ung** *f* admission

einlösen *vt sep* cash <*Scheck*>; redeem <*Pfand*>; (*fig*) keep

einmachen *vt sep* preserve

einmal *adv* once; (*eines Tages*) one *or* some day; **noch/schon e~** again/before; **noch e~ so teuer** twice as expensive; **auf e~** at the same time; (*plötzlich*) suddenly; **nicht e~** not even. **E~eins** *nt* **-** [multiplication] tables *pl*. **e~ig** *a* (*einzigartig*) unique; (! *großartig*) fantastic

einmarschieren *vi sep* (*sein*) march in

einmisch|en (sich) *vr sep* interfere. **E~ung** *f* interference

Einnahme *f* **-, -n** taking; (*Mil*) capture; **E~n** *pl* income *sg*; (*Einkünfte*) revenue *sg*; (*Comm*) receipts; (*eines Ladens*) takings

einnehmen† *vt sep* take; have <*Mahlzeit*>; (*Mil*) capture; take up <*Platz*>

einordnen *vt sep* put in its proper place; (*klassifizieren*) classify; **sich e~** fit in; (*Auto*) get in lane

einpacken *vt sep* pack

einparken *vt sep* park

einpflanzen *vt sep* plant; implant <*Organ*>

einplanen *vt sep* allow for

einprägen *vt sep* impress (**jdm** [up]on s.o.); **sich** (*dat*) **etw e~en** memorize sth.

einrahmen *vt sep* frame

einrasten *vi sep* (*sein*) engage

einräumen *vt sep* put away; (*zugeben*) admit; (*zugestehen*) grant

einrechnen *vt sep* include

einreden *v sep* ● *vt* **jdm/sich** (*dat*) **etw e~** persuade s.o./oneself of sth.

einreiben† *vt sep* rub (**mit** with)

einreichen *vt sep* submit; **die Scheidung e~** file for divorce

Einreih|er *m* **-s,-** single-breasted suit. **e~ig** *a* single-breasted

Einreise *f* entry. **e~n** *vi sep* (*sein*) enter (**nach Irland** Ireland)

einrenken *vt sep* (*Med*) set

einricht|en *vt sep* fit out; (*möblieren*) furnish; (*anordnen*) arrange; (*Med*) set <*Bruch*>; (*eröffnen*) set up; **sich e~en** furnish one's home; (*sich einschränken*) economize; (*sich vorbereiten*) prepare (**auf** + *acc* for). **E~ung** *f* furnishing; (*Möbel*) furnishings *pl*; (*Techn*) equipment; (*Vorrichtung*) device; (*Eröffnung*) setting up; (*Institution*) institution; (*Gewohnheit*) practice

einrosten *vi sep* (*sein*) rust; (*fig*) get rusty

eins *inv a & pron* one; **noch e~** one other thing; **mir ist alles e~** [!] it's all the same to me. **E~** *f* **-, -en** one; (*Sch*) ≈ A

einsam *a* lonely; (*allein*) solitary; (*abgelegen*) isolated. **E~keit** *f* **-** loneliness; solitude; isolation

einsammeln *vt sep* collect

Einsatz *m* use; (*Mil*) mission; (*Wett-*) stake; (*E~teil*) insert; **im E~** in action

einschalt|en *vt sep* switch on; (*einschieben*) interpolate; (*fig: beteiligen*) call in; **sich e~en** (*fig*) intervene. **E~quote** *f* (*TV*) viewing figures *pl*; ≈ ratings *pl*

einschätzen *vt sep* assess; (*bewerten*) rate

einschenken *vt sep* pour

einscheren *vi sep* (*sein*) pull in

einschicken *vt sep* send in

einschieben† *vt sep* push in; (*einfügen*) insert

einschiff|en (sich) *vr sep* embark. **E~ung** *f* **-** embarkation

einschlafen† *vi sep* (*sein*) go to sleep; (*aufhören*) peter out

einschläfern *vt sep* lull to sleep; (*betäuben*) put out; (*töten*) put to sleep. **e~d** *a* soporific

Einschlag *m* impact. **e~en**† *v sep* ● *vt* knock in; (*zerschlagen*) smash; (*drehen*) turn; take <*Weg*>; take up <*Laufbahn*> ● *vi* (*haben*) hit/<*Blitz:*> strike (**in etw** *acc* sth); (*Erfolg haben*) be a hit

einschleusen *vt sep* infiltrate

einschließ|en† *vt sep* lock in; (*umgeben*) enclose; (*einkreisen*) surround; (*einbeziehen*) include; **sich e~en** lock oneself in; **Bedienung eingeschlossen** service included. **e~lich** *adv* inclusive ● *prep* (+ *gen*) including

einschneiden† *vt/i sep* (*haben*) **[in] etw** *acc* **e~** cut into sth. **e~d** *a* (*fig*) drastic

Einschnitt *m* cut; (*Med*) incision; (*Lücke*) gap; (*fig*) decisive event

einschränk|en *vt sep* restrict; (*reduzieren*) cut back; **sich e~en** economize. **E~ung** *f* **-, -en** restriction; (*Reduzierung*) reduction; (*Vorbehalt*) reservation

Einschreib|[e]brief *m* registered letter. **e~en**† *vt sep* enter; register <*Brief*>; **sich e~en** put one's name down; (*sich anmelden*) enrol. **E~en** *nt* registered letter/packet; **als** *od* **per E~en** by registered post

einschüchtern *vt sep* intimidate

Einsegnung *f* **-, -en** confirmation

einsehen† *vt sep* inspect; (*lesen*) consult; (*begreifen*) see

einseitig *a* one-sided; (*Pol*) unilateral ● *adv* on one side; (*fig*) one-sidedly; (*Pol*) unilaterally

einsenden† *vt sep* send in

einsetzen *v sep* ● *vt* put in; (*einfügen*) insert; (*verwenden*) use; put on <*Zug*>; call out <*Truppen*>; (*Mil*) deploy; (*ernennen*) appoint; (*wetten*) stake; (*riskieren*) risk ● *vi*

(*haben*) start; <*Winter, Regen:*> set in
Einsicht *f* insight; (*Verständnis*) understanding; (*Vernunft*) reason. **e~ig** *a* understanding
Einsiedler *m* hermit
einsinken† *vi sep* (*sein*) sink in
einspannen *vt sep* harness; **jdn e~** [!] rope s.o. in
einsparen *vt sep* save
einsperren *vt sep* shut/(*im Gefängnis*) lock up
einsprachig *a* monolingual
einspritzen *vt sep* inject
Einspruch *m* objection; **E~ erheben** object; (*Jur*) appeal
einspurig *a* single-track; (*Auto*) single-lane
einst *adv* once; (*Zukunft*) one day
Einstand *m* (*Tennis*) deuce
einstecken *vt sep* put in; post <*Brief*>; (*Electr*) plug in; ([!] *behalten*) pocket; ([!] *hinnehmen*) take; suffer <*Niederlage*>; **etw e~** put sth in one's pocket
einsteigen† *vi sep* (*sein*) get in; (*in Bus/Zug*) get on
einstell|en *vt sep* put in; (*anstellen*) employ; (*aufhören*) stop; (*regulieren*) adjust, set; (*Optik*) focus; tune <*Motor, Zündung*>; tune to <*Sender*>; **sich e~en** turn up; <*Schwierigkeiten:*> arise; **sich e~en auf** (+ *acc*) adjust to; (*sich vorbereiten*) prepare for. **E~ung** *f* employment; (*Regulierung*) adjustment; (*TV, Auto*) tuning; (*Haltung*) attitude
einstig *a* former
einstimmig *a* unanimous. **E~keit** *f* - unanimity
einstöckig *a* single-storey
einstudieren *vt sep* rehearse
einstufen *vt sep* classify
Ein|sturz *m* collapse. **e~stürzen** *vi sep* (*sein*) collapse
einstweilen *adv* for the time being; (*inzwischen*) meanwhile
eintasten *vt sep* key in
eintauchen *vt/i sep* (*sein*) dip in
eintauschen *vt sep* exchange
eintausend *inv a* one thousand
einteil|en *vt sep* divide (**in** + *acc* into); (*Biol*) classify; **sich** (*dat*) **seine Zeit gut e~en** organize one's time well. **e~ig** *a* one piece. **E~ung** *f* division
eintönig *a* monotonous. **E~keit** *f* - monotony
Eintopf *m*, **E~gericht** *nt* stew
Eintracht *f* - harmony
Eintrag *m* **-[e]s,¨e** entry. **e~en**† *vt sep* enter; (*Admin*) register; **sich e~en** put one's name down
einträglich *a* profitable
Eintragung *f* **-, -en** registration
eintreffen† *vi sep* (*sein*) arrive; (*fig*) come true
eintreiben† *vt sep* drive in; (*einziehen*) collect
eintreten† *v sep* ● *vi* (*sein*) enter; (*geschehen*) occur; **in einen Klub e~** join a club; **e~ für** (*fig*) stand up for ● *vt* kick in
Eintritt *m* entrance; (*zu Veranstaltung*) admission; (*Beitritt*) joining; (*Beginn*) beginning. **E~skarte** *f* [admission] ticket
einüben *vt sep* practise
einundachtzig *inv a* eighty-one
Einvernehmen *nt* **-s** understanding; (*Übereinstimmung*) agreement
einverstanden *a* **e~ sein** agree
Einverständnis *nt* agreement; (*Zustimmung*) consent
Einwand *m* **-[e]s,¨e** objection
Einwander|er *m* immigrant. **e~n** *vi sep* (*sein*) immigrate. **E~ung** *f* immigration
einwandfrei *a* perfect
einwärts *adv* inwards
einwechseln *vt sep* change
einwecken *vt sep* preserve, bottle
Einweg- *pref* non-returnable
einweichen *vt sep* soak

einweih|en *vt sep* inaugurate; (*Relig*) consecrate; (*einführen*) initiate; **in ein Geheimnis e~en** let into a secret. **E~ung** *f* **-, -en** inauguration; consecration; initiation

einweisen† *vt sep* direct; (*einführen*) initiate; **ins Krankenhaus e~** send to hospital

einwerfen† *vt sep* insert; post <*Brief*>; (*Sport*) throw in

einwickeln *vt sep* wrap [up]

einwillig|en *vi sep* (*haben*) consent, agree (**in** + *acc* to). **E~ung** *f* **-** consent

Einwohner|(in) *m* **-s,-** (*f* **-, -nen**) inhabitant. **E~zahl** *f* population

Einwurf *m* interjection; (*Einwand*) objection; (*Sport*) throw-in; (*Münz-*) slot

Einzahl *f* (*Gram*) singular

einzahl|en *vt sep* pay in. **E~ung** *f* payment; (*Einlage*) deposit

einzäunen *vt sep* fence in

Einzel *nt* **-s,-** (*Tennis*) singles *pl*. **E~bett** *nt* single bed. **E~gänger** *m* **-s,-** loner. **E~haft** *f* solitary confinement. **E~handel** *m* retail trade. **E~händler** *m* retailer. **E~haus** *nt* detached house. **E~heit** *f* **-, -en** detail. **E~karte** *f* single ticket. **E~kind** *nt* only child

einzeln *a* single; (*individuell*) individual; (*gesondert*) separate; odd <*Handschuh, Socken*>; **e~e Fälle** some cases. **E~e(r,s)** *pron* **der/die E~e** the individual; **E~e** *pl* some; **im E~en** in detail

Einzel|teil *nt* [component] part. **E~zimmer** *nt* single room

einziehen† *v sep* ● *vt* pull in; draw in <*Atem, Krallen*>; (*Zool, Techn*) retract; indent <*Zeile*>; (*aus dem Verkehr ziehen*) withdraw; (*beschlagnahmen*) confiscate; (*eintreiben*) collect; make <*Erkundigungen*>; (*Mil*) call up ● *vi* (*sein*) enter; (*umziehen*) move in; (*eindringen*) penetrate

einzig *a* only; (*einmalig*) unique; **eine e~e Frage** a a single question ● *adv* only; **e~ und allein** solely. **E~e(r,s)** *pron* **der/die/das E~e** the only one; **ein/kein E~er** a/not a single one; **das E~e, was mich stört** the only thing that bothers me

Eis *nt* **-es** ice; (*Speise-*) ice-cream; **Eis am Stiel** ice lolly; **Eis laufen** skate. **E~bahn** *f* ice rink. **E~bär** *m* polar bear. **E~becher** *m* ice-cream sundae. **E~berg** *m* iceberg. **E~diele** *f* ice-cream parlour

Eisen *nt* **-s,-** iron. **E~bahn** *f* railway

eisern *a* iron; (*fest*) resolute; **e~er Vorhang** (*Theat*) safety curtain; (*Pol*) Iron Curtain

Eis|fach *nt* freezer compartment. **e~gekühlt** *a* chilled. **e~ig** *a* icy. **E~kaffee** *m* iced coffee. **E~lauf** *m* skating. **E~läufer(in)** *m(f)* skater. **E~pickel** *m* ice-axe. **E~scholle** *f* ice-floe. **E~vogel** *m* kingfisher. **E~würfel** *m* icecube. **E~zapfen** *m* icicle. **E~zeit** *f* ice age

eitel *a* vain; (*rein*) pure. **E~keit** *f* **-** vanity

Eiter *m* **-s** pus. **e~n** *vi* (*haben*) discharge pus

Eiweiß *nt* **-es, -e** egg-white

Ekel *m* **-s** disgust; (*Widerwille*) revulsion. **e~haft** *a* nauseating; (*widerlich*) repulsive. **e~n** *vt/i* (*haben*) **mich od mir e~t [es] davor** it makes me feel sick ● *vr* **sich e~n vor** (+ *dat*) find repulsive

eklig *a* disgusting, repulsive

Ekzem *nt* **-s, -e** eczema

elastisch *a* elastic; (*federnd*) springy; (*fig*) flexible

Elch *m* **-[e]s, -e** elk

Elefant *m* **-en, -en** elephant

E

eleganlt *a* elegant. **E~z** *f* - elegance
Elektrilker *m* **-s,-** electrician. **e~sch** *a* electric
Elektrizität *f* - electricity. **E~swerk** *nt* power station
Elektrloartikel *mpl* electrical appliances. **E~ode** *f* **-, -n** electrode. **E~onik** *f* - electronics *sg*. **e~onisch** *a* electronic
Elend *nt* **-s** misery; (*Armut*) poverty. **e~** *a* miserable; (*krank*) poorly; (*gemein*) contemptible. **E~sviertel** *nt* slum
elf *inv a*, **E~** *f* **-, -en** eleven
Elfe *f* **-, -n** fairy
Elfenbein *nt* ivory
Elfmeter *m* (*Fußball*) penalty
elfte(r,s) *a* eleventh
Ell[en]bogen *m* elbow
Ellip|se *f* **-, -n** ellipse. **e~tisch** *a* elliptical
Elsass *nt* - Alsace
elsässisch *a* Alsatian
Elster *f* **-, -n** magpie
elter|lich *a* parental. **E~n** *pl* parents. **e~nlos** *a* orphaned. **E~nteil** *m* parent
Email /e'mai/ *nt* **-s, -s**, **E~le** /e'maljə/ *f* **-, -n** enamel
E-Mail /'i:me:l/ *f* **-, -s** e-mail; e-mail message
Emanzi|pation /-'tsio:n/ *f* - emancipation. **e~piert** *a* emancipated
Embargo *nt* **-s, -s** embargo
Embryo *m* **-s, -s** embryo
Emigr|ant(in) *m* **-en, -en** (*f* **-, -nen**) emigrant. **E~ation** /-'tsio:n/ *f* - emigration. **e~ieren** *vi* (*sein*) emigrate
Empfang *m* **-[e]s,¨e** reception; (*Erhalt*) receipt; **in E~ nehmen** receive; (*annehmen*) accept. **e~en**† *vt* receive; (*Biol*) conceive
Empfäng|er *m* **-s,-** recipient; (*Post-*) addressee; (*Zahlungs-*) payee; (*Radio, TV*) receiver. **E~nis** *f* - (*Biol*) conception
Empfängnisverhütung *f* contraception. **E~smittel** *nt* contraceptive
Empfangs|bestätigung *f* receipt. **E~dame** *f* receptionist. **E~halle** *f* [hotel] foyer
empfehl|en† *vt* recommend. **E~ung** *f* **-, -en** recommendation; (*Gruß*) regards *pl*
empfind|en† *vt* feel. **e~lich** *a* sensitive (**gegen** to); (*zart*) delicate. **E~lichkeit** *f* - sensitivity; delicacy; tenderness; touchiness. **E~ung** *f* **-, -en** sensation; (*Regung*) feeling
empor *adv* (*liter*) up[wards]
empören *vt* incense; **sich e~** be indignant; (*sich auflehnen*) rebel
Emporkömmling *m* **-s, -e** upstart
empör|t *a* indignant. **E~ung** *f* - indignation; (*Auflehnung*) rebellion
Ende *nt* **-s, -n** end; (*eines Films, Romans*) ending; (Ⓘ *Stück*) bit; **zu E~ sein** be finished; **etw zu E~ schreiben** finish writing sth; **am E~** at the end; (*schließlich*) in the end; (Ⓘ *vielleicht*) perhaps; (Ⓘ *erschöpft*) at the end of one's tether
end|en *vi* (*haben*) end. **e~gültig** *a* final; (*bestimmt*) definite
Endivie /-iə/ *f* **-, -n** endive
end|lich *adv* at last, finally; (*schließlich*) in the end. **e~los** *a* endless. **E~station** *f* terminus. **E~ung** *f* **-, -en** (*Gram*) ending
Energie *f* - energy
energisch *a* resolute; (*nachdrücklich*) vigorous
eng *a* narrow; (*beengt*) cramped; (*anliegend*) tight; (*nah*) close; **e~ anliegend** tight-fitting
Engagement /ãgaʒə'mã:/ *nt* **-s, -s** (*Theat*) engagement; (*fig*) commitment
Engel *m* **-s,-** angel
England *nt* **-s** England

Engländer *m* **-s,-** Englishman; (*Techn*) monkey-wrench; **die E~** the English *pl*. **E~in** *f* **-, -nen** Englishwoman

englisch *a* English. **E~** *nt* **-[s]** (*Lang*) English; **auf E~** in English

Engpass *m* (*fig*) bottle-neck

en gros /ã'gro:/ *adv* wholesale

Enkel *m* **-s,-** grandson; **E~** *pl* grandchildren. **E~in** *f* **-, -nen** granddaughter. **E~kind** *nt* grandchild. **E~sohn** *m* grandson. **E~tochter** *f* granddaughter

Ensemble /ã'sã:bəl/ *nt* **-s, -s** ensemble; (*Theat*) company

entart|en *vi* (*sein*) degenerate. **e~et** *a* degenerate

entbehren *vt* do without; (*vermissen*) miss

entbind|en† *vt* release (**von** from); (*Med*) deliver (**von** of) ● *vi* (*haben*) give birth. **E~ung** *f* delivery. **E~ungsstation** *f* maternity ward

entdeck|en *vt* discover. **E~er** *m* **-s,-** discoverer; (*Forscher*) explorer. **E~ung** *f* **-, -en** discovery

Ente *f* **-, -n** duck

entehren *vt* dishonour

enteignen *vt* dispossess; expropriate <*Eigentum*>

enterben *vt* disinherit

Enterich *m* **-s, -e** drake

entfallen† *vi* (*sein*) not apply; **auf jdn e~** be s.o.'s share

entfern|en *vt* remove; **sich e~en** leave. **e~t** *a* distant; (*schwach*) vague; **2 Kilometer e~t** 2 kilometres away; **e~t verwandt** distantly related. **E~ung** *f* **-, -en** removal; (*Abstand*) distance; (*Reichweite*) range

entfliehen† *vi* (*sein*) escape

entfremden *vt* alienate

entfrosten *vt* defrost

entführ|en *vt* abduct, kidnap; hijack <*Flugzeug*>. **E~er** *m* abductor, kidnapper; hijacker. **E~ung** *f* abduction, kidnapping; hijacking

entgegen *adv* towards ● *prep* (+ *dat*) contrary to. **e~gehen**† *vi sep* (*sein*) (+ *dat*) go to meet; (*fig*) be heading for. **e~gesetzt** *a* opposite; (*gegensätzlich*) opposing. **e~kommen**† *vi sep* (*sein*) (+ *dat*) come to meet; (*zukommen auf*) come towards; (*fig*) oblige. **E~kommen** *nt* **-s** helpfulness; (*Zugeständnis*) concession. **e~kommend** *a* approaching; <*Verkehr*> oncoming; (*fig*) obliging. **e~nehmen**† *vt sep* accept. **e~wirken** *vi sep* (*haben*) (+ *dat*) counteract; (*fig*) oppose

entgegn|en *vt* reply (**auf** + *acc* to). **E~ung** *f* **-, -en** reply

entgehen† *vi sep* (*sein*) (+ *dat*) escape; **jdm e~** (*unbemerkt bleiben*) escape s.o.'s notice; **sich** (*dat*) **etw e~ lassen** miss sth

Entgelt *nt* **-[e]s** payment; **gegen E~** for money

entgleis|en *vi* (*sein*) be derailed; (*fig*) make a gaffe. **E~ung** *f* **-, -en** derailment; (*fig*) gaffe

entgräten *vt* fillet, bone

Enthaarungsmittel *nt* depilatory

enthalt|en† *vt* contain; **in etw** (*dat*) **e~en sein** be contained/ (*eingeschlossen*) included in sth; **sich der Stimme e~en** (*Pol*) abstain. **e~sam** *a* abstemious. **E~ung** *f* (*Pol*) abstention

enthaupten *vt* behead

entheben† *vt* **jdn seines Amtes e~** relieve s.o. of his post

Enthüllung *f* **-, -en** revelation

Enthusias|mus *m* **-** enthusiast. **E~t** *m* **-en, -en** enthusiast

entkernen *vt* stone; core <*Apfel*>

entkleiden *vt* undress; **sich e~en** undress

entkommen† *vi* (*sein*) escape

entkorken *vt* uncork

entladen† *vt* unload; (*Electr*) discharge; **sich e∼** discharge; <*Gewitter:*> break; <*Zorn:*> explode

entlang *adv & prep* (+ *preceding acc or following dat*) along; **die Straße e∼** along the road; **an etw** (*dat*) **e∼** along sth. **e∼fahren**† *vi sep* (*sein*) drive along. **e∼gehen**† *vi sep* (*sein*) walk along

entlarven *vt* unmask

entlass|en† *vt* dismiss; (*aus Krankenhaus*) discharge; (*aus der Haft*) release. **E∼ung** *f* **-, -en** dismissal; discharge; release

entlast|en *vt* relieve the strain on; ease <*Gewissen, Verkehr*>; relieve (**von** of); (*Jur*) exonerate. **E∼ung** *f* **-** relief; exoneration

entlaufen† *vi* (*sein*) run away

entleeren *vt* empty

entlegen *a* remote

entlohnen *vt* pay

entlüft|en *vt* ventilate. **E∼er** *m* **-s,-** extractor fan. **E∼ung** *f* ventilation

entmündigen *vt* declare incapable of managing his own affairs

entmutigen *vt* discourage

entnehmen† *vt* take (*dat* from); (*schließen*) gather (*dat* from)

entpuppen (sich) *vr* (*fig*) turn out (**als etw** to be sth)

entrahmt *a* skimmed

entrichten *vt* pay

entrinnen† *vi* (*sein*) escape

entrüst|en *vt* fill with indignation; **sich e∼en** be indignant (**über** + *acc* at). **e∼et** *a* indignant. **E∼ung** *f* **-** indignation

entsaft|en *vt* extract the juice from. **E∼er** *m* **-s,-** juice extractor

entsagen *vi* (*haben*) (+ *dat*) renounce

entschädig|en *vt* compensate. **E∼ung** *f* **-, -en** compensation

entschärfen *vt* defuse

entscheid|en† *vt/i* (*haben*) decide; **sich e∼en** decide; <*Sache:*> be decided. **e∼end** *a* decisive; (*kritisch*) crucial. **E∼ung** *f* decision

entschließen† **(sich)** *vr* decide, make up one's mind; **sich anders e∼** change one's mind

entschlossen *a* determined; (*energisch*) resolute; **kurz e∼** without hesitation. **E∼heit** *f* **-** determination

Entschluss *m* decision

entschlüsseln *vt* decode

entschuld|bar *a* excusable. **e∼igen** *vt* excuse; **sich e∼igen** apologize (**bei** to); **e∼igen Sie [bitte]!** sorry! (*bei Frage*) excuse me. **E∼igung** *f* **-, -en** apology; (*Ausrede*) excuse; **um E∼igung bitten** apologize

entsetz|en *vt* horrify. **E∼en** *nt* **-s** horror. **e∼lich** *a* horrible; (*schrecklich*) terrible

Entsorgung *f* **-** waste disposal

entspann|en *vt* relax; **sich e∼en** relax; <*Lage:*> ease. **E∼ung** *f* **-** relaxation; easing; (*Pol*) détente

entsprech|en† *vi* (*haben*) (+ *dat*) correspond to; (*übereinstimmen*) agree with. **e∼end** *a* corresponding; (*angemessen*) appropriate; (*zuständig*) relevant ● *adv* correspondingly; appropriately; (*demgemäß*) accordingly ● *prep* (+ *dat*) in accordance with

entspringen† *vi* (*sein*) <*Fluss:*> rise; (*fig*) arise, spring (*dat* from)

entstammen *vi* (*sein*) come/ (*abstammen*) be descended (*dat* from)

entsteh|en† *vi* (*sein*) come into being; (*sich bilden*) form; (*sich entwickeln*) develop; <*Brand:*> start; (*stammen*) originate. **E∼ung** *f* **-** origin; formation; development

entstell|en *vt* disfigure; (*verzerren*) distort. **E~ung** *f* disfigurement; distortion
entstört *a* (*Electr*) suppressed
enttäusch|en *vt* disappoint. **E~ung** *f* disappointment
entwaffnen *vt* disarm
entwässer|n *vt* drain. **E~ung** *f* - drainage
entweder *conj & adv* either
entwerfen† *vt* design; (*aufsetzen*) draft; (*skizzieren*) sketch
entwert|en *vt* devalue; (*ungültig machen*) cancel. **E~er** *m* **-s,-** ticket-cancelling machine. **E~ung** *f* devaluation; cancelling
entwick|eln *vt* develop; **sich e~eln** develop. **E~lung** *f* **-, -en** development; (*Biol*) evolution. **E~lungsland** *nt* developing country
entwöhnen *vt* wean (*gen* from); cure <*Süchtige*>
entwürdigend *a* degrading
Entwurf *m* design; (*Konzept*) draft; (*Skizze*) sketch
entwurzeln *vt* uproot
entzie|hen† *vt* take away (*dat* from); **jdm den Führerschein e~hen** disqualify s.o. from driving; **sich e~hen** (+ *dat*) withdraw from. **E~hungskur** *f* treatment for drug/alcohol addiction
entziffern *vt* decipher
Entzug *m* withdrawal; (*Vorenthaltung*) deprivation
entzünd|en *vt* ignite; (*anstecken*) light; (*fig: erregen*) inflame; **sich e~en** ignite; (*Med*) become inflamed. **e~et** *a* (*Med*) inflamed. **e~lich** *a* inflammable. **E~ung** *f* (*Med*) inflammation
entzwei *a* broken
Enzian *m* **-s, -e** gentian
Enzyklo|pädie *f* **-, -en** encyclopaedia. **e~pädisch** *a* encyclopaedic
Enzym *nt* **-s, -e** enzyme
Epidemie *f* **-, -n** epidemic
Epi|lepsie *f* **-** epilepsy. **E~leptiker(in)** *m* **-s,-** (*f* **-, -nen**) epileptic. **e~leptisch** *a* epileptic
Epilog *m* **-s, -e** epilogue
Episode *f* **-, -n** episode
Epoche *f* **-, -n** epoch
Epos *nt* **-/Epen** epic
er *pron* he; (*Ding, Tier*) it
erachten *vt* consider (**für nötig** necessary). **E~** *nt* **-s meines E~s** in my opinion
erbarmen (sich) *vr* have pity/ <*Gott:*> mercy (*gen* on). **E~** *nt* **-s** pity; mercy
erbärmlich *a* wretched
erbauen *vt* build; (*fig*) edify; **nicht erbaut von** [!] not pleased about
Erbe[1] *m* **-n, -n** heir
Erbe[2] *nt* **-s** inheritance; (*fig*) heritage. **e~n** *vt* inherit
erbeuten *vt* get; (*Mil*) capture
Erbfolge *f* (*Jur*) succession
erbieten† **(sich)** *vr* offer (**zu** to)
Erbin *f* **-, -nen** heiress
erbitten† *vt* ask for
erbittert *a* bitter; (*heftig*) fierce
erblassen *vi* (*sein*) turn pale
erblich *a* hereditary
erblicken *vt* catch sight of
erblinden *vi* (*sein*) go blind
erbrechen† *vt* vomit ● *vi/r* **[sich] e~** vomit. **E~** *nt* **-s** vomiting
Erbschaft *f* **-, -en** inheritance
Erbse *f* **-, -n** pea
Erb|stück *nt* heirloom. **E~teil** *nt* inheritance
Erd|apfel *m* (*Aust*) potato. **E~beben** *nt* **-s,-** earthquake. **E~beere** *f* strawberry
Erde *f* **-, -n** earth; (*Erdboden*) ground; (*Fußboden*) floor. **e~n** *vt* (*Electr*) earth
erdenklich *a* imaginable
Erd|gas *nt* natural gas. **E~geschoss** *nt* ground floor. **E~kugel** *f* globe. **E~kunde** *f* geography. **E~nuss** *f* peanut. **E~öl** *nt* [mineral] oil

erdrosseln *vt* strangle

erdrücken *vt* crush to death

Erd|rutsch *m* landslide. **E~teil** *m* continent

erdulden *vt* endure

ereignen (sich) *vr* happen

Ereignis *nt* **-ses, -se** event. **e~los** *a* uneventful. **e~reich** *a* eventful

Eremit *m* **-en, -en** hermit

erfahr|en† *vt* learn, hear; (*erleben*) experience ● *a* experienced. **E~ung** *f* **-, -en** experience; **in E~ung bringen** find out

erfassen *vt* seize; (*begreifen*) grasp; (*einbeziehen*) include; (*aufzeichnen*) record

erfind|en† *vt* invent. **E~er** *m* **-s,-** inventor. **e~erisch** *a* inventive. **E~ung** *f* **-, -en** invention

Erfolg *m* **-[e]s, -e** success; (*Folge*) result; **E~ haben** be successful. **e~en** *vi* (*sein*) take place; (*geschehen*) happen. **e~los** *a* unsuccessful. **e~reich** *a* successful

erforder|lich *a* required, necessary. **e~n** *vt* require, demand

erforsch|en *vt* explore; (*untersuchen*) investigate. **E~ung** *f* exploration; investigation

erfreu|en *vt* please. **e~lich** *a* pleasing. **e~licherweise** *adv* happily. **e~t** *a* pleased

erfrier|en† *vi* (*sein*) freeze to death; <*Glied:*> become frostbitten; <*Pflanze:*> be killed by the frost. **E~ung** *f* **-, -en** frostbite

erfrisch|en *vt* refresh. **E~ung** *f* **-, -en** refreshment

erfüll|en *vt* fill; (*nachkommen*) fulfil; serve <*Zweck*>; discharge <*Pflicht:*> **sich e~en** come true. **E~ung** *f* fulfilment

erfunden *a* invented

ergänz|en *vt* complement; (*hinzufügen*) add. **E~ung** *f* complement; supplement; (*Zusatz*) addition

ergeben† *vt* produce; (*zeigen*) show, establish; **sich e~en** result; <*Schwierigkeit:*> arise; (*kapitulieren*) surrender; (*sich fügen*) submit ● *a* devoted; (*resigniert*) resigned

Ergebnis *nt* **-ses, -se** result. **e~los** *a* fruitless

ergiebig *a* productive; (*fig*) rich

ergreifen† *vt* seize; take <*Maßnahme, Gelegenheit*>; take up <*Beruf*>; (*rühren*) move; **die Flucht e~** flee. **e~d** *a* moving

ergriffen *a* deeply moved. **E~heit** *f* **-** emotion

ergründen *vt* (*fig*) get to the bottom of

erhaben *a* raised; (*fig*) sublime

Erhalt *m* **-[e]s** receipt. **e~en**† *vt* receive, get; (*gewinnen*) obtain; (*bewahren*) preserve, keep; (*instand halten*) maintain; (*unterhalten*) support; **am Leben e~en** keep alive ● *a* **gut/schlecht e~en** in good/bad condition; **e~en bleiben** survive

erhältlich *a* obtainable

Erhaltung *f* **-** preservation; maintenance

erhängen (sich) *vr* hang oneself

erheb|en† *vt* raise; levy <*Steuer*>; charge <*Gebühr*>; **Anspruch e~en** lay claim (**auf** + *acc* to); **Protest e~en** protest; **sich e~en** rise; <*Frage:*> arise. **e~lich** *a* considerable. **E~ung** *f* **-, -en** elevation; (*Anhöhe*) rise; (*Aufstand*) uprising; (*Ermittlung*) survey

erheiter|n *vt* amuse. **E~ung** *f* **-** amusement

erhitzen *vt* heat

erhöh|en *vt* raise; (*fig*) increase; **sich e~en** rise, increase. **E~ung** *f* **-, -en** increase

erhol|en (sich) *vr* recover (**von** from); (*nach Krankheit*) convalesce; (*sich ausruhen*) have a rest. **e∼sam** *a* restful. **E∼ung** *f* **-** recovery; (*Ruhe*) rest

erinner|n *vt* remind (**an** + *acc* of); **sich e∼n** remember (**an jdn/etw** s.o./sth). **E∼ung** *f* **-, -en** memory; (*Andenken*) souvenir

erkält|en (sich) *vr* catch a cold; **e∼et sein** have a cold. **E∼ung** *f* **-, -en** cold

erkenn|bar *a* recognizable; (*sichtbar*) visible. **e∼en†** *vt* recognize; (*wahrnehmen*) distinguish. **E∼tnis** *f* **-, -se** recognition; realization; (*Wissen*) knowledge; **die neuesten E∼tnisse** the latest findings

Erker *m* **-s,-** bay

erklär|en *vt* declare; (*erläutern*) explain; **sich bereit e∼en** agree (**zu** to). **e∼end** *a* explanatory. **e∼lich** *a* explicable; (*verständlich*) understandable. **e∼licherweise** *adv* understandably. **E∼ung** *f* **-, -en** declaration; explanation; **öffentliche E∼ung** public statement

erkrank|en *vi* (*sein*) fall ill; be taken ill (**an** + *dat* with). **E∼ung** *f* **-, -en** illness

erkundig|en (sich) *vr* enquire (**nach jdm/etw** after s.o./about sth). **E∼ung** *f* **-, -en** enquiry

erlangen *vt* attain, get

Erlass *m* **-es,¨-e** (*Admin*) decree; (*Befreiung*) exemption; (*Straf-*) remission

erlassen† *vt* (*Admin*) issue; **jdm etw e∼** exempt s.o. from sth; let s.o. off <*Strafe*>

erlauben *vt* allow, permit; **ich kann es mir nicht e∼** I can't afford it

Erlaubnis *f* **-** permission. **E∼schein** *m* permit

erläutern *vt* explain

Erle *f* **-, -n** alder

erleb|en *vt* experience; (*mit-*) see; have <*Überraschung*>. **E∼nis** *nt* **-ses, -se** experience

erledigen *vt* do; (*sich befassen mit*) deal with; (*beenden*) finish; (*entscheiden*) settle; (*töten*) kill

erleichter|n *vt* lighten; (*vereinfachen*) make easier; (*befreien*) relieve; (*lindern*) ease. **e∼t** *a* relieved. **E∼ung** *f* **-** relief

erleiden† *vt* suffer

erleuchten *vt* illuminate; **hell erleuchtet** brightly lit

erlogen *a* untrue, false

Erlös *m* **-es** proceeds *pl*

erlöschen† *vi* (*sein*) go out; (*vergehen*) die; (*aussterben*) die out; (*ungültig werden*) expire; **erloschener Vulkan** extinct volcano

erlös|en *vt* save; (*befreien*) release (**von** from); (*Relig*) redeem. **e∼t** *a* relieved. **E∼ung** *f* release; (*Erleichterung*) relief; (*Relig*) redemption

ermächtig|en *vt* authorize. **E∼ung** *f* **-, -en** authorization

Ermahnung *f* exhortation; admonition

ermäßig|en *vt* reduce. **E∼ung** *f* **-, -en** reduction

ermessen† *vt* judge; (*begreifen*) appreciate. **E∼** *nt* **-s** discretion; (*Urteil*) judgement; **nach eigenem E∼** at one's own discretion

ermitt|eln *vt* establish; (*herausfinden*) find out ● *vi* (*haben*) investigate (**gegen jdn** s.o.). **E∼lungen** *fpl* investigations. **E∼lungsverfahren** *nt* (*Jur*) preliminary inquiry

ermöglichen *vt* make possible

ermord|en *vt* murder. **E∼ung** *f* **-, -en** murder

ermüd|en *vt* tire ● *vi* (*sein*) get tired. **E∼ung** *f* **-** tiredness

ermutigen *vt* encourage. **e∼d** *a* encouraging

ernähr|en *vt* feed; (*unterhalten*) support, keep; **sich e∼en von**

live/<*Tier:*> feed on. **E~er** *m* **-s,-** breadwinner. **E~ung** *f* **-** nourishment; nutrition; (*Kost*) diet

ernenn|en† *vt* appoint. **E~ung** *f* **-, -en** appointment

erneu|ern *vt* renew; (*auswechseln*) replace; change <*Verband*>; (*renovieren*) renovate. **E~erung** *f* renewal; replacement; renovation. **e~t** *a* renewed; (*neu*) new ● *adv* again

ernst *a* serious; **e~ nehmen** take seriously. **E~** *m* **-es** seriousness; **im E~** seriously; **mit einer Drohung E~ machen** carry out a threat; **ist das dein E~?** are you serious? **e~haft** *a* serious. **e~lich** *a* serious

Ernte *f* **-, -n** harvest; (*Ertrag*) crop. **E~dankfest** *nt* harvest festival. **e~n** *vt* harvest; (*fig*) reap, win

ernüchter|n *vt* sober up; (*fig*) bring down to earth. **e~nd** *a* (*fig*) sobering

Erober|er *m* **-s,-** conqueror. **e~n** *vt* conquer. **E~ung** *f* **-, -en** conquest

eröffn|en *vt* open; **jdm etw e~en** announce sth to s.o. **E~ung** *f* opening; (*Mitteilung*) announcement

erörter|n *vt* discuss. **E~ung** *f* **-, -en** discussion

Erot|ik *f* **-** eroticism. **e~isch** *a* erotic

Erpel *m* **-s,-** drake

erpicht *a* **e~ auf** (+ *acc*) keen on

erpress|en *vt* extort; blackmail <*Person*>. **E~er** *m* **-s,-** blackmailer. **E~ung** *f* **-** extortion; blackmail

erprob|en *vt* test. **e~t** *a* proven

erraten† *vt* guess

erreg|bar *a* excitable. **e~en** *vt* excite; (*hervorrufen*) arouse; **sich e~en** get worked up. **e~end** *a* exciting. **E~er** *m* **-s,-** (*Med*) germ. **e~t** *a* agitated; (*hitzig*) heated. **E~ung** *f* **-** excitement

erreich|bar *a* within reach; <*Ziel*> attainable; <*Person*> available. **e~en** *vt* reach; catch <*Zug*>; live to <*Alter*>; (*durchsetzen*) achieve

errichten *vt* erect

erringen† *vt* gain, win

erröten *vi* (*sein*) blush

Errungenschaft *f* **-, -en** achievement; (![] *Anschaffung*) acquisition

Ersatz *m* **-es** replacement, substitute; (*Entschädigung*) compensation. **E~reifen** *m* spare tyre. **E~teil** *nt* spare part

erschaffen† *vt* create

erschein|en† *vi* (*sein*) appear; <*Buch:*> be published. **E~ung** *f* **-, -en** appearance; (*Person*) figure; (*Phänomen*) phenomenon; (*Symptom*) symptom; (*Geist*) apparition

erschieß|en† *vt* shoot [dead]. **E~ungskommando** *nt* firing squad

erschlaffen *vi* (*sein*) go limp

erschlagen† *vt* beat to death; (*tödlich treffen*) strike dead; **vom Blitz e~ werden** be killed by lightning

erschließen† *vt* develop

erschöpf|en *vt* exhaust. **e~t** *a* exhausted. **E~ung** *f* **-** exhaustion

erschrecken† *vi* (*sein*) get a fright ● *vt* (*reg*) startle; (*beunruhigen*) alarm; **du hast mich erschreckt** you gave me a fright

erschrocken *a* frightened; (*erschreckt*) startled

erschütter|n *vt* shake; (*ergreifen*) upset deeply. **E~ung** *f* **-, -en** shock

erschwinglich *a* affordable

ersehen† *vt* (*fig*) see (**aus** from)

ersetzen *vt* replace; make good <*Schaden*>; refund <*Kosten*>; **jdm etw e~** compensate s.o. for sth

ersichtlich *a* obvious, apparent

erspar|en *vt* save. **E~nis** *f* **-, -se** saving; **E~nisse** savings
erst *adv* (*zuerst*) first; (*noch nicht mehr als*) only; (*nicht vor*) not until; **e~ dann** only then; **eben e~** [only] just
erstarren *vi* (*sein*) solidify; (*gefrieren*) freeze; (*steif werden*) go stiff; (*vor Schreck*) be paralysed
erstatten *vt* (*zurück-*) refund; **Bericht e~** report (**jdm** to s.o.)
Erstaufführung *f* first performance, première
erstaun|en *vt* amaze, astonish. **E~en** *nt* amazement, astonishment. **e~lich** *a* amazing
Erst|ausgabe *f* first edition. **e~e(r,s)** *a* first; (*beste*) best; **e~e Hilfe** first aid. **E~e(r)** *m/f* first; (*Beste*) best; **fürs E~e** for the time being; **als E~es** first of all; **er kam als E~er** he arrived first
erstechen† *vt* stab to death
ersteigern *vt* buy at an auction
erstens *adv* firstly, in the first place. **e~ere(r,s)** *a* the former; **der/die/das E~ere** the former
ersticken *vt* suffocate; smother <*Flammen*> ● *vi* (*sein*) suffocate. **E~** *nt* **-s** suffocation; **zum E~** stifling
erstklassig *a* first-class
ersuchen *vt* ask, request. **E~** *nt* **-s** request
ertappen *vt* [!] catch
erteilen *vt* give (**jdm** s.o.)
ertönen *vi* (*sein*) sound; (*erschallen*) ring out
Ertrag *m* **-[e]s,¨e** yield. **e~en**† *vt* bear
erträglich *a* bearable; (*leidlich*) tolerable
ertränken *vt* drown
ertrinken† *vi* (*sein*) drown
erübrigen (sich) *vr* be unnecessary
erwachsen *a* grown-up. **E~e(r)** *m/f* adult, grown-up
erwäg|en† *vt* consider. **E~ung** *f* **-, -en** consideration; **in E~ung ziehen** consider
erwähn|en *vt* mention. **E~ung** *f* **-, -en** mention
erwärmen *vt* warm; **sich e~** warm up; (*fig*) warm (**für** to)
erwart|en *vt* expect; (*warten auf*) wait for. **E~ung** *f* **-, -en** expectation
erweisen† *vt* prove; (*bezeigen*) do <*Gefallen, Dienst, Ehre*>; **sich e~ als** prove to be
erweitern *vt* widen; dilate <*Pupille*>; (*fig*) extend, expand
Erwerb *m* **-[e]s** acquisition; (*Kauf*) purchase; (*Brot-*) livelihood; (*Verdienst*) earnings *pl*. **e~en**† *vt* acquire; (*kaufen*) purchase. **e~slos** *a* unemployed. **e~stätig** *a* employed
erwider|n *vt* reply; return <*Besuch, Gruß*>. **E~ung** *f* **-, -en** reply
erwirken *vt* obtain
erwürgen *vt* strangle
Erz *nt* **-es, -e** ore
erzähl|en *vt* tell (**jdm** s.o.) ● *vi* (*haben*) talk (**von** about). **E~er** *m* **-s,-** narrator. **E~ung** *f* **-, -en** story, tale
Erzbischof *m* archbishop
erzeug|en *vt* produce; (*Electr*) generate. **E~er** *m* **-s,-** producer. **E~nis** *nt* **-ses, -se** product; **landwirtschaftliche E~nisse** farm produce *sg*.
erzieh|en† *vt* bring up; (*Sch*) educate. **E~er** *m* **-s,-** [private] tutor. **E~erin** *f* **-, -nen** governess. **E~ung** *f* **-** upbringing; education
erzielen *vt* achieve; score <*Tor*>
erzogen *a* **gut/schlecht e~** well/badly brought up

es
● *pronoun*
····➤ (*Sache*) it; (*weibliche Person*) she/her; (*männliche Person*)

he/him. **ich bin es** it's me. **wir sind traurig, ihr seid es auch** we are sad, and so are you. **er ist es, der ...** he is the one who .... **es sind Studenten** they are students

····➤ (*impers*) it. **es hat geklopft** there was a knock. **es klingelt** someone is ringing. **es wird schöner** the weather is improving. **es geht ihm gut/ schlecht** he is well/unwell. **es lässt sich aushalten** it is bearable. **es gibt** there is *or* (*pl*) are

····➤ (*als formales Objekt*) **er hat es gut** he has it made; he's well off. **er meinte es gut** he meant well. **ich hoffe/glaube es** I hope/think so

Esche *f* **-, -n** ash

Esel *m* **-s,-** donkey; (! *Person*) ass

Eskimo *m* **-[s], -[s]** Eskimo

Eskort|e *f* **-, -n** (*Mil*) escort. **e∼ieren** *vt* escort

essbar *a* edible

essen† *vt/i* (*haben*) eat; **zu Mittag/Abend e∼** have lunch/supper; **e∼ gehen** eat out. **E∼** *nt* **-s,-** food; (*Mahl*) meal; (*festlich*) dinner

Esser(in) *m* **-s,-** (*f* **-, -nen**) eater

Essig *m* **-s** vinegar. **E∼gurke** *f* [pickled] gherkin

Esslöffel *m* ≈ dessertspoon. **Essstäbchen** *ntpl* chopsticks. **Esstisch** *m* dining-table. **Esswaren** *fpl* food *sg*; (*Vorräte*) provisions. **Esszimmer** *nt* dining-room

Estland *nt* **-s** Estonia

Estragon *m* **-s** tarragon

etablieren (sich) *vr* establish oneself/<*Geschäft:*> itself

Etage /e'ta:ʒə/ *f* **-, -n** storey. **E∼nbett** *nt* bunk-beds *pl*. **E∼nwohnung** *f* flat

Etappe *f* **-, -n** stage

Etat /e'ta:/ *m* **-s, -s** budget

Eth|ik *f* **-** ethic; (*Sittenlehre*) ethics *sg*. **e∼isch** *a* ethical

ethnisch *a* ethnic; **e∼e Säuberung** ethnic cleansing

Etikett *nt* **-[e]s, -e[n]** label; (*Preis-*) tag. **e∼ieren** *vt* label

Etui /e'tvi:/ *nt* **-s, -s** case

etwa *adv* (*ungefähr*) about; (*zum Beispiel*) for instance; (*womöglich*) perhaps; **nicht e∼, dass** ... not that ...; **denkt nicht e∼** ... don't imagine ...

etwas *pron* something; (*fragend/ verneint*) anything; (*ein bisschen*) some, a little; **sonst noch e∼?** anything else? **so e∼ Ärgerliches!** what a nuisance! ● *adv* a bit

Etymologie *f* **-** etymology

euch *pron* (*acc of* **ihr** *pl*) you; (*dat*) [to] you; (*refl*) yourselves; (*einander*) each other

euer *poss pron pl* your. **e∼e, e∼t-** *s*. **eure, euret-**

Eule *f* **-, -n** owl

Euphorie *f* **-** euphoria

eur|e *poss pron pl* your. **e∼e(r,s)** *poss pron* yours. **e∼etwegen** *adv* for your sake; (*wegen euch*) because of you, on your account. **e∼etwillen** *adv* **um e∼etwillen** for your sake. **e∼ige** *poss pron* **der/ die/das e∼ige** yours

Euro *m* **-[s], -[s]** euro. **E∼-** *pref* Euro-

Europa *nt* **-s** Europe. **E∼-** *pref* European

Europä|er(in) *m* **-s,-** (*f* **-, -nen**) European. **e∼isch** *a* European

Euter *nt* **-s,-** udder

evakuier|en *vt* evacuate. **E∼ung** *f* **-** evacuation

evan|gelisch *a* Protestant. **E∼gelium** *nt* **-s, -ien** gospel

eventuell *a* possible ● *adv* possibly; (*vielleicht*) perhaps

Evolution /-'tsio:n/ *f* **-** evolution

ewig *a* eternal; (*endlos*) never-ending; **e∼ dauern** ! take ages. **E∼keit** *f* **-** eternity

Examen *nt* **-s,-** & **-mina** (*Sch*) examination

Exemplar *nt* **-s, -e** specimen; (*Buch*) copy. **e~isch** *a* exemplary

exerzieren *vt/i* (*haben*) (*Mil*) drill; (*üben*) practise

exhumieren *vt* exhume

Exil *nt* **-s** exile

Existenz *f* **-, -en** existence; (*Lebensgrundlage*) livelihood

existieren *vi* (*haben*) exist

exklusiv *a* exclusive. **e~e** *prep* (+ *gen*) excluding

exkommunizieren *vt* excommunicate

Exkremente *npl* excrement *sg*

Expedition /-'tsio:n/ *f* **-, -en** expedition

Experiment *nt* **-[e]s, -e** experiment. **e~ieren** *vi* (*haben*) experiment

Experte *m* **-n, -n** expert

explo|dieren *vi* (*sein*) explode. **E~sion** *f* **-, -en** explosion

Expor|t *m* **-[e]s, -e** export. **E~teur** /-'tø:ɐ̯/ *m* **-s, -e** exporter. **e~tieren** *vt* export

extra *adv* separately; (*zusätzlich*) extra; (*eigens*) specially; (! *absichtlich*) on purpose

extravagan|t *a* flamboyant; (*übertrieben*) extravagant

extravertiert *a* extrovert

extrem *a* extreme. **E~ist** *m* **-en, -en** extremist

Exzellenz *f* **-** (*title*) Excellency

Exzentr|iker *m* **-s,-** eccentric. **e~isch** *a* eccentric

Ff

Fabel *f* **-, -n** fable. **f~haft** *a* ! fantastic

Fabrik *f* **-, -en** factory. **F~ant** *m* **-en, -en** manufacturer. **F~at** *nt* **-[e]s, -e** product; (*Marke*) make. **F~ation** /-'tsio:n/ *f* **-** manufacture

Fach *nt* **-[e]s,¨er** compartment; (*Schub-*) drawer; (*Gebiet*) field; (*Sch*) subject. **F~arbeiter** *m* skilled worker. **F~arzt** *m*, **F~ärztin** *f* specialist. **F~ausdruck** *m* technical term

Fächer *m* **-s,-** fan

Fach|gebiet *nt* field. **f~kundig** *a* expert. **f~lich** *a* technical; (*beruflich*) professional. **F~mann** *m* (*pl* **-leute**) expert. **f~männisch** *a* expert. **F~schule** *f* technical college. **F~werkhaus** *nt* half-timbered house. **F~wort** *nt* (*pl* **-wörter**) technical term

Fackel *f* **-, -n** torch

fade *a* insipid; (*langweilig*) dull

Faden *m* **-s,¨** thread; (*Bohnen-*) string; (*Naut*) fathom

Fagott *nt* **-[e]s, -e** bassoon

fähig *a* capable (**zu**/*gen* of); (*tüchtig*) able, competent. **F~keit** *f* **-, -en** ability; competence

fahl *a* pale

fahnd|en *vi* (*haben*) search (**nach** for). **F~ung** *f* **-, -en** search

Fahne *f* **-, -n** flag; (*Druck-*) galley [proof]; **eine F~ haben** ! reek of alcohol. **F~nflucht** *f* desertion

Fahr|ausweis *m* ticket. **F~bahn** *f* carriageway; (*Straße*) road. **f~bar** *a* mobile

Fähre *f* **-, -n** ferry

fahr|en† *vi* (*sein*) go, travel; <*Fahrer:*> drive; <*Radfahrer:*> ride; (*verkehren*) run, (*ab-*) leave;

<*Schiff*:> sail; **mit dem Auto/Zug f~en** go by car/train; **was ist in ihn gefahren?** [!] what has got into him? ● *vt* drive; ride <*Fahrrad*>; take <*Kurve*>. **f~end** *a* moving; (*f~bar*) mobile; (*nicht sesshaft*) travelling. **F~er** *m* **-s,-** driver. **F~erflucht** *f* failure to stop after an accident. **F~erhaus** *nt* driver's cab. **F~erin** *f* **-, -nen** woman driver. **F~gast** *m* passenger. **F~geld** *nt* fare. **F~gestell** *nt* chassis; (*Aviat*) undercarriage. **F~karte** *f* ticket. **F~kartenschalter** *m* ticket office. **f~lässig** *a* negligent. **F~lässigkeit** *f* **-** negligence. **F~lehrer** *m* driving instructor. **F~plan** *m* timetable. **f~planmäßig** *a* scheduled ● *adv* according to/(*pünktlich*) on schedule. **F~preis** *m* fare. **F~prüfung** *f* driving test. **F~rad** *nt* bicycle. **F~schein** *m* ticket. **F~schule** *f* driving school. **F~schüler(in)** *m*(*f*) learner driver. **F~stuhl** *m* lift

Fahrt *f* **-, -en** journey; (*Auto*) drive; (*Ausflug*) trip; (*Tempo*) speed

Fährte *f* **-, -n** track; (*Witterung*) scent

Fahr|tkosten *pl* travelling expenses. **F~werk** *nt* undercarriage. **F~zeug** *nt* **-[e]s, -e** vehicle; (*Wasser-*) craft, vessel

fair /fɛːɐ̯/ *a* fair

Fakultät *f* **-, -en** faculty

Falke *m* **-n, -n** falcon

Fall *m* **-[e]s,⸚e** fall; (*Jur, Med, Gram*) case; **im F~[e]** in case (*gen* of); **auf jeden F~** in any case; (*bestimmt*) definitely; **für alle F⸚e** just in case; **auf keinen F~** on no account

Falle *f* **-, -n** trap

fallen† *vi* (*sein*) fall; (*sinken*) go down; **[im Krieg] f~** be killed in the war; **f~ lassen** drop <*etw, fig: Plan, jdn*>; make <*Bemerkung*>

fällen *vt* fell; (*fig*) pass <*Urteil*>

fällig *a* due; <*Wechsel*> mature; **längst f~** long overdue. **F~keit** *f* **-** (*Comm*) maturity

falls *conj* in case; (*wenn*) if

Fallschirm *m* parachute. **F~jäger** *m* paratrooper. **F~springer** *m* parachutist

Falltür *f* trapdoor

falsch *a* wrong; (*nicht echt, unaufrichtig*) false; (*gefälscht*) forged; <*Geld*> counterfeit; <*Schmuck*> fake ● *adv* wrongly; falsely; <*singen*> out of tune; **f~ gehen** <*Uhr*:> be wrong

fälschen *vt* forge, fake

Falschgeld *nt* counterfeit money

fälschlich *a* wrong; (*irrtümlich*) mistaken

Falsch|meldung *f* false report; (*absichtlich*) hoax report. **F~münzer** *m* **-s,-** counterfeiter

Fälschung *f* **-, -en** forgery, fake

Falte *f* **-, -n** fold; (*Rock-*) pleat; (*Knitter-*) crease; (*im Gesicht*) line; wrinkle

falten *vt* fold

Falter *m* **-s,-** butterfly; moth

faltig *a* creased; <*Gesicht*> lined; wrinkled

familiär *a* family ...; (*vertraut, zudringlich*) familiar; (*zwanglos*) informal

Familie /-i̯ə/ *f* **-, -n** family. **F~nforschung** *f* genealogy. **F~nname** *m* surname. **F~nplanung** *f* family planning. **F~nstand** *m* marital status

Fan /fɛn/ *m* **-s, -s** fan

Fana|tiker *m* **-s,-** fanatic. **f~tisch** *a* fanatical

Fanfare *f* **-, -n** trumpet; (*Signal*) fanfare

Fang *m* **-[e]s,⸚e** capture; (*Beute*) catch; **F⸚e** (*Krallen*) talons; (*Zähne*) fangs. **F~arm** *m* tentacle. **f~en**† *vt* catch; (*ein-*) capture;

gefangen nehmen take prisoner. **F~en** *nt* **-s F~en spielen** play tag. **F~frage** *f* catch question

Fantasie *f* **-, -n** = **Phantasie**

Farb|aufnahme *f* colour photograph. **F~band** *nt* (*pl* **-bänder**) typewriter ribbon. **F~e** *f* **-, -n** colour; (*Maler-*) paint; (*zum Färben*) dye; (*Karten*) suit. **f~echt** *a* colour-fast

färben *vt* colour; dye <*Textilien, Haare*> ● *vi* (*haben*) not be colour-fast

farb|enblind *a* colour-blind. **f~enfroh** *a* colourful. **F~film** *m* colour film. **f~ig** *a* coloured ● *adv* in colour. **F~ige(r)** *m/f* coloured man/woman. **F~kasten** *m* box of paints. **f~los** *a* colourless. **F~stift** *m* crayon. **F~stoff** *m* dye; (*Lebensmittel-*) colouring. **F~ton** *m* shade

Färbung *f* **-, -en** colouring

Farn *m* **-[e]s, -e** fern

Färse *f* **-, -n** heifer

Fasan *m* **-[e]s, -e[n]** pheasant

Faschierte(s) *nt* (*Aust*) mince

Fasching *m* **-s** (*SGer*) carnival

Faschis|mus *m* **-** fascism. **F~t** *m* **-en, -en** fascist. **f~tisch** *a* fascist

Faser *f* **-, -n** fibre

Fass *nt* **-es,¨er** barrel, cask; **Bier vom F~** draught beer

Fassade *f* **-, -n** façade

fassbar *a* comprehensible; (*greifbar*) tangible

fassen *vt* take [hold of], grasp; (*ergreifen*) seize; (*fangen*) catch; (*ein-*) set; (*enthalten*) hold; (*fig: begreifen*) take in, grasp; conceive <*Plan*>; make <*Entschluss*>; **sich f~** compose oneself; **sich kurz f~** be brief; **nicht zu f~** (*fig*) unbelievable ● *vi* (*haben*) **f~ an** (+ *acc*) touch

Fassung *f* **-, -en** mount; (*Edelstein-*) setting; (*Electr*) socket; (*Version*) version; (*Beherrschung*) composure; **aus der F~ bringen** disconcert. **f~slos** *a* shaken; (*erstaunt*) flabbergasted. **F~svermögen** *nt* capacity

fast *adv* almost, nearly; **f~ nie** hardly ever

fast|en *vi* (*haben*) fast. **F~enzeit** *f* Lent. **F~nacht** *f* Shrovetide; (*Karneval*) carnival. **F~nachtsdienstag** *m* Shrove Tuesday

fatal *a* fatal; (*peinlich*) embarrassing

Fata Morgana *f* **- -/- -nen** mirage

fauchen *vi* (*haben*) spit, hiss ● *vt* snarl

faul *a* lazy; (*verdorben*) rotten, bad; <*Ausrede*> lame

faul|en *vi* (*sein*) rot; <*Zahn:*> decay; (*verwesen*) putrefy. **f~enzen** *vi* (*haben*) be lazy. **F~enzer** *m* **-s,-** lazy-bones *sg*. **F~heit** *f* **-** laziness

Fäulnis *f* **-** decay

Fauna *f* **-** fauna

Faust *f* **-,Fäuste** fist; **auf eigene F~** (*fig*) off one's own bat. **F~handschuh** *m* mitten. **F~schlag** *m* punch

Fauxpas /fo'pa/ *m* **-,-** /-[s], -s/ gaffe

Favorit(in) /favo'ri:t(ɪn)/ *m* **-en, -en** (*f* **-, -nen**) (*Sport*) favourite

Fax *nt* **-, -[e]** fax. **f~en** *vt* fax

Faxen *fpl* [!] antics; **F~ machen** fool about

Faxgerät *nt* fax machine

Februar *m* **-s, -e** February

fecht|en† *vi* (*haben*) fence. **F~er** *m* **-s,-** fencer

Feder *f* **-, -n** feather; (*Schreib-*) pen; (*Spitze*) nib; (*Techn*) spring. **F~ball** *m* shuttlecock; (*Spiel*) badminton. **F~busch** *m* plume. **f~leicht** *a* as light as a feather. **f~n** *vi* (*haben*) be springy; (*nachgeben*) give; (*hoch-*) bounce. **f~nd** *a* springy; (*elastisch*)

F

elastic. **F~ung** *f* **-** (*Techn*) springs *pl*; (*Auto*) suspension
Fee *f* **-, -n** fairy
Fegefeuer *nt* purgatory
fegen *vt* sweep
Fehde *f* **-, -n** feud
fehl *a* **f~ am Platze** out of place. **F~betrag** *m* deficit. **f~en** *vi* (*haben*) be missing/(*Sch*) absent; (*mangeln*) be lacking; **mir f~t die Zeit** I haven't got the time; **was f~t ihm?** what's the matter with him? **das hat uns noch gefehlt!** that's all we need! **f~end** *a* missing; (*Sch*) absent
Fehler *m* **-s,-** mistake, error; (*Sport & fig*) fault; (*Makel*) flaw. **f~frei** *a* faultless. **f~haft** *a* faulty. **f~los** *a* flawless
Fehl|geburt *f* miscarriage. **F~griff** *m* mistake. **F~kalkulation** *f* miscalculation. **F~schlag** *m* failure. **f~schlagen**† *vi sep* (*sein*) fail. **F~start** *m* (*Sport*) false start. **F~zündung** *f* (*Auto*) misfire
Feier *f* **-, -n** celebration; (*Zeremonie*) ceremony; (*Party*) party. **F~abend** *m* end of the working day; **F~abend machen** stop work. **f~lich** *a* solemn; (*fömlich*) formal. **f~n** *vt* celebrate; hold <*Fest*> ● *vi* (*haben*) celebrate. **F~tag** *m* [public] holiday; (*kirchlicher*) feast-day; **erster/zweiter F~tag** Christmas Day / Boxing Day. **f~tags** *adv* on public holidays
feige *a* cowardly; **f~ sein** be a coward ● *adv* in a cowardly way
Feige *f* **-, -n** fig
Feig|heit *f* **-** cowardice. **F~ling** *m* **-s, -e** coward
Feile *f* **-, -n** file. **f~n** *vt/i* (*haben*) file
feilschen *vi* (*haben*) haggle
fein *a* fine; (*zart*) delicate; <*Strümpfe*> sheer; <*Unterschied*> subtle; (*scharf*) keen; (*vornehm*) refined; (*prima*) great; **sich f~ machen** dress up. **F~arbeit** *f* precision work
Feind(in) *m* **-es, -e** (*f* **-, -nen**) enemy. **f~lich** *a* enemy; (*f~selig*) hostile. **F~schaft** *f* **-, -en** enmity
fein|fühlig *a* sensitive. **F~gefühl** *nt* sensitivity; (*Takt*) delicacy. **F~heit** *f* **-, -en** fineness; delicacy; subtlety; refinement; **F~heiten** subtleties. **F~kostgeschäft** *nt* delicatessen [shop]
feist *a* fat
Feld *nt* **-[e]s, -er** field; (*Fläche*) ground; (*Sport*) pitch; (*Schach-*) square; (*auf Formular*) box. **F~bett** *nt* camp-bed. **F~forschung** *f* fieldwork. **F~herr** *m* commander. **F~stecher** *m* **-s,-** field-glasses *pl*. **F~webel** *m* **-s,-** (*Mil*) sergeant. **F~zug** *m* campaign
Felge *f* **-, -n** [wheel] rim
Fell *nt* **-[e]s, -e** (*Zool*) coat; (*Pelz*) fur; (*abgezogen*) skin, pelt
Fels *m* **-en, -en** rock. **F~block** *m* boulder. **F~en** *m* **-s,-** rock
Femininum *nt* **-s, -na** (*Gram*) feminine
Feminist|(in) *m* **-en, -en** (*f* **-, -nen**) feminist. **f~isch** *a* feminist
Fenchel *m* **-s** fennel
Fenster *nt* **-s,-** window. **F~brett** *nt* window-sill. **F~scheibe** *f* [window-]pane
Ferien /'fe:riə̯n/ *pl* holidays; (*Univ*) vacation *sg*; **F~ haben** be on holiday. **F~ort** *m* holiday resort
Ferkel *nt* **-s,-** piglet
fern *a* distant; **der F~e Osten** the Far East; **sich f~ halten** keep away ● *adv* far away; **von f~** from a distance ● *prep* (+ *dat*) far [away] from. **F~bedienung** *f* remote control. **F~e** *f* **-** distance; **in weiter F~e** far away; (*zeitlich*) in the distant future. **f~er** *a* further ● *adv* (*außerdem*) furthermore; (*in Zukunft*) in

future. **f∼gelenkt** *a* remote-controlled; <*Rakete*> guided. **F∼gespräch** *nt* long-distance call. **F∼glas** *nt* binoculars *pl*. **F∼kurs[us]** *m* correspondence course. **F∼licht** *nt* (*Auto*) full beam. **F∼meldewesen** *nt* telecommunications *pl*. **F∼rohr** *nt* telescope. **F∼schreiben** *nt* telex

Fernseh|apparat *m* television set. **f∼en**† *vi sep* (*haben*) watch television. **F∼en** *nt* **-s** television. **F∼er** *m* **-s,-** [television] viewer; (*Gerät*) television set

Fernsprech|amt *nt* telephone exchange. **F∼er** *m* telephone

Fernsteuerung *f* remote control

Ferse *f* **-, -n** heel

fertig *a* finished; (*bereit*) ready; (*Comm*) ready-made; <*Gericht*> ready-to-serve; **f∼ werden mit** finish; (*bewältigen*) cope with; **f∼ sein** have finished; (*fig*) be through (**mit jdm** with s.o.); ([!] *erschöpft*) be all in/(*seelisch*) shattered; **etw f∼ bringen** manage to do sth; (*beenden*) finish sth; **etw/jdn f∼ machen** finish sth; (*bereitmachen*) get sth/s.o. ready; ([!] *erschöpfen*) wear s.o. out; (*seelisch*) shatter s.o.; **sich f∼ machen** get ready; **etw f∼ stellen** complete sth ● *adv* **f∼ essen/lesen** finish eating/reading. **F∼bau** *m* (*pl* **-bauten**) prefabricated building. **f∼en** *vt* make. **F∼gericht** *nt* ready-to-serve meal. **F∼haus** *nt* prefabricated house. **F∼keit** *f* **-, -en** skill. **F∼stellung** *f* completion. **F∼ung** *f* **-** manufacture

fesch *a* [!] attractive

Fessel *f* **-, -n** ankle

fesseln *vt* tie up; tie (**an** + *acc* to); (*fig*) fascinate

fest *a* firm; (*nicht flüssig*) solid; (*erstarrt*) set; (*haltbar*) strong; (*nicht locker*) tight; (*feststehend*) fixed; (*ständig*) steady; <*Anstellung*> permanent; <*Schlaf*> sound; <*Blick, Stimme*> steady; **f∼ werden** harden; <*Gelee:*> set; **f∼e Nahrung** solids *pl* ● *adv* firmly; tightly; steadily; soundly; (*kräftig, tüchtig*) hard; **f∼ schlafen** be fast asleep; **f∼ angestellt** permanent

Fest *nt* **-[e]s, -e** celebration; (*Party*) party; (*Relig*) festival; **frohes F∼!** happy Christmas!

fest|binden† *vt sep* tie (**an** + *dat* to). **f∼bleiben**† *vi sep* (*sein*) (*fig*) remain firm. **f∼halten**† *v sep* ● *vt* hold on to; (*aufzeichnen*) record; **sich f∼halten** hold on ● *vi* (*haben*) **f∼halten an** (+ *dat*) (*fig*) stick to; cling to <*Tradition*>. **f∼igen** *vt* strengthen. **F∼iger** *m* **-s,-** styling lotion/(*Schaum-*) mousse. **F∼igkeit** *f* **-** firmness; solidity; strength; steadiness. **F∼land** *nt* mainland; (*Kontinent*) continent. **f∼legen** *vt sep* (*fig*) fix, settle; lay down <*Regeln*>; tie up <*Geld*>; **sich f∼legen** commit oneself

festlich *a* festive **F∼keiten** *fpl* festivities

fest|liegen† *vi sep* (*haben*) be fixed, settled. **f∼machen** *v sep* ● *vt* fasten/(*binden*) tie (**an** + *dat* to); (*f∼legen*) fix, settle ● *vi* (*haben*) (*Naut*) moor. **F∼mahl** *nt* feast. **F∼nahme** *f* **-, -n** arrest. **f∼nehmen**† *vt sep* arrest. **f∼setzen** *vt sep* fix, settle; (*inhaftieren*) gaol; **sich f∼setzen** collect. **f∼sitzen**† *vi sep* (*haben*) be firm/<*Schraube:*> tight; (*haften*) stick; (*nicht weiterkommen*) be stuck. **F∼spiele** *npl* festival *sg*. **f∼stehen**† *vi sep* (*haben*) be certain. **f∼stellen** *vt sep* fix; (*ermitteln*) establish; (*bemerken*) notice; (*sagen*) state. **F∼tag** *m* special day

Festung *f* **-, -en** fortress
Festzug *m* [grand] procession
Fete /'fe:tə, 'fɛ:tə/ *f* **-, -n** party
fett *a* fat; fatty; (*fettig*) greasy; (*üppig*) rich; <*Druck*> bold. **F~** *nt* **-[e]s, -e** fat; (*flüssig*) grease. **f~arm** *a* low-fat. **f~en** *vt* grease ● *vi* (*haben*) be greasy. **F~fleck** *m* grease mark. **f~ig** *a* greasy
Fetzen *m* **-s,-** scrap; (*Stoff*) rag
feucht *a* damp, moist; <*Luft*> humid. **F~igkeit** *f* **-** dampness; (*Nässe*) moisture; (*Luft-*) humidity. **F~igkeitscreme** *f* moisturizer
Feuer *nt* **-s,-** fire; (*für Zigarette*) light; (*Begeisterung*) passion; **F~ machen** light a fire. **F~alarm** *m* fire alarm. **f~gefährlich** *a* [in]flammable. **F~leiter** *f* fire-escape. **F~löscher** *m* **-s,-** fire extinguisher. **F~melder** *m* **-s,-** fire alarm. **f~n** *vi* (*haben*) fire (**auf** + *acc* on). **F~probe** *f* (*fig*) test. **f~rot** *a* crimson. **F~stein** *m* flint. **F~stelle** *f* hearth. **F~treppe** *f* fire-escape. **F~wache** *f* fire station. **F~waffe** *f* firearm. **F~wehr** *f* **-, -en** fire brigade. **F~wehrauto** *nt* fire-engine. **F~wehrmann** *m* (*pl* **-männer** & **-leute**) fireman. **F~werk** *nt* firework display, fireworks *pl*. **F~zeug** *nt* lighter
feurig *a* fiery; (*fig*) passionate
Fiaker *m* **-s,-** (*Aust*) horse-drawn cab
Fichte *f* **-, -n** spruce
Fieber *nt* **-s** [raised] temperature; **F~ haben** have a temperature. **f~n** *vi* (*haben*) be feverish. **F~thermometer** *nt* thermometer
fiebrig *a* feverish
Figur *f* **-, -en** figure; (*Roman-, Film-*) character; (*Schach-*) piece
Filet /fi'le:/ *nt* **-s, -s** fillet
Filiale *f* **-, -n** (*Comm*) branch
Filigran *nt* **-s** filigree
Film *m* **-[e]s, -e** film; (*Kino-*) film; (*Schicht*) coating. **f~en** *vt/i* (*haben*) film. **F~kamera** *f* cine/ (*für Kinofilm*) film camera
Filt|er *m* & (*Techn*) *nt* **-s,-** filter; (*Zigaretten-*) filter-tip. **f~ern** *vt* filter. **F~erzigarette** *f* filter-tipped cigarette. **f~rieren** *vt* filter
Filz *m* **-es** felt. **F~stift** *m* felt-tipped pen
Fimmel *m* **-s,-** [!] obsession
Finale *nt* **-s,-** (*Mus*) finale; (*Sport*) final
Finanz *f* **-, -en** finance. **F~amt** *nt* tax office. **f~iell** *a* financial. **f~ieren** *vt* finance. **F~minister** *m* minister of finance
find|en† *vt* find; (*meinen*) think; **den Tod f~en** meet one's death; **wie f~est du das?** what do you think of that? **es wird sich f~en** it'll turn up; (*fig*) it'll be all right ● *vi* (*haben*) find one's way. **F~er** *m* **-s,-** finder. **F~erlohn** *m* reward. **f~ig** *a* resourceful
Finesse *f* **-, -n** (*Kniff*) trick; **F~n** (*Techn*) refinements
Finger *m* **-s,-** finger; **die F~ lassen von** [!] leave alone. **F~abdruck** *m* finger-mark; (*Admin*) fingerprint. **F~hut** *m* thimble. **F~nagel** *m* finger-nail. **F~spitze** *f* finger-tip. **F~zeig** *m* **-[e]s, -e** hint
Fink *m* **-en, -en** finch
Finn|e *m* **-n, -n, F~in** *f* **-, -nen** Finn. **f~isch** *a* Finnish. **F~land** *nt* **-s** Finland
finster *a* dark; (*düster*) gloomy; (*unheildrohend*) sinister. **F~nis** *f* **-** darkness; (*Astr*) eclipse
Firma *f* **-, -men** firm, company
Firmen|wagen *m* company car. **F~zeichen** *nt* trade mark, logo
Firmung *f* **-, -en** (*Relig*) confirmation
Firnis *m* **-ses, -se** varnish. **f~sen** *vt* varnish
First *m* **-[e]s, -e** [roof] ridge

Fisch *m* **-[e]s, -e** fish; **F~e** (*Astr*) Pisces. **F~dampfer** *m* trawler. **f~en** *vt/i* (*haben*) fish. **F~er** *m* **-s,-** fisherman. **F~erei** *f* **-** fishing. **F~händler** *m* fishmonger. **F~reiher** *m* heron

Fiskus *m* **- der F~** the Treasury

fit *a* fit. **Fitness** *f* **-** fitness

fix *a* [!] quick; (*geistig*) bright; **f~e Idee** obsession; **fix und fertig** all finished; (*bereit*) all ready; ([!] *erschöpft*) shattered. **F~er** *m* **-s,-** [x] junkie

fixieren *vt* stare at; (*Phot*) fix

Fjord *m* **-[e]s, -e** fiord

flach *a* flat; (*eben*) level; (*niedrig*) low; (*nicht tief*) shallow

Fläche *f* **-, -n** area; (*Ober-*) surface; (*Seite*) face. **F~nmaß** *nt* square measure

Flachs *m* **-es** flax. **f~blond** *a* flaxen-haired; <*Haar*> flaxen

flackern *vi* (*haben*) flicker

Flagge *f* **-, -n** flag

Flair /flɛ:ɐ̯/ *nt* **-s** air, aura

Flak *f* **-, -[s]** anti-aircraft artillery/ (*Geschütz*) gun

flämisch *a* Flemish

Flamme *f* **-, -n** flame; (*Koch-*) burner

Flanell *m* **-s** (*Tex*) flannel

Flank|e *f* **-, -n** flank. **f~ieren** *vt* flank

Flasche *f* **-, -n** bottle. **F~nbier** *nt* bottled beer. **F~nöffner** *m* bottle-opener

flatter|haft *a* fickle. **f~n** *vi* (*sein/ haben*) flutter; <*Segel:*> flap

flau *a* (*schwach*) faint; (*Comm*) slack

Flaum *m* **-[e]s** down. **f~ig** *a* downy; **f~ig rühren** (*Aust Culin*) cream

flauschig *a* fleecy; <*Spielzeug*> fluffy

Flausen *fpl* [!] silly ideas

Flaute *f* **-, -n** (*Naut*) calm; (*Comm*) slack period; (*Schwäche*) low

fläzen (sich) *vr* [!] sprawl

Flechte *f* **-, -n** (*Med*) eczema; (*Bot*) lichen; (*Zopf*) plait. **f~n†** *vt* plait; weave <*Korb*>

Fleck *m* **-[e]s, -e[n]** spot; (*größer*) patch; (*Schmutz-*) stain, mark; **blauer F~** bruise. **f~en** *vi* (*haben*) stain. **f~enlos** *a* spotless. **F~entferner** *m* **-s,-** stain remover. **f~ig** *a* stained

Fledermaus *f* bat

Flegel *m* **-s,-** lout. **f~haft** *a* loutish

flehen *vi* (*haben*) beg (**um** for)

Fleisch *nt* **-[e]s** flesh; (*Culin*) meat; (*Frucht-*) pulp; **F~ fressend** carnivorous. **F~er** *m* **-s,-** butcher. **F~fresser** *m* **-s,-** carnivore. **f~ig** *a* fleshy. **f~lich** *a* carnal. **F~wolf** *m* mincer

Fleiß *m* **-es** diligence; **mit F~** diligently; (*absichtlich*) on purpose. **f~ig** *a* diligent; (*arbeitsam*) industrious

fletschen *vt* **die Zähne f~** <*Tier:*> bare its teeth

flex|ibel *a* flexible; <*Einband*> limp. **F~ibilität** *f* **-** flexibility

flicken *vt* mend; (*mit Flicken*) patch. **F~** *m* **-s,-** patch

Flieder *m* **-s** lilac

Fliege *f* **-, -n** fly; (*Schleife*) bow-tie. **f~n†** *vi* (*sein*) fly; (*geworfen werden*) be thrown; ([!] *fallen*) fall; ([!] *entlassen werden*) be fired/(*von der Schule*) expelled; **in die Luft f~n** blow up ●*vt* fly. **f~nd** *a* flying. **F~r** *m* **-s,-** airman; (*Pilot*); pilot; ([!] *Flugzeug*) plane. **F~rangriff** *m* air raid

flieh|en† *vi* (*sein*) flee (**vor** + *dat* from); (*entweichen*) escape ●*vt* shun. **f~end** *a* fleeing; <*Kinn, Stirn*> receding

Fliese *f* **-, -n** tile

Fließ|band *nt* assembly line. **f~en†** *vi* (*sein*) flow; (*aus Wasserhahn*) run. **f~end** *a* flowing; <*Wasser*> running; <*Verkehr*> moving; (*geläufig*) fluent

F

flimmern *vi* (*haben*) shimmer; (*TV*) flicker
flink *a* nimble; (*schnell*) quick
Flinte *f* **-, -n** shotgun
Flirt /flœɐt/ *m* **-s, -s** flirtation. **f~en** *vi* (*haben*) flirt
Flitter *m* **-s** sequins *pl*. **F~wochen** *fpl* honeymoon *sg*
flitzen *vi* (*sein*) [!] dash
Flock|e *f* **-, -n** flake; (*Wolle*) tuft. **f~ig** *a* fluffy
Floh *m* **-[e]s,¨e** flea. **F~spiel** *nt* tiddly-winks *sg*
Flora *f* **-** flora
Florett *nt* **-[e]s, -e** foil
florieren *vi* (*haben*) flourish
Floskel *f* **-, -n** [empty] phrase
Floß *nt* **-es,¨e** raft
Flosse *f* **-, -n** fin; (*Seehund-, Gummi-*) flipper; ([✖] *Hand*) paw
Flöt|e *f* **-, -n** flute; (*Block-*) recorder. **f~en** *vi* (*haben*) play the flute/recorder; ([!] *pfeifen*) whistle ● *vt* play on the flute/recorder. **F~ist(in)** *m* **-en, -en** (*f* **-, -nen**) flautist
flott *a* quick; (*lebhaft*) lively; (*schick*) smart
Flotte *f* **-, -n** fleet
flottmachen *vt sep* **wieder f~** (*Naut*) refloat; get going again <*Auto*>; put back on its feet <*Unternehmen*>
Flöz *nt* **-es, -e** [coal] seam
Fluch *m* **-[e]s,¨e** curse. **f~en** *vi* (*haben*) curse, swear
Flucht *f* **-** flight; (*Entweichen*) escape; **die F~ ergreifen** take flight. **f~artig** *a* hasty
flücht|en *vi* (*sein*) flee (**vor** + *dat* from); (*entweichen*) escape ● *vr* **sich f~en** take refuge. **f~ig** *a* fugitive; (*kurz*) brief; <*Blick*> fleeting; <*Bekanntschaft*> passing; (*oberflächlich*) cursory; (*nicht sorgfältig*) careless. **f~ig kennen** know slightly. **F~igkeitsfehler** *m* slip. **F~ling** *m* **-s, -e** fugitive; (*Pol*) refugee
Fluchwort *nt* (*pl* **-wörter**) swear-word
Flug *m* **-[e]s,¨e** flight. **F~abwehr** *f* anti-aircraft defence
Flügel *m* **-s,-** wing; (*Fenster-*) casement; (*Mus*) grand piano
Fluggast *m* [air] passenger
flügge *a* fully-fledged
Flug|gesellschaft *f* airline. **F~hafen** *m* airport. **F~lotse** *m* air-traffic controller. **F~platz** *m* airport; (*klein*) airfield. **F~preis** *m* air fare. **F~schein** *m* air ticket. **F~schneise** *f* flight path. **F~schreiber** *m* **-s,-** flight recorder. **F~schrift** *f* pamphlet. **F~steig** *m* **-[e]s, -e** gate. **F~zeug** *nt* **-[e]s, -e** aircraft, plane
Flunder *f* **-, -n** flounder
flunkern *vi* (*haben*) [!] tell fibs
Flur *m* **-[e]s, -e** [entrance] hall; (*Gang*) corridor
Fluss *m* **-es,¨e** river; (*Fließen*) flow; **im F~** (*fig*) in a state of flux. **f~abwärts** *adv* downstream. **f~aufwärts** *adv* upstream
flüssig *a* liquid; <*Lava*> molten; (*fließend*) fluent; <*Verkehr*> freely moving. **F~keit** *f* **-, -en** liquid; (*Anat*) fluid
Flusspferd *nt* hippopotamus
flüstern *vt/i* (*haben*) whisper
Flut *f* **-, -en** high tide; (*fig*) flood
Föderation /-ˈtsi̯o:n/ *f* **-, -en** federation
Fohlen *nt* **-s,-** foal
Föhn *m* **-s** föhn [wind]; (*Haartrockner*) hair-drier. **f~en** *vt* [blow-]dry
Folg|e *f* **-, -n** consequence; (*Reihe*) succession; (*Fortsetzung*) instalment; (*Teil*) part. **f~en** *vi* (*sein*) follow (**jdm/etw** s.o./sth); (*zuhören*) listen (*dat* to); **wie f~t** as follows ● (*haben*) (*gehorchen*) obey (**jdm** s.o.). **f~end** *a* following; **F~endes** the following

folger|n *vt* conclude (**aus** from). **F~ung** *f* **-, -en** conclusion

folg|lich *adv* consequently. **f~sam** *a* obedient

Folie /'fo:li̯ə/ *f* **-, -n** foil; (*Plastik-*) film

Folklore *f* **-** folklore

Folter *f* **-, -n** torture. **f~n** *vt* torture

Fön (P) *m* **-s, -e** hair-drier

Fonds /fõ:/ *m* **-,-** /**-[s], -s**/ fund

fönen* *vt s.* **föhnen**

Förder|band *nt* (*pl* **-bänder**) conveyor belt. **f~lich** *a* beneficial

fordern *vt* demand; (*beanspruchen*) claim; (*zum Kampf*) challenge

fördern *vt* promote; (*unterstützen*) encourage; (*finanziell*) sponsor; (*gewinnen*) extract

Forderung *f* **-, -en** demand; (*Anspruch*) claim

Förderung *f* **-** promotion; encouragement; (*Techn*) production

Forelle *f* **-, -n** trout

Form *f* **-, -en** form; (*Gestalt*) shape; (*Culin, Techn*) mould; (*Back-*) tin; **[gut] in F~** in good form

Formalität *f* **-, -en** formality

Format *nt* **-[e]s, -e** format; (*Größe*) size; (*fig: Bedeutung*) stature

formatieren *vt* format

Formel *f* **-, -n** formula

formen *vt* shape, mould; (*bilden*) form; **sich f~** take shape

förmlich *a* formal

form|los *a* shapeless; (*zwanglos*) informal. **F~sache** *f* formality

Formular *nt* **-s, -e** [printed] form

formulier|en *vt* formulate, word. **F~ung** *f* **-, -en** wording

forsch|en *vi* (*haben*) search (**nach** for). **f~end** *a* searching. **F~er** *m* **-s,-** research scientist; (*Reisender*) explorer. **F~ung** *f* **-, -en** research

Forst *m* **-[e]s, -e** forest

Förster *m* **-s,-** forester

Forstwirtschaft *f* forestry

Fort *nt* **-s, -s** (*Mil*) fort

fort *adv* away; **f~ sein** be away; (*gegangen/verschwunden*) have gone; **und so f~** and so on; **in einem f~** continuously. **F~bewegung** *f* locomotion. **F~bildung** *f* further education/training. **f~bleiben**† *vi sep* (*sein*) stay away. **f~bringen**† *vt sep* take away. **f~fahren**† *vi sep* (*sein*) go away ● (*haben/sein*) continue (**zu** to). **f~fallen**† *vi sep* (*sein*) be dropped/(*ausgelassen*) omitted; (*entfallen*) no longer apply; (*aufhören*) cease. **f~führen** *vt sep* continue. **f~gehen**† *vi sep* (*sein*) leave, go away; (*ausgehen*) go out; (*andauern*) go on. **f~geschritten** *a* advanced; (*spät*) late. **F~geschrittene(r)** *m/f* advanced student. **f~lassen**† *vt sep* let go; (*auslassen*) omit. **f~laufen**† *vi sep* (*sein*) run away; (*sich f~setzen*) continue. **f~laufend** *a* consecutive. **f~pflanzen (sich)** *vr sep* reproduce; <*Ton, Licht:*> travel. **F~pflanzung** *f* **-** reproduction. **F~pflanzungsorgan** *nt* reproductive organ. **f~schicken** *vt sep* send away; (*abschicken*) send off. **f~schreiten**† *vi sep* (*sein*) continue; (*Fortschritte machen*) progress, advance. **f~schreitend** *a* progressive; <*Alter*> advancing. **F~schritt** *m* progress; **F~schritte machen** make progress. **f~schrittlich** *a* progressive. **f~setzen** *vt sep* continue; **sich f~setzen** continue. **F~setzung** *f* **-, -en** continuation; (*Folge*) instalment; **F~setzung folgt** to be continued. **F~setzungsroman** *m* serialized novel, serial. **f~während** *a* constant. **f~ziehen**† *v sep* ● *vt* pull away ● *vi* (*sein*) move away

Fossil *nt* **-, -ien** /-i̯ən/ fossil

F

Foto *nt* **-s, -s** photo. **F~apparat** *m* camera. **f~gen** *a* photogenic

Fotograf|(in) *m* **-en, -en** (*f* **-, -nen**) photographer. **F~ie** *f* **-, -n** photography; (*Bild*) photograph. **f~ieren** *vt* take a photo[graph] of ● *vi* (*haben*) take photographs. **f~isch** *a* photographic

Fotokopie *f* photocopy. **f~ren** *vt* photocopy. **F~rgerät** *nt* photocopier

Fötus *m* **-, -ten** foetus

Foul /faul/ *nt* **-s, -s** (*Sport*) foul. **f~en** *vt* foul

Fracht *f* **-, -en** freight. **F~er** *m* **-s,-** freighter. **F~gut** *nt* freight. **F~schiff** *nt* cargo boat

Frack *m* **-[e]s,¨e & -s** tailcoat

Frage *f* **-, -n** question; **nicht in F~ kommen** *s.* **infrage**. **F~bogen** *m* questionnaire. **f~n** *vt* (*haben*) ask; **sich f~n** wonder (**ob** whether). **f~nd** *a* questioning. **F~zeichen** *nt* question mark

frag|lich *a* doubtful; <*Person, Sache*> in question. **f~los** *adv* undoubtedly

Fragment *nt* **-[e]s, -e** fragment

fragwürdig *a* questionable; (*verdächtig*) dubious

Fraktion /-'tsio:n/ *f* **-, -en** parliamentary party

Franken[1] *m* **-s,-** (*Swiss*) franc

Franken[2] *nt* **-s** Franconia

frankieren *vt* stamp, frank

Frankreich *nt* **-s** France

Fransen *fpl* fringe *sg*

Franz|ose *m* **-n, -n** Frenchman; **die F~osen** the French *pl.* **F~ösin** *f* **-, -nen** Frenchwoman. **f~ösisch** *a* French. **F~ösisch** *nt* **-[s]** French

Fraß *m* **-es** feed; (*pej: Essen*) muck

Fratze *f* **-, -n** grotesque face; (*Grimasse*) grimace

Frau *f* **-, -en** woman; (*Ehe-*) wife; **F~Thomas** Mrs Thomas; **Unsere Liebe F~** (*Relig*) Our Lady

Frauen|arzt *m*, **F~ärztin** *f* gynaecologist. **F~rechtlerin** *f* **-, -nen** feminist

Fräulein *nt* **-s,-** single woman; (*jung*) young lady; (*Anrede*) Miss

frech *a* cheeky; (*unverschämt*) impudent. **F~heit** *f* **-, -en** cheekiness; impudence; (*Äußerung*) impertinence

frei *a* free; (*freischaffend*) freelance; <*Künstler*> independent; (*nicht besetzt*) vacant; (*offen*) open; (*bloß*) bare; **f~er Tag** day off; **sich** (*dat*) **f~ nehmen** take time off; **f~ machen** (*räumen*) clear; vacate <*Platz*>; (*befreien*) liberate; **f~ lassen** leave free; **ist dieser Platz f~?** is this seat taken? '**Zimmer f~**' 'vacancies' ● *adv* freely; (*ohne Notizen*) without notes; (*umsonst*) free

Frei|bad *nt* open-air swimming pool. **f~beruflich** *a & adv* freelance. **F~e** *nt* **im F~en** in the open air, out of doors. **F~gabe** *f* release. **f~geben**† *v sep* ● *vt* release; (*eröffnen*) open; **jdm einen Tag f~geben** give s.o. a day off ● *vi* (*haben*) **jdm f~geben** give s.o. time off. **f~gebig** *a* generous. **F~gebigkeit** *f* **-** generosity. **f~haben**† *v sep* ● *vt* **eine Stunde f~haben** have an hour off; (*Sch*) have a free period ● *vi* (*haben*) be off work/(*Sch*) school; (*beurlaubt sein*) have time off. **f~händig** *adv* without holding on

Freiheit *f* **-, -en** freedom, liberty. **F~sstrafe** *f* prison sentence

Frei|herr *m* baron. **F~körperkultur** *f* naturism. **F~lassung** *f* **-** release. **F~lauf** *m* free-wheel. **f~legen** *vt sep* expose. **f~lich** *adv* admittedly; (*natürlich*) of course. **F~lichttheater** *nt* open-air theatre. **f~machen** *vt sep* (*frankieren*) frank; (*entkleiden*) bare; **einen Tag f~machen** take a day off. **F~maurer** *m* Freemason. **f~schaffend** *a* freelance. **f~schwimmen**† **(sich)** *v sep* pass one's swimming test. **F~sprecheinrichtung** *f* hands-free kit. **f~sprechen**† *vt sep* acquit. **F~spruch** *m* acquittal. **f~stehen**† *vi sep* (*haben*) stand empty; **es steht ihm f~** (*fig*) he is free (**zu** to). **f~stellen** *vt sep* exempt (**von** from); **jdm etw f~stellen** leave sth up to s.o. **F~stil** *m* freestyle. **F~stoß** *m* free kick

Freitag *m* Friday. **f~s** *adv* on Fridays

Frei|tod *m* suicide. **F~umschlag** *m* stamped envelope. **f~weg** *adv* freely; (*offen*) openly. **f~willig** *a* voluntary. **F~willige(r)** *m/f* volunteer. **F~zeichen** *nt* ringing tone; (*Rufzeichen*) dialling tone. **F~zeit** *f* free *or* spare time; (*Muße*) leisure. **F~zeit-** *pref* leisure … **F~zeitbekleidung** *f* casual wear. **f~zügig** *a* unrestricted; (*großzügig*) liberal

fremd *a* foreign; (*unbekannt*) strange; (*nicht das eigene*) other people's; **ein f~er Mann** a stranger; **f~e Leute** strangers; **unter f~em Namen** under an assumed name; **ich bin hier f~** I'm a stranger here. **F~e** *f* - **in der F~e** away from home; (*im Ausland*) in a foreign country. **F~e(r)** *m/f* stranger; (*Ausländer*) foreigner; (*Tourist*) tourist **F~enführer** *m* [tourist] guide **F~enverkehr** *m* tourism. **F~enzimmer** *nt* room [to let]; (*Gäste-*) guest room. **f~gehen**† *vi sep* (*sein*) ⊡ be unfaithful. **F~sprache** *f* foreign language. **F~wort** *nt* (*pl* **-wörter**) foreign word

Freske *f* **-, -n**, **Fresko** *nt* **-s, -ken** fresco

Fresse *f* **-, -n** ☒ (*Mund*) gob; (*Gesicht*) mug. **f~n**† *vt/i* (*haben*) eat. **F~n** *nt* **-s** feed; (☒ *Essen*) grub

Freud|e *f* **-, -n** pleasure; (*innere*) joy; **mit F~en** with pleasure; **jdm eine F~e machen** please s.o. **f~ig** *a* joyful

freuen *vt* please; **sich f~** be pleased (**über** + *acc* about); **sich f~ auf** (+ *acc*) look forward to; **es freut mich** I'm glad (**dass** that)

Freund *m* **-es, -e** friend; (*Verehrer*) boyfriend. **F~in** *f* **-, -nen** friend; (*Liebste*) girlfriend. **f~lich** *a* kind; (*umgänglich*) friendly; (*angenehm*) pleasant. **f~licherweise** *adv* kindly. **F~lichkeit** *f* **-, -en** kindness; friendliness; pleasantness

Freund|schaft *f* **-, -en** friendship; **F~schaft schließen** become friends. **f~lich** *a* friendly

Frieden *m* **-s** peace; **F~ schließen** make peace; **im F~** in peacetime; **lass mich in F~!** leave me alone! **F~svertrag** *m* peace treaty

Fried|hof *m* cemetery. **f~lich** *a* peaceful

frieren† *vi* (*haben*) <*Person:*> be cold; *impers* **es friert/hat gefroren** it is freezing/there has been a frost; **frierst du?** are you cold? ● (*sein*) (*gefrieren*) freeze

Fries *m* **-es, -e** frieze

frisch *a* fresh; (*sauber*) clean; (*leuchtend*) bright; (*munter*) lively; (*rüstig*) fit; **sich f~ machen** freshen up ● *adv* freshly, newly; **ein Bett f~ beziehen** put clean sheets on a bed; **f~ gestrichen!** wet paint! **F~e** *f* - freshness; brightness; liveliness; fitness. **F~haltepackung** *f* vacuum pack

Fri|seur /fri'zø:ɐ/ *m* **-s, -e** hairdresser; (*Herren-*) barber. **F~seursalon** *m* hairdressing salon. **F~seuse** /-'zø:zə/ *f* **-, -n** hairdresser

frisier|en *vt* **jdn/sich f~en** do s.o.'s/one's hair; **die Bilanz/einen Motor f~en** [!] fiddle the accounts/soup up an engine
Frisör *m* **-s, -e** = **Friseur**
Frist *f* **-, -en** period; (*Termin*) deadline; (*Aufschub*) time; **drei Tage F~** three days' grace. **f~los** *a* instant
Frisur *f* **-, -en** hairstyle
frittieren *vt* deep-fry
frivol /fri'vo:l/ *a* frivolous
froh *a* happy; (*freudig*) joyful; (*erleichtert*) glad
fröhlich *a* cheerful; (*vergnügt*) merry. **F~keit** *f* **-** cheerfulness; merriment
fromm *a* devout; (*gutartig*) docile
Frömmigkeit *f* **-** devoutness
Fronleichnam *m* Corpus Christi
Front *f* **-, -en** front. **f~al** *a* frontal; <*Zusammenstoß*> head-on ● *adv* from the front; <*zusammenstoßen*> head-on. **F~alzusammenstoß** *m* head-on collision
Frosch *m* **-[e]s,¨-e** frog. **F~laich** *m* frog-spawn. **F~mann** *m* (*pl* **-männer**) frogman
Frost *m* **-[e]s,¨-e** frost. **F~beule** *f* chilblain
frösteln *vi* (*haben*) shiver
frost|ig *a* frosty. **F~schutzmittel** *nt* antifreeze
Frottee *nt & m* **-s** towelling
frottier|en *vt* rub down. **F~[hand]tuch** *nt* terry towel
Frucht *f* **-,¨-e** fruit; **F~ tragen** bear fruit. **f~bar** *a* fertile; (*fig*) fruitful. **F~barkeit** *f* **-** fertility
früh *a* early ● *adv* early; (*morgens*) in the morning; **heute f~** this morning; **von f~ an** *od* **auf** from an early age. **F~aufsteher** *m* **-s,-** early riser. **F~e** *f* **-** **in aller F~e** bright and early; **in der F~e** (*SGer*) in the morning. **f~er** *adv* earlier; (*eher*) sooner; (*ehemals*) formerly; (*vor langer Zeit*) in the old days; **f~er oder später** sooner or later; **ich wohnte f~er in X** I used to live in X. **f~ere(r,s)** *a* earlier; (*ehemalig*) former; (*vorige*) previous; **in f~eren Zeiten** in former times. **f~estens** *adv* at the earliest. **F~geburt** *f* premature birth/(*Kind*) baby. **F~jahr** *nt* spring. **F~ling** *m* **-s, -e** spring. **f~morgens** *adv* early in the morning. **f~reif** *a* precocious
Frühstück *nt* breakfast. **f~en** *vi* (*haben*) have breakfast
frühzeitig *a & adv* early; (*vorzeitig*) premature
Frustr|ation /-'tsi̯o:n/ *f* **-, -en** frustration. **f~ieren** *vt* frustrate
Fuchs *m* **-es,¨-e** fox; (*Pferd*) chestnut. **f~en** *vt* [!] annoy
Füchsin *f* **-, -nen** vixen
Fuge[1] *f* **-, -n** joint
Fuge[2] *f* **-, -n** (*Mus*) fugue
füg|en *vt* fit (**in** + *acc* into); (*an-*) join (**an** + *acc* on to); (*dazu-*) add (**zu** to); **sich f~en** fit (**in** + *acc* into); adjoin/(*folgen*) follow (**an etw** *acc* sth); (*fig: gehorchen*) submit (*dat* to). **f~sam** *a* obedient. **F~ung** *f* **-, -en eine F~ung des Schicksals** a stroke of fate
fühl|bar *a* noticeable. **f~en** *vt/i* (*haben*) feel; **sich f~en** feel (**krank/einsam** ill/lonely); ([!] *stolz sein*) fancy oneself. **F~er** *m* **-s,-** feeler. **F~ung** *f* **-** contact
Fuhre *f* **-, -n** load
führ|en *vt* lead; guide <*Tourist*>; (*geleiten*) take; (*leiten*) run; (*befehligen*) command; (*verkaufen*) stock; bear <*Namen*>; keep <*Liste, Bücher*>; **bei** *od* **mit sich f~en** carry ● *vi* (*haben*) lead; (*verlaufen*) go, run; **zu etw f~en** lead to sth. **f~end** *a* leading. **F~er** *m* **-s,-** leader; (*Fremden-*) guide; (*Buch*) guide[book]. **F~erhaus** *nt* driver's cab. **F~erschein** *m* driving licence;

den F~erschein machen take one's driving test. **F~erscheinentzug** *m* disqualification from driving. **F~ung** *f* **-, -en** leadership; (*Leitung*) management; (*Mil*) command; (*Betragen*) conduct; (*Besichtigung*) guided tour; (*Vorsprung*) lead; **in F~ung gehen** go into the lead

Fuhr|unternehmer *m* haulage contractor. **F~werk** *nt* cart

Fülle *f* **-, -n** abundance, wealth (**an** + *dat* of); (*Körper-*) plumpness. **f~n** *vt* fill; (*Culin*) stuff

Füllen *nt* **-s,-** foal

Füll|er *m* **-s,-** [!], **F~federhalter** *m* fountain pen. **F~ung** *f* **-, -en** filling; (*Braten-*) stuffing

fummeln *vi* (*haben*) fumble (**an** + *dat* with)

Fund *m* **-[e]s, -e** find

Fundament *nt* **-[e]s, -e** foundations *pl*. **f~al** *a* fundamental

Fundbüro *nt* lost-property office

fünf *inv a*, **F~** *f* **-, -en** five; (*Sch*) ≈ fail mark. **F~linge** *mpl* quintuplets. **f~te(r,s)** *a* fifth. **f~zehn** *inv a* fifteen. **f~zehnte(r,s)** *a* fifteenth. **f~zig** *inv a* fifty. **f~zigste(r,s)** *a* fiftieth

fungieren *vi* (*haben*) act (**als** as)

Funk *m* **-s** radio. **F~e** *m* **-n, -n** spark. **f~eln** *vi* (*haben*) sparkle; <*Stern:*> twinkle. **F~en** *m* **-s,-** spark. **f~en** *vt* radio. **F~sprechgerät** *nt* walkie-talkie. **F~spruch** *m* radio message. **F~streife** *f* [police] radio patrol

Funktion /-ˈtsi̯oːn/ *f* **-, -en** function; (*Stellung*) position; (*Funktionieren*) working; **außer F~** out of action. **F~är** *m* **-s, -e** official. **f~ieren** *vi* (*haben*) work

für *prep* (+ *acc*) for; **Schritt für Schritt** step by step; **was für [ein]** what [a]! (*fragend*) what sort of [a]? **Für** *nt* **das Für und Wider** the pros and cons *pl*

Furche *f* **-, -n** furrow

Furcht *f* **-** fear (**vor** + *dat* of); **F~erregend** terrifying. **f~bar** *a* terrible

fürcht|en *vt/i* (*haben*) fear; **sich f~en** be afraid (**vor** + *dat* of). **f~erlich** *a* dreadful

füreinander *adv* for each other

Furnier *nt* **-s, -e** veneer. **f~t** *a* veneered

Fürsorg|e *f* care; (*Admin*) welfare; ([!] *Geld*) ≈ social security. **F~er(in)** *m* **-s,-** (*f* **-, -nen**) social worker. **f~lich** *a* solicitous

Fürst *m* **-en, -en** prince. **F~entum** *nt* **-s,¨er** principality. **F~in** *f* **-, -nen** princess

Furt *f* **-, -en** ford

Furunkel *m* **-s,-** (*Med*) boil

Fürwort *nt* (*pl* **-wörter**) pronoun

Furz *m* **-es, -e** (*vulg*) fart

Fusion *f* **-, -en** fusion; (*Comm*) merger

Fuß *m* **-es,¨e** foot; (*Aust: Bein*) leg; (*Lampen-*) base; (*von Weinglas*) stem; **zu Fuß** on foot; **zu Fuß gehen** walk; **auf freiem Fuß** free. **F~abdruck** *m* footprint. **F~abtreter** *m* **-s,-** doormat. **F~ball** *m* football. **F~ballspieler** *m* footballer. **F~balltoto** *nt* football pools *pl*. **F~bank** *f* footstool. **F~boden** *m* floor

Fussel *f* **-, -n** & *m* **-s, -[n]** piece of fluff; **F~n** fluff *sg*. **f~n** *vi* (*haben*) shed fluff

fußen *vi* (*haben*) be based (**auf** + *dat* on)

Fußgänger|(in) *m* **-s,-** (*f* **-, -nen**) pedestrian. **F~brücke** *f* footbridge. **F~zone** *f* pedestrian precinct

Fuß|geher *m* **-s,-** (*Aust*) = **F~gänger**. **F~gelenk** *nt* ankle. **F~hebel** *m* pedal. **F~nagel** *m* toenail. **F~note** *f* footnote. **F~pflege** *f* chiropody. **F~rücken** *m* instep. **F~sohle** *f* sole of the foot. **F~tritt** *m* kick. **F~weg** *m*

footpath; **eine Stunde F~weg** an hour's walk
futsch *pred a* [!] gone
Futter[1] *nt* **-s** feed; (*Trocken-*) fodder
Futter[2] *nt* **-s,-** (*Kleider-*) lining
Futteral *nt* **-s, -e** case
füttern[1] *vt* feed
füttern[2] *vt* line
Futur *nt* **-s** (*Gram*) future

Gg

Gabe *f* **-, -n** gift; (*Dosis*) dose
Gabel *f* **-, -n** fork. **g~n (sich)** *vr* fork. **G~stapler** *m* **-s,-** fork-lift truck. **G~ung** *f* **-, -en** fork
gackern *vi* (*haben*) cackle
gaffen *vi* (*haben*) gape, stare
Gage /ˈgaːʒə/ *f* **-, -n** (*Theat*) fee
gähnen *vi* (*haben*) yawn
Gala *f* **-** ceremonial dress
Galavorstellung *f* gala performance
Galerie *f* **-, -n** gallery
Galgen *m* **-s,-** gallows *sg*. **G~frist** *f* [!] reprieve
Galionsfigur *f* figurehead
Galle *f* **-** bile; (*G~nblase*) gall-bladder. **G~nblase** *f* gall-bladder. **G~nstein** *m* gallstone
Galopp *m* **-s** gallop; **im G~** at a gallop. **g~ieren** *vi* (*sein*) gallop
gamm|eln *vi* (*haben*) [!] loaf around. **G~ler(in)** *m* **-s,-** (*f* **-, -nen**) drop-out
Gams *f* **-, -en** (*Aust*) chamois
Gämse *f* **-, -n** chamois
Gang *m* **-[e]s,¨-e** walk; (*G~art*) gait; (*Boten-*) errand; (*Funktionieren*) running; (*Verlauf, Culin*) course; (*Durch-*) passage; (*Korridor*) corridor; (*zwischen Sitzreihen*) aisle, gangway; (*Anat*) duct; (*Auto*) gear; **in G~ bringen** get going; **im G~e sein** be in progress; **Essen mit vier G~̈en** four-course meal
gängig *a* common; (*Comm*) popular
Gangschaltung *f* gear change
Gangster /ˈgɛŋstɐ/ *m* **-s,-** gangster
Ganove *m* **-n, -n** [!] crook
Gans *f* **-,¨-e** goose
Gänse|blümchen *nt* **-s,-** daisy. **G~füßchen** *ntpl* inverted commas. **G~haut** *f* goose-pimples *pl*. **G~rich** *m* **-s, -e** gander
ganz *a* whole, entire; (*vollständig*) complete; ([!] *heil*) undamaged, intact; **die g~e Zeit** all the time, the whole time; **eine g~e Weile/Menge** quite a while/lot; *inv* **g~ Deutschland** the whole of Germany; **wieder g~ machen** [!] mend; **im Großen und G~en** on the whole ● *adv* quite; (*völlig*) completely, entirely; (*sehr*) very; **nicht g~** not quite; **g~ allein** all on one's own; **g~ und gar** completely, totally; **g~ und gar nicht** not at all. **G~e(s)** *nt* whole. **g~jährig** *adv* all the year round. **g~tägig** *a & adv* full-time; <*geöffnet*> all day. **g~tags** *adv* all day; <*arbeiten*> full-time
gar[1] *a* done, cooked
gar[2] *adv* **gar nicht/nichts/niemand** not/nothing/no one at all
Garage /gaˈraːʒə/ *f* **-, -n** garage
Garantie *f* **-, -n** guarantee. **g~ren** *vt/i* (*haben*) **[für] etw g~ren** guarantee sth. **G~schein** *m* guarantee
Garderobe *f* **-, -n** (*Kleider*) wardrobe; (*Ablage*) cloakroom; (*Künstler-*) dressing-room. **G~nfrau** *f* cloakroom attendant
Gardine *f* **-, -n** curtain
garen *vt/i* (*haben*) cook

gären† *vi* (*haben*) ferment; (*fig*) seethe
Garn *nt* **-[e]s, -e** yarn; (*Näh-*) cotton
Garnele *f* **-, -n** shrimp; prawn
garnieren *vt* decorate; (*Culin*) garnish
Garnison *f* **-, -en** garrison
Garnitur *f* **-, -en** set; (*Möbel-*) suite
Garten *m* **-s,¨** garden. **G~arbeit** *f* gardening. **G~bau** *m* horticulture. **G~haus** *nt*, **G~laube** *f* summerhouse. **G~schere** *f* secateurs *pl*
Gärtner|(in) *m* **-s,-** (*f* **-, -nen**) gardener. **G~ei** *f* **-, -en** nursery
Gärung *f* **-** fermentation
Gas *nt* **-es, -e** gas; **Gas geben** [!] accelerate. **G~maske** *f* gas mask. **G~pedal** *nt* (*Auto*) accelerator
Gasse *f* **-, -n** alley; (*Aust*) street
Gast *m* **-[e]s,¨e** guest; (*Hotel-*) visitor; (*im Lokal*) patron; **zum Mittag G~̈e haben** have people to lunch; **bei jdm zu G~ sein** be staying with s.o. **G~arbeiter** *m* foreign worker. **G~bett** *nt* spare bed
Gäste|bett *nt* spare bed. **G~buch** *nt* visitors' book. **G~zimmer** *nt* [hotel] room; (*privat*) spare room
gast|freundlich *a* hospitable. **G~freundschaft** *f* hospitality. **G~geber** *m* **-s,-** host. **G~geberin** *f* **-, -nen** hostess. **G~haus** *nt*, **G~hof** *m* inn, hotel
gastlich *a* hospitable
Gastronomie *f* **-** gastronomy
Gast|spiel *nt* guest performance. **G~spielreise** *f* (*Theat*) tour. **G~stätte** *f* restaurant. **G~wirt** *m* landlord. **G~wirtin** *f* landlady. **G~wirtschaft** *f* restaurant
Gas|werk *nt* gasworks *sg*. **G~zähler** *m* gas-meter
Gatte *m* **-n, -n** husband
Gattin *f* **-, -nen** wife
Gattung *f* **-, -en** kind; (*Biol*) genus; (*Kunst*) genre
Gaudi *f* **-** (*Aust, fam*) fun
Gaumen *m* **-s,-** palate
Gauner *m* **-s,-** crook, swindler. **G~ei** *f* **-, -en** swindle
Gaze /'ga:zə/ *f* **-** gauze
Gazelle *f* **-, -n** gazelle
Gebäck *nt* **-s** [cakes and] pastries *pl*; (*Kekse*) biscuits *pl*
Gebälk *nt* **-s** timbers *pl*
geballt *a* <*Faust*> clenched
Gebärde *f* **-, -n** gesture
gebär|en† *vt* give birth to, bear; **geboren werden** be born. **G~mutter** *f* womb, uterus
Gebäude *nt* **-s,-** building
Gebeine *ntpl* [mortal] remains
Gebell *nt* **-s** barking
geben† *vt* give; (*tun, bringen*) put; (*Karten*) deal; (*aufführen*) perform; (*unterrichten*) teach; **etw verloren g~** give sth up as lost; **viel/wenig g~ auf** (+ *acc*) set great/little store by; **sich g~** (*nachlassen*) wear off; (*besser werden*) get better; (*sich verhalten*) behave ● *impers* **es gibt** there is/are; **was gibt es Neues/zum Mittag/im Kino?** what's the news/for lunch/on at the cinema? **es wird Regen g~** it's going to rain ● *vi* (*haben*) (*Karten*) deal
Gebet *nt* **-[e]s, -e** prayer
Gebiet *nt* **-[e]s, -e** area; (*Hoheits-*) territory; (*Sach-*) field
gebieten† *vt* command; (*erfordern*) demand ● *vi* (*haben*) rule
Gebilde *nt* **-s,-** structure
gebildet *a* educated; (*kultiviert*) cultured
Gebirg|e *nt* **-s,-** mountains *pl*. **g~ig** *a* mountainous
Gebiss *nt* **-es, -e** teeth *pl*; (*künstliches*) false teeth *pl*; dentures *pl*, (*des Zaumes*) bit
geblümt *a* floral, flowered
gebogen *a* curved

geboren *a* born; **g~er Deutscher** German by birth; **Frau X, g~e Y** Mrs X, née Y
Gebot *nt* **-[e]s, -e** rule
gebraten *a* fried
Gebrauch *m* use; (*Sprach-*) usage; **Gebräuche** customs; **in G~** in use; **G~ machen von** make use of. **g~en** *vt* use; **zu nichts zu g~en** useless
gebräuchlich *a* common; <*Wort*> in common use
Gebrauch|sanleitung, G~sanweisung *f* directions *pl* for use. **g~t** *a* used; (*Comm*) secondhand. **G~twagen** *m* used car
gebrechlich *a* frail, infirm
gebrochen *a* broken ●*adv* **g~ Englisch sprechen** speak broken English
Gebrüll *nt* **-s** roaring
Gebühr *f* **-, -en** charge, fee; **über G~** excessively. **g~end** *a* due; (*geziemend*) proper. **g~enfrei** *a* free ●*adv* free of charge. **g~enpflichtig** *a & adv* subject to a charge; **g~enpflichtige Straße** toll road
Geburt *f* **-, -en** birth; **von G~** by birth. **G~enkontrolle, G~enregelung** *f* birth-control. **G~enziffer** *f* birth-rate
gebürtig *a* native (**aus** of); **g~er Deutscher** German by birth
Geburts|datum *nt* date of birth. **G~helfer** *m* obstetrician. **G~hilfe** *f* obstetrics *sg*. **G~ort** *m* place of birth. **G~tag** *m* birthday. **G~urkunde** *f* birth certificate
Gebüsch *nt* **-[e]s, -e** bushes *pl*
Gedächtnis *nt* **-ses** memory; **aus dem G~** from memory
Gedanke *m* **-ns, -n** thought (**an +** *acc* of); (*Idee*) idea; **sich** (*dat*) **G~n machen** worry (**über +** *acc* about). **g~nlos** *a* thoughtless; (*zerstreut*) absent-minded. **G~nstrich** *m* dash
Gedärme *ntpl* intestines; (*Tier-*) entrails
Gedeck *nt* **-[e]s, -e** place setting; (*auf Speisekarte*) set meal
gedeihen† *vi* (*sein*) thrive, flourish
gedenken† *vi* (*haben*) propose (**etw zu tun** to do sth); **jds g~** remember s.o. **G~** *nt* **-s** memory
Gedenk|feier *f* commemoration. **G~gottesdienst** *m* memorial service
Gedicht *nt* **-[e]s, -e** poem
Gedräng|e *nt* **-s** crush, crowd. **g~t** *a* (*knapp*) concise ●*adv* **g~t voll** packed
Geduld *f* **-** patience; **G~ haben** be patient. **g~en (sich)** *vr* be patient. **g~ig** *a* patient. **G~[s]spiel** *nt* puzzle
gedunsen *a* bloated
geehrt *a* honoured; **Sehr g~er Herr X** Dear Mr X
geeignet *a* suitable; **im g~en Moment** at the right moment
Gefahr *f* **-, -en** danger; **in G~** in danger; **auf eigene G~** at one's own risk; **G~ laufen** run the risk (**etw zu tun** of doing sth)
gefähr|den *vt* endanger; (*fig*) jeopardize. **g~lich** *a* dangerous
gefahrlos *a* safe
Gefährt *nt* **-[e]s, -e** vehicle
Gefährte *m* **-n, -n, Gefährtin** *f* **-, -nen** companion
gefahrvoll *a* dangerous, perilous
Gefälle *nt* **-s,-** slope; (*Straßen-*) gradient
gefallen† *vi* (*haben*) **jdm g~** please s.o.; **er/es gefällt mir** I like him/it; **sich** (*dat*) **etw g~ lassen** put up with sth
Gefallen[1] *m* **-s,-** favour
Gefallen[2] *nt* **-s** pleasure (**an +** *dat* in); **dir zu G~** to please you
Gefallene(r) *m* soldier killed in the war
gefällig *a* pleasing; (*hübsch*) attractive; (*hilfsbereit*) obliging;

noch etwas g~? will there be anything else? **G~keit** *f* **-, -en** favour; (*Freundlichkeit*) kindness
Gefangen|e(r) *m/f* prisoner. **G~nahme** *f* **-** capture. **g~nehmen*** *vt sep* **g~ nehmen**, *s.* **fangen**. **G~schaft** *f* **-** captivity
Gefängnis *nt* **-ses, -se** prison; (*Strafe*) imprisonment. **G~strafe** *f* imprisonment; (*Urteil*) prison sentence. **G~wärter** *m* [prison] warder
Gefäß *nt* **-es, -e** container; (*Blut-*) vessel
gefasst *a* composed; (*ruhig*) calm; **g~ sein auf** (+ *acc*) be prepared for
gefedert *a* sprung
gefeiert *a* celebrated
Gefieder *nt* **-s** plumage
gefleckt *a* spotted
Geflügel *nt* **-s** poultry. **G~klein** *nt* **-s** giblets *pl*. **g~t** *a* winged
Geflüster *nt* **-s** whispering
Gefolge *nt* **-s** retinue, entourage
gefragt *a* popular
Gefreite(r) *m* lance-corporal
gefrier|en† *vi* (*sein*) freeze. **G~fach** *nt* freezer compartment. **G~punkt** *m* freezing point. **G~schrank** *m* upright freezer. **G~truhe** *f* chest freezer
gefroren *a* frozen
gefügig *a* compliant; (*gehorsam*) obedient
Gefühl *nt* **-[e]s, -e** feeling; (*Empfindung*) sensation; (*G~sregung*) emotion; **im G~ haben** know instinctively. **g~los** *a* insensitive; (*herzlos*) unfeeling; (*taub*) numb. **g~smäßig** *a* emotional; (*instinktiv*) instinctive. **G~sregung** *f* emotion. **g~voll** *a* sensitive; (*sentimental*) sentimental
gefüllt *a* filled; (*voll*) full
gefürchtet *a* feared, dreaded
gefüttert *a* lined
gegeben *a* given; (*bestehend*) present; (*passend*) appropriate. **g~enfalls** *adv* if need be
gegen *prep* (+ *acc*) against; (*Sport*) versus; (*g~über*) to[-wards]; (*Vergleich*) compared with; (*Richtung, Zeit*) towards; (*ungefähr*) around; **ein Mittel g~** a remedy for ● *adv* **g~ 100 Leute** about 100 people. **G~angriff** *m* counter-attack
Gegend *f* **-, -en** area, region; (*Umgebung*) neighbourhood
gegeneinander *adv* against/ (*gegenüber*) towards one another
Gegen|fahrbahn *f* opposite carriageway. **G~gift** *nt* antidote. **G~maßnahme** *f* countermeasure. **G~satz** *m* contrast; (*Widerspruch*) contradiction; (*G~teil*) opposite; **im G~satz zu** unlike. **g~seitig** *a* mutual; **sich g~seitig hassen** hate one another. **G~stand** *m* object; (*Gram, Gesprächs-*) subject. **G~stück** *nt* counterpart; (*G~teil*) opposite. **G~teil** *nt* opposite, contrary; **im G~teil** on the contrary. **g~teilig** *a* opposite
gegenüber *prep* (+ *dat*) opposite; (*Vergleich*) compared with; **jdm g~ höflich sein** be polite to s.o. ● *adv* opposite. **G~** *nt* **-s** person opposite. **g~liegend** *a* opposite. **g~stehen**† *vi sep* (*haben*) (+ *dat*) face; **feindlich g~stehen** (+ *dat*) be hostile to. **g~stellen** *vt sep* confront; (*vergleichen*) compare
Gegen|verkehr *m* oncoming traffic. **G~vorschlag** *m* counter-proposal. **G~wart** *f* **-** present; (*Anwesenheit*) presence. **g~wärtig** *a* present ● *adv* at present. **G~wehr** *f* **-** resistance. **G~wert** *m* equivalent. **G~wind** *m* head wind. **g~zeichnen** *vt sep* countersign
geglückt *a* successful

G

Gegner|(in) *m* **-s,-** (*f* **-, -nen**) opponent. **g~isch** *a* opposing
Gehabe *nt* **-s** affected behaviour
Gehackte(s) *nt* mince
Gehalt *nt* **-[e]s,¨-er** salary. **G~serhöhung** *f* rise
gehässig *a* spiteful
gehäuft *a* heaped
Gehäuse *nt* **-s,-** case; (*TV, Radio*) cabinet; (*Schnecken-*) shell
Gehege *nt* **-s,-** enclosure
geheim *a* secret; **g~ halten** keep secret; **im G~en** secretly. **G~dienst** *m* Secret Service. **G~nis** *nt* **-ses, -se** secret. **g~nisvoll** *a* mysterious
gehemmt *a* (*fig*) inhibited

gehen†
- *intransitive verb* (*sein*)

····➤ (*sich irgendwohin begeben*) go; (*zu Fuß*) walk. **tanzen/schwimmen/einkaufen gehen** go dancing/swimming/shopping. **schlafen gehen** go to bed. **zum Arzt gehen** go to the doctor's. **in die Schule gehen** go to school. **auf und ab gehen** walk up and down. **über die Straße gehen** cross the street

····➤ (*weggehen; fam: abfahren*) go; leave. **ich muss bald gehen** I must go soon. **Sie können gehen** you may go. **der Zug geht um zehn Uhr** [!] the train leaves *or* goes at ten o'clock

····➤ (*funktionieren*) work. **der Computer geht wieder/nicht mehr** the computer is working again/has stopped working. **meine Uhr geht falsch/richtig** my watch is wrong/right

····➤ (*möglich sein*) be possible. **ja, das geht** yes, I *or* we can manage that. **das geht nicht** that can't be done; ([!] *ist nicht akzeptabel*) it's not good enough, it's not on [!]. **es geht einfach nicht, dass du so spät nach Hause kommst** it simply won't do for you to come home so late

····➤ ([!] *gerade noch angehen*) **es geht [so]** it is all right. **Wie war die Party? — Es ging so** How was the party? – Not bad *or* So-so

····➤ (*sich entwickeln*) do; go. **der Laden geht gut** the shop is doing well. **es geht alles nach Wunsch** everything is going to plan

····➤ (*impers*) **wie geht es Ihnen?** how are you? **es geht ihm gut/schlecht** (*gesundheitlich*) he is well/not well; (*geschäftlich*) he is doing well/badly; **ein gut g~des Geschäft** a thriving business

····➤ (*impers; sich um etw handeln*) **es geht um** it concerns. **worum geht es hier?** what is this all about? **es geht ihr nur ums Geld** she is only interested in money

Geheul *nt* **-s** howling
Gehilfe *m* **-n, -n, Gehilfin** *f* **-, -nen** trainee; (*Helfer*) assistant
Gehirn *nt* **-s** brain; (*Verstand*) brains *pl* **G~erschütterung** *f* concussion. **G~hautentzündung** *f* meningitis. **G~wäsche** *f* brainwashing
gehoben *a* (*fig*) superior
Gehöft *nt* **-[e]s, -e** farm
Gehör *nt* **-s** hearing
gehorchen *vi* (*haben*) (+ *dat*) obey
gehören *vi* (*haben*) belong (*dat* to); **dazu gehört Mut** that takes courage; **es gehört sich nicht** it isn't done
gehörlos *a* deaf
Gehörn *nt* **-s, -e** horns *pl*; (*Geweih*) antlers *pl*
gehorsam *a* obedient. **G~** *m* **-s** obedience
Geh|steig *m* **-[e]s, -e** pavement. **G~weg** *m* = **Gehsteig;** (*Fußweg*) footpath

Geier *m* **-s,-** vulture
Geig|e *f* **-, -n** violin. **g~en** *vi* (*haben*) play the violin ● *vt* play on the violin. **G~er(in)** *m* **-s,-** (*f* **-, -nen**) violinist
geil *a* lecherous; randy; (! *toll*) great
Geisel *f* **-, -n** hostage
Geiß *f* **-, -en** (*SGer*) [nanny-]goat. **G~blatt** *nt* honeysuckle
Geist *m* **-[e]s, -er** mind; (*Witz*) wit; (*Gesinnung*) spirit; (*Gespenst*) ghost; **der Heilige G~** the Holy Ghost *or* Spirit
geistes|abwesend *a* absent-minded. **G~blitz** *m* brainwave. **g~gegenwärtig** *adv* with great presence of mind. **g~gestört** *a* [mentally] deranged. **g~krank** *a* mentally ill. **G~krankheit** *f* mental illness. **G~wissenschaften** *fpl* arts. **G~zustand** *m* mental state
geist|ig *a* mental; (*intellektuell*) intellectual. **g~lich** *a* spiritual; (*religiös*) religious; <*Musik*> sacred; <*Tracht*> clerical. **G~liche(r)** *m* clergyman. **G~lichkeit** *f* **-** clergy. **g~reich** *a* clever; (*witzig*) witty
Geiz *m* **-es** meanness. **g~en** *vi* (*haben*) be mean (**mit** with). **G~hals** *m* ! miser. **g~ig** *a* mean, miserly. **G~kragen** *m* ! miser
Gekicher *nt* **-s** giggling
geknickt *a* ! dejected
gekonnt *a* accomplished ● *adv* expertly
gekränkt *a* offended, hurt
Gekritzel *nt* **-s** scribble
Gelächter *nt* **-s** laughter
geladen *a* loaded
gelähmt *a* paralysed
Geländer *nt* **-s,-** railings *pl*; (*Treppen-*) banisters
gelangen *vi* (*sein*) reach/(*fig*) attain (**zu etw/an etw** *acc* sth)
gelassen *a* composed; (*ruhig*) calm. **G~heit** *f* **-** equanimity; (*Fassung*) composure
Gelatine /ʒela-/ *f* **-** gelatine
geläufig *a* common, current; (*fließend*) fluent; **jdm g~ sein** be familiar to s.o.
gelaunt *a* **gut/schlecht g~ sein** be in a good/bad mood
gelb *a* yellow; (*bei Ampel*) amber; **das G~e vom Ei** the yolk of the egg. **G~** *nt* **-s,-** yellow. **g~lich** *a* yellowish. **G~sucht** *f* jaundice
Geld *nt* **-es, -er** money; **öffentliche G~er** public funds. **G~automat** *m* cashpoint machine. **G~beutel** *m*, **G~börse** *f* purse. **G~geber** *m* **-s,-** backer. **g~lich** *a* financial. **G~mittel** *ntpl* funds. **G~schein** *m* banknote. **G~schrank** *m* safe. **G~strafe** *f* fine. **G~stück** *nt* coin
Gelee /ʒeˈleː/ *nt* **-s, -s** jelly
gelegen *a* situated; (*passend*) convenient
Gelegenheit *f* **-, -en** opportunity, chance; (*Anlass*) occasion; (*Comm*) bargain; **bei G~** some time. **G~sarbeit** *f* casual work. **G~skauf** *m* bargain
gelegentlich *a* occasional ● *adv* occasionally; (*bei Gelegenheit*) some time
Gelehrte(r) *m/f* scholar
Geleit *nt* **-[e]s** escort; **freies G~** safe conduct. **g~en** *vt* escort
Gelenk *nt* **-[e]s, -e** joint. **g~ig** *a* supple; (*Techn*) flexible
gelernt *a* skilled
Geliebte(r) *m/f* lover
gelingen† *vi* (*sein*) succeed, be successful. **G~** *nt* **-s** success
gellend *a* shrill
geloben *vt* promise [solemnly]; **das Gelobte Land** the Promised Land
gelöst *a* (*fig*) relaxed
gelten† *vi* (*haben*) be valid; <*Regel:*> apply; **g~ als** be regarded as; **etw nicht g~ lassen**

G

not accept sth; **wenig/viel g~** be worth/(*fig*) count for little/a lot; **jdm g~** be meant for s.o.; **das gilt nicht** that doesn't count. **g~d** *a* valid; <*Preise*> current; <*Meinung*> prevailing

Geltung *f* - validity; (*Ansehen*) prestige; **zur G~ bringen** set off

gelungen *a* successful

Gelüst *nt* **-[e]s, -e** desire

gemächlich *a* leisurely ● *adv* in a leisurely manner

Gemahl *m* **-s, -e** husband. **G~in** *f* **-, -nen** wife

Gemälde *nt* **-s,-** painting. **G~galerie** *f* picture gallery

gemäß *prep* (+ *dat*) in accordance with

gemäßigt *a* moderate; <*Klima*> temperate

gemein *a* common; (*unanständig*) vulgar; (*niederträchtig*) mean; **g~er Soldat** private

Gemeinde *f* **-, -n** [local] community; (*Admin*) borough; (*Pfarr-*) parish; (*bei Gottesdienst*) congregation. **G~rat** *m* local council/(*Person*) councillor. **G~wahlen** *fpl* local elections

gemein|gefährlich *a* dangerous. **G~heit** *f* **-, -en** commonness; vulgarity; meanness; (*Bemerkung, Handlung*) mean thing [to say/do]; **so eine G~heit!** how mean! **G~kosten** *pl* overheads. **g~nützig** *a* charitable. **g~sam** *a* common ● *adv* together

Gemeinschaft *f* **-, -en** community. **g~lich** *a* joint; <*Besitz*> communal ● *adv* jointly; (*zusammen*) together. **G~sarbeit** *f* teamwork

Gemenge *nt* **-s,-** mixture

Gemisch *nt* **-[e]s, -e** mixture. **g~t** *a* mixed

Gemme *f* **-, -n** engraved gem

Gemse* *f* **-, -n** *s.* **Gämse**

Gemurmel *nt* **-s** murmuring

Gemüse *nt* **-s,-** vegetable; (*coll*) vegetables *pl*. **G~händler** *m* greengrocer

gemustert *a* patterned

Gemüt *nt* **-[e]s, -er** nature, disposition; (*Gefühl*) feelings *pl*

gemütlich *a* cosy; (*gemächlich*) leisurely; (*zwanglos*) informal; <*Person*> genial; **es sich** (*dat*) **g~ machen** make oneself comfortable. **G~keit** *f* - cosiness

Gen *nt* **-s, -e** gene

genau *a* exact, precise; <*Waage, Messung*> accurate; (*sorgfältig*) meticulous; (*ausführlich*) detailed; **nichts G~es wissen** not know any details; **g~ genommen** strictly speaking; **g~!** exactly! **G~igkeit** *f* - exactitude; precision; accuracy; meticulousness

genauso *adv* just the same; (*g~sehr*) just as much; **g~ teuer** just as expensive; **g~ gut** just as good; *adv* just as well; **g~ sehr** just as much; **g~ viel** just as much/many; **g~ wenig** just as little/few; (*noch*) no more

Gendarm /ʒã'darm/ *m* **-en, -en** (*Aust*) policeman

Genealogie *f* - genealogy

genehmig|en *vt* grant; approve <*Plan*>. **G~ung** *f* **-, -en** permission; (*Schein*) permit

geneigt *a* sloping, inclined; (*fig*) well-disposed (*dat* towards)

General *m* **-s,¨-e** general. **G~direktor** *m* managing director. **G~probe** *f* dress rehearsal. **G~streik** *m* general strike

Generation /-'tsio:n/ *f* **-, -en** generation

Generator *m* **-s, -en** /-'to:rən/ generator

generell *a* general

genes|en† *vi* (*sein*) recover. **G~ung** *f* - recovery; (*Erholung*) convalescence

Genetik *f* - genetics *sg*

genetisch *a* genetic
Genf *nt* **-s** Geneva. **G~er** *a* Geneva ...; **G~er See** Lake Geneva
genial *a* brilliant. **G~ität** *f* genius
Genick *nt* **-s, -e** [back of the] neck; **sich** (*dat*) **das G~ brechen** break one's neck
Genie /ʒe'ni:/ *nt* **-s, -s** genius
genieren /ʒe'ni:rən/ *vt* embarrass; **sich g~** feel *or* be embarrassed
genieß|bar *a* fit to eat/drink. **g~en**† *vt* enjoy; (*verzehren*) eat/drink
Genitiv *m* **-s, -e** genitive
genmanipuliert *a* genetically modified
Genom *nt* **-s, -e** genome
Genosse *m* **-n, -n** (*Pol*) comrade. **G~nschaft** *f* **-, -en** cooperative
Gentechnologie *f* genetic engineering
genug *inv a & adv* enough
Genüge *f* **zur G~** sufficiently. **g~n** *vi* (*haben*) be enough. **g~nd** *inv a* sufficient, enough; (*Sch*) fair ● *adv* sufficiently, enough
Genuss *m* **-es, ¨-e** enjoyment; (*Vergnügen*) pleasure; (*Verzehr*) consumption
geöffnet *a* open
Geo|graphie, G~grafie *f* **-** geography. **g~graphisch, g~grafisch** *a* geographical. **G~logie** *f* **-** geology. **g~logisch** *a* geological. **G~meter** *m* **-s,-** surveyor. **G~metrie** *f* **-** geometry. **g~metrisch** *a* geometric[al]
geordnet *a* well-ordered; (*stabil*) stable; **alphabetisch g~** in alphabetical order
Gepäck *nt* **-s** luggage, baggage. **G~ablage** *f* luggage-rack. **G~aufbewahrung** *f* left-luggage office. **G~schein** *m* left-luggage ticket; (*Aviat*) baggage check. **G~träger** *m* porter; (*Fahrrad-*) luggage carrier; (*Dach-*) roof-rack
gepflegt *a* well-kept; <*Person*> well-groomed; <*Hotel*> first-class
gepunktet *a* spotted
gerade *a* straight; (*direkt*) direct; (*aufrecht*) upright; (*aufrichtig*) straightforward; <*Zahl*> even ● *adv* straight; directly; (*eben*) just; (*genau*) exactly; (*besonders*) especially; **g~ sitzen/stehen** sit/stand [up] straight; **g~ erst** only just. **G~** *f* **-, -n** straight line. **g~aus** *adv* straight ahead/on. **g~heraus** *adv* (*fig*) straight out. **g~so** *adv* just the same; **g~so gut** just as good; *adv* just as well. **g~stehen**† *vi sep* (*haben*) (*fig*) accept responsibility (**für** for). **g~zu** *adv* virtually; (*wirklich*) absolutely
Geranie /-iə/ *f* **-, -n** geranium
Gerät *nt* **-[e]s, -e** tool; (*Acker-*) implement; (*Küchen-*) utensil; (*Elektro-*) appliance; (*Radio-, Fernseh-*) set; (*Turn-*) piece of apparatus; (*coll*) equipment
geraten† *vi* (*sein*) get; **in Brand g~** catch fire; **in Wut g~** get angry; **gut g~** turn out well
Geratewohl *nt* **aufs G~** at random
geräuchert *a* smoked
geräumig *a* spacious, roomy
Geräusch *nt* **-[e]s, -e** noise. **g~los** *a* noiseless
gerben *vt* tan
gerecht *a* just; (*fair*) fair. **g~fertigt** *a* justified. **G~igkeit** *f* **-** justice; fairness
Gerede *nt* **-s** talk
geregelt *a* regular
gereizt *a* irritable
Geriatrie *f* **-** geriatrics *sg*
Gericht[1] *nt* **-[e]s, -e** (*Culin*) dish
Gericht[2] *nt* **-[e]s, -e** court [of law]; **vor G~** in court; **das Jüngste G~** the Last Judgement. **g~lich** *a* judicial; <*Verfahren*> legal ● *adv* **g~lich vorgehen** take legal action. **G~shof** *m* court of justice.

G~smedizin *f* forensic medicine. **G~ssaal** *m* court-room. **G~svollzieher** *m* **-s,-** bailiff

gerieben *a* grated; ([!] *schlau*) crafty

gering *a* small; (*niedrig*) low; (*g~fügig*) slight. **g~fügig** *a* slight. **g~schätzig** *a* contemptuous; <*Bemerkung*> disparaging. **g~ste(r,s)** *a* least; **nicht im G~sten** not in the least

gerinnen† *vi* (*sein*) curdle; <*Blut:*> clot

Gerippe *nt* **-s,-** skeleton; (*fig*) framework

gerissen *a* [!] crafty

Germ *m* **-[e]s** & (*Aust*) *f* **-** yeast

German|e *m* **-n, -n** [ancient] German. **g~isch** *a* Germanic. **G~istik** *f* **-** German [language and literature]

gern[e] *adv* gladly; **g~ haben** like; (*lieben*) be fond of; **ich tanze g~** I like dancing; **willst du mit?—g~!** do you want to come?—I'd love to!

Gerste *f* **-** barley. **G~nkorn** *nt* (*Med*) stye

Geruch *m* **-[e]s,¨e** smell (**von/nach** of). **g~los** *a* odourless. **G~ssinn** *m* sense of smell

Gerücht *nt* **-[e]s, -e** rumour

gerührt *a* (*fig*) moved, touched

Gerümpel *nt* **-s** lumber, junk

Gerüst *nt* **-[e]s, -e** scaffolding; (*fig*) framework

gesammelt *a* collected; (*gefasst*) composed

gesamt *a* entire, whole. **G~ausgabe** *f* complete edition. **G~eindruck** *m* overall impression. **G~heit** *f* **-** whole. **G~schule** *f* comprehensive school. **G~summe** *f* total

Gesandte(r) *m/f* envoy

Gesang *m* **-[e]s,¨e** singing; (*Lied*) song; (*Kirchen-*) hymn. **G~verein** *m* choral society

Gesäß *nt* **-es** buttocks *pl*

Geschäft *nt* **-[e]s, -e** business; (*Laden*) shop, store; (*Transaktion*) deal; **schmutzige G~e** shady dealings; **ein gutes G~machen** do very well (**mit** out of). **g~ig** *a* busy; <*Treiben*> bustling. **G~igkeit** *f* **-** activity. **g~lich** *a* business ... ●*adv* on business

Geschäfts|brief *m* business letter. **G~führer** *m* manager; (*Vereins-*) secretary. **G~mann** *m* (*pl* **-leute**) businessman. **G~stelle** *f* office; (*Zweigstelle*) branch. **g~tüchtig** *a* **g~tüchtig sein** be a good businessman/-woman. **G~zeiten** *fpl* hours of business

geschehen† *vi* (*sein*) happen (*dat* to); **das geschieht dir recht!** it serves you right! **gern g~!** you're welcome! **G~** *nt* **-s** events *pl*

gescheit *a* clever

Geschenk *nt* **-[e]s, -e** present, gift

Geschicht|e *f* **-, -n** history; (*Erzählung*) story; ([!] *Sache*) business. **g~lich** *a* historical

Geschick *nt* **-[e]s** fate; (*Talent*) skill. **G~lichkeit** *f* **-** skilfulness, skill. **g~t** *a* skilful; (*klug*) clever

geschieden *a* divorced

Geschirr *nt* **-s, -e** (*coll*) crockery; (*Porzellan*) china; (*Service*) service; (*Pferde-*) harness; **schmutziges G~** dirty dishes *pl*. **G~spülmaschine** *f* dishwasher. **G~tuch** *nt* tea-towel

Geschlecht *nt* **-[e]s, -er** sex; (*Gram*) gender; (*Generation*) generation. **g~lich** *a* sexual. **G~skrankheit** *f* venereal disease. **G~steile** *ntpl* genitals. **G~sverkehr** *m* sexual intercourse. **G~swort** *nt* (*pl* **-wörter**) article

geschliffen *a* (*fig*) polished

Geschmack *m* **-[e]s,¨e** taste; (*Aroma*) flavour; (*G~ssinn*) sense of taste; **einen guten G~ haben** (*fig*) have good taste.

g~los *a* tasteless; **g~los sein** (*fig*) be in bad taste. **g~voll** *a* (*fig*) tasteful
Geschoss *nt* **-es, -e** missile; (*Stockwerk*) storey, floor
Geschrei *nt* **-s** screaming; (*fig*) fuss
Geschütz *nt* **-es, -e** gun, cannon
geschützt *a* protected; <*Stelle*> sheltered
Geschwader *nt* **-s,-** squadron
Geschwätz *nt* **-es** talk
geschweige *conj* **g~ denn** let alone
Geschwindigkeit *f* **-, -en** speed; (*Phys*) velocity. **G~sbegrenzung, G~sbeschränkung** *f* speed limit
Geschwister *pl* brother[s] and sister[s]; siblings
geschwollen *a* swollen; (*fig*) pompous
Geschworene|(r) *m/f* juror; **die G~n** the jury *sg*
Geschwulst *f* **-,¨e** swelling; (*Tumor*) tumour
geschwungen *a* curved
Geschwür *nt* **-s, -e** ulcer
gesellig *a* sociable; (*Zool*) gregarious; (*unterhaltsam*) convivial; **g~er Abend** social evening
Gesellschaft *f* **-, -en** company; (*Veranstaltung*) party; **die G~** society; **jdm G~ leisten** keep s.o. company. **g~lich** *a* social. **G~sspiel** *nt* party game
Gesetz *nt* **-es, -e** law. **G~entwurf** *m* bill. **g~gebend** *a* legislative. **G~gebung** *f* **-** legislation. **g~lich** *a* legal. **g~mäßig** *a* lawful; (*gesetzlich*) legal. **g~widrig** *a* illegal
gesichert *a* secure
Gesicht *nt* **-[e]s, -er** face; (*Aussehen*) appearance. **G~sfarbe** *f* complexion. **G~spunkt** *m* point of view. **G~szüge** *mpl* features
Gesindel *nt* **-s** riff-raff
Gesinnung *f* **-, -en** mind; (*Einstellung*) attitude
gesondert *a* separate
Gespann *nt* **-[e]s, -e** team; (*Wagen*) horse and cart/carriage
gespannt *a* taut; (*fig*) tense; <*Beziehungen*> strained; (*neugierig*) eager; (*erwartungsvoll*) expectant; **g~ sein, ob** wonder whether; **auf etw g~ sein** look forward eagerly to sth
Gespenst *nt* **-[e]s, -er** ghost. **g~isch** *a* ghostly; (*unheimlich*) eerie
Gespött *nt* **-[e]s** mockery; **zum G~ werden** become a laughing-stock
Gespräch *nt* **-[e]s-e** conversation; (*Telefon-*) call; **ins G~ kommen** get talking; **im G~ sein** be under discussion. **g~ig** *a* talkative, **G~sthema** *nt* topic of conversation
Gestalt *f* **-, -en** figure; (*Form*) shape, form; **G~ annehmen** (*fig*) take shape. **g~en** *vt* shape; (*organisieren*) arrange; (*schaffen*) create; (*entwerfen*) design; **sich g~en** turn out
Geständnis *nt* **-ses, -se** confession
Gestank *m* **-s** stench, [bad] smell
gestatten *vt* allow, permit; **nicht gestattet** prohibited; **g~ Sie?** may I?
Geste /ˈgɛ-, ˈgeːstə/ *f* **-, -n** gesture
Gesteck *nt* **-[e]s, -e** flower arrangement
gestehen† *vt/i* (*haben*) confess; confess to <*Verbrechen*>
Gestein *nt* **-[e]s, -e** rock
Gestell *nt* **-[e]s, -e** stand; (*Flaschen-*) rack; (*Rahmen*) frame
gesteppt *a* quilted
gestern *adv* yesterday; **g~ Nacht** last night
gestrandet *a* stranded
gestreift *a* striped
gestrichelt *a* <*Linie*> dotted
gestrichen *a* **g~er Teelöffel** level teaspoon[ful]

G

gestrig /ˈgɛstrɪç/ *a* yesterday's; **am g~en Tag** yesterday
Gestrüpp *nt* **-s, -e** undergrowth
Gestüt *nt* **-[e]s, -e** stud [farm]
Gesuch *nt* **-[e]s, -e** request; (*Admin*) application. **g~t** *a* sought-after
gesund *a* healthy; **g~ sein** be in good health; <*Sport, Getränk:*> be good for one; **wieder g~ werden** get well again
Gesundheit *f* **-** health; **G~!** (*bei Niesen*) bless you! **g~lich** *a* health ...; **g~licher Zustand** state of health ● *adv* **es geht ihm g~lich gut/schlecht** he is in good/poor health. **g~sschädlich** *a* harmful
getäfelt *a* panelled
Getöse *nt* **-s** racket, din
Getränk *nt* **-[e]s, -e** drink. **G~ekarte** *f* wine-list
getrauen *vt* **sich** (*dat*) **etw g~** dare [to] do sth; **sich g~** dare
Getreide *nt* **-s** (*coll*) grain
getrennt *a* separate; **g~ leben** live apart; **g~ schreiben** write as two words
getreu *a* faithful ● *prep* (+ *dat*) true to. **g~lich** *adv* faithfully
Getriebe *nt* **-s,-** bustle; (*Techn*) gear; (*Auto*) transmission; (*Gehäuse*) gearbox
getrost *adv* with confidence
Getto *nt* **-s, -s** ghetto
Getue *nt* **-s** [!] fuss
Getümmel *nt* **-s** tumult
geübt *a* skilled
Gewächs *nt* **-es, -e** plant
gewachsen *a* **jdm g~ sein** be a match for s.o.
Gewächshaus *nt* greenhouse
gewagt *a* daring
gewählt *a* refined
gewahr *a* **g~ werden** become aware (*acc*/*gen* of)
Gewähr *f* **-** guarantee
gewähr|en *vt* grant; (*geben*) offer. **g~leisten** *vt* guarantee
Gewahrsam *m* **-s** safekeeping; (*Haft*) custody
Gewalt *f* **-, -en** power; (*Kraft*) force; (*Brutalität*) violence; **mit G~** by force. **G~herrschaft** *f* tyranny. **g~ig** *a* powerful; ([!] *groß*) enormous; (*stark*) tremendous. **g~sam** *a* forcible; <*Tod*> violent. **g~tätig** *a* violent. **G~tätigkeit** *f* **-, -en** violence; (*Handlung*) act of violence
Gewand *nt* **-[e]s,⸚er** robe
gewandt *a* skilful. **G~heit** *f* **-** skill
Gewebe *nt* **-s,-** fabric; (*Anat*) tissue
Gewehr *nt* **-s, -e** rifle, gun
Geweih *nt* **-[e]s, -e** antlers *pl*
Gewerb|e *nt* **-s,-** trade. **g~lich** *a* commercial. **g~smäßig** *a* professional
Gewerkschaft *f* **-, -en** trade union. **G~ler(in)** *m* **-s,-** (*f* **-, -nen**) trade unionist
Gewicht *nt* **-[e]s, -e** weight; (*Bedeutung*) importance. **G~heben** *nt* **-s** weight-lifting
Gewinde *nt* **-s,-** [screw] thread
Gewinn *m* **-[e]s, -e** profit; (*fig*) gain, benefit; (*beim Spiel*) winnings *pl*; (*Preis*) prize; (*Los*) winning ticket. **G~beteiligung** *f* profit-sharing. **g~en**† *vt* win; (*erlangen*) gain; (*fördern*) extract ● *vi* (*haben*) win; **g~en an** (+ *dat*) gain in. **g~end** *a* engaging. **G~er(in)** *m* **-s,-** (*f* **-, -nen**) winner
Gewirr *nt* **-s, -e** tangle; (*Straßen-*) maze
gewiss *a* certain
Gewissen *nt* **-s,-** conscience. **g~haft** *a* conscientious. **g~los** *a* unscrupulous. **G~sbisse** *mpl* pangs of conscience
gewissermaßen *adv* to a certain extent; (*sozusagen*) as it were
Gewissheit *f* **-** certainty
Gewitt|er *nt* **-s,-** thunderstorm. **g~rig** *a* thundery

gewogen *a* (*fig*) well-disposed (*dat* towards)
gewöhnen *vt* **jdn/sich g~ an** (+ *acc*) get s.o. used to/get used to; **[an] jdn/etw gewöhnt sein** be used to s.o./sth
Gewohnheit *f* **-, -en** habit. **G~srecht** *nt* common law
gewöhnlich *a* ordinary; (*üblich*) usual; (*ordinär*) common
gewohnt *a* customary; (*vertraut*) familiar; (*üblich*) usual; **etw** (*acc*) **g~ sein** be used to sth
Gewölbe *nt* **-s,-** vault
Gewühl *nt* **-[e]s** crush
gewunden *a* winding
Gewürz *nt* **-es, -e** spice. **G~nelke** *f* clove
gezackt *a* serrated
gezähnt *a* serrated; <*Säge*> toothed
Gezeiten *fpl* tides
gezielt *a* specific; <*Frage*> pointed
geziert *a* affected
gezwungen *a* forced. **g~ermaßen** *adv* of necessity
Gicht *f* **-** gout
Giebel *m* **-s,-** gable
Gier *f* **-** greed (**nach** for). **g~ig** *a* greedy
gieß|en† *vt* pour; water <*Blumen, Garten*>; (*Techn*) cast ● *v impers* **es g~t** it is pouring [with rain]. **G~kanne** *f* watering-can
Gift *nt* **-[e]s, -e** poison; (*Schlangen-*) venom; (*Biol, Med*) toxin. **g~ig** *a* poisonous; <*Schlange*> venomous; (*Med, Chem*) toxic; (*fig*) spiteful. **G~müll** *m* toxic waste. **G~pilz** *m* toadstool
Gilde *f* **-, -n** guild
Gin /dʒɪn/ *m* **-s** gin
Ginster *m* **-s** (*Bot*) broom
Gipfel *m* **-s,-** summit, top; (*fig*) peak. **G~konferenz** *f* summit conference. **g~n** *vi* (*haben*) culminate (**in** + *dat* in)
Gips *m* **-es** plaster. **G~verband** *m* (*Med*) plaster cast
Giraffe *f* **-, -n** giraffe
Girlande *f* **-, -n** garland
Girokonto /ˈʒiːro-/ *nt* current account
Gischt *m* **-[e]s** & *f* **-** spray
Gitar|re *f* **-, -n** guitar. **G~rist(in)** *m* **-en, -en** (*f* **-, -nen**) guitarist
Gitter *nt* **-s,-** bars *pl*; (*Rost*) gratting, grid; (*Geländer, Zaun*) railings *pl*; (*Fenster-*) grille; (*Draht-*) wire screen
Glanz *m* **-es** shine; (*von Farbe, Papier*) gloss; (*Seiden-*) sheen; (*Politur*) polish; (*fig*) brilliance; (*Pracht*) splendour
glänzen *vi* (*haben*) shine. **g~d** *a* shining, bright; <*Papier*> glossy; (*fig*) brilliant
glanz|los *a* dull. **G~stück** *nt* masterpiece
Glas *nt* **-es,¨er** glass; (*Brillen-*) lens; (*Fern-*) binoculars *pl*; (*Marmeladen-*) [glass] jar. **G~er** *m* **-s,-** glazier
glasieren *vt* glaze; ice <*Kuchen*>
glas|ig *a* glassy; (*durchsichtig*) transparent. **G~scheibe** *f* pane
Glasur *f* **-, -en** glaze; (*Culin*) icing
glatt *a* smooth; (*eben*) even; <*Haar*> straight; (*rutschig*) slippery; (*einfach*) straightforward; <*Absage*> flat; **g~ streichen** smooth out; **g~ rasiert** clean-shaven; **g~ gehen** go off smoothly; **das ist g~ gelogen** it's a downright lie
Glätte *f* **-** smoothness; (*Rutschigkeit*) slipperiness
Glatt|eis *nt* [black] ice. **g~weg** *adv* **I** outright
Glatz|e *f* **-, -n** bald patch; (*Voll-*) bald head; **eine G~e bekommen** go bald. **g~köpfig** *a* bald
Glaube *m* **-ns** belief (**an** + *acc* in); (*Relig*) faith; **G~n schenken** (+ *dat*) believe. **g~n** *vt/i* (*haben*) believe (**an** + *acc* in); (*vermuten*)

G

think; **jdm g~n** believe s.o; **nicht zu g~n** unbelievable, incredible. **G~nsbekenntnis** *nt* creed

gläubig *a* religious; (*vertrauend*) trusting. **G~e(r)** *m/f* (*Relig*) believer; **die G~en** the faithful. **G~er** *m* **-s,-** (*Comm*) creditor

glaub|lich *a* **kaum g~lich** scarcely believable. **g~würdig** *a* credible; <*Person*> reliable

gleich *a* same; (*identisch*) identical; (*g~wertig*) equal; **g~ bleibend** constant; **2 mal 5 [ist] g~ 10** two times 5 equals 10; **das ist mir g~** it's all the same to me; **ganz g~, wo/wer** no matter where/who ●*adv* equally; (*übereinstimmend*) identically, the same; (*sofort*) immediately; (*in Kürze*) in a minute; (*fast*) nearly; (*direkt*) right. **g~altrig** *a* [of] the same age. **g~bedeutend** *a* synonymous. **g~berechtigt** *a* equal. **G~berechtigung** *f* equality

gleichen† *vi* (*haben*) **jdm/etw g~** be like *or* resemble s.o./sth

gleich|ermaßen *adv* equally. **g~falls** *adv* also, likewise; **danke g~falls** thank you, the same to you. **G~gewicht** *nt* balance; (*Phys & fig*) equilibrium. **g~gültig** *a* indifferent; (*unwichtig*) unimportant. **G~gültigkeit** *f* indifference. **g~machen** *vt sep* make equal; **dem Erdboden g~machen** raze to the ground. **g~mäßig** *a* even, regular; (*beständig*) constant. **G~mäßigkeit** *f* **-** regularity

Gleichnis *nt* **-ses, -se** parable

Gleich|schritt *m* **im G~schritt** in step. **g~setzen** *vt sep* equate/ (*g~stellen*) place on a par (*dat*/ **mit** with). **g~stellen** *vt sep* place on a par (*dat* with). **G~strom** *m* direct current

Gleichung *f* **-, -en** equation

gleichwertig *adv a* of equal value. **g~zeitig** *a* simultaneous

Gleis *nt* **-es, -e** track; (*Bahnsteig*) platform; **G~ 5** platform 5

gleiten† *vi* (*sein*) glide; (*rutschen*) slide. **g~d** *a* sliding; **g~de Arbeitszeit** flexitime

Gleitzeit *f* flexitime

Gletscher *m* **-s,-** glacier

Glied *nt* **-[e]s, -er** limb; (*Teil*) part; (*Ketten-*) link; (*Mitglied*) member; (*Mil*) rank. **g~ern** *vt* arrange; (*einteilen*) divide. **G~maßen** *fpl* limbs

glitschig *a* slippery

glitzern *vi* (*haben*) glitter

globalisier|en *vt* globalize. **G~ung** *f* **-, -en** globalization

Globus *m* **-** *&* **-busses, -ben** *&* **-busse** globe

Glocke *f* **-, -n** bell. **G~nturm** *m* bell-tower, belfry

glorreich *a* glorious

Glossar *nt* **-s, -e** glossary

Glosse *f* **-, -n** comment

glotzen *vi* (*haben*) stare

Glück *nt* **-[e]s** [good] luck; (*Zufriedenheit*) happiness; **G~ bringend** lucky; **G~/kein G~ haben** be lucky/unlucky; **zum G~** luckily, fortunately; **auf gut G~** on the off chance; (*wahllos*) at random. **g~en** *vi* (*sein*) succeed

glücklich *a* lucky, fortunate; (*zufrieden*) happy; (*sicher*) safe ●*adv* happily; safely. **g~erweise** *adv* luckily, fortunately

Glücksspiel *nt* game of chance; (*Spielen*) gambling

Glückwunsch *m* good wishes *pl*; (*Gratulation*) congratulations *pl*; **herzlichen G~!** congratulations! (*zum Geburtstag*) happy birthday! **G~karte** *f* greetings card

Glüh|birne *f* light-bulb. **g~en** *vi* (*haben*) glow. **g~end** *a* glowing; (*rot-*) red-hot; <*Hitze*> scorching; (*leidenschaftlich*) fervent. **G~faden** *m* filament. **G~wein** *m*

mulled wine. **G~würmchen** *nt* **-s,-** glow-worm

Glukose *f* **-** glucose

Glut *f* **-** embers *pl;* (*Röte*) glow; (*Hitze*) heat; (*fig*) ardour

Glyzinie /-iə/ *f* **-, -n** wisteria

GmbH *abbr* (**Gesellschaft mit beschränkter Haftung**) ≈ plc

Gnade *f* **-** mercy; (*Gunst*) favour; (*Relig*) grace. **G~nfrist** *f* reprieve

gnädig *a* gracious; (*mild*) lenient; **g~e Frau** Madam

Gnom *m* **-en, -en** gnome

Gobelin /gobə'lɛ̃:/ *m* **-s, -s** tapestry

Gold *nt* **-[e]s** gold. **g~en** *a* gold ...; (*g~farben*) golden. **G~fisch** *m* goldfish. **g~ig** *a* sweet, lovely. **G~lack** *m* wallflower. **G~regen** *m* laburnum. **G~schmied** *m* goldsmith

Golf[1] *m* **-[e]s, -e** (*Geog*) gulf

Golf[2] *nt* **-s** golf. **G~platz** *m* golf-course. **G~schläger** *m* golf-club. **G~spieler(in)** *m(f)* golfer

Gondel *f* **-, -n** gondola; (*Kabine*) cabin

gönnen *vt* **jdm etw g~** not begrudge s.o. sth; **jdm etw nicht g~** begrudge s.o. sth

Gör *nt* **-s, -en, Göre** *f* **-, -n** [!] kid

Gorilla *m* **-s, -s** gorilla

Gosse *f* **-, -n** gutter

Gotlik *f* **-** Gothic. **g~isch** *a* Gothic

Gott *m* **-[e]s,¨er** God; (*Myth*) god

Götterspeise *f* jelly

Gottes|dienst *m* service. **G~lästerung** *f* blasphemy

Gottheit *f* **-, -en** deity

Göttin *f* **-, -nen** goddess

göttlich *a* divine

gottlos *a* ungodly; (*atheistisch*) godless

Grab *nt* **-[e]s,¨er** grave

graben† *vi* (*haben*) dig

Graben *m* **-s,¨** ditch; (*Mil*) trench

Grab|mal *nt* tomb. **G~stein** *m* gravestone, tombstone

Grad *m* **-[e]s, -e** degree

Graf *m* **-en, -en** count

Grafik *f* **-, -en** graphics *sg;* (*Kunst*) graphic arts *pl;* (*Druck*) print

Gräfin *f* **-, -nen** countess

grafisch *a* graphic; **g~e Darstellung** diagram

Grafschaft *f* **-, -en** county

Gram *m* **-s** grief

grämen (sich) *vr* grieve

Gramm *nt* **-s, -e** gram

Gram|matik *f* **-, -en** grammar. **g~matikalisch** *a* grammatical

Granat *m* **-[e]s, -e** (*Miner*) garnet. **G~e** *f* **-, -n** shell; (*Hand-*) grenade

Granit *m* **-s, -e** granite

Gras *nt* **-es,¨er** grass. **g~en** *vi* (*haben*) graze. **G~hüpfer** *m* **-s,-** grasshopper

grässlich *a* dreadful

Grat *m* **-[e]s, -e** [mountain] ridge

Gräte *f* **-, -n** fishbone

Gratifikation /-'tsio:n/ *f* **-, -en** bonus

gratis *adv* free [of charge]. **G~probe** *f* free sample

Gratu|lant(in) *m* **-en, -en** (*f* **-, -nen**) well-wisher. **G~lation** /-'tsio:n/ *f* **-, -en** congratulations *pl;* (*Glückwünsche*) best wishes *pl.* **g~lieren** *vi* (*haben*) **jdm g~lieren** congratulate s.o. (**zu** on); (*zum Geburtstag*) wish s.o. happy birthday

grau *a*, **G~** *nt* **-s,-** grey

Gräuel *m* **-s,-** horror

grauen *v impers* **mir graut [es] davor** I dread it. **G~** *nt* **-s** dread. **g~haft** *a* gruesome; (*grässlich*) horrible

gräulich *a* horrible

grausam *a* cruel. **G~keit** *f* **-, -en** cruelty

graus|en *v impers* **mir graust davor** I dread it. **G~en** *nt* **-s** horror, dread. **g~ig** *a* gruesome

gravieren *vt* engrave. **g~d** *a* (*fig*) serious

graziös *a* graceful

greifen† *vt* take hold of; (*fangen*) catch ● *vi* (*haben*) reach (**nach** for); **um sich g~** (*fig*) spread

Greis *m* **-es, -e** old man. **G~in** *f* **-, -nen** old woman

grell *a* glaring; <*Farbe*> garish; (*schrill*) shrill

Gremium *nt* **-s, -ien** committee

Grenz|e *f* **-, -n** border; (*Staats-*) frontier; (*Grundstücks-*) boundary; (*fig*) limit. **g~en** *vi* (*haben*) border (**an** + *acc* on). **g~enlos** *a* boundless; (*maßlos*) infinite

Griech|e *m* **-n, -n** Greek. **G~enland** *nt* **-s** Greece. **G~in** *f* **-, -nen** Greek woman. **g~isch** *a* Greek. **G~isch** *nt* **-[s]** (*Lang*) Greek

Grieß *m* **-es** semolina

Griff *m* **-[e]s, -e** grasp, hold; (*Hand-*) movement of the hand; (*Tür-, Messer-*) handle; (*Schwert-*) hilt. **g~bereit** *a* handy

Grill *m* **-s, -s** grill; (*Garten-*) barbecue

Grille *f* **-, -n** (*Zool*) cricket

grill|en *vt* grill; (*im Freien*) barbecue ● *vi* (*haben*) have a barbecue. **G~fest** *nt* barbecue

Grimasse *f* **-, -n** grimace; **G~n schneiden** pull faces

grimmig *a* furious; <*Kälte*> bitter

grinsen *vi* (*haben*) grin

Grippe *f* **-, -n** influenza, [!] flu

grob *a* coarse; (*unsanft, ungefähr*) rough; (*unhöflich*) rude; (*schwer*) gross; <*Fehler*> bad; **g~ geschätzt** roughly. **G~ian** *m* **-s, -e** brute

Groll *m* **-[e]s** resentment. **g~en** *vi* (*haben*) be angry (*dat* with); <*Donner:*> rumble

Grönland *nt* **-s** Greenland

Gros *nt* **-ses,-** (*Maß*) gross

Groschen *m* **-s,-** (*Aust*) groschen; [!] ten-pfennig piece

groß *a* big; <*Anzahl, Summe*> large; (*bedeutend, stark*) great; (*g~artig*) grand; <*Buchstabe*> capital; **g~e Ferien** summer holidays; **der größte Teil** the majority *or* bulk; **g~ werden** <*Person:*> grow up; **g~ in etw** (*dat*) **sein** be good at sth; **G~ und Klein** young and old; **im G~en und Ganzen** on the whole ● *adv* <*feiern*> in style; ([!] *viel*) much

groß|artig *a* magnificent. **G~aufnahme** *f* close-up. **G~britannien** *nt* **-s** Great Britain. **G~buchstabe** *m* capital letter. **G~e(r)** *m/f* **unser G~er** our eldest; **die G~en** the grown-ups; (*fig*) the great *pl*

Größe *f* **-, -n** size; (*Ausmaß*) extent; (*Körper-*) height; (*Bedeutsamkeit*) greatness; (*Math*) quantity; (*Person*) great figure

Großeltern *pl* grandparents

Groß|handel *m* wholesale trade. **G~händler** *m* wholesaler. **G~macht** *f* superpower. **g~mütig** *a* magnanimous. **G~mutter** *f* grandmother. **G~schreibung** *f* capitalization. **g~spurig** *a* pompous; (*überheblich*) arrogant. **G~stadt** *f* [large] city. **g~städtisch** *a* city … **G~teil** *m* large proportion; (*Hauptteil*) bulk

größtenteils *adv* for the most part

groß|tun† **(sich)** *vr sep* brag. **G~vater** *m* grandfather. **g~ziehen**† *vt sep* bring up; rear <*Tier*>. **g~zügig** *a* generous. **G~zügigkeit** *f* **-** generosity

Grotte *f* **-, -n** grotto

Grübchen *nt* **-s,-** dimple

Grube *f* **-, -n** pit

grübeln *vi* (*haben*) brood

Gruft *f* **-,⸚e** [burial] vault

grün *a* green; **im G~en** out in the country; **die G~en** the Greens

Grund *m* **-[e]s,⸚e** ground; (*Boden*) bottom; (*Hinter-*) background; (*Ursache*) reason; **aus diesem**

G~e for this reason; **im G~e [genommen]** basically; **auf G~ laufen** (*Naut*) run aground; **zu G~e richten/gehen** *s.* **zugrunde**. **G~begriffe** *mpl* basics. **G~besitzer** *m* landowner
gründ|en *vt* found, set up; start <*Familie*>; (*fig*) base (**auf** + *acc* on); **sich g~en** be based (**auf** + *acc* on). **G~er(in)** *m* **-s,-** (*f* **-, -nen**) founder
Grund|farbe *f* primary colour. **G~form** *f* (*Gram*) infinitive. **G~gesetz** *nt* (*Pol*) constitution. **G~lage** *f* basis, foundation
gründlich *a* thorough. **G~keit** *f* **-** thoroughness
Gründonnerstag *m* Maundy Thursday
Grund|regel *f* basic rule. **G~riss** *m* ground-plan; (*fig*) outline. **G~satz** *m* principle. **g~sätzlich** *a* fundamental; (*im Allgemeinen*) in principle; (*prinzipiell*) on principle; **G~schule** *f* primary school. **G~stück** *nt* plot [of land]
Gründung *f* **-, -en** foundation
Grün|span *m* verdigris. **G~streifen** *m* grass verge; (*Mittel-*) central reservation
grunzen *vi* (*haben*) grunt
Gruppe *f* **-, -n** group; (*Reise-*) party
gruppieren *vt* group
Grusel|geschichte *f* horror story. **g~ig** *a* creepy
Gruß *m* **-es,¨-e** greeting; (*Mil*) salute; **einen schönen G~ an X** give my regards to X; **viele/herzliche G¨~e** regards; **Mit freundlichen G¨~en** Yours sincerely/faithfully
grüßen *vt/i* (*haben*) say hallo (**jdn** to s.o.); (*Mil*) salute; **g~Sie X von mir** give my regards to X; **grüß Gott!** (*SGer, Aust*) good morning/afternoon/evening!
gucken *vi* (*haben*) [!] look
Guerilla /ge'rɪlja/ *f* **-** guerrilla warfare. **G~kämpfer** *m* guerrilla
Gulasch *nt* & *m* **-[e]s** goulash
gültig *a* valid
Gummi *m* & *nt* **-s, -[s]** rubber; (*Harz*) gum. **G~band** *nt* (*pl* **-bänder**) elastic *or* rubber band
gummiert *a* gummed
Gummi|knüppel *m* truncheon. **G~stiefel** *m* gumboot, wellington. **G~zug** *m* elastic
Gunst *f* **-** favour
günstig *a* favourable; (*passend*) convenient
Gurgel *f* **-, -n** throat. **g~n** *vi* (*haben*) gargle
Gurke *f* **-, -n** cucumber; (*Essig-*) gherkin
Gurt *m* **-[e]s, -e** strap; (*Gürtel*) belt; (*Auto*) safety-belt. **G~band** *nt* (*pl* **-bänder**) waistband
Gürtel *m* **-s,-** belt. **G~linie** *f* waistline. **G~rose** *f* shingles *sg*
Guss *m* **-es,¨-e** (*Techn*) casting; (*Strom*) stream; (*Regen-*) downpour; (*Torten-*) icing. **G~eisen** *nt* cast iron
gut *a* good; <*Gewissen*> clear; (*gütig*) kind (**zu** to); **jdm gut sein** be fond of s.o.; **im G~en** amicably; **schon gut** that's all right ● *adv* well; <*schmecken, riechen*> good; (*leicht*) easily; **gut zu sehen** clearly visible, **gut drei Stunden** a good three hours
Gut *nt* **-[e]s,¨-er** possession, property; (*Land-*) estate; **Gut und Böse** good and evil; **Güter** (*Comm*) goods
Gutacht|en *nt* **-s,-** expert's report. **G~er** *m* **-s,-** expert
gutartig *a* good-natured; (*Med*) benign
Gute|(s) *nt* **etwas/nichts G~s** something/nothing good; **G~s tun** do good; **alles G~!** all the best!
Güte *f* **-, -n** goodness, kindness; (*Qualität*) quality
Güterzug *m* goods train

G

gut|gehen* *vi sep* (*sein*) **gut gehen**, *s.* **gehen**. **g~gehend*** *a* **gut gehend**, *s.* **gehen. g~gläubig** *a* trusting. **g~haben†** *vt sep* **fünfzig Euro g~haben** have fifty euros credit (**bei** with). **G~haben** *nt* **-s,-** [credit] balance; (*Kredit*) credit

gut|machen *vt sep* make up for; make good <*Schaden*>. **g~mütig** *a* good-natured. **G~mütigkeit** *f* **-** good nature. **G~schein** *m* credit note; (*Bon*) voucher; (*Geschenk-*) gift token. **g~schreiben†** *vt sep* credit. **G~schrift** *f* credit

Guts|haus *nt* manor house

gut|tun* *vi sep* (*haben*) **gut tun**, *s.* **tun**. **g~willig** *a* willing

Gymnasium *nt* **-s, -ien** ≈ grammar school

Gymnastik *f* **-** [keep-fit] exercises *pl;* (*Turnen*) gymnastics *sg*

Gynäko|loge *m* **-n, -n** gynaecologist. **G~logie** *f* **-** gynaecology

Hh

H, h /ha:/ *nt,* **-,-** (*Mus*) B, b

Haar *nt* **-[e]s, -e** hair; **sich** (*dat*) **die Haare** *od* **das H~ waschen** wash one's hair; **um ein H~** [!] very nearly. **H~bürste** *f* hairbrush. **h~en** *vi* (*haben*) shed hairs; <*Tier:*> moult ● *vr* **sich h~en** moult. **h~ig** *a* hairy; [!] tricky. **H~klemme** *f* hair-grip. **H~nadelkurve** *f* hairpin bend. **H~schnitt** *m* haircut. **H~spange** *f* slide. **H~waschmittel** *nt* shampoo

Habe *f* **-** possessions *pl*

haben†

● *transitive verb*

····➤ have; (*im Präsens*) have got [!]. **er hat kein Geld** he has no money *or* [!] he hasn't got any money. **ich habe/hatte die Grippe** I've got flu/had flu. **was haben Sie da?** what have you got there? **wenn ich die Zeit hätte** if I had the time

····➤ (*empfinden*) **Angst/Hunger/Durst haben** be frightened/hungry/thirsty. **was hat er?** what's wrong with him?

····➤ (+ *Adj., es*) **es gut/schlecht haben** be well/badly off. **es schwer haben** be having a difficult time

····➤ (+ *zu*) (*müssen*) **du hast zu gehorchen** you must obey

● *auxiliary verb*

····➤ have. **ich habe/hatte ihn eben gesehen** I have *or* I've/I had *or* I'd just seen him. **er hat es gewusst** he knew it. **er hätte ihr geholfen** he would have helped her

● *reflexive verb*

····➤ ([!] *sich aufregen*) make a fuss. **hab dich nicht so!** don't make such a fuss!

Habgier *f* greed. **h~ig** *a* greedy

Habicht *m* **-[e]s, -e** hawk

Hachse *f* **-, -n** (*Culin*) knuckle

Hackbraten *m* meat loaf

Hacke¹ *f* **-, -n** hoe; (*Spitz-*) pick

Hacke² *f* **-, -n, Hacken** *m* **-s,-** heel

hack|en *vt* hoe; (*schlagen, zerkleinern*) chop; <*Vogel:*> peck. **H~fleisch** *nt* mince

Hafen *m* **-s,¨** harbour; (*See-*) port. **H~arbeiter** *m* docker. **H~stadt** *f* port

Hafer *m* **-s** oats *pl.* **H~flocken** *fpl* [rolled] oats

Haft *f* **-** (*Jur*) custody; (*H~strafe*) imprisonment. **h~bar** *a* (*Jur*) liable. **H~befehl** *m* warrant

haften *vi* (*haben*) cling; (*kleben*) stick; (*bürgen*) vouch/(*Jur*) be liable (**für** for)

Häftling *m* **-s, -e** detainee

Haftpflicht *f* (*Jur*) liability. **H~versicherung** *f* (*Auto*) third-party insurance

Haftung *f* **-** (*Jur*) liability

Hagebutte *f* **-, -n** rose-hip

Hagel *m* **-s** hail. **h~n** *vi* (*haben*) hail

hager *a* gaunt

Hahn *m* **-[e]s,¨-e** cock; (*Techn*) tap

Hähnchen *nt* **-,s-** (*Culin*) chicken

Hai[fisch] *m* **-[e]s, -e** shark

Häkchen *nt* **-s,-** tick

häkel|n *vt/i* (*haben*) crochet. **H~nadel** *f* crochet-hook

Haken *m* **-s,-** hook; (*Häkchen*) tick; (! *Schwierigkeit*) snag. **h~** *vt* hook (**an** + *acc* to). **H~kreuz** *nt* swastika

halb *a* half; **auf h~em Weg** half-way ●*adv* half; **h~drei** half past two; **fünf [Minuten] vor/nach h~vier** twenty-five [minutes] past three/to four. **H~e(r,s)** *f/m/nt* half [a litre]

halber *prep* (+ *gen*) for the sake of; **Geschäfte h~** on business

Halbfinale *nt* semifinal

halbieren *vt* halve, divide in half; (*Geom*) bisect

Halb|insel *f* peninsula. **H~kreis** *m* semicircle. **H~kugel** *f* hemisphere. **h~laut** *a* low ●*adv* in an undertone. **h~mast** *adv* at half-mast. **H~mond** *m* half moon. **H~pension** *f* half-board. **h~rund** *a* semicircular. **H~schuh** *m* [flat] shoe. **h~tags** *adv* [for] half a day; **h~tags arbeiten** ≈ work part-time. **H~ton** *m* semitone. **h~wegs** *adv* half-way; (*ziemlich*) more or less. **h~wüchsig** *a* adolescent. **H~zeit** *f* (*Sport*) half-time; (*Spielzeit*) half

Halde *f* **-, -n** dump, tip

Hälfte *f* **-, -n** half; **zur H~** half

Halfter *f* **-, -n** & *nt* **-s,-** holster

Halle *f* **-, -n** hall; (*Hotel-*) lobby; (*Bahnhofs-*) station concourse

hallen *vi* (*haben*) resound; (*wider-*) echo

Hallen- *pref* indoor

hallo *int* hallo

Halluzination /-ˈt͜si̯oːn/ *f* **-, -en** hallucination

Halm *m* **-[e]s, -e** stalk; (*Gras-*) blade

Hals *m* **-es,¨-e** neck; (*Kehle*) throat; **aus vollem H~e** at the top of one's voice; <*lachen*> out loud. **H~band** *nt* (*pl* **-bänder**) collar. **H~schmerzen** *mpl* sore throat *sg*

halt *int* stop! (*Mil*) halt! ! wait a minute!

Halt *m* **-[e]s, -e** hold; (*Stütze*) support; (*innerer*) stability; (*Anhalten*) stop; **H~ machen** stop. **h~bar** *a* durable; (*Tex*) hard-wearing; (*fig*) tenable; **h~bar bis ...** (*Comm*) use by ...

halten† *vt* hold; make <*Rede*>; give <*Vortrag*>; (*einhalten, bewahren*) keep; **[sich** (*dat*)**] etw h~** keep <*Hund*>; take <*Zeitung*>; **h~ für** regard as; **viel h~ von** think highly of; **sich links h~** keep left; **sich h~ an** (+ *acc*) (*fig*) keep to ●*vi* (*haben*) hold; (*haltbar sein, bestehen bleiben*) keep; <*Freundschaft, Blumen:*> last; (*Halt machen*) stop; **auf sich** (*acc*) **h~** take pride in oneself; **zu jdm h~** be loyal to s.o.

Halte|stelle *f* stop. **H~verbot** *nt* waiting restriction; **'H~verbot'** 'no waiting'

Haltung *f* **-, -en** (*Körper-*) posture; (*Verhalten*) manner; (*Einstellung*) attitude; (*Fassung*) composure; (*Halten*) keeping

Hammel *m* **-s,-** ram; (*Culin*) mutton. **H~fleisch** *nt* mutton

Hammer *m* **-s,¨-** hammer

hämmern *vt/i* (*haben*) hammer

Hamster *m* **-s,-** hamster. **h~n** *vt/i* [!] hoard

Hand *f* **-,¨-e** hand; **jdm die H~ geben** shake hands with s.o.; **rechter/linker H~** on the right/left; **zweiter H~** second-hand; **unter der H~** unofficially; (*geheim*) secretly; **H~ und Fuß haben** (*fig*) be sound. **H~arbeit** *f* manual work; (*handwerklich*) handicraft; (*Nadelarbeit*) needlework; (*Gegenstand*) hand-made article. **H~ball** *m* [German] handball. **H~bewegung** *f* gesture. **H~bremse** *f* handbrake. **H~buch** *nt* handbook, manual

Händedruck *m* handshake

Handel *m* **-s** trade, commerce; (*Unternehmen*) business; (*Geschäft*) deal; **H~ treiben** trade. **h~n** *vi* (*haben*) act; (*Handel treiben*) trade (**mit** in); **von etw** *od* **über etw** (*acc*) **h~n** deal with sth; **sich h~n um** be about, concern. **H~smarine** *f* merchant navy. **H~sschiff** *nt* merchant vessel. **H~sschule** *f* commercial college. **H~sware** *f* merchandise

Hand|feger *m* **-s,-** brush. **H~fläche** *f* palm. **H~gelenk** *nt* wrist. **H~gemenge** *nt* **-s,-** scuffle. **H~gepäck** *nt* hand-luggage. **h~geschrieben** *a* hand-written. **h~greiflich** *a* tangible; **h~greiflich werden** become violent. **H~griff** *m* handle

handhaben *vt insep* (*reg*) handle

Handikap /ˈhɛndikɛp/ *nt* **-s, -s** handicap

Handkuss *m* kiss on the hand

Händler *m* **-s,-** dealer, trader

handlich *a* handy

Handlung *f* **-, -en** act; (*Handeln*) action; (*Roman-*) plot; (*Geschäft*) shop. **H~sweise** *f* conduct

Hand|schellen *fpl* handcuffs. **H~schlag** *m* handshake. **H~schrift** *f* handwriting; (*Text*) manuscript. **H~schuh** *m* glove. **H~stand** *m* handstand. **H~tasche** *f* handbag. **H~tuch** *nt* towel

Handwerk *nt* craft, trade. **H~er** *m* **-s,-** craftsman; (*Arbeiter*) workman

Handy /ˈhɛndi/ *nt* **-s, -s** mobile phone

Hanf *m* **-[e]s** hemp

Hang *m* **-[e]s,¨-e** slope; (*fig*) inclination

Hänge|brücke *f* suspension bridge. **H~matte** *f* hammock

hängen[1] *vt* (*reg*) hang

hängen[2]† *vi* (*haben*) hang; **h~ an** (+ *dat*) (*fig*) be attached to; **h~ lassen** leave

Hannover *nt* **-s** Hanover

hänseln *vt* tease

hantieren *vi* (*haben*) busy oneself

Happen *m* **-s,-** mouthful; **einen H~ essen** have a bite to eat

Harfe *f* **-, -n** harp

Harke *f* **-, -n** rake. **h~n** *vt/i* (*haben*) rake

harmlos *a* harmless; (*arglos*) innocent

Harmonie *f* **-, -n** harmony

Harmonika *f* **-, -s** accordion; (*Mund-*) mouth-organ

harmonisch *a* harmonious

Harn *m* **-[e]s** urine. **H~blase** *f* bladder

Harpune *f* **-, -n** harpoon

hart *a* hard; (*heftig*) violent; (*streng*) harsh

Härte *f* **-, -n** hardness; (*Strenge*) harshness; (*Not*) hardship. **h~n** *vt* harden

Hart|faserplatte *f* hardboard. **h~näckig** *a* stubborn; (*ausdauernd*) persistent. **H~näckigkeit** *f* **-** stubbornness; persistence

Harz *nt* **-es, -e** resin

Haschee *nt* **-s, -s** (*Culin*) hash
Haschisch *nt & m* **-[s]** hashish
Hase *m* **-n, -n** hare
Hasel *f* **-, -n** hazel. **H~maus** *f* dormouse. **H~nuss** *f* hazel-nut
Hass *m* **-es** hatred
hassen *vt* hate
hässlich *a* ugly; (*unfreundlich*) nasty. **H~keit** *f* **-** ugliness; nastiness
Hast *f* **-** haste. **h~ig** *a* hasty, hurried
hast, hat, hatte, hätte *s.* **haben**
Haube *f* **-, -n** cap; (*Trocken-*) drier; (*Kühler-*) bonnet
Hauch *m* **-[e]s** breath; (*Luft-*) breeze; (*Duft*) whiff; (*Spur*) tinge. **h~dünn** *a* very thin
Haue *f* **-, -n** pick; (! *Prügel*) beating. **h~n**† *vt* beat; (*hämmern*) knock; (*meißeln*) hew; **sich h~n** fight; **übers Ohr h~n** ! cheat ● *vi* (*haben*) bang (**auf** + *acc* on); **jdm ins Gesicht h~n** hit s.o. in the face
Haufen *m* **-s,-** heap, pile; (*Leute*) crowd
häufen *vt* heap *or* pile [up]; **sich h~** pile up; (*zunehmen*) increase
häufig *a* frequent
Haupt *nt* **-[e]s, Häupter** head. **H~bahnhof** *m* main station. **H~fach** *nt* main subject. **H~gericht** *nt* main course
Häuptling *m* **-s, -e** chief
Haupt|mahlzeit *f* main meal **H~mann** *m* (*pl* **-leute**) captain. **H~post** *f* main post office. **H~quartier** *nt* headquarters *pl.* **H~rolle** *f* lead; (*fig*) leading role. **H~sache** *f* main thing; **in der H~sache** in the main. **h~sächlich** *a* main. **H~satz** *m* main clause. **H~stadt** *f* capital. **H~verkehrsstraße** *f* main road. **H~verkehrszeit** *f* rush-hour. **H~wort** *nt* (*pl* **-wörter**) noun
Haus *nt* **-es, Häuser** house; (*Gebäude*) building; (*Schnecken-*) shell; **zu H~e** at home; **nach H~e** home. **H~arbeit** *f* housework; (*Sch*) homework. **H~arzt** *m* family doctor. **H~aufgaben** *fpl* homework *sg*. **H~besetzer** *m* **-s,-** squatter
hausen *vi* (*haben*) live; (*wüten*) wreak havoc
Haus|frau *f* housewife. **h~gemacht** *a* home-made. **H~halt** *m* **-[e]s, -e** household; (*Pol*) budget. **h~halten**† *vi sep* (*haben*) **h~halten mit** manage carefully; conserve <*Kraft*>. **H~hälterin** *f* **-, -nen** housekeeper. **H~haltsgeld** *nt* housekeeping [money]. **H~haltsplan** *m* budget. **H~herr** *m* head of the household; (*Gastgeber*) host
Hausierer *m* **-s,-** hawker
Haus|lehrer *m* [private] tutor **H~in** *f* governess
häuslich *a* domestic, <*Person*> domesticated
Haus|meister *m* caretaker. **H~ordnung** *f* house rules *pl.* **H~putz** *m* cleaning. **H~rat** *m* **-[e]s** household effects *pl.* **H~schlüssel** *m* front-door key. **H~schuh** *m* slipper. **H~suchung** *f* [police] search. **H~suchungsbefehl** *m* search-warrant. **H~tier** *nt* domestic animal; (*Hund, Katze*) pet. **H~tür** *f* front door. **H~wirt** *m* landlord. **H~wirtin** *f* landlady
Haut *f* **-,Häute** skin; (*Tier-*) hide. **H~arzt** *m* dermatologist
häuten *vt* skin; **sich h~** moult
haut|eng *a* skin-tight. **H~farbe** *f* colour; (*Teint*) complexion
Hebamme *f* **-, -n** midwife
Hebel *m* **-s,-** lever
heben† *vt* lift; (*hoch-, steigern*) raise; **sich h~** rise; <*Nebel:*> lift; (*sich verbessern*) improve
hebräisch *a* Hebrew
hecheln *vi* (*haben*) pant
Hecht *m* **-[e]s, -e** pike

H

Heck *nt* **-s, -s** (*Naut*) stern; (*Aviat*) tail; (*Auto*) rear
Hecke *f* **-, -n** hedge
Heck|fenster *nt* rear window. **H~tür** *f* hatchback
Heer *nt* **-[e]s, -e** army
Hefe *f* **-** yeast
Heft *nt* **-[e]s, -e** booklet; (*Sch*) exercise book; (*Zeitschrift*) issue. **h~en** *vt* (*nähen*) tack; (*stecken*) pin/(*klammern*) clip/(*mit Heftmaschine*) staple (**an** + *acc* to). **H~er** *m* **-s,-** file
heftig *a* fierce, violent; <*Regen*> heavy; <*Schmerz, Gefühl*> intense
Heft|klammer *f* staple; (*Büro-*) paper-clip. **H~maschine** *f* stapler. **H~zwecke** *f* **-, -n** drawing-pin
Heide[1] *m* **-n, -n** heathen
Heide[2] *f* **-, -n** heath; (*Bot*) heather. **H~kraut** *nt* heather
Heidelbeere *f* bilberry
Heidin *f* **-, -nen** heathen
heikel *a* difficult, tricky
heil *a* undamaged, intact; <*Person*> unhurt; **mit h~er Haut** [!] unscathed
Heil *nt* **-s** salvation
Heiland *m* **-s** (*Relig*) Saviour
Heil|anstalt *f* sanatorium; (*Nerven-*) mental hospital. **H~bad** *nt* spa. **h~bar** *a* curable
Heilbutt *m* **-[e]s, -e** halibut
heilen *vt* cure; heal <*Wunde*> ● *vi* (*sein*) heal
Heilgymnastik *f* physiotherapy
heilig *a* holy; (*geweiht*) sacred; **der H~e Abend** Christmas Eve; **die h~e Anna** Saint Anne; **h~ sprechen** canonize. **H~abend** *m* Christmas Eve. **H~e(r)** *m/f* saint. **H~enschein** *m* halo. **H~keit** *f* **-** sanctity, holiness. **H~tum** *nt* **-s,¨er** shrine
heil|kräftig *a* medicinal. **H~kräuter** *ntpl* medicinal herbs. **H~mittel** *nt* remedy. **H~praktiker** *m* **-s,-** practitioner of alternative medicine. **H~sarmee** *f* Salvation Army. **H~ung** *f* **-** cure
Heim *nt* **-[e]s, -e** home; (*Studenten-*) hostel. **h~** *adv* home
Heimat *f* **-, -en** home; (*Land*) native land. **H~stadt** *f* home town
heim|begleiten *vt sep* see home. **H~computer** *m* home computer. **h~fahren**† *v sep* ● *vi* (*sein*) go/drive home ● *vt* take/drive home. **H~fahrt** *f* way home. **h~gehen**† *vi sep* (*sein*) go home
heimisch *a* native, indigenous; (*Pol*) domestic
Heim|kehr *f* **-** return [home]. **h~kehren** *vi sep* (*sein*) return home. **h~kommen**† *vi sep* (*sein*) come home
heimlich *a* secret; **etw h~ tun** do sth secretly. **H~keit** *f* **-, -en** secrecy; **H~keiten** secrets
Heim|reise *f* journey home. **H~spiel** *nt* home game. **h~suchen** *vt sep* afflict. **h~tückisch** *a* treacherous; <*Krankheit*> insidious. **h~wärts** *adv* home. **H~weg** *m* way home. **H~weh** *nt* **-s** homesickness; **H~weh haben** be homesick. **H~werker** *m* **-s,-** [home] handyman. **h~zahlen** *vt sep* **jdm etw h~zahlen** (*fig*) pay s.o. back for sth
Heirat *f* **-, -en** marriage. **h~en** *vt/i* (*haben*) marry. **H~santrag** *m* proposal; **jdm einen H~santrag machen** propose to s.o.
heiser *a* hoarse. **H~keit** *f* **-** hoarseness
heiß *a* hot; (*hitzig*) heated; (*leidenschaftlich*) fervent
heißen† *vi* (*haben*) be called; (*bedeuten*) mean; **ich heiße** … my name is …; **wie h~Sie?** what is your name? **wie heißt … auf Englisch?** what's the English for …? ● *vt* call; **jdn etw tun h~** tell s.o. to do sth

heiter *a* cheerful; <*Wetter*> bright; (*amüsant*) amusing; **aus h~em Himmel** (*fig*) out of the blue

Heiz|anlage *f* heating; (*Auto*) heater. **H~decke** *f* electric blanket. **h~en** *vt* heat; light <*Ofen*> ● *vi* (*haben*) put the heating on; <*Ofen:*> give out heat. **H~gerät** *nt* heater. **H~kessel** *m* boiler. **H~körper** *m* radiator. **H~lüfter** *m* **-s,-** fan heater. **H~material** *nt* fuel. **H~ung** *f* **-, -en** heating; (*Heizkörper*) radiator

Hektar *nt & m* **-s,-** hectare

Held *m* **-en, -en** hero. **h~enhaft** *a* heroic. **H~entum** *nt* **-s** heroism. **H~in** *f* **-, -nen** heroine

helf|en† *vi* (*haben*) help (**jdm** s.o.); (*nützen*) be effective; **sich** (*dat*) **nicht zu h~en wissen** not know what to do; **es hilft nichts** it's no use. **H~er(in)** *m* **-s,-** (*f* **-, -nen**) helper, assistant

hell *a* light; (*Licht ausstrahlend, klug*) bright; <*Stimme*> clear; ([!] *völlig*) utter; **h~es Bier** ≈ lager ● *adv* brightly

Hell|igkeit *f* **-** brightness. **H~seher(in)** *m* **-s,-** (*f* **-, -nen**) clairvoyant

Helm *m* **-[e]s, -e** helmet

Hemd *nt* **-[e]s, -en** vest; (*Ober-*) shirt

Hemisphäre *f* **-, -n** hemisphere

hemm|en *vt* check; (*verzögern*) impede; (*fig*) inhibit. **H~ung** *f* **-, -en** (*fig*) inhibition; (*Skrupel*) scruple. **H~ungen haben** be inhibited. **h~ungslos** *a* unrestrained

Hendl *nt* **-s, -[n]** (*Aust*) chicken

Hengst *m* **-[e]s, -e** stallion

Henkel *m* **-s,-** handle

Henne *f* **-, -n** hen

her *adv* here; (*zeitlich*) ago; **her mit ...!** give me ...! **von Norden/weit her** from the north/far away; **vom Thema her** as far as the subject is concerned; **her sein** come (**von** from); **es ist schon lange her** it was a long time ago

herab *adv* down [here]; **von oben h~** from above; (*fig*) condescending

herablassen† *vt sep* let down; **sich h~** condescend (**zu** to)

herab|sehen† *vi sep* (*haben*) look down (**auf** + *acc* on). **h~setzen** *vt sep* reduce, cut; (*fig*) belittle

Heraldik *f* **-** heraldry

heran *adv* near; **[bis] h~ an** (+ *acc*) up to. **h~kommen**† *vi sep* (*sein*) approach; **h~kommen an** (+ *acc*) come up to; (*erreichen*) get at; (*fig*) measure up to. **h~machen (sich)** *vr sep* **sich h~machen an** (+ *acc*) approach; get down to <*Arbeit*>. **h~wachsen**† *vi sep* (*sein*) grow up. **h~ziehen**† *v sep* ● *vt* pull up (**an** + *acc* to); (*züchten*) raise; (*h~bilden*) train; (*hinzuziehen*) call in ● *vi* (*sein*) approach

herauf *adv* up [here]; **die Treppe h~** up the stairs. **h~setzen** *vt sep* raise, increase

heraus *adv* out (**aus** of); **h~ damit** *od* **mit der Sprache!** out with it! **h~bekommen**† *vt sep* get out; (*ausfindig machen*) find out; (*lösen*) solve; **Geld h~bekommen** get change. **h~finden**† *v sep* ● *vt* find out ● *vi* (*haben*) find one's way out. **h~fordern** *vt sep* provoke; challenge <*Person*>. **H~forderung** *f* provocation; challenge. **H~gabe** *f* handing over; (*Admin*) issue; (*Veröffentlichung*) publication. **h~geben**† *vt sep* hand over; (*Admin*) issue; (*veröffentlichen*) publish; edit <*Zeitschrift*>; **jdm Geld h~geben** give s.o. change ● *vi* (*haben*) give change (**auf** + *acc* for). **H~geber** *m* **-s,-** publisher; editor. **h~halten**† **(sich)** *vr sep* (*fig*) keep out (**aus**

of). **h~kommen**† *vi sep* (*sein*) come out; (*aus Schwierigkeit, Takt*) get out; **auf eins** *od* **dasselbe h~kommen** [!] come to the same thing. **h~lassen**† *vt sep* let out. **h~nehmen**† *vt sep* take out; **sich zu viel h~nehmen** (*fig*) take liberties. **h~reden (sich)** *vr sep* make excuses. **h~rücken** *v sep* ● *vt* move out; (*hergeben*) hand over ● *vi* (*sein*) **h~rücken mit** hand over; (*fig: sagen*) come out with. **h~schlagen**† *vt sep* knock out; (*fig*) gain. **h~stellen** *vt sep* put out; **sich h~stellen** turn out (**als** to be; **dass** that). **h~ziehen**† *vt sep* pull out

herb *a* sharp; <*Wein*> dry; (*fig*) harsh

herbei *adv* here. **h~führen** *vt sep* (*fig*) bring about. **h~schaffen** *vt sep* get. **h~sehnen** *vt sep* long for

Herberg|e *f* **-, -n** [youth] hostel; (*Unterkunft*) lodging. **H~svater** *m* warden

herbestellen *vt sep* summon

herbitten† *vt sep* ask to come

herbringen† *vt sep* bring [here]

Herbst *m* **-[e]s, -e** autumn. **h~lich** *a* autumnal

Herd *m* **-[e]s, -e** stove, cooker

Herde *f* **-, -n** herd; (*Schaf-*) flock

herein *adv* in [here]; **h~!** come in! **h~bitten**† *vt sep* ask in. **h~fallen**† *vi sep* (*sein*) [!] be taken in (**auf** + *acc* by). **h~kommen**† *vi sep* (*sein*) come in. **h~lassen**† *vt sep* let in. **h~legen** *vt sep* [!] take for a ride

Herfahrt *f* journey/drive here

herfallen† *vi sep* (*sein*) ~ **über** (+ *acc*) attack; fall upon <*Essen*>

hergeben† *vt sep* hand over; (*fig*) give up

hergehen† *vi sep* (*sein*) **h~ vor** (+ *dat*) walk along in front of; **es ging lustig her** [!] there was a lot of merriment

herholen *vt sep* fetch; **weit hergeholt** (*fig*) far-fetched

Hering *m* **-s, -e** herring; (*Zeltpflock*) tent-peg

her|kommen† *vi sep* (*sein*) come here; **wo kommt das her?** where does it come from? **h~kömmlich** *a* traditional. **H~kunft** *f* **-** origin

herleiten *vt sep* derive

hermachen *vt sep* **viel/wenig h~** be impressive/unimpressive; (*wichtig nehmen*) make a lot of/little fuss (**von** of); **sich h~ über** (+ *acc*) fall upon; tackle <*Arbeit*>

Hermelin[1] *nt* **-s, -e** (*Zool*) stoat

Hermelin[2] *m* **-s, -e** (*Pelz*) ermine

Hernie /ˈhɛrni̯ə/ *f* **-, -n** hernia

Heroin *nt* **-s** heroin

heroisch *a* heroic

Herr *m* **-n, -en** gentleman; (*Gebieter*) master (**über** + *acc* of); **[Gott,] der H~** the Lord [God]; **H~ Meier** Mr Meier; **Sehr geehrte H~en** Dear Sirs. **H~enhaus** *nt* manor [house]. **h~enlos** *a* ownerless; <*Tier*> stray

Herrgott *m* **der H~** the Lord

herrichten *vt sep* prepare; **wieder h~** renovate

Herrin *f* **-, -nen** mistress

herrlich *a* marvellous; (*großartig*) magnificent

Herrschaft *f* **-, -en** rule; (*Macht*) power; (*Kontrolle*) control; **meine H~en!** ladies and gentlemen!

herrsch|en *vi* (*haben*) rule; (*verbreitet sein*) prevail; **es h~te Stille** there was silence. **H~er(in)** *m* **-s,-** (*f* **-, -nen**) ruler

herrühren *vi sep* (*haben*) stem (**von** from)

herstammen *vi sep* (*haben*) come (**aus/von** from)

herstell|en *vt sep* establish; (*Comm*) manufacture, make. **H~er** *m* **-s,-** manufacturer, maker. **H~ung** *f* **-** establishment; manufacture

herüber *adv* over [here]

herum *adv* **im Kreis h~** [round] in a circle; **falsch h~** the wrong way round; **um ... h~** round ...; (*ungefähr*) [round] about ...; **h~ sein** be over. **h~drehen** *vt sep* turn round/(*wenden*) over; turn <*Schlüssel*>. **h~gehen**† *vi sep* (*sein*) walk around; <*Zeit:*> pass; **h~gehen um** go round. **h~kommen**† *vi sep* (*sein*) get about; **h~kommen um** get round; come round <*Ecke*>; **um etw [nicht] h~kommen** (*fig*) [not] get out of sth. **h~sitzen**† *vi sep* (*haben*) sit around; **h~sitzen um** sit round. **h~sprechen**† **(sich)** *vr sep* <*Gerücht:*> get about. **h~treiben**† **(sich)** *vr sep* hang around. **h~ziehen**† *vi sep* (*sein*) move around; (*ziellos*) wander about

herunter *adv* down [here]; **die Treppe h~** down the stairs. **h~fallen**† *vi* fall off. **h~gekommen** *a* (*fig*) run-down; <*Gebäude*> dilapidated; <*Person*> down-at-heel. **h~kommen**† *vi sep* (*sein*) come down; (*fig*) go to rack and ruin; <*Firma, Person:*> go downhill; (*gesundheitlich*) get run down. **h~lassen**† *vt sep* let down, lower. **h~machen** *vt sep* [!] reprimand; (*herabsetzen*) run down. **h~spielen** *vt sep* (*fig*) play down

hervor *adv* out (**aus** of). **h~bringen**† *vt sep* produce; utter <*Wort*>. **h~gehen**† *vi sep* (*sein*) come/(*sich ergeben*) emerge/(*folgen*) follow (**aus** from). **h~heben**† *vt sep* (*fig*) stress, emphasize. **h~ragen** *vi sep* (*haben*) jut out; (*fig*) stand out. **h~ragend** *a* (*fig*) outstanding. **h~rufen**† *vt sep* (*fig*) cause. **h~stehen**† *vi sep* (*haben*) protrude. **h~treten**† *vi sep* (*sein*) protrude, bulge; (*fig*) stand out. **h~tun**† **(sich)** *vr sep* (*fig*) distinguish oneself; (*angeben*) show off

Herweg *m* way here

Herz *nt* **-ens, -en** heart; (*Kartenspiel*) hearts *pl*; **sich** (*dat*) **ein H~ fassen** pluck up courage. **H~anfall** *m* heart attack

herzhaft *a* hearty; (*würzig*) savoury

herziehen† *v sep* ● *vt* **hinter sich** (*dat*) **h~** pull along [behind one] ● *vi* (*sein*) **hinter jdm h~** follow along behind s.o.; **über jdn h~** [!] run s.o. down

herz|ig *a* sweet, adorable. **H~infarkt** *m* heart attack. **H~klopfen** *nt* **-s** palpitations *pl*

herzlich *a* cordial; (*warm*) warm; (*aufrichtig*) sincere; **h~en Dank!** many thanks! **h~e Grüße** kind regards

herzlos *a* heartless

Herzog *m* **-s,¨e** duke. **H~in** *f* **-, -nen** duchess. **H~tum** *nt* **-s,¨er** duchy

Herzschlag *m* heartbeat; (*Med*) heart failure

Hessen *nt* **-s** Hesse

heterosexuell *a* heterosexual

Hetze *f* **-** rush; (*Kampagne*) virulent campaign (**gegen** against). **h~n** *vt* chase; **sich h~n** hurry

Heu *nt* **-s** hay

Heuchelei *f* **-** hypocrisy

heuch|eln *vt* feign ● *vi* (*haben*) pretend. **H~ler(in)** *m* **-s,-** (*f* **-, -nen**) hypocrite. **h~lerisch** *a* hypocritical

heuer *adv* (*Aust*) this year

heulen *vi* (*haben*) howl; ([!] *weinen*) cry

Heu|schnupfen *m* hay fever. **H~schober** *m* **-s,-** haystack. **H~schrecke** *f* **-, -n** grasshopper

heut|e *adv* today; (*heutzutage*) nowadays; **h~e früh** *od* **Morgen** this morning; **von h~e auf morgen** from one day to the next. **h~ig** *a* today's ...; (*gegenwärtig*) present; **der h~ige Tag** today. **h~zutage** *adv* nowadays

Hexe *f* **-, -n** witch. **h~n** *vi* (*haben*) work magic. **H~nschuss** *m* lumbago

Hieb *m* **-[e]s, -e** blow; (*Peitschen-*) lash; **H~e** hiding *sg*

hier *adv* here; **h~ sein/bleiben/lassen/behalten** be/stay/leave/keep here; **h~ und da** here and there; (*zeitlich*) now and again

hier|auf *adv* on this/these; (*antworten*) to this; (*zeitlich*) after this. **h~aus** *adv* out of *or* from this/these. **h~durch** *adv* through this/these; (*Ursache*) as a result of this. **h~her** *adv* here. **h~hin** *adv* here. **h~in** *adv* in this/these. **h~mit** *adv* with this/these; (*Comm*) herewith; (*Admin*) hereby. **h~nach** *adv* after this/these; (*demgemäß*) according to this/these. **h~über** *adv* over/(*höher*) above this/these; <*sprechen, streiten*> about this/these. **h~von** *adv* from this/these; (*h~über*) about this/these; (*Menge*) of this/these. **h~zu** *adv* to this/these; (*h~für*) for this/these. **h~zulande** *adv* here

hiesig *a* local. **H~e(r)** *m/f* local

Hilf|e *f* **-, -n** help, aid; **um H~e rufen** call for help. **h~los** *a* helpless. **H~losigkeit** *f* **-** helplessness. **h~reich** *a* helpful

Hilfs|arbeiter *m* unskilled labourer. **h~bedürftig** *a* needy; **h~bedürftig sein** be in need of help. **h~bereit** *a* helpful. **H~kraft** *f* helper. **H~mittel** *nt* aid. **H~verb** *nt* auxiliary verb

Himbeere *f* raspberry

Himmel *m* **-s,-** sky; (*Relig & fig*) heaven; (*Bett-*) canopy; **unter freiem H~** in the open air. **H~bett** *nt* four-poster [bed]. **H~fahrt** *f* Ascension

himmlisch *a* heavenly

hin *adv* there; **hin und her** to and fro; **hin und zurück** there and back; (*Rail*) return; **hin und wieder** now and again; **an** (+ *dat*) ... **hin** along; **auf** (+ *acc*) ... **hin** in reply to <*Brief, Anzeige*>; on <*jds Rat*>; **zu** *od* **nach ... hin** towards; **hin sein** [!] be gone; **es ist noch lange hin** it's a long time yet

hinauf *adv* up [there]. **h~gehen**† *vi sep* (*sein*) go up. **h~setzen** *vt sep* raise

hinaus *adv* out [there]; (*nach draußen*) outside; **zur Tür h~** out of the door; **auf Jahre h~** for years to come; **über etw** (*acc*) **h~** beyond sth; (*Menge*) [over and] above sth; **über etw** (*acc*) **h~ sein** (*fig*) be past sth. **h~gehen**† *vi sep* (*sein*) go out; <*Zimmer:*> face (**nach Norden** north); **h~gehen über** (+ *acc*) go beyond, exceed. **h~laufen**† *vi sep* (*sein*) run out; **h~laufen auf** (+ *acc*) (*fig*) amount to. **h~lehnen (sich)** *vr sep* lean out. **h~schieben**† *vt sep* push out; (*fig*) put off. **h~werfen**† *vt sep* throw out; ([!] *entlassen*) fire. **h~wollen**† *vi sep* (*haben*) want to go out; **h~wollen auf** (+ *acc*) (*fig*) aim at. **h~ziehen**† *v sep* ● *vt* pull out; (*in die Länge ziehen*) drag out; (*verzögern*) delay; **sich h~ziehen** drag on; be delayed ● *vi* (*sein*) move out. **h~zögern** *vt* delay; **sich h~zögern** be delayed

Hinblick *m* **im H~ auf** (+ *acc*) in view of; (*hinsichtlich*) regarding

hinder|lich *a* awkward; **jdm h~lich sein** hamper s.o. **h~n** *vt* hamper; (*verhindern*) prevent. **H~nis** *nt* **-ses, -se** obstacle. **H~nisrennen** *nt* steeplechase

Hindu *m* **-s, -s** Hindu. **H~ismus** *m* **-** Hinduism

hindurch *adv* through it/them

hinein *adv* in [there]; (*nach drinnen*) inside; **h~ in** (+ *acc*) into. **h~fallen**† *vi sep* (*sein*) fall in. **h~gehen**† *vi sep* (*sein*) go in; **h~gehen in** (+ *acc*) go into. **h~reden** *vi sep* (*haben*) **jdm h~reden** interrupt s.o.; (*sich einmischen*) interfere in s.o.'s affairs. **h~versetzen (sich)** *vr sep* **sich in jds Lage h~versetzen** put oneself in s.o.'s position. **h~ziehen**† *vt sep* pull in; **h~ziehen in** (+ *acc*) pull into; **in etw** (*acc*) **h~gezogen werden** (*fig*) become involved in sth

hin|fahren† *v sep* ● *vi* (*sein*) go/drive there ● *vt* take/drive there. **H~fahrt** *f* journey/drive there; (*Rail*) outward journey. **h~fallen**† *vi sep* (*sein*) fall. **h~fliegen**† *v sep* ● *vi* (*sein*) fly there; [!] fall ● *vt* fly there. **H~flug** *m* flight there; (*Admin*) outward flight

Hingeb|ung *f* - devotion. **h~ungsvoll** *a* devoted

hingehen† *vi sep* (*sein*) go/(*zu Fuß*) walk there; (*vergehen*) pass; **h~ zu** go up to; **wo gehst du hin**? where are you going?

hingerissen *a* rapt; **h~ sein** be carried away (**von** by)

hinhalten† *vt sep* hold out; (*warten lassen*) keep waiting

hinken *vi* (*haben/sein*) limp

hin|knien (sich) *vr sep* kneel down. **h~kommen**† *vi sep* (*sein*) get there; (*h~gehören*) belong, go; ([!] *auskommen*) manage (**mit** with); ([!] *stimmen*) be right. **h~laufen**† *vi sep* (*sein*) run/(*gehen*) walk there. **h~legen** *vt sep* lay *or* put down; **sich h~legen** lie down. **h~nehmen**† *vt sep* (*fig*) accept

hinreichen *v sep* ● *vt* hand (*dat* to) ● *vi* (*haben*) extend (**bis** to); (*ausreichen*) be adequate. **h~d** *a* adequate

Hinreise *f* journey there; (*Rail*) outward journey

hinreißen† *vt sep* (*fig*) carry away; **sich h~ lassen** get carried away. **h~d** *a* ravishing

hinricht|en *vt sep* execute. **H~ung** *f* execution

hinschreiben† *vt sep* write there; (*aufschreiben*) write down

hinsehen† *vi sep* (*haben*) look

hinsetzen *vt sep* put down; **sich h~** sit down

Hinsicht *f* - **in dieser H~** in this respect; **in finanzieller H~** financially. **h~lich** *prep* (+ *gen*) regarding

hinstellen *vt sep* put *or* set down; park <*Auto*>

hinstrecken *vt sep* hold out; **sich h~** extend

hinten *adv* at the back; **dort h~** back there; **nach/von h~** to the back/from behind. **h~herum** *adv* round the back; [!] by devious means

hinter *prep* (+ *dat/acc*) behind; (*nach*) after; **h~ jdm/etw herlaufen** run after s.o./sth; **h~ etw** (*dat*) **stecken** (*fig*) be behind sth; **h~ etw** (*acc*) **kommen** (*fig*) get to the bottom of sth; **etw h~ sich** (*acc*) **bringen** get sth over [and done] with

Hinterbliebene *pl* (*Admin*) surviving dependants; **die H~n** the bereaved family *sg*

hintere|(r,s) *a* back, rear; **h~s Ende** far end

hintereinander *adv* one behind/(*zeitlich*) after the other; **dreimal h~** three times in succession

Hintergedanke *m* ulterior motive

hintergehen† *vt* deceive

Hinter|grund *m* background. **H~halt** *m* -[e]s, -e ambush. **h~hältig** *a* underhand

hinterher *adv* behind, after; (*zeitlich*) afterwards

Hinter|hof *m* back yard. **H~kopf** *m* back of the head

H

hinterlassen† *vt* leave [behind]; (*Jur*) leave, bequeath (*dat* to). **H~schaft** *f* **-, -en** (*Jur*) estate

hinterlegen *vt* deposit

Hinter|leib *m* (*Zool*) abdomen. **H~list** *f* deceit. **h~listig** *a* deceitful. **H~n** *m* **-s,-** [!] bottom, backside. **H~rad** *nt* rear *or* back wheel. **h~rücks** *adv* from behind. **h~ste(r,s)** *a* last; **h~ste Reihe** back row. **H~teil** *nt* [!] behind. **H~treppe** *f* back stairs *pl*

hinterziehen† *vt* (*Admin*) evade

hinüber *adv* over *or* across [*there*]; **h~ sein** ([!] *unbrauchbar, tot*) have had it. **h~gehen**† *vi sep* (*sein*) go over *or* across; **h~gehen über** (+ *acc*) cross

hinunter *adv* down [there]. **h~gehen**† *vi sep* (*sein*) go down. **h~schlucken** *vt sep* swallow

Hinweg *m* way there

hinweg *adv* away, off; **h~ über** (+ *acc*) over; **über eine Zeit h~** over a period. **h~kommen**† *vt sep* (*sein*) **h~kommen über** (+ *acc*) (*fig*) get over. **h~sehen**† *vi sep* (*haben*) **h~sehen über** (+ *acc*) see over; (*fig*) overlook. **h~setzen** (sich) *vr sep* **sich h~setzen über** (+ *acc*) ignore

Hinweis *m* **-es, -e** reference; (*Andeutung*) hint; (*Anzeichen*) indication; **unter H~ auf** (+ *acc*) with reference to. **h~en**† *v sep* ● *vi* (*haben*) point (**auf** + *acc* to) ● *vt* **jdn auf etw** (*acc*) **h~en** point sth out to s.o.

hinwieder *adv* on the other hand

hin|zeigen *vi sep* (*haben*) point (**auf** + *acc* to). **h~ziehen**† *vt sep* pull; (*fig: in die Länge ziehen*) drag out; (*verzögern*) delay; **sich h~ziehen** drag on

hinzu *adv* in addition. **h~fügen** *vt sep* add. **h~kommen**† *vt sep* (*sein*) be added; (*ankommen*) arrive [on the scene]; join (**zu jdm** s.o.). **h~ziehen**† *vt sep* call in

Hiobsbotschaft *f* bad news *sg*

Hirn *nt* **-s** brain; (*Culin*) brains *pl*. **H~hautentzündung** *f* meningitis

Hirsch *m* **-[e]s, -e** deer; (*männlich*) stag; (*Culin*) venison

Hirse *f* **-** millet

Hirt *m* **-en, -en**, **Hirte** *m* **-n, -n** shepherd

hissen *vt* hoist

Histor|iker *m* **-s,-** historian. **h~isch** *a* historical; (*bedeutend*) historic

Hitz|e *f* **-** heat. **h~ig** *a* (*fig*) heated; <*Person*> hot-headed; (*jähzornig*) hot-tempered. **H~schlag** *m* heat-stroke

H-Milch /'ha:-/ *f* long-life milk

Hobby *nt* **-s, -s** hobby

Hobel *m* **-s,-** (*Techn*) plane; (*Culin*) slicer. **h~n** *vt/i* (*haben*) plane. **H~späne** *mpl* shavings

hoch *a* (*attrib* **hohe(r,s)**) high; <*Baum, Mast*> tall; <*Offizier*> high-ranking; <*Alter*> great; <*Summe*> large; <*Strafe*> heavy; **hohe Schuhe** ankle boots ● *adv* high; (*sehr*) highly; **h~ gewachsen** tall; **h~ begabt** highly gifted; **h~ gestellte Persönlichkeit** important person; **die Treppe h~** up the stairs; **sechs Mann h~** six of us/them. **H~** *nt* **-s, -s** cheer; (*Meteorol*) high

Hoch|achtung *f* high esteem. **H~achtungsvoll** *adv* Yours faithfully. **H~betrieb** *m* great activity; **in den Geschäften herrscht H~betrieb** the shops are terribly busy. **H~deutsch** *nt* High German. **H~druck** *m* high pressure. **H~ebene** *f* plateau. **h~fahren**† *vi sep* (*sein*) go up; (*auffahren*) start up; (*aufbrausen*) flare up. **h~gehen**† *vi sep* (*sein*) go up; (*explodieren*) blow up; (*aufbrausen*) flare up. **h~gestellt** *attrib a* <*Zahl*> superior; (*fig*) ***h~ gestellt**, *s.* **hoch**. **H~glanz** *m* high gloss. **h~gradig** *a* extreme.

h~hackig *a* high-heeled. **h~halten**† *vt sep* hold up; (*fig*) uphold. **H~haus** *nt* high-rise building. **h~heben**† *vt sep* lift up; raise <*Hand*>. **h~kant** *adv* on end. **h~kommen**† *vi sep* (*sein*) come up; (*aufstehen*) get up; (*fig*) get on [in the world]. **H~konjunktur** *f* boom. **h~krempeln** *vt sep* roll up. **h~leben** *vi sep* (*haben*) **h~leben lassen** give three cheers for; **H~mut** *m* pride, arrogance. **h~näsig** *a* 🗉 snooty. **H~ofen** *m* blast-furnace. **h~ragen** *vi sep* rise [up]; <*Turm:*> soar. **H~ruf** *m* cheer. **H~saison** *f* high season. **h~schlagen**† *vt sep* turn up <*Kragen*>. **H~schule** *f* university; (*Musik-, Kunst-*) academy. **H~sommer** *m* midsummer. **H~spannung** *f* high/(*fig*) great tension. **h~spielen** *vt sep* (*fig*) magnify. **H~sprung** *m* high jump

höchst *adv* extremely, most

Hochstapler *m* **-s,-** confidence trickster

höchst|e(r,s) *a* highest; <*Baum, Turm*> tallest; (*oberste, größte*) top; **es ist h~e Zeit** it is high time. **h~ens** *adv* at most; (*es sei denn*) except perhaps. **H~geschwindigkeit** *f* top or maximum speed. **H~maß** *nt* maximum. **h~persönlich** *adv* in person. **H~preis** *m* top price. **H~temperatur** *f* maximum temperature

Hoch|verrat *m* high treason. **H~wasser** *nt* high tide; (*Überschwemmung*) floods *pl*. **H~würden** *m* **-s** Reverend; (*Anrede*) Father

Hochzeit *f* **-, -en** wedding. **H~skleid** *nt* wedding dress. **H~sreise** *f* honeymoon [trip]. **H~stag** *m* wedding day/(*Jahrestag*) anniversary

Hocke *f* **- in der H~sitzen** squat. **h~n** *vi* (*haben*) squat ● *vr* **sich h~n** squat down

Hocker *m* **-s,-** stool

Höcker *m* **-s,-** bump; (*Kamel-*) hump

Hockey /hɔki/ *nt* **-s** hockey

Hode *f* **-, -n, Hoden** *m* **-s,-** testicle

Hof *m* **-[e]s,¨e** [court]yard; (*Bauern-*) farm; (*Königs-*) court; (*Schul-*) playground; (*Astr*) halo

hoffen *vt/i* (*haben*) hope (**auf** + *acc* for). **h~tlich** *adv* I hope, let us hope

Hoffnung *f* **-, -en** hope. **h~slos** *a* hopeless. **h~svoll** *a* hopeful

höflich *a* polite. **H~keit** *f* **-, -en** politeness, courtesy

hohe(r,s) *a s.* **hoch**

Höhe *f* **-, -n** height; (*Aviat, Geog*) altitude; (*Niveau*) level; (*einer Summe*) size; (*An-*) hill

Hoheit *f* **-, -en** (*Staats-*) sovereignty; (*Titel*) Highness. **H~sgebiet** *nt* [sovereign] territory. **H~szeichen** *nt* national emblem

Höhe|nlinie *f* contour line. **H~nsonne** *f* sun-lamp. **H~punkt** *m* (*fig*) climax, peak. **h~r** *a & adv* higher; **h~re Schule** secondary school

hohl *a* hollow; (*leer*) empty

Höhle *f* **-, -n** cave; (*Tier-*) den; (*Hohlraum*) cavity; (*Augen-*) socket

Hohl|maß *nt* measure of capacity. **H~raum** *m* cavity

Hohn *m* **-s** scorn, derision

höhnen *vt* deride

holen *vt* fetch, get; (*kaufen*) buy; (*nehmen*) take (**aus** from)

Holland *nt* **-s** Holland

Holländ|er *m* **-s,-** Dutchman; **die H~er** the Dutch *pl*. **H~erin** *f* **-, -nen** Dutchwoman. **h~isch** *a* Dutch

Höll|e *f* **-** hell. **h~isch** *a* infernal; (*schrecklich*) terrible

Holunder *m* **-s** (*Bot*) elder
Holz *nt* **-es,¨-er** wood; (*Nutz-*) timber. **H~blasinstrument** *nt* woodwind instrument
hölzern *a* wooden
Holz|hammer *m* mallet. **h~ig** *a* woody. **H~kohle** *f* charcoal. **H~schnitt** *m* woodcut. **H~wolle** *f* wood shavings *pl*
Homöopathie *f* **-** homoeopathy
homosexuell *a* homosexual. **H~e(r)** *m/f* homosexual
Honig *m* **-s** honey. **H~wabe** *f* honeycomb
Hono|rar *nt* **-s, -e** fee. **h~rieren** *vt* remunerate; (*fig*) reward
Hopfen *m* **-s** hops *pl*; (*Bot*) hop
hopsen *vi* (*sein*) jump
horchen *vi* (*haben*) listen (**auf** + *acc* to); (*heimlich*) eavesdrop
hören *vt* hear; (*an-*) listen to ● *vi* (*haben*) hear; (*horchen*) listen; (*gehorchen*) obey; **h~ auf** (+ *acc*) listen to
Hör|er *m* **-s,-** listener; (*Teleph*) receiver. **H~funk** *m* radio. **H~gerät** *nt* hearing-aid
Horizon|t *m* **-[e]s** horizon. **h~tal** *a* horizontal
Hormon *nt* **-s, -e** hormone
Horn *nt* **-s,¨-er** horn. **H~haut** *f* hard skin; (*Augen-*) cornea
Hornisse *f* **-, -n** hornet
Horoskop *nt* **-[e]s, -e** horoscope
Horrorfilm *m* horror film
Hör|saal *m* (*Univ*) lecture hall. **H~spiel** *nt* radio play
Hort *m* **-[e]s, -e** (*Schatz*) hoard; (*fig*) refuge. **h~en** *vt* hoard
Hortensie /-iə/ *f* **-, -n** hydrangea
Hose *f* **-, -n, Hosen** *pl* trousers *pl*. **H~nrock** *m* culottes *pl*. **H~nschlitz** *m* fly, flies *pl*. **H~nträger** *mpl* braces
Hostess *f* **-, -tessen** hostess; (*Aviat*) air hostess
Hostie /ˈhɔstiə/ *f* **-, -n** (*Relig*) host
Hotel *nt* **-s, -s** hotel
hübsch *a* pretty; (*nett*) nice
Hubschrauber *m* **-s,-** helicopter
Huf *m* **-[e]s, -e** hoof. **H~eisen** *nt* horseshoe
Hüft|e *f* **-, -n** hip. **H~gürtel** *m* **-s,-** girdle
Hügel *m* **-s,-** hill. **h~ig** *a* hilly
Huhn *nt* **-s,¨-er** chicken; (*Henne*) hen
Hühn|chen *nt* **-s,-** chicken. **H~erauge** *nt* corn **H~erstall** *m* henhouse
Hülle *f* **-, -n** cover; (*Verpackung*) wrapping; (*Platten-*) sleeve. **h~n** *vt* wrap
Hülse *f* **-, -n** (*Bot*) pod; (*Etui*) case. **H~nfrüchte** *fpl* pulses
human *a* humane. **H~ität** *f* **-** humanity
Hummel *f* **-, -n** bumble-bee
Hummer *m* **-s,-** lobster
Hum|or *m* **-s** humour; **H~or haben** have a sense of humour. **h~orvoll** *a* humorous
humpeln *vi* (*sein/haben*) hobble
Humpen *m* **-s,-** tankard
Hund *m* **-[e]s, -e** dog; (*Jagd-*) hound. **H~ehütte** *f* kennel
hundert *inv a* one/a hundred. **H~** *nt* **-s, -e** hundred; **H~e** *od* **h~e von** hundreds of. **H~jahrfeier** *f* centenary. **h~prozentig** *a & adv* one hundred per cent. **h~ste(r,s)** *a* hundredth. **H~stel** *nt* **-s,-** hundredth
Hündin *f* **-, -nen** bitch
Hüne *m* **-n, -n** giant
Hunger *m* **-s** hunger; **H~ haben** be hungry. **h~n** *vi* (*haben*) starve. **H~snot** *f* famine
hungrig *a* hungry
Hupe *f* **-, -n** (*Auto*) horn. **h~n** *vi* (*haben*) sound one's horn
hüpfen *vi* (*sein*) skip; <*Frosch:*> hop; <*Grashüpfer:*> jump
Hürde *f* **-, -n** (*Sport & fig*) hurdle; (*Schaf-*) pen, fold
Hure *f* **-, -n** whore
hurra *int* hurray

husten *vi* (*haben*) cough. **H~** *m* **-s** cough. **H~saft** *m* cough mixture

Hut[1] *m* **-[e]s,¨-e** hat; (*Pilz-*) cap

Hut[2] *f* **-** **auf der H~sein** be on one's guard (**vor** + *dat* against)

hüten *vt* watch over; tend <*Tiere*>; (*aufpassen*) look after; **das Bett h~ müssen** be confined to bed; **sich h~** be on one's guard (**vor** + *dat* against); **sich h~, etw zu tun** take care not to do sth

Hütte *f* **-, -n** hut; (*Hunde-*) kennel; (*Techn*) iron and steel works. **H~nkäse** *m* cottage cheese. **H~nkunde** *f* metallurgy

Hyäne *f* **-, -n** hyena

hydraulisch *a* hydraulic

Hygien|e /hy'gie:nə/ *f* **-** hygiene. **h~isch** *a* hygienic

Hypno|se *f* **-** hypnosis. **h~tisch** *a* hypnotic. **H~tiseur** /-'zø:ɐ/ *m* **-s, -e** hypnotist. **h~tisieren** *vt* hypnotize

Hypochonder /hypo'xɔndɐ/ *m* **-s,-** hypochondriac

Hypothek *f* **-, -en** mortgage

Hypothese *f* **-, -n** hypothesis

Hys|terie *f* **-** hysteria. **h~terisch** *a* hysterical

Ii

ich *pron* I; **ich bins** it's me. **Ich** *nt* **-[s], -[s]** self; (*Psych*) ego

IC-Zug /i'tse:-/ *m* inter-city train

ideal *a* ideal. **I~** *nt* **-s, -e** ideal. **I~ismus** *m* **-** idealism. **I~ist(in)** *m* **-en, -en** (*f* **-, -nen**) idealist. **i~istisch** *a* idealistic

Idee *f* **-, -n** idea; **fixe I~** obsession

identifizieren *vt* identify

identisch *a* identical

Ideo|logie *f* **-, -n** ideology. **i~logisch** *a* ideological

idiomatisch *a* idiomatic

Idiot *m* **-en, -en** idiot. **i~isch** *a* idiotic

idyllisch /i'dʏlɪʃ/ *a* idyllic

Igel *m* **-s,-** hedgehog

ihm *pron* (*dat of* **er, es**) [to] him; (*Ding, Tier*) [to] it

ihn *pron* (*acc of* **er**) him; (*Ding, Tier*) it. **i~en** *pron* (*dat of* **sie** *pl*) [to] them. **I~en** *pron* (*dat of* **Sie**) [to] you

ihr *pron* (*2nd pers pl*) you ● (*dat of* **sie** *sg*) [to] her; (*Ding, Tier*) [to] it ● *poss pron* her; (*Ding, Tier*) its; (*pl*) their. **Ihr** *poss pron* your. **i~e(r,s)** *poss pron* hers; (*pl*) theirs. **I~e(r,s)** *poss pron* yours. **i~erseits** *adv* for her/(*pl*) their part. **I~erseits** *adv* on your part. **i~etwegen** *adv* for her/(*Ding, Tier*) its/(*pl*) their sake; (*wegen*) because of her/it/them, on her/its/their account. **I~etwegen** *adv* for your sake; (*wegen*) because of you, on your account. **I~ige** *poss pron* **der/die/das i~ige** hers; (*pl*) theirs. **I~ige** *poss pron* **der/die/das I~ige** yours. **i~s** *poss pron* hers; (*pl*) theirs. **I~s** *poss pron* yours

Ikone *f* **-, -n** icon

illegal *a* illegal

Illus|ion *f* **-, -en** illusion. **i~orisch** *a* illusory

Illustr|ation /-'tsio:n/ *f* **-, -en** illustration. **I~ieren** *vt* illustrate. **I~ierte** *f* **-n, -[n]** [illustrated] magazine

Iltis *m* **-ses, -se** polecat

im *prep* = **in dem**

Imbiss *m* snack. **I~stube** *f* snack-bar

Imit|ation /-'tsio:n/ *f* **-, -en** imitation. **i~ieren** *vt* imitate

Imker *m* **-s,-** bee-keeper

Immatrikul|ation /-'tsio:n/ *f* - (*Univ*) enrolment. **i~ieren** *vt* (*Univ*) enrol; **sich i~ieren** enrol

immer *adv* always; **für i~** for ever; (*endgültig*) for good; **i~ noch** still; **i~ mehr** more and more; **was i~** whatever. **i~hin** *adv* (*wenigstens*) at least; (*trotzdem*) all the same; (*schließlich*) after all. **i~zu** *adv* all the time

Immobilien /-iən/ *pl* real estate *sg*. **I~makler** *m* estate agent

immun *a* immune (**gegen** to)

Imperialismus *m* - imperialism

impf|en *vt* vaccinate, inoculate. **I~stoff** *m* vaccine. **I~ung** *f* -, **-en** vaccination, inoculation

imponieren *vi* (*haben*) impress (**jdm** s.o.)

Impor|t *m* **-[e]s, -e** import. **I~teur** /-'tø:ɐ/ *m* **-s, -e** importer. **i~tieren** *vt* import

impoten|t *a* (*Med*) impotent. **I~z** *f* - (*Med*) impotence

imprägnieren *vt* waterproof

Impressionismus *m* - impressionism

improvisieren *vt/i* (*haben*) improvise

imstande *pred a* able (**zu** to); capable (**etw zu tun** of doing sth)

in *prep* (+ *dat*) in; (+ *acc*) into, in; (*bei Bus, Zug*) on; **in der Schule** at school; **in die Schule** to school ● *a* **in sein** be in

Inbegriff *m* embodiment

indem *conj* (*während*) while; (*dadurch*) by (+ -ing)

Inder(in) *m* **-s,-** (*f* **-, -nen**) Indian

indessen *conj* while ● *adv* (*unterdessen*) meanwhile

Indian|er(in) *m* **-s,-** (*f* **-, -nen**) (American) Indian. **i~isch** *a* Indian

Indien /'ɪndiən/ *nt* **-s** India

indirekt *a* indirect

indisch *a* Indian

indiskret *a* indiscreet

indiskutabel *a* out of the question

Individu|alist *m* **-en, -en** individualist. **I~alität** *f* - individuality. **i~ell** *a* individual

Indizienbeweis /ɪn'di:tsiən-/ *m* circumstantial evidence

industr|ialisiert *a* industrialized. **I~ie** *f* **-, -n** industry. **i~iell** *a* industrial

ineinander *adv* in/into one another

Infanterie *f* - infantry

Infektion /-'tsio:n/ *f* **-, -en** infection. **I~skrankheit** *f* infectious disease

infizieren *vt* infect; **sich i~** become/ <*Person:*> be infected

Inflation /-'tsio:n/ *f* - inflation. **i~är** *a* inflationary

infolge *prep* (+ *gen*) as a result of. **i~dessen** *adv* consequently

Inform|atik *f* - information science. **I~ation** /-'tsio:n/ *f* **-, -en** information; **I~ationen** information *sg*. **i~ieren** *vt* inform; **sich i~ieren** find out (**über** + *acc* about)

infrage *adv* **etw i~ stellen** question sth; (*ungewiss machen*) make sth doubtful; **nicht i~ kommen** be out of the question

infrarot *a* infra-red

Ingenieur /ɪnʒe'niø:ɐ/ *m* **-s, -e** engineer

Ingwer *m* **-s** ginger

Inhaber(in) *m* **-s,-** (*f* **-, -nen**) holder; (*Besitzer*) proprietor; (*Scheck-*) bearer

inhaftieren *vt* take into custody

inhalieren *vt/i* (*haben*) inhale

Inhalt *m* **-[e]s, -e** contents *pl*; (*Bedeutung, Gehalt*) content; (*Geschichte*) story. **I~sangabe** *f* summary. **I~sverzeichnis** *nt* list/(*in Buch*) table of contents

Initiative /initsia'ti:və/ *f* **-, -n** initiative

inklusive *prep* (+ *gen*) including ● *adv* inclusive

inkonsequent *a* inconsistent

inkorrekt *a* incorrect

Inkubationszeit /-'tsi̯o:ns-/ *f* (*Med*) incubation period

Inland *nt* **-[e]s** home country; (*Binnenland*) interior. **I~sgespräch** *nt* inland call

inmitten *prep* (+ *gen*) in the middle of; (*unter*) amongst

innen *adv* inside; **nach i~** inwards. **I~architekt(in)** *m*(*f*) interior designer. **I~minister** *m* Minister of the Interior; (*in UK*) Home Secretary. **I~politik** *f* domestic policy. **I~stadt** *f* town centre

inner|e(r,s) *a* inner; (*Med, Pol*) internal. **I~e(s)** *nt* interior; (*Mitte*) centre; (*fig: Seele*) inner being. **I~eien** *fpl* (*Culin*) offal *sg*. **i~halb** *prep* (+ *gen*) inside; (*zeitlich & fig*) within; (*während*) during ● *adv* **i~halb von** within. **i~lich** *a* internal

innig *a* sincere

innovativ *a* innovative

Innung *f* **-, -en** guild

ins *prep* = **in das**

Insasse *m* **-n, -n** inmate; (*im Auto*) occupant; (*Passagier*) passenger

insbesondere *adv* especially

Inschrift *f* inscription

Insekt *nt* **-[e]s, -en** insect. **I~envertilgungsmittel** *nt* insecticide

Insel *f* **-, -n** island

Inser|at *nt* **-[e]s, -e** [newspaper] advertisement. **i~ieren** *vt/i* (*haben*) advertise

insge|heim *adv* secretly. **i~samt** *adv* [all] in all

insofern, insoweit *adv* /-'zo:-/ in this respect; **i~ als** in as much as

Insp|ektion /ɪnspɛk'tsi̯o:n/ *f* **-, -en** inspection. **I~ektor** *m* **-en, -en** /-'to:rən/ inspector

Install|ateur /ɪnstala'tø:ɐ̯/ *m* **-s, -e** fitter; (*Klempner*) plumber. **i~ieren** *vt* install

instand *adv* **i~ halten** maintain; (*pflegen*) look after. **I~haltung** *f* **-** maintenance, upkeep

Instandsetzung *f* **-** repair

Instanz /-st-/ *f* **-, -en** authority

Instinkt /-st-/ *m* **-[e]s, -e** instinct. **i~iv** *a* instinctive

Institut /-st-/ *nt* **-[e]s, -e** institute

Instrument /-st-/ *nt* **-[e]s, -e** instrument. **I~almusik** *f* instrumental music

Insulin *nt* **-s** insulin

inszenier|en *vt* (*Theat*) produce. **I~ung** *f* **-, -en** production

Integr|ation /-'tsi̯o:n/ *f* **-** integration. **i~ieren** *vt* integrate; **sich i~ieren** integrate

Intellekt *m* **-[e]s** intellect. **i~uell** *a* intellectual

intelligen|t *a* intelligent. **I~z** *f* **-** intelligence

Intendant *m* **-en, -en** director

Intensivstation *f* intensive-care unit

interaktiv *a* interactive

inter|essant *a* interesting. **I~esse** *nt* **-s, -n** interest; **I~esse haben** be interested (**an** + *dat* in). **I~essengruppe** *f* pressure group. **I~essent** *m* **-en, -en** interested party; (*Käufer*) prospective buyer. **i~essieren** *vt* interest; **sich i~essieren** be interested (**für** in)

Inter|nat *nt* **-[e]s, -e** boarding school. **i~national** *a* international. **I~nist** *m* **-en, -en** specialist in internal diseases. **I~pretation** /-'tsi̯o:n/ *f* **-, -en** interpretation. **i~pretieren** *vt* interpret. **I~vall** *nt* **-s, -e** interval. **I~vention** /-'tsi̯o:n/ *f* **-, -en** intervention

Internet *nt* **-s, -s** Internet; **im I~** on the Internet

I

Interview /ˈɪntɐvjuː/ *nt* **-s, -s** interview. **i~en** /-ˈvjuːən/ *vt* interview
intim *a* intimate
intoleran|t *a* intolerant. **I~z** *f* **-** intolerance
intravenös *a* intravenous
Intrige *f* **-, -n** intrigue
introvertiert *a* introverted
Invalidenrente *f* disability pension
Invasion *f* **-, -en** invasion
Inven|tar *nt* **-s, -e** furnishings and fittings *pl*; (*Techn*) equipment; (*Bestand*) stock; (*Liste*) inventory. **I~tur** *f* **-, -en** stock-taking
investieren *vt* invest
inwie|fern *adv* in what way. **i~weit** *adv* how far, to what extent
Inzest *m* **-[e]s** incest
inzwischen *adv* in the meantime
Irak (der) -[s] Iraq. **i~isch** *a* Iraqi
Iran (der) -[s] Iran. **i~isch** *a* Iranian
irdisch *a* earthly
Ire *m* **-n, -n** Irishman; **die I~n** the Irish *pl*
irgend *adv* **wenn i~ möglich** if at all possible. **i~ein** *indef art* some/any; **i~ein anderer** someone/anyone else. **i~eine(r,s)** *pron* any one; (*jemand*) someone/anyone. **i~etwas** *pron* something; anything. **i~jemand** *pron* someone; anyone. **i~wann** *pron* at some time [or other]/at any time. **i~was** *pron* [!] something [or other]/anything. **i~welche(r,s)** *pron* any. **i~wer** *pron* someone/anyone. **i~wie** *adv* somehow [or other]. **i~wo** *adv* somewhere/anywhere
Irin *f* **-, -nen** Irishwoman
irisch *a* Irish
Irland *nt* **-s** Ireland
Ironie *f* **-** irony
ironisch *a* ironic
irre *a* mad, crazy; ([!] *gewaltig*) incredible. **I~(r)** *m/f* lunatic. **i~führen** *vt sep* (*fig*) mislead
irre|machen *vt sep* confuse. **i~n** *vi/r* (*haben*) **[sich] i~n** be mistaken ● *vi* (*sein*) wander. **I~nanstalt** *f*, **I~nhaus** *nt* lunatic asylum. **i~werden**† *vi sep* (*sein*) get confused
Irrgarten *m* maze
irritieren *vt* irritate
Irr|sinn *m* madness, lunacy. **i~sinnig** *a* mad; ([!] *gewaltig*) incredible. **I~tum** *m* **-s,¨er** mistake
Ischias *m & nt* **-** sciatica
Islam (der) -[s] Islam. **islamisch** *a* Islamic
Island *nt* **-s** Iceland
Isolier|band *nt* insulating tape. **i~en** *vt* isolate; (*Phys, Electr*) insulate; (*gegen Schall*) soundproof. **I~ung** *f* **-** isolation; insulation; soundproofing
Isra|el /ˈɪsraeːl/ *nt* **-s** Israel. **I~eli** *m* **-[s], -s** & *f* **-, -[s]** Israeli. **i~elisch** *a* Israeli
ist *s.* **sein; er ist** he is
Ital|ien /-iən/ *nt* **-s** Italy. **I~iener(in)** *m* **-s,-** (*f* **-, -nen**) Italian. **i~ienisch** *a* Italian. **I~ienisch** *nt* **-[s]** (*Lang*) Italian

Jj

ja *adv*, **Ja** *nt* **-[s]** yes; **ich glaube ja** I think so; **ja nicht!** not on any account! **da seid ihr ja!** there you are!
Jacht *f* **-, -en** yacht
Jacke *f* **-, -n** jacket; (*Strick-*) cardigan

Jackett /ʒaˈkɛt/ *nt* -s, -s jacket
Jade *m* -[s] & *f* - jade
Jagd *f* -, -en hunt; (*Schießen*) shoot; (*Jagen*) hunting; shooting; (*fig*) pursuit (nach of); auf die J~ gehen go hunting/shooting. J~gewehr *nt* sporting gun. J~hund *m* gun-dog: (*Hetzhund*) hound
jagen *vt* hunt; (*schießen*) shoot; (*verfolgen, wegjagen*) chase; (*treiben*) drive; sich j~ chase each other; in die Luft j~ blow up ● *vi* (*haben*) hunt, go hunting/shooting; (*fig*) chase (nach after) ● *vi* (*sein*) race, dash
Jäger *m* -s,- hunter
Jahr *nt* -[e]s, -e year. j~elang *adv* for years. J~eszahl *f* year. J~eszeit *f* season. J~gang *m* year; (*Wein*) vintage. J~hundert *nt* century
jährlich *a* annual, yearly
Jahr|markt *m* fair. J~tausend *nt* millennium. J~zehnt *nt* -[e]s, -e decade
Jähzorn *m* violent temper. j~ig *a* hot-tempered
Jalousie /ʒaluˈziː/ *f* -, -n venetian blind
Jammer *m* -s misery
jämmerlich *a* miserable; (*Mitleid erregend*) pitiful
jammern *vi* (*haben*) lament ● *vt* jdn j~n arouse s.o.'s pity
Jänner *m* -s,- (*Aust*) January
Januar *m* -s, -e January
Jap|an *nt* -s Japan. J~aner(in) *m* -s,- (*f* -, -nen) Japanese. j~anisch *a* Japanese. J~anisch *nt* -[s] (*Lang*) Japanese
jäten *vt/i* (*haben*) weed
jaulen *vi* (*haben*) yelp
Jause *f* -, -n (*Aust*) snack
jawohl *adv* yes
Jazz /jats, dʒɛs/ *m* - jazz
je *adv* (*jemals*) ever; (*jeweils*) each; (*pro*) per; je nach according to; seit eh und je always ● *conj* je mehr, desto besser the more the better ● *prep* (+ *acc*) per
Jeans /dʒiːns/ *pl* jeans
jed|e(r,s) *pron* every; (*j~er Einzelne*) each; (*j~er Beliebige*) any; (*substantivisch*) everyone; each one; anyone; ohne j~en Grund without any reason. j~enfalls *adv* in any case; (*wenigstens*) at least. j~ermann *pron* everyone. j~erzeit *adv* at any time. j~esmal *adv* every time
jedoch *adv & conj* however
jemals *adv* ever
jemand *pron* someone, somebody; (*fragend, verneint*) anyone, anybody
jen|e(r,s) *pron* that; (*pl*) those; (*substantivisch*) that one; (*pl*) those. j~seits *prep* (+ *gen*) [on] the other side of
jetzt *adv* now
jiddisch *a*, J~ *nt* -[s] Yiddish
Job /dʒɔp/ *m* -s, -s job. j~ben *vi* (*haben*) [!] work
Joch *nt* -[e]s, -e yoke
Jockei, Jockey /ˈdʒɔki/ *m* -s, -s jockey
Jod *nt* -[e]s iodine
jodeln *vi* (*haben*) yodel
Joga *m & nt* -[s] yoga
joggen /ˈdʒɔgən/ *vi* (*haben/sein*) jog
Joghurt, Jogurt *m & nt* -[s] yoghurt
Johannisbeere *f* redcurrant
Joker *m* -s,- (*Karte*) joker
Jolle *f* -, -n dinghy
Jongleur /ʒõˈgløːɐ̯/ *m* -s, -s juggler
Jordanien /-iən/ *nt* -s Jordan
Journalis|mus /ʒʊrnaˈlɪsmʊs/ *m* - journalism. J~t(in) *m* -en, -en (*f* -, -nen) journalist
Jubel *m* -s rejoicing, jubilation. j~n *vi* (*haben*) rejoice
Jubiläum *nt* -s,-äen jubilee; (*Jahrestag*) anniversary

J

jucken *vi* (*haben*) itch; **sich j~en** scratch; **es j~t mich** I have an itch

Jude *m* **-n, -n** Jew. **J~ntum** *nt* **-s** Judaism; (*Juden*) Jewry

Jüd|in *f* **-, -nen** Jewess. **j~isch** *a* Jewish

Judo *nt* **-[s]** judo

Jugend *f* **-** youth; (*junge Leute*) young people *pl*. **J~herberge** *f* youth hostel. **J~kriminalität** *f* juvenile delinquency. **j~lich** a youthful. **J~liche(r)** *m/f* young man/woman. **J~liche** *pl* young people. **J~stil** *m* art nouveau

Jugoslaw|ien /-iən/ *nt* **-s** Yugoslavia. **j~isch** a Yugoslav

Juli *m* **-[s], -s** July

jung *a* young; <*Wein*> new ● *pron* **J~ und Alt** young and old. **J~e** *m* **-n, -n** boy. **J~e(s)** *nt* young animal/bird; (*Katzen-*) kitten; (*Bären-*) cub; (*Hunde-*) pup; **die J~en** the young *pl*

Jünger *m* **-s,-** disciple

Jung|frau *f* virgin; (*Astr*) Virgo. **J~geselle** *m* bachelor

Jüngling *m* **-s, -e** youth

jüngst|e(r,s) *a* youngest; (*neueste*) latest; **in j~er Zeit** recently

Juni *m* **-[s], -s** June

Jura *pl* law *sg*

Jurist|(in) *m* **-en, -en** (*f* **-, -nen**) lawyer. **j~isch** *a* legal

Jury /ʒy'ri:/ *f* **-, -s** jury; (*Sport*) judges *pl*

Justiz *f* **- die J~** justice

Juwel *nt* **-s, -en** & (*fig*) **-e** jewel. **J~ier** *m* **-es, -e** jeweller

Jux *m* **-es, -e** [!] joke; **aus Jux** for fun

Kk

Kabarett *nt* **-s, -s** & **-e** cabaret

Kabel *nt* **-s,-** cable. **K~fernsehen** *nt* cable television

Kabeljau *m* **-s, -e** & **-s** cod

Kabine *f* **-, -n** cabin; (*Umkleide-*) cubicle; (*Telefon-*) booth; (*einer K~nbahn*) car. **K~nbahn** *f* cable-car

Kabinett *nt* **-s, -e** (*Pol*) Cabinet

Kabriolett *nt* **-s, -s** convertible

Kachel *f* **-, -n** tile. **k~n** *vt* tile

Kadenz *f* **-, -en** (*Mus*) cadence

Käfer *m* **-s,-** beetle

Kaffee /'kafe:, ka'fe:/ *m* **-s, -s** coffee. **K~kanne** *f* coffee-pot. **K~maschine** *f* coffee-maker. **K~mühle** *f* coffee-grinder

Käfig *m* **-s, -e** cage

kahl *a* bare; (*haarlos*) bald; **k~ geschoren** shaven

Kahn *m* **-s,¨-e** boat; (*Last-*) barge

Kai *m* **-s, -s** quay

Kaiser *m* **-s,-** emperor. **K~in** *f* **-, -nen** empress. **k~lich** *a* imperial. **K~reich** *nt* empire. **K~schnitt** *m* Caesarean [section]

Kajüte *f* **-, -n** (*Naut*) cabin

Kakao /ka'kau/ *m* **-s** cocoa

Kakerlak *m* **-s** & **-en, -en** cockroach

Kaktus *m* **-, -teen** /-'te:ən/ cactus

Kalb *nt* **-[e]s,¨-er** calf. **K~fleisch** *nt* veal

Kalender *m* **-s,-** calendar; (*Termin-*) diary

Kaliber *nt* **-s,-** calibre; (*Gewehr-*) bore

Kalium *nt* **-s** potassium

Kalk *m* **-[e]s, -e** lime; (*Kalzium*) calcium. **k~en** *vt* whitewash. **K~stein** *m* limestone

Kalkul|ation /-'tsi̯o:n/ *f* **-, -en** calculation. **k~ieren** *vt/i* (*haben*) calculate
Kalorie *f* **-, -n** calorie
kalt *a* cold; **mir ist k~** I am cold
Kälte *f* **-** cold; (*Gefühls-*) coldness; **10 Grad K~** 10 degrees below zero
Kalzium *nt* **-s** calcium
Kamel *nt* **-s, -e** camel
Kamera *f* **-, -s** camera
Kamerad(in) *m* **-en, -en** (*f* **-, -nen**) companion; (*Freund*) mate; (*Mil, Pol*) comrade
Kameramann *m* (*pl* **-männer** & **-leute**) cameraman
Kamille *f* **-** camomile
Kamin *m* **-s, -e** fireplace; (*SGer: Schornstein*) chimney
Kamm *m* **-[e]s,¨-e** comb; (*Berg-*) ridge; (*Zool, Wellen-*) crest
kämmen *vt* comb; **jdn/sich k~** comb s.o.'s/one's hair
Kammer *f* **-, -n** small room; (*Techn, Biol, Pol*) chamber. **K~musik** *f* chamber music
Kammgarn *nt* (*Tex*) worsted
Kampagne /kam'panjə/ *f* **-, -n** (*Pol, Comm*) campaign
Kampf *m* **-es,¨-e** fight; (*Schlacht*) battle; (*Wett-*) contest; (*fig*) struggle
kämpf|en *vi* (*haben*) fight; **sich k~en durch** fight one's way through. **K~er(in)** *m* **-s,-** (*f* **-, -nen**) fighter
Kampfrichter *m* (*Sport*) judge
Kanada *nt* **-s** Canada
Kanad|ier(in) /-i̯ɐ, -i̯ərın/ *m* **-s,-** (*f* **-, -nen**) Canadian. **k~isch** *a* Canadian
Kanal *m* **-s,¨-e** canal; (*Abfluss-*) drain, sewer; (*Radio, TV*) channel; **der K~** the [English] Channel
Kanalisation /-'tsi̯o:n/ *f* **-** sewerage system, drains *pl*
Kanarienvogel /-i̯ən-/ *m* canary
Kanarisch *a* **K~e Inseln** Canaries

Kandidat(in) *m* **-en, -en** (*f* **-, -nen**) candidate
kandiert *a* candied
Känguru *nt* **-s, -s** kangaroo
Kaninchen *nt* **-s,-** rabbit
Kanister *m* **-s,-** canister; (*Benzin-*) can
Kännchen *nt* **-s,-** [small] jug; (*Kaffee-*) pot
Kanne *f* **-, -n** jug; (*Tee-*) pot; (*Öl-*) can; (*große Milch-*) churn
Kannibal|e *m* **-n, -n** cannibal. **K~ismus** *m* **-** cannibalism
Kanon *m* **-s, -s** canon; (*Lied*) round
Kanone *f* **-, -n** cannon, gun
kanonisieren *vt* canonize
Kantate *f* **-, -n** cantata
Kante *f* **-, -n** edge
Kanten *m* **-s,-** crust [of bread]
Kanter *m* **-s,-** canter
kantig *a* angular
Kantine *f* **-, -n** canteen
Kanton *m* **-s, -e** (*Swiss*) canton
Kanu *nt* **-s, -s** canoe
Kanzel *f* **-, -n** pulpit; (*Aviat*) cockpit
Kanzler *m* **-s,-** chancellor
Kap *nt* **-s, -s** (*Geog*) cape
Kapazität *f* **-, -en** capacity
Kapelle *f* **-, -n** chapel; (*Mus*) band
kapern *vt* (*Naut*) seize
kapieren *vt* [!] understand
Kapital *nt* **-s** capital. **K~ismus** *m* **-** capitalism. **K~ist** *m* **-en, -en** capitalist. **k~istisch** *a* capitalist
Kapitän *m* **-s, -e** captain
Kapitel *nt* **-s,-** chapter
Kaplan *m* **-s, -e** curate
Kappe *f* **-, -n** cap
Kapsel *f* **-, -n** capsule; (*Flaschen-*) top
kaputt *a* [!] broken; (*zerrissen*) torn; (*defekt*) out of order; (*ruiniert*) ruined; (*erschöpft*) worn out. **k~gehen**† *vi sep* (*sein*) [!] break; (*zerreißen*) tear; (*defekt werden*) pack up; <*Ehe, Freundschaft*:> break up.

K

k~lachen (sich) *vr sep* [!] be in stitches. **k~machen** *vt sep* [!] break; (*zerreißen*) tear; (*defekt machen*) put out of order; (*erschöpfen*) wear out; **sich k~machen** wear oneself out
Kapuze *f* **-, -n** hood
Kapuzinerkresse *f* nasturtium
Karaffe *f* **-, -n** carafe; (*mit Stöpsel*) decanter
Karamell *m* **-s** caramel. **K~bonbon** *m & nt* ≈ toffee
Karat *nt* **-[e]s, -e** carat
Karawane *f* **-, -n** caravan
Kardinal *m* **-s,¨-e** cardinal. **K~zahl** *f* cardinal number
Karfreitag *m* Good Friday
karg *a* meagre; (*frugal*) frugal; (*spärlich*) sparse; (*unfruchtbar*) barren; (*gering*) scant
Karibik *f* **-** Caribbean
kariert *a* check[ed]; <*Papier*> squared; **schottisch k~** tartan
Karik|atur *f* **-, -en** caricature; (*Journ*) cartoon. **k~ieren** *vt* caricature
Karneval *m* **-s, -e & -s** carnival
Kärnten *nt* **-s** Carinthia
Karo *nt* **-s, -s** (*Raute*) diamond; (*Viereck*) square; (*Muster*) check (*Kartenspiel*) diamonds *pl*
Karosserie *f* **-, -n** bodywork
Karotte *f* **-, -n** carrot
Karpfen *m* **-s,-**, carp
Karren *m* **-s,-** cart; (*Hand-*) barrow. **k~** *vt* cart
Karriere /ka'rie:rə/ *f* **-, -n** career; **K~ machen** get to the top
Karte *f* **-, -n** card; (*Eintritts-, Fahr-*) ticket; (*Speise-*) menu; (*Land-*) map
Kartei *f* **-, -en** card index
Karten|spiel *nt* card-game; (*Spielkarten*) pack of cards. **K~vorverkauf** *m* advance booking
Kartoffel *f* **-, -n** potato. **K~brei** *m nt* mashed potatoes
Karton /kar'tɔŋ/ *m* **-s, -s** cardboard; (**Schachtel**) carton
Karussell *nt* **-s, -s & -e** roundabout
Käse *m* **-s,-** cheese
Kaserne *f* **-, -n** barracks *pl*
Kasino *nt* **-s, -s** casino
Kasperle *nt & m* **-s,-** Punch. **K~theater** *nt* Punch and Judy show
Kasse *f* **-, -n** till; (*Registrier-*) cash register; (*Zahlstelle*) cash desk; (*im Supermarkt*) check-out; (*Theater-*) box-office; (*Geld*) pool [of money], [!] kitty; (*Kranken-*) health insurance scheme; **knapp bei K~ sein** [!] be short of cash. **K~nwart** *m* **-[e]s, -e** treasurer. **K~nzettel** *m* receipt
Kasserolle *f* **-, -n** saucepan
Kassette *f* **-, -n** cassette; (*Film-, Farbband-*) cartridge. **K~nrekorder** /-rəkɔrdɐ/ *m* **-s,-** cassette recorder
kassier|en *vi* (*haben*) collect the money/(*im Bus*) the fares ●*vt* collect. **K~er(in)** *m* **-s,-** (*f* **-, -nen**) cashier
Kastanie /kas'ta:ni̯ə/ *f* **-, -n** [horse] chestnut, [!] conker
Kasten *m* **-s,¨** box; (*Brot-*) bin; (*Flaschen-*) crate; (*Brief-*) letter-box; (*Aust: Schrank*) cupboard
kastrieren *vt* castrate; neuter
Katalog *m* **-[e]s, -e** catalogue
Katalysator *m* **-s, -en** /-'to:rən/ catalyst; (*Auto*) catalytic converter
Katapult *nt* **-[e]s, -e** catapult
Katarrh, Katarr *m* **-s, -e** catarrh
Katastrophe *f* **-, -n** catastrophe
Katechismus *m* **-** catechism
Kategorie *f* **-, -n** category
Kater *m* **-s,-** tom-cat; ([!] *Katzenjammer*) hangover
Kathedrale *f* **-, -n** cathedral
Kath|olik(in) *m* **-en, -en** (*f* **-, -nen**) Catholic. **k~olisch** *a* Catholic. **K~olizismus** *m* **-** Catholicism

Kätzchen *nt* **-s,-** kitten; (*Bot*) catkin
Katze *f* **-, -n** cat. **K~njammer** *m* [!] hangover. **K~nsprung** *m* **ein K~nsprung** [!] a stone's throw
Kauderwelsch *nt* **-[s]** gibberish
kauen *vt/i* (*haben*) chew; bite <*Nägel*>
Kauf *m* **-[e]s, Käufe** purchase; **guter K~** bargain; **in K~nehmen** (*fig*) put up with. **k~en** *vt/i* (*haben*) buy; **k~en bei** shop at
Käufer(in) *m* **-s,-** (*f* **-, -nen**) buyer; (*im Geschäft*) shopper
Kauf|haus *nt* department store. **K~laden** *m* shop
käuflich *a* saleable; (*bestechlich*) corruptible; **k~ erwerben** buy
Kauf|mann *m* (*pl* **-leute**) businessman; (*Händler*) dealer; (*dial*) grocer. **K~preis** *m* purchase price
Kaugummi *m* chewing-gum
Kaulquappe *f* **-, -n** tadpole
kaum *adv* hardly
Kaution /-ˈtsio:n/ *f* **-, -en** surety; (*Jur*) bail; (*Miet-*) deposit
Kautschuk *m* **-s** rubber
Kauz *m* **-es, Käuze** owl
Kavalier *m* **-s, -e** gentleman
Kavallerie *f* **-** cavalry
Kaviar *m* **-s** caviare
keck *a* bold; cheeky
Kegel *m* **-s,-** skittle; (*Geom*) cone. **K~bahn** *f* skittle-alley. **k~n** *vi* (*haben*) play skittles
Kehl|e *f* **-, -n** throat; **aus voller K~e** at the top of one's voice. **K~kopf** *m* larynx. **K~kopfentzündung** *f* laryngitis
Kehr|e *f* **-, -n** [hairpin] bend. **k~en** *vi* (*haben*) (*fegen*) sweep ● *vt* sweep; (*wenden*) turn; **sich nicht k~en an** (+ *acc*) not care about. **K~icht** *m* **-[e]s** sweepings *pl*. **K~reim** *m* refrain. **K~seite** *f* (*fig*) drawback. **k~tmachen** *vi sep* (*haben*) turn back; (*sich umdrehen*) turn round
Keil *m* **-[e]s, -e** wedge
Keilriemen *m* fan belt
Keim *m* **-[e]s, -e** (*Bot*) sprout; (*Med*) germ. **k~en** *vi* (*haben*) germinate; (*austreiben*) sprout. **k~frei** *a* sterile
kein *pron* no; not a; **k~e fünf Minuten** less than five minutes. **k~e(r,s)** *pron* no one, nobody; (*Ding*) none, not one. **k~esfalls** *adv* on no account. **k~eswegs** *adv* by no means. **k~mal** *adv* not once. **k~s** *pron* none, not one
Keks *m* **-[es], -[e]** biscuit
Kelch *m* **-[e]s, -e** goblet, cup; (*Relig*) chalice; (*Bot*) calyx
Kelle *f* **-, -n** ladle; (*Maurer*) trowel
Keller *m* **-s,-** cellar. **K~ei** *f* **-, -en** winery. **K~wohnung** *f* basement flat
Kellner *m* **-s,-** waiter. **K~in** *f* **-, -nen** waitress
keltern *vt* press
keltisch *a* Celtic
Kenia *nt* **-s** Kenya
kenn|en† *vt* know; **k~en lernen** get to know; (*treffen*) meet; **sich k~en lernen** meet; (*näher*) get to know one another. **K~er** *m* **-s,-**, **K~erin** *f* **-, -nen** connoisseur; (*Experte*) expert. **k~tlich** *a* recognizable; **k~tlich machen** mark. **K~tnis** *f* **-, -se** knowledge; **zur K~tnis nehmen** take note of; **in K~tnis setzen** inform (**von** of). **K~wort** *nt* (*pl* **-wörter**) reference; (*geheimes*) password. **K~zeichen** *nt* distinguishing mark *or* feature; (*Merkmal*) characteristic, (*Markierung*) marking; (*Auto*) registration. **k~zeichnen** *vt* distinguish; (*markieren*) mark
kentern *vi* (*sein*) capsize
Keramik *f* **-, -en** pottery
Kerbe *f* **-, -n** notch
Kerker *m* **-s,-** dungeon; (*Gefängnis*) prison
Kerl *m* **-s, -e & -s** [!] fellow, bloke

K

Kern *m* **-s, -e** pip; (*Kirsch-*) stone; (*Nuss-*) kernel; (*Techn*) core; (*Atom-, Zell- & fig*) nucleus; (*Stadt-*) centre; (*einer Sache*) heart. **K~energie** *f* nuclear energy. **K~gehäuse** *nt* core. **k~los** *a* seedless. **K~physik** *f* nuclear physics *sg*
Kerze *f* **-, -n** candle. **K~nhalter** *m* **-s,-** candlestick
kess *a* pert
Kessel *m* **-s,-** kettle
Kette *f* **-, -n** chain; (*Hals-*) necklace. **k~n** *vt* chain (**an** + *acc* to). **K~nladen** *m* chain store
Ketze|r(in) *m* **-s,-** (*f* **-, -nen**) heretic. **K~rei** *f* **-** heresy
keuch|en *vi* (*haben*) pant. **K~husten** *m* whooping cough
Keule *f* **-, -n** club; (*Culin*) leg; (*Hühner-*) drumstick
keusch *a* chaste
Khaki *nt* **-** khaki
kichern *vi* (*haben*) giggle
Kiefer[1] *f* **-, -n** pine[-tree]
Kiefer[2] *m* **-s,-** jaw
Kiel *m* **-s, -e** (*Naut*) keel
Kiemen *fpl* gills
Kies *m* **-es** gravel. **K~el** *m* **-s,-**, **K~elstein** *m* pebble
Kilo *nt* **-s, -[s]** kilo. **K~gramm** *nt* kilogram. **K~hertz** *nt* kilohertz. **K~meter** *m* kilometre. **K~meterstand** *m* ≈ mileage. **K~watt** *nt* kilowatt
Kind *nt* **-es, -er** child; **von K~ auf** from childhood
Kinder|arzt *m*, **K~ärztin** *f* paediatrician. **K~bett** *nt* child's cot. **K~garten** *m* nursery school. **K~geld** *nt* child benefit. **K~lähmung** *f* polio. **k~leicht** *a* very easy. **k~los** *a* childless. **K~mädchen** *nt* nanny. **K~reim** *m* nursery rhyme. **K~spiel** *nt* children's game. **K~tagesstätte** *f* day nursery. **K~teller** *m* children's menu. **K~wagen** *m* pram. **K~zimmer** *nt* child's/children's room; (*für Baby*) nursery
Kind|heit *f* **-** childhood. **k~isch** *a* childish. **k~lich** *a* childlike
kinetisch *a* kinetic
Kinn *nt* **-[e]s, -e** chin. **K~lade** *f* jaw
Kino *nt* **-s, -s** cinema
Kiosk *m* **-[e]s, -e** kiosk
Kippe *f* **-, -n** (*Müll-*) dump; (! *Zigaretten-*) fag-end. **k~n** *vt* tilt; (*schütten*) tip (**in** + *acc* into) ● *vi* (*sein*) topple
Kirch|e *f* **-, -n** church. **K~enbank** *f* pew. **K~endiener** *m* verger. **K~enlied** *nt* hymn. **K~enschiff** *nt* nave. **K~hof** *m* churchyard. **k~lich** *a* church ... ● *adv* **k~lich getraut werden** be married in church. **K~turm** *m* church tower, steeple. **K~weih** *f* **-, -en** [village] fair
Kirmes *f* **-, -sen** = **Kirchweih**
Kirsche *f* **-, -n** cherry
Kissen *nt* **-s,-** cushion; (*Kopf-*) pillow
Kiste *f* **-, -n** crate; (*Zigarren-*) box
Kitsch *m* **-es** sentimental rubbish; (*Kunst*) kitsch
Kitt *m* **-s** [adhesive] cement; (*Fenster-*) putty
Kittel *m* **-s,-** overall, smock
Kitz *nt* **-es, -e** (*Zool*) kid
Kitz|el *m* **-s,-** tickle; (*Nerven-*) thrill. **k~eln** *vt/i* (*haben*) tickle. **k~lig** *a* ticklish
kläffen *vi* (*haben*) yap
Klage *f* **-, -n** lament; (*Beschwerde*) complaint; (*Jur*) action. **k~n** *vi* (*haben*) lament; (*sich beklagen*) complaint; (*Jur*) sue
Kläger(in) *m* **-s,-** (*f* **-, -nen**) (*Jur*) plaintiff
klamm *a* cold and damp; (*steif*) stiff. **K~** *f* **-, -en** (*Geog*) gorge
Klammer *f* **-, -n** (*Wäsche-*) peg; (*Büro-*) paper-clip; (*Heft-*) staple; (*Haar-*) grip; (*für Zähne*) brace;

(*Techn*) clamp; (*Typ*) bracket. **k~n (sich)** *vr* cling (**an** + *acc* to)

Klang *m* **-[e]s,¨-e** sound; (*K~farbe*) tone

Klapp|e *f* **-, -n** flap; (! *Mund*) trap. **k~en** *vt* fold; (*hoch-*) tip up ● *vi* (*haben*) ! work out

Klapper *f* **-, -n** rattle. **k~n** *vi* (*haben*) rattle. **K~schlange** *f* rattlesnake

klapp|rig *a* rickety; (*schwach*) decrepit. **K~stuhl** *m* folding chair

Klaps *m* **-es, -e** pat, smack

klar *a* clear; **sich** (*dat*) **k~ werden** make up one's mind; (*erkennen*) realize (**dass** that); **sich** (*dat*) **k~** *od* **im K~en sein** realize (**dass** that) ● *adv* clearly; (! *natürlich*) of course

klären *vt* clarify; **sich k~** clear; (*fig: sich lösen*) resolve itself

Klarheit *f* **-,-** clarity

Klarinette *f* **-, -n** clarinet

klar|machen *vt sep* make clear (*dat* to); **sich** (*dat*) **etw k~machen** understand sth. **k~stellen** *vt sep* clarify

Klärung *f* **-** clarification

Klasse *f* **-, -n** class; (*Sch*) class, form; (*Zimmer*) classroom. **k~** *inv a* ! super. **K~narbeit** *f* [written] test. **K~nzimmer** *nt* classroom

Klass|ik *f* **-** classicism; (*Epoche*) classical period. **K~iker** *m* **-s,-** classical author/(*Mus*) composer. **k~isch** *a* classical; (*typisch*) classic

Klatsch *m* **-[e]s** gossip. **K~base** *f* ! gossip. **k~en** *vt* slap; **Beifall k~en** applaud ● *vi* (*haben*) make a slapping sound; (*im Wasser*) splash; (*tratschen*) gossip; (*applaudieren*) clap. **k~nass** *a* ! soaking wet

klauen *vt/i* (*haben*) ! steal

Klausel *f* **-, -n** clause

Klaustrophobie *f* **-** claustrophobia

Klausur *f* **-, -en** (*Univ*) paper

Klavier *nt* **-s, -e** piano. **K~spieler(in)** *m(f)* pianist

kleb|en *vt* stick/(*mit Klebstoff*) glue (**an** + *acc* to) ● *vi* (*haben*) stick (**an** + *dat* to). **k~rig** *a* sticky. **K~stoff** *m* adhesive, glue. **K~streifen** *m* adhesive tape

Klecks *m* **-es, -e** stain; (*Tinten-*) blot; (*kleine Menge*) dab. **k~en** *vi* (*haben*) make a mess

Klee *m* **-s** clover

Kleid *nt* **-[e]s, -er** dress; **K~er** dresses; (*Kleidung*) clothes. **k~en** *vt* dress; (*gut stehen*) suit. **K~erbügel** *m* coat-hanger. **K~erbürste** *f* clothes-brush. **K~erhaken** *m* coat-hook. **K~erschrank** *m* wardrobe. **k~sam** *a* becoming. **K~ung** *f* **-** clothes *pl*, clothing. **K~ungsstück** *nt* garment

Kleie *f* **-** bran

klein *a* small, little; (*von kleinem Wuchs*) short; **k~ schneiden** cut up small. **von k~ auf** from childhood. **K~arbeit** *f* painstaking work. **K~e(r,s)** *m/f/nt* little one. **K~geld** *nt* [small] change. **K~handel** *m* retail trade. **K~heit** *f* **-** smallness; (*Wuchs*) short stature. **K~holz** *nt* firewood. **K~igkeit** *f* **-, -en** trifle; (*Mahl*) snack. **K~kind** *nt* infant. **k~laut** *a* subdued. **k~lich** *a* petty

klein|schreiben† *vt sep* write with a small [initial] letter. **K~stadt** *f* small town. **k~städtisch** *a* provincial

Kleister *m* **-s** paste. **k~n** *vt* paste

Klemme *f* **-, -n** [hair-]grip. **k~n** *vt* jam; **sich** (*dat*) **den Finger k~n** get one's finger caught ● *vi* (*haben*) jam, stick

Klempner *m* **-s,-** plumber

Klerus (der) **-** the clergy

Klette *f* **-, -n** burr

K

klettern|n *vi* (*sein*) climb. **K~pflanze** *f* climber
Klettverschluss *m* Velcro (P) fastening
klicken *vi* (*haben*) click
Klient(in) /kli'ɛnt(ɪn)/ *m* **-en, -en** (*f* **-, -nen**) (*Jur*) client
Kliff *nt* **-[e]s, -e** cliff
Klima *nt* **-s** climate. **K~anlage** *f* air-conditioning
klimat|isch *a* climatic. **k~isiert** *a* air-conditioned
klimpern *vi* (*haben*) jingle; **k~ auf** (+ *dat*) tinkle on <*Klavier*>; strum <*Gitarre*>
Klinge *f* **-, -n** blade
Klingel *f* **-, -n** bell. **k~n** *vi* (*haben*) ring; **es k~t** there's a ring at the door
klingen† *vi* (*haben*) sound
Klinik *f* **-, -en** clinic
Klinke *f* **-, -n** [door] handle
Klippe *f* **-, -n** [submerged] rock
Klips *m* **-es, -e** clip; (*Ohr-*) clip-on ear-ring
klirren *vi* (*haben*) rattle <*Glas:*> chink
Klo *nt* **-s, -s** [!] loo
Klon *m* **-s, -e** clone. **k~en** *vt* clone
klopfen *vi* (*haben*) knock; (*leicht*) tap; <*Herz:*> pound; **es k~te** there was a knock at the door
Klops *m* **-es, -e** meatball
Klosett *nt* **-s, -s** lavatory
Kloß *m* **-es,¨-e** dumpling
Kloster *nt* **-s,¨** monastery; (*Nonnen-*) convent
klösterlich *a* monastic
Klotz *m* **-es,¨-e** block
Klub *m* **-s, -s** club
Kluft *f* **-,¨-e** cleft; (*fig: Gegensatz*) gulf
klug *a* intelligent; (*schlau*) clever. **K~heit** *f* **-** cleverness
Klump|en *m* **-s,-** lump
knabbern *vt/i* (*haben*) nibble
Knabe *m* **-n, -n** boy. **k~nhaft** *a* boyish
Knäckebrot *nt* crispbread
knack|en *vt/i* (*haben*) crack. **K~s** *m* **-es, -e** crack
Knall *m* **-[e]s, -e** bang. **K~bonbon** *m* cracker. **k~en** *vi* (*haben*) go bang; <*Peitsche:*> crack ● *vt* ([!] *werfen*) chuck; **jdm eine k~en** [!] clout s.o. **k~ig** *a* [!] gaudy
knapp *a* (*gering*) scant; (*kurz*) short; (*mangelnd*) scarce; (*gerade ausreichend*) bare; (*eng*) tight. **K~heit** *f* **-** scarcity
knarren *vi* (*haben*) creak
Knast *m* **-[e]s** [!] prison
knattern *vi* (*haben*) crackle; <*Gewehr:*> stutter
Knäuel *m & nt* **-s,-** ball
Knauf *m* **-[e]s, Knäufe** knob
knauserig *a* [!] stingy
knautschen *vt* [!] crumple ● *vi* (*haben*) crease
Knebel *m* **-s,-** gag. **k~n** *vt* gag
Knecht *m* **-[e]s, -e** farm-hand; (*fig*) slave
kneif|en† *vt* pinch ● *vi* (*haben*) pinch; ([!] *sich drücken*) chicken out. **K~zange** *f* pincers *pl*
Kneipe *f* **-, -n** [!] pub
knet|en *vt* knead; (*formen*) mould. **K~masse** *f* Plasticine(P)
Knick *m* **-[e]s, -e** bend; (*Kniff*) crease. **k~en** *vt* bend; (*kniffen*) fold; **geknickt sein** [!] be dejected
Knicks *m* **-es, -e** curtsy. **k~en** *vi* (*haben*) curtsy
Knie *nt* **-s,-** /'kni:ə/ knee
knien /'kni:ən/ *vi* (*haben*) kneel ● *vr* **sich k~** kneel [down]
Kniescheibe *f* kneecap
Kniff *m* **-[e]s, -e** pinch; (*Falte*) crease; ([!] *Trick*) trick. **k~en** *vt* fold
knipsen *vt* (*lochen*) punch; (*Phot*) photograph ● *vi* (*haben*) take a photograph/photographs
Knirps *m* **-es, -e** [!] little chap; **(P)** (*Schirm*) telescopic umbrella
knirschen *vi* (*haben*) grate; <*Schnee, Kies:*> crunch

knistern *vi* (*haben*) crackle; <*Papier*:> rustle

Knitter|falte *f* crease. **k~frei** *a* crease-resistant. **k~n** *vi* (*haben*) crease

knobeln *vi* (*haben*) toss (**um** for)

Knoblauch *m* **-s** garlic

Knöchel *m* **-s,-** ankle; (*Finger-*) knuckle

Knochen *m* **-s,-** bone. **K~mark** *nt* bone marrow

knochig *a* bony

Knödel *m* **-s,-** (*SGer*) dumpling

Knoll|e *f* **-, -n** tuber

Knopf *m* **-[e]s,¨e** button; (*Griff*) knob

knöpfen *vt* button

Knopfloch *nt* buttonhole

Knorpel *m* **-s** gristle; (*Anat*) cartilage

Knospe *f* bud

Knoten *m* **-s,-** knot; (*Med*) lump; (*Haar-*) bun, chignon. **k~** *vt* knot. **K~punkt** *m* junction

knüll|en *vt* crumple ● *vi* (*haben*) crease. **K~er** *m* **-s,-** [!] sensation

knüpfen *vt* knot; (*verbinden*) attach (**an** + *acc* to)

Knüppel *m* **-s,-** club; (*Gummi-*) truncheon

knurren *vi* (*haben*) growl; <*Magen*:> rumble

knusprig *a* crunchy, crisp

knutschen *vi* (*haben*) [!] smooch

k.o. /ka'ʔo:/ *a* **k.o. schlagen** knock out; **k.o. sein** [!] be worn out

Koalition /koali'tsi̯o:n/ *f* **-, -en** coalition

Kobold *m* **-[e]s, -e** goblin, imp

Koch *m* **-[e]s,¨e** cook; (*im Restaurant*) chef. **K~buch** *nt* cookery book. **k~en** *vt* cook; (*sieden*) boil; make <*Kaffee, Tee*>; **hart gekochtes Ei** hard boiled egg ● *vi* (*haben*) cook; (*sieden*) boil; [!] seethe (**vor** + *dat* with). **K~en** *nt* **-s** cooking; (*Sieden*) boiling. **k~end** *a* boiling. **K~herd** *m* cooker, stove

Köchin *f* **-, -nen** [woman] cook

Koch|löffel *m* wooden spoon. **K~nische** *f* kitchenette. **K~platte** *f* hotplate. **K~topf** *m* saucepan

Köder *m* **-s,-** bait

Koffein /kɔfe'i:n/ *nt* **-s** caffeine. **k~frei** *a* decaffeinated

Koffer *m* **-s,-** suitcase. **K~kuli** *m* luggage trolley. **K~raum** *m* (*Auto*) boot

Kognak /'kɔnjak/ *m* **-s, -s** brandy

Kohl *m* **-[e]s** cabbage

Kohle *f* **-, -n** coal. **K~[n]hydrat** *nt* **-[e]s, -e** carbohydrate. **K~nbergwerk** *nt* coal-mine, colliery. **K~ndioxid** *nt* carbon dioxide. **K~nsäure** *f* carbon dioxide. **K~nstoff** *m* carbon

Koje *f* **-, -n** (*Naut*) bunk

Kokain /koka'i:n/ *nt* **-s** cocaine

kokett *a* flirtatious. **k~ieren** *vi* (*haben*) flirt

Kokon /ko'kõ:/ *m* **-s, -s** cocoon

Kokosnuss (*f*) coconut

Koks *m* **-es** coke

Kolben *m* **-s,-** (*Gewehr-*) butt; (*Mais-*) cob; (*Techn*) piston; (*Chem*) flask

Kolibri *m* **-s, -s** humming-bird

Kolik *f* **-, -en** colic

Kollaborateur /-'tø:ɐ̯/ *m* **-s, -e** collaborator

Kolleg *nt* **-s, -s & -ien** /-i̯ən/ (*Univ*) course of lectures

Kolleg|e *m* **-n, -n, K~in** *f* **-, -nen** colleague. **K~ium** *nt* **-s, -ien** staff

Kollek|te *f* **-, -n** (*Relig*) collection. **K~tion** /-'tsi̯o:n/ *f* **-, -en** collection

Köln *nt* **-s** Cologne. **K~ischwasser, K~isch Wasser** *nt* eau-de-Cologne

Kolonie *f* **-, -n** colony

Kolonne *f* **-, -n** column; (*Mil*) convoy

Koloss *m* **-es, -e** giant

Koma *nt* **-s, -s** coma

Kombi *m* **-s, -s** = **K~wagen**. **K~nation** /-'tsi̯o:n/ *f* **-, -en**

combination; (*Folgerung*) deduction; (*Kleidung*) co-ordinating outfit. **k~nieren** *vt* combine; (*fig*) reason; (*folgern*) deduce. **K~wagen** *m* estate car

Kombüse *f* **-, -n** (*Naut*) galley

Komet *m* **-en, -en** comet

Komfort /kɔm'foːɐ̯/ *m* **-s** comfort; (*Luxus*) luxury

Komik *f* **-** humour. **K~er** *m* **-s,-** comic, comedian

komisch *a* funny; <*Oper*> comic; (*sonderbar*) odd, funny. **k~erweise** *adv* funnily enough

Komitee *nt* **-s, -s** committee

Komma *nt* **-s, -s** & **-ta** comma; (*Dezimal-*) decimal point; **drei K~ fünf** three point five

Kommando *nt* **-s, -s** order; (*Befehlsgewalt*) command; (*Einheit*) detachment. **K~brücke** *f* bridge

kommen† *vi* (*sein*) come; (*eintreffen*) arrive; (*gelangen*) get (**nach** to); **k~ lassen** send for; **auf/hinter etw** (*acc*) **k~** think of/find out about sth; **um/zu etw k~** lose/acquire sth; **wieder zu sich k~** come round; **wie kommt das?** why is that? **k~d** *a* coming; **k~den Montag** next Monday

Kommen|tar *m* **-s, -e** commentary; (*Bemerkung*) comment. **k~tieren** *vt* comment on

kommerziell *a* commercial

Kommissar *m* **-s, -e** commissioner; (*Polizei-*) superintendent

Kommission *f* **-, -en** commission; (*Gremium*) committee

Kommode *f* **-, -n** chest of drawers

Kommunalwahlen *fpl* local elections

Kommunion *f* **-, -en** [Holy] Communion

Kommun|ismus *m* **-** Communism. **K~ist(in)** *m* **-en, -en** (*f* **-, -nen**) Communist. **k~istisch** *a* Communist

kommunizieren *vi* (*haben*) receive [Holy] Communion

Komödie /ko'møːdi̯ə/ *f* **-, -n** comedy

Kompagnon /'kɔmpanjõː/ *m* **-s, -s** (*Comm*) partner

Kompanie *f* **-, -n** (*Mil*) company

Komparse *m* **-n, -n** (*Theat*) extra

Kompass *m* **-es, -e** compass

komplett *a* complete

Komplex *m* **-es, -e** complex

Komplikation /-'tsi̯oːn/ *f* **-, -en** complication

Kompliment *nt* **-[e]s, -e** compliment

Komplize *m* **-n, -n** accomplice

komplizier|en *vt* complicate. **k~t** *a* complicated

Komplott *nt* **-[e]s, -e** plot

kompo|nieren *vt/i* (*haben*) compose. **K~nist** *m* **-en, -en** composer

Kompost *m* **-[e]s** compost

Kompott *nt* **-[e]s, -e** stewed fruit

Kompromiss *m* **-es, -e** compromise; **einen K~ schließen** compromise. **k~los** *a* uncompromising

Konden|sation /-'tsi̯oːn/ *f* **-** condensation. **k~sieren** *vt* condense

Kondensmilch *f* evaporated/(*gesüßt*) condensed milk

Kondition /-'tsi̯oːn/ *f* **-** (*Sport*) fitness; **in K~** in form

Konditor *m* **-s, -en** /-'toːrən/ confectioner. **K~ei** *f* **-, -en** patisserie

Kondo|lenzbrief *m* letter of condolence. **k~lieren** *vi* (*haben*) express one's condolences

Kondom *nt* & *m* **-s, -e** condom

Konfekt *nt* **-[e]s** confectionery; (*Pralinen*) chocolates *pl*

Konfektion /-'tsi̯oːn/ *f* **-** ready-to-wear clothes *pl*

Konferenz *f* **-, -en** conference; (*Besprechung*) meeting

Konfession *f* **-, -en** [religious] denomination. **k~ell** *a* denominational

Konfetti *nt* **-s** confetti

Konfirm|and(in) *m* **-en, -en** (*f* **-, -nen**) candidate for confirmation. **K~ation** /-ˈtsi̯oːn/ *f* **-, -en** (*Relig*) confirmation. **k~ieren** *vt* (*Relig*) confirm

Konfitüre *f* **-, -n** jam

Konflikt *m* **-[e]s, -e** conflict

Konföderation /-ˈtsi̯oːn/ *f* confederation

konfus *a* confused

Kongress *m* **-es, -e** congress

König *m* **-s, -e** king. **K~in** *f* **-, -nen** queen. **k~lich** *a* royal; (*hoheitsvoll*) regal; (*großzügig*) handsome. **K~reich** *nt* kingdom

Konjunktiv *m* **-s, -e** subjunctive

Konjunktur *f* **-** economic situation; (*Hoch-*) boom

konkret *a* concrete

Konkurren|t(in) *m* **-en, -en** (*f* **-, -nen**) competitor, rival. **K~z** *f* **-** competition; **jdm K~z machen** compete with s.o. **K~zkampf** *m* competition, rivalry

konkurrieren *vi* (*haben*) compete

Konkurs *m* **-es, -e** bankruptcy

---

können†

● *auxiliary verb*

····➤ (*vermögen*) be able to; (*Präsens*) can; (*Vergangenheit, Konditional*) could. **ich kann nicht schlafen** I cannot *or* can't sleep. **kann ich Ihnen helfen?** can I help you? **kann/könnte das explodieren?** can/could it explode? **es kann sein, dass er kommt** he may come

! Distinguish **konnte** and **könnte** (both can be 'could'): **er konnte sie nicht retten** he couldn't *or* was unable to rescue them. **er konnte sie noch retten** he was able to rescue them. **er könnte sie noch retten, wenn ...** he could still rescue them if ...

····➤ (*dürfen*) can, may. **kann ich gehen?** can *or* may I go? **können wir mit[kommen]?** can *or* may we come too?

● *transitive verb*

····➤ (*beherrschen*) know <language>; be able to play <game>. **können Sie Deutsch?** do you know any German? **sie kann das [gut]** she can do that [well]. **ich kann nichts dafür** I can't help that, I'm not to blame

● *intransitive verb*

····➤ (*fähig sein*) **ich kann [heute] nicht** I can't [today]. **er kann nicht anders** there's nothing else he can do; (*es ist seine Art*) he can't help it. **er kann nicht mehr** ! he can't go on; (*nicht mehr essen*) he can't eat any more

····➤ (*irgendwohin gehen können*) be able to go; can go. **ich kann nicht ins Kino** I can't go to the cinema. **er konnte endlich nach Florenz** at last he was able to go to Florence

---

konsequen|t *a* consistent; (*logisch*) logical. **K~z** *f* **-, -en** consequence

konservativ *a* conservative

Konserv|en *fpl* tinned or canned food *sg*. **K~endose** *f* tin, can. **K~ierungsmittel** *nt* preservative

Konsonant *m* **-en, -en** consonant

Konstitution /-ˈtsi̯oːn/ *f* **-, -en** constitution. **k~ell** *a* constitutional

konstruieren *vt* construct, (*entwerfen*) design

Konstruk|tion /-ˈtsi̯oːn/ *f* **-, -en** construction; (*Entwurf*) design. **k~tiv** *a* constructive

Konsul *m* **-s, -n** consul. **K~at** *nt* **-[e]-s, -e** consulate

Konsum *m* **-s** consumption. **K∼güter** *npl* consumer goods

Kontakt *m* **-[e]s, -e** contact. **K∼linsen** *fpl* contact lenses. **K∼person** *f* contact

kontern *vt/i* (*haben*) counter

Kontinent /'kɔn-, kɔnti'nɛnt/ *m* **-[e]s, -e** continent

Konto *nt* **-s, -s** account. **K∼auszug** *m* [bank] statement. **K∼nummer** *f* account number. **K∼stand** *m* [bank] balance

Kontrabass *m* double-bass

Kontroll|abschnitt *m* counterfoil. **K∼e** *f* **-, -n** control; (*Prüfung*) check. **K∼eur** /-'lø:ɐ̯/ *m* **-s, -e** [ticket] inspector. **k∼ieren** *vt* check; inspect <*Fahrkarten*>; (*beherrschen*) control

Kontroverse *f* **-, -n** controversy

Kontur *f* **-, -en** contour

konventionell *a* conventional

Konversationslexikon *nt* encyclopaedia

konvert|ieren *vi* (*haben*) (*Relig*) convert. **K∼it** *m* **-en, -en** convert

Konzentration /-'tsio:n/ *f* **-, -en** concentration. **K∼slager** *nt* concentration camp

konzentrieren *vt* concentrate; **sich k∼** concentrate (**auf** + *acc* on)

Konzept *nt* **-[e]s, -e** [rough] draft; **jdn aus dem K∼bringen** put s.o. off his stroke

Konzern *m* **-s, -e** (*Comm*) group [of companies]

Konzert *nt* **-[e]s, -e** concert; (*Klavier-*) concerto

Konzession *f* **-, -en** licence; (*Zugeständnis*) concession

Konzil *nt* **-s, -e** (*Relig*) council

Kooperation /koˀɔpera'tsio:n/ *f* co-operation

Koordin|ation /koˀɔrdina'tsio:n/ *f* **-** co-ordination. **k∼ieren** *vt* co-ordinate

Kopf *m* **-[e]s,̈-e** head; **ein K∼ Kohl/Salat** a cabbage/lettuce; **aus dem K∼** from memory; (*auswendig*) by heart; **auf dem K∼** (*verkehrt*) upside down; **K∼ stehen** stand on one's head; **sich** (*dat*) **den K∼ waschen** wash one's hair; **sich** (*dat*) **den K∼ zerbrechen** rack one's brains. **K∼ball** *m* header

köpfen *vt* behead; (*Fußball*) head

Kopf|ende *nt* head. **K∼haut** *f* scalp. **K∼hörer** *m* headphones *pl*. **K∼kissen** *nt* pillow. **k∼los** *a* panic-stricken. **K∼rechnen** *nt* mental arithmetic. **K∼salat** *m* lettuce. **K∼schmerzen** *mpl* headache *sg*. **K∼sprung** *m* header, dive. **K∼stand** *m* headstand. **K∼steinpflaster** *nt* cobble-stones *pl*. **K∼tuch** *nt* headscarf. **k∼über** *adv* head first; (*fig*) headlong. **K∼wäsche** *f* shampoo. **K∼weh** *nt* headache

Kopie *f* **-, -n** copy. **k∼ren** *vt* copy

Koppel[1] *f* **-, -n** enclosure; (*Pferde-*) paddock

Koppel[2] *nt* **-s,-** (*Mil*) belt. **k∼n** *vt* couple

Koralle *f* **-, -n** coral

Korb *m* **-[e]s,̈-e** basket; **jdm einen K∼ geben** (*fig*) turn s.o. down. **K∼ball** *m* [kind of] netball

Kord *m* **-s** (*Tex*) corduroy

Kordel *f* **-, -n** cord

Korinthe *f* **-, -n** currant

Kork *m* **-s,-** cork. **K∼en** *m* **-s,-** cork. **K∼enzieher** *m* **-s,-** corkscrew

Korn *nt* **-[e]s,̈-er** grain, (*Samen-*) seed; (*am Visier*) front sight

Körn|chen *nt* **-s,-** granule. **k∼ig** *a* granular

Körper *m* **-s,-** body; (*Geom*) solid. **K∼bau** *m* build, physique. **k∼behindert** *a* physically disabled. **k∼lich** *a* physical; <*Strafe*> corporal. **K∼pflege** *f* personal hygiene. **K∼schaft** *f* **-, -en** corporation, body

korrekt *a* correct. **K∼or** *m* **-s, -en** /-'to:rən/ proof-reader. **K∼ur** *f* **-,**

-**en** correction. **K~urabzug** *m* proof

Korrespon|dent(in) *m* **-en, -en** (*f* **-, -nen**) correspondent. **K~denz** *f* **-, -en** correspondence

Korridor *m* **-s, -e** corridor

korrigieren *vt* correct

Korrosion *f* **-** corrosion

korrup|t *a* corrupt. **K~tion** /-'tsio:n/ *f* **-** corruption

Korsett *nt* **-[e]s, -e** corset

koscher *a* kosher

Kosename *m* pet name

Kosmet|ik *f* **-** beauty culture. **K~ika** *ntpl* cosmetics. **K~ikerin** *f* **-, -nen** beautician. **k~isch** *a* cosmetic; <*Chirurgie*> plastic

kosm|isch *a* cosmic. **K~onaut(in)** *m* **-en, -en** (*f* **-, -nen**) cosmonaut

Kosmos *m* **-** cosmos

Kost *f* **-** food; (*Ernährung*) diet; (*Verpflegung*) board

kostbar *a* precious. **K~keit** *f* **-, -en** treasure

kosten[1] *vt/i* (*haben*) **[von] etw k~** taste sth

kosten[2] *vt* cost; (*brauchen*) take; **wie viel kostet es?** how much is it? **K~** *pl* expense *sg*, cost *sg*; (*Jur*) costs; **auf meine K~** at my expense. **K~[vor]anschlag** *m* estimate. **k~los** *a* free ● *adv* free [of charge]

köstlich *a* delicious; (*entzückend*) delightful

Kostprobe *f* taste; (*fig*) sample

Kostüm *nt* **-s, -e** (*Theat*) costume; (*Verkleidung*) fancy dress; (*Schneider-*) suit. **k~iert** *a* **k~iert sein** be in fancy dress

Kot *m* **-[e]s** excrement

Kotelett /kɔt'lɛt/ *nt* **-s, -s** chop, cutlet. **K~en** *pl* sideburns

Köter *m* **-s,-** (*pej*) dog

Kotflügel *m* (*Auto*) wing

kotzen *vi* (*haben*) ☒ throw up

Krabbe *f* **-, -n** crab, shrimp

krabbeln *vi* (*sein*) crawl

Krach *m* **-[e]s,¨-e** din, racket; (*Knall*) crash; (! *Streit*) row; (! *Ruin*) crash. **k~en** *vi* (*haben*) crash; **es hat gekracht** there was a bang/(! *Unfall*) a crash ● (*sein*) break, crack; (*auftreffen*) crash (**gegen** into)

krächzen *vi* (*haben*) croak

Kraft *f* **-,¨-e** strength; (*Gewalt*) force; (*Arbeits-*) worker; **in/außer K~** in/no longer in force. **K~fahrer** *m* driver. **K~fahrzeug** *nt* motor vehicle. **K~fahrzeugbrief** *m* [vehicle] registration document

kräftig *a* strong; (*gut entwickelt*) sturdy; (*nahrhaft*) nutritious; (*heftig*) hard

kraft|los *a* weak. **K~probe** *f* trial of strength. **K~stoff** *m* (*Auto*) fuel. **K~wagen** *m* motor car. **K~werk** *nt* power station

Kragen *m* **-s,-** collar

Krähe *f* **-, -n** crow

krähen *vi* (*haben*) crow

Kralle *f* **-, -n** claw

Kram *m* **-s** ! things *pl*, ! stuff; (*Angelegenheiten*) business. **k~en** *vi* (*haben*) rummage about (**in** + *dat* in; **nach** for)

Krampf *m* **-[e]s,¨-e** cramp. **K~adern** *fpl* varicose veins. **k~haft** *a* convulsive; (*verbissen*) desperate

Kran *m* **-[e]s,¨-e** (*Techn*) crane

Kranich *m* **-s, -e** (*Zool*) crane

krank *a* sick; <*Knie, Herz*> bad; **k~ sein/werden** be/fall ill. **K~e(r)** *m/f* sick man/woman, invalid; **die K~en** the sick *pl*

kränken *vt* offend, hurt

Kranken|bett *nt* sick-bed. **K~geld** *nt* sickness benefit. **K~gymnast(in)** *m* **-en, -en** (*f* **-, -nen**) physiotherapist. **K~gymnastik** *f* physiotherapy. **K~haus** *nt* hospital. **K~kasse** *f* health insurance scheme/(*Amt*) office. **K~pflege** *f* nursing.

K

K~saal *m* [hospital] ward. **K~schein** *m* certificate of entitlement to medical treatment. **K~schwester** *f* nurse. **K~versicherung** *f* health insurance. **K~wagen** *m* ambulance

Krankheit *f* **-, -en** illness, disease

kränklich *a* sickly

krank|melden *vt sep* **jdn k~melden** report s.o. sick; **sich k~melden** report sick

Kranz *m* **-es,¨-e** wreath

Krapfen *m* **-s,-** doughnut

Krater *m* **-s,-** crater

kratzen *vt/i* (*haben*) scratch. **K~er** *m* **-s,-** scratch

Kraul *nt* **-s** (*Sport*) crawl. **k~en**[1] *vi* (*haben/sein*) (*Sport*) do the crawl

kraulen[2] *vt* tickle; **sich am Kopf k~** scratch one's head

kraus *a* wrinkled; <*Haar*> frizzy; (*verworren*) muddled. **K~e** *f* **-, -n** frill

kräuseln *vt* wrinkle; frizz <*Haar*>; gather <*Stoff*>; **sich k~** wrinkle; (*sich kringeln*) curl; <*Haar:*> go frizzy

Kraut *nt* **-[e]s, Kräuter** herb; (*SGer*) cabbage; (*Sauer-*) sauerkraut

Krawall *m* **-s, -e** riot; (*Lärm*) row

Krawatte *f* **-, -n** [neck]tie

krea|tiv /krea'ti:f/ *a* creative. **K~tur** *f* **-, -en** creature

Krebs *m* **-es, -e** crayfish; (*Med*) cancer; (*Astr*) Cancer

Kredit *m* **-s, -e** credit; (*Darlehen*) loan; **auf K~** on credit. **K~karte** *f* credit card

Kreid|e *f* **-** chalk. **k~ig** *a* chalky

kreieren /kre'i:rən/ *vt* create

Kreis *m* **-es, -e** circle; (*Admin*) district

kreischen *vt/i* (*haben*) screech; (*schreien*) shriek

Kreisel *m* **-s,-** [spinning] top

kreis|en *vi* (*haben*) circle; revolve (**um** around). **k~förmig** *a* circular. **K~lauf** *m* cycle; (*Med*) circulation. **K~säge** *f* circular saw. **K~verkehr** *m* [traffic] roundabout

Krem *f* **-, -s** & *m* **-s, -e** cream

Krematorium *nt* **-s, -ien** crematorium

Krempe *f* **-, -n** [hat] brim

krempeln *vt* turn (**nach oben** up)

Krepp *m* **-s, -s** & **-e** crêpe

Krepppapier *nt* crêpe paper

Kresse *f* **-, -n** cress; (*Kapuziner-*) nasturtium

Kreta *nt* **-s** Crete

Kreuz *nt* **-es, -e** cross; (*Kreuzung*) intersection; (*Mus*) sharp; (*Kartenspiel*) clubs *pl*; (*Anat*) small of the back; **über K~** crosswise; **das K~ schlagen** cross oneself. **k~en** *vt* cross; **sich k~en** cross; <*Straßen:*> intersect; <*Meinungen:*> clash ●*vi* (*haben/sein*) cruise. **K~fahrt** *f* (*Naut*) cruise. **K~gang** *m* cloister

kreuzig|en *vt* crucify. **K~ung** *f* **-, -en** crucifixion

Kreuz|otter *f* adder, common viper. **K~ung** *f* **-, -en** intersection; (*Straßen-*) crossroads *sg*. **K~verhör** *nt* cross-examination. **k~weise** *adv* crosswise. **K~worträtsel** *nt* crossword [puzzle]. **K~zug** *m* crusade

kribbel|ig *a* [!] edgy. **k~n** *vi* (*haben*) tingle; (*kitzeln*) tickle

kriech|en† *vi* (*sein*) crawl; (*fig*) grovel (**vor** + *dat* to). **K~spur** *f* (*Auto*) crawler lane. **K~tier** *nt* reptile

Krieg *m* **-[e]s, -e** war

kriegen *vt* [!] get; **ein Kind k~** have a baby

kriegs|beschädigt *a* war-disabled. **K~dienstverweigerer** *m* **-s,-** conscientious objector. **K~gefangene(r)** *m* prisoner of war. **K~gefangenschaft** *f* captivity. **K~gericht** *nt* court martial. **K~list** *f* stratagem.

K~rat *m* council of war. **K~recht** *nt* martial law

Krimi *m* **-s, -s** [!] crime story/film. **K~nalität** *f* **-** crime; (*Vorkommen*) crime rate. **K~nalpolizei** *f* criminal investigation department. **K~nalroman** *m* crime novel. **k~nell** *a* criminal

Krippe *f* **-, -n** manger; (*Weihnachts-*) crib; (*Kinder-*) crèche. **K~nspiel** *nt* Nativity play

Krise *f* **-, -n** crisis

Kristall *nt* **-s** crystal; (*geschliffen*) cut glass

Kritik *f* **-, -en** criticism; (*Rezension*) review; **unter aller K~** [!] abysmal

Kriti|ker *m* **-s,-** critic; (*Rezensent*) reviewer. **k~sch** *a* critical. **k~sieren** *vt* criticize; review

kritzeln *vt/i* (*haben*) scribble

Krokodil *nt* **-s, -e** crocodile

Krokus *m* **-, -[se]** crocus

Krone *f* **-, -n** crown; (*Baum-*) top

krönen *vt* crown

Kronleuchter *m* chandelier

Krönung *f* **-, -en** coronation; (*fig: Höhepunkt*) crowning event

Kropf *m* **-[e]s,⸚e** (*Zool*) crop; (*Med*) goitre

Kröte *f* **-, -n** toad

Krücke *f* **-, -n** crutch

Krug *m* **-[e]s,⸚e** jug; (*Bier-*) tankard

Krümel *m* **-s,-** crumb. **k~ig** *a* crumbly. **k~n** *vt* crumble ● *vi* (*haben*) be crumbly

krumm *a* crooked; (*gebogen*) curved; (*verbogen*) bent

krümmen *vt* bend; crook <*Finger*>; **sich k~** bend; (*sich winden*) writhe; (*vor Lachen*) double up

Krümmung *f* **-, -en** bend, curve

Krüppel *m* **-s,-** cripple

Kruste *f* **-, -n** crust; (*Schorf*) scab

Kruzifix *nt* **-es, -e** crucifix

Kub|a *nt* **-s** Cuba. **k~anisch** *a* Cuban

Kübel *m* **-s,-** tub; (*Eimer*) bucket; (*Techn*) skip

Küche *f* **-, -n** kitchen; (*Kochkunst*) cooking; **kalte/warme K~** cold/hot food

Kuchen *m* **-s,-** cake

Küchen|herd *m* cooker, stove. **K~maschine** *f* food processor, mixer. **K~schabe** *f* **-, -n** cockroach

Kuckuck *m* **-s, -e** cuckoo

Kufe *f* **-, -n** [sledge] runner

Kugel *f* **-, -n** ball; (*Geom*) sphere; (*Gewehr-*) bullet; (*Sport*) shot. **k~förmig** *a* spherical. **K~lager** *nt* ball-bearing. **k~n** *vt/i* (*haben*) roll; **sich k~n** (*vor Lachen*) fall about. **K~schreiber** *m* **-s,-**, ballpoint [pen]. **k~sicher** *a* bullet-proof. **K~stoßen** *nt* **-s** shot-putting

Kuh *f* **-,⸚e** cow

kühl *a* cool; (*kalt*) chilly. **K~box** *f* **-, -en** cool-box. **K~e** *f* **-** coolness; chilliness. **k~en** *vt* cool; refrigerate <*Lebensmittel*>; chill <*Wein*>. **K~er** *m* **-s,-**; (*Auto*) radiator. **K~erhaube** *f* bonnet. **K~fach** *nt* frozen-food compartment. **K~raum** *m* cold store. **K~schrank** *m* refrigerator. **K~truhe** *f* freezer. **K~wasser** *nt* [radiator] water

kühn *a* bold

Kuhstall *m* cowshed

Küken *nt* **-s,-** chick; (*Enten-*) duckling

Kulissen *fpl* (*Theat*) scenery *sg*; (*seitlich*) wings, **hinter den K~** (*fig*) behind the scenes

Kult *m* **-[e]s, -e** cult

kultivier|en *vt* cultivate. **k~t** *a* cultured

Kultur *f* **-, -en** culture. **K~beutel** *m* toiletbag. **k~ell** *a* cultural. **K~film** *m* documentary film

Kultusminister *m* Minister of Education and Arts

K

Kümmel *m* **-s** caraway; (*Getränk*) kümmel
Kummer *m* **-s** sorrow, grief; (*Sorge*) worry; (*Ärger*) trouble
kümmer|lich *a* puny; (*dürftig*) meagre; (*armselig*) wretched. **k~n** *vt* concern; **sich k~n um** look after; (*sich befassen*) concern oneself with; (*beachten*) take notice of
kummervoll *a* sorrowful
Kumpel *m* **-s,-** [!] mate
Kunde *m* **-n, -n** customer. **K~ndienst** *m* [after-sales] service
Kundgebung *f* **-, -en** (*Pol*) rally
kündig|en *vt* cancel <*Vertrag*>; give notice of withdrawal for <*Geld*>; give notice to quit <*Wohnung*>; **seine Stellung k~en** give [in one's] notice ● *vi* (*haben*) give [in one's] notice; **jdm k~en** give s.o. notice. **K~ung** *f* **-, -en** cancellation; notice [of withdrawal/dismissal/to quit]; (*Entlassung*) dismissal. **K~ungsfrist** *f* period of notice
Kund|in *f* **-, -nen** [woman] customer. **K~schaft** *f* **-** clientele, customers *pl*
künftig *a* future ● *adv* in future
Kunst *f* **-,¨e** art; (*Können*) skill. **K~faser** *f* synthetic fibre. **K~galerie** *f* art gallery. **K~geschichte** *f* history of art. **K~gewerbe** *nt* arts and crafts *pl*. **K~griff** *m* trick
Künstler *m* **-s,-** artist; (*Könner*) master. **K~in** *f* **-, -nen** [woman] artist. **k~isch** *a* artistic
künstlich *a* artificial
Kunst|stoff *m* plastic. **K~stück** *nt* trick; (*große Leistung*) feat. **k~voll** *a* artistic; (*geschickt*) skilful
kunterbunt *a* multicoloured; (*gemischt*) mixed
Kupfer *nt* **-s** copper
Kupon /ku'põ:/ *m* **-s, -s** voucher; (*Zins-*) coupon; (*Stoff-*) length
Kuppe *f* **-, -n** [rounded] top
Kuppel *f* **-, -n** dome
kupp|eln *vt* couple (**an** + *acc* to) ● *vi* (*haben*) (*Auto*) operate the clutch. **K~lung** *f* **-, -en** coupling; (*Auto*) clutch
Kur *f* **-, -en** course of treatment, cure
Kür *f* **-, -en** (*Sport*) free exercise; (*Eislauf*) free programme
Kurbel *f* **-, -n** crank. **K~welle** *f* crankshaft
Kürbis *m* **-ses, -se** pumpkin
Kurier *m* **-s, -e** courier
kurieren *vt* cure
kurios *a* curious, odd. **K~ität** *f* **-, -en** oddness; (*Objekt*) curiosity
Kurort *m* health resort; (*Badeort*) spa
Kurs *m* **-es, -e** course; (*Aktien-*) price. **K~buch** *nt* timetable
kursieren *vi* (*haben*) circulate
kursiv *a* italic ● *adv* in italics. **K~schrift** *f* italics *pl*
Kursus *m* **-,Kurse** course
Kurswagen *m* through carriage
Kurtaxe *f* visitors' tax
Kurve *f* **-, -n** curve; (*Straßen-*) bend
kurz *a* short; (*knapp*) brief; (*rasch*) quick; (*schroff*) curt; **k~e Hosen** shorts; **vor k~em** a short time ago; **seit k~em** lately; **den Kürzeren ziehen** get the worst of it; **k~ vor** shortly before; **sich k~ fassen** be brief; **k~ und gut** in short; **zu k~ kommen** get less than one's fair share. **k~ärmelig** *a* short-sleeved. **k~atmig** *a* **k~atmig sein** be short of breath
Kürze *f* **-** shortness; (*Knappheit*) brevity; **in K~** shortly. **k~n** *vt* shorten; (*verringern*) cut
kurzfristig *a* short-term ● *adv* at short notice
kürzlich *adv* recently

Kurz|meldung *f* newsflash. **K~schluss** *m* short circuit. **K~schrift** *f* shorthand. **k~sichtig** *a* short-sighted. **K~sichtigkeit** *f* - short-sightedness. **K~streckenrakete** *f* short-range missile
Kürzung *f* **-, -en** shortening; (*Verringerung*) cut (*gen* in)
Kurz|waren *fpl* haberdashery *sg*. **K~welle** *f* short wave
kuscheln (sich) *vr* snuggle (**an** + *acc* up to)
Kusine *f* **-, -n** [female] cousin
Kuss *m* **-es,¨e** kiss
küssen *vt/i* (*haben*) kiss; **sich k~** kiss
Küste *f* **-, -n** coast
Küster *m* **-s,-** verger
Kutsch|e *f* **-, -n** [horse-drawn] carriage/(*geschlossen*) coach. **K~er** *m* **-s,-** coachman, driver
Kutte *f* **-, -n** (*Relig*) habit
Kutter *m* **-s,-** (*Naut*) cutter
Kuvert /ku've:ɐ̯/ *nt* **-s, -s** envelope

Ll

Labor *nt* **-s, -s** & **-e** laboratory. **L~ant(in)** *m* **-en, -en** (*f* **-, -nen**) laboratory assistant
Labyrinth *nt* **-[e]s, -e** maze, labyrinth
Lache *f* **-, -n** puddle; (*Blut-*) pool
lächeln *vi* (*haben*) smile. **L~** *nt* **-s** smile. **l~d** *a* smiling
lachen *vi* (*haben*) laugh. **L~** *nt* **-s** laugh; (*Gelächter*) laughter
lächerlich *a* ridiculous; **sich l~ machen** make a fool of oneself. **L~keit** *f* **-, -en** ridiculousness; (*Kleinigkeit*) triviality
Lachs *m* **-es, -e** salmon
Lack *m* **-[e]s, -e** varnish; (*Japan-*) lacquer; (*Auto*) paint. **l~en** *vt* varnish. **l~ieren** *vt* varnish; (*spritzen*) spray. **L~schuhe** *mpl* patent-leather shoes
laden† *vt* load; (*Electr*) charge; (*Jur: vor-*) summon
Laden *m* **-s,¨** shop; (*Fenster-*) shutter. **L~dieb** *m* shop-lifter. **L~schluss** *m* [shop] closing-time. **L~tisch** *m* counter
Laderaum *m* (*Naut*) hold
lädieren *vt* damage
Ladung *f* **-, -en** load; (*Naut, Aviat*) cargo; (*elektrische*) charge
Lage *f* **-, -n** position, situation; (*Schicht*) layer; **nicht in der L~ sein** not be in a position (**zu** to)
Lager *nt* **-s,-** camp; (*L~haus*) warehouse; (*Vorrat*) stock; (*Techn*) bearing; (*Erz-, Ruhe-*) bed; (*eines Tieres*) lair; **[nicht] auf L~** [not] in stock. **L~haus** *nt* warehouse. **l~n** *vt* store; (*legen*) lay; **sich l~n** settle. **L~raum** *m* store-room. **L~ung** *f* **-** storage
Lagune *f* **-, -n** lagoon
lahm *a* lame. **l~en** *vi* (*haben*) be lame
lähmen *vt* paralyse
Lähmung *f* **-, -en** paralysis
Laib *m* **-[e]s, -e** loaf
Laich *m* **-[e]s** (*Zool*) spawn
Laie *m* **-n, -n** layman; (*Theat*) amateur. **l~nhaft** *a* amateurish
Laken *nt* **-s,-** sheet
Lakritze *f* **-** liquorice
lallen *vt/i* (*haben*) mumble; <*Baby:*> babble
Lametta *nt* **-s** tinsel
Lamm *nt* **-[e]s,¨er** lamb
Lampe *f* **-, -n** lamp; (*Decken-, Wand-*) light; (*Glüh-*) bulb. **L~nfieber** *nt* stage fright
Lampion /lam'pi̯ɔŋ/ *m* **-s, -s** Chinese lantern
Land *nt* **-[e]s,¨er** country; (*Fest-*) land; (*Bundes-*) state, Land;

(*Aust*) province; **auf dem L~e** in the country; **an L~ gehen** (*Naut*) go ashore. **L~arbeiter** *m* agricultural worker. **L~ebahn** *f* runway. **l~en** *vt/i* (*sein*) land; (! *gelangen*) end up
Ländereien *pl* estates
Länderspiel *nt* international
Landesverrat *m* treason
Landkarte *f* map
ländlich *a* rural
Land|schaft *f* **-, -en** scenery; (*Geog, Kunst*) landscape; (*Gegend*) country[side]. **l~schaftlich** *a* scenic; (*regional*) regional. **L~streicher** *m* **-s,-** tramp. **L~tag** *m* state/(*Aust*) provincial parliament
Landung *f* **-, -en** landing
Land|vermesser *m* **-s,-** surveyor. **L~weg** *m* country lane; **auf dem L~weg** overland. **L~wirt** *m* farmer. **L~wirtschaft** *f* agriculture; (*Hof*) farm. **l~wirtschaftlich** *a* agricultural
lang¹ *adv & prep* (+ *preceding acc or preceding* **an** + *dat*) along; **den** *od* **am Fluss l~** along the river
lang² *a* long; (*groß*) tall; **seit l~em** for a long time ● *adv* **eine Stunde l~** for an hour; **mein Leben l~** all my life. **l~ärmelig** *a* long-sleeved. **l~atmig** *a* long-winded. **l~e** *adv* a long time; <*schlafen*> late; **schon l~e** [for] a long time; (*zurückliegend*) a long time ago; **l~e nicht** not for a long time; (*bei weitem nicht*) nowhere near
Länge *f* **-, -n** length; (*Geog*) longitude; **der L~nach** lengthways
Läng|engrad *m* degree of longitude. **l~er** *a & adv* longer; (*längere Zeit*) [for] some time
Langeweile *f* **-** boredom; **L~ haben** be bored
lang|fristig *a* long-term; <*Vorhersage*> long-range. **l~jährig** *a* long-standing; <*Erfahrung*> long
länglich *a* oblong; **l~ rund** oval
längs *adv & prep* (+ *gen/dat*) along; (*der Länge nach*) lengthways
lang|sam *a* slow. **L~samkeit** *f* **-** slowness
längst *adv* **[schon] l~** for a long time; (*zurückliegend*) a long time ago; **l~ nicht** nowhere near
Lang|strecken- *pref* long-distance; (*Mil, Aviat*) long-range. **l~weilen** *vt* bore; **sich l~weilen** be bored. **l~weilig** *a* boring
Lanze *f* **-, -n** lance
Lappalie /la'pa:liə/ *f* **-, -n** trifle
Lappen *m* **-s,-** cloth; (*Anat*) lobe
Lärche *f* **-, -n** larch
Lärm *m* **-s** noise. **l~end** *a* noisy
Larve /'larfə/ *f* **-, -n** larva; (*Maske*) mask
lasch *a* listless; (*schlaff*) limp
Lasche *f* **-, -n** tab, flap
Laser /'le:-, 'la:zɐ/ *m* **-s,-** laser

lassen†
● *transitive verb*
····➤ (+ *inf; veranlassen*) **etw tun lassen** have *or* get sth done. **jdn etw tun lassen** make s.o. do sth.; get s.o. to do sth. **sich** *dat* **die Haare schneiden lassen** have *or* get one's hair cut. **jdn warten lassen** make *or* let s.o. wait; keep s.o. waiting. **jdn grüßen lassen** send one's regards to s.o. **jdn kommen/rufen lassen** send for s.o.
····➤ (+ *inf; erlauben*) let; allow; (*hineinlassen/herauslassen*) let *or* allow (**in** + *acc* into, **aus** + *dat* out of). **jdn etw tun lassen** let s.o. do sth; allow s.o. to do sth. **er ließ mich nicht ausreden** he didn't let me finish [what I was saying]
····➤ (*belassen, bleiben lassen*) leave. **jdn in Frieden lassen** leave s.o. in peace. **etw ungesagt lassen** leave sth unsaid

····➤ (*unterlassen*) stop. **das Rauchen lassen** stop smoking. **er kann es nicht lassen, sie zu quälen** he can't stop *or* he is forever tormenting her

····➤ (*überlassen*) **jdm etw lassen** let s.o. have sth

····➤ (*als Aufforderung*) **lass/lasst uns gehen/fahren!** let's go!

● *reflexive verb*

····➤ **das lässt sich machen** that can be done. **das lässt sich nicht beweisen** it can't be proved. **die Tür lässt sich leicht öffnen** the door opens easily

● *intransitive verb*

····➤ [!] **Lass mal. Ich mache das schon** Leave it. I'll do it

lässig *a* casual. **L~keit** *f* - casualness

Lasso *nt* **-s, -s** lasso

Last *f* **-, -en** load; (*Gewicht*) weight; (*fig*) burden; **L~en** charges; (*Steuern*) taxes. **L~auto** *nt* lorry. **l~en** *vi* (*haben*) weigh heavily/(*liegen*) rest (**auf** + *dat* on)

Laster[1] *m* **-s,-** [!] lorry

Laster[2] *nt* **-s,-** vice

läster|n *vt* blaspheme ● *vi* (*haben*) make disparaging remarks (**über** + *acc* about). **L~ung** *f* **-, -en** blasphemy

lästig *a* troublesome; **l~ sein/werden** be/become a nuisance

Last|kahn *m* barge. **L~[kraft]wagen** *m* lorry

Latein *nt* **-[s]** Latin. **L~amerika** *nt* Latin America. **l~isch** *a* Latin

Laterne *f* **-, -n** lantern; (*Straßen-*) street lamp. **L~npfahl** *m* lamp post

latschen *vi* (*sein*) [!] traipse

Latte *f* **-, -n** slat; (*Tor-, Hochsprung-*) bar

Latz *m* **-es,¨-e** bib

Lätzchen *nt* **-s,-** [baby's] bib

Latzhose *f* dungarees *pl*

Laub *nt* **-[e]s** leaves *pl*; (*L~werk*) foliage. **L~baum** *m* deciduous tree

Laube *f* **-, -n** summer-house

Laub|säge *f* fretsaw. **L~wald** *m* deciduous forest

Lauch *m* **-[e]s** leeks *pl*

Lauer *f* **auf der L~ liegen** lie in wait. **l~n** *vi* (*haben*) lurk; **l~n auf** (+ *acc*) lie in wait for

Lauf *m* **-[e]s, Läufe** run; (*Laufen*) running; (*Verlauf*) course; (*Wett-*) race; (*Sport: Durchgang*) heat; (*Gewehr-*) barrel; **im L~[e]** (+ *gen*) in the course of. **L~bahn** *f* career. **l~en**† *vi* (*sein*) run; (*zu Fuß gehen*) walk; (*gelten*) be valid; **Ski/Schlittschuh l~en** ski/skate. **l~end** *a* running; (*gegenwärtig*) current; (*regelmäßig*) regular; **auf dem L~enden sein** be up to date ● *adv* continually

Läufer *m* **-s,-** (*Person, Teppich*) runner; (*Schach*) bishop

Lauf|gitter *nt* play-pen. **L~masche** *f* ladder. **L~zettel** *m* circular

Lauge *f* **-, -n** soapy water

Laun|e *f* **-, -n** mood; (*Einfall*) whim; **guter L~e sein, gute L~e haben** be in a good mood. **l~isch** *a* moody

Laus *f* **-,Läuse** louse; (*Blatt-*) greenfly

lauschen *vi* (*haben*) listen

laut *a* loud; (*geräuschvoll*) noisy; **l~ lesen** read aloud; **l~er stellen** turn up ● *prep* (+ *gen/dat*) according to. **L~** *m* **-es, -e** sound

Laute *f* **-, -n** (*Mus*) lute

lauten *vi* (*haben*) <*Text:*> run, read

läuten *vt/i* (*haben*) ring

lauter *a* pure; (*ehrlich*) honest; <*Wahrheit*> plain ● *a inv* sheer; (*nichts als*) nothing but

laut|hals *adv* at the top of one's voice, <*lachen*> out loud. **l~los** *a*

L

silent, <*Stille*> hushed. **L~schrift** *f* phonetics *pl.* **L~sprecher** *m* loudspeaker. **L~stärke** *f* volume
lauwarm *a* lukewarm
Lava *f* **-, -ven** lava
Lavendel *m* **-s** lavender
lavieren *vi* (*haben*) manœuvre
Lawine *f* **-, -n** avalanche
Lazarett *nt* **-[e]s, -e** military hospital
leasen /ˈliːsən/ *vt* rent
Lebehoch *nt* cheer
leben *vt/i* (*haben*) live (**von** on); **leb wohl!** farewell! **L~** *nt* **-s,-** life, (*Treiben*) bustle; **am L~** alive. **l~d** *a* living
lebendig *a* live; (*lebhaft*) lively; (*anschaulich*) vivid; **l~ sein** be alive. **L~keit** *f* **-** liveliness; vividness
Lebens|abend *m* old age. **L~alter** *nt* age. **l~fähig** *a* viable. **L~gefahr** *f* mortal danger; **in L~gefahr** in mortal danger; <*Patient*> critically ill. **l~gefährlich** *a* extremely dangerous; <*Verletzung*> critical. **L~haltungskosten** *pl* cost of living *sg.* **l~länglich** *a* life ... ● *adv* for life. **L~lauf** *m* curriculum vitae. **L~mittel** *ntpl* food *sg.* **L~mittelgeschäft** *nt* food shop. **L~mittelhändler** *m* grocer. **L~retter** *m* rescuer; (*beim Schwimmen*) life-guard. **L~unterhalt** *m* livelihood; **seinen L~unterhalt verdienen** earn one's living. **L~versicherung** *f* life assurance. **L~wandel** *m* conduct. **l~wichtig** *a* vital. **L~zeit** *f* **auf L~zeit** for life
Leber *f* **-, -n** liver. **L~fleck** *m* mole
Lebe|wesen *nt* living being. **L~wohl** *nt* **-s, -s** & **-e** farewell
leb|haft *a* lively; <*Farbe*> vivid. **L~kuchen** *m* gingerbread. **l~los** *a* lifeless. **L~zeiten** *fpl* **zu jds L~zeiten** in s.o.'s lifetime
leck *a* leaking. **L~** *nt* **-s, -s** leak. **l~en**¹ *vi* (*haben*) leak
lecken² *vi* (*haben*) lick
lecker *a* tasty. **L~ bissen** *m* delicacy
Leder *nt* **-s,-** leather
ledig *a* single
leer *a* empty; (*unbesetzt*) vacant; **l~ laufen** (*Auto*) idle. **l~en** *vt* empty; **sich l~en** empty. **L~lauf** *m* (*Auto*) neutral. **L~ung** *f* **-, -en** (*Post*) collection
legal *a* legal. **l~isieren** *vt* legalize. **L~ität** *f* **-** legality
Legas|thenie *f* **-** dyslexia **L~theniker** *m* **-s,-** dyslexic
legen *vt* put; (*hin-, ver-*) lay; set <*Haare*>; **sich l~** lie down; (*nachlassen*) subside
Legende *f* **-, -n** legend
leger /leˈʒeːɐ/ *a* casual
Legierung *f* **-, -en** alloy
Legion *f* **-, -en** legion
Legislative *f* **-** legislature
legitim *a* legitimate. **L~ität** *f* **-** legitimacy
Lehm *m* **-s** clay
Lehn|e *f* **-, -n** (*Rücken-*) back; (*Arm-*) arm. **l~en** *vt* lean (**an** + *acc against*); **sich l~en** lean (**an** + *acc against*) ● *vi* (*haben*) be leaning (**an** + *acc against*)
Lehr|buch *nt* textbook. **L~e** *f* **-, -n** apprenticeship; (*Anschauung*) doctrine; (*Theorie*) theory; (*Wissenschaft*) science; (*Erfahrung*) lesson. **l~en** *vt/i* (*haben*) teach. **L~er** *m* **-s,-** teacher; (*Fahr-*) instructor. **L~erin** *f* **-, -nen** teacher. **L~erzimmer** *nt* staff-room. **L~fach** *nt* (*Sch*) subject. **L~gang** *m* course. **L~kraft** *f* teacher. **L~ling** *m* **-s, -e** apprentice; (*Auszubildender*) trainee. **L~plan** *m* syllabus. **l~reich** *a* instructive. **L~stelle** *f* apprenticeship. **L~stuhl** *m* (*Univ*) chair. **L~zeit** *f* apprenticeship

Leib *m* **-es, -er** body; (*Bauch*) belly. **L∼eserziehung** *f* (*Sch*) physical education. **L∼gericht** *nt* favourite dish. **l∼lich** *a* physical; (*blutsverwandt*) real, natural. **L∼wächter** *m* bodyguard

Leiche *f* **-, -n** [dead] body; corpse. **L∼nbestatter** *m* **-s,-** undertaker. **L∼nhalle** *f* mortuary. **L∼nwagen** *m* hearse. **L∼nzug** *m* funeral procession, cortège

Leichnam *m* **-s, -e** [dead] body

leicht *a* light; <*Stoff*> lightweight; (*gering*) slight; (*mühelos*) easy; **jdm l∼ fallen** be easy for s.o.; **etw l∼ machen** make sth easy **(dat** for); **es sich** (*dat*) **l∼ machen** take the easy way out; **etw l∼ nehmen** (*fig*) take sth lightly. **L∼athletik** *f* [track and field] athletics *sg*. **L∼gewicht** *nt* (*Boxen*) lightweight. **l∼gläubig** *a* gullible. **l∼hin** *adv* casually. **L∼igkeit** *f* - lightness; (*Mühelosigkeit*) ease; (*L∼sein*) easiness; **mit L∼igkeit** with ease. **L∼sinn** *m* carelessness; recklessness; (*Frivolität*) frivolity. **l∼sinnig** *a* careless; (*unvorsichtig*) reckless

Leid *nt* **-[e]s** sorrow, grief; (*Böses*) harm; **es tut mir L∼** I am sorry; **er tut mir L∼** I feel sorry for him. **l∼** *a* **jdn/etw l∼ sein/werden** be/get tired of s.o./sth

Leide|form *f* passive. **l∼n†** *vt/i* (*haben*) suffer **(an** + *dat* from); **jdn/etw nicht l∼n können** dislike s.o./sth. **L∼n** *nt* **-s,-** suffering; (*Med*) complaint, (*Krankheit*) disease. **l∼nd** *a* suffering. **L∼nschaft** *f* **-, -en** passion. **l∼nschaftlich** *a* passionate

leider *adv* unfortunately; **l∼er ja/nicht** I'm afraid so/not

Leier|kasten *m* barrel-organ. **l∼n** *vt/i* (*haben*) wind; (*herunter-*) drone out

Leih|e *f* **-, -n** loan. **l∼en†** *vt* lend; **sich** (*dat*) **etw l∼en** borrow sth. **L∼gabe** *f* loan. **L∼gebühr** *f* rental; lending charge. **L∼haus** *nt* pawnshop. **L∼wagen** *m* hire-car. **l∼weise** *adv* on loan

Leim *m* **-s** glue. **l∼en** *vt* glue

Leine *f* **-, -n** rope; (*Wäsche-*) line; (*Hunde-*) lead, leash

Lein|en *nt* **-s** linen. **L∼wand** *f* linen; (*Kunst*) canvas; (*Film*) screen

leise *a* quiet; <*Stimme, Berührung*> soft; (*schwach*) faint; (*leicht*) light; **l∼r stellen** turn down

Leiste *f* **-, -n** strip; (*Holz-*) batten; (*Anat*) groin

leist|en *vt* achieve, accomplish; **sich** (*dat*) **etw l∼en** treat oneself to sth; (⁈ *anstellen*) get up to sth; **ich kann es mir nicht l∼en** I can't afford it. **L∼ung** *f* **-, -en** achievement; (*Sport, Techn*) performance; (*Produktion*) output; (*Zahlung*) payment

Leit|artikel *m* leader, editorial. **l∼en** *vt* run, manage; (*an-/hinführen*) lead; (*Mus, Techn, Phys*) conduct; (*lenken, schicken*) direct. **l∼end** *a* leading; <*Posten*> executive

Leiter¹ *f* **-, -n** ladder

Leit|er² *m* **-s,-** director; (*Comm*) manager; (*Führer*) leader; (*Mus, Phys*) conductor. **L∼erin** *f* **-, -nen** director; manageress; leader. **L∼planke** *f* crash barrier. **L∼spruch** *m* motto. **L∼ung** *f* **-, -en** (*Führung*) direction; (*Comm*) management; (*Aufsicht*) control; (*Electr: Schnur*) lead, flex; (*Kabel*) cable; (*Telefon-*) line; (*Rohr-*) pipe; (*Haupt-*) main. **L∼ungswasser** *nt* tap water

Lektion /-ˈtsi̯o:n/ *f* **-, -en** lesson

Lekt|or *m* **-s, -en** /-ˈto:rən/, **L∼orin** *f* **-, -nen** (*Univ*) assistant lecturer; (*Verlags-*) editor. **L∼üre** *f* **-, -n** reading matter

Lende *f* **-, -n** loin

L

lenk|en *vt* guide; (*steuern*) steer; (*regeln*) control; **jds Aufmerksamkeit auf sich** (*acc*) **l~en** attract s.o.'s attention. **L~rad** *nt* steering-wheel. **L~stange** *f* handlebars *pl*. **L~ung** *f* **-** steering

Leopard *m* **-en, -en** leopard

Lepra *f* **-** leprosy

Lerche *f* **-, -n** lark

lernen *vt/i* (*haben*) learn; (*für die Schule*) study

Lesb|ierin /'lɛsbiərɪn/ *f* **-, -nen** lesbian. **l~isch** *a* lesbian

les|en† *vt/i* (*haben*) read; (*Univ*) lecture ● *vt* pick, gather. **L~en** *nt* **-s** reading. **L~er(in)** *m* **-s,-** (*f* **-, -nen**) reader. **l~erlich** *a* legible. **L~ezeichen** *nt* bookmark

lethargisch *a* lethargic

Lettland *nt* **-s** Latvia

letzt|e(r,s) *a* last; (*neueste*) latest; **in l~er Zeit** recently; **l~en Endes** in the end. **l~ens** *adv* recently; (*zuletzt*) lastly. **l~ere(r,s)** *a* the latter; **der/die/das L~ere** the latter

Leucht|e *f* **-, -n** light. **l~en** *vi* (*haben*) shine. **l~end** *a* shining. **L~er** *m* **-s,-** candlestick. **L~feuer** *nt* beacon. **L~rakete** *f* flare. **L~reklame** *f* neon sign. **L~röhre** *f* fluorescent tube. **L~turm** *m* lighthouse

leugnen *vt* deny

Leukämie *f* **-** leukaemia

Leumund *m* **-s** reputation

Leute *pl* people; (*Mil*) men; (*Arbeiter*) workers

Leutnant *m* **-s, -s** second lieutenant

Lexikon *nt* **-s, -ka** encyclopaedia; (*Wörterbuch*) dictionary

Libanon **(der) -s** Lebanon

Libelle *f* **-, -n** dragonfly

liberal *a* (*Pol*) Liberal

Libyen *nt* **-s** Libya

Licht *nt* **-[e]s, -er** light; (*Kerze*) candle; **L~ machen** turn on the light. **l~** *a* bright; (*Med*) lucid; (*spärlich*) sparse. **L~bild** *nt* [passport] photograph; (*Dia*) slide. **L~blick** *m* (*fig*) ray of hope. **l~en** *vt* thin out; **den Anker l~en** (*Naut*) weigh anchor; **sich l~en** become less dense; thin. **L~hupe** *f* headlight flasher; **die L~hupe betätigen** flash one's headlights. **L~maschine** *f* dynamo. **L~ung** *f* **-, -en** clearing

Lid *nt* **-[e]s, -er** [eye]lid. **L~schatten** *m* eye-shadow

lieb *a* dear; (*nett*) nice; (*artig*) good; **jdn l~ haben** be fond of s.o.; (*lieben*) love s.o.; **es wäre mir l~er** I should prefer it (**wenn** if)

Liebe *f* **-, -n** love. **l~n** *vt* love; (*mögen*) like; **sich l~n** love each other; (*körperlich*) make love. **l~nd** *a* loving. **l~nswert** *a* lovable. **l~nswürdig** *a* kind. **l~nswürdigerweise** *adv* very kindly

lieber *adv* rather; (*besser*) better; **l~ mögen** like better; **ich trinke l~ Tee** I prefer tea

Liebes|brief *m* love letter. **L~dienst** *m* favour. **L~kummer** *m* heartache. **L~paar** *nt* [pair of] lovers *pl*

lieb|evoll *a* loving, affectionate. **L~haber** *m* **-s,-** lover; (*Sammler*) collector. **L~haberei** *f* **-, -en** hobby. **L~kosung** *f* **-, -en** caress. **l~lich** *a* lovely; (*sanft*) gentle; (*süß*) sweet. **L~ling** *m* **-s, -e** darling; (*Bevorzugte*) favourite. **L~lings-** *pref* favourite. **l~los** *a* loveless; <*Eltern*> uncaring; (*unfreundlich*) unkind. **L~schaft** *f* **-, -en** [love] affair. **l~ste(r,s)** *a* dearest; (*bevorzugt*) favourite ● *adv* **am l~sten** best [of all]; **jdn/etw am l~sten mögen** like s.o./sth best [of all]. **L~ste(r)** *m/f* beloved; (*Schatz*) sweetheart

Lied *nt* **-[e]s, -er** song

liederlich *a* slovenly; (*unordentlich*) untidy. **L~keit** *f* **-** slovenliness; untidiness

Lieferant *m* **-en, -en** supplier

liefer|bar *a* (*Comm*) available. **l~n** *vt* supply; (*zustellen*) deliver; (*hervorbringen*) yield. **L~ung** *f* **-, -en** delivery; (*Sendung*) consignment

Liege *f* **-, -n** couch. **l~n**† *vi* (*haben*) lie; (*gelegen sein*) be situated; **l~n bleiben** remain lying [there]; (*im Bett*) stay in bed; <*Ding:*> be left; <*Schnee:*> settle; <*Arbeit:*> remain undone; (*zurückgelassen werden*) be left behind; **l~n lassen** leave; (*zurücklassen*) leave behind; (*nicht fortführen*) leave undone; **l~n an** (+ *dat*) (*fig*) be due to; (*abhängen*) depend on; **jdm [nicht] l~n** [not] suit s.o.; **mir liegt viel daran** it is very important to me. **L~stuhl** *m* deck-chair. **L~stütz** *m* **-es, -e** press-up, (*Amer*) push-up. **L~wagen** *m* couchette car

Lift *m* **-[e]s, -e & -s** lift

Liga *f* **-, -gen** league

Likör *m* **-s, -e** liqueur

lila *inv a* mauve; (*dunkel*) purple

Lilie /ˈliːli̯ə/ *f* **-, -n** lily

Liliputaner(in) *m* **-s,-** (*f* **-, -nen**) dwarf

Limo *f* **-, -[s]** [I], **L~nade** *f* **-, -n** fizzy drink; lemonade

Limousine /limuˈziːnə/ *f* **-, -n** saloon

lind *a* mild

Linde *f* **-, -n** lime tree

linder|n *vt* relieve, ease. **L~ung** *f* **-** relief

Lineal *nt* **-s, -e** ruler

Linie /-i̯ə/ *f* **-, -n** line; (*Zweig*) branch; (*Bus-*) route; **L~ 4** number 4 [bus/tram]; **in erster L~** primarily. **L~nflug** *m* scheduled flight. **L~nrichter** *m* linesman

lin[i]iert *a* lined, ruled

Link|e *f* **-n, -n** left side; (*Hand*) left hand; (*Boxen*) left; **die L~e** (*Pol*) the left. **l~e(r,s)** *a* left; (*Pol*) leftwing; **l~e Masche** purl

links *adv* on the left; (*bei Stoff*) on the wrong side; (*verkehrt*) inside out; **l~ stricken** purl. **L~händer(in)** *m* **-s,-** (*f* **-, -nen**) lefthander. **l~händig** *a & adv* lefthanded

Linoleum /-leʊm/ *nt* **-s** lino, linoleum

Linse *f* **-, -n** lens; (*Bot*) lentil

Lippe *f* **-, -n** lip. **L~nstift** *m* lipstick

Liquid|ation /-ˈt͡si̯oːn/ *f* **-, -en** liquidation. **l~ieren** *vt* liquidate

lispeln *vt/i* (*haben*) lisp

List *f* **-, -en** trick, ruse

Liste *f* **-, -n** list

listig *a* cunning, crafty

Litanei *f* **-, -en** litany

Litauen *nt* **-s** Lithuania

Liter *m & nt* **-s,-** litre

Literatur *f* **-** literature

Liturgie *f* **-, -n** liturgy

Litze *f* **-, -n** braid

Lizenz *f* **-, -en** licence

Lob *nt* **-[e]s** praise

Lobby /ˈlɔbi/ *f* **-** (*Pol*) lobby

loben *vt* praise

löblich *a* praiseworthy

Lobrede *f* eulogy

Loch *nt* **-[e]s,¨er** hole. **l~en** *vt* punch a hole/holes in; punch <*Fahrkarte*>. **L~er** *m* **-s,-** punch

löcherig *a* full of holes

Locke *f* **-, -n** curl. **l~n**[1] *vt* curl; **sich l~n** curl

locken[2] *vt* lure, entice; (*reizen*) tempt. **l~d** *a* tempting

Lockenwickler *m* **-s,-** curler; (*Rolle*) roller

locker *a* loose; <*Seil*> slack; <*Erde*> light; (*zwanglos*) casual; (*zu frei*) lax. **l~n** *vt* loosen; slacken <*Seil*>; break up <*Boden*>; relax <*Griff*>; **sich l~n** become loose; <*Seil:*> slacken; (*sich entspannen*) relax

lockig *a* curly

Lockmittel *nt* bait

Loden *m* **-s** (*Tex*) loden

L

Löffel *m* **-s,-** spoon; (*L~ voll*) spoonful. **l~n** *vt* spoon up
Logarithmus *m* **-, -men** logarithm
Logbuch *nt* (*Naut*) log-book
Loge /'lo:ʒə/ *f* **-, -n** lodge; (*Theat*) box
Log|ik *f* **-** logic. **l~isch** *a* logical
Logo *nt* **-s, -s** logo
Lohn *m* **-[e]s,¨e** wages *pl*, pay; (*fig*) reward. **L~empfänger** *m* wage-earner. **l~en** *vi|r* (*haben*) **[sich] l~en** be worth it *or* worth while ● *vt* be worth. **l~end** *a* worthwhile; (*befriedigend*) rewarding. **L~erhöhung** *f* [pay] rise. **L~steuer** *f* income tax
Lok *f* **-, -s** [!] = **Lokomotive**
Lokal *nt* **-s, -e** restaurant; (*Trink-*) bar
Lokomotiv|e *f* **-, -n** engine, locomotive. **L~führer** *m* engine driver
London *nt* **-s** London. **L~er** *a* London ... ● *m* **-s,-** Londoner
Lorbeer *m* **-s, -en** laurel. **L~blatt** *nt* (*Culin*) bay-leaf
Lore *f* **-, -n** (*Rail*) truck
Los *nt* **-es, -e** lot; (*Lotterie-*) ticket; (*Schicksal*) fate
los *pred a* **los sein** be loose; **jdn/etw los sein** be rid of s.o./sth; **was ist [mit ihm] los?** what's the matter [with him]? ● *adv* **los!** go on! **Achtung, fertig, los!** ready, steady, go!
lösbar *a* soluble
losbinden† *vt sep* untie
Lösch|blatt *nt* sheet of blotting-paper. **l~en** *vt* put out, extinguish; quench *<Durst>*; blot *<Tinte>*; (*tilgen*) cancel; (*streichen*) delete
Löschfahrzeug *nt* fire-engine
lose *a* loose
Lösegeld *nt* ransom
losen *vt* (*haben*) draw lots (**um** for)
lösen *vt* undo; (*lockern*) loosen; (*entfernen*) detach; (*klären*) solve; (*auflösen*) dissolve; cancel *<Vertrag>*; break off *<Beziehung>*; (*kaufen*) buy; **sich l~** come off; (*sich trennen*) detach oneself/itself; (*lose werden*) come undone; (*sich klären*) resolve itself; (*sich auflösen*) dissolve
los|fahren† *vi sep* (*sein*) start; *<Auto:>* drive off; **l~fahren auf** (+ *acc*) head for. **l~gehen**† *vi sep* (*sein*) set off; ([!] *anfangen*) start; *<Bombe:>* go off; **l~gehen auf** (+ *acc*) head for; (*fig: angreifen*) go for. **l~kommen**† *vi sep* (*sein*) get away (**von** from). **l~lassen**† *vt sep* let go of; (*freilassen*) release
löslich *a* soluble
los|lösen *vt sep* detach; **sich l~lösen** become detached; (*fig*) break away (**von** from). **l~machen** *vt sep* detach; untie. **l~reißen**† *vt sep* tear off; **sich l~reißen** break free; (*fig*) tear oneself away. **l~schicken** *vt sep* send off. **l~sprechen**† *vt sep* absolve (**von** from)
Losung *f* **-, -en** (*Pol*) slogan; (*Mil*) password
Lösung *f* **-, -en** solution. **L~smittel** *nt* solvent
loswerden† *vt sep* get rid of
Lot *nt* **-[e]s, -e** perpendicular; (*Blei-*) plumb[-bob]. **l~en** *vt* plumb
löt|en *vt* solder. **L~lampe** *f* blow-lamp
lotrecht *a* perpendicular
Lotse *m* **-n, -n** (*Naut*) pilot. **l~n** *vt* (*Naut*) pilot; (*fig*) guide
Lotterie *f* **-, -n** lottery
Lotto *nt* **-s, -s** lotto; (*Lotterie*) lottery
Löw|e *m* **-n, -n** lion; (*Astr*) Leo. **L~enzahn** *m* (*Bot*) dandelion. **L~in** *f* **-, -nen** lioness
loyal /loa'ja:l/ *a* loyal. **L~ität** *f* **-** loyalty
Luchs *m* **-es, -e** lynx

Lücke *f* **-, -n** gap. **l∼nhaft** *a* incomplete; <*Wissen*> patchy. **l∼nlos** *a* complete; <*Folge*> unbroken

Luder *nt* **-s,-** ⊠ (*Frau*) bitch

Luft *f* **-,¨e** air; **tief L∼ holen** take a deep breath; **in die L∼ gehen** explode. **L∼angriff** *m* air raid. **L∼aufnahme** *f* aerial photograph. **L∼ballon** *m* balloon. **L∼blase** *f* air bubble. **L∼druck** *m* atmospheric pressure

lüften *vt* air; raise <*Hut*>; reveal <*Geheimnis*>

Luft|fahrt *f* aviation. **L∼fahrtgesellschaft** *f* airline. **L∼gewehr** *nt* airgun. **l∼ig** *a* airy; <*Kleid*> light. **L∼kissenfahrzeug** *nt* hovercraft. **L∼krieg** *m* aerial warfare. **l∼leer** *a* **l∼leerer Raum** vacuum. **L∼linie** *f* **100 km L∼linie** 100 km as the crow flies. **L∼matratze** *f* air-bed, inflatable mattress. **L∼pirat** *m* hijacker. **L∼post** *f* airmail. **L∼röhre** *f* windpipe. **L∼schiff** *nt* airship. **L∼schlange** *f* [paper] streamer. **L∼schutzbunker** *m* air-raid shelter

Lüftung *f* **-** ventilation

Luft|veränderung *f* change of air. **L∼waffe** *f* air force. **L∼zug** *m* draught

Lüg|e *f* **-, -n** lie. **l∼en**† *vt/i* (*haben*) lie. **L∼ner(in)** *m* **-s,-** (*f* **-, -nen**) liar. **l∼nerisch** *a* untrue; <*Person*> untruthful

Luke *f* **-, -n** hatch; (*Dach-*) skylight

Lümmel *m* **-s,-** lout

Lump *m* **-en, -en** scoundrel. **L∼en** *m* **-s,-** rag; **in L∼en** in rags. **L∼enpack** *nt* riff-raff. **L∼ensammler** *m* rag-and-bone man. **l∼ig** *a* mean, shabby

Lunge *f* **-, -n** lungs *pl*; (*L∼nflügel*) lung. **L∼nentzündung** *f* pneumonia

Lupe *f* **-, -n** magnifying glass

Lurch *m* **-[e]s, -e** amphibian

Lust *f* **-,¨e** pleasure; (*Verlangen*) desire; (*sinnliche Begierde*) lust; **L∼ haben** feel like (**auf etw** *acc* sth); **ich habe keine L∼** I don't feel like it; (*will nicht*) I don't want to

lustig *a* jolly; (*komisch*) funny; **sich l∼ machen über** (+ *acc*) make fun of

Lüstling *m* **-s, -e** lecher

lust|los *a* listless. **L∼mörder** *m* sex killer. **L∼spiel** *nt* comedy

lutsch|en *vt/i* (*haben*) suck. **L∼er** *m* **-s,-** lollipop

Lüttich *nt* **-s** Liège

Luv *f & nt* **- nach Luv** (*Naut*) to windward

luxuriös *a* luxurious

Luxus *m* **-** luxury

Lymph|drüse /ˈlʏmf-/ *f*, **L∼knoten** *m* lymph gland

lynchen /ˈlʏnçən/ *vt* lynch

Lyr|ik *f* **-** lyric poetry. **L∼iker** *m* **-s,-** lyric poet. **l∼isch** *a* lyrical

Mm

Machart *f* style

machen

● *transitive verb*

····➤(*herstellen, zubereiten*) make <*money, beds, music, exception, etc*>. **aus Plastik/Holz gemacht** made of plastic/wood. **sich** (*dat*) **etw machen lassen** have sth made. **etw aus jdm machen** make s.o. into sth. **jdn zum Präsidenten machen** make s.o. president. **er machte sich** (*dat*) **viele Freunde/Feinde** he made a lot of friends/enemies. **jdm/sich** (*dat*) **[einen]**

Kaffee machen make [some] coffee for s.o./oneself. **ein Foto machen** take a photo

····➤(*verursachen*) make, cause <*difficulties*>; cause <*pain, anxiety*>. **jdm Arbeit machen** make [extra] work for s.o., cause s.o. extra work. **jdm Mut/Hoffnung machen** give s.o. courage/hope. **das macht Hunger/Durst** this makes you hungry/thirsty. **das macht das Wetter** that's [because of] the weather

····➤(*ausführen, ordnen*) do <*job, repair* ⊡: *room, washing, etc.*>.; take <*walk, trip, exam, course*>. **sie machte mir die Haare** ⊡ she did my hair for me. **einen Besuch [bei jdm] machen** pay [s.o.] a visit

····➤(*tun*) do <*nothing, everything*>. **was machst du [da]?** what are you doing? **so etwas macht man nicht** that [just] isn't done

····➤**was macht ...?** (*wie ist es um ... bestellt?*) how is ...? **was macht die Gesundheit/Arbeit?** how are you keeping/how is the job [getting on]?

····➤(*Math: ergeben*) be. **zwei mal zwei macht vier** two times two is four. **das macht 6 Euro [zusammen]** that's *or* that comes to six euros [altogether]

····➤(*schaden*) **was macht das schon?** what does it matter? **[das] macht nichts!** ⊡ it doesn't matter

····➤**machs gut!** ⊡ look after yourself!; (*auf Wiedersehen*) so long!

● *reflexive verb*

····➤**sich machen** ⊡ do well

····➤**sich an etw** (*acc*) **machen** get down to sth. **sie machte sich an die Arbeit** she got down to work

● *intransitive verb*

····➤**das macht hungrig/durstig** it makes you hungry/thirsty. **das macht dick** it's fattening

Macht *f* **-,⸚e** power. **M∼haber** *m* **-s,-** ruler

mächtig *a* powerful ●*adv* ⊡ terribly

machtlos *a* powerless

Mädchen *nt* **-s,-** girl; (*Dienst-*) maid. **m∼haft** *a* girlish. **M∼name** *m* girl's name; (*vor der Ehe*) maiden name

Made *f* **-, -n** maggot

madig *a* maggoty

Madonna *f* **-, -nen** madonna

Magazin *nt* **-s, -e** magazine; (*Lager*) warehouse; store-room

Magd *f* **-,⸚e** maid

Magen *m* **-s,⸚** stomach. **M∼verstimmung** *f* stomach upset

mager *a* thin; <*Fleisch*> lean; <*Boden*> poor; (*dürftig*) meagre. **M∼keit** *f* **-** thinness; leanness. **M∼sucht** *f* anorexia

Magie *f* **-** magic

Mag|ier /'ma:giɐ/ *m* **-s,-** magician. **m∼isch** *a* magic

Magistrat *m* **-s, -e** city council

Magnet *m* **-en & -[e]s, -e** magnet. **m∼isch** *a* magnetic

Mahagoni *nt* **-s** mahogany

Mäh|drescher *m* **-s,-** combine harvester. **m∼en** *vt/i* (*haben*) mow

Mahl *nt* **-[e]s,⸚er** *&* **-e** meal

mahlen† *vt* grind

Mahlzeit *f* meal; **M∼!** enjoy your meal!

Mähne *f* **-, -n** mane

mahn|en *vt/i* (*haben*) remind (**wegen** about); (*ermahnen*) admonish; (*auffordern*) urge (**zu** to). **M∼ung** *f* **-, -en** reminder; admonition

Mai *m* **-[e]s, -e** May; **der Erste Mai** May Day. **M∼glöckchen** *nt* **-s,-** lily of the valley

Mailand *nt* **-s** Milan

Mais *m* **-es** maize; (*Culin*) sweet corn
Majestät *f* **-, -en** majesty. **m~isch** *a* majestic
Major *m* **-s, -e** major
Majoran *m* **-s** marjoram
makaber *a* macabre
Makel *m* **-s,-** blemish; (*Defekt*) flaw
Makkaroni *pl* macaroni *sg*
Makler *m* **-s,-** (*Comm*) broker
Makrele *f* **-, -n** mackerel
Makrone *f* **-, -n** macaroon
mal *adv* (*Math*) times; (*bei Maßen*) by; ([!] *einmal*) once; (*eines Tages*) one day; **nicht mal** not even
Mal *nt* **-[e]s, -e** time; **zum ersten/letzten Mal** for the first/last time; **ein für alle Mal** once and for all; **jedes Mal** every time; **jedes Mal, wenn** whenever
Mal|buch *nt* colouring book. **m~en** *vt/i* (*haben*) paint. **M~er** *m* **-s,-** painter. **M~erei** *f* **-, -en** painting. **M~erin** *f* **-, -nen** painter. **m~erisch** *a* picturesque
Mallorca /ma'lɔrka, -'jɔrka/ *nt* **-s** Majorca
malnehmen† *vt sep* multiply (**mit** by)
Malz *nt* **-es** malt
Mama /'mama, ma'ma:/ *f* **-s, -s** mummy
Mammut *nt* **-s, -e** & **-s** mammoth
mampfen *vt* [!] munch
man *pron* one, you; (*die Leute*) people, they; **man sagt** they say, it is said
manch|e(r,s) *pron* many a; **[so] m~es Mal** many a time; **m~e Leute** some people ● (*substantivisch*) **m~er/m~e** many a man/woman; **m~e** *pl* some; (*Leute*) some people; (*viele*) many [people]; **m~es** some things; (*vieles*) many things. **m~erlei** *inv a* various ● *pron* various things
manchmal *adv* sometimes
Mandant(in) *m* **-en, -en** (*f* **-, -nen**) (*Jur*) client
Mandarine *f* **-, -n** mandarin
Mandat *nt* **-[e]s, -e** mandate; (*Jur*) brief; (*Pol*) seat
Mandel *f* **-, -n** almond; (*Anat*) tonsil. **M~entzündung** *f* tonsillitis
Manege /ma'ne:ʒə/ *f* **-, -n** ring; (*Reit-*) arena
Mangel[1] *m* **-s,¨** lack; (*Knappheit*) shortage; (*Med*) deficiency; (*Fehler*) defect
Mangel[2] *f* **-, -n** mangle
mangel|haft *a* faulty, defective; (*Sch*) unsatisfactory. **m~n**[1] *vi* (*haben*) **es m~t an** (+ *dat*) there is a lack/(*Knappheit*) shortage of
mangeln[2] *vt* put through the mangle
Manie *f* **-, -n** mania
Manier *f* **-, -en** manner; **M~en** manners. **m~lich** *a* well-mannered ● *adv* properly
Manifest *nt* **-[e]s, -e** manifesto
Maniküre *f* **-, -n** manicure; (*Person*) manicurist. **m~n** *vt* manicure
Manko *nt* **-s, -s** disadvantage; (*Fehlbetrag*) deficit
Mann *m* **-[e]s,¨er** man; (*Ehe-*) husband
Männchen *nt* **-s,-** little man; (*Zool*) male
Mannequin /'manəkɛ̃/ *nt* **-s, -s** model
männlich *a* male; (*Gram & fig*) masculine; (*mannhaft*) manly; <*Frau*> mannish. **M~keit** *f* **-** masculinity, (*fig*) manhood
Mannschaft *f* **-, -en** team; (*Naut*) crew
Manöv|er *nt* **-s,-** manœuvre; (*Winkelzug*) trick. **m~rieren** *vt/i* (*haben*) manœuvre
Mansarde *f* **-, -n** attic room; (*Wohnung*) attic flat
Manschette *f* **-, -n** cuff. **M~nknopf** *m* cuff-link

M

Mantel *m* **-s,¨** coat; overcoat
Manuskript *nt* **-[e]s, -e** manuscript
Mappe *f* **-, -n** folder; (*Akten-*) briefcase; (*Schul-*) bag
Märchen *nt* **-s,-** fairy-tales
Margarine *f* **-** margarine
Marienkäfer /ma'ri:ən-/ *m* lady-bird
Marihuana *nt* **-s** marijuana
Marine *f* marine; (*Kriegs-*) navy. **m~blau** *a* navy [blue]
marinieren *vt* marinade
Marionette *f* **-, -n** puppet, marionette
Mark¹ *f* **-,-** (*alte Währung*) mark; **drei M~** three marks
Mark² *nt* **-[e]s** (*Knochen-*) marrow (*Bot*)pith; (*Frucht-*) pulp
markant *a* striking
Marke *f* **-, -n** token; (*rund*) disc; (*Erkennungs-*) tag; (*Brief-*) stamp; (*Lebensmittel-*) coupon; (*Spiel-*) counter; (*Markierung*) mark; (*Fabrikat*) make; (*Tabak-*) brand. **M~nartikel** *m* branded article
markieren *vt* mark; (⁝ *vortäuschen*) fake
Markise *f* **-, -n** awning
Markstück *nt* one-mark piece
Markt *m* **-[e]s,¨e** market; (*M~platz*) market-place. **M~forschung** *f* market research
Marmelade *f* **-, -n** jam; (*Orangen-*) marmalade
Marmor *m* **-s** marble
Marokko *nt* **-s** Morocco
Marone *f* **-, -n** [sweet] chestnut
Marsch *m* **-[e]s,¨e** march. **m~** *int* (*Mil*) march!
Marschall *m* **-s,¨e** marshal
marschieren *vi* (*sein*) march
Marter *f* **-, -n** torture. **m~n** *vt* torture
Märtyrer(in) *m* **-s,-** (*f* **-, -nen**) martyr
Marxismus *m* **-** Marxism
März *m* **-, -e** March
Marzipan *nt* **-s** marzipan
Masche *f* **-, -n** stitch; (*im Netz*) mesh; (⁝ *Trick*) dodge. **M~ndraht** *m* wire netting
Maschin|e *f* **-, -n** machine; (*Flugzeug*) plane; (*Schreib-*) typewriter; **M~e schreiben** type. **m~egeschrieben** *a* typewritten, typed. **m~ell** *a* machine ... ● *adv* by machine. **M~enbau** *m* mechanical engineering. **M~engewehr** *nt* machine-gun. **M~ist** *m* **-en, -en** machinist; (*Naut*) engineer
Masern *pl* measles *sg*
Maserung *f* **-, -en** [wood] grain
Maske *f* **-, -n** mask; (*Theat*) make-up
maskieren *vt* mask; **sich m~** dress up (**als** as)
maskulin *a* masculine
Masochist *m* **-en, -en** masochist
Maß¹ *nt* **-es, -e** measure; (*Abmessung*) measurement; (*Grad*) degree; (*Mäßigung*) moderation; **in hohem Maße** to a high degree
Maß² *f* **-,-** (*SGer*) litre [of beer]
Massage /ma'sa:ʒə/ *f* **-, -n** massage
Massaker *nt* **-s,-** massacre
Maßband *nt* (*pl* **-bänder**) tape-measure
Masse *f* **-, -n** mass; (*Culin*) mixture; (*Menschen-*) crowd; **eine M~ Arbeit** ⁝ masses of work. **m~nhaft** *adv* in huge quantities. **M~nproduktion** *f* mass production. **m~nweise** *adv* in huge numbers
Masseu|r /ma'sø:ɐ/ *m* **-s, -e** masseur. **M~se** /-'sø:zə/ *f* **-, -n** masseuse
maß|gebend *a* authoritative; (*einflussreich*) influential. **m~geblich** *a* decisive. **m~geschneidert** *a* made-to-measure
massieren *vt* massage
massig *a* massive

mäßig *a* moderate; (*mittelmäßig*) indifferent. **m~en** *vt* moderate; **sich m~en** moderate; (*sich beherrschen*) restrain oneself. **M~ung** *f* - moderation

massiv *a* solid; (*stark*) heavy

Maß|krug *m* beer mug. **m~los** *a* excessive; (*grenzenlos*) boundless; (*äußerst*) extreme. **M~nahme** *f* -, -n measure

Maßstab *m* scale; (*Norm & fig*) standard. **m~sgerecht, m~sgetreu** *a* scale ... ● *adv* to scale

Mast[1] *m* -[e]s, -en pole; (*Überland-*) pylon; (*Naut*) mast

Mast[2] *f* - fattening

mästen *vt* fatten

masturbieren *vi* (*haben*) masturbate

Material *nt* -s, -ien /-iən/ material; (*coll*) materials *pl*. **M~ismus** *m* - materialism. **m~istisch** *a* materialistic

Mathe *f* - [!] maths *sg*

Mathe|matik *f* - mathematics *sg*. **M~matiker** *m* -s,- mathematician. **m~matisch** *a* mathematical

Matinee *f* -, -n (*Theat*) morning performance

Matratze *f* -, -n mattress

Matrose *m* -n, -n sailor

Matsch *m* -[e]s mud; (*Schnee-*) slush

matt *a* weak; (*gedämpft*) dim; (*glanzlos*) dull; <*Politur, Farbe*> matt. **M~** *nt* -s (*Schach*) mate

Matte *f* -, -n mat

Mattglas *nt* frosted glass

Matura *f* - (*Aust*) ≈ A levels *pl*

Mauer *f* -, -n wall. **M~werk** *nt* masonry

Maul *nt* -[e]s, **Mäuler** (*Zool*) mouth; **halts M~!** [!] shut up! **M~- und Klauenseuche** *f* foot-and-mouth disease. **M~korb** *m* muzzle. **M~tier** *nt* mule. **M~wurf** *m* mole

Maurer *m* -s,- bricklayer

Maus *f* -,**Mäuse** mouse

Maut *f* -, -en (*Aust*) toll. **M~straße** *f* toll road

maximal *a* maximum

Maximum *nt* -s, -ma maximum

Mayonnaise /majɔ'nɛ:zə/ *f* -, -n mayonnaise

Mechan|ik /me'ça:nɪk/ *f* - mechanics *sg*; (*Mechanismus*) mechanism. **M~iker** *m* -s,- mechanic. **m~isch** *a* mechanical. **m~isieren** *vt* mechanize. **M~ismus** *m* -, -men mechanism

meckern *vi* (*haben*) bleat; ([!] *nörgeln*) grumble

Medaill|e /me'daljə/ *f* -, -n medal. **M~on** /-'jõ:/ *nt* -s, -s medallion; (*Schmuck*) locket

Medikament *nt* -[e]s, -e medicine

Medit|ation /-'tsio:n/ *f* -, -en meditation. **m~ieren** *vi* (*haben*) meditate

Medium *nt* -s, -ien medium; **die Medien** the media

Medizin *f* -, -en medicine. **M~er** *m* -s,- doctor; (*Student*) medical student. **m~isch** *a* medical; (*heilkräftig*) medicinal

Meer *nt* -[e]s, -e sea. **M~enge** *f* strait. **M~esspiegel** *m* sea-level. **M~jungfrau** *f* mermaid. **M~rettich** *m* horseradish. **M~schweinchen** *nt* -s,- guinea-pig

Mehl *nt* -[e]s flour. **M~schwitze** *f* (*Culin*) roux

mehr *pron & adv* more; **nicht m~** no more; (*zeitlich*) no longer; **nichts m~** no more; (*nichtsweiter*) nothing else; **nie m~** never again. **m~eres** *pron* several things *pl*. **m~fach** *a* multiple; (*mehrmalig*) repeated ● *adv* several times. **M~fahrtenkarte** *f* book of tickets. **M~heit** *f* -, -en majority. **m~malig** *a* repeated. **m~mals** *adv* several times. **m~sprachig** *a* multilingual. **M~wertsteuer** *f* value-added tax, VAT. **M~zahl** *f*

M

majority; (*Gram*) plural. **M~zweck-** *pref* multi-purpose

meiden† *vt* avoid, shun

Meile *f* **-, -n** mile. **m~nweit** *adv* [for] miles

mein *poss pron* my. **m~e(r,s)** *poss pron* mine; **die M~en** *od* **m~en** *pl* my family *sg*

Meineid *m* perjury

meinen *vt* mean; (*glauben*) think; (*sagen*) say

mein|erseits *adv* for my part. **m~etwegen** *adv* for my sake; (*wegen mir*) because of me; (! *von mir aus*) as far as I'm concerned

Meinung *f* **-, -en** opinion; **jdm die M~ sagen** give s.o. a piece of one's mind. **M~sumfrage** *f* opinion poll

Meise *f* **-, -n** (*Zool*) tit

Meißel *m* **-s,-** chisel. **m~n** *vt/i* (*haben*) chisel

meist *adv* mostly; (*gewöhnlich*) usually. **m~e** *a* **der/die/das m~e** most; **die m~en Leute** most people; **am m~en** [the] most ● *pron* **das m~e** most [of it]; **die m~en** most. **m~ens** *adv* mostly; (*gewöhnlich*) usually

Meister *m* **-s,-** master craftsman; (*Könner*) master; (*Sport*) champion. **m~n** *vt* master. **M~schaft** *f* **-, -en** mastery; (*Sport*) championship

meld|en *vt* report; (*anmelden*) register; (*ankündigen*) announce; **sich m~en** report (**bei** to); (*zum Militär*) enlist; (*freiwillig*) volunteer; (*Teleph*) answer; (*Sch*) put up one's hand; (*von sich hören lassen*) get in touch (**bei** with). **M~ung** *f* **-, -en** report; (*Anmeldung*) registration

melken† *vt* milk

Melodie *f* **-, -n** tune, melody

melodisch *a* melodic; melodious

Melone *f* **-, -n** melon

Memoiren /me'moa:rən/ *pl* memoirs

Menge *f* **-, -n** amount, quantity; (*Menschen-*) crowd; (*Math*) set; **eine M~ Geld** a lot of money. **m~n** *vt* mix

Mensa *f* **-, -sen** (*Univ*) refectory

Mensch *m* **-en, -en** human being; **der M~** man; **die M~en** people; **jeder/kein M~** everybody/nobody. **M~enaffe** *m* ape. **m~enfeindlich** *a* antisocial. **M~enfresser** *m* **-s,-** cannibal; (*Zool*) man-eater. **m~enfreundlich** *a* philanthropic. **M~enleben** *nt* human life; (*Lebenszeit*) lifetime. **m~enleer** *a* deserted. **M~enmenge** *f* crowd. **M~enraub** *m* kidnapping. **M~enrechte** *ntpl* human rights. **m~enscheu** *a* unsociable. **m~enwürdig** *a* humane. **M~heit** *f* **- die M~heit** mankind, humanity. **m~lich** *a* human; (*human*) humane. **M~lichkeit** *f* **-** humanity

Menstru|ation /-'tsio:n/ *f* **-** menstruation. **m~ieren** *vi* (*haben*) menstruate

Mentalität *f* **-, -en** mentality

Menü *nt* **-s, -s** menu; (*festes M~*) set meal

Meridian *m* **-s, -e** meridian

merk|bar *a* noticeable. **M~blatt** *nt* [explanatory] leaflet. **m~en** *vt* notice; **sich** (*dat*) **etw m~en** remember sth. **M~mal** *nt* feature

merkwürdig *a* odd, strange

Messe[1] *f* **-, -n** (*Relig*) mass; (*Comm*) [trade] fair

Messe[2] *f* **-, -n** (*Mil*) mess

messen† *vt/i* (*haben*) measure; (*ansehen*) look at; **[bei jdm] Fieber m~** take s.o.'s temperature; **sich mit jdm m~ können** be a match for s.o.

Messer *nt* **-s,-** knife

Messias *m* **-** Messiah

Messing *nt* **-s** brass

Messung *f* **-, -en** measurement

Metabolismus *m* **-** metabolism

Metall *nt* **-s, -e** metal. **m~isch** *a* metallic

Metamorphose *f* **-, -n** metamorphosis

metaphorisch *a* metaphorical

Meteor *m* **-s, -e** meteor. **M~ologie** *f* **-** meteorology

Meter *m & nt* **-s,-** metre. **M~maß** *nt* tape-measure

Method|e *f* **-, -n** method. **m~isch** *a* methodical

Metropole *f* **-, -n** metropolis

Metzger *m* **-s,-** butcher. **M~ei** *f* **-, -en** butcher's shop

Meuterei *f* **-, -en** mutiny

meutern *vi* (*haben*) mutiny; ([!] *schimpfen*) grumble

Mexikan|er(in) *m* **-s,-** (*f* **-, -nen**) Mexican. **m~isch** *a* Mexican

Mexiko *nt* **-s** Mexico

miauen *vi* (*haben*) mew, miaow

mich *pron* (*acc of* **ich**) me; (*refl*) myself

Mieder *nt* **-s,-** bodice

Miene *f* **-, -n** expression

mies *a* [!] lousy

Miet|e *f* **-, -n** rent; (*Mietgebühr*) hire charge; **zur M~e wohnen** live in rented accommodation. **m~en** *vt* rent <*Haus, Zimmer*>; hire <*Auto, Boot*>. **M~er(in)** *m* **-s,-** (*f* **-, -nen**) tenant. **m~frei** *a & adv* rent-free. **M~shaus** *nt* block of rented flats. **M~vertrag** *m* lease. **M~wagen** *m* hire-car. **M~wohnung** *f* rented flat; (*zu vermieten*) flat to let

Migräne *f* **-, -n** migraine

Mikro|chip *m* microchip. **M~computer** *m* microcomputer. **M~film** *m* microfilm

Mikro|fon, M~phon *nt* **-s, -e** microphone. **M~skop** *nt* **-s, -e** microscope. **m~skopisch** *a* microscopic

Mikrowelle *f* microwave. **M~nherd** *m* microwave oven

Milbe *f* **-, -n** mite

Milch *f* **-** milk. **M~glas** *nt* opal glass. **m~ig** *a* milky. **M~mann** *m* (*pl* **-männer**) milkman. **M~straße** *f* Milky Way

mild *a* mild; (*nachsichtig*) lenient. **M~e** *f* **-** mildness; leniency. **m~ern** *vt* make milder; (*mäßigen*) moderate; (*lindern*) ease; **sich m~ern** become milder; (*sich mäßigen*) moderate; <*Schmerz:*> ease; **m~ernde Umstände** mitigating circumstances

Milieu /mi'li̯ø:/ *nt* **-s, -s** [social] environment

Militär *nt* **-s** army; (*Soldaten*) troops *pl*; **beim M~** in the army. **m~isch** *a* military

Miliz *f* **-, -en** militia

Milliarde /mɪ'li̯ardə/ *f* **-, -n** thousand million, billion

Milli|gramm *nt* milligram. **M~meter** *m & nt* millimetre. **M~meterpapier** *nt* graph paper

Million /mɪ'li̯o:n/ *f* **-, -en** million. **M~är** *m* **-s, -e** millionaire

Milz *f* **-** (*Anat*) spleen. **~brand** *m* anthrax

mimen *vt* ([!] *vortäuschen*) act

Minderheit *f* **-, -en** minority

minderjährig *a* (*Jur*) under-age. **M~e(r)** *m/f* (*Jur*) minor

mindern *vt* diminish; decrease

minderwertig *a* inferior. **M~keit** *f* **-** inferiority. **M~keitskomplex** *m* inferiority complex

Mindest- *pref* minimum. **m~e** *a & pron* **der/die/das M~e** *od* **m~e** the least; **nicht im M~en** not in the least. **m~ens** *adv* at least. **M~lohn** *m* minimum wage. **M~maß** *nt* minimum

Mine *f* **-, -n** mine; (*Bleistift-*) lead; (*Kugelschreiber-*) refill. **M~nräumboot** *nt* minesweeper

Mineral *nt* **-s, -e** & **-ien** /-i̯ən/ mineral. **m~isch** *a* mineral. **M~wasser** *nt* mineral water

Miniatur *f* **-, -en** miniature

Minigolf *nt* miniature golf
minimal *a* minimal
Minimum *nt* **-s, -ma** minimum
Mini|ster *m*, **-s,-** minister. **m~steriell** *a* ministerial. **M~sterium** *nt* **-s, -ien** ministry
minus *conj, adv & prep* (+ *gen*) minus. **M~** *nt* **-** deficit; (*Nachteil*) disadvantage. **M~zeichen** *nt* minus [sign]
Minute *f* **-, -n** minute
mir *pron* (*dat of* **ich**) [to] me; (*refl*) myself
Misch|ehe *f* mixed marriage. **m~en** *vt* mix; blend <*Tee, Kaffee*>; toss <*Salat*>; shuffle <*Karten*>; **sich m~en** mix; <*Person;*> mingle (**unter** + *acc* with); **sich m~en in** (+ *acc*) join in <*Gespräch*>; meddle in <*Angelegenheit*> ● *vi* (*haben*) shuffle the cards. **M~ling** *m* **-s, -e** half-caste. **M~ung** *f* **-, -en** mixture; blend
miserabel *a* abominable
missachten *vt* disregard
Miss|achtung *f* disregard. **M~bildung** *f* deformity
missbilligen *vt* disapprove of
Miss|billigung *f* disapproval. **M~brauch** *m* abuse
missbrauchen *vt* abuse; (*vergewaltigen*) rape
Misserfolg *m* failure
Misse|tat *f* misdeed. **M~täter** *m* [!] culprit
missfallen† *vi* (*haben*) displease (**jdm** s.o.)
Miss|fallen *nt* **-s** displeasure; (*Missbilligung*) disapproval. **M~geburt** *f* freak; (*fig*) monstrosity. **M~geschick** *nt* mishap; (*Unglück*) misfortune
miss|glücken *vi* (*sein*) fail. **m~gönnen** *vt* begrudge
misshandeln *vt* ill-treat
Misshandlung *f* ill-treatment
Mission *f* **-, -en** mission
Missionar(in) *m* **-s, -e** (*f* **-, -nen**) missionary
Missklang *m* discord
misslingen† *vi* (*sein*) fail; **es misslang ihr** she failed. **M~** *nt* **-s** failure
Missmut *m* ill humour. **m~ig** *a* morose
missraten† *vi* (*sein*) turn out badly
Miss|stand *m* abuse; (*Zustand*) undesirable state of affairs. **M~stimmung** *f* discord; (*Laune*) bad mood
misstrauen *vi* (*haben*) **jdm/etw m~** mistrust s.o./sth; (*Argwohn hegen*) distrust s.o./sth
Misstrau|en *nt* **-s** mistrust; (*Argwohn*) distrust. **M~ensvotum** *nt* vote of no confidence. **m~isch** *a* distrustful; (*argwöhnisch*) suspicious
Miss|verständnis *nt* misunderstanding. **m~verstehen**† *vt* misunderstand. **M~wirtschaft** *f* mismanagement
Mist *m* **-[e]s** manure; [!] rubbish
Mistel *f* **-, -n** mistletoe
Misthaufen *m* dungheap
mit *prep* (+ *dat*) with; <*sprechen*> to; (*mittels*) by; (*inklusive*) including; (*bei*) at; **mit Bleistift** in pencil; **mit lauter Stimme** in a loud voice; **mit drei Jahren** at the age of three ● *adv* (*auch*) as well; **mit anfassen** (*fig*) lend a hand
Mitarbeit *f* collaboration. **m~en** *vi sep* collaborate (**an** + *dat* on). **M~er(in)** *m(f)* collaborator; (*Kollege*) colleague; employee
Mitbestimmung *f* co-determination
mitbringen† *vt sep* bring [along]
miteinander *adv* with each other
Mitesser *m* (*Med*) blackhead
mitfahren† *vi sep* (*sein*) go/come along; **mit jdm m~** go with s.o.; (*mitgenommen werden*) be given a lift by s.o.

mịtfühlen *vi sep* (*haben*) sympathize

mịtgeben† *vt sep* **jdm etw m~** give s.o. sth to take with him

Mịtgefühl *nt* sympathy

mịtgehen† *vi sep* (*sein*) **mit jdm m~** go with s.o.

Mịtgift *f* **-, -en** dowry

Mịtglied *nt* member. **M~schaft** *f* **-** membership

mithịlfe *prep* (+ *gen*) with the aid of

Mịthilfe *f* assistance

mịtkommen† *vi sep* (*sein*) come [along] too; (*fig: folgen können*) keep up; (*verstehen*) follow

Mịtlaut *m* consonant

Mịtleid *nt* pity, compassion; **M~ erregend** pitiful. **m~ig** *a* pitying; (*mitfühlend*) compassionate. **m~slos** *a* pitiless

mịtmachen *v sep* ● *vt* take part in; (*erleben*) go through ● *vi* (*haben*) join in

Mịtmensch *m* fellow man

mịtnehmen† *vt sep* take along; (*mitfahren lassen*) give a lift to; (*fig: schädigen*) affect badly; (*erschöpfen*) exhaust; **'zum M~'** 'to take away'

mịtreden *vi sep* (*haben*) join in [the conversation]; (*mit entscheiden*) have a say (**bei** in)

mịtreißen† *vt sep* sweep along; (*fig: begeistern*) carry away; **m~d** rousing

mitsạmt *prep* (+ *dat*) together with

mịtschreiben† *vt sep* (*haben*) take down

Mịtschuld *f partial blame*. **m~ig** *a* **m~ig sein** be partly to blame

Mịtschüler(in) *m*(*f*) fellow pupil

mịtspielen *vi sep* (*haben*) join in; (*Theat*) be in the cast; (*beitragen*) play a part

Mịttag *m* midday, noon; (*Mahlzeit*) lunch; (*Pause*) lunch-break; **heute/gestern M~** at lunch-time today/yesterday; **[zu] M~ essen** have lunch. **M~essen** *nt* lunch. **m~s** *adv* at noon; (*als Mahlzeit*) for lunch; **um 12 Uhr m~s** at noon. **M~spause** *f* lunch-hour; (*Pause*) lunch-break. **M~sschlaf** *m* after-lunch nap

Mịttäter|(in) *m*(*f*) accomplice. **M~schaft** *f* **-** complicity

Mịtte *f* **-, -n** middle; (*Zentrum*) centre; **die goldene M~** the golden mean; **M~ Mai** in mid-May; **in unserer M~** in our midst

mịtteil|en *vt sep* **jdm etw m~en** tell s.o. sth; (*amtlich*) inform s.o. of sth. **M~ung** *f* **-, -en** communication; (*Nachricht*) piece of news

Mịttel *nt* **-s,-** means *sg*; (*Heil*) remedy; (*Medikament*) medicine; (*M~wert*) mean; (*Durchschnitt*) average; **M~** *pl* (*Geld-*) funds, resources. **m~** *pred a* medium; (*m~mäßig*) middling. **M~alter** *nt* Middle Ages *pl*. **m~alterlich** *a* medieval. **M~ding** *nt* (*fig*) cross. **m~europäisch** *a* Central European. **M~finger** *m* middle finger. **m~los** *a* destitute. **m~mäßig** *a* middling; **[nur] m~mäßig** mediocre. **M~meer** *nt* Mediterranean. **M~punkt** *m* centre; (*fig*) centre of attention

mịttels *prep* (+ *gen*) by means of

Mịttel|schule *f* = **Realschule**. **M~smann** *m* (*pl* **-männer**) intermediary, go-between. **M~stand** *m* middle class. **m~ste(r,s)** *a* middle. **M~streifen** *m* (*Auto*) central reservation. **M~stürmer** *m* centre-forward. **M~welle** *f* medium wave. **M~wort** *nt* (*pl* **-wörter**) participle

mịtten *adv* **m~ in/auf** (*dat/acc*) in the middle of. **m~dụrch** *adv* [right] through the middle

Mịtternacht *f* midnight

mịttler|e(r,s) *a* middle; <*Größe, Qualität*> medium;

(*durchschnittlich*) mean, average. **m~weile** *adv* meanwhile; (*seitdem*) by now
Mittwoch *m* **-s, -e** Wednesday. **m~s** *adv* on Wednesdays
mitunter *adv* now and again
mitwirk|en *vi sep* (*haben*) take part; (*helfen*) contribute. **M~ung** *f* participation
mix|en *vt* mix. **M~er** *m* **-s,-** (*Culin*) liquidizer, blender
Möbel *pl* furniture *sg*. **M~stück** *nt* piece of furniture. **M~wagen** *m* removal van
Mobiliar *nt* **-s** furniture
mobilisier|en *vt* mobilize. **M~ung** *f* **-** mobilization
Mobil|machung *f* **-** mobilization. **M~telefon** *nt* mobile phone
möblier|en *vt* furnish; **m~tes Zimmer** furnished room
mochte, möchte *s.* **mögen**
Mode *f* **-, -n** fashion; **M~ sein** be fashionable
Modell *nt* **-s, -e** model. **m~ieren** *vt* model
Modenschau *f* fashion show
Modera|tor *m* **-s, -en** /-'to:rən/, **M~torin** *f* **-, -nen** (*TV*) presenter
modern *a* modern; (*modisch*) fashionable. **m~isieren** *vt* modernize
Mode|schmuck *m* costume jewellery. **M~schöpfer** *m* fashion designer
modisch *a* fashionable
Modistin *f* **-, -nen** milliner
modrig *a* musty
modulieren *vt* modulate
Mofa *nt* **-s, -s** moped
mogeln *vi* (*haben*) [!] cheat

---

mögen†

● *transitive verb*

····➤ like. **sie mag ihn sehr [gern]** she likes him very much. **möchten Sie ein Glas Wein?** would you like a glass of wine? **lieber mögen** prefer. **ich möchte lieber Tee** I would prefer tea

● *auxiliary verb*

····➤ (*wollen*) want to. **sie mochte nicht länger bleiben** she didn't want to stay any longer. **ich möchte ihn [gerne] sprechen** I'd like to speak to him. **möchtest du nach Hause?** do you want to go home? *or* would you like to go home?

····➤ (*Vermutung, Möglichkeit*) may. **ich mag mich irren** I may be wrong. **wer/was mag das sein?** whoever/whatever can it be? **[das] mag sein** that may well be. **mag kommen, was da will** come what may

---

möglich *a* possible; **alle m~en** all sorts of; **über alles M~e sprechen** talk about all sorts of things. **m~erweise** *adv* possibly. **M~keit** *f* **-, -en** possibility. **M~keitsform** *f* subjunctive. **m~st** *adv* if possible; **m~st viel** as much as possible
Mohammedan|er(in) *m* **-s,-** (*f* **-, -nen**) Muslim. **m~isch** *a* Muslim
Mohn *m* **-s** poppy
Möhre, Mohrrübe *f* **-, -n** carrot
Mokka *m* **-s** mocha; (*Geschmack*) coffee
Molch *m* **-[e]s, -e** newt
Mole *f* **-, -n** (*Naut*) mole
Molekül *nt* **-s, -e** molecule
Molkerei *f* **-, -en** dairy
Moll *nt* **-** (*Mus*) minor
mollig *a* cosy; (*warm*) warm; (*rundlich*) plump
Moment *m* **-s, -e** moment; **M~[mal]!** just a moment! **m~an** *a* momentary; (*gegenwärtig*) at the moment
Monarch *m* **-en, -en** monarch. **M~ie** *f* **-, -n** monarchy
Monat *m* **-s, -e** month. **m~elang** *adv* for months. **m~lich** *a & adv* monthly

Mönch *m* **-[e]s, -e** monk
Mond *m* **-[e]s, -e** moon
mondän *a* fashionable
Mond|finsternis *f* lunar eclipse. **m~hell** *a* moonlit. **M~sichel** *f* crescent moon. **M~schein** *m* moonlight
monieren *vt* criticize
Monitor *m* **-s, -en** /-'to:rən/ (*Techn*) monitor
Monogramm *nt* **-s, -e** monogram
Mono|log *m* **-s, -e** monologue. **M~pol** *nt* **-s, -e** monopoly. **m~ton** *a* monotonous
Monster *nt* **-s,-** monster
Monstrum *nt* **-s, -stren** monster
Monsun *m* **-s, -e** monsoon
Montag *m* Monday
Montage /mɔn'ta:ʒə/ *f* **-, -n** fitting; (*Zusammenbau*) assembly; (*Film-*) editing; (*Kunst*) montage
montags *adv* on Mondays
Montanindustrie *f* coal and steel industry
Monteur /mɔn'tø:ɐ̯/ *m* **-s, -e** fitter. **M~anzug** *m* overalls *pl*
montieren *vt* fit; (*zusammenbauen*) assemble
Monument *nt* **-[e]s, -e** monument. **m~al** *a* monumental
Moor *nt* **-[e]s, -e** bog; (*Heide-*) moor
Moos *nt* **es, -e** moss **m~ig** *a* mossy
Moped *nt* **-s, -s** moped
Mopp *m* **-s, -s** mop
Moral *f* **-** morals *pl*, (*Selbstvertrauen*) morale; (*Lehre*) moral. **m~isch** *a* moral
Mord *m* **-[e]s, -e** murder, (*Pol*) assassination. **M~anschlag** *m* murder/assassination attempt. **m~en** *vt/i* (*haben*) murder, kill
Mörder *m* **-s,-** murderer, (*Pol*) assassin. **M~in** *f* **-, -nen** murderess. **m~isch** *a* murderous; (! *schlimm*) dreadful
morgen *adv* tomorrow; **m~ Abend** tomorrow evening
Morgen *m* **-s,-** morning; (*Maß*) ≈ acre; **am M~** in the morning; **heute/Montag M~** this/Monday morning. **M~dämmerung** *f* dawn. **M~rock** *m* dressing-gown. **M~rot** *nt* red sky in the morning. **m~s** *a* in the morning
morgig *a* tomorrow's; **der m~e Tag** tomorrow
Morphium *nt* **-s** morphine
morsch *a* rotten
Morsealphabet *nt* Morse code
Mörtel *m* **-s** mortar
Mosaik /moza'i:k/ *nt* **-s, -e[n]** mosaic
Moschee *f* **-, -n** mosque
Mosel *f* **-** Moselle
Moskau *nt* **-s** Moscow
Moskito *m* **-s, -s** mosquito
Moslem *m* **-s, -s** Muslim
Motiv *nt* **-s, -e** motive; (*Kunst*) motif
Motor /'mo:tɔr, mo'to:ɐ̯/ *m* **-s, -en** /-'to:rən/ engine; (*Elektro-*) motor. **M~boot** *nt* motor boat
motorisieren *vt* motorize
Motor|rad *nt* motor cycle. **M~roller** *m* motor scooter
Motte *f* **-, -n** moth. **M~nkugel** *f* mothball
Motto *nt* **-s, -s** motto
Möwe *f* **-, -n** gull
Mücke *f* **-, -n** gnat; (*kleine*) midge; (*Stech-*) mosquito
müd|e *a* tired; **es m~e sein** be tired (**etw zu tun** of doing sth). **M~igkeit** *f* **-** tiredness
muffig *a* musty, (! *mürrisch*) grumpy
Mühe *f* **-, -n** effort; (*Aufwand*) trouble; **sich** (*dat*) **M~ geben** make an effort; (*sich bemühen*) try; nicht der **M~ wert** not worth while; mit **M~ und** Not with great difficulty; (*gerade noch*) only just. **m~los** *a* effortless
muhen *vi* (*haben*) moo

M

Mühl|e *f* **-, -n** mill; (*Kaffee-*) grinder. **M~stein** *m* millstone

Müh|sal *f* **-, -e** (*liter*) toil; (*Mühe*) trouble. **m~sam** *a* laborious; (*beschwerlich*) difficult

Mulde *f* **-, -n** hollow

Müll *m* **-s** refuse. **M~abfuhr** *f* refuse collection

Mullbinde *f* gauze bandage

Mülleimer *m* waste bin; (*Mülltonne*) dustbin

Müller *m* **-s,-** miller

Müll|halde *f* [rubbish] dump. **M~schlucker** *m* refuse chute. **M~tonne** *f* dustbin

multi|national *a* multinational. **M~plikation** /-'tsi̯o:n/ *f* **-, -en** multiplication. **m~plizieren** *vt* multiply

Mumie /'mu:mi̯ə/ *f* **-, -n** mummy

Mumm *m* **-s** [!] energy

Mumps *m* **-** mumps

Mund *m* **-[e]s,¨er** mouth; **ein M~ voll Suppe** a mouthful of soup; **halt den M~!** [✖] shut up! **M~art** *f* dialect. **m~artlich** *a* dialect

Mündel *nt & m* **-s,-** (*Jur*) ward. **m~sicher** *a* gilt-edged

münden *vi* (*sein*) flow/<*Straße:*> lead (**in** + *acc* into)

Mundharmonika *f* mouth-organ

mündig *a* **m~ sein/werden** (*Jur*) be/come of age. **M~keit** *f* **-** (*Jur*) majority

mündlich *a* verbal; **m~e** Prüfung oral

Mündung *f* **-, -en** (*Fluss-*) mouth; (*Gewehr-*) muzzle

Mundwinkel *m* corner of the mouth

Munition /-'tsi̯o:n/ *f* **-** ammunition

munkeln *vt/i* (*haben*) talk (**von** of); **es wird gemunkelt** rumour has it (**dass** that)

Münster *nt* **-s,-** cathedral

munter *a* lively; (*heiter*) merry; **m~ sein** (*wach*) be wide awake ; **gesund und m~** fit and well

Münz|e *f* **-, -n** coin; (*M~stätte*) mint. **M~fernsprecher** *m* payphone

mürbe *a* crumbly; <*Obst*> mellow; <*Fleisch*> tender. **M~teig** *m* short pastry

Murmel *f* **-, -n** marble

murmeln *vt/i* (*haben*) murmur; (*undeutlich*) mumble

Murmeltier *nt* marmot

murren *vt/i* (*haben*) grumble

mürrisch *a* surly

Mus *nt* **-es** purée

Muschel *f* **-, -n** mussel; [sea] shell

Museum /mu'ze:ʊm/ *nt* **-s, -seen** /-'ze:ən/ museum

Musik *f* **-** music. **m~alisch** *a* musical

Musiker(in) *m* **-s,-** (*f* **-, -nen**) musician

Musik|instrument *nt* musical instrument. **M~kapelle** *f* band. **M~pavillon** *m* bandstand

musisch *a* artistic

musizieren *vi* (*haben*) make music

Muskat *m* **-[e]s** nutmeg

Muskel *m* **-s, -n** muscle. **M~kater** *m* stiff and aching muscles *pl*

muskulös *a* muscular

muss *s.* **müssen**

Muße *f* **-** leisure

müssen†

● *auxiliary verb*

····➤ (*gezwungen/verpflichtet/notwendig sein*) have to; must. **er muss es tun** he must *or* has to do it; [!] he's got to do it. **ich musste schnell fahren** I had to drive fast. **das muss 1968 gewesen sein** it must have been in 1968. **er muss gleich hier sein** he must be here at any moment

····➤ (*in negativen Sätzen; ungezwungen*) **sie muss es nicht tun** she does not have to *or* [!] she hasn't got to do it. **es musste**

nicht so sein it didn't have to be like that

····➤ **es müsste** (*sollte*) **doch möglich sein** it ought to *or* should be possible. **du müsstest es mal versuchen** you ought to *or* should try it

● *intransitive verb*

····➤ (*irgendwohin gehen müssen*) have to *or* must go. **ich muss nach Hause/zum Arzt** I have to *or* must go home/to the doctor. **ich musste mal [aufs Klo]** I had to go [to the loo]

müßig *a* idle

musste, müsste *s.* **müssen**

Muster *nt* **-s,-** pattern; (*Probe*) sample; (*Vorbild*) model. **M~beispiel** *nt* typical example; (*Vorbild*) perfect example. **m~gültig, m~haft** *a* exemplary. **m~n** *vt* eye; (*inspizieren*) inspect. **M~ung** *f* **-, -en** inspection; (*Mil*) medical; (*Muster*) pattern

Mut *m* **-[e]s** courage; **jdm Mut machen** encourage s.o.; **zu M~e sein** = **zumute sein**, *s.* **zumute**

mut|ig *a* courageous. **m~los** *a* despondent

mutmaßen *vt* presume; (*Vermutungen anstellen*) speculate

Mutprobe *f* test of courage

Mutter[1] *f* **-,¨** mother

Mutter[2] *f* **-, -n** (*Techn*) nut

Muttergottes *f* **-,-** madonna

Mutterland *nt* motherland

mütterlich *a* maternal; (*fürsorglich*) motherly. **m~erseits** *adv* on one's/the mother's side

Mutter|mal *nt* birthmark; (*dunkel*) mole. **M~schaft** *f* **-** motherhood. **m~seelenallein** *a & adv* all alone. **M~sprache** *f* mother tongue. **M~tag** *m* Mother's Day

Mütze *f* **-, -n** cap; **wollene M~** woolly hat

MwSt. *abbr* (**Mehrwertsteuer**) VAT

mysteriös *a* mysterious

Mystik /ˈmʏstɪk/ *f* **-** mysticism

myth|isch *a* mythical. **M~ologie** *f* **-** mythology

Nn

na *int* well; **na gut** all right then

Nabel *m* **-s,-** navel. **N~schnur** *f* umbilical cord

nach

● *preposition* (+ *dative*)

····➤ (*räumlich*) to. **nach London fahren** go to London. **der Zug nach München** the train to Munich; (*noch nicht abgefahren*) the train for Munich; the Munich train. **nach Hause gehen** go home. **nach Osten [zu]** eastwards; towards the east

····➤ (*zeitlich*) after; (*Uhrzeit*) past. **nach fünf Minuten/dem Frühstück** after five minutes/breakfast. **zehn [Minuten] nach zwei** ten [minutes] past two

····➤ (*[räumliche und zeitliche] Reihenfolge*) after. **nach Ihnen/dir!** after you!

····➤ (*mit bestimmten Verben*) for. **greifen/streben/schicken nach** grasp/strive/send for

····➤ (*gemäß*) according to. **nach der neuesten Mode gekleidet** dressed in [accordance with] the latest fashion. **dem Gesetz nach** in accordance with the law; by law. **nach meiner Ansicht** *od* **Meinung, meiner Ansicht** *od* **Meinung nach** in my view *or* opinion. **nach etwas schmecken/riechen** taste/smell of sth

● *adverb*

···➤ (*zeitlich*) **nach und nach** little by little; gradually. **nach wie vor** still

nachahm|en *vt sep* imitate. **N~ung** *f* -, -en imitation

Nachbar|(in) *m* -n, -n (*f* -, -nen) neighbour. **N~haus** *nt* house next door. **n~lich** *a* neighbourly; (*Nachbar-*) neighbouring. **N~schaft** *f* - neighbourhood

nachbestell|en *vt sep* reorder. **N~ung** *f* repeat order

nachbild|en *vt sep* copy, reproduce. **N~ung** *f* copy, reproduction

nachdatieren *vt sep* backdate

nachdem *conj* after; **je n~** it depends

nachdenk|en† *vi sep* (*haben*) think (**über** + *acc* about). **n~lich** *a* thoughtful

nachdrücklich *a* emphatic

nacheinander *adv* one after the other

Nachfahre *m* -n, -n descendant

Nachfolg|e *f* succession. **N~er(in)** *m* -s,- (*f* -, -nen) successor

nachforsch|en *vi sep* (*haben*) make enquiries. **N~ung** *f* enquiry

Nachfrage *f* (*Comm*) demand. **n~n** *vi sep* (*haben*) enquire

nachfüllen *vt sep* refill

nachgeben† *v sep* ●*vi* (*haben*) give way; (*sich fügen*) give in, yield ●*vt* **jdm Suppe n~** give s.o. more soup

Nachgebühr *f* surcharge

nachgehen† *vi sep* (*sein*) <*Uhr:*> be slow; **jdm/etw n~** follow s.o./sth; follow up <*Spur, Angelegenheit*>; pursue <*Angelegenheit*>

Nachgeschmack *m* after-taste

nachgiebig *a* indulgent; (*gefällig*) compliant. **N~keit** *f* - indulgence; compliance

nachgrübeln *vi sep* (*haben*) ponder (**über** + *acc* on)

nachhaltig *a* lasting

nachhelfen† *vi sep* (*haben*) help

nachher *adv* later; (*danach*) afterwards; **bis n~!** see you later!

Nachhilfeunterricht *m* coaching

Nachhinein *adv* **im N~** afterwards

nachhinken *vi sep* (*sein*) (*fig*) lag behind

nachholen *vt sep* (*später holen*) fetch later; (*mehr holen*) get more; (*später machen*) do later; (*aufholen*) catch up on

Nachkomme *m* -n, -n descendant. **n~n**† *vi sep* (*sein*) follow [later], come later; **etw** (*dat*) **n~n** (*fig*) comply with <*Bitte*>; carry out <*Pflicht*>. **N~nschaft** *f* - descendants *pl*, progeny

Nachkriegszeit *f* post-war period

Nachlass *m* -es,¨-e discount; (*Jur*) [deceased's] estate

nachlassen† *v sep* ●*vi* (*haben*) decrease; <*Regen, Hitze:*> let up; <*Schmerz:*> ease; <*Sturm:*> abate; <*Augen, Leistungen:*> deteriorate ●*vt* **etw vom Preis n~** take sth off the price

nachlässig *a* careless; (*leger*) casual; (*unordentlich*) sloppy. **N~keit** *f* - carelessness; sloppiness

nachlesen† *vt sep* look up

nachlöse|n *vi sep* (*haben*) pay one's fare on the train/on arrival. **N~schalter** *m* excess-fare office

nachmachen *vt sep* (*später machen*) do later; (*imitieren*) imitate, copy; (*fälschen*) forge

Nachmittag *m* afternoon; **heute/gestern N~** this/yesterday afternoon. **n~s** *adv* in the afternoon

Nachnahme *f* **etw per N~ schicken** send sth cash on delivery *or* COD
Nachname *m* surname
Nachporto *nt* excess postage
nachprüfen *vt sep* check, verify
Nachricht *f* **-, -en** [piece of] news *sg*; **N~en** news *sg*; **eine N~ hinterlassen** leave a message; **jdm N~ geben** inform s.o. **N~endienst** *m* (*Mil*) intelligence service
nachrücken *vi sep* (*sein*) move up
Nachruf *m* obituary
nachsagen *vt sep* repeat (**jdm** after s.o.); **jdm Schlechtes/Gutes n~** speak ill/well of s.o.
Nachsaison *f* late season
nachschicken *vt sep* (*später schicken*) send later; (*hinterher-*) send after (**jdm** s.o.); send on <*Post*> (**jdm** to s.o.)
nachschlagen† *v sep* ●*vt* look up ●*vi* (*haben*) **in einem Wörterbuch n~en** consult a dictionary; **jdm n~en** take after s.o.
Nachschrift *f* transcript; (*Nachsatz*) postscript
Nachschub *m* (*Mil*) supplies *pl*
nachsehen† *v sep* ●*vt* (*prüfen*) check; (*nachschlagen*) look up; (*hinwegsehen über*) overlook ●*vi* (*haben*) have a look; (*prüfen*) check; **im Wörterbuch n~** consult a dictionary
nachsenden† *vt sep* forward <*Post*> (**jdm** to s.o.); **'bitte n~'** 'please forward'
nachsichtig *a* forbearing; lenient; indulgent
Nachsilbe *f* suffix
nachsitzen† *vi sep* (*haben*) **n~ müssen** be kept in [after school]; **jdn n~ lassen** give s.o. detention. **N~** *nt* **-s** (*Sch*) detention
Nachspeise *f* dessert, sweet
nachsprechen† *vt sep* repeat (**jdm** after s.o.)
nachspülen *vt sep* rinse
nächst /-çst/ *prep* (+ *dat*) next to. **n~beste(r,s)** *a* first [available]; (*zweitbeste*) next best. **n~e(r,s)** *a* next; (*nächstgelegene*) nearest; <*Verwandte*> closest; **in n~er Nähe** close by; **am n~en sein** be nearest *or* closest ●*pron* **der/die/das N~e** the next; **der N~e bitte** next please; **als N~es** next; **fürs N~e** for the time being. **N~e(r)** *m* fellow man
nachstehend *a* following ●*adv* below
Nächst|enliebe *f* charity. **n~ens** *adv* shortly. **n~gelegen** *a* nearest
nachsuchen *vi sep* (*haben*) search; **n~ um** request
Nacht *f* **-,¨e** night; **über/bei N~** overnight/at night; **morgen N~** tomorrow night; **heute N~** tonight; (*letzte Nacht*) last night; **gestern N~** last night; (*vorletzte Nacht*) the night before last. **N~dienst** *m* night duty
Nachteil *m* disadvantage; **zum N~** to the detriment (*gen* of)
Nacht|falter *m* moth. **N~hemd** *nt* night-dress; (*Männer-*) night-shirt
Nachtigall *f* **-, -en** nightingale
Nachtisch *m* dessert
Nachtklub *m* night-club
nächtlich *a* nocturnal, night ...
Nacht|lokal *nt* night-club. **N~mahl** *nt* (*Aust*) supper
Nachtrag *m* postscript; (*Ergänzung*) supplement. **n~en**† *vt sep* add; **jdm etw n~en** (*fig*) bear a grudge against s.o. for sth. **n~end** *a* vindictive; **n~end sein** bear grudges
nachträglich *a* subsequent, later; (*verspätet*) belated ●*adv* later; (*nachher*) afterwards; (*verspätet*) belatedly
Nacht|ruhe *f* night's rest; **angenehme N~ruhe!** sleep well! **n~s** *adv* at night; **2 Uhr n~s** 2

N

o'clock in the morning. **N~schicht** *f* night-shift. **N~tisch** *m* bedside table. **N~tischlampe** *f* bedside lamp. **N~topf** *m* chamber-pot. **N~wächter** *m* night-watchman. **N~zeit** *f* night-time

Nachuntersuchung *f* check-up

Nachwahl *f* by-election

Nachweis *m* **-es, -e** proof. **n~bar** *a* demonstrable. **n~en**† *vt sep* prove; (*aufzeigen*) show; (*vermitteln*) give details of; **jdm nichts n~en können** have no proof against s.o.

Nachwelt *f* posterity

Nachwirkung *f* after-effect

Nachwuchs *m* new generation; (! *Kinder*) offspring. **N~spieler** *m* young player

nachzahlen *vt/i sep* (*haben*) pay extra; (*später zahlen*) pay later; **Steuern n~** pay tax arrears

nachzählen *vt/i sep* (*haben*) count again; (*prüfen*) check

Nachzahlung *f* extra/later payment; (*Gehalts-*) back-payment

nachzeichnen *vt sep* copy

Nachzügler *m* **-s,-** late-comer; (*Zurückgebliebener*) straggler

Nacken *m* **-s,-** nape *or* back of the neck

nackt *a* naked; (*bloß, kahl*) bare; <*Wahrheit*> plain. **N~heit** *f* **-** nakedness, nudity. **N~kultur** *f* nudism. **N~schnecke** *f* slug

Nadel *f* **-, -n** needle; (*Häkel-*) hook; (*Schmuck-, Hut-*) pin. **N~arbeit** *f* needlework. **N~baum** *m* conifer. **N~stich** *m* stitch; (*fig*) pinprick. **N~wald** *m* coniferous forest

Nagel *m* **-s,¨** nail. **N~haut** *f* cuticle. **N~lack** *m* nail varnish. **n~n** *vt* nail. **n~neu** *a* brand-new

nagen *vt/i* (*haben*) gnaw (**an** + *dat* at); **n~d** (*fig*) nagging

Nagetier *nt* rodent

nah *a, adv & prep* = **nahe**

Näharbeit *f* sewing

Nahaufnahme *f* close-up

nahe *a* nearby; (*zeitlich*) imminent; (*eng*) close; **der N~ Osten** the Middle East; **in n~r Zukunft** in the near future; **von n~m** [from] close to; **n~ sein** be close (*dat* to) ● *adv* near, close; <*verwandt*> closely; **n~ an** (+ *acc/dat*) near [to], close to; **n~ daran sein, etw zu tun** nearly do sth; **n~ liegen** be close; (*fig*) be highly likely; **n~ legen** (*fig*) recommend (**dat** to); **jdm n~ legen, etw zu tun** urge s.o. to do sth; **jdm n~ gehen** (*fig*) affect s.o. deeply; **jdm zu n~ treten** (*fig*) offend s.o. ● *prep* (+ *dat*) near [to], close to

Nähe *f* **-** nearness, proximity; **aus der N~** [from] close to; **in der N~** near *or* close by

nahe|gehen* *vi sep* (*sein*) **n~ gehen**, *s.* **nahe**. **n~legen*** *vt sep* **n~ legen**, *s.* **nahe**. **n~liegen*** *vi sep* (*haben*) **n~ liegen**, *s.* **nahe**

nähen *vt/i* (*haben*) sew; (*anfertigen*) make; (*Med*) stitch [up]

näher *a* closer; <*Weg*> shorter; <*Einzelheiten*> further ● *adv* closer; (*genauer*) more closely; **n~ kommen** come closer; (*fig*) get closer (**dat** to); **sich n~ erkundigen** make further enquiries; **n~ an** (+ *acc/dat*) nearer [to], closer to ● *prep* (+ *dat*) nearer [to], closer to. **N~e[s]** *nt* [further] details *pl*. **n~n (sich)** *vr* approach

nahezu *adv* almost

Nähgarn *nt* [sewing] cotton

Nahkampf *m* close combat

Näh|maschine *f* sewing machine. **N~nadel** *f* sewing-needle

nähren *vt* feed; (*fig*) nurture

nahrhaft *a* nutritious

Nährstoff *m* nutrient

Nahrung *f* **-** food, nourishment. **N~smittel** *nt* food

Nährwert *m* nutritional value

Naht *f* **-,¨e** seam; (*Med*) suture. **n~los** *a* seamless

Nahverkehr *m* local service

Nähzeug *nt* sewing; (*Zubehör*) sewing kit

naiv /na'i:f/ *a* naïve. **N~ität** /-vi'tɛ:t/ *f* **-** naïvety

Name *m* **-ns, -n** name; **im N~n** (+ *gen*) in the name of; <*handeln*> on behalf of. **n~nlos** *a* nameless; (*unbekannt*) unknown, anonymous. **N~nstag** *m* name-day. **N~nsvetter** *m* namesake. **N~nszug** *m* signature. **n~ntlich** *adv* by name; (*besonders*) especially

namhaft *a* noted; (*ansehnlich*) considerable; **n~ machen** name

nämlich *adv* (*und zwar*) namely; (*denn*) because

nanu *int* hallo

Napf *m* **-[e]s,¨e** bowl

Narbe *f* **-, -n** scar

Narkose *f* **-, -n** general anaesthetic. **N~arzt** *m* anaesthetist. **N~mittel** *nt* anaesthetic

Narr *m* **-en, -en** fool; **zum N~en halten** make a fool of. **n~en** *vt* fool

Närr|in *f* **-, -nen** fool. **n~isch** *a* foolish; (! *verrückt*) crazy (**auf** + *acc* about)

Narzisse *f* **-, -n** narcissus

naschen *vt/i* (*haben*) nibble (**an** + *dat* at)

Nase *f* **-, -n** nose

näseln *vi* (*haben*) speak through one's nose; **n~d** nasal

Nasen|bluten *nt* **-s** nosebleed. **N~loch** *nt* nostril

Nashorn *nt* rhinoceros

nass *a* wet

Nässe *f* **-** wet; wetness. **n~n** *vt* wet

Nation /na'tsi̯o:n/ *f* **-, -en** nation. **n~al** *a* national. **N~alhymne** *f* national anthem. **N~alismus** *m* **-** nationalism. **N~alität** *f* **-, -en** nationality. **N~alspieler** *m* international

Natrium *nt* **-s** sodium

Natron *nt* **-s doppeltkohlensaures N~** bicarbonate of soda

Natter *f* **-, -n** snake; (*Gift-*) viper

Natur *f* **-, -en** nature; **von N~ aus** by nature. **n~alisieren** *vt* naturalize. **N~alisierung** *f* **-, -en** naturalization

Naturell *nt* **-s, -e** disposition

Natur|erscheinung *f* natural phenomenon. **N~forscher** *m* naturalist. **N~kunde** *f* natural history

natürlich *a* natural ● *adv* naturally; (*selbstverständlich*) of course. **N~keit** *f* **-** naturalness

natur|rein *a* pure. **N~schutz** *m* nature conservation; **unter N~schutz stehen** be protected. **N~schutzgebiet** *nt* nature reserve. **N~wissenschaft** *f* [natural] science. **N~wissenschaftler** *m* scientist

nautisch *a* nautical

Navigation /-'tsi̯o:n/ *f* **-** navigation

Nazi *m* **-s, -s** Nazi

n.Chr. *abbr* (**nach Christus**) AD

Nebel *m* **-s,-** fog; (*leicht*) mist

neben *prep* (+ *dat/acc*) next to, beside; (+ *dat*) (*außer*) apart from. **n~an** *adv* next door

Neben|anschluss *m* (*Teleph*) extension. **N~ausgaben** *fpl* incidental expenses

nebenbei *adv* in addition; (*beiläufig*) casually

Neben|bemerkung *f* passing remark. **N~beruf** *m* second job

nebeneinander *adv* next to each other, side by side

Neben|eingang *m* side entrance. **N~fach** *nt* (*Univ*) subsidiary subject. **N~fluss** *m* tributary

nebenher *adv* in addition

nebenhin *adv* casually

Neben|höhle *f* sinus. **N~kosten** *pl* additional costs. **N~produkt** *nt* by-product. **N~rolle** *f* supporting role; (*Kleine*) minor role. **N~sache** *f* unimportant matter. **n~sächlich** *a* unimportant. **N~satz** *m* subordinate clause. **N~straße** *f* minor road; (*Seiten-*) side street. **N~wirkung** *f* side-effect. **N~zimmer** *nt* room next door

neblig *a* foggy; (*leicht*) misty

neck|en *vt* tease. **N~erei** *f* - teasing. **n~isch** *a* teasing

Neffe *m* **-n, -n** nephew

negativ *a* negative. **N~** *nt* **-s, -e** (*Phot*) negative

Neger *m* **-s,-** Negro

nehmen† *vt* take (*dat* from); **sich** (*dat*) **etw n~** take sth; help oneself to <*Essen*>

Neid *m* **-[e]s** envy, jealousy. **n~isch** *a* envious, jealous (**auf** + *acc* of); **auf jdn n~isch sein** envy s.o.

neig|en *vt* incline; (*zur Seite*) tilt; (*beugen*) bend; **sich n~en** incline; <*Boden:*> slope; <*Person:*> bend (**über** + *acc* over) ● *vi* (*haben*) **n~en zu** (*fig*) have a tendency towards; be prone to <*Krankheit*>; incline towards <*Ansicht*>; **dazu n~en, etw zu tun** tend to do sth. **N~ung** *f* **-, -en** inclination; (*Gefälle*) slope; (*fig*) tendency

nein *adv*, **N~** *nt* **-s** no

Nektar *m* **-s** nectar

Nelke *f* **-, -n** carnation; (*Culin*) clove

nenn|en† *vt* call; (*taufen*) name; (*angeben*) give; (*erwähnen*) mention; **sich n~en** call oneself. **n~enswert** *a* significant

Neon *nt* **-s** neon. **N~beleuchtung** *f* fluorescent lighting

Nerv *m* **-s, -en** /-fən/ nerve; **die N~en verlieren** lose control of oneself. **n~en** *vt* **jdn n~en** ⊠ get on s.o.'s nerves. **N~enarzt** *m* neurologist. **n~enaufreibend** *a* nerve-racking. **N~enkitzel** *m* [!] thrill. **N~ensystem** *nt* nervous system. **N~enzusammenbruch** *m* nervous breakdown

nervös *a* nervy, edgy; (*Med*) nervous; **n~ sein** be on edge

Nervosität *f* **-** nerviness, edginess

Nerz *m* **-es, -e** mink

Nessel *f* **-, -n** nettle

Nest *nt* **-[e]s, -er** nest; ([!] *Ort*) small place

nett *a* nice; (*freundlich*) kind

netto *adv* net

Netz *nt* **-es, -e** net; (*Einkaufs-*) string bag; (*Spinnen-*) web; (*auf Landkarte*) grid; (*System*) network; (*Electr*) mains *pl*. **N~haut** *f* retina. **N~karte** *f* area season ticket. **N~werk** *nt* network

neu *a* new; (*modern*) modern; **wie neu** as good as new; **das ist mir neu** it's news to me; **von n~em** all over again ● *adv* newly; (*gerade erst*) only just; (*erneut*) again; **etw neu schreiben** rewrite sth; **neu vermähltes Paar** newly-weds *pl*. **N~auflage** *f* new edition; (*unverändert*) reprint. **N~bau** *m* (*pl* **-ten**) new house/building

Neu|e(r) *m/f* new person, newcomer; (*Schüler*) new boy/girl. **N~e(s)** *nt* **das N~e** the new; **etwas N~es** something new; (*Neuigkeit*) a piece of news; **was gibts N~es?** what's the news?

neuerdings *adv* [just] recently

neuest|e(r,s) *a* newest; (*letzte*) latest; **seit n~em** just recently. **N~e** *nt* **das N~e** the latest thing; (*Neuigkeit*) the latest news *sg*

neugeboren *a* newborn

Neugier, Neugierde *f* **-** curiosity; (*Wissbegierde*) inquisitiveness
neugierig *a* curious (**auf** + *acc* about); (*wissbegierig*) inquisitive
Neuheit *f* **-, -en** novelty; newness
Neuigkeit *f* **-, -en** piece of news; **N∼en** news *sg*
Neujahr *nt* New Year's Day; **über N∼** over the New Year
neulich *adv* the other day
Neumond *m* new moon
neun *inv a,* **N∼** *f* **-, -en** nine. **n∼te(r,s)** *a* ninth. **n∼zehn** *inv a* nineteen. **n∼zehnte(r,s)** *a* nineteenth. **n∼zig** *inv a* ninety. **n∼zigste(r,s)** *a* ninetieth
Neuralgie *f* **-, -n** neuralgia
neureich *a* nouveau riche
Neurologe *m* **-n, -n** neurologist
Neurose *f* **-, -n** neurosis
Neuschnee *m* fresh snow
Neuseeland *nt* **-s** New Zealand
neuste(r,s) *a* = **neueste(r,s)**
neutral *a* neutral. **N∼ität** *f* **-** neutrality
Neutrum *nt* **-s, -tra** neuter noun
neu|vermählt* *a* **n∼ vermählt,** *s.* **neu. N∼zeit** *f* modern times *pl*
nicht *adv* not; **ich kann n∼** I cannot *or* can't; **er ist n∼ gekommen** he hasn't come; **bitte n∼!** please don't! **n∼ berühren!** do not touch! **du kennst ihn doch, n∼?** you know him, don't you?
Nichte *f* **-, -n** niece
Nichtraucher *m* non-smoker
nichts *pron & a* nothing; **n∼ mehr** no more; **n∼ ahnend** unsuspecting; **n∼ sagend** meaningless; (*uninteressant*) nondescript. **N∼** *nt* **-** nothingness; (*fig: Leere*) void
Nichtschwimmer *m* non-swimmer
nichts|nutzig *a* good-for-nothing; ([!] *unartig*) naughty. **n∼sagend*** *a* **n∼ sagend,** *s.* **nichts. N∼tun** *nt* **-s** idleness
Nickel *nt* **-s** nickel
nicken *vi* (*haben*) nod
Nickerchen *nt* **-s,-,** [!] nap
nie *adv* never
nieder *a* low ● *adv* down. **n∼brennen†** *vt/i sep* (*sein*) burn down. **N∼deutsch** *nt* Low German. **N∼gang** *m* (*fig*) decline. **n∼gedrückt** *a* (*fig*) depressed. **n∼geschlagen** *a* dejected, despondent. **N∼kunft** *f* **-,¨e** confinement. **N∼lage** *f* defeat
Niederlande (die) *pl* the Netherlands
Niederländ|er *m* **-s,-** Dutchman; **die N∼er** the Dutch *pl*. **N∼erin** *f* **-, -nen** Dutchwoman. **n∼isch** *a* Dutch
nieder|lassen† *vt sep* let down; **sich n∼lassen** settle; (*sich setzen*) sit down. **N∼lassung** *f* **-, -en** settlement; (*Zweigstelle*) branch. **n∼legen** *vt sep* put *or* lay down; resign <*Amt*>; **die Arbeit n∼legen** go on strike. **n∼metzeln** *vt sep* massacre. **N∼sachsen** *nt* Lower Saxony. **N∼schlag** *m* precipitation; (*Regen*) rainfall; (*radioaktiver*) fallout. **n∼schlagen†** *vt sep* knock down; lower <*Augen*>; (*unterdrücken*) crush. **n∼schmettern** *vt sep* (*fig*) shatter. **n∼setzen** *vt sep* put *or* set down; **sich n∼setzen** sit down. **n∼strecken** *vt sep* fell; (*durch Schuss*) gun down. **n∼trächtig** *a* base, vile. **n∼walzen** *vt sep* flatten
niedlich *a* pretty; sweet
niedrig *a* low; (*fig: gemein*) base ● *adv* low
niemals *adv* never
niemand *pron* nobody, no one
Niere *f* **-, -n** kidney; **künstliche N∼** kidney machine
niesel|n *vi* (*haben*) drizzle. **N∼regen** *m* drizzle
niesen *vi* (*haben*) sneeze. **N∼** *nt* **-s** sneezing; (*Nieser*) sneeze
Niete[1] *f* **-, -n** rivet; (*an Jeans*) stud

Niete² *f* **-, -n** blank; [!] failure
nieten *vt* rivet
Nikotin *nt* **-s** nicotine
Nil *m* **-[s]** Nile. **N~pferd** *nt* hippopotamus
nimmer *adv* (*SGer*) not any more; **nie und n~** never
nirgend|s, n~wo *adv* nowhere
Nische *f* **-, -n** recess, niche
nisten *vi* (*haben*) nest
Nitrat *nt* **-[e]s, -e** nitrate
Niveau /ni'vo:/ *nt* **-s, -s** level; (*geistig, künstlerisch*) standard
nix *adv* [!] nothing
Nixe *f* **-, -n** mermaid
nobel *a* noble; ([!] *luxuriös*) luxurious; ([!] *großzügig*) generous
noch *adv* still; (*zusätzlich*) as well; (*mit Komparativ*) even; **n~ nicht** not yet; **gerade n~** only just; **n~ immer** *od* **immer n~** still; **n~ letzte Woche** only last week; **wer n~?** who else? **n~ etwas** something else; (*Frage*) anything else? **n~ einmal** again; **n~ ein Bier** another beer; **n~ größer** even bigger; **n~ so sehr** however much ● *conj* **weder ... n~** neither ... nor
nochmals *adv* again
Nomad|e *m* **-n, -n** nomad. **n~isch** *a* nomadic
nominier|en *vt* nominate. **N~ung** *f* **-, -en** nomination
Nonne *f* **-, -n** nun. **N~nkloster** *nt* convent
Nonstopflug *m* direct flight
Nord *m* **-[e]s** north. **N~amerika** *nt* North America
Norden *m* **-s** north
nordisch *a* Nordic
nördlich *a* northern; <*Richtung*> northerly ● *adv & prep* (+ *gen*) **n~ [von] der Stadt** [to the] north of the town
Nordosten *m* north-east
Nord|pol *m* North Pole. **N~see** *f* **-** North Sea. **N~westen** *m* north-west
Nörgelei *f* **-, -en** grumbling
nörgeln *vi* (*haben*) grumble
Norm *f* **-, -en** norm; (*Techn*) standard; (*Soll*) quota
normal *a* normal. **n~erweise** *adv* normally
normen *vt* standardize
Norwe|gen *nt* **-s** Norway. **N~ger(in)** *m* **-s,-** (*f* **-, -nen**) Norwegian. **n~gisch** *a* Norwegian
Nost|algie *f* **-** nostalgia. **n~algisch** *a* nostalgic
Not *f* **-,¨e** need; (*Notwendigkeit*) necessity; (*Entbehrung*) hardship; (*seelisch*) trouble; **Not leiden** be in need, suffer hardship; **Not leidende Menschen** needy people; **zur Not** if need be; (*äußerstenfalls*) at a pinch
Notar *m* **-s, -e** notary public
Not|arzt *m* emergency doctor. **N~ausgang** *m* emergency exit. **N~behelf** *m* **-[e]s, -e** makeshift. **N~bremse** *f* emergency brake. **N~dienst** *m* **N~dienst haben** be on call
Note *f* **-, -n** note; (*Zensur*) mark; **ganze/halbe N~** (*Mus*) semi-breve/minim; **N~n lesen** read music; **persönliche N~** personal touch. **N~nblatt** *nt* sheet of music. **N~nschlüssel** *m* clef
Notfall *m* emergency; **für den N~** just in case. **n~s** *adv* if need be
notieren *vt* note down; (*Comm*) quote; **sich** (*dat*) **etw n~** make a note of sth
nötig *a* necessary; **n~ haben** need; **das N~ste** the essentials *pl* ● *adv* urgently. **n~enfalls** *adv* if need be. **N~ung** *f* **-** coercion
Notiz *f* **-, -en** note; (*Zeitungs-*) item; **[keine] N~ nehmen von** take [no] notice of. **N~buch** *nt* notebook. **N~kalender** *m* diary
Not|lage *f* plight. **n~landen** *vi* (*sein*) make a forced landing. **N~landung** *f* forced landing.

n~leidend* *a* **Not leidend**, *s.* **Not**. **N~lösung** *f* stopgap
Not|ruf *m* emergency call; (*Naut, Aviat*) distress call; (*Nummer*) emergency services number. **N~signal** *nt* distress signal. **N~stand** *m* state of emergency. **N~unterkunft** *f* emergency accommodation. **N~wehr** *f* **-** (*Jur*) self-defence
notwendig *a* necessary; essential ● *adv* urgently. **N~keit** *f* **-, -en** necessity
Notzucht *f* **-** (*Jur*) rape
Nougat /'nu:gat/ *m & nt* **-s** nougat
Novelle *f* **-, -n** novella; (*Pol*) amendment
November *m* **-s,-** November
Novize *m* **-n, -n, Novizin** *f* **-, -nen** (*Relig*) novice
Nu *m* **im Nu** [!] in a flash
nüchtern *a* sober; (*sachlich*) matter-of-fact; (*schmucklos*) bare; (*ohne Würze*) bland; **auf n~en Magen** on an empty stomach
Nudel *f* **-, -n** piece of pasta; **N~n** pasta *sg*; (*Band-*) noodles. **N~holz** *nt* rolling-pin
Nudist *m* **-en, -en** nudist
nuklear *a* nuclear
null *inv a* zero, nought; (*Teleph*) O; (*Sport*) nil; (*Tennis*) love; **n~ Fehler** no mistakes; **n~ und nichtig** (*Jur*) null and void. **N~** *f* **-, -en** nought, zero; (*fig: Person*) nonentity. **N~punkt** *m* zero
numerieren* *vt s.* **nummerieren**
Nummer *f* **-, -n** number; (*Ausgabe*) issue; (*Darbietung*) item; (*Zirkus-*) act; (*Größe*) size. **n~ieren** *vt* number. **N~nschild** *nt* number-plate
nun *adv* now; (*na*) well; (*halt*) just; **nun gut!** very well then!
nur *adv* only, just; **wo kann sie nur sein?** wherever can she be? **er soll es nur versuchen!** just let him try!

Nürnberg *nt* **-s** Nuremberg
nuscheln *vt/i* (*haben*) mumble
Nuss *f* **-,¨e** nut. **N~knacker** *m* **-s,-** nutcrackers *pl*
Nüstern *fpl* nostrils
Nut *f* **-, -en, Nute** *f* **-, -n** groove
Nutte *f* **-, -n** ⊠ tart ⊠
nutz|bar *a* usable; **n~bar machen** utilize; cultivate <*Boden*>. **n~bringend** *a* profitable
nutzen *vt* use, utilize; (*aus-*) take advantage of ● *vi* (*haben*) = **nützen. N~** *m* **-s** benefit; (*Comm*) profit; **N~ ziehen aus** benefit from; **von N~ sein** be useful
nützen *vi* (*haben*) be useful *or* of use (*dat* to); <*Mittel:*> be effective; **nichts n~** be useless *or* no use; **was nützt mir das?** what good is that to me? ● *vt* = **nutzen**
nützlich *a* useful. **N~keit** *f* **-** usefulness
nutz|los *a* useless; (*vergeblich*) vain. **N~losigkeit** *f* **-** uselessness. **N~ung** *f* **-** use, utilization
Nylon /'nailɔn/ *nt* **-s** nylon
Nymphe /'nʏmfə/ *f* **-, -n** nymph

Oo

o *int* **o ja/nein!** oh yes/no!
Oase *f* **-, -n** oasis
ob *conj* whether; **ob reich, ob arm** rich or poor; **und ob!** [!] you bet!
Obacht *f* **O~ geben** pay attention; **O~!** look out!
Obdach *nt* **-[e]s** shelter. **o~los** *a* homeless. **O~lose(r)** *m/f* homeless person; **die O~losen** the homeless *pl*
Obduktion /-'tsi̯o:n/ *f* **-, -en** post-mortem

O-Beine *ntpl* [!] bow-legs, bandy legs
oben *adv* at the top; (*auf der Oberseite*) on top; (*eine Treppe hoch*) upstairs; (*im Text*) above; **da o~** up there; **o~ im Norden** up in the north; **siehe o~** see above; **o~ auf** (+ *acc/dat*) on top of; **nach o~** up[wards]; (*die Treppe hinauf*) upstairs; **von o~** from above/upstairs; **von o~ bis unten** from top to bottom/<*Person*> to toe; **jdn von o~ bis unten mustern** look s.o. up and down; **o~ erwähnt** *od* **genannt** above-mentioned. **o~drein** *adv* on top of that
Ober *m* **-s,-** waiter
Ober|arm *m* upper arm. **O~arzt** *m* ≈ senior registrar. **O~deck** *nt* upper deck. **o~e(r,s)** *a* upper; (*höhere*) higher. **O~fläche** *f* surface. **o~flächlich** *a* superficial. **O~geschoss** *nt* upper storey. **o~halb** *adv & prep* (+ *gen*) above. **O~haupt** *nt* (*fig*) head. **O~haus** *nt* (*Pol*) upper house; (*in UK*) House of Lords. **O~hemd** *nt* [man's] shirt. **o~irdisch** *a* surface ... ● *adv* above ground. **O~kiefer** *m* upper jaw. **O~körper** *m* upper part of the body. **O~leutnant** *m* lieutenant. **O~lippe** *f* upper lip
Obers *nt* **-** (*Aust*) cream
Ober|schenkel *m* thigh. **O~schule** *f* grammar school. **O~seite** *f* upper/(*rechte Seite*) right side
Oberst *m* **-en** & **-s, -en** colonel
oberste(r,s) *a* top; (*höchste*) highest; <*Befehlshaber, Gerichtshof*> supreme; (*wichtigste*) first
Ober|stimme *f* treble. **O~teil** *nt* top. **O~weite** *f* chest/(*der Frau*) bust size
obgleich *conj* although
Obhut *f* **-** care
obig *a* above
Objekt *nt* **-[e]s, -e** object; (*Haus, Grundstück*) property
Objektiv *nt* **-s, -e** lens. **o~** *a* objective. **O~ität** *f* **-** objectivity
Oblate *f* **-, -n** (*Relig*) wafer
Obmann *m* (*pl* **-männer**) [jury] foreman; (*Sport*) referee
Oboe /o'bo:ə/ *f* **-, -n** oboe
Obrigkeit *f* **-** authorities *pl*
obschon *conj* although
Observatorium *nt* **-s, -ien** observatory
obskur *a* obscure; dubious
Obst *nt* **-es** (*coll*) fruit. **O~baum** *m* fruit-tree. **O~garten** *m* orchard. **O~händler** *m* fruiterer
obszön *a* obscene
O-Bus *m* trolley bus
obwohl *conj* although
Ochse *m* **-n, -n** ox
öde *a* desolate; (*unfruchtbar*) barren; (*langweilig*) dull. **Öde** *f* **-** desolation; barrenness; dullness
oder *conj* or; **du kennst ihn doch, o~?** you know him, don't you?
Ofen *m* **-s,⸚** stove; (*Heiz-*) heater; (*Back-*) oven; (*Techn*) furnace
offen *a* open; <*Haar*> loose; <*Flamme*> naked; (*o~herzig*) frank; (*o~ gezeigt*) overt; (*unentschieden*) unsettled; **o~e Stelle** vacancy; **Wein o~ verkaufen** sell wine by the glass; **o~ bleiben** remain open; **o~ halten** hold open <*Tür*>; keep open <*Mund, Augen*>; **o~ lassen** leave open; leave vacant <*Stelle*>; **o~ stehen** be open; <*Rechnung:*> be outstanding; **jdm o~ stehen** (*fig*) be open to s.o.; *adv* **o~ gesagt** *od* **gestanden** to be honest. **o~bar** *a* obvious ● *adv* apparently. **o~baren** *vt* reveal. **O~barung** *f* **-, -en** revelation. **O~heit** *f* **-** frankness, openness. **o~sichtlich** *a* obvious
offenstehen* *vi sep* (*haben*) **offen stehen**, *s.* **offen**

öffentlich *a* public. **Ö~keit** *f* - public; **in aller Ö~keit** in public, publicly
Offerte *f* -, **-n** (*Comm*) offer
offiziell *a* official
Offizier *m* **-s, -e** (*Mil*) officer
öffn|en *vt/i* (*haben*) open; **sich ö~en** open. **Ö~er** *m* **-s,-** opener. **Ö~ung** *f* -, **-en** opening. **Ö~ungszeiten** *fpl* opening hours
oft *adv* often
öfter *adv* quite often. **ö~e(r,s)** *a* frequent; **des Ö~en** frequently. **ö~s** *adv* [!] quite often
oh *int* oh!
ohne *prep* (+ *acc*) without; **o~ mich!** count me out! **oben o~** topless ● *conj* **o~ zu überlegen** without thinking; **o~ dass ich es merkte** without my noticing it. **o~dies** *adv* anyway. **o~gleichen** *pred a* unparalleled. **o~hin** *adv* anyway
Ohn|macht *f* -, **-en** faint; (*fig*) powerlessness; **in O~macht fallen** faint. **o~mächtig** *a* unconscious; (*fig*) powerless; **o~mächtig werden** faint
Ohr *nt* **-[e]s, -en** ear
Öhr *nt* **-[e]s, -e** eye
Ohrenschmalz *nt* ear-wax. **O~schmerzen** *mpl* earache *sg*
Ohrfeige *f* slap in the face. **o~n** *vt* **jdn o~n** slap s.o.'s face
Ohr|läppchen *nt* **-s,-** ear-lobe. **O~ring** *m* ear-ring. **O~wurm** *m* earwig
oje *int* oh dear!
okay /o'ke:/ *a & adv* [!] OK
Öko|logie *f* - ecology. **ö~logisch** *a* ecological. **Ö~nomie** *f* - economy; (*Wissenschaft*) economics *sg*. **ö~nomisch** *a* economic; (*sparsam*) economical
Oktave *f* -, **-n** octave
Oktober *m* **-s,-** October
ökumenisch *a* ecumenical
Öl *nt* **-[e]s, -e** oil; **in Öl malen** paint in oils. **Ölbaum** *m* olivetree. **ölen** *vt* oil. **Ölfarbe** *f* oil-paint. **Ölfeld** *nt* oilfield. **Ölgemälde** *nt* oil-painting. **ölig** *a* oily
Oliv|e *f* -, **-n** olive. **O~enöl** *nt* olive oil
Ölmessstab *m* dip-stick. **Ölsardinen** *fpl* sardines in oil. **Ölstand** *m* oil-level. **Öltanker** *m* oil-tanker. **Ölteppich** *m* oil-slick
Olympiade *f* -, **-n** Olympic Games *pl*, Olympics *pl*
Olymp|iasieger(in) /o'lympia-/ *m(f)* Olympic champion. **o~isch** *a* Olympic; **O~ische Spiele** Olympic Games
Ölzeug *nt* oilskins *pl*
Oma *f* -, **-s** [!] granny
Omnibus *m* bus; (*Reise-*) coach
onanieren *vi* (*haben*) masturbate
Onkel *m* **-s,-** uncle
Opa *m* **-s, -s** [!] grandad
Opal *m* **-s, -e** opal
Oper *f* -, **-n** opera
Operation /-'tsio:n/ *f* -, **-en** operation. **O~ssaal** *m* operating theatre
Operette *f* -, **-n** operetta
operieren *vt* operate on <*Patient, Herz*>; **sich o~ lassen** have an operation ● *vi* (*haben*) operate
Opernglas *nt* opera-glasses *pl*
Opfer *nt* **-s,-** sacrifice; (*eines Unglücks*) victim; **ein O~ bringen** make a sacrifice; **jdm/etw zum O~ fallen** fall victim to s.o./sth. **o~n** *vt* sacrifice
Opium *nt* **-s** opium
Opposition /-'tsio:n/ *f* - opposition. **O~spartei** *f* opposition party
Optik *f* - optics *sg*, ([!] *Objektiv*) lens. **O~er** *m* **-s,-** optician
optimal *a* optimum
Optimis|mus *m* - optimism. **O~t** *m* **-en, -en** optimist. **o~tisch** *a* optimistic
optisch *a* optical; <*Eindruck*> visual
Orakel *nt* **-s,-** oracle

O

Orange /oˈrãːʒə/ *f* **-, -n** orange. **o~** *inv a* orange. **O~ade** /orãˈʒaːdə/ *f* **-, -n** orangeade. **O~nmarmelade** *f* [orange] marmalade

Oratorium *nt* **-s, -ien** oratorio

Orchester /ɔrˈkɛstɐ/ *nt* **-s,-** orchestra

Orchidee /ɔrçiˈdeːə/ *f* **-, -n** orchid

Orden *m* **-s,-** (*Ritter-, Kloster-*) order; (*Auszeichnung*) medal, decoration

ordentlich *a* neat. tidy; (*anständig*) respectable; (*ordnungsgemäß* [!]: *richtig*) proper; <*Mitglied, Versammlung*> ordinary; ([!] *gut*) decent; ([!] *gehörig*) good

Order *f* **-, -s & -n** order

ordinär *a* common

Ordination /-ˈtsi̯oːn/ *f* **-, -en** (*Relig*) ordination; (*Aust*) surgery

ordn|en *vt* put in order; tidy; (*an-*) arrange. **O~er** *m* **-s,-** steward; (*Akten-*) file

Ordnung *f* **-** order; **O~ machen** tidy up; **in O~ bringen** put in order; (*aufräumen*) tidy; (*reparieren*) mend; (*fig*) put right; **in O~ sein** be in order; (*ordentlich sein*) be tidy; (*fig*) be all right; **[geht] in O~!** OK! **o~sgemäß** *a* proper. **O~sstrafe** *f* (*Jur*) fine. **o~swidrig** *a* improper

Ordonnanz, Ordonanz *f* **-, -en** (*Mil*) orderly

Organ *nt* **-s, -e** organ; voice

Organisation /-ˈtsi̯oːn/ *f* **-, -en** organization

organisch *a* organic

organisieren *vt* organize; ([!] *beschaffen*) get [hold of]

Organismus *m* **-, -men** organism; (*System*) system

Organspenderkarte *f* donor card

Orgasmus *m* **-, -men** orgasm

Orgel *f* **-, -n** (*Mus*) organ. **O~pfeife** *f* organ-pipe

Orgie /ˈɔrgi̯ə/ *f* **-, -n** orgy

Orien|t /ˈoːri̯ɛnt/ *m* **-s** Orient. **o~talisch** *a* Oriental

orientier|en /ori̯ɛnˈtiːrən/ *vt* inform (**über** + *acc* about); **sich o~en** get one's bearings, orientate oneself; (*unterrichten*) inform oneself (**über** + *acc* about). **O~ung** *f* **-** orientation; **die O~ung verlieren** lose one's bearings

original *a* original. **O~** *nt* **-s, -e** original. **O~übertragung** *f* live transmission

originell *a* original; (*eigenartig*) unusual

Orkan *m* **-s, -e** hurricane

Ornament *nt* **-[e]s, -e** ornament

Ort *m* **-[e]s, -e** place; (*Ortschaft*) [small] town; **am Ort** locally; **am Ort des Verbrechens** at the scene of the crime

ortho|dox *a* orthodox. **O~graphie, O~grafie** *f* **-** spelling. **O~päde** *m* **-n, -n** orthopaedic specialist

örtlich *a* local

Ortschaft *f* **-, -en** [small] town; (*Dorf*) village; **geschlossene O~** (*Auto*) built-up area

Orts|gespräch *nt* (*Teleph*) local call. **O~verkehr** *m* local traffic. **O~zeit** *f* local time

Öse *f* **-, -n** eyelet; (*Schlinge*) loop; **Haken und Öse** hook and eye

Ost *m* **-[e]s** east

Osten *m* **-s** east; **nach O~** east

ostentativ *a* pointed

Osteopath *m* **-en, -en** osteopath

Oster|ei /ˈoːstɐʔai̯/ *nt* Easter egg. **O~fest** *nt* Easter. **O~glocke** *f* daffodil. **O~n** *nt* **-,-** Easter; **frohe O~n!** happy Easter!

Österreich *nt* **-s** Austria. **Ö~er** *m*, **-s,-, Ö~erin** *f* **-, -nen** Austrian. **ö~isch** *a* Austrian

östlich *a* eastern; <*Richtung*> easterly ●*adv & prep* (+ *gen*) **ö~ [von] der Stadt** [to the] east of the town

Ostsee *f* Baltic [Sea]

Otter[1] *m* **-s,-** otter
Otter[2] *f* **-, -n** adder
Ouverture /uvɛrˈtyːrə/ *f* **-, -n** overture
oval *a* oval. **O~** *nt* **-s, -e** oval
Oxid, Oxyd *nt* **-[e]s, -e** oxide
Ozean *m* **-s, -e** ocean
Ozon *nt* **-s** ozone. **O~loch** *nt* hole in the ozone layer. **O~schicht** *f* ozone layer

Pp

paar *pron inv* **ein p~** a few; **ein p~ Mal** a few times; **alle p~ Tage** every few days. **P~** *nt* **-[e]s, -e** pair; (*Ehe-, Liebes-*) couple. **p~en** *vt* mate; (*verbinden*) combine; **sich p~en** mate. **P~ung** *f* **-, -en** mating. **p~weise** *adv* in pairs, in twos
Pacht *f* **-, -en** lease; (*P~summe*) rent. **p~en** *vt* lease
Pächter *m* **-s,-** lessee; (*eines Hofes*) tenant
Pachtvertrag *m* lease
Päckchen *nt* **-s,-** package, small packet
pack|en *vt/i* (*haben*) pack; (*ergreifen*) seize; (*fig: fesseln*) grip. **P~en** *m* **-s,-** bundle. **p~end** *a* (*fig*) gripping. **P~papier** *nt* [strong] wrapping paper. **P~ung** *f* **-, -en** packet; (*Med*) pack
Pädagog|e *m* **-n, -n** educationalist; (*Lehrer*) teacher. **P~ik** *f* **-** educational science
Paddel *nt* **-s,-** paddle. **P~boot** *nt* canoe. **p~n** *vt/i* (*haben/sein*) paddle. **P~sport** *m* canoeing
Page /ˈpaːʒə/ *m* **-n, -n** page
Paillette /paiˈjɛtə/ *f* **-, -n** sequin
Paket *nt* **-[e]s, -e** packet; (*Post-*) parcel
Pakist|an *nt* **-s** Pakistan. **P~aner(in)** *m* **-s,-** (*f* **-, -nen**) Pakistani. **p~anisch** *a* Pakistani
Palast *m* **-[e]s,⸚e** palace
Paläst|ina *nt* **-s** Palestine. **P~inenser(in)** *m* **-s,-** (*f* **-, -nen**) Palestinian. **p~inensisch** *a* Palestinian
Palette *f* **-, -n** palette
Palme *f* **-, -n** palm[-tree]
Pampelmuse *f* **-, -n** grapefruit
Panier|mehl *nt* (*Culin*) breadcrumbs *pl*. **p~t** *a* (*Culin*) breaded
Panik *f* **-** panic
Panne *f* **-, -n** breakdown; (*Reifen-*) flat tyre; (*Missgeschick*) mishap
Panther, Panter *m* **-s,-** panther
Pantine *f* **-, -n** [wooden] clog
Pantoffel *m* **-s, -n** slipper; mule
Pantomime[1] *f* **-, -n** mime
Pantomime[2] *m* **-n, -n** mime artist
Panzer *m* **-s,-** armour; (*Mil*) tank; (*Zool*) shell. **p~n** *vt* armourplate. **P~schrank** *m* safe
Papa /ˈpapa, paˈpaː/ *m* **-s, -s** daddy
Papagei *m* **-s** & **-en, -en** parrot
Papier *nt* **-[e]s, -e** paper. **P~korb** *m* waste-paper basket. **P~schlange** *f* streamer. **P~waren** *fpl* stationery *sg*
Pappe *f* **-** cardboard
Pappel *f* **-, -n** poplar
pappig *a* ⓘ sticky
Papp|karton *m*, **P~schachtel** *f* cardboard box
Paprika *m* **-s, -[s]** [sweet] pepper; (*Gewürz*) paprika
Papst *m* **-[e]s,⸚e** pope
päpstlich *a* papal
Parade *f* **-, -n** parade
Paradies *nt* **-es, -e** paradise
Paraffin *nt* **-s** paraffin
Paragraph, Paragraf *m* **-en, -en** section
parallel *a* & *adv* parallel. **P~e** *f* **-, -n** parallel

Paranuss *f* Brazil nut
Parasit *m* **-en, -en** parasite
parat *a* ready
Parcours /par'kuːɐ̯/ *m* **-,-** /**-[s], -s**/ (*Sport*) course
Pardon /par'dõː/ *int* sorry!
Parfüm *nt* **-s, -e** & **-s** perfume, scent. **p~iert** *a* perfumed, scented
parieren *vi* (*haben*) [!] obey
Park *m* **-s, -s** park. **p~en** *vt/i* (*haben*) park. **P~en** *nt* **-s** parking; '**P~en verboten**' 'no parking'
Parkett *nt* **-[e]s, -e** parquet floor; (*Theat*) stalls *pl*
Park|haus *nt* multi-storey car park. **P~kralle** *f* wheel clamp. **P~lücke** *f* parking space. **P~platz** *m* car park; parking space. **P~scheibe** *f* parking-disc. **P~schein** *m* car-park ticket. **P~uhr** *f* parking-meter. **P~verbot** *nt* parking ban; '**P~verbot**' 'no parking'
Parlament *nt* **-[e]s, -e** parliament. **p~arisch** *a* parliamentary
Parodie *f* **-, -n** parody
Parole *f* **-, -n** slogan; (*Mil*) password
Partei *f* **-, -en** (*Pol, Jur*) party; (*Miet-*) tenant; **für jdn P~ ergreifen** take s.o.'s part. **p~isch** *a* biased
Parterre /par'tɛr/ *nt* **-s, -s** ground floor; (*Theat*) rear stalls *pl*
Partie *f* **-, -n** part; (*Tennis, Schach*) game; (*Golf*) round; (*Comm*) batch
Partikel *nt* **-s,-** particle
Partitur *f* **-, -en** (*Mus*) full score
Partizip *nt* **-s, -ien** /-i̯ən/ participle
Partner|(in) *m* **-s,-** (*f* **-, -nen**) partner. **P~schaft** *f* **-, -en** partnership. **P~stadt** *f* twin town
Party /'paːɐ̯ti/ *f* **-, -s** party
Parzelle *f* **-, -n** plot [of ground]
Pass *m* **-es,¨e** passport; (*Geog, Sport*) pass
Passage /pa'saːʒə/ *f* **-, -n** passage; (*Einkaufs-*) shopping arcade
Passagier /pasa'ʒiːɐ̯/ *m* **-s, -e** passenger
Passant(in) *m* **-en, -en** (*f* **-, -nen**) passer-by
Passe *f* **-, -n** yoke
passen *vi* (*haben*) fit; (*geeignet sein*) be right (**für** for); (*Sport*) pass the ball; (*aufgeben*) pass; **p~ zu** go [well] with; (*übereinstimmen*) match; **jdm p~** fit s.o.; (*gelegen sein*) suit s.o.; **[ich] passe** pass. **p~d** *a* suitable; (*angemessen*) appropriate; (*günstig*) convenient; (*übereinstimmend*) matching
passier|en *vt* **pass; cross** <*Grenze*>; (*Culin*) rub through a sieve ● *vi* (*sein*) happen (**jdm** to s.o.); **es ist ein Unglück p~t** there has been an accident. **P~schein** *m* pass
Passiv *nt* **-s, -e** (*Gram*) passive
Passstraße *f* pass
Paste *f* **-, -n** paste
Pastell *nt* **-[e]s, -e** pastel
Pastete *f* **-, -n** pie; (*Gänseleber-*) pâté
pasteurisieren /pastøri'ziːrən/ *vt* pasteurize
Pastor *m* **-s, -en** /-'toːrən/ pastor
Pate *m* **-n, -n** godfather; (*fig*) sponsor; **P~n** godparents. **P~nkind** *nt* godchild
Patent *nt* **-[e]s, -e** patent; (*Offiziers-*) commission. **p~** *a* [!] clever; <*Person*> resourceful. **p~ieren** *vt* patent
Pater *m* **-s,-** (*Relig*) Father
Patholog|e *m* **-n, -n** pathologist. **p~isch** *a* pathological
Patience /pa'si̯ãːs/ *f* **-, -n** patience
Patient(in) /pa'tsi̯ɛnt(ɪn)/ *m* **-en, -en** (*f* **-, -nen**) patient
Patin *f* **-, -nen** godmother
Patriot|(in) *m* **-en, -en** (*f* **-, -nen**) patriot. **p~isch** *a* patriotic. **P~ismus** *m* **-** patriotism

Patrone *f* **-, -n** cartridge

Patrouille /pa'trʊljə/ *f* **-, -n** patrol

Patsch|e *f* **in der P~e sitzen** [!] be in a jam. **p~nass** *a* [!] soaking wet

Patt *nt* **-s** stalemate

Patz|er *m* **-s,-** [!] slip. **p~ig** *a* [!] insolent

Pauk|e *f* **-, -n** kettledrum; **auf die P~e hauen** [!] have a good time; (*prahlen*) boast. **p~en** *vt/i* (*haben*) [!] swot

pauschal *a* all-inclusive; (*einheitlich*) flat-rate; (*fig*) sweeping <*Urteil*>; **p~e Summe** lump sum. **P~e** *f* **-, -n** lump sum. **P~reise** *f* package tour. **P~summe** *f* lump sum

Pause[1] *f* **-, -n** break; (*beim Sprechen*) pause; (*Theat*) interval; (*im Kino*) intermission; (*Mus*) rest; **P~ machen** have a break

Pause[2] *f* **-, -n** tracing. **p~n** *vt* trace

pausenlos *a* incessant

pausieren *vi* (*haben*) have a break; (*ausruhen*) rest

Pauspapier *nt* tracing-paper

Pavian *m* **-s, -e** baboon

Pavillon /'pavɪljõ/ *m* **-s, -s** pavilion

Pazifi|k *m* **-s** Pacific [Ocean]. **p~sch** *a* Pacific

Pazifist *m* **-en, -en** pacifist

Pech *nt* **-s** pitch; (*Unglück*) bad luck; **P~ haben** be unlucky

Pedal *nt* **-s, -e** pedal

Pedant *m* **-en, -en** pedant

Pediküre *f* **-, -n** pedicure

Pegel *m* **-s,-** level; (*Gerät*) water-level indicator. **P~stand** *m* [water] level

peilen *vt* take a bearing on

peinigen *vt* torment

peinlich *a* embarrassing, awkward; (*genau*) scrupulous; **es war mir sehr p~** I was very embarrassed

Peitsche *f* **-, -n** whip. **p~n** *vt* whip; (*fig*) lash ● *vi* (*sein*) lash (**an** + *acc* against). **P~nhieb** *m* lash

Pelikan *m* **-s, -e** pelican

Pell|e *f* **-, -n** skin. **p~en** *vt* peel; shell <*Ei*>; **sich p~en** peel

Pelz *m* **-es, -e** fur

Pendel *nt* **-s,-** pendulum. **p~n** *vi* (*haben*) swing ● *vi* (*sein*) commute. **P~verkehr** *m* shuttle-service; (*für Pendler*) commuter traffic

Pendler *m* **-s,-** commuter

penetrant *a* penetrating; (*fig*) obtrusive

Penis *m* **-, -se** penis

Penne *f* **-, -n** [!] school

Pension /pã'zio:n/ *f* **-, -en** pension; (*Hotel*) guest-house; **bei voller/halber P~** with full/half board. **P~är(in)** *m* **-s, -e** (*f* **-, -nen**) pensioner. **P~at** *nt* **-[e]s, -e** boarding-school. **p~ieren** *vt* retire. **P~ierung** *f* **-** retirement

Pensum *nt* **-s** [allotted] work

Peperoni *f* **-,-** chilli

per *prep* (+ *acc*) by

Perfekt *nt* **-s** (*Gram*) perfect

Perfektion /-'tsio:n/ *f* **-** perfection

perforiert *a* perforated

Pergament *nt* **-[e]s, -e** parchment. **P~papier** *nt* grease-proof paper

Period|e *f* **-, -n** period. **p~isch** *a* periodic

Perl|e *f* **-, -n** pearl; (*Glas-, Holz-*) bead; (*Sekt-*) bubble. **P~mutt** *nt* **-s** mother-of-pearl

Pers|ien /-iən/ *nt* **-s** Persia. **p~isch** *a* Persian

Person *f* **-, -en** person; (*Theat*) character; **für vier P~en** for four people

Personal *nt* **-s** personnel, staff. **P~ausweis** *m* identity card. **P~chef** *m* personnel manager. **P~ien** /-iən/ *pl* personal particulars. **P~mangel** *m* staff shortage

persönlich *a* personal ● *adv* personally, in person. **P~keit** *f* -, -en personality

Perücke *f* -, -n wig

pervers *a* [sexually] perverted. **P~ion** *f* -, -en perversion

Pessimis|mus *m* - pessimism. **P~t** *m* -en, -en pessimist. **p~tisch** *a* pessimistic

Pest *f* - plague

Petersilie /-iə/ *f* - parsley

Petroleum /-leʊm/ *nt* -s paraffin

Petze *f* -, -n ! sneak. **p~n** *vi* (*haben*) ! sneak

Pfad *m* -[e]s, -e path. **P~finder** *m* -s,- [Boy] Scout. **P~finderin** *f* -, -nen [Girl] Guide

Pfahl *m* -[e]s,¨-e stake, post

Pfalz (die) - the Palatinate

Pfand *nt* -[e]s,¨-er pledge; (*beim Spiel*) forfeit; (*Flaschen-*) deposit

pfänd|en *vt* (*Jur*) seize. **P~erspiel** *nt* game of forfeits

Pfandleiher *m* -s,- pawnbroker

Pfändung *f* -, -en (*Jur*) seizure

Pfann|e *f* -, -n [frying-]pan. **P~kuchen** *m* pancake

Pfarr|er *m* -s,- vicar, parson; (*katholischer*) priest. **P~haus** *nt* vicarage

Pfau *m* -s, -en peacock

Pfeffer *m* -s pepper. **P~kuchen** *m* gingerbread. **P~minze** *f* - (*Bot*) peppermint. **p~n** *vt* pepper; (! *schmeißen*) chuck. **P~streuer** *m* -s,- pepperpot

Pfeif|e *f* -, -n whistle; (*Tabak-, Orgel-*) pipe. **p~en**† *vt/i* (*haben*) whistle; (*als Signal*) blow the whistle

Pfeil *m* -[e]s, -e arrow

Pfeiler *m* -s,- pillar; (*Brücken-*) pier

Pfennig *m* -s, -e pfennig

Pferch *m* -[e]s, -e [sheep] pen

Pferd *nt* -es, -e horse; **zu P~e** on horseback. **P~erennen** *nt* horse-race; (*als Sport*) [horse-] racing. **P~eschwanz** *m* horse's tail; (*Frisur*) pony-tail. **P~estall** *m* stable. **P~estärke** *f* horsepower

Pfiff *m* -[e]s, -e whistle

Pfifferling *m* -s, -e chanterelle

pfiffig *a* smart

Pfingst|en *nt* -s Whitsun. **P~rose** *f* peony

Pfirsich *m* -s, -e peach

Pflanz|e *f* -, -n plant. **p~en** *vt* plant. **P~enfett** *nt* vegetable fat. **p~lich** *a* vegetable

Pflaster *nt* -s,- pavement; (*Heft-*) plaster. **p~n** *vt* pave

Pflaume *f* -, -n plum

Pflege *f* - care; (*Kranken-*) nursing; **in P~ nehmen** look after; (*Admin*) foster <*Kind*>. **p~bedürftig** *a* in need of care. **P~eltern** *pl* foster-parents. **P~kind** *nt* foster-child. **p~leicht** *a* easy-care. **p~n** *vt* look after, care for; nurse <*Kranke*>; cultivate <*Künste, Freundschaft*>. **P~r(in)** *m* -s,- (*f* -, -nen) nurse; (*Tier-*) keeper

Pflicht *f* -, -en duty; (*Sport*) compulsory exercise/routine. **p~bewusst** *a* conscientious. **P~gefühl** *nt* sense of duty

pflücken *vt* pick

Pflug *m* -[e]s,¨-e plough

pflügen *vt/i* (*haben*) plough

Pforte *f* -, -n gate

Pförtner *m* -s,- porter

Pfosten *m* -s,- post

Pfote *f* -, -n paw

Pfropfen *m* -s,- stopper; (*Korken*) cork. **p~** *vt* graft (**auf** + *acc* on [to]); (! *pressen*) cram (**in** + *acc* into)

pfui *int* ugh

Pfund *nt* -[e]s, -e & - pound

Pfusch|arbeit *f* ! shoddy work. **p~en** *vi* (*haben*) ! botch one's work. **P~erei** *f* -, -en ! botch-up

Pfütze *f* -, -n puddle

Phantasie *f* -, -n imagination; **P~n** fantasies; (*Fieber-*)

hallucinations. **p~los** *a* unimaginative. **p~ren** *vi* (*haben*) fantasize; (*im Fieber*) be delirious. **p~voll** *a* imaginative
phantastisch *a* fantastic
pharma|zeutisch *a* pharmaceutical. **P~zie** *f* - pharmacy
Phase *f* -, **-n** phase
Philologie *f* - [study of] language and literature
Philosoph *m* **-en, -en** philosopher. **P~ie** *f* -, **-n** philosophy
philosophisch *a* philosophical
Phobie *f* -, **-n** phobia
Phonet|ik *f* - phonetics *sg*. **p~isch** *a* phonetic
Phosphor *m* **-s** phosphorus
Photo *nt*, **Photo-** = **Foto, Foto-**
Phrase *f* -, **-n** empty phrase
Physik *f* - physics *sg*. **p~alisch** *a* physical
Physiker(in) *m* **-s,-** (*f* -, **-nen**) physicist
Physiologie *f* - physiology
physisch *a* physical
Pianist(in) *m* **-en, -en** (*f* -, **-nen**) pianist
Pickel *m* **-s,-** pimple, spot; (*Spitzhacke*) pick. **p~ig** *a* spotty
Picknick *nt* **-s, -s** picnic
piep[s]|en *vi* (*haben*) <*Vogel:*> cheep; <*Maus:*> squeak; (*Techn*) bleep. **P~er** *m* **-s,-** bleeper
Pier *m* **-s, -e** [harbour] pier
Pietät /pie'tɛ:t/ *f* - reverence. **p~los** *a* irreverent
Pigment *nt* **-[e]s, -e** pigment. **P~ierung** *f* - pigmentation
Pik *nt* **-s, -s** (*Karten*) spades *pl*
pikant *a* piquant; (*gewagt*) racy
piken *vt* [!] prick
pikiert *a* offended, hurt
Pilger|(in) *m* **-s,-** (*f* -, **-nen**) pilgrim. **P~fahrt** *f* pilgrimage. **p~n** *vi* (*sein*) make a pilgrimage
Pille *f* -, **-n** pill
Pilot *m* **-en, -en** pilot
Pilz *m* **-es, -e** fungus; (*essbarer*) mushroom
pingelig *a* [!] fussy
Pinguin *m* **-s, -e** penguin
Pinie /-iə/ *f* -, **-n** stone-pine
pinkeln *vi* (*haben*) [!] pee
Pinsel *m* **-s,-** [paint]brush
Pinzette *f* -, **-n** tweezers *pl*
Pionier *m* **-s, -e** (*Mil*) sapper; (*fig*) pioneer
Pirat *m* **-en, -en** pirate
Piste *f* -, **-n** (*Ski-*) run, piste; (*Renn-*) track; (*Aviat*) runway
Pistole *f* -, **-n** pistol
pitschnass *a* [!] soaking wet
pittoresk *a* picturesque
Pizza *f* -, **-s** pizza
Pkw /'pe:kave:/ *m* **-s, -s** car
plädieren *vi* (*haben*) plead (**für** for); **auf Freispruch p~** (*Jur*) ask for an acquittal
Plädoyer /plɛdoa'je:/ *nt* **-s, -s** (*Jur*) closing speech; (*fig*) plea
Plage *f* -, **-n** [hard] labour; (*Mühe*) trouble; (*Belästigung*) nuisance. **p~n** *vt* torment, plague; (*bedrängen*) pester; **sich p~n** struggle
Plakat *nt* **-[e]s, -e** poster
Plakette *f* -, **-n** badge
Plan *m* **-[e]s,⸚e** plan
Plane *f* -, **-n** tarpaulin; (*Boden-*) groundsheet
planen *vt/i* (*haben*) plan
Planet *m* **-en, -en** planet
planier|en *vt* level. **P~raupe** *f* bulldozer
Planke *f* -, **-n** plank
plan|los *a* unsystematic. **p~mäßig** *a* systematic; <*Ankunft*> scheduled
Plansch|becken *nt* paddling pool. **p~en** *vi* (*haben*) splash about
Plantage /plan'ta:ʒə/ *f* -, **-n** plantation
Planung *f* - planning
plappern *vi* (*haben*) chatter ● *vt* talk <*Unsinn*>

plärren *vi* (*haben*) bawl
Plasma *nt* **-s** plasma
Plastik[1] *f* **-, -en** sculpture
Plast|ik[2] *nt* **-s** plastic. **p~isch** *a* three-dimensional; (*formbar*) plastic; (*anschaulich*) graphic
Plateau /pla'to:/ *nt* **-s, -s** plateau
Platin *nt* **-s** platinum
platonisch *a* platonic
plätschern *vi* (*haben*) splash; <*Bach:*> babble ● *vi* (*sein*) <*Bach:*> babble along
platt *a & adv* flat. **P~** *nt* **-[s]** (*Lang*) Low German
Plättbrett *nt* ironing-board
Platte *f* **-, -n** slab; (*Druck-*) plate; (*Metall-, Glas-*) sheet; (*Fliese*) tile; (*Koch-*) hotplate; (*Tisch-*) top; (*Schall-*) record, disc; (*zum Servieren*) [flat] dish, platter; **kalte P~** assorted cold meats and cheeses *pl*
Plätt|eisen *nt* iron. **p~en** *vt/i* (*haben*) iron
Plattenspieler *m* record-player
Platt|form *f* **-, -en** platform. **P~füße** *mpl* flat feet
Platz *m* **-es,¨-e** place; (*von Häusern umgeben*) square; (*Sitz-*) seat; (*Sport-*) ground; (*Fußball-*) pitch; (*Tennis-*) court; (*Golf-*) course; (*freier Raum*) room, space; **P~ nehmen** take a seat; **P~ machen** make room; **vom P~ stellen** (*Sport*) send off. **P~anweiserin** *f* **-, -nen** usherette
Plätzchen *nt* **-s,-** spot; (*Culin*) biscuit
platzen *vi* (*sein*) burst; (*auf-*) split; (! *scheitern*) fall through; <*Verlobung:*> be off
Platz|karte *f* seat reservation ticket. **P~mangel** *m* lack of space. **P~patrone** *f* blank. **P~verweis** *m* (*Sport*) sending off. **P~wunde** *f* laceration
Plauderei *f* **-, -en** chat
plaudern *vi* (*haben*) chat
plausibel *a* plausible

pleite *a* ! **p~ sein** be broke: <*Firma:*> be bankrupt. **P~** *f* **-, -n** ! bankruptcy; (*Misserfolg*) flop; **P~ gehen** *od* **machen** go bankrupt
plissiert *a* [finely] pleated
Plomb|e *f* **-, -n** seal; (*Zahn-*) filling. **p~ieren** *vt* seal; fill <*Zahn*>
plötzlich *a* sudden
plump *a* plump; clumsy
plumpsen *vi* (*sein*) ! fall
plündern *vt/i* (*haben*) loot
Plunderstück *nt* Danish pastry
Plural *m* **-s, -e** plural
plus *adv, conj & prep* (+ *dat*) plus. **P~** *nt* **-** surplus; (*Gewinn*) profit (*Vorteil*) advantage, plus. **P~punkt** *m* (*Sport*) point; (*fig*) plus
Po *m* **-s, -s** ! bottom
Pöbel *m* **-s** mob, rabble. **p~haft** *a* loutish
pochen *vi* (*haben*) knock, <*Herz:*> pound; **p~ auf** (+ *acc*) (*fig*) insist on
pochieren /pɔ'ʃi:rən/ *vt* poach
Pocken *pl* smallpox *sg*
Podest *nt* **-[e]s, -e** rostrum
Podium *nt* **-s, -ien** /-i̯ən/ platform; (*Podest*) rostrum
Poesie /poe'zi:/ *f* **-** poetry
poetisch *a* poetic
Pointe /'po̯ɛ̃:tə/ *f* **-, -n** point (*of a joke*)
Pokal *m* **-s, -e** goblet; (*Sport*) cup
pökeln *vt* (*Culin*) salt
Poker *nt* **-s** poker
Pol *m* **-s, -e** pole. **p~ar** *a* polar
Polarstern *m* pole-star
Pole *m,* **-n, -n** Pole. **P~n** *nt* **-s** Poland
Police /po'li:sə/ *f* **-, -n** policy
Polier *m* **-s, -e** foreman
polieren *vt* polish
Polin *f* **-, -nen** Pole
Politesse *f* **-, -n** [woman] traffic warden
Politik *f* **-** politics *sg*; (*Vorgehen, Maßnahme*) policy

Polit|iker(in) *m* **-s,-** (*f*, **-**, **-nen**) politician. **p~isch** *a* political

Politur *f* **-**, **-en** polish

Polizei *f* **-** police *pl*. **p~lich** *a* police ... ● *adv* by the police; <*sich anmelden*> with the police. **P~streife** *f* police patrol. **P~stunde** *f* closing time. **P~wache** *f* police station

Polizist *m* **-en**, **-en** policeman. **P~in** *f* **-**, **-nen** policewoman

Pollen *m* **-s** pollen

polnisch *a* Polish

Polster *nt* **-s,-** pad; (*Kissen*) cushion; (*Möbel-*) upholstery. **p~n** *vt* pad; upholster <*Möbel*>. **P~ung** *f* **-** padding; upholstery

Polter|abend *m* wedding-eve party. **p~n** *vi* (*haben*) thump bang

Polyäthylen *nt* **-s** polythene

Polyester *m* **-s** polyester

Polyp *m* **-en**, **-en** polyp. **P~en** adenoids *pl*

Pommes frites /pɔm'fri:t/ *pl* chips; (*dünner*) French fries

Pomp *m* **-s** pomp

Pompon /põ'põ:/ *m* **-s**, **-s** pompon

pompös *a* ostentatious

Pony[1] *nt* **-s**, **-s** pony

Pony[2] *m* **-s**, **-s** fringe

Pop *m* **-[s]** pop

Popo *m* **-s**, **-s** [!] bottom

populär *a* popular

Pore *f* **-**, **-n** pore

Porno|graphie, Pornografie *f* **-** pornography. **p~graphisch, p~grafisch** *a* pornographic

Porree *m* **-s** leeks *pl*

Portal *nt* **-s**, **-e** portal

Portemonnaie /pɔrtmɔ'ne:/ *nt* **-s**, **-s** purse

Portier /pɔr'ti̯e:/ *m* **-s**, **-s** doorman, porter

Portion /-'tsi̯o:n/ *f* **-**, **-en** helping, portion

Portmonee *nt* **-s**, **-s** = **Portemonnaie**

Porto *nt* **-s** postage. **p~frei** *adv* post free, post paid

Porträ|t /pɔr'trɛ:/ *nt* **-s**, **-s** portrait. **p~tieren** *vt* paint a portrait of

Portugal *nt* **-s** Portugal

Portugies|e *m* **-n**, **-n**, **P~in** *f* **-**, **-nen** Portuguese. **p~isch** *a* Portuguese

Portwein *m* port

Porzellan *nt* **-s** china, porcelain

Posaune *f* **-**, **-n** trombone

Position /-'tsi̯o:n/ *f* **-**, **-en** position

positiv *a* positive. **P~** *nt* **-s**, **-e** (*Phot*) positive

Post *f* **-** post office; (*Briefe*) mail, post; **mit der P~** by post

postalisch *a* postal

Post|amt *nt* post office. **P~anweisung** *f* postal money order. **P~bote** *m* postman

Posten *m* **-s,-** post; (*Wache*) sentry; (*Waren-*) batch; (*Rechnungs-*) item, entry

Poster *nt* & *m* **-s,-** poster

Postfach *nt* post-office *or* PO box

Post|karte *f* postcard. **p~lagernd** *adv* poste restante. **P~leitzahl** *f* postcode. **P~scheckkonto** *nt* ≈ National Girobank account. **P~stempel** *m* postmark

postum *a* posthumous

post|wendend *adv* by return of post. **P~wertzeichen** *nt* [postage] stamp

Potenz *f* **-**, **-en** potency; (*Math & fig*) power

Pracht *f* **-** magnificence, splendour

prächtig *a* magnificent; splendid

prachtvoll *a* magnificent

Prädikat *nt* **-[e]s**, **-e** rating; (*Comm*) grade; (*Gram*) predicate

prägen *vt* stamp (**auf** + *acc* on); emboss <*Leder*>; mint <*Münze*>; coin <*Wort*>; (*fig*) shape

prägnant *a* succinct

prähistorisch *a* prehistoric

prahl|en *vi* (*haben*) boast, brag (**mit** about)

Praktik|k *f* **-, -en** practice. **P~kant(in)** *m* **-en, -en** (*f* **-, -nen**) trainee

Prakti|kum *nt* **-s, -ka** practical training. **p~sch** *a* practical; (*nützlich*) handy; (*tatsächlich*) virtual; **p~scher Arzt** general practitioner ● *adv* practically; virtually; (*in der Praxis*) in practice. **p~zieren** *vt/i* (*haben*) practise; (*anwenden*) put into practice; ([!] *bekommen*) get

Praline *f* **-, -n** chocolate

prall *a* bulging; (*dick*) plump; <*Sonne*> blazing ● *adv* **p~ gefüllt** full to bursting. **p~en** *vi* (*sein*) **p~ auf** (+ *acc*)/**gegen** collide with, hit; <*Sonne:*> blaze down on

Prämie /-i̯ə/ *f* **-, -n** premium; (*Preis*) award

präm[i]ieren *vt* award a prize to

Pranger *m* **-s,-** pillory

Pranke *f* **-, -n** paw

Präparat *nt* **-[e]s, -e** preparation

Präsens *nt* **-** (*Gram*) present

präsentieren *vt* present

Präsenz *f* **-** presence

Präservativ *nt* **-s, -e** condom

Präsident|(in) *m* **-en, -en** (*f* **-, -nen**) president. **P~schaft** *f* **-** presidency

Präsidium *nt* **-s** presidency; (*Gremium*) executive committee; (*Polizei-*) headquarters *pl*

prasseln *vi* (*haben*) <*Regen:*> beat down; <*Feuer:*> crackle

Präteritum *nt* **-s** imperfect

Praxis *f* **-, -xen** practice; (*Erfahrung*) practical experience; (*Arzt-*) surgery; **in der P~** in practice

Präzedenzfall *m* precedent

präzis[e] *a* precise

predig|en *vt/i* (*haben*) preach. **P~t** *f* **-, -en** sermon

Preis *m* **-es, -e** price; (*Belohnung*) prize. **P~ausschreiben** *nt* competition

Preiselbeere *f* (*Bot*) cowberry; (*Culin*) ≈ cranberry

preisen† *vt* praise

preisgeben† *vt sep* abandon (*dat* to); reveal <*Geheimnis*>

preis|gekrönt *a* award-winning. **p~günstig** *a* reasonably priced ● *adv* at a reasonable price. **P~lage** *f* price range. **p~lich** *a* price ... ● *adv* in price. **P~richter** *m* judge. **P~schild** *nt* price-tag. **P~träger(in)** *m(f)* prize-winner. **p~wert** *a* reasonable

Prell|bock *m* buffers *pl*. **p~en** *vt* bounce; (*verletzen*) bruise; ([!] *betrügen*) cheat. **P~ung** *f* **-, -en** bruise

Premiere /prəˈmi̯e:rə/ *f* **-, -n** première

Premierminister(in) /prəˈmi̯e:-/ *m(f)* Prime Minister

Presse *f* **-, -n** press. **p~n** *vt* press

Pressluftbohrer *m* pneumatic drill

Preuß|en *nt* **-s** Prussia. **p~isch** *a* Prussian

prickeln *vi* (*haben*) tingle

Priester *m* **-s,-** priest

prima *inv a* first-class, first-rate; ([!] *toll*) fantastic

primär *a* primary

Primel *f* **-, -n** primula

primitiv *a* primitive

Prinz *m* **-en, -en** prince. **P~essin** *f* **-, -nen** princess

Prinzip *nt* **-s, -ien** /-i̯ən/ principle. **p~iell** *a* <*Frage*> of principle ● *adv* on principle

Prise *f* **-, -n P~ Salz** pinch of salt

Prisma *nt* **-s, -men** prism

privat *a* private, personal. **P~adresse** *f* home address. **p~isieren** *vt* privatize

Privileg *nt* **-[e]s, -ien** /-i̯ən/ privilege. **p~iert** *a* privileged

pro *prep* (+ *dat*) per. **Pro** *nt* **- das Pro und Kontra** the pros and cons *pl*

Probe *f* **-, -n** test, trial; (*Menge, Muster*) sample; (*Theat*) rehearsal; **auf die P~ stellen** put to the test; **ein Auto P~ fahren** test-drive a car. **p~n** *vt/i* (*haben*) (*Theat*) rehearse. **p~weise** *adv* on a trial basis. **P~zeit** *f* probationary period

probieren *vt/i* (*haben*) try; (*kosten*) taste; (*proben*) rehearse

Problem *nt* **-s, -e** problem. **p~atisch** *a* problematic

problemlos *a* problem-free ● *adv* without any problems

Produkt *nt* **-[e]s, -e** product

Produk|tion /-'tsio:n/ *f* **-, -en** production. **p~tiv** *a* productive

Produ|zent *m* **-en, -en** producer. **p~zieren** *vt* produce

Professor *m* **-s, -en** /-'so:rən/ professor

Profi *m* **-s, -s** (*Sport*) professional

Profil *nt* **-s, -e** profile; (*Reifen-*) tread; (*fig*) image

Profit *m* **-[e]s, -e** profit. **p~ieren** *vi* (*haben*) profit (**von** from)

Prognose *f* **-, -n** forecast; (*Med*) prognosis

Programm *nt* **-s, -e** programme; (*Computer-*) program; (*TV*) channel; (*Comm: Sortiment*) range. **p~ieren** *vt/i* (*haben*) (*Computer*) program. **P~ierer(in)** *m* **-s,-** (*f* **-, -nen**) [computer] programmer

Projekt *nt* **-[e]s, -e** project

Projektor *m* **-s, -en** /-'to:rən/ projector

Prolet *m* **-en, -en** boor. **P~ariat** *nt* **-[e]s** proletariat

Prolog *m* **-s, -e** prologue

Promenade *f* **-, -n** promenade

Promille *pl* 🄸 alcohol level *sg* in the blood; **zu viel P~ haben** 🄸 be over the limit

Prominenz *f* **-** prominent figures *pl*

Promiskuität *f* **-** promiscuity

promovieren *vi* (*haben*) obtain one's doctorate

prompt *a* prompt

Pronomen *nt* **-s,-** pronoun

Propaganda *f* **-** propaganda; (*Reklame*) publicity

Propeller *m* **-s,-** propeller

Prophet *m* **-en, -en** prophet

prophezei|en *vt* prophesy. **P~ung** *f* **-, -en** prophecy

Proportion /-'tsio:n/ *f* **-, -en** proportion

Prosa *f* **-** prose

prosit *int* cheers!

Prospekt *m* **-[e]s, -e** brochure; (*Comm*) prospectus

prost *int* cheers!

Prostitu|ierte *f* **-n, -n** prostitute. **P~tion** /-'tsio:n/ *f* **-** prostitution

Protest *m* **-[e]s, -e** protest

Protestant|(in) *m* **-en, -en** (*f* **-, -nen**) (*Relig*) Protestant. **p~isch** *a* (*Relig*) Protestant

protestieren *vi* (*haben*) protest

Prothese *f* **-, -n** artificial limb; (*Zahn-*) denture

Protokoll *nt* **-s, -e** record; (*Sitzungs-*) minutes *pl*; (*diplomatisches*) protocol

protz|en *vi* (*haben*) show off (**mit etw** sth). **p~ig** *a* ostentatious

Proviant *m* **-s** provisions *pl*

Provinz *f* **-, -en** province

Provision *f* **-, -en** (*Comm*) commission

provisorisch *a* provisional, temporary

Provokation /-'tsio:n/ *f* **-, -en** provocation

provozieren *vt* provoke

Prozedur *f* **-, -en** [lengthy] business

Prozent *nt* **-[e]s, -e & -** per cent; 5 **P~** 5 per cent. **P~satz** *m* percentage. **p~ual** *a* percentage ...

Prozess *m* **-es, -e** process; (*Jur*) lawsuit; (*Kriminal-*) trial

Prozession *f* **-, -en** procession

P

prüde *a* prudish
prüf|en *vt* test/(*über-*) check (**auf** + *acc* for); audit <*Bücher*>; (*Sch*) examine; **p~ender Blick** searching look. **P~er** *m* **-s,-** inspector; (*Buch-*) auditor; (*Sch*) examiner. **P~ling** *m* **-s, -e** examination candidate. **P~ung** *f* **-, -en** examination; (*Test*) test; (*Bücher-*) audit; (*fig*) trial
Prügel *m* **-s,-** cudgel; **P~** *pl* hiding *sg*, beating *sg*. **P~ei** *f* **-, -en** brawl, fight. **p~n** *vt* beat, thrash
Prunk *m* **-[e]s** magnificence, splendour
Psalm *m* **-s, -en** psalm
Pseudonym *nt* **-s, -e** pseudonym
pst *int* shush!
Psychi|ater *m* **-s,-** psychiatrist. **P~atrie** *f* **-** psychiatry. **p~atrisch** *a* psychiatric
psychisch *a* psychological
Psycho|analyse *f* psychoanalysis. **P~loge** *m* **-n, -n** psychologist. **P~logie** *f* **-** psychology. **p~logisch** *a* psychological
Pubertät *f* **-** puberty
Publi|kum *nt* **-s** public; (*Zuhörer*) audience; (*Zuschauer*) spectators *pl*. **p~zieren** *vt* publish
Pudding *m* **-s, -s** blancmange; (*im Wasserbad gekocht*) pudding
Pudel *m* **-s,-** poodle
Puder *m* & [!] *nt* **-s,-** powder. **P~dose** *f* [powder] compact. **p~n** *vt* powder. **P~zucker** *m* icing sugar
Puff *m* & *nt* **-s, -s** [x] brothel
Puffer *m* **-s,-** (*Rail*) buffer; (*Culin*) pancake. **P~zone** *f* buffer zone
Pull|i *m* **-s, -s** jumper. **P~over** *m* **-s,-** jumper; (*Herren-*) pullover
Puls *m* **-es** pulse. **P~ader** *f* artery
Pult *nt* **-[e]s, -e** desk
Pulver *nt* **-s,-** powder. **p~ig** *a* powdery
Pulverkaffee *m* instant coffee
pummelig *a* [!] chubby
Pumpe *f* **-, -n** pump. **p~n** *vt/i* (*haben*) pump; ([!] *leihen*) lend; **[sich** (*dat*)**] etw p~n** ([!] *borgen*) borrow sth
Pumps /pœmps/ *pl* court shoes
Punkt *m* **-[e]s, -e** dot; (*Tex*) spot; (*Geom, Sport & fig*) point; (*Gram*) full stop, period; **P~ sechs Uhr** at six o'clock sharp
pünktlich *a* punctual. **P~keit** *f* **-** punctuality
Pupille *f* **-, -n** (*Anat*) pupil
Puppe *f* **-, -n** doll; (*Marionette*) puppet; (*Schaufenster-, Schneider-*) dummy; (*Zool*) chrysalis
pur *a* pure; ([!] *bloß*) sheer
Püree *nt* **-s, -s** purée; (*Kartoffel-*) mashed potatoes *pl*
purpurrot *a* crimson
Purzel|baum *m* [!] somersault. **p~n** *vi* (*sein*) [!] tumble
Puste *f* **-** [!] breath. **p~n** *vt/i* (*haben*) [!] blow
Pute *f* **-, -n** turkey
Putsch *m* **-[e]s, -e** coup
Putz *m* **-es** plaster; (*Staat*) finery. **p~en** *vt* clean; (*Aust*) dry-clean; (*zieren*) adorn; **sich p~en** dress up; **sich** (*dat*) **die Zähne/Nase p~en** clean one's teeth/blow one's nose. **P~frau** *f* cleaner, charwoman. **p~ig** *a* [!] amusing, cute; (*seltsam*) odd
Puzzlespiel /'pazl-/ *nt* jigsaw
Pyramide *f* **-, -n** pyramid

Qq

Quacksalber *m* **-s,-** quack
Quadrat *nt* **-[e]s, -e** square. **q~isch** *a* square

quaken *vi* (*haben*) quack; <*Frosch:*> croak
Quäker(in) *m* **-s,-** (*f* **-, -nen**) Quaker
Qual *f* **-, -en** torment; (*Schmerz*) agony
quälen *vt* torment; (*foltern*) torture; (*bedrängen*) pester; **sich q~** torment oneself; (*leiden*) suffer; (*sich mühen*) struggle
Quälerei *f* **-, -en** torture
Qualifi|kation /-'tsio:n/ *f* **-, -en** qualification. **q~zieren** *vt* qualify. **q~ziert** *a* qualified; (*fähig*) competent; <*Arbeit*> skilled
Qualität *f* **-, -en** quality
Qualle *f* **-, -n** jellyfish
Qualm *m* **-s** [thick] smoke
qualvoll *a* agonizing
Quantum *nt* **-s, -ten** quantity; (*Anteil*) share, quota
Quarantäne *f* **-** quarantine
Quark *m* **-s** quark, ≈ curd cheese
Quartal *nt* **-s, -e** quarter
Quartett *nt* **-[e]s, -e** quartet
Quartier *nt* **-s, -e** accommodation; (*Mil*) quarters *pl*
Quarz *m* **-es** quartz
quasseln *vi* (*haben*) [!] jabber
Quaste *f* **-, -n** tassel
Quatsch *m* **-[e]s** [!] nonsense, rubbish; **Q~ machen** (*Unfug machen*) fool around; (*etw falsch machen*) do a silly thing. **q~en** [!] *vi* (*haben*) talk; <*Wasser, Schlamm:*> squelch ● *vt* talk
Quecksilber *nt* mercury
Quelle *f* **-, -n** spring; (*Fluss- & fig*) source
quengeln *vi* [!] whine
quer *adv* across, crosswise; (*schräg*) diagonally; **q~ gestreift** horizontally striped
Quere *f* **- der Q~ nach** across, crosswise; **jdm in die Q~ kommen** get in s.o.'s way
Quer|latte *f* crossbar. **Q~schiff** *nt* transept. **Q~schnitt** *m* cross-section. **q~schnittsgelähmt** *a* paraplegic. **Q~straße** *f* side-street. **Q~verweis** *m* cross-reference
quetschen *vt* squash; (*drücken*) squeeze; (*zerdrücken*) crush; (*Culin*) mash; **sich q~ in** (+ *acc*) squeeze into
Queue /kø:/ *nt* **-s, -s** cue
quieken *vi* (*haben*) squeal; <*Maus:*> squeak
quietschen *vi* (*haben*) squeal; <*Tür, Dielen:*> creak
Quintett *nt* **-[e]s, -e** quintet
quirlen *vt* mix
Quitte *f* **-, -n** quince
quittieren *vt* receipt <*Rechnung*>; sign for <*Geldsumme, Sendung*>; **den Dienst q~** resign
Quittung *f* **-, -en** receipt
Quiz /kvɪs/ *nt* **-,-** quiz
Quote *f* **-, -n** proportion

Rr

Rabatt *m* **-[e]s, -e** discount
Rabatte *f* **-, -n** (*Hort*) border
Rabattmarke *f* trading stamp
Rabbiner *m* **-s,-** rabbi
Rabe *m* **-n, -n** raven
Rache *f* **-** revenge, vengeance
Rachen *m* **-s,-** pharynx
rächen *vt* avenge; **sich r~** take revenge (**an** + *dat* on); <*Fehler:*> cost s.o. dear
Rad *nt* **-[e]s,⸚er** wheel; (*Fahr-*) bicycle, [!] bike; **Rad fahren** cycle
Radar *m & nt* **-s** radar
Radau *m* **-s** [!] din, racket
radeln *vi* (*sein*) [!] cycle
Rädelsführer *m* ringleader

radfahr|en* *vi sep (sein)* **Rad fahren**, *s.* **Rad**. **R~er(in)** *m(f)* **-s,-** (*f* **-, -nen**) cyclist
radier|en *vt/i (haben)* rub out; (*Kunst*) etch. **R~gummi** *m* eraser, rubber. **R~ung** *f* **-, -en** etching
Radieschen /-'di:sçən/ *nt* **-s,-** radish
radikal *a* radical, drastic
Radio *nt* **-s, -s** radio
radioaktiv *a* radioactive. **R~ität** *f* **-** radioactivity
Radius *m* **-, -ien** /-i̯ən/ radius
Rad|kappe *f* hub-cap. **R~ler** *m* **-s,-** cyclist; (*Getränk*) shandy
raffen *vt* grab; (*kräuseln*) gather; (*kürzen*) condense
Raffin|ade *f* **-** refined sugar. **R~erie** *f* **-, -n** refinery. **R~esse** *f* **-, -n** refinement; (*Schlauheit*) cunning. **r~iert** *a* ingenious; (*durchtrieben*) crafty
ragen *vi (haben)* rise [up]
Rahm *m* **-s** (*SGer*) cream
rahmen *vt* frame. **R~** *m* **-s,-** frame; (*fig*) framework; (*Grenze*) limits *pl*; (*einer Feier*) setting
Rakete *f* **-, -n** rocket; (*Mil*) missile
Rallye /'rali/ *nt* **-s, -s** rally
rammen *vt* ram
Rampe *f* **-, -n** ramp; (*Theat*) front of the stage
Ramsch *m* **-[e]s** junk
ran *adv* = **heran**
Rand *m* **-[e]s,¨er** edge; (*Teller-, Gläser-, Brillen-*) rim; (*Zier-*) border, edging; (*Brief-*) margin; (*Stadt-*) outskirts *pl*; (*Ring*) ring
randalieren *vi (haben)* rampage
Randstreifen *m* (*Auto*) hard shoulder
Rang *m* **-[e]s,¨e** rank; (*Theat*) tier; **erster/zweiter R~** (*Theat*) dress/ upper circle; **ersten R~es** first-class
rangieren /raŋ'ʒi:rən/ *vt* shunt ● *vi (haben)* rank (**vor** + *dat* before)

Rangordnung *f* order of importance; (*Hierarchie*) hierarchy
Ranke *f* **-, -n** tendril; (*Trieb*) shoot
ranken (sich) *vr* (*Bot*) trail; (*in die Höhe*) climb
Ranzen *m* **-s,-** (*Sch*) satchel
ranzig *a* rancid
Rappe *m* **-n, -n** black horse
Raps *m* **-es** (*Bot*) rape
rar *a* rare; **er macht sich rar** [!] we don't see much of him. **R~ität** *f* **-, -en** rarity
rasant *a* fast; (*schnittig, schick*) stylish
rasch *a* quick
rascheln *vi (haben)* rustle
Rasen *m* **-s,-** lawn
rasen *vi (sein)* tear [along]; <*Puls:*> race; <*Zeit:*> fly; **gegen eine Mauer r~** career into a wall ● *vi (haben)* rave; <*Sturm:*> rage. **r~d** *a* furious; (*tobend*) raving; <*Sturm, Durst*> raging; <*Schmerz*> excruciating; <*Beifall*> tumultuous
Rasenmäher *m* lawn-mower
Rasier|apparat *m* razor. **r~en** *vt* shave; **sich r~en** shave. **R~klinge** *f* razor blade. **R~wasser** *nt* aftershave [lotion]
Raspel *f* **-, -n** rasp; (*Culin*) grater. **r~n** *vt* grate
Rasse *f* **-, -n** race. **R~hund** *m* pedigree dog
Rassel *f* **-, -n** rattle. **r~n** *vi (haben)* rattle; <*Schlüssel:*> jangle; <*Kette:*> clank
Rassendiskriminierung *f* racial discrimination
Rassepferd *nt* thoroughbred.
rassisch *a* racial
Rassis|mus *m* **-** racism. **r~tisch** *a* racist
Rast *f* **-, -en** rest. **R~platz** *m* picnic area. **R~stätte** *f* motorway restaurant [and services]
Rasur *f* **-, -en** shave

Rat *m* **-[e]s** [piece of] advice; **sich** (*dat*) **keinen Rat wissen** not know what to do; **zu Rat[e] ziehen** = **zurate ziehen**, *s.* **zurate**

Rate *f* **-, -n** instalment

raten† *vt* guess; (*empfehlen*) advise ● *vi* (*haben*) guess; **jdm r∼** advise s.o.

Ratenzahlung *f* payment by instalments

Rat|geber *m* **-s,-** adviser; (*Buch*) guide. **R∼haus** *nt* town hall

ratifizier|en *vt* ratify. **R∼ung** *f* **-, -en** ratification

Ration /ra'tsi̯o:n/ *f* **-, -en** ration. **r∼ell** *a* efficient. **r∼ieren** *vt* ration

rat|los *a* helpless; **r∼los sein** not know what to do. **r∼sam** *pred a* advisable; prudent. **R∼schlag** *m* piece of advice; **R∼schläge** advice *sg*

Rätsel *nt* **-s,-** riddle; (*Kreuzwort-*) puzzle; (*Geheimnis*) mystery. **r∼haft** *a* puzzling, mysterious. **r∼n** *vi* (*haben*) puzzle

Ratte *f* **-, -n** rat

rau *a* rough; (*unfreundlich*) gruff; <*Klima*> harsh, raw; (*heiser*) husky; <*Hals*> sore

Raub *m* **-[e]s** robbery; (*Menschen-*) abduction; (*Beute*) loot, booty. **r∼en** *vt* steal; abduct <*Menschen*>

Räuber *m* **-s,-** robber

Raub|mord *m* robbery with murder. **R∼tier** *nt* predator. **R∼vogel** *m* bird of prey

Rauch *m* **-[e]s** smoke. **r∼en** *vt/i* (*haben*) smoke. **R∼en** *nt* **-s** smoking; '**R∼en verboten**' 'no smoking'. **R∼er** *m* **-s,** -smoker

Räucher|lachs *m* smoked salmon. **r∼n** *vt* (*Culin*) smoke

rauf *adv* = **herauf, hinauf**

rauf|en *vt* pull ● *vr/i* (*haben*) **[sich] r∼en** fight. **R∼erei** *f* **-,-en** fight

rauh* *a s.* **rau**

Raum *m* **-[e]s, Räume** room; (*Gebiet*) area; (*Welt-*) space

räumen *vt* clear; vacate <*Wohnung*>; evacuate <*Gebäude, Gebiet, (Mil) Stellung*>; (*bringen*) put (**in/auf** + *acc* into/on); (*holen*) get (**aus** out of)

Raum|fahrer *m* astronaut. **R∼fahrt** *f* space travel. **R∼inhalt** *m* volume

räumlich *a* spatial

Raum|pflegerin *f* cleaner. **R∼schiff** *nt* spaceship

Räumung *f* **-** clearing; vacating; evacuation. **R∼sverkauf** *m* clearance/closing-down sale

Raupe *f* **-, -n** caterpillar

raus *adv* = **heraus, hinaus**

Rausch *m* **-[e]s, Räusche** intoxication; (*fig*) exhilaration; **einen R∼haben** be drunk

rauschen *vi* (*haben*) <*Wasser, Wind:*> rush; <*Bäume Blätter:*> rustle ● *vi* (*sein*) rush [along]

Rauschgift *nt* [narcotic] drug; (*coll*) drugs *pl*. **R∼süchtige(r)** *m/f* drug addict

räuspern (sich) *vr* clear one's throat

rausschmeißen† *vt sep* ! throw out; (*entlassen*) sack

Raute *f* **-, -n** diamond

Razzia *f* **-, -ien** /-i̯ən/ [police] raid

Reagenzglas *nt* test-tube

reagieren *vi* (*haben*) react (**auf** + *acc* to)

Reaktion /-'tsi̯o:n/ *f* **-, -en** reaction. **r∼är** *a* reactionary

Reaktor *m* **-s, -en** /-'to:rən/ reactor

realisieren *vt* realize

Realis|mus *m* **-** realism. **R∼t** *m* **-en, -en** realist. **r∼tisch** *a* realistic

Realität *f* **-, -en** reality

Realschule *f* ≈ secondary modern school

Rebe *f* **-, -n** vine

Rebell *m* **-en, -en** rebel. **r∼ieren** *vi* (*haben*) rebel. **R∼ion** *f* **-, -en** rebellion

R

rebellisch *a* rebellious
Rebhuhn *nt* partridge
Rebstock *m* vine
Rechen *m* **-s-** rake
Rechen|aufgabe *f* arithmetical problem; (*Sch*) sum. **R~maschine** *f* calculator
recherchieren /reʃɛr'ʃi:rən/ *vt/i* (*haben*) investigate; (*Journ*) research
rechnen *vi* (*haben*) do arithmetic; (*schätzen*) reckon; (*zählen*) count (**zu** among; **auf** + *acc* on); **r~ mit** reckon with; (*erwarten*) expect ● *vt* calculate, work out; (*fig*) count (**zu** among). **R~** *nt* **-s** arithmetic
Rechner *m* **-s,-** calculator; (*Computer*) computer
Rechnung *f* **-, -en** bill; (*Comm*) invoice; (*Berechnung*) calculation; **R~ führen über** (+ *acc*) keep account of. **R~sjahr** *nt* financial year. **R~sprüfer** *m* auditor
Recht *nt* **-[e]s, -e** law; (*Berechtigung*) right (**auf** + *acc* to); **im R~ sein** be in the right; **R~ haben/behalten** be right; **jdm R~ geben** agree with s.o.; **mit** *od* **zu R~** rightly
recht *a* right; (*wirklich*) real; **ich habe keine r~e Lust** I don't really feel like it; **es jdm r~ machen** please s.o.; **jdm r~ sein** be all right with s.o. **r~ vielen Dank** many thanks
Recht|e *f* **-n, -[n]** right side; (*Hand*) right hand; (*Boxen*) right; **die R~e** (*Pol*) the right; **zu meiner R~en** on my right. **r~e(r,s)** *a* right; (*Pol*) right-wing; **r~e Masche** plain stitch. **R~e(r)** *m/f* **der/die R~e** the right man/woman; **R~e(s)** *nt* **das R~e** the right thing; **etwas R~es lernen** learn something useful; **nach dem R~en sehen** see that everything is all right
Rechteck *nt* **-[e]s, -e** rectangle. **r~ig** *a* rectangular
rechtfertigen *vt* justify; **sich r~en** justify oneself
recht|haberisch *a* opinionated. **r~lich** *a* legal. **r~mäßig** *a* legitimate
rechts *adv* on the right; (*bei Stoff*) on the right side; **von/nach r~** from/to the right; **zwei r~, zwei links stricken** knit two, purl two. **R~anwalt** *m*, **R~anwältin** *f* lawyer
Rechtschreib|programm *nt* spell checker. **R~ung** *f* **-** spelling
Rechts|händer(in) *m* **-s,-** (*f* **-, -nen**) right-hander. **r~händig** *a & adv* right-handed. **r~kräftig** *a* legal. **R~streit** *m* law suit. **R~verkehr** *m* driving on the right. **r~widrig** *a* illegal. **R~wissenschaft** *f* jurisprudence
rechtzeitig *a & adv* in time
Reck *nt* **-[e]s, -e** horizontal bar
recken *vt* stretch
Redakteur /redak'tø:ɐ̯/ *m* **-s, -e** editor; (*Radio, TV*) producer
Redaktion /-'tsi̯o:n/ *f* **-, -en** editing; (*Radio, TV*) production; (*Abteilung*) editorial/production department
Rede *f* **-, -n** speech; **zur R~ stellen** demand an explanation from; **nicht der R~ wert** not worth mentioning
reden *vi* (*haben*) talk (**von** about; **mit** to); (*eine Rede halten*) speak ● *vt* talk; speak <*Wahrheit*>. **R~sart** *f* saying
Redewendung *f* idiom
redigieren *vt* edit
Redner *m* **-s,-** speaker
reduzieren *vt* reduce
Reeder *m* **-s,-** shipowner. **R~ei** *f* **-, -en** shipping company
Refer|at *nt* **-[e]s, -e** report; (*Abhandlung*) paper; (*Abteilung*) section. **R~ent(in)** *m* **-en, -en** (*f* **-, -nen**) speaker; (*Sachbearbeiter*) expert. **R~enz** *f* **-, -en** reference

Reflex *m* **-es, -e** reflex; (*Widerschein*) reflection. **R~ion** *f* **-, -en** reflection. **r~iv** *a* reflexive

Reform *f* **-, -en** reform. **R~ation** /-'tsi̯o:n/ *f* **-** (*Relig*) Reformation

Reform|haus *nt* health-food shop. **r~ieren** *vt* reform

Refrain /rə'frɛ̃:/ *m* **-s, -s** refrain

Regal *nt* **-s, -e** [set of] shelves *pl*

Regatta *f* **-, -ten** regatta

rege *a* active; (*lebhaft*) lively; (*geistig*) alert; <*Handel*> brisk

Regel *f* **-, -n** rule; (*Monats-*) period. **r~mäßig** *a* regular. **r~n** *vt* regulate; direct <*Verkehr*>; (*erledigen*) settle. **r~recht** *a* real, proper ● *adv* really. **R~ung** *f* **-, -en** regulation; settlement

regen *vt* move; **sich r~** move; (*wach werden*) stir

Regen *m* **-s,-** rain. **R~bogen** *m* rainbow. **R~bogenhaut** *f* iris

Regener|ation /-'tsi̯o:n/ *f* **-** regeneration. **r~ieren** *vt* regenerate

Regen|mantel *m* raincoat. **R~schirm** *m* umbrella. **R~tag** *m* rainy day. **R~wetter** *nt* wet weather. **R~wurm** *m* earthworm

Regie /re'ʒi:/ *f* **-** direction; **R~ führen** direct

regier|en *vt/i* (*haben*) govern, rule; <*Monarch:*> reign [over]; (*Gram*) take. **R~ung** *f* **-, -en** government; (*Herrschaft*) rule; (*eines Monarchen*) reign

Regiment *nt* **-[e]s, -er** regiment

Region *f* **-, -en** region. **r~al** *a* regional

Regisseur /reʒɪ'sø:ɐ̯/ *m* **-s, -e** director

Register *nt* **-s,-** register; (*Inhaltsverzeichnis*) index; (*Orgel-*) stop

Regler *m* **-s,-** regulator

reglos *a* & *adv* motionless

regn|en *vi* (*haben*) rain; **es r~et** it is raining. **r~erisch** *a* rainy

regul|är *a* normal; (*rechtmäßig*) legitimate. **r~ieren** *vt* regulate

Regung *f* **-, -en** movement; (*Gefühls-*) emotion. **r~slos** *a* & *adv* motionless

Reh *nt* **-[e]s, -e** roe-deer; (*Culin*) venison

Rehbock *m* roebuck

reib|en† *vt* rub; (*Culin*) grate ● *vi* (*haben*) rub. **R~ung** *f* **-** friction. **r~ungslos** *a* (*fig*) smooth

reich *a* rich (**an** + *dat* in)

Reich *nt* **-[e]s, -e** empire; (*König-*) kingdom; (*Bereich*) realm

Reiche(r) *m/f* rich man/woman; **die R~en** the rich *pl*

reichen *vt* hand; (*anbieten*) offer ● *vi* (*haben*) be enough; (*in der Länge*) be long enough; **r~ bis zu** reach [up to]; (*sich erstrecken*) extend to; **mit dem Geld r~** have enough money

reich|haltig *a* extensive, large <*Mahlzeit*> substantial. **r~lich** *a* ample; <*Vorrat*> abundant. **R~tum** *m* **-s, -tümer** wealth (**an** + *dat* of); **R~tümer** riches. **R~weite** *f* reach; (*Techn, Mil*) range

Reif *m* **-[e]s** [hoar-]frost

reif *a* ripe; (*fig*) mature; **r~ für** ready for. **r~en** *vi* (*sein*) ripen; <*Wein, Käse & fig*> mature

Reifen *m* **-s,-** hoop; (*Arm-*) bangle; (*Auto-*) tyre. **R~druck** *m* tyre pressure. **R~panne** *f* puncture, flat tyre

reiflich *a* careful

Reihe *f* **-, -n** row; (*Anzahl & Math*) series; **der R~ nach** in turn; **wer ist an der R~?** whose turn is it? **r~n (sich)** *vr* **sich r~n an** (+ *acc*) follow. **R~nfolge** *f* order. **R~nhaus** *nt* terraced house

Reiher *m* **-s,-** heron

Reim *m* **-[e]s, -e** rhyme. **r~en** *vt* rhyme; **sich r~en** rhyme

rein[1] *a* pure; (*sauber*) clean; <*Unsinn, Dummheit*> sheer; **ins**

R~e schreiben make a fair copy of

rein² *adv* = **herein, hinein**

Reineclaude /rɛ:nə'klo:də/ *f* **-, -n** greengage

Reinfall *m* [!] let-down; (*Misserfolg*) flop

Rein|gewinn *m* net profit. **R~heit** *f* **-** purity

reinig|en *vt* clean; (*chemisch*) dry-clean. **R~ung** *f* **-, -en** cleaning; (*chemische*) dry-cleaning; (*Geschäft*) dry cleaner's

reinlegen *vt sep* put in; [!] dupe; (*betrügen*) take for a ride

reinlich *a* clean. **R~keit** *f* **-** cleanliness

Reis *m* **-es** rice

Reise *f* **-, -n** journey; (*See-*) voyage; (*Urlaubs-, Geschäfts-*) trip. **R~andenken** *nt* souvenir. **R~büro** *nt* travel agency. **R~bus** *m* coach. **R~führer** *m* tourist guide; (*Buch*) guide. **R~gesellschaft** *f* tourist group. **R~leiter(in)** *m(f)* courier. **r~n** *vi* (*sein*) travel. **R~nde(r)** *m/f* traveller. **R~pass** *m* passport. **R~scheck** *m* traveller's cheque. **R~veranstalter** *m* **-s,-** tour operator. **R~ziel** *nt* destination

Reisig *nt* **-s** brushwood

Reißaus *m* **R~ nehmen** [!] run away

Reißbrett *nt* drawing-board

reißen† *vt* tear; (*weg-*) snatch; (*töten*) kill; **Witze r~** crack jokes; **an sich** (*acc*) r~snatch; seize <*Macht*>; **sich r~ um** [!] fight for ● *vi* (*sein*) tear; <*Seil, Faden:*> break ● *vi* (*haben*) **r~ an** (+ *dat*) pull at

Reißer *m* **-s,-** [!] thriller; (*Erfolg*) big hit

Reiß|nagel *m* = **R~zwecke. R~verschluss** *m* zip [fastener]. **R~wolf** *m* shredder. **R~zwecke** *f* **-, -n** drawing-pin

reit|en† *vt/i* (*sein*) ride. **R~er(in)** *m* **-s,-** (*f* **-, -nen**) rider. **R~hose** *f* riding breeches *pl*. **R~pferd** *nt* saddle-horse. **R~weg** *m* bridle-path

Reiz *m* **-es, -e** stimulus; (*Anziehungskraft*) attraction, appeal; (*Charme*) charm. **r~bar** *a* irritable. **R~barkeit** *f* **-** irratability. **r~en** *vt* provoke; (*Med*) irritate; (*interessieren, locken*) appeal to, attract; arouse <*Neugier*>; (*beim Kartenspiel*) bid. **R~ung** *f* **-, -en** (*Med*) irritation. **r~voll** *a* attractive

rekeln (sich) *vr* stretch

Reklamation /-'tsi̯:o:n/ *f* **-, -en** (*Comm*) complaint

Reklam|e *f* **-, -n** advertising, publicity; (*Anzeige*) advertisement; (*TV, Radio*) commercial; **R~e machen** advertise (**für etw** sth). **r~ieren** *vt* complain about; (*fordern*) claim ● *vi* (*haben*) complain

Rekord *m* **-[e]s, -e** record

Rekrut *m* **-en, -en** recruit

Rek|tor *m* **-s, -en** /-'to:rən/ (*Sch*) head[master]; (*Univ*) vice-chancellor. **R~torin** *f* **-, -nen** head, headmistress; vice-chancellor

Relais /rə'lɛ:/ *nt* **-,-** /-s, -s/ (*Electr*) relay

relativ *a* relative

Religi|on *f* **-, -en** religion; (*Sch*) religious education. **r~ös** *a* religious

Reling *f* **-, -s** (*Naut*) rail

Reliquie /re'li:kvi̯ə/ *f* **-, -n** relic

rempeln *vt* jostle; (*stoßen*) push

Reneklode *f* **-, -n** greengage

Renn|bahn *f* race-track; (*Pferde-*) racecourse. **R~boot** *nt* speed-boat. **r~en†** *vt/i* (*sein*) run; **um die Wette r~en** have a race. **R~en** *nt* **-s,-** race. **R~pferd** *nt* racehorse. **R~sport** *m* racing. **R~wagen** *m* racing car

renommiert *a* renowned; <*Hotel, Firma*> of repute
renovier|en *vt* renovate; redecorate <*Zimmer*>. **R~ung** *f* - renovation; redecoration
rentabel *a* profitable
Rente *f* -, -n pension; **in R~ gehen** 🄸 retire. **R~nversicherung** *f* pension scheme
Rentier *nt* reindeer
rentieren (sich) *vr* be profitable; (*sich lohnen*) be worth while
Rentner(in) *m* **-s,-** (*f* **-, -nen**) [old-age] pensioner
Reparatur *f* **-, -en** repair. **R~werkstatt** *f* repair workshop; (*Auto*) garage
reparieren *vt* repair, mend
Reportage /-'ta:ʒə/ *f* **-, -n** report
Reporter(in) *m* **-s,-** (*f* **-, -nen**) reporter
repräsentativ *a* representative (**für** of); (*eindrucksvoll*) imposing
Reprodu|ktion /-'tsi̯o:n/ *f* **-, -en** reproduction. **r~zieren** *vt* reproduce
Reptil *nt* **-s, -ien** /-i̯ən/ reptile
Republik *f* **-, -en** republic. **r~anisch** *a* republican
Requisiten *pl* (*Theat*) properties, 🄸 props
Reservat *nt* **-[e]s, -e** reservation
Reserve *f* **-, -n** reserve; (*Mil, Sport*) reserves *pl*. **R~rad** *nt* spare wheel
reservier|en *vt* reserve; **r~en lassen** book. **r~t** *a* reserved. **R~ung** *f* **-, -en** reservation
Reservoir /rezɛr'vo̯a:ɐ̯/ *nt* **-s, -s** reservoir
Residenz *f* **-, -en** residence
Resign|ation /-'tsi̯o:n/ *f* - resignation. **r~ieren** *vi* (*haben*) (*fig*) give up. **r~iert** *a* resigned
resolut *a* resolute
Resonanz *f* **-, -en** resonanance
Respekt /-sp-, -ʃp-/ *m* **-[e]s** respect (**vor** + *dat* for). **r~ieren** *vt* respect
respektlos *a* disrespectful
Ressort /rɛ'so:ɐ̯/ *nt* **-s, -s** department
Rest *m* **-[e]s, -e** remainder, rest; **R~e** remains; (*Essens-*) leftovers
Restaurant /rɛsto'rã:/ *nt* **-s, -s** restaurant
Restaur|ation /rɛstau̯ra'tsi̯o:n/ *f* - restoration. **r~ieren** *vt* restore
Rest|betrag *m* balance. **r~lich** *a* remaining
Resultat *nt* **-[e]s, -e** result
rett|en *vt* save (**vor** + *dat* from); (*aus Gefahr befreien*) rescue; **sich r~en** save oneself; (*flüchten*) escape. **R~er** *m* **-s,-** rescuer; (*fig*) saviour
Rettich *m* **-s, -e** white radish
Rettung *f* **-, -en** rescue; (*fig*) salvation; **jds letzte R~** s.o.'s last hope. **R~sboot** *nt* lifeboat. **R~sdienst** *m* rescue service. **R~sgürtel** *m* lifebelt. **r~slos** *adv* hopelessly. **R~sring** *m* lifebelt. **R~swagen** *m* ambulance
retuschieren *vt* (*Phot*) retouch
Reue *f* - remorse; (*Relig*) repentance
Revanch|e /re'vã:ʃə/ *f* **-, -n** revenge; **R~e fordern** (*Sport*) ask for a return match. **r~ieren (sich)** *vr* take revenge; (*sich erkenntlich zeigen*) reciprocate (**mit** with)
Revers /re've:ɐ̯/ *nt* **-,-** /-[s], -s/ lapel
Revier *nt* **-s, -e** district; (*Zool & fig*) territory; (*Polizei-*) [police] station
Revision *f* **-, -en** revision; (*Prüfung*) check; (*Jur*) appeal
Revolution /-'tsi̯o:n/ *f* **-, -en** revolution. **r~är** *a* revolutionary. **r~ieren** *vt* revolutionize
Revolver *m* **-s,-** revolver
rezen|sieren *vt* review. **R~sion** *f* **-, -en** review
Rezept *nt* **-[e]s, -e** prescription; (*Culin*) recipe
Rezession *f* **-, -en** recession

R

R-Gespräch *nt* reverse-charge call
Rhabarber *m* **-s** rhubarb
Rhein *m* **-s** Rhine. **R~land** *nt* **-s** Rhineland. **R~wein** *m* hock
Rhetorik *f* **-** rhetoric
Rheum|a *nt* **-s**, **R~atismus** *m* **-** rheumatism
Rhinozeros *nt* **-[ses], -se** rhinoceros
rhyth|misch /ˈrʏt-/ *a* rhythmic[al]. **R~mus** *m* **-, -men** rhythm
richten *vt* direct (**auf** + *acc* at); address <*Frage*> (**an** + *acc* to); aim <*Waffe*> (**auf** + *acc* at); (*einstellen*) set; (*vorbereiten*) prepare; (*reparieren*) mend; **in die Höhe r~** raise [up]; **sich r~** be directed (**auf** + *acc* at; **gegen** against); <*Blick:*> turn (**auf** + *acc* on); **sich r~ nach** comply with <*Vorschrift*>; fit in with <*jds Plänen*>; (*abhängen*) depend on ● *vi* (*haben*) **r~ über** (+ *acc*) judge
Richter *m* **-s,-** judge
richtig *a* right, correct; (*wirklich, echt*) real; **das R~e** the right thing ● *adv* correctly; really; **r~ stellen** put right <*Uhr*>; (*fig*) correct <*Irrtum*>; **die Uhr geht r~** the clock is right
Richtlinien *fpl* guidelines
Richtung *f* **-, -en** direction
riechen† *vt/i* (*haben*) smell (**nach** of; **an etw** *dat* sth)
Riegel *m* **-s,-** bolt; (*Seife*) bar
Riemen *m* **-s,-** strap; (*Ruder*) oar
Riese *m* **-n, -n** giant
rieseln *vi* (*sein*) trickle; <*Schnee:*> fall lightly
riesengroß *a* huge, enormous
riesig *a* huge; (*gewaltig*) enormous ● *adv* [!] terribly
Riff *nt* **-[e]s, -e** reef
Rille *f* **-, -n** groove
Rind *nt* **-es, -er** ox; (*Kuh*) cow; (*Stier*) bull; (*R~fleisch*) beef; **R~er** cattle *pl*
Rinde *f* **-, -n** bark; (*Käse-*) rind; (*Brot-*) crust
Rinder|braten *m* roast beef. **R~wahnsinn** *m* [!] mad cow disease
Rindfleisch *nt* beef
Ring *m* **-[e]s, -e** ring
ringeln (sich) *vr* curl
ring|en† *vi* (*haben*) wrestle; (*fig*) struggle (**um/nach** for) ● *vt* wring <*Hände*>. **R~er** *m* **-s,-** wrestler. **R~kampf** *m* wrestling match; (*als Sport*) wrestling
rings|herum, r~um *adv* all around
Rinn|e *f* **-, -n** channel; (*Dach-*) gutter. **r~en†** *vi* (*sein*) run; <*Sand:*> trickle. **R~stein** *m* gutter
Rippe *f* **-, -n** rib
Risiko *nt* **-s, -s** *&* **-ken** risk
risk|ant *a* risky. **r~ieren** *vt* risk
Riss *m* **-es, -e** tear; (*Mauer-*) crack; (*fig*) rift
rissig *a* cracked; <*Haut*> chapped
Rist *m* **-[e]s, -e** instep
Ritt *m* **-[e]s, -e** ride
Ritter *m* **-s,-** knight
Ritual *nt* **-s, -e** ritual
Ritz *m* **-es, -e** scratch. **R~e** *f* **-, -n** crack; (*Fels-*) cleft; (*zwischen Betten, Vorhängen*) gap. **r~en** *vt* scratch
Rival|e *m* **-n, -n, R~in** *f* **-, -nen** rival. **R~ität** *f* **-, -en** rivalry
Robbe *f* **-, -n** seal
Robe *f* **-, -n** gown; (*Talar*) robe
Roboter *m* **-s,-** robot
robust *a* robust
röcheln *vi* (*haben*) breathe stertorously
Rock[1] *m* **-[e]s,¨e** skirt; (*Jacke*) jacket
Rock[2] *m* **-[s]** (*Mus*) rock
rodel|n *vi* (*sein/haben*) toboggan. **R~schlitten** *m* toboggan
roden *vt* clear <*Land*>; grub up <*Stumpf*>
Roggen *m* **-s** rye

roh *a* rough; (*ungekocht*) raw; <*Holz*> bare; (*brutal*) brutal. **R~bau** *m* **-[e]s, -ten** shell. **R~kost** *f* raw [vegetarian] food. **R~ling** *m* **-s, -e** brute. **R~öl** *nt* crude oil

Rohr *nt* **-[e]s, -e** pipe; (*Geschütz-*) barrel; (*Bot*) reed; (*Zucker-, Bambus-*) cane

Röhre *f* **-, -n** tube; (*Radio-*) valve; (*Back-*) oven

Rohstoff *m* raw material

Rokoko *nt* **-s** rococo

Roll|bahn *f* taxiway; (*Start-/Landebahn*) runway. **R~balken** *m* scroll bar

Rolle *f* **-, -n** roll; (*Garn-*) reel; (*Draht-*) coil; (*Techn*) roller; (*Seil-*) pulley; (*Lauf-*) castor; (*Theat*) part, role; **das spielt keine R~** (*fig*) that doesn't matter. **r~n** *vt* roll; (*auf-*) roll up; (*Computer*) scroll; **sich r~n** roll ●*vi* (*sein*) roll; <*Flugzeug:*> taxi. **R~r** *m* **-s,-** scooter. **R~rblades (P)** /-ble:ds/ *mpl* Rollerblades (P)

Roll|feld *nt* airfield. **R~kragen** *m* polo-neck. **R~mops** *m* rollmop[s] *sg*

Rollo *nt* **-s, -s** [roller] blind

Roll|schuh *m* roller-skate; **R~schuh laufen** roller-skate. **R~stuhl** *m* wheelchair. **R~treppe** *f* escalator

Rom *nt* **-s** Rome

Roman *m* **-s, -e** novel. **r~isch** *a* Romanesque; <*Sprache*> Romance

Romant|ik *f* **-** romanticism. **r~isch** *a* romantic

Röm|er(in) *m* **-s,-** (*f* **-, -nen**) Roman. **r~isch** *a* Roman

Rommé, Rommee /'rɔme:/ *nt* **-s** rummy

röntgen *vt* X-ray. **R~aufnahme** *f*, **R~bild** *nt* X-ray. **R~strahlen** *mpl* X-rays

rosa *inv a*, **R~** *nt* **-[s],-** pink

Rose *f* **-, -n** rose. **R~nkohl** *m* [Brussels] sprouts *pl*. **R~nkranz** *m* (*Relig*) rosary

Rosine *f* **-, -n** raisin

Rosmarin *m* **-s** rosemary

Ross *nt* **-es,¨-er** horse

Rost[1] *m* **-[e]s, -e** grating; (*Kamin-*) grate; (*Brat-*) grill

Rost[2] *m* **-[e]s** rust. **r~en** *vi* (*haben*) rust

rösten *vt* roast; toast <*Brot*>

rostfrei *a* stainless

rostig *a* rusty

rot *a*, **Rot** *nt* **-s,-** red; **rot werden** turn red; (*erröten*) go red, blush

Röte *f* **-** redness; (*Scham-*) blush

Röteln *pl* German measles *sg*

röten *vt* redden; **sich r~** turn red

rothaarig *a* red-haired

rotieren *vi* (*haben*) rotate

Rot|kehlchen *nt* **-s,-** robin. **R~kohl** *m* red cabbage

rötlich *a* reddish

Rotwein *m* red wine

Rou|lade /ru'la:də/ *f* **-, -n** beef olive. **R~leau** /-'lo:/ *nt* **-s, -s** [roller] blind

Routin|e /ru'ti:nə/ *f* **-, -n** routine; (*Erfahrung*) experience. **r~emäßig** *a* routine ... ●*adv* routinely. **r~iert** *a* experienced

Rowdy /'raudi/ *m* **-s, -s** hooligan

Rübe *f* **-, -n** beet; **rote R~** beetroot

Rubin *m* **-s, -e** ruby

Ruck *m* **-[e]s, -e** jerk

ruckartig *a* jerky

rück|bezüglich *a* (*Gram*) reflexive. **R~blende** *f* flashback. **R~blick** *m* (*fig*) review (**auf** + *acc* of). **r~blickend** *adv* in retrospect. **r~datieren** *vt* (*inf & pp only*) backdate

Rücken *m* **-s,-** back; (*Buch-*) spine; (*Berg-*) ridge. **R~lehne** *f* back. **R~mark** *nt* spinal cord. **R~schwimmen** *nt* backstroke. **R~wind** *m* following wind; (*Aviat*) tail wind

rückerstatten *vt* (*inf & pp only*) refund

Rückfahr|karte *f* return ticket. **R~t** *f* return journey

R

Rück|fall *m* relapse. **R~flug** *m* return flight. **R~frage** *f* [further] query. **r~fragen** *vi* (*haben*) (*inf & pp only*) check (**bei** with). **R~gabe** *f* return. **r~gängig** *a* **r~gängig machen** cancel; break off <*Verlobung*>. **R~grat** *nt* **-[e]s, -e** spine, backbone. **R~hand** *f* backhand. **R~kehr** return. **R~lagen** *fpl* reserves. **R~licht** *nt* rear-light. **R~reise** *f* return journey

Rucksack *m* rucksack

Rück|schau *f* review. **R~schlag** *m* (*Sport*) return; (*fig*) set-back. **r~schrittlich** *a* retrograde. **R~seite** *f* back; (*einer Münze*) reverse

Rücksicht *f* **-, -en** consideration. **R~nahme** *f* **-** consideration. **r~slos** *a* inconsiderate; (*schonungslos*) ruthless. **r~svoll** *a* considerate

Rück|sitz *m* back seat; (*Sozius*) pillion. **R~spiegel** *m* rear-view mirror. **R~spiel** *nt* return match. **R~stand** *m* (*Chem*) residue; (*Arbeits-*) backlog; **im R~stand sein** be behind. **r~ständig** *a* (*fig*) backward. **R~stau** *m* (*Auto*) tailback. **R~strahler** *m* **-s,-** reflector. **R~tritt** *m* resignation; (*Fahrrad*) back pedalling

rückwärt|ig *a* back ..., rear ... **r~s** *adv* backwards. **R~sgang** *m* reverse [gear]

Rückweg *m* way back

rück|wirkend *a* retrospective. **R~wirkung** *f* retrospective force; **mit R~wirkung vom** backdated to. **R~zahlung** *f* repayment

Rüde *m* **-n, -n** [male] dog

Rudel *nt* **-s,-** herd; (*Wolfs-*) pack; (*Löwen-*) pride

Ruder *nt* **-s,-** oar; (*Steuer-*) rudder; **am R~** (*Naut & fig*) at the helm. **R~boot** *nt* rowing boat. **r~n** *vt/i* (*haben/sein*) row

Ruf *m* **-[e]s, -e** call; (*laut*) shout; (*Telefon*) telephone number; (*Ansehen*) reputation. **r~en†** *vt/i* (*haben*) call (**nach** for); **r~en lassen** send for

Ruf|name *m* forename by which one is known. **R~nummer** *f* telephone number. **R~zeichen** *nt* dialling tone

Rüge *f* **-, -n** reprimand. **r~n** *vt* reprimand; (*kritisieren*) criticize

Ruhe *f* **-** rest; (*Stille*) quiet; (*Frieden*) peace; (*innere*) calm; (*Gelassenheit*) composure; **R~ [da]!** quiet! **r~los** *a* restless. **r~n** *vi* (*haben*) rest (**auf** + *dat* on); <*Arbeit, Verkehr:*> have stopped. **R~pause** *f* rest, break. **R~stand** *m* retirement; **im R~stand** retired. **R~störung** *f* disturbance of the peace. **R~tag** *m* day of rest; **'Montag R~tag'** 'closed on Mondays'

ruhig *a* quiet; (*erholsam*) restful; (*friedlich*) peaceful; (*unbewegt, gelassen*) calm; **man kann r~ darüber sprechen** there's no harm in talking about it

Ruhm *m* **-[e]s** fame; (*Ehre*) glory

rühmen *vt* praise

ruhmreich *a* glorious

Ruhr *f* **-** (*Med*) dysentery

Rühr|ei *nt* scrambled eggs *pl*. **r~en** *vt* move; (*Culin*) stir; **sich r~en** move ● *vi* (*haben*) stir; **r~en an** (+ *acc*) touch; (*fig*) touch on. **r~end** *a* touching

Rührung *f* **-** emotion

Ruin *m* **-s** ruin. **R~e** *f* **-, -n** ruin; ruins *pl* (*gen* of). **r~ieren** *vt* ruin

rülpsen *vi* (*haben*) [!] belch

Rum *m* **-s** rum

Rumän|ien /-iən/ *nt* **-s** Romania. **r~isch** *a* Romanian

Rummel *m* **-s** [!] hustle and bustle; (*Jahrmarkt*) funfair

Rumpelkammer *f* junk-room

Rumpf *m* **-[e]s,¨-e** body, trunk; (*Schiffs-*) hull; (*Aviat*) fuselage

rund *a* round ● *adv* approximately; **r~ um** [a]round. **R~blick** *m* panoramic view. **R~brief** *m* circular [letter]

Runde *f* **-, -n** round; (*Kreis*) circle; (*eines Polizisten*) beat; (*beim Rennen*) lap; **eine R~ Bier** a round of beer

Rund|fahrt *f* tour. **R~frage** *f* poll

Rundfunk *m* radio; **im R~** on the radio. **R~gerät** *nt* radio [set]

Rund|gang *m* round; (*Spaziergang*) walk (**durch** round). **r~heraus** *adv* straight out. **r~herum** *adv* all around. **r~lich** *a* rounded; (*mollig*) plump. **R~reise** *f* [circular] tour. **R~schreiben** *nt* circular. **r~um** *adv* all round. **R~ung** *f* **-, -en** curve

Runzel *f* **-, -n** wrinkle

runzlig *a* wrinkled

Rüpel *m* **-s,-** [!] lout

rupfen *vt* pull out; pluck <*Geflügel*>

Rüsche *f* **-, -n** frill

Ruß *m* **-es** soot

Russe *m* **-n, -n** Russian

Rüssel *m* **-s,-** (*Zool*) trunk

Russ|in *f* **-, -nen** Russian. **r~isch** *a* Russian. **R~isch** *nt* **-[s]** (*Lang*) Russian

Russland *nt* **-s** Russia

rüsten *vi* (*haben*) prepare (**zu/für** for) ● *vr* **sich r~** get ready

rüstig *a* sprightly

rustikal *a* rustic

Rüstung *f* **-, -en** armament; (*Harnisch*) armour. **R~skontrolle** *f* arms control

Rute *f* **-, -n** twig; (*Angel-, Wünschel-*) rod; (*zur Züchtigung*) birch; (*Schwanz*) tail

Rutsch *m* **-[e]s, -e** slide. **R~bahn** *f* slide. **R~e** *f* **-, -n** chute. **r~en** *vt* slide; (*rücken*) move ● *vi* (*sein*) slide; (*aus-, ab-*) slip; (*Auto*) skid. **r~ig** *a* slippery

rütteln *vt* shake ● *vi* (*haben*) **r~ an** (+ *dat*) rattle

Ss

Saal *m* **-[e]s,Säle** hall; (*Theat*) auditorium; (*Kranken-*) ward

Saat *f* **-, -en** seed; (*Säen*) sowing; (*Gesätes*) crop

sabbern *vi* (*haben*) [!] slobber; <*Baby:*> dribble; (*reden*) jabber

Säbel *m* **-s,-** sabre

Sabo|tage /zabo'ta:ʒə/ *f* **-** sabotage. **S~teur** /-'tø:ɐ̯/ *m* **-s, -e** saboteur. **s~tieren** *vt* sabotage

Sach|bearbeiter *m* expert. **S~buch** *nt* non-fiction book

Sache *f* **-, -n** matter, business; (*Ding*) thing; (*fig*) cause

Sach|gebiet *nt* (*fig*) area, field. **s~kundig** *a* expert. **s~lich** *a* factual; (*nüchtern*) matter-of-fact

sächlich *a* (*Gram*) neuter

Sachse *m* **-n, -n** Saxon. **S~n** *nt* **-s** Saxony

sächsisch *a* Saxon

Sach|verhalt *m* **-[e]s** facts *pl*. **S~verständige(r)** *m/f* expert

Sack *m* **-[e]s,¨e** sack

Sack|gasse *f* cul-de-sac; (*fig*) impasse. **S~leinen** *nt* sacking

Sadis|mus *m* **-** sadism. **S~t** *m* **-en, -en** sadist

säen *vt/i* (*haben*) sow

Safe /ze:f/ *m* **-s, -s** safe

Saft *m* **-[e]s,¨e** juice; (*Bot*) sap. **s~ig** *a* juicy

Sage *f* **-, -n** legend

Säge *f* **-, -n** saw. **S~mehl** *nt* sawdust

sagen *vt* say; (*mitteilen*) tell; (*bedeuten*) mean

sägen *vt/i* (*haben*) saw
sagenhaft *a* legendary
Säge|späne *mpl* wood shavings. **S~werk** *nt* sawmill
Sahn|e *f* - cream. **S~ebonbon** *m & nt* ≈ toffee. **s~ig** *a* creamy
Saison /zɛ'zõ:/ *f* -, -s season
Saite *f* -, -n (*Mus, Sport*) string. **S~ninstrument** *nt* stringed instrument
Sakko *m & nt* -s, -s sports jacket
Sakrament *nt* -[e]s, -e sacrament
Sakristei *f* -, -en vestry
Salat *m* -[e]s, -e salad. **S~soße** *f* salad-dressing
Salbe *f* -, -n ointment
Salbei *m* -s & *f* - sage
salben *vt* anoint
Saldo *m* -s, -dos & -den balance
Salon /za'lõ:/ *m* -s, -s salon
salopp *a* casual; <*Benehmen*> informal
Salto *m* -s, -s somersault
Salut *m* -[e]s, -e salute. **s~ieren** *vi* (*haben*) salute
Salve *f* -, -n volley; (*Geschütz-*) salvo, (*von Gelächter*) burst
Salz *nt* -es, -e salt. **s~en**† *vt* salt. **S~fass** *nt* salt-cellar. **s~ig** *a* salty. **S~kartoffeln** *fpl* boiled potatoes. **S~säure** *f* hydrochloric acid
Samen *m* -s,- seed; (*Anat*) semen, sperm
Sammel|becken *nt* reservoir. **s~n** *vt/i* (*haben*) collect; (*suchen, versammeln*) gather; **sich s~n** collect; (*sich versammeln*) gather; (*sich fassen*) collect oneself. **S~name** *m* collective noun
Samm|ler(in) *m* -s,- (*f* -, -nen) collector. **S~lung** *f* -, -en collection; (*innere*) composure
Samstag *m* -s, -e Saturday. **s~s** *adv* on Saturdays
samt *prep* (+ *dat*) together with
Samt *m* -[e]s velvet
sämtlich *indef pron inv* all. **s~e(r,s)** *indef pron* all the; **s~e Werke** complete works
Sanatorium *nt* -s, -ien sanatorium
Sand *m* -[e]s sand
Sandale *f* -, -n sandal
Sand|bank *f* sandbank. **S~kasten** *m* sand-pit. **S~papier** *nt* sandpaper
sanft *a* gentle
Sänger(in) *m* -s,-(*f* -, -nen) singer
sanieren *vt* clean up; redevelop <*Gebiet*>; (*modernisieren*) modernize; make profitable <*Industrie, Firma*>; **sich s~** become profitable
sanitär *a* sanitary
Sanität|er *m* -s,- first-aid man; (*Fahrer*) ambulance man; (*Mil*) medical orderly. **S~swagen** *m* ambulance
Sanktion /zaŋk'tsio:n/ *f* -, -en sanction. **s~ieren** *vt* sanction
Saphir *m* -s, -e sapphire
Sardelle *f* -, -n anchovy
Sardine *f* -, -n sardine
Sarg *m* -[e]s,¨-e coffin
Sarkasmus *m* - sarcasm
Satan *m* -s Satan; (! *Teufel*) devil
Satellit *m* -en, -en satellite. **S~enfernsehen** *nt* satellite television. **S~enschüssel** *f* satellite dish
Satin /za'tɛŋ/ *m* -s satin
Satire *f* -, -n satire
satt *a* full; <*Farbe*> rich; **s~ sein** have had enough [to eat]; **etw s~ haben** ! be fed up with sth
Sattel *m* -s,¨ saddle. **s~n** *vt* saddle. **S~zug** *m* articulated lorry
sättigen *vt* satisfy; (*Chem & fig*) saturate ● *vi* (*haben*) be filling
Satz *m* -es,¨-e sentence; (*Teil-*) clause; (*These*) proposition; (*Math*) theorem; (*Mus*) movement; (*Tennis, Zusammengehöriges*) set;

(*Boden-*) sediment; (*Kaffee-*) grounds *pl*; (*Steuer-, Zins-*) rate; (*Druck-*) setting; (*Schrift-*) type; (*Sprung*) leap, bound. **S~aussage** *f* predicate. **S~gegenstand** *m* subject. **S~zeichen** *nt* punctuation mark

Sau *f* **-,Säue** sow

sauber *a* clean; (*ordentlich*) neat; (*anständig*) decent; **s~ machen** clean. **S~keit** *f* **-** cleanliness; neatness

säuberlich *a* neat

Sauce /'zo:sə/ *f* **-, -n** sauce; (*Braten-*) gravy

Saudi-Arabien /-i̯ən/ *nt* **-s** Saudi Arabia

sauer *a* sour; (*Chem*) acid; (*eingelegt*) pickled; (*schwer*) hard; **saurer Regen** acid rain

Sauerkraut *nt* sauerkraut

säuerlich *a* slightly sour

Sauerstoff *m* oxygen

saufen† *vt/i* (*haben*) drink; ☒ booze

Säufer *m* **-s,-** ☒ boozer

saugen† *vt/i* (*haben*) suck; (*staub-*) vacuum, hoover; **sich voll Wasser s~** soak up water

säugen *vt* suckle

Säugetier *nt* mammal

saugfähig *a* absorbent

Säugling *m* **-s, -e** infant

Säule *f* **-, -n** column

Saum *m* **-[e]s,Säume** hem; (*Rand*) edge

säumen *vt* hem; (*fig*) line

Sauna *f* **-, -nas & -nen** sauna

Säure *f* **-, -n** acidity; (*Chem*) acid

sausen *vi* (*haben*) rush; <*Ohren:*> buzz ● *vi* (*sein*) rush [along]

Saxophon, Saxofon *nt* **-s, -e** saxophone

S-Bahn *f* city and suburban railway

Scanner *m* **-s,-** scanner

sch *int* shush! (*fort*) shoo!

Schabe *f* **-, -n** cockroach

schaben *vt/i* (*haben*) scrape

schäbig *a* shabby

Schablone *f* **-, -n** stencil; (*Muster*) pattern; (*fig*) stereotype

Schach *nt* **-s** chess; **S~!** check! **S~brett** *nt* chessboard

Schachfigur *f* chess-man

schachmatt *a* **s~ setzen** checkmate; **s~!** checkmate!

Schachspiel *nt* game of chess

Schacht *m* **-[e]s,¨-e** shaft

Schachtel *f* **-, -n** box; (*Zigaretten-*) packet

Schachzug *m* move

schade *a* **s~ sein** be a pity *or* shame: **zu s~ für** too good for

Schädel *m* **-s,** skull. **S~bruch** *m* fractured skull

schaden *vi* (*haben*) (+ *dat*) damage; (*nachteilig sein*) hurt. **S~** *m* **-s,¨** damage; (*Defekt*) defect; (*Nachteil*) disadvantage. **S~ersatz** *m* damages *pl*. **S~freude** *f* malicious glee. **s~froh** *a* gloating

schädig|en *vt* damage, harm. **S~ung** *f* **-, -en** damage

schädlich *a* harmful

Schädling *m* **-s, -e** pest. **S~sbekämpfungsmittel** *nt* pesticide

Schaf *nt* **-[e]s, -e** sheep. **S~bock** *m* ram

Schäfer *m* **-s,-** shepherd. **S~hund** *m* sheepdog; **Deutscher S~hund** alsatian

schaffen[1]† *vt* create; (*herstellen*) establish; make <*Platz*>

schaffen[2] *v* (*reg*) ● *vt* manage [to do]; pass <*Prüfung*>; catch <*Zug*>; (*bringen*) take

Schaffner *m* **-s,-** conductor; (*Zug-*) ticket-inspector

Schaffung *f* creation

Schaft *m* **-[e]s,¨-e** shaft; (*Gewehr-*) stock; (*Stiefel-*) leg

Schal *m* **-s, -s** scarf

Schale *f* **-, -n** skin; (*abgeschält*) peel; (*Eier-, Nuss-, Muschel-*) shell; (*Schüssel*) dish

S

schälen *vt* peel; **sich s~** peel

Schall *m* **-[e]s** sound. **S~dämpfer** *m* silencer. **s~dicht** *a* soundproof. **s~en** *vi* (*haben*) ring out: (*nachhallen*) resound. **S~mauer** *f* sound barrier. **S~platte** *f* record, disc

schalt|en *vt* switch ● *vi* (*haben*) switch/<*Ampel:*> turn (**auf** + *acc* to); (*Auto*) change gear; ([!] *begreifen*) catch on. **S~er** *m* **-s,-** switch; (*Post-, Bank-*) counter; (*Fahrkarten-*) ticket window. **S~hebel** *m* switch; (*Auto*) gear lever. **S~jahr** *nt* leap year. **S~ung** *f* **-, -en** circuit: (*Auto*) gear change

Scham *f* **-** shame; (*Anat*) private parts *pl*

schämen (sich) *vr* be ashamed

scham|haft *a* modest. **s~los** *a* shameless

Schampon *nt* **-s** shampoo. **s~ieren** *vt* shampoo

Schande *f* **-** disgrace, shame

schändlich *a* disgraceful

Schanktisch *m* bar

Schanze *f*, **-, -n** [ski-]jump

Schar *f* **-, -en** crowd; (*Vogel-*) flock

Scharade *f* **-, -n** charade

scharen *vt* **um sich s~** gather round one; **sich s~ um** flock round. **s~weise** *adv* in droves

scharf *a* sharp; (*stark*) strong; (*stark gewürzt*) hot; <*Geruch*> pungent; <*Wind, Augen, Verstand*> keen; (*streng*) harsh; <*Galopp*> hard; <*Munition*> live; <*Hund*> fierce; **s~ einstellen** (*Phot*) focus; **s~ sein** (*Phot*) be in focus; **s~ sein auf** (+ *acc*) [!] be keen on

Schärfe *f* sharpness; strength; hotness; pungency; keenness; harshness. **s~n** *vt* sharpen

Scharf|richter *m* executioner. **S~schütze** *m* marksman. **S~sinn** *m* astutenes

Scharlach *m* **-s** scarlet fever

Scharlatan *m* **-s, -e** charlatan

Scharnier *nt* **-s, -e** hinge

Schärpe *f* **-, -n** sash

scharren *vi* (*haben*) scrape; <*Huhn*> scratch ● *vt* scrape

Schaschlik *m & nt* **-s, -s** kebab

Schatten *m* **-s,-** shadow; (*schattige Stelle*) shade. **S~riss** *m* silhouette. **S~seite** *f* shady side; (*fig*) disadvantage

schattier|en *vt* shade. **S~ung** *f* **-, -en** shading

schattig *a* shady

Schatz *m* **-es,¨-e** treasure; (*Freund, Freundin*) sweetheart

schätzen *vt* estimate; (*taxieren*) value; (*achten*) esteem; (*würdigen*) appreciate

Schätzung *f* **-, -en** estimate; (*Taxierung*) valuation

Schau *f* **-, -en** show. **S~ bild** *nt* diagram

Schauder *m* **-s** shiver; (*vor Abscheu*) shudder. **s~ haft** *a* dreadful. **s~n** *vi* (*haben*) shiver; (*vor Abscheu*) shudder

schauen *vi* (*haben*) (*SGer, Aust*) look; **s~, dass** make sure that

Schauer *m* **-s,-** shower; (*Schauder*) shiver. **S~geschichte** *f* horror story. **s~lich** *a* ghastly

Schaufel *f* **-, -n** shovel; (*Kehr-*) dustpan. **s~n** *vt* shovel; (*graben*) dig

Schaufenster *nt* shop-window. **S~puppe** *f* dummy

Schaukel *f* **-, -n** swing. **s~n** *vt* rock ● *vi* (*haben*) rock; (*auf einer Schaukel*) swing; (*schwanken*) sway. **S~pferd** *nt* rocking-horse. **S~stuhl** *m* rocking-chair

Schaum *m* **-[e]s** foam; (*Seifen-*) lather; (*auf Bier*) froth; (*als Frisier-, Rasiermittel*) mousse

schäumen *vi* (*haben*) foam, froth; <*Seife:*> lather

Schaum|gummi *m* foam rubber. **s~ig** *a* frothy; **s~ig rühren** (*Culin*) cream. **S~stoff** *m* [synthetic] foam. **S~wein** *m* sparkling wine

Schauplatz *m* scene

schaurig *a* dreadful; (*unheimlich*) eerie

Schauspiel *nt* play; (*Anblick*) spectacle. **S~er** *m* actor. **S~erin** *f* actress

Scheck *m* **-s, -s** cheque. **S~buch, S~heft** *nt* cheque-book. **S~karte** *f* cheque card

Scheibe *f* **-, -n** disc; (*Schieß-*) target; (*Glas-*) pane; (*Brot-, Wurst-*) slice. **S~nwischer** *m* **-s,-** windscreen-wiper

Scheich *m* **-s, -e** & **-s** sheikh

Scheide *f* **-, -n** sheath; (*Anat*) vagina

scheid|en† *vt* separate; (*unterscheiden*) distinguish; dissolve <*Ehe*>; **sich s~en lassen** get divorced ● *vi* (*sein*) leave; (*voneinander*) part. **S~ung** *f* **-, -en** divorce

Schein *m* **-[e]s, -e** light; (*Anschein*) appearance; (*Bescheinigung*) certificate; (*Geld-*) note. **s~bar** *a* apparent. **s~en**† *vi* (*haben*) shine; (*den Anschein haben*) seem, appear

scheinheilig *a* hypocritical

Scheinwerfer *m* **-s,-** floodlight; (*Such-*) searchlight; (*Auto*) headlight; (*Theat*) spotlight

Scheiße *f* **-** (*vulg*) shit. **s~n**† *vi* (*haben*) (*vulg*) shit

Scheit *nt* **-[e]s, -e** log

Scheitel *m* **-s,-** parting

scheitern *vi* (*sein*) fail

Schelle *f* **-, -n** bell. **s~n** *vi* (*haben*) ring

Schellfisch *m* haddock

Schelm *m* **-s, -e** rogue

Schelte *f* **-** scolding

Schema *nt* **-s, -mata** model, pattern; (*Skizze*) diagram

Schemel *m* **-s,-** stool

Schenke *f* **-, -n** tavern

Schenkel *m* **-s,-** thigh

schenken *vt* give [as a present]; **jdm Vertrauen s~** trust s.o.

Scherbe *f* **-, -n** [broken] piece

Schere *f* **-, -n** scissors *pl*; (*Techn*) shears *pl*; (*Hummer-*) claw. **s~n**[1]† *vt* shear; crop <*Haar*>

scheren[2] *vt* (*reg*) [!] bother; **sich nicht s~ um** not care about

Scherenschnitt *m* silhouette

Scherereien *fpl* [!] trouble *sg*

Scherz *m* **-es, -e** joke; **im/zum S~** as a joke. **s~en** *vi* (*haben*) joke

scheu *a* shy; <*Tier*> timid; **s~ werden** <*Pferd:*> shy

scheuchen *vt* shoo

scheuen *vt* be afraid of; (*meiden*) shun; **keine Mühe/Kosten s~** spare no effort/expense; **sich s~** be afraid (**vor** + *dat* of); shrink (**etw zu tun** from doing sth)

scheuern *vt* scrub; (*reiben*) rub; **[wund] s~n** chafe ● *vi* (*haben*) rub, chafe

Scheuklappen *fpl* blinkers

Scheune *f* **-, -n** barn

Scheusal *nt* **-s, -e** monster

scheußlich *a* horrible

Schi *m* **-s, -er** ski; **S~ fahren** *od* **laufen** ski

Schicht *f* **-, -en** layer; (*Geol*) stratum; (*Gesellschafts-*) class; (*Arbeits-*) shift. **S~arbeit** *f* shift work. **s~en** *vt* stack [up]

schick *a* stylish; <*Frau*> chic. **S~** *m* **-[e]s** style

schicken *vt/i* (*haben*) send; **s~ nach** send for

Schicksal *nt* **-s, -e** fate. **S~sschlag** *m* misfortune

Schieb|edach *nt* (*Auto*) sun-roof. **s~en**† *vt* push; (*gleitend*) slide; ([!] *handeln mit*) traffic in; **etw s~en auf** (+ *acc*) (*fig*) put sth down to; shift <*Schuld*> on to ● *vi* (*haben*) push. **S~etür** *f* sliding door. **S~ung** *f* **-, -en** [!] illicit deal; (*Betrug*) rigging, fixing

Schieds|gericht *nt* panel of judges; (*Jur*) arbitration tribunal. **S~richter** *m* referee; (*Tennis*) umpire; (*Jur*) arbitrator

schief *a* crooked; (*unsymmetrisch*) lopsided; (*geneigt*) slanting, sloping; (*nicht senkrecht*) leaning; <*Winkel*> oblique; (*fig*) false; suspicious ● *adv* not straight; **s~ gehen** [!] go wrong

Schiefer *m* **-s** slate

schielen *vi* (*haben*) squint

Schienbein *nt* shin

Schiene *f* **-, -n** rail; (*Gleit-*) runner; (*Med*) splint. **s~n** *vt* (*Med*) put in a splint

Schieß|bude *f* shooting-gallery. **s~en**† *vt* shoot; fire <*Kugel*>; score <*Tor*> ● *vi* (*haben*) shoot, fire (**auf** + *acc* at). **S~scheibe** *f* target. **S~stand** *m* shooting-range

Schifahr|en *nt* skiing. **S~er(in)** *m(f)* skier

Schiff *nt* **-[e]s, -e** ship; (*Kirchen-*) nave; (*Seiten-*) aisle

Schiffahrt* *f s.* **Schifffahrt**

schiff|bar *a* navigable. **S~bruch** *m* shipwreck. **s~brüchig** *a* shipwrecked. **S~fahrt** *f* shipping

Schikan|e *f* **-, -n** harassment; **mit allen S~en** [!] with every refinement. **s~ieren** *vt* harass

Schi|laufen *nt* **-s** skiing. **S~läufer(in)** *m(f)* **-s,-** (*f* **-, -nen**) skier

Schild¹ *m* **-[e]s, -e** shield

Schild² *nt* **-[e]s, -er** sign; (*Nummern-*) plate; (*Mützen-*) badge; (*Etikett*) label

Schilddrüse *f* thyroid [gland]

schilder|n *vt* describe. **S~ung** *f* **-, -en** description

Schild|kröte *f* tortoise; (*See-*) turtle. **S~patt** *nt* **-[e]s** tortoiseshell

Schilf *nt* **-[e]s** reeds *pl*

schillern *vi* (*haben*) shimmer

Schimmel *m* **-s,-** mould; (*Pferd*) white horse. **s~n** *vi* (*haben/sein*) go mouldy

schimmern *vi* (*haben*) gleam

Schimpanse *m* **-n, -n** chimpanzee

schimpf|en *vi* (*haben*) grumble (**mit** at; **über** + *acc* about); scold (**mit jdm** s.o.) ● *vt* call. **S~wort** *nt* (*pl* **-wörter**) swear-word

Schinken *m* **-s,-** ham. **S~speck** *m* bacon

Schippe *f* **-, -n** shovel. **s~n** *vt* shovel

Schirm *m* **-[e]s, -e** umbrella; (*Sonnen-*) sunshade; (*Lampen-*) shade; (*Augen-*) visor; (*Mützen-*) peak; (*Ofen-, Bild-*) screen; (*fig: Schutz*) shield. **S~herrschaft** *f* patronage. **S~mütze** *f* peaked cap

schizophren *a* schizophrenic. **S~ie** *f* **-** schizophrenia

Schlacht *f* **-, -en** battle

schlachten *vt* slaughter, kill

Schlacht|feld *nt* battlefield. **S~hof** *m* abattoir

Schlacke *f* **-, -n** slag

Schlaf *m* **-[e]s** sleep; **im S~** in one's sleep. **S~anzug** *m* pyjamas *pl*

Schläfe *f* **-, -n** (*Anat*) temple

schlafen† *vi* (*haben*) sleep; **s~ gehen** go to bed; **er schläft noch** he is still asleep

schlaff *a* limp; <*Seil*> slack; <*Muskel*> flabby

Schlaf|lied *nt* lullaby. **s~los** *a* sleepless. **S~losigkeit** *f* **-** insomnia. **S~mittel** *nt* sleeping drug

schläfrig *a* sleepy

Schlaf|saal *m* dormitory. **S~sack** *m* sleeping-bag. **S~tablette** *f* sleeping-pill. **S~wagen** *m* sleeping-car, sleeper. **s~wandeln** *vi* (*haben/sein*) sleep-walk. **S~zimmer** *nt* bedroom

Schlag *m* **-[e]s,⸚e** blow; (*Faust-*) punch; (*Herz-, Puls-, Trommel-*) beat; (*einer Uhr*) chime; (*Glocken-, Gong- & Med*) stroke; (*elektrischer*) shock; (*Art*) type; **S⸚e bekommen** get a beating; **S~ auf S~** in rapid succession. **S~ader** *f* artery. **S~anfall** *m* stroke. **S~baum** *m* barrier

schlagen† *vt* hit, strike; (*fällen*) fell; knock <*Loch, Nagel*> (**in** + *acc* into); (*prügeln, besiegen*) beat; (*Culin*) whisk <*Eiweiß*>; whip <*Sahne*>; (*legen*) throw; (*wickeln*) wrap; **sich s~** fight ● *vi* (*haben*) beat; <*Tür:*> bang; <*Uhr:*> strike; (*melodisch*) chime; **mit den Flügeln s~** flap its wings ● *vi* (*sein*) **in etw** (*acc*) **s~** <*Blitz, Kugel:*> strike sth; **nach jdm s~** (*fig*) take after s.o.

Schlager *m* **-s,-** popular song; (*Erfolg*) hit

Schläger *m* **-s,-** racket; (*Tischtennis-*) bat; (*Golf-*) club; (*Hockey-*) stick. **S~ei** *f* **-, -en** fight, brawl

schlag|fertig *a* quick-witted. **S~loch** *nt* pot-hole. **S~sahne** *f* whipped cream; (*ungeschlagen*) whipping cream. **S~seite** *f* (*Naut*) list. **S~stock** *m* truncheon. **S~wort** *nt* (*pl* **-worte**) slogan. **S~zeile** *f* headline. **S~zeug** *nt* (*Mus*) percussion. **S~zeuger** *m* **-s,-** percussionist; (*in Band*) drummer

Schlamm *m* **-[e]s** mud. **s~ig** *a* muddy

Schlamp|e *f* **-, -n** [!] slut. **s~en** *vi* (*haben*) [!] be sloppy (**bei** in). **s~ig** *a* slovenly; <*Arbeit*> sloppy

Schlange *f* **-, -n** snake; (*Menschen-, Auto-*) queue; **S~ stehen** queue

schlängeln (sich) *vr* wind; <*Person:*> weave (**durch** through)

schlank *a* slim. **S~heitskur** *f* slimming diet

schlapp *a* tired; (*schlaff*) limp

schlau *a* clever; (*gerissen*) crafty; **ich werde nicht s~ daraus** I can't make head or tail of it

Schlauch *m* **-[e]s,Schläuche** tube; (*Wasser-*) hose[pipe]. **S~boot** *nt* rubber dinghy

Schlaufe *f* **-, -n** loop

schlecht *a* bad; (*böse*) wicked; (*unzulänglich*) poor; **s~ werden** go bad; <*Wetter:*> turn bad; **mir ist s~** I feel sick; **s~ machen** [!] run down. **s~gehen*** *vi sep* (*sein*) **s~ gehen**, *s.* **gehen**

schlecken *vt/i* (*haben*) lick (**an etw** *dat* sth); (*auf-*) lap up

Schlegel *m* **-s,-** (*SGer: Keule*) leg; (*Hühner-*) drumstick

schleichen† *vi* (*sein*) creep; (*langsam gehen/fahren*) crawl ● *vr* **sich s~** creep. **s~d** *a* creeping

Schleier *m* **-s,-** veil; (*fig*) haze

Schleife *f* **-, -n** bow; (*Fliege*) bowtie; (*Biegung*) loop

schleifen¹ *v* (*reg*) ● *vt* drag ● *vi* (*haben*) trail, drag

schleifen²† *vt* grind; (*schärfen*) sharpen; cut <*Edelstein, Glas*>

Schleim *m* **-[e]s** slime; (*Anat*) mucus; (*Med*) phlegm. **s~ig** *a* slimy

schlendern *vi* (*sein*) stroll

schlenkern *vt/i* (*haben*) swing; **s~ mit** swing; dangle <*Beine*>

Schlepp|dampfer *m* tug. **S~e** *f* **-, -n** train. **s~en** *vt* drag; (*tragen*) carry; (*ziehen*) tow; **sich s~en** drag oneself; (*sich hinziehen*) drag on; **sich s~en mit** carry. **S~er** *m* **-s,-** tug; (*Traktor*) tractor. **S~kahn** *m* barge. **S~lift** *m* T-bar lift. **S~tau** *nt* tow-rope; **ins S~tau nehmen** take in tow

Schleuder *f* **-, -n** catapult; (*Wäsche-*) spin-drier. **s~n** *vt* hurl; spin <*Wäsche*> ● *vi* (*sein*) skid; **ins S~n geraten** skid. **S~sitz** *m* ejector seat

Schleuse *f* **-, -n** lock; (*Sperre*) sluice[-gate]. **s~n** *vt* steer
Schliche *pl* tricks
schlicht *a* plain; simple
Schlichtung *f* **-** settlement; (*Jur*) arbitration
Schließe *f* **-, -n** clasp; buckle
schließen† *vt* close (*ab-*) lock; fasten <*Kleid, Verschluss*>; (*stilllegen*) close down; (*beenden, folgern*) conclude; enter into <*Vertrag*>; **sich s~** close; **etw s~ an** (+ *acc*) connect sth to; **sich s~ an** (+ *acc*) follow ● *vi* (*haben*) close, (*den Betrieb einstellen*) close down; (*den Schlüssel drehen*) turn the key; (*enden, folgern*) conclude
Schließ|fach *nt* locker. **s~lich** *adv* finally, in the end; (*immerhin*) after all. **S~ung** *f* **-, -en** closure
Schliff *m* **-[e]s** cut; (*Schleifen*) cutting; (*fig*) polish
schlimm *a* bad
Schlinge *f* **-, -n** loop; (*Henkers-*) noose; (*Med*) sling; (*Falle*) snare
Schlingel *m* **-s,-** [!] rascal
schlingen† *vt* wind, wrap; tie <*Knoten*> ● *vi* (*haben*) bolt one's food
Schlips *m* **-es, -e** tie
Schlitten *m* **-s,-** sledge; (*Rodel-*) toboggan; (*Pferde-*) sleigh; **S~ fahren** toboggan
schlittern *vi* (*haben*/ *sein*) slide
Schlittschuh *m* skate; **S~ laufen** skate. **S~läufer(in)** *m*(*f*) **-s,-** (*f* **-, -nen**) skater
Schlitz *m* **-es, -e** slit; (*für Münze*) slot; (*Jacken-*) vent; (*Hosen-*) flies *pl*. **s~en** *vt* slit
Schloss *nt* **-es,¨-er** lock; (*Vorhänge-*) padlock; (*Verschluss*) clasp; (*Gebäude*) castle; palace
Schlosser *m* **-s,-** locksmith; (*Auto-*) mechanic
Schlucht *f* **-, -en** ravine, gorge
schluchzen *vi* (*haben*) sob
Schluck *m* **-[e]s, -e** mouthful; (*klein*) sip
Schluckauf *m* **-s** hiccups *pl*
schlucken *vt*/*i* (*haben*) swallow
Schlummer *m* **-s** slumber
Schlund *m* **-[e]s** [back of the] throat; (*fig*) mouth
schlüpf|en *vi* (*sein*) slip; **[aus dem Ei] s~en** hatch. **S~er** *m* **-s,-** knickers *pl*. **s~rig** *a* slippery
schlürfen *vt*/*i* (*haben*) slurp
Schluss *m* **-es,¨-e** end; (*S~folgerung*) conclusion; **zum S~** finally; **S~ machen** stop (**mit etw** sth); finish (**mit jdm** with s.o.)
Schlüssel *m* **-s,-** key; (*Schrauben-*) spanner; (*Geheim-*) code; (*Mus*) clef. **S~bein** *nt* collar-bone. **S~bund** *m & nt* bunch of keys. **S~loch** *nt* keyhole
Schlussfolgerung *f* conclusion
schlüssig *a* conclusive
Schluss|licht *nt* rear-light. **S~verkauf** *m* sale
schmächtig *a* slight
schmackhaft *a* tasty
schmal *a* narrow; (*dünn*) thin; (*schlank*) slender; (*karg*) meagre
schmälern *vt* diminish; (*herabsetzen*) belittle
Schmalz[1] *nt* **-es** lard; (*Ohren-*) wax
Schmalz[2] *m* **-es** [!] schmaltz
Schmarotzer *m* **-s,-** parasite; (*Person*) sponger
schmatzen *vi* (*haben*) eat noisily
schmausen *vi* (*haben*) feast
schmecken *vi* (*haben*) taste (**nach** of); **[gut] s~** taste good ● *vt* taste
Schmeichelei *f* **-, -en** flattery; (*Kompliment*) compliment
schmeichel|haft *a* complimentary, flattering. **s~n** *vi* (*haben*) (+ *dat*) flatter
schmeißen† *vt*/*i* (*haben*) **s~ [mit]** [!] chuck
Schmeißfliege *f* bluebottle

schmelz|en† *vt/i* (*sein*) melt; smelt <*Erze*>. **S~wasser** *nt* melted snow and ice
Schmerbauch *m* [!] paunch
Schmerz *m* **-es, -en** pain; (*Kummer*) grief; **S~en haben** be in pain. **s~en** *vt* hurt; (*fig*) grieve ● *vi* (*haben*) hurt, be painful. **S~ensgeld** *nt* compensation for pain and suffering. **s~haft** *a* painful. **s~los** *a* painless **s~stillend** *a* pain-killing; **s~stillendes Mittel** analgesic, pain-killer. **S~tablette** *f* pain-killer
Schmetterball *m* (*Tennis*) smash
Schmetterling *m* **-s, -e** butterfly
schmettern *vt* hurl; (*Tennis*) smash; (*singen*) sing ● *vi* (*haben*) sound
Schmied *m* **-[e]s, -e** blacksmith
Schmiede *f* **-, -n** forge. **S~eisen** *nt* wrought iron. **s~n** *vt* forge
Schmier|e *f* **-, -n** grease; (*Schmutz*) mess. **s~en** *vt* lubricate; (*streichen*) spread; (*schlecht schreiben*) scrawl ● *vi* (*haben*) smudge; (*schreiben*) scrawl. **S~geld** *nt* [!] bribe. **s~ig** *a* greasy; (*schmutzig*) grubby. **S~mittel** *nt* lubricant
Schminke *f* **-, -n** make-up. **s~n** *vt* make up; **sich s~n** put on make-up; **sich** (*dat*) **die Lippen s~n** put on lipstick
schmirgel|n *vt* sand down. **S~papier** *nt* emery-paper
schmollen *vi* (*haben*) sulk
schmor|en *vt/i* (*haben*) braise. **S~topf** *m* casserole
Schmuck *m* **-[e]s** jewellery; (*Verzierung*) ornament, decoration
schmücken *vt* decorate, adorn
schmuck|los *a* plain. **S~stück** *nt* piece of jewellery
Schmuggel *m* **-s** smuggling. **s~n** *vt* smuggle. **S~ware** *f* contraband
Schmuggler *m* **-s,-** smuggler
schmunzeln *vi* (*haben*) smile
schmusen *vi* (*haben*) cuddle
Schmutz *m* **-es** dirt. **s~en** *vi* (*haben*) get dirty. **s~ig** *a* dirty
Schnabel *m* **-s,⸚** beak, bill; (*eines Kruges*) lip; (*Tülle*) spout
Schnalle *f* **-, -n** buckle. **s~n** *vt* strap; (*zu-*) buckle
schnalzen *vi* (*haben*) **mit der Zunge s~** click one's tongue
schnapp|en *vi* (*haben*) **s~en nach** snap at; gasp for <*Luft*> ● *vt* snatch, grab; ([!] *festnehmen*) nab. **S~schloss** *nt* spring lock. **S~schuss** *m* snapshot
Schnaps *m* **-es,⸚e** schnapps
schnarchen *vi* (*haben*) snore
schnaufen *vi* (*haben*) puff, pant
Schnauze *f* **-, -n** muzzle; (*eines Kruges*) lip; (*Tülle*) spout
schnäuzen (sich) *vr* blow one's nose
Schnecke *f* **-, -n** snail; (*Nackt-*) slug; (*Spirale*) scroll. **S~nhaus** *nt* snail-shell
Schnee *m* **-s** snow; (*Eier-*) beaten egg-white. **S~besen** *m* whisk. **S~brille** *f* snow-goggles *pl*. **S~fall** *m* snow-fall. **S~flocke** *f* snowflake. **S~glöckchen** *nt* **-s,-** snowdrop. **S~kette** *f* snow chain. **S~mann** *m* (*pl* **-männer**) snowman. **S~pflug** *m* snowplough. **S~schläger** *m* whisk. **S~sturm** *m* snowstorm, blizzard. **S~wehe** *f* **-, -n** snowdrift
Schneide *f* **-, -n** [cutting] edge; (*Klinge*) blade
schneiden† *vt* cut; (*in Scheiben*) slice; (*kreuzen*) cross; (*nicht beachten*) cut dead; **Gesichter s~** pull faces; **sich s~** cut oneself; (*über-*) intersect
Schneider *m* **-s,-** tailor. **S~in** *f* **-, -nen** dressmaker. **s~n** *vt* make <*Anzug, Kostüm*>
Schneidezahn *m* incisor
schneien *vi* (*haben*) snow; **es schneit** it is snowing

Schneise *f* **-, -n** path
schnell *a* quick; <*Auto, Tempo*> fast ● *adv* quickly; (*in s~em Tempo*) fast; (*bald*) soon; **mach s~!** hurry up! **S~igkeit** *f* **-** rapidity; (*Tempo*) speed. **S~kochtopf** *m* pressure-cooker. **s~stens** *adv* as quickly as possible. **S~zug** *m* express [train]
schnetzeln *vt* cut into thin strips
Schnipsel *m & nt* **-s,-** scrap
Schnitt *m* **-[e]s, -e** cut; (*Film-*) cutting; (*S~muster*) [paper] pattern; **im S~** (*durchschnittlich*) on average
Schnitte *f* **-, -n** slice [of bread]
schnittig *a* stylish; (*stromlinienförmig*) streamlined
Schnitt|lauch *m* chives *pl*. **S~muster** *nt* [paper] pattern. **S~punkt** *m* [point of] intersection. **S~wunde** *f* cut
Schnitzel *nt* **-s,-** scrap; (*Culin*) escalope. **s~n** *vt* shred
schnitzen *vt/i* (*haben*) carve
schnodderig *a* [!] brash
Schnorchel *m* **-s,-** snorkel
Schnörkel *m* **-s,-** flourish; (*Kunst*) scroll. **s~ig** *a* ornate
schnüffeln *vi* (*haben*) sniff (**an etw** *dat* sth); ([!] *spionieren*) snoop [around]
Schnuller *m* **-s,-** [baby's] dummy
Schnupf|en *m* **-s,-** [head] cold. **S~tabak** *m* snuff
schnuppern *vt/i* (*haben*) sniff (**an etw** *dat* sth)
Schnur *f* **-,¨-e** string; (*Kordel*) cord; (*Electr*) flex
schnüren *vt* tie; lace [up] <*Schuhe*>
Schnurr|bart *m* moustache. **s~en** *vi* (*haben*) hum; <*Katze:*> purr
Schnürsenkel *m* [shoe-]lace
Schock *m* **-[e]s, -s** shock. **s~en** *vt* [!] shock. **s~ieren** *vt* shock
Schöffe *m* **-n, -n** lay judge
Schokolade *f* **-** chocolate
Scholle *f* **-, -n** clod [of earth]; (*Eis-*) [ice-]floe; (*Fisch*) plaice
schon *adv* already; (*allein*) just; (*sogar*) even; (*ohnehin*) anyway; **s~ einmal** before; (*jemals*) ever; **s~ immer/oft/wieder** always/often/again; **s~ deshalb** for that reason alone; **das ist s~ möglich** that's quite possible; **ja s~, aber** well yes, but
schön *a* beautiful; <*Wetter*> fine; (*angenehm, nett*) nice; (*gut*) good; ([!] *beträchtlich*) pretty; **s~en Dank!** thank you very much!
schonen *vt* spare; (*gut behandeln*) look after. **s~d** *a* gentle
Schönheit *f* **-, -en** beauty. **S~sfehler** *m* blemish. **S~skonkurrenz** *f* beauty contest
Schonung *f* **-, -en** gentle care; (*nach Krankheit*) rest; (*Baum-*) plantation. **s~slos** *a* ruthless
Schonzeit *f* close season
schöpf|en *vt* scoop [up]; ladle <*Suppe*>; **Mut s~en** take heart. **s~erisch** *a* creative. **S~kelle** *f*. **S~löffel** *m* ladle. **S~ung** *f* **-, -en** creation
Schoppen *m* **-s,-** (*SGer*) ≈ pint
Schorf *m* **-[e]s** scab
Schornstein *m* chimney. **S~feger** *m* **-s,-** chimney-sweep
Schoß *m* **-es,¨-e** lap; (*Frack-*) tail
Schössling *m* **-s, -e** (*Bot*) shoot
Schote *f* **-, -n** pod; (*Erbse*) pea
Schotte *m* **-n, -n** Scot, Scotsman
Schotter *m* **-s** gravel
schott|isch *a* Scottish, Scots. **S~land** *nt* **-s** Scotland
schraffieren *vt* hatch
schräg *a* diagonal; (*geneigt*) sloping; **s~ halten** tilt. **S~strich** *m* oblique stroke
Schramme *f* **-, -n** scratch
Schrank *m* **-[e]s,¨-e** cupboard; (*Kleider-*) wardrobe; (*Akten-, Glas-*) cabinet
Schranke *f* **-, -n** barrier

Schraube *f* **-, -n** screw; (*Schiffs-*) propeller. **s~n** *vt* screw; (*ab-*) unscrew; (*drehen*) turn. **S~nschlüssel** *m* spanner. **S~nzieher** *m* **-s,-** screwdriver

Schraubstock *m* vice

Schreck *m* **-[e]s, -e** fright. **S~en** *m* **-s,-** fright; (*Entsetzen*) horror

Schreck|gespenst *nt* spectre. **s~haft** *a* easily frightened; (*nervös*) jumpy. **s~lich** *a* terrible. **S~schuss** *m* warning shot

Schrei *m* **-[e]s, -e** cry, shout; (*gellend*) scream; **der letzte S~** [!] the latest thing

schreib|en† *vt/i* (*haben*) write; (*auf der Maschine*) type; **richtig/falsch s~en** spell right/wrong; **sich s~en** <*Wort*:> be spelt; (*korrespondieren*) correspond. **S~en** *nt* **-s,-** writing; (*Brief*) letter. **S~fehler** *m* spelling mistake. **S~heft** *nt* exercise book. **S~kraft** *f* clerical assistant; (*für Maschineschreiben*) typist. **S~maschine** *f* typewriter. **S~tisch** *m* desk. **S~ung** *f* **-, -en** spelling. **S~waren** *fpl* stationery *sg*.

schreien† *vt/i* (*haben*) cry; (*gellend*) scream; (*rufen, laut sprechen*) shout

Schreiner *m* **-s,-** joiner

schreiten† *vi* (*sein*) walk

Schrift *f* **-, -en** writing; (*Druck-*) type; (*Abhandlung*) paper; **die Heilige S~** the Scriptures *pl*. **S~führer** *m* secretary. **s~lich** *a* written ● *adv* in writing. **S~sprache** *f* written language. **S~steller(in)** *m* **-s,-** (*f* **-, -nen**) writer. **S~stück** *nt* document. **S~zeichen** *nt* character

schrill *a* shrill

Schritt *m* **-[e]s, -e** step; (*Entfernung*) pace; (*Gangart*) walk; (*der Hose*) crotch. **S~macher** *m* **-s,-** pace-maker. **s~weise** *adv* step by step

schroff *a* precipitous; (*abweisend*) brusque; (*unvermittelt*) abrupt; <*Gegensatz*> stark

Schrot *m & nt* **-[e]s** coarse meal; (*Blei-*) small shot. **S~flinte** *f* shotgun

Schrott *m* **-[e]s** scrap[-metal]; **zu S~ fahren** [!] write off. **S~platz** *m* scrap-yard

schrubben *vt/i* (*haben*) scrub

Schrull|e *f* **-, -n** whim; **alte S~e** [!] old crone. **s~ig** *a* cranky

schrumpfen *vi* (*sein*) shrink

schrump[e]lig *a* wrinkled

Schub *m* **-[e]s,¨e** (*Phys*) thrust; (*S~fach*) drawer; (*Menge*) batch. **S~fach** *nt* drawer. **S~karre** *f*, **S~karren** *m* wheelbarrow. **S~lade** *f* drawer

Schubs *m* **-es, -e** push, shove **s~en** *vt* push, shove

schüchtern *a* shy. **S~heit** *f* **-** shyness

Schuft *m* **-[e]s, -e** (*pej*) swine

Schuh *m* **-[e]s, -e** shoe. **S~anzieher** *m* **-s,-** shoehorn. **S~band** *nt* (*pl* **-bänder**) shoe-lace. **S~creme** *f* shoe-polish. **S~löffel** *m* shoehorn. **S~macher** *m* **-s,-** shoemaker

Schul|abgänger *m* **-s,-** schoolleaver. **S~arbeiten, S~aufgaben** *fpl* homework *sg*.

Schuld *f* **-, -en** guilt; (*Verantwortung*) blame; (*Geld-*) debt; **S~en machen** get into debt; **S~ haben** be to blame (**an** + *dat* for); **jdm S~ geben** blame s.o. ● **s~ sein** be to blame (**an** + *dat* for). **s~en** *vt* owe

schuldig *a* guilty (*gen* of); (*gebührend*) due; **jdm etw s~ sein** owe s.o. sth. **S~keit** *f* - duty

schuld|los *a* innocent. **S~ner** *m* **-s,-** debtor. **S~spruch** *m* guilty verdict

Schule *f* **-, -n** school; **in der/die S~** at/to school. **s~n** *vt* train

Schüler(in) *m* **-s,-** (*f* **-, -nen**) pupil

S

schul|frei *a* **s~freier Tag** day without school; **wir haben morgen s~frei** there's no school tomorrow. **S~hof** *m* [school] playground. **S~jahr** *nt* school year; (*Klasse*) form. **S~kind** *nt* schoolchild. **S~stunde** *f* lesson

Schulter *f* **-, -n** shoulder. **S~blatt** *nt* shoulder-blade

Schulung *f* **-** training

schummeln *vi* (*haben*) [!] cheat

Schund *m* **-[e]s** trash

Schuppe *f* **-, -n** scale; **S~n** *pl* dandruff *sg*. **s~n (sich)** *vr* flake [off]

Schuppen *m* **-s,-** shed

schürf|en *vt* mine; **sich** (*dat*) **das Knie s~en** graze one's knee ● *vi* (*haben*) **s~en nach** prospect for. **S~wunde** *f* abrasion, graze

Schürhaken *m* poker

Schurke *m* **-n, -n** villain

Schürze *f* **-, -n** apron

Schuss *m* **-es,¨-e** shot; (*kleine Menge*) dash

Schüssel *f* **-, -n** bowl; (*TV*) dish

Schuss|fahrt *f* (*Ski*) schuss. **S~waffe** *f* firearm

Schuster *m* **-s,-** = **Schuhmacher**

Schutt *m* **-[e]s** rubble. **S~abladeplatz** *m* rubbish dump

Schüttel|frost *m* shivering fit. **s~n** *vt* shake; **sich s~n** shake oneself/itself; (*vor Ekel*) shudder; **jdm die Hand s~n** shake s.o.'s hand

schütten *vt* pour; (*kippen*) tip; (*ver-*) spill ● *vi* (*haben*) **es schüttet** it is pouring [with rain]

Schutz *m* **-es** protection; (*Zuflucht*) shelter; (*Techn*) guard; **S~ suchen** take refuge. **S~anzug** *m* protective suit. **S~blech** *nt* mudguard. **S~brille** *f* goggles *pl*

Schütze *m* **-n, -n** marksman; (*Tor-*) scorer; (*Astr*) Sagittarius

schützen *vt* protect/(*Zuflucht gewähren*) shelter (**vor** + *dat* from) ● *vi* (*haben*) give protection/shelter (**vor** + *dat* from)

Schutz|engel *m* guardian angel. **S~heilige(r)** *m*/*f* patron saint

Schützling *m* **-s, -e** charge

schutz|los *a* defenceless, helpless. **S~mann** *m* (*pl* **-männer** & **-leute**) policeman. **S~umschlag** *m* dust-jacket

Schwaben *nt* **-s** Swabia

schwäbisch *a* Swabian

schwach *a* weak; (*nicht gut; gering*) poor; (*leicht*) faint

Schwäche *f* **-, -n** weakness. **s~n** *vt* weaken

schwäch|lich *a* delicate. **S~ling** *m* **-s, -e** weakling

Schwachsinn *m* mental deficiency. **s~ig** *a* mentally deficient; [!] idiotic

Schwager *m* **-s,¨-** brother-in-law

Schwägerin *f* **-, -nen** sister-in-law

Schwalbe *f* **-, -n** swallow

Schwall *m* **-[e]s** torrent

Schwamm *m* **-[e]s,¨-e** sponge; (*SGer: Pilz*) fungus; (*essbar*) mushroom. **s~ig** *a* spongy

Schwan *m* **-[e]s,¨-e** swan

schwanger *a* pregnant

Schwangerschaft *f* **-, -en** pregnancy

Schwank *m* **-[e]s,¨-e** (*Theat*) farce

schwank|en *vi* (*haben*) sway; <*Boot:*> rock; (*sich ändern*) fluctuate; (*unentschieden sein*) be undecided ● (*sein*) stagger. **S~ung** *f* **-, -en** fluctuation

Schwanz *m* **-es,¨-e** tail

schwänzen *vt* [!] skip; **die Schule s~** play truant

Schwarm *m* **-[e]s,¨-e** swarm; (*Fisch-*) shoal; ([!] *Liebe*) idol

schwärmen *vi* (*haben*) swarm; **s~ für** [!] adore; (*verliebt sein*) have a crush on

Schwarte *f* **-, -n** (*Speck-*) rind

schwarz *a* black; ([!] *illegal*) illegal; **s~er Markt** black market; **s~ gekleidet** dressed in black; **s~**

auf weiß in black and white; **s~ sehen** (*fig*) be pessimistic; **ins S~e treffen** score a bull's-eye. **S~** *nt* **-[e]s,-** black. **S~arbeit** *f* moonlighting. **s~arbeiten** *vi sep* (*haben*) moonlight. **S~e(r)** *m/f* black

Schwärze *f* **-** blackness. **s~n** *vt* blacken

Schwarz|fahrer *m* fare-dodger. **S~handel** *m* black market (**mit** in). **S~händler** *m* black marketeer. **S~markt** *m* black market. **S~wald** *m* Black Forest. **s~weiß** *a* black and white

schwatzen, (*SGer*) **schwätzen** *vi* (*haben*) chat; (*klatschen*) gossip; (*Sch*) talk [in class] ● *vt* talk

Schwebe *f* **- in der S~** (*fig*) undecided. **S~bahn** *f* cable railway. **s~n** *vi* (*haben*) float; (*fig*) be undecided; <*Verfahren:*> be pending; **in Gefahr s~n** be in danger ● (*sein*) float

Schwed|e *m* **-n, -n** Swede. **S~en** *nt* **-s** Sweden. **S~in** *f* **-, -nen** Swede. **s~isch** *a* Swedish

Schwefel *m* **-s** sulphur

schweigen† *vi* (*haben*) be silent; **ganz zu s~ von** let alone. **S~** *nt* **-s** silence; **zum S~ bringen** silence

schweigsam *a* silent; (*wortkarg*) taciturn

Schwein *nt* **-[e]s, -e** pig; (*Culin*) pork; (☒ *Schuft*) swine; **S~ haben** [!] be lucky. **S~ebraten** *m* roast pork. **S~efleisch** *nt* pork. **S~erei** *f* **-, -en** ☒ [dirty] mess; (*Gemeinheit*) dirty trick. **S~estall** *m* pigsty. **S~sleder** *nt* pigskin

Schweiß *m* **-es** sweat

schweißen *vt* weld

Schweiz (die) - Switzerland. **S~er** *a & m* **-s,-, S~erin** *f* **-, -nen** Swiss. **s~erisch** *a* Swiss

Schwelle *f* **-, -n** threshold; (*Eisenbahn-*) sleeper

schwell|en† *vi* (*sein*) swell. **S~ung** *f* **-, -en** swelling

schwer *a* heavy; (*schwierig*) difficult; (*mühsam*) hard; (*ernst*) serious; (*schlimm*) bad; **3 Pfund s~ sein** weigh 3 pounds ● *adv* heavily; with difficulty; (*mühsam*) hard; (*schlimm, sehr*) badly, seriously; **s~ krank/verletzt** seriously ill/injured; **s~ hören** be hard of hearing; **etw s~ nehmen** take sth seriously; **jdm s~ fallen** be hard for s.o.; **es jdm s~ machen** make it *or* things difficult for s.o.; **sich s~ tun** have difficulty (**mit** with); **s~ zu sagen** difficult *or* hard to say

Schwere *f* **-** heaviness; (*Gewicht*) weight; (*Schwierigkeit*) difficulty; (*Ernst*) gravity. **S~losigkeit** *f* **-** weightlessness

schwer|fällig *a* ponderous, clumsy. **S~gewicht** *nt* heavyweight. **s~hörig** *a* **s~hörig sein** be hard of hearing. **S~kraft** *f* (*Phys*) gravity. **s~mütig** *a* melancholic. **S~punkt** *m* centre of gravity; (*fig*) emphasis

Schwert *nt* **-[e]s, -er** sword. **S~lilie** *f* iris

Schwer|verbrecher *m* serious offender. **s~wiegend** *a* weighty

Schwester *f* **-, -n** sister; (*Kranken-*) nurse. **s~lich** *a* sisterly

Schwieger|eltern *pl* parents-in-law. **S~mutter** *f* mother-in-law. **S~sohn** *m* son-in-law. **S~tochter** *f* daughter-in-law. **S~vater** *m* father-in-law

schwierig *a* difficult. **S~keit** *f* **-, -en** difficulty

Schwimm|bad *nt* swimming-baths *pl*. **S~becken** *nt* swimming-pool. **s~en**† *vt/i* (*sein/haben*) swim; (*auf dem Wasser treiben*) float. **S~weste** *f* life-jacket

Schwindel *m* **-s** dizziness, vertigo; ([!] *Betrug*) fraud; (*Lüge*) lie. **S~anfall** *m* dizzy spell. **s~frei** *a*

S

s~frei sein have a good head for heights. **s~n** *vi* (*haben*) lie

Schwindl|er *m* **-s,-** liar; (*Betrüger*) fraud, con-man. **s~ig** *a* dizzy; **mir ist** *od* **wird s~ig** I feel dizzy

schwing|en† *vi* (*haben*) swing; (*Phys*) oscillate; (*vibrieren*) vibrate ● *vt* swing; wave <*Fahne*>; (*drohend*) brandish. **S~ung** *f* **-, -en** oscillation; vibration

Schwips *m* **-es, -e einen S~ haben** [!] be tipsy

schwitzen *vi* (*haben*) sweat; **ich schwitze** I am hot

schwören† *vt/i* (*haben*) swear (**auf** + *acc* by)

schwul *a* ([!] *homosexuell*) gay

schwül *a* close. **S~e** *f* **-** closeness

Schwung *m* **-[e]s,¨e** swing; (*Bogen*) sweep; (*Schnelligkeit*) momentum; (*Kraft*) vigour. **s~los** *a* dull. **s~voll** *a* vigorous; <*Bogen, Linie*> sweeping; (*mitreißend*) spirited

Schwur *m* **-[e]s,¨e** vow; (*Eid*) oath. **S~gericht** *nt* jury [court]

sechs *inv a*, **S~** *f* **-, -en** six; (*Sch*) ≈ fail mark. **s~eckig** *a* hexagonal. **s~te(r,s)** *a* sixth

sech|zehn *inv a* sixteen. **s~zehnte(r,s)** *a* sixteenth. **s~zig** *inv a* sixty. **s~zigste(r,s)** *a* sixtieth

See[1] *m* **-s, -n** /ˈzeːən/ lake

See[2] *f* **-** sea; **an die/der See** to/at the seaside; **auf See** at sea. **S~fahrt** *f* [sea] voyage; (*Schifffahrt*) navigation. **S~gang** *m* **schwerer S~gang** rough sea. **S~hund** *m* seal. **s~krank** *a* seasick

Seele *f* **-, -n** soul

seelisch *a* psychological; (*geistig*) mental

See|macht *f* maritime power. **S~mann** *m* (*pl* **-leute**) seaman, sailor. **S~not** *f* **in S~not** in distress. **S~räuber** *m* pirate. **S~reise** *f* [sea] voyage. **S~rose** *f* water-lily. **S~sack** *m* kitbag. **S~stern** *m* starfish. **S~tang** *m* seaweed. **s~tüchtig** *a* seaworthy. **S~zunge** *f* sole

Segel *nt* **-s,-** sail. **S~boot** *nt* sailing-boat. **S~flugzeug** *nt* glider. **s~n** *vt/i* (*sein/haben*) sail. **S~schiff** *nt* sailing-ship. **S~sport** *m* sailing. **S~tuch** *nt* canvas

Segen *m* **-s** blessing

Segler *m* **-s,-** yachtsman

segnen *vt* bless

sehen† *vt* see; watch <*Fernsehsendung*>; **jdn/etw wieder s~** see s.o./sth again; **sich s~ lassen** show oneself ● *vi* (*haben*) see; (*blicken*) look (**auf** + *acc* at); (*ragen*) show (**aus** above); **gut/schlecht s~** have good/bad eyesight; **vom S~ kennen** know by sight; **s~ nach** keep an eye on; (*betreuen*) look after; (*suchen*) look for. **s~swert, s~swürdig** *a* worth seeing. **S~swürdigkeit** *f* **-, -en** sight

Sehne *f* **-, -n** tendon; (*eines Bogens*) string

sehnen (sich) *vr* long (**nach** for)

Sehn|sucht *f* **-** longing (**nach** for). **s~süchtig** *a* longing; <*Wunsch*> dearest

sehr *adv* very; (*mit Verb*) very much; **so s~, dass** so much that

seicht *a* shallow

seid *s.* **sein**[1]

Seide *f* **-, -n** silk

Seidel *nt* **-s,-** beer-mug

seiden *a* silk ... **S~papier** *nt* tissue paper. **S~raupe** *f* silk-worm

seidig *a* silky

Seife *f* **-, -n** soap. **S~npulver** *nt* soap powder. **S~nschaum** *m* lather

Seil *nt* **-[e]s, -e** rope; (*Draht-*) cable. **S~bahn** *f* cable railway. **s~springen**† *vi* (*sein*) (*inf & pp*

only) skip. **S~tänzer(in)** *m(f)* tightrope walker

sein†[1]

- *intransitive verb (sein)*

····➤ be. **ich bin glücklich** I am happy. **er ist Lehrer/Schwede** he is a teacher/Swedish. **bist du es?** is that you? **sei still!** be quiet! **sie waren in Paris** they were in Paris. **morgen bin ich zu Hause** I shall be at home tomorrow. **er ist aus Berlin** he is *or* comes from Berlin

····➤ (*impers + dat*) **mir ist kalt/besser** I am cold/better. **ihr ist schlecht** she feels sick

····➤ (*existieren*) be. **es ist/sind ...** there is/are .... **es ist keine Hoffnung mehr** there is no more hope. **es sind vier davon** there are four of them. **es war einmal ein Prinz** once upon a time there was a prince

- *auxiliary verb*

····➤ (*zur Perfektumschreibung*) have. **er ist gestorben** he has died. **sie sind angekommen** they have arrived. **sie war dort gewesen** she had been there. **ich wäre gefallen** I would have fallen

····➤ (*zur Bildung des Passivs*) be. **wir sind gerettet worden/wir waren gerettet** we were saved

····➤ (+ *zu + Infinitiv*) be to be. **es war niemand zu sehen** there was no one to be seen. **das war zu erwarten** that was to be expected. **er ist zu bemitleiden** he is to be pitied. **die Richtlinien sind strengstens zu beachten** the guidelines are to be strictly followed

sein[2] *poss pron* his; (*Ding, Tier*) its; (*nach man*) one's; **sein Glück versuchen** try one's luck. **s~e(r,s)** *poss pron* his; (*nach man*) one's own; **das S~e tun** do one's share. **s~erseits** *adv* for his part. **s~erzeit** *adv* in those days. **s~etwegen** *adv* for his sake; (*wegen ihm*) because of him, on his account. **s~ige** *poss pron* **der/die/das s~ige** his

seins *poss pron* his; (*nach man*) one's own

seit *conj & prep* (+ *dat*) since; **s~ einiger** Zeit for some time [past]; **ich wohne s~ zehn Jahren hier** I've lived here for ten years. **s~dem** *conj* since ● *adv* since then

Seite *f* **-, -n** side; (*Buch-*) page; **zur S~ treten** step aside; **auf der einen/anderen S~** (*fig*) on the one/other hand

seitens *prep* (+ *gen*) on the part of

Seiten|schiff *nt* [side] aisle. **S~sprung** *m* infidelity. **S~stechen** *nt* **-s** (*Med*) stitch. **S~straße** *f* side-street. **S~streifen** *m* verge; (*Autobahn-*) hard shoulder

seither *adv* since then

seit|lich *a* side ... ● *adv* at/on the side; **s~lich von** to one side of ● *prep* (+ *gen*) to one side of. **s~wärts** *adv* on/to one side; (*zur Seite*) sideways

Sekret|är *m* **-s, -e** secretary; (*Schrank*) bureau. **S~ariat** *nt* **-[e]s, -e** secretary's office. **S~ärin** *f* **-, -nen** secretary

Sekt *m* **-[e]s** [German] sparkling wine

Sekte *f* **-, -n** sect

Sektor *m* **-s, -en** /-ˈtoːrən/ sector

Sekunde *f* **-, -n** second

selber *pron* [!] = **selbst**

selbst *pron* oneself; **ich/du/er/sie s~** I myself /you yourself/ he himself/she herself; **wir/ihr/sie s~** we ourselves/you yourselves/ they themselves; **ich schneide mein Haar s~** I cut my own hair; **von s~** of one's own accord;

S

(*automatisch*) automatically; **s~ gemacht** home-made ● *adv* even
selbständig *a* = **selbstständig**. **S~keit** *f* - = **Selbstständigkeit**
Selbst|bedienung *f* self-service. **S~befriedigung** *f* masturbation. **s~bewusst** *a* self-confident. **S~bewusstsein** *nt* self-confidence. **S~bildnis** *nt* self-portrait. **S~erhaltung** *f* self-preservation. **s~gemacht*** *a* **s~ gemacht**, *s.* **selbst**. **s~haftend** *a* self-adhesive. **S~hilfe** *f* self-help. **s~klebend** *a* self-adhesive. **S~kostenpreis** *m* cost price. **S~laut** *m* vowel. **s~los** *a* selfless. **S~mord** *m* suicide. **S~mörder(in)** *m(f)* suicide. **s~mörderisch** *a* suicidal. **S~porträt** *nt* self-portrait. **s~sicher** *a* self assured. **s~ständig** *a* independent; self-employed <*Handwerker*>; **sich s~ständig machen** set up on one's own. **S~ständigkeit** *f* - independence. **s~süchtig** *a* selfish. **S~tanken** *nt* self-service (*for petrol*). **s~tätig** *a* automatic. **S~versorgung** *f* self-catering. **s~verständlich** *a* natural; **etw für s~ halten** take sth for granted; **das ist s~** that goes without saying; **s~!** of course! **S~verteidigung***f* self-defence. **S~vertrauen** *nt* self-confidence. **S~verwaltung** *f* self-government
selig *a* blissfully happy; (*Relig*) blessed; (*verstorben*) late. **S~keit** *f* - bliss
Sellerie *m* **-s, -s** & *f* **-,-** celeriac; (*Stangen-*) celery
selten *a* rare ● *adv* rarely, seldom; (*besonders*) exceptionally. **S~heit** *f* **-, -en** rarity
seltsam *a* odd, strange. **s~erweise** *adv* oddly
Semester *nt* **-s,-** (*Univ*) semester
Semikolon *nt* **-s, -s** semicolon
Seminar *nt* **-s, -e** seminar; (*Institut*) department; (*Priester-*) seminary
Semmel *f* **-, -n** [bread] roll. **S~brösel** *pl* breadcrumbs
Senat *m* **-[e]s, -e** senate. **S~or** *m* **-s, -en** /-'to:rən/ senator
senden[1]† *vt* send
sende|n[2] *vt* (*reg*) broadcast; (*über Funk*) transmit, send. **S~r** *m* **-s,-** [broadcasting] station; (*Anlage*) transmitter. **S~reihe** *f* series
Sendung *f* **-, -en** consignment, shipment; (*TV*) programme
Senf *m* **-s** mustard
senil *a* senile. **S~ität** *f* - senility
Senior *m* **-s, -en** /-'o:rən/ senior; **S~en** senior citizens. **S~enheim** *nt* old people's home
senken *vt* lower; bring down <*Fieber, Preise*>; bow <*Kopf*>; **sich s~** come down, fall; (*absinken*) subside
senkrecht *a* vertical. **S~e** *f* **-n, -n** perpendicular
Sensation /-'tsi̯o:n/ *f* **-, -en** sensation. **s~ell** *a* sensational
Sense *f* **-, -n** scythe
sensibel *a* sensitive
sentimental *a* sentimental
September *m* **-s,-** September
Serie /'ze:ri̯ə/ *f* **-, -n** series; (*Briefmarken*) set; (*Comm*) range. **S~nnummer** *f* serial number
seriös *a* respectable; (*zuverlässig*) reliable
Serpentine *f* **-, -n** winding road; (*Kehre*) hairpin bend
Serum *nt* **-s,Sera** serum
Service[1] /zɛr'vi:s/ *nt* **-[s],-** /-'vi:s[əs], -'vi:sə/ service, set
Service[2] /'zø:ɐ̯vɪs/ *m* & *nt* **-s** /-vɪs[əs]/ (*Comm, Tennis*) service
servier|en *vt/i* (*haben*) serve. **S~erin** *f* **-, -nen** waitress
Serviette *f* **-, -n** napkin, serviette
Servus *int* (*Aust*) cheerio; (*Begrüßung*) hallo

Sessel *m* **-s,-** armchair. **S~bahn** *f*, **S~lift** *m* chair-lift

sesshaft *a* settled

Set /zɛt/ *nt & m* **-[s], -s** set; (*Deckchen*) place-mat

setz|en *vt* put; (*abstellen*) set down; (*hin-*) sit down <*Kind*>; move <*Spielstein*>; (*pflanzen*) plant; (*schreiben, wetten*) put; **sich s~en** sit down; (*sinken*) settle ● *vi* (*sein*) leap ● *vi* (*haben*) **s~en auf** (+ *acc*) back

Seuche *f* **-, -n** epidemic

seufz|en *vi* (*haben*) sigh. **S~er** *m* **-s,-** sigh

Sex /zɛks/ *m* **-[es]** sex

Sexu|alität *f* **-** sexuality. **s~ell** *a* sexual

sezieren *vt* dissect

Shampoo /ʃam'pu:/, **Shampoon** /ʃam'po:n/ *nt* **-s** shampoo

siamesisch *a* Siamese

sich *refl pron* oneself; (*mit er/sie/es*) himself/herself/itself; (*mit sie pl*) themselves; (*mit Sie*) yourself; (*pl*) yourselves; (*einander*) each other; **s~ kennen** know oneself/(*einander*) each other; **s~ waschen** have a wash; **s~** (*dat*) **die Haare kämmen** comb one's hair; **s~ wundern** be surprised; **s~ gut verkaufen** sell well; **von s~ aus** of one's own accord

Sichel *f* **-, -n** sickle

sicher *a* safe; (*gesichert*) secure; (*gewiss*) certain; (*zuverlässig*) reliable; sure <*Urteil*>; steady <*Hand*>; (*selbstbewusst*) self-confident; **bist du s~?** are you sure? ● *adv* safely; securely; certainly; reliably; self-confidently; (*wahrscheinlich*) most probably; **s~!** certainly! **s~gehen**† *vi sep* (*sein*) (*fig*) be sure

Sicherheit *f* **-** safety; (*Pol, Psych, Comm*) security; (*Gewissheit*) certainty; (*Zuverlässigkeit*) reliability; (*des Urteils*) surety; (*Selbstbewusstsein*) self-confidence. **S~sgurt** *m* safety-belt; (*Auto*) seat-belt. **S~snadel** *f* safety-pin

sicherlich *adv* certainly; (*wahrscheinlich*) most probably

sicher|n *vt* secure; (*garantieren*) safeguard; (*schützen*) protect; put the safety-catch on <*Pistole*>. **S~ung** *f* **-, -en** safeguard, protection; (*Gewehr-*) safety-catch; (*Electr*) fuse

Sicht *f* **-** view; (*S~weite*) visibility; **auf lange S~** in the long term. **s~bar** *a* visible. **S~vermerk** *m* visa. **S~weite** *f* visibility; **außer S~weite** out of sight

sie *pron* (*nom*) (*sg*) she; (*Ding, Tier*) it; (*pl*) they; (*acc*) (*sg*) her; (*Ding, Tier*) it; (*pl*) them

Sie *pron* you; **gehen/warten Sie!** go/wait!

Sieb *nt* **-[e]s, -e** sieve; (*Tee-*) strainer. **s~en¹** *vt* sieve, sift

sieben² *inv a*, **S~** *f* **-, -en** seven. **S~sachen** *fpl* [!] belongings. **s~te(r,s)** *a* seventh

sieb|te(r,s) *a* seventh. **s~zehn** *inv a* seventeen. **s~zehnte(r,s)** *a* seventeenth. **s~zig** *inv a* seventy. **s~zigste(r,s)** *a* seventieth

siede|n† *vt/i* (*haben*) boil. **S~punkt** *m* boiling point

Siedlung *f* **-, -en** [housing] estate; (*Niederlassung*) settlement

Sieg *m* **-[e]s, -e** victory

Siegel *nt* **-s,-** seal. **S~ring** *m* signet-ring

sieg|en *vi* (*haben*) win. **S~er(in)** *m* **-s,-** (*f* **-, -nen**) winner. **s~reich** *a* victorious

siezen *vt* **jdn s~** call s.o. 'Sie'

Signal *nt* **-s, -e** signal

Silbe *f* **-, -n** syllable

Silber *nt* **-s** silver. **s~n** *a* silver

Silhouette /zi'luɛtə/ *f* **-, -n** silhouette

Silizium *nt* **-s** silicon
Silo *m & nt* **-s, -s** silo
Silvester *nt* **-s** New Year's Eve
Sims *m & nt* **-es, -e** ledge
simultan *a* simultaneous
sind *s.* **sein**[1]
Sinfonie *f* **-, -n** symphony
singen† *vt/i* (*haben*) sing
Singvogel *m* songbird
sinken† *vi* (*sein*) sink; (*nieder-*) drop; (*niedriger werden*) go down, fall
Sinn *m* **-[e]s, -e** sense; (*Denken*) mind; (*Zweck*) point; **in gewissem S~e** in a sense; **es hat keinen S~** it is pointless. **S~bild** *nt* symbol
sinnlich *a* sensory; (*sexuell*) sensual; <*Genüsse*> sensuous. **S~keit** *f* - sensuality; sensuousness
sinn|los *a* senseless; (*zwecklos*) pointless. **s~voll** *a* meaningful; (*vernünftig*) sensible
Sintflut *f* flood
Siphon /'zi:fõ/ *m* **-s, -s** siphon
Sippe *f* **-, -n** clan
Sirene *f* **-, -n** siren
Sirup *m* **-s, -e** syrup; treacle
Sitte *f* **-, -n** custom; **S~n** manners
sittlich *a* moral. **S~keit** *f* - morality. **S~keitsverbrecher** *m* sex offender
sittsam *a* well-behaved; (*züchtig*) demure
Situ|ation /-'tsi̯o:n/ *f* **-, -en** situation. **s~iert** *a* **gut/schlecht s~iert** well/badly off
Sitz *m* **-es, -e** seat; (*Passform*) fit
sitzen† *vi* (*haben*) sit; (*sich befinden*) be; (*passen*) fit; (! *treffen*) hit home; **[im Gefängnis] s~** ! be in jail; **s~ bleiben** remain seated; ! (*Sch*) stay *or* be kept down; (*nicht heiraten*) be left on the shelf; **s~ bleiben auf** (+ *dat*) be left with
Sitz|gelegenheit *f* seat. **S~platz** *m* seat. **S~ung** *f* **-, -en** session
Sizilien /-i̯ən/ *nt* **-s** Sicily
Skala *f* **-, -len** scale; (*Reihe*) range
Skalpell *nt* **-s, -e** scalpel
skalpieren *vt* scalp
Skandal *m* **-s, -e** scandal. **s~ös** *a* scandalous
Skandinav|ien /-i̯ən/ *nt* **-s** Scandinavia. **s~isch** *a* Scandinavian
Skat *m* **-s** skat
Skateboard /'ske:tbo:ɐ̯t/ *nt* **-s, -s** skateboard
Skelett *nt* **-[e]s, -e** skeleton
Skep|sis *f* - scepticism. **s~tisch** *a* sceptical
Ski /ʃi:/ *m* **-s, -er** ski; **Ski fahren** *od* **laufen** ski. **S~fahrer(in), S~läufer(in)** *m(f)* **-s,-** (*f* **-, -nen**) skier. **S~sport** *m* skiing
Skizz|e *f* **-, -n** sketch. **s~ieren** *vt* sketch
Sklav|e *m* **-n, -n** slave. **S~erei** *f* - slavery. **S~in** *f* **-, -nen** slave
Skorpion *m* **-s, -e** scorpion; (*Astr*) Scorpio
Skrupel *m* **-s,-** scruple. **s~los** *a* unscrupulous
Skulptur *f* **-, -en** sculpture
Slalom *m* **-s, -s** slalom
Slaw|e *m* **-n, -n, S~in** *f* **-, -nen** Slav. **s~isch** *a* Slav; (*Lang*) Slavonic
Slip *m* **-s, -s** briefs *pl*
Smaragd *m* **-[e]s, -e** emerald
Smoking *m* **-s, -s** dinner jacket
Snob *m* **-s, -s** snob. **S~ismus** *m* - snobbery **s~istisch** *a* snobbish
so *adv* so; (*so sehr*) so much; (*auf diese Weise*) like this/that; (*solch*) such; (! *sowieso*) anyway; (! *umsonst*) free; (! *ungefähr*) about; **so viel** so much; **so gut/bald wie** as good/soon as; **so ein Zufall!** what a coincidence! **mir ist so, als ob** I feel as if; **so oder so** in any case; **so um zehn Euro** ! about ten euros; **so?** really? ● *conj* (*also*) so; (*dann*) then; **so dass = sodass**
sobald *conj* as soon as
Söckchen *nt* **-s,-** [ankle] sock

Socke *f* **-, -n** sock
Sockel *m* **-s,-** plinth, pedestal
Socken *m* **-s,-** sock
sodass *conj* so that
Sodawasser *nt* soda water
Sodbrennen *nt* **-s** heartburn
soeben *adv* just [now]
Sofa *nt* **-s, -s** settee, sofa
sofern *adv* provided [that]
sofort *adv* at once, immediately; (*auf der Stelle*) instantly
Software /'zɔftvɛːɐ̯/ *f* **-** software
sogar *adv* even
sogenannt *a* so-called
sogleich *adv* at once
Sohle *f* **-, -n** sole, (*Tal*) bottom
Sohn *m* **-[e]s,¨-e** son
Sojabohne *f* soya bean
solange *conj* as long as
solch *inv pron* such; **s~ ein(e)** such a; **s~ einer/eine/eins** one/(*Person*) someone like that. **s~e(r,s)** *pron* such
● (*substantivisch*) **ein s~er/eine s~e/ein s~es** one/(*Person*) someone like that; **s~e** *pl* those; (*Leute*) people like that
Soldat *m* **-en, -en** soldier
Söldner *m* **-s,-** mercenary
Solidarität *f* **-** solidarity
solide *a* solid; (*haltbar*) sturdy; (*sicher*) sound; (*anständig*) respectable
Solist(in) *m* **-en, -en** (*f* **-, -nen**) soloist
Soll *nt* **-s** (*Comm*) debit; (*Produktions-*) quota

sollen†
● *auxiliary verb*
····➤ (*Verpflichtung*) be [supposed or meant] to. **er soll morgen zum Arzt gehen** he is [supposed] to go to the doctor tomorrow. **die beiden Flächen sollen fluchten** the two surfaces are meant to be *or* should be in alignment. **du solltest ihn anrufen** you were meant to phone him *or* should have phoned him
····➤ (*Befehl*) **du sollst sofort damit aufhören** you're to stop that at once. **er soll hereinkommen** he is to come in; (*sagen Sie es ihm*) tell him to come in
····➤ **sollte** (*subjunctive*) should; ought to. **wir sollten früher aufstehen** we ought to *or* should get up earlier. **das hätte er nicht tun/sagen sollen** he shouldn't have done/said that
····➤ (*Zukunft, Geplantes*) be to. **ich soll die Abteilung übernehmen** I am to take over the department. **du sollst dein Geld zurückbekommen** you are to *or* shall get your money back. **es soll nicht wieder vorkommen** it won't happen again. **sie sollten ihr Reiseziel nie erreichen** they were never to reach their destination
····➤ (*Ratlosigkeit*) be to; shall. **was soll man nur machen?** what is one to do?; what shall I/we do? **ich weiß nicht, was ich machen soll** I don't know what I should do *or* what to do
····➤ (*nach Bericht*) be supposed to. **er soll sehr reich sein** he is supposed *or* is said to be very rich. **sie soll geheiratet haben** they say *or* I gather she has got married
····➤ (*Absicht*) be meant *or* supposed to. **was soll dieses Bild darstellen?** what is this picture supposed to represent? **das sollte ein Witz sein** that was meant *or* supposed to be a joke
····➤ (*in Bedingungssätzen*) should. **sollte er anrufen, falls** *od* **wenn er anrufen sollte** should he *or* if he should telephone
● *intransitive verb*
····➤ (*irgendwohin gehen sollen*) be [supposed] to go. **er soll morgen**

S

zum Arzt/nach Berlin he is [supposed] to go to the doctor/ to Berlin tomorrow. **ich sollte ins Theater** I was supposed to go to the theatre

····➤ (*sonstige Wendungen*) **soll er doch!** let him! **was soll das?** what's that in aid of? [!]

Solo *nt* **-s, -los** & **-li** solo

somit *adv* therefore, so

Sommer *m* **-s,-** summer. **s~lich** *a* summery; (*Sommer-*) summer ... ● *adv* **s~lich warm** as warm as summer. **S~sprossen** *fpl* freckles

Sonate *f* **-, -n** sonata

Sonde *f* **-, -n** probe

Sonder|angebot *nt* special offer. **s~bar** *a* odd. **S~fahrt** *f* special excursion. **S~fall** *m* special case. **s~gleichen** *adv* **eine Gemeinheit s~gleichen** unparalleled meanness. **S~ling** *m* **-s, -e** crank. **S~marke** *f* special stamp

sondern *conj* but; **nicht nur ... s~ auch** not only ... but also

Sonder|preis *m* special price. **S~schule** *f* special school

Sonett *nt* **-[e]s, -e** sonnet

Sonnabend *m* **-s, -e** Saturday. **s~s** *adv* on Saturdays

Sonne *f* **-, -n** sun. **s~n (sich)** *vr* sun oneself

Sonnen|aufgang *m* sunrise. **s~baden** *vi* (*haben*) sunbathe. **S~bank** *f* sun-bed. **S~blume** *f* sunflower. **S~brand** *m* sun-burn. **S~brille** *f* sun-glasses *pl*. **S~energie** *f* solar energy. **S~finsternis** *f* solar eclipse. **S~milch** *f* sun-tan lotion. **S~öl** *nt* sun-tan oil. **S~schein** *m* sunshine. **S~schirm** *m* sunshade. **S~stich** *m* sunstroke. **S~uhr** *f* sundial. **S~untergang** *m* sunset. **S~wende** *f* solstice

sonnig *a* sunny

Sonntag *m* **-s, -e** Sunday. **s~s** *adv* on Sundays

sonst *adv* (*gewöhnlich*) usually; (*im Übrigen*) apart from that; (*andernfalls*) otherwise, or [else]; **wer/was/wie/wo s~?** who/what/ how/where else? **s~ niemand** no one else; **s~ noch etwas?** anything else? **s~ noch Fragen?** any more questions? **s~ jemand** *od* **wer** someone/(*fragend, verneint*) anyone else; (*irgendjemand*) [just] anyone; **s~ wo** somewhere/(*fragend, verneint*) anywhere else; (*irgendwo*) [just] anywhere. **s~ig** *a* other

sooft *conj* whenever

Sopran *m* **-s, -e** soprano

Sorge *f* **-, -n** worry (**um** about); (*Fürsorge*) care; **sich** (*dat*) **S~n machen** worry. **s~n** *vi* (*haben*) **s~n für** look after, care for; (*vorsorgen*) provide for; (*sich kümmern*) see to; **dafür s~n, dass** see *or* make sure that ● *vr* **sich s~n** worry. **s~nfrei** *a* carefree. **s~nvoll** *a* worried. **S~recht** *nt* (*Jur*) custody

Sorg|falt *f* **-** care. **s~fältig** *a* careful

Sorte *f* **-, -n** kind, sort; (*Comm*) brand

sort|ieren *vt* sort [out]; (*Comm*) grade. **S~iment** *nt* **-[e]s, -e** range

sosehr *conj* however much

Soße *f* **-, -n** sauce; (*Braten-*) gravy; (*Salat-*) dressing

Souvenir /zuvəˈniːɐ̯/ *nt* **-s, -s** souvenir

souverän /zuvəˈrɛːn/ *a* sovereign

soviel *conj* however much; **s~ ich weiß** as far as I know ● *adv* ***so viel**, *s.* **viel**

soweit *conj* as far as; (*insoweit*) [in] so far as ● *adv* ***so weit**, *s.* **weit**

sowenig *conj* however little ● *adv* ***so wenig**, *s.* **wenig**

sowie *conj* as well as; (*sobald*) as soon as

sowieso *adv* anyway, in any case
sowjetisch *a* Soviet. **S~union** *f* - Soviet Union
sowohl *adv* **s~ ... als** *od* **wie auch ...** ... as well as ...
sozial *a* social; <*Einstellung, Beruf*> caring. **S~arbeit** *f* social work. **S~demokrat** *m* social democrat. **S~hilfe** *f* social security
Sozialis|mus *m* - socialism. **S~t** *m* **-en, -en** socialist
Sozial|versicherung *f* National Insurance. **S~wohnung** *f* ≈ council flat
Soziologie *f* - sociology
Sozius *m* **-, -se** (*Comm*) partner; (*Beifahrersitz*) pillion
Spachtel *m* **-s,-** & *f* **-, -n** spatula
Spagat *m* **-[e]s, -e** (*Aust*) string; **S~ machen** do the splits *pl*
Spaghetti, Spagetti *pl* spaghetti *sg*
Spalier *nt* **-s, -e** trellis
Spalt|e *f* **-, -n** crack; (*Gletscher-*) crevasse; (*Druck-*) column; (*Orangen-*) segment. **s~en**† *vt* split. **S~ung** *f* **-, -en** splitting; (*Kluft*) split; (*Phys*) fission
Span *m* **-[e]s,¨e** [wood] chip
Spange *f* **-, -n** clasp; (*Haar-*) slide; (*Zahn-*) brace
Span|ien /-iən/ *nt* **-s** Spain. **S~ier** *m* **-s,-**, **S~ierin** *f* **-, -nen** Spaniard. **s~isch** *a* Spanish. **S~isch** *nt* **-[s]** (*Lang*) Spanish
Spann *m* **-[e]s** instep
Spanne *f* **-, -n** span; (*Zeit-*) space; (*Comm*) margin
spann|en *vt* stretch; put up <*Leine*>; (*straffen*) tighten; (*an-*) harness (**an** + *acc* to); **sich s~en** tighten ● *vi* (*haben*) be too tight. **s~end** *a* exciting. **S~ung** *f* **-, -en** tension; (*Erwartung*) suspense; (*Electr*) voltage
Spar|buch *nt* savings book. **S~büchse** *f* money-box. **s~en** *vt/i* (*haben*) save; (*sparsam sein*) economize (**mit/an** + *dat* on). **S~er** *m* **-s,-** saver
Spargel *m* **-s,-** asparagus
Spar|kasse *f* savings bank. **S~konto** *nt* deposit account
sparsam *a* economical; <*Person*> thrifty. **S~keit** *f* - economy; thrift
Sparschwein *nt* piggy bank
Sparte *f* **-, -n** branch; (*Zeitungs-*) section; (*Rubrik*) column
Spaß *m* **-es,¨e** fun; (*Scherz*) joke; **im/aus/zum S~** for fun; **S~ machen** be fun; <*Person:*> be joking; **viel S~!** have a good time! **s~en** *vi* (*haben*) joke. **S~vogel** *m* joker
Spastiker *m* **-s,-** spastic
spät *a* & *adv* late; **wie s~ ist es?** what time is it? **zu s~ kommen** be late
Spaten *m* **-s,-** spade
später *a* later; (*zukünftig*) future ● *adv* later
spätestens *adv* at the latest
Spatz *m* **-en, -en** sparrow
Spätzle *pl* (*Culin*) noodles
spazieren *vi* (*sein*) stroll; **s~ gehen** go for a walk
Spazier|gang *m* walk; **einen S~gang machen** go for a walk. **S~gänger(in)** *m* **-s,-** (*f* **-, -nen**) walker. **S~stock** *m* walking-stick
Specht *m* **-[e]s, -e** woodpecker
Speck *m* **-s** bacon. **s~ig** *a* greasy
Spedi|teur /ʃpedi'tø:ɐ̯/ *m* **-s, -e** haulage/(*für Umzüge*) removals contractor. **S~tion** /-'tsi̯o:n/ *f* **-, -en** carriage, haulage; (*Firma*) haulage/(*für Umzüge*) removals firm
Speer *m* **-[e]s, -e** spear; (*Sport*) javelin
Speiche *f* **-, -n** spoke
Speichel *m* **-s** saliva
Speicher *m* **-s,-** warehouse; (*dial: Dachboden*) attic; (*Computer*) memory. **s~n** *vt* store
Speise *f* **-, -n** food; (*Gericht*) dish; (*Pudding*) blancmange. **S~eis** *nt*

ice-cream. **S~kammer** *f* larder. **S~karte** *f* menu. **s~n** *vi* (*haben*) eat ● *vt* feed. **S~röhre** *f* oesophagus. **S~saal** *m* dining-room. **S~wagen** *m* dining-car

Spektrum *nt* **-s, -tra** spectrum

Spekul|ant *m* **-en, -en** speculator. **s~ieren** *vi* (*haben*) speculate; **s~ieren auf** (+ *acc*) ! hope to get

Spelze *f* **-, -n** husk

spendabel *a* generous

Spende *f* **-, -n** donation. **s~n** *vt* donate; give <*Blut, Schatten*>; **Beifall s~n** applaud. **S~r** *m* **-s,-** donor; (*Behälter*) dispenser

spendieren *vt* pay for

Sperling *m* **-s, -e** sparrow

Sperre *f* **-, -n** barrier; (*Verbot*) ban; (*Comm*) embargo. **s~n** *vt* close; (*ver-*) block; (*verbieten*) ban; cut off <*Strom, Telefon*>; stop <*Scheck, Kredit*>; **s~n in** (+ *acc*) put in <*Gefängnis, Käfig*>

Sperr|holz *nt* plywood. **S~müll** *m* bulky refuse. **S~stunde** *f* closing time

Spesen *pl* expenses

spezial|isieren (sich) *vr* specialize (**auf** + *acc* in). **S~ist** *m* **-en, -en** specialist. **S~ität** *f* **-, -en** speciality

spicken *vt* (*Culin*) lard; **gespickt mit** (*fig*) full of

Spiegel *m* **-s,-** mirror; (*Wasser-, Alkohol-*) level. **S~bild** *nt* reflection. **S~ei** *nt* fried egg. **s~n** *vt* reflect; **sich s~n** be reflected ● *vi* (*haben*) reflect [the light]; (*glänzen*) gleam. **S~ung** *f* **-, -en** reflection

Spiel *nt* **-[e]s, -e** game; (*Spielen*) playing; (*Glücks-*) gambling; (*Schau-*) play; (*Satz*) set; **auf dem S~ stehen** be at stake; **aufs S~ setzen** risk. **S~automat** *m* fruit machine. **S~bank** *f* casino. **S~dose** *f* musical box. **s~en** *vt/i* (*haben*) play; (*im Glücksspiel*) gamble; (*vortäuschen*) act; <*Roman:*> be set (**in** + *dat* in); **s~en mit** (*fig*) toy with

Spieler(in) *m* **-s,-** (*f* **-, -nen**) player; (*Glücks-*) gambler

Spiel|feld *nt* field, pitch. **~konsole** *f* games console. **S~marke** *f* chip. **S~plan** *m* programme. **S~platz** *m* playground. **S~raum** *m* (*fig*) scope; (*Techn*) clearance. **S~regeln** *fpl* rules [of the game]. **S~sachen** *fpl* toys. **S~verderber** *m* **-s,-** spoilsport. **S~waren** *fpl* toys. **S~warengeschäft** *nt* toyshop. **S~zeug** *nt* toy; (*S~sachen*) toys *pl*

Spieß *m* **-es, -e** spear; (*Brat-*) spit; skewer; (*Fleisch-*) kebab. **S~er** *m* **-s,-** [petit] bourgeois. **s~ig** *a* bourgeois

Spike[s]reifen /ˈʃpai̯k[s]-/ *m* studded tyre

Spinat *m* **-s** spinach

Spindel *f* **-, -n** spindle

Spinne *f* **-, -n** spider

spinn|en† *vt/i* (*haben*) spin; **er spinnt** ! he's crazy. **S~[en]gewebe** *nt*, **S~webe** *f* **-, -n** cobweb

Spion *m* **-s, -e** spy

Spionage /ʃpi̯oˈnaːʒə/ *f* **-** espionage, spying. **S~abwehr** *f* counter-espionage

spionieren *vi* (*haben*) spy

Spionin *f* **-, -nen** [woman] spy

Spiral|e *f* **-, -n** spiral. **s~ig** *a* spiral

Spirituosen *pl* spirits

Spiritus *m* **-** alcohol; (*Brenn-*) methylated spirits *pl*. **S~kocher** *m* spirit stove

spitz *a* pointed; (*scharf*) sharp; (*schrill*) shrill; <*Winkel*> acute. **S~bube** *m* scoundrel

Spitze *f* **-, -n** point; (*oberer Teil*) top; (*vorderer Teil*) front; (*Pfeil-, Finger-, Nasen-*) tip; (*Schuh-, Strumpf-*) toe; (*Zigarren-, Zigaretten-*) holder; (*Höchstleistung*) maximum; (*Tex*)

lace; ([!] *Anspielung*) dig; **an der S~ liegen** be in the lead

Spitzel *m* **-s,-** informer

spitzen *vt* sharpen; purse <*Lippen*>; prick up <*Ohren*>. **S~geschwindigkeit** *f* top speed

Spitzname *m* nickname

Spleen /ʃpli:n/ *m* **-s, -e** obsession

Splitter *m* **-s,-** splinter. **s~n** *vi* (*sein*) shatter

sponsern *vt* sponsor

Spore *f* **-, -n** (*Biol*) spore

Sporn *m* **-[e]s, Sporen** spur

Sport *m* **-[e]s** sport; (*Hobby*) hobby. **S~art** *f* sport. **S~ler** *m* **-s,-** sportsman. **S~lerin** *f* **-, -nen** sportswoman. **s~lich** *a* sports ...; (*fair*) sporting; (*schlank*) sporty. **S~platz** *m* sports ground. **S~verein** *m* sports club. **S~wagen** *m* sports car; (*Kinder-*) push-chair, (*Amer*) stroller

Spott *m* **-[e]s** mockery

spotten *vi* (*haben*) mock; **s~ über** (+ *acc*) make fun of; (*höhnend*) ridicule

spöttisch *a* mocking

Sprach|e *f* **-, -n** language; (*Sprechfähigkeit*) speech; **zur S~e bringen** bring up. **S~fehler** *m* speech defect. **S~labor** *nt* language laboratory. **s~lich** *a* linguistic. **s~los** *a* speechless

Spray /ʃpre:/ *nt & m* **-s, -s** spray. **S~dose** *f* aerosol [can]

Sprechanlage *f* intercom

sprechen† *vi* (*haben*) speak/(*sich unterhalten*) talk (**über** + *acc*/**von** about/of); **Deutsch s~** speak German ● *vt* speak; (*sagen*) say; pronounce <*Urteil*>; **schuldig s~** find guilty; **Herr X ist nicht zu s~** Mr X is not available

Sprecher(in) *m* **-s,-** (*f* **-, -nen**) speaker; (*Radio, TV*) announcer; (*Wortführer*) spokesman, *f* spokeswoman

Sprechstunde *f* consulting hours *pl*; (*Med*) surgery. **S~nhilfe** *f* (*Med*) receptionist

Sprechzimmer *nt* consulting room

spreizen *vt* spread

spreng|en *vt* blow up; blast <*Felsen*>; (*fig*) burst; (*begießen*) water; (*mit Sprenger*) sprinkle; dampen <*Wäsche*>. **S~er** *m* **-s,-** sprinkler. **S~kopf** *m* warhead. **S~körper** *m* explosive device. **S~stoff** *m* explosive

Spreu *f* **-** chaff

Sprich|wort *nt* (*pl* **-wörter**) proverb. **s~wörtlich** *a* proverbial

Springbrunnen *m* fountain

spring|en† *vi* (*sein*) jump; (*Schwimmsport*) dive; <*Ball:*> bounce; (*spritzen*) spurt; (*zer-*) break; (*rissig werden*) crack; (*SGer: laufen*) run. **S~er** *m* **-s,-** jumper; (*Kunst-*) diver; (*Schach*) knight. **S~reiten** *nt* show-jumping

Sprint *m* **-s, -s** sprint

Spritz|e *f* **-, -n** syringe; (*Injektion*) injection; (*Feuer-*) hose. **s~en** *vt* spray; (*be-, ver-*) splash; (*Culin*) pipe; (*Med*) inject ● *vi* (*haben*) splash; <*Fett:*> spit ● *vi* (*sein*) splash; (*hervor-*) spurt. **S~er** *m* **-s,-** splash; (*Schuss*) dash

spröde *a* brittle; (*trocken*) dry

Sprosse *f* **-, -n** rung

Sprotte *f* **-, -n** sprat

Spruch *m* **-[e]s,⸚e** saying; (*Denk-*) motto; (*Zitat*) quotation. **S~band** *nt* (*pl* **-bänder**) banner

Sprudel *m* **-s,-** sparkling mineral water. **s~n** *vi* (*haben/sein*) bubble

Sprüh|dose *f* aerosol [can]. **s~en** *vt* spray ● *vi* (*sein*) <*Funken:*> fly; (*fig*) sparkle

Sprung *m* **-[e]s,⸚e** jump, leap; (*Schwimmsport*) dive; ([!] *Katzen-*) stone's throw; (*Riss*) crack. **S~brett** *nt* springboard.

S~schanze *f* ski-jump. **S~seil** *nt* skipping-rope
Spucke *f* **-** spit. **s~n** *vt/i* (*haben*) spit; (*sich übergeben*) be sick
Spuk *m* **-[e]s, -e** [ghostly] apparition. **s~en** *vi* (*haben*) <*Geist:*> walk; **in diesem Haus s~t es** this house is haunted
Spülbecken *nt* sink
Spule *f* **-, -n** spool
Spüle *f* **-, -n** sink
spulen *vt* spool
spül|en *vt* rinse; (*schwemmen*) wash; **Geschirr s~en** wash up ●*vi* (*haben*) flush [the toilet]. **S~kasten** *m* cistern. **S~mittel** *nt* washing-up liquid
Spur *f* **-, -en** track; (*Fahr-*) lane; (*Fährte*) trail; (*Anzeichen*) trace; (*Hinweis*) lead
spürbar *a* noticeable
spür|en *vt* feel; (*seelisch*) sense. **S~hund** *m* tracker dog
spurlos *adv* without trace
spurten *vi* (*sein*) put on a spurt
sputen (sich) *vr* hurry
Staat *m* **-[e]s, -en** state; (*Land*) country; (*Putz*) finery. **s~lich** *a* state ... ●*adv* by the state
Staatsangehörig|e(r) *m/f* national. **S~keit** *f* **-** nationality
Staats|anwalt *m* state prosecutor. **S~beamte(r)** *m* civil servant. **S~besuch** *m* state visit. **S~bürger(in)** *m(f)* national. **S~mann** *m* (*pl* **-männer**) statesman. **S~streich** *m* coup
Stab *m* **-[e]s,⸚e** rod; (*Gitter-*) bar (*Sport*) baton; (*Mil*) staff
Stäbchen *ntpl* chopsticks
Stabhochsprung *m* pole-vault
stabil *a* stable; (*gesund*) robust; (*solide*) sturdy
Stachel *m* **-s,-** spine; (*Gift-*) sting; (*Spitze*) spike. **S~beere** *f* gooseberry. **S~draht** *m* barbed wire. **S~schwein** *nt* porcupine
Stadion *nt* **-s, -ien** stadium
Stadium *nt* **-s, -ien** stage
Stadt *f* **-,⸚e** town; (*Groß-*) city
städtisch *a* urban; (*kommunal*) municipal
Stadt|mitte *f* town centre. **S~plan** *m* street map. **S~teil** *m* district
Staffel *f* **-, -n** team; (*S~lauf*) relay; (*Mil*) squadron
Staffelei *f* **-, -en** easel
Staffel|lauf *m* relay race. **s~n** *vt* stagger; (*abstufen*) grade
Stahl *m* **-s** steel. **S~beton** *m* reinforced concrete
Stall *m* **-[e]s,⸚e** stable; (*Kuh-*) shed; (*Schweine-*) sty; (*Hühner-*) coop; (*Kaninchen-*) hutch
Stamm *m* **-[e]s⸚e** trunk; (*Sippe*) tribe; (*Wort-*) stem. **S~baum** *m* family tree; (*eines Tieres*) pedigree
stammeln *vt/i* (*haben*) stammer
stammen *vi* (*haben*) come/ (*zeitlich*) date (**von**/**aus** from)
stämmig *a* sturdy
Stamm|kundschaft *f* regulars *pl*. **S~lokal** *nt* favourite pub
stampfen *vi* (*haben*) stamp; <*Maschine:*> pound ●*vi* (*sein*) tramp ●*vt* pound; mash <*Kartoffeln*>
Stand *m* **-[e]s,⸚e** standing position; (*Zustand*) state; (*Spiel-*) score; (*Höhe*) level; (*gesellschaftlich*) class; (*Verkaufs-*) stall; (*Messe-*) stand; (*Taxi-*) rank; **auf den neuesten S~ bringen** up-date
Standard *m* **-s, -s** standard
Standbild *nt* statue
Ständer *m* **-s,-** stand; (*Geschirr-*) rack; (*Kerzen-*) holder
Standes|amt *nt* registry office. **S~beamte(r)** *m* registrar
standhaft *a* steadfast
ständig *a* constant; (*fest*) permanent
Stand|licht *nt* sidelights *pl*. **S~ort** *m* position; (*Firmen-*) location; (*Mil*) garrison. **S~punkt** *m* point

of view. **S~uhr** *f* grandfather clock

Stange *f* **-, -n** bar; (*Holz-*) pole; (*Gardinen-*) rail; (*Hühner-*) perch; (*Zimt-*) stick; **von der S~** [!] off the peg

Stängel *m* **-s,-** stalk, stem

Stangenbohne *f* runner bean

Stanniol *nt* **-s** tin foil. **S~papier** *nt* silver paper

stanzen *vt* stamp; punch <*Loch*>

Stapel *m* **-s,-** stack, pile. **S~lauf** *m* launch[ing]. **s~n** *vt* stack *or* pile up

Star[1] *m* **-[e]s, -e** starling

Star[2] *m* **-[e]s** (*Med*) **[grauer] S~** cataract; **grüner S~** glaucoma

Star[3] *m* **-s, -s** (*Theat, Sport*) star

stark *a* strong; <*Motor*> powerful; <*Verkehr, Regen*> heavy; <*Hitze, Kälte*> severe; (*groß*) big; (*schlimm*) bad; (*dick*) thick; (*korpulent*) stout ● *adv* (*sehr*) very much

Stärk|e *f* **-, -n** strength; power; thickness; stoutness; (*Größe*) size; (*Mais-, Wäsche-*) starch. **S~emehl** *nt* cornflour. **s~en** *vt* strengthen; starch <*Wäsche*>; **sich s~en** fortify oneself. **S~ung** *f* **-, -en** strengthening; (*Erfrischung*) refreshment

starr *a* rigid; (*steif*) stiff

starren *vi* (*haben*) stare

Starr|sinn *m* obstinacy. **s~sinnig** *a* obstinate

Start *m* **-s, -s** start; (*Aviat*) take-off. **S~bahn** *f* runway. **s~en** *vi* (*sein*) start; (*Aviat*) take off ● *vt* start; (*fig*) launch

Station /-'tsjo:n/ *f* **-, -en** station; (*Haltestelle*) stop; (*Abschnitt*) stage; (*Med*) ward; **S~ machen** break one's journey. **s~är** *adv* as an inpatient. **s~ieren** *vt* station

statisch *a* static

Statist(in) *m* **-en, -en** (*f* **-, -nen**) (*Theat*) extra

Statisti|k *f* **-, -en** statistics *sg*; (*Aufstellung*) statistics *pl*. **s~sch** *a* statistical

Stativ *nt* **-s, -e** (*Phot*) tripod

statt *prep* (+ *gen*) instead of; **an seiner s~** in his place; **an Kindes s~ annehmen** adopt ● *conj* **s~ etw zu tun** instead of doing sth. **s~dessen** *adv* instead

statt|finden† *vi sep* (*haben*) take place. **s~haft** *a* permitted

Statue /'ʃta:tuə/ *f* **-, -n** statue

Statur *f* **-** build, stature

Status *m* **-** status. **S~symbol** *nt* status symbol

Statut *nt* **-[e]s, -en** statute

Stau *m* **-[e]s, -s** congestion; (*Auto*) [traffic] jam; (*Rück-*) tailback

Staub *m* **-[e]s** dust; **S~ wischen** dust; **S~ saugen** vacuum, hoover

Staubecken *nt* reservoir

staub|ig *a* dusty. **s~saugen** *vt/i* (*haben*) vacuum, hoover. **S~sauger** *m* vacuum cleaner, Hoover (P)

Staudamm *m* dam

stauen *vt* dam up; **sich s~** accumulate; <*Autos:*> form a tailback

staunen *vi* (*haben*) be amazed *or* astonished

Stau|see *m* reservoir. **S~ung** *f* **-, -en** congestion; (*Auto*) [traffic] jam

Steak /ʃte:k, ste:k/ *nt* **-s, -s** steak

stechen† *vt* stick (**in** + *acc* in); (*verletzen*) prick; (*mit Messer*) stab; <*Insekt:*> sting; <*Mücke:*> bite ● *vi* (*haben*) prick; <*Insekt:*> sting; <*Mücke:*> bite; (*mit Stechuhr*) clock in/out; **in See s~** put to sea

Stech|ginster *m* gorse. **S~kahn** *m* punt. **S~palme** *f* holly. **S~uhr** *f* time clock

Steck|brief *m* 'wanted' poster. **S~dose** *f* socket. **s~en** *vt* put; (*mit Nadel, Reißzwecke*) pin; (*pflanzen*) plant ● *vi* (*haben*) be;

S

(*fest-*) be stuck; **s~ bleiben** get stuck; **den Schlüssel s~ lassen** leave the key in the lock
Steckenpferd *nt* hobby-horse
Steck|er *m* **-s,-** (*Electr*) plug. **S~nadel** *f* pin
Steg *m* **-[e]s, -e** foot-bridge; (*Boots-*) landing-stage; (*Brillen-*) bridge
stehen† *vi* (*haben*) stand; (*sich befinden*) be; (*still-*) be stationary; <*Maschine, Uhr:*> have stopped; **s~ bleiben** remain standing; <*Gebäude:*> be left standing; (*anhalten*) stop; <*Motor:*> stall; <*Zeit:*> stand still; **vor dem Ruin s~** face ruin; **zu jdm/etw s~** (*fig*) stand by s.o./sth; **jdm [gut] s~** suit s.o.; **sich gut s~** be on good terms; **es steht 3 zu 1** the score is 3–1. **s~d** *a* standing; (*sich nicht bewegend*) stationary; <*Gewässer*> stagnant
Stehlampe *f* standard lamp
stehlen† *vt/i* (*haben*) steal; **sich s~** steal, creep
Steh|platz *m* standing place. **S~vermögen** *nt* stamina, staying-power
steif *a* stiff
Steig|bügel *m* stirrup. **S~eisen** *nt* crampon
steigen† *vi* (*sein*) climb; (*hochgehen*) rise, go up; <*Schulden, Spannung:*> mount; **s~ auf** (+ *acc*) climb on [to] <*Stuhl*>; climb <*Berg, Leiter*>; get on <*Pferd, Fahrrad*>; **s~ in** (+ *acc*) climb into; get in <*Auto*>; get on <*Bus, Zug*>; **s~ aus** climb out of; get out of <*Bett, Auto*>; get off <*Bus, Zug*>; **s~de Preise** rising prices
steiger|n *vt* increase; **sich s~n** increase; (*sich verbessern*) improve. **S~ung** *f* **-, -en** increase; improvement; (*Gram*) comparison
steil *a* steep. **S~küste** *f* cliffs *pl*
Stein *m* **-[e]s, -e** stone; (*Ziegel-*) brick; (*Spiel-*) piece. **S~bock** *m* ibex; (*Astr*) Capricorn. **S~bruch** *m* quarry. **S~garten** *m* rockery. **S~gut** *nt* earthenware. **s~ig** *a* stony. **s~igen** *vt* stone. **S~kohle** *f* [hard] coal. **S~schlag** *m* rock fall
Stelle *f* **-, -n** place; (*Fleck*) spot; (*Abschnitt*) passage; (*Stellung*) job, post; (*Behörde*) authority; **auf der S~** immediately
stellen *vt* put; (*aufrecht*) stand; set <*Wecker, Aufgabe*>; ask <*Frage*>; make <*Antrag, Forderung, Diagnose*>; **zur Verfügung s~** provide; **lauter/leiser s~** turn up/down; **kalt/warm s~** chill/keep hot; **sich s~** [go and] stand; give oneself up (**der Polizei** to the police); **sich tot s~** pretend to be dead; **gut gestellt sein** be well off
Stellen|anzeige *f* job advertisement. **S~vermittlung** *f* employment agency. **s~weise** *adv* in places
Stellung *f* **-, -en** position; (*Arbeit*) job; **S~ nehmen** make a statement (**zu** on). **S~suche** *f* job-hunting
Stellvertreter *m* deputy
Stelzen *fpl* stilts. **s~** *vi* (*sein*) stalk
stemmen *vt* press; lift <*Gewicht*>
Stempel *m* **-s,-** stamp; (*Post-*) post-mark; (*Präge-*) die; (*Feingehalts-*) hallmark. **s~n** *vt* stamp; hallmark <*Silber*>; cancel <*Marke*>
Stengel* *m* **-s,-** *s.* **Stängel**
Steno *f* **-** [!] shorthand
Steno|gramm *nt* **-[e]s, -e** shorthand text. **S~grafie** *f* **-** shorthand. **s~grafieren** *vt* take down in shorthand ● *vi* (*haben*) do shorthand
Steppdecke *f* quilt
Steppe *f* **-, -n** steppe

Stepptanz *m* tap-dance
sterben† *vi* (*sein*) die (**an** + *dat* of); **im S~ liegen** be dying
sterblich *a* mortal. **S~keit** *f* - mortality
stereo *adv* in stereo. **S~anlage** *f* stereo [system]
steril *a* sterile. **s~isieren** *vt* sterilize. **S~ität** *f* - sterility
Stern *m* **-[e]s, -e** star. **S~bild** *nt* constellation. **S~chen** *nt* **-s,-** asterisk. **S~kunde** *f* astronomy. **S~schnuppe** *f* **-, -n** shooting star. **S~warte** *f* **-, -n** observatory
stets *adv* always
Steuer[1] *nt* **-s,-** steering-wheel; (*Naut*) helm; **am S~** at the wheel
Steuer[2] *f* **-, -n** tax
Steuer|bord *nt* **-[e]s** starboard [side]. **S~erklärung** *f* tax return. **s~frei** *a* & *adv* tax-free. **S~mann** *m* (*pl* **-leute**) helmsman; (*beim Rudern*) cox. **s~n** *vt* steer; (*Aviat*) pilot; (*Techn*) control ● *vi* (*haben*) be at the wheel/(*Naut*) helm. **s~pflichtig** *a* taxable. **S~rad** *nt* steering-wheel. **S~ruder** *nt* helm. **S~ung** *f* - steering; (*Techn*) controls *pl*. **S~zahler** *m* **-s,-** taxpayer
Stewardess /ˈstjuːɐdɛs/ *f* **-, -en** air hostess, stewardess
Stich *m* **-[e]s, -e** prick; (*Messer-*) stab; (*S~wunde*) stab wound; (*Bienen-*) sting; (*Mücken-*) bite; (*Schmerz*) stabbing pain; (*Näh-*) stitch; (*Kupfer-*) engraving; (*Kartenspiel*) trick
stick|en *vt/i* (*haben*) embroider. **S~erei** *f* - embroidery
Stickstoff *m* nitrogen
Stiefel *m* **-s,-** boot
Stief|kind *nt* stepchild. **S~mutter** *f* stepmother. **S~mütterchen** *nt* **-s,-** pansy. **S~sohn** *m* stepson. **S~tochter** *f* stepdaughter. **S~vater** *m* stepfather
Stiege *f* **-, -n** stairs *pl*
Stiel *m* **-[e]s, -e** handle; (*Blumen-, Gläser-*) stem; (*Blatt-*) stalk
Stier *m* **-[e]s, -e** bull; (*Astr*) Taurus
Stierkampf *m* bullfight
Stift[1] *m* **-[e]s, -e** pin; (*Nagel*) tack; (*Blei-*) pencil; (*Farb-*) crayon
Stift[2] *nt* **-[e]s, -e** [endowed] foundation. **s~en** *vt* endow; (*spenden*) donate; create <*Unheil, Verwirrung*>; bring about <*Frieden*>. **S~ung** *f* **-, -en** foundation; (*Spende*) donation
Stil *m* **-[e]s, -e** style
still *a* quiet; (*reglos, ohne Kohlensäure*) still; (*heimlich*) secret; **der S~e Ozean** the Pacific; **im S~en** secretly. **S~e** *f* - quiet; (*Schweigen*) silence
Stilleben* *nt s*. **Stillleben**
stillen *vt* satisfy; quench <*Durst*>; stop <*Schmerzen, Blutung*>; breast-feed <*Kind*>
still|halten† *vi sep* (*haben*) keep still. **S~leben** *nt* still life. **s~legen** *vt sep* close down. **S~schweigen** *nt* silence. **S~stand** *m* standstill; **zum S~stand bringen/kommen** stop. **s~stehen**† *vi sep* (*haben*) stand still; (*anhalten*) stop; <*Verkehr:*> be at a standstill
Stimm|bänder *ntpl* vocal cords. **s~berechtigt** *a* entitled to vote. **S~bruch** *m* **er ist im S~bruch** his voice is breaking
Stimme *f* **-, -n** voice; (*Wahl-*) vote
stimmen *vi* (*haben*) be right; (*wählen*) vote ● *vt* tune
Stimmung *f* **-, -en** mood; (*Atmosphäre*) atmosphere
Stimmzettel *m* ballot-paper
stink|en† *vi* (*haben*) smell/(*stark*) stink (**nach** of). **S~tier** *nt* skunk
Stipendium *nt* **-s, -ien** scholarship; (*Beihilfe*) grant
Stirn *f* **-, -en** forehead
stochern *vi* (*haben*) **s~ in** (+ *dat*) poke <*Feuer*>; pick at <*Essen*>

Stock[1] *m* **-[e]s,⸚e** stick; (*Ski-*) pole; (*Bienen-*) hive; (*Rosen-*) bush; (*Reb-*) vine

Stock[2] *m* **-[e]s,-** storey, floor. **S~bett** *nt* bunk-beds *pl.*

stock|en *vi* (*haben*) stop; <*Verkehr:*> come to a standstill; <*Person:*> falter. **S~ung** *f* **-, -en** hold-up

Stockwerk *nt* storey, floor

Stoff *m* **-[e]s, -e** substance; (*Tex*) fabric, material; (*Thema*) subject [matter]; (*Gesprächs-*) topic. **S~wechsel** *m* metabolism

stöhnen *vi* (*haben*) groan, moan

Stola *f* **-, -len** stole

Stollen *m* **-s,-** gallery; (*Kuchen*) stollen

stolpern *vi* (*sein*) stumble; **s~ über** (+ *acc*) trip over

stolz *a* proud (**auf** + *acc* of). **S~** *m* **-es** pride

stopfen *vt* stuff; (*stecken*) put; (*ausbessern*) darn ● *vi* (*haben*) be constipating

Stopp *m* **-s, -s** stop. **s~** *int* stop!

stoppelig *a* stubbly

stopp|en *vt* stop; (*Sport*) time ● *vi* (*haben*) stop. **S~uhr** *f* stop-watch

Stöpsel *m* **-s,-** plug; (*Flaschen-*) stopper

Storch *m* **-[e]s,⸚e** stork

Store /ʃtoːɐ/ *m* **-s, -s** net curtain

stören *vt* disturb; disrupt <*Rede*>; jam <*Sender*>; (*missfallen*) bother ● *vi* (*haben*) be a nuisance

stornieren *vt* cancel

störrisch *a* stubborn

Störung *f* **-, -en** disturbance; disruption; (*Med*) trouble; (*Radio*) interference; **technische S~** technical fault

Stoß *m* **-es,⸚e** push, knock; (*mit Ellbogen*) dig; (*Hörner-*) butt; (*mit Waffe*) thrust; (*Schwimm-*) stroke; (*Ruck*) jolt; (*Erd-*) shock; (*Stapel*) stack, pile. **S~dämpfer** *m* **-s,-** shock absorber

stoßen† *vt* push, knock; (*mit Füßen*) kick; (*mit Kopf*) butt; (*an-*) poke, nudge; (*treiben*) thrust; **sich s~** knock oneself; **sich** (*dat*) **den Kopf s~** hit one's head ● *vi* (*haben*) push; **s~ an** (+ *acc*) knock against; (*angrenzen*) adjoin ● *vi* (*sein*) **s~ gegen** knock against; bump into <*Tür*>; **s~ auf** (+ *acc*) bump into; (*entdecken*) come across; strike <*Öl*>

Stoß|stange *f* bumper. **S~verkehr** *m* rush-hour traffic. **S~zahn** *m* tusk. **S~zeit** *f* rush-hour

stottern *vt/i* (*haben*) stutter, stammer

Str. *abbr* (**Straße**) St

Strafanstalt *f* prison

Strafe *f* **-, -n** punishment; (*Jur & fig*) penalty; (*Geld-*) fine; (*Freiheits-*) sentence. **s~n** *vt* punish

straff *a* tight, taut. **s~en** *vt* tighten

Strafgesetz *nt* criminal law

sträf|lich *a* criminal. **S~ling** *m* **-s, -e** prisoner

Straf|mandat *nt* (*Auto*) [parking/ speeding] ticket. **S~porto** *nt* excess postage. **S~raum** *m* penalty area. **S~stoß** *m* penalty. **S~tat** *f* crime

Strahl *m* **-[e]s, -en** ray; (*einer Taschenlampe*) beam; (*Wasser-*) jet. **s~en** *vi* (*haben*) shine; (*funkeln*) sparkle; (*lächeln*) beam. **S~enbehandlung** *f* radiotherapy. **S~ung** *f* **-** radiation

Strähne *f* **-, -n** strand

stramm *a* tight

Strampel|höschen /-sç-/ *nt* **-s,-** rompers *pl.* **s~n** *vi* (*haben*) <*Baby:*> kick

Strand *m* **-[e]s,⸚e** beach. **s~en** *vi* (*sein*) run aground

Strang *m* **-[e]s,⸚e** rope

Strapaz|e *f* **-, -n** strain. **s~ieren** *vt* be hard on; tax <*Nerven*>

Strass *m* **-** *&* **-es** paste
Straße *f* **-, -n** road; (*in der Stadt auch*) street; (*Meeres-*) strait. **S~nbahn** *f* tram. **S~nkarte** *f* road-map. **S~nsperre** *f* road-block
Strat|ogie *f* **-, -n** strategy. **s~egisch** *a* strategic
Strauch *m* **-[e]s, Sträucher** bush
Strauß[1] *m* **-es, Sträuße** bunch [of flowers]; (*Bukett*) bouquet
Strauß[2] *m* **-es, -e** ostrich
streben *vi* (*haben*) strive (**nach** for) ● *vi* (*sein*) head (**nach/zu** for)
Streber *m* **-s,-** pushy person
Strecke *f* **-, -n** stretch, section; (*Entfernung*) distance; (*Rail*) line; (*Route*) route
strecken *vt* stretch; (*aus-*) stretch out; (*gerade machen*) straighten; (*Culin*) thin down; **den Kopf aus dem Fenster s~** put one's head out of the window
Streich *m* **-[e]s, -e** prank, trick
streicheln *vt* stroke
streichen† *vt* spread; (*weg-*) smooth; (*an-*) paint; (*aus-*) delete; (*kürzen*) cut ● *vi* (*haben*) **s~ über** (+ *acc*) stroke
Streichholz *nt* match
Streich|instrument *nt* stringed instrument. **S~käse** *m* cheese spread. **S~orchester** *nt* string orchestra. **S~ung** *f* **-, -en** deletion; (*Kürzung*) cut
Streife *f* **-, -n** patrol
streifen *vt* brush against; (*berühren*) touch; (*verletzen*) graze; (*fig*) touch on <*Thema*>
Streifen *m* **-s,-** stripe; (*Licht-*) streak; (*auf der Fahrbahn*) line; (*schmales Stück*) strip
Streifenwagen *m* patrol car
Streik *m* **-s, -s** strike; **in den S~ treten** go on strike. **S~brecher** *m* strike-breaker, (*pej*) scab. **s~en** *vi* (*haben*) strike; [!] refuse; (*versagen*) pack up
Streit *m* **-[e]s, -e** quarrel; (*Auseinandersetzung*) dispute. **s~en**† *vr/i* (*haben*) **[sich] s~en** quarrel. **S~igkeiten** *fpl* quarrels. **S~kräfte** *fpl* armed forces
streng *a* strict; <*Blick, Ton*> stern; (*rau, nüchtern*) severe; <*Geschmack*> sharp; **s~ genommen** strictly speaking. **S~e** *f* **-** strictness; sternness; severity
Stress *m* **-es, -e** stress
streuen *vt* spread; (*ver-*) scatter; sprinkle <*Zucker, Salz*>; **die Straßen s~** grit the roads
streunen *vi* (*sein*) roam
Strich *m* **-[e]s, -e** line; (*Feder-, Pinsel-*) stroke; (*Morse-, Gedanken-*) dash. **S~kode** *m* bar code. **S~punkt** *m* semicolon
Strick *m* **-[e]s, -e** cord; (*Seil*) rope
strick|en *vt/i* (*haben*) knit. **S~jacke** *f* cardigan. **S~leiter** *f* rope-ladder. **S~nadel** *f* knitting-needle. **S~waren** *fpl* knitwear *sg*. **S~zeug** *nt* knitting
striegeln *vt* groom
strittig *a* contentious
Stroh *nt* **-[e]s** straw. **S~blumen** *fpl* everlasting flowers. **S~dach** *nt* thatched roof. **S~halm** *m* straw
Strolch *m* **-[e]s, -e** [!] rascal
Strom *m* **-[e]s,¨e** river; (*Menschen-, Auto-, Blut-*) stream; (*Tränen-*) flood; (*Schwall*) torrent; (*Electr*) current, power; **gegen den S~** (*fig*) against the tide. **s~abwärts** *adv* downstream. **s~aufwärts** *adv* upstream
strömen *vi* (*sein*) flow; <*Menschen, Blut*> stream, pour
Strom|kreis *m* circuit. **s~linienförmig** *a* streamlined. **S~sperre** *f* power cut
Strömung *f* **-, -en** current
Strophe *f* **-, -n** verse
Strudel *m* **-s,-** whirlpool; (*SGer Culin*) strudel
Strumpf *m* **-[e]s,¨e** stocking; (*Knie-*) sock. **S~band** *nt* (*pl*

-bänder) suspender. **S~hose** *f* tights *pl*
struppig *a* shaggy
Stube *f* **-, -n** room. **s~nrein** *a* house-trained
Stuck *m* **-s** stucco
Stück *nt* **-[e]s, -e** piece; (*Zucker-*) lump; (*Seife*) tablet; (*Theater-*) play; (*Gegenstand*) item; (*Exemplar*) specimen; **ein S~** (*Entfernung*) some way. **S~chen** *nt* **-s,-** [little] bit
Student|(in) *m* **-en, -en** (*f* **-, -nen**) student. **s~isch** *a* student ...
Studie /-i̯ə/ *f* **-, -n** study
studieren *vt/i* (*haben*) study
Studio *nt* **-s, -s** studio
Studium *nt* **-s, -ien** studies *pl*
Stufe *f* **-, -n** step; (*Treppen-*) stair; (*Raketen-*) stage; (*Niveau*) level. **s~n** *vt* terrace; (*staffeln*) grade
Stuhl *m* **-[e]s,¨-e** chair; (*Med*) stools *pl*. **S~gang** *m* bowel movement
stülpen *vt* put (**über** + *acc* over)
stumm *a* dumb; (*schweigsam*) silent
Stummel *m* **-s,-** stump; (*Zigaretten-*) butt; (*Bleistift-*) stub
Stümper *m* **-s,-** bungler
stumpf *a* blunt; <*Winkel*> obtuse; (*glanzlos*) dull; (*fig*) apathetic. **S~** *m* **-[e]s,¨-e** stump
Stumpfsinn *m* apathy; tedium
Stunde *f* **-, -n** hour; (*Sch*) lesson
stunden *vt* **jdm eine Schuld s~** give s.o. time to pay a debt
Stunden|kilometer *mpl* kilometres per hour. **s~lang** *adv* for hours. **S~lohn** *m* hourly rate. **S~plan** *m* timetable. **s~weise** *adv* by the hour
stündlich *a & adv* hourly
stur *a* pigheaded
Sturm *m* **-[e]s,¨-e** gale; storm; (*Mil*) assault
stürm|en *vi* (*haben*) <*Wind:*> blow hard ● *vi* (*sein*) rush ● *vt* storm; (*bedrängen*) besiege. **S~er** *m* **-s,-** forward. **s~isch** *a* stormy; <*Überfahrt*> rough
Sturz *m* **-es,¨-e** [heavy] fall; (*Preis-*) sharp drop; (*Pol*) overthrow
stürzen *vi* (*sein*) fall [heavily]; (*in die Tiefe*) plunge; <*Preise:*> drop sharply; <*Regierung:*> fall; (*eilen*) rush ● *vt* throw; (*umkippen*) turn upside down; turn out <*Speise, Kuchen*>; (*Pol*) overthrow, topple; **sich s~** throw oneself (**aus/in** + *acc* out of/into)
Sturzhelm *m* crash-helmet
Stute *f* **-, -n** mare
Stütze *f* **-, -n** support
stützen *vt* support; (*auf-*) rest; **sich s~ auf** (+ *acc*) lean on
stutzig *a* puzzled; (*misstrauisch*) suspicious
Stützpunkt *m* (*Mil*) base
Substantiv *nt* **-s, -e** noun
Substanz *f* **-, -en** substance
Subvention /-ˈt͡si̯o:n/ *f* **-, -en** subsidy. **s~ieren** *vt* subsidize
Such|e *f* **-** search; **auf der S~e nach** looking for. **s~en** *vt* look for; (*intensiv*) search for; seek <*Hilfe, Rat*>; **'Zimmer gesucht'** 'room wanted' ● *vi* (*haben*) look, search (**nach** for). **S~er** *m* **-s,-** (*Phot*) viewfinder. **S~maschine** *f* search engine
Sucht *f* **-,¨-e** addiction; (*fig*) mania
süchtig *a* addicted. **S~e(r)** *m/f* addict
Süd *m* **-[e]s** south. **S~afrika** *nt* South Africa. **S~amerika** *nt* South America. **s~deutsch** *a* South German
Süden *m* **-s** south; **nach S~** south
Süd|frucht *f* tropical fruit. **s~lich** *a* southern; <*Richtung*> southerly ● *adv & prep* (+ *gen*) **s~lich der Stadt** south of the town. **S~pol** *m* South Pole. **s~wärts** *adv* southwards
Sühne *f* **-, -n** atonement; (*Strafe*) penalty. **s~n** *vt* atone for

Sultanine *f* **-, -n** sultana
Sülze *f* **-, -n** [meat] jelly
Summe *f* **-, -n** sum
summen *vi* (*haben*) hum; *<Biene:>* buzz ● *vt* hum
summieren (sich) *vr* add up
Sumpf *m* **-[e]s,¨e** marsh, swamp
Sünd|e *f* **-, -n** sin. **S∼enbock** *m* scapegoat. **S∼er(in)** *m* **-s,-** (*f* **-, -nen**) sinner. **s∼igen** *vi* (*haben*) sin
super *inv a* 🅵 great. **S∼markt** *m* supermarket
Suppe *f* **-, -n** soup. **S∼nlöffel** *m* soup-spoon. **S∼nteller** *m* soup-plate. **S∼nwürfel** *m* stock cube
Surf|brett /ˈsøːɐ̯f-/ *nt* surfboard. **s∼en** *vi* (*haben*) surf. **S∼en** *nt* **-s** surfing
surren *vi* (*haben*) whirr
süß *a* sweet. **S∼e** *f* **-** sweetness. **s∼en** *vt* sweeten. **S∼igkeit** *f* **-, -en** sweet. **s∼lich** *a* sweetish; (*fig*) sugary. **S∼speise** *f* sweet. **S∼stoff** *m* sweetener. **S∼waren** *fpl* confectionery *sg*, sweets *pl*. **S∼wasser-** *pref* freshwater …
Sylvester *nt* **-s** = **Silvester**
Symbol *nt* **-s, -e** symbol. **S∼ik** *f* **-** symbolism. **s∼isch** *a* symbolic
Sym|metrie *f* **-** symmetry. **s∼metrisch** *a* symmetrical
Sympathie *f* **-, -n** sympathy
sympathisch *a* agreeable; *<Person>* likeable
Symptom *nt* **-s, -e** symptom. **s∼atisch** *a* symptomatic
Synagoge *f* **-, -n** synagogue
synchronisieren /zynkroniˈziːrən/ *vt* synchronize; dub *<Film>*
Syndikat *nt* **-[e]s, -e** syndicate
Syndrom *nt* **-s, -e** syndrome
synonym *a* synonymous
Synthese *f* **-, -n** synthesis
Syrien /-iən/ *nt* **-s** Syria
System *nt* **-s, -e** system. **s∼atisch** *a* systematic
Szene *f* **-, -n** scene

Tt

Tabak *m* **-s, -e** tobacco
Tabelle *f* **-, -n** table; (*Sport*) league table
Tablett *nt* **-[e]s, -s** tray
Tablette *f* **-, -n** tablet
tabu *a* taboo. **T∼** *nt* **-s, -s** taboo
Tacho *m* **-s, -s**, **Tachometer** *m & nt* speedometer
Tadel *m* **-s,-** reprimand; (*Kritik*) censure; (*Sch*) black mark. **t∼los** *a* impeccable. **t∼n** *vt* reprimand; censure
Tafel *f* **-, -n** (*Tisch, Tabelle*) table; (*Platte*) slab; (*Anschlag-, Hinweis-*) board; (*Gedenk-*) plaque; (*Schiefer-*) slate; (*Wand-*) blackboard; (*Bild-*) plate; (*Schokolade*) bar
Täfelung *f* **-** panelling
Tag *m* **-[e]s, -e** day; **unter T∼e** underground; **es wird Tag** it is getting light; **guten Tag!** good morning/afternoon!
Tage|buch *nt* diary. **t∼lang** *adv* for days
Tages|anbruch *m* daybreak. **T∼ausflug** *m* day trip. **T∼decke** *f* bedspread. **T∼karte** *f* day ticket; (*Speise-*) menu of the day. **T∼licht** *nt* daylight. **T∼mutter** *f* child-minder. **T∼ordnung** *f* agenda. **T∼rückfahrkarte** *f* day return [ticket]. **T∼zeit** *f* time of the day. **T∼zeitung** *f* daily [news]paper
täglich *a & adv* daily; **zweimal t∼** twice a day
tags *adv* by day; **t∼ zuvor/darauf** the day before/after
tagsüber *adv* during the day

tag|täglich *a* daily ●*adv* every single day. **T~ung** *f* **-, -en** meeting; conference

Taill|e /ˈtaljə/ *f* **-, -n** waist. **t~iert** /taˈjiːɐ̯t/ *a* fitted

Takt *m* **-[e]s, -e** tact; (*Mus*) bar; (*Tempo*) time; (*Rhythmus*) rhythm; **im T~** in time

Taktik *f* **-** tactics *pl.*

takt|los *a* tactless. **T~losigkeit** *f* **-** tactlessness. **T~stock** *m* baton. **t~voll** *a* tactful

Tal *nt* **-[e]s, ¨er** valley

Talar *m* **-s, -e** robe; (*Univ*) gown

Talent *nt* **-[e]s, -e** talent. **t~iert** *a* talented

Talg *m* **-s** tallow; (*Culin*) suet

Talsperre *f* dam

Tampon /tamˈpõː/ *m* **-s, -s** tampon

Tank *m* **-s, -s** tank. **t~en** *vt* fill up with <*Benzin*> ●*vi* (*haben*) fill up with petrol; (*Aviat*) refuel. **T~er** *m* **-s,-** tanker. **T~stelle** *f* petrol station. **T~wart** *m* **-[e]s, -e** petrol-pump attendant

Tanne *f* **-, -n** fir [tree]. **T~nbaum** *m* fir tree; (*Weihnachtsbaum*) Christmas tree. **T~nzapfen** *m* fir cone

Tante *f* **-, -n** aunt

Tantiemen /tanˈti̯eːmən/ *pl* royalties

Tanz *m* **-es,¨e** dance. **t~en** *vt/i* (*haben*) dance

Tänzer(in) *m* **-s,-** (*f* **-, -nen**) dancer

Tapete *f* **-, -n** wallpaper

tapezieren *vt* paper

tapfer *a* brave. **T~keit** *f* **-** bravery

Tarif *m* **-s, -e** rate; (*Verzeichnis*) tariff

tarn|en *vt* disguise; (*Mil*) camouflage. **T~ung** *f* **-** disguise; camouflage

Tasche *f* **-, -n** bag; (*Hosen-, Mantel-*) pocket. **T~nbuch** *nt* paper-back. **T~ndieb** *m* pickpocket. **T~ngeld** *nt* pocket-money. **T~nlampe** *f* torch. **T~nmesser** *nt* penknife. **T~ntuch** *nt* handkerchief

Tasse *f* **-, -n** cup

Tastatur *f* **-, -en** keyboard

Tast|e *f* **-, -n** key; (*Druck-*) push-button. **t~en** *vi* (*haben*) feel, grope (**nach** for) ●*vt* key in <*Daten*>; **sich t~en** feel one's way (zu to)

Tat *f* **-, -en** action; (*Helden-*) deed; (*Straf-*) crime; **auf frischer Tat ertappt** caught in the act

Täter(in) *m* **-s,-** (*f* **-, -nen**) culprit; (*Jur*) offender

tätig *a* active; **t~ sein** work. **T~keit** *f* **-, -en** activity; (*Arbeit*) work, job

Tatkraft *f* energy

Tatort *m* scene of the crime

tätowier|en *vt* tattoo. **T~ung** *f* **-, -en** tattooing; (*Bild*) tattoo

Tatsache *f* fact. **T~nbericht** *m* documentary

tatsächlich *a* actual

Tatze *f* **-, -n** paw

Tau[1] *m* **-[e]s** dew

Tau[2] *nt* **-[e]s, -e** rope

taub *a* deaf; (*gefühllos*) numb

Taube *f* **-, -n** pigeon; dove. **T~nschlag** *m* pigeon-loft

Taub|heit *f* **-** deafness. **t~stumm** *a* deaf and dumb

tauch|en *vt* dip, plunge; (*unter-*) duck ●*vi* (*haben/sein*) dive/(*ein-*) plunge (**in** + *acc* into); (*auf-*) appear (**aus** out of). **T~er** *m* **-s,-** diver. **T~eranzug** *m* diving-suit

tauen *vi* (*sein*) melt, thaw ●*impers* **es taut** it is thawing

Tauf|becken *nt* font. **T~e** *f* **-, -n** christening, baptism. **t~en** *vt* christen, baptize. **T~pate** *m* godfather

taugen *vi* (*haben*) **etwas/nichts t~n** be good/no good

tauglich *a* suitable; (*Mil*) fit

Tausch *m* **-[e]s, -e** exchange, [!] swap. **t~en** *vt* exchange/ (*handeln*) barter (*gegen* for) ●*vi* (*haben*) swap (**mit etw** sth; **mit jdm** with s.o.)

täuschen *vt* deceive, fool; betray <*Vertrauen*>; **sich t~** delude oneself; (*sich irren*) be mistaken ● *vi* (*haben*) be deceptive. **t~d** *a* deceptive; <*Ähnlichkeit*> striking

Täuschung *f* **-, -en** deception; (*Irrtum*) mistake; (*Illusion*) delusion

tausend *inv a* one/a thousand. **T~** *nt* **-s, -e** thousand. **T~füßler** *m* **-s,-** centipede. **t~ste(r, s)** *a* thousandth. **T~stel** *nt* **-s,-** thousandth

Tau|tropfen *m* dewdrop. **T~wetter** *nt* thaw

Taxe *f* **-, -n** charge; (*Kur-*) tax; (*Taxi*) taxi

Taxi *nt* **-s, -s** taxi, cab

Taxi|fahrer *m* taxi driver. **T~stand** *m* taxi rank

Teakholz /ˈtiːk-/ *nt* teak

Team /tiːm/ *nt* **-s, -s** team

Techni|k *f* **-, -en** technology; (*Methode*) technique. **T~ker** *m* **-s,-** technician. **t~sch** *a* technical; (*technologisch*) technological; **T~sche Hochschule** Technical University

Techno|logie *f* **-, -n** technology. **t~logisch** *a* technological

Teddybär *m* teddy bear

Tee *m* **-s, -s** tea. **T~beutel** *m* tea-bag. **T~kanne** *f* teapot. **T~löffel** *m* teaspoon

Teer *m* **-s** tar. **t~en** *vt* tar

Tee|sieb *nt* tea-strainer. **T~wagen** *m* [tea] trolley

Teich *m* **-[e]s, -e** pond

Teig *m* **-[e]s, -e** pastry; (*Knet-*) dough; (*Rühr-*) mixture; (*Pfannkuchen-*) batter. **T~rolle** *f* rolling-pin. **T~waren** *fpl* pasta *sg*

Teil *m* **-[e]s, -e** part; (*Bestand-*) component; (*Jur*) party; **zum T~** partly; **zum großen/größten T~** for the most part ● *m & nt* **-[e]s** (*Anteil*) share; **ich für mein[en] T~** for my part ● *nt* **-[e]s, -e** part; (*Ersatz-*) spare part; (*Anbau-*) unit

teil|bar *a* divisible. **T~chen** *nt* **-s,-** particle. **t~en** *vt* divide; (*auf-*) share out; (*gemeinsam haben*) share; (*Pol*) partition <*Land*>; **sich** (*dat*) **etw t~en** share sth; **sich t~en** divide; <*Meinungen:*> differ ● *vi* (*haben*) share

Teilhaber *m* **-s,-** (*Comm*) partner

Teilnahme *f* **-** participation; (*innere*) interest; (*Mitgefühl*) sympathy

teilnehm|en† *vi sep* (*haben*) **t~en an** (+ *dat*) take part in; (*mitfühlen*) share [in]. **T~er(in)** *m* **-s,-** (*f* **-, -nen**) participant; (*an Wettbewerb*) competitor

teil|s *adv* partly. **T~ung** *f* **-, -en** division; (*Pol*) partition. **t~weise** *a* partial ● *adv* partially, partly. **T~zahlung** *f* part-payment; (*Rate*) instalment. **T~zeitbeschäftigung** *f* part-time job

Teint /tɛ̃ː/ *m* **-s, -s** complexion

Telearbeit *f* teleworking

Telefax *nt* fax

Telefon *nt* **-s, -e** [tele]phone. **T~anruf** *m*, **T~at** *nt* **-[e]s, -e** [tele]phone call. **T~buch** *nt* [tele]phone book. **t~ieren** *vi* (*haben*) [tele]phone

telefon|isch *a* [tele]phone ... ● *adv* by [tele]phone. **T~ist(in)** *m* **-en, -en** (*f* **-, -nen**) telephonist. **T~karte** *f* phone card. **T~nummer** *f* [tele]phone number. **T~zelle** *f* [tele]phone box

Telegraf *m* **-en, -en** telegraph. **T~enmast** *m* telegraph pole. **t~ieren** *vi* (*haben*) send a telegram. **t~isch** *a* telegraphic ● *adv* by telegram

Telegramm *nt* **-s, -e** telegram

Teleobjektiv *nt* telephoto lens

Telepathie *f* **-** telepathy

T

Teleskop *nt* **-s, -e** telescope
Telex *nt* **-, -[e]** telex. **t~en** *vt* telex
Teller *m* **-s,-** plate
Tempel *m* **-s,-** temple
Temperament *nt* **-s, -e** temperament; (*Lebhaftigkeit*) vivacity
Temperatur *f* **-, -en** temperature
Tempo *nt* **-s, -s** speed; **T~ [T~]!** hurry up!
Tendenz *f* **-, -en** trend; (*Neigung*) tendency
Tennis *nt* **-** tennis. **T~platz** *m* tennis-court. **T~schläger** *m* tennis-racket
Teppich *m* **-s,e** carpet. **T~boden** *m* fitted carpet
Termin *m* **-s, -e** date; (*Arzt-*) appointment. **T~kalender** *m* [appointments] diary
Terrasse *f* **-, -n** terrace
Terrier /ˈtɛriɐ/ *m* **-s,-** terrier
Terrine *f* **-, -n** tureen
Territorium *nt* **-s, -ien** territory
Terror *m* **-s** terror. **t~isieren** *vt* terrorize. **T~ismus** *m* **-** terrorism. **T~ist** *m* **-en, -en** terrorist
Tesafilm (P) *m* ≈ Sellotape (P)
Test *m* **-[e]s, -s** & **-e** test
Testament *nt* **-[e]s, -e** will; **Altes/Neues T~** Old/New Testament. **T~svollstrecker** *m* **-s,-** executor
testen *vt* test
Tetanus *m* **-** tetanus
teuer *a* expensive; (*lieb*) dear; **wie t~?** how much?
Teufel *m* **-s,-** devil. **T~skreis** *m* vicious circle
teuflisch *a* fiendish
Text *m* **-[e]s, -e** text; (*Passage*) passage; (*Bild-*) caption; (*Lied-*) lyrics *pl*. **T~er** *m* **-s,-** copy-writer; (*Schlager-*) lyricist
Textilien /-iən/ *pl* textiles; (*Textilwaren*) textile goods
Text|nachricht *f* text message. **T~verarbeitungssystem** *nt* word processor
Theater *nt* **-s,-** theatre; (🅵 *Getue*) fuss. **T~kasse** *f* box-office. **T~stück** *nt* play
Theke *f* **-, -n** bar; (*Ladentisch*) counter
Thema *nt* **-s, -men** subject
Themse *f* **-** Thames
Theolo|ge *m* **-n, -n** theologian. **T~gie** *f* **-** theology
theor|etisch *a* theoretical. **T~ie** *f* **-, -n** theory
Therapeut(in) *m* **-en, -en** (*f* **-, -nen**) therapist
Therapie *f* **-, -n** therapy
Thermalbad *nt* thermal bath
Thermometer *nt* **-s,-** thermometer
Thermosflasche (P) *f* Thermos flask (P)
Thermostat *m* **-[e]s, -e** thermostat
These *f* **-, -n** thesis
Thrombose *f* **-, -n** thrombosis
Thron *m* **-[e]s, -e** throne. **t~en** *vi* (*haben*) sit [in state]. **T~folge** *f* succession. **T~folger** *m* **-s,-** heir to the throne
Thunfisch *m* tuna
Thymian *m* **-s** thyme
ticken *vi* (*haben*) tick
tief *a* deep; (*t~ liegend, niedrig*) low; (*t~gründig*) profound; **t~er Teller** soup-plate ●*adv* deep; low; (*sehr*) deeply, profoundly; <*schlafen*> soundly. **T~** *nt* **-s, -s** (*Meteorol*) depression. **T~bau** *m* civil engineering. **T~e** *f* **-, -n** depth. **T~garage** *f* underground car park. **t~gekühlt** *a* [deep-] frozen
Tiefkühl|fach *nt* freezer compartment. **T~kost** *f* frozen food. **T~truhe** *f* deep-freeze
Tiefsttemperatur *f* minimum temperature
Tier *nt* **-[e]s, -e** animal. **T~arzt** *m*, **T~ärztin** *f* vet, veterinary surgeon. **T~garten** *m* zoo. **T~kreis** *m* zodiac. **T~kunde** *f* zoology. **T~quälerei** *f* cruelty to animals

Tiger *m* **-s,-** tiger
tilgen *vt* pay off <*Schuld*>; (*streichen*) delete; (*fig: auslöschen*) wipe out
Tinte *f* **-, -n** ink. **T~nfisch** *m* squid
Tipp *m* **-s, -s** [!] tip
tipp|en *vt* [!] type ● *vi* (*haben*) (*berühren*) touch (**auf/an etw** *acc* sth); ([!] *Maschine schreiben*) type; **t~en auf** (+ *acc*) ([!] *wetten*) bet on. **T~schein** *m* pools/lottery coupon
tipptopp *a* [!] immaculate
Tirol *nt* **-s** [the] Tyrol
Tisch *m* **-[e]s, -e** table; (*Schreib-*) desk; **nach T~** after the meal. **T~decke** *f* table-cloth. **T~gebet** *nt* grace. **T~ler** *m* **-s,-** joiner; (*Möbel-*) cabinet-maker. **T~rede** *f* after-dinner speech. **T~tennis** *nt* table tennis
Titel *m* **-s,-** title
Toast /to:st/ *m* **-[e]s, -e** toast; (*Scheibe*) piece of toast. **T~er** *m* **-s,-** toaster
toben *vi* (*haben*) rave; <*Sturm:*> rage; <*Kinder:*> play boisterously
Tochter *f* **-,⸚** daughter. **T~gesellschaft** *f* subsidiary
Tod *m* **-es** death
Todes|angst *f* mortal fear. **T~anzeige** *f* death announcement; (*Zeitungs-*) obituary. **T~fall** *m* death. **T~opfer** *nt* fatality, casualty. **T~strafe** *f* death penalty. **T~urteil** *nt* death sentence
todkrank *a* dangerously ill
tödlich *a* fatal; <*Gefahr*> mortal
Toilette /toa'lɛtə/ *f* **-, -n** toilet. **T~npapier** *nt* toilet paper
toler|ant *a* tolerant. **T~anz** *f* **-** tolerance. **t~ieren** *vt* tolerate
toll *a* crazy, mad; ([!] *prima*) fantastic; (*schlimm*) awful ● *adv* (*sehr*) very; (*schlimm*) badly. **t~kühn** *a* foolhardy. **T~wut** *f* rabies. **t~wütig** *a* rabid
Tölpel *m* **-s,-** fool
Tomate *f* **-, -n** tomato. **T~nmark** *nt* tomato purée
Tombola *f* **-, -s** raffle
Ton[1] *m* **-[e]s** clay
Ton[2] *m* **-[e]s,⸚e** tone; (*Klang*) sound; (*Note*) note; (*Betonung*) stress; (*Farb-*) shade; **der gute Ton** (*fig*) good form. **T~abnehmer** *m* **-s,-** pick-up. **t~angebend** *a* (*fig*) leading. **T~art** *f* tone [of voice]; (*Mus*) key. **T~band** *nt* (*pl* **-bänder**) tape. **T~bandgerät** *nt* tape recorder
tönen *vi* (*haben*) sound ● *vt* tint
Tonleiter *f* scale
Tonne *f* **-, -n** barrel, cask; (*Müll-*) bin; (*Maß*) tonne, metric ton
Topf *m* **-[e]s,⸚e** pot; (*Koch-*) pan
Topfen *m* **-s** (Aust) ≈ curd cheese
Töpferei *f* **-, -en** pottery
Topf|lappen *m* oven-cloth. **T~pflanze** *f* potted plant
Tor *nt* **-[e]s, -e** gate; (*Einfahrt*) gateway; (*Sport*) goal
Torf *m* **-s** peat
torkeln *vi* (*sein/habe*) stagger
Tornister *m* **-s,-** knapsack; (*Sch*) satchel
Torpedo *m* **-s, -s** torpedo
Torpfosten *m* goal-post
Torte *f* **-, -n** gateau; (*Obst-*) flan
Tortur *f* **-, -en** torture
Torwart *m* **-s, -e** goalkeeper
tot *a* dead; **tot geboren** stillborn; **sich tot stellen** pretend to be dead
total *a* total. **T~schaden** *m* ≈ write-off
Tote|(r) *m/f* dead man/woman; (*Todesopfer*) fatality; **die T~n** the dead *pl*
töten *vt* kill
Toten|gräber *m* **-s,-** grave digger. **T~kopf** *m* skull. **T~schein** *m* death certificate
totfahren† *vt sep* run over and kill
Toto *nt & m* **-s** football pools *pl*. **T~schein** *m* pools coupon

tot|schießen† *vt sep* shoot dead. **T~schlag** *m* (*Jur*) manslaughter. **t~schlagen**† *vt sep* kill

Tötung *f* **-, -en** killing; **fahrlässige T~** (*Jur*) manslaughter

Toup|et /tu'pe:/ *nt* **-s, -s** toupee. **t~ieren** *vt* back-comb

Tour /tu:ɐ̯/ *f* **-, -en** tour; (*Ausflug*) trip; (*Auto-*) drive; (*Rad-*) ride; (*Strecke*) distance; (*Techn*) revolution; (⊡ *Weise*) way

Touris|mus /tu'rɪsmʊs/ *m* **-** tourism. **T~t** *m* **-en, -en** tourist

Tournee /tʊr'ne:/ *f* **-, -n** tour

Trab *m* **-[e]s** trot

Trabant *m* **-en, -en** satellite

traben *vi* (*haben/sein*) trot

Tracht *f* **-, -en** [national] costume

Tradition /-'tsi̯o:n/ *f* **-, -en** tradition. **t~ell** *a* traditional

Trag|bahre *f* stretcher. **t~bar** *a* portable; <*Kleidung*> wearable

tragen† *vt* carry; (*an-/ aufhaben*) wear; (*fig*) bear ● *vi* (*haben*) carry; **gut t~** <*Baum:*> produce a good crop

Träger *m* **-s,-** porter; (*Inhaber*) bearer; (*eines Ordens*) holder; (*Bau-*) beam; (*Stahl-*) girder; (*Achsel-*) [shoulder] strap. **T~kleid** *nt* pinafore dress

Trag|etasche *f* carrier bag. **T~flächenboot, T~flügelboot** *nt* hydrofoil

Trägheit *f* **-** sluggishness; (*Faulheit*) laziness; (*Phys*) inertia

Trag|ik *f* **-** tragedy. **t~isch** *a* tragic

Tragödie /-i̯ə/ *f* **-, -n** tragedy

Train|er /'trɛ:nɐ/ *m* **-s,-** trainer; (*Tennis-*) coach. **t~ieren** *vt/i* (*haben*) train

Training /'trɛ:nɪŋ/ *nt* **-s** training. **T~sanzug** *m* tracksuit. **T~s-schuhe** *mpl* trainers

Traktor *m* **-s, -en** /-'to:rən/ tractor

trampeln *vi* (*haben*) stamp one's feet ● *vi* (*sein*) trample (**auf** + *acc* on) ● *vt* trample

trampen /'trɛmpən/ *vi* (*sein*) ⊡ hitch-hike

Tranchiermesser /trã'ʃi:ɐ̯-/ *nt* carving-knife

Träne *f* **-, -n** tear. **t~n** *vi* (*haben*) water. **T~ngas** *nt* tear-gas

Tränke *f* **-, -n** watering-place; (*Trog*) drinking-trough. **t~n** *vt* water <*Pferd*>; (*nässen*) soak (**mit** with)

Trans|formator *m* **-s, -en** /-'to:rən/ transformer. **T~fusion** *f* **-, -en** [blood] transfusion

Transit /tran'zi:t/ *m* **-s** transit

Transparent *nt* **-[e]s, -e** banner; (*Bild*) transparency

transpirieren *vi* (*haben*) perspire

Transport *m* **-[e]s, -e** transport; (*Güter-*) consignment. **t~ieren** *vt* transport

Trapez *nt* **-es, -e** trapeze

Tratte *f* **-, -n** (*Comm*) draft

Traube *f* **-, -n** bunch of grapes; (*Beere*) grape; (*fig*) cluster. **T~nzucker** *m* glucose

trauen *vi* (*haben*) (+ *dat*) trust ● *vt* marry; **sich t~** dare (**etw zu tun** [to] do sth); venture (**in** + *acc*/**aus** into/out of)

Trauer *f* **-** mourning; (*Schmerz*) grief (**um** for); **T~ tragen** be [dressed] in mourning. **T~fall** *m* bereavement. **T~feier** *f* funeral service. **t~n** *vi* (*haben*) grieve; **t~n um** mourn [for]. **T~spiel** *nt* tragedy. **T~weide** *f* weeping willow

Traum *m* **-[e]s, Träume** dream

Trauma *nt* **-s, -men** trauma

träumen *vt/i* (*haben*) dream

traumhaft *a* dreamlike; (*schön*) fabulous

traurig *a* sad; (*erbärmlich*) sorry. **T~keit** *f* **-** sadness

Trau|ring *m* wedding-ring. **T~schein** *m* marriage certificate. **T~ung** *f* **-, -en** wedding [ceremony]

Treff *nt* **-s, -s** (*Karten*) spades *pl*

treff|en† *vt* hit; <*Blitz:*> strike; (*fig: verletzen*) hurt; (*zusammenkommen mit*) meet; take <*Maßnahme*>; **sich t~en** meet (**mit jdm** s.o.); **sich gut t~en** be convenient; **es gut/schlecht t~en** be lucky/unlucky ● *vi* (*haben*) hit the target; **t~en auf** (+ *acc*) meet; (*fig*) meet with. **T~en** *nt* **-s,-** meeting. **T~er** *m* **-s,-** hit; (*Los*) winner. **T~punkt** *m* meeting-place

treiben† *vt* drive; (*sich befassen mit*) do; carry on <*Gewerbe*>; indulge in <*Luxus*>; get up to <*Unfug*>; **Handel t~** trade ● *vi* (*sein*) drift; (*schwimmen*) float ● *vi* (*haben*) (*Bot*) sprout. **T~** *nt* **-s** activity

Treib|haus *nt* hothouse. **T~hauseffekt** *m* greenhouse effect. **T~holz** *nt* driftwood. **T~riemen** *m* transmission belt. **T~sand** *m* quicksand. **T~stoff** *m* fuel

trenn|bar *a* separable. **t~en** *vt* separate/(*abmachen*) detach (**von** from); divide, split <*Wort*>; **sich t~en** separate; (*auseinander gehen*) part; **sich t~en von** leave; (*fortgeben*) part with. **T~ung** *f* **-, -en** separation; (*Silben-*) division. **T~ungsstrich** *m* hyphen. **T~wand** *f* partition

trepp|ab *adv* downstairs. **t~auf** *adv* upstairs

Treppe *f* **-, -n** stairs *pl*; (*Außen-*) steps *pl*. **T~ngeländer** *nt* banisters *pl*

Tresor *m* **-s, -e** safe

Tresse *f* **-, -n** braid

Treteimer *m* pedal bin

treten† *vi* (*sein/haben*) step; (*versehentlich*) tread; (*ausschlagen*) kick (**nach** at); **in Verbindung t~** get in touch ● *vt* tread; (*mit Füßen*) kick

treu *a* faithful; (*fest*) loyal. **T~e** *f* **-** faithfulness; loyalty; (*eheliche*) fidelity. **T~ekarte** *f* loyalty card. **T~händer** *m* **-s,-** trustee. **t~los** *a* disloyal; (*untreu*) unfaithful

Tribüne *f* **-, -n** platform; (*Zuschauer-*) stand

Trichter *m* **-s,-** funnel; (*Bomben-*) crater

Trick *m* **-s, -s** trick. **T~film** *m* cartoon. **t~reich** *a* clever

Trieb *m* **-[e]s, -e** drive, urge; (*Instinkt*) instinct; (*Bot*) shoot. **T~verbrecher** *m* sex offender. **T~werk** *nt* (*Aviat*) engine; (*Uhr-*) mechanism

triefen† *vi* (*haben*) drip; (*nass sein*) be dripping (**von/vor** + *dat* with)

Trigonometrie *f* **-** trigonometry

Trikot[1] /tri'ko:/ *m* **-s** (*Tex*) jersey

Trikot[2] *nt* **-s, -s** (*Sport*) jersey; (*Fußball-*) shirt

Trimester *nt* **-s,-** term

Trimm-dich *nt* **-s** keep-fit

trimmen *vt* trim; tune <*Motor*>; **sich t~** keep fit

trink|en† *vt/i* (*haben*) drink. **T~er(in)** *m* **-s,-** (*f* **-, -nen**) alcoholic. **T~geld** *nt* tip

trist *a* dreary

Tritt *m* **-[e]s, -e** step; (*Fuß-*) kick. **T~brett** *nt* step

Triumph *m* **-s, -e** triumph. **t~ieren** *vi* (*haben*) rejoice

trocken *a* dry. **T~haube** *f* drier. **T~heit** *f* **-, -en** dryness; (*Dürre*) drought. **t~legen** *vt sep* change <*Baby*>; drain <*Sumpf*>. **T~milch** *f* powdered milk

trockn|en *vt/i* (*sein*) dry. **T~er** *m* **-s,-** drier

Trödel *m* **-s** [!] junk. **t~n** *vi* (*haben*) dawdle

Trödler *m* **-s,-** [!] slowcoach; (*Händler*) junk-dealer

Trog *m* **-[e]s,¨-e** trough

Trommel *f* **-, -n** drum. **T~fell** *nt* ear-drum. **t~n** *vi* (*haben*) drum

Trommler *m* **-s,-** drummer

T

Trompete *f* **-, -n** trumpet. **T~r** *m* **-s,-** trumpeter
Tropen *pl* tropics
Tropf *m* **-[e]s, -e** (*Med*) drip
tröpfeln *vt/i* (*sein/haben*) drip
tropfen *vt/i* (*sein/haben*) drip. **T~** *m* **-s,-** drop; (*fallend*) drip. **t~weise** *adv* drop by drop
Trophäe /tro'fɛ:ə/ *f* **-, -n** trophy
tropisch *a* tropical
Trost *m* **-[e]s** consolation, comfort
tröst|en *vt* console, comfort; **sich t~en** console oneself. **t~lich** *a* comforting
trost|los *a* desolate; (*elend*) wretched; (*reizlos*) dreary. **T~preis** *m* consolation prize
Trott *m* **-s** amble; (*fig*) routine
Trottel *m* **-s,-** ! idiot
Trottoir /trɔ'to̯a:ɐ̯/ *nt* **-s, -s** pavement
trotz *prep* (+ *gen*) despite, in spite of. **T~** *m* **-es** defiance. **t~dem** *adv* nevertheless. **t~ig** *a* defiant; stubborn
trübe *a* dull; <*Licht*> dim; <*Flüssigkeit*> cloudy; (*fig*) gloomy
Trubel *m* **-s** bustle
trüben *vt* dull; make cloudy <*Flüssigkeit*>; (*fig*) spoil; strain <*Verhältnis*> **sich t~** <*Flüssigkeit:*> become cloudy; <*Himmel:*> cloud over; <*Augen:*> dim
Trüb|sal *f* **-** misery. **T~sinn** *m* melancholy. **t~sinnig** *a* melancholy
trügen† *vt* deceive ● *vi* (*haben*) be deceptive
Trugschluss *m* fallacy
Truhe *f* **-, -n** chest
Trümmer *pl* rubble *sg*; (*T~teile*) wreckage *sg*, (*fig*) ruins
Trumpf *m* **-[e]s,¨-e** trump [card]. **t~en** *vi* (*haben*) play trumps
Trunk *m* **-[e]s** drink. **T~enheit** *f* **-** drunkenness; **T~enheit am Steuer** drink-driving
Trupp *m* **-s, -s** group; (*Mil*) squad. **T~e** *f* **-, -n** (*Mil*) unit; (*Theat*) troupe; **T~en** troops
Truthahn *m* turkey
Tschech|e *m* **-n, -n, T~in** *f* **-, -nen** Czech. **t~isch** *a* Czech. **T~oslowakei (die) -** Czechoslovakia
tschüs, tschüss *int* bye, cheerio
Tuba *f* **-, -ben** (*Mus*) tuba
Tube *f* **-, -n** tube
Tuberkulose *f* **-** tuberculosis
Tuch *nt* **-[e]s,¨-er** cloth; (*Hals-, Kopf-*) scarf; (*Schulter-*) shawl
tüchtig *a* competent; (*reichlich, beträchtlich*) good; (*groß*) big ● *adv* competently; (*ausreichend*) well
Tück|e *f* **-, -n** malice. **t~isch** *a* malicious; (*gefährlich*) treacherous
Tugend *f* **-,en** virtue. **t~haft** *a* virtuous
Tülle *f* **-, -n** spout
Tulpe *f* **-, -n** tulip
Tümmler *m* **-s,-** porpoise
Tumor *m* **-s, -en** /-'mo:rən/ tumour
Tümpel *m* **-[e]s,-** pond
Tumult *m* **-[e]s, -e** commotion; (*Aufruhr*) riot
tun† *vt* do; take <*Schritt, Blick*>; work <*Wunder*>; (*bringen*) put (**in** + *acc* into); **sich tun** happen; **jdm etwas tun** hurt s.o.; **das tut nichts** it doesn't matter ● *vi* (*haben*) act (**als ob** as if); **er tut nur so** he's just pretending; **jdm/etw gut tun** do s.o./sth. good; **zu tun haben** have things/work to do; **[es] zu tun haben mit** have to deal with. **Tun** *nt* **-s** actions *pl*
Tünche *f* **-, -n** whitewash; (*fig*) veneer. **t~n** *vt* whitewash
Tunesien /-i̯ən/ *nt* **-s** Tunisia
Tunfisch *m* = **Thunfisch**
Tunnel *m* **-s,-** tunnel
tupf|en *vt* dab ● *vi* (*haben*) **t~en an/auf** (+ *acc*) touch. **T~en** *m* **-s,-**

spot. **T~er** *m* **-s,-** spot; (*Med*) swab

Tür *f* **-, -en** door

Turban *m* **-s, -e** turban

Turbine *f* **-, -n** turbine

Türk|e *m* **-n, -n** Turk. **T~ei (die) -** Turkey. **T~in** *f* **-, -nen** Turk

türkis *inv a* turquoise

türkisch *a* Turkish

Turm *m* **-[e]s,¨e** tower; (*Schach*) rook, castle

Türm|chen *nt* **-s,-** turret. **t~en** *vt* pile [up]; **sich t~en** pile up

Turmspitze *f* spire

turn|en *vi* (*haben*) do gymnastics. **T~en** *nt* **-s** gymnastics *sg*; (*Sch*) physical education, [!] gym. **T~er(in)** *m* **-s,-** (*f* **-, -nen**) gymnast. **T~halle** *f* gymnasium

Turnier *nt* **-s, -e** tournament; (*Reit-*) show

Turnschuhe *mpl* gym shoes; trainers

Türschwelle *f* doorstep, threshold

Tusche *f* **-, -n** [drawing] ink

tuscheln *vt/i* (*haben*) whisper

Tüte *f* **-, -n** bag; (*Comm*) packet; (*Eis-*) cornet; **in die T~ blasen** [!] be breathalysed

TÜV *m* **-** ≈ MOT [test]

Typ *m* **-s, -en** type; ([!] *Kerl*) bloke. **T~e** *f* **-, -n** type

Typhus *m* **-** typhoid

typisch *a* typical (**für** of)

Typus *m* **-, Typen** type

Tyrann *m* **-en, -en** tyrant. **T~ei** *f* **-** tyranny. **t~isch** *a* tyrannical. **t~isieren** *vt* tyrannize

Uu

U-Bahn *f* underground

übel *a* bad; (*hässlich*) nasty; **mir ist ü~** I feel sick; **jdm etw ü~ nehmen** hold sth against s.o. **Ü~keit** *f* **-** nausea

üben *vt/i* (*haben*) practise

über *prep* (+ *dat/acc*) over; (*höher als*) above; (*betreffend*) about; <*Buch, Vortrag*> on; <*Scheck, Rechnung*> for; (*quer ü~*) across; **ü~ Köln fahren** go via Cologne; **ü~ Ostern** over Easter; **die Woche ü~** during the week; **Fehler ü~ Fehler** mistake after mistake ● *adv* **ü~ und ü~** all over; **jdm ü~ sein** be better/(*stärker*) stronger than s.o. ● *a* [!] **ü~ sein** be left over; **etw ü~ sein** be fed up with sth

überall *adv* everywhere

überanstrengen *vt insep* overtax; strain <*Augen*>

überarbeiten *vt insep* revise; **sich ü~en** overwork

überbieten† *vt insep* outbid; (*übertreffen*) surpass

Überblick *m* overall view; (*Abriss*) summary

überblicken *vt insep* overlook; (*abschätzen*) assess

überbringen† *vt insep* deliver

überbrücken *vt insep* (*fig*) bridge

überdies *adv* moreover

überdimensional *a* oversized

Überdosis *f* overdose

überdrüssig *a* **ü~ sein/werden** be/grow tired (*gen* of)

übereignen *vt insep* transfer

übereilt *a* over-hasty

übereinander *adv* one on top of/ above the other; <*sprechen*> about each other

überein|kommen† *vi sep* (*sein*) agree. **Ü~kunft** *f* **-** agreement. **ü~stimmen** *vi sep* (*haben*) agree; <*Zahlen:*> tally; <*Ansichten:*> coincide; <*Farben:*> match. **Ü~stimmung** *f* agreement

überfahren† *vt insep* run over

Überfahrt *f* crossing

Überfall *m* attack; (*Bank-*) raid

überfallen† *vt insep* attack; raid <*Bank*>; (*bestürmen*) bombard (**mit** with)

Überfluss *m* abundance; (*Wohlstand*) affluence

überflüssig *a* superfluous

überfordern *vt insep* overtax

überführ|en *vt insep* transfer; (*Jur*) convict (*gen* of). **Ü~ung** *f* transfer; (*Straße*) flyover; (*Fußgänger-*) foot-bridge

überfüllt *a* overcrowded

Übergabe *f* handing over; transfer

Übergang *m* crossing; (*Wechsel*) transition

übergeben† *vt insep* hand over; (*übereignen*) transfer; **sich ü~** be sick

übergehen† *vt insep* (*fig*) pass over; (*nicht beachten*) ignore; (*auslassen*) leave out

Übergewicht *nt* excess weight; (*fig*) predominance; **Ü~ haben** be overweight

über|greifen† *vi sep* (*haben*) spread (**auf** + *acc* to). **Ü~griff** *m* infringement

über|groß *a* outsize; (*übertrieben*) exaggerated. **Ü~größe** *f* outsize

überhand *adv* **ü~ nehmen** increase alarmingly

überhäufen *vt insep* inundate (**mit** with)

überhaupt *adv* (*im Allgemeinen*) altogether; (*eigentlich*) anyway; (*überdies*) besides; **ü~ nicht/nichts** not/nothing at all

überheblich *a* arrogant. **Ü~keit** *f* **-** arrogance

überhol|en *vt insep* overtake; (*reparieren*) overhaul. **ü~t** *a* out-dated. **Ü~ung** *f* **-, -en** overhaul. **Ü~verbot** *nt* '**Ü~verbot**' 'no overtaking'

überhören *vt insep* fail to hear; (*nicht beachten*) ignore

überirdisch *a* supernatural

überkochen *vi sep* (*sein*) boil over

überlassen† *vt insep* **jdm etw ü~** leave sth to s.o.; (*geben*) let s.o. have sth; **sich** (*dat*) **selbst ü~ sein** be left to one's own devices

Überlauf *m* overflow

überlaufen† *vi sep* (*sein*) overflow; (*Mil, Pol*) defect

Überläufer *m* defector

überleben *vt/i insep* (*haben*) survive. **Ü~de(r)** *m/f* survivor

überlegen[1] *vt sep* put over

überlegen[2] *v insep* ● *vt* [**sich** *dat*] **ü~** think over, consider; **es sich** (*dat*) **anders ü~** change one's mind ● *vi* (*haben*) think, reflect

überlegen[3] *a* superior. **Ü~heit** *f* **-** superiority

Überlegung *f* **-, -en** reflection

überliefer|n *vt insep* hand down. **Ü~ung** *f* tradition

überlisten *vt insep* outwit

Übermacht *f* superiority

übermäßig *a* excessive

Übermensch *m* superman. **ü~lich** *a* superhuman

übermitteln *vt insep* convey; (*senden*) transmit

übermorgen *adv* the day after tomorrow

übermüdet *a* overtired

Über|mut *m* high spirits *pl*. **ü~mütig** *a* high-spirited

übernächst|e(r,s) *a* next … but one; **ü~es Jahr** the year after next

übernacht|en *vi insep* (*haben*) stay overnight. **Ü~ung** *f* **-, -en** overnight stay; **Ü~ung und Frühstück** bed and breakfast

Übernahme *f* **-** taking over; (*Comm*) take-over

übernatürlich *a* supernatural

übernehmen† *vt insep* take over; (*annehmen*) take on; **sich ü~** overdo things; (*finanziell*) overreach oneself

überqueren *vt insep* cross

überrasch|en *vt insep* surprise. **ü~end** *a* surprising; (*unerwartet*) unexpected. **Ü~ung** *f* **-, -en** surprise

überreden *vt insep* persuade

Überreste *mpl* remains

Überschall- *pref* supersonic

überschätzen *vt insep* overestimate

Überschlag *m* rough estimate; (*Sport*) somersault

überschlagen¹† *vt sep* cross <*Beine*>

überschlagen²† *vt insep* estimate roughly; (*auslassen*) skip; **sich ü~** somersault; <*Ereignisse:*> happen fast ● *a* tepid

überschneiden† **(sich)** *vr insep* intersect, cross; (*zusammenfallen*) overlap

überschreiten† *vt insep* cross; (*fig*) exceed

Überschrift *f* heading; (*Zeitungs-*) headline

Über|schuss *m* surplus. **ü~schüssig** *a* surplus

überschwemm|en *vt insep* flood; (*fig*) inundate. **Ü~ung** *f* **-, -en** flood

Übersee in/nach Ü~ overseas; **aus/von Ü~** from overseas. **Ü~dampfer** *m* ocean liner. **ü~isch** *a* overseas

übersehen† *vt insep* look out over; (*abschätzen*) assess; (*nicht sehen*) overlook, miss; (*ignorieren*) ignore

übersenden† *vt insep* send

übersetzen¹ *vi sep* (*haben/sein*) cross [over]

übersetz|en² *vt insep* translate. **Ü~er(in)** *m* **-s,-** (*f* **-, -nen**) translator. **Ü~ung** *f* **-, -en** translation

Übersicht *f* overall view; (*Abriss*) summary; (*Tabelle*) table. **ü~lich** *a* clear

Übersiedlung *f* move

überspielen *vt insep* (*fig*) cover up; **auf Band ü~** tape

überstehen† *vt insep* come through; get over <*Krankheit*>; (*überleben*) survive

übersteigen† *vt insep* climb [over]; (*fig*) exceed

überstimmen *vt insep* outvote

Überstunden *fpl* overtime *sg*; **Ü~ machen** work overtime

überstürz|en *vt insep* rush; **sich ü~en** <*Ereignisse:*> happen fast. **ü~t** *a* hasty

übertrag|bar *a* transferable; (*Med*) infectious. **ü~en**† *vt insep* transfer; (*übergeben*) assign (*dat* to); (*Techn, Med*) transmit; (*Radio, TV*) broadcast; (*übersetzen*) translate; (*anwenden*) apply (**auf** + *acc* to) ● *a* transferred, figurative. **Ü~ung** *f* **-, -en** transfer; transmission; broadcast; translation, application

übertreffen† *vt insep* surpass; (*übersteigen*) exceed; **sich selbst ü~** excel oneself

übertreib|en† *vt insep* exaggerate; (*zu weit treiben*) overdo. **Ü~ung** *f* **-, -en** exaggeration

übertreten¹† *vi sep* (*sein*) step over the line; (*Pol*) go over/ (*Relig*) convert (**zu** to)

übertret|en²† *vt insep* infringe; break <*Gesetz*>. **Ü~ung** *f* **-, -en** infringement; breach

übertrieben *a* exaggerated

übervölkert *a* overpopulated

überwachen *vt insep* supervise; (*kontrollieren*) monitor;

(*bespitzeln*) keep under surveillance

überwältigen *vt insep* overpower; (*fig*) overwhelm

überweis|en† *vt insep* transfer; refer <*Patienten*>. **Ü~ung** *f* transfer; (*ärztliche*) referral

überwiegen† *v insep* ● *vi* (*haben*) predominate, ● *vt* outweigh

überwind|en† *vt insep* overcome; **sich ü~en** force oneself

Über|zahl *f* majority. **ü~zählig** *a* spare

überzeug|en *vt insep* convince; **sich [selbst] ü~en** satisfy oneself. **ü~end** *a* convincing. **Ü~ung** *f* **-, -en** conviction

überziehen[1]† *vt sep* put on

überziehen[2]† *vt insep* cover; overdraw <*Konto*>

Überzug *m* cover; (*Schicht*) coating

üblich *a* usual; (*gebräuchlich*) customary

U-Boot *nt* submarine

übrig *a* remaining; (*andere*) other; **alles Ü~e** [all] the rest; **im Ü~en** besides; (*ansonsten*) apart from that; **ü~ sein** *od* **bleiben** be left [over]; **etw ü~ lassen** leave sth [over]; **uns blieb nichts anderes ü~** we had no choice

Übung *f* **-, -en** exercise; (*Üben*) practice; **außer** *od* **aus der Ü~** out of practice

Ufer *nt* **-s,-** shore; (*Fluss-*) bank

Uhr *f* **-, -en** clock; (*Armband-*) watch; (*Zähler*) meter; **um ein U~** at one o'clock; **wie viel U~ ist es?** what's the time? **U~macher** *m* **-s,-** watch and clockmaker. **U~werk** *nt* clock/watch mechanism. **U~zeiger** *m* [clock-/watch-]hand. **U~zeit** *f* time

Uhu *m* **-s, -s** eagle owl

UKW *abbr* (*Ultrakurzwelle*) VHF

ulkig *a* funny; (*seltsam*) odd

Ulme *f* **-, -n** elm

Ultimatum *nt* **-s, -ten** ultimatum

Ultra|kurzwelle *f* very high frequency. **U~leichtflugzeug** *nt* microlight [aircraft]

Ultraschall *m* ultrasound

ultraviolett *a* ultraviolet

um *prep* (+ *acc*) [a]round; (*Uhrzeit*) at; <*bitten*> for; <*streiten*> over; <*sich sorgen*> about; <*betrügen*> out of; (*bei Angabe einer Differenz*) by; **um [... herum]** around, [round] about; **Tag um Tag** day after day; **um seinetwillen** for his sake ● *adv* (*ungefähr*) around, about; **um sein** [!] be over; <*Zeit*> be up ● *conj* **um zu** to; (*Absicht*) [in order] to; **zu müde, um zu ...** too tired to ...

umarm|en *vt insep* embrace, hug. **U~ung** *f* **-, -en** embrace, hug

Umbau *m* rebuilding; conversion (**zu** into). **u~en** *vt sep* rebuild; convert (**zu** into)

Umbildung *f* reorganization; (*Pol*) reshuffle

umbinden† *vt sep* put on

umblättern *v sep* ● *vt* turn [over] ● *vi* (*haben*) turn the page

umbringen† *vt sep* kill; **sich u~** kill oneself

umbuchen *v sep* ● *vt* change; (*Comm*) transfer ● *vi* (*haben*) change one's booking

umdrehen *v sep* ● *vt* turn round/ (*wenden*) over; turn <*Schlüssel*>; (*umkrempeln*) turn inside out; **sich u~** turn round; (*im Liegen*) turn over ● *vi* (*haben/sein*) turn back

Umdrehung *f* turn; (*Motor-*) revolution

umeinander *adv* around each other; **sich u~ sorgen** worry about each other

umfahren[1]† *vt sep* run over

umfahren[2]† *vt insep* go round; bypass <*Ort*>

umfallen† *vi sep* (*sein*) fall over; <*Person:*> fall down

Umfang *m* girth; (*Geom*) circumference; (*Größe*) size

umfangreich *a* extensive; (*dick*) big

umfassen *vt insep* consist of, comprise; (*umgeben*) surround. **u~d** *a* comprehensive

Umfrage *f* survey, poll

umfüllen *vt sep* transfer

umfunktionieren *vt sep* convert

Umgang *m* [social] contact; (*Umgehen*) dealing (**mit** with)

Umgangssprache *f* colloquial language

umgeb|en† *vt/i insep* (*haben*) surround ● *a* **u~en von** surrounded by. **U~ung** *f* **-, -en** surroundings *pl*

umgehen† *vt insep* avoid; (*nicht beachten*) evade; <*Straße:*> bypass

umgehend *a* immediate

Umgehungsstraße *f* bypass

umgekehrt *a* inverse; <*Reihenfolge*> reverse; **es war u~** it was the other way round

umgraben† *vt sep* dig [over]

Umhang *m* cloak

umhauen† *vt sep* knock down; (*fällen*) chop down

umhören (sich) *vr sep* ask around

Umkehr *f* - turning back. **u~en** *v sep* ● *vi* (*sein*) turn back ● *vt* turn round; turn inside out <*Tasche*>; (*fig*) reverse

umkippen *v sep* ● *vt* tip over; (*versehentlich*) knock over ● *vi* (*sein*) fall over; <*Boot:*> capsize

Umkleide|kabine *f* changing-cubicle. **u~n (sich)** *vr sep* change. **U~raum** *m* changing-room

umknicken *v sep* ● *vt* bend; (*falten*) fold ● *vi* (*sein*) bend; (*mit dem Fuß*) go over on one's ankle

umkommen† *vi sep* (*sein*) perish

Umkreis *m* surroundings *pl*; **im U~ von** within a radius of

umkreisen *vt insep* circle; (*Astr*) revolve around; <*Satellit:*> orbit

umkrempeln *vt sep* turn up; (*von innen nach außen*) turn inside out; (*ändern*) change radically

Umlauf *m* circulation; (*Astr*) revolution. **U~bahn** *f* orbit

Umlaut *m* umlaut

umlegen *vt sep* lay *or* put down; flatten <*Getreide*>; turn down <*Kragen*>; put on <*Schal*>; throw <*Hebel*>; (*verlegen*) transfer; (! *töten*) kill

umleit|en *vt sep* divert. **U~ung** *f* diversion

umliegend *a* surrounding

umpflanzen *vt sep* transplant

umranden *vt insep* edge

umräumen *vt sep* rearrange

umrechn|en *vt sep* convert. **U~ung** *f* conversion

umreißen† *vt insep* outline

Umriss *m* outline

umrühren *vt/i sep* (*haben*) stir

ums *pron* = **um das**

Umsatz *m* (*Comm*) turnover

umschalten *vt/i sep* (*haben*) switch over; **auf Rot u~** <*Ampel:*> change to red

Umschau *f* **U~ halten nach** look out for

Umschlag *m* cover; (*Schutz-*) jacket; (*Brief-*) envelope; (*Med*) compress; (*Hosen-*) turn-up. **u~en**† *v sep* ● *vt* turn up; turn over <*Seite*>; (*fällen*) chop down ● *vi* (*sein*) topple over; <*Wetter:*> change; <*Wind:*> veer

umschließen† *vt insep* enclose

umschreiben *vt insep* define; (*anders ausdrücken*) paraphrase

umschulen *vt sep* retrain; (*Sch*) transfer to another school

Umschwung *m* (*fig*) change; (*Pol*) U-turn

umsehen† **(sich)** *vr sep* look round; (*zurück*) look back; **sich u~ nach** look for

U

ụmsein* *vi sep* (*sein*) **um sein**, *s.* **um**

ụmseitig *a & adv* overleaf

ụmsetzen *vt sep* move; (*umpflanzen*) transplant; (*Comm*) sell

ụmsied|eln *v sep* ● *vt* resettle ● *vi* (*sein*) move. **U∼lung** *f* resettlement

ụmso *conj* ∼ **besser**/**mehr** all the better/more; **je mehr, ∼ besser** the more the better

umsọnst *adv* in vain; (*grundlos*) without reason; (*gratis*) free

Ụmstand *m* circumstance; (*Tatsache*) fact; (*Aufwand*) fuss; (*Mühe*) trouble; **unter U∼̈en** possibly; **jdm U∼̈e machen** put s.o. to trouble; **in andern U∼̈en** pregnant

ụmständlich *a* laborious; (*kompliziert*) involved

Ụmstands|kleid *nt* maternity dress. **U∼wort** *nt* (*pl* **-wörter**) adverb

Ụmstehende *pl* bystanders

ụmsteigen† *vi sep* (*sein*) change

umstẹllen¹ *vt insep* surround

ụmstell|en² *vt sep* rearrange; transpose <*Wörter*>; (*anders einstellen*) reset; (*Techn*) convert; (*ändern*) change; **sich u∼en** adjust. **U∼ung** *f* rearrangement; transposition; resetting; conversion; change; adjustment

umstrịtten *a* controversial; (*ungeklärt*) disputed

ụmstülpen *vt sep* turn upside down; (*von innen nach außen*) turn inside out

Ụm|sturz *m* coup. **u∼stürzen** *v sep* ● *vt* overturn; (*Pol*) overthrow ● *vi* (*sein*) fall over

ụmtaufen *vt sep* rename

Ụmtausch *m* exchange. **u∼en** *vt sep* change; exchange (**gegen** for)

ụmwechseln *vt sep* change

Ụmweg *m* detour; **auf U∼en** (*fig*) in a roundabout way

Ụmwelt *f* environment. **u∼freundlich** *a* environmentally friendly. **U∼schutz** *m* protection of the environment

ụmwerfen† *vt sep* knock over; (*fig*) upset <*Plan*>

ụmziehen† *v sep* ● *vi* (*sein*) move ● *vt* change; **sich u∼** change

umzịngeln *vt insep* surround

Ụmzug *m* move; (*Prozession*) procession

unabạnderlich *a* irrevocable; <*Tatsache*> unalterable

ụnabhängig *a* independent; **u∼ davon, ob** irrespective of whether. **U∼keit** *f* - independence

ụnablässig *a* incessant

unabsehbar *a* incalculable

ụnabsichtlich *a* unintentional

ụnachtsam *a* careless

ụnangebracht *a* inappropriate

ụnangenehm *a* unpleasant; (*peinlich*) embarrassing

Ụnannehmlichkeiten *fpl* trouble *sg*

ụnansehnlich *a* shabby

ụnanständig *a* indecent

ụnappetitlich *a* unappetizing

Ụnart *f* **-, -en** bad habit. **u∼ig** *a* naughty

ụnauffällig *a* inconspicuous; unobtrusive

ụnaufgefordert *adv* without being asked

unauf|hạltsam *a* inexorable. **u∼hörlich** *a* incessant

ụnaufmerksam *a* inattentive

ụnaufrichtig *a* insincere

unausbleiblich *a* inevitable

unausstehlich *a* insufferable

ụnbarmherzig *a* merciless

ụnbeabsichtigt *a* unintentional

ụnbedenklich *a* harmless ● *adv* without hesitation

ụnbedeutend *a* insignificant; (*geringfügig*) slight

ụnbedingt *a* absolute; **nicht u∼** not necessarily

unbefriedig|end *a* unsatisfactory. **u~t** *a* dissatisfied
unbefugt *a* unauthorized ●*adv* without authorization
unbegreiflich *a* incomprehensible
unbegrenzt *a* unlimited ●*adv* indefinitely
unbegründet *a* unfounded
Unbehagen *nt* unease; (*körperlich*) discomfort
unbekannt *a* unknown; (*nicht vertraut*) unfamiliar. **U~e(r)** *m/f* stranger
unbekümmert *a* unconcerned; (*unbeschwert*) carefree
unbeliebt *a* unpopular. **U~heit** *f* unpopularity
unbemannt *a* unmanned
unbemerkt *a & adv* unnoticed
unbenutzt *a* unused
unbequem *a* uncomfortable; (*lästig*) awkward
unberechenbar *a* unpredictable
unberechtigt *a* unjustified; (*unbefugt*) unauthorized
unberührt *a* untouched; (*fig*) virgin; <*Landschaft*> unspoilt
unbescheiden *a* presumptuous
unbeschrankt *a* unguarded
unbeschränkt *a* unlimited ●*adv* without limit
unbeschwert *a* carefree
unbesiegt *a* undefeated
unbespielt *a* blank
unbeständig *a* inconsistent; <*Wetter*> unsettled
unbestechlich *a* incorruptible
unbestimmt *a* indefinite; <*Alter*> indeterminate; (*ungewiss*) uncertain; (*unklar*) vague
unbestritten *a* undisputed ●*adv* indisputably
unbeteiligt *a* indifferent; **u~ an** (+ *dat*) not involved in
unbetont *a* unstressed
unbewacht *a* unguarded
unbewaffnet *a* unarmed
unbeweglich *a & adv* motionless, still
unbewohnt *a* uninhabited
unbewusst *a* unconscious
unbezahlbar *a* priceless
unbrauchbar *a* useless
und *conj* and; **und so weiter** and so on; **nach und nach** bit by bit
Undank *m* ingratitude. **u~bar** *a* ungrateful; (*nicht lohnend*) thankless. **U~barkeit** *f* ingratitude
undeutlich *a* indistinct; vague
undicht *a* leaking; **u~e Stelle** leak
Unding *nt* absurdity
undiplomatisch *a* undiplomatic
unduldsam *a* intolerant
undurch|dringlich *a* impenetrable; <*Miene*> inscrutable. **u~führbar** *a* impracticable
undurch|lässig *a* impermeable. **u~sichtig** *a* opaque; (*fig*) doubtful
uneben *a* uneven. **U~heit** *f* **-, -en** unevenness; (*Buckel*) bump
unecht *a* false; **u~er Schmuck** imitation jewellery
unehelich *a* illegitimate
uneinig *a* (*fig*) divided; **[sich** (*dat*)**] u~ sein** disagree
uneins *a* **u~ sein** be at odds
unempfindlich *a* insensitive (**gegen** to); (*widerstandsfähig*) tough; (*Med*) immune
unendlich *a* infinite; (*endlos*) endless. **U~keit** *f* **-** infinity
unentbehrlich *a* indispensable
unentgeltlich *a* free, <*Arbeit*> unpaid ●*adv* free of charge
unentschieden *a* undecided; (*Sport*) drawn; **u~ spielen** draw. **U~** *nt* **-s,-** draw
unentschlossen *a* indecisive; (*unentschieden*) undecided
unentwegt *a* persistent; (*unaufhörlich*) incessant
unerfahren *a* inexperienced. **U~heit** *f* **-** inexperience

unerfreulich *a* unpleasant
unerhört *a* enormous; (*empörend*) outrageous
unerklärlich *a* inexplicable
unerlässlich *a* essential
unerlaubt *a* unauthorized ● *adv* without permission
unerschwinglich *a* prohibitive
unersetzlich *a* irreplaceable; <*Verlust*> irreparable
unerträglich *a* unbearable
unerwartet *a* unexpected
unerwünscht *a* unwanted; <*Besuch*> unwelcome
unfähig *a* incompetent; **u~, etw zu tun** incapable of doing sth; (*nicht in der Lage*) unable to do sth. **U~keit** *f* incompetence; inability (**zu** to)
unfair *a* unfair
Unfall *m* accident. **U~flucht** *f* failure to stop after an accident. **U~station** *f* casualty department
unfassbar *a* incomprehensible
Unfehlbarkeit *f* **-** infallibility
unfolgsam *a* disobedient
unförmig *a* shapeless
unfreiwillig *a* involuntary; (*unbeabsichtigt*) unintentional
unfreundlich *a* unfriendly; (*unangenehm*) unpleasant. **U~keit** *f* unfriendliness; unpleasantness
Unfriede[n] *m* discord
unfruchtbar *a* infertile; (*fig*) unproductive. **U~keit** *f* infertility
Unfug *m* **-s** mischief; (*Unsinn*) nonsense
Ungar|(in) *m* **-n, -n** (*f* **-, -nen**) Hungarian. **u~isch** *a* Hungarian. **U~n** *nt* **-s** Hungary
ungeachtet *prep* (+ *gen*) in spite of; **dessen u~** notwithstanding [this]. **ungebraucht** *a* unused. **ungedeckt** *a* uncovered; (*Sport*) unmarked; <*Tisch*> unlaid
Ungeduld *f* impatience. **u~ig** *a* impatient
ungeeignet *a* unsuitable
ungefähr *a* approximate, rough
ungefährlich *a* harmless
ungeheuer *a* enormous. **U~** *nt* **-s,-** monster
ungehorsam *a* disobedient. **U~** *m* disobedience
ungeklärt *a* unsolved; <*Frage*> unsettled; <*Ursache*> unknown
ungelegen *a* inconvenient
ungelernt *a* unskilled
ungemütlich *a* uncomfortable; (*unangenehm*) unpleasant
ungenau *a* inaccurate; vague. **U~igkeit** *f* **-, -en** inaccuracy
ungeniert /ˈʊnʒeniːɐ̯t/ *a* uninhibited ● *adv* openly
ungenießbar *a* inedible; <*Getränk*> undrinkable. **ungenügend** *a* inadequate; (*Sch*) unsatisfactory. **ungepflegt** *a* neglected; <*Person*> unkempt. **ungerade** *a* <*Zahl*> odd
ungerecht *a* unjust. **U~igkeit** *f* **-, -en** injustice
ungern *adv* reluctantly
ungesalzen *a* unsalted
Ungeschick|lichkeit *f* clumsiness. **u~t** *a* clumsy
ungeschminkt *a* without make-up; <*Wahrheit*> unvarnished. **ungesetzlich** *a* illegal. **ungestört** *a* undisturbed. **ungesund** *a* unhealthy. **ungesüßt** *a* unsweetened. **ungetrübt** *a* perfect
Ungetüm *nt* **-s, -e** monster
ungewiss *a* uncertain; **im Ungewissen sein/lassen** be/leave in the dark. **U~heit** *f* uncertainty
ungewöhnlich *a* unusual. **ungewohnt** *a* unaccustomed; (*nicht vertraut*) unfamiliar
Ungeziefer *nt* **-s** vermin
ungezogen *a* naughty
ungezwungen *a* informal; (*natürlich*) natural
ungläubig *a* incredulous
unglaublich *a* incredible, unbelievable

ungleich *a* unequal; (*verschieden*) different. **U~heit** *f* - inequality. **u~mäßig** *a* uneven

Unglück *nt* **-s, -e** misfortune; (*Pech*) bad luck; (*Missgeschick*) mishap; (*Unfall*) accident. **u~lich** *a* unhappy; (*ungünstig*) unfortunate. **u~licherweise** *adv* unfortunately

ungültig *a* invalid; (*Jur*) void

ungünstig *a* unfavourable; (*unpassend*) inconvenient

Unheil *nt* **-s** disaster; **U~ anrichten** cause havoc

unheilbar *a* incurable

unheimlich *a* eerie; (*gruselig*) creepy; ([!] *groß*) terrific ● *adv* eerily; ([!] *sehr*) terribly

unhöflich *a* rude. **U~keit** *f* rudeness

unhygienisch *a* unhygienic

Uni *f* **-, -s** [!] university

uni /y'ni:/ *inv a* plain

Uniform *f* **-, -en** uniform

uninteressant *a* uninteresting

Union *f* **-, -en** union

universell *a* universal

Universität *f* **-, -en** university

Universum *nt* **-s** universe

unkenntlich *a* unrecognizable

unklar *a* unclear; (*ungewiss*) uncertain; (*vage*) vague; **im U~en sein** be in the dark

unkompliziert *a* uncomplicated

Unkosten *pl* expenses

Unkraut *nt* weed; (*coll*) weeds *pl*; **U~ jäten** weed. **U~vertilgungsmittel** *nt* weed-killer

unlängst *adv* recently

unlauter *a* dishonest; (*unfair*) unfair

unleserlich *a* illegible

unleugbar *a* undeniable

unlogisch *a* illogical

Unmenge *f* enormous amount/ (*Anzahl*) number

Unmensch *m* [!] brute. **u~lich** *a* inhuman

unmerklich *a* imperceptible

unmittelbar *a* immediate; (*direkt*) direct

unmöbliert *a* unfurnished

unmodern *a* old-fashioned

unmöglich *a* impossible. **U~keit** *f* - impossibility

Unmoral *f* immorality. **u~isch** *a* immoral

unmündig *a* under-age

Unmut *m* displeasure

unnatürlich *a* unnatural

unnormal *a* abnormal

unnötig *a* unnecessary

unord|entlich *a* untidy; (*nachlässig*) sloppy. **U~nung** *f* disorder; (*Durcheinander*) muddle

unorthodox *a* unorthodox ● *adv* in an unorthodox manner

unparteiisch *a* impartial

unpassend *a* inappropriate; <*Moment*> inopportune

unpersönlich *a* impersonal

unpraktisch *a* impractical

unpünktlich *a* unpunctual ● *adv* late

unrealistisch *a* unrealistic

unrecht *a* wrong ● *n* **jdm u~ tun** do s.o. an injustice. **U~** *nt* wrong; **zu U~** wrongly; **U~ haben** be wrong; **jdm U~ geben** disagree with s.o. **u~mäßig** *a* unlawful

unregelmäßig *a* irregular

unreif *a* unripe; (*fig*) immature

unrein *a* impure; <*Luft*> polluted; <*Haut*> bad; **ins U~e schreiben** make a rough draft of

unrentabel *a* unprofitable

Unruh|e *f* **-, -n** restlessness; (*Erregung*) agitation; (*Besorgnis*) anxiety; **U~en** (*Pol*) unrest *sg*. **u~ig** *a* restless; (*laut*) noisy; (*besorgt*) anxious

uns *pron* (*acc/dat of* **wir**) us; (*refl*) ourselves; (*einander*) each other

unsauber *a* dirty; (*nachlässig*) sloppy

unschädlich *a* harmless

U

unscharf *a* blurred
unschätzbar *a* inestimable
unscheinbar *a* inconspicuous
unschlagbar *a* unbeatable
unschlüssig *a* undecided
Unschuld *f* **-** innocence; (*Jungfräulichkeit*) virginity. **u~ig** *a* innocent
unselbstständig, unselbständig *a* dependent ● *adv* **u~ denken** not think for oneself
unser *poss pron* our. **u~e(r,s)** *poss pron* ours. **u~erseits** *adv* for our part. **u~twegen** *adv* for our sake; (*wegen uns*) because of us, on our account
unsicher *a* unsafe; (*ungewiss*) uncertain; (*nicht zuverlässig*) unreliable; <*Schritte, Hand*> unsteady; <*Person*> insecure ● *adv* unsteadily. **U~heit** *f* uncertainty; unreliability; insecurity
unsichtbar *a* invisible
Unsinn *m* nonsense. **u~ig** *a* nonsensical, absurd
Unsitt|e *f* bad habit. **u~lich** *a* indecent
unsportlich *a* not sporty; (*unfair*) unsporting
uns|re(r,s) *poss pron* = **unsere(r,s)**. **u~rige** *poss pron* **der/die/das u~rige** ours
unsterblich *a* immortal. **U~keit** *f* immortality
Unsumme *f* vast sum
unsympathisch *a* unpleasant; **er ist mir u~** I don't like him
untätig *a* idle
untauglich *a* unsuitable; (*Mil*) unfit
unten *adv* at the bottom; (*auf der Unterseite*) underneath; (*eine Treppe tiefer*) downstairs; (*im Text*) below; **hier/da u~** down here/there; **nach u~** down[wards]; (*die Treppe hinunter*) downstairs; **siehe u~** see below
unter *prep* (+ *dat*/*acc*) under; (*niedriger als*) below; (*inmitten, zwischen*) among; **u~ anderem** among other things; **u~ der Woche** during the week; **u~ sich** by themselves
Unter|arm *m* forearm. **U~bewusstsein** *nt* subconscious
unterbieten† *vt insep* undercut; beat <*Rekord*>
unterbinden† *vt insep* stop
unterbrech|en† *vt insep* interrupt; break <*Reise*>. **U~ung** *f* **-, -en** interruption, break
unterbringen† *vt sep* put; (*beherbergen*) put up
unterdessen *adv* in the meantime
Unterdrückung *f* **-** suppression; oppression
untere(r,s) *a* lower
untereinander *adv* one below the other; (*miteinander*) among ourselves/yourselves/themselves
unterernähr|t *a* undernourished. **U~ung** *f* malnutrition
Unterführung *f* underpass; (*Fußgänger-*) subway
Untergang *m* (*Astr*) setting; (*Naut*) sinking; (*Zugrundegehen*) disappearance; (*der Welt*) end
Untergebene(r) *m*/*f* subordinate
untergehen† *vi sep* (*sein*) (*Astr*) set; (*versinken*) go under; <*Schiff:*> go down, sink; (*zugrunde gehen*) disappear; <*Welt:*> come to an end
Untergeschoss *nt* basement
Untergrund *m* foundation; (*Hintergrund*) background. **U~bahn** *f* underground [railway]
unterhaken *vt sep* **jdn u~** take s.o.'s arm; **untergehakt** arm in arm
unterhalb *adv & prep* (+ *gen*) below
Unterhalt *m* maintenance
unterhalt|en† *vt insep* maintain; (*ernähren*) support; (*betreiben*) run; (*erheitern*) entertain; **sich**

u~en talk; (*sich vergnügen*) enjoy oneself. **U~ung** *f* **-, -en** maintenance; (*Gespräch*) conversation; (*Zeitvertreib*) entertainment

Unter|haus *nt* (*Pol*) lower house; (*in UK*) House of Commons. **U~hemd** *nt* vest. **U~hose** *f* underpants *pl*. **u~irdisch** *a & adv* underground

Unterkiefer *m* lower jaw

unterkommen† *vi sep* (*sein*) find accommodation; (*eine Stellung finden*) get a job

Unterkunft *f* **-, -künfte** accommodation

Unterlage *f* pad; **U~n** papers

Unterlass *m* **ohne U~** incessantly

Unterlassung *f* **-, -en** omission

unterlegen *a* inferior; (*Sport*) losing; **zahlenmäßig u~** outnumbered (*dat* by). **U~e(r)** *m/f* loser

Unterleib *m* abdomen

unterliegen† *vi insep* (*sein*) lose (*dat* to); (*unterworfen sein*) be subject (*dat* to)

Unterlippe *f* lower lip

Untermiete *f* **zur U~ wohnen** be a lodger. **U~r(in)** *m(f)* lodger

unternehm|en† *vt insep* undertake; take <*Schritte*>; **etw/nichts u~en** do sth/nothing. **U~en** *nt* **-s,-** undertaking, enterprise (*Betrieb*) concern. **U~er** *m* **-s,-** employer; (*Bau-*) contractor; (*Industrieller*) industrialist. **u~ungslustig** *a* enterprising

Unteroffizier *m* non commissioned officer

unterordnen *vt sep* subordinate

Unterredung *f* **-, -en** talk

Unterricht *m* **-[e]s** teaching; (*Privat-*) tuition; (*U~sstunden*) lessons *pl*

unterrichten *vt/i insep* (*haben*) teach; (*informieren*) inform; **sich u~** inform oneself

Unterrock *m* slip

untersagen *vt insep* forbid

Untersatz *m* mat; (*mit Füßen*) stand; (*Gläser-*) coaster

unterscheid|en† *vt/i insep* (*haben*) distinguish; (*auseinander halten*) tell apart; **sich u~en** differ. **U~ung** *f* **-, -en** distinction

Unterschied *m* **-[e]s, -e** difference; (*Unterscheidung*) distinction; **im U~ zu ihm** unlike him. **u~lich** *a* different; (*wechselnd*) varying

unterschlag|en† *vt insep* embezzle; (*verheimlichen*) suppress. **U~ung** *f* **-, -en** embezzlement; suppression

Unterschlupf *m* **-[e]s** shelter; (*Versteck*) hiding-place

unterschreiben† *vt/i insep* (*haben*) sign

Unter|schrift *f* signature; (*Bild-*) caption. **U~seeboot** *nt* submarine

Unterstand *m* shelter

unterste(r,s) *a* lowest, bottom

unterstehen† *v insep* ● *vi* (*haben*) be answerable (*dat* to); (*unterliegen*) be subject (*dat* to)

unterstellen¹ *vt sep* put underneath; (*abstellen*) store; **sich u~** shelter

unterstellen² *vt insep* place under the control (*dat* of); (*annehmen*) assume; (*fälschlich zuschreiben*) impute (*dat* to)

unterstreichen† *vt insep* underline

unterstütz|en *vt insep* support; (*helfen*) aid. **U~ung** *f* **-, -en** support; (*finanziell*) aid; (*regelmäßiger Betrag*) allowance; (*Arbeitslosen-*) benefit

untersuch|en *vt insep* examine; (*Jur*) investigate; (*prüfen*) test; (*überprüfen*) check; (*durchsuchen*) search. **U~ung** *f* **-, -en** examination; investigation; test; check; search. **U~ungshaft** *f* detention on remand

Untertan *m* **-s** *&* **-en, -en** subject
Untertasse *f* saucer
Unterteil *nt* bottom (part)
Untertitel *m* subtitle
untervermieten *vt/i insep* (*haben*) sublet
Unterwäsche *f* underwear
unterwegs *adv* on the way; (*außer Haus*) out; (*verreist*) away
Unterwelt *f* underworld
unterzeichnen *vt insep* sign
unterziehen† *vt insep* **etw einer Untersuchung/Überprüfung u~** examine/ check sth; **sich einer Operation/Prüfung u~** have an operation/take a test
Untier *nt* monster
untragbar *a* intolerable
untrennbar *a* inseparable
untreu *a* disloyal; (*in der Ehe*) unfaithful. **U~e** *f* disloyalty; infidelity
untröstlich *a* inconsolable
unübersehbar *a* obvious; (*groß*) immense
ununterbrochen *a* incessant
unveränderlich *a* invariable; (*gleichbleibend*) unchanging
unverändert *a* unchanged
unverantwortlich *a* irresponsible
unverbesserlich *a* incorrigible
unverbindlich *a* non-committal; (*Comm*) not binding ● *adv* without obligation
unverdaulich *a* indigestible
unver|gesslich *a* unforgettable. **u~gleichlich** *a* incomparable. **u~heiratet** *a* unmarried. **u~käuflich** *a* not for sale; *<Muster>* free
unverkennbar *a* unmistakable
unverletzt *a* unhurt
unvermeidlich *a* inevitable
unver|mindert *a & adv* undiminished. **u~mutet** *a* unexpected
Unver|nunft *f* folly. **u~nünftig** *a* foolish
unverschämt *a* insolent; (❗ *ungeheuer*) outrageous. **U~heit** *f* **-, -en** insolence
unver|sehens *adv* suddenly. **u~sehrt** *a* unhurt; (*unbeschädigt*) intact
unverständlich *a* incomprehensible; (*undeutlich*) indistinct
unverträglich *a* incompatible; *<Person>* quarrelsome; (*unbekömmlich*) indigestible
unver|wundbar *a* invulnerable. **u~wüstlich** *a* indestructible; *<Person, Humor>* irrepressible; *<Gesundheit>* robust. **u~zeihlich** *a* unforgivable
unverzüglich *a* immediate
unvollendet *a* unfinished
unvollkommen *a* imperfect; (*unvollständig*) incomplete
unvollständig *a* incomplete
unvor|bereitet *a* unprepared. **u~hergesehen** *a* unforeseen
unvorsichtig *a* careless
unvorstellbar *a* unimaginable
unvorteilhaft *a* unfavourable; (*nicht hübsch*) unattractive
unwahr *a* untrue. **U~heit** *f* **-, -en** untruth. **u~scheinlich** *a* unlikely; (*unglaublich*) improbable; (❗ *groß*) incredible
unweit *adv & prep* (+ *gen*) not far
unwesentlich *a* unimportant
Unwetter *nt* **-s,-** storm
unwichtig *a* unimportant
unwider|legbar *a* irrefutable. **u~stehlich** *a* irresistible
Unwill|e *m* displeasure. **u~ig** *a* angry; (*widerwillig*) reluctant
unwirklich *a* unreal
unwirksam *a* ineffective
unwirtschaftlich *a* uneconomic
unwissen|d *a* ignorant. **U~heit** *f* **-** ignorance
unwohl *a* unwell; (*unbehaglich*) uneasy
unwürdig *a* unworthy (*gen* of)

Unzahl *f* vast number. **unzählig** *a* innumerable, countless
unzerbrechlich *a* unbreakable
unzerstörbar *a* indestructible
unzertrennlich *a* inseparable
Unzucht *f* sexual offence; **gewerbsmäßige U~** prostitution
unzüchtig *a* indecent; <*Schriften*> obscene
unzufrieden *a* dissatisfied; (*innerlich*) discontented. **U~heit** *f* dissatisfaction
unzulässig *a* inadmissible
unzurechnungsfähig *a* insane. **U~keit** *f* insanity
unzusammenhängend *a* incoherent
unzutreffend *a* inapplicable; (*falsch*) incorrect
unzuverlässig *a* unreliable
unzweifelhaft *a* undoubted
üppig *a* luxuriant; (*überreichlich*) lavish
uralt *a* ancient
Uran *nt* **-s** uranium
Uraufführung *f* first performance
Urenkel *m* great-grandson; (*pl*) great-grandchildren
Urgroß|mutter *f* great-grandmother. **U~vater** *m* great-grandfather
Urheber *m* **-s,-** originator; (*Verfasser*) author. **U~recht** *nt* copyright
Urin *m* **-s, -e** urine
Urkunde *f* **-, -n** certificate; (*Dokument*) document
Urlaub *m* **-s** holiday; (*Mil, Admin*) leave; **auf U~** on holiday/leave; **U~ haben** be on holiday/leave. **U~er(in)** *m* **-s,-** (*f* **-, -nen**) holiday-maker. **U~sort** *m* holiday resort
Urne *f* **-, -n** urn; (*Wahl-*) ballot-box
Ursache *f* cause; (*Grund*) reason; **keine U~!** don't mention it!
Ursprung *m* origin
ursprünglich *a* original; (*anfänglich*) initial; (*natürlich*) natural
Urteil *nt* **-s, -e** judgement; (*Meinung*) opinion; (*U~sspruch*) verdict; (*Strafe*) sentence. **u~en** *vi* (*haben*) judge
Urwald *m* primeval forest; (*tropischer*) jungle
Urzeit *f* primeval times *pl*
USA *pl* USA *sg*
usw. *abbr* (**und so weiter**) etc.
utopisch *a* Utopian

Vv

Vakuum /'va:kuʊm/ *nt* **-s** vacuum. **v~verpackt** *a* vacuum-packed
Vanille /va'nɪljə/ *f* **-** vanilla
variieren *vt/i* (*haben*) vary
Vase /'va:zə/ *f* **-, -n** vase
Vater *m* **-s,⸚** father. **V~land** *nt* fatherland
väterlich *a* paternal; (*fürsorglich*) fatherly. **v~erseits** *adv* on one's/the father's side
Vater|schaft *f* **-** fatherhood; (*Jur*) paternity. **V~unser** *nt* **-s,-** Lord's Prayer
v. Chr. *abbr* (**vor Christus**) BC
Vegetar|ier(in) /vege'ta:ri̯ɐ, -i̯ərɪn/ *m(f)* **-s,-** (*f* **-, -nen**) vegetarian. **v~isch** *a* vegetarian
Veilchen *nt* **-s, -n** violet
Vene /'ve:nə/ *f* **-, -n** vein
Venedig /ve'ne:dɪç/ *nt* **-s** Venice
Ventil /vɛn'ti:l/ *nt* **-s, -e** valve. **V~ator** *m* **-s, -en** /-'to:rən/ fan
verabred|en *vt* arrange; **sich [mit jdm] v~en** arrange to meet [s.o.]. **V~ung** *f* **-, -en** arrangement; (*Treffen*) appointment

verabschieden *vt* say goodbye to; (*aus dem Dienst*) retire; pass <*Gesetz*>; **sich v~** say goodbye
verachten *vt* despise
Verachtung *f* **-** contempt
verallgemeinern *vt/i* (*haben*) generalize
veränder|lich *a* changeable; (*Math*) variable. **v~n** *vt* change; **sich v~n** change; (*beruflich*) change one's job. **V~ung** *f* change
verängstigt *a* frightened, scared
verankern *vt* anchor
veranlag|t *a* **künstlerisch/ musikalisch v~t sein** have an artistic/a musical bent; **praktisch v~t** practically minded. **V~ung** *f* **-, -en** disposition; (*Neigung*) tendency; (*künstlerisch*) bent
veranlassen *vt* (*reg*) arrange for; (*einleiten*) institute; **jdn v~** prompt s.o. (**zu** to)
veranschlagen *vt* (*reg*) estimate
veranstalt|en *vt* organize; hold, give <*Party*>; make <*Lärm*>. **V~er** *m* **-s,-** organizer. **V~ung** *f* **-, -en** event
verantwort|lich *a* responsible; **v~lich machen** hold responsible. **V~ung** *f* **-** responsibility. **v~ungsbewusst** *a* responsible. **v~ungslos** *a* irresponsible. **v~ungsvoll** *a* responsible
verarbeiten *vt* use; (*Techn*) process; (*verdauen & fig*) digest
verärgern *vt* annoy
verausgaben (sich) *vr* spend all one's money
veräußern *vt* sell
Verb /vɛrp/ *nt* **-s, -en** verb
Verband *m* **-[e]s,¨e** association; (*Mil*) unit; (*Med*) bandage; (*Wund-*) dressing. **V~szeug** *nt* first-aid kit
verbann|en *vt* exile; (*fig*) banish. **V~ung** *f* **-** exile
verbergen† *vt* hide; **sich v~** hide
verbesser|n *vt* improve; (*berichtigen*) correct. **V~ung** *f* **-, -en** improvement; correction
verbeug|en (sich) *vr* bow. **V~ung** *f* bow
verbeulen *vt* dent
verbiegen† *vt* bend
verbieten† *vt* forbid; (*Admin*) prohibit, ban
verbillig|en *vt* reduce [in price]. **v~t** *a* reduced
verbinden† *vt* connect (**mit** to); (*zusammenfügen*) join; (*verknüpfen*) combine; (*in Verbindung bringen*) associate; (*Med*) bandage; dress <*Wunde*>; **jdm verbunden sein** (*fig*) be obliged to s.o.
verbindlich *a* friendly; (*bindend*) binding
Verbindung *f* connection; (*Verknüpfung*) combination; (*Kontakt*) contact; (*Vereinigung*) association; **chemiche V~** chemical compound; **in V~ stehen/sich in V~ setzen** be/get in touch
verbissen *a* grim
verbitter|n *vt* make bitter. **v~t** *a* bitter. **V~ung** *f* **-** bitterness
verblassen *vi* (*sein*) fade
Verbleib *m* **-s** whereabouts *pl*
verbleit *a* <*Benzin*> leaded
verblüff|en *vt* amaze, astound. **V~ung** *f* **-** amazement
verblühen *vi* (*sein*) wither, fade
verbluten *vi* (*sein*) bleed to death
verborgen *vt* lend
Verbot *nt* **-[e]s, -e** ban. **v~en** *a* forbidden; (*Admin*) prohibited
Verbrauch *m* **-[e]s** consumption. **v~en** *vt* use; consume <*Lebensmittel*>; (*erschöpfen*) use up. **V~er** *m* **-s,-** consumer
Verbrechen *nt* **-s,-** crime
Verbrecher *m* **-s,-** criminal
verbreit|en *vt* spread. **v~et** *a* widespread. **V~ung** *f* **-** spread; (*Verbreiten*) spreading

verbrenn|en† *vt/i* (*sein*) burn; cremate <*Leiche*>. **V~ung** *f* **-, -en** burning; cremation; (*Wunde*) burn

verbringen† *vt* spend

verbrühen *vt* scald

verbuchen *vt* enter

verbünd|en (sich) *vr* form an alliance. **V~ete(r)** *m/f* ally

verbürgen *vt* guarantee; **sich v~ für** vouch for

Verdacht *m* **-[e]s** suspicion; **in** *or* **im V~ haben** suspect

verdächtig *a* suspicious. **v~en** *vt* suspect (*gen* of). **V~te(r)** *m/f* suspect

verdamm|en *vt* condemn; (*Relig*) damn. **v~t** *a & adv* [x] damned; **v~t!** damn!

verdampfen *vt/i* (*sein*) evaporate

verdanken *vt* owe (*dat* to)

verdau|en *vt* digest. **v~lich** *a* digestible. **V~ung** *f* **-** digestion

Verdeck *nt* **-[e]s, -e** hood; (*Oberdeck*) top deck

verderb|en† *vi* (*sein*) spoil; <*Lebensmittel*:> go bad ● *vt* spoil; **ich habe mir den Magen verdorben** I have an upset stomach. **V~en** *nt* **-s** ruin. **v~lich** *a* perishable; (*schädlich*) pernicious

verdien|en *vt/i* (*haben*) earn; (*fig*) deserve. **V~er** *m* **-s,-** wage-earner

Verdienst[1] *m* **-[e]s** earnings *pl*

Verdienst[2] *nt* **-[e]s, -e** merit

verdient *a* well-deserved

verdoppeln *vt* double

verdorben *a* spoilt, ruined; <*Magen*> upset; (*moralisch*) corrupt; (*verkommen*) depraved

verdreh|en *vt* twist, roll <*Augen*>; (*fig*) distort. **v~t** *a* [!] crazy

verdreifachen *vt* treble, triple

verdrücken *vt* crumple; ([!] *essen*) polish off; **sich v~** [!] slip away

Verdruss *m* **-es** annoyance

verdünnen *vt* dilute; **sich v~** taper off

verdunst|en *vi* (*sein*) evaporate. **V~ung** *f* **-** evaporation

verdursten *vi* (*sein*) die of thirst

veredeln *vt* refine; (*Hort*) graft

verehr|en *vt* revere; (*Relig*) worship; (*bewundern*) admire; (*schenken*) give. **V~er(in)** *m* **-s,-** (*f* **-, -nen**) admirer. **V~ung** *f* **-** veneration; worship; admiration

vereidigen *vt* swear in

Verein *m* **-s, -e** society; (*Sport-*) club

vereinbar *a* compatible. **v~en** *vt* arrange. **V~ung** *f* **-, -en** agreement

vereinfachen *vt* simplify

vereinheitlichen *vt* standardize

vereinig|en *vt* unite; merge <*Firmen*>; **wieder v~en** reunite; reunify <*Land*>; **sich v~en** unite; **V~te Staaten [von Amerika]** United States *sg* [of America]. **V~ung** *f* **-, -en** union; (*Organisation*) organization

vereinzelt *a* isolated ● *adv* occasionally

vereist *a* frozen; <*Straße*> icy

vereitert *a* septic

verenden *vi* (*sein*) die

verengen *vt* restrict; **sich v~** narrow; <*Pupille*:> contract

vererb|en *vt* leave (*dat* to); (*Biol & fig*) pass on (*dat* to). **V~ung** *f* **-** heredity

verfahren† *vi* (*sein*) proceed; **v~ mit** deal with ● *vr* **sich v~** lose one's way ● *a* muddled. **V~** *nt* **-s,-** procedure; (*Techn*) process; (*Jur*) proceedings *pl*

Verfall *m* decay; (*eines Gebäudes*) dilapidation; (*körperlich & fig*) decline; (*Ablauf*) expiry. **v~en**† *vi* (*sein*) decay; <*Person, Sitten*:> decline; (*ablaufen*) expire; **v~en in** (+ *acc*) lapse into; **v~en auf** (+ *acc*) hit on <*Idee*>

verfärben (sich) *vr* change colour; <*Stoff*:> discolour

verfass|en *vt* write; (*Jur*) draw up; (*entwerfen*) draft. **V~er** *m* **-s,-** author. **V~ung** *f* (*Pol*) constitution; (*Zustand*) state
verfaulen *vi* (*sein*) rot, decay
verfechten† *vt* advocate
verfehlen *vt* miss
verfeinde|n (sich) *vr* become enemies; **v~t sein** be enemies
verfeinern *vt* refine; (*verbessern*) improve
verfilmen *vt* film
verfluch|en *vt* curse. **v~t** *a & adv* ! damned; **v~t!** damn!
verfolg|en *vt* pursue; (*folgen*) follow; (*bedrängen*) pester; (*Pol*) persecute; **strafrechtlich v~en** prosecute. **V~er** *m* **-s,-** pursuer. **V~ung** *f* **-** pursuit; persecution
verfrüht *a* premature
verfügbar *a* available
verfüg|en *vt* order; (*Jur*) decree ● *vi* (*haben*) **v~en über** (+ *acc*) have at one's disposal. **V~ung** *f* **-, -en** order; (*Jur*) decree; **jdm zur V~ung stehen** be at s.o.'s disposal
verführ|en *vt* seduce; tempt. **V~ung** *f* seduction; temptation
vergangen *a* past; (*letzte*) last. **V~heit** *f* **-** past; (*Gram*) past tense
vergänglich *a* transitory
vergas|en *vt* gas. **V~er** *m* **-s,-** carburettor
vergeb|en† *vt* award (**an** + *dat* to); (*weggeben*) give away; (*verzeihen*) forgive. **v~lich** *a* futile, vain ● *adv* in vain. **V~ung** *f* **-** forgiveness
vergehen† *vi* (*sein*) pass; **sich v~** violate (**gegen etw** sth). **V~** *nt* **-s,-** offence
vergelt|en† *vt* repay. **V~ung** *f* **-** retaliation; (*Rache*) revenge
vergessen† *vt* forget; (*liegen lassen*) leave behind
vergesslich *a* forgetful. **V~keit** *f* **-** forgetfulness
vergeuden *vt* waste, squander
vergewaltig|en *vt* rape. **V~ung** *f* **-, -en** rape
vergießen† *vt* spill; shed <*Tränen, Blut*>
vergift|en *vt* poison. **V~ung** *f* **-, -en** poisoning
Vergissmeinnicht *nt* **-[e]s, -[e]** forget-me-not
vergittert *a* barred
verglasen *vt* glaze
Vergleich *m* **-[e]s, -e** comparison; (*Jur*) settlement. **v~bar** *a* comparable. **v~en**† *vt* compare (**mit** with/to)
vergnüg|en (sich) *vr* enjoy oneself. **V~en** *nt* **-s,-** pleasure; (*Spaß*) fun; **viel V~en!** have a good time! **v~t** *a* cheerful; (*zufrieden*) happy. **V~ungen** *fpl* entertainments
vergolden *vt* gild; (*plattieren*) gold-plate
vergraben† *vt* bury
vergriffen *a* out of print
vergrößer|n *vt* enlarge; <*Linse:*> magnify; (*vermehren*) increase; (*erweitern*) extend; expand <*Geschäft*>; **sich v~n** grow bigger; <*Firma:*> expand; (*zunehmen*) increase. **V~ung** *f* **-, -en** magnification; increase; expansion; (*Phot*) enlargement. **V~ungsglas** *nt* magnifying glass
vergüt|en *vt* pay for; **jdm etw v~en** reimburse s.o. for sth. **V~ung** *f* **-, -en** remuneration; (*Erstattung*) reimbursement
verhaft|en *vt* arrest. **V~ung** *f* **-, -en** arrest
verhalten† **(sich)** *vr* behave; (*handeln*) act; (*beschaffen sein*) be. **V~** *nt* **-s** behaviour, conduct
Verhältnis *nt* **-ses, -se** relationship; (*Liebes-*) affair; (*Math*) ratio; **V~se** circumstances; conditions. **v~mäßig** *adv* comparatively, relatively

verhand|eln *vt* discuss; (*Jur*) try ● *vi* (*haben*) negotiate. **V∼lung** *f* (*Jur*) trial; **V∼lungen** negotiations

Verhängnis *nt* **-ses** fate, doom

verhärten *vt/i* (*sein*) harden

verhasst *a* hated

verhätscheln *vt* spoil

verhauen† *vt* [!] beat; make a mess of <*Prüfung*>

verheilen *vi* (*sein*) heal

verheimlichen *vt* keep secret

verheirat|en (sich) *vr* get married (**mit** to); **sich wieder v∼en** remarry. **v∼et** *a* married

verhelfen† *vi* (*haben*) **jdm zu etw v∼** help s.o. get sth

verherrlichen *vt* glorify

verhexen *vt* bewitch

verhinder|n *vt* prevent; **v∼t sein** be unable to come

Verhör *nt* **-s, -e** interrogation; **ins V∼ nehmen** interrogate. **v∼en** *vt* interrogate; **sich v∼en** mishear

verhungern *vi* (*sein*) starve

verhüt|en *vt* prevent. **V∼ung** *f* **-** prevention. **V∼ungsmittel** *nt* contraceptive

verirren (sich) *vr* get lost

verjagen *vt* chase away

verjüngen *vt* rejuvenate

verkalkt *a* [!] senile

verkalkulieren (sich) *vr* miscalculate

Verkauf *m* sale; **zum V∼** for sale. **v∼en** *vt* sell; **zu v∼en** for sale

Verkäufer(in) *m(f)* seller; (*im Geschäft*) shop assistant

Verkehr *m* **-s** traffic; (*Kontakt*) contact; (*Geschlechts-*) intercourse; **aus dem V∼ ziehen** take out of circulation. **v∼en** *vi* (*haben*) operate; <*Bus, Zug:*> run; (*Umgang haben*) associate, mix (**mit** with); (*Gast sein*) visit (**bei jdm** s.o.)

Verkehrs|ampel *f* traffic lights *pl*. **V∼unfall** *m* road accident. **V∼verein** *m* tourist office. **V∼zeichen** *nt* traffic sign

verkehrt *a* wrong; **v∼ herum** *adv* the wrong way round; (*links*) inside out

verklagen *vt* sue (**auf** + *acc* for)

verkleid|en *vt* disguise; (*Techn*) line; **sich v∼en** disguise oneself; (*für Kostümfest*) dress up. **V∼ung** *f* **-, -en** disguise; (*Kostüm*) fancy dress; (*Techn*) lining

verkleiner|n *vt* reduce [in size]. **V∼ung** *f* **-** reduction

verknittern *vt/i* (*sein*) crumple

verknüpfen *vt* knot together

verkommen† *vi* (*sein*) be neglected; (*sittlich*) go to the bad; (*verfallen*) decay; <*Haus:*> fall into disrepair; <*Gegend:*> become run-down; <*Lebensmittel:*> go bad ● *a* neglected; (*sittlich*) depraved; <*Haus*> dilapidated; <*Gegend*> run-down

verkörpern *vt* embody, personify

verkraften *vt* cope with

verkrampft *a* (*fig*) tense

verkriechen† (sich) *vr* hide

verkrümmt *a* crooked, bent

verkrüppelt *a* crippled; <*Glied*> deformed

verkühl|en (sich) *vr* catch a chill. **V∼ung** *f* **-, -en** chill

verkümmern *vi* (*sein*) waste/ <*Pflanze:*> wither away

verkünden *vt* announce; pronounce <*Urteil*>

verkürzen *vt* shorten; (*verringern*) reduce; (*abbrechen*) cut short; while away <*Zeit*>

Verlag *m* **-[e]s, -e** publishing firm

verlangen *vt* ask for; (*fordern*) demand; (*berechnen*) charge. **V∼** *nt* **-s** desire; (*Bitte*) request

verlänger|n *vt* extend; lengthen <*Kleid*>, (*zeitlich*) prolong; renew <*Pass, Vertrag*>; (*Culin*) thin down. **V∼ung** *f* **-, -en** extension; renewal. **V∼ungsschnur** *f* extension cable

verlassen† *vt* leave; (*im Stich lassen*) desert; **sich v∼ auf** (+ *acc*) rely *or* depend on ● *a* deserted. **V~heit** *f* **-** desolation

verlässlich *a* reliable

Verlauf *m* course; **im V~** (+ *gen*) in the course of. **v~en**† *vi* (*sein*) run; (*ablaufen*) go; **gut v~en** go [off] well ● *vr* **sich v~en** lose one's way

verlegen *vt* move; (*verschieben*) postpone; (*vor-*) bring forward; (*verlieren*) mislay; (*versperren*) block; (*legen*) lay <*Teppich, Rohre*>; (*veröffentlichen*) publish; **sich v~ auf** (+ *acc*) take up <*Beruf*>; resort to <*Bitten*> ● *a* embarrassed. **V~heit** *f* **-** embarrassment

Verleger *m* **-s,-** publisher

verleihen† *vt* lend; (*gegen Gebühr*) hire out; (*überreichen*) award, confer; (*fig*) give

verlernen *vt* forget

verletz|en *vt* injure; (*kränken*) hurt; (*verstoßen gegen*) infringe; violate <*Grenze*>. **v~end** *a* hurtful, wounding. **V~te(r)** *m/f* injured person; (*bei Unfall*) casualty. **V~ung** *f* **-, -en** (*Verstoß*) infringement; violation

verleugnen *vt* deny; disown <*Freund*>

verleumd|en *vt* slander; (*schriftlich*) libel. **v~erisch** *a* slanderous; libellous. **V~ung** *f* **-, -en** slander; (*schriftlich*) libel

verlieben (sich) *vr* fall in love (**in** + *acc* with); **verliebt sein** be in love (**in** + *acc* with)

verlier|en† *vt* lose; shed <*Laub*> ● *vi* (*haben*) lose (**an etw** *dat* sth). **V~er** *m* **-s,-** loser

verlob|en (sich) *vr* get engaged (**mit** to); **v~t sein** be engaged. **V~te** *f* fiancée. **V~te(r)** *m* fiancé. **V~ung** *f* **-, -en** engagement

verlock|en *vt* tempt. **V~ung** *f* **-, -en** temptation

verloren *a* lost; **v~ gehen** get lost

verlos|en *vt* raffle. **V~ung** *f* **-, -en** raffle; (*Ziehung*) draw

Verlust *m* **-[e]s, -e** loss

vermachen *vt* leave, bequeath

Vermächtnis *nt* **-ses, -se** legacy

vermähl|en (sich) *vr* marry. **V~ung** *f* **-, -en** marriage

vermehren *vt* increase; propagate <*Pflanzen*>; **sich v~** increase; (*sich fortpflanzen*) breed

vermeiden† *vt* avoid

Vermerk *m* **-[e]s, -e** note. **v~en** note [down]

vermessen† *vt* measure; survey <*Gelände*> ● *a* presumptuous

vermiet|en *vt* let, rent [out]; hire out <*Boot, Auto*>; **zu v~en** to let; <*Boot:*> for hire. **V~er** *m* landlord. **V~erin** *f* landlady

vermindern *vt* reduce

vermischen *vt* mix

vermissen *vt* miss

vermisst *a* missing

vermitteln *vi* (*haben*) mediate ● *vt* arrange; (*beschaffen*) find; place <*Arbeitskräfte*>

Vermittl|er *m* **-s,-** agent; (*Schlichter*) mediator. **V~ung** *f* **-, -en** arrangement; (*Agentur*) agency; (*Teleph*) exchange; (*Schlichtung*) mediation

Vermögen *nt* **-s,-** fortune. **v~d** *a* wealthy

vermut|en *vt* suspect; (*glauben*) presume. **v~lich** *a* probable ● *adv* presumably. **V~ung** *f* **-, -en** supposition; (*Verdacht*) suspicion

vernachlässigen *vt* neglect

vernehm|en† *vt* hear; (*verhören*) question; (*Jur*) examine. **V~ung** *f* **-, -en** questioning

verneigen (sich) *vr* bow

verneinen *vt* answer in the negative; (*ablehnen*) reject. **v~end** *a* negative. **V~ung** *f* **-, -en** negative answer

vernicht|en *vt* destroy; (*ausrotten*) exterminate. **V~ung** *f* **-** destruction; extermination

Vernunft *f* - reason
vernünftig *a* reasonable, sensible
veröffentlich|en *vt* publish. **V~ung** *f* -, -en publication
verordn|en *vt* prescribe (*dat* for). **V~ung** *f* -, -en prescription; (*Verfügung*) decree
verpachten *vt* lease [out]
verpack|en *vt* pack; (*einwickeln*) wrap. **V~ung** *f* packaging; wrapping
verpassen *vt* miss; ([!] *geben*) give
verpfänden *vt* pawn
verpflanzen *vt* transplant
verpfleg|en *vt* feed: **sich selbst v~en** cater for oneself. **V~ung** *f* - board; (*Essen*) food; **Unterkunft und V~ung** board and lodging
verpflicht|en *vt* oblige; (*einstellen*) engage; (*Sport*) sign; **sich v~en** undertake/(*versprechen*) promise (**zu** to); (*vertraglich*) sign a contract. **V~ung** *f* -, -en obligation, commitment
verprügeln *vt* beat up, thrash
Verputz *m* -es plaster. **v~en** *vt* plaster
Verrat *m* -[e]s betrayal, treachery. **v~en**† *vt* betray; give away <*Geheimnis*>
Verräter *m* -s,- traitor
verrech|nen *vt* settle; clear <*Scheck*>; **sich v~nen** make a mistake; (*fig*) miscalculate. **V~nungsscheck** *m* crossed cheque
verreisen *vi* (*sein*) go away, **verreist sein** be away
verrenken *vt* dislocate
verrichten *vt* perform, do
verriegeln *vt* bolt
verringer|n *vt* reduce; **sich v~n** decrease. **V~ung** *f* - reduction; decrease
verrost|en *vi* (*sein*) rust. **v~et** *a* rusty
verrückt *a* crazy, mad. **V~e(r)** *m/f* lunatic, **V~heit** *f* -, -en madness; (*Torheit*) folly
verrühren *vt* mix
verrunzelt *a* wrinkled
verrutschen *vt* (*sein*) slip
Vers /fɛrs/ *m* -es, -e verse
versag|en *vi* (*haben*) fail ● *vt* **sich etw v~en** deny oneself sth. **V~en** *nt* -s,- failure. **V~er** *m* -s,- failure
versalzen† *vt* put too much salt in/on; (*fig*) spoil
versamm|eln *vt* assemble. **V~lung** *f* assembly, meeting
Versand *m* -[e]s dispatch. **V~haus** *nt* mail-order firm
versäumen *vt* miss; lose <*Zeit*>; (*unterlassen*) neglect; **[es] v~, etw zu tun** fail to do sth
verschärfen *vt* intensify; tighten <*Kontrolle*>; increase <*Tempo*>; aggravate <*Lage*>; **sich v~** intensify; increase; <*Lage*:> worsen
verschätzen (sich) *vr* **sich v~ in** (+ *dat*) misjudge
verschenken *vt* give away
verscheuchen *vt* shoo/(*jagen*) chase away
verschicken *vt* send; (*Comm*) dispatch
verschieb|en† *vt* move; (*aufschieben*) put off, postpone; **sich v~en** move, shift; (*verrutschen*) slip; (*zeitlich*) be postponed. **V~ung** *f* shift; postponement
verschieden *a* different; **v~e** *pl* different; (*mehrere*) various; **V~es** some things; (*dieses und jenes*) various things; **das ist v~** it varies ● *adv* differently; **v~ groß** of different sizes. **v~artig** *a* diverse
verschimmel|n *vi* (*sein*) go mouldy. **v~t** *a* mouldy
verschlafen† *vi* (*haben*) oversleep ● *vt* sleep through

<*Tag*>; **sich v~** oversleep ● *a* sleepy

verschlagen† *vt* lose <*Seite*>; **jdm die Sprache/den Atem v~** leave s.o. speechless/take s.o.'s breath away ● *a* sly

verschlechter|n *vt* make worse; **sich v~n** get worse, deteriorate. **V~ung** *f* **-, -en** deterioration

Verschleiß *m* **-es** wear and tear

verschleppen *vt* carry off; (*entführen*) abduct; spread <*Seuche*>; neglect <*Krankheit*>; (*hinausziehen*) delay

verschleudern *vt* sell at a loss

verschließen† *vt* close; (*abschließen*) lock; (*einschließen*) lock up

verschlimmer|n *vt* make worse; aggravate <*Lage*>; **sich v~n** get worse, deteriorate. **V~ung** *f* **-, -en** deterioration

verschlossen *a* reserved. **V~heit** *f* **-** reserve

verschlucken *vt* swallow; **sich v~** choke (**an** + *dat* on)

Verschluss *m* **-es,¨-e** fastener, clasp; (*Koffer-*) catch; (*Flaschen-*) top; (*luftdicht*) seal; (*Phot*) shutter

verschlüsselt *a* coded

verschmelzen† *vt/i* (*sein*) fuse

verschmerzen *vt* get over

verschmutz|en *vt* soil; pollute <*Luft*> ● *vi* (*sein*) get dirty. **V~ung** *f* **-** pollution

verschneit *a* snow-covered

verschnörkelt *a* ornate

verschnüren *vt* tie up

verschollen *a* missing

verschonen *vt* spare

verschossen *a* faded

verschränken *vt* cross

verschreiben† *vt* prescribe; **sich v~** make a slip of the pen

verschulden *vt* be to blame for. **V~** *nt* **-s** fault

verschuldet *a* **v~ sein** be in debt

verschütten *vt* spill; (*begraben*) bury

verschweigen† *vt* conceal, hide

verschwend|en *vt* waste. **V~ung** *f* **-** extravagance; (*Vergeudung*) waste

verschwiegen *a* discreet

verschwinden† *vi* (*sein*) disappear; **[mal] v~** 🄵 spend a penny

verschwommen *a* blurred

verschwör|en† **(sich)** *vr* conspire. **V~ung** *f* **-, -en** conspiracy

versehen† *vt* perform; hold <*Posten*>; keep <*Haushalt*>; **v~ mit** provide with; **sich v~** make a mistake. **V~** *nt* **-s,-** oversight; (*Fehler*) slip; **aus V~** by mistake. **v~tlich** *adv* by mistake

Versehrte(r) *m* disabled person

versengen *vt* singe; (*stärker*) scorch

versenken *vt* sink

versessen *a* keen (**auf** + *acc* on)

versetz|en *vt* move; transfer <*Person*>; (*Sch*) move up; (*verpfänden*) pawn; (*verkaufen*) sell; (*vermischen*) blend; **jdn v~en** (🄵 *warten lassen*) stand s.o. up; **jdm in Angst/Erstaunen v~en** frighten/astonish s.o.; **sich in jds Lage v~en** put oneself in s.o.'s place. **V~ung** *f* **-, -en** move; transfer; (*Sch*) move to a higher class

verseuchen *vt* contaminate

versicher|n *vt* insure; (*bekräftigen*) affirm; **jdm v~n** assure s.o (**dass** that). **V~ung** *f* **-, -en** insurance; assurance

versiegeln *vt* seal

versiert /vɛr'ʒiːɐt/ *a* experienced

versilbert *a* silver-plated

Versmaß /'fɛrs-/ *nt* metre

versöhn|en *vt* reconcile; **sich v~en** become reconciled. **V~ung** *f* **-, -en** reconciliation

versorg|en *vt* provide, supply (**mit** with); provide for <*Familie*>;

(*betreuen*) look after. **V~ung** *f* **-** provision, supply; (*Betreuung*) care

verspät|en (sich) *vr* be late. **v~et** *a* late; <*Zug*> delayed; <*Dank*> belated. **V~ung** *f* **-** lateness; **V~ung haben** be late

versperren *vt* block; bar <*Weg*>

verspiel|en *vt* gamble away. **v~t** *a* playful

verspotten *vt* mock, ridicule

versprech|en† *vt* promise; **sich v~en** make a slip of the tongue; **sich** (*dat*) **viel v~en von** have high hopes of; **ein viel v~ender Anfang** a promising start. **V~en** *nt* **-s,-** promise. **V~ungen** *fpl* promises

verstaatlich|en *vt* nationalize. **V~ung** *f* **-** nationalization

Verstand *m* **-[e]s** mind; (*Vernunft*) reason; **den V~ verlieren** go out of one's mind

verständig *a* sensible; (*klug*) intelligent. **v~en** *vt* notify, inform; **sich v~en** communicate; (*sich verständlich machen*) make oneself understood. **V~ung** *f* **-** notification; communication; (*Einigung*) agreement

verständlich *a* comprehensible; (*deutlich*) clear; (*begreiflich*) understandable; **sich v~ machen** make oneself understood. **v~erweise** *adv* understandably

Verständnis *nt* **-ses** understanding

verstärk|en *vt* strengthen, reinforce; (*steigern*) intensify, increase; amplify <*Ton*>. **V~er** *m* **-s,-** amplifier. **V~ung** *f* reinforcement; increase; amplification; (*Truppen*) reinforcements *pl*

verstaubt *a* dusty

verstauchen *vt* sprain

Versteck *nt* **-[e]s, -e** hiding-place; **V~ spielen** play hide-and-seek. **v~en** *vt* hide; **sich v~en** hide

verstehen† *vt* understand; (*können*) know; **falsch v~** misunderstand; **sich v~** understand one another; (*auskommen*) get on

versteiger|n *vt* auction. **V~ung** *f* auction

versteinert *a* fossilized

verstell|en *vt* adjust; (*versperren*) block; (*verändern*) disguise; **sich v~en** pretend. **V~ung** *f* **-** pretence

versteuern *vt* pay tax on

verstimm|t *a* disgruntled; <*Magen*> upset; (*Mus*) out of tune. **V~ung** *f* **-** ill humour; (*Magen-*) upset

verstockt *a* stubborn

verstopf|en *vt* plug; (*versperren*) block; **v~t** blocked; <*Person*> constipated. **V~ung** *f* **-, -en** blockage; (*Med*) constipation

verstorben *a* late, deceased. **V~e(r)** *m/f* deceased

verstört *a* bewildered

Verstoß *m* infringement. **v~en**† *vt* disown ● *vi* (*haben*) **v~en gegen** contravene, infringe

verstreuen *vt* scatter

verstümmeln *vt* mutilate; garble <*Text*>

Versuch *m* **-[e]s, -e** attempt; (*Experiment*) experiment. **v~en** *vt/i* (*haben*) try; **v~t sein** be tempted (**zu** to). **V~ung** *f* **-, -en** temptation

vertagen *vt* adjourn; (*aufschieben*) postpone; **sich v~** adjourn

vertauschen *vt* exchange; (*verwechseln*) mix up

verteidig|en *vt* defend. **V~er** *m* **-s,-** defender; (*Jur*) defence counsel. **V~ung** *f* **-, -en** defence

verteil|en *vt* distribute; (*zuteilen*) allocate; (*ausgeben*) hand out; (*verstreichen*) spread. **V~ung** *f* **-** distribution; allocation

vertief|en *vt* deepen; **v~t sein in** (+ *acc*) be engrossed in. **V~ung** *f* **-, -en** hollow, depression
vertikal /vɛrti'ka:l/ *a* vertical
vertilgen *vt* exterminate; kill [off] <*Unkraut*>
vertippen (sich) *vr* make a typing mistake
vertonen *vt* set to music
Vertrag *m* **-[e]s,⸚e** contract; (*Pol*) treaty
vertragen† *vt* tolerate, stand; take <*Kritik, Spaß*>; **sich v~** get on
vertraglich *a* contractual
verträglich *a* good-natured; (*bekömmlich*) digestible
vertrauen *vi* (*haben*) trust (**jdm/etw** s.o./sth; **auf** + *acc* in). **V~** *nt* **-s** trust, confidence (**zu** in); **im V~** in confidence. **v~swürdig** *a* trustworthy
vertraulich *a* confidential; (*intim*) familiar
vertraut *a* intimate; (*bekannt*) familiar. **V~heit** *f* **-** intimacy; familiarity
vertreib|en† *vt* drive away; drive out <*Feind*>; (*Comm*) sell; **sich** (*dat*) **die Zeit v~en** pass the time. **V~ung** *f* **-, -en** expulsion
vertret|en† *vt* represent; (*einspringen für*) stand in *or* deputize for; (*verfechten*) support; hold <*Meinung*>; **sich** (*dat*) **den Fuß v~en** twist one's ankle. **V~er** *m* **-s,-** representative; deputy; (*Arzt-*) locum; (*Verfechter*) supporter. **V~ung** *f* **-, -en** representation; (*Person*) deputy; (*eines Arztes*) locum; (*Handels-*) agency
Vertrieb *m* **-[e]s** (*Comm*) sale
vertrocknen *vi* (*sein*) dry up
verüben *vt* commit
verunglücken *vi* (*sein*) be involved in an accident; (**!** *missglücken*) go wrong; **tödlich v~** be killed in an accident
verunreinigen *vt* pollute; (*verseuchen*) contaminate
verursachen *vt* cause
verurteil|en *vt* condemn; (*Jur*) convict (**wegen** of); sentence (**zum Tode** to death). **V~ung** *f* **-** condemnation; (*Jur*) conviction
vervielfachen *vt* multiply
vervielfältigen *vt* duplicate
vervollständigen *vt* complete
verwählen (sich) *vr* misdial
verwahren *vt* keep; (*verstauen*) put away
verwahrlost *a* neglected; <*Haus*> dilapidated
Verwahrung *f* **-** keeping; **in V~ nehmen** take into safe keeping
verwaist *a* orphaned
verwalt|en *vt* administer; (*leiten*) manage; govern <*Land*>. **V~er** *m* **-s,-** administrator; manager. **V~ung** *f* **-, -en** administration; management; government
verwand|eln *vt* transform, change (**in** + *acc* into) **sich v~eln** change, turn (**in** + *acc* into). **V~lung** *f* transformation
verwandt *a* related (**mit** to). **V~e(r)** *m/f* relative. **V~schaft** *f* **-** relationship; (*Menschen*) relatives *pl*
verwarn|en *vt* warn, caution. **V~ung** *f* warning, caution
verwechs|eln *vt* mix up, confuse; (*halten für*) mistake (**mit** for). **V~lung** *f* **-, -en** mix-up
verweiger|n *vt/i* (*haben*) refuse (**jdm etw** s.o sth). **V~ung** *f* refusal
Verweis *m* **-es, -e** reference (**auf** + *acc* to); (*Tadel*) reprimand; **v~en**† *vt* refer (**auf/an** + *acc* to); (*tadeln*) reprimand; **von der Schule v~en** expel
verwelken *vi* (*sein*) wilt
verwend|en† *vt* use; spend <*Zeit, Mühe*>. **V~ung** *f* use
verwerten *vt* utilize, use
verwesen *vi* (*sein*) decompose

verwick|eln *vt* involve (**in** + *acc* in); **sich v~eln** get tangled up. **v~elt** *a* complicated
verwildert *a* wild; <*Garten*> overgrown; <*Aussehen*> unkempt
verwinden† *vt* (*fig*) get over
verwirklichen *vt* realize
verwirr|en *vt* tangle up; (*fig*) confuse; **sich v~en** get tangled; (*fig*) become confused. **v~t** *a* confused. **V~ung** *f* **-** confusion
verwischen *vt* smudge
verwittert *a* weathered
verwitwet *a* widowed
verwöhn|en *vt* spoil. **v~t** *a* spoilt
verworren *a* confused
verwund|bar *a* vulnerable. **v~en** *vt* wound
verwunder|lich *a* surprising. **v~n** *vt* surprise; **sich v~n** be surprised. **V~ung** *f* **-** surprise
Verwund|ete(r) *m* wounded soldier; **die V~eten** the wounded *pl*. **V~ung** *f* **-, -en** wound
verwüst|en *vt* devastate, ravage. **V~ung** *f* **-, -en** devastation
verzählen (sich) *vr* miscount
verzaubern *vt* bewitch; (*fig*) enchant; **v~ in** (+ *acc*) turn into
Verzehr *m* **-s** consumption. **v~en** *vt* eat
verzeih|en† *vt* forgive; **v~en Sie!** excuse me! **V~ung** *f* **-** forgiveness; **um V~ung bitten** apologize; **V~ung!** sorry! (*bei Frage*) excuse me!
Verzicht *m* **-[e]s** renunciation (**auf** + *acc* of). **v~en** *vi* (*haben*) do without; **v~en auf** (+ *acc*) give up; renounce <*Recht, Erbe*>
verziehen† *vt* pull out of shape; (*verwöhnen*) spoil; **sich v~** lose shape; <*Holz:*> warp; <*Gesicht:*> twist; (*verschwinden*) disappear; <*Nebel:*> disperse; <*Gewitter:*> pass ● *vi* (*sein*) move [away]
verzier|en *vt* decorate. **V~ung** *f* **-, -en** decoration
verzinsen *vt* pay interest on
verzöger|n *vt* delay; (*verlangsamen*) slow down. **V~ung** *f* **-, -en** delay
verzollen *vt* pay duty on; **haben Sie etwas zu v~?** have you anything to declare?
verzweif|eln *vi* (*sein*) despair. **v~elt** *a* desperate. **V~lung** *f* **-** despair; (*Ratlosigkeit*) desperation
verzweigen (sich) *vr* branch [out]
Veto /'ve:to/ *nt* **-s, -s** veto
Vetter *m* **-s, -n** cousin
vgl. *abbr* (**vergleiche**) cf.
Viadukt /vi̯a'dʊkt/ *nt* **-[e]s, -e** viaduct
Video /'vi:deo/ *nt* **-s, -s** video. **V~kassette** *f* video cassette. **V~recorder** /-rəkɔrdɐ/ *m* **-s,-** video recorder. **~spiel** *nt* video game
Vieh *nt* **-[e]s** livestock; (*Rinder*) cattle *pl*; ([!] *Tier*) creature
viel *pron* a great deal/[!] a lot of; (*pl*) many, [!] a lot of; (*substantivisch*) **v~[es]** much, [!] a lot; **nicht/so/wie/zu v~** not/so/how/too much/ (*pl*) many; **v~e** *pl* many; **das v~e Geld** all that money ● *adv* much, [!] a lot; **v~ mehr/weniger** much more/less; **v~ zu groß/klein** much *or* far too big/small; **so v~ wie möglich** as much as possible
viel|deutig *a* ambiguous. **v~fach** *a* multiple ● *adv* many times; ([!] *oft*) frequently. **V~falt** *f* **-** diversity, [great] variety
vielleicht *adv* perhaps, maybe; ([!] *wirklich*) really
vielmals *adv* very much
vielmehr *adv* rather; (*im Gegenteil*) on the contrary
vielseitig *a* varied; <*Person*> versatile. **V~keit** *f* **-** versatility
vielversprechend* *a* **viel versprechend**, *s*. **versprechen**
vier *inv a*, **V~** *f* **-, -en** four; (*Sch*) ≈ fair. **V~eck** *nt* **-[e]s, -e** oblong,

rectangle; (*Quadrat*) square. **v~eckig** *a* oblong, rectangular; square. **V~linge** *mpl* quadruplets
viertel /'fɪrtəl/ *inv a* quarter; **um v~ neun** at [a] quarter past eight; **um drei v~ neun** at [a] quarter to nine. **V~** *nt* **-s,-** quarter; (*Wein*) quarter litre; **V~ vor/nach sechs** [a] quarter to/past six. **V~finale** *nt* quarter-final. **V~jahr** *nt* three months *pl*; (*Comm*) quarter. **v~jährlich** *a & adv* quarterly. **V~stụnde** *f* quarter of an hour
vier|zehn/'fɪr-/ *inv a* fourteen. **v~zehnte(r,s)** *a* fourteenth. **v~zig** *inv a* forty. **v~zigste(r,s)** *a* fortieth
Villa /'vɪla/ *f* **-, -len** villa
violett /vio'lɛt/ *a* violet
Vio|line /vio'li:nə/ *f* **-, -n** violin. **V~linschlüssel** *m* treble clef
Virus /'vi:rʊs/ *nt* **-, -ren** virus
Visier /vi'zi:ɐ/ *nt* **-s, -e** visor
Visite /vi'zi:tə/ *f* **-, -n** round; **V~ machen** do one's round
Visum /'vi:zʊm/ *nt* **-s, -sa** visa
Vitamin /vita'mi:n/ *nt* **-s, -e** vitamin
Vitrine /vi'tri:nə/ *f* **-, -n** display cabinet/(*im Museum*) case
Vizepräsident /'fi:tsə-/ *m* vice president
Vogel *m* **-s,¨** bird; **einen V~ haben** [!] have a screw loose. **V~scheuche** *f* **-, -n** scarecrow
Vokabeln /vo'ka:bəln/ *fpl* vocabulary *sg*
Vokal /vo'ka:l/ *m* **-s, -e** vowel
Volant /vo'lã:/ *m* **-s, -s** flounce
Vọlk *nt* **-[e]s,¨er** people *sg*; (*Bevölkerung*) people *pl*
Vö̩lker|kunde *f* ethnology. **V~mord** *m* genocide. **V~recht** *nt* international law
Vọlks|abstimmung *f* plebiscite. **V~fest** *nt* public festival. **V~hochschule** *f* adult education classes *pl*/(*Gebäude*) centre. **V~lied** *nt* folk-song. **V~tanz** *m* folk-dance. **v~tümlich** *a* popular. **V~wirt** *m* economist. **V~wirtschaft** *f* economics *sg*. **V~zählung** *f* [national] census
vọll *a* full (**von** *od* **mit** of); <*Haar*> thick; <*Erfolg, Ernst*> complete; <*Wahrheit*> whole; **v~ machen** fill up; **v~ tanken** fill up with petrol ● *adv* (*ganz*) completely; <*arbeiten*> full-time; <*auszahlen*> in full; **v~ und ganz** completely
Vọllblut *nt* thoroughbred
vollẹnde|n *vt insep* complete. **v~t** *a* perfect
Vollẹndung *f* completion; (*Vollkommenheit*) perfection
vọller *inv a* full of
Volleyball /'vɔli-/ *m* volleyball
vollführen *vt insep* perform
vọllfüllen *vt sep* fill up
Vọllgas *nt* **V~ geben** put one's foot down; **mit V~** flat out
vö̩llig *a* complete
vọlljährig *a* **v~ sein** (*Jur*) be of age. **V~keit** *f* **-** (*Jur*) majority
Vọllkaskoversicherung *f* fully comprehensive insurance
vollkọmmen *a* perfect; (*völlig*) complete
Vọll|kornbrot *nt* wholemeal bread. **V~macht** *f* **-, -en** authority; (*Jur*) power of attorney. **V~mond** *m* full moon. **V~pension** *f* full board
vọllständig *a* complete
vollstrẹcken *vt insep* execute; carry out <*Urteil*>
vọlltanken* *vi sep* (*haben*) **voll tanken**, *s.* **voll**
Vọlltreffer *m* direct hit
vọllzählig *a* complete
vollziehen† *vt insep* carry out; perform <*Handlung*>; consummate <*Ehe*>; **sich v~** take place
Volt /vɔlt/ *nt* **-[s],-** volt
Volumen /vo'lu:mən/ *nt* **-s,-** volume
vọm *prep* = **von dem**

von

● *preposition (+ dative)*

! Note that **von dem** can become **vom**

····➤ (*räumlich*) from; (*nach Richtungen*) of. **von hier an** from here on[ward]. **von Wien aus** [starting] from Vienna. **nördlich/südlich von Mannheim** [to the] north/south of Mannheim. **rechts/links von mir** to the right/left of me; on my right/left

····➤ (*zeitlich*) from. **von jetzt an** from now on. **von heute/morgen an** [as] from today/tomorrow; starting today/tomorrow

····➤ (*zur Angabe des Urhebers, der Ursache; nach Passiv*) by. **der Roman ist von Fontane** the novel is by Fontane. **sie hat ein Kind von ihm**. she has a child by him. **er ist vom Blitz erschlagen worden** he was killed by lightning

····➤ (*anstelle eines Genitivs; Zugehörigkeit, Beschaffenheit, Menge etc.*) of. **ein Stück von dem Kuchen** a piece of the cake. **einer von euch** one of you. **eine Fahrt von drei Stunden** a drive of three hours; a three-hour drive. **das Brot von gestern** yesterday's bread. **ein Tal von erstaunlicher Schönheit** a valley of extraordinary beauty

····➤ (*beftreffend*) about. **handeln/wissen/erzählen** *od* **reden von ...** be/know/talk about .... **eine Geschichte von zwei Elefanten** a story about *or* of two elephants

voneinander *adv* from each other; *<abhängig>* on each other

vonseiten *prep* (+ *gen*) on the part of

vonstatten *adv* **v~ gehen** take place

vor *prep* (+ *dat*/*acc*) in front of; (*zeitlich, Reihenfolge*) before; (+ *dat*) (*bei Uhrzeit*) to; *<warnen, sich fürchten>* of; *<schützen, davonlaufen>* from; *<Respekt haben>* for; **vor Angst zittern** tremble with fear; **vor drei Tagen** three days ago; **vor allen Dingen** above all ● *adv* forward; **vor und zurück** backwards and forwards

Vorabend *m* eve

voran *adv* at the front; (*voraus*) ahead; (*vorwärts*) forward. **v~gehen**† *vi sep* (*sein*) lead the way; (*Fortschritte machen*) make progress. **v~kommen**† *vi sep* (*sein*) make progress; (*fig*) get on

Vor|anschlag *m* estimate. **V~anzeige** *f* advance notice. **V~arbeiter** *m* foreman

voraus *adv* ahead (*dat* of); (*vorn*) at the front; (*vorwärts*) forward ● **im Voraus** in advance. **v~bezahlen** *vt sep* pay in advance. **v~gehen**† *vi sep* (*sein*) go on ahead; **jdm/etw v~gehen** precede s.o./sth. **V~sage** *f* **-, -n** prediction. **v~sagen** *vt sep* predict

voraussetz|en *vt sep* take for granted; (*erfordern*) require; **vorausgesetzt, dass** provided that. **V~ung** *f* **-, -en** assumption; (*Erfordernis*) prerequisite

voraussichtlich *a* anticipated, expected ● *adv* probably

Vorbehalt *m* **-[e]s, -e** reservation

vorbei *adv* past (**an jdm/etw** s.o./sth); (*zu Ende*) over. **v~fahren**† *vi sep* (*sein*) drive/go past. **v~gehen**† *vi sep* (*sein*) go past; (*verfehlen*) miss; (*vergehen*) pass; (**!** *besuchen*) drop in (**bei** on)

vorbereit|en *vt sep* prepare; prepare for *<Reise>*; **sich v~en** prepare [oneself] (**auf** + *acc* for). **V~ung** *f* **-, -en** preparation

vorbestellen *vt sep* order/(*im Theater, Hotel*) book in advance

vorbestraft *a* **v~ sein** have a [criminal] record
Vorbeugung *f* **-** prevention
Vorbild *nt* model. **v~lich** *a* exemplary, model ● *adv* in an exemplary manner
vorbringen† *vt sep* put forward; offer <*Entschuldigung*>
vordatieren *vt sep* post-date
Vorder|bein *nt* foreleg. **v~e(r,s)** *a* front. **V~grund** *m* foreground. **V~rad** *nt* front wheel. **V~seite** *f* front; (*einer Münze*) obverse. **v~ste(r,s)** *a* front, first. **V~teil** *nt* front
vor|drängeln (sich) *vr sep* [!] jump the queue. **v~drängen (sich)** *vr sep* push forward. **v~dringen**† *vi sep* (*sein*) advance
voreilig *a* rash
voreingenommen *a* biased, prejudiced. **V~heit** *f* **-** bias
vorenthalten† *vt sep* withhold
vorerst *adv* for the time being
Vorfahr *m* **-en, -en** ancestor
Vorfahrt *f* right of way; **'V~ beachten'** 'give way'. **V~sstraße** *f* ≈ major road
Vorfall *m* incident. **v~en**† *vi sep* (*sein*) happen
vorfinden† *vt sep* find
Vorfreude *f* [happy] anticipation
vorführ|en *vt sep* present, show; (*demonstrieren*) demonstrate; (*aufführen*) perform. **V~ung** *f* presentation; demonstration; performance
Vor|gabe *f* (*Sport*) handicap. **V~gang** *m* occurrence; (*Techn*) process. **V~gänger(in)** *m* **-s,-** (*f* **-, -nen**) predecessor
vorgehen† *vi sep* (*sein*) go forward; (*voraus-*) go on ahead; <*Uhr:*> be fast; (*wichtig sein*) take precedence; (*verfahren*) act, proceed; (*geschehen*) happen, go on. **V~** *nt* **-s** action
vor|geschichtlich *a* prehistoric. **V~geschmack** *m* foretaste. **V~gesetzte(r)** *m*/*f* superior. **v~gestern** *adv* the day before yesterday; **v~gestern Abend** the evening before last
vorhaben† *vt sep* propose, intend (**zu** to); **etw v~** have sth planned. **V~** *nt* **-s,-** plan
Vorhand *f* (*Sport*) forehand
vorhanden *a* existing; **v~ sein** exist; be available
Vorhang *m* curtain
Vorhängeschloss *nt* padlock
vorher *adv* before[hand]
vorhergehend *a* previous
vorherrschend *a* predominant
Vorher|sage *f* **-, -n** prediction: (*Wetter-*) forecast. **v~sagen** *vt sep* predict; forecast <*Wetter*>. **v~sehen**† *vt sep* foresee
vorhin *adv* just now
vorige(r,s) *a* last, previous
Vor|kehrungen *fpl* precautions. **V~kenntnisse** *fpl* previous knowledge *sg*
vorkommen† *vi sep* (*sein*) happen; (*vorhanden sein*) occur; (*nach vorn kommen*) come forward; (*hervorkommen*) come out; (*zu sehen sein*) show; **jdm bekannt v~** seem familiar to s.o.
Vorkriegszeit *f* pre-war period
vorlad|en† *vt sep* (*Jur*) summons. **V~ung** *f* summons
Vorlage *f* model; (*Muster*) pattern; (*Gesetzes-*) bill
vorlassen† *vt sep* admit; **jdn v~** [!] let s.o. pass; (*den Vortritt lassen*) let s.o. go first
Vor|lauf *m* (*Sport*) heat. **V~läufer** *m* forerunner. **v~läufig** *a* provisional; (*zunächst*) for the time being. **v~laut** *a* forward. **V~leben** *nt* past
vorleg|en *vt sep* put on <*Kette*>; (*unterbreiten*) present; (*vorzeigen*) show. **V~er** *m* **-s,-** mat; (*Bett-*) rug
vorles|en† *vt sep* read [out]; **jdm v~en** read to s.o. **V~ung** *f* lecture

vorletzt|e(r,s) *a* last ... but one; **v~es Jahr** the year before last
Vorliebe *f* preference
vorliegen† *vt sep* (*haben*) be present/(*verfügbar*) available; (*bestehen*) exist, be
vorlügen† *vt sep* lie (*dat* to)
vormachen *vt sep* put up; put on <*Kette*>; push <*Riegel*>; (*zeigen*) demonstrate; **jdm etwas v~** (! *täuschen*) kid s.o.
Vormacht *f* supremacy
vormals *adv* formerly
vormerken *vt sep* make a note of; (*reservieren*) reserve
Vormittag *m* morning; **gestern/heute V~** yesterday/this morning. **v~s** *adv* in the morning
Vormund *m* **-[e]s, -munde** & **-münder** guardian
vorn *adv* at the front; **nach v~** to the front; **von v~** from the front/(*vom Anfang*) beginning; **von v~ anfangen** start afresh
Vorname *m* first name
vorne *adv* = **vorn**
vornehm *a* distinguished; smart
vornehmen† *vt sep* carry out; **sich** (*dat*) **v~, etw zu tun** plan to do sth
vornherein *adv* **von v~herein** from the start
Vor|ort *m* suburb. **V~rang** *m* priority, precedence (**vor** + *dat* over). **V~rat** *m* **-[e]s, ¨e** supply, stock (**an** + *dat* of). **v~rätig** *a* available; **v~rätig haben** have in stock. **V~ratskammer** *f* larder. **V~recht** *nt* privilege. **V~richtung** *f* device
Vorrunde *f* qualifying round
vorsagen *vt/i sep* (*haben*) recite; **jdm v~** tell s.o. the answer
Vor|satz *m* resolution. **v~sätzlich** *a* deliberate; (*Jur*) premeditated
Vorschau *f* preview; (*Film-*) trailer
Vorschein *m* **zum V~kommen** appear
Vorschlag *m* suggestion, proposal. **v~en**† *vt sep* suggest, propose
vorschnell *a* rash
vorschreiben† *vt sep* lay down; dictate (*dat* to); **vorgeschriebene Dosis** prescribed dose
Vorschrift *f* regulation; (*Anweisung*) instruction; **jdm V~en machen** tell s.o. what to do. **v~smäßig** *a* correct
Vorschule *f* nursery school
Vorschuss *m* advance
vorseh|en† *v sep* ● *vt* intend (**für/als** for/as); (*planen*) plan; **sich v~en** be careful (**vor** + *dat* of) ● *vi* (*haben*) peep out. **V~ung** *f* - providence
Vorsicht *f* - care; (*bei Gefahr*) caution; **V~!** careful! (*auf Schild*) 'caution'. **v~ig** *a* careful; cautious. **V~smaßnahme** *f* precaution
Vorsilbe *f* prefix
Vorsitz *m* chairmanship; **den V~ führen** be in the chair. **V~ende(r)** *m/f* chairman
Vorsorge *f* **V~ treffen** take precautions; make provisions (**für** for). **v~n** *vi sep* (*haben*) provide (**für** for)
Vorspeise *f* starter
Vorspiel *nt* prelude. **v~en** *v sep* ● *vt* perform/ (*Mus*) play (*dat* for) ● *vi* (*haben*) audition
vorsprechen† *v sep* ● *vt* recite; (*zum Nachsagen*) say (*dat* to) ● *vi* (*haben*) (*Theat*) audition; **bei jdm v~** call on s.o.
Vor|sprung *m* projection; (*Fels-*) ledge; (*Vorteil*) lead (**vor** + *dat* over). **V~stadt** *f* suburb. **V~stand** *m* board [of directors]; (*Vereins-*) committee; (*Partei-*) executive
vorsteh|en† *vi sep* (*haben*) project, protrude; **einer Abteilung v~en** be in charge of a department. **V~er** *m* **-s,-** head

vorstell|en *vt sep* put forward <*Bein, Uhr*>; (*darstellen*) represent; (*bekanntmachen*) introduce; **sich v~en** introduce oneself; (*als Bewerber*) go for an interview; **sich** (*dat*) **etw v~en** imagine sth. **V~ung** *f* introduction; (*bei Bewerbung*) interview; (*Aufführung*) performance; (*Idee*) idea; (*Phantasie*) imagination. **V~ungsgespräch** *nt* interview

Vorstoß *m* advance

Vorstrafe *f* previous conviction

Vortag *m* day before

vortäuschen *vt sep* feign, fake

Vorteil *m* advantage. **v~haft** *a* advantageous; flattering

Vortrag *m* **-[e]s,¨-e** talk; (*wissenschaftlich*) lecture. **v~en**† *vt sep* perform; (*aufsagen*) recite; (*singen*) sing; (*darlegen*) present (*dat* to)

vortrefflich *a* excellent

Vortritt *m* precedence; **jdm den V~ lassen** let s.o. go first

vorüber *adv* **v~ sein** be over; **an etw** (*dat*) **v~** past sth. **v~gehend** *a* temporary

Vor|urteil *nt* prejudice. **V~verkauf** *m* advance booking

vorverlegen *vt sep* bring forward

Vor|wahl[nummer] *f* dialling code. **V~wand** *m* **-[e]s,¨-e** pretext; (*Ausrede*) excuse

vorwärts *adv* forward[s]; **v~ kommen** make progress; (*fig*) get on *or* ahead

vorwegnehmen† *vt sep* anticipate

vorweisen† *vt sep* show

vorwiegend *adv* predominantly

Vorwort *nt* (*pl* **-worte**) preface

Vorwurf *m* reproach; **jdm Vorwürfe machen** reproach s.o. **v~svoll** *a* reproachful

Vorzeichen *nt* sign; (*fig*) omen

vorzeigen *vt sep* show

vorzeitig *a* premature

vorziehen† *vt sep* pull forward; draw <*Vorhang*>; (*lieber mögen*) prefer; favour

Vor|zimmer *nt* ante-room; (*Büro*) outer office. **V~zug** *m* preference; (*gute Eigenschaft*) merit, virtue; (*Vorteil*) advantage

vorzüglich *a* excellent

vulgär /vʊlˈgɛːɐ̯/ *a* vulgar ● *adv* in a vulgar way

Vulkan /vʊlˈkaːn/ *m* **-s, -e** volcano

Ww

Waage *f* **-, -n** scales *pl*; (*Astr*) Libra. **w~recht** *a* horizontal

Wabe *f* **-, -n** honeycomb

wach *a* awake; (*aufgeweckt*) alert; **w~ werden** wake up

Wach|e *f* **-, -n** guard; (*Posten*) sentry; (*Dienst*) guard duty; (*Naut*) watch; (*Polizei-*) station; **W~e halten** keep watch. **W~hund** *m* guard-dog

Wacholder *m* **-s** juniper

Wachposten *m* sentry

Wachs *nt* **-es** wax

wachsam *a* vigilant. **W~keit** *f* **-** vigilance

wachsen†[1] *vi* (*sein*) grow

wachs|en[2] *vt* (*reg*) wax. **W~figur** *f* waxwork

Wachstum *nt* **-s** growth

Wächter *m* **-s,-** guard; (*Park-*) keeper; (*Parkplatz-*) attendant

Wacht|meister *m* [police] constable. **W~posten** *m* sentry

wackel|ig *a* wobbly; <*Stuhl*> rickety; <*Person*> shaky. **W~kontakt** *m* loose connection. **w~n** *vi* (*haben*) wobble; (*zittern*) shake

Wade *f* **-, -n** (*Anat*) calf

Waffe *f* **-, -n** weapon; **W~n** arms

Waffel *f* **-, -n** waffle; (*Eis-*) wafer

Waffen|ruhe *f* cease-fire. **W~schein** *m* firearms licence. **W~stillstand** *m* armistice

Wagemut *m* daring

wagen *vt* risk; **es w~, etw zu tun** dare [to] do sth; **sich w~** (*gehen*) venture

Wagen *m* **-s,-** cart; (*Eisenbahn-*) carriage, coach; (*Güter-*) wagon; (*Kinder-*) pram; (*Auto*) car. **W~heber** *m* **-s,-** jack

Waggon /va'gõ:/ *m* **-s, -s** wagon

Wahl *f* **-, -en** choice; (*Pol, Admin*) election; (*geheime*) ballot; **zweite W~** (*Comm*) seconds *pl*

wähl|en *vt/i* (*haben*) choose; (*Pol, Admin*) elect; (*stimmen*) vote; (*Teleph*) dial. **W~er(in)** *m* **-s,-** (*f* **-, -nen**) voter. **w~erisch** *a* choosy, fussy

Wahl|fach *nt* optional subject. **w~frei** *a* optional. **W~kampf** *m* election campaign. **W~kreis** *m* constituency. **W~lokal** *nt* polling-station. **w~los** *a* indiscriminate

Wahl|spruch *m* motto. **W~urne** *f* ballot-box

Wahn *m* **-[e]s** delusion; (*Manie*) mania

Wahnsinn *m* madness. **w~ig** *a* mad, insane; (! *unsinnig*) crazy; (! *groß*) terrible; **w~ig werden** go mad ● *adv* ! terribly. **W~ige(r)** *m/f* maniac

wahr *a* true; (*echt*) real; **du kommst doch, nicht w~?** you are coming, aren't you?

während *prep* (+ *gen*) during ● *conj* while, (*wohingegen*) whereas

Wahrheit *f* **-, -en** truth. **w~sgemäß** *a* truthful

wahrnehm|en† *vt sep* notice; (*nutzen*) take advantage of; exploit <*Vorteil*>; look after <*Interessen*>. **W~ung** *f* **-, -en** perception

Wahrsagerin *f* **-, -nen** fortune teller

wahrscheinlich *a* probable. **W~keit** *f* **-** probability

Währung *f* **-, -en** currency

Wahrzeichen *nt* symbol

Waise *f* **-, -n** orphan. **W~nhaus** *nt* orphanage. **W~nkind** *nt* orphan

Wal *m* **-[e]s, -e** whale

Wald *m* **-[e]s,⸚er** wood; (*groß*) forest. **w~ig** *a* wooded

Walis|er *m* **-s,-** Welshman. **w~isch** *a* Welsh

Wall *m* **-[e]s,⸚e** mound

Wallfahr|er(in) *m*(*f*) pilgrim. **W~t** *f* pilgrimage

Walnuss *f* walnut

Walze *f* **-, -n** roller. **w~n** *vt* roll

Walzer *m* **-s,-** waltz

Wand *f* **-,⸚e** wall; (*Trenn-*) partition; (*Seite*) side; (*Fels-*) face

Wandel *m* **-s** change

Wander|er *m* **-s,-, W~in** *f* **-, -nen** hiker, rambler. **w~n** *vi* (*sein*) hike, ramble; (*ziehen*) travel; (*gemächlich gehen*) wander; (*ziellos*) roam. **W~schaft** *f* **-** travels *pl*. **W~ung** *f* **-, -en** hike, ramble. **W~weg** *m* footpath

Wandlung *f* **-, -en** change, transformation

Wand|malerei *f* mural. **W~tafel** *f* blackboard. **W~teppich** *m* tapestry

Wange *f* **-, -n** cheek

wann *adv* when

Wanne *f* **-, -n** tub

Wanze *f* **-, -n** bug

Wappen *nt* **-s,-** coat of arms. **W~kunde** *f* heraldry

war, wäre *s.* **sein**¹

Ware *f* **-, -n** article; (*Comm*) commodity; (*coll*) merchandise; **W~n** goods. **W~nhaus** *nt* department store. **W~nprobe** *f* sample. **W~nzeichen** *nt* trademark

warm *a* warm; <*Mahlzeit*> hot; **w~ machen** heat ●*adv* warmly; **w~ essen** have a hot meal
Wärm|e *f* **-** warmth; (*Phys*) heat; **10 Grad W~e** 10 degrees above zero. **w~en** *vt* warm; heat <*Essen, Wasser*>. **W~flasche** *f* hot-water bottle
Warn|blinkanlage *f* hazard [warning] lights *pl*. **w~en** *vt/i* (*haben*) warn (**vor** + *dat* of). **W~ung** *f* **-, -en** warning
Warteliste *f* waiting list
warten *vi* (*haben*) wait (**auf** + *acc* for) ●*vt* service
Wärter(in) *m* **-s,-** (*f* **-, -nen**) keeper; (*Museums-*) attendant; (*Gefängnis-*) warder; (*Kranken-*) orderly
Warte|raum, W~saal *m* waiting-room. **W~zimmer** *nt* (*Med*) waiting-room
Wartung *f* **-** (*Techn*) service
warum *adv* why
Warze *f* **-, -n** wart
was *pron* what ●*rel pron* that; **alles, was ich brauche** all [that] I need ●*indef pron* ([!] *etwas*) something; (*fragend, verneint*) anything; **so was Ärgerliches!** what a nuisance! ●*adv* [!] (*warum*) why; (*wie*) how
wasch|bar *a* washable. **W~becken** *nt* wash-basin
Wäsche *f* **-** washing; (*Unter-*) underwear
waschecht *a* colour-fast
Wäscheklammer *f* clothes-peg
waschen† *vt* wash; **sich w~** have a wash; **W~ und Legen** shampoo and set ●*vi* (*haben*) do the washing
Wäscherei *f* **-, -en** laundry
Wäsche|schleuder *f* spin-drier. **W~trockner** *m* tumble-drier
Wasch|küche *f* laundry-room. **W~lappen** *m* face-flannel. **W~maschine** *f* washing machine. **W~mittel** *nt* detergent. **W~pulver** *nt* washing-powder. **W~zettel** *m* blurb
Wasser *nt* **-s** water. **W~ball** *m* beach-ball; (*Spiel*) water polo. **w~dicht** *a* watertight; <*Kleidung*> waterproof. **W~fall** *m* waterfall. **W~farbe** *f* water-colour. **W~hahn** *m* tap. **W~kraft** *f* water-power. **W~kraftwerk** *nt* hydroelectric power-station. **W~leitung** *f* water-main; **aus der W~leitung** from the tap. **W~mann** *m* (*Astr*) Aquarius
wässern *vt* soak; (*begießen*) water ●*vi* (*haben*) water
Wasser|ski *nt* **-s** water-skiing. **W~stoff** *m* hydrogen. **W~straße** *f* waterway. **W~waage** *f* spirit-level
wässrig *a* watery
watscheln *vi* (*sein*) waddle
Watt *nt* **-s,-** (*Phys*) watt
Watt|e *f* **-** cotton wool. **w~iert** *a* padded; (*gesteppt*) quilted
WC /ve'tse:/ *nt* **-s, -s** WC
web|en *vt/i* (*haben*) weave. **W~er** *m* **-s,-** weaver
Web|seite /'vɛp-/ *f* web page. **W~site** /-sait/ *f* **-, -s** website
Webstuhl *m* loom
Wechsel *m* **-s,-** change; (*Tausch*) exchange; (*Comm*) bill of exchange. **W~geld** *nt* change. **w~haft** *a* changeable. **W~jahre** *npl* menopause *sg*. **W~kurs** *m* exchange rate. **w~n** *vt* change; (*tauschen*) exchange ●*vi* (*haben*) change; vary. **w~nd** *a* changing; varying. **W~strom** *m* alternating current. **W~stube** *f* bureau de change
weck|en *vt* wake [up]; (*fig*) awaken ●*vi* (*haben*) <*Wecker:*> go off. **W~er** *m* **-s,-** alarm [clock]
wedeln *vi* (*haben*) wave; **mit dem Schwanz w~** wag its tail
weder *conj* **w~ ... noch** neither ... nor

Weg *m* **-[e]s, -e** way; (*Fuß-*) path; (*Fahr-*) track; (*Gang*) errand; **sich auf den Weg machen** set off

weg *adv* away, off; (*verschwunden*) gone; **weg sein** be away; (*gegangen/verschwunden*) have gone; **Hände weg!** hands off!

wegen *prep* (+ *gen*) because of, (*um ... willen*) for the sake of

weg|fahren† *vi sep* (*sein*) go away; (*abfahren*) leave. **W∼fahrsperre** *f* immobilizer. **w∼fallen**† *vi sep* (*sein*) be dropped/(*ausgelassen*) omitted; (*entfallen*) no longer apply. **w∼geben**† *vt sep* give away. **w∼gehen**† *vi sep* (*sein*) leave, go away; (*ausgehen*) go out. **w∼kommen**† *vi sep* (*sein*) get away; (*verloren gehen*) disappear; **schlecht w∼kommen** [!] get a raw deal. **w∼lassen**† *vt sep* let go; (*auslassen*) omit. **w∼laufen**† *vi sep* (*sein*) run away. **w∼räumen** *vt sep* put away; (*entfernen*) clear away. **w∼schicken** *vt sep* send away; (*abschicken*) send off. **w∼tun**† *vt sep* put away; (*wegwerfen*) throw away

Wegweiser *m* **-s,-** signpost

weg|werfen† *vt sep* throw away. **w∼ziehen**† *v sep* ● *vt* pull away ● *vi* (*sein*) move away

weh *a* sore; **weh tun** hurt; <*Kopf, Rücken:*> ache; **jdm weh tun** hurt s.o.

wehe *int* alas; **w∼ [dir/euch]!** (*drohend*) don't you dare!

wehen *vi* (*haben*) blow, (*flattern*) flutter ● *vt* blow

Wehen *fpl* contractions

Wehr[1] *nt* **-[e]s, -e** weir

Wehr[2] *f* **sich zur W∼ setzen** resist. **W∼dienst** *m* military service. **W∼dienstverweigerer** *m* **-s,-** conscientious objector

wehren (sich) *vr* resist; (*gegen Anschuldigung*) protest; (*sich sträuben*) refuse

wehr|los *a* defenceless. **W∼macht** *f* armed forces *pl*. **W∼pflicht** *f* conscription

Weib *nt* **-[e]s, -er** woman; (*Ehe-*) wife. **W∼chen** *nt* **-s,-** (*Zool*) female. **w∼lich** *a* feminine; (*Biol*) female

weich *a* soft; (*gar*) done

Weiche *f* **-, -n** (*Rail*) points *pl*

Weich|heit *f* **-** softness. **w∼lich** *a* soft; <*Charakter*> weak. **W∼spüler** *m* **-s,-** (*Tex*) conditioner. **W∼tier** *nt* mollusc

Weide[1] *f* **-, -n** (*Bot*) willow

Weide[2] *f* **-, -n** pasture. **w∼n** *vt/i* (*haben*) graze

weiger|n (sich) *vr* refuse. **W∼ung** *f* **-, -en** refusal

Weihe *f* **-, -n** consecration; (*Priester-*) ordination. **w∼n** *vt* consecrate; (*zum Priester*) ordain

Weiher *m* **-s,-** pond

Weihnacht|en *nt* **-s** & *pl* Christmas. **w∼lich** *a* Christmassy. **W∼sbaum** *m* Christmas tree. **W∼slied** *nt* Christmas carol. **W∼smann** *m* (*pl* **-männer**) Father Christmas. **W∼stag** *m* **erster/zweiter W∼stag** Christmas Day/Boxing Day

Weih|rauch *m* incense. **W∼wasser** *nt* holy water

weil *conj* because; (*da*) since

Weile *f* **-** while

Wein *m* **-[e]s, -e** wine; (*Bot*) vines *pl*; (*Trauben*) grapes *pl*. **W∼bau** *m* wine-growing. **W∼berg** *m* vineyard. **W∼brand** *m* **-[e]s** brandy

weinen *vt/i* (*haben*) cry, weep

Wein|glas *nt* wineglass. **W∼karte** *f* wine-list. **W∼lese** *f* grape harvest. **W∼liste** *f* wine-list. **W∼probe** *f* wine-tasting. **W∼rebe** *f*, **W∼stock** *m* vine. **W∼stube** *f* wine-bar. **W∼traube** *f* bunch of grapes; (*W∼beere*) grape

weise *a* wise

Weise *f* **-, -n** way; (*Melodie*) tune
Weisheit *f* **-, -en** wisdom. **W~szahn** *m* wisdom tooth
weiß *a*, **W~** *nt* **-,-** white
weissag|en *vt/i insep* (*haben*) prophesy. **W~ung** *f* **-, -en** prophecy
Weiß|brot *nt* white bread. **W~e(r)** *m/f* white man/woman. **w~en** *vt* whitewash. **W~wein** *m* white wine
Weisung *f* **-, -en** instruction; (*Befehl*) order
weit *a* wide; (*ausgedehnt*) extensive; (*lang*) long ● *adv* widely; <*offen, öffnen*> wide; (*lang*) far; **von w~em** from a distance; **bei w~em** by far; **w~ und breit** far and wide; **ist es noch w~?** is it much further? **so w~ wie möglich** as far as possible; **ich bin so w~** I'm ready; **w~ verbreitet** widespread; **w~ reichende Folgen** far-reaching consequences
Weite *f* **-, -n** expanse; (*Entfernung*) distance; (*Größe*) width. **w~n** *vt* widen; stretch <*Schuhe*>
weiter *a* further ● *adv* further; (*außerdem*) in addition; (*anschließend*) then; **etw w~ tun** go on doing sth; **w~ nichts/ niemand** nothing/no one else; **und so w~** and so on
weiter|e(r,s) *a* further; **ohne w~es** just like that; (*leicht*) easily
weiter|erzählen *vt sep* go on with; (*w~sagen*) repeat. **w~fahren**† *vi sep* (*sein*) go on. **w~geben**† *vt sep* pass on. **w~hin** *adv* (*immer noch*) still; (*in Zukunft*) in future; (*außerdem*) furthermore; **etw w~hin tun** go on doing sth. **w~machen** *vi sep* (*haben*) carry on
weit|gehend *a* extensive ● *adv* to a large extent. **w~sichtig** *a* long-sighted; (*fig*) far-sighted. **W~sprung** *m* long jump.
w~verbreitet* *a* **w~ verbreitet**, *s.* **weit**
Weizen *m* **-s** wheat
welch *inv pron* what; **w~ ein(e)** what a. **w~e(r,s)** *pron* which; **um w~e Zeit?** at what time? ● *rel pron* which; (*Person*) who ● *indef pron* some; (*fragend*) any; **was für w~e?** what sort of?
Wellblech *nt* corrugated iron
Well|e *f* **-, -n** wave; (*Techn*) shaft. **W~enlänge** *f* wavelength. **W~enlinie** *f* wavy line. **W~enreiten** *nt* surfing. **W~ensittich** *m* **-s, -e** budgerigar. **w~ig** *a* wavy
Welt *f* **-, -en** world; **auf der W~** in the world; **auf die** *od* **zur W~ kommen** be born. **W~all** *nt* universe. **w~berühmt** *a* world-famous. **w~fremd** *a* unworldly. **W~kugel** *f* globe. **w~lich** *a* worldly; (*nicht geistlich*) secular
Weltmeister|(in) *m*(*f*) world champion. **W~schaft** *f* world championship
Weltraum *m* space. **W~fahrer** *m* astronaut
Weltrekord *m* world record
wem *pron* (*dat of* **wer**) to whom
wen *pron* (*acc of* **wer**) whom
Wende *f* **-, -n** change. **W~kreis** *m* (*Geog*) tropic
Wendeltreppe *f* spiral staircase
wenden[1] *vt* (*reg*) turn ● *vi* (*haben*) turn [round]
wenden[2]† (*& reg*) *vt* turn; **sich w~** turn; **sich an jdn w~** turn/ (*schriftlich*) write to s.o.
Wend|epunkt *m* (*fig*) turning-point. **W~ung** *f* **-, -en** turn; (*Biegung*) bend; (*Veränderung*) change
wenig *pron* little; (*pl*) few; **so/zu w~** so/too little/(*pl*) few; **w~e** *pl* few ● *adv* little; (*kaum*) not much; **so w~ wie möglich** as little as possible. **w~er** *pron* less; (*pl*) fewer; **immer w~er** less and less

● *adv & conj* less. **w~ste(r,s)** least; **am w~sten** least [of all]. **w~stens** *adv* at least

wẹnn *conj* if; (*sobald*) when; **immer w~** whenever; **w~ nicht** *od* **außer w~** unless; **w~ auch** even though

wer *pron* who; (! *jemand*) someone; (*fragend*) anyone

Wẹrbe|agentur *f* advertising agency. **w~n**† *vt* recruit; attract <*Kunden, Besucher*> ● *vi* (*haben*) **w~n für** advertise; canvass for <*Partei*>. **W~spot** /-sp-/ *m* **-s, -s** commercial

Wẹrbung *f* **-** advertising

werden†

● *intransitive verb* (*sein*)

····➤ (+ *adjective*) become; get; (*allmählich*) grow. **müde/alt/länger werden** become *or* get/grow tired/old/longer. **taub/blind/wahnsinnig werden** go deaf/blind/mad. **blass werden** become *or* turn pale. **krank werden** become *or* fall ill. **es wird warm/dunkel** it is getting warm/dark. **mir wurde schlecht** I began to feel sick

····➤ (+ *noun*) become. **Arzt/Lehrer/Mutter werden** become a doctor/teacher/mother. **er will Lehrer werden** he wants to be a teacher. **was ist aus ihm geworden?** what has become of him?

····➤ **werden zu** become; turn into. **das Erlebnis wurde zu einem Albtraum** the experience became *or* turned into a nightmare. **zu Eis werden** turn into ice

● *auxiliary verb*

····➤ (*Zukunft*) will; shall. **er wird bald hier sein** he will *or* he'll soon be here. **wir werden sehen** we shall see. **es wird bald regnen** it's going to rain soon

····➤ (*Konjunktiv*) **würde(n)** would. **ich würde es kaufen, wenn ...** I would buy it if .... **würden Sie so nett sein?** would you be so kind?

····➤ (*beim Passiv; pp* **worden**) be. **geliebt/geboren werden** be loved/born. **du wirst gerufen** you are being called. **er wurde gebeten** he was asked. **es wurde gemunkelt** it was rumoured. **mir wurde gesagt, dass ...** I was told that .... **das Haus ist soeben/1995 renoviert worden** the house has just been renovated/was renovated in 1995

wẹrfen† *vt* throw; cast <*Blick, Schatten*>; **sich w~** <*Holz:*> warp

Wẹrft *f* **-, -en** shipyard

Wẹrk *nt* **-[e]s, -e** work; (*Fabrik*) works *sg*, factory; (*Trieb-*) mechanism. **W~en** *nt* **-s** (*Sch*) handicraft. **W~statt** *f* **-,¨en** workshop; (*Auto-*) garage. **W~tag** *m* weekday. **w~tags** *adv* on weekdays. **w~tätig** *a* working

Wẹrkzeug *nt* tool; (*coll*) tools *pl*. **W~leiste** *f* toolbar

Wermut *m* **-s** vermouth

wert *a* **viel w~** worth a lot; **nichts w~ sein** be worthless; **jds w~ sein** be worthy of s.o. **W~** *m* **-[e]s, -e** value; (*Nenn-*) denomination; **im W~ von** worth. **w~en** *vt* rate

Wert|gegenstand *m* object of value. **w~los** *a* worthless. **W~minderung** *f* depreciation. **W~papier** *nt* (*Comm*) security. **W~sachen** *fpl* valuables. **w~voll** *a* valuable

Wesen *nt* **-s,-** nature; (*Lebe-*) being; (*Mensch*) creature

wesentlich *a* essential; (*grundlegend*) fundamental ● *adv* considerably, much

weshạlb *adv* why

Wẹspe *f* **-, -n** wasp

wẹssen *pron* (*gen of* **wer**) whose

wẹstdeutsch *a* West German

Wẹste *f* **-, -n** waistcoat

Westen *m* **-s** west
Western *m* **-[s],-** western
Westfalen *nt* **-s** Westphalia
Westindien *nt* West Indies *pl*
west|lich *a* western; <*Richtung*> westerly ● *adv & prep* (+ *gen*) **w~lich [von] der Stadt** [to the] west of the town. **w~wärts** *adv* westwards
weswegen *adv* why
Wettbewerb *m* **-s, -e** competition
Wette *f* **-, -n** bet; **um die W~ laufen** race (**mit jdm** s.o.)
wetten *vt/i* (*haben*) bet (**auf** + *acc* on); **mit jdm w~** have a bet with s.o.
Wetter *nt* **-s,-** weather; (*Un-*) storm. **W~bericht** *m* weather report. **W~vorhersage** *f* weather forecast. **W~warte** *f* **-, -n** meteorological station
Wett|kampf *m* contest. **W~kämpfer(in)** *m(f)* competitor. **W~lauf** *m* race. **W~rennen** *nt* race. **W~streit** *m* contest
Whisky *m* **-s** whisky
wichtig *a* important; **w~ nehmen** take seriously. **W~keit** *f* **-** importance
Wicke *f* **-, -n** sweet pea
Wickel *m* **-s,-** compress
wickeln *vt* wind; (*ein-*) wrap; (*bandagieren*) bandage; **ein Kind frisch w~** change a baby
Widder *m* **-s,-** ram; (*Astr*) Aries
wider *prep* (+ *acc*) against; (*entgegen*) contrary to; **w~ Willen** against one's will
widerlegen *vt insep* refute
wider|lich *a* repulsive. **W~rede** *f* contradiction; **keine W~rede!** don't argue!
widerrufen† *vt/i insep* (*haben*) retract; revoke <*Befehl*>
Widersacher *m* **-s,-** adversary
widersetzen (sich) *vr insep* resist (**jdm/etw** s.o./sth)
widerspiegeln *vt sep* reflect
widersprechen† *vi insep* (*haben*) contradict (**jdm/etw** s.o./sth)
Wider|spruch *m* contradiction; (*Protest*) protest. **w~sprüchlich** *a* contradictory. **w~spruchslos** *adv* without protest
Widerstand *m* resistance; **W~ leisten** resist. **w~sfähig** *a* resistant; (*Bot*) hardy
widerstehen† *vi insep* (*haben*) resist (**jdm/etw** s.o/sth); (*anwidern*) be repugnant (**jdm** to s.o.)
Widerstreben *nt* **-s** reluctance
widerwärtig *a* disagreeable
Widerwill|e *m* aversion, repugnance. **w~ig** *a* reluctant
widm|en *vt* dedicate (*dat* to); (*verwenden*) devote (*dat* to); **sich w~en** (+ *dat*) devote oneself to. **W~ung** *f* **-, -en** dedication
wie *adv* how; **wie viel** how much/ (*pl*) many; **um wie viel Uhr?** at what time? **wie viele?** how many? **wie ist Ihr Name?** what is your name? **wie ist das Wetter?** what is the weather like? ● *conj* as; (*gleich wie*) like; (*sowie*) as well as; (*als*) when, as; **so gut wie** as good as; **nichts wie** nothing but
wieder *adv* again; **jdn/etw w~ erkennen** recognize s.o./sth; **etw w~ verwenden/verwerten** reuse/ recycle sth; **etw w~ gutmachen** make up for <*Schaden*>; redress <*Unrecht*>; (*bezahlen*) pay for sth
Wiederaufbau *m* reconstruction
wieder|bekommen† *vt sep* get back. **W~belebung** *f* **-** resuscitation. **w~bringen**† *vt sep* bring back. **w~erkennen*** *vt sep* **w~ erkennen,** *s.* **wieder**. **w~geben**† *vt sep* give back, return; (*darstellen*) portray; (*ausdrücken, übersetzen*) render; (*zitieren*) quote. **W~geburt** *f* reincarnation

Wiedergutmachung *f* **-** reparation; (*Entschädigung*) compensation

wiederherstellen *vt sep* re-establish; restore <*Gebäude*>; restore to health <*Kranke*>

wiederhol|en *vt insep* repeat; (*Sch*) revise; **sich w~en** recur; <*Person:*> repeat oneself. **w~t** *a* repeated. **W~ung** *f* **-, -en** repetition; (*Sch*) revision

Wieder|hören *nt* **auf W~hören!** goodbye! **W~käuer** *m* **-s,-** ruminant. **W~kehr** *f* **-** return; (*W~holung*) recurrence. **w~kommen**† *vi sep* (*sein*) come back

wiedersehen* *vt sep* **wieder sehen**, *s.* **sehen**. **W~** *nt* **-s,-** reunion; **auf W~!** goodbye!

wiedervereinig|en* *vt sep* **wieder vereinigen**, *s.* **vereinigen**. **W~ung** *f* reunification

wieder|verwenden* *vt sep* **w~ verwenden**, *s.* **wieder**. **w~verwerten*** *vt sep* **w~ verwerten**, *s.* **wieder**

Wiege *f* **-, -n** cradle

wiegen¹† *vt/i* (*haben*) weigh

wiegen² *vt* (*reg*) rock. **W~lied** *nt* lullaby

wiehern *vi* (*haben*) neigh

Wien *nt* **-s** Vienna. **W~er** *a* Viennese ● *m* **-s,-** Viennese ● *f* **-,-** ≈ frankfurter. **w~erisch** *a* Viennese

Wiese *f* **-, -n** meadow

Wiesel *nt* **-s,-** weasel

wieso *adv* why

wieviel* *pron* **wie viel**, *s.* **wie**. **w~te(r,s)** *a* which; **der W~te ist heute?** what is the date today?

wieweit *adv* how far

wild *a* wild; <*Stamm*> savage; **w~er Streik** wildcat strike; **w~ wachsen** grow wild. **W~** *nt* **-[e]s** game; (*Rot-*) deer; (*Culin*) venison. **W~e(r)** *m/f* savage

Wilder|er *m* **-s,-** poacher. **w~n** *vt/i* (*haben*) poach

Wild|heger, W~hüter *m* **-s,-** gamekeeper. **W~leder** *nt* suede. **W~nis** *f* **-** wilderness. **W~schwein** *nt* wild boar. **W~westfilm** *m* western

Wille *m* **-ns** will

Willenskraft *f* will-power

willig *a* willing

willkommen *a* welcome; **w~ heißen** welcome. **W~** *nt* **-s** welcome

wimmeln *vi* (*haben*) swarm

wimmern *vi* (*haben*) whimper

Wimpel *m* **-s,-** pennant

Wimper *f* **-, -n** [eye]lash; **W~ntusche** *f* mascara

Wind *m* **-[e]s, -e** wind

Winde *f* **-, -n** (*Techn*) winch

Windel *f* **-, -n** nappy

winden† *vt* wind; make <*Kranz*>, **in die Höhe w~** winch up; **sich w~** wind; (*sich krümmen*) writhe

Wind|hund *m* greyhound. **w~ig** *a* windy. **W~mühle** *f* windmill. **W~park** *m* wind farm. **W~pocken** *fpl* chickenpox *sg*. **W~schutzscheibe** *f* windscreen. **W~stille** *f* calm. **W~stoß** *m* gust of wind. **W~surfen** *nt* windsurfing

Windung *f* **-, -en** bend; (*Spirale*) spiral

Winkel *m* **-s,-** angle; (*Ecke*) corner. **W~messer** *m* **-s,-** protractor

winken *vi* (*haben*) wave

Winter *m* **-s,-** winter. **w~lich** *a* wintry; (*Winter-*) winter ... **W~schlaf** *m* hibernation; **W~sport** *m* winter sports *pl*

Winzer *m* **-s,-** winegrower

winzig *a* tiny, minute

Wipfel *m* **-s,-** [tree-]top

Wippe *f* **-, -n** see-saw

wir *pron* we; **wir sind es** it's us

Wirbel *m* **-s,-** eddy; (*Drehung*) whirl; (*Trommel-*) roll; (*Anat*) vertebra; (*Haar-*) crown; (*Aufsehen*) fuss. **w~n** *vt/i* (*sein/haben*) whirl. **W~säule** *f* spine. **W~sturm** *m* cyclone. **W~tier** *nt* vertebrate. **W~wind** *m* whirlwind

wird *s.* **werden**

wirken *vi* (*haben*) have an effect (**auf** + *acc* on); (*zur Geltung kommen*) be effective; (*tätig sein*) work; (*scheinen*) seem ● *vt* (*Tex*) knit

wirklich *a* real. **W~keit** *f* **-, -en** reality

wirksam *a* effective

Wirkung *f* **-, -en** effect. **w~slos** *a* ineffective. **w~svoll** *a* effective

wirr *a* tangled; <*Haar*> tousled; (*verwirrt, verworren*) confused

Wirt *m* **-[e]s, -e** landlord. **W~in** *f* **-, -nen** landlady

Wirtschaft *f* **-, -en** economy; (*Gast-*) restaurant; (*Kneipe*) pub. **w~en** *vi* (*haben*) manage one's finances. **w~lich** *a* economic; (*sparsam*) economical. **W~sgeld** *nt* housekeeping [money]. **W~sprüfer** *m* auditor

Wirtshaus *nt* inn; (*Kneipe*) pub

wischen *vt/i* (*haben*) wipe; wash <*Fußboden*>

wissen† *vt/i* (*haben*) know; **weißt du noch?** do you remember? **nichts w~ wollen von** not want anything to do with. **W~** *nt* **-s** knowledge; **meines W~s** to my knowledge

Wissenschaft *f* **-, -en** science. **W~ler** *m* **-s,-** academic; (*Natur-*) scientist. **w~lich** *a* academic; scientific

wissenswert *a* worth knowing

witter|n *vt* scent; (*ahnen*) sense. **W~ung** *f* **-** scent; (*Wetter*) weather

Witwe *f* **-, -n** widow. **W~r** *m* **-s,-** widower

Witz *m* **-es, -e** joke; (*Geist*) wit. **W~bold** *m* **-[e]s, -e** joker. **w~ig** *a* funny; witty

wo *adv* where; (*als*) when; (*irgendwo*) somewhere; **wo immer** wherever ● *conj* seeing that; (*obwohl*) although; (*wenn*) if

woanders *adv* somewhere else

wobei *adv* how; (*relativ*) during the course of which

Woche *f* **-, -n** week. **W~nende** *nt* weekend. **W~nkarte** *f* weekly ticket. **w~nlang** *adv* for weeks. **W~ntag** *m* day of the week; (*Werktag*) weekday. **w~tags** *adv* on weekdays

wöchentlich *a & adv* weekly

Wodka *m* **-s** vodka

wofür *adv* what ... for; (*relativ*) for which

Woge *f* **-, -n** wave

woher *adv* where from; **woher weißt du das?** how do you know that? **wohin** *adv* where [to]; **wohin gehst du?** where are you going?

wohl *adv* well; (*vermutlich*) probably; (*etwa*) about; (*zwar*) perhaps; **w~ kaum** hardly; **sich w~ fühlen** feel well/(*behaglich*) comfortable; **jdm w~ tun** do s.o. good. **W~** *nt* **-[e]s** welfare, well-being; **zum W~** (+ *gen*) for the good of; **zum W~!** cheers!

Wohl|befinden *nt* well-being. **W~behagen** *nt* feeling of well-being. **W~ergehen** *nt* **-s** welfare. **w~erzogen** *a* well brought-up

Wohlfahrt *f* **-** welfare. **W~sstaat** *m* Welfare State

wohl|habend *a* prosperous, well-to-do. **w~ig** *a* comfortable. **w~schmeckend** *a* tasty

Wohlstand *m* prosperity. **W~sgesellschaft** *f* affluent society

Wohltat *f* [act of] kindness; (*Annehmlichkeit*) treat; (*Genuss*) bliss

Wohltät|er *m* benefactor. **w~ig** *a* charitable

wohl|tuend *a* agreeable. **w~tun*** *vi sep* (*haben*) **w~ tun**, *s.* **wohl**

Wohlwollen *nt* **-s** goodwill; (*Gunst*) favour. **w~d** *a* benevolent

Wohn|block *m* block of flats. **w~en** *vi* (*haben*) live; (*vorübergehend*) stay. **W~gegend** *f* residential area. **w~haft** *a* resident. **W~haus** *nt* house. **W~heim** *nt* hostel; (*Alten-*) home. **w~lich** *a* comfortable. **W~mobil** *nt* **-s, -e** camper. **W~ort** *m* place of residence. **W~sitz** *m* place of residence

Wohnung *f* **-, -en** flat; (*Unterkunft*) accommodation. **W~snot** *f* housing shortage

Wohn|wagen *m* caravan. **W~zimmer** *nt* living-room

wölb|en *vt* curve; arch <*Rücken*>. **W~ung** *f* **-, -en** curve; (*Archit*) vault

Wolf *m* **-[e]s,¨e** wolf; (*Fleisch-*) mincer; (*Reiß-*) shredder

Wolk|e *f* **-, -n** cloud. **W~enbruch** *m* cloudburst. **W~enkratzer** *m* skyscraper. **w~enlos** *a* cloudless. **w~ig** *a* cloudy

Woll|decke *f* blanket. **W~e** *f* **-, -n** wool

wollen†¹

● *auxiliary verb*

····➤ (*den Wunsch haben*) want to. **ich will nach Hause gehen** I want to go home. **ich wollte Sie fragen, ob ...** I wanted to ask you if ...

····➤ (*im Begriff sein*) be about to. **wir wollten gerade gehen** we were just about to go

····➤ (*sich in der gewünschten Weise verhalten*) **will nicht** refuses to. **der Motor will nicht anspringen** the engine won't *or* refuses to start

● *intransitive verb*

····➤ want to. **ob du willst oder nicht** whether you want to or not. **ganz wie du willst** just as you like

····➤ ([!] *irgendwohin zu gehen wünschen*) **ich will nach Hause** I want to go home. **zu wem wollen Sie?** who[m] do you want to see?

····➤ ([!] *funktionieren*) **will nicht** won't go. **meine Beine wollen nicht mehr** my legs are giving up [!]

● *transitive verb*

····➤ want; (*beabsichtigen*) intend. **er will nicht, dass du ihm hilfst** he does not want you to help him. **das habe ich nicht gewollt** I never intended *or* meant that to happen

wollen² *a* woollen. **w~ig** *a* woolly. **W~sachen** *fpl* woollens.

womit *adv* what ... with; (*relativ*) with which. **wonach** *adv* what ... after/<*suchen*> for/<*riechen*> of; (*relativ*) after/for/of which

woran *adv* what ... on/<*denken, sterben*> of; (*relativ*) on/of which; **woran hast du ihn erkannt?** how did you recognize him? **worauf** *adv* what ... on/<*warten*> for; (*relativ*) on/for which; (*woraufhin*) whereupon. **woraus** *adv* what ... from; (*relativ*) from which

Wort *nt* **-[e]s,¨er & -e** word; **jdm ins W~ fallen** interrupt s.o.

Wörterbuch *nt* dictionary

Wort|führer *m* spokesman. **w~getreu** *a & adv* word-for-word. **w~karg** *a* taciturn. **W~laut** *m* wording

wörtlich *a* literal, (*wortgetreu*) word-for-word

wort|los *a* silent ● *adv* without a word. **W~schatz** *m* vocabulary. **W~spiel** *nt* pun, play on words

worüber *adv* what ... over/<*lachen, sprechen*> about; (*relativ*) over/

about which. **worum** *adv* what … round/<*bitten, kämpfen*> for; (*relativ*) round/for which; **worum geht es?** what is it about? **wovon** *adv* what … from/<*sprechen*> about; (*relativ*) from/about which. **wovor** *adv* what … in front of; <*sich fürchten*> what … of; (*relativ*) in front of which; of which. **wozu** *adv* what … to/ <*brauchen, benutzen*> for; (*relativ*) to/for which; **wozu?** what for?

Wrack *nt* **-s, -s** wreck

wringen† *vt* wring

Wucher|preis *m* extortionate price. **W~ung** *f* **-, -en** growth

Wuchs *m* **-es** growth; (*Gestalt*) stature

Wucht *f* **-** force

wühlen *vi* (*haben*) rummage; (*in der Erde*) burrow ● *vt* dig

Wulst *m* **-[e]s,⸚e** bulge; (*Fett-*) roll

wund *a* sore; **w~ reiben** chafe; **sich w~ liegen** get bedsores. **W~brand** *m* gangrene

Wunde *f* **-, -n** wound

Wunder *nt* **-s,-** wonder, marvel; (*übernatürliches*) miracle; **kein W~!** no wonder! **w~bar** *a* miraculous; (*herrlich*) wonderful. **W~kind** *nt* infant prodigy. **w~n** *vt* surprise; **sich w~n** be surprised (**über** + *acc* at). **w~schön** *a* beautiful

Wundstarrkrampf *m* tetanus

Wunsch *m* **-[e]s,⸚e** wish; (*Verlangen*) desire; (*Bitte*) request

wünschen *vt* want; **sich** (*dat*) **etw w~** want sth; (*bitten um*) ask for sth; **jdm Glück/gute Nacht w~** wish s.o. luck/good night; **Sie w~?** can I help you? **w~swert** *a* desirable

Wunschkonzert *nt* musical request programme

wurde, würde *s.* **werden**

Würde *f* **-, -n** dignity; (*Ehrenrang*) honour. **w~los** *a* undignified. **W~nträger** *m* dignitary. **w~voll** *a* dignified ● *adv* with dignity

würdig *a* dignified; (*wert*) worthy

Wurf *m* **-[e]s,⸚e** throw; (*Junge*) litter

Würfel *m* **-s,-** cube; (*Spiel-*) dice; (*Zucker-*) lump. **w~n** *vi* (*haben*) throw the dice; **w~n um** play dice for ● *vt* throw; (*in Würfel schneiden*) dice. **W~zucker** *m* cube sugar

würgen *vt* choke ● *vi* (*haben*) retch; choke (**an** + *dat* on)

Wurm *m* **-[e]s,⸚er** worm; (*Made*) maggot. **w~en** *vi* (*haben*) **jdn w~en** [!] rankle [with s.o.]

Wurst *f* **-,⸚e** sausage; **das ist mir W~** [!] I couldn't care less

Würze *f* **-, -n** spice; (*Aroma*) aroma

Wurzel *f* **-, -n** root; **W~n schlagen** take root. **w~n** *vi* (*haben*) root

würz|en *vt* season. **w~ig** *a* tasty; (*aromatisch*) aromatic; (*pikant*) spicy

wüst *a* chaotic; (*wirr*) tangled; (*öde*) desolate; (*wild*) wild; (*schlimm*) terrible

Wüste *f* **-, -n** desert

Wut *f* **-** rage, fury. **W~anfall** *m* fit of rage

wüten *vi* (*haben*) rage. **w~d** *a* furious; **w~d machen** infuriate

Xx

x /ɪks/ *inv a* (*Math*) x; [!] umpteen. **X-Beine** *ntpl* knock-knees. **x-beinig, X-beinig** *a* knock-kneed. **x-beliebig** *a* [!] any. **x-mal** *adv* [!] umpteen times

Yy

Yoga /ˈjo:ga/ *m & nt* **-[s]** yoga

Zz

Zack|e *f* **-, -n** point; (*Berg-*) peak; (*Gabel-*) prong. **z~ig** *a* jagged; (*gezackt*) serrated

zaghaft *a* timid; (*zögernd*) tentative

zäh *a* tough; (*hartnäckig*) tenacious. **z~flüssig** *a* viscous; <*Verkehr*> slow-moving. **Z~igkeit** *f* **-** toughness; tenacity

Zahl *f* **-, -en** number; (*Ziffer, Betrag*) figure

zahlen *vt/i* (*haben*) pay; (*bezahlen*) pay for; **bitte z~!** the bill please!

zählen *vi* (*haben*) count; **z~ zu** (*fig*) be one/(*pl*) some of ● *vt* count; **z~ zu** add to; (*fig*) count among

zahlenmäßig *a* numerical

Zähler *m* **-s,-** meter

Zahl|grenze *f* fare-stage. **Z~karte** *f* paying-in slip. **z~los** *a* countless. **z~reich** *a* numerous; <*Anzahl, Gruppe*> large ● *adv* in large numbers. **Z~ung** *f* **-, -en** payment; **in Z~ung nehmen** take in part-exchange

Zählung *f* **-, -en** count

Zahlwort *nt* (*pl* **-wörter**) numeral

zahm *a* tame

zähmen *vt* tame; (*fig*) restrain

Zahn *m* **-[e]s,¨e** tooth; (*am Zahnrad*) cog. **Z~arzt** *m*, **Z~ärztin** *f* dentist. **Z~belag** *m* plaque. **Z~bürste** *f* toothbrush. **Z~fleisch** *nt* gums *pl*. **z~los** *a* toothless. **Z~pasta** *f* **-, -en** toothpaste. **Z~rad** *nt* cog-wheel. **Z~schmelz** *m* enamel. **Z~schmerzen** *mpl* toothache *sg*. **Z~spange** *f* brace. **Z~stein** *m* tartar. **Z~stocher** *m* **-s,-** toothpick

Zange *f* **-, -n** pliers *pl*; (*Kneif-*) pincers *pl*; (*Kohlen-, Zucker-*) tongs *pl*; (*Geburts-*) forceps *pl*

Zank *m* **-[e]s** squabble. **z~en** *vr* **sich z~en** squabble

Zäpfchen *nt* **-s,-** (*Anat*) uvula; (*Med*) suppository

zapfen *vt* tap, draw. **Z~streich** *m* (*Mil*) tattoo

Zapf|hahn *m* tap. **Z~säule** *f* petrol-pump

zappeln *vi* (*haben*) wriggle; <*Kind:*> fidget

zart *a* delicate; (*weich, zärtlich*) tender; (*sanft*) gentle. **Z~gefühl** *nt* tact

zärtlich *a* tender; (*liebevoll*) loving. **Z~keit** *f* **-, -en** tenderness; (*Liebkosung*) caress

Zauber *m* **-s** magic; (*Bann*) spell. **Z~er** *m* **-s,-** magician. **z~haft** *a* enchanting. **Z~künstler** *m* conjuror. **z~n** *vi* (*haben*) do magic; (*Zaubertricks ausführen*) do conjuring tricks ● *vt* produce as if by magic. **Z~stab** *m* magic wand. **Z~trick** *m* conjuring trick

Zaum *m* **-[e]s,Zäume** bridle

Zaun *m* **-[e]s,Zäune** fence

z.B. *abbr* (**zum Beispiel**) e.g.

Zebra *nt* **-s, -s** zebra. **Z~streifen** *m* zebra crossing

Zeche *f* **-, -n** bill; (*Bergwerk*) pit

zechen *vi* (*haben*) [!] drink

Zeder *f* **-, -n** cedar

Zeh *m* **-[e]s, -en** toe. **Z~e** *f* **-, -n** toe; (*Knoblauch-*) clove

zehn *inv a*, **Z~** *f* **-, -en** ten. **z~te(r,s)** *a* tenth. **Z~tel** *nt* **-s,-** tenth

Zeichen *nt* **-s,-** sign; (*Signal*) signal. **Z~setzung** *f* **-** punctuation. **Z~trickfilm** *m* cartoon

zeichn|en *vt/i* (*haben*) draw; (*kenn-*) mark; (*unter-*) sign. **Z~ung** *f* **-, -en** drawing

Zeige|finger *m* index finger. **z~n** *vt* show; **sich z~n** appear; (*sich herausstellen*) become clear ● *vi* (*haben*) point (**auf** + *acc* to). **Z~r** *m* **-s,-** pointer; (*Uhr-*) hand

Zeile *f* **-, -n** line; (*Reihe*) row

Zeit *f* **-, -en** time; **sich** (*dat*) **Z~ lassen** take one's time; **es hat Z~** theres's no hurry; **mit der Z~** in time; **in nächster Z~** in the near future; **zur Z~** (*rechtzeitig*) in time; *(*derzeit*) *s.* **zurzeit**; **eine Z~ lang** for a time *or* while

Zeit|alter *nt* age, era. **z~gemäß** *a* modern, up-to-date. **Z~genosse** *m*, **Z~genossin** *f* contemporary. **z~genössisch** *a* contemporary. **z~ig** *a & adv* early

zeitlich *a* <*Dauer*> in time; <*Folge*> chronological. ● *adv* **z~ begrenzt** for a limited time

zeit|los *a* timeless. **Z~lupe** *f* slow motion. **Z~punkt** *m* time. **z~raubend** *a* time-consuming. **Z~raum** *m* period. **Z~schrift** *f* magazine, periodical

Zeitung *f* **-, -en** newspaper. **Z~spapier** *nt* newspaper

Zeit|verschwendung *f* waste of time. **Z~vertreib** *m* pastime. **z~weise** *adv* at times. **Z~wort** *nt* (*pl* **-wörter**) verb. **Z~zünder** *m* time fuse

Zelle *f* **-, -n** cell; (*Telefon-*) box

Zelt *nt* **-[e]s, -e** tent; (*Fest-*) marquee. **z~en** *vi* (*haben*) camp. **Z~en** *nt* **-s** camping. **Z~plane** *f* tarpaulin. **Z~platz** *m* campsite

Zement *m* **-[e]s** cement

zen|sieren *vt* (*Sch*) mark; censor <*Presse, Film*>. **Z~sur** *f* **-, -en** (*Sch*) mark; (*Presse-*) censorship

Zentimeter *m & nt* centimetre. **Z~maß** *nt* tape-measure

Zentner *m* **-s,-** [metric] hundredweight (*50 kg*)

zentral *a* central. **Z~e** *f* **-, -n** central office; (*Partei-*) headquarters *pl*; (*Teleph*) exchange. **Z~heizung** *f* central heating

Zentrum *nt* **-s, -tren** centre

zerbrech|en† *vt/i* (*sein*) break. **z~lich** *a* fragile

zerdrücken *vt* crush

Zeremonie *f* **-, -n** ceremony

Zerfall *m* disintegration; (*Verfall*) decay. **z~en**† *vi* (*sein*) disintegrate; (*verfallen*) decay

zergehen† *vi* (*sein*) melt; (*sich auflösen*) dissolve

zerkleinern *vt* chop/(*schneiden*) cut up; (*mahlen*) grind

zerknüllen *vt* crumple [up]

zerkratzen *vt* scratch

zerlassen† *vt* melt

zerlegen *vt* take to pieces, dismantle; (*zerschneiden*) cut up; (*tranchieren*) carve

zerlumpt *a* ragged

zermalmen *vt* crush

zermürben *vt* (*fig*) wear down

zerplatzen *vi* (*sein*) burst

zerquetschen *vt* squash; crush

Zerrbild *nt* caricature

zerreißen† *vt* tear; (*in Stücke*) tear up; break <*Faden, Seil*> ● *vi* (*sein*) tear; break

zerren *vt* drag; pull <*Muskel*> ● *vi* (*haben*) pull (**an** + *dat* at)

zerrissen *a* torn

zerrütten *vt* ruin, wreck; shatter <*Nerven*>

zerschlagen† *vt* smash; smash up <*Möbel*>; **sich z~** (*fig*) fall through; <*Hoffnung:*> be dashed

zerschmettern *vt/i* (*sein*) smash

zerschneiden† *vt* cut; (*in Stücke*) cut up

zersplittern *vi* (*sein*) splinter; <*Glas:*> shatter ● *vt* shatter

zerspringen† *vi* (*sein*) shatter; (*bersten*) burst

Zerstäuber *m* **-s,-** atomizer

zerstör|en *vt* destroy; (*zunichte machen*) wreck. **Z~er** *m* **-s,-** destroyer. **Z~ung** *f* destruction

zerstreu|en *vt* scatter; disperse <*Menge*>; dispel <*Zweifel*>; **sich z~en** disperse; (*sich unterhalten*) amuse oneself. **z~t** *a* absent-minded

Zertifikat *nt* **-[e]s, -e** certificate

zertrümmern *vt* smash [up]; wreck <*Gebäude, Stadt*>

Zettel *m* **-s,-** piece of paper; (*Notiz*) note; (*Bekanntmachung*) notice

Zeug *nt* **-s** [!] stuff; (*Sachen*) things *pl*; (*Ausrüstung*) gear; **dummes Z~** nonsense

Zeuge *m* **-n, -n** witness. **z~n** *vi* (*haben*) testify; **z~n von** (*fig*) show ● *vt* father. **Z~naussage** *f* testimony. **Z~nstand** *m* witness box

Zeugin *f* **-, -nen** witness

Zeugnis *nt* **-ses, -se** certificate; (*Sch*) report; (*Referenz*) reference; (*fig: Beweis*) evidence

Zickzack *m* **-[e]s, -e** zigzag

Ziege *f* **-, -n** goat

Ziegel *m* **-s,-** brick; (*Dach-*) tile. **Z~stein** *m* brick

ziehen† *vt* pull; (*sanfter; zücken; zeichnen*) draw; (*heraus-*) pull out; extract <*Zahn*>; raise <*Hut*>, put on <*Bremse*>; move <*Schachfigur*>, (*dehnen*) stretch; make <*Grimasse, Scheitel*>; (*züchten*) breed; grow <*Rosen*>; **nach sich z~** (*fig*) entail ● *vr* **sich z~** (*sich erstrecken*) run; (*sich verziehen*) warp ● *vi* (*haben*) pull (**an** + *dat* on/at); <*Tee, Ofen:*> draw; (*Culin*) simmer; **es zieht** there is a draught; **solche Filme z~ nicht mehr** films like that are no longer popular ● *vi* (*sein*) (*um-*) move (**nach** to); <*Menge:*> march; <*Vögel:*> migrate; <*Wolken, Nebel:*> drift

Ziehharmonika *f* accordion

Ziehung *f* **-, -en** draw

Ziel *nt* **-[e]s, -e** destination; (*Sport*) finish; (*Z~scheibe & Mil*) target; (*Zweck*) aim, goal. **z~bewusst** *a* purposeful. **z~en** *vi* (*haben*) aim (**auf** + *acc* at). **z~los** *a* aimless. **Z~scheibe** *f* target

ziemlich *a* [!] fair ● *adv* rather, fairly

Zier|de *f* **-, -n** ornament. **z~en** *vt* adorn

zierlich *a* dainty

Ziffer *f* **-, -n** figure, digit; (*Zahlzeichen*) numeral. **Z~blatt** *nt* dial

Zigarette *f* **-, -n** cigarette

Zigarre *f* **-, -n** cigar

Zigeuner(in) *m* **-s,-** (*f* **-, -nen**) gypsy

Zimmer *nt* **-s,-** room. **Z~mädchen** *nt* chambermaid. **Z~mann** *m* (*pl* **-leute**) carpenter. **Z~nachweis** *m* accommodation bureau. **Z~pflanze** *f* house plant

Zimt *m* **-[e]s** cinnamon

Zink *nt* **-s** zinc

Zinn *m* **-s** tin; (*Gefäße*) pewter

Zins|en *mpl* interest *sg*; **Z~en tragen** earn interest. **Z~eszins** *m* **-es, -en** compound interest. **Z~fuß, Z~satz** *m* interest rate

Zipfel *m* **-s,-** corner; (*Spitze*) point

zirka *adv* about

Zirkel *m* **-s,-** [pair of] compasses *pl*; (*Gruppe*) circle

Zirkul|ation /-ˈtsi̯o:n/ *f* - circulation. **z~ieren** *vi* (*sein*) circulate

Zirkus *m* **-, -se** circus

zirpen *vi* (*haben*) chirp

zischen *vi* (*haben*) hiss; <*Fett:*> sizzle ● *vt* hiss

Zit|at *nt* **-[e]s, -e** quotation. **z~ieren** *vt/i* (*haben*) quote

Zitr|onat *nt* **-[e]s** candied lemon-peel. **Z~one** *f* **-, -n** lemon

zittern *vi* (*haben*) tremble; (*vor Kälte*) shiver; (*beben*) shake

zittrig *a* shaky

Zitze *f* **-, -n** teat

zivil *a* civilian; <*Ehe, Recht*> civil. **Z~** *nt* **-s** civilian clothes *pl*. **Z~dienst** *m* community service

Zivili|sation /-'tsio:n/ *f* **-, -en** civilization. **z~sieren** *vt* civilize. **z~siert** *a* civilized ● *adv* in a civilized manner

Zivilist *m* **-en, -en** civilian

zögern *vi* (*haben*) hesitate. **Z~** *nt* **-s** hesitation. **z~d** *a* hesitant

Zoll[1] *m* **-[e]s,-** inch

Zoll[2] *m* **-[e]s,¨-e** [customs] duty; (*Behörde*) customs *pl*. **Z~abfertigung** *f* customs clearance. **Z~beamte(r)** *m* customs officer. **z~frei** *a & adv* duty-free. **Z~kontrolle** *f* customs check

Zone *f* **-, -n** zone

Zoo *m* **-s, -s** zoo

zoologisch *a* zoological

Zopf *m* **-[e]s,¨-e** plait

Zorn *m* **-[e]s** anger. **z~ig** *a* angry

---

zu

● *preposition (+ dative)*

> **!** Note that **zu dem** can become **zum** and **zu der zur**

····➤ (*Richtung*) to; (*bei Beruf*) into. **wir gehen zur Schule** we are going to school. **ich muss zum Arzt** I must go to the doctor's. **zu ... hin** towards. **er geht zum Theater/Militär** he is going into the theatre/army

····➤ (*zusammen mit*) with. **zu dem Käse gab es Wein** there was wine with the cheese. **zu etw passen** go with sth

····➤ (*räumlich; zeitlich*) at. **zu Hause** at home. **zu ihren Füßen** at her feet. **zu Ostern** at Easter. **zur Zeit** (+ *gen*) at the time of

····➤ (*preislich*) at; for. **zum halben Preis** at half price. **das Stück zu zwei Euro** at *or* for two euros each. **eine Marke zu 60 Cent** a 60-cent stamp

····➤ (*Zweck, Anlass*) for. **zu diesem Zweck** for this purpose. **zum Spaß** for fun. **zum Lesen** for reading. **zum Geburtstag bekam ich ...** for my birthday I got .... **zum ersten Mal** for the first time

····➤ (*Art und Weise*) **zu meinem Erstaunen/Entsetzen** to my surprise/horror. **zu Fuß/Pferde** on foot/horseback. **zu Dutzenden** by the dozen. **wir waren zu dritt/viert** there were three/four of us

····➤ (*Zahlenverhältnis*) to. **es steht 5 zu 3** the score is 5–3

····➤ (*Ziel, Ergebnis*) into. **zu etw werden** turn into sth

····➤ (*gegenüber*) to; towards. **freundlich/hässlich zu jdm sein** be friendly/nasty to s.o.

····➤ (*über*) on; about. **sich zu etw äußern** to comment on sth

● *adverb*

····➤ (*allzu*) too. **zu groß/viel/weit** too big/much/far

····➤ (*Richtung*) towards. **nach dem Fluss zu** towards the river

····➤ (*geschlossen*) closed; (*an Schalter, Hahn*) off. **zu sein** be closed. **Augen zu!** close your eyes! **Tür zu!** shut the door!

● *conjunction*

····➤ to. **etwas zu essen** something to eat. **nicht zu glauben** unbelievable. **zu erörternde Probleme** problems to be discussed

---

zualler|erst *adv* first of all. **z~letzt** *adv* last of all

Zubehör *nt* **-s** accessories *pl*

zubereit|en *vt sep* prepare. **Z~ung** *f* **-** preparation; (*in Rezept*) method

zubinden† *vt sep* tie [up]

zubring|en† *vt sep* spend. **Z~er** *m* **-s,-** access road; (*Bus*) shuttle

Zucchini /tsu'ki:ni/ *pl* courgettes

Zucht *f* **-, -en** breeding; (*Pflanzen-*) cultivation; (*Art, Rasse*) breed; (*von Pflanzen*) strain; (*Z~farm*) farm; (*Pferde-*) stud

zücht|en *vt* breed; cultivate, grow <*Rosen*>. **Z~er** *m* **-s,-** breeder; grower

Zuchthaus *nt* prison

Züchtung *f* **-, -en** breeding; (*Pflanzen-*) cultivation; (*Art, Rasse*) breed; (*von Pflanzen*) strain

zucken *vi* (*haben*) twitch; (*sich z~d bewegen*) jerk; <*Blitz:*> flash; <*Flamme:*> flicker ● *vt* **die Achseln z~** shrug one's shoulders

Zucker *m* **-s** sugar. **Z~dose** *f* sugar basin. **Z~guss** *m* icing. **z~krank** *a* diabetic. **Z~krankheit** *f* diabetes. **z~n** *vt* sugar. **Z~rohr** *nt* sugar cane. **Z~rübe** *f* sugar beet. **Z~watte** *f* candyfloss

zudecken *vt sep* cover up; (*im Bett*) tuck up; cover <*Topf*>

zudem *adv* moreover

zudrehen *vt sep* turn off

zueinander *adv* to one another; **z~ passen** go together; **z~ halten** (*fig*) stick together

zuerkennen† *vt sep* award (*dat* to)

zuerst *adv* first; (*anfangs*) at first

zufahr|en† *vi sep* (*sein*) **z~en auf** (+ *acc*) drive towards. **Z~t** *f* access; (*Einfahrt*) drive

Zufall *m* chance; (*Zusammentreffen*) coincidence; **durch Z~** by chance/coincidence. **z~en**† *vi sep* (*sein*) close, shut; **jdm z~en** <*Aufgabe:*> fall/<*Erbe:*> go to s.o.

zufällig *a* chance, accidental ● *adv* by chance

Zuflucht *f* refuge; (*Schutz*) shelter

zufolge *prep* (+ *dat*) according to

zufrieden *a* contented; (*befriedigt*) satisfied; **sich z~ geben** be satisfied; **jdn z~ lassen** leave s.o. in peace; **jdn z~ stellen** satisfy s.o.; **z~ stellend** satisfactory. **Z~heit** *f* **-** contentment; satisfaction

zufrieren† *vi sep* (*sein*) freeze over

zufügen *vt sep* inflict (*dat* on); do <*Unrecht*> (*dat* to)

Zufuhr *f* **-** supply

Zug *m* **-[e]s,¨e** train; (*Kolonne*) column; (*Um-*) procession; (*Mil*) platoon; (*Vogelschar*) flock; (*Ziehen, Zugkraft*) pull; (*Wandern, Ziehen*) migration; (*Schluck, Luft-*) draught; (*Atem-*) breath; (*beim Rauchen*) puff; (*Schach-*) move; (*beim Schwimmen, Rudern*) stroke; (*Gesichts-*) feature; (*Wesens-*) trait

Zugabe *f* (*Geschenk*) [free] gift; (*Mus*) encore

Zugang *m* access

zugänglich *a* accessible; <*Mensch:*> approachable

Zugbrücke *f* drawbridge

zugeben† *vt sep* add; (*gestehen*) admit; (*erlauben*) allow

zugehen† *vi sep* (*sein*) close; **jdm z~** be sent to s.o.; **z~ auf** (+ *acc*) go towards; **dem Ende z~** draw to a close; <*Vorräte:*> run low; **auf der Party ging es lebhaft zu** the party was pretty lively

Zugehörigkeit *f* **-** membership

Zügel *m* **-s,-** rein

zugelassen *a* registered

zügel|los *a* unrestrained. **z~n** *vt* rein in; (*fig*) curb

Zuge|ständnis *nt* concession. **z~stehen**† *vt sep* grant

zügig *a* quick

Zugkraft *f* pull; (*fig*) attraction
zugleich *adv* at the same time
Zugluft *f* draught
zugreifen† *vi sep* (*haben*) grab it/them; (*bei Tisch*) help oneself; (*bei Angebot*) jump at it; (*helfen*) lend a hand
zugrunde *adv* **z~ richten** destroy; **z~ gehen** be destroyed; (*sterben*) die; **z~ liegen** form the basis (*dat* of)
zugunsten *prep* (+ *gen*) in favour of; <*Sammlung*> in aid of
zugute *adv* **jdm/etw z~ kommen** benefit s.o./sth
Zugvogel *m* migratory bird
zuhalten† *v sep* ● *vt* keep closed; (*bedecken*) cover; **sich** (*dat*) **die Nase z~** hold one's nose
Zuhälter *m* **-s,-** pimp
zuhause *adv* = **zu Hause**, *s.* **Haus**. **Z~** *nt* **-s,-** home
zuhör|en *vi sep* (*haben*) listen (*dat* to). **Z~er(in)** *m*(*f*) listener
zujubeln *vi sep* (*haben*) **jdm z~** cheer s.o.
zukleben *vt sep* seal
zuknöpfen *vt sep* button up
zukommen† *vi sep* (*sein*) **z~ auf** (+ *acc*) come towards; (*sich nähern*) approach; **z~ lassen** send (**jdm** s.o.); devote <*Pflege*> (*dat* to); **jdm z~** be s.o.'s right
Zukunft *f* **-** future. **zukünftig** *a* future ● *adv* in future
zulächeln *vi sep* (*haben*) smile (*dat* at)
zulangen *vi sep* (*haben*) help oneself
zulassen† *vt sep* allow, permit; (*teilnehmen lassen*) admit; (*Admin*) license, register; (*geschlossen lassen*) leave closed; leave unopened <*Brief*>
zulässig *a* permissible
Zulassung *f* **-, -en** admission; registration; (*Lizenz*) licence
zuleide *adv* **jdm etwas z~ tun** hurt s.o.
zuletzt *adv* last; (*schließlich*) in the end
zuliebe *adv* **jdm/etw z~** for the sake of s.o./sth
zum *prep* = **zu dem; zum Spaß** for fun; **etw zum Lesen** sth to read
zumachen *v sep* ● *vt* close, shut; do up <*Jacke*>; seal <*Umschlag*>; turn off <*Hahn*>; (*stilllegen*) close down ● *vi* (*haben*) close, shut; (*stillgelegt werden*) close down
zumal *adv* especially ● *conj* especially since
zumindest *adv* at least
zumutbar *a* reasonable
zumute *adv* **mir ist nicht danach z~** I don't feel like it
zumut|en *vt sep* **jdm etw z~en** ask *or* expect sth of s.o.; **sich** (*dat*) **zu viel z~en** overdo things. **Z~ung** *f* **-** imposition
zunächst *adv* first [of all]; (*anfangs*) at first; (*vorläufig*) for the moment ● *prep* (+ *dat*) nearest to
Zunahme *f* **-, -n** increase
Zuname *m* surname
zünd|en *vt*/*i* (*haben*) ignite. **Z~er** *m* **-s,-** detonator, fuse. **Z~holz** *nt* match. **Z~kerze** *f* sparking-plug. **Z~schlüssel** *m* ignition key. **Z~schnur** *f* fuse. **Z~ung** *f* **-, -en** ignition
zunehmen† *vi sep* (*haben*) increase (**an** + *dat* in); <*Mond:*> wax; (*an Gewicht*) put on weight. **z~d** *a* increasing
Zuneigung *f* **-** affection
Zunft *f* **-,¨-e** guild
Zunge *f* **-, -n** tongue. **Z~nbrecher** *m* tongue-twister
zunutze *a* **sich** (*dat*) **etw z~ machen** make use of sth; (*ausnutzen*) take advantage of sth
zuoberst *adv* right at the top
zuordnen *vt sep* assign (*dat* to)
zupfen *vt*/*i* (*haben*) pluck (**an** + *dat* at); pull out <*Unkraut*>

zur *prep* = **zu der; zur Schule** to school; **zur Zeit** at present
zurate *adv* **z~ ziehen** consult
zurechnungsfähig *a* of sound mind
zurecht|finden† (sich) *vr sep* find one's way. **z~kommen†** *vi sep* (*sein*) cope (**mit** with); (*rechtzeitig kommen*) be in time. **z~legen** *vt sep* put out ready; **sich** (*dat*) **eine Ausrede z~legen** have an excuse all ready. **z~machen** *vt sep* get ready. **Z~weisung** *f* reprimand
zureden *vi sep* (*haben*) **jdm z~** try to persuade s.o.
zurichten *vt sep* prepare; (*beschädigen*) damage; (*verletzen*) injure
zuriegeln *vt sep* bolt
zurück *adv* back; **Berlin, hin und z~** return to Berlin. **z~bekommen†** *vt sep* get back. **z~bleiben†** *vi sep* (*sein*) stay behind, (*nicht mithalten*) lag behind. **z~bringen†** *vt sep* bring back; (*wieder hinbringen*) take back. **z~erstatten** *vt sep* refund. **z~fahren†** *v sep* ● *vt* drive back ● *vi* (*sein*) return, go back; (*im Auto*) drive back; (*z~weichen*) recoil. **z~finden†** *vi sep* (*haben*) find one's way back. **z~führen** *v sep* ● *vt* take back; (*fig*) attribute (**auf** + *acc* to) ● *vi* (*haben*) lead back. **z~geben†** *vt sep* give back, return. **z~geblieben** *a* retarded. **z~gehen†** *vi sep* (*sein*) go back, return; (*abnehmen*) go down; **z~gehen auf** (+ *acc*) (*fig*) go back to
zurückgezogen *a* secluded. **Z~heit** *f* - seclusion
zurückhalt|en† *vt sep* hold back; (*abhalten*) stop; **sich z~en** restrain oneself. **z~end** *a* reserved. **Z~ung** *f* - reserve
zurück|kehren *vi sep* (*sein*) return. **z~kommen†** *vi sep* (*sein*) come back, return; (*ankommen*) get back. **z~lassen†** *vt sep* leave behind; (*z~kehren lassen*) allow back. **z~legen** *vt sep* put back; (*reservieren*) keep; (*sparen*) put by; cover <*Strecke*>. **z~liegen†** *vi sep* (*haben*) be in the past; (*Sport*) be behind; **das liegt lange zurück** that was long ago. **z~melden (sich)** *vr sep* report back. **z~schicken** *vt sep* send back. **z~schlagen†** *v sep* ● *vi* (*haben*) hit back ● *vt* hit back; (*umschlagen*) turn back. **z~schrecken†** *vi sep* (*sein*) shrink back, recoil; (*fig*) shrink (**vor** + *dat* from). **z~stellen** *vt sep* put back; (*reservieren*) keep; (*fig*) put aside; (*aufschieben*) postpone. **z~stoßen†** *v sep* ● *vt* push back ● *vi* (*sein*) reverse, back. **z~treten†** *vi sep* (*sein*) step back; (*vom Amt*) resign; (*verzichten*) withdraw. **z~weisen†** *vt sep* turn away; (*fig*) reject. **z~zahlen** *vt sep* pay back. **z~ziehen†** *vt sep* draw back; (*fig*) withdraw; **sich z~ziehen** withdraw; (*vom Beruf*) retire
Zuruf *m* shout. **z~en†** *vt sep* shout (*dat* to)
zurzeit *adv* at present
Zusage *f* -, **-n** acceptance; (*Versprechen*) promise. **z~n** *v sep* ● *vt* promise ● *vi* (*haben*) accept
zusammen *adv* together; (*insgesamt*) altogether; **z~ sein** be together. **Z~arbeit** *f* co-operation. **z~arbeiten** *vi sep* (*haben*) co-operate. **z~bauen** *vt sep* assemble. **z~bleiben†** *vi sep* (*sein*) stay together. **z~brechen†** *vi sep* (*sein*) collapse. **Z~bruch** *m* collapse; (*Nerven-* & *fig*) breakdown. **z~fallen†** *vi sep* (*sein*) collapse; (*zeitlich*) coincide. **z~fassen** *vt sep* summarize, sum up. **Z~fassung** *f* summary.

Z

z~fügen *vt sep* fit together. **z~gehören** *vi sep* (*haben*) belong together; (*z~passen*) go together. **z~gesetzt** *a* (*Gram*) compound. **z~halten**† *v sep* ● *vt* hold together; (*beisammenhalten*) keep together ● *vi* (*haben*) (*fig*) stick together. **Z~hang** *m* connection; (*Kontext*) context. **z~hanglos** *a* incoherent. **z~klappen** *v sep* ● *vt* fold up ● *vi* (*sein*) collapse. **z~kommen**† *vi sep* (*sein*) meet; (*sich sammeln*) accumulate. **Z~kunft** *f* **-,¨e** meeting. **z~laufen**† *vi sep* (*sein*) gather; <*Flüssigkeit:*> collect; <*Linien:*> converge. **z~leben** *vi sep* (*haben*) live together. **z~legen** *v sep* ● *vt* put together; (*z~falten*) fold up; (*vereinigen*) amalgamate; pool <*Geld*> ● *vi* (*haben*) club together. **z~nehmen**† *vt sep* gather up; summon up <*Mut*>; collect <*Gedanken*>; **sich z~nehmen** pull oneself together. **z~passen** *vi sep* (*haben*) go together, match. **Z~prall** *m* collision. **z~rechnen** *vt sep* add up. **z~schlagen**† *vt sep* smash up; (*prügeln*) beat up. **z~schließen**† **(sich)** *vr sep* join together; <*Firmen:*> merge. **Z~schluss** *m* union; (*Comm*) merger

Zusammensein *nt* **-s** get-together

zusammensetz|en *vt sep* put together; (*Techn*) assemble; **sich z~en** sit [down] together; (*bestehen*) be made up (**aus** from). **Z~ung** *f* **-, -en** composition; (*Techn*) assembly; (*Wort*) compound

zusammen|stellen *vt sep* put together; (*gestalten*) compile. **Z~stoß** *m* collision; (*fig*) clash. **z~treffen**† *vi sep* (*sein*) meet; (*zeitlich*) coincide. **z~zählen** *vt sep* add up. **z~ziehen**† *v sep* ● *vt* draw together; (*addieren*) add up; (*konzentrieren*) mass; **sich z~ziehen** contract; <*Gewitter:*> gather ● *vi* (*sein*) move in together; move in (**mit** with)

Zusatz *m* addition; (*Jur*) rider; (*Lebensmittel-*) additive.

zusätzlich *a* additional ● *adv* in addition

zuschau|en *vi sep* (*haben*) watch. **Z~er(in)** *m* **-s,-** (*f* **-, -nen**) spectator; (*TV*) viewer

Zuschlag *m* surcharge; (*D-Zug-*) supplement. **z~pflichtig** *a* <*Zug*> for which a supplement is payable

zuschließen† *v sep* ● *vt* lock ● *vi* (*haben*) lock up

zuschneiden† *vt sep* cut out; cut to size <*Holz*>

zuschreiben† *vt sep* attribute (*dat* to); **jdm die Schuld z~** blame s.o.

Zuschrift *f* letter; (*auf Annonce*) reply

zuschulden *adv* **sich** (*dat*) **etwas z~ kommen lassen** do wrong

Zuschuss *m* contribution; (*staatlich*) subsidy

zusehends *adv* visibly

zusein* *vi sep* (*sein*) **zu sein**, *s.* **zu**

zusenden† *vt sep* send (*dat* to)

zusetzen *v sep* ● *vt* add; (*einbüßen*) lose

zusicher|n *vt sep* promise. **Z~ung** *f* promise.

zuspielen *vt sep* (*Sport*) pass

zuspitzen (sich) *vr sep* (*fig*) become critical

Zustand *m* condition, state

zustande *adv* **z~ bringen/kommen** bring/come about

zuständig *a* competent; (*verantwortlich*) responsible

zustehen† *vi sep* (*haben*) **jdm z~** be s.o.'s right; <*Urlaub:*> be due to s.o.

zusteigen† *vi sep* (*sein*) get on; **noch jemand zugestiegen?** tickets please; (*im Bus*) any more fares please?

zustell|en *vt sep* block; (*bringen*) deliver. **Z~ung** *f* delivery
zusteuern *v sep* ● *vi* (*sein*) head (**auf** + *acc* for) ● *vt* contribute
zustimm|en *vi sep* (*haben*) agree; (*billigen*) approve (*dat* of). **Z~ung** *f* consent; approval
zustoßen† *vi sep* (*sein*) happen (*dat* to)
Zustrom *m* influx
Zutat *f* (*Culin*) ingredient
zuteil|en *vt sep* allocate; assign <*Aufgabe*>. **Z~ung** *f* allocation
zutiefst *adv* deeply
zutragen† *vt sep* carry/(*fig*) report (*dat* to); **sich z~** happen
zutrau|en *vt sep* **jdm etw z~** believe s.o. capable of sth. **Z~en** *nt* **-s** confidence
zutreffen† *vi sep* (*haben*) be correct; **z~ auf** (+ *acc*) apply to
Zutritt *m* admittance
zuunterst *adv* right at the bottom
zuverlässig *a* reliable. **Z~keit** *f* **-** reliability
Zuversicht *f* **-** confidence. **z~lich** *a* confident
zuviel* *pron & adv* **zu viel**, *s.* **viel**
zuvor *adv* before; (*erst*) first
zuvorkommen† *vi sep* (*sein*) (+ *dat*) anticipate. **z~d** *a* obliging
Zuwachs *m* **-es** increase
zuwege *adv* **z~ bringen** achieve
zuweilen *adv* now and then
zuweisen† *vt sep* assign
Zuwendung *f* donation; (*Fürsorge*) care
zuwenig* *pron & adv* **zu wenig**, *s.* **wenig**
zuwerfen† *vt sep* slam <*Tür*>; **jdm etw z~** throw s.o. sth
zuwider *adv* **jdm z~ sein** be repugnant to s.o. ● *prep* (+ *dat*) contrary to
zuzahlen *vt sep* pay extra
zuziehen† *v sep* ● *vt* pull tight; draw <*Vorhänge*>; (*hinzu-*) call in; **sich** (*dat*) **etw z~** contract <*Krankheit*>; sustain <*Verletzung*>; incur <*Zorn*> ● *vi* (*sein*) move into the area
zuzüglich *prep* (+ *gen*) plus
Zwang *m* **-[e]s,⸚e** compulsion; (*Gewalt*) force; (*Verpflichtung*) obligation
zwängen *vt* squeeze
zwanglos *a* informal. **Z~igkeit** *f* **-** informality
Zwangsjacke *f* straitjacket
zwanzig *inv a* twenty. **z~ste(r,s)** *a* twentieth
zwar *adv* admittedly
Zweck *m* **-[e]s, -e** purpose; (*Sinn*) point. **z~los** *a* pointless. **z~mäßig** *a* suitable; (*praktisch*) functional
zwei *inv a*, **Z~** *f* **-, -en** two; (*Sch*) ≈ B. **Z~bettzimmer** *nt* twin-bedded room
zweideutig *a* ambiguous
zwei|erlei *inv a* two kinds of ● *pron* two things. **z~fach** *a* double
Zweifel *m* **-s,-** doubt. **z~haft** *a* doubtful; (*fragwürdig*) dubious. **z~los** *adv* undoubtedly. **z~n** *vi* (*haben*) doubt (**an etw** *dat* sth)
Zweig *m* **-[e]s, -e** branch. **Z~stelle** *f* branch [office]
Zwei|kampf *m* duel. **z~mal** *adv* twice. **z~reihig** *a* <*Anzug*> double-breasted. **z~sprachig** *a* bilingual
zweit *adv* **zu z~** in twos; **wir waren zu z~** there were two of us. **z~beste(r,s)** *a* second-best. **z~e(r,s)** *a* second
zweitens *adv* secondly
Zwerchfell *nt* diaphragm
Zwerg *m* **-[e]s, -e** dwarf
Zwickel *m* **-s,-** gusset
zwicken *vt/i* (*haben*) pinch
Zwieback *m* **-[e]s,⸚e** rusk
Zwiebel *f* **-, -n** onion; (*Blumen-*)bulb
Zwielicht *nt* half-light; (*Dämmerlicht*) twilight. **z~ig** *a* shady

Zwiespalt *m* conflict
Zwilling *m* **-s, -e** twin; **Z~e** (*Astr*) Gemini
zwingen† *vt* force; **sich z~** force oneself. **z~d** *a* compelling
Zwinger *m* **-s,-** run; (*Zucht-*) kennels *pl*
zwinkern *vi* (*haben*) blink; (*als Zeichen*) wink
Zwirn *m* **-[e]s** button thread
zwischen *prep* (+ *dat*/*acc*) between; (*unter*) among[st]. **Z~bemerkung** *f* interjection. **z~durch** *adv* in between; (*in der Z~zeit*) in the meantime. **Z~fall** *m* incident. **Z~landung** *f* stopover. **Z~raum** *m* gap, space. **Z~wand** *f* partition. **Z~zeit** *f* **in der Z~zeit** in the meantime
Zwist *m* **-[e]s, -e** discord; (*Streit*) feud
zwitschern *vi* (*haben*) chirp
zwo *inv a* two
zwölf *inv a* twelve. **z~te(r,s)** *a* twelfth
Zylind|er *m* **-s,-** cylinder; (*Hut*) top hat. **z~risch** *a* cylindrical
Zyn|iker *m* **-s,-** cynic. **z~isch** *a* cynical. **Z~ismus** *m* **-** cynicism
Zypern *nt* **-s** Cyprus
Zypresse *f* **-, -n** cypress
Zyste /ˈt͡sʏstə/ *f* **-, -n** cyst

Test yourself with word games

This section contains a number of word games which will help you to use your dictionary more effectively and to build up your knowledge of German vocabulary and usage an entertaining way. You will find answers to all puzzles and games at the end of the section.

1 Join Up the Nouns

These German nouns are all made up of two separate words, but they have split apart. Draw a line between two pieces of paper that make up a noun. Watch out: one of the first words goes with two of the second words!

When you've made all the German words, do the same for the English translations and match them up with the German.

Flug
Wetter
Auto
Stadt
Post
Blumen

karte
bericht
mitte
topf
hafen
bahn
plan

street
town
motor
post
weather
flower
air

pot
card
centre
way
map
report
port

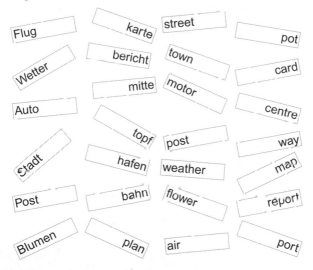

2 Wordsearch

Fifteen German words are hidden among the letters in the grid. Can you find them all? Watch out: six of the words read downwards, while all the others read across.

To help you, here are the English meanings of the German words. You can tick them off as you find the German.

ace	rough
almost	save
also	speak
better	ten
daughter	under
opera	village
powder	wide
quay	

M	W	N	B	U	N	T	E	R	V
Z	E	H	N	C	X	Z	L	K	J
H	I	G	F	P	U	L	V	E	R
D	T	O	C	H	T	E	R	S	A
D	S	P	R	E	C	H	E	N	P
O	B	E	S	S	E	R	A	O	I
R	U	R	K	U	F	A	S	T	A
F	Y	T	A	R	E	W	S	Q	U
Z	X	C	I	V	B	R	A	U	C
N	R	E	T	T	E	N	M	L	H

3 Odd Meaning Out

One word can have several different meanings. In the following exercise, only two of the three English translations given for each German word are correct. Use the dictionary to spot the odd one out, and then look up the right German translation for it:

fordern	demand challenge convince	**Pilz**	mushroom fungus beer
Schnee	snow icing beaten egg-white	**schwer**	swift difficult heavy
patent	obvious resourceful clever	**gerade**	straight grand even
Haken	tick hake hook	**drehen**	turn shoot catch
Brause	bruise fizzy drink shower	**Strom**	power storm stream
neben	next to apart from foggy	**Blase**	blanket blister bladder

4 Troubleshooting

Our computer has developed some annoying little problems. Can you help put them right?

First, when we type any three-letter word beginning with d, the computer shows three d's on the screen! The problem words are all highlighted in our "Recipe of the Week". Can you correct them in the box above each word?

Ddd Rezept ddd Woche

Für ddd Kuchenteig ddd Butter in Stückchen schneiden und mit ddd Mehl vermischen. Ddd Gemisch mit ddd Honig und ddd Milch zu einem festen Teig verarbeiten. Ddd Äpfel waschen, halbieren und in ddd Pfanne mit ddd Butter, ddd Zimt und ddd Zitronensaft aufkochen lassen. Ddd Teig in ddd Form geben und mit ddd Obst belegen. Ddd Kuchen in ddd Backofen schieben und 35 Minuten backen.

5 Crossword

If you need to, you can use the dictionary to solve this crossword. Just translate the clues into German, and write the translations in capital letters.

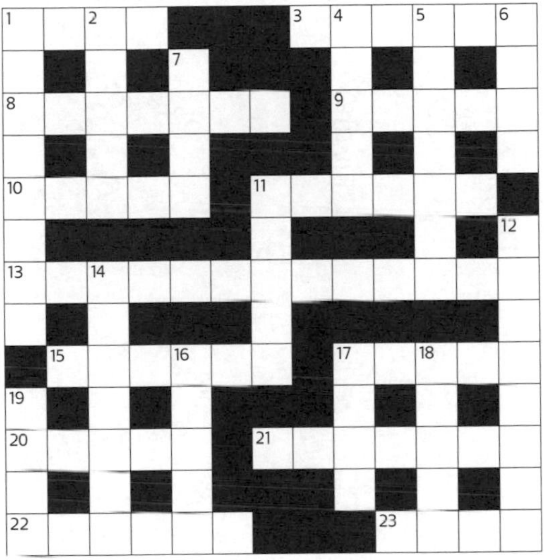

Across

1 mature (4)
3 journeys (6)
8 advertisement, small ad (7)
9 pale (adjective) (5)
10 to hurry (5)
11 few (6)
13 a (male) industrialist (13)
15 to catch (6)
17 (male) Russian (5)
20 price or prize (5)
21 bags or pockets (7)
22 saddle (noun) (6)
23 stove (4)

Down

1 (female) rider (8)
2 island (5)
4 heiress (5)
5 asparagus (7)
6 nest (4)
7 crane (machine) (4)
11 goods, or (they) wore (5)
12 to appoint (8)
14 dialect (7)
16 alley (5)
17 pink (4)
18 sheep (5)
19 epic (noun) (4)

6 Curly Words

One word is missing in each of the curly lists. Which day, month, capital city, and number are missing?

Can you write out the four lists in the right order?

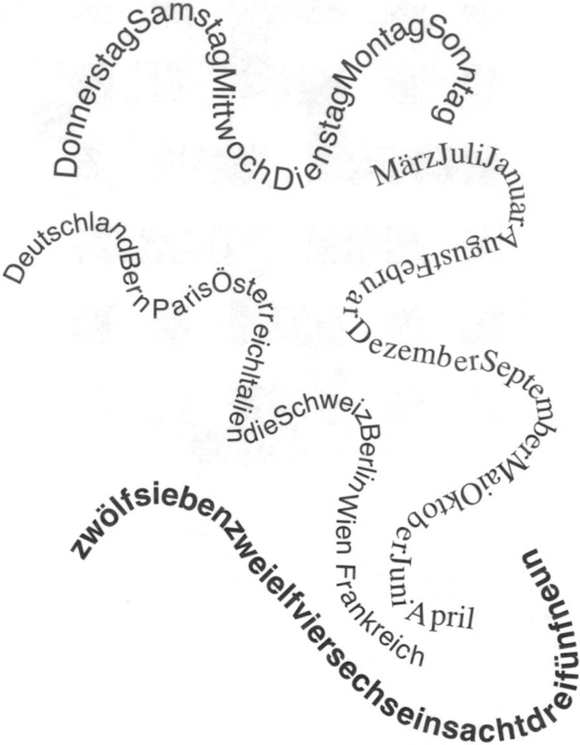

7 Sporting Links

Can you match each piece of sporting equipment to the right sport?
Can you translate the sports into German?

das Seil	**archery**
die Zielscheibe	**tennis**
der Schlittschuh	**skittles**
der Tennisschläger	**surfing**
der Kegel	**mountaineering**
der Ski	**football**
der Federball	**swimming**
das Segel	**golf**
die Kugel	**skating**
der Fußball	**riding**
die Flosse	**cycling**
der Zügel	**gymnastics**
das Sprungbrett	**skiing**
das Fahrrad	**fencing**
der Golfschläger	**diving**
die Turnschuhe	**shot-put**
das Florett	**sailing**
das Surfbrett	**badminton**

Answers

1

Flughafen	airport
Wetterbericht	weather report
Autobahn	motorway
Stadtmitte	town centre
Stadtplan	street map
Postkarte	postcard
Blumentopf	flowerpot

2

Ass	ace	rau	rough
fast	almost	retten	save
auch	also	sprechen	speak
besser	better	zehn	ten
Tochter	daughter	unter	under
Oper	opera	Dorf	village
Pulver	powder	weit	wide
Kai	quay		

3

convince	überzeugen
icing	Zuckerguss
obvious	offensichtlich
hake	Seehecht
bruise	blauer Fleck
foggy	neblig
beer	Bier
swift	schnell
grand	großartig
catch	fangen
storm	Sturm
blanket	Decke

4

Das Rezept *der* Woche
Für *den* Kuchenteig *die* Butter in Stückchen schneiden und mit *dem* Mehl vermischen. *Das* Gemisch mit *dem* Honig und *der* Milch zu einem festen Teig verarbeiten. *Die* Äpfel waschen, halbieren und in *der* Pfanne mit *der* Butter, *dem* Zimt und *dem* Zitronensaft aufkochen lassen. *Den* Teig in *die* Form geben und mit *dem* Obst belegen. *Den* Kuchen in *den* Backofen schieben und 35 Minuten backen.

5

R	E	I	F	■	■	■	R	E	I	S	E	N
E	■	N	■	K	■	■	■	R	■	P	■	E
I	N	S	E	R	A	T	■	B	L	A	S	S
T	■	E	■	A	■	■	■	I	■	R	■	T
E	I	L	E	N	■	W	E	N	I	G	E	■
R	■	■	■	■	■	A	■	■	■	E	■	E
I	N	D	U	S	T	R	I	E	L	L	E	R
N	■	I	■	■	■	E	■	■	■	■	■	N
■	F	A	N	G	E	N	■	R	U	S	S	E
E	■	L	■	A	■	■	■	O	■	C	■	N
P	■	E	■	S	■	T	A	S	C	H	E	N
O	■	K	■	S	■	■	■	A	■	A	■	E
S	A	T	T	E	L	■	■	■	O	F	E	N

6

Freitag; Sonntag, Montag, Dienstag, Mittwoch, Donnerstag, Freitag, Samstag;
November; Januar, Februar, März, April, Mai, Juni, Juli, August, September, Oktober, November, Dezember;
Rom; Deutschland/Berlin, Österreich/Wien, die Schweiz/Bern, Frankreich/Paris, Italien/Rom;
zehn; eins, zwei, drei, vier, fünf, sechs, sieben, acht, neun, zehn, elf, zwölf.

7

das Fahrrad	bicycle	cycling	das Radfahren
der Federball	shuttlecock	badminton	der Federball
das Florett	foil	fencing	das Fechten
die Flosse	flipper	swimming	das Schwimmen
der Fußball	football	football	der Fußball
der Golfschläger	golf-club	golf	das Golf
der Kegel	skittle	skittles	das Kegeln
die Kugel	shot	shot-put	das Kugelstoßen
der Schlittschuh	ice-skate	skating	das Eislaufen
das Segel	sail	sailing	der Segelsport
das Seil	rope	mountaineering	das Bergsteigen
der Ski	ski	skiing	das Skilaufen
das Sprungbrett	springboard	diving	das Kunstspringen
das Surfbrett	surfboard	surfing	das Surfen
der Tennisschläger	tennis-racket	tennis	das Tennis
die Turnschuhe	gym shoes	gymnastics	das Turnen
die Zielscheibe	target	archery	das Bogenschießen
der Zügel	rein	riding	das Reiten

Calendar of traditions, festivals, and holidays in German-speaking countries

January

1	8	15	22	29
2	9	16	23	30
3	10	17	24	31
4	11	18	25	
5	12	19	26	
6	13	20	27	
7	14	21	28	

February

1	8	15	22
2	9	16	23
3	10	17	24
4	11	18	25
5	12	19	26
6	13	20	27
7	**14**	21	28

March

1	8	15	22	29
2	9	16	23	30
3	10	17	24	31
4	11	18	25	
5	12	19	26	
6	13	20	27	
7	14	21	28	

April

1	8	15	22	29
2	9	16	23	30
3	10	17	24	31
4	11	18	25	
5	12	19	26	
6	13	20	27	
7	14	21	28	

May

1	8	15	22	29
2	9	16	23	30
3	10	17	24	31
4	11	18	25	
5	12	19	26	
6	13	20	27	
7	14	21	28	

June

1	8	15	22	29
2	9	16	23	30
3	10	17	24	
4	11	18	25	
5	12	19	26	
6	13	20	27	
7	14	21	28	

July

1	8	15	22	29
2	9	16	23	30
3	10	17	24	31
4	11	18	25	
5	12	19	26	
6	13	20	27	
7	14	21	28	

August

1	8	15	22	29
2	9	16	23	30
3	10	17	24	31
4	11	18	25	
5	12	19	26	
6	13	20	27	
7	14	21	28	

September

1	8	15	22	29
2	9	16	23	30
3	10	17	24	
4	11	18	25	
5	12	19	26	
6	13	20	27	
7	14	21	28	

October

1	8	15	22	29
2	9	16	23	30
3	10	17	24	**31**
4	11	18	25	
5	12	19	**26**	
6	13	20	27	
7	14	21	28	

November

1	8	15	22	29
2	9	16	23	30
3	10	17	24	
4	**11**	18	25	
5	12	19	26	
6	13	20	27	
7	14	21	28	

December

1	8	15	22	29
2	9	16	23	30
3	10	17	**24**	**31**
4	11	18	**25**	
5	12	19	**26**	
6	13	20	27	
7	14	21	28	

1 January

Neujahr New Year's Day is always a public holiday and tends to be a quiet day when people are recovering from the *Silvester* celebrations.

6 January

Heilige Drei Könige Epiphany or Twelfth Night is a public holiday in Austria and some parts of southern Germany. In some areas, children dressed up as the Three Kings go from house to house to bless the homes for the coming year and collect money for charity. This is also traditionally the day when the Christmas tree is taken down.

2 February

Mariä Lichtmess Candlemas is celebrated in the Catholic church but is not a public holiday.

1 April

Erster April April Fool's Day is the time to make an April fool of your family and friends (*jdn. in den April schicken*) or to play an April fool trick (*Aprilscherz*).

1 May

Erster Mai May Day is a public holiday in Germany, Austria, and Switzerland. It is celebrated by trade unions as *Labour Day*, often with rallies and demonstrations. Many people simply use the day for a family outing or picnic, and in rural areas maypoles are put up in the villages.

3 October

Tag der deutschen Einheit Germany's national holiday, the *Day of German Unity* commemorates German reunification on 3 October 1990.

26 October

Nationalfeiertag Austria's national holiday.

31 October

Reformationstag Reformation Day is a public holiday in some mainly Protestant parts of Germany and commemorates the Reformation.

1 November

Allerheiligen All Saints' Day is a public holiday in Catholic parts of Germany and Austria.

2 November

Allerseelen All Souls' Day is the day when Catholics remember their dead by visiting the cemeteries to pray and place wreaths, flowers, and lighted candles on the graves. This is often done on 1 November as *Allerseelen* is not a public holiday.

11 November

Martinstag St Martin's day is not a public holiday, but in Catholic areas the charitable Saint is commemorated with processions where children carry lanterns and sing songs. Traditional food includes the *Martinsgans* (roast goose) and *Martinsbrezel* (a kind of soft pretzel).

6 December

Nikolaustag On the eve of St Nicholas' Day, children put out their boots in the hope of finding presents and fruit, nuts, and sweets in the morning. The Saint may also turn up in person, looking much like Santa Claus or Father Christmas.

24 December

Heiligabend Christmas Eve is not a public holiday but many firms and shops close early for the Christmas period. This is the day when traditionally the Christmas tree is put up and decorated. Christmas presents are given in the evening, and many people attend midnight mass.

25 December

Erster Weihnachtstag Christmas Day is a public holiday in Germany, Austria, and Switzerland. It tends to be a quiet day for family get-togethers, often with a traditional lunch of goose or carp.

26 December

Zweiter Weihnachtstag Boxing Day is a public holiday in Germany, Austria, and Switzerland. In Austria and Switzerland it is called *Stephanstag* (St Stephen's day).

31 December

Silvester New Year's Eve is not a bank holiday, but firms and shops tend to close early. A party, or at least a meal with friends, is a must for *Silvester* evening. At midnight, the new year is toasted in Sekt (German sparkling wine), and everybody goes outside to admire the fireworks.

Movable feasts

Rosenmontag The day before Shrove Tuesday is not an official public holiday but many people, especially in the Rhineland, get the day off work or school to take part in the *Karneval* celebrations, which involve masked balls, fancy-dress parties, and parades. The street parades in Düsseldorf, Cologne, Mainz, and other cities are attended by thousands of revellers and shown live on television.

Faschingsdienstag Shrove Tuesday is the final day of *Fasching* (Carnival) in Southern Germany, with processions and fancy dress parties similar to Rosenmontag in the Northwest. In the far south, ancient customs to drive out the winter with bells and drums survive. The pre-Lent carnival in and around the Rhineland is called Karneval. Almost every town has its own carnival prince and princess, and organizes a street parade with decorated floats, which is watched by thousands of revellers in fancy dress.

Aschermittwoch Ash Wednesday marks the end of the carnival season and the beginning of Lent. This day is celebrated in the Catholic Church but is not a public holiday.

Karfreitag Good Friday is a public holiday and generally a very quiet day. Catholics traditionally eat fish on this day.

Ostern Easter traditions include hiding Easter eggs (often dyed hardboiled eggs, or the chocolate variety) in the garden for the children. The *Osterhase* (Easter bunny) is supposed to have brought them. Ostermontag (Easter Monday) is also a public holiday.

Weißer Sonntag (Sunday after Easter) In the Catholic Church, first communion is traditionally taken on this Sunday.

Muttertag (second Sunday in May) On Mothers' Day, children of all ages give their mothers small gifts, cards, or flowers.

Christi Himmelfahrt (40 days after Easter) Ascension day is a public holiday in Germany, Austria, and Switzerland. This day is also Fathers' day when fathers traditionally go out on daytrips or pub crawls.

Pfingsten (seventh Sunday after Easter) As *Pfingstmontag* (Whit Monday) is also a public holiday in Germany, Austria, and Switzerland, Whitsun is a popular time to have a long weekend away.

Fronleichnam (second Thursday after Whitsun) Corpus Christi is a public holiday in Austria and in parts of Germany and Switzerland. In Catholic areas, processions and open-air masses are held.

Buß- und Bettag (third Wednesday in November, 11 days before the first Advent Sunday) This 'day of repentance and prayer' is a public holiday only in some parts of Germany.

Volkstrauertag (second Sunday before the beginning of Advent) In Germany, this is a national day of mourning to commemorate the dead of both world wars, and the victims of the Nazis.

Totensonntag (last Sunday before the beginning of Advent) Protestants remember their dead on this day.

Advent The four weeks leading up to Christmas, beginning with the **1. Adventssonntag** (first Sunday in Advent) in late November or early December, still have a special significance in Germany, even for non-religious people. An Advent wreath with four candles is present in almost every German household during this time, and on each Sunday of Advent one more candle is lit.

A–Z of German life and culture

Abendbrot, Abendessen
For most Germans, MITTAGESSEN is still the main meal of the day. *Abendbrot* or *Abendessen* normally consists of bread, cheese, meats, perhaps a salad, and a hot drink. It is eaten by the whole family at about 6 or 7 p.m. *Abendessen* can also refer to a cooked meal, especially for people who are out at work all day.

Abitur
This is the final exam taken by pupils at a GYMNASIUM, usually when they are about 19. The result is based on continuous assessment during the last two years before the *Abitur*, plus examinations in four subjects. The *Abitur* is the obligatory qualification for university entrance.

Ampel-Koalition
A term describing any coalition between the SPD (the party colour is red), the FDP (yellow), and the Green Party. This type of coalition has become increasingly common in local government over the last ten years, with some LÄNDER ruled in this way.

AOK - Allgemeine Ortskrankenkasse
The largest health insurance organization in Germany. Foreign visitors to Germany who need medical assistance can get the necessary forms at the local *AOK* office.

Arbeitsamt
The local employment office to be found in every German town. It provides career guidance, helps the unemployed find new jobs, and processes all claims for ARBEITSLOSENGELD and related benefits. Unemployed people have to report to the *Arbeitsamt* once every three months to prove they are still looking for work.

Arbeitslosengeld
This is the benefit paid to all unemployed people who are looking for a new job and have already made a minimum contribution to the ARBEITSLOSENVERSICHERUNG. The benefit is a proportion of the person's previous pay, and is higher for people supporting children. After one year, it is reduced and called *Arbeitslosenhilfe*.

Arbeitslosenversicherung

This is the compulsory state-run insurance against unemployment. All *Arbeiter* and *Angestellte* have to pay into this scheme and in return are entitled to ARBEITSLOSENGELD and related benefits. This area has been subject to wide-ranging reforms in recent years.

ARD
An umbrella organization for the regional broadcasting stations of the various German LÄNDER, financed by licence fees plus a certain amount of advertising. The *ARD* broadcasts DAS ERSTE.

Autobahn
Germany's motorway network is very extensive and not subject to a general speed limit, other than a recommended limit of about 80 mph. Many motorways have only two lanes. To ease congestion, lorries are not allowed to use the *Autobahn* on Sundays.

BAföG - Bundesausbildungsförderungsgesetz
The grant which about a quarter of German students receive from the state. Whether they are entitled to *BAföG*, and how much they get, depends on the students' and their parents' financial circumstances. Half of the money is given in the form of a loan which has to be repaid later.

Bayern
Bayern (Bavaria), Germany's largest and southernmost LAND, is known for its beautiful scenery (the Alps and their foothills, as well as forests, rivers, and lakes, picturesque towns and villages), its excellent beer and food, and its lively cosmopolitan capital München (Munich). The Bavarians are said to be warm and hospitable, but also fiercely independent and very conservative.

Beamte
This term covers civil servants and other officials, but also occupations like teachers and lecturers. *Beamte* are legally obliged to support the democratic system in Germany and are not allowed to go on strike. In return, they enjoy many privileges, such as total job security, private health insurance, and exemption from social security contributions.

Berlin
After WIEDERVEREINIGUNG, Berlin took over from Bonn as

the capital of Germany, but the German government did not start moving there until 1998. This vibrant city in the heart of Europe lies on the river Spree. It has about 3.5 million inhabitants and is a major cultural and industrial centre.

Berufsausbildung
▶ LEHRE.

Berufsschule
A college for young people who are doing a LEHRE. They attend *Berufsschule* 2 days a week (or sometimes in blocks of several weeks) to continue their general education and receive formal training in their chosen type of job.

Biergarten
A rustic open-air pub which is traditional in Bavaria but can now be found throughout Germany. It is usually set up for the summer in the yard of a pub or restaurant. A *Biergarten* is the best place to enjoy a beer and a simple meal on a summer's day.

Bild Zeitung
Germany's largest-selling daily newspaper, *Bild* is a typical tabloid with huge headlines, lots of photos, scandal stories, gossip, and nude models. It is known for its right-wing views. *Bild* sells about 4.5 million copies every day, almost eight times more than any other newspaper in Germany. Its Sunday edition is called *Bild am Sonntag*.

Bodensee
This is the German name for Lake Constance, Germany's biggest lake, bordered by Germany, Switzerland, and Austria. The river Rhine flows through it. This popular recreation area enjoys a particularly mild climate, especially on the three islands Lindau, Mainau, and Reichenau.

Bonn
Bonn was the capital of the Federal Republic of Germany from 1949 until BERLIN was made the capital of a reunified Germany and it remains home to a number of government institutions. This relatively small, quiet city of about 300,000 inhabitants enjoys a picturesque location on the river Rhine.

Bund
This term refers to the federal state as the top level of government, as opposed to the individual LÄNDER which make up the Federal Republic. *Bund* and *Länder* have different responsibilities, with the *Bund* in charge of foreign policy, defence,

transport, health, employment, etc.

Bundesbank
Properly called the *Deutsche Bundesbank*, Germany's central bank is located in Frankfurt/Main. With the introduction of the Euro in 1999, some of its functions have passed to the European Central Bank (also in Frankfurt).

Bundeskanzler
The Chancellor is the head of government in Germany and Austria. The German chancellor is normally elected for 4 years by the MPs in the BUNDESTAG after being proposed by the BUNDESPRÄSIDENT. He chooses the ministers and decides on government policies.

Bundesland
▶ LAND.

Bundespräsident
The President is the head of state in Germany and Austria. The German president is elected for 5 years by the MPs and delegates from the LÄNDER. He (so far there have not been any women) acts mainly as a figurehead, representing Germany abroad, and does not get involved in party politics, although he often takes a moral lead in major issues like the reform of the education system.

Bundesrat
This is the upper house of the German parliamentary system, where the LÄNDER are represented. The *Bundesrat* members are appointed by the Länder governments. It has to approve laws affecting the *Länder*, and also any changes to the GRUNDGESETZ. Sometimes the opposition parties actually hold a majority in the *Bundesrat*, which allows them to influence German legislation.

Bundestag
The lower house of the German parliament, which is elected every four years by the German people. The *Bundestag* is responsible for federal legislation, the federal budget, and electing the BUNDESKANZLER. Half of the MPs are elected directly and half by proportional representation, in a complicated voting system where each voter has two votes.

Bundeswehr
This is the name for the German armed forces, which come under the control of the defence minister. The

Bundeswehr consists of professional soldiers and conscripts serving their WEHRDIENST. Until 1994, the GRUNDGESETZ did not allow German forces to be deployed abroad, but they now take part in certain operations, notably UN peacekeeping missions.

Bündnis 90/Die Grünen

This party came into being in 1993 as the result of a merger of the West German Green party and civil rights movements of the former GDR. It is the third largest force in the German parliament, committed to environmental and social issues.

CDU - Christlich-Demokratische Union

One of the main German political parties. It was founded in 1945 and is committed to Christian and conservative values. The *CDU* is not active in Bavaria.
▶ CSU.

Christkind

Traditionally, it is *Das Christkind* (the Christ Child) who brings Christmas presents to children on Christmas Eve. The concept of *der Weihnachtsmann* (Father Christmas) is relatively new in Germany.

CSU - Christlich-Soziale Union

The Bavarian sister party of the CDU. It was founded in 1946 and has enjoyed an absolute majority in Bavaria for over 30 years. Politically, it stands to the right of the *CDU*.

Das Erste

Also called ERSTES PROGRAMM, this is the first German public TV channel, broadcast by ARD. Programming includes news, information, films, and entertainment. There is a limited amount of advertising, which is concentrated in 'blocks' at certain times of day and not after 8 p.m.

Der Spiegel

One of Germany's best-selling weekly news and current affairs magazines, *Der Spiegel* was founded in 1947 and is published in Hamburg. It has a liberal to left-wing outlook and has become synonymous with investigative journalism in Germany, as it has brought to light a number of major scandals in German business and politics over the years.

Deutsche Post

The previously state-run German postal system has undergone wide-ranging reforms in recent years which effectively removed the *Deutsche Post* monopoly in

2002. The number of post offices has been reduced, but small post office agencies can now be found in shops, newsagents, and petrol stations. German letter boxes are yellow. Postal charges are relatively high, but the service is very reliable.

Deutsche Telekom
The previously state-run German telecommunications service has undergone extensive reforms and gradual privatization and is now a public limited company. Since 1998 when the market was opened up to competition, *Deutsche Telekom* has ceased to have a monopoly.

Deutsche Welle
The German equivalent of the BBC World Service, this radio station is financed and controlled by the German government and broadcasts programmes on German politics, business, arts, and culture, aimed at listeners abroad.

Die Republikaner
This ultra right-wing party was founded in 1983 and quickly became notorious for its xenophobic and nationalistic aims. After some success in the early 90s it now has very little support and is not represented in the BUNDESTAG.

Die Welt
A national daily newspaper which was founded in 1946 and is published in Hamburg. It has a large business section and is considered to be right-wing in its views.

Die Zeit
Germany's 'heaviest' weekly newspaper is published in Hamburg and is considered essential reading for academics and intellectuals. Former BUNDESKANZLER Helmut Schmidt is a joint editor. The paper offers in-depth analysis of current issues in politics, society, culture, and the arts.

Drittes Programm
One of the eight regional television channels run by the ARD and focussing on regional affairs and educational programmes.

Duales System
This is a waste disposal and recycling system which was introduced in Germany in 1993 and is operated by the private company *DSD*. All packaging materials marked with the GRÜNER PUNKT symbol are collected separately, and sorted into plastics, glass, paper, and metal for recycling. Non-recyclable and compostable

waste is still collected by the local refuse collection service.

Eigenheim

The level of home ownership in Germany is rising but still far lower than in Britain. Many people happily live in rented flats or houses, but most dream of buying or building their *Eigenheim* (own home) one day and save up towards it through the system of BAUSPAREN. German houses tend to be large and solidly built, usually with cellars, and are therefore relatively expensive. First-time buyers are usually middle-aged and expect to stay in their home for the rest of their lives.

Einwohnermeldeamt

Anybody who moves to Germany or relocates within Germany is legally obliged to register their address with the *Einwohnermeldeamt* within a week.

Entwerter

When travelling on buses and trams in Germany it is important to remember that you have to cancel (*entwerten*) your ticket in one of the *Entwerter* machines located inside the bus or tram. Your ticket, even if you have just bought it from the driver, is not valid without the stamp from the *Entwerter*.

Erste, Das

▶ DAS ERSTE.

Eurocheque

The Eurocheque is the standard cheque issued by banks in Germany. It is backed up by the *Eurochequekarte* which can also be used at cash machines and for payments in shops. Although plastic cards have become more popular in Germany, many people (and shops and restaurants) still prefer cash.

Fachhochschule

This type of university provides shorter, more vocational and practically-based courses than those available at a HOCHSCHULE.

Fahrschule

Learner drivers in Germany have to take lessons from a qualified driving instructor at a *Fahrschule* (driving school) in a specially adapted car with dual controls. It is quite common to have 20 or 30 driving lessons before sitting the driving test, as there is no other way of getting driving practice on the road.

FDP - Freie Demokratische Partei

The German Liberal party, which was founded in 1948. This relatively small party tends to gain only 5 to 10% of the vote at general elections, but it has held the balance of power in various coalition governments both with the SPD and the CDU/CSU. It supports a free-market economy and the freedom of the individual.

Focus

A relatively new weekly news and current affairs magazine published in Munich. It was set up in 1993 and is aimed at a centre-right readership, especially businesspeople and professionals. *Focus* has become a serious competitor of DER SPIEGEL, with shorter, easier-to-read articles and a more modern presentation.

Frankfurter Allgemeine Zeitung (FAZ)

One of Germany's most serious and widely respected daily newspapers. It was founded in 1945 and is published in Frankfurt/Main. It tends to have a centre-left to liberal outlook.

Frühstück

Breakfast in Germany typically consists of strong coffee, slices of bread or fresh rolls with butter, jam, honey, sliced cheese and meat, and maybe a boiled egg. For working people and schoolchildren, who have little time for breakfast first thing in the morning, a *zweites Frühstück* is common at around 10 a.m.

Gastarbeiter

The term used for foreign workers from southern European countries, mainly Turkey, former Yugoslavia, and Italy, many of whom came to Germany in the 60s and 70s. Despite the time that they have lived in Germany and the fact that their children have grown up there, integration is still a widely discussed issue.

Gemeinde

The lowest level of local government, run by a local council chaired by the *Bürgermeister* (mayor). *Gemeinden* have their own budget, with income from local taxes. They pass local legislation and administer local affairs.

Gesamthochschule

A type of university established in some LÄNDER following reforms in the 60s and combining HOCHSCHULE and FACHHOCHSCHULE under one roof, thereby offering greater flexibility and a wider choice of subjects to the student.

Gesamtschule

A comprehensive secondary school introduced in the 70s and designed to replace the traditional division into GYMNASIUM, REALSCHULE, and HAUPTSCHULE. Pupils are taught different subjects at their own level and may take any of the school-leaving exams, including the ABITUR.

Goethe-Institut
An organization for promoting German language and culture abroad. It is based in Munich and runs about 140 institutes in over 70 countries, offering German language classes, cultural events such as exhibitions, films and seminars, and a library of German books and magazines and other documentation, which is open to the public.

Grundgesetz
The written German constitution which came into force in May 1949. It lays down the basic rights of German citizens, the relationship between BUND and LÄNDER, and the legal framework of the German state.

Grundschule
The primary school which all German children attend for four years from the age of 6 (some children do not start until they are 7). Lessons are intense but pupils only attend school for about 4 hours a day. At the end of the *Grundschule*, teachers and parents decide together which type of secondary school the child should attend.

Grüner Punkt
A symbol used to mark packaging materials which can be recycled. Any packaging carrying this logo is collected separately under the DUALES SYSTEM recycling scheme. Manufacturers have to buy a licence from the recycling company *DSD* to entitle them to use this symbol.

Gymnasium
The secondary school which prepares pupils for the ABITUR. The *Gymnasium* is attended after the GRUNDSCHULE by the most academically-inclined pupils. They spend nine years at this school, and during the last three years, they have some choice as to which subjects they study.
▶ SCHULE.

Hauptschule
The secondary school which prepares pupils for the HAUPTSCHULABSCHLUSS (school-leaving certificate). The *Hauptschule* aims to give the least academically-inclined children a sound educational grounding. Pupils stay at the *Hauptschule* for 5 or 6 years after the

GRUNDSCHULE. ▶ SCHULE, LEHRE.

Hochschule
German *Hochschulen* (universities) do not charge fees, and anybody who has passed the ABITUR is entitled to go to university (except for some subjects which have a NUMERUS CLAUSUS). They tend to be very large and impersonal institutions. Students may receive a BAFÖG grant and often take more than the minimum 8 semesters (4 years) to complete their course.

ICE - Intercityexpresszug
This high-speed train runs at two-hour intervals on a number of main routes in Germany, offering shorter journey times and better facilities than ordinary trains. A futuristic new *ICE* station has been built at Frankfurt airport.

Internet
A wealth of useful information on German politics, culture, and so on can be obtained on the Internet, which is very popular in Germany. All the main German newspapers have web sites (e.g. http://www.focus.de), as do the television channels (e.g. http://www.ard.de) and organizations like the *Goethe-Institut* (http://goethe.de). In addition, many German towns and cities have web sites (e.g. http://www.berlin.de).

Kaffee
This refers not only to coffee as a drink but also to the small meal taken at about 4 in the afternoon, consisting of coffee and cakes or biscuits. It is often a social occasion as it is common to invite family or friends for *Kaffee und Kuchen* (rather than for lunch or dinner), especially on birthdays and other family occasions.

Kanton
The name for the individual autonomous states that make up Switzerland. There are 26 *Kantone*, with the largest having just over 1 million inhabitants. Each *Kanton* has its own government and its own constitution.

Kindergarten
Every German pre-school child has the right to attend *Kindergarten* (nursery or play school) between the ages of 3 and 6. Kindergarten concentrates on play, crafts, singing etc., and aims to foster the child's social and emotional development. There is no formal teaching at all, this being reserved for the

GRUNDSCHULE.

Kindertagesstätte
Often called *Kita* for short, this is a day nursery intended for the children of working parents. The age range is usually from babies to 6, although some *Kitas* also offer after-school care for older children.

Krankenkasse
There are many different health insurance organizations in Germany with the AOK being the largest. Contributions are high, due to the high standard (and cost) of health care in Germany. The *Krankenkassen* issue their members with plastic cards which entitle them to treatment by the doctor of their choice.

Ladenschlusszeit
The strict regulations governing shop closing times in Germany were relaxed in 1996. Shops are allowed to stay open until 8 p.m. on weekdays and 4 p.m. on Saturdays, and bakeries may open for 3 hours on Sundays. However, the actual opening times vary, depending on the location and size of the shop.

Land
Germany is a federal republic consisting of 16 member states called *Länder* or *Bundesländer*. Five so-called neue *Bundesländer* were added after reunification in 1990. The Land has a degree of autonomy and is responsible for all educational and cultural affairs, the police, the environment, and local government. Austria is a federal state consisting of 9 *Länder*, and the Swiss equivalent is a KANTON.

Landtag
The parliament of a LAND, which is elected every 4 to 5 years using a similar mixed system of voting as for the BUNDESTAG elections.

Lehre
This type of apprenticeship is still the normal way to learn a trade or train for a practical career in Germany. A *Hauptschulabschluss* is the minimum requirement, although many young people with a *Realschulabschluss* or even *Lehre* opt to train in this way. A Lehre takes about 2 to 3 years and involves practial training by a MEISTER(IN) backed up by lessons at a BERUFSSCHULE, with an exam at the end.

Love Parade
A festival of techno music and dance which takes place in Berlin every summer, with

about 1 million mainly young people attending. Originally a celebration of youth culture, it has become a major tourist attraction.

Markt

Weekly markets are still held in most German cities and towns, usually laid out very attractively in the picturesque market squares. Fresh fruit and vegetables, flowers, eggs, cheese and other dairy products, bread, meat and fish are available directly from the producer. Many Germans still buy most of their provisions *auf dem Markt*.

Meister(in)

A master craftsman or craftswoman who has completed rigorous training in his/her trade or vocation and has passed a final exam after several years' experience in a job. A *Meister(in)* is allowed to set up in business and train young people who are doing their LEHRE.

Mittagessen

This is a cooked meal eaten in the middle of the day and is the main meal of the day for most Germans. Schoolchildren come home from school in time for *Mittagessen* and most large companies have canteens where hot meals are served at lunchtime. On a Sunday, *Mittagessen* might consist of a starter like a clear broth, followed by a roast with gravy, boiled potatoes and vegetables, and a dessert.

Namenstag

This day is celebrated by many Germans, especially Catholics, in the same way as a birthday. It is the day dedicated to the saint whose name the person carries so, for example, someone called Martin would celebrate their *Namenstag* on *Martinstag* (November 11).

Numerus clausus

The *Numerus clausus* system is used to limit the number of students studying certain oversubscribed subjects such as medicine at German universities. It means that only those students who have achieved a minimum average mark in their ABITUR are admitted.

Orientierungsstufe

The name given to the first two years at a HAUPTSCHULE, a REALSCHULE, or a GYMNASIUM. During this time pupils can find out if they are suited to the type of school they are attending, and at the end of the two years they may transfer to a different school.

Ossi
A colloquial and sometimes derogatory term for someone from East Germany, as opposed to a WESSI (someone from West Germany).

Polterabend
This is Germany's answer to stag and hen nights. The *Polterabend* usually takes place a few days before the wedding and takes the form of a large party for the family and friends of both bride and groom. Traditionally, the guests smash some crockery, as this is supposed to bring luck to the couple.

Post
▶ DEUTSCHE POST

Premiere
Germany's main Pay-TV channel was introduced in 1991 and can be received via satellite or cable. *Premiere* subscribers can watch the latest feature films, sports events, cultural programmes, and documentaries uninterrupted by advertising.

Realschule
The secondary school which prepares pupils for the *Realschulabschluss* (school-leaving certificate). This type of school is in between HAUPTSCHULE and GYMNASIUM, catering for less academic children who will probably train for a practical career. Pupils stay at the *Realschule* for 6 years after the GRUNDSCHULE. ▶ SCHULE, LEHRE.

Rechtschreibreform
After much controversy, a reform aiming to simplify the strict rules governing German spelling and punctuation was finally implemented in 1998. The old spelling is still acceptable for a transitional period until 2005, but most newspapers and some new books already use the new spelling.

Reichstag
This historic building in the centre of Berlin became the seat of the BUNDESTAG in 1999. The refurbishment of the *Reichstag* included the addition of a glass cupola, with a walkway open to visitors, which provides a spectacular viewing platform and addition to the Berlin skyline.

Republikaner
▶ DIE REPUBLIKANER

RTL
Germany's largest privately-owned television channel is the market leader in commercial television. It broadcasts films, sport, news, and entertainment and

regularly achieves the highest viewing figures.

SAT 1
Germany's second largest privately-owned television channel broadcasts films, news, sport, and entertainment. It was the first commercial channel in the country.

3SAT
This satellite TV channel is run jointly by ARD, ZDF, and Swiss and Austrian TV.

Schule
German children do not start school until they are 6, and they are not allowed to leave school until they are at least 15. All children attend the GRUNDSCHULE for four years (six in Berlin) and either a HAUPTSCHULE, REALSCHULE, GYMNASIUM, or GESAMTSCHULE, depending on their ability. Some students stay at school until they are over 20 due to the system of "SITZEN BLEIBEN".

Schultag - 1. Schultag
The first day at school is a big event for a German child, involving a ceremony at school and sometimes at church. The child is given a *Schultüte*, a large cardboard cone containing pens, small gifts, and sweets, to mark this special occasion.

Schützenfest
An annual festival celebrated in most towns, involving a shooting competition, parade, and fair. The winners of the shooting competition are crowned *Schützenkönig* and *Schützenkönigin* for the year.

Schwarzwald
This is the German name for the Black Forest, a mountainous area in south-western Germany and a popular holiday destination for Germans and foreign tourists alike. The name refers to the large coniferous forests in the area.

sitzen bleiben
If German pupils fail more than one subject in their end-of-year school report, they have to repeat the year. This is colloquially referred to as *sitzen bleiben*, and it means that some pupils do not manage to sit their ABITUR until they are 20.

Skat
A popular card game for three players playing with 32 German cards. Keen players meet regularly for a game or even join a *Skat* club.

Sozialabgaben
This term refers to the contributions every German taxpayer has to make towards

the four main state insurance schemes: pension, health, nursing care, and unemployment. Altogether this amounts to over 40% of gross income, with employee and employer paying half each.

SPD - Sozialdemokratische Partei Deutschlands
One of the main German political parties and the party with the biggest membership. Re-formed after the war in 1945, it is a workers' party supporting social democratic values.

Spiegel
▶ DER SPIEGEL.

Stammtisch
A large table reserved for regulars in most German pubs. The word is also used to refer to the group of people who meet around this table for a drink and lively discussion.

Stasi - Staatssicherheitsdienst
The secret service in the former GDR. With the help of an extensive network of informers, the *Stasi* built up personal files on over 6 million people, that is one third of the population. It was disbanded a year before re-unification.
▶ IM.

Süddeutsche Zeitung
This respected daily national newspaper was founded in 1945 and is published in Munich. It has a liberal outlook and is read mainly in southern Germany.

Volkshochschule (VHS)
A local adult education centre that can be found in every German town. The *VHS* offers low-cost daytime and evening classes in a wide range of subjects, including crafts, languages, music, and exercise.

Waldorfschule
An increasingly popular type of private school originally founded by the Austrian anthroposophist Rudolf Steiner in the 1920s. The main aim of these schools is to develop pupils' creative and cognitive abilities through music, art, and crafts.

Wehrdienst
Compulsory military service for young men in Germany (10 months), Switzerland (3 months), and Austria (6 months). Young Germans are generally called up when they are 19, although there are certain exemptions. Conscientious objectors may apply to do ZIVILDIENST instead.

Weihnachtsmarkt
During the weeks of Advent, these Christmas markets take place in most German towns, selling Christmas decorations, handmade toys and crib figures, traditional Christmas biscuits, and mulled wine to sustain the shoppers.

Weinstube
A cosy wine bar which offers a wide choice of wines and usually also serves a few dishes which are considered to go well with wine. A *Weinstube* tends to be more upmarket than an ordinary pub, or else fairly rustic, especially in wine-growing areas.

Welt
▶ DIE WELT

Wende
This word can refer to any major political or social change or turning point, but it is used especially to refer to the collapse of Communism in 1989, which was symbolized by the fall of the Berlin wall and eventually led to the WIEDERVEREINIGUNG in 1990.

Wessi
A colloquial and sometimes derogatory term for someone from West Germany, as opposed to an OSSI. The expression *Besserwessi*, a pun on *Besserwisser* ('know-all') is used by East Germans to describe a *Wessi* who thinks he knows it all.

Westdeutsche Allgemeine Zeitung (WAZ)
Germany's highest-circulation serious national paper. It was founded in 1948 and is published in Essen, catering mainly for the densely populated Ruhr area.

Wiedervereinigung
This is the German word for the reunification of Germany which officially took place on 3 October 1990, when the former GDR was incorporated into the Federal Republic. The huge financial and social costs of reunification are still being felt throughout Germany.

ZDF - Zweites Deutsches Fernsehen
The second German public TV channel which was founded in 1961 and broadcasts the *Zweites Programm* with entertainment, news, information, and a limited amount of advertising.

Zeit
▶ DIE ZEIT.

Zivildienst
Community service which recognized conscientious

objectors in Germany and Austria can choose to carry out instead of WEHRDIENST. It lasts 3 months longer than *Wehrdienst* (2 months longer in Austria) and usually involves caring for children, the elderly, the disabled, or the sick.

Letter-writing in German

Holiday postcard

- Address: Note that the title (*Herrn, Frau, Fräulein*) stands on the line above the name. *Herr* always has an n on the end in addresses.

  The house number comes after the street name.

  The postcode comes before the place, and if you're writing from outside the country put a D- for Germany, A- for Austria or CH- for Switzerland in front of it.

- Beginnings (informal): *'Lieber'* here because it's a man; if it's a woman, use e.g. *Liebe Elke*.

  To two people, repeat *'Liebe(r)'*: *Lieber Hans, liebe Elke*.

  To a family: *Liebe Schmidts, Liebe Familie Schmidt*, or just *Liebe Leute*.

Heidelberg, den 6.8. 2001

Lieber Hans!

Einen schönen Gruß aus Alt-Heidelberg! Wir sind erst zwei Tage hier, aber schon sehr angetan von der Stadt und Umgebung, trotz der vielen Touristen. Wir waren gestern abend in einem Konzert im Schlosshof, eine wunderbare Stimmung! Morgen machen wir eine Bootsfahrt, dann geht's am Donnerstag wieder nach Hause. Hoffentlich ist deine Mutter inzwischen wieder gesund.

Bis bald

Max und Sophie

Herrn

Hans Matthäus

Brucknerstr. 26

91052 Erlangen

- Endings (informal): *Herzlich* or *Herzlichst, Herzliche Grüße*; more affectionately: *Alles Liebe*; *Bis bald* = See you soon .

Christmas and New Year wishes

On a card:

Frohe Weihnachten und viel Glück im neuen Jahr

A bit more formal: Ein gesegnetes Weihnachtsfest und die besten Wünsche zum neuen Jahr

A bit less formal: Fröhliche Weihnachten und einen guten Rutsch ins neue Jahr

In a letter:

- On most personal letters German speakers don't put their address at the top, but just the name of the place and the date

Würzburg, den 20.12.2001

Liebe Karin, lieber Ferdinand,

euch und euren Kindern wünschen wir von Herzen frohe Weihnachten und ein glückliches neues Jahr. Wir hoffen, es geht euch allen gut, und dass wir uns bald mal wieder sehen werden. Es kommt uns so vor, als hätten wir uns eine Ewigkeit nicht gesehen.

Das vergangene Jahr war für uns sehr ereignisreich. Thomas hatte im Sommer einen Unfall mit dem Fahrrad, und brach sich den Arm und das Schlüsselbein. Sabine hat das Abitur gerade noch bestanden und ist jetzt an der Uni in Erlangen, studiert Sport. Der arme Michael ist im Oktober arbeitslos geworden und sucht immer noch nach einer Stelle.

Ihr müsst unbedingt vorbeikommen, wenn ihr das nächste Mal in der Gegend seid. Ruft doch einfach ein paar Tage vorher an, damit wir etwas ausmachen können.

Mit herzlichen Grüßen

Eure Gabi und Michael

Invitation (informal)

Hamm, den 22.4.2001

Liebe Jennie,

wäre es möglich, dass du 1 in den Sommerferien zu uns kommst? Katrin und Gottfried würden sich riesig freuen (ich und mein Mann natürlich auch). Wir planen eine Reise zum Bodensee Ende Juli/Anfang August, du 1 könntest gerne mitfahren. Es ist wirklich sehr schön dort unten. Wir werden wahrscheinlich zelten – hoffentlich hast du 1 nichts dagegen!

Schreib bald, ob das für dich 1 in Frage kommt.

Herzliche Grüße

Monika Pfortner

- Beginning: if you put a comma after the name on the first line (which is usual), the letter proper should start with a small letter.

1 *du, dich, dein* etc.: although many people still write these with a capital in letters, this is not necessary. But the formal *Sie, Ihnen, Ihr* must always have a capital.

Invitation (formal)

Invitations to parties are usually by word of mouth, while for weddings, announcements rather than invitations are usually sent out:

Irene Brinkmann — Stefan Hopf

Wir heiraten am Samstag, den 20. April 2001, um 14 Uhr in der Pfarrkirche Landsberg.

Goethestraße 12	Ulrichsweg 4
Landsberg	Altötting

Accepting an invitation

Edinburgh, den 2.5.2001

Liebe Frau Pfortner,

recht herzlichen Dank für Ihre liebe Einladung. Da ich noch keine festen Pläne für die Sommerferien habe, möchte ich sie sehr gerne annehmen. Allerdings darf ich nicht mehr als vier bis fünf Tage weg sein, da es meiner Mutter nicht sehr gut geht. Sie **1** *müssen mir sagen, was ich mitbringen soll (außer Edinburgh Rock!). Ist es sehr warm am Bodensee? Kann man im See schwimmen?*

Natürlich habe ich nichts gegen Zelten. Auch hier in Schottland bei Wind und Regen macht es mir Spaß!

Ich freue mich auf ein baldiges Wiedersehen.

Herzliche Grüße

Jennie Stewart

1 Since this is a letter from a younger person writing to the mother of a friend, she uses the formal *Sie* form and possessive *Ihr* (always with capitals), and writes to her as "*Frau Pfortner*". On the other hand it was quite natural for Frau Pfortner to use the *du* form to her.

Enquiry to a tourist office

- A simple business-style letter. The recipient's address is on the left and the sender's on the right, with the date below.
- The subject of the letter is centred.

Verkehrsverein Heidelberg e.V.
Friedrich-Ebert-Anlage 2
69117 Heidelberg

Silvia Sommer
Tannenweg 23
48149 Münster

24. April 2001

Hotels und Pensionen in Heidelberg

Sehr geehrte Damen und Herren,

würden Sie mir bitte freundlicherweise eine Liste der Hotels und Pensionen (der mittleren Kategorie) am Ort zusenden?

Ich möchte bitte auch Informationen über Busfahrten zu den Sehenswürdigkeiten der Umgebung in der zweiten Augusthälfte haben.

Mit freundlichen Grüßen

Silvia Sommer

- This is the standard formula for starting a business letter addressed to a firm or organization, and not to a particular person.
- "*Mit freundlichen Grüßen*" is the standard ending for a formal or business letter; another possibility is "*Mit besten Grüßen*".

Booking a hotel room

Hotel Goldener Pflug
Ortsstraße 7
69235 Steinbach

Tobias Schwarz
Gartenstr. 19
76530 Baden-Baden

16. Juli 2001

Sehr geehrte Damen und Herren,

Ich wurde durch die Broschüre "Hotels und Pensionen im Naturpark Odenwald (Ausgabe 2000)" auf ihr Hotel aufmerksam.

Ich möchte für mich und meine Frau für die Zeit vom 2. bis 11. August (neun Nächte) ein ruhiges Doppelzimmer mit Dusche reservieren, sowie ein Einzelzimmer für unseren Sohn.

Falls Sie für diese Zeit etwas Passendes haben, informieren Sie mich doch bitte über den Preis und darüber, ob Sie eine Anzahlung wünschen.

Mit freundlichen Grüßen

Tobias Schwarz

Booking a campsite

- For a business letter to a particular person, use "*Sehr geehrte(r)*" and the name. (If this letter were to a man, it would start "*Sehr geehrter Herr Sattler*").

Camilla Stumpf
Saalgasse 10
60311 Frankfurt

Camping am See
Frau Bettina Sattler
Auweg 6-10
87654 Waldenkirchen

Frankfurt, den 16.04.2001

Sehr geehrte Frau Sattler,

Ihr Campingplatz wurde mir von Herrn Stephan Seidel empfohlen, der schon mehrmals bei Ihnen war. **1** Ich würde nun gerne vom 18. bis 25. Juli mit zwei Freunden eine Woche bei Ihnen verbringen. Könnten Sie uns bitte einen Zeltplatz **2** möglichst in unmittelbarer Nähe des Sees **3** reservieren?

Würden Sie mir freundlicherweise mitteilen, ob Sie meine Reservierung annehmen können und ob Sie eine Anzahlung wünschen?

Außerdem wäre ich Ihnen dankbar für eine kurze Wegbeschreibung von der Autobahn.

Mit vielem Dank im Voraus und freundlichen Grüßen

Camilla Stumpf

1 Or if you have found the campsite in a guide, say e.g.: "*Ich habe Ihre Anschrift dem ADAC-Campingführer 2000 entnommen*".

2 Or if you have a caravan: "*einen Stellplatz für einen Wohnwagen*".

3 Alternatives: "*in schattiger/geschützter Lage*".

Cancelling a reservation

Herrn
Hans Knauer
Gasthaus Sonnenblick
Hauptstr. 6
D-94066 Bad Füssing
Germany

Aberdeen, den 2.6.2001

Sehr geehrter Herr Knauer,

leider muss ich meine Reservierung für die Woche vom 7. bis 13. August **1** rückgängig machen. Wegen unvorhergesehener Umstände **2** muss ich auf meinen Urlaub verzichten.

Es tut mir aufrichtig Leid, dass ich so spät abbestellen muss, und hoffe, dass Sie deswegen keine Unannehmlichkeiten haben.

Mit freundlichen Grüßen

Robert McDonald

1 Or: "*für die Zeit vom 7. bis 20. August*" etc.

2 Or more precisely: "*Durch den überraschenden Tod meines Vaters/die Krankheit meines Mannes*" etc.

Sending an e-mail

The illustration shows a typical interface for sending e-mail.

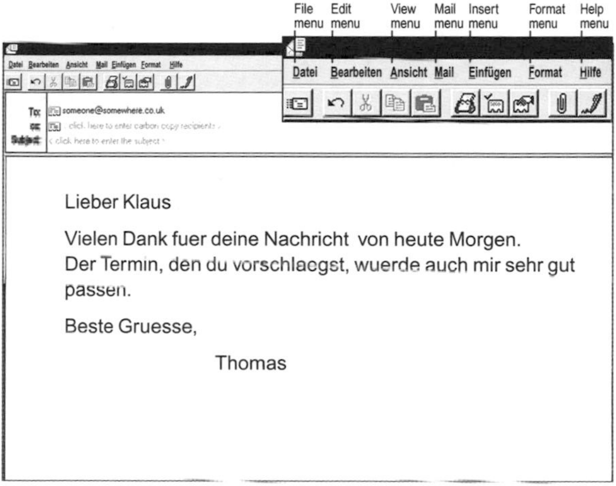

English–German Dictionary

Aa

a

vor einem Vokal **an**

● *indefinite article*

····➤ ein (*m*), eine (*f*), ein (*nt*). **a problem** ein Problem. **an apple** ein Apfel. **a cat** eine Katze. **have you got a pencil?** hast du einen Bleistift? **I gave it to a beggar** ich gab es einem Bettler

! There are some cases where **a** is not translated, such as when talking about people's professions or nationalities: **she is a lawyer** sie ist Rechsanwältin. **he's an Italian** er ist Italiener

····➤ (*with 'not'*) kein (*m*), keine (*f*), kein (*nt*), keine (*pl*). **that's not a problem/not a good idea** das ist kein Problem/keine gute Idee. **there was not a chance that ...** es bestand keine Möglichkeit, dass .... **she did not say a word** sie sagte kein Wort. **I didn't tell a soul** ich habe es keinem Menschen gesagt

····➤ (*per; each*) pro. **£300 a week** 300 Pfund pro Woche. **30 miles an hour** 30 Meilen pro Stunde. (*in prices*) **it costs 90p a pound** es kostet 90 Pence das Pfund.

aback *adv* **be taken ~** verblüfft sein

abandon *vt* verlassen; (*give up*) aufgeben

abate *vi* nachlassen

abattoir *n* Schlachthof *m*

abb|ey *n* Abtei *f*. **~ot** *n* Abt *m*

abbreviat|e *vt* abkürzen. **~ion** *n* Abkürzung *f*

abdicat|e *vi* abdanken. **~ion** *n* Abdankung *f*

abdom|en *n* Unterleib *m*. **~inal** *a* Unterleibs-

abduct *vt* entführen. **~ion** *n* Entführung *f*

aberration *n* Abweichung *f*; (*mental*) Verwirrung *f*

abeyance *n* **in ~** [zeitweilig] außer Kraft

abhor *vt* (*pt/pp* **abhorred**) verabscheuen. **~rent** *a* abscheulich

abid|e *vt* (*pt/pp* **abided**) (*tolerate*) aushalten; ausstehen <*person*>

ability *n* Fähigkeit *f*; (*talent*) Begabung *f*

abject *a* erbärmlich; (*humble*) demütig

ablaze *a* in Flammen

able *a* (**-r, -st**) fähig; **be ~ to do sth** etw tun können. **~-bodied** *a* körperlich gesund

ably *adv* gekonnt

abnormal *a* anormal; (*Med*) abnorm. **~ity** *n* Abnormität *f*. **~ly** *adv* ungewöhnlich

aboard *adv & prep* an Bord (+ *gen*)

abol|ish *vt* abschaffen. **~ition** *n* Abschaffung *f*

abominable *a*, **-bly** *adv* abscheulich

aborigines *npl* Ureinwohner *pl*

abort *vt* abtreiben. **~ion** *n* Abtreibung *f*. **~ive** *a* <*attempt*> vergeblich

about *adv* umher, herum; (*approximately*) ungefähr; **be ~** (*in circulation*) umgehen; (*in existence*) vorhanden sein; **be ~ to do sth** im Begriff sein, etw zu tun; **there was no one ~** es war kein Mensch da; **run/play ~** herumlaufen/-spielen ●*prep* um (+ *acc*) [... herum]; (*concerning*) über (+ *acc*); **what is it ~?** worum geht es? <*book:*> wovon handelt es? **I know nothing ~ it** ich weiß nichts davon; **talk/know ~** reden/wissen von

about: ~-face *n*, **-turn** *n* Kehrtwendung *f*

above *adv* oben ● *prep* über (+ *dat*/*acc*); **~ all** vor allem

above: ~-board *a* legal. **~-mentioned** *a* oben erwähnt

abrasive *a* Scheuer-; <*remark*> verletzend ● *n* Scheuermittel *nt*; (*Techn*) Schleifmittel *nt*

abreast *adv* nebeneinander; **keep ~ of** Schritt halten mit

abridge *vt* kürzen

abroad *adv* im Ausland; **go ~** ins Ausland fahren

abrupt *a*, **-ly** *adv* abrupt; (*sudden*) plötzlich; (*curt*) schroff

abscess *n* Abszess *m*

absence *n* Abwesenheit *f*

absent *a* abwesend; **be ~** fehlen

absentee *n* Abwesende(r) *m*/*f*

absent-minded *a*, **-ly** *adv* geistesabwesend; (*forgetful*) zerstreut

absolute *a*, **-ly** *adv* absolut

absorb *vt* absorbieren, aufsaugen; **~ed in** vertieft in (+ *acc*). **~ent** *a* saugfähig

absorption *n* Absorption *f*

abstain *vi* sich enthalten (**from** *gen*)

abstemious *a* enthaltsam

abstention *n* (*Pol*) [Stimm]enthaltung *f*

abstract *a* abstrakt ● *n* (*summary*) Abriss *m*

absurd *a*, **-ly** *adv* absurd. **~ity** *n* Absurdität *f*

abundan|ce *n* Fülle *f* (**of** an + *dat*). **~t** *a* reichlich

abuse[1] *vt* missbrauchen; (*insult*) beschimpfen

abus|e[2] *n* Missbrauch *m*; (*insults*) Beschimpfungen *pl*. **~ive** ausfallend

abysmal *a* [!] katastrophal

abyss *n* Abgrund *m*

academic *a*, **-ally** *adv* akademisch

academy *n* Akademie *f*

accelerat|e *vt*/*i* beschleunigen. **~ion** *n* Beschleunigung *f*. **~or** *n* (*Auto*) Gaspedal *nt*

accent *n* Akzent *m*

accept *vt* annehmen; (*fig*) akzeptieren ● *vi* zusagen. **~able** *a* annehmbar. **~ance** *n* Annahme *f*; (*of invitation*) Zusage *f*

access *n* Zugang *m*. **~ible** *a* zugänglich

accessor|y *n* (*Jur*) Mitschuldige(r) *m*/*f*; **~ies** *pl* (*fashion*) Accessoires *pl*; (*Techn*) Zubehör *nt*

accident *n* Unfall *m*; (*chance*) Zufall *m*; **by ~** zufällig; (*unintentionally*) versehentlich. **~al** *a*, **-ly** *adv* zufällig; (*unintentional*) versehentlich

acclaim *vt* feiern (**as** als)

acclimatize *vt* **become ~d** sich akklimatisieren

accommodat|e *vt* unterbringen. **~ing** *a* entgegenkommend. **~ion** *n* (*rooms*) Unterkunft *f*

accompan|iment *n* Begleitung *f*. **~ist** *n* (*Mus*) Begleiter(in) *m(f)*

accompany *vt* (*pt*/*pp* **-ied**) begleiten

accomplice *n* Komplize/-zin *m*/*f*

accomplish *vt* erfüllen <*task*>; (*achieve*) erreichen. **~ed** *a* fähig. **~ment** *n* Fertigkeit *f*; (*achievement*) Leistung *f*

accord *n* **of one's own ~** aus eigenem Antrieb. **~ance** *n* **in ~ance with** entsprechend (+ *dat*)

according *adv* **~ to** nach (+ *dat*). **~ly** *adv* entsprechend

accordion *n* Akkordeon *nt*

account *n* Konto *nt*; (*bill*) Rechnung *f*; (*description*) Darstellung *f*; (*report*) Bericht *m*; **~s** *pl* (*Comm*) Bücher *pl*; **on ~ of**

A

wegen (+ *gen*); **on no ~** auf keinen Fall; **take into ~** in Betracht ziehen, berücksichtigen ● *vi* **~ for** Rechenschaft ablegen für; (*explain*) erklären

accountant *n* Buchhalter(in) *m(f)*; (*chartered*) Wirtschaftsprüfer *m*

accumulat|e *vt* ansammeln, anhäufen ● *vi* sich ansammeln, sich anhäufen. **~ion** *n* Ansammlung *f*, Anhäufung *f*

accura|cy *n* Genauigkeit *f*. **~te** *a*, **-ly** *adv* genau

accusation *n* Anklage *f*

accusative *a & n* **~ [case]** (*Gram*) Akkusativ *m*

accuse *vt* (*Jur*) anklagen (**of** *gen*); **~ s.o. of doing sth** jdn beschuldigen, etw getan zu haben

accustom *vt* gewöhnen (**to** an + *dat*); **grow** *or* **get ~ed to** sich gewöhnen an (+ *acc*). **~ed** *a* gewohnt

ace *n* (*Cards, Sport*) Ass *nt*

ache *n* Schmerzen *pl* ● *vi* weh tun, schmerzen

achieve *vt* leisten; (*gain*) erzielen; (*reach*) erreichen. **~ment** *n* (*feat*) Leistung *f*

acid *a* sauer; (*fig*) beißend ● *n* Säure *f*. **~ity** *n* Säure *f*. **~ rain** *n* saurer Regen *m*

acknowledge *vt* anerkennen; (*admit*) zugeben; erwidern <*greeting*>; **~ receipt of** den Empfang bestätigen (+ *gen*). **~ment** *n* Anerkennung *f*; (*of letter*) Empfangsbestätigung *f*

acne *n* Akne *f*

acorn *n* Eichel *f*

acoustic *a*, **-ally** *adv* akustisch. **~s** *npl* Akustik *f*

acquaint *vt* **be ~ed with** kennen; vertraut sein mit <*fact*>. **~ance** *n* (*person*) Bekannte(r) *m/f*; **make s.o.'s ~ance** jdn kennen lernen

acquire *vt* erwerben

acquisit|ion *n* Erwerb *m*; (*thing*) Erwerbung *f*. **~ive** *a* habgierig

acquit *vt* (*pt/pp* **acquitted**) freisprechen

acre *n* ≈ Morgen *m*

acrimonious *a* bitter

acrobat *n* Akrobat(in) *m(f)*. **~ic** *a* akrobatisch

across *adv* hinüber/herüber; (*wide*) breit; (*not lengthwise*) quer; (*in crossword*) waagerecht; **come ~ sth** auf etw (*acc*) stoßen; **go ~** hinübergehen; **bring ~** herüberbringen ● *prep* über (+ *acc*); (*on the other side of*) auf der anderen Seite (+ *gen*)

act *n* Tat *f*; (*action*) Handlung *f*; (*law*) Gesetz *nt*; (*Theat*) Akt *m*; (*item*) Nummer *f* ● *vi* handeln; (*behave*) sich verhalten; (*Theat*) spielen; (*pretend*) sich verstellen; **~ as** fungieren als ● *vt* spielen <*role*>. **~ing** *a* (*deputy*) stellvertretend ● *n* (*Theat*) Schauspielerei *f*

action *n* Handlung *f*; (*deed*) Tat *f*; (*Mil*) Einsatz *m*; (*Jur*) Klage *f*; (*effect*) Wirkung *f*; (*Techn*) Mechanismus *m*; **out of ~** <*machine:*> außer Betrieb; **take ~** handeln; **killed in ~** gefallen

activate *vt* betätigen

activ|e *a*, **-ly** *adv* aktiv; **on ~e service** im Einsatz. **~ity** *n* Aktivität *f*

act|or *n* Schauspieler *m*. **~ress** *n* Schauspielerin *f*

actual *a*, **-ly** *adv* eigentlich; (*real*) tatsächlich

acupuncture *n* Akupunktur *f*

acute *a* scharf; <*angle*> spitz; <*illness*> akut. **~ly** *adv* sehr

ad *n* ! = **advertisement**

AD *abbr* (**Anno Domini**) n.Chr.

adamant *a* **be ~ that** darauf bestehen, dass

adapt *vt* anpassen; bearbeiten <*play*> ● *vi* sich anpassen. **~able** *a* anpassungsfähig

adaptation *n* (*Theat*) Bearbeitung *f*

add *vt* hinzufügen; (*Math*) addieren ● *vi* zusammenzählen, addieren; ~ **to** hinzufügen zu; (*fig: increase*) steigern; (*compound*) verschlimmern. ~ **up** *vt* zusammenzählen <*figures*> ● *vi* zusammenzählen, addieren

adder *n* Kreuzotter *f*

addict *n* Süchtige(r) *m/f*

addict|ed *a* süchtig; ~**ed to drugs** drogensüchtig. ~**ion** *n* Sucht *f*

addition *n* Hinzufügung *f*; (*Math*) Addition *f*; (*thing added*) Ergänzung *f*; **in** ~ zusätzlich. ~**al** *a*, **-ly** *adv* zusätzlich

additive *n* Zusatz *m*

address *n* Adresse *f*, Anschrift *f*; (*speech*) Ansprache *f* ● *vt* adressieren (**to** an + *acc*); (*speak to*) anreden <*person*>; sprechen vor (+ *dat*) <*meeting*>. ~**ee** *n* Empfänger *m*

adequate *a*, **-ly** *adv* ausreichend

adhere *vi* kleben/(*fig*) festhalten (**to** an + *dat*)

adhesive *a* klebend ● *n* Klebstoff *m*

adjacent *a* angrenzend

adjective *n* Adjektiv *nt*

adjoin *vt* angrenzen an (+ *acc*). ~**ing** *a* angrenzend

adjourn *vt* vertagen (**until** auf + *acc*) ● *vi* sich vertagen. ~**ment** *n* Vertagung *f*

adjudicate *vi* (*in competition*) Preisrichter sein

adjust *vt* einstellen; (*alter*) verstellen ● *vi* sich anpassen (**to** *dat*). ~**able** *a* verstellbar. ~**ment** *n* Einstellung *f*; Anpassung *f*

ad lib *adv* aus dem Stegreif ● *vi* (*pt/pp* **ad libbed**) [!] improvisieren

administer *vt* verwalten; verabreichen <*medicine*>

administration *n* Verwaltung *f*; (*Pol*) Regierung *f*

admirable *a* bewundernswert

admiral *n* Admiral *m*

admiration *n* Bewunderung *f*

admire *vt* bewundern. ~**r** *n* Verehrer(in) *m(f)*

admission *n* Eingeständnis *nt*; (*entry*) Eintritt *m*

admit *vt* (*pt/pp* **admitted**) (*let in*) hereinlassen; (*acknowledge*) zugeben; ~ **to sth** etw zugeben. ~**tance** *n* Eintritt *m*. ~**tedly** *adv* zugegebenermaßen

admonish *vt* ermahnen

adolescen|ce *n* Jugend *f*, Pubertät *f*. ~**t** *a* Jugend-; <*boy, girl*> halbwüchsig ● *n* Jugendliche(r) *m/f*

adopt *vt* adoptieren; ergreifen <*measure*>; (*Pol*) annehmen <*candidate*>. ~**ion** *n* Adoption *f*

ador|able *a* bezaubernd. ~**ation** *n* Anbetung *f*

adore *vt* (*worship*) anbeten; ([!] *like*) lieben

adorn *vt* schmücken. ~**ment** *n* Schmuck *m*

Adriatic *a* & *n* ~ **[Sea]** Adria *f*

adrift *a* **be** ~ treiben

adroit *a*, **-ly** *adv* gewandt, geschickt

adulation *n* Schwärmerei *f*

adult *n* Erwachsene(r) *m/f*

adulterate *vt* verfälschen; panschen <*wine*>

adultery *n* Ehebruch *m*

advance *n* Fortschritt *m*; (*Mil*) Vorrücken *nt*; (*payment*) Vorschuss *m*; **in** ~ im Voraus ● *vi* vorankommen; (*Mil*) vorrücken; (*make progress*) Fortschritte machen ● *vt* fördern <*cause*>; vorbringen <*idea*>; vorschießen <*money*>. ~**d** *a* fortgeschritten; (*progressive*) fortschrittlich. ~**ment** *n* Förderung *f*; (*promotion*) Beförderung *f*

advantage *n* Vorteil *m*; **take** ~ **of** ausnutzen. ~**ous** *a* vorteilhaft

adventur|e *n* Abenteuer *nt*. **~er** *n* Abenteurer *m*. **~ous** *a* abenteuerlich; <*person*> abenteuerlustig

adverb *n* Adverb *nt*

adverse *a* ungünstig

advert *n* [!] = **advertisement**

advertise *vt* Reklame machen für; (*by small ad*) inserieren ● *vi* Reklame machen; inserieren

advertisement *n* Anzeige *f*; (*publicity*) Reklame *f*; (*small ad*) Inserat *nt*

advertis|er *n* Inserent *m*. **~ing** *n* Werbung *f*

advice *n* Rat *m*

advisable *a* ratsam

advis|e *vt* raten (**s.o.** jdm); (*counsel*) beraten; (*inform*) benachrichtigen; **~e s.o. against sth** jdm von etw abraten ● *vi* raten. **~er** *n* Berater(in) *m(f)*. **~ory** *a* beratend

advocate¹ *n* (*supporter*) Befürworter *m*

advocate² *vt* befürworten

aerial *a* Luft- ● *n* Antenne *f*

aerobics *n* Aerobic *nt*

aero|drome *n* Flugplatz *m*. **~plane** *n* Flugzeug *nt*

aerosol *n* Spraydose *f*

aesthetic *a* ästhetisch

affair *n* Angelegenheit *f*, Sache *f*; (*scandal*) Affäre *f*; **[love-]~** [Liebes]verhältnis *nt*

affect *vt* sich auswirken auf (+ *acc*); (*concern*) betreffen; (*move*) rühren; (*pretend*) vortäuschen. **~ation** *n* Affektiertheit *f*. **~ed** *a* affektiert

affection *n* Liebe *f*. **~ate** *a*, **-ly** *adv* liebevoll

affirm *vt* behaupten

affirmative *a* bejahend ● *n* Bejahung *f*

afflict *vt* **be ~ed with** behaftet sein mit. **~ion** *n* Leiden *nt*

affluen|ce *n* Reichtum *m*. **~t** *a* wohlhabend. **~t society** *n* Wohlstandsgesellschaft *f*

afford *vt* **be able to ~ sth** sich (*dat*) etw leisten können. **~able** *a* erschwinglich

affront *n* Beleidigung *f* ● *vt* beleidigen

afloat *a* **be ~** <*ship:*> flott sein; **keep ~** <*person:*> sich über Wasser halten

afraid *a* **be ~** Angst haben (**of** vor + *dat*); **I'm ~ not** leider nicht; **I'm ~ so** [ja] leider

Africa *n* Afrika *nt*. **~n** *a* afrikanisch ● *n* Afrikaner(in) *m(f)*

after *adv* danach ● *prep* nach (+ *dat*); **~ that** danach; **~ all** schließlich; **the day ~ tomorrow** übermorgen; **be ~** aus sein auf (+ *acc*) ● *conj* nachdem

after: ~-effect *n* Nachwirkung *f*. **~math** *n* Auswirkungen *pl*. **~noon** *n* Nachmittag *m*; **good ~noon!** guten Tag! **~-sales service** *n* Kundendienst *m*. **~shave** *n* Rasierwasser *nt*. **~thought** *n* nachträglicher Einfall *m*. **~wards** *adv* nachher

again *adv* wieder; (*once more*) noch einmal; **~ and ~** immer wieder

against *prep* gegen (+ *acc*)

age *n* Alter *nt*; (*era*) Zeitalter *nt*; **~s** [!] ewig; **under ~** minderjährig; **of ~** volljährig; **two years of ~** zwei Jahre alt ● *v* (*pres p* **ageing**) ● *vt* älter machen ● *vi* altern; (*mature*) reifen

aged¹ *a* **~ two** zwei Jahre alt

aged² *a* betagt ● *n* **the ~** *pl* die Alten

ageless *a* ewig jung

agency *n* Agentur *f*; (*office*) Büro *nt*

agenda *n* Tagesordnung *f*

agent *n* Agent(in) *m(f)*; (*Comm*) Vertreter(in) *m(f)*; (*substance*) Mittel *nt*

aggravat|e *vt* verschlimmern; ([!] *annoy*) ärgern. **~ion** *n* [!] Ärger *m*

aggregate *a* gesamt ● *n* Gesamtzahl *f*; (*sum*) Gesamtsumme *f*

aggress|ion *n* Aggression *f*. **~ive** *a*, **-ly** *adv* aggressiv. **~or** *n* Angreifer(in) *m(f)*

aggro *n* [!] Ärger *m*

aghast *a* entsetzt

agil|e *a* flink, behände; <*mind*> wendig. **~ity** *n* Flinkheit *f*, Behändigkeit *f*

agitat|e *vt* bewegen; (*shake*) schütteln ● *vi* (*fig*) **~ for** agitieren für. **~ed** *a*, **-ly** *adv* erregt. **~ion** *n* Erregung *f*; (*Pol*) Agitation *f*

ago *adv* vor (+ *dat*); **a long time ~** vor langer Zeit; **how long ~ is it?** wie lange ist es her?

agony *n* Qual *f*; **be in ~** furchtbare Schmerzen haben

agree *vt* vereinbaren; (*admit*) zugeben; **~ to do sth** sich bereit erklären, etw zu tun ● *vi* <*people, figures:*> übereinstimmen; (*reach agreement*) sich einigen; (*get on*) gut miteinander auskommen; (*consent*) einwilligen (**to** in + *acc*); **~ with s.o.** jdm zustimmen; <*food:*> jdm bekommen; **~ with sth** (*approve of*) mit etw einverstanden sein

agreeable *a* angenehm

agreed *a* vereinbart

agreement *n* Übereinstimmung *f*; (*consent*) Einwilligung *f*; (*contract*) Abkommen *nt*; **reach ~** sich einigen

agricultur|al *a* landwirtschaftlich. **~e** *n* Landwirtschaft *f*

aground *a* gestrandet; **run ~** <*ship:*> stranden

ahead *adv* **straight ~** geradeaus; **be ~ of s.o./sth** vor jdm/etw sein; (*fig*) voraus sein; **go on ~** vorgehen; **get ~** vorankommen; **go ~!** [!] bitte! **look/plan ~** vorausblicken/-planen

aid *n* Hilfe *f*; (*financial*) Unterstützung *f*; **in ~ of** zugunsten (+ *gen*) ● *vt* helfen (+ *dat*)

Aids *n* Aids *nt*

aim *n* Ziel *nt*; **take ~** zielen ● *vt* richten (**at** auf + *acc*); ● *vi* zielen (**at** auf + *acc*); **~ to do sth** beabsichtigen, etw zu tun. **~less** *a*, **-ly** *adv* ziellos

air *n* Luft *f*; (*expression*) Miene *f*; (*appearance*) Anschein *m*; **be on the ~** <*programme:*> gesendet werden; <*person:*> auf Sendung sein; **by ~** auf dem Luftweg; (*airmail*) mit Luftpost ● *vt* lüften; vorbringen <*views*>

air: ~ bag *n* (*Auto*) Airbag *m*. **~-conditioned** *a* klimatisiert. **~-conditioning** *n* Klimaanlage *f*. **~craft** *n* Flugzeug *nt*. **~field** *n* Flugplatz *m*. **~ force** *n* Luftwaffe *f*. **~ freshener** *n* Raumspray *nt*. **~gun** *n* Luftgewehr *nt*. **~ hostess** *n* Stewardess *f*. **~ letter** *n* Aerogramm *nt*. **~line** *n* Fluggesellschaft *f*. **~mail** *n* Luftpost *f*. **~man** *n* Flieger *m*. **~plane** *n* (*Amer*) Flugzeug *nt*. **~port** *n* Flughafen *m*. **~ rage** *n* ausfälliges Fluggastverhalten. **~-raid** *n* Luftangriff *m*. **~-raid shelter** *n* Luftschutzbunker *m*. **~ship** *n* Luftschiff *nt*. **~ ticket** *n* Flugschein *m*. **~tight** *a* luftdicht. **~-traffic controller** *n* Fluglotse *m*

airy *a* (**-ier, -iest**) luftig; <*manner*> nonchalant

aisle *n* Gang *m*

ajar *a* angelehnt

alarm *n* Alarm *m*; (*device*) Alarmanlage *f*; (*clock*) Wecker *m*; (*fear*) Unruhe *f* ● *vt* erschrecken

A

alas *int* ach!
album *n* Album *nt*
alcohol *n* Alkohol *m*. **~ic** *a* alkoholisch ● *n* Alkoholiker(in) *m(f)*. **~ism** *n* Alkoholismus *m*
alert *a* aufmerksam ● *n* Alarm *m*
algebra *n* Algebra *f*
Algeria *n* Algerien *nt*
alias *n* Deckname *m* ● *adv* alias
alibi *n* Alibi *nt*
alien *a* fremd ● *n* Ausländer(in) *m(f)*
alienate *vt* entfremden
alight[1] *vi* aussteigen (**from** aus)
alight[2] *a* **be ~** brennen; **set ~** anzünden
align *vt* ausrichten
alike *a & adv* ähnlich; (*same*) gleich; **look ~** sich (*dat*) ähnlich sehen
alive *a* lebendig; **be ~** leben; **be ~ with** wimmeln von

all
● *adjective*
····➤ (*plural*) alle. **all [the] children** alle Kinder. **all our children** alle unsere Kinder. **all the books** alle Bücher
····➤ (*singular = whole*) ganz. **all the wine** der ganze Wein. **all the town** die ganze Stadt. **all my money** mein ganzes Geld; all mein Geld. **all day** den ganzen Tag. **all Germany** ganz Deutschland
● *pronoun*
····➤ (*plural = all persons/things*) alle. **all are welcome** alle sind willkommen. **they all came** sie sind alle gekommen. **are we all here?** sind wir alle da? **the best pupils of all** die besten Schüler (von allen). **the most beautiful of all** der/die/das schönste von allen
····➤ (*singular = everything*) alles. **that is all** das ist alles. **all that I possess** alles, was ich besitze
····➤ **all of** ganz; (*with plural*) alle. **all of the money** das ganze Geld. **all of the paintings** alle Gemälde. **all of you/them** Sie/sie alle
····➤ (*in phrases*) **all in all** alles in allem. **in all** insgesamt. **most of all** am meisten. **once and for all** ein für alle Mal. **not at all** gar nicht
● *adverb*
····➤ (*completely*) ganz. **she was all alone** sie war ganz allein. **I was all dirty** ich war ganz schmutzig
····➤ (*in scores*) **four all** vier zu vier
····➤ **all right** (*things*) in Ordnung. **is everything all right?** ist alles in Ordnung? **is that all right for you?** passt das Ihnen? **I'm all right** mir geht es gut. **did you get home all right?** sind Sie gut nach Hause gekommen? **is it all right to go in?** kann ich reingehen? **yes, all right** ja, gut. **work out all right** gut gehen; klappen [!]
····➤ (*in phrases*) **all but** (*almost*) fast. **all at once** auf einmal. **all the better** umso besser. **all the same** (*nevertheless*) trotzdem

allege *vt* behaupten
allegiance *n* Treue *f*
allerg|ic *a* allergisch (**to** gegen). **~y** *n* Allergie *f*
alleviate *vt* lindern
alley *n* Gasse *f*; (*for bowling*) Bahn *f*
alliance *n* Verbindung *f*; (*Pol*) Bündnis *nt*
allied *a* alliiert
alligator *n* Alligator *m*
allocat|e *vt* zuteilen; (*share out*) verteilen. **~ion** *n* Zuteilung *f*
allot *vt* (*pt/pp* **allotted**) zuteilen (**s.o.** jdm)
allow *vt* erlauben; (*give*) geben; (*grant*) gewähren; (*reckon*) rechnen; (*agree, admit*) zugeben; **~ for** berücksichtigen; **~ s.o. to**

do sth jdm erlauben, etw zu tun; **be ~ed to do sth** etw tun dürfen
allowance *n* [finanzielle] Unterstützung *f*; **make ~s for** berücksichtigen
alloy *n* Legierung *f*
allude *vi* anspielen (**to** auf + *acc*)
allusion *n* Anspielung *f*
ally[1] *n* Verbündete(r) *m/f*; **the Allies** *pl* die Alliierten
ally[2] *vt* (*pt/pp* **-ied**) verbinden; **~ oneself with** sich verbünden mit
almighty *a* allmächtig; (🅘 *big*) Riesen- ● *n* **the A~** der Allmächtige
almond *n* (*Bot*) Mandel *f*
almost *adv* fast, beinahe
alone *a & adv* allein; **leave me ~** lass mich in Ruhe; **leave that ~!** lass die Finger davon! **let ~** ganz zu schweigen von
along *prep* entlang (+ *acc*); **~ the river** den Fluss entlang ● *adv* **~ with** zusammen mit; **all ~** die ganze Zeit; **come ~** komm doch; **I'll bring it ~** ich bringe es mit
alongside *adv* daneben ● *prep* neben (+ *dat*)
aloud *adv* laut
alphabet *n* Alphabet *nt*. **~ical** *a*, **-ly** *adv* alphabetisch
alpine *a* alpin; **A ~** Alpen-
Alps *npl* Alpen *pl*
already *adv* schon
Alsace *n* Elsass *nt*
Alsatian *n* (*dog*) [deutscher] Schäferhund *m*
also *adv* auch
altar *n* Altar *m*
alter *vt* ändern ● *vi* sich verändern. **~ation** *n* Änderung *f*
alternate[1] *vi* [sich] abwechseln ● *vt* abwechseln
alternate[2] *a*, **-ly** *adv* abwechselnd; **on ~ days** jeden zweiten Tag
alternative *a* andere(r,s); **~ medicine** Alternativmedizin *f* ● *n* Alternative *f*. **~ly** *adv* oder aber
although *conj* obgleich, obwohl
altitude *n* Höhe *f*
altogether *adv* insgesamt; (*on the whole*) alles in allem
aluminium *n*, (*Amer*) **aluminum** *n* Aluminium *nt*
always *adv* immer
am *see* **be**
a.m. *abbr* (**ante meridiem**) vormittags
amass *vt* anhäufen
amateur *n* Amateur *m* ● *attrib* Amateur-; (*Theat*) Laien-. **~ish** *a* laienhaft
amaze *vt* erstaunen. **~d** *a* erstaunt. **~ment** *n* Erstaunen *nt*
amazing *a*, **-ly** *adv* erstaunlich
ambassador *n* Botschafter *m*
amber *n* Bernstein *m* ● *a* (*colour*) gelb
ambigu|ity *n* Zweideutigkeit *f*. **~ous** *a* **-ly** *adv* zweideutig
ambiti|on *n* Ehrgeiz *m*; (*aim*) Ambition *f*. **~ous** *a* ehrgeizig
amble *vi* schlendern
ambulance *n* Krankenwagen *m*. **~ man** *n* Sanitäter *m*
ambush *n* Hinterhalt *m* ● *vt* aus dem Hinterhalt überfallen
amen *int* amen
amend *vt* ändern. **~ment** *n* Änderung *f*
amenities *npl* Einrichtungen *pl*
America *n* Amerika *nt*. **~n** *a* amerikanisch ● *n* Amerikaner(in) *m(f)*. **~nism** *n* Amerikanismus *m*
amiable *a* nett
amicable *a*, **-bly** *adv* freundschaftlich; *<agreement>* gütlich
amid[st] *prep* inmitten (+ *gen*)
ammonia *n* Ammoniak *nt*
ammunition *n* Munition *f*
amnesty *n* Amnestie *f*
among[st] *prep* unter (+ *dat/acc*); **~ yourselves** untereinander
amoral *a* amoralisch
amorous *a* zärtlich

amount *n* Menge *f*; (*sum of money*) Betrag *m*; (*total*) Gesamtsumme *f* ● *vi* ~ **to** sich belaufen auf (+ *acc*); (*fig*) hinauslaufen auf (+ *acc*)

amphibi|an *n* Amphibie *f*. ~**ous** *a* amphibisch

amphitheatre *n* Amphitheater *nt*

ample *a* (**-r, -st**), **-ly** *adv* reichlich; (*large*) füllig

amplif|ier *n* Verstärker *m*. ~**y** *vt* (*pt/pp* **-ied**) weiter ausführen; verstärken <*sound*>

amputat|e *vt* amputieren. ~**ion** *n* Amputation *f*

amuse *vt* amüsieren, belustigen; (*entertain*) unterhalten. ~**ment** *n* Belustigung *f*; Unterhaltung *f*

amusing *a* amüsant

an *see* **a**

anaem|ia *n* Blutarmut *f*, Anämie *f*. ~**ic** *a* blutarm

anaesthetic *n* Narkosemittel *nt*, Betäubungsmittel *nt*; **under [an]** ~ in Narkose

anaesthetist *n* Narkosearzt *m*

analogy *n* Analogie *f*

analyse *vt* analysieren

analysis *n* Analyse *f*

analyst *n* Chemiker(in) *m(f)*; (*Psych*) Analytiker *m*

analytical *a* analytisch

anarch|ist *n* Anarchist *m*. ~**y** *n* Anarchie *f*

anatom|ical *a*, **-ly** *adv* anatomisch. ~**y** *n* Anatomie *f*

ancest|or *n* Vorfahr *m*. ~**ry** *n* Abstammung *f*

anchor *n* Anker *m* ● *vi* ankern ● *vt* verankern

ancient *a* alt

and *conj* und; ~ **so on** und so weiter; **six hundred** ~ **two** sechshundertzwei; **more** ~ **more** immer mehr; **nice** ~ **warm** schön warm

anecdote *n* Anekdote *f*

angel *n* Engel *m*. ~**ic** *a* engelhaft

anger *n* Zorn *m* ● *vt* zornig machen

angle *n* Winkel *m*; (*fig*) Standpunkt *m*; **at an** ~ schräg

angler *n* Angler *m*

Anglican *a* anglikanisch ● *n* Anglikaner(in) *m(f)*

Anglo-Saxon *a* angelsächsich ● *n* Angelsächsisch *nt*

angry *a* (**-ier, -iest**), **-ily** *adv* zornig; **be** ~ **with** böse sein auf (+ *acc*)

anguish *n* Qual *f*

angular *a* eckig; <*features*> kantig

animal *n* Tier *nt* ● *a* tierisch

animat|e *vt* beleben. ~**ed** *a* lebhaft

animosity *n* Feindseligkeit *f*

ankle *n* [Fuß]knöchel *m*

annex[e] *n* Nebengebäude *nt*; (*extension*) Anbau *m*

annihilate *vt* vernichten

anniversary *n* Jahrestag *m*

annotate *vt* kommentieren

announce *vt* bekannt geben; (*over loudspeaker*) durchsagen; (*at reception*) ankündigen; (*Radio, TV*) ansagen; (*in newspaper*) anzeigen. ~**ment** *n* Bekanntgabe *f*, Bekanntmachung *f*; Durchsage *f*; Ansage *f*; Anzeige *f*. ~**r** *n* Ansager(in) *m(f)*

annoy *vt* ärgern; (*pester*) belästigen; **get** ~**ed** sich ärgern. ~**ance** *n* Ärger *m*. ~**ing** *a* ärgerlich

annual *a*, **-ly** *adv* jährlich ● *n* (*book*) Jahresalbum *nt*

anonymous *a*, **-ly** *adv* anonym

anorak *n* Anorak *m*

anorexi|a *n* Magersucht *f*. ~**c** *a* **be** ~**c** an Magersucht leiden

another *a & pron* ein anderer/eine andere/ein anderes, (*additional*) noch ein(e); ~ **[one]** noch einer/eine/eins; ~ **time** ein andermal; **one** ~ einander

answer *n* Antwort *f*; (*solution*) Lösung *f* ● *vt* antworten (**s.o.** jdm); beantworten <*question,* *letter*>; ~ **the door/telephone** an die Tür/ans Telefon gehen ● *vi* antworten; (*Teleph*) sich melden; ~ **back** eine freche Antwort geben. ~**ing machine** *n* (*Teleph*) Anrufbeantworter *m*

ant *n* Ameise *f*

antagonis|m *n* Antagonismus *m*. ~**tic** *a* feindselig

Antarctic *n* Antarktis *f*

antelope *n* Antilope *f*

antenatal *a* ~ **care** Schwangerschaftsfürsorge *f*

antenna *n* Fühler *m*; (*Amer: aerial*) Antenne *f*

anthem *n* Hymne *f*

anthology *n* Anthologie *f*

anthrax *n* Milzbrand *m*, Anthrax *m*

anthropology *n* Anthropologie *f*

antibiotic *n* Antibiotikum *nt*

anticipat|e *vt* vorhersehen; (*forestall*) zuvorkommen (+ *dat*); (*expect*) erwarten. ~**ion** *n* Erwartung *f*

anticlimax *n* Enttäuschung *f*

anticlockwise *a & adv* gegen den Uhrzeigersinn

antics *npl* Mätzchen *pl*

antidote *n* Gegengift *nt*

antifreeze *n* Frostschutzmittel *nt*

antipathy *n* Abneigung *f*, Antipathie *f*

antiquated *a* veraltet

antique *a* antik ● *n* Antiquität *f*. ~ **dealer** *n* Antiquitätenhändler *m*

antiquity *n* Altertum *nt*

antiseptic *a* antiseptisch ● *n* Antiseptikum *nt*

antisocial *a* asozial; [!] ungesellig

antlers *npl* Geweih *nt*

anus *n* After *m*

anvil *n* Amboss *m*

anxiety *n* Sorge *f*

anxious *a*, **-ly** *adv* ängstlich; (*worried*) besorgt; **be** ~ **to do sth** etw gerne machen wollen

any *a* irgendein(e); *pl* irgendwelche; (*every*) jede(r,s); *pl* alle; (*after negative*) kein(e); *pl* keine; ~ **colour/number you like** eine beliebige Farbe/Zahl; **have you** ~ **wine/apples?** haben Sie Wein/Äpfel? ● *pron* [irgend]einer/eine/eins; *pl* [irgend]welche; (*some*) welche(r,s); *pl* welche; (*all*) alle *pl*; (*negative*) keiner/keine/keins; *pl* keine; **I don't want** ~ **of it** ich will nichts davon; **there aren't** ~ es gibt keine ● *adv* noch; ~ **quicker/slower** noch schneller/langsamer; **is it** ~ **better?** geht es etwas besser? **I can't eat** ~ **more** ich kann nichts mehr essen

anybody *pron* [irgend]jemand; (*after negative*) niemand; ~ **can do that** das kann jeder

anyhow *adv* jedenfalls; (*nevertheless*) trotzdem; (*badly*) irgendwie

anyone *pron* = **anybody**

anything *pron* [irgend]etwas; (*after negative*) nichts; (*everything*) alles

anyway *adv* jedenfalls; (*in any case*) sowieso

anywhere *adv* irgendwo; (*after negative*) nirgendwo; <*be, live*> überall; <*go*> überallhin

apart *adv* auseinander; **live** ~ getrennt leben; ~ **from** abgesehen von

apartment *n* Zimmer *nt*; (*flat*) Wohnung *f*

ape *n* [Menschen]affe *m* ● *vt* nachäffen

aperitif *n* Aperitif *m*

apologetic *a*, **-ally** *adv* entschuldigend; **be** ~ sich entschuldigen

apologize *vi* sich entschuldigen (**to** bei)

apology *n* Entschuldigung *f*

apostle *n* Apostel *m*

apostrophe *n* Apostroph *m*

appal *vt* (*pt/pp* **appalled**) entsetzen. **~ling** *a* entsetzlich

apparatus *n* Apparatur *f*; (*Sport*) Geräte *pl*; (*single piece*) Gerät *nt*

apparent *a* offenbar; (*seeming*) scheinbar. **~ly** *adv* offenbar, anscheinend

appeal *n* Appell *m*, Aufruf *m*; (*request*) Bitte *f*; (*attraction*) Reiz *m*; (*Jur*) Berufung *f* ● *vi* appellieren (**to** an + *acc*); (*ask*) bitten (**for** um); (*be attractive*) zusagen (**to** *dat*); (*Jur*) Berufung einlegen. **~ing** *a* ansprechend

appear *vi* erscheinen; (*seem*) scheinen; (*Theat*) auftreten. **~ance** *n* Erscheinen *nt*; (*look*) Aussehen *nt*; **to all ~ances** allem Anschein nach

appendicitis *n* Blinddarmentzündung *f*

appendix *n* (*pl* **-ices**) (*of book*) Anhang *m* ● (*pl* **-es**) (*Anat*) Blinddarm *m*

appetite *n* Appetit *m*

appetizing *a* appetitlich

applau|d *vt/i* Beifall klatschen (+ *dat*). **~se** *n* Beifall *m*

apple *n* Apfel *m*

appliance *n* Gerät *nt*

applicable *a* anwendbar (**to** auf + *acc*); (*on form*) **not ~** nicht zutreffend

applicant *n* Bewerber(in) *m(f)*

application *n* Anwendung *f*; (*request*) Antrag *m*; (*for job*) Bewerbung *f*; (*diligence*) Fleiß *m*

applied *a* angewandt

apply *vt* (*pt/pp* **-ied**) auftragen <*paint*>; anwenden <*force, rule*> ● *vi* zutreffen (**to** auf + *acc*); **~ for** beantragen, sich bewerben um <*job*>

appoint *vt* ernennen; (*fix*) festlegen. **~ment** *n* Ernennung *f*; (*meeting*) Verabredung *f*; (*at doctor's, hairdresser's*) Termin *m*; (*job*) Posten *m*; **make an ~ment** sich anmelden

appreciable *a* merklich; (*considerable*) beträchtlich

appreciat|e *vt* zu schätzen wissen; (*be grateful for*) dankbar sein für; (*enjoy*) schätzen; (*understand*) verstehen ● *vi* (*increase in value*) im Wert steigen. **~ion** *n* (*gratitude*) Dankbarkeit *f*. **~ive** *a* dankbar

apprehens|ion *n* Festnahme *f*; (*fear*) Angst *f*. **~ive** *a* ängstlich

apprentice *n* Lehrling *m*. **~ship** *n* Lehre *f*

approach *n* Näherkommen *nt*; (*of time*) Nahen *nt*; (*access*) Zugang *m*; (*road*) Zufahrt *f* ● *vi* sich nähern; <*time*:> nahen ● *vt* sich nähern (+ *dat*); (*with request*) herantreten an (+ *acc*); (*set about*) sich heranmachen an (+ *acc*). **~able** *a* zugänglich

appropriate *a* angebracht, angemessen

approval *n* Billigung *f*; **on ~** zur Ansicht

approv|e *vt* billigen ● *vi* **~e of sth/s.o.** mit etw/jdm einverstanden sein. **~ing** *a*, **-ly** *adv* anerkennend

approximate *a*, **-ly** *adv* ungefähr

approximation *n* Schätzung *f*

apricot *n* Aprikose *f*

April *n* April *m*; **make an ~ fool of** in den April schicken

apron *n* Schürze *f*

apt *a*, **-ly** *adv* passend; **be ~ to do sth** dazu neigen, etw zu tun

aqualung *n* Tauchgerät *nt*

aquarium *n* Aquarium *nt*

aquatic *a* Wasser-

Arab *a* arabisch ● *n* Araber(in) *m(f)*. **~ian** *a* arabisch

Arabic *a* arabisch

arbitrary *a*, **-ily** *adv* willkürlich

arbitrat|e *vi* schlichten. **~ion** *n* Schlichtung *f*

arc *n* Bogen *m*

arcade *n* Laubengang *m*; (*shops*) Einkaufspassage *f*

arch *n* Bogen *m*; (*of foot*) Gewölbe *nt* ● *vt* ~ **its back** <*cat:*> einen Buckel machen
archaeological *a* archäologisch
archaeolog|ist *n* Archäologe *m*/ -login *f*. ~**y** *n* Archäologie *f*
archaic *a* veraltet
archbishop *n* Erzbischof *m*
archer *n* Bogenschütze *m*. ~**y** *n* Bogenschießen *nt*
architect *n* Architekt(in) *m(f)*. ~**ural** *a*, **-ly** *adv* architektonisch
architecture *n* Architektur *f*
archives *npl* Archiv *nt*
archway *n* Torbogen *m*
Arctic *a* arktisch ● *n* **the** ~ die Arktis
ardent *a*, **-ly** *adv* leidenschaftlich
ardour *n* Leidenschaft *f*
arduous *a* mühsam
are *see* **be**
area *n* (*surface*) Fläche *f*; (*Geom*) Flächeninhalt *m*; (*region*) Gegend *f*; (*fig*) Gebiet *nt*
arena *n* Arena *f*
Argentina *n* Argentinien *nt*
Argentin|e, ~**ian** *a* argentinisch
argue *vi* streiten (**about** über + *acc*); <*two people:*> sich streiten; (*debate*) diskutieren; **don't** ~! keine Widerrede! ● *vt* (*debate*) diskutieren; (*reason*) ~ **that** argumentieren, dass
argument *n* Streit *m*, Auseinandersetzung *f*; (*reasoning*) Argument *nt*; **have an** ~ sich streiten. ~**ative** *a* streitlustig
aria *n* Arie *f*
arise *vi* (*pt* **arose**, *pp* **arisen**) sich ergeben (**from** aus)
aristocracy *n* Aristokratie *f*
aristocrat *n* Aristokrat(in) *m(f)*. ~**ic** *a* aristokratisch
arithmetic *n* Rechnen *nt*
arm *n* Arm *m*; (*of chair*) Armlehne *f*; ~**s** *pl* (*weapons*) Waffen *pl*; (*Heraldry*) Wappen *nt* ● *vt* bewaffnen
armament *n* Bewaffnung *f*; ~**s** *pl* Waffen *pl*
armchair *n* Sessel *m*
armed *a* bewaffnet; ~ **forces** Streitkräfte *pl*
armour *n* Rüstung *f*. ~**ed** *a* Panzer-
armpit *n* Achselhöhle *f*
army *n* Heer *nt*; (*specific*) Armee *f*; **join the** ~ zum Militär gehen
aroma *n* Aroma *nt*, Duft *m*. ~**tic** *a* aromatisch
arose *see* **arise**
around *adv* **[all]** ~ rings herum; **he's not** ~ er ist nicht da; **travel** ~ herumreisen ● *prep* um (+ *acc*) ... herum; (*approximately*) gegen
arouse *vt* aufwecken; (*excite*) erregen
arrange *vt* arrangieren; anordnen <*furniture, books*>; (*settle*) abmachen. ~**ment** *n* Anordnung *f*; (*agreement*) Vereinbarung *f*; (*of flowers*) Gesteck *nt*; **make** ~**ments** Vorkehrungen treffen
arrest *n* Verhaftung *f*; **under** ~ verhaftet ● *vt* verhaften
arrival *n* Ankunft *f*; **new** ~**s** *pl* Neuankömmlinge *pl*
arrive *vi* ankommen; ~ **at** (*fig*) gelangen zu
arrogan|ce *n* Arroganz *f*. ~**t** *a*, **-ly** *adv* arrogant
arrow *n* Pfeil *m*
arse *n* (*vulg*) Arsch *m*
arson *n* Brandstiftung *f*. ~**ist** *n* Brandstifter *m*
art *n* Kunst *f*; **work of** ~ Kunstwerk *nt*; ~**s and crafts** *pl* Kunstgewerbe *nt*; **A**~**s** *pl* (*Univ*) Geisteswissenschaften *pl*
artery *n* Schlagader *f*, Arterie *f*
art gallery *n* Kunstgalerie *f*
arthritis *n* Arthritis *f*
artichoke *n* Artischocke *f*
article *n* Artikel *m*; (*object*) Gegenstand *m*; ~ **of clothing** Kleidungsstück *nt*
artificial *a*, **-ly** *adv* künstlich

artillery *n* Artillerie *f*
artist *n* Künstler(in) *m(f)*
artiste *n* (*Theat*) Artist(in) *m(f)*
artistic *a*, **-ally** *adv* künstlerisch
as *conj* (*because*) da; (*when*) als; (*while*) während ● *prep* als; **as a child/foreigner** als Kind/Ausländer ● *adv* **as well** auch; **as soon as** sobald; **as much as** so viel wie; **as quick as you** so schnell wie du; **as you know** wie Sie wissen; **as far as I'm concerned** was mich betrifft
asbestos *n* Asbest *m*
ascend *vi* [auf]steigen ● *vt* besteigen <*throne*>
ascent *n* Aufstieg *m*
ascertain *vt* ermitteln
ash¹ *n* (*tree*) Esche *f*
ash² *n* Asche *f*
ashamed *a* beschämt; **be ~** sich schämen (**of** über + *acc*)
ashore *adv* an Land
ashtray *n* Aschenbecher *m*
Asia *n* Asien *nt*. **~n** *a* asiatisch ● *n* Asiat(in) *m(f)*. **~tic** *a* asiatisch
aside *adv* beiseite
ask *vt/i* fragen; stellen <*question*>; (*invite*) einladen; **~ for** bitten um; verlangen <*s.o.*>; **~ after** sich erkundigen nach; **~ s.o. in** jdn hereinbitten; **~ s.o. to do sth** jdn bitten, etw zu tun
asleep *a* **be ~** schlafen; **fall ~** einschlafen
asparagus *n* Spargel *m*
aspect *n* Aspekt *m*
asphalt *n* Asphalt *m*
aspire *vi* **~ to** streben nach
ass *n* Esel *m*
assail *vt* bestürmen. **~ant** *n* Angreifer(in) *m(f)*
assassin *n* Mörder(in) *m(f)*. **~ate** *vt* ermorden. **~ation** *n* [politischer] Mord *m*
assault *n* (*Mil*) Angriff *m*; (*Jur*) Körperverletzung *f* ● *vt* [tätlich] angreifen
assemble *vi* sich versammeln ● *vt* versammeln; (*Techn*) montieren
assembly *n* Versammlung *f*; (*Sch*) Andacht *f*; (*Techn*) Montage *f*. **~ line** *n* Fließband *nt*
assent *n* Zustimmung *f*
assert *vt* behaupten; **~ oneself** sich durchsetzen. **~ion** *n* Behauptung *f*
assess *vt* bewerten; (*fig & for tax purposes*) einschätzen; schätzen <*value*>. **~ment** *n* Einschätzung *f*; (*of tax*) Steuerbescheid *m*
asset *n* Vorteil *m*; **~s** *pl* (*money*) Vermögen *nt*; (*Comm*) Aktiva *pl*
assign *vt* zuweisen (**to** *dat*). **~ment** *n* (*task*) Aufgabe *f*
assist *vt/i* helfen (+ *dat*). **~ance** *n* Hilfe *f*. **~ant** *a* Hilfs- ● *n* Assistent(in) *m(f)*; (*in shop*) Verkäufer(in) *m(f)*
associat|e¹ *vt* verbinden; (*Psych*) assoziieren ● *vi* **~ with** verkehren mit. **~ion** *n* Verband *m*
associate² *a* assoziiert ● *n* Kollege *m*/-gin *f*
assort|ed *a* gemischt. **~ment** *n* Mischung *f*
assum|e *vt* annehmen; übernehmen <*office*>; **~ing that** angenommen, dass
assumption *n* Annahme *f*; **on the ~** in der Annahme (**that** dass)
assurance *n* Versicherung *f*; (*confidence*) Selbstsicherheit *f*
assure *vt* versichern (**s.o.** jdm); **I ~ you [of that]** das versichere ich Ihnen. **~d** *a* sicher
asterisk *n* Sternchen *nt*
asthma *n* Asthma *nt*
astonish *vt* erstaunen. **~ing** *a* erstaunlich. **~ment** *n* Erstaunen *nt*
astray *adv* **go ~** verloren gehen; <*person:*> sich verlaufen
astride *adv* rittlings ● *prep* rittlings auf (+ *dat/acc*)

astrolog|er *n* Astrologe *m*/-gin *f*. **~y** *n* Astrologie *f*
astronaut *n* Astronaut(in) *m(f)*
astronom|er *n* Astronom *m*. **~ical** *a* astronomisch. **~y** *n* Astronomie *f*
astute *a* scharfsinnig
asylum *n* Asyl *nt*; **[lunatic] ~** Irrenanstalt *f*. **~-seeker** *n* Asylant *m*

at
● *preposition*
····➤ (*expressing place*) an (+ *dat*). **at the station** am Bahnhof. **at the end** am Ende. **at the corner** an der Ecke. **at the same place** an der gleichen Stelle
····➤ (*at s.o.'s house or shop*) bei (+ *dat*). **at Lisa's** bei Lisa. **at my uncle's** bei meinem Onkel. **at the baker's/butcher's** beim Bäcker/ Fleischer
····➤ (*inside a building*) in (+ *dat*). **at the theatre/supermarket** im Theater/Supermarkt. **we spent the night at a hotel** wir übernachteten in einem Hotel. **he is still at the office** er ist noch im Büro
····➤ (*expressing time*) (*with clock time*) um; (*with main festivals*) zu. **at six o'clock** um sechs Uhr. **at midnight** um Mitternacht. **at midday** um zwölf Uhr mittags. **at Christmas/Easter** zu Weihnachten/Ostern
····➤ (*expressing age*) mit. **at [the age of] forty** mit vierzig; im Alter von vierzig
····➤ (*expressing price*) zu. **at £2.50 [each]** zu *od* für [je] 2,50 Pfund
····➤ (*expressing speed*) mit. **at 30 m.p.h.** mit dreißig Meilen pro Stunde
····➤ (*in phrases*) **good/bad at languages** gut/schlecht in Sprachen. **two at a time** zwei auf einmal. **at that** (*at that point*) dabei; (*at that provocation*) daraufhin; (*moreover*) noch dazu

ate *see* **eat**
atheist *n* Atheist(in) *m(f)*
athlet|e *n* Athlet(in) *m(f)*. **~ic** *a* sportlich. **~ics** *n* Leichtathletik *f*
Atlantic *a* & *n* **the ~ [Ocean]** der Atlantik
atlas *n* Atlas *m*
atmosphere *n* Atmosphäre *f*
atom *n* Atom *nt*. **~ bomb** *n* Atombombe *f*
atomic *a* Atom-
atrocious *a* abscheulich
atrocity *n* Gräueltat *f*
attach *vt* befestigen (**to** an + *dat*); beimessen <*importance*> (**to** *dat*); **be ~ed to** (*fig*) hängen an (+ *dat*)
attack *n* Angriff *m*; (*Med*) Anfall *m* ● *vt/i* angreifen
attain *vt* erreichen. **~able** *a* erreichbar
attempt *n* Versuch *m* ● *vt* versuchen
attend *vt* anwesend sein bei; (*go regularly to*) besuchen; (*take part in*) teilnehmen an (+ *dat*); (*accompany*) begleiten; <*doctor:*> behandeln ● *vi* anwesend sein; (*pay attention*) aufpassen; **~ to** sich kümmern um; (*in shop*) bedienen. **~ance** *n* Anwesenheit *f*; (*number*) Besucherzahl *f*. **~ant** *n* Wärter(in) *m(f)*; (*in car park*) Wächter *m*
attention *n* Aufmerksamkeit *f*; **~!** (*Mil*) stillgestanden! **pay ~** aufpassen; **pay ~ to** beachten, achten auf (+ *acc*)
attentive *a*, **-ly** *adv* aufmerksam
attic *n* Dachboden *m*
attitude *n* Haltung *f*
attorney *n* (*Amer: lawyer*) Rechtsanwalt *m*; **power of ~** Vollmacht *f*
attract *vt* anziehen; erregen <*attention*>; **~ s.o.'s attention** jds

Aufmerksamkeit auf sich (*acc*) lenken. **~ion** *n* Anziehungskraft *f*; (*charm*) Reiz *m*; (*thing*) Attraktion *f*. **~ive** *a*, **-ly** *adv* attraktiv
attribute *vt* zuschreiben (**to** *dat*)
aubergine *n* Aubergine *f*
auburn *a* kastanienbraun
auction *n* Auktion *f* Versteigerung *f* ● *vt* versteigern. **~eer** *n* Auktionator *m*
audaci|ous *a*, **-ly** *adv* verwegen. **~ty** *n* Verwegenheit *f*; (*impudence*) Dreistigkeit *f*
audible *a*, **-bly** *adv* hörbar
audience *n* Publikum *nt*; (*Theat*, *TV*) Zuschauer *pl*; (*Radio*) Zuhörer *pl*; (*meeting*) Audienz *f*
audit *n* Bücherrevision *f* ● *vt* (*Comm*) prüfen
audition *n* (*Theat*) Vorsprechen *nt*; (*Mus*) Vorspielen *nt*; (*for singer*) Vorsingen *nt* ● *vi* vorsprechen; vorspielen; vorsingen
auditor *n* Buchprüfer *m*
auditorium *n* Zuschauerraum *m*
August *n* August *m*
aunt *n* Tante *f*
au pair *n* ~ **[girl]** Au-pair-Mädchen *nt*
aura *n* Fluidum *nt*
auspicious *a* günstig; <*occasion*> freudig
auster|e *a* streng; (*simple*) nüchtern. **~ity** *n* Strenge *f*; (*hardship*) Entbehrung *f*
Australia *n* Australien *nt*. **~n** *a* australisch ● *n* Australier(in) *m(f)*
Austria *n* Österreich *nt* **~n** *a* österreichisch ● *n* Österreicher(in) *m(f)*
authentic *a* echt, authentisch. **~ate** *vt* beglaubigen. **~ity** *n* Echtheit *f*
author *n* Schriftsteller *m*, Autor *m*; (*of document*) Verfasser *m*
authoritarian *a* autoritär
authoritative *a* maßgebend
authority *n* Autorität *f*; (*public*) Behörde *f*; **in ~** verantwortlich
authorization *n* Ermächtigung *f*
authorize *vt* ermächtigen <*s.o.*>; genehmigen <*sth*>
autobiography *n* Autobiographie *f*
autograph *n* Autogramm *nt*
automatic *a*, **-ally** *adv* automatisch
automation *n* Automation *f*
automobile *n* Auto *nt*
autonom|ous *a* autonom. **~y** *n* Autonomie *f*
autumn *n* Herbst *m*. **~al** *a* herbstlich
auxiliary *a* Hilfs- ● *n* Helfer(in) *m(f)*, Hilfskraft *f*
avail *n* **to no ~** vergeblich
available *a* verfügbar; (*obtainable*) erhältlich
avalanche *n* Lawine *f*
avenge *vt* rächen
avenue *n* Allee *f*
average *a* Durchschnitts-, durchschnittlich ● *n* Durchschnitt *m*; **on ~** im Durchschnitt, durchschnittlich ● *vt* durchschnittlich schaffen
averse *a* **not be ~e to sth** etw (*dat*) nicht abgeneigt sein
avert *vt* abwenden
aviary *n* Vogelhaus *nt*
aviation *n* Luftfahrt *f*
avocado *n* Avocado *f*
avoid *vt* vermeiden; **~ s.o.** jdm aus dem Weg gehen. **~able** *a* vermeidbar. **~ance** *n* Vermeidung *f*
await *vt* warten auf (+ *acc*)
awake *a* wach; **wide ~** hellwach ● *vi* (*pt* **awoke**, *pp* **awoken**) erwachen
awaken *vt* wecken ● *vi* erwachen. **~ing** *n* Erwachen *nt*
award *n* Auszeichnung *f*; (*prize*) Preis *m* ● *vt* zuerkennen (**to s.o.** *dat*); verleihen <*prize*>

aware *a* **become ~** gewahr werden (**of** *gen*); **be ~ that** wissen, dass. **~ness** *n* Bewusstsein *nt*
away *adv* weg, fort; (*absent*) abwesend; **four kilometres ~** vier Kilometer entfernt; **play ~** (*Sport*) auswärts spielen. **~ game** *n* Auswärtsspiel *nt*
awful *a*, **-ly** *adv* furchtbar
awkward *a* schwierig; (*clumsy*) ungeschickt; (*embarrassing*) peinlich; (*inconvenient*) ungünstig. **~ly** *adv* ungeschickt; (*embarrassedly*) verlegen
awning *n* Markise *f*
awoke(n) *see* **awake**
axe *n* Axt *f* ● *vt* (*pres p* **axing**) streichen
axle *n* (*Techn*) Achse *f*

Bb

B *n* (*Mus*) H *nt*
baboon *n* Pavian *m*
baby *n* Baby *nt*; (*Amer* [!]) Schätzchen *nt*
baby: ~ish *a* kindisch. **~-sit** *vi* babysitten. **~-sitter** *n* Babysitter *m*
bachelor *n* Junggeselle *m*
back *n* Rücken *m*; (*reverse*) Rückseite *f*; (*of chair*) Rückenlehne *f*; (*Sport*) Verteidiger *m*; **at**/(*Auto*) **in the ~** hinten; **on the ~** auf der Rückseite; **~ to front** verkehrt ● *a* Hinter- ● *adv* zurück; **~ here/there** hier/da hinten; **~ at home** zu Hause; **go/pay ~** zurückgehen/-zahlen ● *vt* (*support*) unterstützen; (*with money*) finanzieren; (*Auto*) zurücksetzen; (*Betting*) [Geld] setzen auf (+ *acc*); (*cover the back of*) mit einer Verstärkung versehen ● *vi* (*Auto*) zurücksetzen. **~ down** *vi* klein beigeben. **~ in** *vi* rückwärts hineinfahren. **~ out** *vi* rückwärts hinaus-/herausfahren; (*fig*) aussteigen (**of** aus). **~ up** *vt* unterstützen; (*confirm*) bestätigen ● *vi* (*Auto*) zurücksetzen
back: ~ache *n* Rückenschmerzen *pl*. **~biting** *n* gehässiges Gerede *nt*. **~bone** *n* Rückgrat *nt*. **~date** *vt* rückdatieren; **~dated to** rückwirkend von. **~ door** *n* Hintertür *f*
backer *n* Geldgeber *m*
back: ~fire *vi* (*Auto*) fehlzünden; (*fig*) fehlschlagen. **~ground** *n* Hintergrund *m*; **family ~ground** Familienverhältnisse *pl*. **~hand** *n* (*Sport*) Rückhand *f*. **~handed** *a* <*compliment*> zweifelhaft
backing *n* (*support*) Unterstützung *f*; (*material*) Verstärkung *f*
back: ~lash *n* (*fig*) Gegenschlag *m*. **~log** *n* Rückstand *m* (**of** an + *dat*). **~pack** *n* Rucksack *m*. **~ seat** *n* Rücksitz *m*. **~side** *n* [!] Hintern *m*. **~stroke** *n* Rückenschwimmen *nt*. **~-up** *n* Unterstützung *f*; (*Amer: traffic jam*) Stau *m*
backward *a* zurückgeblieben; <*country*> rückständig ● *adv* rückwärts. **~s** rückwärts; **~s and forwards** hin und her
back yard *n* Hinterhof *m*; **not in my ~ yard** [!] nicht vor meiner Haustür
bacon *n* [Schinken]speck *m*
bacteria *npl* Bakterien *pl*
bad *a* (**worse, worst**) schlecht; (*serious*) schwer, schlimm; (*naughty*) unartig; **~ language**

gemeine Ausdrucksweise *f*; **feel ~** sich schlecht fühlen; (*feel guilty*) ein schlechtes Gewissen haben
badge *n* Abzeichen *nt*
badger *n* Dachs *m* ● *vt* plagen
badly *adv* schlecht; (*seriously*) schwer; **~ off** schlecht gestellt; **~ behaved** unerzogen; **want ~** sich (*dat*) sehnsüchtig wünschen; **need ~** dringend brauchen
bad-mannered *a* mit schlechten Manieren
badminton *n* Federball *m*
bad-tempered *a* schlecht gelaunt
baffle *vt* verblüffen
bag *n* Tasche *f*; (*of paper*) Tüte *f*; (*pouch*) Beutel *m*; **~s of** [!] jede Menge ● *vt* ([!] *reserve*) in Beschlag nehmen
baggage *n* [Reise]gepäck *nt*
baggy *a* <*clothes*> ausgebeult
bagpipes *npl* Dudelsack *m*
bail *n* Kaution *f*; **on ~** gegen Kaution ● *vt* **~ s.o. out** jdn gegen Kaution freibekommen; (*fig*) jdm aus der Patsche helfen
bait *n* Köder *m* ● *vt* mit einem Köder versehen; (*fig: torment*) reizen
bake *vt/i* backen
baker *n* Bäcker *m*; **~'s [shop]** Bäckerei *f*. **~y** *n* Bäckerei *f*
baking *n* Backen *nt*. **~-powder** *n* Backpulver *nt*
balance *n* (*equilibrium*) Gleichgewicht *nt*, Balance *f*; (*scales*) Waage *f*; (*Comm*) Saldo *m*; (*outstanding sum*) Restbetrag *m*; **[bank] ~** Kontostand *m*; **in the ~** (*fig*) in der Schwebe ● *vt* balancieren; (*equalize*) ausgleichen; (*Comm*) abschließen <*books*> ● *vi* balancieren; (*fig & Comm*) sich ausgleichen. **~d** *a* ausgewogen
balcony *n* Balkon *m*
bald *a* (**-er, -est**) kahl; <*person*> kahlköpfig
bald|ly *adv* unverblümt. **~ness** *n* Kahlköpfigkeit *f*
ball¹ *n* Ball *m*; (*Billiards, Croquet*) Kugel *f*; (*of yarn*) Knäuel *m & nt*; **on the ~** [!] auf Draht
ball² *n* (*dance*) Ball *m*
ball-bearing *n* Kugellager *nt*
ballerina *n* Ballerina *f*
ballet *m* Ballett *nt*. **~ dancer** *n* Balletttänzer(in) *m(f)*
balloon *n* Luftballon *m*; (*Aviat*) Ballon *m*
ballot *n* [geheime] Wahl *f*; (*on issue*) [geheime] Abstimmung *f*. **~-box** *n* Wahlurne *f*. **~-paper** *n* Stimmzettel *m*
ball: ~point [pen] *n* Kugelschreiber *m*. **~room** *n* Ballsaal *m*
balm *n* Balsam *m*
balmy *a* (**-ier, -iest**) *a* sanft
Baltic *a & n* **the ~ [Sea]** die Ostsee
bamboo *n* Bambus *m*
ban *n* Verbot *nt* ● *vt* (*pt/pp* **banned**) verbieten
banal *a* banal. **~ity** *n* Banalität *f*
banana *n* Banane *f*
band *n* Band *nt*; (*stripe*) Streifen *m*; (*group*) Schar *f*; (*Mus*) Kapelle *f*
bandage *n* Verband *m*; (*for support*) Bandage *f* ● *vt* verbinden; bandagieren <*limb*>
b. & b. *abbr of* **bed and breakfast**
bandit *n* Bandit *m*
band: ~stand *n* Musikpavillon *m*. **~wagon** *n* **jump on the ~wagon** (*fig*) sich einer erfolgreichen Sache anschließen
bang *n* (*noise*) Knall *m*; (*blow*) Schlag *m* ● *adv* **go ~** knallen ● *int* bums! peng! ● *vt* knallen; (*shut noisily*) zuknallen; (*strike*) schlagen auf (+ *acc*); **~ one's head** sich (*dat*) den Kopf stoßen (**on** an + *acc*) ● *vi* schlagen; <*door:*> zuknallen

banger *n (firework)* Knallfrosch *m*; ([!] *sausage*) Wurst *f*; **old ~** ([!] *car*) Klapperkiste *f*
bangle *n* Armreifen *m*
banish *vt* verbannen
banisters *npl* [Treppen]geländer *nt*
banjo *n* Banjo *nt*
bank[1] *n (of river)* Ufer *nt*; *(slope)* Hang *m* ● *vi (Aviat)* in die Kurve gehen
bank[2] *n* Bank *f* ● **~ on** *vt* sich verlassen auf (+ *acc*)
bank account *n* Bankkonto *nt*
banker *n* Bankier *m*
bank: ~ holiday *n* gesetzlicher Feiertag *m*. **~ing** *n* Bankwesen *nt*. **~note** *n* Banknote *f*
bankrupt *a* bankrott; **go ~** Bankrott machen ● *n* Bankrotteur *m* ● *vt* Bankrott machen. **~cy** *n* Bankrott *m*
banner *n* Banner *nt*; *(carried by demonstrators)* Transparent *nt*, Spruchband *nt*
banquet *n* Bankett *nt*
baptism *n* Taufe *f*
baptize *vt* taufen
bar *n* Stange *f*; *(of cage)* [Gitter]stab *m*; *(of gold)* Barren *m*; *(of chocolate)* Tafel *f*; *(of soap)* Stück *nt*; *(long)* Riegel *m*; *(café)* Bar *f*; *(counter)* Theke *f*; *(Mus)* Takt *m*; *(fig: obstacle)* Hindernis *nt*; **parallel ~s** *(Sport)* Barren *m*; **behind ~s** [!] hinter Gittern ● *vt* (*pt/pp* **barred**) versperren <*way, door*>; ausschließen <*person*>
barbar|ic *a* barbarisch. **~ity** *n* Barbarei *f*. **~ous** *a* barbarisch
barbecue *n* Grill *m*; *(party)* Grillfest *nt* ● *vt* [im Freien] grillen
barbed *a* **~ wire** Stacheldraht *m*
barber *n* [Herren]friseur *m*
bar code *n* Strichkode *m*
bare *a* (**-r, -st**) nackt, bloß; <*tree*> kahl; *(empty)* leer; *(mere)* bloß
bare: ~back *adv* ohne Sattel. **~faced** *a* schamlos. **~foot** *adv* barfuß. **~headed** *a* mit unbedecktem Kopf
barely *adv* kaum
bargain *n (agreement)* Geschäft *nt*; *(good buy)* Gelegenheitskauf *m*; **into the ~** noch dazu; **make a ~** sich einigen ● *vi* handeln; *(haggle)* feilschen; **~ for** *(expect)* rechnen mit
barge *n* Lastkahn *m*; *(towed)* Schleppkahn *m* ● *vi* **~ in** [!] hereinplatzen
baritone *n* Bariton *m*
bark[1] *n (of tree)* Rinde *f*
bark[2] *n* Bellen *nt* ● *vi* bellen
barley *n* Gerste *f*
bar: ~maid *n* Schankmädchen *nt*. **~man** Barmann *m*
barmy *a* [!] verrückt
barn *n* Scheune *f*
barometer *n* Barometer *nt*
baron *n* Baron *m*. **~ess** *n* Baronin *f*
barracks *npl* Kaserne *f*
barrage *n (in river)* Wehr *nt*; *(Mil)* Sperrfeuer *nt*; *(fig)* Hagel *m*
barrel *n* Fass *nt*; *(of gun)* Lauf *m*; *(of cannon)* Rohr *nt*. **~-organ** *n* Drehorgel *f*
barren *a* unfruchtbar; <*landscape*> öde
barricade *n* Barrikade *f* ● *vt* verbarrikadieren
barrier *n* Barriere *f*; *(across road)* Schranke *f*; *(Rail)* Sperre *f*; *(fig)* Hindernis *nt*
barrow *n* Karre *f*, Karren *m*
base *n* Fuß *m*; *(fig)* Basis *f*; *(Mil)* Stützpunkt *m* ● *vt* stützen (**on** auf + *acc*); **be ~d on** basieren auf (+ *dat*)
base: ~ball *n* Baseball *m*. **~less** *a* unbegründet. **~ment** *n* Kellergeschoss *nt*
bash *n* Schlag *m*; **have a ~!** [!] probier es mal! ● *vt* hauen

basic *a* Grund-; (*fundamental*) grundlegend; (*essential*) wesentlich; (*unadorned*) einfach; **the ~s** das Wesentliche. **~ally** *adv* grundsätzlich
basin *n* Becken *nt;* (*for washing*) Waschbecken *nt;* (*for food*) Schüssel *f*
basis *n* (*pl* **-ses**) Basis *f*
bask *vi* sich sonnen
basket *n* Korb *m.* **~ball** *n* Basketball *m*
Basle *n* Basel *nt*
bass *a* Bass-; **~ voice** Bassstimme *f* ●*n* Bass *m;* (*person*) Bassist *m*
bassoon *n* Fagott *nt*
bastard *n* ⊠ Schuft *m*
bat¹ *n* Schläger *m;* **off one's own ~** ! auf eigene Faust ●*vt* (*pt/pp* **batted**) schlagen; **not ~ an eyelid** (*fig*) nicht mit der Wimper zucken
bat² *n* (*Zool*) Fledermaus *f*
batch *n* (*of people*) Gruppe *f;* (*of papers*) Stoß *m;* (*of goods*) Sendung *f;* (*of bread*) Schub *m*
bath *n* (*pl* **-s**) Bad *nt;* (*tub*) Badewanne *f;* **~s** *pl* Badeanstalt *f;* **have a ~** baden
bathe *n* Bad *nt* ●*vt/i* baden. **~r** *n* Badende(r) *m/f*
bathing *n* Baden *nt.* **~-cap** *n* Bademütze *f.* **~-costume** *n* Badeanzug *m*
bath: ~-mat *n* Bădematte *f.* **~room** *n* Badezimmer *nt.* **~-towel** *n* Badetuch *nt*
battalion *n* Bataillon *nt*
batter *n* (*Culin*) flüssiger Teig *m* ●*vt* schlagen. **~ed** *a* <*car*> verbeult; <*wife*> misshandelt
battery *n* Batterie *f*
battle *n* Schlacht *f;* (*fig*) Kampf *m* ●*vi* (*fig*) kämpfen (**for** um)
battle: ~field *n* Schlachtfeld *nt.* **~ship** *n* Schlachtschiff *nt*
batty *a* ! verrückt
Bavaria *n* Bayern *nt.* **~n** *a* bayrisch ●*n* Bayer(in) *m(f)*
bawl *vt/i* brüllen
bay¹ *n* (*Geog*) Bucht *f;* (*Archit*) Erker *m*
bay² *n* (*Bot*) [echter] Lorbeer *m.* **~-leaf** *n* Lorbeerblatt *nt*
bayonet *n* Bajonett *nt*
bay window *n* Erkerfenster *nt*
bazaar *n* Basar *m*
BC *abbr* (**before Christ**) v. Chr.

be

(*pres* **am, are, is**, *pl* **are**; *pt* **was**, *pl* **were**; *pp* **been**)

● *intransitive verb*

····➤ (*expressing identity, nature, state, age etc.*) sein. **he is a teacher** er ist Lehrer. **she is French** sie ist Französin. **he is very nice** er ist sehr nett. **I am tall** ich bin groß. **you are thirty** du bist dreißig. **it was very cold** es war sehr kalt

····➤ (*expressing general position*) sein; (*lie*) liegen; (*stand*) stehen. **where is the bank?** wo ist die Bank? **the book is on the table** das Buch liegt auf dem Tisch. **the vase is on the shelf** die Vase steht auf dem Brett

····➤ (*feel*) **I am cold/hot** mir ist kalt/heiß. **I am ill** ich bin krank. **I am well** mir geht es gut. **how are you?** wie geht es Ihnen?

····➤ (*date*) **it is the 5th today** heute haben wir den Fünften

····➤ (*go, come, stay*) sein. **I have been to Vienna** ich bin in Wien gewesen. **have you ever been to London?** bist du schon einmal in London gewesen? **has the postman been?** war der Briefträger schon da? **I've been here for an hour** ich bin seit einer Stunde hier

····➤ (*origin*) **where are you from?** woher stammen *od* kommen Sie? **she is from Australia** sie stammt *od* ist aus Australien

····▶ (*cost*) kosten. **how much are the eggs?** was kosten die Eier?

····▶ (*in calculations*) **two threes are six** zweimal drei ist *od* sind sechs

····▶ (*exist*) **there is**/**are** es gibt (+ *acc*). **there's no fish left** es gibt keinen Fisch mehr

● *auxiliary verb*

····▶ (*forming continuous tenses: not translated*) **I'm working** ich arbeite. **I'm leaving tomorrow** ich reise morgen [ab]. **they were singing** sie sangen. **they will be coming on Tuesday** sie kommen am Dienstag

····▶ (*forming passive*) werden. **the child was found** das Kind wurde gefunden. **German is spoken here** hier wird Deutsch gesprochen; hier spricht man Deutsch

····▶ (*expressing arrangement, obligation, destiny*) sollen. **I am to go**/**inform you** ich soll gehen/Sie unterrichten. **they were to fly today** sie sollten heute fliegen. **you are to do that immediately** das sollst du sofort machen. **you are not to ...** (*prohibition*) du darfst nicht .... **they were never to meet again** (*destiny*) sie sollten sich nie wieder treffen

····▶ (*in short answers*) **Are you disappointed? — Yes I am** Bist du enttäuscht? – Ja. (*negating previous statement*) **Aren't you coming? — Yes I am!** Kommst du nicht? – Doch!

····▶ (*in tag questions*) **isn't it? wasn't she? aren't they?** *etc.* nicht wahr. **it's a beautiful house, isn't it?** das Haus ist sehr schön, nicht wahr?

beach *n* Strand *m*

bead *n* Perle *f*

beak *n* Schnabel *m*

beam *n* Balken *m*; (*of light*) Strahl *m* ● *vi* strahlen. **~ing** *a* [freude]strahlend

bean *n* Bohne *f*

bear¹ *n* Bär *m*

bear² *vt/i* (*pt* **bore**, *pp* **borne**) tragen; (*endure*) ertragen; gebären <*child*>; **~ right** sich rechts halten. **~able** *a* erträglich

beard *n* Bart *m*. **~ed** *a* bärtig

bearer *n* Träger *m*; (*of news, cheque*) Überbringer *m*; (*of passport*) Inhaber(in) *m*(*f*)

bearing *n* Haltung *f*; (*Techn*) Lager *nt*; **get one's ~s** sich orientieren

beast *n* Tier *nt*; ([!] *person*) Biest *nt*

beastly *a* (**-ier, -iest**) [!] scheußlich; <*person*> gemein

beat *n* Schlag *m*; (*of policeman*) Runde *f*; (*rhythm*) Takt *m* ● *vt/i* (*pt* **beat**, *pp* **beaten**) schlagen; (*thrash*) verprügeln; klopfen <*carpet*>; (*hammer*) hämmern (**on** an + *acc*); **~ it!** [!] hau ab! **it ~s me** [!] das begreife ich nicht. **~ up** *vt* zusammenschlagen

beat|en *a* **off the ~en track** abseits. **~ing** *n* Prügel *pl*

beauti|ful *a*, **-ly** *adv* schön. **~fy** *vt* (*pt/pp* **-ied**) verschönern

beauty *n* Schönheit *f*. **~ parlour** *n* Kosmetiksalon *m*. **~ spot** *n* Schönheitsfleck *m*; (*place*) landschaftlich besonders reizvolles Fleckchen *nt*.

beaver *n* Biber *m*

became *see* **become**

because *conj* weil ● *adv* **~ of** wegen (+ *gen*)

becom|e *vt/i* (*pt* **became**, *pp* **become**) werden. **~ing** *a* <*clothes*> kleidsam

bed *n* Bett *nt*; (*layer*) Schicht *f*; (*of flowers*) Beet *nt*; **in ~** im Bett; **go to ~** ins *od* zu Bett gehen; **~ and breakfast** Zimmer mit Frühstück.

~**clothes** *npl*, ~**ding** *n* Bettzeug *nt*. ~**room** *n* Schlafzimmer *nt*
bedside *n* **at his** ~ an seinem Bett. ~ **lamp** *n* Nachttischlampe *f*. ~ **table** *n* Nachttisch *m*
bed: ~**sitter** *n*, ~**-sitting-room** *n* Wohnschlafzimmer *nt*. ~**spread** *n* Tagesdecke *f*. ~**time** *n* **at** ~**time** vor dem Schlafengehen
bee *n* Biene *f*
beech *n* Buche *f*
beef *n* Rindfleisch *nt*. ~**burger** *n* Hamburger *m*
bee: ~**hive** *n* Bienenstock *m*. ~**-line** *n* **make a** ~**-line for** [!] zusteuern auf (+ *acc*)
been *see* **be**
beer *n* Bier *nt*
beet *n* (*Amer: beetroot*) Rote Bete *f*; **[sugar]** ~ Zuckerrübe *f*
beetle *n* Käfer *m*
beetroot *n* Rote Bete *f*
before *prep* vor (+ *dat/acc*); **the day** ~ **yesterday** vorgestern; ~ **long** bald ● *adv* vorher; (*already*) schon; **never** ~ noch nie; ~ **that** davor ● *conj* (*time*) ehe, bevor. ~**hand** *adv* vorher, im Voraus
beg *v* (*pt/pp* **begged**) ● *vi* betteln ● *vt* (*entreat*) anflehen; (*ask*) bitten (**for** um)
began *see* **begin**
beggar *n* Bettler(in) *m(f)*; [!] Kerl *m*
begin *vt/i* (*pt* **began**, *pp* **begun**, *pres p* **beginning**) anfangen, beginnen; **to** ~ **with** anfangs. ~**ner** *n* Anfänger(in) *m(f)*. ~**ning** *n* Anfang *m*, Beginn *m*
begun *see* **begin**
behalf *n* **on** ~ **of** im Namen von; **on my** ~ meinetwegen
behave *vi* sich verhalten; ~ **oneself** sich benehmen
behaviour *n* Verhalten *nt*; **good/bad** ~ gutes/schlechtes Benehmen *nt*
behind *prep* hinter (+ *dat/acc*); **be** ~ **sth** hinter etw (*dat*) stecken ● *adv* hinten; (*late*) im Rückstand; **a long way** ~ weit zurück ● *n* [!] Hintern *m*. ~**hand** *adv* im Rückstand
beige *a* beige
being *n* Dasein *nt*; **living** ~ Lebewesen *nt*; **come into** ~ entstehen
belated *a*, **-ly** *adv* verspätet
belfry *n* Glockenstube *f*; (*tower*) Glockenturm *m*
Belgian *a* belgisch ● *n* Belgier(in) *m(f)*
Belgium *n* Belgien *nt*
belief *n* Glaube *m*
believable *a* glaubhaft
believe *vt/i* glauben (**s.o.** jdm; **in** an + *acc*). ~**r** *n* (*Relig*) Gläubige(r) *m/f*
belittle *vt* herabsetzen
bell *n* Glocke *f*; (*on door*) Klingel *f*
bellow *vt/i* brüllen
belly *n* Bauch *m*
belong *vi* gehören (**to** *dat*); (*be member*) angehören (**to** *dat*). ~**ings** *npl* Sachen *pl*
beloved *a* geliebt ● *n* Geliebte(r) *m/f*
below *prep* unter (+ *dat/acc*) ● *adv* unten; (*Naut*) unter Deck
belt *n* Gürtel *m*; (*area*) Zone *f*; (*Techn*) [Treib]riemen *m* ● *vi* ([!] *rush*) rasen ● *vt* ([!] *hit*) hauen
bench *n* Bank *f*; (*work-*) Werkbank *f*
bend *n* Biegung *f*; (*in road*) Kurve *f*; **round the** ~ [!] verrückt ● *v* (*pt/pp* **bent**) ● *vt* biegen; beugen <*arm, leg*> ● *vi* sich bücken; <*thing:*> sich biegen; <*road:*> eine Biegung machen. ~ **down** *vi* sich bücken. ~ **over** *vi* sich vornüberbeugen
beneath *prep* unter (+ *dat/acc*); ~ **him** (*fig*) unter seiner Würde ● *adv* darunter
benefactor *n* Wohltäter(in) *m(f)*
beneficial *a* nützlich

B

benefit *n* Vorteil *m*; (*allowance*) Unterstützung *f*; (*insurance*) Leistung *f*; **sickness ~** Krankengeld *nt* ●*v* (*pt/pp* **-fited**, *pres p* **-fiting**) ●*vt* nützen (+ *dat*) ●*vi* profitieren (**from** von)

benevolen|ce *n* Wohlwollen *nt*. **~t** *a*, **-ly** *adv* wohlwollend

bent *see* **bend** ●*a* <*person*> gebeugt; (*distorted*) verbogen; ([!] *dishonest*) korrupt; **be ~ on doing sth** darauf erpicht sein, etw zu tun ●*n* Hang *m*, Neigung *f* (**for** zu); **artistic ~** künstlerische Ader *f*

bequeath *vt* vermachen (**to** *dat*)

bereave|d *n* **the ~d** *pl* die Hinterbliebenen

beret *n* Baskenmütze *f*

Berne *n* Bern *nt*

berry *n* Beere *f*

berth *n* (*on ship*) [Schlaf]koje *f*; (*ship's anchorage*) Liegeplatz *m*; **give a wide ~ to** [!] einen großen Bogen machen um

beside *prep* neben (+ *dat/acc*); **~ oneself** außer sich (*dat*)

besides *prep* außer (+ *dat*) ●*adv* außerdem

besiege *vt* belagern

best *a & n* beste(r,s); **the ~** der/die/das Beste; **at ~** bestenfalls; **all the ~!** alles Gute! **do one's ~** sein Bestes tun; **the ~ part of a year** fast ein Jahr; **to the ~ of my knowledge** so viel ich weiß; **make the ~ of it** das Beste daraus machen ●*adv* am besten; **as ~ I could** so gut ich konnte. **~ man** *n* ≈ Trauzeuge *m*. **~seller** *n* Bestseller *m*

bet *n* Wette *f* ●*v* (*pt/pp* **bet** *or* **betted**) ●*vt* **~ s.o. £5** mit jdm um £5 wetten ●*vi* wetten; **~ on** [Geld] setzen auf (+ *acc*)

betray *vt* verraten. **~al** *n* Verrat *m*

better *a* besser; **get ~** sich bessern; (*after illness*) sich erholen ●*adv* besser; **~ off** besser dran; **~ not** lieber nicht; **all the ~** umso besser; **the sooner the ~** je eher, desto besser; **think ~ of it** sich eines Besseren besinnen; **you'd ~ stay** du bleibst am besten hier ●*vt* verbessern; (*do better than*) übertreffen; **~ oneself** sich verbessern

between *prep* zwischen (+ *dat/acc*); **~ you and me** unter uns; **~ us** (*together*) zusammen ●*adv* **[in] ~** dazwischen

beware *vi* sich in Acht nehmen (**of** vor + *dat*); **~ of the dog!** Vorsicht, bissiger Hund!

bewilder *vt* verwirren. **~ment** *n* Verwirrung *f*

bewitch *vt* verzaubern; (*fig*) bezaubern

beyond *prep* über (+ *acc*) … hinaus; (*further*) weiter als; **~ reach** außer Reichweite; **~ doubt** ohne jeden Zweifel; **it's ~ me** [!] das geht über meinen Horizont ●*adv* darüber hinaus

bias *n* Voreingenommenheit *f*; (*preference*) Vorliebe *f*; (*Jur*) Befangenheit *f* ●*vt* (*pt/pp* **biased**) (*influence*) beeinflussen. **~ed** *a* voreingenommen; (*Jur*) befangen

bib *n* Lätzchen *nt*

Bible *n* Bibel *f*

biblical *a* biblisch

bibliography *n* Bibliographie *f*

bicycle *n* Fahrrad *nt* ●*vi* mit dem Rad fahren

bid *n* Gebot *nt*; (*attempt*) Versuch *m* ●*vt/i* (*pt/pp* **bid**, *pres p* **bidding**) bieten (**for** auf + *acc*); (*Cards*) reizen

bidder *n* Bieter(in) *m(f)*

bide *vt* **~ one's time** den richtigen Moment abwarten

big *a* (**bigger, biggest**) groß ●*adv* **talk ~** [!] angeben

bigam|ist *n* Bigamist *m*. **~y** *n* Bigamie *f*

big-headed *a* [!] eingebildet

bigot *n* Eiferer *m*. **~ed** *a* engstirnig
bigwig *n* [!] hohes Tier *nt*
bike *n* [!] [Fahr]rad *nt*
bikini *n* Bikini *m*
bile *n* Galle *f*
bilingual *a* zweisprachig
bill¹ *n* Rechnung *f*; (*poster*) Plakat *nt*; (*Pol*) Gesetzentwurf *m*; (*Amer: note*) Banknote *f*; **~ of exchange** Wechsel *m* ● *vt* eine Rechnung schicken (+ *dat*)
bill² *n* (*beak*) Schnabel *m*
billfold *n* (*Amer*) Brieftasche *f*
billiards *n* Billard *nt*
billion *n* (*thousand million*) Milliarde *f*; (*million million*) Billion *f*
bin *n* Mülleimer *m*; (*for bread*) Kasten *m*
bind *vt* (*pt/pp* **bound**) binden (**to** an + *acc*); (*bandage*) verbinden; (*Jur*) verpflichten; (*cover the edge of*) einfassen. **~ing** *a* verbindlich ● *n* Einband *m*; (*braid*) Borte *f*; (*on ski*) Bindung *f*
binge *n* [!] **go on the ~** eine Sauftour machen
binoculars *npl* **[pair of] ~** Fernglas *nt*
bio|chemistry *n* Biochemie *f*. **~degradable** *a* biologisch abbaubar
biograph|er *n* Biograph(in) *m(f)*. **~y** *n* Biographie *f*
biological *a* biologisch
biolog|ist *n* Biologe *m*. **~y** *n* Biologie *f*
bioterrorism *n* Bioterrorismus *m*
birch *n* Birke *f*; (*whip*) Rute *f*
bird *n* Vogel *m*; ([!] *girl*) Mädchen *nt*; **kill two ~s with one stone** zwei Fliegen mit einer Klappe schlagen
Biro (P) *n* Kugelschreiber *m*
birth *n* Geburt *f*
birth: ~ certificate *n* Geburtsurkunde *f*. **~-control** *n* Geburtenregelung *f*. **~day** *n* Geburtstag *m*. **~-rate** *n* Geburtenziffer *f*
biscuit *n* Keks *m*
bishop *n* Bischof *m*
bit¹ *n* Stückchen *nt*; (*for horse*) Gebiss *nt*; (*Techn*) Bohreinsatz *m*; **a ~** ein bisschen; **~ by ~** nach und nach; **a ~ of bread** ein bisschen Brot; **do one's ~** sein Teil tun
bit² *see* **bite**
bitch *n* Hündin *f*; [x] Luder *nt*. **~y** *a* gehässig
bit|e *n* Biss *m*; **[insect] ~** Stich *m*; (*mouthful*) Bissen *m* ● *vt/i* (*pt* **bit**, *pp* **bitten**) beißen; <*insect:*> stechen; kauen <*one's nails*>. **~ing** *a* beißend
bitten *see* **bite**
bitter *a*, **-ly** *adv* bitter; **~ly cold** bitterkalt ● *n* bitteres Bier *nt*. **~ness** *n* Bitterkeit *f*
bitty *a* zusammengestoppelt
bizarre *a* bizarr
black *a* (**-er, -est**) schwarz; **be ~ and blue** grün und blau sein ● *n* Schwarz *nt*; (*person*) Schwarze(r) *m/f* ● *vt* schwärzen; boykottieren <*goods*>
black: ~berry *n* Brombeere *f*. **~bird** *n* Amsel *f*. **~board** *n* (*Sch*) [Wand]tafel *f*. **~currant** *n* schwarze Johannisbeere *f*
blacken *vt/i* schwärzen
black: ~ eye *n* blaues Auge *nt*. **B~ Forest** *n* Schwarzwald *m*. **~ ice** *n* Glatteis *nt*. **~list** *vt* auf die schwarze Liste setzen. **~mail** *n* Erpressung *f* ● *vt* erpressen. **~mailer** *n* Erpresser(in) *m(f)*. **~ market** *n* schwarzer Markt *m*. **~-out** *n* **have a ~-out** (*Med*) das Bewusstsein verlieren. **~ pudding** *n* Blutwurst *f*
bladder *n* (*Anat*) Blase *f*
blade *n* Klinge *f*; (*of grass*) Halm *m*

blame *n* Schuld *f* ● *vt* die Schuld geben (+ *dat*); **no one is to ~** keiner ist schuld daran. **~less** *a* schuldlos
bland *a* (**-er, -est**) mild
blank *a* leer; <*look*> ausdruckslos ● *n* Lücke *f*; (*cartridge*) Platzpatrone *f*. **~ cheque** *n* Blankoscheck *m*
blanket *n* Decke *f*; **wet ~** [!] Spielverderber(in) *m*(*f*)
blare *vt*/*i* schmettern
blasé *a* blasiert
blast *n* (*gust*) Luftstoß *m*; (*sound*) Schmettern *nt*; (*of horn*) Tuten *nt* ● *vt* sprengen ● *int* [✖] verdammt. **~ed** *a* [✖] verdammt
blast-off *n* (*of missile*) Start *m*
blatant *a* offensichtlich
blaze *n* Feuer *nt* ● *vi* brennen
blazer *n* Blazer *m*
bleach *n* Bleichmittel *nt* ● *vt*/*i* bleichen
bleak *a* (**-er, -est**) öde; (*fig*) trostlos
bleary-eyed *a* mit trüben/(*on waking up*) verschlafenen Augen
bleat *vi* blöken
bleed *v* (*pt*/*pp* **bled**) ● *vi* bluten ● *vt* entlüften <*radiator*>
bleep *n* Piepton *m* ● *vi* piepsen ● *vt* mit dem Piepser rufen. **~er** *n* Piepser *m*
blemish *n* Makel *m*
blend *n* Mischung *f* ● *vt* mischen ● *vi* sich vermischen
bless *vt* segnen. **~ed** *a* heilig; [✖] verflixt. **~ing** *n* Segen *m*
blew *see* **blow**[2]
blight *n* (*Bot*) Brand *m*
blind *a* blind; <*corner*> unübersichtlich; **~ man/woman** Blinde(r) *m*/*f* ● *n* **[roller] ~** Rouleau *nt* ● *vt* blenden
blind: ~ alley *n* Sackgasse *f*. **~fold** *a & adv* mit verbundenen Augen ● *n* Augenbinde *f* ● *vt* die Augen verbinden (+ *dat*). **~ly** *adv* blindlings. **~ness** *n* Blindheit *f*
blink *vi* blinzeln; <*light:*> blinken
bliss *n* Glückseligkeit *f*. **~ful** *a* glücklich
blister *n* (*Med*) Blase *f*
blitz *n* [!] Großaktion *f*
blizzard *n* Schneesturm *m*
bloated *a* aufgedunsen
blob *n* Klecks *m*
block *n* Block *m*; (*of wood*) Klotz *m*; (*of flats*) [Wohn]block *m* ● *vt* blockieren. **~ up** *vt* zustopfen
blockade *n* Blockade *f* ● *vt* blockieren
blockage *n* Verstopfung *f*
block: ~head *n* [!] Dummkopf *m*. **~ letters** *npl* Blockschrift *f*
bloke *n* [!] Kerl *m*
blonde *a* blond ● *n* Blondine *f*
blood *n* Blut *nt*
blood: ~-curdling *a* markerschütternd. **~ donor** *n* Blutspender *m*. **~ group** *n* Blutgruppe *f*. **~hound** *n* Bluthund *m*. **~-poisoning** *n* Blutvergiftung *f*. **~ pressure** *n* Blutdruck *m*. **~shed** *n* Blutvergießen *nt*. **~shot** *a* blutunterlaufen. **~ sports** *npl* Jagdsport *m*. **~-stained** *a* blutbefleckt. **~ test** *n* Blutprobe *f*. **~thirsty** *a* blutdürstig. **~-vessel** *n* Blutgefäß *nt*
bloody *a* (**-ier, -iest**) blutig; [✖] verdammt. **~-minded** *a* [✖] stur
bloom *n* Blüte *f* ● *vi* blühen
blossom *n* Blüte *f* ● *vi* blühen
blot *n* [Tinten]klecks *m*; (*fig*) Fleck *m* ● **~ out** *vt* (*fig*) auslöschen
blotch *n* Fleck *m*. **~y** *a* fleckig
blotting-paper *n* Löschpapier *nt*
blouse *n* Bluse *f*
blow[1] *n* Schlag *m*
blow[2] *v* (*pt* **blew**, *pp* **blown**) ● *vt* blasen; (*fam; squander*) verpulvern; **~ one's nose** sich (*dat*) die Nase putzen ● *vi* blasen; <*fuse:*> durchbrennen. **~ away** *vt* wegblasen ● *vi*

wegfliegen. ~ **down** *vt* umwehen ● *vi* umfallen. ~ **out** *vt* (*extinguish*) ausblasen. ~ **over** *vi* umfallen; (*fig: die down*) vorübergehen. ~ **up** *vt* (*inflate*) aufblasen; (*enlarge*) vergrößern; (*shatter by explosion*) sprengen ● *vi* explodieren

blowlamp *n* Lötlampe *f*

blown *see* **blow²**

blowtorch *n* (*Amer*) Lötlampe *f*

blowy *a* windig

blue *a* (**-r, -st**) blau; **feel ~** deprimiert sein ● *n* Blau *nt*; **have the ~s** deprimiert sein; **out of the ~** aus heiterem Himmel

blue: ~bell *n* Sternhyazinthe *f*. **~berry** *n* Heidelbeere *f*. **~bottle** *n* Schmeißfliege *f*. ~ **film** *n* Pornofilm *m*. **~print** *n* (*fig*) Entwurf *m*

bluff *n* Bluff *m* ● *vi* bluffen

blunder *n* Schnitzer *m* ● *vi* einen Schnitzer machen

blunt *a* stumpf; <*person*> geradeheraus. **~ly** *adv* unverblümt, geradeheraus

blur *n* **it's all a ~** alles ist verschwommen ● *vt* (*pt/pp* **blurred**) verschwommen machen; **~red** verschwommen

blush *n* Erröten *nt* ● *vi* erröten

bluster *n* Großtuerei *f*. **~y** *a* windig

boar *n* Eber *m*

board *n* Brett *nt*; (*for notices*) schwarzes Brett *nt*; (*committee*) Ausschuss *m*; (*of directors*) Vorstand *m*; **on ~** an Bord; **full ~** Vollpension *f*; **~ and lodging** Unterkunft und Verpflegung *pl* ● *vt* einsteigen in (+ *acc*); (*Naut, Aviat*) besteigen ● *vi* an Bord gehen. ~ **up** *vt* mit Brettern verschlagen

boarder *n* Pensionsgast *m*; (*Sch*) Internatsschüler(in) *m*(*f*)

board: ~-game *n* Brettspiel *nt*. **~ing-house** *n* Pension *f*. **~ing-school** *n* Internat *nt*

boast *vt* sich rühmen (+ *gen*) ● *vi* prahlen (**about** mit). **~ful** *a*, **-ly** *adv* prahlerisch

boat *n* Boot *nt*; (*ship*) Schiff *nt*

bob *vi* (*pt/pp* **bobbed**) ~ **up and down** sich auf und ab bewegen

bob-sleigh *n* Bob *m*

bodily *a* körperlich ● *adv* (*forcibly*) mit Gewalt

body *n* Körper *m*; (*corpse*) Leiche *f*; (*corporation*) Körperschaft *f*. **~guard** *n* Leibwächter *m*. **~work** *n* (*Auto*) Karosserie *f*

bog *n* Sumpf *m*

bogus *a* falsch

boil¹ *n* Furunkel *m*

boil² *n* **bring/come to the ~** zum Kochen bringen/kommen ● *vt/i* kochen; **~ed potatoes** Salzkartoffeln *pl*. ~ **down** *vi* (*fig*) hinauslaufen (**to** auf + *acc*). ~ **over** *vi* überkochen

boiler *n* Heizkessel *m*

boiling point *n* Siedepunkt *m*

boisterous *a* übermütig

bold *a* (**-er, -est**), **-ly** *adv* kühn; (*Typ*) fett. **~ness** *n* Kühnheit *f*

bolster *n* Nackenrolle *f* ● *vt* ~ **up** Mut machen (+ *dat*)

bolt *n* Riegel *m*; (*Techn*) Bolzen *m* ● *vt* schrauben (**to** an + *acc*); verriegeln <*door*>; hinunterschlingen <*food*> ● *vi* abhauen; <*horse*:> durchgehen

bomb *n* Bombe *f* ● *vt* bombardieren

bombard *vt* beschießen; (*fig*) bombardieren

bombastic *a* bombastisch

bomber *n* (*Aviat*) Bomber *m*; (*person*) Bombenleger(in) *m*(*f*)

bond *n* (*fig*) Band *nt*; (*Comm*) Obligation *f*

bone *n* Knochen *m*; (*of fish*) Gräte *f* ● *vt* von den Knochen lösen <*meat*>; entgräten <*fish*>. **~-dry** *a* knochentrocken

bonfire *n* Gartenfeuer *nt;* (*celebratory*) Freudenfeuer *nt*

bonus *n* Prämie *f;* (*gratuity*) Gratifikation *f;* (*fig*) Plus *nt*

bony *a* (**-ier, -iest**) knochig; <*fish*> grätig

boo *int* buh! ● *vt* ausbuhen ● *vi* buhen

boob *n* (! *mistake*) Schnitzer *m*

book *n* Buch *nt;* (*of tickets*) Heft *nt;* **keep the ~s** (*Comm*) die Bücher führen ● *vt/i* buchen; (*reserve*) [vor]bestellen; (*for offence*) aufschreiben

book: ~case *n* Bücherregal *nt.* **~-ends** *npl* Buchstützen *pl.* **~ing-office** *n* Fahrkartenschalter *m.* **~keeping** *n* Buchführung *f.* **~let** *n* Broschüre *f.* **~maker** *n* Buchmacher *m.* **~mark** *n* Lesezeichen *nt.* **~seller** *n* Buchhändler(in) *m(f).* **~shop** *n* Buchhandlung *f.* **~stall** *n* Bücherstand *m*

boom *n* (*Comm*) Hochkonjunktur *f;* (*upturn*) Aufschwung *m* ● *vi* dröhnen; (*fig*) blühen

boon *n* Segen *m*

boost *n* Auftrieb *m* ● *vt* Auftrieb geben (+ *dat*)

boot *n* Stiefel *m;* (*Auto*) Kofferraum *m*

booth *n* Bude *f;* (*cubicle*) Kabine *f*

booty *n* Beute *f*

booze *n* ! Alkohol *m* ● *vi* ! saufen

border *n* Rand *m;* (*frontier*) Grenze *f;* (*in garden*) Rabatte *f* ● *vi* **~ on** grenzen an (+ *acc*). **~line case** *n* Grenzfall *m*

bore[1] *see* **bear**[2]

bor|e[2] *n* (*of gun*) Kaliber *nt;* (*person*) langweiliger Mensch *m;* (*thing*) langweilige Sache *f* ● *vt* langweilen; **be ~ed** sich langweilen. **~edom** *n* Langeweile *f.* **~ing** *a* langweilig

born *pp* **be ~** geboren werden ● *a* geboren

borne *see* **bear**[2]

borrow *vt* [sich (*dat*)] borgen *od* leihen (**from** von)

bosom *n* Busen *m*

boss *n* ! Chef *m* ● *vt* herumkommandieren. **~y** *a* herrschsüchtig

botanical *a* botanisch

botan|ist *n* Botaniker(in) *m(f).* **~y** *n* Botanik *f*

both *a & pron* beide; **~[of] the children** beide Kinder; **~ of them** beide [von ihnen] ● *adv* **~ men and women** sowohl Männer als auch Frauen

bother *n* Mühe *f;* (*minor trouble*) Ärger *m* ● *int* ! verflixt! ● *vt* belästigen; (*disturb*) stören ● *vi* sich kümmern (**about** um)

bottle *n* Flasche *f* ● *vt* auf Flaschen abfüllen; (*preserve*) einmachen

bottle: ~-neck *n* (*fig*) Engpass *m.* **~-opener** *n* Flaschenöffner *m*

bottom *a* unterste(r,s) ● *n* (*of container*) Boden *m;* (*of river*) Grund *m;* (*of page, hill*) Fuß *m;* (*buttocks*) Hintern *m;* **at the ~** unten; **get to the ~ of sth** (*fig*) hinter etw (*acc*) kommen

bought *see* **buy**

bounce *vi* [auf]springen; <*cheque:*> ! nicht gedeckt sein ● *vt* aufspringen lassen <*ball*>

bouncer *n* ! Rausschmeißer *m*

bound[1] *n* Sprung *m* ● *vi* springen

bound[2] *see* **bind** ● *a* **~ for** <*ship*> mit Kurs auf (+ *acc*); **be ~ to do sth** etw bestimmt machen; (*obliged*) verpflichtet sein, etw zu machen

boundary *n* Grenze *f*

bounds *npl* (*fig*) Grenzen *pl;* **out of ~** verboten

bouquet *n* [Blumen]strauß *m;* (*of wine*) Bukett *nt*

bourgeois *a* (*pej*) spießbürgerlich

bout *n* (*Med*) Anfall *m*; (*Sport*) Kampf *m*
bow¹ *n* (*weapon & Mus*) Bogen *m*; (*knot*) Schleife *f*
bow² *n* Verbeugung *f* ● *vi* sich verbeugen ● *vt* neigen <*head*>
bow³ *n* (*Naut*) Bug *m*
bowel *n* Darm *m*. **~s** *pl* Eingeweide *pl*
bowl¹ *n* Schüssel *f*; (*shallow*) Schale *f*
bowl² *n* (*ball*) Kugel *f* ● *vt/i* werfen. **~ over** *vt* umwerfen
bowler *n* (*Sport*) Werfer *m*
bowling *n* Kegeln *nt*. **~-alley** *n* Kegelbahn *f*
bowls *n* Bowlsspiel *nt*
bow-tie *n* Fliege *f*
box¹ *n* Schachtel *f*; (*wooden*) Kiste *f*; (*cardboard*) Karton *m*, (*Theat*) Loge *f*
box² *vt/i* (*Sport*) boxen
box|er *n* Boxer *m*. **~ing** *n* Boxen *nt*. **B~ing Day** *n* zweiter Weihnachtstag *m*
box: ~-office *n* (*Theat*) Kasse *f*. **~-room** *n* Abstellraum *m*
boy *n* Junge *m*
boycott *n* Boykott *m* ● *vt* boykottieren
boy: ~friend *n* Freund *m*. **~ish** *a* jungenhaft
bra *n* BH *m*
brace *n* Strebe *f*, Stütze *f*; (*dental*) Zahnspange *f*; **~s** *npl* Hosenträger *mpl*
bracelet *n* Armband *nt*
bracing *a* stärkend
bracket *n* Konsole *f*; (*group*) Gruppe *f*; (*Typ*) **round/square ~s** runde/eckige Klammern ● *vt* einklammern
brag *vi* (*pt/pp* **bragged**) prahlen (**about** mit)
braille *n* Blindenschrift *f*
brain *n* Gehirn *nt*; **~s** (*fig*) Intelligenz *f*
brain: ~less *a* dumm. **~wash** *vt* einer Gehirnwäsche unterziehen. **~wave** *n* Geistesblitz *m*
brainy *a* (**-ier, -iest**) klug
brake *n* Bremse *f* ● *vt/i* bremsen. **~-light** *n* Bremslicht *nt*
bramble *n* Brombeerstrauch *m*
branch *n* Ast *m*; (*fig*) Zweig *m*; (*Comm*) Zweigstelle *f*; (*shop*) Filiale *f* ● *vi* sich gabeln
brand *n* Marke *f* ● *vt* (*fig*) brandmarken als
brandish *vt* schwingen
brand-new *a* nagelneu
brandy *n* Weinbrand *m*
brash *a* nassforsch
brass *n* Messing *nt*; (*Mus*) Blech *nt*; **top ~** [!] hohe Tiere *pl*. **~ band** *n* Blaskapelle *f*
brassy *a* (**-ier, -iest**) [!] ordinär
brat *n* (*pej*) Balg *nt*
bravado *n* Forschheit *f*
brave *a* (**-r, -st**), **-ly** *adv* tapfer ● *vt* die Stirn bieten (+ *dat*). **~ry** *n* Tapferkeit *f*
bravo *int* bravo!
brawl *n* Schlägerei *f*
brawn *n* (*Culin*) Sülze *f*
brawny *a* muskulös
bray *vi* iahen
brazen *a* unverschämt
Brazil *n* Brasilien *nt*. **~ian** *a* brasilianisch. **~ nut** *n* Paranuss *f*
breach *n* Bruch *m*; (*Mil & fig*) Bresche *f*; **~ of contract** Vertragsbruch *m*
bread *n* Brot *nt*; **slice of ~ and butter** Butterbrot *nt*. **~crumbs** *npl* Brotkrümel *pl*; (*Culin*) Paniermehl *nt*
breadth *n* Breite *f*
break *n* Bruch *m*; (*interval*) Pause *f*; (*interruption*) Unterbrechung *f*; ([!] *chance*) Chance *f* ● *v* (*pt* **broke**, *pp* **broken**) ● *vt* brechen; (*smash*) zerbrechen; (*damage*) kaputtmachen [!]; (*interrupt*) unterbrechen; **~ one's arm** sich (*dat*) den Arm brechen ● *vi*

brechen; <*day:*> anbrechen; <*storm:*> losbrechen; <*thing:*> kaputtgehen [!]; <*rope, thread:*> reißen; <*news:*> bekannt werden; **his voice is ~ing** er ist im Stimmbruch. **~ away** *vi* sich losreißen/(*fig*) sich absetzen (**from** von). **~ down** *vi* zusammenbrechen; (*Techn*) eine Panne haben; <*negotiations:*> scheitern ● *vt* aufbrechen <*door*>; aufgliedern <*figures*>. **~ in** *vi* einbrechen. **~ off** *vt/i* abbrechen; lösen <*engagement*>. **~ out** *vi* ausbrechen. **~ up** *vt* zerbrechen ● *vi* <*crowd:*> sich zerstreuen; <*marriage, couple:*> auseinander gehen; (*Sch*) Ferien bekommen

break|able *a* zerbrechlich. **~age** *n* Bruch *m*. **~down** *n* (*Techn*) Panne *f*; (*Med*) Zusammenbruch *m*; (*of figures*) Aufgliederung *f*. **~er** *n* (*wave*) Brecher *m*

breakfast *n* Frühstück *nt*

break: ~through *n* Durchbruch *m*. **~water** *n* Buhne *f*

breast *n* Brust *f*. **~bone** *n* Brustbein *nt*. **~-feed** *vt* stillen. **~-stroke** *n* Brustschwimmen *nt*

breath *n* Atem *m*; **out of ~** außer Atem; **under one's ~** vor sich (*acc*) hin

breathe *vt/i* atmen. **~ in** *vt/i* einatmen. **~ out** *vt/i* ausatmen

breathing *n* Atmen *nt*

breath: : ~less *a* atemlos. **~-taking** *a* atemberaubend

bred *see* **breed**

breed *n* Rasse *f* ● *v* (*pt/pp* **bred**) ● *vt* züchten; (*give rise to*) erzeugen ● *vi* sich vermehren. **~er** *n* Züchter *m*. **~ing** *n* Zucht *f*; (*fig*) [gute] Lebensart *f*

breez|e *n* Lüftchen *nt*; (*Naut*) Brise *f*. **~y** *a* windig

brevity *n* Kürze *f*

brew *n* Gebräu *nt* ● *vt* brauen; kochen <*tea*>. **~er** *n* Brauer *m*. **~ery** *n* Brauerei *f*

bribe *n* (*money*) Bestechungsgeld *nt* ● *vt* bestechen. **~ry** *n* Bestechung *f*

brick *n* Ziegelstein *m*, Backstein *m*

bricklayer *n* Maurer *m*

bridal *a* Braut-

bride *n* Braut *f*. **~groom** *n* Bräutigam *m*. **~smaid** *n* Brautjungfer *f*

bridge[1] *n* Brücke *f*; (*of nose*) Nasenrücken *m*; (*of spectacles*) Steg *m*

bridge[2] *n* (*Cards*) Bridge *nt*

bridle *n* Zaum *m*

brief[1] *a* (**-er, -est**) kurz; **be ~** <*person:*> sich kurz fassen

brief[2] *n* Instruktionen *pl*; (*Jur: case*) Mandat *nt*. **~case** *n* Aktentasche *f*

brief|ing *n* Informationsgespräch *nt*. **~ly** *adv* kurz. **~ness** *n* Kürze *f*

briefs *npl* Slip *m*

brigade *n* Brigade *f*

bright *a* (**-er, -est**), **-ly** *adv* hell; <*day*> heiter; **~ red** hellrot

bright|en *v* **~en [up]** ● *vt* aufheitern ● *vi* sich aufheitern. **~ness** *n* Helligkeit *f*

brilliance *n* Glanz *m*; (*of person*) Genialität *f*

brilliant *a*, **-ly** *adv* glänzend; <*person*> genial

brim *n* Rand *m*; (*of hat*) Krempe *f*

bring *vt* (*pt/pp* **brought**) bringen; **~ them with you** bring sie mit; **I can't ~ myself to do it** ich bringe es nicht fertig. **~ about** *vt* verursachen. **~ along** *vt* mitbringen. **~ back** *vt* zurückbringen. **~ down** *vt* herunterbringen; senken <*price*>. **~ off** *vt* vollbringen. **~ on** *vt* (*cause*) verursachen. **~ out** *vt* herausbringen. **~ round** *vt* vorbeibringen; (*persuade*) überreden; wieder zum Bewusstsein bringen <*unconscious person*>. **~ up** *vt* heraufbringen; (*vomit*) erbrechen; aufziehen <*children*>

brink *n* Rand *m*

brisk *a* (**-er, -est,**) **-ly** *adv* lebhaft; (*quick*) schnell

bristle *n* Borste *f*

Brit|ain *n* Großbritannien *nt*. **~ish** *a* britisch; **the ~ish** die Briten *pl*. **~on** *n* Brite *m*/Britin *f*

brittle *a* brüchig, spröde

broad *a* (**-er, -est**) breit; <*hint*> deutlich; **in ~ daylight** am helllichten Tag. **~ beans** *npl* dicke Bohnen *pl*

broadcast *n* Sendung *f* ● *vt/i* (*pt/pp* **-cast**) senden. **~er** *n* Rundfunk- und Fernsehpersönlichkeit *f*. **~ing** *n* Funk und Fernsehen *pl*

broaden *vt* verbreitern; (*fig*) erweitern ● *vi* sich verbreitern

broadly *adv* breit; **~ speaking** allgemein gesagt

broadminded *a* tolerant

broccoli *n inv* Brokkoli *pl*

brochure *n* Broschüre *f*

broke *see* **break** ● *a* [!] pleite

broken *see* **break** ● *a* zerbrochen, [!] kaputt. **~-hearted** *a* untröstlich

broker *n* Makler *m*

bronchitis *n* Bronchitis *f*

bronze *n* Bronze *f*

brooch *n* Brosche *f*

brood *vi* (*fig*) grübeln

broom *n* Besen *m*; (*Bot*) Ginster *m*

broth *n* Brühe *f*

brothel *n* Bordell *nt*

brother *n* Bruder *m*

brother: ~-in-law *n* (*pl* **-s-in-law**) Schwager *m*. **~ly** *a* brüderlich

brought *see* **bring**

brow *n* Augenbraue *f*; (*forehead*) Stirn *f*; (*of hill*) [Berg]kuppe *f*

brown *a* (**-er, -est**) braun; **~ paper** Packpapier *nt* ● *n* Braun *nt* ● *vt* bräunen ● *vi* braun werden

browse *vi* (*read*) schmökern; (*in shop*) sich umsehen. **~r** *n* (*Computing*) Browser *m*

bruise *n* blauer Fleck *m* ● *vt* beschädigen <*fruit*>; **~ one's arm** sich (*dat*) den Arm quetschen

brunette *n* Brünette *f*

brush *n* Bürste *f*; (*with handle*) Handfeger *m*; (*for paint, pastry*) Pinsel *m*; (*bushes*) Unterholz *nt*; (*fig: conflict*) Zusammenstoß *m* ● *vt* bürsten; putzen <*teeth*>; **~ against** streifen [gegen]; **~ aside** (*fig*) abtun. **~ off** *vt* abbürsten. **~ up** *vt/i* (*fig*) **~ up [on]** auffrischen

brusque *a*, **-ly** *adv* brüsk

Brussels *n* Brüssel *nt*. **~ sprouts** *npl* Rosenkohl *m*

brutal *a*, **-ly** *adv* brutal. **~ity** *n* Brutalität *f*

brute *n* Unmensch *m*. **~ force** *n* rohe Gewalt *f*

BSE *abbr* (**bovine spongiform encephalopathy**) BSE *f*

bubble *n* [Luft]blase *f* ● *vi* sprudeln

buck[1] *n* (*deer & Gym*) Bock *m*; (*rabbit*) Rammler *m* ● *vi* <*horse:*> bocken

buck[2] *n* (*Amer* [!]) Dollar *m*

buck[3] *n* **pass the ~** die Verantwortung abschieben

bucket *n* Eimer *m*

buckle *n* Schnalle *f* ● *vt* zuschnallen ● *vi* sich verbiegen

bud *n* Knospe *f*

buddy *n* [!] Freund *m*

budge *vt* bewegen ● *vi* sich [von der Stelle] rühren

budget *n* Budget *nt*; (*Pol*) Haushaltsplan *m*; (*money available*) Etat *m* ● *vi* (*pt/pp* **budgeted**) **~ for sth** etw einkalkulieren

B

buff *a* (*colour*) sandfarben ● *n* Sandfarbe *f*; [!] Fan *m* ● *vt* polieren
buffalo *n* (*inv or pl* **-es**) Büffel *m*
buffer *n* (*Rail*) Puffer *m*
buffet[1] *n* Büfett *nt*; (*on station*) Imbissstube *f*
buffet[2] *vt* (*pt/pp* **buffeted**) hin und her werfen
bug *n* Wanze *f*; ([!] *virus*) Bazillus *m*; ([!] *device*) Abhörgerät *nt*, [!] Wanze *f* ● *vt* (*pt/pp* **bugged**) [!] verwanzen <*room*>; abhören <*telephone*>; (*Amer: annoy*) ärgern
bugle *n* Signalhorn
build *n* (*of person*) Körperbau *m* ● *vt/i* (*pt/pp* **built**) bauen. ~ **on** *vt* anbauen (**to** an + *acc*). ~ **up** *vt* aufbauen ● *vi* zunehmen
builder *n* Bauunternehmer *m*
building *n* Gebäude *nt*. ~ **site** *n* Baustelle *f*. ~ **society** *n* Bausparkasse *f*
built *see* **build.** ~**-in** *a* eingebaut. ~**-in cupboard** *n* Einbauschrank *m*. ~**-up area** *n* bebautes Gebiet *nt*; (*Auto*) geschlossene Ortschaft *f*
bulb *n* [Blumen]zwiebel *f*; (*Electr*) [Glüh]birne *f*
bulbous *a* bauchig
Bulgaria *n* Bulgarien *nt*
bulg|e *n* Ausbauchung *f* ● *vi* sich ausbauchen. ~**ing** *a* prall; <*eyes*> hervorquellend
bulk *n* Masse *f*; (*greater part*) Hauptteil *m*. ~**y** *a* sperrig; (*large*) massig
bull *n* Bulle *m*, Stier *m*
bulldog *n* Bulldogge *f*
bulldozer *n* Planierraupe *f*
bullet *n* Kugel *f*
bulletin *n* Bulletin *nt*
bullet-proof *a* kugelsicher
bullfight *n* Stierkampf *m*. ~**er** *n* Stierkämpfer *m*
bullfinch *n* Dompfaff *m*
bullock *n* Ochse *m*
bull: ~**ring** *n* Stierkampfarena *f*. ~**'s-eye** *n* **score a** ~**'s-eye** ins Schwarze treffen
bully *n* Tyrann *m* ● *vt* tyrannisieren
bum *n* [x] Hintern *m*
bumble-bee *n* Hummel *f*
bump *n* Bums *m*; (*swelling*) Beule *f*; (*in road*) holperige Stelle *f* ● *vt* stoßen; ~ **into** stoßen gegen; (*meet*) zufällig treffen. ~ **off** *vt* [!] um die Ecke bringen
bumper *a* Rekord- ● *n* (*Auto*) Stoßstange *f*
bumpy *a* holperig
bun *n* Milchbrötchen *nt*; (*hair*) [Haar]knoten *m*
bunch *n* (*of flowers*) Strauß *m*; (*of radishes, keys*) Bund *m*; (*of people*) Gruppe *f*; ~ **of grapes** [ganze] Weintraube *f*
bundle *n* Bündel *nt* ● *vt* ~ **[up]** bündeln
bungalow *n* Bungalow *m*
bungle *vt* verpfuschen
bunk *n* [Schlaf]koje *f*. ~**-beds** *npl* Etagenbett *nt*
bunker *n* Bunker *m*
bunny *n* [!] Kaninchen *nt*
buoy *n* Boje *f*
buoyan|cy *n* Auftrieb *m*. ~**t** *a* **be** ~**t** schwimmen
burden *n* Last *f*
bureau *n* (*pl* **-x** *or* **-s**) (*desk*) Sekretär *m*; (*office*) Büro *nt*
bureaucracy *n* Bürokratie *f*
bureaucratic *a* bürokratisch
burger *n* Hamburger *m*
burglar *n* Einbrecher *m*. ~ **alarm** *n* Alarmanlage *f*
burglary *n* Einbruch *m*
burgle *vt* einbrechen in (+ *acc*); **they have been** ~**d** bei ihnen ist eingebrochen worden
burial *n* Begräbnis *nt*
burly *a* (**-ier, -iest**) stämmig
Burm|a *n* Birma *nt*. ~**ese** *a* birmanisch

burn *n* Verbrennung *f*; (*on skin*) Brandwunde *f*; (*on material*) Brandstelle *f* ● *v* (*pt/pp* **burnt** *or* **burned**) ● *vt* verbrennen ● *vi* brennen; <*food:*> anbrennen. **~ down** *vt/i* niederbrennen

burnt *see* **burn**

burp *vi* [!] aufstoßen

burrow *n* Bau *m* ● *vi* wühlen

burst *n* Bruch *m*; (*surge*) Ausbruch *m* ● *v* (*pt/pp* **burst**) ● *vt* platzen machen ● *vi* platzen; <*bud:*> aufgehen; **~ into tears** in Tränen ausbrechen

bury *vt* (*pt/pp* **-ied**) begraben; (*hide*) vergraben

bus *n* [Auto]bus *m*

bush *n* Strauch *m*; (*land*) Busch *m*. **~y** *a* (**-ier, -iest**) buschig

busily *adv* eifrig

business *n* Angelegenheit *f*; (*Comm*) Geschäft *nt*; **on ~** geschäftlich; **he has no ~** er hat kein Recht (**to** zu); **mind one's own ~** sich um seine eigenen Angelegenheiten kümmern; **that's none of your ~** das geht Sie nichts an. **~-like** *a* geschäftsmäßig. **~man** *n* Geschäftsmann *m*

bus-stop *n* Bushaltestelle *f*

bust[1] *n* Büste *f*

bust[2] *a* [!] kaputt; **go ~** Pleite gehen ● *v* (*pt/pp* **busted** *or* **bust**) [!] ● *vt* kaputtmachen ● *vi* kaputtgehen

busy *a* (**-ier, -iest**) beschäftigt; <*day*> voll; <*street*> belebt; (*with traffic*) stark befahren; (*Amer Teleph*) besetzt; **be ~** zu tun haben ● *vt* **~ oneself** sich beschäftigen (**with** mit)

but *conj* aber; (*after negative*) sondern ● *prep* außer (+ *dat*); **~ for** (*without*) ohne (+ *acc*); **the last ~ one** der/die/das vorletzte; **the next ~ one** der/die/das übernächste ● *adv* nur

butcher *n* Fleischer *m*, Metzger *m*; **~'s [shop]** Fleischerei *f*, Metzgerei *f* ● *vt* [ab]schlachten

butler *n* Butler *m*

butt *n* (*of gun*) [Gewehr]kolben *m*; (*fig: target*) Zielscheibe *f*; (*of cigarette*) Stummel *m*; (*for water*) Regentonne *f* ● *vi* **~ in** unterbrechen

butter *n* Butter *f* ● *vt* mit Butter bestreichen. **~ up** *vt* [!] schmeicheln (+ *dat*)

butter: ~cup *a* Butterblume *f*, Hahnenfuß *m*. **~fly** *n* Schmetterling *m*

buttocks *npl* Gesäß *nt*

button *n* Knopf *m* ● *vt* **~ [up]** zuknöpfen. **~hole** *n* Knopfloch *nt*

buy *n* Kauf *m* ● *vt* (*pt/pp* **bought**) kaufen. **~er** *n* Käufer(in) *m(f)*

buzz *n* Summen *nt* ● *vi* summen

buzzer *n* Summer *m*

by *prep* (*close to*) bei (+ *dat*); (*next to*) neben (+ *dat/acc*); (*past*) an (+ *dat*) … vorbei; (*to the extent of*) um (+ *acc*); (*at the latest*) bis; (*by means of*) durch; **by Mozart/Dickens** von Mozart/Dickens; **~ oneself** allein; **~ the sea** am Meer; **~ car/bus** mit dem Auto/Bus; **~ sea** mit dem Schiff; **~ day/night** bei Tag/Nacht; **~ the hour** pro Stunde; **~ the metre** meterweise; **six metres ~ four** sechs mal vier Meter; **win ~ a length** mit einer Länge Vorsprung gewinnen; **miss the train ~ a minute** den Zug um eine Minute verpassen ● *adv* **~ and large** im Großen und Ganzen; **put ~** beiseite legen; **go/pass ~** vorbeigehen

bye *int* [!] tschüs

by: ~-election *n* Nachwahl *f*. **~pass** *n* Umgehungsstraße *f*; (*Med*) Bypass *m* ● *vt* umfahren. **~-product** *n* Nebenprodukt *m*. **~stander** *n* Zuschauer(in) *m(f)*

Cc

cab *n* Taxi *nt*; (*of lorry, train*) Führerhaus *nt*
cabaret *n* Kabarett *nt*
cabbage *n* Kohl *m*
cabin *n* Kabine *f*; (*hut*) Hütte *f*
cabinet *n* Schrank *m*; **[display] ~** Vitrine *f*; **C~** (*Pol*) Kabinett *nt*
cable *n* Kabel *nt*; (*rope*) Tau *nt*. **~ railway** *n* Seilbahn *f*. **~ television** *n* Kabelfernsehen *nt*
cackle *vi* gackern
cactus *n* (*pl* **-ti** *or* **-tuses**) Kaktus *m*
cadet *n* Kadett *m*
cadge *vt/i* [!] schnorren
Caesarean *a & n* **~ [section]** Kaiserschnitt *m*
café *n* Café *nt*
cafeteria *n* Selbstbedienungsrestaurant *nt*
cage *n* Käfig *m*
cagey *a* [!] **be ~** mit der Sprache nicht herauswollen
cake *n* Kuchen *m*; (*of soap*) Stück *nt*. **~d** *a* verkrustet (**with** mit)
calculat|e *vt* berechnen; (*estimate*) kalkulieren. **~ing** *a* (*fig*) berechnend. **~ion** *n* Rechnung *f*, Kalkulation *f*. **~or** *n* Rechner *m*
calendar *n* Kalender *m*
calf[1] *n* (*pl* **calves**) Kalb *nt*
calf[2] *n* (*pl* **calves**) (*Anat*) Wade *f*
calibre *n* Kaliber *nt*
call *n* Ruf *m*; (*Teleph*) Anruf *m*; (*visit*) Besuch *m* ● *vt* rufen; (*Teleph*) anrufen; (*wake*) wecken; ausrufen <*strike*>; (*name*) nennen; **be ~ed** heißen ● *vi* rufen; **~ [in** *or* **round]** vorbeikommen. **~ back** *vt* zurückrufen ● *vi* noch einmal vorbeikommen. **~ for** *vt* rufen nach; (*demand*) verlangen; (*fetch*) abholen. **~ off** *vt* zurückrufen <*dog*>; (*cancel*) absagen. **~ on** *vt* bitten (**for** um); (*appeal to*) appellieren an (+ *acc*); (*visit*) besuchen. **~ out** *vt* rufen; aufrufen <*names*> ● *vi* rufen. **~ up** *vt* (*Mil*) einberufen; (*Teleph*) anrufen
call: ~-box *n* Telefonzelle *f*. **~er** *n* Besucher *m*; (*Teleph*) Anrufer *m*. **~ing** *n* Berufung *f*. **~-up** *n* (*Mil*) Einberufung *f*
calm *a* (**-er, -est**), **-ly** *adv* ruhig ● *n* Ruhe *f* ● *vt* **~ [down]** beruhigen ● *vi* **~ down** sich beruhigen. **~ness** *n* Ruhe *f*; (*of sea*) Stille *f*
calorie *n* Kalorie *f*
calves *npl see* **calf**[1] *&* [2]
camcorder *n* Camcorder *m*
came *see* **come**
camel *n* Kamel *nt*
camera *n* Kamera *f*
camouflage *n* Tarnung *f* ● *vt* tarnen
camp *n* Lager *nt* ● *vi* campen; (*Mil*) kampieren
campaign *n* Feldzug *m*; (*Comm, Pol*) Kampagne *f* ● *vi* (*Pol*) im Wahlkampf arbeiten
camp: ~-bed *n* Feldbett *nt*. **~er** *n* Camper *m*; (*Auto*) Wohnmobil *nt*. **~ing** *n* Camping *nt*. **~site** *n* Campingplatz *m*
can[1] *n* (*for petrol*) Kanister *m*; (*tin*) Dose *f*, Büchse *f*; **a ~ of beer** eine Dose Bier

---

can[2]
pres **can**, *pt* **could**
● *auxiliary verb*
····➤ (*be able to*) können. **I can't** *or* **cannot go** ich kann nicht gehen. **she couldn't** *or* **could not go** (*was unable to*) sie konnte nicht gehen; (*would not be able to*) sie könnte nicht gehen. **he could go if he had time** er könnte gehen,

wenn er Zeit hätte. **if I could go** wenn ich gehen könnte. **that cannot be true** das kann nicht stimmen

····➤ (*know how to*) können. **can you swim?** können Sie schwimmen? **she can drive** sie kann Auto fahren

····➤ (*be allowed to*) dürfen. **you can't smoke here** hier dürfen Sie nicht rauchen. **can I go?** kann *od* darf ich gehen?

····➤ (*in requests*) können. **can I have a glass of water, please?** kann ich ein Glas Wasser haben, bitte? **could you ring me tomorrow?** könnten Sie mich morgen anrufen?

····➤ **could** (*expressing possibility*) könnte. **that could be so** das könnte *od* kann sein. **I could have killed him** ich hätte ihn umbringen können

Canad|a *n* Kanada *nt*. **~ian** *a* kanadisch ● *n* Kanadier(in) *m(f)*

canal *n* Kanal *m*

canary *n* Kanarienvogel *m*

cancel *vt/i* (*pt/pp* **cancelled**) absagen; abbestellen <*newspaper*>; (*Computing*) abbrechen; **be ~led** ausfallen. **~lation** *n* Absage *f*

cancer *n*, & (*Astr*) **C~** Krebs *m*. **~ous** *a* krebsig

candid *a*, **-ly** *adv* offen

candidate *n* Kandidat(in) *m(f)*

candle *n* Kerze *f*. **~stick** *n* Kerzenständer *m*, Leuchter *m*

candy *n* (*Amer*) Süßigkeiten *pl*; **[piece of] ~** Bonbon *m*

cane *n* Rohr *nt*; (*stick*) Stock *m* ● *vt* mit dem Stock züchtigen

canine *a* Hunde-. **~ tooth** *n* Eckzahn *m*

cannabis *n* Haschisch *nt*

canned *a* Dosen-, Büchsen-

cannibal *n* Kannibale *m*. **~ism** *n* Kannibalismus *m*

cannon *n inv* Kanone *f*

cannot *see* **can²**

canoe *n* Paddelboot *nt*; (*Sport*) Kanu *nt*

can-opener *n* Dosenöffner *m*

can't = **cannot.** *See* **can²**

canteen *n* Kantine *f*

canter *n* Kanter *m* ● *vi* kantern

canvas *n* Segeltuch *nt*; (*Art*) Leinwand *f*; (*painting*) Gemälde *nt*

canvass *vi* um Stimmen werben

canyon *n* Cañon *m*

cap *n* Kappe *f*, Mütze *f*; (*nurse's*) Haube *f*; (*top, lid*) Verschluss *m*

capability *n* Fähigkeit *f*

capable *a*, **-bly** *adv* fähig; **be ~ of doing sth** fähig sein, etw zu tun

capacity *n* Fassungsvermögen *nt*; (*ability*) Fähigkeit *f*; **in my ~ as** in meiner Eigenschaft als

cape¹ *n* (*cloak*) Cape *nt*

cape² *n* (*Geog*) Kap *nt*

capital *a* <*letter*> groß ● *n* (*town*) Hauptstadt *f*; (*money*) Kapital *nt*; (*letter*) Großbuchstabe *m*

capital|ism *n* Kapitalismus *m*. **~ist** *a* kapitalistisch ● *n* Kapitalist *m*. **~ letter** *n* Großbuchstabe *m*. **~ punishment** *n* Todesstrafe *f*

capsize *vi* kentern ● *vt* zum Kentern bringen

captain *n* Kapitän *m*; (*Mil*) Hauptmann *m* ● *vt* anführen <*team*>

caption *n* Überschrift *f*; (*of illustration*) Bildtext *m*

captivate *vt* bezaubern

captiv|e *a* **hold/take ~e** gefangen halten/nehmen ● *n* Gefangene(r) *m/f*. **~ity** *n* Gefangenschaft *f*

capture *n* Gefangennahme *f* ● *vt* gefangen nehmen; [ein]fangen <*animal*>; (*Mil*) einnehmen <*town*>

car *n* Auto *nt*, Wagen *m*; **by ~** mit dem Auto *od* Wagen

caramel *n* Karamell *m*

carat *n* Karat *nt*
caravan *n* Wohnwagen *m*; (*procession*) Karawane *f*
carbon *n* Kohlenstoff *m*; (*paper*) Kohlepapier *nt*; (*copy*) Durchschlag *m*
carbon: ~ copy *n* Durchschlag *m*. **~ paper** *n* Kohlepapier *nt*
carburettor *n* Vergaser *m*
carcass *n* Kadaver *m*
card *n* Karte *f*
cardboard *n* Pappe *f*, Karton *m*. **~ box** *n* Pappschachtel *f*; (*large*) [Papp]karton *m*
card-game *n* Kartenspiel *nt*
cardigan *n* Strickjacke *f*
cardinal *a* Kardinal- ●*n* (*Relig*) Kardinal *m*
card index *n* Kartei *f*
care *n* Sorgfalt *f*; (*caution*) Vorsicht *f*; (*protection*) Obhut *f*; (*looking after*) Pflege *f*; (*worry*) Sorge *f*; **~ of** (*on letter abbr* **c/o**) bei; **take ~** vorsichtig sein; **take into ~** in Pflege nehmen; **take ~ of** sich kümmern um ●*vi* **~ for** (*like*) mögen; (*look after*) betreuen; **I don't ~** das ist mir gleich
career *n* Laufbahn *f*; (*profession*) Beruf *m* ●*vi* rasen
care: ~free *a* sorglos. **~ful** *a*, **-ly** *adv* sorgfältig; (*cautious*) vorsichtig. **~less** *a*, **-ly** *adv* nachlässig. **~lessness** *n* Nachlässigkeit *f*
caretaker *n* Hausmeister *m*
car ferry *n* Autofähre *f*
cargo *n* (*pl* **-es**) Ladung *f*
Caribbean *n* **the ~** die Karibik
caricature *n* Karikatur *f* ●*vt* karikieren
caring *a* <*parent*> liebevoll; <*profession, attitude*> sozial
carnation *n* Nelke *f*
carnival *n* Karneval *m*
carol *n* **[Christmas] ~** Weihnachtslied *nt*
carp[1] *n inv* Karpfen *m*
carp[2] *vi* nörgeln
car park *n* Parkplatz *m*; (*multi-storey*) Parkhaus *nt*; (*underground*) Tiefgarage *f*
carpent|er *n* Zimmermann *m*; (*joiner*) Tischler *m*. **~ry** *n* Tischlerei *f*
carpet *n* Teppich *m*
carriage *n* Kutsche *f*; (*Rail*) Wagen *m*; (*of goods*) Beförderung *f*; (*cost*) Frachtkosten *pl*; (*bearing*) Haltung *f*
carrier *n* Träger(in) *m*(*f*); (*Comm*) Spediteur *m*; **~ [-bag]** Tragetasche *f*
carrot *n* Möhre *f*, Karotte *f*
carry *vt/i* (*pt/pp* **-ied**) tragen; **be carried away** [!] hingerissen sein. **~ off** *vt* wegtragen; gewinnen <*prize*>. **~ on** *vi* weitermachen; **~ on with** [!] eine Affäre haben mit ●*vt* führen; (*continue*) fortführen. **~ out** *vt* hinaus-/heraustragen; (*perform*) ausführen
cart *n* Karren *m*; **put the ~ before the horse** das Pferd beim Schwanz aufzäumen ●*vt* karren; ([!] *carry*) schleppen
carton *n* [Papp]karton *m*; (*for drink*) Tüte *f*; (*of cream, yoghurt*) Becher *m*
cartoon *n* Karikatur *f*; (*joke*) Witzzeichnung *f*; (*strip*) Comic Strips *pl*; (*film*) Zeichentrickfilm *m*. **~ist** *n* Karikaturist *m*
cartridge *n* Patrone *f*; (*for film*) Kassette *f*
carve *vt* schnitzen; (*in stone*) hauen; (*Culin*) aufschneiden
carving *n* Schnitzerei *f*. **~-knife** *n* Tranchiermesser *nt*
car wash *n* Autowäsche *f*; (*place*) Autowaschanlage *f*
case[1] *n* Fall *m*; **in any ~** auf jeden Fall; **just in ~** für alle Fälle; **in ~ he comes** falls er kommt

case² *n* Kasten *m*; (*crate*) Kiste *f*; (*for spectacles*) Etui *nt*; (*suitcase*) Koffer *m*; (*for display*) Vitrine *f*

cash *n* Bargeld *nt*; **pay [in] ~** [in] bar bezahlen; **~ on delivery** per Nachnahme ● *vt* einlösen <*cheque*>. **~ desk** *n* Kasse *f*

cashier *n* Kassierer(in) *m(f)*

cash: ~point [machine] *n* Geldautomat *m*. **~ register** *n* Registrierkasse *f*

cassette *n* Kassette *f*. **~ recorder** *n* Kassettenrecorder *m*

cast *n* (*mould*) Form *f*; (*model*) Abguss *m*; (*Theat*) Besetzung *f*; **[plaster] ~** (*Med*) Gipsverband *m* ● *vt* (*pt/pp* **cast**) (*throw*) werfen; (*shed*) abwerfen; abgeben <*vote*>; gießen <*metal*>; (*Theat*) besetzen <*role*>. **~ off** *vi* (*Naut*) ablegen

castle *n* Schloss *nt*; (*fortified*) Burg *f*; (*Chess*) Turm *m*

cast-offs *npl* abgelegte Kleidung *f*

castor *n* (*wheel*) [Lauf]rolle *f*

castor sugar *n* Streuzucker *m*

casual *a*, **-ly** *adv* (*chance*) zufällig; (*offhand*) lässig; (*informal*) zwanglos; (*not permanent*) Gelegenheits-; **~ wear** Freizeitbekleidung *f*

casualty *n* [Todes]opfer *nt*; (*injured person*) Verletzte(r) *m/f*; **~ [department]** Unfallstation *f*

cat *n* Katze *f*

catalogue *n* Katalog *m* ● *vt* katalogisieren

catapult *n* Katapult *nt* ● *vt* katapultieren

cataract *n* (*Med*) grauer Star *m*

catarrh *n* Katarrh *m*

catastroph|e *n* Katastrophe *f*. **~ic** *a* katastrophal

catch *n* (*of fish*) Fang *m*; (*fastener*) Verschluss *m*; (*on door*) Klinke *f*; ([!] *snag*) Haken *m* [!] ● *v* (*pt/pp* **caught**) ● *vt* fangen; (*be in time for*) erreichen; (*travel by*) fahren mit; bekommen <*illness*>; **~ a cold** sich erkälten; **~ sight of** erblicken; **~ s.o. stealing** jdn beim Stehlen erwischen; **~ one's finger in the door** sich (*dat*) den Finger in der Tür [ein]klemmen ● *vi* (*burn*) anbrennen; (*get stuck*) klemmen. **~ on** *vi* [!] (*understand*) kapieren; (*become popular*) sich durchsetzen. **~ up** *vt* einholen ● *vi* aufholen; **~ up with** einholen <*s.o.*>; nachholen <*work*>

catching *a* ansteckend

catch: ~-phrase *n*, **~word** *n* Schlagwort *nt*

catchy *a* (**-ier, -iest**) einprägsam

categor|ical *a*, **-ly** *adv* kategorisch. **~y** *n* Kategorie *f*

cater *vi* **~ for** beköstigen; <*firm:*> das Essen liefern für <*party*>; (*fig*) eingestellt sein auf (+ *acc*)

caterpillar *n* Raupe *f*

cathedral *n* Dom *m*, Kathedrale *f*

Catholic *a* katholisch ● *n* Katholik(in) *m(f)*

cattle *npl* Vieh *nt*

catty *a* (**-ier, -iest**) boshaft

caught *see* **catch**

cauliflower *n* Blumenkohl *m*

cause *n* Ursache *f*; (*reason*) Grund *m*; **good ~** gute Sache *f* ● *vt* verursachen; **~ s.o. to do sth** jdn veranlassen, etw zu tun

caution *n* Vorsicht *f*; (*warning*) Verwarnung *f* ● *vt* (*Jur*) verwarnen

cautious *a*, **-ly** *adv* vorsichtig

cavalry *n* Kavallerie *f*

cave *n* Höhle *f* ● *vi* **~ in** einstürzen

cavern *n* Höhle *f*

caviare *n* Kaviar *m*

cavity *n* Hohlraum *m*; (*in tooth*) Loch *nt*

CCTV *abbr* (**closed-circuit television**) CCTV *nt*; (*surveillance*) Videoüberwachung *f*

CD *abbr* (**compact disc**) CD *f*; **~-ROM** CD-ROM *f*

cease *vt/i* aufhören. **~-fire** *n* Waffenruhe *f*. **~less** *a*, **-ly** *adv* unaufhörlich
cedar *n* Zeder *f*
ceiling *n* [Zimmer]decke *f*; (*fig*) oberste Grenze *f*
celebrat|e *vt/i* feiern. **~ed** *a* berühmt (**for** wegen). **~ion** *n* Feier *f*
celebrity *n* Berühmtheit *f*
celery *n* [Stangen]sellerie *m & f*
cell *n* Zelle *f*
cellar *n* Keller *m*
cellist *n* Cellist(in) *m(f)*
cello *n* Cello *nt*
Celsius *a* Celsius
Celt *n* Kelte *m*/ Keltin *f*. **~ic** *a* keltisch
cement *n* Zement *m*; (*adhesive*) Kitt *m*
cemetery *n* Friedhof *m*
censor *n* Zensor *m* ● *vt* zensieren. **~ship** *n* Zensur *f*
census *n* Volkszählung *f*
cent *n* Cent *m*
centenary *n*, (*Amer*) **centennial** *n* Hundertjahrfeier *f*
center *n* (*Amer*) = **centre**
centi|grade *a* Celsius. **~metre** *n* Zentimeter *m & nt*
central *a*, **-ly** *adv* zentral. **~ heating** *n* Zentralheizung *f*. **~ize** *vt* zentralisieren
centre *n* Zentrum *nt*; (*middle*) Mitte *f* ● *v* (*pt/pp* **centred**) ● *vt* zentrieren. **~-forward** *n* Mittelstürmer *m*
century *n* Jahrhundert *nt*
ceramic *a* Keramik-
cereal *n* Getreide *nt*; (*breakfast food*) Frühstücksflocken *pl*
ceremon|ial *a*, **-ly** *adv* zeremoniell, feierlich ● *n* Zeremoniell *nt*. **~ious** *a*, **-ly** *adv* formell
ceremony *n* Zeremonie *f*, Feier *f*
certain *a* sicher; (*not named*) gewiss; **for ~** mit Bestimmtheit; **make ~** (*check*) sich vergewissern (**that** dass); (*ensure*) dafür sorgen (**that** dass); **he is ~ to win** er wird ganz bestimmt siegen. **~ly** *adv* bestimmt, sicher; **~ly not!** auf keinen Fall! **~ty** *n* Sicherheit *f*, Gewissheit *f*; **it's a ~ty** es ist sicher
certificate *n* Bescheinigung *f*; (*Jur*) Urkunde *f*; (*Sch*) Zeugnis *nt*
certify *vt* (*pt/pp* **-ied**) bescheinigen; (*declare insane*) für geisteskrank erklären
cf. *abbr* (*compare*) vgl.
chafe *vt* wund reiben
chaffinch *n* Buchfink *m*
chain *n* Kette *f* ● *vt* ketten (**to** an + *acc*). **~ up** *vt* anketten
chain: ~ reaction *n* Kettenreaktion *f*. **~-smoker** *n* Kettenraucher *m*. **~ store** *n* Kettenladen *m*
chair *n* Stuhl *m*; (*Univ*) Lehrstuhl *m*; (*Adm*) Vorsitzende(r) *m/f*. **~-lift** *n* Sessellift *m*. **~man** *n* Vorsitzende(r) *m/f*
chalet *n* Chalet *nt*
chalk *n* Kreide *f*
challeng|e *n* Herausforderung *f*; (*Mil*) Anruf *m* ● *vt* herausfordern; (*Mil*) anrufen; (*fig*) anfechten <*statement*>. **~er** *n* Herausforderer *m*. **~ing** *a* herausfordernd; (*demanding*) anspruchsvoll
chamber *n* Kammer *f*; **C~ of Commerce** Handelskammer *f*. **~ music** *n* Kammermusik *f*
chamber music *n* Kammermusik *f*
chamois *n* **~[-leather]** Ledertuch *nt*
champagne *n* Champagner *m*
champion *n* (*Sport*) Meister(in) *m(f)*; (*of cause*) Verfechter *m* ● *vt* sich einsetzen für. **~ship** *n* (*Sport*) Meisterschaft *f*
chance *n* Zufall *m*; (*prospect*) Chancen *pl*; (*likelihood*) Aussicht *f*; (*opportunity*) Gelegenheit *f*; **by**

~ zufällig; **take a ~** ein Risiko eingehen; **give s.o. a ~** jdm eine Chance geben ● *attrib* zufällig ● *vt* **~ it** es riskieren

chancellor *n* Kanzler *m*; (*Univ*) Rektor *m*

chancy *a* riskant

change *n* Veränderung *f*; (*alteration*) Änderung *f*; (*money*) Wechselgeld *nt*; **for a ~** zur Abwechslung ● *vt* wechseln; (*alter*) ändern; (*exchange*) umtauschen (**for** gegen); (*transform*) verwandeln; trocken legen <*baby*>; **~ one's clothes** sich umziehen; **~ trains** umsteigen ● *vi* sich verändern; (**~** *clothes*) sich umziehen; (**~** *trains*) umsteigen; **all ~!** alles aussteigen!

changeable *a* wechselhaft

changing-room *n* Umkleideraum *m*

channel *n* Rinne *f*; (*Radio, TV*) Kanal *m*; (*fig*) Weg *m*; **the [English] C~** der Ärmelkanal; **the C~ Islands** die Kanalinseln

chant *vt* singen; <*demonstrators:*> skandieren

chao|s *n* Chaos *nt*. **~tic** *a* chaotisch

chap *n* [!] Kerl *m*

chapel *n* Kapelle *f*

chaplain *n* Geistliche(r) *m*

chapped *a* <*skin*> aufgesprungen

chapter *n* Kapitel *nt*

character *n* Charakter *m*; (*in novel, play*) Gestalt *f*; (*Typ*) Schriftzeichen *nt*; **out of ~** uncharakteristisch; **quite a ~** [!] ein Original

characteristic *a*, **-ally** *adv* charakteristisch (**of** für) ● *n* Merkmal *nt*

characterize *vt* charakterisieren

charge *n* (*price*) Gebühr *f*; (*Electr*) Ladung *f*; (*attack*) Angriff *m*; (*Jur*) Anklage *f*; **free of ~** kostenlos; **be in ~** verantwortlich sein (**of** für); **take ~** die Aufsicht übernehmen (**of** über + *acc*) ● *vt* berechnen <*fee*>; (*Electr*) laden; (*attack*) angreifen; (*Jur*) anklagen (**with** *gen*); **~ s.o. for sth** jdm etw berechnen

charitable *a* wohltätig; (*kind*) wohlwollend

charity *n* Nächstenliebe *f*; (*organization*) wohltätige Einrichtung *f*; **for ~** für Wohltätigkeitszwecke

charm *n* Reiz *m*; (*of person*) Charme *f*; (*object*) Amulett *nt* ● *vt* bezaubern. **~ing** *a*, **-ly** *adv* reizend; <*person, smile*> charmant

chart *n* Karte *f*; (*table*) Tabelle *f*

charter *n* **~ [flight]** Charterflug *m* ● *vt* chartern; **~ed accountant** Wirtschaftsprüfer(in) *m(f)*

chase *n* Verfolgungsjagd *f* ● *vt* jagen, verfolgen. **~ away** *or* **off** *vt* wegjagen

chassis *n* (*pl* **chassis**) Chassis *nt*

chaste *a* keusch

chat *n* Plauderei *f*; **have a ~ with** plaudern mit ● *vi* (*pt/pp* **chatted**) plaudern. **~ show** *n* Talkshow *f*

chatter *n* Geschwätz *nt* ● *vi* schwatzen; <*child:*> plappern; <*teeth:*> klappern. **~box** *n* [!] Plappermaul *nt*

chatty *a* (**-ier, -iest**) geschwätzig

chauffeur *n* Chauffeur *m*

cheap *a* & *adv* (**-er, -est**), **-ly** *adv* billig. **~en** *vt* entwürdigen

cheat *n* Betrüger(in) *m(f)*; (*at games*) Mogler *m* ● *vt* betrügen ● *vi* (*at games*) mogeln [!]

check[1] *a* (*squared*) kariert ● *n* Karo *nt*

check[2] *n* Überprüfung *f*; (*inspection*) Kontrolle *f*; (*Chess*) Schach *nt*; (*Amer: bill*) Rechnung *f*; (*Amer: cheque*) Scheck *m*; (*Amer: tick*) Haken *m*; **keep a ~ on** kontrollieren ● *vt* [über]prüfen; (*inspect*) kontrollieren; (*restrain*) hemmen; (*stop*) aufhalten ● *vi* **[go and] ~** nachsehen. **~ in** *vi* sich anmelden; (*Aviat*) einchecken ● *vt* abfertigen; einchecken. **~ out** *vi* sich abmelden. **~ up** *vi* prüfen, kontrollieren; **~ up on** überprüfen

checked *a* kariert

check: ~-out *n* Kasse *f*. **~room** *n* (*Amer*) Garderobe *f*. **~-up** *n* (*Med*) [Kontroll]untersuchung *f*

cheek *n* Backe *f*; (*impudence*) Frechheit *f*. **~y** *a*, **-ily** *adv* frech

cheer *n* Beifallsruf *m*; **three ~s** ein dreifaches Hoch (**for** auf + *acc*); **~s!** prost! (*goodbye*) tschüs! ● *vt* zujubeln (+ *dat*) ● *vi* jubeln. **~ up** *vt* aufmuntern; aufheitern ● *vi* munterer werden. **~ful** *a*, **-ly** *adv* fröhlich. **~fulness** *n* Fröhlichkeit *f*

cheerio *int* [!] tschüs!

cheese *n* Käse *m*. **~cake** *n* Käsekuchen *m*

chef *n* Koch *m*

chemical *a*, **-ly** *adv* chemisch ● *n* Chemikalie *f*

chemist *n* (*pharmacist*) Apotheker(in) *m(f)*; (*scientist*) Chemiker(in) *m(f)*; **~'s [shop]** Drogerie *f*; (*dispensing*) Apotheke *f*. **~ry** *n* Chemie *f*

cheque *n* Scheck *m*. **~-book** *n* Scheckbuch *nt*. **~ card** *n* Scheckkarte *f*

cherish *vt* lieben; (*fig*) hegen

cherry *n* Kirsche *f* ● *attrib* Kirsch-

chess *n* Schach *nt*

chess: ~board *n* Schachbrett *nt*. **~-man** *n* Schachfigur *f*

chest *n* Brust *f*; (*box*) Truhe *f*

chestnut *n* Esskastanie *f*, Marone *f*; (*horse-*) [Ross]kastanie *f*

chest of drawers *n* Kommode *f*

chew *vt* kauen. **~ing-gum** *n* Kaugummi *m*

chick *n* Küken *nt*

chicken *n* Huhn *nt* ● *attrib* Hühner- ● *a* [!] feige

chief *a* Haupt- ● *n* Chef *m*; (*of tribe*) Häuptling *m*. **~ly** *adv* hauptsächlich

child *n* (*pl* **~ren**) Kind *nt*

child: ~birth *n* Geburt *f*. **~hood** *n* Kindheit *f*. **~ish** *a* kindisch. **~less** *a* kinderlos. **~like** *a* kindlich. **~-minder** *n* Tagesmutter *f*

children *npl see* **child**

Chile *n* Chile *nt*

chill *n* Kälte *f*; (*illness*) Erkältung *f* ● *vt* kühlen

chilly *a* kühl; **I felt ~** mich fröstelte [es]

chime *vi* läuten; <*clock:*> schlagen

chimney *n* Schornstein *m*. **~-pot** *n* Schornsteinaufsatz *m*. **~-sweep** *n* Schornsteinfeger *m*

chin *n* Kinn *nt*

china *n* Porzellan *nt*

Chin|a *n* China *nt*. **~ese** *a* chinesisch ● *n* (*Lang*) Chinesisch *nt*; **the ~ese** *pl* die Chinesen

chink[1] *n* (*slit*) Ritze *f*

chink[2] *n* Geklirr *nt* ● *vi* klirren; <*coins:*> klimpern

chip *n* (*fragment*) Span *m*; (*in china, paintwork*) angeschlagene Stelle *f*; (*Computing, Gambling*) Chip *m*; **~s** *pl* (*Culin*) Pommes frites *pl*; (*Amer: crisps*) Chips *pl* ● *vt* (*pt/pp* **chipped**) (*damage*) anschlagen. **~ped** *a* angeschlagen

chirp *vi* zwitschern; <*cricket:*> zirpen. **~y** *a* [!] munter

chit *n* Zettel *m*

chocolate *n* Schokolade *f*; (*sweet*) Praline *f*

choice *n* Wahl *f*; (*variety*) Auswahl *f* ● *a* auserlesen

choir *n* Chor *m*. **~boy** *n* Chorknabe *m*

choke *n* (*Auto*) Choke *m* ● *vt* würgen; (*to death*) erwürgen ● *vi* sich verschlucken; ~ **on** [fast] ersticken an (+ *dat*)

choose *vt/i* (*pt* **chose**, *pp* **chosen**) wählen; (*select*) sich (*dat*) aussuchen; ~ **to do/go** [freiwillig] tun/gehen; **as you** ~ wie Sie wollen

choos[e]y *a* [!] wählerisch

chop *n* (*blow*) Hieb *m*; (*Culin*) Kotelett *nt* ● *vt* (*pt/pp* **chopped**) hacken. ~ **down** *vt* abhacken; fällen <*tree*>. ~ **off** *vt* abhacken

chop|per *n* Beil *nt*; [!] (*helicopter*) Hubschrauber *m*. ~**py** *a* kabbelig

chopsticks *npl* Essstäbchen *pl*

choral *a* Chor-

chord *n* (*Mus*) Akkord *m*

chore *n* lästige Pflicht *f*; **[household]** ~**s** Hausarbeit *f*

chorus *n* Chor *m*; (*of song*) Refrain *m*

chose, chosen *see* **choose**

Christ *n* Christus *m*

christen *vt* taufen

Christian *a* christlich ● *n* Christ(in) *m(f)*. ~**ity** *n* Christentum *nt*. ~ **name** *n* Vorname *m*

Christmas *n* Weihnachten *nt*. ~ **card** *n* Weihnachtskarte *f*. ~ **Day** *n* erster Weihnachtstag *m*. ~ **Eve** *n* Heiligabend *m*. ~ **tree** *n* Weihnachtsbaum *m*

chrome *n*, **chromium** *n* Chrom *nt*

chronic *a* chronisch

chronicle *n* Chronik *f*

chrysanthemum *n* Chrysantheme *f*

chubby *a* (**-ier, -iest**) mollig

chuck *vt* [!] schmeißen. ~ **out** *vt* [!] rausschmeißen

chuckle *vi* in sich (*acc*) hineinlachen

chum *n* Freund(in) *m(f)*

chunk *n* Stück *nt*

church *n* Kirche *f*. ~**yard** *n* Friedhof *m*

churn *vt* ~ **out** am laufenden Band produzieren

cider *n* ≈ Apfelwein *m*

cigar *n* Zigarre *f*

cigarette *n* Zigarette *f*

cine-camera *n* Filmkamera *f*

cinema *n* Kino *nt*

cinnamon *n* Zimt *m*

circle *n* Kreis *m*; (*Theat*) Rang *m* ● *vt* umkreisen ● *vi* kreisen

circuit *n* Runde *f*; (*racetrack*) Rennbahn *f*; (*Electr*) Stromkreis *m*. ~**ous** *a* ~ **route** Umweg *m*

circular *a* kreisförmig ● *n* Rundschreiben *nt*. ~ **saw** *n* Kreissäge *f*. ~ **tour** *n* Rundfahrt *f*

circulat|e *vt* in Umlauf setzen ● *vi* zirkulieren. ~**ion** *n* Kreislauf *m*; (*of newspaper*) Auflage *f*

circumference *n* Umfang *m*

circumstance *n* Umstand *m*; ~**s** *pl* Umstände *pl*; (*financial*) Verhältnisse *pl*

circus *n* Zirkus *m*

cistern *n* (*tank*) Wasserbehälter *m*; (*of WC*) Spülkasten *m*

cite *vt* zitieren

citizen *n* Bürger(in) *m(f)*. ~**ship** *n* Staatsangehörigkeit *f*

citrus *n* ~ **[fruit]** Zitrusfrucht *f*

city *n* [Groß]stadt *f*

civic *a* Bürger-

civil *a* bürgerlich; <*aviation, defence*> zivil; (*polite*) höflich. ~ **engineering** *n* Hoch- und Tiefbau *m*

civilian *a* Zivil-; **in** ~ **clothes** in Zivil ● *n* Zivilist *m*

civiliz|ation *n* Zivilisation *f*. ~**e** *vt* zivilisieren

civil: ~ **servant** *n* Beamte(r) *m*/Beamtin *f*. **C**~ **Service** *n* Staatsdienst *m*

claim *n* Anspruch *m*; (*application*) Antrag *m*; (*demand*) Forderung *f*; (*assertion*) Behauptung *f* ● *vt* beanspruchen; (*apply for*) beantragen; (*demand*) fordern; (*assert*) behaupten; (*collect*) abholen

clam *n* Klaffmuschel *f*

clamber *vi* klettern

clammy *a* (**-ier, -iest**) feucht

clamour *n* Geschrei *nt* ● *vi* ~ **for** schreien nach

clamp *n* Klammer *f*; **[wheel]** ~ Parkkralle *f* ● *vt* [ein]spannen ● *vi* [!] ~ **down on** vorgehen gegen

clan *n* Clan *m*

clang *n* Schmettern *nt*. ~**er** *n* [!] Schnitzer *m*

clank *vi* klirren

clap *n* **give s.o. a** ~ jdm Beifall klatschen; ~ **of thunder** Donnerschlag *m* ● *vt/i* (*pt/pp* **clapped**) Beifall klatschen (+ *dat*); ~ **one's hands** [in die Hände] klatschen

clari|fication *n* Klärung *f*. ~**fy** *vt/i* (*pt/pp* **-ied**) klären

clarinet *n* Klarinette *f*

clarity *n* Klarheit *f*

clash *n* Geklirr *nt*; (*fig*) Konflikt *m* ● *vi* klirren; <*colours:*> sich beißen; <*events:*> ungünstig zusammenfallen

clasp *n* Verschluss *m* ● *vt* ergreifen; (*hold*) halten

class *n* Klasse *f*; **travel first/second** ~ erster/zweiter Klasse reisen ● *vt* einordnen

classic *a* klassisch ● *n* Klassiker *m*. ~**al** *a* klassisch

classi|fication *n* Klassifikation *f*. ~**fy** *vt* (*pt/pp* **-ied**) klassifizieren

classroom *n* Klassenzimmer *nt*

classy *a* (**-ier, -iest**) [!] schick

clatter *n* Geklapper *nt* ● *vi* klappern

clause *n* Klausel *f*; (*Gram*) Satzteil *m*

claw *n* Kralle *f*; (*of bird of prey & Techn*) Klaue *f*; (*of crab, lobster*) Schere *f* ● *vt* kratzen

clay *n* Lehm *m*; (*pottery*) Ton *m*

clean *a* (**-er, -est**) sauber ● *adv* glatt ● *vt* sauber machen; putzen <*shoes, windows*>; ~ **one's teeth** sich (*dat*) die Zähne putzen; **have sth** ~**ed** etw reinigen lassen. ~ **up** *vt* sauber machen

cleaner *n* Putzfrau *f*; (*substance*) Reinigungsmittel *nt*; **[dry]** ~**'s** chemische Reinigung *f*

cleanliness *n* Sauberkeit *f*

cleanse *vt* reinigen

clear *a* (**-er, -est**), **-ly** *adv* klar; (*obvious*) eindeutig; (*distinct*) deutlich; <*conscience*> rein; (*without obstacles*) frei; **make sth** ~ etw klarmachen (**to** *dat*) ● *adv* **stand** ~ zurücktreten; **keep** ~ **of** aus dem Wege gehen (+ *dat*) ● *vt* räumen; abräumen <*table*>; (*acquit*) freisprechen; (*authorize*) genehmigen; (*jump over*) überspringen; ~ **one's throat** sich räuspern ● *vi* <*fog:*> sich auflösen. ~ **away** *vt* wegräumen. ~ **off** *vi* [!] abhauen. ~ **out** *vt* ausräumen ● *vi* [!] abhauen. ~ **up** *vt* (*tidy*) aufräumen; (*solve*) aufklären ● *vi* <*weather:*> sich aufklären

clearance *n* Räumung *f*; (*authorization*) Genehmigung *f*; (*customs*) [Zoll]abfertigung *f*; (*Techn*) Spielraum *m*. ~ **sale** *n* Räumungsverkauf *m*

clench *vt* ~ **one's fist** die Faust ballen; ~ **one's teeth** die Zähne zusammenbeißen

clergy *npl* Geistlichkeit *f*. ~**man** *n* Geistliche(r) *m*

clerk *n* Büroangestellte(r) *m/f*; (*Amer: shop assistant*) Verkäufer(in) *m(f)*

clever *a* (**-er, -est**), -ly *adv* klug; (*skilful*) geschickt

cliché *n* Klischee *nt*

click *vi* klicken

client *n* Kunde *m*/ Kundin *f*; (*Jur*) Klient(in) *m(f)*

cliff *n* Kliff *nt*

climate *n* Klima *nt*

climax *n* Höhepunkt *m*

climb *n* Aufstieg *m* ● *vt* besteigen <*mountain*>; steigen auf (+ *acc*)

<ladder, tree> ● *vi* klettern; (*rise*) steigen; *<road:>* ansteigen. **~ down** *vi* hinunter-/herunterklettern; (*from ladder, tree*) heruntersteigen

climber *n* Bergsteiger *m*; (*plant*) Kletterpflanze *f*

cling *vi* (*pt/pp* **clung**) sich klammern (**to** an + *acc*); (*stick*) haften (**to** an + *dat*). **~ film** *n* Sichtfolie *f* mit Hafteffekt

clinic *n* Klinik *f*. **~al** *a*, **-ly** *adv* klinisch

clink *vi* klirren

clip[1] *n* Klammer *f*; (*jewellery*) Klipp *m* ● *vt* (*pt/pp* **clipped**) anklammern (**to** an + *acc*)

clip[2] *n* (*extract*) Ausschnitt *m* ● *vt* schneiden; knipsen *<ticket>*. **~ping** *n* (*extract*) Ausschnitt *m*

cloak *n* Umhang *m*. **~room** *n* Garderobe *f*; (*toilet*) Toilette *f*

clobber *n* [!] Zeug *nt* ● *vt* ([!] *hit, defeat*) schlagen

clock *n* Uhr *f*; ([!] *speedometer*) Tacho *m* ● *vi* **~ in/out** stechen

clock: ~wise *a & adv* im Uhrzeigersinn. **~work** *n* Uhrwerk *nt*; (*of toy*) Aufziehmechanismus *m*; **like ~work** [!] wie am Schnürchen

clod *n* Klumpen *m*

clog *vt/i* (*pt/pp* **clogged**) **~ [up]** verstopfen

cloister *n* Kreuzgang *m*

clone *n* Klon *m* ● *vt* klonen

close[1] *a* (**-r, -st**) nah[e] (**to** *dat*); *<friend>* eng; *<weather>* schwül; **have a ~ shave** [!] mit knapper Not davonkommen ● *adv* nahe ● *n* (*street*) Sackgasse *f*

close[2] *n* Ende *nt*; **draw to a ~** sich dem Ende nähern ● *vt* zumachen, schließen; (*bring to an end*) beenden; sperren *<road>* ● *vi* sich schließen; *<shop:>* schließen, zumachen; (*end*) enden. **~ down** *vt* schließen; stilllegen *<factory>* ● *vi* schließen; *<factory:>* stillgelegt werden

closely *adv* eng, nah[e]; (*with attention*) genau

closet *n* (*Amer*) Schrank *m*

close-up *n* Nahaufnahme *f*

closure *n* Schließung *f*; (*of factory*) Stilllegung *f*; (*of road*) Sperrung *f*

clot *n* [Blut]gerinnsel *nt*; ([!] *idiot*) Trottel *m*

cloth *n* Tuch *nt*

clothe *vt* kleiden

clothes *npl* Kleider *pl*. **~-line** *n* Wäscheleine *f*

clothing *n* Kleidung *f*

cloud *n* Wolke *f* ● *vi* **~ over** sich bewölken

cloudy *a* (**-ier, -iest**) wolkig, bewölkt; *<liquid>* trübe

clout *n* [!] Schlag *m*; (*influence*) Einfluss *m*

clove *n* [Gewürz]nelke *f*; **~ of garlic** Knoblauchzehe *f*

clover *n* Klee *m*. **~ leaf** *n* Kleeblatt *nt*

clown *n* Clown *m* ● *vi* **~ [about]** herumalbern

club *n* Klub *m*; (*weapon*) Keule *f*; (*Sport*) Schläger *m*; **~s** *pl* (*Cards*) Kreuz *nt*, Treff *nt*

clue *n* Anhaltspunkt *m*; (*in crossword*) Frage *f*; **I haven't a ~** [!] ich habe keine Ahnung

clump *n* Gruppe *f*

clumsiness *n* Ungeschicklichkeit *f*

clumsy *a* (**-ier, -iest**), **-ily** *adv* ungeschickt; (*unwieldy*) unförmig

clung *see* **cling**

clutch *n* Griff *m*; (*Auto*) Kupplung *f*; **be in s.o.'s ~es** [!] in jds Klauen sein ● *vt* festhalten; (*grab*) ergreifen ● *vi* **~ at** greifen nach

clutter *n* Kram *m* ● *vt* **~ [up]** vollstopfen

c/o *abbr* (**care of**) bei

coach *n* [Reise]bus *m*; (*Rail*) Wagen *m*; (*horse-drawn*) Kutsche *f*; (*Sport*) Trainer *m* ● *vt* Nachhilfestunden geben (+ *dat*); (*Sport*) trainieren

coal *n* Kohle *f*

coalition *n* Koalition *f*

coal-mine *n* Kohlenbergwerk *nt*

coarse *a* (**-r, -st**), **-ly** *adv* grob

coast *n* Küste *f* ● *vi* (*freewheel*) im Freilauf fahren; (*Auto*) im Leerlauf fahren. **~er** *n* (*mat*) Untersatz *m*

coast: ~guard *n* Küstenwache *f*. **~line** *n* Küste *f*

coat *n* Mantel *m*; (*of animal*) Fell *nt*; (*of paint*) Anstrich *m*; **~ of arms** Wappen *nt* ● *vt* überziehen; (*with paint*) streichen. **~-hanger** *n* Kleiderbügel *m*. **~-hook** *n* Kleiderhaken *m*

coating *n* Überzug *m*, Schicht *f*; (*of paint*) Anstrich *m*

coax *vt* gut zureden (+ *dat*)

cobble¹ *n* Kopfstein *m*; **~s** *pl* Kopfsteinpflaster *nt*

cobble² *vt* flicken. **~r** *n* Schuster *m*

cobweb *n* Spinnengewebe *nt*

cock *n* Hahn *m*; (*any male bird*) Männchen *nt* ● *vt* <*animal:*> **~ its ears** die Ohren spitzen; **~ the gun** den Hahn spannen

cockerel *n* [junger] Hahn *m*

cockney *n* (*dialect*) Cockney *nt*; (*person*) Cockney *m*

cock: ~pit *n* (*Aviat*) Cockpit *nt*. **~roach** *n* Küchenschabe *f*. **~tail** *n* Cocktail *m*. **~-up** *n* ☒ **make a ~-up** Mist bauen (**of** bei)

cocky *a* (**-ier, -iest**) [!] eingebildet

cocoa *n* Kakao *m*

coconut *n* Kokosnuß *f*

cod *n inv* Kabeljau *m*

COD *abbr* (**cash on delivery**) per Nachnahme

coddle *vt* verhätscheln

code *n* Kode *m*; (*Computing*) Code *m*; (*set of rules*) Kodex *m*. **~d** *a* verschlüsselt

coerc|e *vt* zwingen. **~ion** *n* Zwang *m*

coffee *n* Kaffee *m*

coffee: ~-grinder *n* Kaffeemühle *f*. **~-pot** *n* Kaffeekanne *f*. **~-table** *n* Couchtisch *m*

coffin *n* Sarg *m*

cogent *a* überzeugend

coherent *a* zusammenhängend; (*comprehensible*) verständlich

coil *n* Rolle *f*; (*Electr*) Spule *f*; (*one ring*) Windung *f* ● *vt* **~[up]** zusammenrollen

coin *n* Münze *f* ● *vt* prägen

coincide *vi* zusammenfallen; (*agree*) übereinstimmen

coinciden|ce *n* Zufall *m*. **~tal** *a*, **-ly** *adv* zufällig

coke *n* Koks *m*

Coke (P) *n* (*drink*) Cola *f*

cold *a* (**-er, -est**) kalt; **I am or feel ~** mir ist kalt ● *n* Kälte *f*; (*Med*) Erkältung *f*

cold: ~-blooded *a* kaltblütig. **~-hearted** *a* kaltherzig. **~ly** *adv* (*fig*) kalt, kühl. **~ness** *n* Kälte *f*

collaborat|e *vi* zusammenarbeiten (**with** mit); **~e on sth** mitarbeiten bei etw. **~ion** *n* Zusammenarbeit *f*, Mitarbeit *f*; (*with enemy*) Kollaboration *f*. **~or** *n* Mitarbeiter(in) *m*(*f*); Kollaborateur *m*

collaps|e *n* Zusammenbruch *m*; Einsturz *m* ● *vi* zusammenbrechen; <*roof, building*> einstürzen. **~ible** *a* zusammenklappbar

collar *n* Kragen *m*; (*for animal*) Halsband *nt*. **~-bone** *n* Schlüsselbein *nt*

colleague *n* Kollege *m*/Kollegin *f*

collect *vt* sammeln; (*fetch*) abholen; einsammeln <*tickets*>; einziehen <*taxes*> ● *vi* sich

[an]sammeln ● *adv* **call ~** (*Amer*) ein R-Gespräch führen
collection *n* Sammlung *f*; (*in church*) Kollekte *f*; (*of post*) Leerung *f*; (*designer's*) Kollektion *f*
collector *n* Sammler(in) *m(f)*
college *n* College *nt*
collide *vi* zusammenstoßen
colliery *n* Kohlengrube *f*
collision *n* Zusammenstoß *m*
colloquial *a*, **-ly** *adv* umgangssprachlich
Cologne *n* Köln *nt*
colon *n* Doppelpunkt
colonel *n* Oberst *m*
colonial *a* Kolonial-
colony *n* Kolonie *f*
colossal *a* riesig
colour *n* Farbe *f*; (*complexion*) Gesichtsfarbe *f*; (*race*) Hautfarbe *f*; **off ~** [!] nicht ganz auf der Höhe ● *vt* färben; **~ [in]** ausmalen
colour: ~-blind *a* farbenblind. **~ed** *a* farbig ● *n* (*person*) Farbige(r) *m/f*. **~-fast** *a* farbecht. **~ film** *n* Farbfilm *m*. **~ful** *a* farbenfroh. **~less** *a* farblos. **~ photo[graph]** *n* Farbaufnahme *f*. **~ television** *n* Farbfernsehen *nt*
column *n* Säule *f*; (*of soldiers, figures*) Kolonne *f*; (*Typ*) Spalte *f*; (*Journ*) Kolumne *f*
comb *n* Kamm *m* ● *vt* kämmen; (*search*) absuchen; **~ one's hair** sich (*dat*) [die Haare] kämmen
combat *n* Kampf *m*
combination *n* Kombination *f*
combine[1] *vt* verbinden ● *vi* sich verbinden; <*people:*> sich zusammenschließen
combine[2] *n* (*Comm*) Konzern *m*
combustion *n* Verbrennung *f*
come *vi* (*pt* **came**, *pp* **come**) kommen; (*reach*) reichen (**to** an + *acc*); **that ~ s to £10** das macht £10; **~ into money** zu Geld kommen; **~ true** wahr werden; **~ in two sizes** in zwei Größen erhältlich sein; **the years to ~** die kommenden Jahre; **how ~?** [!] wie das? **~ about** *vi* geschehen. **~ across** *vi* herüberkommen; [!] klar werden ● *vt* stoßen auf (+ *acc*). **~ apart** *vi* sich auseinander nehmen lassen; (*accidentally*) auseinander gehen. **~ away** *vi* weggehen; <*thing:*> abgehen. **~ back** *vi* zurückkommen. **~ by** *vi* vorbeikommen ● *vt* (*obtain*) bekommen. **~ in** *vi* hereinkommen. **~ off** *vi* abgehen; (*take place*) stattfinden; (*succeed*) klappen [!]. **~ out** *vi* herauskommen; <*book:*> erscheinen; <*stain:*> herausgehen. **~ round** *vi* vorbeikommen; (*after fainting*) [wieder] zu sich kommen; (*change one's mind*) sich umstimmen lassen. **~ to** *vi* [wieder] zu sich kommen. **~ up** *vi* heraufkommen; <*plant:*> aufgehen; (*reach*) reichen (**to** bis); **~ up with** sich (*dat*) einfallen lassen
come-back *n* Comeback *nt*
comedian *n* Komiker *m*
come-down *n* Rückschritt *m*
comedy *n* Komödie *f*
comet *n* Komet *m*
comfort *n* Bequemlichkeit *f*; (*consolation*) Trost *m* ● *vt* trösten
comfortable *a*, **-bly** *adv* bequem
comfort station *n* (*Amer*) öffentliche Toilette *f*
comfy *a* [!] bequem
comic *a* komisch ● *n* Komiker *m*; (*periodical*) Comic-Heft *nt*
coming *a* kommend ● *n* Kommen *nt*
comma *n* Komma *nt*
command *n* Befehl *m*; (*Mil*) Kommando *nt*; (*mastery*) Beherrschung *f* ● *vt* befehlen (+ *dat*); kommandieren <*army*>

command|er *n* Befehlshaber *m*. **~ing officer** *n* Befehlshaber *m*

commemorat|e *vt* gedenken (+ *gen*). **~ion** *n* Gedenken *nt*

commence *vt/i* anfangen, beginnen

commend *vt* loben; (*recommend*) empfehlen (**to** *dat*)

comment *n* Bemerkung *f*; **no ~!** kein Kommentar! ● *vi* sich äußern (**on** zu); **~ on** (*Journ*) kommentieren

commentary *n* Kommentar *m*; **[running] ~** (*Radio, TV*) Reportage *f*

commentator *n* Kommentator *m*; (*Sport*) Reporter *m*

commerce *n* Handel *m*

commercial *a*, **-ly** *adv* kommerziell ● *n* (*Radio, TV*) Werbespot *m*

commission *n* (*order for work*) Auftrag *m*; (*body of people*) Kommission *f*; (*payment*) Provision *f*; (*Mil*) [Offiziers]patent *nt*; **out of ~** außer Betrieb ● *vt* beauftragen <*s.o.*>; in Auftrag geben <*thing*>; (*Mil*) zum Offizier ernennen

commit *vt* (*pt/pp* **committed**) begehen; (*entrust*) anvertrauen (**to** *dat*); (*consign*) einweisen (**to** in + *acc*); **~ oneself** sich festlegen; (*involve oneself*) sich engagieren. **~ment** *n* Verpflichtung *f*; (*involvement*) Engagement *nt*. **~ted** *a* engagiert

committee *n* Ausschuss *m*, Komitee *nt*

common *a* (**-er, -est**) gemeinsam; (*frequent*) häufig; (*ordinary*) gewöhnlich; (*vulgar*) ordinär ● *n* Gemeindeland *nt*; **have in ~** gemeinsam haben; **House of C~s** Unterhaus *nt*

common: ~ly *adv* allgemein. **C~ Market** *n* Gemeinsamer Markt *m*. **~place** *a* häufig. **~-room** *n* Aufenthaltsraum *m*. **~ sense** *n* gesunder Menschenverstand *m*

commotion *n* Tumult *m*

communal *a* gemeinschaftlich

communicate *vt* mitteilen (**to** *dat*); übertragen <disease> ● *vi* sich verständigen

communication *n* Verständigung *f*; (*contact*) Verbindung *f*; (*message*) Mitteilung *f*; **~s** *pl* (*technology*) Nachrichtenwesen *nt*

communicative *a* mitteilsam

Communion *n* **[Holy] ~** das [heilige] Abendmahl; (*Roman Catholic*) die [heilige] Kommunion

communis|m *n* Kommunismus *m*. **~t** *a* kommunistisch ● *n* Kommunist(in) *m(f)*

community *n* Gemeinschaft *f*; **local ~** Gemeinde *f*

commute *vi* pendeln. **~r** *n* Pendler(in) *m(f)*

compact *a* kompakt

companion *n* Begleiter(in) *m(f)*. **~ship** *n* Gesellschaft *f*

company *n* Gesellschaft *f*; (*firm*) Firma *f*; (*Mil*) Kompanie *f*; (! *guests*) Besuch *m*. **~ car** *n* Firmenwagen *m*

comparable *a* vergleichbar

comparative *a* vergleichend; (*relative*) relativ ● *n* (*Gram*) Komparativ *m*. **~ly** *adv* verhältnismäßig

compare *vt* vergleichen (**with/to** mit) ● *vi* sich vergleichen lassen

comparison *n* Vergleich *m*

compartment *n* Fach *nt*; (*Rail*) Abteil *nt*

compass *n* Kompass *m*

compassion *n* Mitleid *nt*. **~ate** *a* mitfühlend

compatible *a* vereinbar; <*drugs*> verträglich; (*Techn*) kompatibel; **be ~** <*people:*> [gut] zueinander passen

compatriot *n* Landsmann *m* /-männin *f*

compel *vt* (*pt/pp* **compelled**) zwingen

compensat|e *vt* entschädigen. **~ion** *n* Entschädigung *f*; (*fig*) Ausgleich *m*

compete *vi* konkurrieren; (*take part*) teilnehmen (**in** an + *dat*)

competen|ce *n* Fähigkeit *f*. **~t** *a* fähig

competition *n* Konkurrenz *f*; (*contest*) Wettbewerb *m*; (*in newspaper*) Preisausschreiben *nt*

competitive *a* (*Comm*) konkurrenzfähig

competitor *n* Teilnehmer *m*; (*Comm*) Konkurrent *m*

compile *vt* zusammenstellen

complacen|cy *n* Selbstzufriedenheit *f*. **~t** *a*, **-ly** *adv* selbstzufrieden

complain *vi* klagen (**about/of** über + *acc*); (*formally*) sich beschweren. **~t** *n* Klage *f*; (*formal*) Beschwerde *f*; (*Med*) Leiden *nt*

complement[1] *n* Ergänzung *f*; **full ~** volle Anzahl *f*

complement[2] *vt* ergänzen

complete *a* vollständig; (*finished*) fertig; (*utter*) völlig ● *vt* vervollständigen; (*finish*) abschließen; (*fill in*) ausfüllen. **~ly** *adv* völlig

completion *n* Vervollständigung *f*; (*end*) Abschluss *m*

complex *a* komplex ● *n* Komplex *m*

complexion *n* Teint *m*; (*colour*) Gesichtsfarbe *f*

complexity *n* Komplexität *f*

complicat|e *vt* komplizieren. **~ed** *a* kompliziert. **~ion** *n* Komplikation *f*

compliment *n* Kompliment *nt*; **~s** *pl* Grüße *pl* ● *vt* ein Kompliment machen (+ *dat*). **~ary** *a* schmeichelhaft; (*given free*) Frei-

comply *vi* (*pt/pp* **-ied**) **~ with** nachkommen (+ *dat*)

compose *vt* verfassen; (*Mus*) komponieren; **be ~d of** sich zusammensetzen aus. **~r** *n* Komponist *m*

composition *n* Komposition *f*; (*essay*) Aufsatz *m*

compost *n* Kompost *m*

composure *n* Fassung *f*

compound *a* zusammengesetzt; <*fracture*> kompliziert ● *n* (*Chem*) Verbindung *f*; (*Gram*) Kompositum *nt*

comprehen|d *vt* begreifen, verstehen. **~sible** *a*, **-bly** *adv* verständlich. **~sion** *n* Verständnis *nt*

comprehensive *a* & *n* umfassend; **~ [school]** Gesamtschule *f*. **~ insurance** *n* (*Auto*) Vollkaskoversicherung *f*

compress *vt* zusammenpressen; **~ed air** Druckluft *f*

comprise *vt* umfassen, bestehen aus

compromise *n* Kompromiss *m* ● *vt* kompromittieren <*person*> ● *vi* einen Kompromiss schließen

compuls|ion *n* Zwang *m*. **~ive** *a* zwanghaft. **~ory** *a* obligatorisch

comput|er *n* Computer *m*. **~er game** *n* Computerspiel. **~erize** *vt* computerisieren <*data*>; auf Computer umstellen <*firm*>. **~-literate** *a* mit Computern vertraut. **~ing** *n* Computertechnik *f*

comrade *n* Kamerad *m*; (*Pol*) Genosse *m*/Genossin *f*

con[1] *see* **pro**

con[2] *n* [!] Schwindel *m* ● *vt* (*pt/pp* **conned**) [!] beschwindeln

concave *a* konkav

conceal *vt* verstecken; (*keep secret*) verheimlichen

concede *vt* zugeben; (*give up*) aufgeben
conceit *n* Einbildung *f*. **~ed** *a* eingebildet
conceivable *a* denkbar
conceive *vt* (*Biol*) empfangen; (*fig*) sich (*dat*) ausdenken ● *vi* schwanger werden
concentrat|e *vt* konzentrieren ● *vi* sich konzentrieren. **~ion** *n* Konzentration *f*
concern *n* Angelegenheit *f*; (*worry*) Sorge *f*; (*Comm*) Unternehmen *nt* ● *vt* (*be about, affect*) betreffen; (*worry*) kümmern; **be ~ed about** besorgt sein um; **~ oneself with** sich beschäftigen mit; **as far as I am ~ed** was mich angeht *od* betrifft. **~ing** *prep* bezüglich (+ *gen*)
concert *n* Konzert *nt*
concerto *n* Konzert *nt*
concession *n* Zugeständnis *nt*; (*Comm*) Konzession *f*; (*reduction*) Ermäßigung *f*
concise *a*, **-ly** *adv* kurz
conclude *vt/i* schließen
conclusion *n* Schluss *m*; **in ~** abschließend, zum Schluss
conclusive *a* schlüssig
concoct *vt* zusammenstellen; (*fig*) fabrizieren. **~ion** *n* Zusammenstellung *f*; (*drink*) Gebräu *nt*
concrete *a* konkret ● *n* Beton *m* ● *vt* betonieren
concurrently *adv* gleichzeitig
concussion *n* Gehirnerschütterung *f*
condemn *vt* verurteilen; (*declare unfit*) für untauglich erklären. **~ation** *n* Verurteilung *f*
condensation *n* Kondensation *f*
condense *vt* zusammenfassen
condescend *vi* sich herablassen (**to** zu). **~ing** *a*, **-ly** *adv* herablassend
condition *n* Bedingung *f*; (*state*) Zustand *m*; **~s** *pl* Verhältnisse *pl*; **on ~ that** unter der Bedingung, dass ● *vt* (*Psych*) konditionieren. **~al** *a* bedingt ● *n* (*Gram*) Konditional *m*. **~er** *n* Pflegespülung *f*; (*for fabrics*) Weichspüler *m*
condolences *npl* Beileid *nt*
condom *n* Kondom *nt*
condominium *n* (*Amer*) ≈ Eigentumswohnung *f*
conduct[1] *n* Verhalten *nt*; (*Sch*) Betragen *nt*
conduct[2] *vt* führen; (*Phys*) leiten; (*Mus*) dirigieren. **~or** *n* Dirigent *m*; (*of bus*) Schaffner *m*; (*Phys*) Leiter *m*
cone *n* Kegel *m*; (*Bot*) Zapfen *m*; (*for ice-cream*) [Eis]tüte *f*; (*Auto*) Leitkegel *m*
confectioner *n* Konditor *m*. **~y** *n* Süßwaren *pl*
conference *n* Konferenz *f*
confess *vt/i* gestehen; (*Relig*) beichten. **~ion** *n* Geständnis *nt*; (*Relig*) Beichte *f*
confetti *n* Konfetti *nt*
confide *vt* anvertrauen ● *vi* **~ in s.o.** sich jdm anvertrauen
confidence *n* (*trust*) Vertrauen *nt*; (*self-assurance*) Selbstvertrauen *nt*; (*secret*) Geheimnis *nt*; **in ~** im Vertrauen. **~ trick** *n* Schwindel *m*
confident *a*, **-ly** *adv* zuversichtlich; (*self-assured*) selbstsicher
confidential *a*, **-ly** *adv* vertraulich
confine *vt* beschränken (**to** auf + *acc*). **~d** *a* (*narrow*) eng
confirm *vt* bestätigen; (*Relig*) konfirmieren; (*Roman Catholic*) firmen. **~ation** *n* Bestätigung *f*; Konfirmation *f*; Firmung *f*
confiscat|e *vt* beschlagnahmen. **~ion** *n* Beschlagnahme *f*
conflict[1] *n* Konflikt *m*
conflict[2] *vi* im Widerspruch stehen (**with** zu). **~ing** *a* widersprüchlich

conform *vi* <*person:*> sich anpassen; <*thing:*> entsprechen (**to** *dat*). **~ist** *n* Konformist *m*

confounded *a* [!] verflixt

confront *vt* konfrontieren. **~ation** *n* Konfrontation *f*

confus|e *vt* verwirren; (*mistake for*) verwechseln (**with** mit). **~ing** *a* verwirrend. **~ion** *n* Verwirrung *f*; (*muddle*) Durcheinander *nt*

congenial *a* angenehm

congest|ed *a* verstopft; (*with people*) überfüllt. **~ion** *n* Verstopfung *f*; Überfüllung *f*

congratulat|e *vt* gratulieren (+ *dat*) (**on** zu). **~ions** *npl* Glückwünsche *pl*; **~ions!** [ich] gratuliere!

congregation *n* (*Relig*) Gemeinde *f*

congress *n* Kongress *m*. **~man** *n* Kongressabgeordnete(r) *m*

conical *a* kegelförmig

conifer *n* Nadelbaum *m*

conjecture *n* Mutmaßung *f*

conjunction *n* Konjunktion *f*; **in ~ with** zusammen mit

conjur|e *vi* zaubern ● *vt* **~e up** heraufbeschwören. **~or** *n* Zauberkünstler *m*

conk *vi* **~ out** [!] <*machine:*> kaputtgehen

conker *n* [!] Kastanie *f*

con-man *n* [!] Schwindler *m*

connect *vt* verbinden (**to** mit); (*Electr*) anschließen (**to** an + *acc*); **be ~ed with** zu tun haben mit; (*be related to*) verwandt sein mit ● *vi* verbunden sein; <*train:*> Anschluss haben (**with** an + *acc*)

connection *n* Verbindung *f*; (*Rail, Electr*) Anschluss *m*; **in ~ with** in Zusammenhang mit. **~s** *npl* Beziehungen *pl*

connoisseur *n* Kenner *m*

conquer *vt* erobern; (*fig*) besiegen. **~or** *n* Eroberer *m*

conquest *n* Eroberung *f*

conscience *n* Gewissen *nt*

conscientious *a*, **-ly** *adv* gewissenhaft

conscious *a*, **-ly** *adv* bewusst; **[fully] ~** bei [vollem] Bewusstsein; **be/become ~ of sth** sich (*dat*) etw (*gen*) bewusst sein/werden. **~ness** *n* Bewusstsein *nt*

conscript *n* Einberufene(r) *m*

consecrat|e *vt* weihen; einweihen <*church*>. **~ion** *n* Weihe *f*; Einweihung *f*

consecutive *a* aufeinanderfolgend. **-ly** *adv* fortlaufend

consent *n* Einwilligung *f*, Zustimmung *f* ● *vi* einwilligen (**to** in + *acc*), zustimmen (**to** *dat*)

consequen|ce *n* Folge *f*. **~t** *a* daraus folgend. **~tly** *adv* folglich

conservation *n* Erhaltung *f*, Bewahrung *f*. **~ist** *n* Umweltschützer *m*

conservative *a* konservativ; <*estimate*> vorsichtig. **C~** (*Pol*) *a* konservativ ● *n* Konservative(r) *m*/*f*

conservatory *n* Wintergarten *m*

conserve *vt* erhalten, bewahren; sparen <*energy*>

consider *vt* erwägen; (*think over*) sich (*dat*) überlegen; (*take into account*) berücksichtigen; (*regard as*) betrachten als; **~ doing sth** erwägen, etw zu tun. **~able** *a*, **-bly** *adv* erheblich

consider|ate *a*, **-ly** *adv* rücksichtsvoll. **~ation** *n* Erwägung *f*; (*thoughtfulness*) Rücksicht *f*; (*payment*) Entgelt *nt*; **take into ~ation** berücksichtigen. **~ing** *prep* wenn man bedenkt (**that** dass)

consist *vi* **~ of** bestehen aus

consisten|cy *n* Konsequenz *f*; (*density*) Konsistenz *f*. **~t** *a* konsequent; (*unchanging*) gleichbleibend. **~tly** *adv* konsequent; (*constantly*) ständig

consolation *n* Trost *m*. ~ **prize** *n* Trostpreis *m*

console *vt* trösten

consonant *n* Konsonant *m*

conspicuous *a* auffällig

conspiracy *n* Verschwörung *f*

constable *n* Polizist *m*

constant *a*, **-ly** *adv* beständig; (*continuous*) ständig

constipat|ed *a* verstopft. **~ion** *n* Verstopfung *f*

constituency *n* Wahlkreis *m*

constitut|e *vt* bilden. **~ion** *n* (*Pol*) Verfassung *f*; (*of person*) Konstitution *f*

constraint *n* Zwang *m*; (*restriction*) Beschränkung *f*; (*strained manner*) Gezwungenheit *f*

construct *vt* bauen. **~ion** *n* Bau *m*; (*Gram*) Konstruktion *f*; (*interpretation*) Deutung *f*; **under ~ion** im Bau

consul *n* Konsul *m*. **~ate** *n* Konsulat *nt*

consult *vt* [um Rat] fragen; konsultieren <*doctor*>; nachschlagen in (+ *dat*) <*book*>. **~ant** *n* Berater *m*; (*Med*) Chefarzt *m*. **~ation** *n* Beratung *f*; (*Med*) Konsultation *f*

consume *vt* verzehren; (*use*) verbrauchen. **~r** *n* Verbraucher *m*

consumption *n* Konsum *m*; (*use*) Verbrauch *m*

contact *n* Kontakt *m*; (*person*) Kontaktperson *f* ● *vt* sich in Verbindung setzen mit. ~ **lenses** *npl* Kontaktlinsen *pl*

contagious *a* direkt übertragbar

contain *vt* enthalten; (*control*) beherrschen. **~er** *n* Behälter *m*; (*Comm*) Container *m*

contaminat|e *vt* verseuchen. **~ion** *n* Verseuchung *f*

contemplat|e *vt* betrachten; (*meditate*) nachdenken über (+ *acc*). **~ion** *n* Betrachtung *f*; Nachdenken *nt*

contemporary *a* zeitgenössisch ● *n* Zeitgenosse *m*/ -genossin *f*

contempt *n* Verachtung *f*; **beneath ~** verabscheuungswürdig. **~ible** *a* verachtenswert. **~uous** *a*, **-ly** *adv* verächtlich

content[1] *n* & **contents** *pl* Inhalt *m*

content[2] *a* zufrieden ● *n* **to one's heart's ~** nach Herzenslust ● *vt* **~ oneself** sich begnügen (**with** mit). **~ed** *a*, **-ly** *adv* zufrieden

contentment *n* Zufriedenheit *f*

contest *n* Kampf *m*; (*competition*) Wettbewerb *m*. **~ant** *n* Teilnehmer *m*

context *n* Zusammenhang *m*

continent *n* Kontinent *m*

continental *a* Kontinental-. ~ **breakfast** *n* kleines Frühstück *nt*. ~ **quilt** *n* Daunendecke *f*

continual *a*, **-ly** *adv* dauernd

continuation *n* Fortsetzung *f*

continue *vt* fortsetzen; ~ **doing** *or* **to do sth** fortfahren, etw zu tun; **to be ~d** Fortsetzung folgt ● *vi* weitergehen; (*doing sth*) weitermachen; (*speaking*) fortfahren; <*weather:*> anhalten

continuity *n* Kontinuität *f*

continuous *a*, **-ly** *adv* anhaltend, ununterbrochen

contort *vt* verzerren. **~ion** *n* Verzerrung *f*

contour *n* Kontur *f*; (*line*) Höhenlinie *f*

contracep|tion *n* Empfängnisverhütung *f*. **~tive** *n* Empfängnisverhütungsmittel *nt*

contract[1] *n* Vertrag *m*

contract[2] *vi* sich zusammenziehen. **~or** *n* Unternehmer *m*

contradict *vt* widersprechen (+ *dat*). **~ion** *n* Widerspruch *m*. **~ory** *a* widersprüchlich

contralto *n* Alt *m*; (*singer*) Altistin *f*

contraption *n* [!] Apparat *m*
contrary *a & adv* entgegengesetzt; **~ to** entgegen (+ *dat*) ● *n* Gegenteil *nt*; **on the ~** im Gegenteil
contrast¹ *n* Kontrast *m*
contrast² *vt* gegenüberstellen (**with** *dat*) ● *vi* einen Kontrast bilden (**with** zu). **~ing** *a* gegensätzlich; <*colour*> Kontrast-
contribut|e *vt/i* beitragen; beisteuern <*money*>; (*donate*) spenden. **~ion** *n* Beitrag *m*; (*donation*) Spende *f*. **~or** *n* Beitragende(r) *m/f*
contrivance *n* Vorrichtung *f*
control *n* Kontrolle *f*; (*mastery*) Beherrschung *f*; (*Techn*) Regler *m*; **~s** *pl* (*of car, plane*) Steuerung *f*; **get out of ~** außer Kontrolle geraten ● *vt* (*pt/pp* **controlled**) kontrollieren; (*restrain*) unter Kontrolle halten; **~ oneself** sich beherrschen
controvers|ial *a* umstritten. **~y** *n* Kontroverse *f*
convalesce *vi* sich erholen. **~nce** *n* Erholung *f*
convalescent *a* **~ home** *n* Erholungsheim *nt*
convenience *n* Bequemlichkeit *f*; **[public] ~** öffentliche Toilette *f*; **with all modern ~s** mit allem Komfort
convenient *a*, **-ly** *adv* günstig; **be ~ for s.o.** jdm gelegen sein, jdm passen; **if it is ~ [for you]** wenn es Ihnen passt
convent *n* [Nonnen]kloster *nt*
convention *n* (*custom*) Brauch *m*, Sitte *f*. **~al** *a*, **-ly** *adv* konventionell
converge *vi* zusammenlaufen
conversation *n* Gespräch *nt*; (*Sch*) Konversation *f*
conversion *n* Umbau *m*; (*Relig*) Bekehrung *f*; (*calculation*) Umrechnung *f*
convert¹ *n* Bekehrte(r) *m/f*, Konvertit *m*
convert² *vt* bekehren <*person*>; (*change*) umwandeln (**into** in + *acc*); umbauen <*building*>; (*calculate*) umrechnen; (*Techn*) umstellen. **~ible** *a* verwandelbar ● *n* (*Auto*) Kabrio[lett] *nt*
convex *a* konvex
convey *vt* befördern; vermitteln <*idea, message*>. **~or belt** *n* Förderband *nt*
convict¹ *n* Sträfling *m*
convict² *vt* verurteilen (**of** wegen). **~ion** *n* Verurteilung *f*; (*belief*) Überzeugung *f*; **previous ~ion** Vorstrafe *f*
convinc|e *vt* überzeugen. **~ing** *a*, **-ly** *adv* überzeugend
convoy *n* Konvoi *m*
convulse *vt* **be ~ed** sich krümmen (**with** vor + *dat*)
coo *vi* gurren
cook *n* Koch *m*/ Köchin *f* ● *vt/i* kochen; **is it ~ed?** ist es gar? **~ the books** [!] die Bilanz frisieren. **~book** *n* (*Amer*) Kochbuch *nt*
cooker *n* [Koch]herd *m*; (*apple*) Kochapfel *m*. **~y** *n* Kochen *nt*. **~y book** *n* Kochbuch *nt*
cookie *n* (*Amer*) Keks *m*
cool *a* (**-er, -est**), **-ly** *adv* kühl ● *n* Kühle *f* ● *vt* kühlen ● *vi* abkühlen. **~-box** *n* Kühlbox *f*. **~ness** *n* Kühle *f*
coop *vt* **~ up** einsperren
co-operat|e *vi* zusammenarbeiten. **~ion** *n* Kooperation *f*
co-operative *a* hilfsbereit ● *n* Genossenschaft *f*
cop *n* [!] Polizist *m*
cope *vi* [!] zurechtkommen; **~ with** fertig werden mit
copious *a* reichlich
copper¹ *n* Kupfer *nt* ● *a* kupfern
copper² *n* [!] Polizist *m*
copper beech *n* Blutbuche *f*
coppice *n*, **copse** *n* Gehölz *nt*

copy *n* Kopie *f*; (*book*) Exemplar *nt* ● *vt* (*pt*/*pp* **-ied**) kopieren; (*imitate*) nachahmen; (*Sch*) abschreiben

copy: ~right *n* Copyright *nt*. **~-writer** *n* Texter *m*

coral *n* Koralle *f*

cord *n* Schnur *f*; (*fabric*) Cordsamt *m*; **~s** *pl* Cordhose *f*

cordial *a*, **-ly** *adv* herzlich ● *n* Fruchtsirup *m*

cordon *n* Kordon *m* ● *vt* **~ off** absperren

corduroy *n* Cordsamt *m*

core *n* Kern *m*; (*of apple, pear*) Kerngehäuse *nt*

cork *n* Kork *m*; (*for bottle*) Korken *m*. **~screw** *n* Korkenzieher *m*

corn[1] *n* Korn *nt*; (*Amer: maize*) Mais *m*

corn[2] *n* (*Med*) Hühnerauge *nt*

corned beef *n* Cornedbeef *nt*

corner *n* Ecke *f*; (*bend*) Kurve *f*; (*football*) Eckball *m* ● *vt* (*fig*) in die Enge treiben; (*Comm*) monopolisieren <*market*>. **~-stone** *n* Eckstein *m*

cornet *n* (*Mus*) Kornett *nt*; (*for ice-cream*) [Eis]tüte *f*

corn: ~flour *n*, (*Amer*) **~starch** *n* Stärkemehl *nt*

corny *a* [!] abgedroschen

coronation *n* Krönung *f*

coroner *n* Beamte(r) *m*, der verdächtige Todesfälle untersucht

corporal *n* (*Mil*) Stabsunteroffizier *m*

corps *n* (*pl* **corps**) Korps *nt*

corpse *n* Leiche *f*

correct *a*, **-ly** *adv* richtig; (*proper*) korrekt ● *vt* verbessern; (*Sch, Typ*) korrigieren. **~ion** *n* Verbesserung *f*; (*Typ*) Korrektur *f*

correspond *vi* entsprechen (**to** *dat*); <*two things:*> sich entsprechen; (*write*) korrespondieren. **~ence** *n* Briefwechsel *m*; (*Comm*) Korrespondenz *f*. **~ent** *n* Korrespondent(in) *m*(*f*). **~ing** *a*, **-ly** *adv* entsprechend

corridor *n* Gang *m*; (*Pol, Aviat*) Korridor *m*

corro|de *vt* zerfressen ● *vi* rosten. **~sion** *n* Korrosion *f*

corrugated *a* gewellt. **~ iron** *n* Wellblech *nt*

corrupt *a* korrupt ● *vt* korrumpieren; (*spoil*) verderben. **~ion** *n* Korruption *f*

corset *n* & **-s** *pl* Korsett *nt*

Corsica *n* Korsika *nt*

cosh *n* Totschläger *m*

cosmetic *a* kosmetisch ● *n* **~s** *pl* Kosmetika *pl*

cosset *vt* verhätscheln

cost *n* Kosten *pl*; **~s** *pl* (*Jur*) Kosten; **at all ~s** um jeden Preis ● *vt* (*pt*/*pp* **cost**) kosten; **it ~ me £20** es hat mich £20 gekostet ● *vt* (*pt*/*pp* **costed**) **~ [out]** die Kosten kalkulieren für

costly *a* (**-ier, -iest**) teuer

cost: ~ of living *n* Lebenshaltungskosten *pl*. **~ price** *n* Selbstkostenpreis *m*

costume *n* Kostüm *nt*; (*national*) Tracht *f*. **~ jewellery** *n* Modeschmuck *m*

cosy *a* (**-ier, -iest**) gemütlich ● *n* (*tea-, egg-*) Wärmer *m*

cot *n* Kinderbett *nt*; (*Amer: camp bed*) Feldbett *nt*

cottage *n* Häuschen *nt*. **~ cheese** *n* Hüttenkäse *m*

cotton *n* Baumwolle *f*; (*thread*) Nähgarn *nt* ● *a* baumwollen ● *vi* **~ on** [!] kapieren

cotton wool *n* Watte *f*

couch *n* Liege *f*

couchette *n* (*Rail*) Liegeplatz *m*

cough *n* Husten *m* ● *vi* husten. **~ up** *vt*/*i* husten; ([!] *pay*) blechen

cough mixture *n* Hustensaft *m*

could *see* can[2]

council *n* Rat *m*; (*Admin*) Stadtverwaltung *f*; (*rural*) Gemeindeverwaltung *f*. ~ **house** *n* ≈ Sozialwohnung *f*

councillor *n* Ratsmitglied *nt*

council tax *n* Gemeindesteuer *f*

count¹ *n* Graf *m*

count² *n* Zählung *f*; **keep ~** zählen ● *vt/i* zählen. ~ **on** *vt* rechnen auf (+ *acc*)

counter¹ *n* (*in shop*) Ladentisch *m*; (*in bank*) Schalter *m*; (*in café*) Theke *f*; (*Games*) Spielmarke *f*

counter² *a* Gegen- ● *vt/i* kontern

counteract *vt* entgegenwirken (+ *dat*)

counterfeit *a* gefälscht

counterfoil *n* Kontrollabschnitt *m*

counterpart *n* Gegenstück *nt*

counter-productive *a* **be ~** das Gegenteil bewirken

countersign *vt* gegenzeichnen

countess *n* Gräfin *f*

countless *a* unzählig

country *n* Land *nt*; (*native land*) Heimat *f*; (*countryside*) Landschaft *f*; **in the ~** auf dem Lande. **~man** *n* **[fellow] ~man** Landsmann *m*. **~side** *n* Landschaft *f*

county *n* Grafschaft *f*

coup *n* (*Pol*) Staatsstreich *m*

couple *n* Paar *nt*; **a ~ of** (*two*) zwei ● *vt* verbinden

coupon *n* Kupon *m*; (*voucher*) Gutschein *m*; (*entry form*) Schein *m*

courage *n* Mut *m*. **~ous** *a*, **-ly** *adv* mutig

courgettes *npl* Zucchini *pl*

courier *n* Bote *m*; (*diplomatic*) Kurier *m*; (*for tourists*) Reiseleiter(in) *m(f)*

course *n* (*Naut, Sch*) Kurs *m*; (*Culin*) Gang *m*; (*for golf*) Platz *m*; **~ of treatment** (*Med*) Kur *f*; **of ~** natürlich, selbstverständlich; **in the ~ of** im Lauf[e] (+ *gen*)

court *n* Hof *m*; (*Sport*) Platz *m*; (*Jur*) Gericht *nt*

courteous *a*, **-ly** *adv* höflich

courtesy *n* Höflichkeit *f*

court: ~ martial *n* (*pl* **~s martial**) Militärgericht *nt*. **~yard** *n* Hof *m*

cousin *n* Vetter *m*, Cousin *m*; (*female*) Kusine *f*

cove *n* kleine Bucht *f*

cover *n* Decke *f*; (*of cushion*) Bezug *m*; (*of umbrella*) Hülle *f*; (*of typewriter*) Haube *f*; (*of book, lid*) Deckel *m*; (*of magazine*) Umschlag *m*; (*protection*) Deckung *f*, Schutz *m*; **take ~** Deckung nehmen; **under separate ~** mit getrennter Post ● *vt* bedecken; beziehen <*cushion*>; decken <*costs, needs*>; zurücklegen <*distance*>; (*Journ*) berichten über (+ *acc*); (*insure*) versichern. ~ **up** *vt* zudecken; (*fig*) vertuschen

coverage *n* (*Journ*) Berichterstattung *f* (**of** über + *acc*)

cover: ~ing *n* Decke *f*; (*for floor*) Belag *m*. **~-up** *n* Vertuschung *f*

cow *n* Kuh *f*

coward *n* Feigling *m*. **~ice** *n* Feigheit *f*. **~ly** *a* feige

cowboy *n* Cowboy *m*; [!] unsolider Handwerker *m*

cower *vi* sich [ängstlich] ducken

cowshed *n* Kuhstall *m*

cox *n*, **coxswain** *n* Steuermann *m*

coy *a* (**-er, -est**) gespielt schüchtern

crab *n* Krabbe *f*

crack *n* Riss *m*; (*in china, glass*) Sprung *m*; (*noise*) Knall *m*; ([!] *joke*) Witz *m*; ([!] *attempt*) Versuch *m* ● *a* [!] erstklassig ● *vt* knacken <*nut, code*>; einen Sprung machen in (+ *acc*) <*china, glass*>; [!] reißen <*joke*>; [!] lösen <*problem*> ● *vi* <*china, glass:*> springen; <*whip:*>

knallen. ~ **down** *vi* [!] durchgreifen

cracked *a* gesprungen; <*rib*> angebrochen; ([!] *crazy*) verrückt

cracker *n* (*biscuit*) Kräcker *m*; (*firework*) Knallkörper *m*; **[Christmas]** ~ Knallbonbon *m*. ~**s** *a* **be** ~**s** [!] einen Knacks haben

crackle *vi* knistern

cradle *n* Wiege *f*

craft *n* Handwerk *nt*; (*technique*) Fertigkeit *f*. ~**sman** *n* Handwerker *m*

crafty *a* (**-ier, -iest**), **-ily** *adv* gerissen

crag *n* Felszacken *m*

cram *v* (*pt/pp* **crammed**) ● *vt* hineinstopfen (**into** in + *acc*); vollstopfen (**with** mit) ● *vi* (*for exams*) pauken

cramp *n* Krampf *m*. ~**ed** *a* eng

cranberry *n* (*Culin*) Preiselbeere *f*

crane *n* Kran *m*; (*bird*) Kranich *m*

crank *n* [!] Exzentriker *m*

crankshaft *n* Kurbelwelle *f*

crash *n* (*noise*) Krach *m*; (*Auto*) Zusammenstoß *m*; (*Aviat*) Absturz *m* ● *vi* krachen (**into** gegen); <*cars:*> zusammenstoßen; <*plane:*> abstürzen ● *vt* einen Unfall haben mit <*car*>

crash: ~**-helmet** *n* Sturzhelm *m*. ~**-landing** *n* Bruchlandung *f*

crate *n* Kiste *f*

crater *n* Krater *m*

crawl *n* (*Swimming*) Kraul *nt*; **do the** ~ kraulen; **at a** ~ im Kriechtempo ● *vi* kriechen; <*baby:*> krabbeln; ~ **with** wimmeln von

crayon *n* Wachsstift *m*; (*pencil*) Buntstift *m*

craze *n* Mode *f*

crazy *a* (**-ier, -iest**) verrückt; **be** ~ **about** verrückt sein nach

creak *vi* knarren

cream *n* Sahne *f*; (*Cosmetic, Med, Culin*) Creme *f* ● *a* (*colour*) cremefarben ● *vt* (*Culin*) cremig rühren. ~**y** *a* sahnig; (*smooth*) cremig

crease *n* Falte *f*; (*unwanted*) Knitterfalte *f* ● *vt* falten; (*accidentally*) zerknittern ● *vi* knittern

creat|e *vt* schaffen. ~**ion** *n* Schöpfung *f*. ~**ive** *a* schöpferisch. ~**or** *n* Schöpfer *m*

creature *n* Geschöpf *nt*

crèche *n* Kinderkrippe *f*

credibility *n* Glaubwürdigkeit *f*

credible *a* glaubwürdig

credit *n* Kredit *m*; (*honour*) Ehre *f* ● *vt* glauben; ~ **s.o. with sth** (*Comm*) jdm etw gutschreiben; (*fig*) jdm etw zuschreiben. ~**able** *a* lobenswert

credit: ~ **card** *n* Kreditkarte *f*. ~**or** *n* Gläubiger *m*

creep *vi* (*pt/pp* **crept**) schleichen ● *n* [!] fieser Kerl *m*; **it gives me the** ~**s** es ist mir unheimlich. ~**er** *n* Kletterpflanze *f*. ~**y** *a* gruselig

cremat|e *vt* einäschern. ~**ion** *n* Einäscherung *f*

crêpe *n* Krepp *m*. ~ **paper** *n* Krepppapier *nt*

crept *see* creep

crescent *n* Halbmond *m*

cress *n* Kresse *f*

crest *n* Kamm *m*; (*coat of arms*) Wappen *nt*

crew *n* Besatzung *f*; (*gang*) Bande *f*. ~ **cut** *n* Bürstenschnitt *m*

crib[1] *n* Krippe *f*

crib[2] *vt/i* (*pt/pp* **cribbed**) [!] abschreiben

cricket *n* Kricket *nt*. ~**er** *n* Kricketspieler *m*

crime *n* Verbrechen *nt*; (*rate*) Kriminalität *f*

criminal *a* kriminell, verbrecherisch; <*law, court*> Straf- ● *n* Verbrecher *m*

crimson *a* purpurrot

crinkle *vt/i* knittern

cripple *n* Krüppel *m* ● *vt* zum Krüppel machen; (*fig*) lahmlegen. **~d** *a* verkrüppelt
crisis *n* (*pl* **-ses**) Krise *f*
crisp *a* (**-er, -est**) knusprig. **~bread** *n* Knäckebrot *nt*. **~s** *npl* Chips *pl*
criss-cross *a* schräg gekreuzt
criterion *n* (*pl* **-ria**) Kriterium *nt*
critic *n* Kritiker *m*. **~al** *a* kritisch. **~ally** *adv* kritisch; **~ally ill** schwer krank
criticism *n* Kritik *f*
criticize *vt* kritisieren
croak *vi* krächzen; <*frog:*> quaken
crockery *n* Geschirr *nt*
crocodile *n* Krokodil *nt*
crocus *n* (*pl* **-es**) Krokus *m*
crony *n* Kumpel *m*
crook *n* (*stick*) Stab *m*; ([!] *criminal*) Schwindler *m*, Gauner *m*
crooked *a* schief; (*bent*) krumm; ([!] *dishonest*) unehrlich
crop *n* Feldfrucht *f*; (*harvest*) Ernte *f* ● *v* (*pt/pp* **cropped**) ● *vt* stutzen ● *vi* **~ up** [!] zur Sprache kommen; (*occur*) dazwischenkommen
croquet *n* Krocket *nt*
cross *a*, **-ly** *adv* (*annoyed*) böse (**with** auf + *acc*); **talk at ~ purposes** aneinander vorbeireden ● *n* Kreuz *nt*; (*Bot, Zool*) Kreuzung *f* ● *vt* kreuzen <*cheque, animals*>; überqueren <*road*>; **~ oneself** sich bekreuzigen; **~ one's arms** die Arme verschränken; **~ one's legs** die Beine übereinander schlagen; **keep one's fingers ~ed for s.o.** jdm die Daumen drücken; **it ~ed my mind** es fiel mir ein ● *vi* (*go across*) hinübergehen/ -fahren; <*lines:*> sich kreuzen. **~ out** *vt* durchstreichen
cross: ~-country *n* (*Sport*) Crosslauf *m*. **~-eyed** *a* schielend; **be ~-eyed** schielen. **~fire** *n* Kreuzfeuer *nt*. **~ing** *n* Übergang *m*; (*sea journey*) Überfahrt *f*. **~roads** *n* [Straßen]kreuzung *f*. **~-section** *n* Querschnitt *m*. **~wise** *adv* quer. **~word** *n* **~word [puzzle]** Kreuzworträtsel *nt*
crotchety *a* griesgrämig
crouch *vi* kauern
crow *n* Krähe *f*; **as the ~ flies** Luftlinie
crowd *n* [Menschen]menge *f* ● *vi* sich drängen. **~ed** *a* [gedrängt] voll
crown *n* Krone *f* ● *vt* krönen; überkronen <*tooth*>
crucial *a* höchst wichtig; (*decisive*) entscheidend (**to** für)
crude *a* (**-r, -st**) primitiv; (*raw*) roh
cruel *a* (**crueller, cruellest**), **-ly** *adv* grausam (**to** gegen). **~ty** *n* Grausamkeit *f*
cruis|e *n* Kreuzfahrt *f* ● *vi* kreuzen; <*car:*> fahren. **~er** *n* (*Mil*) Kreuzer *m*; (*motor boat*) Kajütboot *nt*
crumb *n* Krümel *m*
crumble *vt/i* krümeln; (*collapse*) einstürzen
crumple *vt* zerknittern ● *vi* knittern
crunch *n* [!] **when it comes to the ~** wenn es [wirklich] drauf ankommt ● *vt* mampfen ● *vi* knirschen
crusade *n* Kreuzzug *m*; (*fig*) Kampagne *f*. **~r** *n* Kreuzfahrer *m*; (*fig*) Kämpfer *m*
crush *n* (*crowd*) Gedränge *nt* ● *vt* zerquetschen; zerknittern <*clothes*>; (*fig: subdue*) niederschlagen
crust *n* Kruste *f*
crutch *n* Krücke *f*
cry *n* Ruf *m*; (*shout*) Schrei *m*; **a far ~ from** (*fig*) weit entfernt von ● *vi* (*pt/pp* **cried**) (*weep*) weinen; <*baby:*> schreien; (*call*) rufen
crypt *n* Krypta *f*. **~ic** *a* rätselhaft

C

crystal *n* Kristall *m*; (*glass*) Kristall *nt*
cub *n* (*Zool*) Junge(s) *nt*
Cuba *n* Kuba *nt*
cubby-hole *n* Fach *nt*
cub|e *n* Würfel *m*. **~ic** *a* Kubik-
cubicle *n* Kabine *f*
cuckoo *n* Kuckuck *m*. **~ clock** *n* Kuckucksuhr *f*
cucumber *n* Gurke *f*
cuddl|e *vt* herzen ● *vi* **~e up to** sich kuscheln an (+ *acc*). **~y** *a* kuschelig
cue[1] *n* Stichwort *nt*
cue[2] *n* (*Billiards*) Queue *nt*
cuff *n* Manschette *f*; (*Amer: turn-up*) [Hosen]aufschlag *m*; (*blow*) Klaps *m*; **off the ~** [!] aus dem Stegreif. **~-link** *n* Manschettenknopf *m*
cul-de-sac *n* Sackgasse *f*
culinary *a* kulinarisch
culprit *n* Täter *m*
cult *n* Kult *m*
cultivate *vt* anbauen <*crop*>; bebauen <*land*>
cultural *a* kulturell
culture *n* Kultur *f*. **~d** *a* kultiviert
cumbersome *a* hinderlich; (*unwieldy*) unhandlich
cunning *a* listig ● *n* List *f*
cup *n* Tasse *f*; (*prize*) Pokal *m*
cupboard *n* Schrank *m*
Cup Final *n* Pokalendspiel *nt*
curable *a* heilbar
curate *n* Vikar *m*; (*Roman Catholic*) Kaplan *m*
curb *vt* zügeln
curdle *vi* gerinnen
cure *n* [Heil]mittel *nt* ● *vt* heilen; (*salt*) pökeln; (*smoke*) räuchern; gerben <*skin*>
curiosity *n* Neugier *f*; (*object*) Kuriosität *f*
curious *a*, **-ly** *adv* neugierig; (*strange*) merkwürdig, seltsam
curl *n* Locke *f* ● *vt* locken ● *vi* sich locken
curly *a* (**-ier, -iest**) lockig
currant *n* (*dried*) Korinthe *f*
currency *n* Geläufigkeit *f*; (*money*) Währung *f*; **foreign ~** Devisen *pl*
current *a* augenblicklich, gegenwärtig; (*in general use*) geläufig, gebräuchlich ● *n* Strömung *f*; (*Electr*) Strom *m*. **~ affairs** *or* **events** *npl* Aktuelle(s) *nt*. **~ly** *adv* zurzeit
curriculum *n* Lehrplan *m*. **~ vitae** *n* Lebenslauf *m*
curry *n* Curry *nt & m*; (*meal*) Currygericht *nt*
curse *n* Fluch *m* ● *vt* verfluchen ● *vi* fluchen
cursor *n* Cursor *m*
cursory *a* flüchtig
curt *a*, **-ly** *adv* barsch
curtain *n* Vorhang *m*
curtsy *n* Knicks *m* ● *vi* (*pt/pp* **-ied**) knicksen
curve *n* Kurve *f* ● *vi* einen Bogen machen; **~ to the right/left** nach rechts/links biegen. **~d** *a* gebogen
cushion *n* Kissen *nt* ● *vt* dämpfen; (*protect*) beschützen
custard *n* Vanillesoße *f*
custom *n* Brauch *m*; (*habit*) Gewohnheit *f*; (*Comm*) Kundschaft *f*. **~ary** *a* üblich; (*habitual*) gewohnt. **~er** *n* Kunde *m*/Kundin *f*
customs *npl* Zoll *m*. **~ officer** *n* Zollbeamte(r) *m*
cut *n* Schnitt *m*; (*Med*) Schnittwunde *f*; (*reduction*) Kürzung *f*; (*in price*) Senkung *f*; **~ [of meat]** [Fleisch]stück *nt* ● *vt/i* (*pt/pp* **cut**, *pres p* **cutting**) schneiden; (*mow*) mähen; abheben <*cards*>; (*reduce*) kürzen; senken <*price*>; **~ one's finger** sich in den Finger schneiden; **~ s.o.'s hair** jdm die Haare schneiden; **~ short** abkürzen. **~ back** *vt* zurückschneiden; (*fig*)

einschränken, kürzen. **~ down** *vt* fällen; (*fig*) einschränken. **~ off** *vt* abschneiden; (*disconnect*) abstellen; **be ~ off** (*Teleph*) unterbrochen werden. **~ out** *vt* ausschneiden; (*delete*) streichen; **be ~ out for** [!] geeignet sein zu. **~ up** *vt* zerschneiden; (*slice*) aufschneiden

cut-back *n* Kürzung *f*

cute *a* (**-r, -st**) [!] niedlich

cut glass *n* Kristall *nt*

cutlery *n* Besteck *nt*

cutlet *n* Kotelett *nt*

cut-price *a* verbilligt

cutting *a* <*remark*> bissig ● *n* (*from newspaper*) Ausschnitt *m*; (*of plant*) Ableger *m*

CV *abbr of* **curriculum vitae**

cyberspace *n* Cyberspace *m*

cycl|e *n* Zyklus *m*; (*bicycle*) [Fahr]rad *nt* ● *vi* mit dem Rad fahren. **~ing** *n* Radfahren *nt*. **~ist** *n* Radfahrer(in) *m(f)*

cylind|er *n* Zylinder *m*. **~rical** *a* zylindrisch

cynic *n* Zyniker *m*. **~al** *a*, **-ly** *adv* zynisch. **~ism** *n* Zynismus *m*

Cyprus *n* Zypern *nt*

Czech *a* tschechisch; **~ Republic** Tschechische Republik *f* ● *n* Tscheche *m*/ Tschechin *f*

Dd

dab *n* Tupfer *m*; (*of butter*) Klecks *m*

dabble *vi* **~ in sth** (*fig*) sich nebenbei mit etw befassen

dachshund *n* Dackel *m*

dad[dy] *n* [!] Vati *m*

daddy-long-legs *n* [Kohl]schnake *f*; (*Amer: spider*) Weberknecht *m*

daffodil *n* Osterglocke *f*, gelbe Narzisse *f*

daft *a* (**-er, -est**) dumm

dagger *n* Dolch *m*

dahlia *n* Dahlie *f*

daily *a & adv* täglich

dainty *a* (**-ier, -iest**) zierlich

dairy *n* Molkerei *f*; (*shop*) Milchgeschäft *nt*. **~ products** *pl* Milchprodukte *pl*

daisy *n* Gänseblümchen *nt*

dam *n* [Stau]damm *m* ● *vt* (*pt/pp* **dammed**) eindämmen

damage *n* Schaden *m* (**to** an + *dat*); **~s** *pl* (*Jur*) Schadenersatz *m* ● *vt* beschädigen; (*fig*) beeinträchtigen

damn *a, int & adv* [!] verdammt ● *n* **I don't care** *or* **give a ~** [!] ich schere mich einen Dreck darum ● *vt* verdammen. **~ation** *n* Verdammnis *f*

damp *a* (**-er, -est**) feucht ● *n* Feuchtigkeit *f*

damp|en *vt* anfeuchten; (*fig*) dämpfen. **~ness** *n* Feuchtigkeit *f*

dance *n* Tanz *m*; (*function*) Tanzveranstaltung *f* ● *vt/i* tanzen. **~ music** *n* Tanzmusik *f*

dancer *n* Tänzer(in) *m(f)*

dandelion *n* Löwenzahn *m*

dandruff *n* Schuppen *pl*

Dane *n* Däne *m*/Dänin *f*

danger *n* Gefahr *f*; **in/out of ~** in/ außer Gefahr. **~ous** *a*, **-ly** *adv* gefährlich; **~ously ill** schwer erkrankt

dangle *vi* baumeln ● *vt* baumeln lassen

Danish *a* dänisch

Danube *n* Donau *f*

dare *vt/i* (*challenge*) herausfordern (**to** zu); **~ [to] do sth** [es] wagen, etw zu tun. **~devil** *n* Draufgänger *m*

daring *a* verwegen ● *n* Verwegenheit *f*

dark *a* (**-er, -est**) dunkel; ~ **blue/ brown** dunkelblau/ -braun; ~ **horse** (*fig*) stilles Wasser *nt* ● *n* Dunkelheit *f*; **after** ~ nach Einbruch der Dunkelheit; **in the** ~ im Dunkeln

dark|en *vt* verdunkeln ● *vi* dunkler werden. **~ness** *n* Dunkelheit *f*

dark-room *n* Dunkelkammer *f*

darling *a* allerliebst ● *n* Liebling *m*

darn *vt* stopfen

dart *n* Pfeil *m*; **~s** *sg* (*game*) [Wurf]pfeil *m* ● *vi* flitzen

dash *n* (*Typ*) Gedankenstrich *m*; **a ~ of milk** ein Schuss Milch ● *vi* rennen ● *vt* schleudern. ~ **off** *vi* losstürzen ● *vt* (*write quickly*) hinwerfen

dashboard *n* Armaturenbrett *nt*

data *npl & sg* Daten *pl*. ~ **processing** *n* Datenverarbeitung *f*

date[1] *n* (*fruit*) Dattel *f*

date[2] *n* Datum *nt*; [!] Verabredung *f*; **to** ~ bis heute; **out of** ~ überholt; (*expired*) ungültig; **be up to** ~ auf dem Laufenden sein ● *vt/i* datieren; (*Amer* [!]: *go out with*) ausgehen mit

dated *a* altmodisch

dative *a & n* (*Gram*) ~ **[case]** Dativ *m*

daub *vt* beschmieren (**with** mit); schmieren <*paint*>

daughter *n* Tochter *f*. **~-in-law** *n* (*pl* **~s-in-law**) Schwiegertochter *f*

dawdle *vi* trödeln

dawn *n* Morgendämmerung *f*; **at** ~ bei Tagesanbruch ● *vi* anbrechen; **it ~ed on me** (*fig*) es ging mir auf

day *n* Tag *m*; ~ **by** ~ Tag für Tag; ~ **after** ~ Tag um Tag; **these ~s** heutzutage; **in those ~s** zu der Zeit

day: **~-dream** *n* Tagtraum *m* ● *vi* [mit offenen Augen] träumen. **~light** *n* Tageslicht *nt*. **~time** *n* **in the ~time** am Tage

daze *n* **in a** ~ wie benommen. **~d** *a* benommen

dazzle *vt* blenden

dead *a* tot; <*flower*> verwelkt; (*numb*) taub; ~ **body** Leiche *f*; ~ **centre** genau in der Mitte ● *adv* ~ **tired** todmüde; ~ **slow** sehr langsam ● *n* **the** ~ *pl* die Toten

deaden *vt* dämpfen <*sound*>; betäuben <*pain*>

dead: ~ **end** *n* Sackgasse *f*. ~ **heat** *n* totes Rennen *nt*. **~line** *n* [letzter] Termin *m*

deadly *a* (**-ier, -iest**) tödlich; ([!] *dreary*) sterbenslangweilig

deaf *a* (**-er, -est**) taub; ~ **and dumb** taubstumm

deaf|en *vt* betäuben; (*permanently*) taub machen. **~ening** *a* ohrenbetäubend. **~ness** *n* Taubheit *f*

deal *n* (*transaction*) Geschäft *nt*; **whose ~?** (*Cards*) wer gibt? **a good** *or* **great** ~ eine Menge; **get a raw** ~ [!] schlecht wegkommen ● *v* (*pt/pp* **dealt**) ● *vt* (*Cards*) geben; ~ **out** austeilen ● *vi* ~ **in** handeln mit; ~ **with** zu tun haben mit; (*handle*) sich befassen mit; (*cope with*) fertig werden mit; (*be about*) handeln von; **that's been dealt with** das ist schon erledigt

dealer *n* Händler *m*

dean *n* Dekan *m*

dear *a* (**-er, -est**) lieb; (*expensive*) teuer; (*in letter*) liebe(r,s)/ (*formal*) sehr geehrte(r,s) ● *n* Liebe(r) *m/f* ● *int* **oh ~!** oje! **~ly** *adv* <*love*> sehr; <*pay*> teuer

death *n* Tod *m*; **three ~s** drei Todesfälle. ~ **certificate** *n* Sterbeurkunde *f*

deathly *a* ~ **silence** Totenstille *f* ● *adv* ~ **pale** totenblass

death: ~ **penalty** *n* Todesstrafe *f*. ~**-trap** *n* Todesfalle *f*

debatable *a* strittig

debate *n* Debatte *f* ● *vt/i* debattieren

debauchery *n* Ausschweifung *f*

debit *n* ~ **[side]** Soll *nt* ● *vt* (*pt/pp* **debited**) belasten; abbuchen <*sum*>

debris *n* Trümmer *pl*

debt *n* Schuld *f*; **in** ~ verschuldet. ~**or** *n* Schuldner *m*

debut *n* Debüt *nt*

decade *n* Jahrzehnt *nt*

decaden|ce *n* Dekadenz *f*. ~**t** *a* dekadent

decaffeinated *a* koffeinfrei

decay *n* Verfall *m*; (*rot*) Verwesung *f*; (*of tooth*) Zahnfäule *f* ● *vi* verfallen; (*rot*) verwesen; <*tooth:*> schlecht werden

deceased *a* verstorben ● *n* **the** ~**d** der/die Verstorbene

deceit *n* Täuschung *f*. ~**ful** *a*, **-ly** *adv* unaufrichtig

deceive *vt* täuschen; (*be unfaithful to*) betrügen

December *n* Dezember *m*

decency *n* Anstand *m*

decent *a*, **-ly** *adv* anständig

decept|ion *n* Täuschung *f*; (*fraud*) Betrug *m*. ~**ive** *a*, **-ly** *adv* täuschend

decide *vt* entscheiden ● *vi* sich entscheiden (**on** für)

decided *a*, **-ly** *adv* entschieden

decimal *a* Dezimal- ● *n* Dezimalzahl *f*. ~ **point** *n* Komma *nt*

decipher *vt* entziffern

decision *n* Entscheidung *f*; (*firmness*) Entschlossenheit *f*

decisive *a* ausschlaggebend; (*firm*) entschlossen

deck[1] *vt* schmücken

deck[2] *n* (*Naut*) Deck *nt*; **on** ~ an Deck; ~ **of cards** (*Amer*) [Karten]spiel *nt*. ~**-chair** *n* Liegestuhl *m*

declaration *n* Erklärung *f*

declare *vt* erklären; angeben <*goods*>; **anything to** ~**?** etwas zu verzollen?

decline *n* Rückgang *m*; (*in health*) Verfall *m* ● *vt* ablehnen; (*Gram*) deklinieren ● *vi* ablehnen; (*fall*) sinken; (*decrease*) nachlassen

decommission *vt* stilllegen; außer Dienst stellen <*Schiff*>

décor *n* Ausstattung *f*

decorat|e *vt* (*adorn*) schmücken; verzieren <*cake*>; (*paint*) streichen; (*wallpaper*) tapezieren; (*award medal to*) einen Orden verleihen (+ *dat*). ~**ion** *n* Verzierung *f*; (*medal*) Orden *m*; ~**ions** *pl* Schmuck *m*. ~**ive** *a* dekorativ. ~**or** *n* **painter and** ~**or** Maler und Tapezierer *m*

decoy *n* Lockvogel *m*

decrease[1] *n* Verringerung *f*; (*in number*) Rückgang *m*

decrease[2] *vt* verringern; herabsetzen <*price*> ● *vi* sich verringern; <*price:*> sinken

decrepit *a* altersschwach

dedicat|e *vt* widmen; (*Relig*) weihen. ~**ed** *a* hingebungsvoll; <*person*> aufopfernd. ~**ion** *n* Hingabe *f*; (*in book*) Widmung *f*

deduce *vt* folgern (**from** aus)

deduct *vt* abziehen

deduction *n* Abzug *m*; (*conclusion*) Folgerung *f*

deed *n* Tat *f*; (*Jur*) Urkunde *f*

deep *a* (**-er, -est**), **-ly** *adv* tief; **go off the** ~ **end** [!] auf die Palme gehen ● *adv* tief

deepen *vt* vertiefen

deep-freeze *n* Gefriertruhe *f*; (*upright*) Gefrierschrank *m*

deer *n inv* Hirsch *m*; (*roe*) Reh *nt*

deface *vt* beschädigen

default *n* **win by** ~ (*Sport*) kampflos gewinnen

defeat *n* Niederlage *f*; (*defeating*) Besiegung *f*; (*rejection*) Ablehnung *f* ● *vt* besiegen; ablehnen <*motion*>; (*frustrate*) vereiteln
defect *n* Fehler *m*; (*Techn*) Defekt *m*. **~ive** *a* fehlerhaft; (*Techn*) defekt
defence *n* Verteidigung *f*. **~less** *a* wehrlos
defend *vt* verteidigen; (*justify*) rechtfertigen. **~ant** *n* (*Jur*) Beklagte(r) *m/f*; (*in criminal court*) Angeklagte(r) *m/f*
defensive *a* defensiv
defer *vt* (*pt/pp* **deferred**) (*postpone*) aufschieben
deferen|ce *n* Ehrerbietung *f*. **~tial** *a*, **-ly** *adv* ehrerbietig
defian|ce *n* Trotz *m*; **in ~ce of** zum Trotz (+ *dat*). **~t** *a*, **-ly** *adv* aufsässig
deficien|cy *n* Mangel *m*. **~t** *a* mangelhaft
deficit *n* Defizit *nt*
define *vt* bestimmen; definieren <*word*>
definite *a*, **-ly** *adv* bestimmt; (*certain*) sicher
definition *n* Definition *f*; (*Phot, TV*) Schärfe *f*
definitive *a* endgültig; (*authoritative*) maßgeblich
deflat|e *vt* die Luft auslassen aus. **~ion** *n* (*Comm*) Deflation *f*
deflect *vt* ablenken
deform|ed *a* missgebildet. **~ity** *n* Missbildung *f*
defraud *vt* betrügen (**of** um)
defray *vt* bestreiten
defrost *vt* entfrosten; abtauen <*fridge*>; auftauen <*food*>
deft *a* (**-er, -est**), **-ly** *adv* geschickt. **~ness** *n* Geschicklichkeit *f*
defuse *vt* entschärfen
defy *vt* (*pt/pp* **-ied**) trotzen (+ *dat*); widerstehen (+ *dat*) <*attempt*>
degrading *a* entwürdigend
degree *n* Grad *m*; (*Univ*) akademischer Grad *m*; **20 ~s** 20 Grad
de-ice *vt* enteisen
deity *n* Gottheit *f*
dejected *a*, **-ly** *adv* niedergeschlagen
delay *n* Verzögerung *f*; (*of train, aircraft*) Verspätung *f*; **without ~** unverzüglich ● *vt* aufhalten; (*postpone*) aufschieben ● *vi* zögern
delegate[1] *n* Delegierte(r) *m/f*
delegat|e[2] *vt* delegieren. **~ion** *n* Delegation *f*
delet|e *vt* streichen. **~ion** *n* Streichung *f*
deliberate *a*, **-ly** *adv* absichtlich; (*slow*) bedächtig
delicacy *n* Feinheit *f*; Zartheit *f*; (*food*) Delikatesse *f*
delicate *a* fein; <*fabric, health*> zart; <*situation*> heikel; <*mechanism*> empfindlich
delicatessen *n* Delikatessengeschäft *nt*
delicious *a* köstlich
delight *n* Freude *f* ● *vt* entzücken ● *vi* **~ in** sich erfreuen an (+ *dat*). **~ed** *a* hocherfreut; **be ~ed** sich sehr freuen. **~ful** *a* reizend
delinquent *a* straffällig ● *n* Straffällige(r) *m/f*
deli|rious *a* **be ~rious** im Delirium sein. **~rium** *n* Delirium *nt*
deliver *vt* liefern; zustellen <*post, newspaper*>; halten <*speech*>; überbringen <*message*>; versetzen <*blow*>; (*set free*) befreien; **~ a baby** ein Kind zur Welt bringen. **~y** *n* Lieferung *f*; (*of post*) Zustellung *f*; (*Med*) Entbindung *f*; **cash on ~y** per Nachnahme
delta *n* Delta *nt*
deluge *n* Flut *f*; (*heavy rain*) schwerer Guss *m*
delusion *n* Täuschung *f*
de luxe *a* Luxus-

demand *n* Forderung *f*; (*Comm*) Nachfrage *f*; **in ~** gefragt; **on ~** auf Verlangen ● *vt* verlangen, fordern (**of/from** von). **~ing** *a* anspruchsvoll
demented *a* verrückt
demister *n* (*Auto*) Defroster *m*
demo *n* (*pl* **~s**) [!] Demonstration *f*
democracy *n* Demokratie *f*
democrat *n* Demokrat *m*. **~ic** *a*, **-ally** *adv* demokratisch
demo|lish *vt* abbrechen; (*destroy*) zerstören. **~lition** *n* Abbruch *m*
demon *n* Dämon *m*
demonstrat|e *vt* beweisen; vorführen *<appliance>* ● *vi* (*Pol*) demonstrieren. **~ion** *n* Vorführung *f*; (*Pol*) Demonstration *f*
demonstrator *n* Vorführer *m*; (*Pol*) Demonstrant *m*
demoralize *vt* demoralisieren
demote *vt* degradieren
demure *a*, **-ly** *adv* sittsam
den *n* Höhle *f*; (*room*) Bude *f*
denial *n* Leugnen *nt*; **official ~** Dementi *nt*
denim *n* Jeansstoff *m*; **~s** *pl* Jeans *pl*
Denmark *n* Dänemark *nt*
denounce *vt* denunzieren; (*condemn*) verurteilen
dens|e *a* (**-r**, **-st**), **-ly** *adv* dicht; ([!] *stupid*) blöd[e]. **~ity** *n* Dichte *f*
dent *n* Delle *f*, Beule *f* ● *vt* einbeulen; **~ed** verbeult
dental *a* Zahn-; *<treatment>* zahnärztlich. **~ floss** *n* Zahnseide *f*. **~ surgeon** *n* Zahnarzt *m*
dentist *n* Zahnarzt *m*/-ärztin *f*. **~ry** *n* Zahnmedizin *f*
denture *n* Zahnprothese *f*; **~s** *pl* künstliches Gebiss *nt*
deny *vt* (*pt/pp* **-ied**) leugnen; (*officially*) dementieren; **~ s.o. sth** jdm etw verweigern
deodorant *n* Deodorant *nt*
depart *vi* abfahren; (*Aviat*) abfliegen; (*go away*) weggehen/-fahren; (*deviate*) abweichen (**from** von)
department *n* Abteilung *f*; (*Pol*) Ministerium *nt*. **~ store** *n* Kaufhaus *nt*
departure *n* Abfahrt *f*; (*Aviat*) Abflug *m*; (*from rule*) Abweichung *f*
depend *vi* abhängen (**on** von); (*rely*) sich verlassen (**on** auf + *acc*); **it all ~s** das kommt darauf an. **~able** *a* zuverlässig. **~ant** *n* Abhängige(r) *m/f*. **~ence** *n* Abhängigkeit *f*. **~ent** *a* abhängig (**on** von)
depict *vt* darstellen
deplor|able *a* bedauerlich. **~e** *vt* bedauern
deploy *vt* (*Mil*) einsetzen
depopulate *vt* entvölkern
deport *vt* deportieren, ausweisen. **~ation** *n* Ausweisung *f*
depose *vt* absetzen
deposit *n* Anzahlung *f*; (*against damage*) Kaution *f*; (*on bottle*) Pfand *nt*; (*sediment*) Bodensatz *m*; (*Geol*) Ablagerung *f* ● *vt* (*pt/pp* **deposited**) legen; (*for safety*) deponieren; (*Geol*) ablagern. **~ account** *n* Sparkonto *nt*
depot *n* Depot *nt*; (*Amer: railway station*) Bahnhof *m*
deprave *vt* verderben. **~d** *a* verkommen
depreciat|e *vi* an Wert verlieren. **~ion** *n* Wertminderung *f*; (*Comm*) Abschreibung *f*
depress *vt* deprimieren; (*press down*) herunterdrücken. **~ed** *a* deprimiert. **~ing** *a* deprimierend. **~ion** *n* Vertiefung *f*; (*Med*) Depression *f*; (*Meteorol*) Tief *nt*
deprivation *n* Entbehrung *f*
deprive *vt* **~ s.o. of sth** jdm etw entziehen. **~d** *a* benachteiligt

D

depth *n* Tiefe *f*; **in ~** gründlich; **in the ~s of winter** im tiefsten Winter
deputize *vi* **~ for** vertreten
deputy *n* Stellvertreter *m* ● *attrib* stellvertretend
derail *vt* **be ~ed** entgleisen. **~ment** *n* Entgleisung *f*
derelict *a* verfallen; (*abandoned*) verlassen
derisory *a* höhnisch; <*offer*> lächerlich
derivation *n* Ableitung *f*
derivative *a* abgeleitet ● *n* Ableitung *f*
derive *vt/i* (*obtain*) gewinnen (**from** aus); **be ~d from** <*word:*> hergeleitet sein aus
derogatory *a* abfällig
derv *n* Diesel[kraftstoff] *m*
descend *vt/i* hinunter-/heruntergehen; <*vehicle, lift:*> hinunter-/herunterfahren; **be ~ed from** abstammen von. **~ant** *n* Nachkomme *m*
descent *n* Abstieg *m*; (*lineage*) Abstammung *f*
describe *vt* beschreiben
descrip|tion *n* Beschreibung *f*; (*sort*) Art *f*. **~tive** *a* beschreibend; (*vivid*) anschaulich
desecrate *vt* entweihen
desert[1] *n* Wüste *f*. **~ island** verlassene Insel *f*
desert[2] *vt* verlassen ● *vt* desertieren. **~ed** *a* verlassen. **~er** *n* (*Mil*) Deserteur *m*. **~ion** *n* Fahnenflucht *f*
deserv|e *vt* verdienen. **~edly** *adv* verdientermaßen. **~ing** *a* verdienstvoll
design *n* Entwurf *m*; (*pattern*) Muster *nt*; (*construction*) Konstruktion *f*; (*aim*) Absicht *f* ● *vt* entwerfen; (*construct*) konstruieren; **be ~ed for** bestimmt sein für
designer *n* Designer *m*; (*Techn*) Konstrukteur *m*; (*Theat*) Bühnenbildner *m*
desirable *a* wünschenswert; (*sexually*) begehrenswert
desire *n* Wunsch *m*; (*longing*) Verlangen *nt* (**for** nach); (*sexual*) Begierde *f* ● *vt* [sich (*dat*)] wünschen; (*sexually*) begehren
desk *n* Schreibtisch *m*; (*Sch*) Pult *nt*
desolat|e *a* trostlos. **~ion** *n* Trostlosigkeit *f*
despair *n* Verzweiflung *f*; **in ~** verzweifelt ● *vi* verzweifeln
desperat|e *a*, **-ly** *adv* verzweifelt; (*urgent*) dringend; **be ~e for** dringend brauchen. **~ion** *n* Verzweiflung *f*
despicable *a* verachtenswert
despise *vt* verachten
despite *prep* trotz (+ *gen*)
despondent *a* niedergeschlagen
dessert *n* Dessert *nt*, Nachtisch *m*. **~ spoon** *n* Dessertlöffel *m*
destination *n* [Reise]ziel *nt*; (*of goods*) Bestimmungsort *m*
destiny *n* Schicksal *nt*
destitute *a* völlig mittellos
destroy *vt* zerstören; (*totally*) vernichten. **~er** *n* (*Naut*) Zerstörer *m*
destruc|tion *n* Zerstörung *f*; Vernichtung *f*. **-tive** *a* zerstörerisch; (*fig*) destruktiv
detach *vt* abnehmen; (*tear off*) abtrennen. **~able** *a* abnehmbar. **~ed** *a* **~ed house** Einzelhaus *nt*
detail *n* Einzelheit *f*, Detail *nt*; **in ~** ausführlich ● *vt* einzeln aufführen. **~ed** *a* ausführlich
detain *vt* aufhalten; <*police:*> in Haft behalten; (*take into custody*) in Haft nehmen
detect *vt* entdecken; (*perceive*) wahrnehmen. **~ion** *n* Entdeckung *f*
detective *n* Detektiv *m*. **~ story** *n* Detektivroman *m*

detention *n* Haft *f*; (*Sch*) Nachsitzen *nt*
deter *vt* (*pt*/*pp* **deterred**) abschrecken; (*prevent*) abhalten
detergent *n* Waschmittel *nt*
deteriorat|e *vi* sich verschlechtern. **~ion** *n* Verschlechterung *f*
determination *n* Entschlossenheit *f*
determine *vt* bestimmen. **~d** *a* entschlossen
deterrent *n* Abschreckungsmittel *nt*
detest *vt* verabscheuen. **~able** *a* abscheulich
detonate *vt* zünden
detour *n* Umweg *m*
detract *vi* **~ from** beeinträchtigen
detriment *n* **to the ~ (of)** zum Schaden (+ *gen*). **~al** *a* schädlich (**to** *dat*)
deuce *n* (*Tennis*) Einstand *m*
devaluation *n* Abwertung *f*
devalue *vt* abwerten <*currency*>
devastat|e *vt* verwüsten. **~ing** *a* verheerend. **~ion** *n* Verwüstung *f*
develop *vt* entwickeln; bekommen <*illness*>; erschließen <*area*> ● *vi* sich entwickeln (**into** zu). **~er** *n* **[property] ~er** Bodenspekulant *m*
development *n* Entwicklung *f*
deviat|e *vi* abweichen. **~ion** *n* Abweichung *f*
device *n* Gerät *nt*; (*fig*) Mittel *nt*
devil *n* Teufel *m*. **~ish** *a* teuflisch
devious *a* verschlagen
devise *vt* sich (*dat*) ausdenken
devot|e *vt* widmen (**to** *dat*). **~ed** *a*, **-ly** *adv* ergeben; <*care*> liebevoll; **be ~ed to s.o.** sehr an jdm hängen
devotion *n* Hingabe *f*
devour *vt* verschlingen
devout *a* fromm
dew *n* Tau *m*
dexterity *n* Geschicklichkeit *f*
diabet|es *n* Zuckerkrankheit *f*. **~ic** *n* Diabetiker(in) *m*(*f*)
diabolical *a* teuflisch
diagnose *vt* diagnostizieren
diagnosis *n* (*pl* **-oses**) Diagnose *f*
diagonal *a*, **-ly** *adv* diagonal ● *n* Diagonale *f*
diagram *n* Diagramm *nt*
dial *n* (*of clock*) Zifferblatt *nt*; (*Techn*) Skala *f*; (*Teleph*) Wählscheibe *f* ● *vt*/*i* (*pt*/*pp* **dialled**) (*Teleph*) wählen; **~ direct** durchwählen
dialect *n* Dialekt *m*
dialling: ~ code *n* Vorwahlnummer *f*. **~ tone** *n* Amtszeichen *nt*
dialogue *n* Dialog *m*
diameter *n* Durchmesser *m*
diamond *n* Diamant *m*; (*cut*) Brillant *m*; (*shape*) Raute *f*; **~s** *pl* (*Cards*) Karo *nt*
diaper *n* (*Amer*) Windel *f*
diarrhoea *n* Durchfall *m*
diary *n* Tagebuch *nt*; (*for appointments*) [Termin]kalender *m*
dice *n inv* Würfel *m*
dictat|e *vt*/*i* diktieren. **~ion** *n* Diktat *nt*
dictator *n* Diktator *m*. **~ial** *a* diktatorisch. **~ship** *n* Diktatur *f*
dictionary *n* Wörterbuch *nt*
did *see* **do**
didn't = **did not**
die¹ *n* (*Techn*) Prägestempel *m*; (*metal mould*) Gussform *f*
die² *vi* (*pres p* **dying**) sterben (**of** an + *dat*); <*plant, animal:*> eingehen; <*flower:*> verwelken; **be dying to do sth** [!] darauf brennen, etw zu tun; **be dying for sth** [!] sich nach etw sehnen. **~ down** *vi* nachlassen; <*fire:*> herunterbrennen. **~ out** *vi* aussterben
diesel *n* Diesel *m*. **~ engine** *n* Dieselmotor *m*

diet *n* Kost *f*; (*restricted*) Diät *f*; (*for slimming*) Schlankheitskur *f*; **be on a ~** Diät leben; eine Schlankheitskur machen ● *vi* diät leben; eine Schlankheitskur machen

differ *vi* sich unterscheiden; (*disagree*) verschiedener Meinung sein

differen|ce *n* Unterschied *m*; (*disagreement*) Meinungsverschiedenheit *f*. **~t** *a* andere(r,s); (*various*) verschiedene; **be ~t** anders sein (**from** als)

differential *a* Differenzial- ● *n* Unterschied *m*; (*Techn*) Differenzial *nt*

differentiate *vt/i* unterscheiden (**between** zwischen + *dat*)

differently *adv* anders

difficult *a* schwierig, schwer. **~y** *n* Schwierigkeit *f*

diffiden|ce *n* Zaghaftigkeit *f*. **~t** *a* zaghaft

dig *n* (*poke*) Stoß *m*; (*remark*) spitze Bemerkung *f*; (*Archaeol*) Ausgrabung *f* ● *vt/i* (*pt/pp* **dug**, *pres p* **digging**) graben; umgraben <*garden*>. **~ out** *vt* ausgraben. **~ up** *vt* ausgraben; umgraben <*garden*>; aufreißen <*street*>

digest *vt* verdauen. **~ible** *a* verdaulich. **~ion** *n* Verdauung *f*

digit *n* Ziffer *f*; (*finger*) Finger *m*; (*toe*) Zehe *f*

digital *a* Digital-; **~ camera** Digitalkamera *f*; **~ television** Digitalfernsehen *nt*

dignified *a* würdevoll

dignity *n* Würde *f*

dilapidated *a* baufällig

dilemma *n* Dilemma *nt*

diligen|ce *n* Fleiß *m*. **~t** *a*, **-ly** *adv* fleißig

dilute *vt* verdünnen

dim *a* (**dimmer, dimmest**). **-ly** *adv* (*weak*) schwach; (*dark*) trüb[e]; (*indistinct*) undeutlich; ([!] *stupid*) dumm, [!] doof ● *v* (*pt/pp* **dimmed**) ● *vt* dämpfen

dime *n* (*Amer*) Zehncentstück *nt*

dimension *n* Dimension *f*; **~s** *pl* Maße *pl*

diminutive *a* winzig ● *n* Verkleinerungsform *f*

dimple *n* Grübchen *nt*

din *n* Krach *m*, Getöse *nt*

dine *vi* speisen. **~r** *n* Speisende(r) *m/f*; (*Amer: restaurant*) Esslokal *nt*

dinghy *n* Dinghi *nt*; (*inflatable*) Schlauchboot *nt*

dingy *a* (**-ier, -iest**) trübe

dining: ~-car *n* Speisewagen *m*. **~-room** *n* Esszimmer *nt*. **~-table** *n* Esstisch *m*

dinner *n* Abendessen *nt*; (*at midday*) Mittagessen *nt*; (*formal*) Essen *nt*. **~-jacket** *n* Smoking *m*

dinosaur *n* Dinosaurier *m*

diocese *n* Diözese *f*

dip *n* (*in ground*) Senke *f*; (*Culin*) Dip *m* ● *v* (*pt/pp* **dipped**) *vt* [ein]tauchen; **~ one's headlights** (*Auto*) [die Scheinwerfer] abblenden ● *vi* sich senken

diploma *n* Diplom *nt*

diplomacy *n* Diplomatie *f*

diplomat *n* Diplomat *m*. **~ic** *a*, **-ally** *adv* diplomatisch

dip-stick *n* (*Auto*) Ölmessstab *m*

dire *a* (**-r, -st**) bitter; <*consequences*> furchtbar

direct *a* & *adv* direkt ● *vt* (*aim*) richten (**at** auf / (*fig*) an + *acc*); (*control*) leiten; (*order*) anweisen; **~ a film/play** bei einem Film/Theaterstück Regie führen

direction *n* Richtung *f*; (*control*) Leitung *f*; (*of play, film*) Regie *f*; **~s** *pl* Anweisungen *pl*; **~s for use** Gebrauchsanweisung *f*

directly *adv* direkt; (*at once*) sofort

director *n* (*Comm*) Direktor *m*; (*of play, film*) Regisseur *m*

directory *n* Verzeichnis *nt*; (*Teleph*) Telefonbuch *nt*
dirt *n* Schmutz *m*; (*soil*) Erde *f*; **~ cheap** 🄸 spottbillig
dirty *a* (**-ier, -iest**) schmutzig
dis|ability *n* Behinderung *f*. **~abled** *a* [körper]behindert
disadvantage *n* Nachteil *m*; **at a ~** im Nachteil. **~d** *a* benachteiligt
disagree *vi* nicht übereinstimmen (**with** mit); **I ~** ich bin anderer Meinung; **oysters ~ with me** Austern bekommen mir nicht
disagreeable *a* unangenehm
disagreement *n* Meinungsverschiedenheit *f*
disappear *vi* verschwinden. **~ance** *n* Verschwinden *nt*
disappoint *vt* enttäuschen. **~ment** *n* Enttäuschung *f*
disapproval *n* Missbilligung *f*
disapprove *vi* dagegen sein; **~ of** missbilligen
disarm *vt* entwaffnen ● *vi* (*Mil*) abrüsten. **~ament** *n* Abrüstung *f*. **~ing** *a* entwaffnend
disast|er *n* Katastrophe *f*; (*accident*) Unglück *nt*. **~rous** *a* katastrophal
disbelief *n* Ungläubigkeit *f*; **in ~** ungläubig
disc *n* Scheibe *f*; (*record*) [Schall]platte *f*; (*CD*) CD *f*
discard *vt* ablegen; (*throw away*) wegwerfen
discerning *a* anspruchsvoll
discharge¹ *n* Ausstoßen *nt*; (*Naut, Electr*) Entladung *f*; (*dismissal*) Entlassung *f*; (*Jur*) Freispruch *m*; (*Med*) Ausfluss *m*
discharge² *vt* ausstoßen; (*Naut, Electr*) entladen; (*dismiss*) entlassen; (*Jur*) freisprechen <*accused*>
disciplinary *a* disziplinarisch
discipline *n* Disziplin *f* ● *vt* Disziplin beibringen (+ *dat*); (*punish*) bestrafen
disc jockey *n* Diskjockey *m*
disclaim *vt* abstreiten. **~er** *n* Verzichterklärung *f*
disclos|e *vt* enthüllen. **~ure** *n* Enthüllung *f*
disco *n* 🄸 Disko *f*
discolour *vt* verfärben ● *vi* sich verfärben
discomfort *n* Beschwerden *pl*; (*fig*) Unbehagen *nt*
disconnect *vt* trennen; (*Electr*) ausschalten; (*cut supply*) abstellen
discontent *n* Unzufriedenheit *f*. **~ed** *a* unzufrieden
discontinue *vt* einstellen; (*Comm*) nicht mehr herstellen
discord *n* Zwietracht *f*; (*Mus & fig*) Missklang *m*
discothèque *n* Diskothek *f*
discount *n* Rabatt *m*
discourage *vt* entmutigen; (*dissuade*) abraten (+ *dat*)
discourteous *a*, **-ly** *adv* unhöflich
discover *vt* entdecken. **~y** *n* Entdeckung *f*
discreet *a*, **-ly** *adv* diskret
discretion *n* Diskretion *f*; (*judgement*) Ermessen *nt*
discriminat|e *vi* unterscheiden (**between** zwischen + *dat*); **~e against** diskriminieren. **~ing** *a* anspruchsvoll. **~ion** *n* Diskriminierung *f*
discus *n* Diskus *m*
discuss *vt* besprechen; (*examine critically*) diskutieren. **~ion** *n* Besprechung *f*; Diskussion *f*
disdain *n* Verachtung *f*
disease *n* Krankheit *f*
disembark *vi* an Land gehen
disenchant *vt* ernüchtern
disengage *vt* losmachen
disentangle *vt* entwirren
disfigure *vt* entstellen

D

disgrace *n* Schande *f*; **in ~** in Ungnade ● *vt* Schande machen (+ *dat*). **~ful** *a* schändlich
disgruntled *a* verstimmt
disguise *n* Verkleidung *f*; **in ~** verkleidet ● *vt* verkleiden; verstellen <*voice*>
disgust *n* Ekel *m*; **in ~** empört ● *vt* anekeln; (*appal*) empören. **~ing** *a* eklig; (*appalling*) abscheulich
dish *n* Schüssel *f*; (*shallow*) Schale *f*; (*small*) Schälchen *nt*; (*food*) Gericht *nt*. **~ out** *vt* austeilen. **~ up** *vt* auftragen
dishcloth *n* Spültuch *nt*
dishearten *vt* entmutigen
dishonest *a* **-ly** *adv* unehrlich. **~y** *n* Unehrlichkeit *f*
dishonour *n* Schande *f*. **~able** *a*, **-bly** *adv* unehrenhaft
dishwasher *n* Geschirrspülmaschine *f*
disillusion *vt* ernüchtern. **~ment** *n* Ernüchterung *f*
disinfect *vt* desinfizieren. **~ant** *n* Desinfektionsmittel *nt*
disinherit *vt* enterben
disintegrate *vi* zerfallen
disjointed *a* unzusammenhängend
disk *n* = **disc**
dislike *n* Abneigung *f* ● *vt* nicht mögen
dislocate *vt* ausrenken
dislodge *vt* entfernen
disloyal *a*, **-ly** *adv* illoyal. **~ty** *n* Illoyalität *f*
dismal *a* trüb[e]; <*person*> trübselig
dismantle *vt* auseinander nehmen; (*take down*) abbauen
dismay *n* Bestürzung *f*. **~ed** *a* bestürzt
dismiss *vt* entlassen; (*reject*) zurückweisen. **~al** *n* Entlassung *f*; Zurückweisung *f*
disobedien|ce *n* Ungehorsam *m*. **~t** *a* ungehorsam
disobey *vt/i* nicht gehorchen (+ *dat*); nicht befolgen <*rule*>
disorder *n* Unordnung *f*; (*Med*) Störung *f*. **~ly** *a* unordentlich
disorganized *a* unorganisiert
disown *vt* verleugnen
disparaging *a*, **-ly** *adv* abschätzig
dispassionate *a*, **-ly** *adv* gelassen; (*impartial*) unparteiisch
dispatch *n* (*Comm*) Versand *m*; (*Mil*) Nachricht *f*; (*report*) Bericht *m* ● *vt* [ab]senden; (*kill*) töten
dispel *vt* (*pt/pp* **dispelled**) vertreiben
dispensary *n* Apotheke *f*
dispense *vt* austeilen; **~ with** verzichten auf (+ *acc*). **~r** *n* (*device*) Automat *m*
disperse *vt* zerstreuen ● *vi* sich zerstreuen
dispirited *a* entmutigt
display *n* Ausstellung *f*; (*Comm*) Auslage *f*; (*performance*) Vorführung *f* ● *vt* zeigen; ausstellen <*goods*>
displease *vt* missfallen (+ *dat*)
displeasure *n* Missfallen *nt*
disposable *a* Wegwerf-; <*income*> verfügbar
disposal *n* Beseitigung *f*; **be at s.o.'s ~** jdm zur Verfügung stehen
dispose *vi* **~ of** beseitigen; (*deal with*) erledigen
disposition *n* Veranlagung *f*; (*nature*) Wesensart *f*
disproportionate *a*, **-ly** *adv* unverhältnismäßig
disprove *vt* widerlegen
dispute *n* Disput *m*; (*quarrel*) Streit *m* ● *vt* bestreiten
disqualification *n* Disqualifikation *f*
disqualify *vt* disqualifizieren; **~ s.o. from driving** jdm den Führerschein entziehen
disregard *vt* nicht beachten
disrepair *n* **fall into ~** verfallen
disreputable *a* verrufen

disrepute *n* Verruf *m*
disrespect *n* Respektlosigkeit *f*. **~ful** *a*, **-ly** *adv* respektlos
disrupt *vt* stören. **~ion** *n* Störung *f*
dissatisfaction *n* Unzufriedenheit *f*
dissatisfied *a* unzufrieden
dissect *vt* zergliedern; (*Med*) sezieren. **~ion** *n* Zergliederung *f*; (*Med*) Sektion *f*
dissent *n* Nichtübereinstimmung *f* ● *vi* nicht übereinstimmen
dissident *n* Dissident *m*
dissimilar *a* unähnlich (**to** *dat*)
dissociate *vt* **~ oneself** sich distanzieren (**from** von)
dissolute *a* zügellos; <*life*> ausschweifend
dissolve *vt* auflösen ● *vi* sich auflösen
dissuade *vt* abbringen (**from** von)
distance *n* Entfernung *f*; **long/short ~** lange/kurze Strecke *f*; **in the/from a ~** in/aus der Ferne
distant *a* fern; (*aloof*) kühl; <*relative*> entfernt
distasteful *a* unangenehm
distil *vt* (*pt/pp* **distilled**) brennen; (*Chem*) destillieren. **~lery** *n* Brennerei *f*
distinct *a* deutlich; (*different*) verschieden. **~ion** *n* Unterschied *m*; (*Sch*) Auszeichnung *f*. **~ive** *a* kennzeichnend; (*unmistakable*) unverwechselbar. **~ly** *adv* deutlich
distinguish *vt/i* unterscheiden; (*make out*) erkennen; **~ oneself** sich auszeichnen. **~ed** *a* angesehen; <*appearance*> distinguiert
distort *vt* verzerren; (*fig*) verdrehen. **~ion** *n* Verzerrung *f*; (*fig*) Verdrehung *f*
distract *vt* ablenken. **~ion** *n* Ablenkung *f*; (*despair*) Verzweiflung *f*
distraught *a* [völlig] aufgelöst
distress *n* Kummer *m*; (*pain*) Schmerz *m*; (*poverty, danger*) Not *f* ● *vt* Kummer/Schmerz bereiten (+ *dat*); (*sadden*) bekümmern; (*shock*) erschüttern. **~ing** *a* schmerzlich; (*shocking*) erschütternd
distribut|e *vt* verteilen; (*Comm*) vertreiben. **~ion** *n* Verteilung *f*; Vertrieb *m*. **~or** *n* Verteiler *m*
district *n* Gegend *f*; (*Admin*) Bezirk *m*
distrust *n* Misstrauen *nt* ● *vt* misstrauen (+ *dat*). **~ful** *a* misstrauisch
disturb *vt* stören; (*perturb*) beunruhigen; (*touch*) anrühren. **~ance** *n* Unruhe *f*; (*interruption*) Störung *f*. **~ed** *a* beunruhigt; **[mentally] ~ed** geistig gestört. **~ing** *a* beunruhigend
disused *a* stillgelegt; (*empty*) leer
ditch *n* Graben *m* ● *vt* ([!] *abandon*) fallen lassen <*plan*>
dither *vi* zaudern
ditto *n* dito; [!] ebenfalls
dive *n* [Kopf]sprung *m*; (*Aviat*) Sturzflug *m*; ([!] *place*) Spelunke *f* ● *vi* einen Kopfsprung machen; (*when in water*) tauchen; (*Aviat*) einen Sturzflug machen; ([!] *rush*) stürzen
diver *n* Taucher *m*; (*Sport*) [Kunst]springer *m*
diverse *a* verschieden
diversify *vt/i* (*pt/pp* **-ied**) variieren; (*Comm*) diversifizieren
diversion *n* Umleitung *f*; (*distraction*) Ablenkung *f*
diversity *n* Vielfalt *f*
divert *vt* umleiten; ablenken <*attention*>; (*entertain*) unterhalten
divide *vt* teilen; (*separate*) trennen; (*Math*) dividieren (**by** durch) ● *vi* sich teilen
dividend *n* Dividende *f*
divine *a* göttlich

diving *n* (*Sport*) Kunstspringen *nt*. **~-board** *n* Sprungbrett *nt*
divinity *n* Göttlichkeit *f*; (*subject*) Theologie *f*
division *n* Teilung *f*; (*separation*) Trennung *f*; (*Math, Mil*) Division *f*; (*Parl*) Hammelsprung *m*; (*line*) Trennlinie *f*; (*group*) Abteilung *f*
divorce *n* Scheidung *f* ● *vt* sich scheiden lassen von. **~d** *a* geschieden; **get ~d** sich scheiden lassen
DIY *abbr of* **do-it-yourself**
dizziness *n* Schwindel *m*
dizzy *a* (**-ier, -iest**) schwindlig; **I feel ~** mir ist schwindlig

do

3 sg pres tense **does**; *pt* **did**; *pp* **done**

● *transitive verb*

····➤ (*perform*) machen *<homework, housework, exam, handstand etc>*; tun *<duty, favour, something, nothing>*; vorführen *<trick, dance>*; durchführen *<test>*. **what are you doing?** was tust *od* machst du? **what can I do for you?** was kann ich für Sie tun? **do something!** tu doch etwas! **have you nothing better to do?** hast du nichts Besseres zu tun? **do the washing-up /cleaning** abwaschen/sauber machen

····➤ (*as job*) **what does your father do?** was macht dein Vater?; was ist dein Vater von Beruf?

····➤ (*clean*) putzen; (*arrange*) [zurecht]machen *<hair>*

····➤ (*cook*) kochen; (*roast, fry*) braten. **well done** (*meat*) durch[gebraten]. **the potatoes aren't done yet** die Kartoffeln sind noch nicht richtig durch

····➤ (*solve*) lösen *<problem, riddle>*; machen *<puzzle>*

····➤ (! *swindle*) reinlegen. **do s.o. out of sth** jdn um etw bringen

● *intransitive verb*

····➤ (*with as or adverb*) es tun; es machen. **do as they do** mach es wie sie. **he can do as he likes** er kann tun *od* machen, was er will. **you did well** du hast es gut gemacht

····➤ (*get on*) vorankommen; (*in exams*) abschneiden. **do well/ badly at school** gut/schlecht in der Schule sein. **how are you doing?** wie geht's dir? **how do you do?** (*formal*) guten Tag!

····➤ **will do** (*serve purpose*) es tun; (*suffice*) [aus]reichen; (*be suitable*) gehen. **that won't do** das geht nicht. **that will do!** jetzt aber genug!

● *auxiliary verb*

····➤ (*in questions*) **do you know him?** kennst du ihn? **what does he want?** was will er?

····➤ (*in negation*) **I don't** *or* **do not wish to take part** ich will nicht teilnehmen. **don't be so noisy!** seid [doch] nicht so laut!

····➤ (*as verb substitute*) **you mustn't act as he does** du darfst nicht so wie er handeln. **come in, do!** komm doch herein!

····➤ (*in tag questions*) **don't you, doesn't he** *etc.* nicht wahr. **you went to Paris, didn't you?** du warst in Paris, nicht wahr?

····➤ (*in short questions*) **Does he live in London? — Yes, he does** Wohnt er in London? – Ja [, stimmt]

····➤ (*for special emphasis*) **I do love Greece** Griechenland gefällt mir wirklich gut

····➤ (*for inversion*) **little did he know that ...** er hatte keine Ahnung, dass ...

● *noun*

pl **do's** *or* **dos**

····➤ (! *celebration*) Feier *f*

● *phrasal verbs*

● **do away with** *vt* abschaffen.

● **do for** *vt* [!]: **do for s.o.** jdn fertig machen [!]; **be done for** erledigt sein. ● **do in** *vt* ([✖] *kill*) kaltmachen [✖]. ● **do up** *vt* (*fasten*) zumachen; binden <*shoe-lace, bow-tie*>; (*wrap*) einpacken; (*renovate*) renovieren. ● **do with** *vt*: **I could do with ...** ich brauche .... ● **do without** *vt*: **do without sth** auf etw (*acc*) verzichten; *vi* darauf verzichten

docile *a* fügsam
dock¹ *n* (*Jur*) Anklagebank *f*
dock² *n* Dock *nt* ● *vi* anlegen. **~er** *n* Hafenarbeiter *m*. **~yard** *n* Werft *f*
doctor *n* Arzt *m*/ Ärztin *f*; (*Univ*) Doktor *m* ● *vt* kastrieren; (*spay*) sterilisieren
doctrine *n* Lehre *f*
document *n* Dokument *nt*. **~ary** *a* Dokumentar- ● *n* Dokumentarbericht *m*; (*film*) Dokumentarfilm *m*
dodge *n* [!] Trick *m*, Kniff *m* ● *vt/i* ausweichen (+ *dat*)
dodgy *a* (**-ier, -iest**) [!] (*awkward*) knifflig; (*dubious*) zweifelhaft
doe *n* Ricke *f*; (*rabbit*) [Kaninchen]weibchen *nt*
does *see* **do**
doesn't = **does not**
dog *n* Hund *m*
dog: ~-biscuit *n* Hundekuchen *m*. **~-collar** *n* Hundehalsband *nt*; (*Relig* [!]) Kragen *m* eines Geistlichen. **~-eared** *a* **be ~-eared** Eselsohren haben
dogged *a*, **-ly** *adv* beharrlich
dogma *n* Dogma *nt*. **~tic** *a* dogmatisch
do-it-yourself *n* Heimwerken *nt*. **~ shop** *n* Heimwerkerladen *m*
doldrums *npl* **be in the ~** niedergeschlagen sein; <*business:*> daniederliegen
dole *n* [!] Stempelgeld *nt*; **be on the ~** arbeitslos sein ● *vt* **~ out** austeilen
doll *n* Puppe *f* ● *vt* [!] **~ oneself up** sich herausputzen
dollar *n* Dollar *m*
dolphin *n* Delphin *m*
domain *n* Gebiet *nt*
dome *n* Kuppel *m*
domestic *a* häuslich; (*Pol*) Innen-; (*Comm*) Binnen-. **~ animal** *n* Haustier *nt*. **~ flight** *n* Inlandflug *m*
dominant *a* vorherrschend
dominat|e *vt* beherrschen ● *vi* dominieren. **~ion** *n* Vorherrschaft *f*
domineering *a* herrschsüchtig
domino *n* (*pl* **-es**) Dominostein *m*; **~es** *sg* (*game*) Domino *nt*
donat|e *vt* spenden. **~ion** *n* Spende *f*
done *see* **do**
donkey *n* Esel *m*; **~'s years** [!] eine Ewigkeit. **~-work** *n* Routinearbeit *f*
donor *n* Spender(in) *m*(*f*)
don't = **do not**
doom *n* Schicksal *nt*; (*ruin*) Verhängnis *nt*
door *n* Tür *f*; **out of ~s** im Freien
door: ~man *n* Portier *m*. **~mat** *n* [Fuß]abtreter *m*. **~step** *n* Türschwelle *f*; **on the ~step** vor der Tür. **~way** *n* Türöffnung *f*
dope *n* [!] Drogen *pl*; ([!] *information*) Informationen *pl*; ([!] *idiot*) Trottel *m* ● *vt* betäuben; (*Sport*) dopen
dormant *a* ruhend
dormitory *n* Schlafsaal *m*
dormouse *n* Haselmaus *f*
dosage *n* Dosierung *f*
dose *n* Dosis *f*
dot *n* Punkt *m*; **on the ~** pünktlich. **~-com** *n* Dot-com-Firma *f*
dote *vi* **~ on** vernarrt sein in (+ *acc*)

dotted *a* ~ **line** punktierte Linie *f*; **be ~ with** bestreut sein mit
dotty *a* (**-ier, -iest**) [!] verdreht
double *a & adv* doppelt; <*bed, chin*> Doppel-; <*flower*> gefüllt ● *n* das Doppelte; (*person*) Doppelgänger *m*; **~s** *pl* (*Tennis*) Doppel *nt*; ● *vt* verdoppeln; (*fold*) falten ● *vi* sich verdoppeln. **~ up** *vi* sich krümmen (**with** vor + *dat*)
double: ~-bass *n* Kontrabass *m*. **~-breasted** *a* zweireihig. **~-click** *vt/i* doppelklicken (**on** auf + *acc*). **~-cross** *vt* ein Doppelspiel treiben mit. **~-decker** *n* Doppeldecker *m*. **~ glazing** *n* Doppelverglasung *f*. **~ room** *n* Doppelzimmer *nt*
doubly *adv* doppelt
doubt *n* Zweifel *m* ● *vt* bezweifeln. **~ful** *a*, **-ly** *adv* zweifelhaft; (*disbelieving*) skeptisch. **~less** *adv* zweifellos
dough *n* [fester] Teig *m*; ([!] *money*) Pinke *f*. **~nut** *n* Berliner [Pfannkuchen] *m*
dove *n* Taube *f*
down¹ *n* (*feathers*) Daunen *pl*
down² *adv* unten; (*with movement*) nach unten; **go ~** hinuntergehen; **come ~** herunterkommen; **~ there** da unten; **£50 ~** £50 Anzahlung; **~!** (*to dog*) Platz! **~ with ...!** nieder mit ...! ● *prep* **~ the road/stairs** die Straße/Treppe hinunter; **~ the river** den Fluss abwärts ● *vt* [!] (*drink*) runterkippen; **~ tools** die Arbeit niederlegen
down: ~cast *a* niedergeschlagen. **~fall** *n* Sturz *m*; (*ruin*) Ruin *m*. **~-hearted** *a* entmutigt. **~hill** *adv* bergab. **~ payment** *n* Anzahlung *f*. **~pour** *n* Platzregen *m*. **~right** *a & adv* ausgesprochen. **~size** *vt* verschlanken ● *vi* abspecken. **~stairs** *adv* unten; <*go*> nach unten ● *a* im Erdgeschoss. **~stream** *adv* stromabwärts. **~-to-earth** *a* sachlich. **~town** *adv* (*Amer*) im Stadtzentrum. **~ward** *a* nach unten; <*slope*> abfallend ● *adv* **~[s]** abwärts, nach unten
doze *n* Nickerchen *nt* ● *vi* dösen. **~ off** *vi* einnicken
dozen *n* Dutzend *nt*
Dr *abbr of* **doctor**
draft¹ *n* Entwurf *m*; (*Comm*) Tratte *f*; (*Amer Mil*) Einberufung *f* ● *vt* entwerfen; (*Amer Mil*) einberufen
draft² *n* (*Amer*) = **draught**
drag *n* **in ~** [!] <*man*> als Frau gekleidet ● *vt* (*pt/pp* **dragged**) schleppen; absuchen <*river*>. **~ on** *vi* sich in die Länge ziehen
dragon *n* Drache *m*. **~-fly** *n* Libelle *f*
drain *n* Abfluss *m*; (*underground*) Kanal *m*; **the ~s** die Kanalisation ● *vt* entwässern <*land*>; ablassen <*liquid*>; das Wasser ablassen aus <*tank*>; abgießen <*vegetables*>; austrinken <*glass*> ● *vi* **~ [away]** ablaufen
drain|age *n* Kanalisation *f*; (*of land*) Dränage *f*. **~ing board** *n* Abtropfbrett *nt*. **~-pipe** *n* Abflussrohr *nt*
drake *n* Enterich *m*
drama *n* Drama *nt*
dramatic *a*, **-ally** *adv* dramatisch
dramat|ist *n* Dramatiker *m*. **~ize** *vt* für die Bühne bearbeiten; (*fig*) dramatisieren
drank *see* **drink**
drape *n* (*Amer*) Vorhang *m* ● *vt* drapieren
drastic *a*, **-ally** *adv* drastisch
draught *n* [Luft]zug *m*; **~s** *sg* (*game*) Damespiel *nt*; **there is a ~** es zieht
draught beer *n* Bier *nt* vom Fass
draughty *a* zugig
draw *n* Attraktion *f*; (*Sport*) Unentschieden *nt*; (*in lottery*) Ziehung *f* ● *v* (*pt* **drew**, *pp* **drawn**) ● *vt* ziehen; (*attract*) anziehen;

zeichnen <*picture*>; abheben <*money*>; ~ **the curtains** die Vorhänge zuziehen/ (*back*) aufziehen ● *vi* (*Sport*) unentschieden spielen. ~ **back** *vt* zurückziehen ● *vi* (*recoil*) zurückweichen. ~ **in** *vt* einziehen ● *vi* einfahren. ~ **out** *vt* herausziehen; abheben <*money*> ● *vi* ausfahren. ~ **up** *vt* aufsetzen <*document*>; herrücken <*chair*> ● *vi* [an]halten

draw: ~**back** *n* Nachteil *m*. ~**bridge** *n* Zugbrücke *f*

drawer *n* Schublade *f*

drawing *n* Zeichnung *f*

drawing: ~**-board** *n* Reißbrett *nt*. ~**-pin** *n* Reißzwecke *f*

drawl *n* schleppende Aussprache *f*

drawn *see* **draw**

dread *n* Furcht *f* (**of** vor + *dat*) ● *vt* fürchten. ~**ful** *a*, **-fully** *adv* fürchterlich

dream *n* Traum *m* ● *vt/i* (*pt/pp* **dreamt** *or* **dreamed**) träumen (**about/of** von)

dreary *a* (**-ier, -iest**) trüb[e]; (*boring*) langweilig

dregs *npl* Bodensatz *m*

drench *vt* durchnässen

dress *n* Kleid *nt*; (*clothing*) Kleidung *f* ● *vt* anziehen; (*Med*) verbinden; ~ **oneself, get** ~**ed** sich anziehen ● *vi* sich anziehen. ~ **up** *vi* sich schön anziehen; (*in disguise*) sich verkleiden (**as** als)

dress: ~ **circle** *n* (*Theat*) erster Rang *m*. ~**er** *n* (*furniture*) Anrichte *f*; (*Amer: dressing-table*) Frisiertisch *m*

dressing *n* (*Culin*) Soße *f*; (*Med*) Verband *m*

dressing: ~**-gown** *n* Morgenmantel *m*. ~**-room** *n* Ankleidezimmer *nt*; (*Theat*) [Künstler]garderobe *f*. ~**-table** *n* Frisiertisch *m*

dress: ~**maker** *n* Schneiderin *f*. ~ **rehearsal** *n* Generalprobe *f*

drew *see* **draw**

dried *a* getrocknet. ~ **fruit** Dörrobst *nt*

drier *n* Trockner *m*

drift *n* Abtrift *f*; (*of snow*) Schneewehe *f*; (*meaning*) Sinn *m* ● *vi* treiben; (*off course*) abtreiben; <*snow:*> Wehen bilden; (*fig*) <*person:*> sich treiben lassen

drill *n* Bohrer *m*; (*Mil*) Drill *m* ● *vt/i* bohren (**for** nach); (*Mil*) drillen

drily *adv* trocken

drink *n* Getränk *nt*; (*alcoholic*) Drink *m*; (*alcohol*) Alkohol *m* ● *vt/i* (*pt* **drank**, *pp* **drunk**) trinken. ~ **up** *vt/i* austrinken

drink|able *a* trinkbar. ~**er** *n* Trinker *m*

drinking-water *n* Trinkwasser *nt*

drip *n* Tropfen *nt*; (*drop*) Tropfen *m*; (*Med*) Tropf *m*; ([!] *person*) Niete *f* ● *vi* (*pt/pp* **dripped**) tropfen

drive *n* [Auto]fahrt *f*; (*entrance*) Einfahrt *f*; (*energy*) Elan *m*; (*Psych*) Trieb *m*; (*Pol*) Aktion *f*; (*Sport*) Treibschlag *m*; (*Techn*) Antrieb *m* ● *v* (*pt* **drove**, *pp* **driven**) ● *vt* treiben; fahren <*car*>; (*Sport: hit*) schlagen; (*Techn*) antreiben; ~ **s.o. mad** [!] jdn verrückt machen; **what are you driving at?** [!] worauf willst du hinaus? ● *vi* fahren. ~ **away** *vt* vertreiben ● *vi* abfahren. ~ **off** *vt* vertreiben ● *vi* abfahren. ~ **on** *vi* weiterfahren. ~ **up** *vi* vorfahren

drivel *n* [!] Quatsch *m*

driven *see* **drive**

driver *n* Fahrer(in) *m(f)*; (*of train*) Lokführer *m*

driving: ~ **lesson** *n* Fahrstunde *f*. ~ **licence** *n* Führerschein *m*. ~ **school** *n* Fahrschule *f*. ~ **test** Fahrprüfung *f*

drizzle *n* Nieselregen *m* ● *vi* nieseln

drone *n* (*sound*) Brummen *nt*

droop *vi* herabhängen

drop *n* Tropfen *m*; (*fall*) Fall *m*; (*in price, temperature*) Rückgang *m* ● *v* (*pt/pp* **dropped**) ● *vt* fallen lassen; abwerfen <*bomb*>; (*omit*) auslassen; (*give up*) aufgeben ● *vi* fallen; (*fall lower*) sinken; <*wind:*> nachlassen. **~ in** *vi* vorbeikommen. **~ off** *vt* absetzen <*person*> ● *vi* abfallen; (*fall asleep*) einschlafen. **~ out** *vi* herausfallen; (*give up*) aufgeben

drought *n* Dürre *f*

drove *see* **drive**

drown *vi* ertrinken ● *vt* ertränken; übertönen <*noise*>; **be ~ed** ertrinken

drowsy *a* schläfrig

drudgery *n* Plackerei *f*

drug *n* Droge *f* ● *vt* (*pt/pp* **drugged**) betäuben

drug: ~ addict *n* Drogenabhängige(r) *m/f*. **~store** *n* (*Amer*) Drogerie *f*; (*dispensing*) Apotheke *f*

drum *n* Trommel *f*; (*for oil*) Tonne *f* ● *v* (*pt/pp* **drummed**) ● *vi* trommeln ● *vt* **~sth into s.o.** [!] jdm etw einbläuen. **~mer** *n* Trommler *m*; (*in pop-group*) Schlagzeuger *m*. **~stick** *n* Trommelschlegel *m*

drunk *see* **drink** ● *a* betrunken; **get ~** sich betrinken ● *n* Betrunkene(r) *m*

drunk|ard *n* Trinker *m*. **~en** *a* betrunken

dry *a* (**drier, driest**) trocken ● *vt/i* trocknen. **~ up** *vt/i* austrocknen

dry: ~-clean *vt* chemisch reinigen. **~-cleaner's** *n* (*shop*) chemische Reinigung *f*. **~ness** *n* Trockenheit *f*

dual *a* doppelt

dual carriageway *n* ≈ Schnellstraße *f*

dubious *a* zweifelhaft

duchess *n* Herzogin *f*

duck *n* Ente *f* ● *vt* (*in water*) untertauchen ● *vi* sich ducken

duct *n* Rohr *nt*; (*Anat*) Gang *m*

dud *a* [!] nutzlos; <*coin*> falsch; <*cheque*> ungedeckt; (*forged*) gefälscht

due *a* angemessen; **be ~** fällig sein; <*baby:*> erwartet werden; <*train:*> planmäßig ankommen; **~ to** (*owing to*) wegen (+ *gen*); **be ~ to** zurückzuführen sein auf (+ *acc*) ● *adv* **~ west** genau westlich

duel *n* Duell *nt*

duet *n* Duo *nt*; (*vocal*) Duett *nt*

dug *see* **dig**

duke *n* Herzog *m*

dull *a* (**-er, -est**) (*overcast, not bright*) trüb[e]; (*not shiny*) matt; <*sound*> dumpf; (*boring*) langweilig; (*stupid*) schwerfällig

duly *adv* ordnungsgemäß

dumb *a* (**-er, -est**) stumm. **~ down** *vt/i* verflachen

dummy *n* (*tailor's*) [Schneider]puppe *f*; (*for baby*) Schnuller *m*; (*Comm*) Attrappe *f*

dump *n* Abfallhaufen *m*; (*for refuse*) Müllhalde *f*, Deponie *f*; ([!] *town*) Kaff *nt*; **be down in the ~s** [!] deprimiert sein ● *vt* abladen

dumpling *n* Kloß *m*

dunce *n* Dummkopf *m*

dune *n* Düne *f*

dung *n* Mist *m*

dungarees *npl* Latzhose *f*

dungeon *n* Verlies *nt*

dunk *vt* eintunken

duo *n* Paar *nt*; (*Mus*) Duo *nt*

dupe *n* Betrogene(r) *m/f* ● *vt* betrügen

duplicate[1] *n* Doppel *nt*; **in ~** in doppelter Ausfertigung *f*

duplicate[2] *vt* kopieren; (*do twice*) zweimal machen

durable *a* haltbar

duration *n* Dauer *f*

during *prep* während (+ *gen*)

dusk *n* [Abend]dämmerung *f*

dust *n* Staub *m* ● *vt* abstauben; (*sprinkle*) bestäuben (**with** mit)
dust: ~bin *n* Mülltonne *f*. **~-cart** *n* Müllwagen *m*. **~er** *n* Staubtuch *nt*. **~-jacket** *n* Schutzumschlag *m*. **~man** *n* Müllmann *m*. **~pan** *n* Kehrschaufel *f*
dusty *a* (**-ier, -iest**) staubig
Dutch *a* holländisch ● *n* (*Lang*) Holländisch *nt*; **the ~** *pl* die Holländer. **~man** *n* Holländer *m*
dutiful *a*, **-ly** *adv* pflichtbewusst
duty *n* Pflicht *f*; (*task*) Aufgabe *f*; (*tax*) Zoll *m*; **be on ~** Dienst haben. **~-free** *a* zollfrei
duvet *n* Steppdecke *f*
DVD *abbr* (**digital versatile disc**) DVD *f*
dwarf *n* (*pl* **-s** *or* **dwarves**) Zwerg *m*
dwell *vi* (*pt/pp* **dwelt**); **~ on** (*fig*) verweilen bei. **~ing** *n* Wohnung *f*
dwindle *vi* abnehmen, schwinden
dye *n* Farbstoff *m* ● *vt* (*pres p* **dyeing**) färben
dying *see* **die²**
dynamic *a* dynamisch
dynamite *n* Dynamit *nt*
dyslex|ia *n* Legasthenie *f*. **~ic** *a* legasthenisch; **be ~ic** Legastheniker sein

Ee

each *a & pron* jede(r,s); (*per*) je; **~ other** einander; **£1 ~** £1 pro Person; (*for thing*) pro Stück
eager *a*, **-ly** *adv* eifrig; **be ~ to do sth** etw gerne machen wollen. **~ness** *n* Eifer *m*
eagle *n* Adler *m*
ear *n* Ohr *nt*. **~ache** *n* Ohrenschmerzen *pl*. **~-drum** *n* Trommelfell *nt*
earl *n* Graf *m*
early *a & adv* (**-ier, -iest**) früh; <*reply*> baldig; **be ~** früh dran sein
earn *vt* verdienen
earnest *a*, **-ly** *adv* ernsthaft ● *n* **in ~** im Ernst
earnings *npl* Verdienst *m*
ear: ~phones *npl* Kopfhörer *pl*. **~-ring** *n* Ohrring *m*; (*clip-on*) Ohrklips *m*. **~shot** *n* **within/out of ~shot** in/außer Hörweite
earth *n* Erde *f*; (*of fox*) Bau *m* ● *vt* (*Electr*) erden
earthenware *n* Tonwaren *pl*
earthly *a* irdisch; **be no ~ use** [!] völlig nutzlos sein
earthquake *n* Erdbeben *nt*
earthy *a* erdig; (*coarse*) derb
ease *n* Leichtigkeit *f* ● *vt* erleichtern; lindern <*pain*> ● *vi* <*pain:*> nachlassen; <*situation:*> sich entspannen
easily *adv* leicht, mit Leichtigkeit
east *n* Osten *m*; **to the ~ of** östlich von ● *a* Ost-, ost- ● *adv* nach Osten
Easter *n* Ostern *nt* ● *attrib* Oster-. **~ egg** *n* Osterei *nt*
east|erly *a* östlich. **~ern** *a* östlich. **~ward[s]** *adv* nach Osten
easy *a* (**-ier, -iest**) leicht; **take it ~** [!] sich schonen; **go ~ with** [!] sparsam umgehen mit
easy: ~ chair *n* Sessel *m*. **~going** *a* gelassen
eat *vt/i* (*pt* **ate**, *pp* **eaten**) essen; <*animal:*> fressen. **~ up** *vt* aufessen
eatable *a* genießbar
eau-de-Cologne *n* Kölnisch Wasser *nt*
eaves *npl* Dachüberhang *m*. **~drop** *vi* (*pt/pp* **~ dropped**) [heimlich] lauschen

ebb *n* (*tide*) Ebbe *f* ● *vi* zurückgehen; (*fig*) verebben
ebony *n* Ebenholz *nt*
EC *abbr* (**European Community**) EG *f*
eccentric *a* exzentrisch ● *n* Exzentriker *m*
ecclesiastical *a* kirchlich
echo *n* (*pl* **-es**) Echo *nt*, Widerhall *m* ● *v* (*pt/pp* **echoed**, *pres p* **echoing**) ● *vi* widerhallen (**with** von)
eclipse *n* (*Astr*) Finsternis *f*
ecolog|ical *a* ökologisch. **~y** *n* Ökologie *f*
e-commerce *n* E-Commerce *m*
economic *a* wirtschaftlich. **~al** *a* sparsam. **~ally** *adv* wirtschaftlich; (*thriftily*) sparsam. **~s** *n* Volkswirtschaft *f*
economist *n* Volkswirt *m*; (*Univ*) Wirtschaftswissenschaftler *m*
economize *vi* sparen (**on** an + *dat*)
economy *n* Wirtschaft *f*; (*thrift*) Sparsamkeit *f*
ecstasy *n* Ekstase *f*
ecstatic *a*, **-ally** *adv* ekstatisch
eddy *n* Wirbel *m*
edge *n* Rand *m*; (*of table, lawn*) Kante *f*; (*of knife*) Schneide *f*; **on ~** [!] nervös ● *vt* einfassen. **~ forward** *vi* sich nach vorn schieben
edgy *a* [!] nervös
edible *a* essbar
edifice *n* [großes] Gebäude *nt*
edit *vt* (*pt/pp* **edited**) redigieren; herausgeben <*anthology, dictionary*>; schneiden <*film, tape*>
edition *n* Ausgabe *f*; (*impression*) Auflage *f*
editor *n* Redakteur *m*; (*of anthology, dictionary*) Herausgeber *m*; (*of newspaper*) Chefredakteur *m*; (*of film*) Cutter(in) *m*(*f*)
editorial *a* redaktionell, Redaktions- ● *n* (*Journ*) Leitartikel *m*
educate *vt* erziehen. **~d** *a* gebildet
education *n* Erziehung *f*; (*culture*) Bildung *f*. **~al** *a* pädagogisch; <*visit*> kulturell
eel *n* Aal *m*
eerie *a* (**-ier, -iest**) unheimlich
effect *n* Wirkung *f*, Effekt *m*; **take ~** in Kraft treten
effective *a*, **-ly** *adv* wirksam, effektiv; (*striking*) wirkungsvoll, effektvoll; (*actual*) tatsächlich. **~ness** *n* Wirksamkeit *f*
effeminate *a* unmännlich
effervescent *a* sprudelnd
efficiency *n* Tüchtigkeit *f*; (*of machine, organization*) Leistungsfähigkeit *f*
efficient *a* tüchtig; <*machine, organization*> leistungsfähig; <*method*> rationell. **~ly** *adv* gut; <*function*> rationell
effort *n* Anstrengung *f*; **make an ~** sich (*dat*) Mühe geben. **~less** *a*, **-ly** *adv* mühelos
e.g. *abbr* z.B.
egalitarian *a* egalitär
egg *n* Ei *nt*. **~-cup** *n* Eierbecher *m*. **~shell** *n* Eierschale *f*
ego *n* Ich *nt*. **~ism** *n* Egoismus *m*. **~ist** *n* Egoist *m*. **~tism** *n* Ichbezogenheit *f*. **~tist** *n* ichbezogener Mensch *m*
Egypt *n* Ägypten *nt*. **~ian** *a* ägyptisch ● *n* Ägypter(in) *m*(*f*)
eiderdown *n* (*quilt*) Daunendecke *f*
eigh|t *a* acht ● *n* Acht *f*; (*boat*) Achter *m*. **~teen** *a* achtzehn. **~teenth** *a* achtzehnte(r,s)
eighth *a* achte(r,s) ● *n* Achtel *nt*
eightieth *a* achtzigste(r,s)
eighty *a* achtzig
either *a & pron* **~ [of them]** einer von [den] beiden; (*both*) beide; **on ~ side** auf beiden Seiten

● *adv* **I don't ~** ich auch nicht ● *conj* **~ ... or** entweder ... oder
eject *vt* hinauswerfen
elaborate *a*, **-ly** *adv* kunstvoll; (*fig*) kompliziert
elapse *vi* vergehen
elastic *a* elastisch. **~ band** *n* Gummiband *nt*
elasticity *n* Elastizität *f*
elated *a* überglücklich
elbow *n* Ellbogen *m*
elder[1] *n* Holunder *m*
eld|er[2] *a* ältere(r,s) ● *n* **the ~er** der/die Ältere. **~erly** *a* alt. **~est** *a* älteste(r,s) ● *n* **the ~est** der/die Älteste
elect *vt* wählen. **~ion** *n* Wahl *f*
elector *n* Wähler(in) *m(f)*. **~ate** *n* Wählerschaft *f*
electric *a*, **-ally** *adv* elektrisch
electrical *a* elektrisch; **~ engineering** Elektrotechnik *f*
electric: ~ blanket *n* Heizdecke *f*. **~ fire** *n* elektrischer Heizofen *m*
electrician *n* Elektriker *m*
electricity *n* Elektrizität *f*; (*supply*) Strom *m*
electrify *vt* (*pt/pp* **-ied**) elektrifizieren. **~ing** *a* (*fig*) elektrisierend
electrocute *vt* durch einen elektrischen Schlag töten
electrode *n* Elektrode *f*
electronic *a* elektronisch. **~s** *n* Elektronik *f*
elegance *n* Eleganz *f*
elegant *a*, **-ly** *adv* elegant
elegy *n* Elegie *f*
element *n* Element *nt*. **~ary** *a* elementar
elephant *n* Elefant *m*
elevat|e *vt* heben; (*fig*) erheben **~ion** *n* Erhebung *f*
elevator *n* (*Amer*) Aufzug *m*, Fahrstuhl *m*
eleven *a* elf ● *n* Elf *f*. **~th** *a* elfte(r,s); **at the ~th hour** [!] in letzter Minute
eligible *a* berechtigt
eliminate *vt* ausschalten
élite *n* Elite *f*
elm *n* Ulme *f*
elocution *n* Sprecherziehung *f*
elope *vi* durchbrennen [!]
eloquen|ce *n* Beredsamkeit *f*. **~t** *a*, **~ly** *adv* beredt
else *adv* sonst; **nothing ~** sonst nichts; **or ~** oder; (*otherwise*) sonst; **someone/somewhere ~** jemand/irgendwo anders; **anyone ~** jeder andere; (*as question*) sonst noch jemand? **anything ~** alles andere; (*as question*) sonst noch etwas? **~where** *adv* woanders
elucidate *vt* erläutern
elusive *a* **be ~** schwer zu fassen sein
emaciated *a* abgezehrt
e-mail *n* E-Mail *f* ● *vt* per E-Mail übermitteln <*Ergebnisse, Datei usw.*>; **~ s.o.** jdm eine E-Mail schicken ● **~ address** *n* E-Mail-Adresse *f*. **~ message** *n* E-Mail *f*
emancipat|ed *a* emanzipiert. **~ion** *n* Emanzipation *f*; (*of slaves*) Freilassung *f*
embankment *n* Böschung *f*; (*of railway*) Bahndamm *m*
embark *vi* sich einschiffen. **~ation** *n* Einschiffung *f*
embarrass *vt* in Verlegenheit bringen. **~ed** *a* verlegen. **~ing** *a* peinlich. **~ment** *n* Verlegenheit *f*
embassy *n* Botschaft *f*
embellish *vt* verzieren; (*fig*) ausschmücken
embezzle *vt* unterschlagen. **~ment** *n* Unterschlagung *f*
emblem *n* Emblem *nt*
embodiment *n* Verkörperung *f*
embody *vt* (*pt/pp* **-ied**) verkörpern; (*include*) enthalten
embrace *n* Umarmung *f* ● *vt* umarmen; (*fig*) umfassen ● *vi* sich umarmen

embroider *vt* besticken; sticken <*design*> ● *vi* sticken. **~y** *n* Stickerei *f*
embryo *n* Embryo *m*
emerald *n* Smaragd *m*
emer|ge *vi* auftauchen (**from** aus); (*become known*) sich herausstellen; (*come into being*) entstehen. **~gence** *n* Auftauchen *nt*; Entstehung *f*
emergency *n* Notfall *m*. **~ exit** *n* Notausgang *m*
emigrant *n* Auswanderer *m*
emigrat|e *vi* auswandern. **~ion** *n* Auswanderung *f*
eminent *a*, **-ly** *adv* eminent
emission *n* Ausstrahlung *f*; (*of pollutant*) Emission *f*
emit *vt* (*pt/pp* **emitted**) ausstrahlen <*light, heat*>; ausstoßen <*smoke, fumes, cry*>
emotion *n* Gefühl *nt*. **~al** *a* emotional; **become ~al** sich erregen
empathy *n* Einfühlungsvermögen *nt*
emperor *n* Kaiser *m*
emphasis *n* Betonung *f*
emphasize *vt* betonen
emphatic *a*, **-ally** *adv* nachdrücklich
empire *n* Reich *nt*
employ *vt* beschäftigen; (*appoint*) einstellen; (*fig*) anwenden. **~ee** *n* Beschäftigte(r) *m/f*; (*in contrast to employer*) Arbeitnehmer *m*. **~er** *n* Arbeitgeber *m*. **~ment** *n* Beschäftigung *f*; (*work*) Arbeit *f*. **~ment agency** *n* Stellenvermittlung *f*
empress *n* Kaiserin *f*
emptiness *n* Leere *f*
empty *a* leer ● *vt* leeren; ausleeren <*container*> ● *vi* sich leeren
emulsion *n* Emulsion *f*
enable *vt* **~ s.o. to** es jdm möglich machen, zu
enact *vt* (*Theat*) aufführen
enamel *n* Email *nt*; (*on teeth*) Zahnschmelz *m*; (*paint*) Lack *m*
enchant *vt* bezaubern. **~ing** *a* bezaubernd. **~ment** *n* Zauber *m*
encircle *vt* einkreisen
enclos|e *vt* einschließen; (*in letter*) beilegen (**with** *dat*). **~ure** *n* (*at zoo*) Gehege *nt*; (*in letter*) Anlage *f*
encore *n* Zugabe *f* ● *int* bravo!
encounter *n* Begegnung *f* ● *vt* begegnen (+ *dat*); (*fig*) stoßen auf (+ *acc*)
encourag|e *vt* ermutigen; (*promote*) fördern. **~ement** *n* Ermutigung *f*. **~ing** *a* ermutigend
encroach *vi* **~ on** eindringen in (+ *acc*) <*land*>
encyclopaed|ia *n* Enzyklopädie *f*, Lexikon *nt*. **~ic** *a* enzyklopädisch
end *n* Ende *nt*; (*purpose*) Zweck *m*; **in the ~** schließlich; **at the ~ of May** Ende Mai; **on ~** hochkant; **for days on ~** tagelang; **make ~s meet** [!] [gerade] auskommen; **no ~ of** [!] unheimlich viel(e) ● *vt* beenden ● *vi* enden; **~ up in** ([!] *arrive at*) landen in (+ *dat*)
endanger *vt* gefährden
endeavour *n* Bemühung *f* ● *vi* sich bemühen (**to** zu)
ending *n* Schluss *m*, Ende *nt*; (*Gram*) Endung *f*
endless *a*, **-ly** *adv* endlos
endorse *vt* (*Comm*) indossieren; (*confirm*) bestätigen. **~ment** *n* (*Comm*) Indossament *nt*; (*fig*) Bestätigung *f*; (*on driving licence*) Strafvermerk *m*
endow *vt* stiften; **be ~ed with** (*fig*) haben
endurance *n* Durchhaltevermögen *nt*; **beyond ~** unerträglich
endure *vt* ertragen
enemy *n* Feind *m* ● *attrib* feindlich
energetic *a* tatkräftig; **be ~** voller Energie sein

energy *n* Energie *f*
enforce *vt* durchsetzen. **~d** *a* unfreiwillig
engage *vt* einstellen <*staff*>; (*Theat*) engagieren; (*Auto*) einlegen <*gear*> ● *vi* sich beteiligen (**in** an + *dat*); (*Techn*) ineinandergreifen. **~d** *a* besetzt; <*person*> beschäftigt; (*to be married*) verlobt; **get ~d** sich verloben (**to** mit). **~ment** *n* Verlobung *f*; (*appointment*) Verabredung *f*; (*Mil*) Gefecht *nt*
engaging *a* einnehmend
engine *n* Motor *m*; (*Naut*) Maschine *f*; (*Rail*) Lokomotive *f*; (*of jet plane*) Triebwerk *nt*. **~-driver** *n* Lokomotivführer *m*
engineer *n* Ingenieur *m*; (*service, installation*) Techniker *m*; (*Naut*) Maschinist *m*; (*Amer*) Lokomotivführer *m*. **~ing** *n* **[mechanical] ~ing** Maschinenbau *m*
England *n* England *nt*
English *a* englisch; **the ~ Channel** der Ärmelkanal ● *n* (*Lang*) Englisch *nt*; **in ~** auf Englisch; **into ~** ins Englische; **the ~** *pl* die Engländer. **~man** *n* Engländer *m*. **~woman** *n* Engländerin *f*
engrav|e *vt* eingravieren. **~ing** *n* Stich *m*
enhance *vt* verschönern; (*fig*) steigern
enigma *n* Rätsel *nt*. **~tic** *a* rätselhaft
enjoy *vt* genießen; **~ oneself** sich amüsieren; **~ cooking** gern kochen; **I ~ed it** es hat mir gut gefallen/ <*food:*> geschmeckt. **~able** *a* angenehm, nett. **~ment** *n* Vergnügen *nt*
enlarge *vt* vergrößern. **~ment** *n* Vergrößerung *f*
enlist *vt* (*Mil*) einziehen; **~ s.o.'s help** jdn zur Hilfe heranziehen ● *vi* (*Mil*) sich melden
enliven *vt* beleben
enmity *n* Feindschaft *f*
enormity *n* Ungeheuerlichkeit *f*
enormous *a*, **-ly** *adv* riesig
enough *a, adv & n* genug; **be ~** reichen; **funnily ~** komischerweise
enquir|e *vi* sich erkundigen (**about** nach). **~y** *n* Erkundigung *f*; (*investigation*) Untersuchung *f*
enrage *vt* wütend machen
enrich *vt* bereichern
enrol *v* (*pt/pp* **-rolled**) ● *vt* einschreiben ● *vi* sich einschreiben
ensemble *n* (*clothing & Mus*) Ensemble *nt*
enslave *vt* versklaven
ensue *vi* folgen; (*result*) sich ergeben (**from** aus)
ensure *vt* sicherstellen; **~ that** dafür sorgen, dass
entail *vt* erforderlich machen; **what does it ~?** was ist damit verbunden?
entangle *vt* **get ~d** sich verfangen (**in** in + *dat*)
enter *vt* eintreten/ <*vehicle:*> einfahren in (+ *acc*); einreisen in (+ *acc*) <*country*>; (*register*) eintragen; sich anmelden zu <*competition*> ● *vi* eintreten; <*vehicle:*> einfahren; (*Theat*) auftreten; (*register as competitor*) sich anmelden; (*take part*) sich beteiligen (**in** an + *dat*)
enterpris|e *n* Unternehmen *nt*; (*quality*) Unternehmungsgeist *m*. **~ing** *a* unternehmend
entertain *vt* unterhalten; (*invite*) einladen; (*to meal*) bewirten <*guest*> ● *vi* unterhalten; (*have guests*) Gäste haben. **~er** *n* Unterhalter *m*. **~ment** *n* Unterhaltung *f*
enthral *vt* (*pt/pp* **enthralled**) **be ~led** gefesselt sein (**by** von)
enthuse *vi* **~ over** schwärmen von

enthusias|m *n* Begeisterung *f*. **~t** *n* Enthusiast *m*. **~tic** *a*, **-ally** *adv* begeistert

entice *vt* locken. **~ment** *n* Anreiz *m*

entire *a* ganz. **~ly** *adv* ganz, völlig. **~ty** *n* **in its ~ty** in seiner Gesamtheit

entitle *vt* berechtigen; **~d** ... mit dem Titel ...; **be ~d to sth** das Recht auf etw (*acc*) haben. **~ment** *n* Berechtigung *f*; (*claim*) Anspruch *m* (**to** auf + *acc*)

entrance *n* Eintritt *m*; (*Theat*) Auftritt *m*; (*way in*) Eingang *m*; (*for vehicle*) Einfahrt *f*. **~ fee** *n* Eintrittsgebühr *f*

entrant *n* Teilnehmer(in) *m*(*f*)

entreat *vt* anflehen (**for** um)

entrust *vt* **~ s.o. with sth, ~ sth to s.o.** jdm etw anvertrauen

entry *n* Eintritt *m*; (*into country*) Einreise *f*; (*on list*) Eintrag *m*; **no ~** Zutritt/ (*Auto*) Einfahrt verboten

envelop *vt* (*pt*/*pp* **enveloped**) einhüllen

envelope *n* [Brief]umschlag *m*

enviable *a* beneidenswert

envious *a*, **-ly** *adv* neidisch (**of** auf + *acc*)

environment *n* Umwelt *f*

environmental *a* Umwelt-. **~ist** *n* Umweltschützer *m*. **~ly** *adv* **~ly friendly** umweltfreundlich

envisage *vt* sich (*dat*) vorstellen

envoy *n* Gesandte(r) *m*

envy *n* Neid *m* ● *vt* (*pt*/*pp* **-ied**) **~ s.o. sth** jdn um etw beneiden

epic *a* episch ● *n* Epos *nt*

epidemic *n* Epidemie *f*

epilep|sy *n* Epilepsie *f*. **~tic** *a* epileptisch ● *n* Epileptiker(in) *m*(*f*)

epilogue *n* Epilog *m*

episode *n* Episode *f*; (*instalment*) Folge *f*

epitome *n* Inbegriff *m*

epoch *n* Epoche *f*. **~-making** *a* epochemachend

equal *a* gleich (**to** *dat*); **be ~ to a task** einer Aufgabe gewachsen sein ● *n* Gleichgestellte(r) *m*/*f* ● *vt* (*pt*/*pp* **equalled**) gleichen (+ *dat*); (*fig*) gleichkommen (+ *dat*). **~ity** *n* Gleichheit *f*

equalize *vt*/*i* ausgleichen

equally *adv* gleich; <*divide*> gleichmäßig; (*just as*) genauso

equat|e *vt* gleichsetzen (**with** mit). **~ion** *n* (*Math*) Gleichung *f*

equator *n* Äquator *m*

equestrian *a* Reit-

equilibrium *n* Gleichgewicht *nt*

equinox *n* Tagundnachtgleiche *f*

equip *vt* (*pt*/*pp* **equipped**) ausrüsten; (*furnish*) ausstatten. **~ment** *n* Ausrüstung *f*; Ausstattung *f*

equity *n* Gerechtigkeit *f*

equivalent *a* gleichwertig; (*corresponding*) entsprechend ● *n* Äquivalent *nt*; (*value*) Gegenwert *m*; (*counterpart*) Gegenstück *nt*

era *n* Ära *f*, Zeitalter *nt*

eradicate *vt* ausrotten

erase *vt* ausradieren; (*from tape*) löschen

erect *a* aufrecht ● *vt* errichten. **~ion** *n* Errichtung *f*; (*building*) Bau *m*; (*Biol*) Erektion *f*

ero|de *vt* <*water*:> auswaschen; <*acid*:> angreifen. **~sion** *n* Erosion *f*

erotic *a* erotisch

errand *n* Botengang *m*

erratic *a* unregelmäßig; <*person*> unberechenbar

erroneous *a* falsch; <*belief, assumption*> irrig

error *n* Irrtum *m*; (*mistake*) Fehler *m*; **in ~** irrtümlicherweise

erupt *vi* ausbrechen. **~ion** *n* Ausbruch *m*

escalat|e *vt*/*i* eskalieren. **~or** *n* Rolltreppe *f*

escape *n* Flucht *f*; (*from prison*) Ausbruch *m*; **have a narrow ~** gerade noch davonkommen ● *vi* flüchten; <*prisoner:*> ausbrechen; entkommen (**from** aus; **from s.o.** jdm); <*gas:*> entweichen
escapism *n* Eskapismus *m*
escort[1] *n* (*of person*) Begleiter *m*; (*Mil*) Eskorte *f*
escort[2] *vt* begleiten; (*Mil*) eskortieren
Eskimo *n* Eskimo *m*
esoteric *a* esoterisch
especially *adv* besonders
espionage *n* Spionage *f*
essay *n* Aufsatz *m*
essence *n* Wesen *nt*; (*Chem, Culin*) Essenz *f*
essential *a* wesentlich; (*indispensable*) unentbehrlich ● *n* **the ~s** das Wesentliche; (*items*) das Nötigste. **~ly** *adv* im Wesentlichen
establish *vt* gründen; (*form*) bilden; (*prove*) beweisen
estate *n* Gut *nt*; (*possessions*) Besitz *m*; (*after death*) Nachlass *m*; (*housing*) [Wohn]siedlung *f*. **~ agent** *n* Immobilienmakler *m*. **~ car** *n* Kombi[wagen] *m*
esteem *n* Achtung *f* ● *vt* hochschätzen
estimate[1] *n* Schätzung *f*; (*Comm*) [Kosten]voranschlag *m*; **at a rough ~** grob geschätzt
estimat|e[2] *vt* schätzen. **~ion** *n* Einschätzung *f*
estuary *n* Mündung *f*
etc. *abbr* (**et cetera**) und so weiter, usw.
eternal *a*, **-ly** *adv* ewig
eternity *n* Ewigkeit *f*
ethic|al *a* ethisch; (*morally correct*) moralisch einwandfrei. **~s** *n* Ethik *f*
Ethiopia *n* Äthiopien *nt*
ethnic *a* ethnisch. **~ cleansing** *n* ethnische Säuberung
etiquette *n* Etikette *f*
EU *abbr* (**European Union**) EU *f*
eulogy *n* Lobrede *f*
euphemis|m *n* Euphemismus *m*. **~tic** *a*, **-ally** *adv* verhüllend
euro *n* Euro *m*. **E~cheque** *n* Euroscheck *m*. **E~land** *n* Euroland *nt*
Europe *n* Europa *nt*
European *a* europäisch; **~ Union** Europäische Union *f* ● *n* Europäer(in) *m(f)*
eurosceptic *n* Euroskeptiker(in) *m(f)*
evacuat|e *vt* evakuieren; räumen <*building, area*>. **~ion** *n* Evakuierung *f*; Räumung *f*
evade *vt* sich entziehen (+ *dat*); hinterziehen <*taxes*>
evaluate *vt* einschätzen
evange|lical *a* evangelisch. **~list** *n* Evangelist *m*
evaporat|e *vi* verdunsten. **~ion** *n* Verdampfung *f*
evasion *n* Ausweichen *nt*; **tax ~** Steuerhinterziehung *f*
evasive *a*, **-ly** *adv* ausweichend; **be ~** ausweichen
even *a* (*level*) eben; (*same, equal*) gleich; (*regular*) gleichmäßig; <*number*> gerade; **get ~ with** [!] es jdm heimzahlen ● *adv* sogar, selbst; **~ so** trotzdem; **not ~** nicht einmal ● *vt* **~ the score** ausgleichen
evening *n* Abend *m*; **this ~** heute Abend; **in the ~** abends, am Abend. **~ class** *n* Abendkurs *m*
evenly *adv* gleichmäßig
event *n* Ereignis *nt*; (*function*) Veranstaltung *f*; (*Sport*) Wettbewerb *m*. **~ful** *a* ereignisreich
eventual *a* **his ~ success** der Erfolg, der ihm schließlich zuteil wurde. **~ly** *adv* schließlich
ever *adv* je[mals]; **not ~** nie; **for ~** für immer; **hardly ~** fast nie; **~ since** seitdem

E

evergreen *n* immergrüner Strauch *m*/ (*tree*) Baum *m*

everlasting *a* ewig

every *a* jede(r,s); ~ **one** jede(r,s) Einzelne; ~ **other day** jeden zweiten Tag

every: ~body *pron* jeder[mann]; alle *pl.* **~day** *a* alltäglich. ~ **one** *pron* jeder[mann]; alle *pl.* **~thing** *pron* alles. **~where** *adv* überall

evict *vt* [aus der Wohnung] hinausweisen. **~ion** *n* Ausweisung *f*

eviden|ce *n* Beweise *pl*; (*Jur*) Beweismaterial *nt*; (*testimony*) Aussage *f*; **give ~ce** aussagen. **~t** *a*, **-ly** *adv* offensichtlich

evil *a* böse ● *n* Böse *nt*

evoke *vt* heraufbeschwören

evolution *n* Evolution *f*

evolve *vt* entwickeln ● *vi* sich entwickeln

ewe *n* Schaf *nt*

exact *a*, **-ly** *adv* genau; **not ~ly** nicht gerade. **~ness** *n* Genauigkeit *f*

exaggerat|e *vt/i* übertreiben. **~ion** *n* Übertreibung *f*

exam *n* [!] Prüfung *f*

examination *n* Untersuchung *f*; (*Sch*) Prüfung *f*

examine *vt* untersuchen; (*Sch*) prüfen

example *n* Beispiel *nt* (**of** für); **for ~** zum Beispiel; **make an ~ of** ein Exempel statuieren an (+ *dat*)

exasperat|e *vt* zur Verzweiflung treiben. **~ion** *n* Verzweiflung *f*

excavat|e *vt* ausschachten; (*Archaeol*) ausgraben. **~ion** *n* Ausgrabung *f*

exceed *vt* übersteigen. **~ingly** *adv* äußerst

excel *v* (*pt/pp* **excelled**) *vi* sich auszeichnen ● *vt* ~ **oneself** sich selbst übertreffen

excellen|ce *n* Vorzüglichkeit *f*. **~t** *a*, **-ly** *adv* ausgezeichnet, vorzüglich

except *prep* außer (+ *dat*); ~ **for** abgesehen von ● *vt* ausnehmen

exception *n* Ausnahme *f*. **~al** *a*, **-ly** *adv* außergewöhnlich

excerpt *n* Auszug *m*

excess *n* Übermaß *nt* (**of** an + *dat*); (*surplus*) Überschuss *m*; **~es** *pl* Exzesse *pl*

excessive *a*, **-ly** *adv* übermäßig

exchange *n* Austausch *m*; (*Teleph*) Fernsprechamt *nt*; (*Comm*) [Geld]wechsel *m*; **in ~** dafür ● *vt* austauschen (**for** gegen); tauschen <*places*>. ~ **rate** *n* Wechselkurs *m*

excitable *a* [leicht] erregbar

excit|e *vt* aufregen; (*cause*) erregen. **~ed** *a*, **-ly** *adv* aufgeregt; **get ~ed** sich aufregen. **~ement** *n* Aufregung *f*; Erregung *f*. **~ing** *a* aufregend; <*story*> spannend

exclaim *vt/i* ausrufen

exclamation *n* Ausruf *m*. ~ **mark** *n*, (*Amer*) ~ **point** *n* Ausrufezeichen *nt*

exclu|de *vt* ausschließen. **~ding** *prep* ausschließlich (+ *gen*). **~sion** *n* Ausschluss *m*

exclusive *a*, **-ly** *adv* ausschließlich; (*select*) exklusiv

excrement *n* Kot *m*

excrete *vt* ausscheiden

excruciating *a* grässlich

excursion *n* Ausflug *m*

excusable *a* entschuldbar

excuse[1] *n* Entschuldigung *f*; (*pretext*) Ausrede *f*

excuse[2] *vt* entschuldigen; ~ **me!** Entschuldigung!

ex-directory *a* **be ~** nicht im Telefonbuch stehen

execute *vt* ausführen; (*put to death*) hinrichten

execution *n* Ausführung *f*; Hinrichtung *f*

executive *a* leitend ● *n* leitende(r) Angestellte(r) *m/f*; (*Pol*) Exekutive *f*

exemplary *a* beispielhaft

exemplify *vt* (*pt/pp* **-ied**) veranschaulichen

exempt *a* befreit ● *vt* befreien (**from** von). **~ion** *n* Befreiung *f*

exercise *n* Übung *f*; **physical ~** körperliche Bewegung *f* ● *vt* (*use*) ausüben; bewegen <*horse*> ● *vi* sich bewegen. **~ book** *n* [Schul]heft *nt*

exert *vt* ausüben; **~ oneself** sich anstrengen. **~ion** *n* Anstrengung *f*

exhale *vt/i* ausatmen

exhaust *n* (*Auto*) Auspuff *m*; (*fumes*) Abgase *pl* ● *vt* erschöpfen. **~ed** *a* erschöpft. **~ing** *a* anstrengend. **~ion** *n* Erschöpfung *f*. **~ive** *a* (*fig*) erschöpfend

exhibit *n* Ausstellungsstück *nt*; (*Jur*) Beweisstück *nt* ● *vt* ausstellen

exhibition *n* Ausstellung *f*; (*Univ*) Stipendium *nt*. **~ist** *n* Exhibitionist(in) *m*(*f*)

exhibitor *n* Aussteller *m*

exhilarat|ing *a* berauschend. **~ion** *n* Hochgefühl *nt*

exhume *vt* exhumieren

exile *n* Exil *nt*; (*person*) im Exil Lebende(r) *m/f* ● *vt* ins Exil schicken

exist *vi* bestehen, existieren. **~ence** *n* Existenz *f*; **be in ~ence** existieren

exit *n* Ausgang *m*; (*Auto*) Ausfahrt *f*; (*Theat*) Abgang *m*

exorbitant *a* übermäßig hoch

exotic *a* exotisch

expand *vt* ausdehnen; (*explain better*) weiter ausführen ● *vi* sich ausdehnen; (*Comm*) expandieren

expans|e *n* Weite *f*. **~ion** *n* Ausdehnung *f*; (*Techn, Pol, Comm*) Expansion *f*

expect *vt* erwarten; (*suppose*) annehmen; **I ~ so** wahrscheinlich

expectan|cy *n* Erwartung *f*. **~t** *a*, **-ly** *adv* erwartungsvoll; **~t mother** werdende Mutter *f*

expectation *n* Erwartung *f*

expedient *a* zweckdienlich

expedite *vt* beschleunigen

expedition *n* Expedition *f*

expel *vt* (*pt/pp* **expelled**) ausweisen (**from** aus); (*from school*) von der Schule verweisen

expenditure *n* Ausgaben *pl*

expense *n* Kosten *pl*; **business ~s** *pl* Spesen *pl*; **at my ~** auf meine Kosten

expensive *a*, **-ly** *adv* teuer

experience *n* Erfahrung *f*; (*event*) Erlebnis *nt* ● *vt* erleben. **~d** *a* erfahren

experiment *n* Versuch *m*, Experiment *nt* ● *vi* experimentieren. **~al** *a* experimentell

expert *a*, **-ly** *adv* fachmännisch ● *n* Fachmann *m*, Experte *m*

expertise *n* Sachkenntnis *f*

expire *vi* ablaufen

expiry *n* Ablauf *m*

explain *vt* erklären

explana|tion *n* Erklärung *f*. **~tory** *a* erklärend

explicit *a*, **-ly** *adv* deutlich

explode *vi* explodieren ● *vt* zur Explosion bringen

exploit[1] *n* [Helden]tat *f*

exploit[2] *vt* ausbeuten. **~ation** *n* Ausbeutung *f*

exploration *n* Erforschung *f*

explore *vt* erforschen. **~r** *n* Forschungsreisende(r) *m*

explos|ion *n* Explosion *f*. **~ive** *a* explosiv ● *n* Sprengstoff *m*

export[1] *n* Export *m*, Ausfuhr *f*

export[2] *vt* exportieren, ausführen. **~er** *n* Exporteur *m*

expos|e *vt* freilegen; (*to danger*) aussetzen (**to** *dat*); (*reveal*) aufdecken; (*Phot*) belichten. **~ure** *n* Aussetzung *f*; (*Med*) Unterkühlung *f*; (*Phot*)

E

Belichtung *f*; **24 ~ures** 24 Aufnahmen

express *adv* <*send*> per Eilpost ● *n* (*train*) Schnellzug *m* ● *vt* ausdrücken; **~ oneself** sich ausdrücken. **~ion** *n* Ausdruck *m*. **~ive** *a* ausdrucksvoll. **~ly** *adv* ausdrücklich

expulsion *n* Ausweisung *f*; (*Sch*) Verweisung *f* von der Schule

exquisite *a* erlesen

extend *vt* verlängern; (*stretch out*) ausstrecken; (*enlarge*) vergrößern ● *vi* sich ausdehnen; <*table:*> sich ausziehen lassen

extension *n* Verlängerung *f*; (*to house*) Anbau *m*; (*Teleph*) Nebenanschluss *m*

extensive *a* weit; (*fig*) umfassend. **~ly** *adv* viel

extent *n* Ausdehnung *f*; (*scope*) Ausmaß *nt*, Umfang *m*; **to a certain ~** in gewissem Maße

exterior *a* äußere(r,s) ● *n* **the ~** das Äußere

exterminat|e *vt* ausrotten. **~ion** *n* Ausrottung *f*

external *a* äußere(r,s); **for ~ use only** (*Med*) nur äußerlich. **~ly** *adv* äußerlich

extinct *a* ausgestorben; <*volcano*> erloschen. **~ion** *n* Aussterben *nt*

extinguish *vt* löschen. **~er** *n* Feuerlöscher *m*

extort *vt* erpressen. **~ion** *n* Erpressung *f*

extortionate *a* übermäßig hoch

extra *a* zusätzlich ● *adv* extra; (*especially*) besonders ● *n* (*Theat*) Statist(in) *m(f)*; **~s** *pl* Nebenkosten *pl*; (*Auto*) Extras *pl*

extract[1] *n* Auszug *m*

extract[2] *vt* herausziehen; ziehen <*tooth*>

extraordinary *a*, **-ily** *adv* außerordentlich; (*strange*) seltsam

extravagan|ce *n* Verschwendung *f*; **an ~ce** ein Luxus *m*. **~t** *a* verschwenderisch

extrem|e *a* äußerste(r,s); (*fig*) extrem ● *n* Extrem *nt*; **in the ~e** im höchsten Grade. **~ely** *adv* äußerst. **~ist** *n* Extremist *m*

extricate *vt* befreien

extrovert *n* extravertierter Mensch *m*

exuberant *a* überglücklich

exude *vt* absondern; (*fig*) ausstrahlen

exult *vi* frohlocken

eye *n* Auge *nt*; (*of needle*) Öhr *nt*; (*for hook*) Öse *f*; **keep an ~ on** aufpassen auf (+ *acc*) ● *vt* (*pt/pp* **eyed**, *pres p* **ey[e]ing**) ansehen

eye: ~ brow *n* Augenbraue *f*. **~lash** *n* Wimper *f*. **~lid** *n* Augenlid *nt*. **~-shadow** *n* Lidschatten *m*. **~sight** *n* Sehkraft *f*. **~sore** *n* [!] Schandfleck *m*. **~witness** *n* Augenzeuge *m*

Ff

fable *n* Fabel *f*

fabric *n* Stoff *m*

fabrication *n* Erfindung *f*

fabulous *a* [!] phantastisch

façade *n* Fassade *f*

face *n* Gesicht *nt*; (*surface*) Fläche *f*; (*of clock*) Zifferblatt *nt*; **pull ~s** Gesichter schneiden; **in the ~ of** angesichts (+ *gen*); **on the ~ of it** allem Anschein nach ● *vt/i* gegenüberstehen (+ *dat*); **~ north** <*house:*> nach Norden liegen; **~ the fact that** sich damit abfinden, dass

face: ~-flannel *n* Waschlappen *m*. **~less** *a* anonym. **~-lift** *n* Gesichtsstraffung *f*

facet *n* Facette *f*; (*fig*) Aspekt *m*

facetious *a*, **-ly** *adv* spöttisch

facial *a* Gesichts-

facile *a* oberflächlich

facilitate *vt* erleichtern

facility *n* Leichtigkeit *f*; (*skill*) Gewandtheit *f*; **~ies** *pl* Einrichtungen *pl*

facsimile *n* Faksimile *nt*

fact *n* Tatsache *f*; **in ~** tatsächlich; (*actually*) eigentlich

faction *n* Gruppe *f*

factor *n* Faktor *m*

factory *n* Fabrik *f*

factual *a*, **-ly** *adv* sachlich

faculty *n* Fähigkeit *f*; (*Univ*) Fakultät *f*

fad *n* Fimmel *m*

fade *vi* verblassen; <*material:*> verbleichen; <*sound:*> abklingen; <*flower:*> verwelken.

fag *n* (*chore*) Plage *f*; (! *cigarette*) Zigarette *f*

fail *n* **without ~** unbedingt ● *vi* <*attempt:*> scheitern; (*grow weak*) nachlassen; (*break down*) versagen; (*in exam*) durchfallen; **~ to do sth** etw nicht tun ● *vt* nicht bestehen <*exam*>; durchfallen lassen <*candidate*>; (*disappoint*) enttäuschen

failing *n* Fehler *m*

failure *n* Misserfolg *m*; (*breakdown*) Versagen *nt*; (*person*) Versager *m*

faint *a* (**-er, -est**), **-ly** *adv* schwach; **I feel~** mir ist schwach ● *n* Ohnmacht *f* ● *vi* ohnmächtig werden. **~ness** *n* Schwäche *f*

fair¹ *n* Jahrmarkt *m*; (*Comm*) Messe *f*

fair² *a* (**-er, -est**) <*hair*> blond; <*skin*> hell; <*weather*> heiter; (*just*) gerecht, fair; (*quite good*) ziemlich gut; (*Sch*) genügend; **a ~ amount** ziemlich viel ● *adv* **play ~** fair sein. **~ly** *adv* gerecht; (*rather*) ziemlich. **~ness** *n* Blondheit *f*; Helle *f*; Gerechtigkeit *f*; (*Sport*) Fairness *f*

fairy *n* Elfe *f*; **good/wicked ~** gute/böse Fee *f*. **~ story, ~-tale** *n* Märchen *nt*

faith *n* Glaube *m*; (*trust*) Vertrauen *nt* (**in** zu)

faithful *a*, **-ly** *adv* treu; (*exact*) genau; **Yours ~ly** Hochachtungsvoll. **~ness** *n* Treue *f*; Genauigkeit *f*

fake *a* falsch ● *n* Fälschung *f*; (*person*) Schwindler *m* ● *vt* fälschen; (*pretend*) vortäuschen

falcon *n* Falke *m*

fall *n* Fall *m*; (*heavy*) Sturz *m*; (*in prices*) Fallen *nt*; (*Amer: autumn*) Herbst *m*; **have a ~** fallen ● *vi* (*pt* **fell**, *pp* **fallen**) fallen; (*heavily*) stürzen; <*night:*> anbrechen; **~ in love** sich verlieben; **~ back on** zurückgreifen auf (+ *acc*); **~ for s.o.** ! sich in jdn verlieben; **~ for sth** ! auf etw (*acc*) hereinfallen. **~ about** *vi* (*with laughter*) sich [vor Lachen] kringeln. **~ down** *vi* umfallen; <*thing:*> herunterfallen; <*building:*> einstürzen. **~ in** *vi* hineinfallen; (*collapse*) einfallen; (*Mil*) antreten; **~ in with** sich anschließen (+ *dat*). **~ off** *vi* herunterfallen; (*diminish*) abnehmen. **~ out** *vi* herausfallen; <*hair:*> ausfallen; (*quarrel*) sich überwerfen. **~ over** *vi* hinfallen. **~ through** *vi* durchfallen; <*plan:*> ins Wasser fallen

fallacy *n* Irrtum *m*

fallible *a* fehlbar

fall-out *n* [radioaktiver] Niederschlag *m*

false *a* falsch; (*artificial*) künstlich. **~hood** *n* Unwahrheit *f*. **~ly** *adv* falsch

false teeth *npl* [künstliches] Gebiss *nt*
falsify *vt* (*pt/pp* **-ied**) fälschen
falter *vi* zögern
fame *n* Ruhm *m.*
familiar *a* vertraut; (*known*) bekannt; **too ~** familiär. **~ity** *n* Vertrautheit *f.* **~ize** *vt* vertraut machen (**with** mit)
family *n* Familie *f*
family: ~ doctor *n* Hausarzt *m.* **~ life** *n* Familienleben *nt.* **~ planning** *n* Familienplanung *f.* **~ tree** *n* Stammbaum *m*
famine *n* Hungersnot *f*
famished *a* sehr hungrig
famous *a* berühmt
fan[1] *n* Fächer *m*; (*Techn*) Ventilator *m*
fan[2] *n* (*admirer*) Fan *m*
fanatic *n* Fanatiker *m.* **~al** *a*, **-ly** *adv* fanatisch. **~ism** *n* Fanatismus *m*
fanciful *a* phantastisch; (*imaginative*) phantasiereich
fancy *n* Phantasie *f*; **I have taken a real ~ to him** er hat es mir angetan ●*a* ausgefallen ●*vt* (*believe*) meinen; (*imagine*) sich (*dat*) einbilden; (! *want*) Lust haben auf (+ *acc*); **~ that!** stell dir vor! (*really*) tatsächlich! **~ dress** *n* Kostüm *nt*
fanfare *n* Fanfare *f*
fang *n* Fangzahn *m*
fan heater *n* Heizlüfter *m*
fantas|ize *vi* fantasieren. **~tic** *a* fantastisch. **~y** *n* Fantasie *f*
far *adv* weit; (*much*) viel; **by ~** bei weitem; **~ away** weit weg; **as ~ as I know** soviel ich weiß; **as ~ as the church** bis zur Kirche ●*a* **at the ~ end** am anderen Ende; **the F~ East** der Ferne Osten
farc|e *n* Farce *f.* **~ical** *a* lächerlich
fare *n* Fahrpreis *m*; (*money*) Fahrgeld *nt*; (*food*) Kost *f*; **air ~** Flugpreis *m*
farewell *int* (*liter*) lebe wohl! ●*n* Lebewohl *nt*
far-fetched *a* weit hergeholt
farm *n* Bauernhof *m* ●*vi* Landwirtschaft betreiben ●*vt* bewirtschaften <*land*>. **~er** *n* Landwirt *m*
farm: ~house *n* Bauernhaus *nt.* **~ing** *n* Landwirtschaft *f.* **~yard** *n* Hof *m*
far: ~-reaching *a* weit reichend. **~-sighted** *a* (*fig*) umsichtig; (*Amer: long-sighted*) weitsichtig
farther *adv* weiter; **~ off** weiter entfernt
fascinat|e *vt* faszinieren. **~ing** *a* faszinierend. **~ion** *n* Faszination *f*
fascis|m *n* Faschismus *m.* **~t** *n* Faschist *m* ●*a* faschistisch
fashion *n* Mode *f*; (*manner*) Art *f.* **~able** *a*, **-bly** *adv* modisch
fast *a* & *adv* (**-er, -est**) schnell; (*firm*) fest; <*colour*> waschecht; **be ~** <*clock:*> vorgehen; **be ~ asleep** fest schlafen
fasten *vt* zumachen; (*fix*) befestigen (**to an** + *dat*). **~er** *n*, **~ing** *n* Verschluss *m*
fastidious *a* wählerisch; (*particular*) penibel
fat *a* (**fatter, fattest**) dick; <*meat*> fett ●*n* Fett *nt*
fatal *a* tödlich; <*error*> verhängnisvoll. **~ity** *n* Todesopfer *nt.* **~ly** *adv* tödlich
fate *n* Schicksal *nt.* **~ful** *a* verhängnisvoll
fat-head *n* ! Dummkopf *m*
father *n* Vater *m*; **F ~ Christmas** der Weihnachtsmann ●*vt* zeugen
father: ~hood *n* Vaterschaft *f.* **~-in-law** *n* (*pl* **~s-in-law**) Schwiegervater *m.* **~ly** *a* väterlich
fathom *n* (*Naut*) Faden *m* ●*vt* verstehen
fatigue *n* Ermüdung *f*

fatten *vt* mästen *<animal>*
fatty *a* fett; *<foods>* fetthaltig
fatuous *a*, **-ly** *adv* albern
fault *n* Fehler *m*; (*Techn*) Defekt *m*; (*Geol*) Verwerfung *f*; **at ~** im Unrecht; **find ~ with** etwas auszusetzen haben an (+ *dat*); **it's your ~** du bist schuld. **~less** *a*, **-ly** *adv* fehlerfrei
faulty *a* fehlerhaft
favour *n* Gunst *f*; **I am in ~** ich bin dafür; **do s.o. a ~** jdm einen Gefallen tun ● *vt* begünstigen; (*prefer*) bevorzugen. **~able** *a*, **-bly** *adv* günstig; *<reply>* positiv
favourit|e *a* Lieblings- ● *n* Liebling *m*; (*Sport*) Favorit(in) *m(f)*. **~ism** *n* Bevorzugung *f*
fawn *a* rehbraun ● *n* Hirschkalb *nt*
fax *n* Fax *nt* ● *vt* faxen (**s.o.** jdm). **~ machine** *n* Faxgerät *nt*
fear *n* Furcht *f*, Angst *f* (**of** vor + *dat*) ● *vt/i* fürchten
fear|ful *a* besorgt; (*awful*) furchtbar. **~less** *a*, **-ly** *adv* furchtlos
feas|ibility *n* Durchführbarkeit *f*. **~ible** *a* durchführbar; (*possible*) möglich
feast *n* Festmahl *nt*; (*Relig*) Fest *nt* ● *vi* **~ [on]** schmausen
feat *n* Leistung *f*
feather *n* Feder *f*
feature *n* Gesichtszug *m*; (*quality*) Merkmal *nt*; (*Journ*) Feature *nt* ● *vt* darstellen
February *n* Februar *m*
fed ● *a* **be ~ up** [!] die Nase voll haben (**with** von)
federal *a* Bundes-
federation *n* Föderation *f*
fee *n* Gebühr *f*; (*professional*) Honorar *nt*
feeble *a* (**-r, -st**), **-bly** *adv* schwach
feed *n* Futter *nt*; (*for baby*) Essen *nt* ● *v* (*pt/pp* **fed**) ● *vt* füttern; (*support*) ernähren; (*into machine*) eingeben; speisen *<computer>* ● *vi* sich ernähren (**on** von)
feedback *n* Feedback *nt*
feel *v* (*pt/pp* **felt**) ● *vt* fühlen; (*experience*) empfinden; (*think*) meinen ● *vi* sich fühlen; **~ soft/hard** sich weich/hart anfühlen; **I ~ hot/ill** mir ist heiß/schlecht; **~ing** *n* Gefühl *nt*; **no hard ~ings** nichts für ungut
feet *see* **foot**
feline *a* Katzen-; (*catlike*) katzenartig
fell[1] *vt* fällen
fell[2] *see* **fall**
fellow *n* ([!] *man*) Kerl *m*
fellow: ~-countryman *n* Landsmann *m*. **~ men** *pl* Mitmenschen *pl*
felt[1] *see* **feel**
felt[2] *n* Filz *m*. **~[-tipped] pen** *n* Filzstift *m*
female *a* weiblich ● *nt* Weibchen *nt*; (*pej: woman*) Weib *nt*
femin|ine *a* weiblich ● *n* (*Gram*) Femininum *nt*. **~inity** *n* Weiblichkeit *f*. **~ist** *a* feministisch ● *n* Feminist(in) *m(f)*
fenc|e *n* Zaun *m*; ([!] *person*) Hehler *m* ● *vi* (*Sport*) fechten ● *vt* **~e in** einzäunen. **~er** *n* Fechter *m*. **~ing** *n* Zaun *m*; (*Sport*) Fechten *nt*
fender *n* Kaminvorsetzer *m*, (*Naut*) Fender *m*; (*Amer: wing*) Kotflügel *m*
ferment *vi* gären ● *vt* gären lassen
fern *n* Farn *m*
feroc|ious *a* wild. **~ity** *n* Wildheit *f*
ferry *n* Fähre *f*
fertil|e *a* fruchtbar. **~ity** *n* Fruchtbarkeit *f*
fertilize *vt* befruchten; düngen *<land>*. **~r** *n* Dünger *m*
fervent *a* leidenschaftlich
fervour *n* Leidenschaft *f*

festival *n* Fest *nt*; (*Mus, Theat*) Festspiele *pl*
festiv|e *a* festlich. **~ities** *npl* Feierlichkeiten *pl*
festoon *vt* behängen (**with** mit)
fetch *vt* holen; (*collect*) abholen; (*be sold for*) einbringen
fetching *a* anziehend
fête *n* Fest *nt* ● *vt* feiern
feud *n* Fehde *f*
feudal *a* Feudal-
fever *n* Fieber *nt*. **~ish** *a* fiebrig; (*fig*) fieberhaft
few *a* (**-er, -est**) wenige; **every ~ days** alle paar Tage ● *n* **a ~** ein paar; **quite a ~** ziemlich viele
fiancé *n* Verlobte(r) *m*. **fiancée** *n* Verlobte *f*
fiasco *n* Fiasko *nt*
fib *n* kleine Lüge
fibre *n* Faser *f*
fiction *n* Erfindung *f*; **[works of] ~** Erzählungsliteratur *f*. **~al** *a* erfunden
fictitious *a* [frei] erfunden
fiddle *n* [!] Geige *f*; (*cheating*) Schwindel *m* ● *vi* herumspielen (**with** mit) ● *vt* [!] frisieren <*accounts*>
fiddly *a* knifflig
fidelity *n* Treue *f*
fidget *vi* zappeln. **~y** *a* zappelig
field *n* Feld *nt*; (*meadow*) Wiese *f*; (*subject*) Gebiet *nt*
field: ~ events *npl* Sprung- und Wurfdisziplinen *pl*. **F~ Marshal** *n* Feldmarschall *m*
fiendish *a* teuflisch
fierce *a* (**-r, -st**), **-ly** *adv* wild; (*fig*) heftig. **~ness** *n* Wildheit *f*; (*fig*) Heftigkeit *f*
fiery *a* (**-ier, -iest**) feurig
fifteen *a* fünfzehn ● *n* Fünfzehn *f*. **~th** *a* fünfzehnte(r,s)
fifth *a* fünfte(r,s)
fiftieth *a* fünfzigste(r,s)
fifty *a* fünfzig
fig *n* Feige *f*
fight *n* Kampf *m*; (*brawl*) Schlägerei *f*; (*between children, dogs*) Rauferei *f* ● *v* (*pt/pp* **fought**) ● *vt* kämpfen gegen; (*fig*) bekämpfen ● *vi* kämpfen; (*brawl*) sich schlagen; <*children, dogs:*> sich raufen. **~er** *n* Kämpfer *m*; (*Aviat*) Jagdflugzeug *nt*. **~ing** *n* Kampf *m*
figurative *a*, **-ly** *adv* bildlich, übertragen
figure *n* (*digit*) Ziffer *f*; (*number*) Zahl *f*; (*sum*) Summe *f*; (*carving, sculpture, woman's*) Figur *f*; (*form*) Gestalt *f*; (*illustration*) Abbildung *f*; **good at ~s** gut im Rechnen ● *vi* (*appear*) erscheinen ● *vt* (*Amer: think*) glauben
filch *vt* [!] klauen
file[1] *n* Akte *f*; (*for documents*) [Akten]ordner *m* ● *vt* ablegen <*documents*>; (*Jur*) einreichen
file[2] *n* (*line*) Reihe *f*; **in single ~** im Gänsemarsch
file[3] *n* (*Techn*) Feile *f* ● *vt* feilen
fill *n* **eat one's ~** sich satt essen ● *vt* füllen; plombieren <*tooth*> ● *vi* sich füllen. **~ in** *vt* auffüllen; ausfüllen <*form*>. **~ out** *vt* ausfüllen <*form*>. **~ up** *vi* sich füllen ● *vt* vollfüllen; (*Auto*) volltanken; ausfüllen <*form*>
fillet *n* Filet *nt* ● *vt* (*pt/pp* **filleted**) entgräten
filling *n* Füllung *f*; (*of tooth*) Plombe *f*. **~ station** *n* Tankstelle *f*
filly *n* junge Stute *f*
film *n* Film *m* ● *vt/i* filmen; verfilmen <*book*>. **~ star** *n* Filmstar *m*
filter *n* Filter *m* ● *vt* filtern
filth *n* Dreck *m*. **~y** *a* (**-ier, -iest**) dreckig
fin *n* Flosse *f*
final *a* letzte(r,s); (*conclusive*) endgültig ● *n* (*Sport*) Endspiel *nt*; **~s** *pl* (*Univ*) Abschlussprüfung *f*

finale *n* Finale *nt*

final|ist *n* Finalist(in) *m(f)*

final|ize *vt* endgültig festlegen. **~ly** *adv* schließlich

finance *n* Finanz *f* ● *vt* finanzieren

financial *a*, **-ly** *adv* finanziell

find *n* Fund *m* ● *vt* (*pt/pp* **found**) finden; (*establish*) feststellen; **go and ~** holen; **try to ~** suchen. **~ out** *vt* herausfinden; (*learn*) erfahren ● *vi* (*enquire*) sich erkundigen

fine¹ *n* Geldstrafe *f* ● *vt* zu einer Geldstrafe verurteilen

fine² *a* (**-r, -st,**) **-ly** *adv* fein; <*weather*> schön; **he's ~** es geht ihm gut ● *adv* gut; **cut it ~** [!] sich (*dat*) wenig Zeit lassen

finesse *n* Gewandtheit *f*

finger *n* Finger *m* ● *vt* anfassen

finger: ~-nail *n* Fingernagel *m*. **~print** *n* Fingerabdruck *m*. **~tip** *n* Fingerspitze *f*

finicky *a* knifflig; (*choosy*) wählerisch

finish *n* Schluss *m*; (*Sport*) Finish *nt*; (*line*) Ziel *nt*; (*of product*) Ausführung *f* ● *vt* beenden; (*use up*) aufbrauchen; **~ one's drink** austrinken; **~ reading** zu Ende lesen ● *vi* fertig werden; <*performance:*> zu Ende sein; <*runner:*> durchs Ziel gehen

Finland *n* Finnland *nt*

Finn *n* Finne *m*/ Finnin *f*. **~ish** *a* finnisch

fir *n* Tanne *f*

fire *n* Feuer *nt*; (*forest, house*) Brand *m*; **be on ~** brennen; **catch ~** Feuer fangen; **set ~ to** anzünden; <*arsonist:*> in Brand stecken; **under ~** unter Beschuss ● *vt* brennen <*pottery*>; abfeuern <*shot*>; schießen mit <*gun*>; ([!] *dismiss*) feuern ● *vi* schießen (**at** auf + *acc*); <*engine:*> anspringen

fire: ~ alarm *n* Feuermelder *m*. **~ brigade** *n* Feuerwehr *f*. **~-engine** *n* Löschfahrzeug *nt*. **~ extinguisher** *n* Feuerlöscher *m*. **~man** *n* Feuerwehrmann *m*. **~place** *n* Kamin *m*. **~side** *n* **by** *or* **at the ~side** am Kamin. **~ station** *n* Feuerwache *f*. **~wood** *n* Brennholz *nt*. **~work** *n* Feuerwerkskörper *m*; **~works** *pl* (*display*) Feuerwerk *nt*

firm¹ *n* Firma *f*

firm² *a* (**-er, -est**), **-ly** *adv* fest; (*resolute*) entschlossen; (*strict*) streng

first *a & n* erste(r,s); **at ~** zuerst; **at ~ sight** auf den ersten Blick; **from the ~** von Anfang an ● *adv* zuerst; (*firstly*) erstens

first: ~ aid *n* erste Hilfe. **~-aid kit** *n* Verbandkasten *m*. **~-class** *a* erstklassig; (*Rail*) erster Klasse ● *adv* <*travel*> erster Klasse. **~ floor** *n* erster Stock; (*Amer: ground floor*) Erdgeschoss *nt*. **~ly** *adv* erstens. **~name** *n* Vorname *m*. **~-rate** *a* erstklassig

fish *n* Fisch *m* ● *vt/i* fischen; (*with rod*) angeln

fish: ~bone *n* Gräte *f*. **~erman** *n* Fischer *m*. **~ finger** *n* Fischstäbchen *nt*

fishing *n* Fischerei *f*. **~ boat** *n* Fischerboot *nt*. **~-rod** *n* Angel[rute] *f*

fish: ~monger *n* Fischhändler *m*. **~y** *a* Fisch-; ([!] *suspicious*) verdächtig

fission *n* (*Phys*) Spaltung *f*

fist *n* Faust *f*

fit¹ *n* (*attack*) Anfall *m*

fit² *a* (**fitter, fittest**) (*suitable*) geeignet; (*healthy*) gesund; (*Sport*) fit; **~ to eat** essbar

fit³ *n* (*of clothes*) Sitz *m*; **be a good ~** gut passen ● *v* (*pt/pp* **fitted**) ● *vi* (*be the right size*) passen ● *vt* anbringen (**to** an + *dat*); (*install*) einbauen; **~ with** versehen mit. **~ in** *vi* hineinpassen; (*adapt*) sich

einfügen (**with** in + *acc*) ●*vt* (*accommodate*) unterbringen
fit|ness *n* Eignung *f*; **[physical]** **~ness** Gesundheit *f*; (*Sport*) Fitness *f*. **~ted** *a* eingebaut; <*garment*> tailliert
fitted: **~ carpet** *n* Teppichboden *m*. **~ kitchen** *n* Einbauküche *f*. **~ sheet** *n* Spannlaken *nt*
fitting *a* passend ●*n* (*of clothes*) Anprobe *f*; (*of shoes*) Weite *f*; (*Techn*) Zubehörteil *nt*; **~s** *pl* Zubehör *nt*
five *a* fünf ●*n* Fünf *f*. **~r** *n* Fünfpfundschein *m*
fix *n* ([✱] *drugs*) Fix *m*; **be in a ~** [!] in der Klemme sitzen ●*vt* befestigen (**to** an + *dat*); (*arrange*) festlegen; (*repair*) reparieren; (*Phot*) fixieren; **~ a meal** Essen machen
fixed *a* fest
fixture *n* (*Sport*) Veranstaltung *f*; **~s and fittings** zu einer Wohnung gehörende Einrichtungen *pl*
fizz *vi* sprudeln
fizzle *vi* **~ out** verpuffen
fizzy *a* sprudelnd. **~ drink** *n* Brause[limonade] *f*
flabbergasted *a* **be ~** platt sein [!]
flabby *a* schlaff
flag *n* Fahne *f*; (*Naut*) Flagge *f*
flag-pole *n* Fahnenstange *f*
flagrant *a* flagrant
flagstone *n* [Pflaster]platte *f*
flair *n* Begabung *f*
flake *n* Flocke *f* ●*vi* **~ [off]** abblättern
flamboyant *a* extravagant
flame *n* Flamme *f*
flan *n* **[fruit] ~** Obsttorte *f*
flank *n* Flanke *f*
flannel *n* Flanell *m*; (*for washing*) Waschlappen *m*
flap *n* Klappe *f*; **in a ~** [!] aufgeregt ●*v* (*pt/pp* **flapped**) *vi* flattern; [!] sich aufregen ●*vt* **~ its wings** mit den Flügeln schlagen
flare *n* Leuchtsignal *nt*. ●*vi* **~ up** auflodern; ([!] *get angry*) aufbrausen
flash *n* Blitz *m*; **in a ~** [!] im Nu ●*vi* blitzen; (*repeatedly*) blinken; **~ past** vorbeirasen
flash: **~back** *n* Rückblende *f*. **~er** *n* (*Auto*) Blinker *m*. **~light** *n* (*Phot*) Blitzlicht *nt*; (*Amer: torch*) Taschenlampe *f*. **~y** a auffällig
flask *n* Flasche *f*
flat *a* (**flatter, flattest**) flach; <*surface*> eben; <*refusal*> glatt; <*beer*> schal; <*battery*> verbraucht/ (*Auto*) leer; <*tyre*> platt; (*Mus*) **A ~** As *nt*; **B ~** B *nt* ●*n* Wohnung *f*; ([!] *puncture*) Reifenpanne *f*
flat: **~ly** *adv* <*refuse*> glatt. **~ rate** *n* Einheitspreis *m*
flatten *vt* platt drücken
flatter *vt* schmeicheln (+ *dat*). **~y** *n* Schmeichelei *f*
flat tyre *n* Reifenpanne *f*
flaunt *vt* prunken mit
flautist *n* Flötist(in) *m*(*f*)
flavour *n* Geschmack *m* ●*vt* abschmecken. **~ing** *n* Aroma *nt*
flaw *n* Fehler *m*. **~less** *a* tadellos; <*complexion*> makellos
flea *n* Floh *m*
fleck *n* Tupfen *m*
fled *see* **flee**
flee *v* (*pt/pp* **fled**) ●*vi* fliehen (**from** vor + *dat*) ●*vt* flüchten aus
fleece *n* Vlies *nt* ●*vt* [!] schröpfen
fleet *n* Flotte *f*; (*of cars*) Wagenpark *m*
fleeting *a* flüchtig
Flemish *a* flämisch
flesh *n* Fleisch *nt*
flew *see* **fly**[2]
flex[1] *vt* anspannen <*muscle*>
flex[2] *n* (*Electr*) Schnur *f*

flexib|ility *n* Biegsamkeit *f*; (*fig*) Flexibilität *f*. **~le** *a* biegsam; (*fig*) flexibel
flick *vt* schnippen
flicker *vi* flackern
flier *n* = **flyer**
flight[1] *n* (*fleeing*) Flucht *f*
flight[2] *n* (*flying*) Flug *m*; **~ of stairs** Treppe *f*
flight recorder *n* Flugschreiber *m*
flimsy *a* (**-ier, -iest**) dünn; <*excuse*> fadenscheinig
flinch *vi* zurückzucken
fling *vt* (*pt/pp* **flung**) schleudern
flint *n* Feuerstein *m*
flip *vt/i* schnippen; **~ through** durchblättern
flippant *a*, **-ly** *adv* leichtfertig
flirt *n* kokette Frau *f* ● *vi* flirten
flirtat|ion *n* Flirt *m*. **~ious** *a* kokett
flit *vi* (*pt/pp* **flitted**) flattern
float *n* Schwimmer *m*; (*in procession*) Festwagen *m*; (*money*) Wechselgeld *nt* ● *vi* <*thing:*> schwimmen; <*person:*> sich treiben lassen; (*in air*) schweben
flock *n* Herde *f*; (*of birds*) Schwarm *m* ● *vi* strömen
flog *vt* (*pt/pp* **flogged**) auspeitschen; (🅱 *sell*) verkloppen
flood *n* Überschwemmung *f*; (*fig*) Flut *f* ● *vt* überschwemmen
floodlight *n* Flutlicht *nt* ● *vt* (*pt/pp* **floodlit**) anstrahlen
floor *n* Fußboden *m*; (*storey*) Stock *m*
floor: ~ board *n* Dielenbrett *nt*. **~ polish** *n* Bohnerwachs *nt*. **~ show** *n* Kabarettvorstellung *f*
flop *n* 🅱 (*failure*) Reinfall *m*; (*Theat*) Durchfall *m* ● *vi* (*pt/pp* **flopped**) 🅱 (*fail*) durchfallen
floppy *a* schlapp. **~ disc** *n* Diskette *f*
floral *a* Blumen-
florid *a* <*complexion*> gerötet; <*style*> blumig
florist *n* Blumenhändler(in) *m(f)*
flounder *vi* zappeln
flour *n* Mehl *nt*
flourish *n* große Geste *f*; (*scroll*) Schnörkel *m* ● *vi* gedeihen; (*fig*) blühen ● *vt* schwenken
flout *vt* missachten
flow *n* Fluss *m*; (*of traffic, blood*) Strom *m* ● *vi* fließen
flower *n* Blume *f* ● *vi* blühen
flower: ~-bed *n* Blumenbeet *nt*. **~pot** *n* Blumentopf *m*. **~y** *a* blumig
flown *see* **fly**[2]
flu *n* 🅱 Grippe *f*
fluctuat|e *vi* schwanken. **~ion** *n* Schwankung *f*
fluent *a*, **-ly** *adv* fließend
fluff *n* Fusseln *pl*; (*down*) Flaum *m*. **~y** *a* (**-ier, -iest**) flauschig
fluid *a* flüssig, (*fig*) veränderlich ● *n* Flüssigkeit *f*
fluke *n* [glücklicher] Zufall *m*
flung *see* **fling**
fluorescent *a* fluoreszierend
fluoride *n* Fluor *nt*
flush *n* (*blush*) Erröten *nt* ● *vi* rot werden ● *vt* spülen ● *a* in einer Ebene (**with** mit); (🅱 *affluent*) gut bei Kasse
flustered *a* nervös
flute *n* Flöte *f*
flutter *n* Flattern *nt* ● *vi* flattern
fly[1] *n* (*pl* **flies**) Fliege *f*
fly[2] *v* (*pt* **flew**, *pp* **flown**) ● *vi* fliegen; <*flag:*> wehen; (*rush*) sausen ● *vt* fliegen; führen <*flag*>
fly[3] *n* & **flies** *pl* (*on trousers*) Hosenschlitz *m*
flyer *n* Flieger(in) *m(f)*; (*leaflet*) Flugblatt *nt*
foal *n* Fohlen *nt*
foam *n* Schaum *m*; (*synthetic*) Schaumstoff *m* ● *vi* schäumen

F

fob *vt* (*pt/pp* **fobbed**) ~ **sth off** etw andrehen (**on s.o.** jdm); ~ **s.o. off** jdn abspeisen (**with** mit)
focal *n* Brenn-
focus *n* Brennpunkt *m*; **in** ~ scharf eingestellt ● *v* (*pt/pp* **focused** *or* **focussed**) ● *vt* einstellen (**on auf** + *acc*) ● *vi* (*fig*) sich konzentrieren (**on** auf + *acc*)
fog *n* Nebel *m*
foggy *a* (**foggier, foggiest**) neblig
fog-horn *n* Nebelhorn *nt*
foible *n* Eigenart *f*
foil[1] *n* Folie *f*; (*Culin*) Alufolie *f*
foil[2] *vt* (*thwart*) vereiteln
foil[3] *n* (*Fencing*) Florett *nt*
fold *n* Falte *f*; (*in paper*) Kniff *m* ● *vt* falten; ~ **one's arms** die Arme verschränken ● *vi* sich falten lassen; (*fail*) eingehen. ~ **up** *vt* zusammenfalten; zusammenklappen <*chair*> ● *vi* sich zusammenfalten/-klappen lassen; [!] <*business:*> eingehen
fold|er *n* Mappe *f*. ~**ing** *a* Klapp-
foliage *n* Blätter *pl*; (*of tree*) Laub *nt*
folk *npl* Leute *pl*
folk: ~**-dance** *n* Volkstanz *m*. ~**-song** *n* Volkslied *nt*
follow *vt/i* folgen (+ *dat*); (*pursue*) verfolgen; (*in vehicle*) nachfahren (+ *dat*). ~ **up** *vt* nachgehen (+ *dat*)
follow|er *n* Anhänger(in) *m(f)*. ~**ing** *a* folgend ● *n* Folgende(s) *nt*; (*supporters*) Anhängerschaft *f* ● *prep* im Anschluss an (+ *acc*)
folly *n* Torheit *f*
fond *a* (**-er, -est**), **-ly** *adv* liebevoll; **be** ~ **of** gern haben; gern essen <*food*>
fondle *vt* liebkosen
fondness *n* Liebe *f* (**for** zu)
food *n* Essen *nt*; (*for animals*) Futter *nt*; (*groceries*) Lebensmittel *pl*. ~ **poisoning** *n* Lebensmittelvergiftung *f*
food poisoning *n* Lebensmittelvergiftung *f*
fool[1] *n* (*Culin*) Fruchtcreme *f*
fool[2] *n* Narr *m*; **make a** ~ **of oneself** sich lächerlich machen ● *vt* hereinlegen ● *vi* ~ **around** herumalbern
fool|hardy *a* tollkühn. ~**ish** *a*, **-ly** *adv* dumm. ~**ishness** *n* Dummheit *f*. ~**proof** *a* narrensicher
foot *n* (*pl* **feet**) Fuß *m*; (*measure*) Fuß *m* (*30,48 cm*); (*of bed*) Fußende *nt*; **on** ~ zu Fuß; **on one's feet** auf den Beinen; **put one's** ~ **in it** [!] ins Fettnäpfchen treten
foot: ~**-and-mouth [disease]** *n* Maul-und Klauenseuche *f*. ~**ball** *n* Fußball *m*. ~**baller** *n* Fußballspieler *m*. ~**ball pools** *npl* Fußballtoto *nt*. ~**-bridge** *n* Fußgängerbrücke *f*. ~**hills** *npl* Vorgebirge *nt*. ~**hold** *n* Halt *m*. ~**ing** *n* Halt *m*. ~**lights** *npl* Rampenlicht *nt*. ~**note** *n* Fußnote *f*. ~**path** *n* Fußweg *m*. ~**print** *n* Fußabdruck *m*. ~**step** *n* Schritt *m*; **follow in s.o.'s** ~**steps** (*fig*) in jds Fußstapfen treten. ~**wear** *n* Schuhwerk *nt*

---

for

● *preposition*

····➤ (*on behalf of; in place of; in favour of*) für (+ *acc*). **I did it for you** ich habe es für dich gemacht. **I work for him/for a bank** ich arbeite für ihn/für eine Bank. **be for doing sth** dafür sein, etw zu tun. **cheque/bill for £5** Scheck/Rechnung über 5 Pfund. **for nothing** umsonst.

····➤ (*expressing reason*) wegen (+ *gen*); (*with emotion*) aus. **famous for these wines** berühmt wegen dieser Weine *od* für diese Weine. **he was sentenced to death for murder** er wurde wegen

Mordes zum Tode verurteilt. **were it not for you/your help** ohne dich/deine Hilfe. **for fear/love of** aus Angst vor (+ *dat*)/aus Liebe zu (+ *dat*)

····➤ (*expressing purpose*) (*with action, meal*) zu (+ *dat*); (*with object*) für (+ *acc*). **it's for washing the car** es ist zum Autowaschen. **we met for a discussion** wir trafen uns zu einer Besprechung. **for pleasure** zum Vergnügen. **meat for lunch** Fleisch zum Mittagessen. **what is that for?** wofür *od* wozu ist das? **a dish for nuts** eine Schale für Nüsse

····➤ (*expressing direction*) nach (+ *dat*); (*less precise*) in Richtung. **the train for Oxford** der Zug nach Oxford. **they were heading** *or* **making for London** sie fuhren in Richtung London

····➤ (*expressing time*) (*completed process*) ... lang; (*continuing process*) seit (+ *dat*). **I lived here for two years** ich habe zwei Jahre [lang] hier gewohnt. **I have been living here for two years** ich wohne hier seit zwei Jahren. **we are staying for a week** wir werden eine Woche bleiben

····➤ (*expressing difficulty, impossibility, embarrassment etc.*) + *dat*. **it's impossible/inconvenient for her** es ist ihr unmöglich/ungelegen. **it was embarrassing for our teacher** unserem Lehrer war es peinlich

● *conjunction*

····➤ denn. **he's not coming for he has no money** er kommt nicht mit, denn er hat kein Geld

forbade *see* **forbid**

forbid *vt* (*pt* **forbade**, *pp* **forbidden**) verbieten (**s.o.** jdm). **~ding** *a* bedrohlich; (*stern*) streng

force *n* Kraft *f*; (*of blow*) Wucht *f*; (*violence*) Gewalt *f*; **in ~** gültig; (*in large numbers*) in großer Zahl; **come into ~** in Kraft treten; **the ~s** *pl* die Streitkräfte *pl* ● *vt* zwingen; (*break open*) aufbrechen

forced *a* gezwungen; **~ landing** Notlandung *f*

force: ~-feed *vt* (*pt/pp* **-fed**) zwangsernähren. **~ful** *a*, **-ly** *adv* energisch

forceps *n inv* Zange *f*

forcible *a* gewaltsam

ford *n* Furt *f* ● *vt* durchwaten; (*in vehicle*) durchfahren

fore *a* vordere(r,s)

fore: ~arm *n* Unterarm *m*. **~cast** *n* Voraussage *f*; (*for weather*) Vorhersage *f* ● *vt* (*pt/pp* **~cast**) voraussagen, vorhersagen. **~finger** *n* Zeigefinger *m*. **~gone** *a* **be a ~gone conclusion** von vornherein feststehen. **~ground** *n* Vordergrund *m*. **~head** *n* Stirn *f*. **~hand** *n* Vorhand *f*

foreign *a* ausländisch; <*country*> fremd; **he is ~** er ist Ausländer. **~ currency** *n* Devisen *pl*. **~er** *n* Ausländer(in) *m(f)*. **~ language** *n* Fremdsprache *f*

Foreign: ~ Office *n* ≈ Außenministerium *nt*. **~ Secretary** *n* ≈ Außenminister *m*

fore: ~leg *n* Vorderbein *nt*. **~man** *n* Vorarbeiter *m*. **~most** *a* führend ● *adv* **first and ~most** zuallererst. **~name** *n* Vorname *m*. **~runner** *n* Vorläufer *m*

foresee *vt* (*pt* **-saw**, *pp* **-seen**) voraussehen, vorhersehen. **~able** *a* **in the ~able future** in absehbarer Zeit

foresight *n* Weitblick *m*

forest *n* Wald *m*. **~er** *n* Förster *m*

forestry *n* Forstwirtschaft *f*

foretaste *n* Vorgeschmack *m*

forever *adv* für immer

forewarn *vt* vorher warnen

F

foreword *n* Vorwort *nt*
forfeit *n* (*in game*) Pfand *nt* ● *vt* verwirken
forgave *see* **forgive**
forge *n* Schmiede *f* ● *vt* schmieden; (*counterfeit*) fälschen. **~r** *n* Fälscher *m*. **~ry** *n* Fälschung *f*
forget *vt/i* (*pt* **-got**, *pp* **-gotten**) vergessen; verlernen <*language, skill*>. **~ful** *a* vergesslich. **~fulness** *n* Vergesslichkeit *f*. **~-me-not** *n* Vergissmeinnicht *nt*
forgive *vt* (*pt* **-gave**, *pp* **-given**) **~ s.o. for sth** jdm etw vergeben *od* verzeihen
forgot(ten) *see* **forget**
fork *n* Gabel *f*; (*in road*) Gabelung *f* ● *vi* <*road:*> sich gabeln; **~ right** rechts abzweigen
fork-lift truck *n* Gabelstapler *m*
forlorn *a* verlassen; <*hope*> schwach
form *n* Form *f*; (*document*) Formular *nt*; (*bench*) Bank *f*; (*Sch*) Klasse *f* ● *vt* formen (**into** zu); (*create*) bilden ● *vi* sich bilden; <*idea:*> Gestalt annehmen
formal *a*, **-ly** *adv* formell, förmlich. **~ity** *n* Förmlichkeit *f*; (*requirement*) Formalität *f*
format *n* Format *nt* ● *vt* formatieren
formation *n* Formation *f*
former *a* ehemalig; **the ~** der/die/das Erstere. **~ly** *adv* früher
formidable *a* gewaltig
formula *n* (*pl* **-ae** *or* **-s**) Formel *f*
formulate *vt* formulieren
forsake *vt* (*pt* **-sook**, *pp* **-saken**) verlassen
fort *n* (*Mil*) Fort *nt*
forth *adv* **back and ~** hin und her; **and so ~** und so weiter
forth: ~coming *a* bevorstehend; (▣ *communicative*) mitteilsam. **~right** *a* direkt
fortieth *a* vierzigste(r,s)
fortification *n* Befestigung *f*
fortify *vt* (*pt/pp* **-ied**) befestigen; (*fig*) stärken
fortnight *n* vierzehn Tage *pl*. **~ly** *a* vierzehntäglich ● *adv* alle vierzehn Tage
fortress *n* Festung *f*
fortunate *a* glücklich; **be ~** Glück haben. **~ly** *adv* glüklicherweise
fortune *n* Glück *nt*; (*money*) Vermögen *nt*. **~-teller** *n* Wahrsagerin *f*
forty *a* vierzig
forward *adv* vorwärts; (*to the front*) nach vorn ● *a* Vorwärts-; (*presumptuous*) anmaßend ● *n* (*Sport*) Stürmer *m* ● *vt* nachsenden <*letter*>. **~s** *adv* vorwärts
fossil *n* Fossil *nt*
foster *vt* fördern; in Pflege nehmen <*child*>. **~-child** *n* Pflegekind *nt*. **~-mother** *n* Pflegemutter *f*
fought *see* **fight**
foul *a* (**-er, -est**) widerlich; <*language*> unflätig; **~ play** (*Jur*) Mord *m* ● *n* (*Sport*) Foul *nt* ● *vt* verschmutzen; (*obstruct*) blockieren; (*Sport*) foulen
found[1] *see* **find**
found[2] *vt* gründen
foundation *n* (*basis*) Gundlage *f*; (*charitable*) Stiftung *f*; **~s** *pl* Fundament *nt*
founder *n* Gründer(in) *m(f)*
foundry *n* Gießerei *f*
fountain *n* Brunnen *m*
four *a* vier ● *n* Vier *f*
four: ~teen *a* vierzehn ● *n* Vierzehn *f*. **~teenth** *a* vierzehnte(r,s)
fourth *a* vierte(r,s)
fowl *n* Geflügel *nt*
fox *n* Fuchs *m* ● *vt* (*puzzle*) verblüffen
foyer *n* Foyer *nt*; (*in hotel*) Empfangshalle *f*

fraction *n* Bruchteil *m*; (*Math*) Bruch *m*

fracture *n* Bruch *m* ● *vt/i* brechen

fragile *a* zerbrechlich

fragment *n* Bruchstück *nt*, Fragment *nt*

fragran|ce *n* Duft *m*. **~t** *a* duftend

frail *a* (**-er, -est**) gebrechlich

frame *n* Rahmen *m*; (*of spectacles*) Gestell *nt*; (*Anat*) Körperbau *m* ● *vt* einrahmen; (*fig*) formulieren; ⊠ ein Verbrechen anhängen (+ *dat*). **~work** *n* Gerüst *nt*; (*fig*) Gerippe *nt*

franc *n* (*French, Belgian*) Franc *m*; (*Swiss*) Franken *m*

France *n* Frankreich *nt*

franchise *n* (*Pol*) Wahlrecht *nt*; (*Comm*) Franchise *nt*

frank *a*, **-ly** *adv* offen

frankfurter *n* Frankfurter *f*

frantic *a*, **-ally** *adv* verzweifelt; außer sich (*dat*) (**with** vor)

fraternal *a* brüderlich

fraud *n* Betrug *m*; (*person*) Betrüger(in) *m(f)*

fray *vi* ausfransen

freak *n* Missbildung *f*; (*person*) Missgeburt *f* ● *a* anormal

freckle *n* Sommersprosse *f*

free *a* (**freer, freest**) frei; <*ticket, copy, time*> Frei-; (*lavish*) freigebig; **~ [of charge]** kostenlos; **set ~** freilassen; (*rescue*) befreien ● *vt* (*pt/pp* **freed**) freilassen; (*rescue*) befreien; (*disentangle*) freibekommen

free: ~dom *n* Freiheit *f*. **~hold** *n* [freier] Grundbesitz *m*. **~lance** *a* & *adv* freiberuflich. **~ly** *adv* frei; (*voluntarily*) freiwillig; (*generously*) großzügig. **F~mason** *n* Freimaurer *m*. **~-range** *a* **~-range eggs** Landeier *pl*. **~ sample** *n* Gratisprobe *f*. **~style** *n* Freistil *m*. **~way** *n* (*Amer*) Autobahn *f*

freez|e *vt* (*pt* **froze**, *pp* **frozen**) einfrieren; stoppen <*wages*> ● *vi* **it's ~ing** es friert. **~er** *n* Gefriertruhe *f*; (*upright*) Gefrierschrank *m*. **~ing** *a* eiskalt ● *n* **below ~ing** unter Null

freight *n* Fracht *f*. **~er** *n* Frachter *m*. **~ train** *n* Güterzug *m*

French *a* französisch ● *n* (*Lang*) Französisch *nt*; **the ~** *pl* die Franzosen

French: ~ beans *npl* grüne Bohnen *pl*. **~ bread** *n* Stangenbrot *nt*. **~ fries** *npl* Pommes frites *pl*. **~man** *n* Franzose *m*. **~ window** *n* Terrassentür *f*. **~woman** *n* Französin *f*

frenzy *n* Raserei *f*

frequency *n* Häufigkeit *f*; (*Phys*) Frequenz *f*

frequent[1] *a*, **-ly** *adv* häufig

frequent[2] *vt* regelmäßig besuchen

fresh *a* (**-er, -est**), **-ly** *adv* frisch; (*new*) neu; (*cheeky*) frech

freshness *n* Frische *f*

freshwater *a* Süßwasser-

fret *vi* (*pt/pp* **fretted**) sich grämen. **~ful** *a* weinerlich

fretsaw *n* Laubsäge *f*

friction *n* Reibung *f*; (*fig*) Reibereien *pl*

Friday *n* Freitag *m*

fridge *n* Kühlschrank *m*

fried *see* **fry**[2] ● *a* gebraten; **~ egg** Spiegelei *nt*

friend *n* Freund(in) *m(f)*. **~liness** *n* Freundlichkeit *f*. **~ly** *a* (**-ier, -iest**) freundlich; **~ly with** befreundet mit. **~ship** *n* Freundschaft *f*

fright *n* Schreck *m*

frighten *vt* Angst machen (+ *dat*); (*startle*) erschrecken; **be ~ed** Angst haben (**of** vor + *dat*). **~ing** *a* Angst erregend

frightful *a*, **-ly** *adv* schrecklich

frigid *a* frostig; (*Psych*) frigide. **~ity** *n* Frostigkeit *f*; Frigidität *f*

frill *n* Rüsche *f*; (*paper*) Manschette *f*. **~y** *a* rüschenbesetzt

fringe *n* Fransen *pl*; (*of hair*) Pony *m*; (*fig: edge*) Rand *m*

frisk *vi* herumspringen ● *vt* (*search*) durchsuchen

frisky *a* (**-ier, -iest**) lebhaft

fritter *vt* ~ **[away]** verplempern [!]

frivol|ity *n* Frivolität *f*. **~ous** *a*, **-ly** *adv* frivol, leichtfertig

fro *see* **to**

frock *n* Kleid *nt*

frog *n* Frosch *m*. **~man** *n* Froschmann *m*

frolic *vi* (*pt/pp* **frolicked**) herumtollen

from *prep* von (+ *dat*); (*out of*) aus (+ *dat*); (*according to*) nach (+ *dat*); ~ **Monday** ab Montag; ~ **that day** seit dem Tag

front *n* Vorderseite *f*; (*fig*) Fassade *f*; (*of garment*) Vorderteil *nt*; (*sea~*) Strandpromenade *f*; (*Mil, Pol, Meteorol*) Front *f*; **in** ~ **of** vor; **in** or **at the** ~ vorne; **to the** ~ nach vorne ● *a* vordere(r,s); <*page, row*> erste(r,s); <*tooth, wheel*> Vorder-

front: ~ **door** *n* Haustür *f*. ~ **garden** *n* Vorgarten *m*

frontier *n* Grenze *f*

frost *n* Frost *m*; (*hoar-~*) Raureif *m*; **ten degrees of** ~ zehn Grad Kälte. **~bite** *n* Erfrierung *f*. **~bitten** *a* erfroren

frost|ed *a* **~ed glass** Mattglas *nt*. **~ing** *n* (*Amer Culin*) Zuckerguss *m*. **~y** *a*, **-ily** *adv* frostig

froth *n* Schaum *m* ● *vi* schäumen. **~y** *a* schaumig

frown *n* Stirnrunzeln *nt* ● *vi* die Stirn runzeln

froze *see* **freeze**

frozen *see* **freeze** ● *a* gefroren; (*Culin*) tiefgekühlt; **I'm** ~ [!] mir ist eiskalt. ~ **food** *n* Tiefkühlkost *f*

frugal *a*, **-ly** *adv* sparsam; <*meal*> frugal

fruit *n* Frucht *f*; (*collectively*) Obst *nt*. ~ **cake** *n* englischer [Tee]kuchen *m*

fruitful *a* fruchtbar

fruit: ~ **juice** *n* Obstsaft *m*. **~less** *a*, **-ly** *adv* fruchtlos. ~ **salad** *n* Obstsalat *m*

fruity *a* fruchtig

frustrat|e *vt* vereiteln; (*Psych*) frustrieren. **~ion** *n* Frustration *f*

fry *vt/i* (*pt/pp* **fried**) [in der Pfanne] braten. **~ing-pan** *n* Bratpfanne *f*

fuel *n* Brennstoff *m*; (*for car*) Kraftstoff *m*; (*for aircraft*) Treibstoff *m*

fugitive *n* Flüchtling *m*

fulfil *vt* (*pt/pp* **-filled**) erfüllen. **~ment** *n* Erfüllung *f*

full *a & adv* (**-er, -est**) voll; (*detailed*) ausführlich; <*skirt*> weit; ~ **of** voll von (+ *dat*), voller (+ *gen*); **at** ~ **speed** in voller Fahrt ● *n* **in** ~ vollständig

full: ~ **moon** *n* Vollmond *m*. **~-scale** *a* <*model*> in Originalgröße; <*rescue, alert*> großangelegt. ~ **stop** *n* Punkt *m*. **~-time** *a* ganztägig ● *adv* ganztags

fully *adv* völlig; (*in detail*) ausführlich

fumble *vi* herumfummeln (**with** an + *dat*)

fume *vi* vor Wut schäumen

fumes *npl* Dämpfe *pl*; (*from car*) Abgase *pl*

fun *n* Spaß *m*; **for** ~ aus *od* zum Spaß; **make** ~ **of** sich lustig machen über (+ *acc*); **have** ~**!** viel Spaß!

function *n* Funktion *f*; (*event*) Veranstaltung *f* ● *vi* funktionieren; (*serve*) dienen (**as** als). **~al** *a* zweckmäßig

fund *n* Fonds *m*; (*fig*) Vorrat *m*; **~s** *pl* Geldmittel *pl* ● *vt* finanzieren
fundamental *a* grundlegend; (*essential*) wesentlich
funeral *n* Beerdigung *f*; (*cremation*) Feuerbestattung *f*
funeral: ~ march *n* Trauermarsch *m*. **~ service** *n* Trauergottesdienst *m*
funfair *n* Jahrmarkt *m*
fungus *n* (*pl* **-gi**) Pilz *m*
funnel *n* Trichter *m*; (*on ship, train*) Schornstein *m*
funnily *adv* komisch; **~ enough** komischerweise
funny *a* (**-ier, -iest**) komisch
fur *n* Fell *nt*; (*for clothing*) Pelz *m*; (*in kettle*) Kesselstein *m*. **~ coat** *n* Pelzmantel *m*
furious *a*, **-ly** *adv* wütend (**with auf** + *acc*)
furnace *n* (*Techn*) Ofen *m*
furnish *vt* einrichten; (*supply*) liefern. **~ed** *a* **~ed room** möbliertes Zimmer *nt*. **~ings** *npl* Einrichtungsgegenstände *pl*
furniture *n* Möbel *pl*
further *a* weitere(r,s); **at the ~ end** am anderen Ende; **until ~ notice** bis auf weiteres ● *adv* weiter; **~ off** weiter entfernt ● *vt* fördern
furthest *a* am weitesten entfernt ● *adv* am weitesten
fury *n* Wut *f*
fuse[1] *n* (*of bomb*) Zünder *m*; (*cord*) Zündschnur *f*
fuse[2] *n* (*Electr*) Sicherung *f* ● *vt/i* verschmelzen; **the lights have ~d** die Sicherung [für das Licht] ist durchgebrannt. **~-box** *n* Sicherungskasten *m*
fuselage *n* (*Aviat*) Rumpf *m*
fuss *n* Getue *nt*; **make a ~ of** verwöhnen; (*caress*) liebkosen ● *vi* Umstände machen
fussy *a* (**-ier, -iest**) wählerisch; (*particular*) penibel
futil|e *a* zwecklos. **~ity** *n* Zwecklosigkeit *f*
future *a* zukünftig ● *n* Zukunft *f*; (*Gram*) [erstes] Futur *nt*
futuristic *a* futuristisch
fuzzy *a* (**-ier, -iest**) <*hair*> kraus; (*blurred*) verschwommen

Gg

gabble *vi* schnell reden
gable *n* Giebel *m*
gadget *n* [kleines] Gerät *nt*
Gaelic *n* Gälisch *nt*
gag *n* Knebel *m*; (*joke*) Witz *m*; (*Theat*) Gag *m* ● *vt* (*pt/pp* **gagged**) knebeln
gaiety *n* Fröhlichkeit *f*
gaily *adv* fröhlich
gain *n* Gewinn *m*; (*increase*) Zunahme *f* ● *vt* gewinnen; (*obtain*) erlangen; **~ weight** zunehmen ● *vi* <*clock:*> vorgehen
gait *n* Gang *m*
gala *n* Fest *nt* ● *attrib* Gala-
galaxy *n* Galaxie *f*; **the G~** die Milchstraße
gale *n* Sturm *m*
gallant *a*, **-ly** *adv* tapfer; (*chivalrous*) galant. **~ry** *n* Tapferkeit *f*
gall-bladder *n* Gallenblase *f*
gallery *n* Galerie *f*
galley *n* (*ship's kitchen*) Kombüse *f*; **~ [proof]** [Druck]fahne *f*
gallon *n* Gallone *f* (= *4,5 l*; *Amer* = *3,785 l*)
gallop *n* Galopp *m* ● *vi* galoppieren
gallows *n* Galgen *m*
galore *adv* in Hülle und Fülle

gamble *n* (*risk*) Risiko *nt* ● *vi* [um Geld] spielen; **~ on** (*rely*) sich verlassen auf (+ *acc*). **~r** *n* Spieler(in) *m*(*f*)

game *n* Spiel *nt*; (*animals, birds*) Wild *nt*; **~s** (*Sch*) Sport *m* ● *a* (*brave*) tapfer; (*willing*) bereit (**for** zu). **~keeper** *n* Wildhüter *m*. **~s console** *n* Spielkonsole *f*

gammon *n* [geräucherter] Schinken *m*

gang *n* Bande *f*; (*of workmen*) Kolonne *f*

gangling *a* schlaksig

gangrene *n* Wundbrand *m*

gangster *n* Gangster *m*

gangway *n* Gang *m*; (*Naut, Aviat*) Gangway *f*

gaol *n* Gefängnis *nt* ● *vt* ins Gefängnis sperren. **~er** *n* Gefängniswärter *m*

gap *n* Lücke *f*; (*interval*) Pause *f*; (*difference*) Unterschied *m*

gap|e *vi* gaffen; **~e at** anstarren. **~ing** *a* klaffend

garage *n* Garage *f*; (*for repairs*) Werkstatt *f*; (*for petrol*) Tankstelle *f*

garbage *n* Müll *m*. **~ can** *n* (*Amer*) Mülleimer *m*

garbled *a* verworren

garden *n* Garten *m*; **[public] ~s** *pl* [öffentliche] Anlagen *pl* ● *vi* im Garten arbeiten. **~er** *n* Gärtner(in) *m*(*f*). **~ing** *n* Gartenarbeit *f*

gargle *n* (*liquid*) Gurgelwasser *nt* ● *vi* gurgeln

garish *a* grell

garland *n* Girlande *f*

garlic *n* Knoblauch *m*

garment *n* Kleidungsstück *nt*

garnish *n* Garnierung *f* ● *vt* garnieren

garrison *n* Garnison *f*

garter *n* Strumpfband *nt*; (*Amer*: *suspender*) Strumpfhalter *m*

gas *n* Gas *nt*; (*Amer* [!]: *petrol*) Benzin *nt* ● *v* (*pt*/*pp* **gassed**) ● *vt* vergasen ● *vi* [!] schwatzen. **~ cooker** *n* Gasherd *m*. **~ fire** *n* Gasofen *m*

gash *n* Schnitt *m*; (*wound*) klaffende Wunde *f*

gasket *n* (*Techn*) Dichtung *f*

gas: ~ mask *n* Gasmaske *f*. **~-meter** *n* Gaszähler *m*

gasoline *n* (*Amer*) Benzin *nt*

gasp *vi* keuchen; (*in surprise*) hörbar die Luft einziehen

gas station *n* (*Amer*) Tankstelle *f*

gastric *a* Magen-

gastronomy *n* Gastronomie *f*

gate *n* Tor *nt*; (*to field*) Gatter *nt*; (*barrier*) Schranke *f*; (*at airport*) Flugsteig *m*

gate: ~crasher *n* ungeladener Gast *m*. **~way** *n* Tor *nt*

gather *vt* sammeln; (*pick*) pflücken; (*conclude*) folgern (**from** aus) ● *vi* sich versammeln; <*storm*:> sich zusammenziehen. **~ing** *n* **family ~ing** Familientreffen *nt*

gaudy *a* (**-ier, -iest**) knallig

gauge *n* Stärke *f*; (*Rail*) Spurweite *f*; (*device*) Messinstrument *nt*

gaunt *a* hager

gauze *n* Gaze *f*

gave *see* **give**

gay *a* (**-er, -est**) fröhlich; [!] homosexuell, [!] schwul

gaze *n* [langer] Blick *m* ● *vi* sehen; **~ at** ansehen

GB *abbr of* **Great Britain**

gear *n* Ausrüstung *f*; (*Techn*) Getriebe *nt*; (*Auto*) Gang *m*; **change ~** schalten

gear: ~box *n* (*Auto*) Getriebe *nt*. **~-lever** *n*, (*Amer*) **~-shift** *n* Schalthebel *m*

geese *see* **goose**

gel *n* Gel *nt*

gelatine *n* Gelatine *f*

gem *n* Juwel *nt*

gender *n* (*Gram*) Geschlecht *nt*

gene *n* Gen *nt*

genealogy *n* Genealogie *f*

general *a* allgemein ● *n* General *m*; **in ~** im Allgemeinen. **~ election** *n* allgemeine Wahlen *pl*
generaliz|ation *n* Verallgemeinerung *f*. **~e** *vi* verallgemeinern
generally *adv* im Allgemeinen
general practitioner *n* praktischer Arzt *m*
generate *vt* erzeugen
generation *n* Generation *f*
generator *n* Generator *m*
generosity *n* Großzügigkeit *f*
generous *a*, **-ly** *adv* großzügig
genetic *a*, **~ally** *adv* genetisch. **~ally modified** gentechnisch verändert, genmanipuliert. **~ engineering** *n* Gentechnologie *f*
Geneva *n* Genf *nt*
genial *a*, **-ly** *adv* freundlich
genitals *pl* [äußere] Geschlechtsteile *pl*
genitive *a & n* **~ [case]** Genitiv *m*
genius *n* (*pl* **-uses**) Genie *nt*; (*quality*) Genialität *f*
genome *n* Genom *nt*
genre *n* Gattung *f*, Genre *nt*
gent *n* ! Herr *m*; **the ~s** *sg* die Herrentoilette *f*
genteel *a* vornehm
gentle *a* (**-r, -st**) sanft
gentleman *n* Herr *m*; (*well-mannered*) Gentleman *m*
gent|leness *n* Sanftheit *f*. **~ly** *adv* sanft
genuine *a* echt; (*sincere*) aufrichtig. **~ly** *adv* (*honestly*) ehrlich
geograph|ical *a*, **-ly** *adv* geographisch. **~y** *n* Geographie *f*, Erdkunde *f*
geological *a*, **-ly** *adv* geologisch
geolog|ist *n* Geologe *m*/-gin *f*. **~y** *n* Geologie *f*
geometr|ic(al) *a* geometrisch. **~y** *n* Geometrie *f*
geranium *n* Geranie *f*
geriatric *a* geriatrisch ● *n* geriatrischer Patient *m*
germ *n* Keim *m*; **~s** *pl* ! Bazillen *pl*
German *a* deutsch ● *n* (*person*) Deutsche(r) *m*/*f*; (*Lang*) Deutsch *nt*; **in ~** auf Deutsch; **into ~** ins Deutsche
Germanic *a* germanisch
Germany *n* Deutschland *nt*
germinate *vi* keimen
gesticulate *vi* gestikulieren
gesture *n* Geste *f*

get *v*
pt **got**, *pp* **got** (*Amer also* **gotten**), *pres p* **getting**

● *transitive verb*
- (*obtain, receive*) bekommen, ! kriegen; (*procure*) besorgen; (*buy*) kaufen; (*fetch*) holen. **get a job/taxi for s.o.** jdm einen Job verschaffen/ein Taxi besorgen. **I must get some bread** ich muss Brot holen. **get permission** die Erlaubnis erhalten. **I couldn't get her on the phone** ich konnte sie nicht telefonisch erreichen
- (*prepare*) machen <*meal*>. **he got the breakfast** er machte das Frühstück
- (*cause*) **get s.o. to do sth** jdn dazu bringen, etw zu tun. **get one's hair cut** sich (*dat*) die Haare schneiden lassen. **get one's hands dirty** sich (*dat*) die Hände schmutzig machen
- **get the bus/train** (*travel by*) den Bus/Zug nehmen; (*be in time for, catch*) den Bus/Zug erreichen
- **have got** (! *have*) haben. **I've got a cold** ich habe eine Erkältung
- **have got to do sth** etw tun müssen. **I've got to hurry** ich muss mich beeilen
- (! *understand*) kapieren !. **I don't get it** ich kapiere nicht

● *intransitive verb*

G

····➤ (*become*) werden. **get older** älter werden. **the weather got worse** das Wetter wurde schlechter. **get to** kommen zu/nach <*town*>; (*reach*) erreichen. **get dressed** sich anziehen. **get married** heiraten.

● *phrasal verbs*

● **get about** *vi* (*move*) sich bewegen; (*travel*) herumkommen; (*spread*) sich verbreiten. ● **get at** *vt* (*have access*) herankommen an (+ *acc*); ([!] *criticize*) anmachen [!]. (*mean*) **what are you getting at?** worauf willst du hinaus? ● **get away** *vi* (*leave*) wegkommen; (*escape*) entkommen. ● **get back** *vi* zurückkommen; *vt* (*recover*) zurückbekommen; **get one's own back** sich revanchieren. ● **get by** *vi* vorbeikommen; (*manage*) sein Auskommen haben. ● **get down** *vi* heruntersteigen; **get down to** sich [heran]machen an (+ *acc*); *vt* (*depress*) deprimieren. ● **get in** *vi* (*into bus*) einsteigen; *vt* (*fetch*) hereinholen. ● **get off** *vi* (*dismount*) absteigen; (*from bus*) aussteigen; (*leave*) wegkommen; (*Jur*) freigesprochen werden; *vt* (*remove*) abbekommen. ● **get on** *vi* (*mount*) aufsteigen; (*to bus*) einsteigen; (*be on good terms*) gut auskommen (**with** mit + *dat*); (*make progress*) Fortschritte machen; **how are you getting on?** wie geht's? ● **get out** *vi* herauskommen; (*of car*) aussteigen; **get out of** (*avoid doing*) sich drücken um; *vt* (*take out*) herausholen; herausbekommen <*cork, stain*>. ● **get over** *vi* hinübersteigen; *vt* (*fig*) hinwegkommen über (+ *acc*). ● **get round** *vi* herumkommen; **I never get round to it** ich komme nie dazu; *vt* herumkriegen; (*avoid*) umgehen. ● **get through** *vi* durchkommen. ● **get up** *vi* aufstehen

get: ~away *n* Flucht *f*. **~-up** *n* Aufmachung *f*

ghastly *a* (**-ier, -iest**) grässlich; (*pale*) blass

gherkin *n* Essiggurke *f*

ghost *n* Geist *m*, Gespenst *nt*. **~ly** *a* geisterhaft

ghoulish *a* makaber

giant *n* Riese *m* ● *a* riesig

gibberish *n* Kauderwelsch *nt*

giblets *npl* Geflügelklein *nt*

giddiness *n* Schwindel *m*

giddy *a* (**-ier, -iest**) schwindlig

gift *n* Geschenk *nt*; (*to charity*) Gabe *f*; (*talent*) Begabung *f*. **~ed** *a* begabt

gigantic *a* riesig, riesengroß

giggle *n* Kichern *nt* ● *vi* kichern

gild *vt* vergolden

gilt *a* vergoldet ● *n* Vergoldung *f*. **~-edged** *a* (*Comm*) mündelsicher

gimmick *n* Trick *m*

gin *n* Gin *m*

ginger *a* rotblond; <*cat*> rot ● *n* Ingwer *m*. **~bread** *n* Pfefferkuchen *m*

gingerly *adv* vorsichtig

gipsy *n* = **gypsy**

giraffe *n* Giraffe *f*

girder *n* (*Techn*) Träger *m*

girl *n* Mädchen *nt*; (*young woman*) junge Frau *f*. **~friend** *n* Freundin *f*. **~ish** *a*, **-ly** *adv* mädchenhaft

gist *n* **the ~** das Wesentliche

give *n* Elastizität *f* ● *v* (*pt* **gave**, *pp* **given**) ● *vt* geben/(*as present*) schenken (**to** *dat*); (*donate*) spenden; <*lecture*> halten; <*one's name*> angeben ● *vi* geben; (*yield*) nachgeben. **~ away** *vt* verschenken; (*betray*) verraten; (*distribute*) verteilen. **~ back** *vt* zurückgeben. ~ **in** *vt* einreichen ● *vi* (*yield*) nachgeben. ~ **off** *vt* abgeben. ~ **up** *vt/i* aufgeben; ~ **oneself up** sich stellen. ~ **way** *vi* nachgeben; (*Auto*) die Vorfahrt beachten

glacier *n* Gletscher *m*

glad *a* froh (**of** über + *acc*)

gladly *adv* gern[e]

glamorous *a* glanzvoll; <*film star*> glamourös

glamour *n* [betörender] Glanz *m*

glance *n* [flüchtiger] Blick *m* ● *vi* ~ **at** einen Blick werfen auf (+ *acc*). ~ **up** *vi* aufblicken

gland *n* Drüse *f*

glare *n* grelles Licht *nt*; (*look*) ärgerlicher Blick *m* ● *vi* ~ **at** böse ansehen

glaring *a* grell; <*mistake*> krass

glass *n* Glas *nt*; (*mirror*) Spiegel *m*; ~**es** *pl* (*spectacles*) Brille *f*. ~**y** *a* glasig

glaze *n* Glasur *f*

gleam *n* Schein *m* ● *vi* glänzen

glib *a*, **-ly** *adv* (*pej*) gewandt

glid|e *vi* gleiten; (*through the air*) schweben. ~**er** *n* Segelflugzeug *nt*. ~**ing** *n* Segelfliegen *nt*

glimmer *n* Glimmen *nt* ● *vi* glimmen

glimpse *vt* flüchtig sehen

glint *n* Blitzen *nt* ● *vi* blitzen

glisten *vi* glitzern

glitter *vi* glitzern

global *a*, **-ly** *adv* global

globaliz|e *vt* globalisieren. ~**ation** *n* Globalisierung *f*

globe *n* Kugel *f*; (*map*) Globus *m*

gloom *n* Düsterkeit *f*; (*fig*) Pessimismus *m*

gloomy *a* (**-ier, -iest**), **-ily** *adv* düster; (*fig*) pessimistisch

glorify *vt* (*pt/pp* **-ied**) verherrlichen

glorious *a* herrlich; <*deed, hero*> glorreich

glory *n* Ruhm *m*; (*splendour*) Pracht *f* ● *vi* ~ **in** genießen

gloss *n* Glanz *m* ● *a* Glanz- ● *vi* ~ **over** beschönigen

glossary *n* Glossar *nt*

glossy *a* (**-ier, -iest**) glänzend

glove *n* Handschuh *m*

glow *n* Glut *f*; (*of candle*) Schein *m* ● *vi* glühen; <*candle:*> scheinen. ~**ing** *a* glühend; <*account*> begeistert

glucose *n* Traubenzucker *m*, Glukose *f*

glue *n* Klebstoff *m* ● *vt* (*pres p* **gluing**) kleben (**to** an + *acc*)

glum *a* (**glummer, glummest**), **-ly** *adv* niedergeschlagen

glut *n* Überfluss *m* (**of** an + *dat*)

glutton *n* Vielfraß *m*

GM *abbr* (**genetically modified**); ~ **crops/food** gentechnisch veränderte Feldfrüchte/ Nahrungsmittel

gnash *vt* ~ **one's teeth** mit den Zähnen knirschen

gnat *n* Mücke *f*

gnaw *vt/i* nagen (**at** an + *dat*)

go

3 sg pres tense **goes**; *pt* **went**; *pp* **gone**

● *intransitive verb*

····➤ gehen; (*in vehicle*) fahren. **go by air** fliegen. **where are you going?** wo gehst du hin? **I'm going to France** ich fahre nach Frankreich. **go to the doctor's/ dentist's** zum Arzt/Zahnarzt gehen. **go to the theatre/cinema** ins Theater/Kino gehen. **I must go to Paris/to the doctor's** ich muss nach Paris/zum Arzt. **go shopping** einkaufen gehen. **go swimming** schwimmen gehen. **go to see s.o.** jdn besuchen [gehen]

····➤ (*leave*) weggehen; (*on journey*) abfahren. **I must go now** ich muss jetzt gehen. **we're going on Friday** wir fahren am Freitag

····➤ (*work, function*) <*engine, clock*> gehen

····➤ (*become*) werden. **go deaf** taub werden. **go mad** verrückt werden. **he went red** er wurde rot

····➤ (*pass*) <*time*> vergehen

····➤ (*disappear*) weggehen; <*coat, hat, stain*> verschwinden. **my headache/my coat/the stain has gone** mein Kopfweh/mein Mantel/der Fleck ist weg

····➤ (*turn out, progress*) gehen; verlaufen. **everything's going very well** alles geht *od* verläuft sehr gut. **how did the party go?** wie war die Party? **go smoothly/according to plan** reibungslos/planmäßig verlaufen

····➤ (*match*) zusammenpassen. **the two colours don't go [together]** die beiden Farben passen nicht zusammen

····➤ (*cease to function*) kaputtgehen; <*fuse*> durchbrennen. **his memory is going** sein Gedächtnis lässt nach

● *auxiliary verb*

····➤ **be going to** werden + *inf*. **it's going to rain** es wird regnen. **I'm not going to** ich werde es nicht tun

● *noun*
pl **goes**

····➤ (*turn*) **it's your go** du bist jetzt an der Reihe *od* dran

····➤ (*attempt*) Versuch. **have a go at doing sth** versuchen, etw zu tun. **have another go!** versuch's noch mal!

····➤ (*energy, drive*) Energie

····➤ (*in phrases*) **on the go** auf Trab. **make a go of sth** das Beste aus etw machen

● *phrasal verbs*

● **go across** *vi* hinübergehen/-fahren; *vt* überqueren. ● **go after** *vt* (*pursue*) jagen. ● **go away** *vi* weggehen/-fahren; (*on holiday or business*) verreisen. ● **go back** *vi* zurückgehen/-fahren. ● **go back on** *vt* nicht [ein]halten <*promise*>. ● **go by** *vi* vorbeigehen/-fahren; <*time*> vergehen. ● **go down** *vi* hinuntergehen/-fahren; <*sun, ship*> untergehen; <*prices*> fallen; <*temperature, swelling*> zurückgehen. ● **go for** *vt* holen; ([!] *attack*) losgehen auf (+ *acc*). ● **go in** *vi* hineingehen/-fahren; ● **go in for** *vt* teilnehmen an (+ *dat*) <*competition*>; (*take up*) sich verlegen auf (+ *acc*). ● **go off** *vi* weggehen/-fahren; <*alarm clock*> klingeln; <*alarm, gun, bomb*> losgehen; <*light*> ausgehen; (*go bad*) schlecht werden; **go off well** gut verlaufen; *vt*: **go off sth** von etw abkommen. ● **go on** *vi* weitergehen/-fahren; <*light*> angehen; (*continue*) weitermachen; (*talking*) fortfahren; (*happen*) vorgehen. ● **go on at** *vt* [!] herumnörgeln an (+ *dat*). ● **go out** *vi* (*from home*) ausgehen; (*leave*) hinausgehen/-fahren; <*fire, light*> ausgehen; **go out to work/for a meal** arbeiten/essen gehen; **go out with s.o.** ([!] *date s.o.*) mit jdm gehen [!]. ● **go over** *vi* hinübergehen/-fahren; *vt* (*rehearse*) durchgehen. ● **go round** *vi* herumgehen/-fahren; (*visit*) vorbeigehen; (*turn*) sich drehen; (*be enough*) reichen. ● **go through** *vi* durchgehen/-fahren; *vt* (*suffer*) durchmachen; (*rehearse*) durchgehen; <*bags*> durchsuchen. ● **go through with** *vt* zu Ende machen. ● **go under** *vi* untergehen/-fahren; (*fail*) scheitern. ● **go up** *vi* hinaufgehen/-fahren; <*lift*> hochfahren; <*prices*> steigen. ● **go without** *vt*: **go without sth** auf etw (*acc*) verzichten; *vi* darauf verzichten

go-ahead *a* fortschrittlich; (*enterprising*) unternehmend ●*n* (*fig*) grünes Licht *nt*
goal *n* Ziel *nt*; (*sport*) Tor *nt*. **~keeper** *n* Torwart *m*. **~-post** *n* Torpfosten *m*
goat *n* Ziege *f*
gobble *vt* hinunterschlingen
God, god *n* Gott *m*
god: ~child *n* Patenkind *nt*. **~-daughter** *n* Patentochter *f*. **~dess** *n* Göttin *f*. **~father** *n* Pate *m*. **~mother** *n* Patin *f*. **~parents** *npl* Paten *pl*. **~send** *n* Segen *m*. **~son** *n* Patensohn *m*
goggles *npl* Schutzbrille *f*
going *a* <*price, rate*> gängig; <*concern*> gut gehend ●*n* **it is hard ~** es ist schwierig
gold *n* Gold *nt* ●*a* golden
golden *a* golden. **~ wedding** *n* goldene Hochzeit *f*
gold: ~fish *n inv* Goldfisch *m*. **~-mine** *n* Goldgrube *f*. **~-plated** *a* vergoldet. **~smith** *n* Goldschmied *m*
golf *n* Golf *nt*
golf: ~-club *n* Golfklub *m*; (*implement*) Golfschläger *m*. **~-course** *n* Golfplatz *m*. **~er** *m* Golfspieler(in) *m(f)*
gone *see* **go**
good *a* (**better, best**) gut; (*well-behaved*) brav, artig; **~ at** gut in (+ *dat*); **a ~ deal** ziemlich viel; **~ morning/evening** guten Morgen/Abend ●*n* **for ~** für immer; **do ~** Gutes tun; **do s.o. ~** jdm gut tun; **it's no ~** es ist nutzlos; (*hopeless*) da ist nichts zu machen
goodbye *int* auf Wiedersehen; (*Teleph, Radio*) auf Wiederhören
good: G~ Friday *n* Karfreitag *m*. **~-looking** *a* gut aussehend. **~-natured** *a* gutmütig
goodness *n* Güte *f*; **thank ~!** Gott sei Dank!
goods *npl* Waren *pl*. **~ train** *n* Güterzug *m*
goodwill *n* Wohlwollen *nt*; (*Comm*) Goodwill *m*
gooey *a* [!] klebrig
goose *n* (*pl* **geese**) Gans *f*
gooseberry *n* Stachelbeere *f*
goose: ~-flesh *n*, **~-pimples** *npl* Gänsehaut *f*
gorge *n* (*Geog*) Schlucht *f* ●*vt* **~ oneself** sich vollessen
gorgeous *a* prachtvoll; [!] herrlich
gorilla *n* Gorilla *m*
gormless *a* [!] doof
gorse *n inv* Stechginster *m*
gory *a* (**-ier, -iest**) blutig; <*story*> blutrünstig
gosh *int* [!] Mensch!
gospel *n* Evangelium *nt*
gossip *n* Klatsch *m*; (*person*) Klatschbase *f* ●*vi* klatschen
got *see* **get**; **have ~** haben; **have ~ to** müssen; **have ~ to do sth** etw tun müssen
Gothic *a* gotisch
gotten *see* **get**
goulash *n* Gulasch *nt*
gourmet *n* Feinschmecker *m*
govern *vt/i* regieren; (*determine*) bestimmen
government *n* Regierung *f*
governor *n* Gouverneur *m*; (*on board*) Vorstandsmitglied *nt*; (*of prison*) Direktor *m*; ([!] *boss*) Chef *m*
gown *n* [elegantes] Kleid *nt*; (*Univ, Jur*) Talar *m*
GP *abbr of* **general practitioner**
grab *vt* (*pt/pp* **grabbed**) ergreifen; **~ [hold of]** packen
grace *n* Anmut *f*; (*before meal*) Tischgebet *nt*; **three days' ~** drei Tage Frist. **~ful** *a*, **-ly** *adv* anmutig
gracious *a* gnädig; (*elegant*) vornehm
grade *n* Stufe *f*; (*Comm*) Güteklasse *f*; (*Sch*) Note *f*; (*Amer, Sch: class*) Klasse *f*; (*Amer*) = **gradient** ●*vt* einstufen; (*Comm*)

sortieren. ~ **crossing** *n* (*Amer*) Bahnübergang *m*
gradient *n* Steigung *f*; (*downward*) Gefälle *nt*
gradual *a*, **-ly** *adv* allmählich
graduate *n* Akademiker(in) *m*(*f*)
graffiti *npl* Graffiti *pl*
graft *n* (*Bot*) Pfropfreis *nt*; (*Med*) Transplantat *nt*; ([!] *hard work*) Plackerei *f*
grain *n* (*sand, salt, rice*) Korn *nt*; (*cereals*) Getreide *nt*; (*in wood*) Maserung *f*
gram *n* Gramm *nt*
grammar *n* Grammatik *f*. ~ **school** *n* ≈ Gymnasium *nt*
grammatical *a*, **-ly** *adv* grammatisch
grand *a* (**-er, -est**) großartig
grandad *n* [!] Opa *m*
grandchild *n* Enkelkind *nt*
granddaughter *n* Enkelin *f*
grandeur *n* Pracht *f*
grandfather *n* Großvater *m*. ~ **clock** *n* Standuhr *f*
grandiose *a* grandios
grand: ~mother *n* Großmutter *f*. **~parents** *npl* Großeltern *pl*. ~ **piano** *n* Flügel *m*. **~son** *n* Enkel *m*. **~stand** *n* Tribüne *f*
granite *n* Granit *m*
granny *n* [!] Oma *f*
grant *n* Subvention *f*; (*Univ*) Studienbeihilfe *f* ● *vt* gewähren; (*admit*) zugeben; **take sth for ~ed** etw als selbstverständlich hinnehmen
grape *n* [Wein]traube *f*; **bunch of ~s** [ganze] Weintraube *f*
grapefruit *n invar* Grapefruit *f*
graph *n* grafische Darstellung *f*
graphic *a*, **-ally** *adv* grafisch; (*vivid*) anschaulich
graph paper *n* Millimeterpapier *nt*
grapple *vi* ringen
grasp *n* Griff *m* ● *vt* ergreifen; (*understand*) begreifen. **~ing** *a* habgierig
grass *n* Gras *nt*; (*lawn*) Rasen *m*. **~hopper** *n* Heuschrecke *f*
grassy *a* grasig
grate[1] *n* Feuerrost *m*; (*hearth*) Kamin *m*
grate[2] *vt* (*Culin*) reiben
grateful *a*, **-ly** *adv* dankbar (**to** *dat*)
grater *n* (*Culin*) Reibe *f*
gratify *vt* (*pt/pp* **-ied**) befriedigen. **~ing** *a* erfreulich
gratis *adv* gratis
gratitude *n* Dankbarkeit *f*
gratuitous *a* (*uncalled for*) überflüssig
grave[1] *a* (**-r, -st**), **-ly** *adv* ernst; **~ly ill** schwer krank
grave[2] *n* Grab *nt*. **~-digger** *n* Totengräber *m*
gravel *n* Kies *m*
grave: ~stone *n* Grabstein *m*. **~yard** *n* Friedhof *m*
gravity *n* Ernst *m*; (*force*) Schwerkraft *f*
gravy *n* [Braten]soße *f*
gray *a* (*Amer*) = **grey**
graze[1] *vi* <*animal:*> weiden
graze[2] *n* Schürfwunde *f* ● *vt* <*car*> streifen; <*knee*> aufschürfen
grease *n* Fett *nt*; (*lubricant*) Schmierfett *nt* ● *vt* einfetten; (*lubricate*) schmieren
greasy *a* (**-ier, -iest**) fettig
great *a* (**-er, -est**) groß; ([!] *marvellous*) großartig
great: ~-aunt *n* Großtante *f*. **G~ Britain** *n* Großbritannien *nt*. **~-grandchildren** *npl* Urenkel *pl*. **~-grandfather** *n* Urgroßvater *m*. **~-grandmother** *n* Urgroßmutter *f*
great|ly *adv* sehr. **~ness** *n* Größe *f*
great-uncle *n* Großonkel *m*
Greece *n* Griechenland *nt*
greed *n* [Hab]gier *f*
greedy *a* (**-ier, -iest**), **-ily** *adv* gierig
Greek *a* griechisch ● *n* Grieche *m*/Griechin *f*; (*Lang*) Griechisch

nt

green *a* (**-er, -est**) grün; (*fig*) unerfahren ●*n* Grün *nt*; (*grass*) Wiese *f*; **~s** *pl* Kohl *m*; **the G~s** *pl* (*Pol*) die Grünen *pl*

greenery *n* Grün *nt*

green: ~fly *n* Blattlaus *f*. **~grocer** *n* Obst- und Gemüsehändler *m*. **~house** *n* Gewächshaus *nt*

Greenland *n* Grönland *nt*

greet *vt* grüßen; (*welcome*) begrüßen. **~ing** *n* Gruß *m*; (*welcome*) Begrüßung *f*

grew *see* **grow**

grey *a* (**-er, -est**) grau ●*n* Grau *nt* ●*vi* grau werden. **~hound** *n* Windhund *m*

grid *n* Gitter *nt*

grief *n* Trauer *f*

grievance *n* Beschwerde *f*

grieve *vi* trauern (**for** um)

grill *n* Gitter *nt*; (*Culin*) Grill *m*; **mixed ~** Gemischtes *nt* vom Grill ●*vt/i* grillen; (*interrogate*) [streng] verhören

grille *n* Gitter *nt*

grim *a* (**grimmer, grimmest**), **-ly** *adv* ernst; <*determination*> verbissen

grimace *n* Grimasse *f* ●*vi* Grimassen schneiden

grime *n* Schmutz *m*

grimy *a* (**-ier, -iest**) schmutzig

grin *n* Grinsen *nt* ●*vi* (*pt/pp* **grinned**) grinsen

grind *n* (🄵 *hard work*) Plackerei *f* ●*vt* (*pt/pp* **ground**) mahlen; (*smooth, sharpen*) schleifen; (*Amer: mince*) durchdrehen

grip *n* Griff *m*; (*bag*) Reisetasche *f* ●*vt* (*pt/pp* **gripped**) ergreifen; (*hold*) festhalten

gripping *a* fesselnd

grisly *a* (**-ier, -iest**) grausig

gristle *n* Knorpel *m*

grit *n* [grober] Sand *m*; (*for roads*) Streugut *nt*; (*courage*) Mut *m* ●*vt* (*pt/pp* **gritted**) streuen <*road*>

groan *n* Stöhnen *nt* ●*vi* stöhnen

grocer *n* Lebensmittelhändler *m*; **~'s [shop]** Lebensmittelgeschäft *nt*. **~ies** *npl* Lebensmittel *pl*

groin *n* (*Anat*) Leiste *f*

groom *n* Bräutigam *m*; (*for horse*) Pferdepfleger(in) *m(f)* ●*vt* striegeln <*horse*>

groove *n* Rille *f*

grope *vi* tasten (**for** nach)

gross *a* (**-er, -est**) fett; (*coarse*) derb; (*glaring*) grob; (*Comm*) brutto; <*salary, weight*> Brutto-. **~ly** *adv* (*very*) sehr

grotesque *a*, **-ly** *adv* grotesk

ground[1] *see* **grind**

ground[2] *n* Boden *m*; (*terrain*) Gelände *nt*; (*reason*) Grund *m*; (*Amer, Electr*) Erde *f*; **~s** *pl* (*park*) Anlagen *pl*; (*of coffee*) Satz *m*

ground: ~ floor *n* Erdgeschoss *nt*. **~ing** *n* Grundlage *f*. **~less** *a* grundlos. **~sheet** *n* Bodenplane *f*. **~work** *n* Vorarbeiten *pl*

group *n* Gruppe *f* ●*vt* gruppieren ●*vi* sich gruppieren

grouse *vi* 🄵 meckern

grovel *vi* (*pt/pp* **grovelled**) kriechen

grow *v* (*pt* **grew**, *pp* **grown**) ●*vi* wachsen; (*become*) werden; (*increase*) zunehmen ●*vt* anbauen. **~ up** *vi* aufwachsen; <*town:*> entstehen

growl *n* Knurren *nt* ●*vi* knurren

grown *see* **grow**. **~-up** *a* erwachsen ●*n* Erwachsene(r) *m/f*

growth *n* Wachstum *nt*; (*increase*) Zunahme *f*; (*Med*) Gewächs *nt*

grub *n* (*larva*) Made *f*; (*fam: food*) Essen *nt*

grubby *a* (**-ier, -iest**) schmuddelig

grudg|e *n* Groll *m* ●*vt* **~e s.o. sth** jdm etw missgönnen. **~ing** *a*, **-ly** *adv* widerwillig

gruelling *a* strapaziös

gruesome *a* grausig

gruff *a*, **-ly** *adv* barsch

G

grumble *vi* schimpfen (**at** mit)
grumpy *a* (**-ier, -iest**) griesgrämig
grunt *n* Grunzen *nt* ● *vi* grunzen
guarantee *n* Garantie *f*; (*document*) Garantieschein *m* ● *vt* garantieren; garantieren für <*quality, success*>
guard *n* Wache *f*; (*security*) Wächter *m*; (*on train*) ≈ Zugführer *m*; (*Techn*) Schutz *m*; **be on ~** Wache stehen; **on one's ~** auf der Hut ● *vt* bewachen; (*protect*) schützen ● *vi* **~ against** sich hüten vor (+ *dat*). **~-dog** *n* Wachhund *m*
guarded *a* vorsichtig
guardian *n* Vormund *m*
guess *n* Vermutung *f* ● *vt* erraten ● *vi* raten; (*Amer: believe*) glauben. **~work** *n* Vermutung *f*
guest *n* Gast *m*. **~-house** *n* Pension *f*
guidance *n* Führung *f*, Leitung *f*; (*advice*) Beratung *f*
guide *n* Führer(in) *m*(*f*); (*book*) Führer *m*; **[Girl] G~** Pfadfinderin *f* ● *vt* führen, leiten. **~book** *n* Führer *m*
guided *a* **~ tour** Führung *f*
guide: ~-dog *n* Blindenhund *m*. **~lines** *npl* Richtlinien *pl*
guilt *n* Schuld *f*. **~ily** *adv* schuldbewusst
guilty *a* (**-ier, -iest**) *a* schuldig (**of** *gen*); <*look*> schuldbewusst; <*conscience*> schlecht
guinea-pig *n* Meerschweinchen *nt*; (*person*) Versuchskaninchen *nt*
guitar *n* Gitarre *f*. **~ist** *n* Gitarrist(in) *m*(*f*)
gulf *n* (*Geog*) Golf *m*; (*fig*) Kluft *f*
gull *n* Möwe *f*
gullible *a* leichtgläubig
gully *n* Schlucht *f*; (*drain*) Rinne *f*
gulp *n* Schluck *m* ● *vi* schlucken ● *vt* **~ down** hinunterschlucken
gum¹ *n* & **-s** *pl* (*Anat*) Zahnfleisch *nt*
gum² *n* Gummi[harz] *nt*; (*glue*) Klebstoff *m*; (*chewing gum*) Kaugummi *m*
gummed *see* **gum²** ● *a* <*label*> gummiert
gun *n* Schusswaffe *f*; (*pistol*) Pistole *f*; (*rifle*) Gewehr *nt*; (*cannon*) Geschütz *nt*
gun: ~fire *n* Geschützfeuer *nt*. **~man** bewaffneter Bandit *m*
gunner *n* Artillerist *m*
gunpowder *n* Schießpulver *nt*
gurgle *vi* gluckern; (*of baby*) glucksen
gush *vi* strömen; (*enthuse*) schwärmen (**over** von)
gust *n* (*of wind*) Windstoß *m*; (*Naut*) Bö *f*
gusto *n* **with ~** mit Schwung
gusty *a* böig
gut *n* Darm *m*; **~s** *pl* Eingeweide *pl*; ([!] *courage*) Schneid *m* ● *vt* (*pt/pp* **gutted**) (*Culin*) ausnehmen; **~ted by fire** ausgebrannt
gutter *n* Rinnstein *m*; (*fig*) Gosse *f*; (*on roof*) Dachrinne *f*
guy *n* [!] Kerl *m*
guzzle *vt/i* schlingen; (*drink*) schlürfen
gym *n* [!] Turnhalle *f*; (*gymnastics*) Turnen *nt*
gymnasium *n* Turnhalle *f*
gymnast *n* Turner(in) *m*(*f*). **~ics** *n* Turnen *nt*
gym shoes *pl* Turnschuhe *pl*
gynaecolog|ist *n* Frauenarzt *m* /-ärztin *f*. **~y** *n* Gynäkologie *f*
gypsy *n* Zigeuner(in) *m*(*f*)

Hh

habit *n* Gewohnheit *f*; (*Relig: costume*) Ordenstracht *f*; **be in the ~** die Angewohnheit haben (**of** zu)
habitat *n* Habitat *nt*
habitation *n* **unfit for human ~** für Wohnzwecke ungeeignet
habitual *a* gewohnt; (*inveterate*) gewohnheitsmäßig. **~ly** *adv* gewohnheitsmäßig; (*constantly*) ständig
hack¹ *n* (*writer*) Schreiberling *m*; (*hired horse*) Mietpferd *nt*
hack² *vt* hacken; **~ to pieces** zerhacken
hackneyed *a* abgedroschen
hacksaw *n* Metallsäge *f*
had *see* **have**
haddock *n inv* Schellfisch *m*
haggard *a* abgehärmt
haggle *vi* feilschen (**over** um)
hail¹ *vt* begrüßen; herbeirufen <*taxi*> ●*vi* **~ from** kommen aus
hail² *n* Hagel *m* ●*vi* hageln. **~stone** *n* Hagelkorn *nt*
hair *n* Haar *nt*; **wash one's ~** sich (*dat*) die Haare waschen
hair: ~brush *n* Haarbürste *f*. **~cut** *n* Haarschnitt *m*; **have a ~cut** sich (*dat*) die Haare schneiden lassen. **~-do** *n* [I] Frisur *f*. **~dresser** *n* Friseur *m*/Friseuse *f*. **~-drier** *n* Haartrockner *m*; (*hand-held*) Föhn *m*. **~pin** *n* Haarnadel *f*. **~pin bend** *n* Haarnadelkurve *f*. **~-raising** *a* haarsträubend. **~-style** *n* Frisur *f*
hairy *a* (**-ier, -iest**) behaart; (*excessively*) haarig; (*fam; frightening*) brenzlig
hake *n inv* Seehecht *m*
half *n* (*pl* **halves**) Hälfte *f*; **cut in ~** halbieren; **one and a ~** eineinhalb, anderthalb; **~ a dozen** ein halbes Dutzend; **~ an hour** eine halbe Stunde ●*a & adv* halb; **~ past two** halb drei; **[at] ~ price** zum halben Preis
half: ~-hearted *a* lustlos. **~-term** *n* schulfreie Tage nach dem halben Trimester. **~-timbered** *a* Fachwerk-. **~-time** *n* (*Sport*) Halbzeit *f*. **~-way** *a* **the ~-way mark/stage** die Hälfte ●*adv* auf halbem Weg
halibut *n inv* Heilbutt *m*
hall *n* Halle *f*; (*room*) Saal *m*; (*Sch*) Aula *f*; (*entrance*) Flur *m*; (*mansion*) Gutshaus *nt*; **~ of residence** (*Univ*) Studentenheim *nt*
hallmark *n* [Feingehalts]stempel *m*; (*fig*) Kennzeichen *nt* (**of** für)
hallo *int* [guten] Tag! [!] hallo!
hallucination *n* Halluzination *f*
halo *n* (*pl* **-es**) Heiligenschein *m*; (*Astr*) Hof *m*
halt *n* Halt *m*; **come to a ~** stehen bleiben; <*traffic:*> zum Stillstand kommen ●*vi* Halt machen; **~!** halt! **~ing** *a*, *adv* **-ly** zögernd
halve *vt* halbieren; (*reduce*) um die Hälfte reduzieren
ham *n* Schinken *m*
hamburger *n* Hamburger *m*
hammer *n* Hammer *m* ●*vt/i* hämmern (**at** an + *acc*)
hammock *n* Hängematte *f*
hamper *vt* behindern
hamster *n* Hamster *m*
hand *n* Hand *f*; (*of clock*) Zeiger *m*; (*writing*) Handscrift *f*; (*worker*) Arbeiter(in) *m*(*f*); (*Cards*) Blatt *nt*; **on the one/other ~** einer-/andererseits; **out of ~** außer Kontrolle; (*summarily*) kurzerhand; **in ~** unter Kontrolle; (*available*) verfügbar; **give s.o. a ~** jdm behilflich sein ●*vt* reichen (**to** *dat*). **~ in** *vt*

abgeben. ~ **out** *vt* austeilen. ~ **over** *vt* überreichen

hand: ~bag *n* Handtasche *f*. **~book** *n* Handbuch *nt*. **~brake** *n* Handbremse *f*. **~cuffs** *npl* Handschellen *pl*. **~ful** *n* Handvoll *f*; **be [quite] a ~ful** [!] nicht leicht zu haben sein

handicap *n* Behinderung *f*; (*Sport & fig*) Handikap *nt*. **~ped** *a* **mentally/physically ~ped** geistig/körperlich behindert

handkerchief *n* (*pl* **~s** & **-chieves**) Taschentuch *nt*

handle *n* Griff *m*; (*of door*) Klinke *f*; (*of cup*) Henkel *m*; (*of broom*) Stiel *m* ● *vt* handhaben; (*treat*) umgehen mit; (*touch*) anfassen. **~bars** *npl* Lenkstange *f*

hand: ~made *a* handgemacht. **~s-free kit** *n* Freisprecheinrichtung *f*. **~shake** *n* Händerdruck *m*

handsome *a* gut aussehend; (*generous*) großzügig; (*large*) beträchtlich

hand: ~writing *n* Handschrift *f*. **~-written** *a* handgeschrieben

handy *a* (**-ier, -iest**) handlich; <*person*> geschickt; **have/keep ~** griffbereit haben/halten

hang *vt/i* (*pt/pp* **hung**) hängen; **~ wallpaper** tapezieren ● *vt* (*pt/pp* **hanged**) hängen <*criminal*> ● *n* **get the ~ of it** [!] den Dreh herauskriegen. **~ about** *vi* sich herumdrücken. **~ on** *vi* sich festhalten (**to** an + *dat*); ([!] *wait*) warten. **~ out** *vi* heraushängen; ([!] *live*) wohnen ● *vt* draußen aufhängen <*washing*>. **~ up** *vt/i* aufhängen

hangar *n* Flugzeughalle *f*

hanger *n* [Kleider]bügel *m*

hang: ~-glider *n* Drachenflieger *m*. **~-gliding** *n* Drachenfliegen *nt*. **~man** *n* Henker *m*. **~over** *n* [!] Kater *m* [!]. **~-up** *n* [!] Komplex *m*

hanker *vi* **~ after sth** sich (*dat*) etw wünschen

hanky *n* [!] Taschentuch *nt*

haphazard *a*, **-ly** *adv* planlos

happen *vi* geschehen, passieren; **I ~ed to be there** ich war zufällig da; **what has ~ed to him?** was ist mit ihm los? (*become of*) was ist aus ihm geworden? **~ing** *n* Ereignis *nt*

happi|ly *adv* glücklich; (*fortunately*) glücklicherweise. **~ness** *n* Glück *nt*

happy *a* (**-ier, -iest**) glücklich. **~-go-lucky** *a* sorglos

harass *vt* schikanieren. **~ed** *a* abgehetzt. **~ment** *n* Schikane *f*; (*sexual*) Belästigung *f*

harbour *n* Hafen *m*

hard *a* (**-er, -est**) hart; (*difficult*) schwer; **~ of hearing** schwerhörig ● *adv* hart; <*work*> schwer; <*pull*> kräftig; <*rain, snow*> stark; **be ~ up** [!] knapp bei Kasse sein; **be ~ done by** [!] ungerecht behandelt werden

hard: ~back *n* gebundene Ausgabe *f*. **~board** *n* Hartfaserplatte *f*. **~-boiled** *a* hart gekocht

harden *vi* hart werden

hard-hearted *a* hartherzig

hard|ly *adv* kaum; **~ly ever** kaum [jemals]. **~ness** *n* Härte *f*. **~ship** *n* Not *f*

hard: ~ shoulder *n* (*Auto*) Randstreifen *m*. **~ware** *n* Haushaltswaren *pl*; (*Computing*) Hardware *f*. **~-wearing** *a* strapazierfähig. **~-working** *a* fleißig

hardy *a* (**-ier, -iest**) abgehärtet; <*plant*> winterhart

hare *n* Hase *m*

harm *n* Schaden *m*; **it won't do any ~** es kann nichts schaden ● *vt* **~ s.o.** jdm etwas antun. **~ful** *a* schädlich. **~less** *a* harmlos

harmonious *a*, **-ly** *adv* harmonisch

harmon|ize *vi* (*fig*) harmonieren. **~y** *n* Harmonie *f*

harness *n* Geschirr *nt*; (*of parachute*) Gurtwerk *nt* ● *vt* anschirren <*horse*>; (*use*) nutzbar machen

harp *n* Harfe *f*. **~ist** *n* Harfenist(in) *m*(*f*)

harrowing *a* grauenhaft

harsh *a* (**-er, -est**), **-ly** *adv* hart; <*voice*> rau; <*light*> grell. **~ness** *n* Härte *f*; Rauheit *f*

harvest *n* Ernte *f* ● *vt* ernten

has *see* **have**

hassle *n* [!] Ärger *m* ● *vt* schikanieren

haste *n* Eile *f*

hasten *vi* sich beeilen (**to** zu); (*go quickly*) eilen ● *vt* beschleunigen

hasty *a* (**-ier, -iest**), **-ily** *adv* hastig; <*decision*> voreilig

hat *n* Hut *m*; (*knitted*) Mütze *f*

hatch[1] *n* (*for food*) Durchreiche *f*, (*Naut*) Luke *f*

hatch[2] *vi* **~[out]** ausschlüpfen ● *vt* ausbrüten

hatchback *n* (*Auto*) Modell *nt* mit Hecktür

hate *n* Hass *m* ● *vt* hassen. **~ful** *a* abscheulich

hatred *n* Hass *m*

haughty *a* (**-ier, -iest**), **-ily** *adv* hochmütig

haul *n* (*loot*) Beute *f* ● *vt/i* ziehen (**on** an + *dat*)

haunt *n* Lieblingsaufenthalt *m* ● *vt* umgehen in (+ *dat*); **this house is ~ed** in diesem Haus spukt es

have

3 sg pres tense **has**; *pt and pp* **had**

● *transitive verb*

····➤ (*possess*) haben. **he has [got] a car** er hat ein Auto. **she has [got] a brother** sie hat einen Bruder. **we have [got] five minutes** wir haben fünf Minuten

····➤ (*eat*) essen; (*drink*) trinken; (*smoke*) rauchen. **have a cup of tea** eine Tasse Tee trinken. **have a pizza** eine Pizza essen. **have a cigarette** eine Zigarette rauchen. **have breakfast/dinner/lunch** frühstücken/zu Abend essen/zu Mittag essen

····➤ (*take esp. in shop, restaurant*) nehmen. **I'll have the soup/the red dress** ich nehme die Suppe/das rote Kleid. **have a cigarette!** nehmen Sie eine Zigarette!

····➤ (*get, receive*) bekommen. **I had a letter from her** ich bekam einen Brief von ihr. **have a baby** ein Baby bekommen

····➤ (*suffer*) haben <*illness, pain, disappointment*>; erleiden <*shock*>

····➤ (*organize*) **have a party** eine Party veranstalten. **they had a meeting** sie hielten eine Versammlung ab

····➤ (*take part in*) **have a game of football** Fußball spielen. **have a swim** schwimmen

····➤ (*as guest*) **have s.o. to stay** jdn zu Besuch haben

····➤ **have had it** [!] <*thing*> ausgedient haben; <*person*> geliefert sein. **you've had it now** jetzt ist es aus

····➤ **have sth done** etw machen lassen. **we had the house painted** wir haben das Haus malen lassen. **have a dress made** sich (*dat*) ein Kleid machen lassen. **have a tooth out** sich (*dat*) einen Zahn ziehen lassen. **have one's hair cut** sich (*dat*) die Haare schneiden lassen

····➤ **have to do sth** etw tun müssen. **I have to go now** ich muss jetzt gehen

● *auxiliary verb*

····➤ (*forming perfect and past perfect tenses*) haben; (*with verbs of motion and some others*) sein. **I have seen him** ich habe ihn gesehen. **he has never been there** er ist nie da gewesen. **I had gone** ich war gegangen. **if I had known ...** wenn ich gewusst hätte ...

····➤ (*in tag questions*) nicht wahr. **you've met her, haven't you?** du kennst sie, nicht wahr?

····➤ (*in short answers*) **Have you seen the film? — Yes, I have** Hast du den Film gesehen? – Ja [, stimmt]

● ● **have on** *vt* (*be wearing*) anhaben; (*dupe*) anführen

havoc *n* Verwüstung *f*

hawk *n* Falke *m*

hawthorn *n* Hagedorn *m*

hay *n* Heu *nt*. ~ **fever** *n* Heuschnupfen *m*. ~**stack** *n* Heuschober *m*

hazard *n* Gefahr *f*; (*risk*) Risiko *nt* ● *vt* riskieren. ~**ous** *a* gefährlich; (*risky*) riskant

haze *n* Dunst *m*

hazel *n* Haselbusch *m*. ~**-nut** *n* Haselnuss *f*

hazy *a* (**-ier, -iest**) dunstig; (*fig*) unklar

he *pron* er

head *n* Kopf *m*; (*chief*) Oberhaupt *nt*; (*of firm*) Chef(in) *m*(*f*); (*of school*) Schulleiter(in) *m*(*f*); (*on beer*) Schaumkrone *f*; (*of bed*) Kopfende *nt*; ~ **first** kopfüber ● *vt* anführen; (*Sport*) köpfen <*ball*> ● *vi* ~ **for** zusteuern auf (+ *acc*). ~**ache** *n* Kopfschmerzen *pl*

head|er *n* Kopfball *m*; (*dive*) Kopfsprung *m*. ~**ing** *n* Überschrift *f*

head: ~**lamp**, ~**light** *n* (*Auto*) Scheinwerfer *m*. ~**line** *n* Schlagzeile *f*. ~**long** *adv* kopfüber. ~**master** *n* Schulleiter *m*. ~**mistress** *n* Schulleiterin *f*. ~**-on** *a & adv* frontal. ~**phones** *npl* Kopfhörer *m*. ~**quarters** *npl* Hauptquartier *nt*; (*Pol*) Zentrale *f*. ~**-rest** *n* Kopfstütze *f*. ~**room** *n* lichte Höhe *f*. ~**scarf** *n* Kopftuch *nt*. ~**strong** *a* eigenwillig. ~**way** *n* **make** ~**way** Fortschritte machen. ~**word** *n* Stichwort *nt*

heady *a* berauschend

heal *vt/i* heilen

health *n* Gesundheit *f*

health: ~ **farm** *n* Schönheitsfarm *f*. ~ **foods** *npl* Reformkost *f*. ~**-food shop** *n* Reformhaus *nt*. ~ **insurance** *n* Krankenversicherung *f*

healthy *a* (**-ier, -iest**), **-ily** *adv* gesund

heap *n* Haufen *m*; ~**s** [!] jede Menge ● *vt* ~ **[up]** häufen

hear *vt/i* (*pt/pp* **heard**) hören; ~, ~! hört, hört! **he would not ~ of it** er ließ es nicht zu

hearing *n* Gehör *nt*; (*Jur*) Verhandlung *f*. ~**-aid** *n* Hörgerät *nt*

hearse *n* Leichenwagen *m*

heart *n* Herz *nt*; (*courage*) Mut *m*; ~**s** *pl* (*Cards*) Herz *nt*; **by** ~ auswendig

heart: ~**ache** *n* Kummer *m*. ~**attack** *n* Herzanfall *m*. ~**beat** *n* Herzschlag *m*. ~**-breaking** *a* herzzerreißend. ~**-broken** *a* untröstlich. ~**burn** *n* Sodbrennen *nt*. ~**en** *vt* ermutigen. ~**felt** *a* herzlich[st]

hearth *n* Herd *m*; (*fireplace*) Kamin *m*

heart|ily *adv* herzlich; <*eat*> viel. ~**less** *a*, **-ly** *adv* herzlos. ~**y** *a* herzlich; <*meal*> groß; <*person*> burschikos

heat *n* Hitze *f*; (*Sport*) Vorlauf *m* ● *vt* heiß machen; heizen <*room*>. ~**ed** *a* geheizt; <*swimming pool*> beheizt;

<discussion> hitzig. **~er** *n* Heizgerät *nt*; (*Auto*) Heizanlage *f*

heath *n* Heide *f*

heathen *a* heidnisch ● *n* Heide *m*/Heidin *f*

heather *n* Heidekraut *nt*

heating *n* Heizung *f*

heat wave *n* Hitzewelle *f*

heave *vt/i* ziehen; (*lift*) heben; ([!] *throw*) schmeißen

heaven *n* Himmel *m*. **~ly** *a* himmlisch

heavy *a* (**-ier, -iest**), **-ily** *adv* schwer; *<traffic, rain>* stark. **~weight** *n* Schwergewicht *nt*

heckle *vt* [durch Zwischenrufe] unterbrechen. **~r** *n* Zwischenrufer *m*

hectic *a* hektisch

hedge *n* Hecke *f*. **~hog** *n* Igel *m*

heed *vt* beachten

heel[1] *n* Ferse *f*; (*of shoe*) Absatz *m*; **down at ~** heruntergekommen

heel[2] *vi* **~ over** (*Naut*) sich auf die Seite legen

hefty *a* (**-ier, -iest**) kräftig; (*heavy*) schwer

height *n* Höhe *f*; (*of person*) Größe *f*. **~en** *vt* (*fig*) steigern

heir *n* Erbe *m*. **~ess** *n* Erbin *f*. **~loom** *n* Erbstück *nt*

held *see* **hold**[2]

helicopter *n* Hubschrauber *m*

hell *n* Hölle *f*; **go to ~!** [x] geh zum Teufel! ● *int* verdammt!

hello *int* [guten] Tag! [!] hallo!

helm *n* [Steuer]ruder *nt*

helmet *n* Helm *m*

help *n* Hilfe *f*; (*employees*) Hilfskräfte *pl*; **that's no ~** das nützt nichts ● *vt/i* helfen (**s.o.** jdm), **~ oneself to sth** sich (*dat*) etw nehmen; **~ yourself** (*at table*) greif zu; **I could not ~ laughing** ich musste lachen; **it cannot be ~ed** es lässt sich nicht ändern; **I can't ~ it** ich kann nichts dafür

help|er *n* Helfer(in) *m(f)*. **~ful** *a*, -ly *adv* hilfsbereit; *<advice>* nützlich. **~ing** *n* Portion *f*. **~less** *a*, **-ly** *adv* hilflos

hem *n* Saum *m* ● *vt* (*pt/pp* **hemmed**) säumen; **~ in** umzingeln

hemisphere *n* Hemisphäre *f*

hem-line *n* Rocklänge *f*

hen *n* Henne *f*; (*any female bird*) Weibchen *nt*

hence *adv* daher; **five years ~** in fünf Jahren. **~forth** *adv* von nun an

henpecked *a* **~ husband** Pantoffelheld *m*

her *a* ihr ● *pron* (*acc*) sie; (*dat*) ihr

herald *vt* verkünden. **~ry** *n* Wappenkunde *f*

herb *n* Kraut *nt*

herbaceous *a* **~ border** Staudenrabatte *f*

herd *n* Herde *f*. **~ together** *vt* zusammentreiben

here *adv* hier; (*to this place*) hierher; **in ~** hier drinnen; **come/bring ~** herkommen/herbringen

hereditary *a* erblich

here|sy *n* Ketzerei *f*. **~tic** *n* Ketzer(in) *m(f)*

herewith *adv* (*Comm*) beiliegend

heritage *n* Erbe *nt*

hero *n* (*pl* **-es**) Held *m*

heroic *a*, **-ally** *adv* heldenhaft

heroin *n* Heroin *nt*

hero|ine *n* Heldin *f*. **~ism** *n* Heldentum *nt*

heron *n* Reiher *m*

herring *n* Hering *m*

hers *poss pron* ihre(r), ihrs; **a friend of ~** ein Freund von ihr; **that is ~** das gehört ihr

herself *pron* selbst; (*refl*) sich; **by ~** allein

hesitant *a*, **-ly** *adv* zögernd

hesitat|e *vi* zögern. **~ion** *n* Zögern *nt*; **without ~ion** ohne zu zögern

hexagonal *a* sechseckig

H

heyday *n* Glanzzeit *f*
hi *int* he! (*hallo*) Tag!
hiatus *n* (*pl* **-tuses**) Lücke *f*
hibernat|e *vi* Winterschlaf halten. **~ion** *n* Winterschlaf *m*
hiccup *n* Hick *m*; ([!] *hitch*) Panne *f*; **have the ~s** den Schluckauf haben ●*vi* hick machen
hid, hidden *see* **hide**[2]
hide *v* (*pt* **hid**, *pp* **hidden**) ●*vt* verstecken; (*keep secret*) verheimlichen ●*vi* sich verstecken
hideous *a*, **-ly** *adv* hässlich; (*horrible*) grässlich
hide-out *n* Versteck *nt*
hiding[1] *n* [!] **give s.o. a ~** jdn verdreschen
hiding[2] *n* **go into ~** untertauchen
hierarchy *n* Hierarchie *f*
high *a* (**-er, -est**) hoch; *attrib* hohe(r,s); <*meat*> angegangen; <*wind*> stark; (*on drugs*) high; **it's ~ time** es ist höchste Zeit ●*adv* hoch; **~ and low** überall ●*n* Hoch *nt*; (*temperature*) Höchsttemperatur *f*
high: ~brow *a* intellektuell. **~chair** *n* Kinderhochstuhl *m*. **~-handed** *a* selbstherrlich. **~-heeled** *a* hochhackig. **~ jump** *n* Hochsprung *m*
highlight *n* (*fig*) Höhepunkt *m*; **~s** *pl* (*in hair*) helle Strähnen *pl* ●*vt* (*emphasize*) hervorheben
highly *adv* hoch; **speak ~ of** loben; **think ~ of** sehr schätzen. **~-strung** *a* nervös
Highness *n* Hoheit *f*
high: ~ season *n* Hochsaison *f*. **~ street** *n* Hauptstraße *f*. **~ tide** *n* Hochwasser *nt*. **~way** *n* **public ~way** öffentliche Straße *f*
hijack *vt* entführen. **~er** *n* Entführer *m*
hike *n* Wanderung *f* ●*vi* wandern. **~r** *n* Wanderer *m*
hilarious *a* sehr komisch
hill *n* Berg *m*; (*mound*) Hügel *m*; (*slope*) Hang *m*
hill: ~side *n* Hang *m*. **~y** *a* hügelig
him *pron* (*acc*) ihn; (*dat*) ihm. **~self** *pron* selbst; (*refl*) sich; **by ~self** allein
hind *a* Hinter-
hind|er *vt* hindern. **~rance** *n* Hindernis *nt*
hindsight *n* **with ~** rückblickend
Hindu *n* Hindu *m* ●*a* Hindu-. **~ism** *n* Hinduismus *m*
hinge *n* Scharnier *nt*; (*on door*) Angel *f*
hint *n* Wink *m*, Andeutung *f*; (*advice*) Hinweis *m*; (*trace*) Spur *f* ●*vi* **~ at** anspielen auf (+ *acc*)
hip *n* Hüfte *f*
hip pocket *n* Gesäßtasche *f*
hippopotamus *n* (*pl* **-muses** *or* **-mi**) Nilpferd *nt*
hire *vt* mieten <*car*>; leihen <*suit*>; einstellen <*person*>; **~[out]** vermieten; verleihen
his *a* sein ●*poss pron* seine(r), seins; **a friend of ~** ein Freund von ihm; **that is ~** das gehört ihm
hiss *n* Zischen *nt* ●*vt/i* zischen
historian *n* Historiker(in) *m*(*f*)
historic *a* historisch. **~al** *a*, **-ly** *adv* geschichtlich, historisch
history *n* Geschichte *f*
hit *n* (*blow*) Schlag *m*; ([!] *success*) Erfolg *m*; **direct ~** Volltreffer *m* ●*vt/i* (*pt/pp* **hit**, *pres p* **hitting**) schlagen; (*knock against, collide with, affect*) treffen; **~ the target** das Ziel treffen; **~ on** (*fig*) kommen auf (+ *acc*); **~ it off** gut auskommen (**with** mit); **~ one's head on sth** sich (*dat*) den Kopf an etw (*dat*) stoßen
hitch *n* Problem *nt*; **technical ~** Panne *f* ●*vt* festmachen (**to** an + *dat*); **~ up** hochziehen. **~-hike** *vi* [!] trampen. **~-hiker** *n* Anhalter(in) *m*(*f*)
hive *n* Bienenstock *m*

hoard *n* Hort *m* ● *vt* horten, hamstern

hoarding *n* Bauzaun *m*; (*with advertisements*) Reklamewand *f*

hoar-frost *n* Raureif *m*

hoarse *a* (**-r, -st**), **-ly** *adv* heiser. **~ness** *n* Heiserkeit *f*

hoax *n* übler Scherz *m*; (*false alarm*) blinder Alarm *m*

hobble *vi* humpeln

hobby *n* Hobby *nt*. **~-horse** *n* (*fig*) Lieblingsthema *nt*

hockey *n* Hockey *nt*

hoe *n* Hacke *f* ● *vt* (*pres p* **hoeing**) hacken

hog *vt* (*pt/pp* **hogged**) [!] mit Beschlag belegen

hoist *n* Lastenaufzug *m* ● *vt* hochziehen; hissen <*flag*>

hold[1] *n* (*Naut*) Laderaum *m*

hold[2] *n* Halt *m*; (*Sport*) Griff *m*; (*fig: influence*) Einfluss *m*; **get ~ of** fassen; ([!] *contact*) erreichen ● *v* (*pt/pp* **held**) ● *vt* halten; <*container:*> fassen; (*believe*) meinen; (*possess*) haben; anhalten <*breath*> ● *vi* <*rope:*> halten; <*weather:*> sich halten. **~ back** *vt* zurückhalten ● *vi* zögern. **~ on** *vi* (*wait*) warten; (*on telephone*) am Apparat bleiben; **~ on to** (*keep*) behalten; (*cling to*) sich festhalten an (+ *dat*). **~ out** *vt* hinhalten ● *vi* (*resist*) aushalten. **~ up** *vt* hochhalten; (*delay*) aufhalten; (*rob*) überfallen

hold|all *n* Reisetasche *f*. **~er** *n* Inhaber(in) *m(f)*; (*container*) Halter *m*. **~-up** *n* Verzögerung *f*; (*attack*) Überfall *m*

hole *n* Loch *nt*

holiday *n* Urlaub *m*; (*Sch*) Ferien *pl*; (*public*) Feiertag *m*; (*day off*) freier Tag *m*; **go on ~** in Urlaub fahren

holiness *n* Heiligkeit *f*

Holland *n* Holland *nt*

hollow *a* hohl; <*promise*> leer ● *n* Vertiefung *f*; (*in ground*) Mulde *f*. **~ out** *vt* aushöhlen

holly *n* Stechpalme *f*

holster *n* Pistolentasche *f*

holy *a* (**-ier, -est**) heilig. **H~ Ghost** *or* **Spirit** *n* Heiliger Geist *m*

homage *n* Huldigung *f*; **pay ~ to** huldigen (+ *dat*)

home *n* Zuhause *nt* (*house*) Haus *nt*; (*institution*) Heim *nt*; (*native land*) Heimat *f* ● *adv* **at ~** zu Hause; **come/go ~** nach Hause kommen/gehen

home: ~ address *n* Heimatanschrift *f*. **~ game** *n* Heimspiel *nt*. **~land** *n* Heimatland *nt*. **~less** *a* obdachlos

homely *a* (**-ier, -iest**) *a* gemütlich; (*Amer: ugly*) unscheinbar

home: ~-made *a* selbst gemacht. **H~ Office** *n* Innenministerium *nt*. **~ page** *n* Homepage *f*. **H~ Secretary** Innenminister *m*. **~sick** *a* **be ~sick** Heimweh haben (**for** nach). **~sickness** *n* Heimweh *nt*. **~ town** *n* Heimatstadt *f*. **~work** *n* (*Sch*) Hausaufgaben *pl*

homosexual *a* homosexuell ● *n* Homosexuelle(r) *m/f*

honest *a*, **-ly** *adv* ehrlich. **~y** *n* Ehrlichkeit *f*

honey *n* Honig *m*; ([!] *darling*) Schatz *m*

honey: ~comb *n* Honigwabe *f*. **~moon** *n* Flitterwochen *pl*; (*journey*) Hochzeitsreise *f*

honorary *a* ehrenamtlich; <*member, doctorate*> Ehren-

honour *n* Ehre *f* ● *vt* ehren; honorieren <*cheque*>. **~able** *a*, **-bly** *adv* ehrenhaft

hood *n* Kapuze *f*; (*of car, pram*) [Klapp]verdeck *nt*; (*over cooker*) Abzugshaube *f*; (*Auto, Amer*) Kühlerhaube *f*

hoof *n* (*pl* **~s** *or* **hooves**) Huf *m*

hook *n* Haken *m* ● *vt* festhaken (**to** an + *acc*)
hook|ed *a* **~ed nose** Hakennase *f*; **~ed on** [!] abhängig von; (*keen on*) besessen von. **~er** *n* (*Amer* [x]) Nutte *f*
hookey *n* **play ~** (*Amer* [!]) schwänzen
hooligan *n* Rowdy *m*. **~ism** *n* Rowdytum *nt*
hooray *int & n* = **hurrah**
hoot *n* Ruf *m*; **~s of laughter** schallendes Gelächter *nt* ● *vi* <*owl:*> rufen; <*car:*> hupen; (*jeer*) johlen. **~er** *n* (*of factory*) Sirene *f*; (*Auto*) Hupe *f*
hoover *n* **H~** (**P**) Staubsauger *m* ● *vt/i* [staub]saugen
hop¹ *n*, & **~s** *pl* Hopfen *m*
hop² *vi* (*pt/pp* **hopped**) hüpfen; **~ it!** [!] hau ab!
hope *n* Hoffnung *f*; (*prospect*) Aussicht *f* (**of** auf + *acc*) ● *vt/i* hoffen (**for** auf + acc); **I ~ so** hoffentlich
hope|ful *a* hoffnungsvoll; **be ~ful that** hoffen, dass. **~fully** *adv* hoffnungsvoll; (*it is hoped*) hoffentlich. **~less** *a*, **-ly** *adv* hoffnungslos; (*useless*) nutzlos; (*incompetent*) untauglich
horde *n* Horde *f*
horizon *n* Horizont *m*
horizontal *a*, **-ly** *adv* horizontal. **~ bar** *n* Reck *nt*
horn *n* Horn *nt*; (*Auto*) Hupe *f*
hornet *n* Hornisse *f*
horoscope *n* Horoskop *nt*
horrible *a*, **-bly** *adv* schrecklich
horrid *a* grässlich
horrific *a* entsetzlich
horrify *vt* (*pt/pp* **-ied**) entsetzen
horror *n* Entsetzen *nt*
hors-d'œuvre *n* Vorspeise *f*
horse *n* Pferd *nt*
horse: ~back *n* **on ~back** zu Pferde. **~man** *n* Reiter *m*. **~power** *n* Pferdestärke *f*. **~-racing** *n* Pferderennen *nt*. **~radish** *n* Meerrettich *m*. **~shoe** *n* Hufeisen *nt*
horticulture *n* Gartenbau *m*
hose *n* (*pipe*) Schlauch *m* ● *vt* **~ down** abspritzen
hosiery *n* Strumpfwaren *pl*
hospitable *a*, **-bly** *adv* gastfreundlich
hospital *n* Krankenhaus *nt*
hospitality *n* Gastfreundschaft *f*
host *n* Gastgeber *m*
hostage *n* Geisel *f*
hostel *n* [Wohn]heim *nt*
hostess *n* Gastgeberin *f*
hostile *a* feindlich; (*unfriendly*) feindselig
hostilit|y *n* Feindschaft *f*; **~ies** *pl* Feindseligkeiten *pl*
hot *a* (**hotter, hottest**) heiß; <*meal*> warm; (*spicy*) scharf; **I am** *or* **feel ~** mir ist heiß
hotel *n* Hotel *nt*
hot: ~head *n* Hitzkopf *m*. **~house** *n* Treibhaus *nt*. **~ly** *adv* (*fig*) heiß, heftig. **~plate** *n* Tellerwärmer *m*; (*of cooker*) Kochplatte *f*. **~ tap** *n* Warmwasserhahn *m*. **~-tempered** *a* jähzornig. **~-water bottle** *n* Wärmflasche *f*
hound *n* Jagdhund *m* ● *vt* (*fig*) verfolgen
hour *n* Stunde *f*. **~ly** *a & adv* stündlich
house¹ *n* Haus *nt*; **at my ~** bei mir
house² *vt* unterbringen
house: ~breaking *n* Einbruch *m*. **~hold** *n* Haushalt *m*. **~holder** *n* Hausinhaber(in) *m*(*f*). **~keeper** *n* Haushälterin *f*. **~keeping** *n* Hauswirtschaft *f*; (*money*) Haushaltsgeld *nt*. **~-plant** *n* Zimmerpflanze *f*. **~-trained** *a* stubenrein. **~-warming** *n* **have a ~-warming party** Einstand feiern. **~wife** *n* Hausfrau *f*. **~work** *n* Hausarbeit *f*
housing *n* Wohnungen *pl*; (*Techn*) Gehäuse *nt*

hovel *n* elende Hütte *f*
hover *vi* schweben. **~craft** *n* Luftkissenfahrzeug *nt*
how *adv* wie; **~ do you do?** guten Tag!; **and ~!** und ob!
however *adv* (*in question*) wie; (*nevertheless*) jedoch, aber; **~ small** wie klein es auch sein mag
howl *n* Heulen *nt* ● *vi* heulen; <*baby*:> brüllen
hub *n* Nabe *f*
huddle *vi* **~ together** sich zusammendrängen
huff *n* **in a ~** beleidigt
hug *n* Umarmung *f* ● *vt* (*pt/pp* **hugged**) umarmen
huge *a*, **-ly** *adv* riesig
hull *n* (*Naut*) Rumpf *m*
hullo *int* = **hallo**
hum *n* Summen *nt*; Brummen *nt* ● *vt/i* (*pt/pp* **hummed**) summen; <*motor*:> brummen
human *a* menschlich ● *n* Mensch *m*. **~ being** *n* Mensch *m*
humane *a*, **-ly** *adv* human
humanitarian *a* humanitär
humanity *n* Menschheit *f*
humble *a* (**-r, -st**), **-bly** *adv* demütig ● *vt* demütigen
humdrum *a* eintönig
humid *a* feucht. **~ity** *n* Feuchtigkeit *f*
humiliat|e *vt* demütigen. **~ion** *n* Demütigung *f*
humility *n* Demut *f*
humorous *a*, **-ly** *adv* humorvoll; <*story*> humoristisch
humour *n* Humor *m*; (*mood*) Laune *f*; **have a sense of ~** Humor haben
hump *n* Buckel *m*; (*of camel*) Höcker *m* ● *vt* schleppen
hunch *n* (*idea*) Ahnung *f*
hunchback *n* Bucklige(r) *m/f*
hundred *a* **one/a ~** [ein]hundert ● *n* Hundert *nt*; (*written figure*) Hundert *f*. **~th** *a* hundertste(r,s) ● *n* Hundertstel *nt*. **~weight** *n* ≈ Zentner *m*
hung *see* **hang**
Hungarian *a* ungarisch ● *n* Ungar(in) *m(f)*
Hungary *n* Ungarn *nt*
hunger *n* Hunger *m*. **~-strike** *n* Hungerstreik *m*
hungry *a* (**-ier, -iest**), **-ily** *adv* hungrig; **be ~** Hunger haben
hunt *n* Jagd *f*; (*for criminal*) Fahndung *f* ● *vt/i* jagen; fahnden nach <*criminal*>; **~ for** suchen. **~er** *n* Jäger *m*; (*horse*) Jagdpferd *nt*. **~ing** *n* Jagd *f*
hurdle *n* (*Sport & fig*) Hürde *f*
hurl *vt* schleudern
hurrah, hurray *int* hurra! ● *n* Hurra *nt*
hurricane *n* Orkan *m*
hurried *a*, **-ly** *adv* eilig; (*superficial*) flüchtig
hurry *n* Eile *f*; **be in a ~** es eilig haben ● *vi* (*pt/pp* **-ied**) sich beeilen; (*go quickly*) eilen. **~ up** *vi* sich beeilen ● *vt* antreiben
hurt *n* Schmerz *m* ● *vt/i* (*pt/pp* **hurt**) weh tun (+ *dat*); (*injure*) verletzen; (*offend*) kränken
hurtle *vi* **~ along** rasen
husband *n* [Ehe]mann *m*
hush *n* Stille *f* ● *vt* **~ up** vertuschen. **~ed** *a* gedämpft
husky *a* (**-ier, -iest**) heiser; (*burly*) stämmig
hustle *vt* drängen ● *n* Gedränge *nt*
hut *n* Hütte *f*
hutch *n* [Kaninchen]stall *m*
hybrid *a* hybrid ● *n* Hybride *f*
hydraulic *a*, **-ally** *adv* hydraulisch
hydroelectric *a* hydroelektrisch
hydrogen *n* Wasserstoff *m*
hygien|e *n* Hygiene *f*. **~ic** *a*, **-ally** *adv* hygienisch
hymn *n* Kirchenlied *nt*. **~-book** *n* Gesangbuch *nt*
hyphen *n* Bindestrich *m*. **~ate** *vt* mit Bindestrich schreiben
hypno|sis *n* Hypnose *f*. **~tic** *a* hypnotisch

hypno|tism *n* Hypnotik *f*. **~tist** *n* Hypnotiseur *m*. **~tize** *vt* hypnotisieren

hypochondriac *n* Hypochonder *m*

hypocrisy *n* Heuchelei *f*

hypocrite *n* Heuchler(in) *m(f)*

hypodermic *a & n* **~ [syringe]** Injektionsspritze *f*

hypothe|sis *n* Hypothese *f*. **~tical** *a*, **-ly** *adv* hypothetisch

hyster|ia *n* Hysterie *f*. **~ical** *a*, **-ly** *adv* hysterisch. **~ics** *npl* hysterischer Anfall *m*

Ii

I *pron* ich

ice *n* Eis *nt* ● *vt* mit Zuckerguss überziehen <*cake*>

ice: ~berg *n* Eisberg *m*. **~box** *n* (*Amer*) Kühlschrank *m*. **~-cream** *n* [Speise]eis *nt*. **~-cube** *n* Eiswürfel *m*

Iceland *n* Island *nt*

ice: ~lolly *n* Eis *nt* am Stiel. **~ rink** *n* Eisbahn *f*

icicle *n* Eiszapfen *m*

icing *n* Zuckerguss *m*. **~ sugar** *n* Puderzucker *m*

icon *n* Ikone *f*

icy *a* (**-ier, -iest**), **-ily** *adv* eisig; <*road*> vereist

idea *n* Idee *f*; (*conception*) Vorstellung *f*; **I have no ~!** ich habe keine Ahnung!

ideal *a* ideal ● *n* Ideal *nt*. **~ism** *n* Idealismus *m*. **~ist** *n* Idealist(in) *m(f)*. **~istic** *a* idealistisch. **~ize** *vt* idealisieren. **~ly** *adv* ideal; (*in ideal circumstances*) idealerweise

identical *a* identisch; <*twins*> eineiig

identi|fication *n* Identifizierung *f*; (*proof of identity*) Ausweispapiere *pl*. **~fy** *vt* (*pt/pp* **-ied**) identifizieren

identity *n* Identität *f*. **~ card** *n* [Personal]ausweis *m*

idiom *n* [feste] Redewendung *f*. **~atic** *a*, **-ally** *adv* idiomatisch

idiosyncrasy *n* Eigenart *f*

idiot *n* Idiot *m*. **~ic** *a* idiotisch

idle *a* (**-r, -st**), **-ly** *adv* untätig; (*lazy*) faul; (*empty*) leer; <*machine*> nicht in Betrieb ● *vi* faulenzen; <*engine:*> leer laufen. **~ness** *n* Untätigkeit *f*; Faulheit *f*

idol *n* Idol *nt*. **~ize** *vt* vergöttern

idyllic *a* idyllisch

i.e. *abbr* (**id est**) d.h.

if *conj* wenn; (*whether*) ob; **as if** als ob

ignition *n* (*Auto*) Zündung *f*. **~ key** *n* Zündschlüssel *m*

ignoramus *n* Ignorant *m*

ignoran|ce *n* Unwissenheit *f*. **~t** *a* unwissend

ignore *vt* ignorieren

ill *a* krank; (*bad*) schlecht; **feel ~ at ease** sich unbehaglich fühlen ● *adv* schlecht

illegal *a*, **-ly** *adv* illegal

illegible *a*, **-bly** *adv* unleserlich

illegitimate *a* unehelich; <*claim*> unberechtigt

illicit *a*, **-ly** *adv* illegal

illiterate *a* **be ~te** nicht lesen und schreiben können

illness *n* Krankheit *f*

illogical *a*, **-ly** *adv* unlogisch

ill-treat *vt* misshandeln. **~ment** *n* Misshandlung *f*

illuminat|e *vt* beleuchten. **~ion** *n* Beleuchtung *f*

illusion *n* Illusion *f*; **be under the ~ that** sich (*dat*) einbilden, dass

illustrat|e *vt* illustrieren. **~ion** *n* Illustration *f*

illustrious *a* berühmt

image *n* Bild *nt*; (*statue*) Standbild *nt*; (*exact likeness*) Ebenbild *nt*; **[public] ~** Image *nt*
imagin|able *a* vorstellbar. **~ary** *a* eingebildet
imagination *n* Fantasie *f*; (*fancy*) Einbildung *f*. **~ive** *a*, **-ly** *adv* fantasievoll; (*full of ideas*) einfallsreich
imagine *vt* sich (*dat*) vorstellen; (*wrongly*) sich (*dat*) einbilden
imbecile *n* Schwachsinnige(r) *m/f*; (*pej*) Idiot *m*
imitat|e *vt* nachahmen, imitieren. **~ion** *n* Nachahmung *f*, Imitation *f*
immaculate *a*, **-ly** *adv* tadellos; (*Relig*) unbefleckt
immature *a* unreif
immediate *a* sofortig; (*nearest*) nächste(r,s). **~ly** *adv* sofort; **~ly next to** unmittelbar neben ● *conj* sobald
immemorial *a* **from time ~** seit Urzeiten
immense *a*, **-ly** *adv* riesig; [!] enorm
immerse *vt* untertauchen
immigrant *n* Einwanderer *m*
immigration *n* Einwanderung *f*
imminent *a* **be ~** unmittelbar bevorstehen
immobil|e *a* unbeweglich. **~ize** *vt* (*fig*) lähmen; (*Med*) ruhig stellen. **~izer** *n* (*Auto*) Wegfahrsperre *f*
immodest *a* unbescheiden
immoral *a*, **-ly** *adv* unmoralisch. **~ity** *n* Unmoral *f*
immortal *a* unsterblich. **~ity** *n* Unsterblichkeit *f*. **~ize** *vt* verewigen
immune *a* immun (**to/from** gegen)
immunity *n* Immunität *f*
imp *n* Kobold *m*
impact *n* Aufprall *m*; (*collision*) Zusammenprall *m*; (*of bomb*) Einschlag *m*; (*fig*) Auswirkung *f*
impair *vt* beeinträchtigen
impart *vt* übermitteln (**to** *dat*); vermitteln <*knowledge*>
impartial *a* unparteiisch. **~ity** *n* Unparteilichkeit *f*
impassable *a* unpassierbar
impassioned *a* leidenschaftlich
impassive *a*, **-ly** *adv* unbeweglich
impatien|ce *n* Ungeduld *f*. **~t** *a*, **-ly** *adv* ungeduldig
impeccable *a*, **-bly** *adv* tadellos
impede *vt* behindern
impediment *n* Hindernis *nt*; (*in speech*) Sprachfehler *m*
impel *vt* (*pt/pp* **impelled**) treiben
impending *a* bevorstehend
impenetrable *a* undurchdringlich
imperative *a* **be ~** dringend notwendig sein ● *n* (*Gram*) Imperativ *m*
imperceptible *a* nicht wahrnehmbar
imperfect *a* unvollkommen; (*faulty*) fehlerhaft ● *n* (*Gram*) Imperfekt *nt*. **~ion** *n* Unvollkommenheit *f*; (*fault*) Fehler *m*
imperial *a* kaiserlich. **~ism** *n* Imperialismus *m*
impersonal *a* unpersönlich
impersonat|e *vt* sich ausgeben als; (*Theat*) nachahmen, imitieren. **~or** *n* Imitator *m*
impertinen|ce *n* Frechheit *f*. **~t** *a* frech
imperturbable *a* unerschütterlich
impetuous *a*, **-ly** *adv* ungestüm
impetus *n* Schwung *m*
implacable *a* unerbittlich
implant *vt* einpflanzen
implement¹ *n* Gerät *nt*
implement² *vt* ausführen
implication *n* Verwicklung *f*; **~s** *pl* Auswirkungen *pl*; **by ~** implizit
implicit *a*, **-ly** *adv* unausgesprochen; (*absolute*) unbedingt
implore *vt* anflehen

imply *vt* (*pt*/*pp* **-ied**) andeuten; **what are you ~ing?** was wollen Sie damit sagen?
impolite *a*, **-ly** *adv* unhöflich
import¹ *n* Import *m*, Einfuhr *f*
import² *vt* importieren, einführen
importan|ce *n* Wichtigkeit *f*. **~t** *a* wichtig
importer *n* Importeur *m*
impos|e *vt* auferlegen (**on** *dat*) ● *vi* sich aufdrängen (**on** *dat*). **~ing** *a* eindrucksvoll
impossibility *n* Unmöglichkeit *f*
impossible *a*, **-bly** *adv* unmöglich
impostor *n* Betrüger(in) *m*(*f*)
impoten|ce *n* Machtlosigkeit *f*; (*Med*) Impotenz *f*. **~t** *a* machtlos; (*Med*) impotent
impoverished *a* verarmt
impracticable *a* undurchführbar
impractical *a* unpraktisch
imprecise *a* ungenau
impress *vt* beeindrucken; **~ sth [up]on s.o.** jdm etw einprägen
impression *n* Eindruck *m*; (*imitation*) Nachahmung *f*; (*edition*) Auflage *f*. **~ism** *n* Impressionismus *m*
impressive *a* eindrucksvoll
imprison *vt* gefangen halten; (*put in prison*) ins Gefängnis sperren
improbable *a* unwahrscheinlich
impromptu *a* improvisiert ● *adv* aus dem Stegreif
improper *a*, **-ly** *adv* inkorrekt; (*indecent*) unanständig
impropriety *n* Unkorrektheit *f*
improve *vt* verbessern; verschönern <*appearance*> ● *vi* sich bessern; **~ [up]on** übertreffen. **~ment** *n* Verbesserung *f*; (*in health*) Besserung *f*
improvise *vt*/*i* improvisieren
imprudent *a* unklug
impuden|ce *n* Frechheit *f*. **~t** *a*, **-ly** *adv* frech
impuls|e *n* Impuls *m*; **on [an] ~e** impulsiv. **~ive** *a*, **-ly** *adv* impulsiv
impur|e *a* unrein. **~ity** *n* Unreinheit *f*
in *prep* in (+ *dat*/(*into*) + *acc*); **sit in the garden** im Garten sitzen; **go in the garden** in den Garten gehen; **in May** im Mai; **in 1992** [im Jahre] 1992; **in this heat** bei dieser Hitze; **in the evening** am Abend; **in the sky** am Himmel; **in the world** auf der Welt; **in the street** auf der Straße; **deaf in one ear** auf einem Ohr taub; **in the army** beim Militär; **in English/German** auf Englisch/Deutsch; **in ink/pencil** mit Tinte/Bleistift; **in a soft/loud voice** mit leiser/lauter Stimme; **in doing this, he ...** indem er das tut/tat, ... er ● *adv* (*at home*) zu Hause; (*indoors*) drinnen; **he's not in yet** er ist noch nicht da; **all in** alles inbegriffen; ([!] *exhausted*) kaputt; **day in, day out** tagaus, tagein; **have it in for s.o.** [!] es auf jdn abgesehen haben; **send/go in** hineinschicken/-gehen; **come/bring in** hereinkommen/-bringen ● *a* ([!] *in fashion*) in ● *n* **the ins and outs** alle Einzelheiten *pl*
inability *n* Unfähigkeit *f*
inaccessible *a* unzugänglich
inaccura|cy *n* Ungenauigkeit *f*. **~te** *a*, **-ly** *adv* ungenau
inac|tive *a* untätig. **~tivity** *n* Untätigkeit *f*
inadequate *a*, **-ly** *adv* unzulänglich
inadmissible *a* unzulässig
inadvertently *adv* versehentlich
inadvisable *a* nicht ratsam
inane *a*, **-ly** *adv* albern
inanimate *a* unbelebt
inapplicable *a* nicht zutreffend
inappropriate *a* unangebracht
inarticulate *a* undeutlich; **be ~** sich nicht gut ausdrücken können
inattentive *a* unaufmerksam
inaudible *a*, **-bly** *adv* unhörbar

inaugural *a* Antritts-

inauspicious *a* ungünstig

inborn *a* angeboren

inbred *a* angeboren

incalculable *a* nicht berechenbar; (*fig*) unabsehbar

incapable *a* unfähig; **be ~ of doing sth** nicht fähig sein, etw zu tun

incapacitate *vt* unfähig machen

incarnation *n* Inkarnation *f*

incendiary *a* & *n* ~ **[bomb]** Brandbombe *f*

incense¹ *n* Weihrauch *m*

incense² *vt* wütend machen

incentive *n* Anreiz *m*

incessant *a*, **-ly** *adv* unaufhörlich

incest *n* Inzest *m*, Blutschande *f*

inch *n* Zoll *m* ● *vi* ~ **forward** sich ganz langsam vorwärts schieben

incident *n* Zwischenfall *m*

incidental *a* nebensächlich; <*remark*> beiläufig; <*expenses*> Neben-. **~ly** *adv* übrigens

incinerate *vt* verbrennen

incision *n* Einschnitt *m*

incisive *a* scharfsinnig

incite *vt* aufhetzen. **~ment** *n* Aufhetzung *f*

inclement *a* rau

inclination *n* Neigung *f*

incline *vt* neigen; **be ~d to do sth** dazu neigen, etw zu tun ● *vi* sich neigen

inclu|de *vt* einschließen; (*contain*) enthalten; (*incorporate*) aufnehmen (**in** in + *acc*). **~ding** *prep* einschließlich (+ *gen*). **~sion** *n* Aufnahme *f*

inclusive *a* Inklusiv-; ~ **of** einschließlich (+ *gen*)

incognito *adv* inkognito

incoherent *a*, **-ly** *adv* zusammenhanglos; (*incomprehensible*) unverständlich

income *n* Einkommen *nt*. ~ **tax** *n* Einkommensteuer *f*

incoming *a* ankommend; <*mail, call*> eingehend

incomparable *a* unvergleichlich

incompatible *a* unvereinbar; **be ~** <*people:*> nicht zueinander passen

incompeten|ce *n* Unfähigkeit *f*. **~t** *a* unfähig

incomplete *a* unvollständig

incomprehensible *a* unverständlich

inconceivable *a* undenkbar

inconclusive *a* nicht schlüssig

incongruous *a* unpassend

inconsiderate *a* rücksichtslos

inconsistent *a*, **-ly** *adv* widersprüchlich; (*illogical*) inkonsequent; **be ~** <*things:*> nicht übereinstimmen

inconsolable *a* untröstlich

inconspicuous *a* unauffällig

incontinen|ce *n* Inkontinenz *f*. **~t** *a* inkontinent

inconvenien|ce *n* Unannehmlichkeit *f*; (*drawback*) Nachteil *m*. **~t** *a*, **-ly** *adv* ungünstig; **be ~t for s.o.** jdm nicht passen

incorporate *vt* aufnehmen; (*contain*) enthalten

incorrect *a*, **-ly** *adv* inkorrekt

incorrigible *a* unverbesserlich

incorruptible *a* unbestechlich

increase¹ *n* Zunahme *f*; (*rise*) Erhöhung *f*; **be on the ~** zunehmen

increas|e² *vt* vergrößern; (*raise*) erhöhen ● *vi* zunehmen; (*rise*) sich erhöhen. **~ing** *a*, **-ly** *adv* zunehmend

incredible *a*, **-bly** *adv* unglaublich

incredulous *a* ungläubig

incriminate *vt* (*Jur*) belasten

incur *vt* (*pt/pp* **incurred**) sich (*dat*) zuziehen; machen <*debts*>

incurable *a*, **-bly** *adv* unheilbar

indebted *a* verpflichtet (**to** *dat*)

indecent *a*, **-ly** *adv* unanständig

indecision *n* Unentschlossenheit *f*

indecisive *a* ergebnislos; <*person*> unentschlossen

indeed *adv* in der Tat, tatsächlich; **very much ~** sehr

indefatigable *a* unermüdlich

indefinite *a* unbestimmt. **~ly** *adv* unbegrenzt; <*postpone*> auf unbestimmte Zeit

indent *vt* (*Typ*) einrücken. **~ation** *n* Einrückung *f*; (*notch*) Kerbe *f*

independen|ce *n* Unabhängigkeit *f*; (*self-reliance*) Selbstständigkeit *f*. **~t** *a*, **-ly** *adv* unabhängig; selbstständig

indescribable *a*, **-bly** *adv* unbeschreiblich

indestructible *a* unzerstörbar

indeterminate *a* unbestimmt

index *n* Register *nt*

index: ~ card *n* Karteikarte *f*. **~ finger** *n* Zeigefinger *m*. **~-linked** *a* <*pension*> dynamisch

India *n* Indien *nt*. **~n** *a* indisch; (*American*) indianisch ● *n* Inder(in) *m(f)*; (*American*) Indianer(in) *m(f)*

Indian summer *n* Nachsommer *m*

indicat|e *vt* zeigen; (*point at*) zeigen auf (+ *acc*); (*hint*) andeuten; (*register*) anzeigen ● *vi* <*car:*> blinken. **~ion** *n* Anzeichen *nt*

indicative *n* (*Gram*) Indikativ *m*

indicator *n* (*Auto*) Blinker *m*

indifferen|ce *n* Gleichgültigkeit *f*. **~t** *a*, **-ly** *adv* gleichgültig; (*not good*) mittelmäßig

indigest|ible *a* unverdaulich; (*difficult to digest*) schwer verdaulich. **~ion** *n* Magenverstimmung *f*

indigna|nt *a*, **-ly** *adv* entrüstet, empört. **~tion** *n* Entrüstung *f*, Empörung *f*

indignity *n* Demütigung *f*

indirect *a*, **-ly** *adv* indirekt

indiscreet *a* indiskret

indiscretion *n* Indiskretion *f*

indispensable *a* unentbehrlich

indisposed *a* indisponiert

indisputable *a*, **-bly** *adv* unbestreitbar

indistinct *a*, **-ly** *adv* undeutlich

indistinguishable *a* **be ~** nicht zu unterscheiden sein

individual *a*, **-ly** *adv* individuell; (*single*) einzeln ● *n* Individuum *nt*. **~ity** *n* Individualität *f*

indivisible *a* unteilbar

indoctrinate *vt* indoktrinieren

indolen|ce *n* Faulheit *f*. **~t** *a* faul

indomitable *a* unbeugsam

indoor *a* Innen-; <*clothes*> Haus-; <*plant*> Zimmer-; (*Sport*) Hallen-. **~s** *adv* im Haus, drinnen; **go ~s** ins Haus gehen

indulge *vt* frönen (+ *dat*); verwöhnen <*child*> ● *vi* **~ in** frönen (+ *dat*). **~nce** *n* Nachgiebigkeit *f*; (*leniency*) Nachsicht *f*. **~nt** *a* [zu] nachgiebig; nachsichtig

industrial *a* Industrie-. **~ist** *n* Industrielle(r) *m*

industr|ious *a*, **-ly** *adv* fleißig. **~y** *n* Industrie *f*; (*zeal*) Fleiß *m*

inebriated *a* betrunken

inedible *a* nicht essbar

ineffective *a*, **-ly** *adv* unwirksam; <*person*> untauglich

inefficient *a* unfähig; <*organization*> nicht leistungsfähig; <*method*> nicht rationell

ineligible *a* nicht berechtigt

inept *a* ungeschickt

inequality *n* Ungleichheit *f*

inertia *n* Trägheit *f*

inescapable *a* unvermeidlich

inestimable *a* unschätzbar

inevitab|le *a* unvermeidlich. **~ly** *adv* zwangsläufig

inexact *a* ungenau

inexcusable *a* unverzeihlich

inexhaustible *a* unerschöpflich

inexpensive *a*, **-ly** *adv* preiswert

inexperience *n* Unerfahrenheit *f*. **~d** *a* unerfahren
inexplicable *a* unerklärlich
infallible *a* unfehlbar
infamous *a* niederträchtig; (*notorious*) berüchtigt
infan|cy *n* frühe Kindheit *f*; (*fig*) Anfangsstadium *nt*. **~t** *n* Kleinkind *nt*. **~tile** *a* kindisch
infantry *n* Infanterie *f*
infatuated *a* vernarrt (**with** in + *acc*)
infect *vt* anstecken, infizieren; **become ~ed** <*wound:*> sich infizieren. **~ion** *n* Infektion *f*. **~ious** *a* ansteckend
inferior *a* minderwertig; (*in rank*) untergeordnet ● *n* Untergebene(r) *m*/*f*
inferiority *n* Minderwertigkeit *f*. **~ complex** *n* Minderwertigkeitskomplex *m*
infern|al *a* höllisch. **~o** *n* flammendes Inferno *nt*
infertile *a* unfruchtbar
infest *vt* **be ~ed with** befallen sein von; <*place*> verseucht sein mit
infidelity *n* Untreue *f*
infighting *n* (*fig*) interne Machtkämpfe *pl*
infinite *a*, **-ly** *adv* unendlich
infinitive *n* (*Gram*) Infinitiv *m*
infinity *n* Unendlichkeit *f*
inflame *vt* entzünden. **~d** *a* entzündet
inflammable *a* feuergefährlich
inflammation *n* Entzündung *f*
inflammatory *a* aufrührerisch
inflat|e *vt* aufblasen, (*with pump*) aufpumpen. **~ion** *n* Inflation *f*. **~ionary** *a* inflationär
inflexible *a* starr; <*person*> unbeugsam
inflict *vt* zufügen (**on** *dat*); versetzen <*blow*> (**on** *dat*)
influen|ce *n* Einfluss *m* ● *vt* beeinflussen. **~tial** *a* einflussreich
influenza *n* Grippe *f*
inform *vt* benachrichtigen; (*officially*) informieren; **~ s.o. of sth** jdm etw mitteilen; **keep s.o. ~ed** jdn auf dem Laufenden halten ● *vi* **~ against** denunzieren
informal *a*, **-ly** *adv* zwanglos; (*unofficial*) inoffiziell. **~ity** *n* Zwanglosigkeit *f*
informant *n* Gewährsmann *m*
informat|ion *n* Auskunft *f*; **a piece of ~ion** eine Auskunft. **~ive** *a* aufschlussreich; (*instructive*) lehrreich
informer *n* Spitzel *m*; (*Pol*) Denunziant *m*
infra-red *a* infrarot
infrequent *a*, **-ly** *adv* selten
infringe *vt*/*i* **~ [on]** verstoßen gegen. **~ment** *n* Verstoß *m*
infuriat|e *vt* wütend machen. **~ing** *a* ärgerlich
ingenious *a* erfinderisch; <*thing*> raffiniert
ingenuity *n* Geschicklichkeit *f*
ingrained *a* eingefleischt; **be ~** <*dirt:*> tief sitzen
ingratiate *vt* **~ oneself** sich einschmeicheln (**with** bei)
ingratitude *n* Undankbarkeit *f*
ingredient *n* (*Culin*) Zutat *f*
ingrowing *a* <*nail*> eingewachsen
inhabit *vt* bewohnen. **~ant** *n* Einwohner(in) *m*(*f*)
inhale *vt*/*i* einatmen; (*Med & when smoking*) inhalieren
inherent *a* natürlich
inherit *vt* erben. **~ance** *n* Erbschaft *f*, Erbe *nt*
inhibit|ed *a* gehemmt. **~ion** *n* Hemmung *f*
inhospitable *a* ungastlich
inhuman *a* unmenschlich
inimitable *a* unnachahmlich
initial *a* anfänglich, Anfangs- ● *n* Anfangsbuchstabe *m*; **my ~s** meine Initialen. **~ly** *adv* anfangs, am Anfang

initiat|e *vt* einführen. **~ion** *n* Einführung *f*
initiative *n* Initiative *f*
inject *vt* einspritzen, injizieren. **~ion** *n* Spritze *f*, Injektion *f*
injur|e *vt* verletzen. **~y** *n* Verletzung *f*
injustice *n* Ungerechtigkeit *f*; **do s.o. an ~** jdm unrecht tun
ink *n* Tinte *f*
inlaid *a* eingelegt
inland *a* Binnen- ●*adv* landeinwärts
in-laws *npl* [!] Schwiegereltern *pl*
inlay *n* Einlegearbeit *f*
inlet *n* schmale Bucht *f*; (*Techn*) Zuleitung *f*
inmate *n* Insasse *m*
inn *n* Gasthaus *nt*
innate *a* angeboren
inner *a* innere(r,s). **~most** *a* innerste(r,s)
innocen|ce *n* Unschuld *f*. **~t** *a* unschuldig. **~tly** *adv* in aller Unschuld
innocuous *a* harmlos
innovat|ion *n* Neuerung *f*. **~ive** *a* innovativ. **~or** *n* Neuerer *m*
innumerable *a* unzählig
inoculat|e *vt* impfen. **~ion** *n* Impfung *f*
inoffensive *a* harmlos
inoperable *a* nicht operierbar
inopportune *a* unpassend
inorganic *a* anorganisch
in-patient *n* [stationär behandelter] Krankenhauspatient *m*
input *n* Input *m & nt*
inquest *n* gerichtliche Untersuchung *f* der Todesursache
inquir|e *vi* sich erkundigen (**about** nach); **~e into** untersuchen ●*vt* sich erkundigen nach. **~y** *n* Erkundigung *f*; (*investigation*) Untersuchung *f*
inquisitive *a*, **-ly** *adv* neugierig
insane *a* geisteskrank; (*fig*) wahnsinnig
insanitary *a* unhygienisch
insanity *n* Geisteskrankheit *f*
insatiable *a* unersättlich
inscription *n* Inschrift *f*
inscrutable *a* unergründlich; <*expression*> undurchdringlich
insect *n* Insekt *nt*. **~icide** *n* Insektenvertilgungsmittel *nt*
insecur|e *a* nicht sicher; (*fig*) unsicher. **~ity** *n* Unsicherheit *f*
insensitive *a* gefühllos; **~ to** unempfindlich gegen
inseparable *a* untrennbar; (*people*) unzertrennlich
insert¹ *n* Einsatz *m*
insert² *vt* einfügen, einsetzen; einstecken <*key*>; einwerfen <*coin*>. **~ion** *n* (*insert*) Einsatz *m*; (*in text*) Einfügung *f*
inside *n* Innenseite *f*; (*of house*) Innere(s) *nt* ●*attrib* Innen- ●*adv* innen; (*indoors*) drinnen; **go ~** hineingehen; **come ~** hereinkommen; **~ out** links [herum]; **know sth ~ out** etw in- und auswendig kennen ●*prep* **~ [of]** in (+ *dat*/ (*into*) + *acc*)
insight *n* Einblick *m* (**into** in + *acc*); (*understanding*) Einsicht *f*
insignificant *a* unbedeutend
insincere *a* unaufrichtig
insinuat|e *vt* andeuten. **~ion** *n* Andeutung *f*
insipid *a* fade
insist *vi* darauf bestehen; **~ on** bestehen auf (+ *dat*) ●*vt* **~ that** darauf bestehen, dass. **~ence** *n* Bestehen *nt*. **~ent** *a*, **-ly** *adv* beharrlich; **be ~ent** darauf bestehen
insole *n* Einlegesohle *f*
insolen|ce *n* Unverschämtheit *f*. **~t** *a*, **-ly** *adv* unverschämt
insoluble *a* unlöslich; (*fig*) unlösbar
insolvent *a* zahlungsunfähig
insomnia *n* Schlaflosigkeit *f*

inspect *vt* inspizieren; (*test*) prüfen; kontrollieren <*ticket*>. **~ion** *n* Inspektion *f*. **~or** *n* Inspektor *m*; (*of tickets*) Kontrolleur *m*

inspiration *n* Inspiration *f*

inspire *vt* inspirieren

instability *n* Unbeständigkeit *f*; (*of person*) Labilität *f*

install *vt* installieren. **~ation** *n* Installation *f*

instalment *n* (*Comm*) Rate *f*; (*of serial*) Fortsetzung *f*; (*Radio, TV*) Folge *f*

instance *n* Fall *m*; (*example*) Beispiel *nt*; **in the first ~** zunächst; **for ~** zum Beispiel

instant *a* sofortig; (*Culin*) Instant- ● *n* Augenblick *m*, Moment *m*. **~aneous** *a* unverzüglich, unmittelbar

instant coffee *n* Pulverkaffee *m*

instantly *adv* sofort

instead *adv* statt dessen; **~ of** statt (+ *gen*), anstelle von; **~ of me** an meiner Stelle; **~ of going** anstatt zu gehen

instep *n* Spann *m*, Rist *m*

instigat|e *vt* anstiften; einleiten <*proceedings*>. **~ion** *n* Anstiftung *f*; **at his ~ion** auf seine Veranlassung

instil *vt* (*pt/pp* **instilled**) einprägen (**into s.o.** jdm)

instinct *n* Instinkt *m*. **~ive** *a*, **-ly** *adv* instinktiv

institut|e *n* Institut *nt*. **~ion** *n* Institution *f*; (*home*) Anstalt *f*

instruct *vt* unterrichten; (*order*) anweisen. **~ion** *n* Unterricht *m*; Anweisung *f*; **~ions** *pl* **for use** Gebrauchsanweisung *f*. **~ive** *a* lehrreich. **~or** *n* Lehrer(in) *m(f)*; (*Mil*) Ausbilder *m*

instrument *n* Instrument *nt*. **~al** *a* Instrumental-

insubordi|nate *a* ungehorsam. **~nation** *n* Ungehorsam *m*; (*Mil*) Insubordination *f*

insufficient *a*, **-ly** *adv* nicht genügend

insulat|e *vt* isolieren. **~ing tape** *n* Isolierband *nt*. **~ion** *n* Isolierung *f*

insult[1] *n* Beleidigung *f*

insult[2] *vt* beleidigen

insur|ance *n* Versicherung *f*. **~e** *vt* versichern

intact *a* unbeschädigt; (*complete*) vollständig

intake *n* Aufnahme *f*

intangible *a* nicht greifbar

integral *a* wesentlich

integrat|e *vt* integrieren ● *vi* sich integrieren. **~ion** *n* Integration *f*

integrity *n* Integrität *f*

intellect *n* Intellekt *m*. **~ual** *a* intellektuell

intelligen|ce *n* Intelligenz *f*; (*Mil*) Nachrichtendienst *m*; (*information*) Meldungen *pl*. **~t** *a*, **-ly** *adv* intelligent

intelligible *a* verständlich

intend *vt* beabsichtigen; **be ~ed for** bestimmt sein für

intense *a* intensiv; <*pain*> stark. **~ly** *adv* äußerst; <*study*> intensiv

intensify *v* (*pt/pp* **-ied**) ● *vt* intensivieren ● *vi* zunehmen

intensity *n* Intensität *f*

intensive *a*, **-ly** *adv* intensiv; **be in ~ care** auf der Intensivstation sein

intent *a*, **-ly** *adv* aufmerksam; **~ on** (*absorbed in*) vertieft in (+ *acc*) ● *n* Absicht *f*

intention *n* Absicht *f*. **~al** *a*, **-ly** *adv* absichtlich

interacti|on *n* Wechselwirkung *f*. **~ve** *a* interaktiv

intercede *vi* Fürsprache einlegen (**on behalf of** für)

intercept *vt* abfangen

interchange *n* Austausch *m*; (*Auto*) Autobahnkreuz *nt*

intercom *n* [Gegen]sprechanlage *f*

intercourse *n* (*sexual*) Geschlechtsverkehr *m*

interest *n* Interesse *nt;* (*Comm*) Zinsen *pl* ● *vt* interessieren; **be ~ed** sich interessieren (**in** für). **~ing** *a* interessant. **~ rate** *n* Zinssatz *m*

interfere *vi* sich einmischen. **~nce** *n* Einmischung *f;* (*Radio, TV*) Störung *f*

interim *a* Zwischen-; (*temporary*) vorläufig

interior *a* innere(r,s), Innen- ● *n* Innere(s) *nt*

interject *vt* einwerfen. **~ion** *n* Interjektion *f;* (*remark*) Einwurf *m*

interlude *n* Pause *f;* (*performance*) Zwischenspiel *nt*

intermarry *vi* untereinander heiraten; *<different groups:>* Mischehen schließen

intermediary *n* Vermittler(in) *m(f)*

intermediate *a* Zwischen-

interminable *a* endlos [lang]

intermittent *a* in Abständen auftretend

internal *a* innere(r,s); *<matter, dispute>* intern. **~ly** *adv* innerlich; *<deal with>* intern

international *a*, **-ly** *adv* international ● *n* Länderspiel *nt;* (*player*) Nationalspieler(in) *m(f)*

Internet *n* Internet *nt;* **on the ~** im Internet

internment *n* Internierung *f*

interplay *n* Wechselspiel *nt*

interpolate *vt* einwerfen

interpret *vt* interpretieren; auslegen *<text>*; deuten *<dream>*; (*translate*) dolmetschen ● *vi* dolmetschen. **~ation** *n* Interpretation *f*. **~er** *n* Dolmetscher(in) *m(f)*

interrogat|e *vt* verhören. **~ion** *n* Verhör *nt*

interrogative *a* & *n* **~ [pronoun]** Interrogativpronomen *nt*

interrupt *vt/i* unterbrechen; **don't ~!** red nicht dazwischen! **~ion** *n* Unterbrechung *f*

intersect *vi* sich kreuzen; (*Geom*) sich schneiden. **~ion** *n* Kreuzung *f*

interspersed *a* **~ with** durchsetzt mit

intertwine *vi* sich ineinanderschlingen

interval *n* Abstand *m;* (*Theat*) Pause *f;* (*Mus*) Intervall *nt;* **at hourly ~s** alle Stunde; **bright ~s** *pl* Aufheiterungen *pl*

interven|e *vi* eingreifen; (*occur*) dazwischenkommen. **~tion** *n* Eingreifen *nt;* (*Mil, Pol*) Intervention *f*

interview *n* (*Journ*) Interview *nt;* (*for job*) Vorstellungsgespräch *nt* ● *vt* interviewen; ein Vorstellungsgespräch führen mit. **~er** *n* Interviewer(in) *m(f)*

intimacy *n* Vertrautheit *f;* (*sexual*) Intimität *f*

intimate *a*, **-ly** *adv* vertraut; *<friend>* eng; (*sexually*) intim

intimidat|e *vt* einschüchtern. **~ion** *n* Einschüchterung *f*

into *prep* in (+ *acc*); **be ~** [!] sich auskennen mit; **7 ~ 21** 21 [geteilt] durch 7

intolerable *a* unerträglich

intoleran|ce *n* Intoleranz *f*. **~t** *a* intolerant

intonation *n* Tonfall *m*

intoxicat|ed *a* betrunken; (*fig*) berauscht. **~ion** *n* Rausch *m*

intransigent *a* unnachgiebig

intransitive *a*, **-ly** *adv* intransitiv

intrepid *a* kühn, unerschrocken

intricate *a* kompliziert

intrigu|e *n* Intrige *f* ● *vt* faszinieren. **~ing** *a* faszinierend

intrinsic *a* **~ value** Eigenwert *m*

introduce *vt* vorstellen; (*bring in, insert*) einführen

introduct|ion *n* Einführung *f*; (*to person*) Vorstellung *f*; (*to book*) Einleitung *f*. **~ory** *a* einleitend
introvert *n* introvertierter Mensch *m*
intru|de *vi* stören. **~der** *n* Eindringling *m*. **~sion** *n* Störung *f*
intuit|ion *n* Intuition *f*. **~ive** *a*, **-ly** *adv* intuitiv
inundate *vt* überschwemmen
invade *vt* einfallen in (+ *acc*). **~r** *n* Angreifer *m*
invalid[1] *n* Kranke(r) *m/f*
invalid[2] *a* ungültig
invaluable *a* unschätzbar; <*person*> unersetzlich
invariab|le *a* unveränderlich. **~ly** *adv* immer
invasion *n* Invasion *f*
invent *vt* erfinden. **~ion** *n* Erfindung *f*. **~ive** *a* erfinderisch. **~or** *n* Erfinder *m*
inventory *n* Bestandsliste *f*
invert *vt* umkehren. **~ed commas** *npl* Anführungszeichen *pl*
invest *vt* investieren, anlegen; **~ in** (🅘 *buy*) sich (*dat*) zulegen
investigat|e *vt* untersuchen. **~ion** *n* Untersuchung *f*
invest|ment *n* Anlage *f*; **be a good ~ment** (*fig*) sich bezahlt machen. **~or** *n* Kapitalanleger *m*
invidious *a* unerfreulich; (*unfair*) ungerecht
invincible *a* unbesiegbar
inviolable *a* unantastbar
invisible *a* unsichtbar
invitation *n* Einladung *f*
invit|e *vt* einladen. **~ing** *a* einladend
invoice *n* Rechnung *f* ● *vt* **~ s.o.** jdm eine Rechnung schicken
involuntary *a*, **-ily** *adv* unwillkürlich
involve *vt* beteiligen; (*affect*) betreffen; (*implicate*) verwickeln; (*entail*) mit sich bringen; (*mean*) bedeuten; **be ~d in** beteiligt sein an (+ *dat*); (*implicated*) verwickelt sein in (+ *acc*); **get ~d with s.o.** sich mit jdm einlassen. **~d** *a* kompliziert
invulnerable *a* unverwundbar; <*position*> unangreifbar
inward *a* innere(r,s). **~s** *adv* nach innen
iodine *n* Jod *nt*
IOU *abbr* Schuldschein *m*
Iran *n* der Iran
Iraq *n* der Irak
irascible *a* aufbrausend
irate *a* wütend
Ireland *n* Irland *nt*
iris *n* (*Anat*) Regenbogenhaut *f*, Iris *f*; (*Bot*) Schwertlilie *f*
Irish *a* irisch ● *n* **the ~** *pl* die Iren. **~man** *n* Ire *m*. **~woman** *n* Irin *f*
iron *a* Eisen-; (*fig*) eisern ● *n* Eisen *nt*; (*appliance*) Bügeleisen *nt* ● *vt/i* bügeln
ironic[al] *a* ironisch
ironing *n* Bügeln *nt*; (*articles*) Bügelwäsche *f*. **~-board** *n* Bügelbrett *nt*
ironmonger *n* **~'s [shop]** Haushaltswarengeschäft *nt*
irony *n* Ironie *f*
irrational *a* irrational
irreconcilable *a* unversöhnlich
irrefutable *a* unwiderlegbar
irregular *a*, **-ly** *adv* unregelmäßig; (*against rules*) regelwidrig. **~ity** *n* Unregelmäßigkeit *f*; Regelwidrigkeit *f*
irrelevant *a* irrelevant
irreparable *a* nicht wieder gutzumachen
irreplaceable *a* unersetzlich
irrepressible *a* unverwüstlich; **be ~** <*person*> nicht unterzukriegen sein
irresistible *a* unwiderstehlich
irresolute *a* unentschlossen
irrespective *a* **~ of** ungeachtet (+ *gen*)

irresponsible *a*, **-bly** *adv* unverantwortlich; <*person*> verantwortungslos
irreverent *a*, **-ly** *adv* respektlos
irrevocable *a*, **-bly** *adv* unwiderruflich
irrigat|e *vt* bewässern. **~ion** *n* Bewässerung *f*
irritable *a* reizbar
irritant *n* Reizstoff *m*
irritat|e *vt* irritieren; (*Med*) reizen. **~ion** *n* Ärger *m*; (*Med*) Reizung *f*
is *see* **be**
Islam *n* der Islam. **~ic** *a* islamisch
island *n* Insel *f*. **~er** *n* Inselbewohner(in) *m(f)*
isolat|e *vt* isolieren. **~ed** *a* (*remote*) abgelegen; (*single*) einzeln. **~ion** *n* Isoliertheit *f*; (*Med*) Isolierung *f*
Israel *n* Israel *nt*. **~i** *a* israelisch ● *n* Israeli *m/f*
issue *n* Frage *f*; (*outcome*) Ergebnis *nt*; (*of magazine, stamps*) Ausgabe *f*; (*offspring*) Nachkommen *pl* ● *vt* ausgeben; ausstellen <*passport*>; erteilen <*order*>; herausgeben <*book*>; **be ~d with sth** etw erhalten

it
● *pronoun*
····➤ (*as subject*) er (*m*), sie (*f*), es (*nt*); (*in impersonal sentence*) es. **where is the spoon? It's on the table** wo ist der Löffel? Er liegt auf dem Tisch. **it was very kind of you** es war sehr nett von Ihnen. **it's five o'clock** es ist fünf Uhr
····➤ (*as direct object*) ihn (*m*), sie (*f*), es (*nt*). **that's my pencil — give it to me** das ist mein Bleistift – gib ihn mir.
····➤ (*as dative object*) ihm (*m*), ihr (*f*), ihm (*nt*). **he found a track and followed it** er fand eine Spur und folgte ihr.
····➤ (*after prepositions*)

! Combinations such as *with it, from it, to it* are translated by the prepositions with the prefix **da-** (**damit**, **davon**, **dazu**). Prepositions beginning with a vowel insert an 'r' (**daran**, **darauf**, **darüber**). **I can't do anything with it** ich kann nichts damit anfangen. **don't lean on it!** lehn dich nicht daran!

····➤ (*the person in question*) es. **it's me** ich bin's. **is it you, Dad?** bist du es, Vater? **who is it?** wer ist da?

Italian *a* italienisch ● *n* Italiener(in) *m(f)*; (*Lang*) Italienisch *nt*
italics *npl* Kursivschrift *f*; **in ~s** kursiv
Italy *n* Italien *nt*
itch *n* Juckreiz *m*; **I have an ~** es juckt mich ● *vi* jucken; **I'm ~ing** [!] es juckt mich (**to** zu). **~y** *a* **be ~y** jucken
item *n* Gegenstand *m*; (*Comm*) Artikel *m*; (*on agenda*) Punkt *m*; (*on invoice*) Posten *m*; (*act*) Nummer *f*
itinerary *n* [Reise]route *f*
its *poss pron* sein; (*f*) ihr
it's = it is, it has
itself *pron* selbst; (*refl*) sich; **by ~** von selbst; (*alone*) allein
ivory *n* Elfenbein *nt* ● *attrib* Elfenbein-
ivy *n* Efeu *m*

Jj

jab *n* Stoß *m*; ([!] *injection*) Spritze *f* ● *vt* (*pt/pp* **jabbed**) stoßen

jabber *vi* plappern
jack *n* (*Auto*) Wagenheber *m*; (*Cards*) Bube *m* ● *vt* ~ **up** (*Auto*) aufbocken
jacket *n* Jacke *f*; (*of book*) Schutzumschlag *m*
jackpot *n* **hit the** ~ das große Los ziehen
jade *n* Jade *m*
jagged *a* zackig
jail = **gaol**
jam¹ *n* Marmelade *f*
jam² *n* Gedränge *nt*; (*Auto*) Stau *m*; (*fam. difficulty*) Klemme *f* ● *v* (*pt/pp* **jammed**) ● *vt* klemmen (**in** in + *acc*); stören *<broadcast>* ● *vi* klemmen
Jamaica *n* Jamaika *nt*
jangle *vi* klimpern ● *vt* klimpern mit
January *n* Januar *m*
Japan *n* Japan *nt*. ~**ese** *a* japanisch ● *n* Japaner(in) *m(f)*; (*Lang*) Japanisch *nt*
jar *n* Glas *nt*; (*earthenware*) Topf *m*
jargon *n* Jargon *m*
jaunt *n* Ausflug *m*
jaunty *a* (**-ier, -iest**) **-ily** *adv* keck
javelin *n* Speer *m*
jaw *n* Kiefer *m*
jazz *n* Jazz *m*. ~**y** *a* knallig
jealous *a*, **-ly** *adv* eifersüchtig (**of** auf + *acc*). ~**y** *n* Eifersucht *f*
jeans *npl* Jeans *pl*
jeer *vi* johlen; ~ **at** verhöhnen
jelly *n* Gelee *nt*, (*dessert*) Götterspeise *f*. ~**fish** *n* Qualle *f*
jeopar|dize *vt* gefährden. ~**dy** *n* **in** ~**dy** gefährdet
jerk *n* Ruck *m* ● *vt* stoßen; (*pull*) reißen ● *vi* rucken; *<limb, muscle:>* zucken. ~**ily** *adv* ruckweise. ~**y** *a* ruckartig
jersey *n* Pullover *m*; (*Sport*) Trikot *nt*; (*fabric*) Jersey *m*
jest *n* **in** ~ im Spaß
jet *n* (*of water*) [Wasser]strahl *m*; (*nozzle*) Düse *f*; (*plane*) Düsenflugzeug *nt*
jet: ~**-black** *a* pechschwarz. ~**-propelled** *a* mit Düsenantrieb
jetty *n* Landesteg *m*; (*breakwater*) Buhne *f*
Jew *n* Jude *m* /Jüdin *f*
jewel *n* Edelstein *m*; (*fig*) Juwel *nt*. ~**ler** *n* Juwelier *m*; ~**ler's [shop]** Juweliergeschäft *nt*. ~**lery** *n* Schmuck *m*
Jew|ess *n* Jüdin *f*. ~**ish** *a* jüdisch
jib *vi* (*pt/pp* **jibbed**) (*fig*) sich sträuben (**at** gegen)
jigsaw *n* ~ **[puzzle]** Puzzlespiel *nt*
jilt *vt* sitzen lassen
jingle *n* (*rhyme*) Verschen *nt* ● *vi* klimpern
jinx *n* [!] **it's got a** ~ **on it** es ist verhext
jittery *a* [!] nervös
job *n* Aufgabe *f*; (*post*) Stelle *f*, [!] Job *m*; **be a** ~ [!] nicht leicht sein; **it's a good** ~ **that** es ist [nur] gut, dass. ~**less** *a* arbeitslos
jockey *n* Jockei *m*
jocular *a*, **-ly** *adv* spaßhaft
jog *n* Stoß *m* ● *v* (*pt/pp* **jogged**) ● *vt* anstoßen; ~ **s.o.'s memory** jds Gedächtnis nachhelfen ● *vi* (*Sport*) joggen. ~**ging** *n* Jogging *nt*
john *n* (*Amer* [!]) Klo *nt*
join *n* Nahtstelle *f* ● *vt* verbinden (**to** mit); sich anschließen (+ *dat*) *<person>*; (*become member of*) beitreten (+ *dat*); eintreten in (+ *acc*) *<firm>* ● *vi* *<roads:>* sich treffen. ~ **in** *vi* mitmachen. ~ **up** *vi* (*Mil*) Soldat werden ● *vt* zusammenfügen
joint *a*, **-ly** *adv* gemeinsam ● *n* Gelenk *nt*; (*in wood, brickwork*) Fuge *f*; (*Culin*) Braten *m*; ([!] *bar*) Lokal *nt*
jok|e *n* Scherz *m*; (*funny story*) Witz *m*; (*trick*) Streich *m* ● *vi* scherzen. ~**er** *n* Witzbold *m*;

J

(*Cards*) Joker *m*. **~ing** *n* **~ing apart** Spaß beiseite. **~ingly** *adv* im Spaß

jolly *a* (**-ier, -iest**) lustig ● *adv* [!] sehr

jolt *n* Ruck *m* ● *vt* einen Ruck versetzen (+ *dat*) ● *vi* holpern

Jordan *n* Jordanien *nt*

jostle *vt* anrempeln

jot *vt* (*pt/pp* **jotted**) **~ [down]** sich (*dat*) notieren

journal *n* Zeitschrift *f*; (*diary*) Tagebuch *nt*. **~ese** *n* Zeitungsjargon *m*. **~ism** *n* Journalismus *m*. **~ist** *n* Journalist(in) *m(f)*

journey *n* Reise *f*

jovial *a* lustig

joy *n* Freude *f*. **~ful** *a*, **-ly** *adv* freudig, froh. **~ride** *n* [!] Spritztour *f* [im gestohlenen Auto]

jubil|ant *a* überglücklich. **~ation** *n* Jubel *m*

jubilee *n* Jubiläum *nt*

judder *vi* rucken

judge *n* Richter *m*; (*of competition*) Preisrichter *m* ● *vt* beurteilen; (*estimate*) [ein]schätzen ● *vi* urteilen (**by** nach). **~ment** *n* Beurteilung *f*; (*Jur*) Urteil *nt*; (*fig*) Urteilsvermögen *nt*

judic|ial *a* gerichtlich. **~ious** *a* klug

jug *n* Kanne *f*; (*small*) Kännchen *nt*; (*for water, wine*) Krug *m*

juggle *vi* jonglieren. **~r** *n* Jongleur *m*

juice *n* Saft *m*

juicy *a* (**-ier, -iest**) saftig; [!] <*story*> pikant

juke-box *n* Musikbox *f*

July *n* Juli *m*

jumble *n* Durcheinander *nt* ● *vt* **~ [up]** durcheinander bringen. **~ sale** *n* [Wohltätigkeits]basar *m*

jump *n* Sprung *m*; (*in prices*) Anstieg *m*; (*in horse racing*) Hindernis *nt* ● *vi* springen; (*start*) zusammenzucken; **make s.o. ~** jdn erschrecken; **~ at** (*fig*) sofort zugreifen bei <*offer*>; **~ to conclusions** voreilige Schlüsse ziehen ● *vt* überspringen. **~ up** *vi* aufspringen

jumper *n* Pullover *m*, Pulli *m*

jumpy *a* nervös

junction *n* Kreuzung *f*; (*Rail*) Knotenpunkt *m*

June *n* Juni *m*

jungle *n* Dschungel *m*

junior *a* jünger; (*in rank*) untergeordnet; (*Sport*) Junioren- ● *n* Junior *m*

junk *n* Gerümpel *nt*, Trödel *m*

junkie *n* [✖] Fixer *m*

junk-shop *n* Trödelladen *m*

jurisdiction *n* Gerichtsbarkeit *f*

jury *n* **the ~** die Geschworenen *pl*; (*for competition*) die Jury

just *a* gerecht ● *adv* gerade; (*only*) nur; (*simply*) einfach; (*exactly*) genau; **~ as tall** ebenso groß; **I'm ~ going** ich gehe schon

justice *n* Gerechtigkeit *f*; **do ~ to** gerecht werden (+ *dat*)

justifiab|le *a* berechtigt. **~ly** *adv* berechtigterweise

justi|fication *n* Rechtfertigung *f*. **~fy** *vt* (*pt/pp* **-ied**) rechtfertigen

justly *adv* zu Recht

jut *vi* (*pt/pp* **jutted**) **~ out** vorstehen

juvenile *a* jugendlich; (*childish*) kindisch ● *n* Jugendliche(r) *m/f*. **~ delinquency** *n* Jugendkriminalität *f*

Kk

kangaroo *n* Känguru *nt*

kebab *n* Spießchen *nt*

keel *n* Kiel *m* ●*vi* **~ over** umkippen; (*Naut*) kentern

keen *a* (**-er, -est**) (*sharp*) scharf; (*intense*) groß; (*eager*) eifrig, begeistert; **~ on** [!] erpicht auf (+ *acc*); **~ on s.o.** von jdm sehr angetan; **be ~ to do sth** etw gerne machen wollen. **~ly** *adv* tief. **~ness** *n* Eifer *m*, Begeisterung *f*

keep *n* (*maintenance*) Unterhalt *m*; (*of castle*) Bergfried *m*; **for ~s** für immer ●*v* (*pt/pp* **kept**) ●*vt* behalten; (*store*) aufbewahren; (*not throw away*) aufheben; (*support*) unterhalten; (*detain*) aufhalten; freihalten <*seat*>; halten <*promise, animals*>; führen, haben <*shop*>; einhalten <*law, rules*>; **~ s.o. waiting** jdn warten lassen; **~ sth to oneself** etw nicht weitersagen ●*vi* (*remain*) bleiben; <*food*:> sich halten; **~ left/right** sich links/ rechts halten; **~ on doing sth** etw weitermachen; (*repeatedly*) etw dauernd machen; **~ in with** sich gut stellen mit. **~ up** *vi* Schritt halten ●*vt* (*continue*) weitermachen

keep|er *n* Wärter(in) *m*(*f*). **~ing** *n* **be in ~ing with** passen zu

kennel *n* Hundehütte *f*; **~s** *pl* (*boarding*) Hundepension *f*; (*breeding*) Zwinger *m*

Kenya *n* Kenia *nt*

kept *see* **keep**

kerb *n* Bordstein *m*

kernel *n* Kern *m*

ketchup *n* Ketschup *m*

kettle *n* [Wasser]kessel *m*; **put the ~ on** Wasser aufsetzen

key *n* Schlüssel *m*; (*Mus*) Tonart *f*; (*of piano, typewriter*) Taste *f* ●*vt* **~ in** eintasten

key: ~board *n* Tastatur *f*; (*Mus*) Klaviatur *f*. **~hole** *n* Schlüsselloch *nt*. **~-ring** *n* Schlüsselring *m*

khaki *a* khakifarben ●*n* Khaki *nt*

kick *n* [Fuß]tritt *m*; **for ~s** [!] zum Spaß ●*vt* treten; **~ the bucket** [!] abkratzen ●*vi* <*animal*> ausschlagen

kid *n* ([!] *child*) Kind *nt* ●*vt* (*pt/pp* **kidded**) [!] **~ s.o.** jdm etwas vormachen

kidnap *vt* (*pt/pp* **-napped**) entführen. **~per** *n* Entführer *m*. **~ping** *n* Entführung *f*

kidney *n* Niere *f*

kill *vt* töten; [!] totschlagen <*time*>; **~ two birds with one stone** zwei Fliegen mit einer Klappe schlagen. **~er** *n* Mörder(in) *m*(*f*). **~ing** *n* Tötung *f*; (*murder*) Mord *m*

killjoy *n* Spielverderber *m*

kilo *n* Kilo *nt*

kilo: ~gram *n* Kilogramm *nt*. **~metre** *n* Kilometer *m*. **~watt** *n* Kilowatt *nt*

kilt *n* Schottenrock *m*

kind[1] *n* Art *f*; (*brand, type*) Sorte *f*; **what ~ of car?** was für ein Auto? **~ of** [!] irgendwie

kind[2] *a* (**-er, -est**) nett; **~ to animals** gut zu Tieren

kind|ly *a* (**-ler, -lest**) nett ●*adv* netterweise; (*if you please*) gefälligst. **~ness** *n* Güte *f*; (*favour*) Gefallen *m*

king *n* König *m*; (*Draughts*) Dame *f*. **~dom** *n* Königreich *nt*; (*fig & Relig*) Reich *nt*

king: ~fisher *n* Eisvogel *m*. **~-sized** *a* extragroß

kink *n* Knick *m*. **~y** *a* [!] pervers

kiosk *n* Kiosk *m*

kip *n* **have a ~** [!] pennen ● *vi* (*pt/pp* **kipped**) [!] pennen

kipper *n* Räucherhering *m*

kiss *n* Kuss *m* ● *vt/i* küssen

kit *n* Ausrüstung *f*; (*tools*) Werkzeug *nt*; (*construction* ~) Bausatz *m* ● *vt* (*pt/pp* **kitted**) **~out** ausrüsten

kitchen *n* Küche *f* ● *attrib* Küchen-. **~ette** *n* Kochnische *f*

kitchen: ~garden *n* Gemüsegarten *m*. **~sink** *n* Spülbecken *nt*

kite *n* Drachen *m*

kitten *n* Kätzchen *nt*

kitty *n* (*money*) [gemeinsame] Kasse *f*

knack *n* Trick *m*, Dreh *m*

knead *vt* kneten

knee *n* Knie *nt*. **~cap** *n* Kniescheibe *f*

kneel *vi* (*pt/pp* **knelt**) knien; **~ [down]** sich [nieder]knien

knelt *see* **kneel**

knew *see* **know**

knickers *npl* Schlüpfer *m*

knife *n* (*pl* **knives**) Messer *nt* ● *vt* einen Messerstich versetzen (+ *dat*)

knight *n* Ritter *m*; (*Chess*) Springer *m* ● *vt* adeln

knit *vt/i* (*pt/pp* **knitted**) stricken; **~ one's brow** die Stirn runzeln. **~ting** *n* Stricken *nt*; (*work*) Strickzeug *nt*. **~ting-needle** *n* Stricknadel *f*. **~wear** *n* Strickwaren *pl*

knives *npl see* **knife**

knob *n* Knopf *m*; (*on door*) Knauf *m*; (*small lump*) Beule *f*. **~bly** *a* knorrig; (*bony*) knochig

knock *n* Klopfen *nt*; (*blow*) Schlag *m*; **there was a ~** es klopfte ● *vt* anstoßen; ([!] *criticize*) heruntermachen; **~ a hole in sth** ein Loch in etw (*acc*) schlagen; **~ one's head** sich (*dat*) den Kopf stoßen (**on** an + *dat*) ● *vi* klopfen. **~ about** *vt* schlagen ● *vi* [!] herumkommen. **~ down** *vt* herunterwerfen; (*with fist*) niederschlagen; (*in car*) anfahren; (*demolish*) abreißen; ([!] *reduce*) herabsetzen. **~ off** *vt* herunterwerfen; ([!] *steal*) klauen; ([!] *complete quickly*) hinhauen ● *vi* ([!] *cease work*) Feierabend machen. **~ out** *vt* ausschlagen; (*make unconscious*) bewusstlos schlagen; (*Boxing*) k.o. schlagen. **~ over** *vt* umwerfen; (*in car*) anfahren

knock: ~-down *a* **~-down prices** Schleuderpreise *pl*. **~er** *n* Türklopfer *m*. **~-out** *n* (*Boxing*) K.o. *m*

knot *n* Knoten *m* ● *vt* (*pt/pp* **knotted**) knoten

know *vt/i* (*pt* **knew**, *pp* **known**) wissen; kennen <*person*>; können <*language*>; **get to ~** kennen lernen ● *n* **in the ~** [!] im Bild

know: ~-all *n* [!] Alleswisser *m*. **~-how** *n* [!] [Sach]kenntnis *f*. **~ing** *a* wissend. **~ingly** *adv* wissend; (*intentionally*) wissentlich

knowledge *n* Kenntnis *f* (**of** von/*gen*); (*general*) Wissen *nt*; (*specialized*) Kenntnisse *pl*. **~able** *a* **be ~able** viel wissen

knuckle *n* [Finger]knöchel *m*; (*Culin*) Hachse *f*

kosher *a* koscher

kudos *n* [!] Prestige *nt*

Ll

lab *n* [!] Labor *nt*

label *n* Etikett *nt* ● *vt* (*pt/pp* **labelled**) etikettieren
laboratory *n* Labor *nt*
laborious *a*, **-ly** *adv* mühsam
labour *n* Arbeit *f*; (*workers*) Arbeitskräfte *pl*; (*Med*) Wehen *pl*; **L~** (*Pol*) die Labourpartei ● *attrib* Labour- ● *vi* arbeiten ● *vt* (*fig*) sich lange auslassen über (+ *acc*). **~er** *n* Arbeiter *m*
labour-saving *a* arbeitssparend
lace *n* Spitze *f*; (*of shoe*) Schnürsenkel *m* ● *vt* schnüren
lack *n* Mangel *m* (**of** an + *dat*) ● *vt* **I ~ the time** mir fehlt die Zeit ● *vi* **be ~ing** fehlen
laconic *a*, **-ally** *adv* lakonisch
lacquer *n* Lack *m*; (*for hair*) [Haar]spray *m*
lad *n* Junge *m*
ladder *n* Leiter *f*; (*in fabric*) Laufmasche *f*
ladle *n* [Schöpf]kelle *f* ● *vt* schöpfen
lady *n* Dame *f*; (*title*) Lady *f*
lady: ~bird *n*, (*Amer*) **~bug** *n* Marienkäfer *m*. **~like** *a* damenhaft
lag¹ *vi* (*pt/pp* **lagged**) **~ behind** zurückbleiben; (*fig*) nachhinken
lag² *vt* (*pt/pp* **lagged**) umwickeln <*pipes*>
lager *n* Lagerbier *nt*
laid *see* **lay³**
lain *see* **lie²**
lake *n* See *m*
lamb *n* Lamm *nt*
lame *a* (**-r, -st**) lahm
lament *n* Klage *f*; (*song*) Klagelied *nt* ● *vt* beklagen ● *vi* klagen
laminated *a* laminiert
lamp *n* Lampe *f*; (*in street*) Laterne *f*. **~post** *n* Laternenpfahl *m*. **~shade** *n* Lampenschirm *m*
lance *vt* (*Med*) aufschneiden
land *n* Land *nt*; **plot of ~** Grundstück *nt* ● *vt/i* landen; **~ s.o. with sth** [!] jdm etw aufhalsen
landing *n* Landung *f*; (*top of stairs*) Treppenflur *m*. **~-stage** *n* Landesteg *m*
land: ~lady *n* Wirtin *f*. **~lord** *n* Wirt *m*; (*of land*) Grundbesitzer *m*; (*of building*) Hausbesitzer *m*. **~mark** *n* Erkennungszeichen *nt*; (*fig*) Meilenstein *m*. **~owner** *n* Grundbesitzer *m*. **~scape** *n* Landschaft *f*. **~slide** *n* Erdrutsch *m*
lane *n* kleine Landstraße *f*; (*Auto*) Spur *f*; (*Sport*) Bahn *f*; **'get in ~'** (*Auto*) 'bitte einordnen'
language *n* Sprache *f*; (*speech, style*) Ausdrucksweise *f*
languid *a*, **-ly** *adv* träge
languish *vi* schmachten
lanky *a* (**-ier, -iest**) schlaksig
lantern *n* Laterne *f*
lap¹ *n* Schoß *m*
lap² *n* (*Sport*) Runde *f*; (*of journey*) Etappe *f* ● *vi* (*pt/pp* **lapped**) plätschern (**against** gegen)
lap³ *vt* (*pt/pp* **lapped**) **~ up** aufschlecken
lapel *n* Revers *nt*
lapse *n* Fehler *m*; (*moral*) Fehltritt *m*; (*of time*) Zeitspanne *f* ● *vi* (*expire*) erlöschen; **~ into** verfallen in (+ *acc*)
lard *n* [Schweine]schmalz *nt*
larder *n* Speisekammer *f*
large *a* (**-r, -st**) & *adv* groß; **by and ~** im Großen und Ganzen; **at ~** auf freiem Fuß. **~ly** *adv* großenteils
lark¹ *n* (*bird*) Lerche *f*
lark² *n* (*joke*) Jux *m* ● *vi* **~ about** herumalbern
laryngitis *n* Kehlkopfentzündung *f*
larynx *n* Kehlkopf *m*
laser *n* Laser *m*

L

lash *n* Peitschenhieb *m*; (*eyelash*) Wimper *f* ● *vt* peitschen; (*tie*) festbinden (**to** an + *acc*). **~ out** *vi* um sich schlagen; (*spend*) viel Geld ausgeben (**on** für)

lass *n* Mädchen *nt*

lasso *n* Lasso *nt*

last *a & n* letzte(r,s); **~ night** heute *od* gestern Nacht; (*evening*) gestern Abend; **at ~** endlich; **for the ~ time** zum letzten Mal; **the ~ but one** der/die/das vorletzte ● *adv* zuletzt; (*last time*) das letzte Mal; **he/she went ~** er/sie ging als Letzter/Letzte ● *vi* dauern; <*weather:*> sich halten; <*relationship:*> halten. **~ing** *a* dauerhaft. **~ly** *adv* schließlich, zum Schluss

latch *n* [einfache] Klinke *f*

late *a & adv* (**-r, -st**) spät; (*delayed*) verspätet; (*deceased*) verstorben; **the ~st news** die neuesten Nachrichten; **stay up ~** bis spät aufbleiben; **arrive ~** zu spät ankommen; **I am ~** ich komme zu spät *od* habe mich verspätet; **the train is ~** der Zug hat Verspätung. **~comer** *n* Zuspätkommende(r) *m/f*. **~ly** *adv* in letzter Zeit. **~ness** *n* Zuspätkommen *nt*; (*delay*) Verspätung *f*

later *a & adv* später; **~ on** nachher

lateral *a* seitlich

lather *n* [Seifen]schaum *m*

Latin *a* lateinisch ● *n* Latein *nt*. **~ America** *n* Lateinamerika *nt*

latitude *n* (*Geog*) Breite *f*; (*fig*) Freiheit *f*

latter *a & n* **the ~** der/die/das Letztere

Latvia *n* Lettland *nt*

laudable *a* lobenswert

laugh *n* Lachen *nt*; **with a ~** lachend ● *vi* lachen (**at/about** über + *acc*); **~ at s.o.** (*mock*) jdn auslachen. **~able** *a* lachhaft, lächerlich

laughter *n* Gelächter *nt*

launch[1] *n* (*boat*) Barkasse *f*

launch[2] *n* Stapellauf *m*; (*of rocket*) Abschuss *m*; (*of product*) Lancierung *f* ● *vt* vom Stapel lassen <*ship*>; zu Wasser lassen <*lifeboat*>; abschießen <*rocket*>; starten <*attack*>; (*Comm*) lancieren <*product*>

laund(e)rette *n* Münzwäscherei *f*

laundry *n* Wäscherei *f*; (*clothes*) Wäsche *f*

laurel *n* Lorbeer *m*

lava *n* Lava *f*

lavatory *n* Toilette *f*

lavender *n* Lavendel *m*

lavish *a*, **-ly** *adv* großzügig; (*wasteful*) verschwenderisch ● *vt* **~ sth on s.o.** jdn mit etw überschütten

law *n* Gesetz *nt*; (*system*) Recht *nt*; **study ~** Jura studieren; **~ and order** Recht und Ordnung

law: ~-abiding *a* gesetzestreu. **~ court** *n* Gerichtshof *m*. **~ful** *a* rechtmäßig. **~less** *a* gesetzlos

lawn *n* Rasen *m*. **~-mower** *n* Rasenmäher *m*

lawyer *n* Rechtsanwalt *m* /-anwältin *f*

lax *a* lax, locker

laxative *n* Abführmittel *nt*

laxity *n* Laxheit *f*

lay[1] *see* **lie**[2]

lay[2] *vt* (*pt/pp* **laid**) legen; decken <*table*>; **~ a trap** eine Falle stellen. **~ down** *vt* hinlegen; festlegen <*rules, conditions*>. **~ off** *vt* entlassen <*workers*> ● *vi* ([!] *stop*) aufhören. **~ out** *vt* hinlegen; aufbahren <*corpse*>; anlegen <*garden*>; (*Typ*) gestalten

lay-by *n* Parkbucht *f*

layer *n* Schicht *f*

lay: **~man** *n* Laie *m*. **~out** *n* Anordnung *f*; (*design*) Gestaltung *f*; (*Typ*) Layout *nt*

laze *vi* **~[about]** faulenzen

laziness *n* Faulheit *f*

lazy *a* (**-ier, -iest**) faul. **~-bones** *n* Faulenzer *m*

lead[1] *n* Blei *nt*; (*of pencil*) [Bleistift]mine *f*

lead[2] *n* Führung *f*; (*leash*) Leine *f*; (*flex*) Schnur *f*; (*clue*) Hinweis *m*, Spur *f*; (*Theat*) Hauptrolle *f*; (*distance ahead*) Vorsprung *m*; **be in the ~** in Führung liegen ● *vt/i* (*pt/pp* **led**) führen; leiten <*team*>; (*induce*) bringen; (*at cards*) ausspielen; **~ the way** vorangehen; **~ up to sth** (*fig*) etw (*dat*) vorangehen

leader *n* Führer *m*; (*of expedition, group*) Leiter(in) *m(f)*; (*of orchestra*) Konzertmeister *m*; (*in newspaper*) Leitartikel *m*. **~ship** *n* Führung *f*; Leitung *f*

leading *a* führend; **~ lady** Hauptdarstellerin *f*

leaf *n* (*pl* **leaves**) Blatt *nt* ● *vi* **~ through sth** etw durchblättern. **~let** *n* Merkblatt *nt*; (*advertising*) Reklameblatt *nt*; (*political*) Flugblatt *nt*

league *n* Liga *f*

leak *n* (*hole*) undichte Stelle *f*; (*Naut*) Leck *nt*; (*of gas*) Gasausfluss *m* ● *vi* undicht sein; <*ship:*> leck sein, lecken; <*liquid:*> auslaufen; <*gas:*> ausströmen ● *vt* auslaufen lassen; **~ sth to s.o.** (*fig*) jdm etw zuspielen. **~y** *a* undicht; (*Naut*) leck

lean[1] *a* (**-er, -est**) mager

lean[2] *v* (*pt/pp* **leaned** *or* **leant**) ● *vt* lehnen (**against/on** an + *acc*) ● *vi* <*person*> sich lehnen (**against/on** an + *acc*); (*not be straight*) sich neigen; **be ~ing against** lehnen an (+ *dat*). **~ back** *vi* sich zurücklehnen. **~ forward** *vi* sich vorbeugen. **~ out** *vi* sich hinauslehnen. **~ over** *vi* sich vorbeugen

leaning *a* schief ● *n* Neigung *f*

leap *n* Sprung *m* ● *vi* (*pt/pp* **leapt** *or* **leaped**) springen; **he leapt at it** [!] er griff sofort zu. **~ year** *n* Schaltjahr *nt*

learn *vt/i* (*pt/pp* **learnt** *or* **learned**) lernen; (*hear*) erfahren; **~ to swim** schwimmen lernen

learn|ed *a* gelehrt. **~er** *n* Anfänger *m*; **~er [driver]** Fahrschüler(in) *m(f)*. **~ing** *n* Gelehrsamkeit *f*

lease *n* Pacht *f*; (*contract*) Mietvertrag *m* ● *vt* pachten

leash *n* Leine *f*

least *a* geringste(r,s) ● *n* **the ~** das wenigste; **at ~** wenigstens, mindestens; **not in the ~** nicht im Geringsten ● *adv* am wenigsten

leather *n* Leder *nt*

leave *n* Erlaubnis *f*; (*holiday*) Urlaub *m*; **on ~** auf Urlaub; **take one's ~** sich verabschieden ● *v* (*pt/pp* **left**) ● *vt* lassen; (*go out of, abandon*) verlassen; (*forget*) liegen lassen; (*bequeath*) vermachen (**to** *dat*); **~ it to me!** überlassen Sie es mir! **there is nothing left** es ist nichts mehr übrig ● *vi* [weg]gehen/-fahren; <*train, bus:*> abfahren. **~ behind** *vt* zurücklassen; (*forget*) liegen lassen. **~ out** *vt* liegen lassen; (*leave outside*) draußen lassen; (*omit*) auslassen

leaves *see* **leaf**

Lebanon *n* Libanon *m*

lecherous *a* lüstern

lecture *n* Vortrag *m*; (*Univ*) Vorlesung *f*; (*reproof*) Strafpredigt *f* ● *vi* einen Vortrag/eine Vorlesung halten (**on** über + *acc*) ● *vt* **~ s.o.** jdm eine Strafpredigt halten. **~r** *n* Vortragende(r) *m/f*; (*Univ*) Dozent(in) *m(f)*

led *see* **lead²**

ledge *n* Leiste *f*; (*shelf, of window*) Sims *m*; (*in rock*) Vorsprung *m*

ledger *n* Hauptbuch *nt*

leech *n* Blutegel *m*

leek *n* Stange *f* Porree; **~s** *pl* Porree *m*

left¹ *see* **leave**

left² *a* linke(r,s) ● *adv* links; <*go*> nach links ● *n* linke Seite *f*; **on the ~** links; **from/to the ~** von/nach links; **the ~** (*Pol*) die Linke

left: ~-handed *a* linkshändig. **~-luggage [office]** *n* Gepäckaufbewahrung *f*. **~overs** *npl* Reste *pl*. **~-wing** *a* (*Pol*) linke(r,s)

leg *n* Bein *nt*; (*Culin*) Keule *f*; (*of journey*) Etappe *f*

legacy *n* Vermächtnis *nt*, Erbschaft *f*

legal *a*, **-ly** *adv* gesetzlich; <*matters*> rechtlich; <*department, position*> Rechts-; **be ~** [gesetzlich] erlaubt sein

legality *n* Legalität *f*

legend *n* Legende *f*. **~ary** *a* legendär

legible *a*, **-bly** *adv* leserlich

legion *n* Legion *f*

legislat|e *vi* Gesetze erlassen. **~ion** *n* Gesetzgebung *f*; (*laws*) Gesetze *pl*

legislative *a* gesetzgebend

legitimate *a* rechtmäßig; (*justifiable*) berechtigt

leisure *n* Freizeit *f*; **at your ~** wenn Sie Zeit haben. **~ly** *a* gemächlich

lemon *n* Zitrone *f*. **~ade** *n* Zitronenlimonade *f*

lend *vt* (*pt/pp* **lent**) leihen (**s.o. sth** jdm etw)

length *n* Länge *f*; (*piece*) Stück *nt*; (*of wallpaper*) Bahn *f*; (*of time*) Dauer *f*

length|en *vt* länger machen ● *vi* länger werden. **~ways** *adv* der Länge nach

lengthy *a* (**-ier, -iest**) langwierig

lenien|t *a*, **-ly** *adv* nachsichtig

lens *n* Linse *f*; (*Phot*) Objektiv *nt*; (*of spectacles*) Glas *nt*

lent *see* **lend**

Lent *n* Fastenzeit *f*

lentil *n* (*Bot*) Linse *f*

leopard *n* Leopard *m*

leotard *n* Trikot *nt*

lesbian *a* lesbisch ● *n* Lesbierin *f*

less *a, adv, n & prep* weniger; **~ and ~** immer weniger

lessen *vt* verringern ● *vi* nachlassen; <*value:*> abnehmen

lesser *a* geringere(r,s)

lesson *n* Stunde *f*; (*in textbook*) Lektion *f*; (*Relig*) Lesung *f*; **teach s.o. a ~** (*fig*) jdm eine Lehre erteilen

lest *conj* (*liter*) damit ... nicht

let *vt* (*pt/pp* **let**, *pres p* **letting**) lassen; (*rent*) vermieten; **~ alone** (*not to mention*) geschweige denn; **~ us go** gehen wir; **~ me know** sagen Sie mir Bescheid; **~ oneself in for sth** [!] sich (*dat*) etw einbrocken. **~ down** *vt* hinunter-/herunterlassen; (*lengthen*) länger machen; **~ s.o. down** [!] jdn im Stich lassen; (*disappoint*) jdn enttäuschen. **~ in** *vt* hereinlassen. **~ off** *vt* abfeuern <*gun*>; hochgehen lassen <*firework, bomb*>; (*emit*) ausstoßen; (*excuse from*) befreien von; (*not punish*) frei ausgehen lassen. **~ out** *vt* hinaus-/herauslassen; (*make larger*) auslassen. **~ through** *vt* durchlassen. **~ up** *vi* [!] nachlassen

let-down *n* Enttäuschung *f*, [!] Reinfall *m*

lethal *a* tödlich

letharg|ic *a* lethargisch. **~y** *n* Lethargie *f*

letter *n* Brief *m*; (*of alphabet*) Buchstabe *m*. **~-box** *n* Briefkasten *m*. **~-head** *n* Briefkopf *m*. **~ing** *n* Beschriftung *f*

lettuce *n* [Kopf]salat *m*

let-up *n* [!] Nachlassen *nt*

level *a* eben; (*horizontal*) waagerecht; (*in height*) auf gleicher Höhe; <*spoonful*> gestrichen; **one's ~ best** sein Möglichstes ● *n* Höhe *f*; (*fig*) Ebene *f*, Niveau *nt*; (*stage*) Stufe *f*; **on the ~** [!] ehrlich ● *vt* (*pt*/*pp* **levelled**) einebnen

level crossing *n* Bahnübergang *m*

lever *n* Hebel *m* ● *vt* **~ up** mit einem Hebel anheben. **~age** *n* Hebelkraft *f*

lewd *a* (**-er, -est**) anstößig

liabilit|y *n* Haftung *f*; **~ies** *pl* Verbindlichkeiten *pl*

liable *a* haftbar; **be ~ to do sth** etw leicht tun können

liaise *vi* [!] Verbindungsperson sein

liaison *n* Verbindung *f*; (*affair*) Verhältnis *nt*

liar *n* Lügner(in) *m*(*f*)

libel *n* Verleumdung *f* ● *vt* (*pt*/*pp* **libelled**) verleumden. **~lous** *a* verleumderisch

liberal *a*, **-ly** *adv* tolerant; (*generous*) großzügig. **L~** *a* (*Pol*) liberal ● *n* Liberale(r) *m*/*f*

liberat|e *vt* befreien. **~ed** *a* <*woman*> emanzipiert. **~ion** *n* Befreiung *f*. **~or** *n* Befreier *m*

liberty *n* Freiheit *f*; **take liberties** sich (*dat*) Freiheiten erlauben

librarian *n* Bibliothekar(in) *m*(*f*)

library *n* Bibliothek *f*

Libya *n* Libyen *nt*

lice *see* **louse**

licence *n* Genehmigung *f*; (*Comm*) Lizenz *f*; (*for TV*) ≈ Fernsehgebühr *f*; (*for driving*) Führerschein *m*; (*for alcohol*) Schankkonzession *f*

license *vt* eine Genehmigung/(*Comm*) Lizenz erteilen (+ *dat*); **be ~d** <*car:*> zugelassen sein; <*restaurant:*> Schankkonzession haben. **~-plate** *n* (*Amer*) Nummernschild *nt*

lick *n* Lecken *nt*; **a ~ of paint** ein bisschen Farbe ● *vt* lecken; ([!] *defeat*) schlagen

lid *n* Deckel *m*; (*of eye*) Lid *nt*

lie[1] *n* Lüge *f*; **tell a ~** lügen ● *vi* (*pt*/*pp* **lied**, *pres p* **lying**) lügen; **~ to** belügen

lie[2] *vi* (*pt* **lay**, *pp* **lain**, *pres p* **lying**) liegen; **here ~s ...** hier ruht ... **~ down** *vi* sich hinlegen

lie-in *n* **have a ~** [sich] ausschlafen

lieu *n* **in ~ of** statt (+ *gen*)

lieutenant *n* Oberleutnant *m*

life *n* (*pl* **lives**) Leben *nt*; **lose one's ~** ums Leben kommen

life: ~-boat *n* Rettungsboot *nt*. **~-guard** *n* Lebensretter *m*. **~-jacket** *n* Schwimmweste *f*. **~less** *a* leblos. **~like** *a* naturgetreu. **~long** *a* lebenslang. **~ preserver** *n* (*Amer*) Rettungsring *m*. **~-size(d)** *a* ... in Lebensgröße. **~time** *n* Leben *nt*; **in s.o.'s ~time** zu jds Lebzeiten; **the chance of a ~time** eine einmalige Gelegenheit

lift *n* Aufzug *m*, Lift *m*; **give s.o. a ~** jdn mitnehmen; **get a ~** mitgenommen werden ● *vt* heben; aufheben <*restrictions*> ● *vi* <*fog:*> sich lichten. **~ up** *vt* hochheben

light[1] *a* (**-er, -est**) (*not dark*) hell; **~ blue** hellblau ● *n* Licht *nt*; (*lamp*) Lampe *f*; **have you [got] a ~?** haben Sie Feuer? ● *vt* (*pt*/*pp* **lit** *or* **lighted**) anzünden <*fire, cigarette*>; (*illuminate*) beleuchten. **~ up** *vi* <*face:*> sich erhellen

light[2] *a* (**-er, -est**) (*not heavy*) leicht; **~ sentence** milde Strafe *f* ●*adv* **travel ~** mit wenig Gepäck reisen

light-bulb *n* Glühbirne *f*

lighten[1] *vt* heller machen

lighten[2] *vt* leichter machen <*load*>

lighter *n* Feuerzeug *nt*

light: ~-hearted *a* unbekümmert. **~house** *n* Leuchtturm *m*. **~ing** *n* Beleuchtung *f*. **~ly** *adv* leicht; **get off ~ly** glimpflich davonkommen

lightning *n* Blitz *m*

lightweight *a* leicht ●*n* (*Boxing*) Leichtgewicht *nt*

like[1] *a* ähnlich; (*same*) gleich ●*prep* wie; (*similar to*) ähnlich (+ *dat*); **~ this** so; **what's he ~?** wie ist er denn? ●*conj* ([!] *as*) wie; (*Amer: as if*) als ob

like[2] *vt* mögen; **I should/would ~** ich möchte; **I ~ the car** das Auto gefällt mir; **~ dancing/singing** gern tanzen/singen ●*n* **~s and dislikes** *pl* Vorlieben und Abneigungen *pl*

like|able *a* sympathisch. **~lihood** *n* Wahrscheinlichkeit *f*. **~ly** *a* (**-ier, -iest**) & *adv* wahrscheinlich; **not ~ly!** [!] auf gar keinen Fall!

like-minded *a* gleich gesinnt

liken *vt* vergleichen (**to** mit)

like|ness *n* Ähnlichkeit *f*. **~wise** *adv* ebenso

liking *n* Vorliebe *f*; **is it to your ~?** gefällt es Ihnen?

lilac *n* Flieder *m*

lily *n* Lilie *f*

limb *n* Glied *nt*

lime *n* (*fruit*) Limone *f*; (*tree*) Linde *f*. **~light** *n* **be in the ~light** im Rampenlicht stehen

limit *n* Grenze *f*; (*limitation*) Beschränkung *f*; **that's the ~!** [!] das ist doch die Höhe! ●*vt* beschränken (**to** auf + *acc*). **~ation** *n* Beschränkung *f*; **~ed** *a* beschränkt. **~ed company** Gesellschaft *f* mit beschränkter Haftung

limousine *n* Limousine *f*

limp[1] *n* Hinken *nt* ●*vi* hinken

limp[2] *a* (**-er -est**), **-ly** *adv* schlaff

limpid *a* klar

line[1] *n* Linie *f*; (*length of rope, cord*) Leine *f*; (*Teleph*) Leitung *f*; (*of writing*) Zeile *f*; (*row*) Reihe *f*; (*wrinkle*) Falte *f*; (*of business*) Branche *f*; (*Amer: queue*) Schlange *f*; **in ~ with** gemäß (+ *dat*) ●*vt* säumen <*street*>

line[2] *vt* füttern <*garment*>; (*Techn*) auskleiden

lined[1] *a* (*wrinkled*) faltig; <*paper*> liniert

lined[2] *a* <*garment*> gefüttert

line dancing *n* Linedance-Tanzen *nt*

linen *n* Leinen *nt*; (*articles*) Wäsche *f*

liner *n* Passagierschiff *nt*

linesman *n* Linienrichter *m*

linger *vi* [zurück]bleiben

lingerie *n* Damenunterwäsche *f*

linguist *n* Sprachkundige(r) *m/f*

linguistic *a*, **-ally** *adv* sprachlich

lining *n* (*of garment*) Futter *nt*; (*Techn*) Auskleidung *f*

link *n* (*of chain*) Glied *nt* (*fig*) Verbindung *f* ●*vt* verbinden; **~ arms** sich unterhaken

links *n or npl* Golfplatz *m*

lint *n* Verbandstoff *m*

lion *n* Löwe *m*; **~'s share** (*fig*) Löwenanteil *m*. **~ess** *n* Löwin *f*

lip *n* Lippe *f*; (*edge*) Rand *m*; (*of jug*) Schnabel *m*

lip: ~-reading *n* Lippenlesen *nt*. **~-service** *n* **pay ~-service** ein Lippenbekenntnis ablegen (**to** zu). **~stick** *n* Lippenstift *m*

liqueur *n* Likör *m*

liquid *n* Flüssigkeit *f* ●*a* flüssig

liquidation *n* Liquidation *f*

liquidize *vt* [im Mixer] pürieren. **~r** *n* Mixer *m*

liquor *n* Alkohol *m*. **~ store** *n* (*Amer*) Spirituosengeschäft *nt*

lisp *n* Lispeln *nt* ●*vt/i* lispeln
list¹ *n* Liste *f* ●*vt* aufführen
list² *vi* <*ship:*> Schlagseite haben
listen *vi* zuhören (**to** *dat*); ~ **to the radio** Radio hören. **~er** *n* Zuhörer(in) *m(f)*; (*Radio*) Hörer(in) *m(f)*
listless *a*, **-ly** *adv* lustlos
lit *see* **light¹**
literacy *n* Lese- und Schreibfertigkeit *f*
literal *a* wörtlich. **~ly** *adv* buchstäblich
literary *a* literarisch
literate *a* **be** ~ lesen und schreiben können
literature *n* Literatur *f*; [!] Informationsmaterial *nt*
lithe *a* geschmeidig
Lithuania *n* Litauen *nt*
litre *n* Liter *m & nt*
litter *n* Abfall *m*; (*Zool*) Wurf *m*. **~-bin** *n* Abfalleimer *m*
little *a* klein; (*not much*) wenig ●*adv & n* wenig; **a** ~ ein bisschen/wenig; ~ **by** ~ nach und nach
live¹ *a* lebendig; <*ammunition*> scharf; ~ **broadcast** Live-Sendung *f*; **be** ~ (*Electr*) unter Strom stehen
live² *vi* leben; (*reside*) wohnen. ~ **on** *vt* leben von; (*eat*) sich ernähren von ●*vi* weiterleben
liveli|hood *n* Lebensunterhalt *m*. **~ness** *n* Lebendigkeit *f*
lively *a* (**-ier, -iest**) lebhaft, lebendig
liver *n* Leber *f*
lives *see* **life**
livid *a* [!] wütend
living *a* lebend ●*n* **earn one's** ~ seinen Lebensunterhalt verdienen. **~-room** *n* Wohnzimmer *nt*
lizard *n* Eidechse *f*
load *n* Last *f*; (*quantity*) Ladung *f*; (*Electr*) Belastung *f*; **~s of** [!] jede Menge ●*vt* laden <*goods, gun*>; beladen <*vehicle*>; ~ **a camera** einen Film in eine Kamera einlegen. **~ed** *a* beladen; ([!] *rich*) steinreich
loaf *n* (*pl* **loaves**) Brot *nt*
loan *n* Leihgabe *f*; (*money*) Darlehen *nt*; **on** ~ geliehen ●*vt* leihen (*to dat*)
loath *a* **be** ~ **to do sth** etw ungern tun
loath|e *vt* verabscheuen. **~ing** *n* Abscheu *m*
loaves *see* **loaf¹**
lobby *n* Foyer *nt*; (*anteroom*) Vorraum *m*; (*Pol*) Lobby *f*
lobster *n* Hummer *m*
local *a* hiesig; <*time, traffic*> Orts-; ~ **anaesthetic** örtliche Betäubung; **I'm not** ~ ich bin nicht von hier ●*n* Hiesige(r) *m/f*; ([!] *public house*) Stammkneipe *f*. ~ **call** *n* (*Teleph*) Ortsgespräch *nt*
locality *n* Gegend *f*
locally *adv* am Ort
locat|e *vt* ausfindig machen; **be ~ed** sich befinden. **~ion** *n* Lage *f*; **filmed on ~ion** als Außenaufnahme gedreht
lock¹ *n* (*hair*) Strähne *f*
lock² *n* (*on door*) Schloss *nt*; (*on canal*) Schleuse *f* ●*vt* abschließen ●*vi* sich abschließen lassen. ~ **in** *vt* einschließen. ~ **out** *vt* ausschließen. ~ **up** *vt* abschließen; einsperren <*person*>
locker *n* Schließfach *nt*; (*Mil*) Spind *m*
lock: ~-out *n* Aussperrung *f*. **~smith** *n* Schlosser *m*
locomotive *n* Lokomotive *f*
locum *n* Vertreter(in) *m(f)*
locust *n* Heuschrecke *f*
lodge *n* (*porter's*) Pförtnerhaus *nt* ●*vt* (*submit*) einreichen; (*deposit*) deponieren ●*vi* zur Untermiete wohnen (**with** bei);

L

(*become fixed*) stecken bleiben. **~r** *n* Untermieter(in) *m*(*f*)

lodging *n* Unterkunft *f*; **~s** *npl* möbliertes Zimmer *nt*

loft *n* Dachboden *m*

lofty *a* (**-ier, -iest**) hoch

log *n* Baumstamm *m*; (*for fire*) [Holz]scheit *nt*; **sleep like a ~** [!] wie ein Murmeltier schlafen ● *vi* **~ off** sich abmelden; **~ on** sich anmelden

loggerheads *npl* **be at ~** [!] sich in den Haaren liegen

logic *n* Logik *f*. **~al** *a*, **-ly** *adv* logisch

logo *n* Symbol *nt*, Logo *nt*

loiter *vi* herumlungern

loll *vi* sich lümmeln

loll|ipop *n* Lutscher *m*. **~y** *n* Lutscher *m*; ([!] *money*) Moneten *pl*

London *n* London *nt* ● *attrib* Londoner. **~er** *n* Londoner(in) *m*(*f*)

lone *a* einzeln. **~liness** *n* Einsamkeit *f*

lonely *a* (**-ier, -iest**) einsam

lone|r *n* Einzelgänger *m*. **~some** *a* einsam

long[1] *a* (**-er, -est**) lang; <*journey*> weit; **a ~ time** lange; **a ~ way** weit; **in the ~ run** auf lange Sicht; (*in the end*) letzten Endes ● *adv* lange; **all day ~** den ganzen Tag; **not ~ ago** vor kurzem; **before ~** bald; **no ~er** nicht mehr; **as** *or* **so ~as** solange; **so ~!** [!] tschüs!

long[2] *vi* **~ for** sich sehnen nach

long-distance *a* Fern-; (*Sport*) Langstrecken-

longing *a*, **-ly** *adv* sehnsüchtig ● *n* Sehnsucht *f*

longitude *n* (*Geog*) Länge *f*

long: ~ jump *n* Weitsprung *m*. **~-lived** *a* langlebig. **~-range** *a* (*Mil, Aviat*) Langstrecken-; <*forecast*> langfristig. **~-sighted** *a* weitsichtig. **~-sleeved** *a* langärmelig. **~-suffering** *a* langmütig. **~-term** *a* langfristig. **~ wave** *n* Langwelle. **~-winded** *a* langatmig

loo *n* [!] Klo *nt*

look *n* Blick *m*; (*appearance*) Aussehen *nt*; **[good] ~s** *pl* [gutes] Aussehen *nt*; **have a ~ at** sich (*dat*) ansehen; **go and have a ~** sieh mal nach ● *vi* sehen; (*search*) nachsehen; (*seem*) aussehen; **don't ~** sieh nicht hin; **~ here!** hören Sie mal! **~ at** ansehen; **~ for** suchen; **~ forward to** sich freuen auf (+ *acc*); **~ in on** vorbeischauen bei; **~ into** (*examine*) nachgehen (+ *dat*); **~ like** aussehen wie; **~ on to** <*room:*> gehen auf (+ *acc*). **~ after** *vt* betreuen. **~ down** *vi* hinuntersehen; **~ down on s.o.** (*fig*) auf jdn herabsehen. **~ out** *vi* hinaus-/heraussehen; (*take care*) aufpassen; **~ out for** Ausschau halten nach; **~ out!** Vorsicht! **~ round** *vi* sich umsehen. **~ up** *vi* aufblicken; **~ up to s.o.** (*fig*) zu jdm aufsehen ● *vt* nachschlagen <*word*>

look-out *n* Wache *f*; (*prospect*) Aussicht *f*; **be on the ~ for** Ausschau halten nach

loom[1] *n* Webstuhl *m*

loom[2] *vi* auftauchen

loony *a* [!] verrückt

loop *n* Schlinge *f*; (*in road*) Schleife *f*. **~hole** *n* Hintertürchen *nt*; (*in the law*) Lücke *f*

loose *a* (**-r, -st**), **-ly** *adv* lose; (*not tight enough*) locker; (*inexact*) frei; **be at a ~ end** nichts zu tun haben. **~ change** *n* Kleingeld *nt*

loosen *vt* lockern

loot *n* Beute *f* ● *vt/i* plündern. **~er** *n* Plünderer *m*

lop *vt* (*pt/pp* **lopped**) stutzen

lopsided *a* schief

lord *n* Herr *m*; (*title*) Lord *m*; **House of L~s** ≈ Oberhaus *nt*; **the L~'s Prayer** das Vaterunser
lorry *n* Last[kraft]wagen *m*
lose *v* (*pt/pp* **lost**) ● *vt* verlieren; (*miss*) verpassen ● *vi* verlieren; <*clock:*> nachgehen; **get lost** verloren gehen; <*person*> sich verlaufen. **~r** *n* Verlierer *m*
loss *n* Verlust *m*; **be at a ~** nicht mehr weiter wissen
lost *see* **lose**. **~ property office** *n* Fundbüro *nt*
lot[1] Los *nt*; (*at auction*) Posten *m*; **draw ~s** losen (**for** um)
lot[2] *n* **the ~** alle; (*everything*) alles; **a ~ [of]** viel; (*many*) viele; **~s of** [!] eine Menge; **it has changed a ~** es hat sich sehr verändert
lotion *n* Lotion *f*
lottery *n* Lotterie *f*. **~ ticket** *n* Los *nt*
loud *a* (**-er, -est**), **-ly** *adv* laut; <*colours*> grell ● *adv* **[out] ~** laut. **~ speaker** *n* Lautsprecher *m*
lounge *n* Wohnzimmer *nt*; (*in hotel*) Aufenthaltsraum *m*. ● *vi* sich lümmeln
louse *n* (*pl* **lice**) Laus *f*
lousy *a* (**-ier, -iest**) [!] lausig
lout *n* Flegel *m*, Lümmel *m*
lovable *a* liebenswert
love *n* Liebe *f*; (*Tennis*) null; **in ~** verliebt ● *vt* lieben; **~ doing sth** etw sehr gerne machen. **~-affair** *n* Liebesverhältnis *nt*. **~ letter** *n* Liebesbrief *m*
lovely *a* (**-ier, -iest**) schön
lover *n* Liebhaber *m*
love: ~ song *n* Liebeslied *nt*. **~ story** *n* Liebesgeschichte *f*
loving *a*, **-ly** *adv* liebevoll
low *a* (**-er, -est**) niedrig; <*cloud, note*> tief; <*voice*> leise; (*depressed*) niedergeschlagen ● *adv* niedrig; <*fly, sing*> tief; <*speak*> leise ● *n* (*Meteorol*) Tief *nt*; (*fig*) Tiefstand *m*
low: ~brow *a* geistig anspruchslos. **~-cut** *a* <*dress*> tief ausgeschnitten
lower *a & adv see* **low** ● *vt* niedriger machen; (*let down*) herunterlassen; (*reduce*) senken
low: ~-fat *a* fettarm. **~lands** *npl* Tiefland *nt*. **~ tide** *n* Ebbe *f*
loyal *a*, **-ly** *adv* treu. **~ty** *n* Treue *f*. **~ty card** *n* Treuekarte *f*
lozenge *n* Pastille *f*
Ltd *abbr* (**Limited**) GmbH
lubricant *n* Schmiermittel *nt*
lubricat|e *vt* schmieren. **~ion** *n* Schmierung *f*
lucid *a* klar. **~ity** *n* Klarheit *f*
luck *n* Glück *nt*; **bad ~** Pech *nt*; **good ~!** viel Glück! **~ily** *adv* glücklicherweise, zum Glück
lucky *a* (**-ier, -iest**) glücklich; <*day, number*> Glücks-; **be ~** Glück haben; <*thing:*> Glück bringen
lucrative *a* einträglich
ludicrous *a* lächerlich
lug *vt* (*pt/pp* **lugged**) [!] schleppen
luggage *n* Gepäck *nt*
luggage: ~-rack *in* Gepäckablage *f*. **~-van** *n* Gepäckwagen *m*
lukewarm *a* lauwarm
lull *n* Pause *f* ● *vt* **~ to sleep** einschläfern
lullaby *n* Wiegenlied *nt*
lumber *n* Gerümpel *nt*; (*Amer: timber*) Bauholz *nt* ● *vt* **~ s.o. with sth** jdm etw aufhalsen. **~jack** *n* (*Amer*) Holzfäller *m*
luminous *a* leuchtend
lump *n* Klumpen *m*; (*of sugar*) Stück *nt*; (*swelling*) Beule *f*; (*in breast*) Knoten *m*; (*tumour*) Geschwulst *f*; **a ~ in one's throat** [!] ein Kloß im Hals
lump: ~ sugar *n* Würfelzucker *m* **~ sum** *n* Pauschalsumme *f*
lumpy *a* (**-ier, -iest**) klumpig
lunacy *n* Wahnsinn *m*
lunar *a* Mond-
lunatic *n* Wahnsinnige(r) *m/f*

lunch *n* Mittagessen *nt* ●*vi* zu Mittag essen
luncheon *n* Mittagessen *nt*. ~ **voucher** *n* Essensbon *m*
lunch: ~**-hour** *n* Mittagspause *f*. ~**-time** *n* Mittagszeit *f*
lung *n* Lungenflügel *m*; ~**s** *pl* Lunge *f*
lunge *vi* sich stürzen (**at** auf + *acc*)
lurch[1] *n* **leave in the** ~ [!] im Stich lassen
lurch[2] *vi* <*person:*> torkeln
lure *vt* locken
lurid *a* grell; (*sensational*) reißerisch
lurk *vi* lauern
luscious *a* lecker, köstlich
lush *a* üppig
lust *n* Begierde *f*. ~**ful** *a* lüstern
lustre *n* Glanz *m*
lusty *a* (**-ier, -iest**) kräftig
luxuriant *a* üppig
luxurious *a*, **-ly** *adv* luxuriös
luxury *n* Luxus *m* ●*attrib* Luxus-
lying *see* **lie**[1], **lie**[2]
lynch *vt* lynchen
lyric *a* lyrisch. ~**al** *a* lyrisch; (*enthusiastic*) schwärmerisch. ~ **poetry** *n* Lyrik *f*. ~**s** *npl* [Lied]text *m*

Mm

mac *n* [!] Regenmantel *m*
macabre *a* makaber
macaroni *n* Makkaroni *pl*
machine *n* Maschine *f* ●*vt* (*sew*) mit der Maschine nähen; (*Techn*) maschinell bearbeiten. ~**-gun** *n* Maschinengewehr *nt*
machinery *n* Maschinerie *f*
mackerel *n inv* Makrele *f*
mackintosh *n* Regenmantel *m*
mad *a* (**madder, maddest**) verrückt; (*dog*) tollwütig; (*fam: angry*) böse (**at** auf + *acc*)
madam *n* gnädige Frau *f*
mad cow disease *n* [!] Rinderwahnsinn *m*
madden *vt* (*make angry*) wütend machen
madden *vt* (*make angry*) wütend machen
made *see* **make**; ~ **to measure** maßgeschneidert
mad|ly *adv* [!] wahnsinnig. ~**man** *n* Irre(r) *m*. ~**ness** *n* Wahnsinn *m*
madonna *n* Madonna *f*
magazine *n* Zeitschrift *f*; (*Mil, Phot*) Magazin *nt*
maggot *n* Made *f*
magic *n* Zauber *m*; (*tricks*) Zauberkunst *f* ●*a* magisch; <*word, wand*> Zauber-. ~**al** *a* zauberhaft
magician *n* Zauberer *m*; (*entertainer*) Zauberkünstler *m*
magistrate *n* ≈ Friedensrichter *m*
magnet *n* Magnet *m*. ~**ic** *a* magnetisch. ~**ism** *n* Magnetismus *m*
magnification *n* Vergrößerung *f*
magnificen|ce *n* Großartigkeit *f*. ~**t** *a*, **-ly** *adv* großartig
magnify *vt* (*pt/pp* **-ied**) vergrößern; (*exaggerate*) übertreiben. ~**ing glass** *n* Vergrößerungsglas *nt*
magnitude *n* Größe *f*; (*importance*) Bedeutung *f*
magpie *n* Elster *f*
mahogany *n* Mahagoni *nt*
maid *n* Dienstmädchen *nt*; **old** ~ (*pej*) alte Jungfer *f*
maiden *a* <*speech, voyage*> Jungfern-. ~ **name** *n* Mädchenname *m*
mail *n* Post *f* ●*vt* mit der Post schicken

mail: ~-bag *n* Postsack *m*. **~box** *n* (*Amer*) Briefkasten *m*. **~ing list** *n* Postversandliste *f*. **~man** *n* (*Amer*) Briefträger *m*. **~-order firm** *n* Versandhaus *nt*

maim *vt* verstümmeln

main *a* Haupt- ● *n* (*water, gas, electricity*) Hauptleitung *f*

main: ~land *n* Festland *nt*. **~ly** *adv* hauptsächlich. **~stay** *n* (*fig*) Stütze *f*. **~ street** *n* Hauptstraße *f*

maintain *vt* aufrechterhalten; (*keep in repair*) instand halten; (*support*) unterhalten; (*claim*) behaupten

maintenance *n* Aufrechterhaltung *f*; (*care*) Instandhaltung *f*; (*allowance*) Unterhalt *m*

maize *n* Mais *m*

majestic *a*, **-ally** *adv* majestätisch

majesty *n* Majestät *f*

major *a* größer ● *n* (*Mil*) Major *m*; (*Mus*) Dur *nt* ● *vi* **~ in** als Hauptfach studieren

majority *n* Mehrheit *f*; **in the ~** in der Mehrzahl

major road *n* Hauptverkehrsstraße *f*

make *n* (*brand*) Marke *f* ● *v* (*pt*/*pp* **made**) ● *vt* machen; (*force*) zwingen; (*earn*) verdienen; halten <*speech*>; treffen <*decision*>; erreichen <*destination*> ● *vi* **~ do** *vi* zurechtkommen (**with** mit). **~ for** *vi* zusteuern auf (+ *acc*). **~ off** *vi* sich davonmachen (**with** mit). **~ out** *vt* (*distinguish*) ausmachen; (*write out*) ausstellen; (*assert*) behaupten. **~ up** *vt* (*constitute*) bilden; (*invent*) erfinden; (*apply cosmetics to*) schminken; **~ up one's mind** sich entschließen ● *vi* sich versöhnen; **~ up for sth** etw wieder gutmachen; **~ up for lost time** verlorene Zeit aufholen

make-believe *n* Phantasie *f*

maker *n* Hersteller *m*

make: ~ shift *a* behelfsmäßig ● *n* Notbehelf *m*. **~-up** *n* Make-up *nt*

maladjusted *a* verhaltensgestört

male *a* männlich ● *n* Mann *m*; (*animal*) Männchen *nt*. **~ nurse** *n* Krankenpfleger *m*. **~ voice choir** *n* Männerchor *m*

malice *n* Bosheit *f*

malicious *a*, **-ly** *adv* böswillig

malign *vt* verleumden

malignant *a* bösartig

mallet *n* Holzhammer *m*

malnutrition *n* Unterernährung *f*

malpractice *n* Berufsvergehen *nt*

malt *n* Malz *nt*

maltreat *vt* misshandeln. **~ment** *n* Misshandlung *f*

mammal *n* Säugetier *nt*

mammoth *a* riesig

man *n* (*pl* **men**) Mann *m*; (*mankind*) der Mensch; (*chess*) Figur *f*; (*draughts*) Stein *m* ● *vt* (*pt*/*pp* **manned**) bemannen <*ship*>; bedienen <*pump*>; besetzen <*counter*>

manage *vt* leiten; verwalten <*estate*>; (*cope with*) fertig werden mit; **~ to do sth** es schaffen, etw zu tun ● *vi* zurechtkommen; **~ on** auskommen mit. **~able** *a* <*tool*> handlich; <*person*> fügsam. **~ment** *n* Leitung *f*; **the ~ment** die Geschäftsleitung *f*

manager *n* Geschäftsführer *m*; (*of bank*) Direktor *m*; (*of estate*) Verwalter *m*; (*Sport*) [Chef]trainer *m*. **~ess** *n* Geschäftsführerin *f*. **~ial** *a* **~ial staff** Führungskräfte *pl*

managing *a* **~ director** Generaldirektor *m*

mandat|e *n* Mandat *nt*. **~ory** *a* obligatorisch

mane *n* Mähne *f*

manful *a*, **-ly** *adv* mannhaft

man: ~handle *vt* grob behandeln <*person*>. **~hole** *n* Kanalschacht

m. **~hood** *n* Mannesalter *nt*; (*quality*) Männlichkeit *f*. **~-hour** *n* Arbeitsstunde *f*. **~-hunt** *n* Fahndung *f*
mania *n* Manie *f*. **~c** *n* Wahnsinnige(r) *m/f*
manicure *n* Maniküre *f* ● *vt* maniküren
manifest *a*, **-ly** *adv* offensichtlich
manifesto *n* Manifest *nt*
manifold *a* mannigfaltig
manipulat|e *vt* handhaben; (*pej*) manipulieren. **~ion** *n* Manipulation *f*
mankind *n* die Menschheit
manly *a* männlich
man-made *a* künstlich. **~ fibre** *n* Kunstfaser *f*
manner *n* Weise *f*; (*kind, behaviour*) Art *f*; **[good/bad] ~s** [gute/schlechte] Manieren *pl*. **~ism** *n* Angewohnheit *f*
manœuvrable *a* manövrierfähig
manœuvre *n* Manöver *nt* ● *vt/i* manövrieren
manor *n* Gutshof *m*; (*house*) Gutshaus *nt*
manpower *n* Arbeitskräfte *pl*
mansion *n* Villa *f*
manslaughter *n* Totschlag *m*
mantelpiece *n* Kaminsims *m & nt*
manual *a* Hand- ● *n* Handbuch *nt*
manufacture *vt* herstellen ● *n* Herstellung *f*. **~r** *n* Hersteller *m*
manure *n* Mist *m*
manuscript *n* Manuskript *nt*
many *a* viele ● *n* **a good/great ~** sehr viele
map *n* Landkarte *f*; (*of town*) Stadtplan *m*
maple *n* Ahorn *m*
mar *vt* (*pt/pp* **marred**) verderben
marathon *n* Marathon *m*
marble *n* Marmor *m*; (*for game*) Murmel *f*
March *n* März *m*
march *n* Marsch *m* ● *vi* marschieren ● *vt* marschieren lassen; **~ s.o. off** jdn abführen
mare *n* Stute *f*
margarine *n* Margarine *f*
margin *n* Rand *m*; (*leeway*) Spielraum *m*; (*Comm*) Spanne *f*. **~al** *a*, **-ly** *adv* geringfügig
marigold *n* Ringelblume *f*
marina *n* Jachthafen *m*
marine *a* Meeres- ● *n* Marine *f*; (*sailor*) Marineinfanterist *m*
marital *a* ehelich. **~ status** *n* Familienstand *m*
maritime *a* See-
mark[1] *n* (*former German currency*) Mark *f*
mark[2] *n* Fleck *m*; (*sign*) Zeichen *nt*; (*trace*) Spur *f*; (*target*) Ziel *nt*; (*Sch*) Note *f* ● *vt* markieren; (*spoil*) beschädigen; (*characterize*) kennzeichnen; (*Sch*) korrigieren; (*Sport*) decken; **~ time** (*Mil*) auf der Stelle treten; (*fig*) abwarten. **~ out** *vt* markieren
marked *a*, **~ly** *adv* deutlich; (*pronounced*) ausgeprägt
market *n* Markt *m* ● *vt* vertreiben; (*launch*) auf den Markt bringen. **~ing** *n* Marketing *nt*. **~ research** *n* Marktforschung *f*
marking *n* Markierung *f*; (*on animal*) Zeichnung *f*
marksman *n* Scharfschütze *m*
marmalade *n* Orangenmarmelade *f*
maroon *a* dunkelrot
marooned *a* (*fig*) von der Außenwelt abgeschnitten
marquee *n* Festzelt *nt*
marquetry *n* Einlegearbeit *f*
marriage *n* Ehe *f*; (*wedding*) Hochzeit *f*. **~able** *a* heiratsfähig
married *see* **marry** ● *a* verheiratet. **~ life** *n* Eheleben *nt*
marrow *n* (*Anat*) Mark *nt*; (*vegetable*) Kürbis *m*

marr|y *vt/i* (*pt/pp* **married**) heiraten; (*unite*) trauen; **get ~ied** heiraten
marsh *n* Sumpf *m*
marshal *n* Marschall *m*; (*steward*) Ordner *m*
marshy *a* sumpfig
martial *a* kriegerisch. **~ law** *n* Kriegsrecht *nt*
martyr *n* Märtyrer(in) *m*(*f*). **~dom** *n* Martyrium *nt*
marvel *n* Wunder *nt* ● *vi* (*pt/pp* **marvelled**) staunen (**at** über + *acc*). **~lous** a, **-ly** adv wunderbar
Marxis|m *n* Marxismus *m*. **~t** *a* marxistisch ● *n* Marxist(in) *m*(*f*)
marzipan *n* Marzipan *nt*
mascot *n* Maskottchen *nt*
masculin|e *a* männlich ● *n* (*Gram*) Maskulinum *nt*. **~ity** *n* Männlichkeit *f*
mash *n* [!], **~ed potatoes** *npl* Kartoffelpüree *nt*
mask *n* Maske *f* ● *vt* maskieren
masochis|m *n* Masochismus *m*. **~t** *n* Masochist *m*
mason *n* Steinmetz *m*. **~ry** *n* Mauerwerk *nt*
mass¹ *n* (*Relig*) Messe *f*
mass² *n* Masse *f* ● *vi* sich sammeln; (*Mil*) sich massieren
massacre *n* Massaker *nt* ● *vt* niedermetzeln
massage *n* Massage *f* ● *vt* massieren
masseu|r *n* Masseur *m*. **~se** *n* Masseuse *f*
massive *a* massiv; (*huge*) riesig
mass: ~ media *npl* Massenmedien *pl*. **~-produce** *vt* in Massenproduktion herstellen. **~ production** *n* Massenproduktion *f*
mast *n* Mast *m*
master *n* Herr *m*; (*teacher*) Lehrer *m*; (*craftsman, artist*) Meister *m*; (*of ship*) Kapitän *m* ● *vt* meistern; beherrschen <*language*>
master: ~ly *a* meisterhaft. **~mind** *n* führender Kopf *m* ● *vt* der führende Kopf sein von. **~piece** *n* Meisterwerk *nt*. **~y** *n* (*of subject*) Beherrschung *f*
mat *n* Matte *f*; (*on table*) Untersatz *m*
match¹ *n* Wettkampf *m*; (*in ball games*) Spiel *nt*; (*Tennis*) Match *nt*; (*marriage*) Heirat *f*; **be a good ~** <*colours:*> gut zusammenpassen; **be no ~ for s.o.** jdm nicht gewachsen sein ● *vt* (*equal*) gleichkommen (+ *dat*); (*be like*) passen zu; (*find sth similar*) etwas Passendes finden zu ● *vi* zusammenpassen
match² *n* Streichholz *nt*. **~box** *n* Streichholzschachtel *f*
mate¹ *n* Kumpel *m*; (*assistant*) Gehilfe *m*; (*Naut*) Maat *m*; (*Zool*) Männchen *nt*; (*female*) Weibchen *nt* ● *vi* sich paaren
mate² *n* (*Chess*) Matt *nt*
material *n* Material *nt*; (*fabric*) Stoff *m*; **raw ~s** Rohstoffe *pl* ● *a* materiell
material|ism *n* Materialismus *m*. **~istic** *a* materialistisch. **~ize** *vi* sich verwirklichen
maternal *a* mütterlich
maternity *n* Mutterschaft *f*. **~ clothes** *npl* Umstandskleidung *f*. **~ ward** *n* Entbindungsstation *f*
mathematic|al *a*, **-ly** *adv* mathematisch. **~ian** *n* Mathematiker(in) *m*(*f*)
mathematics *n* Mathematik *f*
maths *n* [!] Mathe *f*
matinée *n* (*Theat*) Nachmittagsvorstellung *f*
matrimony *n* Ehe *f*
matron *n* (*of hospital*) Oberin *f*; (*of school*) Hausmutter *f*
matt *a* matt
matted *a* verfilzt
matter *n* (*affair*) Sache *f*; (*Phys: substance*) Materie *f*; **money ~s** Geldangelegenheiten *pl*; **what is**

the ~? was ist los? ● *vi* wichtig sein; **~ to s.o.** jdm etwas ausmachen; **it doesn't ~** es macht nichts. **~-of-fact** *a* sachlich
mattress *n* Matratze *f*
matur|e *a* reif; (*Comm*) fällig ● *vi* reifen; <*person:*> reifer werden; (*Comm*) fällig werden ● *vt* reifen lassen. **~ity** *n* Reife *f*; (*Comm*) Fälligkeit *f*
mauve *a* lila
maximum *a* maximal ● *n* (*pl* **-ima**) Maximum *nt*. **~ speed** *n* Höchstgeschwindigkeit *f*

may
pres **may**, *pt* **might**
● *auxiliary verb*
····➤ (*expressing possibility*) können. **she may come** es kann sein, dass sie kommt; es ist möglich, dass sie kommt. **she might come** (*more distant possibility*) sie könnte kommen. **it may/might rain** es könnte regnen. **I may be wrong** vielleicht irre ich mich. **he may have missed his train** vielleicht hat er seinen Zug verpasst
····➤ (*expressing permission*) dürfen. **may I come in?** darf ich reinkommen? **you may smoke** Sie dürfen rauchen
····➤ (*expressing wish*) **may the best man win!** auf dass der Beste gewinnt!
····➤ (*expressing concession*) **he may be slow but he's accurate** mag *od* kann sein, dass er langsam ist, aber dafür ist er auch genau
····➤ **may/might as well** ebenso gut können. **we may/might as well go** wir könnten eigentlich ebensogut [auch] gehen. **we might as well give up** da können wir gleich aufgeben

May *n* Mai *m*
maybe *adv* vielleicht
May Day *n* der Erste Mai
mayonnaise *n* Mayonnaise *f*
mayor *n* Bürgermeister *m*. **~ess** *n* Bürgermeisterin *f*; (*wife of mayor*) Frau Bürgermeister *f*
maze *n* Irrgarten *m*; (*fig*) Labyrinth *nt*
me *pron* (*acc*) mich; (*dat*) mir; **it's ~** [!] ich bin es
meadow *n* Wiese *f*
meagre *a* dürftig
meal *n* Mahlzeit *f*; (*food*) Essen *nt*; (*grain*) Schrot *m*
mean[1] *a* (**-er, -est**) (*miserly*) geizig; (*unkind*) gemein; (*poor*) schäbig
mean[2] *a* mittlere(r,s) ● *n* (*average*) Durchschnitt *m*
mean[3] *vt* (*pt/pp* **meant**) heißen; (*signify*) bedeuten; (*intend*) beabsichtigen; **I ~ it** das ist mein Ernst; **~ well** es gut meinen; **be meant for** <*present:*> bestimmt sein für; <*remark:*> gerichtet sein an (+ *acc*)
meaning *n* Bedeutung *f*. **~ful** *a* bedeutungsvoll. **~less** *a* bedeutungslos
means *n* Möglichkeit *f*, Mittel *nt*; **~ of transport** Verkehrsmittel *nt*; **by ~ of** durch; **by all ~!** aber natürlich! **by no ~** keineswegs ● *npl* (*resources*) [Geld]mittel *pl*
meant *see* **mean**[3]
meantime *n* **in the ~** in der Zwischenzeit ● *adv* inzwischen
meanwhile *adv* inzwischen
measles *n* Masern *pl*
measure *n* Maß *nt*; (*action*) Maßnahme *f* ● *vt/i* messen; **~ up to** (*fig*) herankommen an (+ *acc*). **~d** *a* gemessen. **~ment** *n* Maß *nt*
meat *n* Fleisch *nt*
mechan|ic *n* Mechaniker *m*. **~ical** *a*, **-ly** *adv* mechanisch. **~ical engineering** Maschinenbau *m*
mechan|ism *n* Mechanismus *m*. **~ize** *vt* mechanisieren

medal *n* Orden *m*; (*Sport*) Medaille *f*

medallist *n* Medaillengewinner(in) *m*(*f*)

meddle *vi* sich einmischen (**in** in + *acc*); (*tinker*) herumhantieren (**with** an + *acc*)

media *see* **medium** ● *n pl* **the ~** die Medien *pl*

mediat|e *vi* vermitteln. **~or** *n* Vermittler(in) *m*(*f*)

medical *a* medizinisch; <*treatment*> ärztlich ● *n* ärztliche Untersuchung *f*. **~ insurance** *n* Krankenversicherung *f*. **~ student** *n* Medizinstudent *m*

medicat|ed *a* medizinisch. **~ion** *n* (*drugs*) Medikamente *pl*

medicinal *a* medizinisch; <*plant*> heilkräftig

medicine *n* Medizin *f*; (*preparation*) Medikament *nt*

medieval *a* mittelalterlich

mediocr|e *a* mittelmäßig. **~ity** *n* Mittelmäßigkeit *f*

meditat|e *vi* nachdenken (**on** über + *acc*). **~ion** *n* Meditation *f*

Mediterranean *n* Mittelmeer *nt* ● *a* Mittelmeer-

medium *a* mittlere(r,s); <*steak*> medium; **of ~ size** von mittlerer Größe ● *n* (*pl* **media**) Medium *nt*: (*means*) Mittel *nt*

medium: ~-sized *a* mittelgroß. **~ wave** *n* Mittelwelle *f*

medley *n* Gemisch *nt*; (*Mus*) Potpourri *nt*

meek *a* (**-er, -est**), **-ly** *adv* sanftmütig; (*unprotesting*) widerspruchslos

meet *v* (*pt/pp* **met**) ● *vt* treffen; (*by chance*) begegnen (+ *dat*); (*at station*) abholen; (*make the acquaintance of*) kennen lernen; stoßen auf (+ *acc*) <*problem*>; bezahlen <*bill*>; erfüllen <*requirements*> ● *vi* sich treffen; (*for the first time*) sich kennen lernen

meeting *n* Treffen *nt*; (*by chance*) Begegnung *f*; (*discussion*) Besprechung *f*; (*of committee*) Sitzung *f*; (*large*) Versammlung *f*

megalomania *n* Größenwahnsinn *m*

megaphone *n* Megaphon *nt*

melancholy *a* melancholisch ● *n* Melancholie *f*

mellow *a* (**-er, -est**) <*fruit*> ausgereift; <*sound, person*> sanft ● *vi* reifer werden

melodious *a* melodiös

melodramatic *a*, **-ally** *adv* melodramatisch

melody *n* Melodie *f*

melon *n* Melone *f*

melt *vt/i* schmelzen

member *n* Mitglied *nt*; (*of family*) Angehörige(r) *m/f*; **M~ of Parliament** Abgeordnete(r) *m/f*. **~ship** *n* Mitgliedschaft *f*; (*members*) Mitgliederzahl *f*

memento *n* Andenken *nt*

memo *n* Mitteilung *f*

memoirs *n pl* Memoiren *pl*

memorable *a* denkwürdig

memorial *n* Denkmal *nt*. **~ service** *n* Gedenkfeier *f*

memorize *vt* sich (*dat*) einprägen

memory *n* Gedächtnis *nt*; (*thing remembered*) Erinnerung *f*; (*of computer*) Speicher *m*; **from ~** auswendig; **in ~ of** zur Erinnerung an (+ *acc*)

men *see* **man**

menac|e *n* Drohung *f*; (*nuisance*) Plage *f* ● *vt* bedrohen. **~ing** *a*, **~ly** *adv* drohend

mend *vt* reparieren; (*patch*) flicken; ausbessern <*clothes*>

menfolk *n pl* Männer *pl*

menial *a* niedrig

menopause *n* Wechseljahre *pl*

mental *a*, **-ly** *adv* geistig; (! *mad*) verrückt. **~ arithmetic** *n* Kopfrechnen *nt*. **~ illness** *n* Geisteskrankheit *f*

mentality *n* Mentalität *f*

mention *n* Erwähnung *f* ● *vt* erwähnen; **don't ~ it** keine Ursache; bitte
menu *n* Speisekarte *f*
merchandise *n* Ware *f*
merchant *n* Kaufmann *m*; (*dealer*) Händler *m*. **~ navy** *n* Handelsmarine *f*
merci|ful *a* barmherzig. **~fully** *adv* [!] glücklicherweise. **~less** *a*, **-ly** *adv* erbarmungslos
mercury *n* Quecksilber *nt*
mercy *n* Barmherzigkeit *f*, Gnade *f*; **be at s.o.'s ~** jdm ausgeliefert sein
mere *a*, **-ly** *adv* bloß
merest *a* kleinste(r,s)
merge *vi* zusammenlaufen; (*Comm*) fusionieren
merger *n* Fusion *f*
meringue *n* Baiser *nt*
merit *n* Verdienst *nt*; (*advantage*) Vorzug *m*; (*worth*) Wert *m* ● *vt* verdienen
merry *a* (**-ier, -iest**) fröhlich
merry-go-round *n* Karussell *nt*
mesh *n* Masche *f*
mesmerized *a* (*fig*) [wie] gebannt
mess *n* Durcheinander *nt*; (*trouble*) Schwierigkeiten *pl*; (*something spilt*) Bescherung *f* [!]; (*Mil*) Messe *f*; **make a ~ of** (*botch*) verpfuschen ● *vt* **~ up** in Unordnung bringen; (*botch*) verpfuschen ● *vi* **~ about** herumalbern; (*tinker*) herumspielen (**with** mit)
message *n* Nachricht *f*; **give s.o. a ~** jdm etwas ausrichten
messenger *n* Bote *m*
Messrs *n pl see* **Mr**; (*on letter*) **~ Smith** Firma Smith
messy *a* (**-ier, -iest**) schmutzig; (*untidy*) unordentlich
met *see* **meet**
metal *n* Metall *nt* ● *a* Metall-. **~lic** *a* metallisch
metaphor *n* Metapher *f*. **~ical** *a*, **-ly** *adv* metaphorisch
meteor *n* Meteor *m*. **~ic** *a* kometenhaft
meteorological *a* Wetter-
meteorolog|ist *n* Meteorologe *m*/-gin *f*. **~y** *n* Meteorologie *f*
meter[1] *n* Zähler *m*
meter[2] *n* (*Amer*) = **metre**
method *n* Methode *f*; (*Culin*) Zubereitung *f*
methodical *a*, **-ly** *adv* systematisch, methodisch
methylated *a* **~ spirit[s]** Brennspiritus *m*
meticulous *a*, **-ly** *adv* sehr genau
metre *n* Meter *m & n*; (*rhythm*) Versmaß *nt*
metric *a* metrisch
metropolis *n* Metropole *f*
mew *n* Miau *nt* ● *vi* miauen
Mexican *a* mexikanisch ● *n* Mexikaner(in) *m(f)*. **Mexico** *n* Mexiko *nt*
miaow *n* Miau *nt* ● *vi* miauen
mice *see* **mouse**
micro: ~film *n* Mikrofilm *m*. **~light [aircraft]** *n* Ultraleichtflugzeug *nt*. **~phone** *n* Mikrofon *nt*. **~scope** *n* Mikroskop *nt*. **~scopic** *a* mikroskopisch. **~wave [oven]** *n* Mikrowellenherd *m*
mid *a* **~ May** Mitte Mai; **in ~ air** in der Luft
midday *n* Mittag *m*
middle *a* mittlere(r,s); **the M~ Ages** das Mittelalter; **the ~ class[es]** der Mittelstand; **the M~ East** der Nahe Osten ● *n* Mitte *f*; **in the ~ of the night** mitten in der Nacht
middle: ~-aged *a* mittleren Alters. **~-class** *a* bürgerlich
midge *n* [kleine] Mücke *f*
midget *n* Liliputaner(in) *m(f)*
Midlands *npl* **the ~** Mittelengland *n*
midnight *n* Mitternacht *f*
midriff *n* [!] Taille *f*

midst *n* **in the ~ of** mitten in (+ *dat*); **in our ~** unter uns

mid: ~summer *n* Hochsommer *m*. **~way** *adv* auf halbem Wege. **~wife** *n* Hebamme *f*. **~winter** *n* Mitte *f* des Winters

might¹ *v aux* **I ~** vielleicht; **it ~ be true** es könnte wahr sein; **he asked if he ~ go** er fragte, ob er gehen dürfte; **you ~ have drowned** du hättest ertrinken können

might² *n* Macht *f*

mighty *a* (**-ier, -iest**) mächtig

migraine *n* Migräne *f*

migrat|e *vi* abwandern; <*birds:*> ziehen. **~ion** *n* Wanderung *f*; (*of birds*) Zug *m*

mike *n* [!] Mikrofon *nt*

mild *a* (**-er, -est**) mild

mild|ly *adv* leicht; **to put it ~ly** gelinde gesagt. **~ness** *n* Milde *f*

mile *n* Meile *f* (= *1,6 km*); **~s too big** [!] viel zu groß

mile|age *n* Meilenzahl *f*; (*of car*) Meilenstand *m*

militant *a* militant

military *a* militärisch. **~ service** *n* Wehrdienst *m*

milk *n* Milch *f* ● *vt* melken

milk: ~man *n* Milchmann *m*. **~ shake** *n* Milchmixgetränk *nt*. **~ tooth** *n* Milchzahn *m*

milky *a* (**-ier, -iest**) milchig. **M~ Way** *n* (*Astr*) Milchstraße *f*

mill *n* Mühle *f*; (*factory*) Fabrik *f*

millennium *n* Jahrtausend *nt*

milli|gram *n* Milligramm *nt*. **~metre** *n* Millimeter *m & nt*

million *n* Million *f*; **a ~ pounds** eine Million Pfund. **~aire** *n* Millionär(in) *m(f)*

mime *n* Pantomime *f* ● *vi* pantomimisch darstellen

mimic *n* Imitator *m* ● *vt* (*pt/pp* **mimicked**) nachahmen

mince *n* Hackfleisch *nt* ● *vt* (*Culin*) durchdrehen; **not ~ words** kein Blatt vor den Mund nehmen

mince: ~meat *n* Masse *f* aus Korinthen, Zitronat *usw*; **make ~meat of** (*fig*) vernichtend schlagen. **~ pie** *n* mit 'mincemeat' gefülltes Pastetchen *nt*

mincer *n* Fleischwolf *m*

mind *n* Geist *m*; (*sanity*) Verstand *m*; **give s.o. a piece of one's ~** jdm gehörig die Meinung sagen; **make up one's ~** sich entschließen; **be out of one's ~** nicht bei Verstand sein; **have sth in ~** etw im Sinn haben; **bear sth in ~** an etw (*acc*) denken; **have a good ~ to** große Lust haben, zu; **I have changed my ~** ich habe es mir anders überlegt ● *vt* aufpassen auf (+ *acc*); **I don't ~ the noise** der Lärm stört mich nicht; **~ the step!** Achtung Stufe! ● *vi* (*care*) sich kümmern (**about** um); **I don't ~** mir macht es nichts aus; **never ~!** macht nichts! **do you ~ if?** haben Sie etwas dagegen, wenn? **~ out** *vi* aufpassen

mindless *a* geistlos

mine¹ *poss pron* meine(r), meins; **a friend of ~** ein Freund von mir; **that is ~** das gehört mir

mine² *n* Bergwerk *nt*; (*explosive*) Mine *f* ● *vt* abbauen; (*Mil*) verminen

miner *n* Bergarbeiter *m*

mineral *n* Mineral *nt*. **~ water** *n* Mineralwasser *nt*

minesweeper *n* Minenräumboot *nt*

mingle *vi* **~ with** sich mischen unter (+ *acc*)

miniature *a* Klein- ● *n* Miniatur *f*

mini|bus *n* Kleinbus *m*. **~cab** *n* Kleintaxi *nt*

minim|al *a* minimal. **~um** *n* (*pl* **-ima**) Minimum *nt* ● *a* Mindest-

mining *n* Bergbau *m*

miniskirt *n* Minirock *m*

minister *n* Minister *m*; (*Relig*) Pastor *m*. **~ial** *a* ministeriell

ministry *n* (*Pol*) Ministerium *nt*
mink *n* Nerz *m*
minor *a* kleiner; (*less important*) unbedeutend ● *n* Minderjährige(r) *m/f*; (*Mus*) Moll *nt*
minority *n* Minderheit *f*
minor road *n* Nebenstraße *f*
mint[1] *n* Münzstätte *f* ● *a* <*stamp*> postfrisch; **in ~ condition** wie neu ● *vt* prägen
mint[2] *n* (*herb*) Minze *f*; (*sweet*) Pfefferminzbonbon *m & nt*
minus *prep* minus, weniger; (🅸 *without*) ohne
minute[1] *n* Minute *f*; **in a ~** (*shortly*) gleich; **~s** *pl* (*of meeting*) Protokoll *nt*
minute[2] *a* winzig
mirac|le *n* Wunder *nt*. **~ulous** *a* wunderbar
mirror *n* Spiegel *m* ● *vt* widerspiegeln
mirth *n* Heiterkeit *f*
misadventure *n* Missgeschick *nt*
misapprehension *n* Missverständnis *nt*; **be under a ~** sich irren
misbehav|e *vi* sich schlecht benehmen. **~iour** *n* schlechtes Benehmen *nt*
miscalcu|late *vt* falsch berechnen ● *vi* sich verrechnen. **~lation** *n* Fehlkalkulation *f*
miscarriage *n* Fehlgeburt *f*
miscellaneous *a* vermischt
mischief *n* Unfug *m*
mischievous *a*, **-ly** *adv* schelmisch; (*malicious*) boshaft
misconception *n* falsche Vorstellung *f*
misconduct *n* unkorrektes Verhalten *nt*; (*adultery*) Ehebruch *m*
miser *n* Geizhals *m*
miserable *a*, **-bly** *adv* unglücklich; (*wretched*) elend
miserly *adv* geizig
misery *n* Elend *nt*; (🅸 *person*) Miesepeter *m*
misfire *vi* fehlzünden; (*go wrong*) fehschlagen
misfit *n* Außenseiter(in) *m(f)*
misfortune *n* Unglück *nt*
misgivings *npl* Bedenken *pl*
misguided *a* töricht
mishap *n* Missgeschick *nt*
misinform *vt* falsch unterrichten
misinterpret *vt* missdeuten
misjudge *vt* falsch beurteilen
mislay *vt* (*pt/pp* **-laid**) verlegen
mislead *vt* (*pt/pp* **-led**) irreführen. **~ing** *a* irreführend
mismanage *vt* schlecht verwalten. **~ment** *n* Misswirtschaft *f*
misnomer *n* Fehlbezeichnung *f*
misprint *n* Druckfehler *m*
misquote *vt* falsch zitieren
misrepresent *vt* falsch darstellen
miss *n* Fehltreffer *m* ● *vt* verpassen; (*fail to hit or find*) verfehlen; (*fail to attend*) versäumen; (*fail to notice*) übersehen; (*feel the loss of*) vermissen ● *vi* (*fail to hit*) nicht treffen. **~ out** *vt* auslassen
Miss *n* (*pl* **-es**) Fräulein *nt*
missile *n* [Wurf]geschoss *nt*; (*Mil*) Rakete *f*
missing *a* fehlend; (*lost*) verschwunden; (*Mil*) vermisst; **be ~** fehlen
mission *n* Auftrag *m*; (*Mil*) Einsatz *m*; (*Relig*) Mission *f*
missionary *n* Missionar(in) *m(f)*
misspell *vt* (*pt/pp* **-spelt** or **-spelled**) falsch schreiben
mist *n* Dunst *m*; (*fog*) Nebel *m*; (*on window*) Beschlag *m* ● *vi* **~ up** beschlagen
mistake *n* Fehler *m*; **by ~** aus Versehen ● *vt* (*pt* **mistook**, *pp* **mistaken**); **~ for** verwechseln mit
mistaken *a* falsch; **be ~** sich irren. **~ly** *adv* irrtümlicherweise
mistletoe *n* Mistel *f*

mistress *n* Herrin *f*; (*teacher*) Lehrerin *f*; (*lover*) Geliebte *f*

mistrust *n* Misstrauen *nt* ● *vt* misstrauen (+ *dat*)

misty *a* (**-ier, -iest**) dunstig; (*foggy*) neblig; (*fig*) unklar

misunderstand *vt* (*pt/pp* **-stood**) missverstehen. **~ing** *n* Missverständnis *nt*

misuse[1] *vt* missbrauchen

misuse[2] *n* Missbrauch *m*

mitigating *a* mildernd

mix *n* Mischung *f* ● *vt* mischen ● *vi* sich mischen; **~ with** (*associate with*) verkehren mit. **~ up** *vt* mischen; (*muddle*) durcheinander bringen; (*mistake for*) verwechseln (**with** mit)

mixed *a* gemischt; **be ~ up** durcheinander sein

mixer *n* Mischmaschine *f*; (*Culin*) Küchenmaschine *f*

mixture *n* Mischung *f*; (*medicine*) Mixtur *f*; (*Culin*) Teig *m*

mix-up *n* Durcheinander *nt*; (*confusion*) Verwirrung *f*; (*mistake*) Verwechslung *f*

moan *n* Stöhnen *nt* ● *vi* stöhnen; (*complain*) jammern

mob *n* Horde *f*; (*rubble*) Pöbel *m*; (! *gang*) Bande *f* ● *vt* (*pt/pp* **mobbed**) herfallen über (+ *acc*); belagern <*celebrity*>

mobile *a* beweglich ● *n* Mobile *nt*; (*telephone*) Handy *nt*. **~ home** *n* Wohnwagen *m*. **~ phone** *n* Handy *nt*

mobility *n* Beweglichkeit *f*

mock *a* Schein- ● *vt* verspotten. **~ery** *n* Spott *m*

mock-up *n* Modell *nt*

mode *n* [Art und] Weise *f*; (*fashion*) Mode *f*

model *n* Modell *nt*; (*example*) Vorbild *nt*; **[fashion] ~** Mannequin *nt* ● *a* Modell-; (*exemplary*) Muster- ● *v* (*pt/pp* **modelled**) ● *vt* formen, modellieren; vorführen <*clothes*> ● *vi* Mannequin sein; (*for artist*) Modell stehen

moderate[1] *vt* mäßigen

moderate[2] *a* mäßig; <*opinion*> gemäßigt. **~ly** *adv* mäßig; (*fairly*) einigermaßen

moderation *n* Mäßigung *f*; **in ~** mit Maß[en]

modern *a* modern. **~ize** *vt* modernisieren. **~ languages** *npl* neuere Sprachen *pl*

modest *a* bescheiden; (*decorous*) schamhaft. **~y** *n* Bescheidenheit *f*

modif|ication *n* Abänderung *f*. **~y** *vt* (*pt/pp* **-fied**) abändern

moist *a* (**-er, -est**) feucht

moisten *vt* befeuchten

moistur|e *n* Feuchtigkeit *f*. **~izer** *n* Feuchtigkeitscreme *f*

molar *n* Backenzahn *m*

mole[1] *n* Leberfleck *m*

mole[2] *n* (*Zool*) Maulwurf *m*

molecule *n* Molekül *nt*

molest *vt* belästigen

mollify *vt* (*pt/pp* **-ied**) besänftigen

mollycoddle *vt* verzärteln

molten *a* geschmolzen

mom *n* (*Amer fam*) Mutti *f*

moment *n* Moment *m*, Augenblick *m*; **at the ~** im Augenblick, augenblicklich. **~ary** *a* vorübergehend

momentous *a* bedeutsam

momentum *n* Schwung *m*

monarch *n* Monarch(in) *m*(*f*). **~y** *n* Monarchie *f*

monastery *n* Kloster *nt*

Monday *n* Montag *m*

money *n* Geld *nt*

money: ~-box *n* Sparbüchse *f*. **~-lender** *n* Geldverleiher *m*. **~ order** *n* Zahlungsanweisung *f*

mongrel *n* Promenadenmischung *f*

monitor *n* (*Techn*) Monitor *m* ● *vt* überwachen <*progress*>; abhören <*broadcast*>

monk *n* Mönch *m*

M

monkey *n* Affe *m*
mono *n* Mono *nt*
monogram *n* Monogramm *nt*
monologue *n* Monolog *m*
monopol|ize *vt* monopolisieren. **~y** *n* Monopol *nt*
monosyllable *n* einsilbiges Wort *nt*
monotone *n* **in a ~** mit monotoner Stimme
monoton|ous *a*, **-ly** *adv* eintönig, monoton; (*tedious*) langweillig. **~y** *n* Eintönigkeit *f*, Monotonie *f*
monster *n* Ungeheuer *nt*; (*cruel person*) Unmensch *m*
monstrosity *n* Monstrosität *f*
monstrous *a* ungeheuer; (*outrageous*) ungeheuerlich
month *n* Monat *m*. **~ly** *a & adv* monatlich ● *n* (*periodical*) Monatszeitschrift *f*
monument *n* Denkmal *nt*. **~al** *a* (*fig*) monumental
moo *n* Muh *nt* ● *vi* (*pt/pp* **mooed**) muhen
mood *n* Laune *f*; **be in a good/bad ~** gute/schlechte Laune haben
moody *a* (**-ier, -iest**) launisch
moon *n* Mond *m*; **over the ~** ! überglücklich
moon: ~light *n* Mondschein *m*. **~lighting** *n* ! ≈ Schwarzarbeit *f*. **~lit** *a* mondhell
moor[1] *n* Moor *nt*
moor[2] *vt* (*Naut*) festmachen ● *vi* anlegen
mop *n* Mopp *m*; **~ of hair** Wuschelkopf *m* ● *vt* (*pt/pp* **mopped**) wischen. **~ up** *vt* aufwischen
moped *n* Moped *nt*
moral *a*, **-ly** *adv* moralisch, sittlich; (*virtuous*) tugendhaft ● *n* Moral *f*; **~s** *pl* Moral *f*
morale *n* Moral *f*
morality *n* Sittlichkeit *f*
morbid *a* krankhaft; (*gloomy*) trübe
more *a, adv & n* mehr; (*in addition*) noch; **a few ~** noch ein paar; **any ~** noch etwas; **once ~** noch einmal; **~ or less** mehr oder weniger; **some ~ tea?** noch etwas Tee? **~ interesting** interessanter; **~ [and ~] quickly** [immer] schneller
moreover *adv* außerdem
morgue *n* Leichenschauhaus *nt*
morning *n* Morgen *m*; **in the ~** morgens, am Morgen; (*tomorrow*) morgen früh
Morocco *n* Marokko *nt*
moron *n* ! Idiot *m*
morose *a*, **-ly** *adv* mürrisch
morsel *n* Happen *m*
mortal *a* sterblich; (*fatal*) tödlich ● *n* Sterbliche(r) *m/f*. **~ity** *n* Sterblichkeit *f*. **~ly** *adv* tödlich
mortar *n* Mörtel *m*
mortgage *n* Hypothek *f* ● *vt* hypothekarisch belasten
mortuary *n* Leichenhalle *f*; (*public*) Leichenschauhaus *nt*; (*Amer: undertaker's*) Bestattungsinstitut *nt*
mosaic *n* Mosaik *nt*
Moscow *n* Moskau *nt*
mosque *n* Moschee *f*
mosquito *n* (*pl* **-es**) [Stech]mücke *f*, Schnake *f*; (*tropical*) Moskito *m*
moss *n* Moos *nt*. **~y** *a* moosig
most *a* der/die/das meiste; (*majority*) die meisten; **for the ~ part** zum größten Teil ● *adv* am meisten; (*very*) höchst; **the ~ interesting day** der interessanteste Tag; **~ unlikely** höchst unwahrscheinlich ● *n* das meiste; **~ of them** die meisten [von ihnen]; **at [the] ~** höchstens; **~ of the time** die meiste Zeit. **~ly** *adv* meist
MOT *n* ≈ TÜV *m*
motel *n* Motel *nt*
moth *n* Nachtfalter *m*; **[clothes-] ~** Motte *f*
mothball *n* Mottenkugel *f*

mother *n* Mutter *f*

mother: ~hood *n* Mutterschaft *f*. **~-in-law** *n* (*pl* **~s-in-law**) Schwiegermutter *f*. **~land** *n* Mutterland *nt*. **~ly** *a* mütterlich. **~-of-pearl** *n* Perlmutter *f*. **~-to-be** *n* werdende Mutter *f*

mothproof *a* mottenfest

motif *n* Motiv *nt*

motion *n* Bewegung *f*; (*proposal*) Antrag *m*. **~less** *a*, **-ly** *adv* bewegungslos

motivat|e *vt* motivieren. **~ion** *n* Motivation *f*

motive *n* Motiv *nt*

motor *n* Motor *m*; (*car*) Auto *nt* ●*a* Motor-; (*Anat*) motorisch ●*vi* [mit dem Auto] fahren

motor: ~bike *n* [!] Motorrad *nt*. **~ boat** *n* Motorboot *nt*. **~ car** *n* Auto *nt*, Wagen *m*. **~cycle** *n* Motorrad *nt*. **~cyclist** *n* Motorradfahrer *m*. **~ing** *n* Autofahren *nt*. **~ist** *n* Autofahrer(in) *m*(*f*). **~ vehicle** *n* Kraftfahrzeug *nt*. **~way** *n* Autobahn *f*

mottled *a* gesprenkelt

motto *n* (*pl* **-es**) Motto *nt*

mould[1] *n* (*fungus*) Schimmel *m*

mould[2] *n* Form *f* ●*vt* formen (**into** zu). **~ing** *n* (*Archit*) Fries *m*

mouldy *a* schimmelig; ([!] *worthless*) schäbig

mound *n* Hügel *m*; (*of stones*) Haufen *m*

mount *n* (*animal*) Reittier *nt*; (*of jewel*) Fassung *f*; (*of photo, picture*) Passepartout *nt* ●*vt* (*get on*) steigen auf (+ *acc*); (*on pedestal*) montieren auf (+ *acc*); besteigen <*horse*>; fassen <*jewel*>; aufziehen <*photo, picture*> ●*vi* aufsteigen, <*tension:*> steigen. **~ up** *vi* sich häufen; (*add up*) sich anhäufen

mountain *n* Berg *m*

mountaineer *n* Bergsteiger(in) *m*(*f*). **~ing** *n* Bergsteigen *nt*

mountainous *a* bergig, gebirgig

mourn *vt* betrauern ●*vi* trauern (**for** um). **~er** *n* Trauernde(r) *m*/*f*. **~ful** *a*, **-ly** *adv* trauervoll. **~ing** *n* Trauer *f*

mouse *n* (*pl* **mice**) Maus *f*. **~trap** *n* Mausefalle *f*

moustache *n* Schnurrbart *m*

mouth[1] *vt* **~ sth** etw lautlos mit den Lippen sagen

mouth[2] *n* Mund *m*; (*of animal*) Maul *nt*; (*of river*) Mündung *f*

mouth: ~ful *n* Mundvoll *m*; (*bite*) Bissen *m*. **~-organ** *n* Mundharmonika *f*. **~wash** *n* Mundwasser *nt*

movable *a* beweglich

move *n* Bewegung *f*; (*fig*) Schritt *m*; (*moving house*) Umzug *m*; (*in board game*) Zug *m*; **on the ~** unterwegs; **get a ~ on** [!] sich beeilen ●*vt* bewegen; (*emotionally*) rühren; (*move along*) rücken; (*in board game*) ziehen; (*take away*) wegnehmen; wegfahren <*car*>; (*rearrange*) umstellen; (*transfer*) versetzen <*person*>; verlegen <*office*>; (*propose*) beantragen; **~ house** umziehen ●*vi* sich bewegen; (*move house*) umziehen; **don't ~!** stillhalten! (*stop*) stillstehen! **~ along** *vt*/*i* weiterrücken. **~ away** *vt*/*i* wegrücken; (*move house*) wegziehen. **~ in** *vi* einziehen. **~ off** *vi* <*vehicle:*> losfahren. **~ out** *vi* ausziehen. **~ over** *vt*/*i* [zur Seite] rücken. **~ up** *vi* aufrücken

movement *n* Bewegung *f*; (*Mus*) Satz *m*; (*of clock*) Uhrwerk *nt*

movie *n* (*Amer*) Film *m*; **go to the ~s** ins Kino gehen

moving *a* beweglich; (*touching*) rührend

mow *vt* (*pt* **mowed**, *pp* **mown** *or* **mowed**) mähen

mower *n* Rasenmäher *m*

MP *abbr see* **Member of Parliament**

Mr *n* (*pl* **Messrs**) Herr *m*

M

Mrs *n* Frau *f*
Ms *n* Frau *f*
much *a, adv & n* viel; **as ~ as** so viel wie; **~ loved** sehr geliebt
muck *n* Mist *m*; ([!] *filth*) Dreck *m*. **~ about** *vi* herumalbern; (*tinker*) herumspielen (**with** mit). **~ out** *vt* ausmisten. **~ up** *vt* [!] vermasseln; (*make dirty*) schmutzig machen
mucky *a* (**-ier, -iest**) dreckig
mud *n* Schlamm *m*
muddle *n* Durcheinander *nt*; (*confusion*) Verwirrung *f* ● *vt* **~ [up]** durcheinander bringen
muddy *a* (**-ier, -iest**) schlammig; <*shoes*> schmutzig
mudguard *n* Kotflügel *m*; (*on bicycle*) Schutzblech *nt*
muffle *vt* dämpfen
muffler *n* Schal *m*; (*Amer, Auto*) Auspufftopf *m*
mug¹ *n* Becher *m*; (*for beer*) Bierkrug *m*; ([!] *face*) Visage *f*; ([!] *simpleton*) Trottel *m*
mug² *vt* (*pt/pp* **mugged**) überfallen. **~ger** *n* Straßenräuber *m*. **~ging** *n* Straßenraub *m*
muggy *a* (**-ier, -iest**) schwül
mule *n* Maultier *nt*
mulled *a* **~ wine** Glühwein *m*
multi: ~coloured *a* vielfarbig, bunt. **~lingual** *a* mehrsprachig. **~national** *a* multinational
multiple *a* vielfach; (*with pl*) mehrere ● *n* Vielfache(s) *nt*
multiplication *n* Multiplikation *f*
multiply *v* (*pt/pp* **-ied**) ● *vt* multiplizieren (**by** mit) ● *vi* sich vermehren
multistorey *a* **~ car park** Parkhaus *nt*
mum *n* [!] Mutti *f*
mumble *vt/i* murmeln
mummy¹ *n* [!] Mutti *f*
mummy² *n* (*Archaeol*) Mumie *f*
mumps *n* Mumps *m*
munch *vt/i* mampfen
municipal *a* städtisch
munitions *npl* Kriegsmaterial *nt*
mural *n* Wandgemälde *nt*
murder *n* Mord *m* ● *vt* ermorden. **~er** *n* Mörder *m*. **~ess** *n* Mörderin *f*. **~ous** *a* mörderisch
murky *a* (**-ier, -iest**) düster
murmur *n* Murmeln *nt* ● *vt/i* murmeln
muscle *n* Muskel *m*
muscular *a* Muskel-; (*strong*) muskulös
museum *n* Museum *nt*
mushroom *n* [essbarer] Pilz *m*, *esp* Champignon *m* ● *vi* (*fig*) wie Pilze aus dem Boden schießen
mushy *a* breiig
music *n* Musik *f*; (*written*) Noten *pl*; **set to ~** vertonen
musical *a* musikalisch ● *n* Musical *nt*. **~ box** *n* Spieldose *f*. **~ instrument** *n* Musikinstrument *nt*
musician *n* Musiker(in) *m(f)*
music-stand *n* Notenständer *m*
Muslim *a* mohammedanisch ● *n* Mohammedaner(in) *m(f)*
must *v aux* (*nur Präsens*) müssen; (*with negative*) dürfen ● *n* **a ~** [!] ein Muss *nt*
mustard *n* Senf *m*
musty *a* (**-ier, -iest**) muffig
mute *a* stumm
mutilat|e *vt* verstümmeln. **~ion** *n* Verstümmelung *f*
mutin|ous *a* meuterisch. **~y** *n* Meuterei *f* ● *vi* (*pt/pp* **-ied**) meutern
mutter *n* Murmeln *nt* ● *vt/i* murmeln
mutton *n* Hammelfleisch *nt*
mutual *a* gegenseitig; ([!] *common*) gemeinsam. **~ly** *adv* gegenseitig
muzzle *n* (*of animal*) Schnauze *f*; (*of firearm*) Mündung *f*; (*for dog*) Maulkorb *m*
my *a* mein

myself *pron* selbst; (*refl*) mich; **by ~** allein; **I thought to ~** ich habe mir gedacht

mysterious *a*, **-ly** *adv* geheimnisvoll; (*puzzling*) mysteriös, rätselhaft

mystery *n* Geheimnis *nt*; (*puzzle*) Rätsel *nt*; **~ [story]** Krimi *m*

mysti|c[al] *a* mystisch. **~cism** *n* Mystik *f*

mystified *a* **be ~** vor einem Rätsel stehen

mystique *n* geheimnisvoller Zauber *m*

myth *n* Mythos *m*; ([!] *untruth*) Märchen *nt*. **~ical** *a* mythisch; (*fig*) erfunden

mythology *n* Mythologie *f*

Nn

nab *vt* (*pt/pp* **nabbed**) [!] erwischen

nag¹ *n* (*horse*) Gaul *m*

nag² *vt/i* (*pp/pp* **nagged**) herumnörgeln (**s.o.** an jdm)

nail *n* (*Anat, Techn*) Nagel *m*; **on the ~** [!] sofort ● *vt* nageln (**to** an + *acc*)

nail: ~-brush *n* Nagelbürste *f*. **~-file** *n* Nagelfeile *f*. **~ scissors** *npl* Nagelschere *f*. **~ varnish** *n* Nagellack *m*

naïve *a*, **-ly** *adv* naiv. **~ty** *n* Naivität *f*

naked *a* nackt; <*flame*> offen; **with the ~ eye** mit bloßem Auge. **~ness** *n* Nacktheit *f*

name *n* Name *m*; (*reputation*) Ruf *m*; **by ~** dem Namen nach; **by the ~ of** namens; **call s.o. ~s** [!] jdn beschimpfen ● *vt* nennen; (*give a name to*) einen Namen geben (+ *dat*); (*announce publicly*) den Namen bekannt geben von. **~less** *a* namenlos. **~ly** *adv* nämlich

name: ~-plate *n* Namensschild *nt*. **~sake** *n* Namensvetter *m*/Namensschwester *f*

nanny *n* Kindermädchen *nt*

nap *n* Nickerchen *nt*

napkin *n* Serviette *f*

nappy *n* Windel *f*

narcotic *n* (*drug*) Rauschgift *nt*

narrat|e *vt* erzählen. **~ion** *n* Erzählung *f*

narrative *n* Erzählung *f*

narrator *n* Erzähler(in) *m*(*f*)

narrow *a* (**-er, -est**) schmal; (*restricted*) eng; <*margin, majority*> knapp; **have a ~ escape** mit knapper Not davonkommen ● *vi* sich verengen. **~-minded** *a* engstirnig

nasal *a* nasal; (*Med & Anat*) Nasen-

nasty *a* (**-ier, -iest**) übel; (*unpleasant*) unangenehm; (*unkind*) boshaft; (*serious*) schlimm

nation *n* Nation *f*; (*people*) Volk *nt*

national *a* national; <*newspaper*> überregional; <*campaign*> landesweit ● *n* Staatsbürger(in) *m*(*f*)

national: ~ anthem *n* Nationalhymne *f*. **N~ Health Service** *n* staatlicher Gesundheitsdienst *m*. **N~ Insurance** *n* Sozialversicherung *f*

nationalism *n* Nationalismus *m*

nationality *n* Staatsangehörigkeit *f*

national|ization *n* Verstaatlichung *f*. **~ize** *vt* verstaatlichen

native *a* einheimisch; (*innate*) angeboren ● *n* Eingeborene(r) *m/f*; (*local inhabitant*)

Einheimische(r) *m/f*; **a ~ of Vienna** ein gebürtiger Wiener

native: ~ land *n* Heimatland *nt*. **~ language** *n* Muttersprache *f*

natter *vi* [!] schwatzen

natural *a*, **-ly** *adv* natürlich; **~[-coloured]** naturfarben

natural: ~ gas *n* Erdgas *nt*. **~ history** *n* Naturkunde *f*

naturalist *n* Naturforscher *m*

natural|ization *n* Einbürgerung *f*. **~ize** *vt* einbürgern

nature *n* Natur *f*; (*kind*) Art *f*; **by ~** von Natur aus. **~ reserve** *n* Naturschutzgebiet *nt*

naughty *a* (**-ier, -iest**), **-ily** *adv* unartig; (*slightly indecent*) gewagt

nausea *n* Übelkeit *f*

nautical *a* nautisch. **~ mile** *n* Seemeile *f*

naval *a* Marine-

nave *n* Kirchenschiff *nt*

navel *n* Nabel *m*

navigable *a* schiffbar

navigat|e *vi* navigieren ●*vt* befahren <*river*>. **~ion** *n* Navigation *f*

navy *n* [Kriegs]marine *f* ●*a* **~ [blue]** marineblau

near *a* (**-er, -est**) nah[e]; **the ~est bank** die nächste Bank ●*adv* nahe; **draw ~** sich nähern ●*prep* nahe an (+ *dat/acc*); in der Nähe von

near: ~by *a* nahe gelegen, nahe liegend. **~ly** *adv* fast, beinahe; **not ~ly** bei weitem nicht. **~ness** *n* Nähe *f*. **~ side** *n* Beifahrerseite *f*. **~-sighted** *a* (*Amer*) kurzsichtig

neat *a* (**-er, -est**), **-ly** *adv* adrett; (*tidy*) ordentlich; (*clever*) geschickt; (*undiluted*) pur. **~ness** *n* Ordentlichkeit *f*

necessarily *adv* notwendigerweise; **not ~** nicht unbedingt

necessary *a* nötig, notwendig

necessit|ate *vt* notwendig machen. **~y** *n* Notwendigkeit *f*; **work from ~y** arbeiten, weil man es nötig hat

neck *n* Hals *m*; **~ and ~** Kopf an Kopf

necklace *n* Halskette *f*

neckline *n* Halsausschnitt *m*

née *a* **~ X** geborene X

need *n* Bedürfnis *nt*; (*misfortune*) Not *f*; **be in ~ of** brauchen; **in case of ~** notfalls; **if ~ be** wenn nötig; **there is a ~ for** es besteht ein Bedarf an (+ *dat*); **there is no ~ for that** das ist nicht nötig ●*vt* brauchen; **you ~ not go** du brauchst nicht zu gehen; **~ I come?** muss ich kommen? **I ~ to know** ich muss es wissen

needle *n* Nadel *f*

needless *a*, **-ly** *adv* unnötig; **~ to say** selbstverständlich, natürlich

needlework *n* Nadelarbeit *f*

needy *a* (**-ier, -iest**) bedürftig

negation *n* Verneinung *f*

negative *a* negativ ●*n* Verneinung *f*; (*photo*) Negativ *nt*

neglect *n* Vernachlässigung *f* ●*vt* vernachlässigen; (*omit*) versäumen (**to** zu). **~ed** *a* verwahrlost. **~ful** *a* nachlässig

negligen|ce *n* Nachlässigkeit *f*. **~t** *a*, **-ly** *adv* nachlässig

negligible *a* unbedeutend

negotiat|e *vt* aushandeln; (*Auto*) nehmen <*bend*> ●*vi* verhandeln. **~ion** *n* Verhandlung *f*. **~or** *n* Unterhändler(in) *m(f)*

Negro *a* Neger- ●*n* (*pl* **-es**) Neger *m*

neigh *vi* wiehern

neighbour *n* Nachbar(in) *m(f)*. **~hood** *n* Nachbarschaft *f*. **~ing** *a* Nachbar-. **~ly** *a* [gut]nachbarlich

neither *a & pron* keine(r, s) [von beiden] ●*adv* **~... nor** weder ... noch ●*conj* auch nicht

neon *n* Neon *nt*

nephew *n* Neffe *m*

nepotism *n* Vetternwirtschaft *f*

nerve *n* Nerv *m*; ([!] *courage*) Mut *m*; ([!] *impudence*) Frechheit *f*. **~-racking** *a* nervenaufreibend
nervous *a*, **-ly** *adv* (*afraid*) ängstlich; (*highly strung*) nervös; (*Anat, Med*) Nerven-. **~ breakdown** *n* Nervenzusammenbruch *m*. **~ness** Ängstlichkeit *f*
nervy *a* (**-ier, -iest**) nervös; (*Amer: impudent*) frech
nest *n* Nest *nt* ● *vi* nisten
nestle *vi* sich schmiegen (**against** an + *acc*)
net[1] *n* Netz *nt*; (*curtain*) Store *m*
net[2] *a* netto; <*salary, weight*> Netto-
netball *n* ≈ Korbball *m*
Netherlands *npl* **the ~** die Niederlande *pl*
nettle *n* Nessel *f*
network *n* Netz *nt*
neurolog|ist *n* Neurologe *m*/ -gin *f*. **~y** *n* Neurologie *f*
neur|osis *n* (*pl* **-oses**) Neurose *f*. **~otic** *a* neurotisch
neuter *a* (*Gram*) sächlich ● *n* (*Gram*) Neutrum *nt* ● *vt* kastrieren; (*spay*) sterilisieren
neutral *a* neutral ● *n* **in ~** (*Auto*) im Leerlauf. **~ity** *n* Neutralität *f*
never *adv* nie, niemals; ([!] *not*) nicht; **~ mind** macht nichts; **well I ~!** ja so was! **~-ending** *a* endlos
nevertheless *adv* dennoch, trotzdem
new *a* (**-er, -est**) neu
new: ~comer *n* Neuankömmling *m*. **~fangled** *a* (*pej*) neumodisch. **~-laid** *a* frisch gelegt
newly *adv* frisch. **~-weds** *npl* Jungverheiratete *pl*
new: ~ moon *n* Neumond *m*. **~ness** *n* Neuheit *f*
news *n* Nachricht *f*; (*Radio, TV*) Nachrichten *pl*; **piece of ~** Neuigkeit *f*
news: ~agent *n* Zeitungshändler *m*. **~ bulletin** *n* Nachrichtensendung *f*. **~letter** *n* Mitteilungsblatt *nt*. **~paper** *n* Zeitung *f*; (*material*) Zeitungspapier *nt*. **~reader** *n* Nachrichtensprecher(in) *m*(*f*)
New: ~ Year's Day *n* Neujahr *nt*. **~ Year's Eve** *n* Silvester *nt*. **~ Zealand** *n* Neuseeland *nt*
next *a* & *n* nächste(r, s); **who's ~?** wer kommt als Nächster dran? **the ~ best** das nächstbeste; **~ door** nebenan; **my ~ of kin** mein nächster Verwandter; **~ to nothing** fast gar nichts; **the week after ~** übernächste Woche ● *adv* als Nächstes; **~ to** neben
nib *n* Feder *f*
nibble *vt/i* knabbern (**at** an + *dat*)
nice *a* (**-r, -st**) nett; <*day, weather*> schön; <*food*> gut; <*distinction*> fein. **~ly** *adv* nett; (*well*) gut
niche *n* Nische *f*; (*fig*) Platz *m*
nick *n* Kerbe *f*; ([!] *prison*) Knast *m*; ([!] *police station*) Revier *nt*; **in good ~** [!] in gutem Zustand ● *vt* einkerben; (*steal*) klauen; ([!] *arrest*) schnappen
nickel *n* Nickel *nt*; (*Amer*) Fünfcentstück *nt*
nickname *n* Spitzname *m*
nicotine *n* Nikotin *nt*
niece *n* Nichte *f*
Nigeria *n* Nigeria *nt*. **~n** *a* nigerianisch ● *n* Nigerianer(in) *m*(*f*)
night *n* Nacht *f*; (*evening*) Abend *m*; **at ~** nachts
night: ~-club *n* Nachtklub *m*. **~-dress** *n* Nachthemd *nt*. **~fall** *n* **at ~fall** bei Einbruch der Dunkelheit. **~-gown** *n*, [!] **~ie** *n* Nachthemd *nt*
nightingale *n* Nachtigall *f*
night: ~-life *n* Nachtleben *nt*. **~ly** *a* nächtlich ● *adv* jede Nacht. **~mare** *n* Albtraum *m*. **~-time** *n* **at ~-time** bei Nacht
nil *n* null
nimble *a* (**-r, -st**), **-bly** *adv* flink

N

nine *a* neun ● *n* Neun *f*. **~teen** *a* neunzehn. **~teenth** *a* neunzehnte(r, s)
ninetieth *a* neunzigste(r, s)
ninety *a* neunzig
ninth *a* neunte(r, s)
nip *vt* kneifen; (*bite*) beißen; **~ in the bud** (*fig*) im Keim ersticken ● *vi* (! *run*) laufen
nipple *n* Brustwarze *f*; (*Amer: on bottle*) Sauger *m*
nitwit *n* ! Dummkopf *m*
no *adv* nein ● *n* (*pl* **noes**) Nein *nt* ● *a* kein(e); (*pl*) keine; **in no time** [sehr] schnell; **no parking/smoking** Parken/Rauchen verboten; **no one** = **nobody**
nobility *n* Adel *m*
noble *a* (**-r, -st**) edel; (*aristocratic*) adlig. **~man** *n* Adlige(r) *m*
nobody *pron* niemand, keiner ● *n* **a ~** ein Niemand *m*
nocturnal *a* nächtlich; <*animal, bird*> Nacht-
nod *n* Nicken *nt* ● *v* (*pt/pp* **nodded**) ● *vi* nicken ● *vt* **~ one's head** mit dem Kopf nicken
noise *n* Geräusch *nt*; (*loud*) Lärm *m*. **~less** *a*, **-ly** *adv* geräuschlos
noisy *a* (**-ier, -iest**), **-ily** *adv* laut; <*eater*> geräuschvoll
nomad *n* Nomade *m*. **~ic** *a* nomadisch; <*life, tribe*> Nomaden-
nominal *a*, **-ly** *adv* nominell
nominat|e *vt* nominieren, aufstellen; (*appoint*) ernennen. **~ion** *n* Nominierung *f*; Ernennung *f*
nominative *a* & *n* (*Gram*) **~[case]** Nominativ *m*
nonchalant *a*, **-ly** *adv* nonchalant; <*gesture*> lässig
nondescript *a* unbestimmbar; <*person*> unscheinbar
none *pron* keine(r)/keins; **~ of it/this** nichts davon ● *adv* **~ too** nicht gerade; **~ too soon** [um] keine Minute zu früh; **~ the less** dennoch
nonentity *n* Null *f*
non-existent *a* nicht vorhanden
non-fiction *n* Sachliteratur *f*
nonplussed *a* verblüfft
nonsens|e *n* Unsinn *m*. **~ical** *a* unsinnig
non-smoker *n* Nichtraucher *m*
non-stop *adv* ununterbrochen; <*fly*> nonstop
non-swimmer *n* Nichtschwimmer *m*
non-violent *a* gewaltlos
noodles *npl* Bandnudeln *pl*
noon *n* Mittag *m*; **at ~** um 12 Uhr mittags
noose *n* Schlinge *f*
nor *adv* noch ● *conj* auch nicht
Nordic *a* nordisch
norm *n* Norm *f*
normal *a* normal. **~ity** *n* Normalität *f*. **~ly** *adv* normal; (*usually*) normalerweise
north *n* Norden *m*; **to the ~ of** nördlich von ● *a* Nord-, nord- ● *adv* nach Norden
north: N~ America *n* Nordamerika *nt*. **~-east** *a* Nordost- ● *n* Nordosten *m*
norther|ly *a* nördlich. **~n** *a* nördlich. **N~n Ireland** *n* Nordirland *nt*
north: N~ Pole *n* Nordpol *m*. **N~ Sea** *n* Nordsee *f*. **~ward[s]** *adv* nach Norden. **~-west** *a* Nordwest- ● *n* Nordwesten *m*
Nor|way *n* Norwegen *nt*. **~wegian** *a* norwegisch ● *n* Norweger(in) *m(f)*
nose *n* Nase
nosebleed *n* Nasenbluten *nt*
nostalg|ia *n* Nostalgie *f*. **~ic** *a* nostalgisch
nostril *n* Nasenloch *nt*
nosy *a* (**-ier, -iest**) ! neugierig

not
● *adverb*

····➤ nicht. **I don't know** ich weiß nicht. **isn't she pretty?** ist sie nicht hübsch?
····➤ **not a** kein. **he is not a doctor** er ist kein Arzt. **she didn't wear a hat** sie trug keinen Hut. **there was not a person to be seen** es gab keinen Menschen zu sehen. **not a thing** gar nichts. **not a bit** kein bisschen
····➤ (*in elliptical phrases*) **I hope not** ich hoffe nicht. **of course not** natürlich nicht. **not at all** überhaupt nicht; (*in polite reply to thanks*) keine Ursache; gern geschehen. **certainly not!** auf keinen Fall! **not I** ich nicht
····➤ **not ... but ...** nicht ... sondern .... **it was not a small town but a big one** es war keine kleine Stadt, sondern eine große

notab|le *a* bedeutend; (*remarkable*) bemerkenswert. **~ly** *adv* insbesondere
notation *n* Notation *f*; (*Mus*) Notenschrift *f*
notch *n* Kerbe *f*
note *n* (*written comment*) Notiz *f*, Anmerkung *f*; (*short letter*) Briefchen *nt*, Zettel *m*; (*bank* ~) Banknote *f*, Schein *m*; (*Mus*) Note *f*; (*sound*) Ton *m*; (*on piano*) Taste *f*; **half/whole** ~ (*Amer*) halbe/ganze Note *f*; **of** ~ von Bedeutung; **make a** ~ **of** notieren ● *vt* beachten; (*notice*) bemerken (**that** dass)
notebook *n* Notizbuch *nt*
noted *a* bekannt (**for** für)
note: ~paper *n* Briefpapier *nt*. **~worthy** *a* beachtenswert
nothing *n, pron & adv* nichts; **for** ~ umsonst; ~ **but** nichts als; ~ **much** nicht viel; ~ **interesting** nichts Interessantes
notice *n* (*on board*) Anschlag *m*, Bekanntmachung *f*; (*announcement*) Anzeige *f*; (*review*) Kritik *f*; (*termination of lease, employment*) Kündigung *f*; **give [in one's]** ~ kündigen; **give s.o.** ~ jdm kündigen; **take no** ~! ignoriere es! ● *vt* bemerken. **~able**, *a*, **-bly** *adv* merklich. **~-board** *n* Anschlagbrett *nt*
noti|fication *n* Benachrichtigung *f*. **~fy** *vt* (*pt/pp* **-ied**) benachrichtigen
notion *n* Idee *f*
notorious *a* berüchtigt
notwithstanding *prep* trotz (+ *gen*) ● *adv* trotzdem, dennoch
nought *n* Null *f*
noun *n* Substantiv *nt*
nourish *vt* nähren. **~ing** *a* nahrhaft. **~ment** *n* Nahrung *f*
novel *a* neu[artig] ● *n* Roman *m*. **~ist** *n* Romanschriftsteller(in) *m(f)*. **~ty** *n* Neuheit *f*
November *n* November *m*
novice *n* Neuling *m*; (*Relig*) Novize *m*/Novizin *f*
now *adv & conj* jetzt; ~ **[that]** jetzt, wo; **just** ~ gerade, eben; **right** ~ sofort; ~ **and again** hin und wieder; **now, now!** na, na!
nowadays *adv* heutzutage
nowhere *adv* nirgendwo, nirgends
nozzle *n* Düse *f*
nuance *n* Nuance *f*
nuclear *a* Kern-. ~ **deterrent** *n* nukleares Abschreckungsmittel *nt*
nucleus *n* (*pl* **-lei**) Kern *m*
nude *a* nackt ● *n* (*Art*) Akt *m*; **in the** ~ nackt
nudge *vt* stupsen
nud|ist *n* Nudist *m*. **~ity** *n* Nacktheit *f*
nuisance *n* Ärgernis *nt*; (*pest*) Plage *f*; **be a** ~ ärgerlich sein
null *a* ~ **and void** null und nichtig
numb *a* gefühllos, taub ● *vt* betäuben
number *n* Nummer *f*; (*amount*) Anzahl *f*; (*Math*) Zahl *f* ● *vt*

N

nummerieren; (*include*) zählen (**among** zu). **~-plate** *n* Nummernschild *nt*

numeral *n* Ziffer *f*

numerical *a*, **-ly** *adv* numerisch; **in ~ order** zahlenmäßig geordnet

numerous *a* zahlreich

nun *n* Nonne *f*

nurse *n* [Kranken]schwester *f*; (*male*) Krankenpfleger *m*; **children's ~** Kindermädchen *nt* ● *vt* pflegen

nursery *n* Kinderzimmer *nt*; (*Hort*) Gärtnerei *f*; **[day] ~** Kindertagesstätte *f*. **~ rhyme** *n* Kinderreim *m*. **~ school** *n* Kindergarten *m*

nursing *n* Krankenpflege *f*. **~ home** *n* Pflegeheim *nt*

nut *n* Nuss *f*; (*Techn*) [Schrauben]mutter *f*; ([!] *head*) Birne *f* [!]; **be ~s** [!] spinnen [!]. **~crackers** *npl* Nussknacker *m*. **~meg** *n* Muskat *m*

nutrient *n* Nährstoff *m*

nutrit|ion *n* Ernährung *f*. **~ious** *a* nahrhaft

nutshell *n* Nussschale *f*; **in a ~** (*fig*) kurz gesagt

nylon *n* Nylon *nt*

Oo

O *n* (*Teleph*) null

oak *n* Eiche *f*

OAP *abbr* (**old-age pensioner**) Rentner(in) *m*(*f*)

oar *n* Ruder *nt*. **~sman** *n* Ruderer *m*

oasis *n* (*pl* **oases**) Oase *f*

oath *n* Eid *m*; (*swear-word*) Fluch *m*

oatmeal *n* Hafermehl *nt*

oats *npl* Hafer *m*; (*Culin*) **[rolled] ~** Haferflocken *pl*

obedien|ce *n* Gehorsam *m*. **~t** *a*, **-ly** *adv* gehorsam

obey *vt*/*i* gehorchen (+ *dat*); befolgen <*instructions, rules*>

obituary *n* Nachruf *m*; (*notice*) Todesanzeige *f*

object[1] *n* Gegenstand *m*; (*aim*) Zweck *m*; (*intention*) Absicht *f*; (*Gram*) Objekt *nt*; **money is no ~** Geld spielt keine Rolle

object[2] *vi* Einspruch erheben (**to** gegen); (*be against*) etwas dagegen haben

objection *n* Einwand *m*; **have no ~** nichts dagegen haben. **~able** *a* anstößig; <*person*> unangenehm

objectiv|e *a*, **-ly** *adv* objektiv ● *n* Ziel *nt*. **~ity** *n* Objektivität *f*

objector *n* Gegner *m*

obligation *n* Pflicht *f*; **without ~** unverbindlich

obligatory *a* obligatorisch; **be ~** Vorschrift sein

oblig|e *vt* verpflichten; (*compel*) zwingen; (*do a small service*) einen Gefallen tun (+ *dat*). **~ing** *a* entgegenkommend

oblique *a* schräg; <*angle*> schief; (*fig*) indirekt

obliterate *vt* auslöschen

oblivion *n* Vergessenheit *f*

oblivious *a* **be ~** sich (*dat*) nicht bewusst sein (**of** *gen*)

oblong *a* rechteckig ● *n* Rechteck *nt*

obnoxious *a* widerlich

oboe *n* Oboe *f*

obscen|e *a* obszön. **~ity** *n* Obszönität *f*

obscur|e *a* dunkel; (*unknown*) unbekannt ● *vt* verdecken; (*confuse*) verwischen. **~ity** *n* Dunkelheit *f*; Unbekanntheit *f*

observa|nce *n* (*of custom*) Einhaltung *f*. **~nt** *a* aufmerksam.

~tion *n* Beobachtung *f*; (*remark*) Bemerkung *f*
observatory *n* Sternwarte *f*
observe *vt* beobachten; (*say, notice*) bemerken; (*keep, celebrate*) feiern; (*obey*) einhalten. **~r** *n* Beobachter *m*
obsess *vt* **be ~ed by** besessen sein von. **~ion** *n* Besessenheit *f*; (*persistent idea*) fixe Idee *f*. **~ive** *a*, **-ly** *adv* zwanghaft
obsolete *a* veraltet
obstacle *n* Hindernis *nt*
obstina|cy *n* Starrsinn *m*. **~te** *a*, **-ly** *adv* starrsinnig; <*refusal*> hartnäckig
obstruct *vt* blockieren; (*hinder*) behindern. **~ion** *n* Blockierung *f*; Behinderung *f*; (*obstacle*) Hindernis *nt*. **~ive** *a* **be ~ive** Schwierigkeiten bereiten
obtain *vt* erhalten. **~able** *a* erhältlich
obtrusive *a* aufdringlich; <*thing*> auffällig
obtuse *a* begriffsstutzig
obvious *a*, **-ly** *adv* offensichtlich, offenbar
occasion *n* Gelegenheit *f*; (*time*) Mal *nt*; (*event*) Ereignis *nt*; (*cause*) Anlass *m*, Grund *m*; **on the ~ of** anlässlich (+ *gen*)
occasional *a* gelegentlich. **~ly** *adv* gelegentlich, hin und wieder
occult *a* okkult
occupant *n* Bewohner(in) *m*(*f*); (*of vehicle*) Insasse *m*
occupation *n* Beschäftigung *f*; (*job*) Beruf *m*; (*Mil*) Besetzung *f*; (*period*) Besatzung *f*. **~al** *a* Berufs-. **~al therapy** *n* Beschäftigungstherapie *f*
occupier *n* Bewohner(in) *m*(*f*)
occupy *vt* (*pt/pp* **occupied**) besetzen <*seat*, (*Mil*) *country*>; einnehmen <*space*>; in Anspruch nehmen <*time*>; (*live in*) bewohnen; (*fig*) bekleiden <*office*>; (*keep busy*) beschäftigen
occur *vi* (*pt/pp* **occurred**) geschehen; (*exist*) vorkommen, auftreten; **it ~red to me that** es fiel mir ein, dass. **~rence** *n* Auftreten *nt*; (*event*) Ereignis *nt*
ocean *n* Ozean *m*
o'clock *adv* **[at] 7 ~** [um] 7 Uhr
octagonal *a* achteckig
October *n* Oktober *m*
octopus *n* (*pl* **-puses**) Tintenfisch *m*
odd *a* (**-er, -est**) seltsam, merkwürdig; <*number*> ungerade; (*not of set*) einzeln; **forty ~** über vierzig; **~ jobs** Gelegenheitsarbeiten *pl*; **the ~ one out** die Ausnahme; **at ~ moments** zwischendurch
odd|ity *n* Kuriosität *f*. **~ly** *adv* merkwürdig; **~ly enough** merkwürdigerweise **~ment** *n* (*of fabric*) Rest *m*
odds *npl* (*chances*) Chancen *pl*; **at ~** uneinig; **~ and ends** Kleinkram *m*
ode *n* Ode *f*
odious *a* widerlich
odour *n* Geruch *m*. **~less** *a* geruchlos

of

● *preposition*

····➤ (*indicating belonging, origin*) von (+ *dat*); genitive. **the mother of twins** die Mutter von Zwillingen. **the mother of the twins** die Mutter der Zwillinge *or* von den Zwillingen. **the Queen of England** die Königin von England. **a friend of mine** ein Freund von mir. **a friend of the teacher's** ein Freund des Lehrers. **the brother of her father** der Bruder ihres Vaters. **the works of Shakespeare** Shakespeares Werke. **it was nice of him** es war nett von ihm

O

····➤ (*made of*) aus (+ *dat*). **a dress of cotton** ein Kleid aus Baumwolle

····➤ (*following number*) **five of us** fünf von uns. **the two of us** wir zwei. **there were four of us waiting** wir waren vier, die warteten

····➤ (*followed by number, description*) von (+ *dat*). **a girl of ten** ein Mädchen von zehn Jahren. **a distance of 50 miles** eine Entfernung von 50 Meilen. **a man of character** ein Mann von Charakter. **a woman of exceptional beauty** eine Frau von außerordentlicher Schönheit. **a person of strong views** ein Mensch mit festen Ansichten

> **!** **of** is not translated after measures and in some other cases: **a pound of apples** ein Pfund Äpfel; **a cup of tea** eine Tasse Tee; **a glass of wine** ein Glas Wein; **the city of Chicago** die Stadt Chicago; **the fourth of January** der vierte Januar

off *prep* von (+ *dat*); **~ the coast** vor der Küste; **get ~ the ladder/bus** von der Leiter/aus dem Bus steigen ● *adv* weg; <*button, lid, handle*> ab; <*light*> aus; <*brake*> los; <*machine*> abgeschaltet; <*tap*> zu; (*on appliance*) **'off'** 'aus'; **2 kilometres ~** 2 Kilometer entfernt; **a long way ~** weit weg; (*time*) noch lange hin; **~ and on** hin und wieder; **with his hat/coat ~** ohne Hut/Mantel; **20% ~** 20% Nachlass; **be ~** (*leave*) [weg]gehen; (*Sport*) starten; <*food:*> schlecht sein; **be well ~** gut dran sein; (*financially*) wohlhabend sein; **have a day ~** einen freien Tag haben

offal *n* (*Culin*) Innereien *pl*

offence *n* (*illegal act*) Vergehen *nt*; **give/take ~** Anstoß erregen/nehmen (**at** an + *dat*)

offend *vt* beleidigen. **~er** *n* (*Jur*) Straftäter *m*

offensive *a* anstößig; (*Mil, Sport*) offensiv ● *n* Offensive *f*

offer *n* Angebot *nt*; **on (special) ~** im Sonderangebot ● *vt* anbieten (**to** *dat*); leisten <*resistance*>; **~ to do sth** sich anbieten, etw zu tun. **~ing** *n* Gabe *f*

offhand *a* brüsk; (*casual*) lässig

office *n* Büro *nt*; (*post*) Amt *nt*

officer *n* Offizier *m*; (*official*) Beamte(r) *m*/ Beamtin *f*; (*police*) Polizeibeamte(r) *m*/-beamtin *f*

official *a* offiziell, amtlich ● *n* Beamte(r) *m*/ Beamtin *f*; (*Sport*) Funktionär *m*. **~ly** *adv* offiziell

officious *a*, **-ly** *adv* übereifrig

off-licence *n* Wein und Spirituosenhandlung *f*

off-load *vt* ausladen

off-putting *a* [!] abstoßend

offset *vt* (*pt/pp* **-set**, *pres p* **-setting**) ausgleichen

offshoot *n* Schössling *m*; (*fig*) Zweig *m*

offshore *a* Offshore-

offside *a* (*Sport*) abseits

offspring *n* Nachwuchs *m*

offstage *adv* hinter den Kulissen

off-white *a* fast weiß

often *adv* oft; **every so ~** von Zeit zu Zeit

oh *int* oh! ach! **oh dear!** o weh!

oil *n* Öl *nt*; (*petroleum*) Erdöl *nt* ● *vt* ölen

oil: ~field *n* Ölfeld *nt*. **~-painting** *n* Ölgemälde *nt*. **~ refinery** *n* [Erd]ölraffinerie *f*. **~-tanker** *n* Öltanker *m*. **~ well** *n* Ölquelle *f*

oily *a* (**-ier, -iest**) ölig

ointment *n* Salbe *f*

OK *a & int* [!] in Ordnung; okay ● *adv* (*well*) gut ● *vt* (*auch* **okay**) (*pt/pp* **okayed**) genehmigen

old *a* (**-er, -est**) alt; (*former*) ehemalig

old: ~ age *n* Alter *nt*. **~-age pensioner** *n* Rentner(in) *m(f)*. **~ boy** *n* ehemaliger Schüler. **~-fashioned** *a* altmodisch. **~ girl** ehemalige Schülerin *f*

olive *n* Olive *f*; (*colour*) Oliv *nt* ● *a* olivgrün. **~ oil** *n* Olivenöl *nt*

Olympic *a* olympisch ● *n* **the ~s** die Olympischen Spiele *pl*

omelette *n* Omelett *nt*

ominous *a* bedrohlich

omission *n* Auslassung *f*; (*failure to do*) Unterlassung *f*

omit *vt* (*pt/pp* **omitted**) auslassen; **~ to do sth** es unterlassen, etw zu tun

omnipotent *a* allmächtig

on *prep* auf (+ *dat*/(*on to*) + *acc*); (*on vertical surface*) an (+ *dat*/(*on to*) + *acc*); (*about*) über (+ *acc*); **on Monday** [am] Montag; **on Mondays** montags; **on the first of May** am ersten Mai; **on arriving** als ich ankam; **on one's finger** am Finger; **on the right/left** rechts/links; **on the Rhine** am Rhein; **on the radio/television** im Radio/Fernsehen; **on the bus/train** im Bus/Zug; **go on the bus/train** mit dem Bus/Zug fahren; **on me** (*with me*) bei mir; **it's on me** [!] das spendiere ich ● *adv* (*further on*) weiter; (*switched on*) an; <*brake*> angezogen; <*machine*> angeschaltet; (*on appliance*) **'on'** 'ein'; **with/without his hat/coat on** mit/ohne Hut/Mantel; **be on** <*film:*> laufen; <*event:*> stattfinden; **be on at** [!] bedrängen (**zu** to); **it's not on** [!] das geht nicht; **on and on** immer weiter; **on and off** hin und wieder; **and so on** und so weiter

once *adv* einmal; (*formerly*) früher; **at ~** sofort; (*at the same time*) gleichzeitig; **~ and for all** ein für alle Mal ● *conj* wenn; (*with past tense*) als

oncoming *a* **~ traffic** Gegenverkehr *m*

one *a* ein(e); (*only*) einzig; **not ~** kein(e); **~ day/evening** eines Tages/Abends ● *n* Eins *f* ● *pron* eine(r)/eins; (*impersonal*) man; **which ~** welche(r,s); **~ another** einander; **~ by ~** einzeln; **~ never knows** man kann nie wissen

one: ~-parent family *n* Einelternfamilie *f*. **~self** *pron* selbst; (*refl*) sich; **by ~self** allein. **~-sided** *a* einseitig. **~-way** *a* <*street*> Einbahn-; <*ticket*> einfach

onion *n* Zwiebel *f*

on-line *adv* online

onlooker *n* Zuschauer(in) *m(f)*

only *a* einzige(r,s); **an ~ child** ein Einzelkind *nt* ● *adv & conj* nur; **~ just** gerade erst; (*barely*) gerade noch

onset *n* Beginn *m*; (*of winter*) Einsetzen *nt*

onward[s] *adv* vorwärts; **from then ~** von der Zeit an

ooze *vi* sickern

opaque *a* undurchsichtig

open *a*, **-ly** *adv* offen; **be ~** <*shop:*> geöffnet sein; **in the ~ air** im Freien ● *n* **in the ~** im Freien ● *vt* öffnen, aufmachen; (*start, set up*) eröffnen ● *vi* sich öffnen; <*flower:*> aufgehen; <*shop:*> öffnen, aufmachen. **~ up** *vt* öffnen, aufmachen

open day *n* Tag *m* der offenen Tür

opener *n* Öffner *m*

opening *n* Öffnung *f*; (*beginning*) Eröffnung *f*; (*job*) Einstiegsmöglichkeit *f*. **~ hours** *npl* Öffnungszeiten *pl*

open: ~-minded *a* aufgeschlossen. **~ sandwich** *n* belegtes Brot *nt*

opera *n* Oper *f*. **~-house** *n* Opernhaus *nt*. **~-singer** *n* Opernsänger(in) *m(f)*

operate *vt* bedienen <*machine, lift*>; betätigen <*lever, brake*>; (*fig: run*) betreiben ● *vi* (*Techn*) funktionieren; (*be in action*) in Betrieb sein; (*Mil & fig*) operieren; **~ [on]** (*Med*) operieren

operatic *a* Opern-

operation *n* (*see* **operate**) Bedienung *f*; Betätigung *f*; Operation *f*; **in ~** (*Techn*) in Betrieb; **come into ~** (*fig*) in Kraft treten; **have an ~** (*Med*) operiert werden. **~al** *a* **be ~al** in Betrieb sein; <*law:*> in Kraft sein

operative *a* wirksam

operator *n* (*user*) Bedienungsperson *f*; (*Teleph*) Vermittlung *f*

operetta *n* Operette *f*

opinion *n* Meinung *f*; **in my ~** meiner Meinung nach. **~ated** *a* rechthaberisch

opponent *n* Gegner(in) *m(f)*

opportun|e *a* günstig. **~ist** *n* Opportunist *m*

opportunity *n* Gelegenheit *f*

oppos|e *vt* Widerstand leisten (+ *dat*); (*argue against*) sprechen gegen; **be ~ed to sth** gegen etw sein; **as ~ed to** im Gegensatz zu. **~ing** *a* gegnerisch

opposite *a* entgegengesetzt; <*house, side*> gegenüberliegend; **~ number** (*fig*) Gegenstück *nt*; **the ~ sex** das andere Geschlecht ● *n* Gegenteil *nt* ● *adv* gegenüber ● *prep* gegenüber (+ *dat*)

opposition *n* Widerstand *m*; (*Pol*) Opposition *f*

oppress *vt* unterdrücken. **~ion** *n* Unterdrücken *f*. **~ive** *a* tyrannisch; <*heat*> drückend

opt *vi* **~ for** sich entscheiden für

optical *a* optisch

optician *n* Optiker *m*

optimis|m *n* Optimismus *m*. **~t** *n* Optimist *m*. **~tic** *a*, **-ally** *adv* optimistisch

optimum *a* optimal

option *n* Wahl *f*; (*Comm*) Option *f*. **~al** *a* auf Wunsch erhältlich; <*subject*> wahlfrei

opu|lence *n* Prunk *m*. **~lent** *a* prunkvoll

or *conj* oder; (*after negative*) noch; **or [else]** sonst; **in a year or two** in ein bis zwei Jahren

oral *a*, **-ly** *adv* mündlich; (*Med*) oral ● *n* Mündliche(s) *nt*

orange *n* Apfelsine *f*, Orange *f*; (*colour*) Orange *nt* ● *a* orangefarben

oratorio *n* Oratorium *nt*

oratory *n* Redekunst *f*

orbit *n* Umlaufbahn *f* ● *vt* umkreisen

orchard *n* Obstgarten *m*

orches|tra *n* Orchester *nt*. **~tral** *a* Orchester-. **~trate** *vt* orchestrieren

ordeal *n* (*fig*) Qual *f*

order *n* Ordnung *f*; (*sequence*) Reihenfolge *f*; (*condition*) Zustand *m*; (*command*) Befehl *m*; (*in restaurant*) Bestellung *f*; (*Comm*) Auftrag *m*; (*Relig, medal*) Orden *m*; **out of ~** <*machine*> außer Betrieb; **in ~ that** damit; **in ~ to help** um zu helfen ● *vt* (*put in ~*) ordnen; (*command*) befehlen (+ *dat*); (*Comm, in restaurant*) bestellen; (*prescribe*) verordnen

orderly *a* ordentlich; (*not unruly*) friedlich ● *n* (*Mil, Med*) Sanitäter *m*

ordinary *a* gewöhnlich, normal

ore *n* Erz *nt*

organ *n* (*Biol & fig*) Organ *nt*; (*Mus*) Orgel *f*

organic *a*, **-ally** *adv* organisch; (*without chemicals*) biodynamisch; <*crop*> biologisch

angebaut; <*food*> Bio-. ~ **farming** *n* biologischer Anbau *m*
organism *n* Organismus *m*
organist *n* Organist *m*
organization *n* Organisation *f*
organize *vt* organisieren; veranstalten <*event*>. ~**r** *n* Organisator *m*; Veranstalter *m*
orgy *n* Orgie *f*
Orient *n* Orient *m*. **o~al** *a* orientalisch ● *n* Orientale *m*/ Orientalin *f*
orientation *n* Orientierung *f*
origin *n* Ursprung *m*; (*of person, goods*) Herkunft *f*
original *a* ursprünglich; (*not copied*) original; (*new*) originell ● *n* Original *nt*. ~**ity** *n* Originalität *f*. ~**ly** *adv* ursprünglich
originate *vi* entstehen
ornament *n* Ziergegenstand *m*; (*decoration*) Verzierung *f*. ~**al** *a* dekorativ
ornate *a* reich verziert
ornithology *n* Vogelkunde *f*
orphan *n* Waisenkind *nt*, Waise *f*. ~**age** *n* Waisenhaus *nt*
orthodox *a* orthodox
ostensible *a*, **-bly** *adv* angeblich
ostentat|ion *n* Protzerei *f* [!]. ~**ious** *a* protzig [!]
osteopath *n* Osteopath *m*
ostrich *n* Strauß *m*
other *a*, *pron* & *n* andere(r,s); **the ~ [one]** der/die/das andere; **the ~ two** die zwei anderen; **no ~s** sonst keine; **any ~ questions?** sonst noch Fragen? **every ~ day** jeden zweiten Tag; **the ~ day** neulich; **the ~ evening** neulich abends; **someone/something or ~** irgendjemand/-etwas ● *adv* anders; **~ than him** außer ihm; **somehow/somewhere or ~** irgendwie/irgendwo
otherwise *adv* sonst; (*differently*) anders
ought *v aux* **I/we ~ to stay** ich sollte/wir sollten eigentlich bleiben; **he ~ not to have done it** er hätte es nicht machen sollen
ounce *n* Unze *f* (*28, 35 g*)
our *a* unser
ours *poss pron* unsere(r,s); **a friend of ~** ein Freund von uns; **that is ~** das gehört uns
ourselves *pron* selbst; (*refl*) uns; **by ~** allein
out *adv* (*not at home*) weg; (*outside*) draußen; (*not alight*) aus; (*unconscious*) bewusstlos; **be ~** <*sun:*> scheinen; <*flower*> blühen; <*workers*> streiken; <*calculation:*> nicht stimmen; (*Sport*) aus sein; (*fig: not feasible*) nicht infrage kommen; **~ and about** unterwegs; **have it ~ with s.o.** [!] jdn zur Rede stellen; **get ~!** [!] raus! **~ with it!** [!] heraus damit! ● *prep* **~ of** aus (+ *dat*); **go ~ (of) the door** zur Tür hinausgehen; **be ~ of bed/ the room** nicht im Bett/im Zimmer sein; **~ of breath/danger** außer Atem/Gefahr; **~ of work** arbeitslos; **nine ~ of ten** neun von zehn; **be ~ of sugar** keinen Zucker mehr haben
outboard *a* **~ motor** Außenbordmotor *m*
outbreak *n* Ausbruch *m*
outbuilding *n* Nebengebäude *nt*
outburst *n* Ausbruch *m*
outcast *n* Ausgestoßene(r) *m*/*f*
outcome *n* Ergebnis *nt*
outcry *n* Aufschrei *m* [der Entrüstung]
outdated *a* überholt
outdo *vt* (*pt* **-did**, *pp* **-done**) übertreffen, übertrumpfen
outdoor *a* <*life, sports*> im Freien; **~ swimming pool** Freibad *nt*
outdoors *adv* draußen; **go ~** nach draußen gehen
outer *a* äußere(r,s)

outfit *n* Ausstattung *f*; (*clothes*) Ensemble *nt*; (! *organization*) Laden *m*

outgoing *a* ausscheidend; <*mail*> ausgehend; (*sociable*) kontaktfreudig. **~s** *npl* Ausgaben *pl*

outgrow *vi* (*pt* **-grew**, *pp* **-grown**) herauswachsen aus

outing *n* Ausflug *m*

outlaw *n* Geächtete(r) *m/f* ● *vt* ächten

outlay *n* Auslagen *pl*

outlet *n* Abzug *m*; (*for water*) Abfluss *m*; (*fig*) Ventil *nt*; (*Comm*) Absatzmöglichkeit *f*

outline *n* Umriss *m*; (*summary*) kurze Darstellung *f* ● *vt* umreißen

outlive *vt* überleben

outlook *n* Aussicht *f*; (*future prospect*) Aussichten *pl*; (*attitude*) Einstellung *f*

outmoded *a* überholt

outnumber *vt* zahlenmäßig überlegen sein (+ *dat*)

out-patient *n* ambulanter Patient *m*

outpost *n* Vorposten *m*

output *n* Leistung *f*; Produktion *f*

outrage *n* Gräueltat *f*; (*fig*) Skandal *m*; (*indignation*) Empörung *f*. **~ous** *a* empörend

outright[1] *a* völlig, total; <*refusal*> glatt

outright[2] *adv* ganz; (*at once*) sofort; (*frankly*) offen

outset *n* Anfang *m*

outside[1] *a* äußere(r,s); **~ wall** Außenwand *f* ● *n* Außenseite *f*; **from the ~** von außen; **at the ~** höchstens

outside[2] *adv* außen; (*out of doors*) draußen; **go ~** nach draußen gehen ● *prep* außerhalb (+ *gen*); (*in front of*) vor (+ *dat/acc*)

outsider *n* Außenseiter *m*

outsize *a* übergroß

outskirts *npl* Rand *m*

outspoken *a* offen; **be ~** kein Blatt vor den Mund nehmen

outstanding *a* hervorragend; (*conspicuous*) bemerkenswert; (*Comm*) ausstehend

outstretched *a* ausgestreckt

outvote *vt* überstimmen

outward *a* äußerlich; **~ journey** Hinreise *f* ● *adv* nach außen. **~ly** *adv* nach außen hin, äußerlich. **~s** *adv* nach außen

outwit *vt* (*pt/pp* **-witted**) überlisten

oval *a* oval ● *n* Oval *nt*

ovation *n* Ovation *f*

oven *n* Backofen *m*

over *prep* über (+ *acc/dat*); **~ dinner** beim Essen; **~ the phone** am Telefon; **~ the page** auf der nächsten Seite ● *adv* (*remaining*) übrig; (*ended*) zu Ende; **~ again** noch einmal; **~ and ~** immer wieder; **~ here/there** hier/da drüben; **all ~** (*everywhere*) überall; **it's all ~** es ist vorbei; **I ache all ~** mir tut alles weh

overall[1] *n* Kittel *m*; **~s** *pl* Overall *m*

overall[2] *a* gesamt; (*general*) allgemein ● *adv* insgesamt

overbalance *vi* das Gleichgewicht verlieren

overbearing *a* herrisch

overboard *adv* (*Naut*) über Bord

overcast *a* bedeckt

overcharge *vt* **~ s.o.** jdm zu viel berechnen ● *vi* zu viel verlangen

overcoat *n* Mantel *m*

overcome *vt* (*pt* **-came**, *pp* **-come**) überwinden; **be ~ by** überwältigt werden von

overcrowded *a* überfüllt

overdo *vt* (*pt* **-did**, *pp* **-done**) übertreiben; (*cook too long*) zu lange kochen; **~ it** (! *do too much*) sich übernehmen

overdose *n* Überdosis *f*

overdraft *n* [Konto]überziehung *f*; **have an ~** sein Konto überzogen haben

overdue *a* überfällig
overestimate *vt* überschätzen
overflow[1] *n* Überschuss *m*; (*outlet*) Überlauf *m*
overflow[2] *vi* überlaufen
overgrown *a* <*garden*> überwachsen
overhang[1] *n* Überhang *m*
overhang[2] *vt/i* (*pt/pp* **-hung**) überhängen (über + *acc*)
overhaul[1] *n* Überholung *f*
overhaul[2] *vt* (*Techn*) überholen
overhead[1] *adv* oben
overhead[2] *a* Ober-; (*ceiling*) Decken-. **~s** *npl* allgemeine Unkosten *pl*
overhear *vt* (*pt/pp* **-heard**) mit anhören <*conversation*>
overheat *vi* zu heiß werden
overjoyed *a* überglücklich
overland *a & adv* auf dem Landweg; **~ route** Landroute *f*
overlap *vi* (*pt/pp* **-lapped**) sich überschneiden
overleaf *adv* umseitig
overload *vt* überladen
overlook *vt* überblicken; (*fail to see, ignore*) übersehen
overnight[1] *adv* über Nacht; **stay ~** übernachten
overnight[2] *a* Nacht-; **~ stay** Übernachtung *f*
overpass *n* Überführung *f*
overpay *vt* (*pt/pp* **-paid**) überbezahlen
overpopulated *a* übervölkert
overpower *vt* überwältigen. **~ing** *a* überwältigend
overpriced *a* zu teuer
overrated *a* überbewertet
overreact *vi* überreagieren. **~ion** *n* Überreaktion *f*
overriding *a* Haupt-
overrule *vt* ablehnen; **we were ~d** wir wurden überstimmt
overrun *vt* (*pt* **-ran**, *pp* **-run**, *pres p* **-running**) überrennen; überschreiten <*time*>; **be ~ with** überlaufen sein von
overseas[1] *adv* in Übersee; **go ~** nach Übersee gehen
overseas[2] *a* Übersee-
oversee *vt* (*pt* **-saw**, *pp* **-seen**) beaufsichtigen
overshadow *vt* überschatten
overshoot *vt* (*pt/pp* **-shot**) hinausschießen über (+ *acc*)
oversight *n* Versehen *nt*
oversleep *vi* (*pt/pp* **-slept**) [sich] verschlafen
overstep *vt* (*pt/pp* **-stepped**) überschreiten
overt *a* offen
overtake *vt/i* (*pt* **-took**, *pp* **-taken**) überholen
overthrow *vt* (*pt* **-threw**, *pp* **-thrown**) (*Pol*) stürzen
overtime *n* Überstunden *pl* ● *adv* **work ~** Überstunden machen
overtired *a* übermüdet
overture *n* (*Mus*) Ouvertüre *f*; **~s** *pl* (*fig*) Annäherungsversuche *pl*
overturn *vt* umstoßen ● *vi* umkippen
overweight *a* übergewichtig; **be ~** Übergewicht haben
overwhelm *vt* überwältigen. **~ing** *a* überwältigend
overwork *n* Überarbeitung *f* ● *vt* überfordern ● *vi* sich überarbeiten
overwrought *a* überreizt
ow|e *vt* schulden/ (*fig*) verdanken (**[to] s.o.** jdm); **~e s.o. sth** jdm etw schuldig sein. **~ing to** *prep* wegen (+ *gen*)
owl *n* Eule *f*
own[1] *a & pron* eigen; **it's my ~** es gehört mir; **a car of my ~** mein eigenes Auto; **on one's ~** allein; **get one's ~ back** [!] sich revanchieren
own[2] *vt* besitzen; **I don't ~ it** es gehört mir nicht. **~ up** *vi* es zugeben
owner *n* Eigentümer(in) *m(f)*, Besitzer(in) *m(f)*; (*of shop*)

Inhaber(in) *m(f)*. ~**ship** *n* Besitz *m*

oxygen *n* Sauerstoff *m*

oyster *n* Auster *f*

Pp

pace *n* Schritt *m*; (*speed*) Tempo *nt*; **keep ~ with** Schritt halten mit ● *vi* **~ up and down** auf und ab gehen. ~**-maker** *n* (*Sport & Med*) Schrittmacher *m*

Pacific *a & n* **the ~ [Ocean]** der Pazifik

pacifist *n* Pazifist *m*

pacify *vt* (*pt/pp* **-ied**) beruhigen

pack *n* Packung *f*; (*Mil*) Tornister *m*; (*of cards*) [Karten]spiel *nt*; (*gang*) Bande *f*; (*of hounds*) Meute *f*; (*of wolves*) Rudel *nt*; **a ~ of lies** ein Haufen Lügen ● *vt/i* packen; einpacken <*article*>; **be ~ed** (*crowded*) [gedrängt] voll sein. **~ up** *vt* einpacken ● *vi* [!] <*machine:*> kaputtgehen

package *n* Paket *nt*. **~ holiday** *n* Pauschalreise *f*

packet *n* Päckchen *nt*

packing *n* Verpackung *f*

pact *n* Pakt *m*

pad *n* Polster *nt*; (*for writing*) [Schreib]block *m* ● *vt* (*pt/pp* **padded**) polstern

padding *n* Polsterung *f*; (*in written work*) Füllwerk *nt*

paddle¹ *n* Paddel *nt* ● *vt* (*row*) paddeln

paddle² *vi* waten

paddock *n* Koppel *f*

padlock *n* Vorhängeschloss *nt* ● *vt* mit einem Vorhängeschloss verschließen

paediatrician *n* Kinderarzt *m* /-ärztin *f*

pagan *a* heidnisch ● *n* Heide *m*/ Heidin *f*

page¹ *n* Seite *f*

page² *n* (*boy*) Page *m* ● *vt* ausrufen <*person*>

paid *see* **pay** ● *a* bezahlt; **put ~ to** [!] zunichte machen

pail *n* Eimer *m*

pain *n* Schmerz *m*; **be in ~** Schmerzen haben; **take ~s** sich (*dat*) Mühe geben; **~ in the neck** [!] Nervensäge *f*

pain: ~ful *a* schmerzhaft; (*fig*) schmerzlich. **~-killer** *n* schmerzstillendes Mittel *nt*. **~less** *a*, **-ly** *adv* schmerzlos

painstaking *a* sorgfältig

paint *n* Farbe *f* ● *vt/i* streichen; <*artist:*> malen. **~brush** *n* Pinsel *m*. **~er** *n* Maler *m*; (*decorator*) Anstreicher *m*. **~ing** *n* Malerei *f*; (*picture*) Gemälde *nt*

pair *n* Paar *nt*; **~ of trousers** Hose *f* ● *vi* **~ off** Paare bilden

pajamas *n pl* (*Amer*) Schlafanzug *m*

Pakistan *n* Pakistan *nt*. **~i** *a* pakistanisch ● *n* Pakistaner(in) *m(f)*

pal *n* Freund(in) *m(f)*

palace *n* Palast *m*

palatable *a* schmackhaft

palate *n* Gaumen *m*

palatial *a* palastartig

pale *a* (**-r, -st**) blass ● *vi* blass werden. **~ness** *n* Blässe *f*

Palestin|e *n* Palästina *nt*. **~ian** *a* palästinensisch ● *n* Palästinenser(in) *m(f)*

palette *n* Palette *f*

palm *n* Handfläche *f*; (*tree, symbol*) Palme *f* ● *vt* **~ sth off on s.o.** jdm etw andrehen. **P~ Sunday** *n* Palmsonntag *m*

palpable *a* tastbar; (*perceptible*) spürbar

palpitations *npl* Herzklopfen *nt*

paltry *a* (**-ier, -iest**) armselig
pamper *vt* verwöhnen
pamphlet *n* Broschüre *f*
pan *n* Pfanne *f*; (*saucepan*) Topf *m*; (*of scales*) Schale *f*
panacea *n* Allheilmittel *nt*
pancake *n* Pfannkuchen *m*
panda *n* Panda *m*
pandemonium *n* Höllenlärm *m*
pane *n* [Glas]scheibe *f*
panel *n* Tafel *f*, Platte *f*; **~ of experts** Expertenrunde *f*; **~ of judges** Jury *f*. **~ling** *n* Täfelung *f*
pang *n* **~s of hunger** Hungergefühl *nt*; **~s of conscience** Gewissensbisse *pl*
panic *n* Panik *f* ● *vi* (*pt/pp* **panicked**) in Panik geraten. **~-stricken** *a* von Panik ergriffen
panoram|a *n* Panorama *nt*. **~ic** *a* Panorama-
pansy *n* Stiefmütterchen *nt*
pant *vi* keuchen; *<dog:>* hecheln
panther *n* Panther *m*
panties *npl* [Damen]slip *m*
pantomime *n* [zu Weihnachten aufgeführte] Märchenvorstellung *f*
pantry *n* Speisekammer *f*
pants *npl* Unterhose *f*; (*woman's*) Schlüpfer *m*; (*trousers*) Hose *f*
pantyhose *n* (*Amer*) Strumpfhose *f*
paper *n* Papier *nt*; (*newspaper*) Zeitung *f*; (*exam* **~**) Testbogen *m*; (*exam*) Klausur *f*; (*treatise*) Referat *nt*; **~s** *pl* (*documents*) Unterlagen *pl*; (*for identification*) [Ausweis]papiere *pl* ● *vt* tapezieren
paper: ~back *n* Taschenbuch *nt*. **~-clip** *n* Büroklammer *f*. **~weight** *n* Briefbeschwerer *m*. **~work** *n* Schreibarbeit *f*
par *n* (*Golf*) Par *nt*; **on a ~** gleichwertig (**with** *dat*)
parable *n* Gleichnis *nt*
parachut|e *n* Fallschirm *m* ● *vi* [mit dem Fallschirm] abspringen. **~ist** *n* Fallschirmspringer *m*
parade *n* Parade *f*; (*procession*) Festzug *m* ● *vt* (*show off*) zur Schau stellen
paradise *n* Paradies *nt*
paradox *n* Paradox *nt*. **~ical** paradox
paraffin *n* Paraffin *nt*
paragraph *n* Absatz *m*
parallel *a & adv* parallel ● *n* (*Geog*) Breitenkreis *m*; (*fig*) Parallele *f*
paralyse *vt* lähmen; (*fig*) lahmlegen
paralysis *n* (*pl* **-ses**) Lähmung *f*
paranoid *a* [krankhaft] misstrauisch
parapet *n* Brüstung *f*
paraphernalia *n* Kram *m*
parasite *n* Parasit *m*, Schmarotzer *m*
paratrooper *n* Fallschirmjäger *m*
parcel *n* Paket *nt*
parch *vt* austrocknen; **be ~ed** *<person:>* einen furchtbaren Durst haben
parchment *n* Pergament *nt*
pardon *n* Verzeihung *f*; (*Jur*) Begnadigung *f*; **~?** [!] bitte? **I beg your ~** wie bitte? (*sorry*) Verzeihung! ● *vt* verzeihen; (*Jur*) begnadigen
parent *n* Elternteil *m*; **~s** *pl* Eltern *pl*. **~al** *a* elterlich
parenthesis *n* (*pl* **-ses**) Klammer *f*
parish *n* Gemeinde *f*. **~ioner** *n* Gemeindemitglied *nt*
park *n* Park *m* ● *vt/i* parken
parking *n* Parken *nt*; **'no ~'** 'Parken verboten'. **~-lot** *n* (*Amer*) Parkplatz *m*. **~-meter** *n* Parkuhr *f*. **~ space** *n* Parkplatz *m*
parliament *n* Parlament *nt*. **~ary** *a* parlamentarisch
parochial *a* Gemeinde-; (*fig*) beschränkt

parody *n* Parodie *f* ● *vt* (*pt/pp* **-ied**) parodieren
parole *n* **on ~** auf Bewährung
parquet *n* **~ floor** Parkett *nt*
parrot *n* Papagei *m*
parsley *n* Petersilie *f*
parsnip *n* Pastinake *f*
parson *n* Pfarrer *m*
part *n* Teil *m*; (*Techn*) Teil *nt*; (*area*) Gegend *f*; (*Theat*) Rolle *f*; (*Mus*) Part *m*; **spare ~** Ersatzteil *nt*; **for my ~** meinerseits; **on the ~ of** vonseiten (+ *gen*); **take s.o.'s ~** für jdn Partei ergreifen; **take ~ in** teilnehmen an (+ *dat*) ● *adv* teils ● *vt* trennen; scheiteln <*hair*> ● *vi* <*people*:> sich trennen; **~ with** sich trennen von
partial *a* Teil-; **be ~ to** mögen. **-ly** *adv* teilweise
particip|ant *n* Teilnehmer(in) *m*(*f*). **~ate** *vi* teilnehmen (**in** an + *dat*). **~ation** *n* Teilnahme *f*
particle *n* Körnchen *nt*; (*Phys*) Partikel *nt*; (*Gram*) Partikel *f*
particular *a* besondere(r,s); (*precise*) genau; (*fastidious*) penibel; **in ~** besonders. **~ly** *adv* besonders. **~s** *npl* nähere Angaben *pl*
parting *n* Abschied *m*; (*in hair*) Scheitel *m*
partition *n* Trennwand *f*; (*Pol*) Teilung *f* ● *vt* teilen
partly *adv* teilweise
partner *n* Partner(in) *m*(*f*); (*Comm*) Teilhaber *m*. **~ship** *n* Partnerschaft *f*; (*Comm*) Teilhaberschaft *f*
partridge *n* Rebhuhn *nt*
part-time *a & adv* Teilzeit-; **be** *or* **work ~** Teilzeitarbeit machen
party *n* Party *f*, Fest *nt*; (*group*) Gruppe *f*; (*Pol, Jur*) Partei *f*
pass *n* Ausweis *m*; (*Geog, Sport*) Pass *m*; (*Sch*) ≈ ausreichend; **get a ~** bestehen ● *vt* vorbeigehen/ -fahren an (+ *dat*); (*overtake*) überholen; (*hand*) reichen; (*Sport*) abgeben, abspielen; (*approve*) annehmen; (*exceed*) übersteigen; bestehen <*exam*>; machen <*remark*>; fällen <*judgement*>; (*Jur*) verhängen <*sentence*>; **~ the time** sich (*dat*) die Zeit vertreiben; **~ one's hand over sth** mit der Hand über etw (*acc*) fahren ● *vi* vorbeigehen/ -fahren; (*get by*) vorbeikommen; (*overtake*) überholen; <*time*:> vergehen; (*in exam*) bestehen; **~ away** *vi* sterben. **~ down** *vt* herunterreichen; (*fig*) weitergeben. **~ out** *vi* ohnmächtig werden. **~ round** *vt* herumreichen. **~ up** *vt* heraufreichen; (! *miss*) vorübergehen lassen
passable *a* <*road*> befahrbar; (*satisfactory*) passabel
passage *n* Durchgang *m*; (*corridor*) Gang *m*; (*voyage*) Überfahrt *f*; (*in book*) Passage *f*
passenger *n* Fahrgast *m*; (*Naut, Aviat*) Passagier *m*; (*in car*) Mitfahrer *m*. **~ seat** *n* Beifahrersitz *m*
passer-by *n* (*pl* **-s-by**) Passant(in) *m*(*f*)
passion *n* Leidenschaft *f*. **~ate** *a*, **-ly** *adv* leidenschaftlich
passive *a* passiv ● *n* Passiv *nt*
pass: ~port *n* [Reise]pass *m*. **~word** *n* Kennwort *nt*; (*Mil*) Losung *f*
past *a* vergangene(r,s); (*former*) ehemalig; **that's all ~** das ist jetzt vorbei ● *n* Vergangenheit *f* ● *prep* an (+ *dat*) … vorbei; (*after*) nach; **at ten ~ two** um zehn nach zwei ● *adv* vorbei; **go ~** vorbeigehen
pasta *n* Nudeln *pl*
paste *n* Brei *m*; (*adhesive*) Kleister *m*; (*jewellery*) Strass *m* ● *vt* kleistern
pastel *n* Pastellfarbe *f*; (*drawing*) Pastell *nt* ● *attrib* Pastell-

pastime *n* Zeitvertreib *m*
pastry *n* Teig *m*; **cakes and ~ies** Kuchen und Gebäck
pasture *n* Weide *f*
pasty *n* Pastete *f*
pat *n* Klaps *m*; (*of butter*) Stückchen *nt* ● *vt* (*pt/pp* **patted**) tätscheln; **~ s.o. on the back** jdm auf die Schulter klopfen
patch *n* Flicken *m*; (*spot*) Fleck *m*; **not a ~ on** [!] gar nicht zu vergleichen mit ● *vt* flicken. **~ up** *vt* [zusammen]flicken; beilegen <*quarrel*>
patchy *a* ungleichmäßig
patent *n* Patent *nt* ● *vt* patentieren. **~ leather** *n* Lackleder *nt*
paternal *a* väterlich
path *n* (*pl* **-s**) [Fuß]weg *m*, Pfad *m*; (*orbit, track*) Bahn *f*; (*fig*) Weg *m*
pathetic *a* mitleiderregend; <*attempt*> erbärmlich
patience *n* Geduld *f*; (*game*) Patience *f*
patient *a*, **-ly** *adv* geduldig ● *n* Patient(in) *m*(*f*)
patio *n* Terrasse *f*
patriot *n* Patriot(in) *m*(*f*). **~ic** *a* patriotisch. **~ism** *n* Patriotismus *m*
patrol *n* Patrouille *f* ● *vt/i* patrouillieren [in (+ *dat*)]; <*police*:> auf Streife gehen/fahren [in (+ *dat*)]. **~ car** *n* Streifenwagen *m*
patron *n* Gönner *m*; (*of charity*) Schirmherr *m*; (*of the arts*) Mäzen *m*; (*customer*) Kunde *m*/Kundin *f*; (*Theat*) Besucher *m*. **~age** *n* Schirmherrschaft *f*
patroniz|e *vt* (*fig*) herablassend behandeln. **~ing** *a*, **-ly** *adv* gönnerhaft
patter *n* (*speech*) Gerede *nt*
pattern *n* Muster *nt*
paunch *n* [Schmer]bauch *m*
pause *n* Pause *f* ● *vi* innehalten
pave *vt* pflastern; **~ the way** den Weg bereiten (**for** *dat*). **~ment** *n* Bürgersteig *m*
paw *n* Pfote *f*; (*of large animal*) Pranke *f*, Tatze *f*
pawn[1] *n* (*Chess*) Bauer *m*; (*fig*) Schachfigur *f*
pawn[2] *vt* verpfänden. **~ broker** *n* Pfandleiher *m*
pay *n* Lohn *m*; (*salary*) Gehalt *nt*; **be in the ~ of** bezahlt werden von ● *v* (*pt/pp* **paid**) ● *vt* bezahlen; zahlen <*money*>; **~ s.o. a visit** jdm einen Besuch abstatten; **~ s.o. a compliment** jdm ein Kompliment machen ● *vi* zahlen; (*be profitable*) sich bezahlt machen; (*fig*) sich lohnen; **~ for sth** etw bezahlen. **~ back** *vt* zurückzahlen. **~ in** *vt* einzahlen. **~ off** *vt* abzahlen <*debt*> ● *vi* (*fig*) sich auszahlen
payable *a* zahlbar; **make ~ to** ausstellen auf (+ *acc*)
payment *n* Bezahlung *f*; (*amount*) Zahlung *f*
pea *n* Erbse *f*
peace *n* Frieden *m*; **for my ~ of mind** zu meiner eigenen Beruhigung
peace|ful *a*, **-ly** *adv* friedlich. **~maker** *n* Friedensstifter *m*
peach *n* Pfirsich *m*
peacock *n* Pfau *m*
peak *n* Gipfel *m*; (*fig*) Höhepunkt *m*. **~ed cap** *n* Schirmmütze *f*. **~ hours** *npl* Hauptbelastungszeit *f*; (*for traffic*) Hauptverkehrszeit *f*
peal *n* (*of bells*) Glockengeläut *nt*; **~s of laughter** schallendes Gelächter *nt*
peanut *n* Erdnuss *f*
pear *n* Birne *f*
pearl *n* Perle *f*
peasant *n* Bauer *m*
peat *n* Torf *m*
pebble *n* Kieselstein *m*

P

peck *n* Schnabelhieb *m*; (*kiss*) flüchtiger Kuss *m* ● *vt/i* picken/ (*nip*) hacken (**at** nach)

peculiar *a* eigenartig, seltsam; ~ **to** eigentümlich (+ *dat*). ~**ity** *n* Eigenart *f*

pedal *n* Pedal *nt* ● *vt* fahren <*bicycle*> ● *vi* treten

pedantic *a*, **-ally** *adv* pedantisch

pedestal *n* Sockel *m*

pedestrian *n* Fußgänger(in) *m*(*f*) ● *a* (*fig*) prosaisch. ~ **crossing** *n* Fußgängerüberweg *m*. ~ **precinct** *n* Fußgängerzone *f*

pedigree *n* Stammbaum *m* ● *attrib* <*animal*> Rasse-

pedlar *n* Hausierer *m*

peek *vi* [!] gucken

peel *n* Schale *f* ● *vt* schälen; ● *vi* <*skin:*> sich schälen; <*paint:*> abblättern. ~**ings** *npl* Schalen *pl*

peep *n* kurzer Blick *m* ● *vi* gucken. ~**-hole** *n* Guckloch *nt*

peer[1] *vi* ~ **at** forschend ansehen

peer[2] *n* Peer *m*; **his** ~**s** *pl* seinesgleichen

peg *n* (*hook*) Haken *m*; (*for tent*) Pflock *m*, Hering *m*; (*for clothes*) [Wäsche]klammer *f*; **off the** ~ [!] von der Stange

pejorative *a*, **-ly** *adv* abwertend

pelican *n* Pelikan *m*

pellet *n* Kügelchen *nt*

pelt[1] *n* (*skin*) Pelz *m*, Fell *nt*

pelt[2] *vt* bewerfen ● *vi* ~ **[down]** <*rain:*> [hernieder]prasseln

pelvis *n* (*Anat*) Becken *nt*

pen[1] *n* (*for animals*) Hürde *f*

pen[2] *n* Federhalter *m*; (*ballpoint*) Kugelschreiber *m*

penal *a* Straf-. ~**ize** *vt* bestrafen; (*fig*) benachteiligen

penalty *n* Strafe *f*; (*fine*) Geldstrafe *f*; (*Sport*) Strafstoß *m*; (*Football*) Elfmeter *m*

penance *n* Buße *f*

pence *see* **penny**

pencil *n* Bleistift *m* ● *vt* (*pt/pp* **pencilled**) mit Bleistift schreiben. ~**-sharpener** *n* Bleistiftspitzer *m*

pendulum *n* Pendel *nt*

penetrat|e *vt* durchdringen; ~**e into** eindringen in (+ *acc*). ~**ing** *a* durchdringend. ~**ion** *n* Durchdringen *nt*

penfriend *n* Brieffreund(in) *m*(*f*)

penguin *n* Pinguin *m*

penicillin *n* Penizillin *nt*

peninsula *n* Halbinsel *f*

penis *n* Penis *m*

penitentiary *n* (*Amer*) Gefängnis *nt*

pen: ~**knife** *n* Taschenmesser *nt*. ~**-name** *n* Pseudonym *nt*

penniless *a* mittellos

penny *n* (*pl* **pence**; *single coins* **pennies**) Penny *m*; (*Amer*) Centstück *nt*; **the** ~**'s dropped** [!] der Groschen ist gefallen

pension *n* Rente *f*; (*of civil servant*) Pension *f*. ~**er** *n* Rentner(in) *m*(*f*); Pensionär(in) *m*(*f*)

pensive *a* nachdenklich

pent-up *a* angestaut

penultimate *a* vorletzte(r,s)

people *npl* Leute *pl*, Menschen *pl*; (*citizens*) Bevölkerung *f*; **the** ~ das Volk; **English** ~ die Engländer; ~ **say** man sagt; **for four** ~ für vier Personen ● *vt* bevölkern

pepper *n* Pfeffer *m*; (*vegetable*) Paprika *m*

pepper: ~**mint** *n* Pfefferminz *nt*; (*Bot*) Pfefferminze *f*. ~**pot** *n* Pfefferstreuer *m*

per *prep* pro; ~ **cent** Prozent *nt*

percentage *n* Prozentsatz *m*; (*part*) Teil *m*

perceptible *a* wahrnehmbar

percept|ion *n* Wahrnehmung *f*. ~**ive** *a* feinsinnig

perch[1] *n* Stange *f* ● *vi* <*bird:*> sich niederlassen

perch[2] *n inv* (*fish*) Barsch *m*

percussion *n* Schlagzeug *nt*. ~ **instrument** *n* Schlaginstrument *nt*

perennial *a* <*problem*> immer wiederkehrend ● *n* (*Bot*) mehrjährige Pflanze *f*

perfect¹ *a* perfekt, vollkommen; ([!] *utter*) völlig ● *n* (*Gram*) Perfekt *nt*

perfect² *vt* vervollkommnen. ~**ion** *n* Vollkommenheit *f*; **to** ~**ion** perfekt

perfectly *adv* perfekt; (*completely*) vollkommen, völlig

perforated *a* perforiert

perform *vt* ausführen; erfüllen <*duty*>; (*Theat*) aufführen <*play*>; spielen <*role*> ● *vi* (*Theat*) auftreten; (*Techn*) laufen. ~**ance** *n* Aufführung *f*; (*at theatre, cinema*) Vorstellung *f*; (*Techn, Sport*) Leistung *f*. ~**er** *n* Künstler(in) *m(f)*

perfume *n* Parfüm *nt*; (*smell*) Duft *m*

perhaps *adv* vielleicht

perilous *a* gefährlich

perimeter *n* [äußere] Grenze *f*; (*Geom*) Umfang *m*

period *n* Periode *f*; (*Sch*) Stunde *f*; (*full stop*) Punkt *m* ● *attrib* <*costume*> zeitgenössisch; <*furniture*> antik. ~**ic** *a*, **-ally** *adv* periodisch. ~**ical** *n* Zeitschrift *f*

peripher|al *a* nebensächlich. ~**y** *n* Peripherie *f*

perish *vi* <*rubber*:> verrotten; <*food*:> verderben; (*liter: die*) ums Leben kommen. ~**able** *a* leicht verderblich. ~**ing** *a* ([!] *cold*) eiskalt

perjur|e *vt* ~**e oneself** einen Meineid leisten. ~**y** *n* Meineid *m*

perk¹ *n* [!] [Sonder]vergünstigung *f*

perk² *vi* ~ **up** munter werden

perm *n* Dauerwelle *f* ● *vt* ~ **s.o.'s hair** jdm eine Dauerwelle machen

permanent *a* ständig; <*job, address*> fest. ~**ly** *adv* ständig; <*work, live*> dauernd, permanent; <*employed*> fest

permissible *a* erlaubt

permission *n* Erlaubnis *f*

permit¹ *vt* (*pt/pp* **-mitted**) erlauben (**s.o.** jdm)

permit² *n* Genehmigung *f*

perpendicular *a* senkrecht ● *n* Senkrechte *f*

perpetual *a*, **-ly** *adv* ständig, dauernd

perpetuate *vt* bewahren; verewigen <*error*>

perplex *vt* verblüffen. ~**ed** *a* verblüfft

persecut|e *vt* verfolgen. ~**ion** *n* Verfolgung *f*

perseverance *n* Ausdauer *f*

persevere *vi* beharrlich weitermachen

Persia *n* Persien *nt*

Persian *a* persisch; <*cat, carpet*> Perser-

persist *vi* beharrlich weitermachen; (*continue*) anhalten; <*view*:> weiter bestehen; ~ **in doing sth** dabei bleiben, etw zu tun. ~**ence** *n* Beharrlichkeit *f*. ~**ent** *a*, **-ly** *adv* beharrlich; (*continuous*) anhaltend

person *n* Person *f*; **in** ~ persönlich

personal *a*, **-ly** *adv* persönlich. ~ **hygiene** *n* Körperpflege *f*

personality *n* Persönlichkeit *f*

personify *vt* (*pt/pp* **-ied**) personifizieren, verkörpern

personnel *n* Personal *nt*

perspective *n* Perspektive *f*

persp|iration *n* Schweiß *m*. ~**ire** *vi* schwitzen

persua|de *vt* überreden; (*convince*) überzeugen. ~**sion** *n* Überredung *f*; (*powers of* ~*sion*) Überredungskunst *f*

persuasive *a*, **-ly** *adv* beredsam; (*convincing*) überzeugend
pertinent *a* relevant (**to** für)
perturb *vt* beunruhigen
peruse *vt* lesen
pervers|e *a* eigensinnig. **~ion** *n* Perversion *f*
pervert[1] *vt* verdrehen; verführen <*person*>
pervert[2] *n* Perverse(r) *m*
pessimis|m *n* Pessimismus *m*. **~t** *n* Pessimist *m*. **~tic** *a*, **-ally** *adv* pessimistisch
pest *n* Schädling *m*; (! *person*) Nervensäge *f*
pester *vt* belästigen
pesticide *n* Schädlingsbekämpfungsmittel *nt*
pet *n* Haustier *nt*; (*favourite*) Liebling *m* ● *vt* (*pt/pp* **petted**) liebkosen
petal *n* Blütenblatt *nt*
peter *vi* **~ out** allmählich aufhören
petition *n* Bittschrift *f*
pet name *n* Kosename *m*
petrified *a* vor Angst wie versteinert
petrol *n* Benzin *nt*
petroleum *n* Petroleum *nt*
petrol: ~-pump *n* Zapfsäule *f*. **~ station** *n* Tankstelle *f*. **~ tank** *n* Benzintank *m*
petticoat *n* Unterrock *m*
petty *a* (**-ier, -iest**) kleinlich. **~ cash** *n* Portokasse *f*
petulant *a* gekränkt
pew *n* [Kirchen]bank *f*
pharmaceutical *a* pharmazeutisch
pharmac|ist *n* Apotheker(in) *m(f)*. **~y** *n* Pharmazie *f*; (*shop*) Apotheke *f*
phase *n* Phase *f* ● *vt* **~ in/out** allmählich einführen/abbauen
Ph.D. (*abbr of* **Doctor of Philosophy**) Dr. phil.
pheasant *n* Fasan *m*
phenomen|al *a* phänomenal. **~on** *n* (*pl* **-na**) Phänomen *nt*
philharmonic *n* (*orchestra*) Philharmoniker *pl*
Philippines *npl* Philippinen *pl*
philistine *n* Banause *m*
philosoph|er *n* Philosoph *m*. **~ical** *a*, **-ly** *adv* philosophisch. **~y** *n* Philosophie *f*
phlegmatic *a* phlegmatisch
phobia *n* Phobie *f*
phone *n* Telefon *nt*; **be on the ~** Telefon haben; (*be phoning*) telefonieren ● *vt* anrufen ● *vi* telefonieren. **~ back** *vt/i* zurückrufen. **~ book** *n* Telefonbuch *nt*. **~ box** *n* Telefonzelle *f*. **~ card** *n* Telefonkarte *f*. **~-in** *n* (*Radio*) Hörersendung *f*. **~ number** *n* Telefonnummer *f*
phonetic *a* phonetisch. **~s** *n* Phonetik *f*
phoney *a* (**-ier, -iest**) falsch; (*forged*) gefälscht
photo *n* Foto *nt*, Aufnahme *f*. **~copier** *n* Fotokopiergerät *nt*. **~copy** *n* Fotokopie *f* ● *vt* fotokopieren
photogenic *a* fotogen
photograph *n* Fotografie *f*, Aufnahme *f* ● *vt* fotografieren
photograph|er *n* Fotograf(in) *m(f)*. **~ic** *a*, **-ally** *adv* fotografisch. **~y** *n* Fotografie *f*
phrase *n* Redensart *f* ● *vt* formulieren. **~-book** *n* Sprachführer *m*
physical *a*, **-ly** *adv* körperlich
physician *n* Arzt *m*/ Ärztin *f*
physic|ist *n* Physiker(in) *m(f)*. **~s** *n* Physik *f*
physiotherap|ist *n* Physiotherapeut(in) *m(f)*. **~y** *n* Physiotherapie *f*
physique *n* Körperbau *m*
pianist *n* Klavierspieler(in) *m(f)*; (*professional*) Pianist(in) *m(f)*
piano *n* Klavier *nt*

pick¹ *n* Spitzhacke *f*

pick² *n* Auslese *f*; **take one's ~** sich (*dat*) aussuchen ● *vt/i* (*pluck*) pflücken; (*select*) wählen, sich (*dat*) aussuchen; **~ and choose** wählerisch sein; **~ a quarrel** einen Streit anfangen; **~ holes in** [!] kritisieren; **~ at one's food** im Essen herumstochern. **~ on** *vt* wählen; ([!] *find fault with*) herumhacken auf (+ *dat*). **~ up** *vt* in die Hand nehmen; (*off the ground*) aufheben; hochnehmen <*baby*>; (*learn*) lernen; (*acquire*) erwerben; (*buy*) kaufen; (*Teleph*) abnehmen <*receiver*>; auffangen <*signal*>; (*collect*) abholen; aufnehmen <*passengers*>; <*police:*> aufgreifen <*criminal*>; sich holen <*illness*>; [!] aufgabeln <*girl*>; **~ oneself up** aufstehen ● *vi* (*improve*) sich bessern

pickaxe *n* Spitzhacke *f*

picket *n* Streikposten *m*

pickle *n* (*Amer: gherkin*) Essiggurke *f*; **~s** *pl* [Mixed] Pickles *pl* ● *vt* einlegen

pick: ~pocket *n* Taschendieb *m*. **~-up** *n* (*truck*) Lieferwagen *m*

picnic *n* Picknick *nt* ● *vi* (*pt/pp* **-nicked**) picknicken

picture *n* Bild *nt*; (*film*) Film *m*; **as pretty as a ~** bildhübsch; **put s.o. in the ~** (*fig*) jdn ins Bild setzen ● *vt* (*imagine*) sich (*dat*) vorstellen

picturesque *a* malerisch

pie *n* Pastete *f*; (*fruit*) Kuchen *m*

piece *n* Stück *nt*; (*of set*) Teil *nt*; (*in game*) Stein *m*; (*Journ*) Artikel *m*; **a ~ of bread/paper** ein Stück Brot/Papier; **a ~ of news/advice** eine Nachricht/ein Rat; **take to ~s** auseinander nehmen ● *vt* **~ together** zusammensetzen; (*fig*) zusammenstückeln. **~meal** *adv* stückweise

pier *n* Pier *m*; (*pillar*) Pfeiler *m*

pierc|e *vt* durchstechen. **~ing** *a* durchdringend

pig *n* Schwein *nt*

pigeon *n* Taube *f*. **~-hole** *n* Fach *nt*

piggy|back *n* **give s.o. a ~back** jdn huckepack tragen. **~ bank** *n* Sparschwein *nt*

pigheaded *a* [!] starrköpfig

pigment *n* Pigment *nt*

pig: ~skin *n* Schweinsleder *nt*. **~sty** *n* Schweinestall *m*. **~tail** *n* [!] Zopf *m*

pilchard *n* Sardine *f*

pile¹ *n* (*of fabric*) Flor *m*

pile² *n* Haufen *m* ● *vt* **~ sth on to sth** etw auf etw (*acc*) häufen. **~ up** *vt* häufen ● *vi* sich häufen

piles *npl* Hämorrhoiden *pl*

pile-up *n* Massenkarambolage *f*

pilgrim *n* Pilger(in) *m*(*f*). **~age** *n* Pilgerfahrt *f*, Wallfahrt *f*

pill *n* Pille *f*

pillar *n* Säule *f*. **~-box** *n* Briefkasten *m*

pillow *n* Kopfkissen *nt*. **~case** *n* Kopfkissenbezug *m*

pilot *n* Pilot *m*; (*Naut*) Lotse *m* ● *vt* fliegen <*plane*>; lotsen <*ship*>. **~-light** *n* Zündflamme *f*

pimple *n* Pickel *m*

pin *n* Stecknadel *f*; (*Techn*) Bolzen *m*, Stift *m*; (*Med*) Nagel *m*; **I have ~s and needles in my leg** [!] mein Bein ist eingeschlafen ● *vt* (*pt/pp* **pinned**) anstecken (**to/on** an + *acc*); (*sewing*) stecken; (*hold down*) festhalten

pinafore *n* Schürze *f*. **~ dress** *n* Kleiderrock *m*

pincers *npl* Kneifzange *f*; (*Zool*) Scheren *pl*

pinch *n* Kniff *m*; (*of salt*) Prise *f*; **at a ~** [!] zur Not ● *vt* kneifen, zwicken; (*fam; steal*) klauen; **~ one's finger** sich (*dat*) den Finger klemmen ● *vi* <*shoe:*> drücken

pine¹ *n* (*tree*) Kiefer *f*

pine² *vi* **~ for** sich sehnen nach

pineapple *n* Ananas *f*
pink *a* rosa
pinnacle *n* Gipfel *m*; (*on roof*) Turmspitze *f*
pin: ~point *vt* genau festlegen. **~stripe** *n* Nadelstreifen *m*
pint *n* Pint *nt* (*0,57 l, Amer: 0,47 l*)
pioneer *n* Pionier *m* ● *vt* bahnbrechende Arbeit leisten für
pious *a*, **-ly** *adv* fromm
pip[1] *n* (*seed*) Kern *m*
pip[2] *n* (*sound*) Tonsignal *nt*
pipe *n* Pfeife *f*; (*for water, gas*) Rohr *nt* ● *vt* in Rohren leiten; (*Culin*) spritzen
pipe: ~-dream *n* Luftschloss *nt*. **~line** *n* Pipeline *f*; **in the ~line** [!] in Vorbereitung
piping *a* **~ hot** kochend heiß
pirate *n* Pirat *m*
piss *vi* [✖] pissen
pistol *n* Pistole *f*
piston *n* (*Techn*) Kolben *m*
pit *n* Grube *f*; (*for orchestra*) Orchestergraben *m*; (*for audience*) Parkett *nt*; (*motor racing*) Box *f*
pitch[1] *n* (*steepness*) Schräge *f*; (*of voice*) Stimmlage *f*; (*of sound*) [Ton]höhe *f*; (*Sport*) Feld *nt*; (*of street trader*) Standplatz *m*; (*fig: degree*) Grad *m* ● *vt* werfen; aufschlagen <*tent*> ● *vi* fallen
pitch[2] *n* (*tar*) Pech *nt*. **~-black** *a* pechschwarz. **~-dark** *a* stockdunkel
pitfall *n* (*fig*) Falle *f*
pith *n* (*Bot*) Mark *nt*; (*of orange*) weiße Haut *f*
pithy *a* (**-ier, -iest**) (*fig*) prägnant
piti|ful *a* bedauernswert. **~less** *a* mitleidslos
pit stop *n* Boxenstopp *m*
pittance *n* Hungerlohn *m*
pity *n* Mitleid *nt*, Erbarmen *nt*; **[what a] ~!** [wie] schade! **take ~ on** sich erbarmen über (+ *acc*) ● *vt* bemitleiden
pivot *n* Drehzapfen *m* ● *vi* sich drehen (**on** um)
pizza *n* Pizza *f*
placard *n* Plakat *nt*
placate *vt* beschwichtigen
place *n* Platz *m*; (*spot*) Stelle *f*; (*town, village*) Ort *m*; ([!] *house*) Haus *nt*; **out of ~** fehl am Platze; **take ~** stattfinden ● *vt* setzen; (*upright*) stellen; (*flat*) legen; (*remember*) unterbringen [!]; **~ an order** eine Bestellung aufgeben; **be ~d** (*in race*) sich platzieren. **~-mat** *n* Set *nt*
placid *a* gelassen
plague *n* Pest *f* ● *vt* plagen
plaice *n inv* Scholle *f*
plain *a* (**-er, -est**) klar; (*simple*) einfach; (*not pretty*) nicht hübsch; (*not patterned*) einfarbig; <*chocolate*> zartbitter; **in ~ clothes** in Zivil ● *adv* (*simply*) einfach ● *n* Ebene *f*. **~ly** *adv* klar, deutlich; (*simply*) einfach; (*obviously*) offensichtlich
plait *n* Zopf *m* ● *vt* flechten
plan *n* Plan *m* ● *vt* (*pt/pp* **planned**) planen; (*intend*) vorhaben
plane[1] *n* (*tree*) Platane *f*
plane[2] *n* Flugzeug *nt*; (*Geom & fig*) Ebene *f*
plane[3] *n* (*Techn*) Hobel *m* ● *vt* hobeln
planet *n* Planet *m*
plank *n* Brett *nt*; (*thick*) Planke *f*
planning *n* Planung *f*
plant *n* Pflanze *f*; (*Techn*) Anlage *f*; (*factory*) Werk *nt* ● *vt* pflanzen; (*place in position*) setzen; **~ oneself** sich hinstellen. **~ation** *n* Plantage *f*
plaque *n* [Gedenk]tafel *f*; (*on teeth*) Zahnbelag *m*
plaster *n* Verputz *m*; (*sticking ~*) Pflaster *nt*; **~ [of Paris]** Gips *m* ● *vt* verputzen <*wall*>; (*cover*) bedecken mit
plastic *n* Kunststoff *m*, Plastik *nt* ● *a* Kunststoff-, Plastik-; (*malleable*) formbar, plastisch

plastic surgery *n* plastische Chirurgie *f*

plate *n* Teller *m*; (*flat sheet*) Platte *f*; (*with name, number*) Schild *nt*; (*gold and silverware*) vergoldete/versilberte Ware *f*; (*in book*) Tafel *f* ● *vt* (*with gold*) vergolden; (*with silver*) versilbern

platform *n* Plattform *f*; (*stage*) Podium *nt*; (*Rail*) Bahnsteig *m*; **~ 5** Gleis 5

platinum *n* Platin *nt*

platitude *n* Plattitüde *f*

plausible *a* plausibel

play *n* Spiel *nt*; [Theater]stück *nt*; (*Radio*) Hörspiel *nt*; (*TV*) Fernsehspiel *nt*; **~ on words** Wortspiel *nt* ● *vt/i* spielen; ausspielen <*card*>; **~ safe** sichergehen. **~ down** *vt* herunterspielen. **~ up** *vi* [!] Mätzchen machen

play: ~er *n* Spieler(in) *m(f)*. **~ful** *a*, **-ly** *adv* verspielt. **~ground** *n* Spielplatz *m*; (*Sch*) Schulhof *m*. **~group** *n* Kindergarten *m*

playing: ~-card *n* Spielkarte *f*. **~-field** *n* Sportplatz *m*

play: ~mate *n* Spielkamerad *m*. **~thing** *n* Spielzeug *nt*. **~wright** *n* Dramatiker *m*

plc *abbr* (**public limited company**) ≈ GmbH

plea *n* Bitte *f*; **make a ~ for** bitten um

plead *vi* flehen (**for** um); **~ guilty** sich schuldig bekennen; **~ with s.o.** jdn anflehen

pleasant *a* angenehm; <*person*> nett. **~ly** *adv* angenehm; <*say, smile*> freundlich

pleas|e *adv* bitte ● *vt* gefallen (+ *dat*); **~e s.o.** jdm eine Freude machen; **~e oneself** tun, was man will. **~ed** *a* erfreut; **be ~ed with/about sth** sich über etw (*acc*) freuen. **~ing** *a* erfreulich

pleasure *n* Vergnügen *nt*; (*joy*) Freude *f*; **with ~** gern[e]

pleat *n* Falte *f* ● *vt* fälteln

pledge *n* Versprechen *nt* ● *vt* verpfänden; versprechen

plentiful *a* reichlich

plenty *n* eine Menge; (*enough*) reichlich; **~ of money/people** viel Geld/viele Leute

pliable *a* biegsam

pliers *npl* [Flach]zange *f*

plight *n* [Not]lage *f*

plinth *n* Sockel *m*

plod *vi* (*pt/pp* **plodded**) trotten; (*work*) sich abmühen

plonk *n* [!] billiger Wein *m*

plot *n* Komplott *nt*; (*of novel*) Handlung *f*; **~ of land** Stück *nt* Land ● *vt* einzeichnen ● *vi* ein Komplott schmieden

plough *n* Pflug *m* ● *vt/i* pflügen

ploy *n* [!] Trick *m*

pluck *n* Mut *m* ● *vt* zupfen; rupfen <*bird*>; pflücken <*flower*>; **~ up courage** Mut fassen

plucky *a* (**-ier, -iest**) tapfer, mutig

plug *n* Stöpsel *m*; (*wood*) Zapfen *m*; (*cotton wool*) Bausch *m*; (*Electr*) Stecker *m*; (*Auto*) Zündkerze *f*; ([!] *advertisement*) Schleichwerbung *f* ● *vt* zustopfen; ([!] *advertise*) Schleichwerbung machen für. **~ in** *vt* (*Electr*) einstecken

plum *n* Pflaume *f*

plumage *n* Gefieder *nt*

plumb|er *n* Klempner *m*. **~ing** *n* Wasserleitungen *pl*

plume *n* Feder *f*

plump *a* (**-er, -est**) mollig, rundlich ● *vt* **~ for** wählen

plunge *n* Sprung *m*; **take the ~** [!] den Schritt wagen ● *vt/i* tauchen

plural *a* pluralisch ● *n* Mehrzahl *f*, Plural *m*

plus *prep* plus (+ *dat*) ● *a* Plus- ● *n* Pluszeichen *nt*; (*advantage*) Plus *nt*

plush[y] *a* luxuriös

P

ply *vt* (*pt/pp* **plied**) ausüben <*trade*>; ~ **s.o. with drink** jdm ein Glas nach dem anderen eingießen. ~**wood** *n* Sperrholz *nt*

p.m. *adv* (*abbr of* **post meridiem**) nachmittags

pneumatic *a* pneumatisch. ~ **drill** *n* Presslufthammer *m*

pneumonia *n* Lungenentzündung *f*

poach *vt* (*Culin*) pochieren; (*steal*) wildern. ~**er** *n* Wilddieb *m*

pocket *n* Tasche *f*; **be out of** ~ [an einem Geschäft] verlieren ● *vt* einstecken. ~**-book** *n* Notizbuch *nt*; (*wallet*) Brieftasche *f*. ~**-money** *n* Taschengeld *nt*

pod *n* Hülse *f*

poem *n* Gedicht *nt*

poet *n* Dichter(in) *m*(*f*). ~**ic** *a* dichterisch

poetry *n* Dichtung *f*

poignant *a* ergreifend

point *n* Punkt *m*; (*sharp end*) Spitze *f*; (*meaning*) Sinn *m*; (*purpose*) Zweck *m*; (*Electr*) Steckdose *f*; ~**s** *pl* (*Rail*) Weiche *f*; ~ **of view** Standpunkt *m*; **good/bad** ~**s** gute/schlechte Seiten; **what is the** ~**?** wozu? **the** ~ **is** es geht darum; **up to a** ~ bis zu einem gewissen Grade; **be on the** ~ **of doing sth** im Begriff sein, etw zu tun ● *vt* richten (**at** auf + *acc*); ausfugen <*brickwork*> ● *vi* deuten (**at/to** auf + *acc*); (*with finger*) mit dem Finger zeigen. ~ **out** *vt* zeigen auf (+ *acc*); ~ **sth out to s.o.** jdn auf etw (*acc*) hinweisen

point-blank *a* aus nächster Entfernung; (*fig*) rundweg

point|ed *a* spitz; <*question*> gezielt. ~**less** *a* zwecklos, sinnlos

poise *n* Haltung *f*

poison *n* Gift *nt* ● *vt* vergiften. ~**ous** *a* giftig

poke *n* Stoß *m* ● *vt* stoßen; schüren <*fire*>; (*put*) stecken

poker[1] *n* Schüreisen *nt*

poker[2] *n* (*Cards*) Poker *nt*

poky *a* (**-ier, -iest**) eng

Poland *n* Polen *nt*

polar *a* Polar-. ~**bear** *n* Eisbär *m*

Pole *n* Pole *m*/Polin *f*

pole[1] *n* Stange *f*

pole[2] *n* (*Geog, Electr*) Pol *m*

pole-vault *n* Stabhochsprung *m*

police *npl* Polizei *f*

police: ~**man** *n* Polizist *m*. ~ **station** *n* Polizeiwache *f*. ~**woman** *n* Polizistin *f*

policy[1] *n* Politik *f*

policy[2] *n* (*insurance*) Police *f*

Polish *a* polnisch

polish *n* (*shine*) Glanz *m*; (*for shoes*) [Schuh]creme *f*; (*for floor*) Bohnerwachs *m*; (*for furniture*) Politur *f*; (*for silver*) Putzmittel *nt*; (*for nails*) Lack *m*; (*fig*) Schliff *m* ● *vt* polieren; bohnern <*floor*>. ~ **off** *vt* [!] verputzen <*food*>; erledigen <*task*>

polite *a*, **-ly** *adv* höflich. ~**ness** *n* Höflichkeit *f*

politic|al *a*, **-ly** *adv* politisch. ~**ian** *n* Politiker(in) *m*(*f*)

politics *n* Politik *f*

poll *n* Abstimmung *f*; (*election*) Wahl *f*; **[opinion]** ~ [Meinungs]umfrage *f*

pollen *n* Blütenstaub *m*, Pollen *m*

polling: ~**-booth** *n* Wahlkabine *f*. ~**-station** *n* Wahllokal *nt*

pollut|e *vt* verschmutzen. ~**ion** *n* Verschmutzung *f*

polo *n* Polo *nt*. ~**-neck** *n* Rollkragen *m*

polystyrene *n* Polystyrol *nt*; (*for packing*) Styropor (P) *nt*

polythene *n* Polyäthylen *nt*. ~ **bag** *n* Plastiktüte *f*

pomp *n* Pomp *m*

pompous *a*, **-ly** *adv* großspurig

pond *n* Teich *m*

ponder *vi* nachdenken

ponderous *a* schwerfällig
pony *n* Pony *nt*. **~-tail** *n* Pferdeschwanz *m*
poodle *n* Pudel *m*
pool *n* [Schwimm]becken *nt*; (*pond*) Teich *m*; (*of blood*) Lache *f*; (*common fund*) [gemeinsame] Kasse *f*; **~s** *pl* [Fußball]toto *nt* ● *vt* zusammenlegen
poor *a* (**-er, -est**) arm; (*not good*) schlecht; **in ~ health** nicht gesund. **~ly** *a* **be ~ly** krank sein ● *adv* ärmlich; (*badly*) schlecht
pop¹ *n* Knall *m* ● *v* (*pt/pp* **popped**) ● *vt* ([!] *put*) stecken (**in** in + *acc*) ● *vi* knallen; (*burst*) platzen. **~ in** *vi* [!] reinschauen. **~ out** *vi* [!] kurz rausgehen
pop² *n* [!] Popmusik *f*, Pop *m* ● *attrib* Pop-
popcorn *n* Puffmais *m*
pope *n* Papst *m*
poplar *n* Pappel *f*
poppy *n* Mohn *m*
popular *a* beliebt, populär; <*belief*> volkstümlich. **~ity** *n* Beliebtheit *f*, Popularität *f*
populat|e *vt* bevölkern. **~ion** *n* Bevölkerung *f*
porcelain *n* Porzellan *nt*
porch *n* Vorbau *m*; (*Amer*) Veranda *f*
porcupine *n* Stachelschwein *nt*
pore *n* Pore *f*
pork *n* Schweinefleisch *nt*
porn *n* [!] Porno *m*
pornograph|ic *a* pornographisch. **~y** *n* Pornographie *f*
porridge *n* Haferbrei *m*
port¹ *n* Hafen *m*; (*town*) Hafenstadt *f*
port² *n* (*Naut*) Backbord *nt*
port³ *n* (*wine*) Portwein *m*
portable *a* tragbar
porter *n* Portier *m*; (*for luggage*) Gepäckträger *m*
porthole *n* Bullauge *nt*
portion *n* Portion *f*; (*part, share*) Teil *nt*
portrait *n* Porträt *nt*
portray *vt* darstellen. **~al** *n* Darstellung *f*
Portug|al *n* Portugal *nt*. **~uese** *a* portugiesisch ● *n* Portugiese *m*/-giesin *f*
pose *n* Pose *f* ● *vt* aufwerfen <*problem*>; stellen <*question*> ● *vi* posieren; (*for painter*) Modell stehen
posh *a* [!] feudal
position *n* Platz *m*; (*posture*) Haltung *f*; (*job*) Stelle *f*; (*situation*) Lage *f*, Situation *f*; (*status*) Stellung *f* ● *vt* platzieren; **~ oneself** sich stellen
positive *a*, **-ly** *adv* positiv; (*definite*) eindeutig; (*real*) ausgesprochen ● *n* Positiv *nt*
possess *vt* besitzen. **~ion** *n* Besitz *m*; **~ions** *pl* Sachen *pl*
possess|ive *a* Possessiv-; **be ~ive about s.o.** zu sehr an jdm hängen
possibility *n* Möglichkeit *f*
possib|le *a* möglich. **~ly** *adv* möglicherweise; **not ~ly** unmöglich
post¹ *n* (*pole*) Pfosten *m*
post² *n* (*place of duty*) Posten *m*; (*job*) Stelle *f*
post³ *n* (*mail*) Post *f*; **by ~** mit der Post ● *vt* aufgeben <*letter*>; (*send by ~*) mit der Post schicken; **keep s.o. ~ed** jdn auf dem Laufenden halten
postage *n* Porto *nt*
postal *a* Post-. **~ order** *n* ≈ Geldanweisung *f*
post: ~-box *n* Briefkasten *m*. **~card** *n* Postkarte *f*; (*picture*) Ansichtskarte *f*. **~code** *n* Postleitzahl *f*. **~-date** *vt* vordatieren
poster *n* Plakat *nt*
posterity *n* Nachwelt *f*
posthumous *a*, **-ly** *adv* postum
post: ~man *n* Briefträger *m*. **~mark** *n* Poststempel *m*
post-mortem *n* Obduktion *f*

post office *n* Post *f*
postpone *vt* aufschieben; **~ until** verschieben auf (+ *acc*). **~ment** *n* Verschiebung *f*
postscript *n* Nachschrift *f*
posture *n* Haltung *f*
pot *n* Topf *m*; (*for tea, coffee*) Kanne *f*; **~s of money** [!] eine Menge Geld
potato *n* (*pl* **-es**) Kartoffel *f*
potent *a* stark
potential *a*, **-ly** *adv* potenziell ● *n* Potenzial *nt*
pot: ~-hole *n* Höhle *f*; (*in road*) Schlagloch *nt*. **~-shot** *n* **take a ~-shot at** schießen auf (+ *acc*)
potter *n* Töpfer(in) *m(f)*. **~y** *n* Töpferei *f*; (*articles*) Töpferwaren *pl*
potty *a* (**-ier, -iest**) [!] verrückt ● *n* Töpfchen *nt*
pouch *n* Beutel *m*
poultry *n* Geflügel *nt*
pounce *vi* zuschlagen; **~ on** sich stürzen auf (+ *acc*)
pound[1] *n* (*money & 0,454 kg*) Pfund *nt*
pound[2] *vi* <*heart:*> hämmern; (*run heavily*) stampfen
pour *vt* gießen; einschenken <*drink*> ● *vi* strömen; (*with rain*) gießen. **~ out** *vi* ausströmen ● *vt* ausschütten; einschenken <*drink*>
pout *vi* einen Schmollmund machen
poverty *n* Armut *f*
powder *n* Pulver *nt*; (*cosmetic*) Puder *m* ● *vt* pudern
power *n* Macht *f*; (*strength*) Kraft *f*; (*Electr*) Strom *m*; (*nuclear*) Energie *f*; (*Math*) Potenz *f*. **~ cut** *n* Stromsperre *f*. **~ed** *a* betrieben (**by** mit); **~ed by electricity** mit Elektroantrieb. **~ful** *a* mächtig; (*strong*) stark. **~less** *a* machtlos. **~-station** *n* Kraftwerk *nt*
practicable *a* durchführbar, praktikabel
practical *a*, **-ly** *adv* praktisch. **~ joke** *n* Streich *m*
practice *n* Praxis *f*; (*custom*) Brauch *m*; (*habit*) Gewohnheit *f*; (*exercise*) Übung *f*; (*Sport*) Training *nt*; **in ~** (*in reality*) in der Praxis; **out of ~** außer Übung; **put into ~** ausführen
practise *vt* üben; (*carry out*) praktizieren; ausüben <*profession*> ● *vi* üben; <*doctor:*> praktizieren. **~d** *a* geübt
praise *n* Lob *nt* ● *vt* loben. **~worthy** *a* lobenswert
pram *n* Kinderwagen *m*
prank *n* Streich *m*
prawn *n* Garnele *f*, Krabbe *f*
pray *vi* beten. **~er** *n* Gebet *nt*
preach *vt/i* predigen. **~er** *n* Prediger *m*
pre-arrange *vt* im Voraus arrangieren
precarious *a*, **-ly** *adv* unsicher
precaution *n* Vorsichtsmaßnahme *f*
precede *vt* vorangehen (+ *dat*)
preceden|ce *n* Vorrang *m*. **~t** *n* Präzedenzfall *m*
preceding *a* vorhergehend
precinct *n* Bereich *m*; (*traffic-free*) Fußgängerzone *f*; (*Amer: district*) Bezirk *m*
precious *a* kostbar; <*style*> preziös ● *adv* [!] **~ little** recht wenig
precipice *n* Steilabfall *m*
precipitation *n* (*Meteorol*) Niederschlag *m*
precis|e *a*, **-ly** *adv* genau. **~ion** *n* Genauigkeit *f*
precocious *a* frühreif
pre|conceived *a* vorgefasst. **~conception** *n* vorgefasste Meinung *f*
predator *n* Raubtier *nt*
predecessor *n* Vorgänger(in) *m(f)*
predicat|e *n* (*Gram*) Prädikat *nt*. **~ive** *a*, **-ly** *adv* prädikativ

predict *vt* voraussagen. **~able** *a* voraussehbar; <*person*> berechenbar. **~ion** *n* Voraussage *f*

predomin|ant *a* vorherrschend. **~antly** *adv* hauptsächlich, überwiegend. **~ate** *vi* vorherrschen

preen *vt* putzen

prefab *n* [!] [einfaches] Fertighaus *nt*. **~ricated** *a* vorgefertigt

preface *n* Vorwort *nt*

prefect *n* Präfekt *m*

prefer *vt* (*pt/pp* **preferred**) vorziehen; **I ~ to walk** ich gehe lieber zu Fuß; **I ~ wine** ich trinke lieber Wein

prefera|ble *a* **be ~ble** vorzuziehen sein (**to** *dat*). **~bly** *adv* vorzugsweise

preferen|ce *n* Vorzug *m*. **~tial** *a* bevorzugt

pregnan|cy *n* Schwangerschaft *f*. **~t** *a* schwanger; <*animal*> trächtig

prehistoric *a* prähistorisch

prejudice *n* Vorurteil *nt*; (*bias*) Voreingenommenheit *f* ● *vt* einnehmen (**against** gegen). **~d** *a* voreingenommen

preliminary *a* Vor-

prelude *n* Vorspiel *nt*

premature *a* vorzeitig; <*birth*> Früh-. **~ly** *adv* zu früh

premeditated *a* vorsätzlich

premier *a* führend ● *n* (*Pol*) Premier[minister] *m*

premiere *n* Premiere *f*

premises *npl* Räumlichkeiten *pl*; **on the ~** im Haus

premium *n* Prämie *f*; **be at a ~** hoch im Kurs stehen

premonition *n* Vorahnung *f*

preoccupied *a* [in Gedanken] beschäftigt

preparation *n* Vorbereitung *f*; (*substance*) Präparat *nt*

preparatory *a* Vor-

prepare *vt* vorbereiten; anrichten <*meal*> ● *vi* sich vorbereiten (**for** auf + *acc*); **~d to** bereit zu

preposition *n* Präposition *f*

preposterous *a* absurd

prerequisite *n* Voraussetzung *f*

Presbyterian *a* presbyterianisch ● *n* Presbyterianer(in) *m(f)*

prescribe *vt* vorschreiben; (*Med*) verschreiben

prescription *n* (*Med*) Rezept *nt*

presence *n* Anwesenheit *f*, Gegenwart *f*; **~ of mind** Geistesgegenwart *f*

present¹ *a* gegenwärtig; **be ~** anwesend sein; (*occur*) vorkommen ● *n* Gegenwart *f*; (*Gram*) Präsens *nt*; **at ~** zurzeit; **for the ~** vorläufig

present² *n* (*gift*) Geschenk *nt*

present³ *vt* überreichen; (*show*) zeigen; vorlegen <*cheque*>; (*introduce*) vorstellen; **~ s.o. with sth** jdm etw überreichen. **~able** *a* **be ~able** sich zeigen lassen können

presentation *n* Überreichung *f*

presently *adv* nachher; (*Amer: now*) zurzeit

preservation *n* Erhaltung *f*

preservative *n* Konservierungsmittel *nt*

preserve *vt* erhalten; (*Culin*) konservieren; (*bottle*) einmachen ● *n* (*Hunting & fig*) Revier *nt*; (*jam*) Konfitüre *f*

preside *vi* den Vorsitz haben (**over** bei)

presidency *n* Präsidentschaft *f*

president *n* Präsident *m*; (*Amer: chairman*) Vorsitzende(r) *m/f*. **~ial** *a* Präsidenten-; <*election*> Präsidentschafts-

press *n* Presse *f* ● *vt/i* drücken; drücken auf (+ *acc*) <*button*>; pressen <*flower*>; (*iron*) bügeln; (*urge*) bedrängen; **~ for** drängen auf (+ *acc*); **be ~ed for time** in Zeitdruck sein. **~ on** *vi*

P

weitergehen/-fahren; (*fig*) weitermachen

press: ~ **cutting** *n* Zeitungsausschnitt *m*. ~**ing** *a* dringend

pressure *n* Druck *m*. ~**-cooker** *n* Schnellkochtopf *m*

pressurize *vt* Druck ausüben auf (+ *acc*). ~**d** *a* Druck-

prestig|e *n* Prestige *nt*. ~**ious** *a* Prestige-

presumably *adv* vermutlich

presume *vt* vermuten

presumpt|ion *n* Vermutung *f*; (*boldness*) Anmaßung *f*. ~**uous** *a*, **-ly** *adv* anmaßend

pretence *n* Verstellung *f*; (*pretext*) Vorwand *m*

pretend *vt* (*claim*) vorgeben; ~ **that** so tun, als ob; ~ **to be** sich ausgeben als

pretentious *a* protzig

pretext *n* Vorwand *m*

pretty *a* (**-ier, -iest**), ~**ily** *adv* hübsch ● *adv* (! *fairly*) ziemlich

prevail *vi* siegen; <*custom:*> vorherrschen; ~ **on s.o. to do sth** jdn dazu bringen, etw zu tun

prevalen|ce *n* Häufigkeit *f*. ~**t** *a* vorherrschend

prevent *vt* verhindern, verhüten; ~ **s.o. [from] doing sth** jdn daran hindern, etw zu tun. ~**ion** *n* Verhinderung *f*, Verhütung *f*. ~**ive** *a* vorbeugend

preview *n* Voraufführung *f*

previous *a* vorhergehend; ~ **to** vor (+ *dat*). ~**ly** *adv* vorher, früher

prey *n* Beute *f*; **bird of** ~ Raubvogel *m*

price *n* Preis *m* ● *vt* (*Comm*) auszeichnen. ~**less** *a* unschätzbar; (*fig*) unbezahlbar

prick *n* Stich *m* ● *vt/i* stechen

prickl|e *n* Stachel *m*; (*thorn*) Dorn *m*. ~**y** *a* stachelig; <*sensation*> stechend

pride *n* Stolz *m*; (*arrogance*) Hochmut *m* ● *vt* ~ **oneself on** stolz sein auf (+ *acc*)

priest *n* Priester *m*

prim *a* (**primmer, primmest**) prüde

primarily *adv* hauptsächlich, in erster Linie

primary *a* Haupt-. ~ **school** *n* Grundschule *f*

prime[1] *a* Haupt-; (*first-rate*) erstklassig

prime[2] *vt* scharf machen <*bomb*>; grundieren <*surface*>

Prime Minister *n* Premierminister(in) *m(f)*

primitive *a* primitiv

primrose *n* gelbe Schlüsselblume *f*

prince *n* Prinz *m*

princess *n* Prinzessin *f*

principal *a* Haupt- ● *n* (*Sch*) Rektor(in) *m(f)*

principally *adv* hauptsächlich

principle *n* Prinzip *nt*, Grundsatz *m*; **in/on** ~ im/aus Prinzip

print *n* Druck *m*; (*Phot*) Abzug *m*; **in** ~ gedruckt; (*available*) erhältlich; **out of** ~ vergriffen ● *vt* drucken; (*write in capitals*) in Druckschrift schreiben; (*Computing*) ausdrucken; (*Phot*) abziehen. ~**ed matter** *n* Drucksache *f*

print|er *n* Drucker *m*. ~**ing** *n* Druck *m*

printout *n* (*Computing*) Ausdruck *m*

prior *a* frühere(r,s); ~ **to** vor (+ *dat*)

priority *n* Priorität *f*, Vorrang *m*

prise *vt* ~ **open/up** aufstemmen/hochstemmen

prison *n* Gefängnis *nt*. ~**er** *n* Gefangene(r) *m/f*

privacy *n* Privatsphäre *f*; **have no** ~ nie für sich sein

private *a*, **-ly** *adv* privat; (*confidential*) vertraulich; <*car, secretary, school*> Privat- ● *n*

(*Mil*) [einfacher] Soldat *m*; **in ~** privat; (*confidentially*) vertraulich

privation *n* Entbehrung *f*

privilege *n* Privileg *nt*. **~d** *a* privilegiert

prize *n* Preis *m* ● *vt* schätzen

pro *n* [!] Profi *m*; **the ~s and cons** das Für und Wider

probability *n* Wahrscheinlichkeit *f*

probable *a*, **-bly** *adv* wahrscheinlich

probation *n* (*Jur*) Bewährung *f*

probe *n* Sonde *f*; (*fig: investigation*) Untersuchung *f*

problem *n* Problem *nt*; (*Math*) Textaufgabe *f*. **~atic** *a* problematisch

procedure *n* Verfahren *nt*

proceed *vi* gehen; (*in vehicle*) fahren; (*continue*) weitergehen/ -fahren; (*speaking*) fortfahren; (*act*) verfahren

proceedings *npl* Verfahren *nt*; (*Jur*) Prozess *m*

proceeds *npl* Erlös *m*

process *n* Prozess *m*; (*procedure*) Verfahren *nt*; **in the ~** dabei ● *vt* verarbeiten; (*Admin*) bearbeiten; (*Phot*) entwickeln

procession *n* Umzug *m*, Prozession *f*

proclaim *vt* ausrufen

proclamation *n* Proklamation *f*

procure *vt* beschaffen

prod *n* Stoß *m* ● *vt* stoßen

prodigy *n* **[infant] ~** Wunderkind *nt*

produce[1] *n* landwirtschaftliche Erzeugnisse *pl*

produce[2] *vt* erzeugen, produzieren; (*manufacture*) herstellen; (*bring out*) hervorholen; (*cause*) hervorrufen; inszenieren <*play*>; (*Radio, TV*) redigieren. **~r** *n* Erzeuger *m*, Produzent *m*; Hersteller *m*; (*Theat*) Regisseur *m*; (*Radio, TV*) Redakteur(in) *m*(*f*)

product *n* Erzeugnis *nt*, Produkt *nt*. **~ion** *n* Produktion *f*; (*Theat*) Inszenierung *f*

productiv|e *a* produktiv; <*land, talks*> fruchtbar. **~ity** *n* Produktivität *f*

profession *n* Beruf *m*. **~al** *a*, **-ly** *adv* beruflich; (*not amateur*) Berufs-; (*expert*) fachmännisch; (*Sport*) professionell ● *n* Fachmann *m*; (*Sport*) Profi *m*

professor *n* Professor *m*

proficien|cy *n* Können *nt*. **~t** *a* **be ~t in** beherrschen

profile *n* Profil *nt*; (*character study*) Porträt *nt*

profit *n* Gewinn *m*, Profit *m* ● *vi* **~ from** profitieren von. **~able** *a*, **-bly** *adv* gewinnbringend; (*fig*) nutzbringend

profound *a*, **-ly** *adv* tief

program (*Amer & Computing*) *n* Programm *nt* ● *vt* (*pt/pp* **programmed**) programmieren

programme *n* Programm *nt*; (*Radio, TV*) Sendung *f*. **~r** *n* (*Computing*) Programmierer(in) *m*(*f*)

progress[1] *n* Vorankommen *nt*; (*fig*) Fortschritt *m*; **in ~** im Gange; **make ~** (*fig*) Fortschritte machen

progress[2] *vi* vorankommen; (*fig*) fortschreiten. **~ion** *n* Folge *f*; (*development*) Entwicklung *f*

progressive *a* fortschrittlich. **~ly** *adv* zunehmend

prohibit *vt* verbieten (**s.o.** jdm). **~ive** *a* unerschwinglich

project[1] *n* Projekt *nt*; (*Sch*) Arbeit *f*

project[2] *vt* projizieren <*film*>; (*plan*) planen ● *vi* (*jut out*) vorstehen

projector *n* Projektor *m*

prolific *a* fruchtbar; (*fig*) produktiv

P

prologue *n* Prolog *m*
prolong *vt* verlängern
promenade *n* Promenade *f* ● *vi* spazieren gehen
prominent *a* vorstehend; (*important*) prominent; (*conspicuous*) auffällig
promiscuous *a* **be ~ous** häufig den Partner wechseln
promis|e *n* Versprechen *nt* ● *vt/i* versprechen (**s.o.** jdm). **~ing** *a* viel versprechend
promot|e *vt* befördern; (*advance*) fördern; (*publicize*) Reklame machen für; **be ~ed** (*Sport*) aufsteigen. **~ion** *n* Beförderung *f*; (*Sport*) Aufstieg *m*; (*Comm*) Reklame *f*
prompt *a* prompt, unverzüglich; (*punctual*) pünktlich ● *adv* pünktlich ● *vt/i* veranlassen (**to** zu); (*Theat*) soufflieren (+ *dat*). **~er** *n* Souffleur *m*/Souffleuse *f*. **~ly** *adv* prompt
prone *a* **be** *or* **lie ~** auf dem Bauch liegen; **be ~ to** neigen zu
pronoun *n* Fürwort *nt*, Pronomen *nt*
pronounce *vt* aussprechen; (*declare*) erklären. **~d** *a* ausgeprägt; (*noticeable*) deutlich. **~ment** *n* Erklärung *f*
pronunciation *n* Aussprache *f*
proof *n* Beweis *m*; (*Typ*) Korrekturbogen *m*. **~-reader** *n* Korrektor *m*
prop[1] *n* Stütze *f* ● *vt* (*pt/pp* **propped**) **~ against** lehnen an (+ *acc*). **~ up** *vt* stützen
prop[2] *n* (*Theat* [!]) Requisit *nt*
propaganda *n* Propaganda *f*
propel *vt* (*pt/pp* **propelled**) [an]treiben. **~ler** *n* Propeller *m*
proper *a*, **-ly** *adv* richtig; (*decent*) anständig
property *n* Eigentum *nt*; (*quality*) Eigenschaft *f*; (*Theat*) Requisit *nt*; (*land*) [Grund]besitz *m*; (*house*) Haus *nt*
prophecy *n* Prophezeiung *f*
prophesy *vt* (*pt/pp* **-ied**) prophezeien
prophet *n* Prophet *m*. **~ic** *a* prophetisch
proportion *n* Verhältnis *nt*; (*share*) Teil *m*; **~s** *pl* Proportionen; (*dimensions*) Maße. **~al** *a*, **-ly** *adv* proportional
proposal *n* Vorschlag *m*; (*of marriage*) [Heirats]antrag *m*
propose *vt* vorschlagen; (*intend*) vorhaben; einbringen <*motion*> ● *vi* einen Heiratsantrag machen
proposition *n* Vorschlag *m*
proprietor *n* Inhaber(in) *m(f)*
propriety *n* Korrektheit *f*; (*decorum*) Anstand *m*
prose *n* Prosa *f*
prosecut|e *vt* strafrechtlich verfolgen. **~ion** *n* strafrechtliche Verfolgung *f*; **the ~ion** die Anklage. **~or** *n* **[Public] P~or** Staatsanwalt *m*
prospect *n* Aussicht *f*
prospect|ive *a* (*future*) zukünftig. **~or** *n* Prospektor *m*
prospectus *n* Prospekt *m*
prosper *vi* gedeihen, florieren; <*person*> Erfolg haben. **~ity** *n* Wohlstand *m*
prosperous *a* wohlhabend
prostitut|e *n* Prostituierte *f*. **~ion** *n* Prostitution *f*
prostrate *a* ausgestreckt
protagonist *n* Kämpfer *m*; (*fig*) Protagonist *m*
protect *vt* schützen (**from** vor + *dat*); beschützen <*person*>. **~ion** *n* Schutz *m*. **~ive** *a* Schutz-; (*fig*) beschützend. **~or** *n* Beschützer *m*
protein *n* Eiweiß *nt*
protest[1] *n* Protest *m*
protest[2] *vi* protestieren
Protestant *a* protestantisch ● *n* Protestant(in) *m(f)*
protester *n* Protestierende(r) *m/f*
prototype *n* Prototyp *m*

protrude *vi* [her]vorstehen

proud *a*, **-ly** *adv* stolz (**of** auf + *acc*)

prove *vt* beweisen ●*vi* ~ **to be** sich erweisen als

proverb *n* Sprichwort *nt*

provide *vt* zur Verfügung stellen; spenden <*shade*>; ~ **s.o. with sth** jdn mit etw versorgen *od* versehen ●*vi* ~ **for** sorgen für

provided *conj* ~ **[that]** vorausgesetzt [dass]

providen|ce *n* Vorsehung *f*. ~**tial** *a* **be** ~**tial** ein Glück sein

provinc|e *n* Provinz *f*; (*fig*) Bereich *m*. ~**ial** *a* provinziell

provision *n* Versorgung *f* (*of* mit); ~**s** *pl* Lebensmittel *pl*. ~**al** *a*, **-ly** *adv* vorläufig

provocat|ion *n* Provokation *f*. ~**ive** *a*, **-ly** *adv* provozierend; (*sexually*) aufreizend

provoke *vt* provozieren; (*cause*) hervorrufen

prow *n* Bug *m*

prowl *vi* herumschleichen

proximity *n* Nähe *f*

pruden|ce *n* Umsicht *f*. ~**t** *a*, **-ly** *adv* umsichtig; (*wise*) klug

prudish *a* prüde

prune[1] *n* Backpflaume *f*

prune[2] *vt* beschneiden

pry *vi* (*pt/pp* **pried**) neugierig sein

psalm *n* Psalm *m*

psychiatric *a* psychiatrisch

psychiatr|ist *n* Psychiater(*in*) *m*(*f*). ~**y** *n* Psychiatrie *f*

psychic *a* übersinnlich

psycho|analysis *n* Psychoanalyse *f*. ~**analyst** *n* Psychoanalytiker(in) *m*(*f*)

psychological *a*, **-ly** *adv* psychologisch; <*illness*> psychisch

psycholog|ist *n* Psychologe *m*/ -login *f*. ~**y** *n* Psychologie *f*

P.T.O. *abbr* (**please turn over**) b.w.

pub *n* [!] Kneipe *f*

puberty *n* Pubertät *f*

public *a*, **-ly** *adv* öffentlich; **make** ~ publik machen ●*n* **the** ~ die Öffentlichkeit

publican *n* [Gast]wirt *m*

publication *n* Veröffentlichung *f*

public: ~ **holiday** *n* gesetzlicher Feiertag *m*. ~ **house** *n* [Gast]wirtschaft *f*

publicity *n* Publicity *f*; (*advertising*) Reklame *f*

publicize *vt* Reklame machen für

public: ~ **school** *n* Privatschule *f*; (*Amer*) staatliche Schule *f*. ~**-spirited** *a* **be** ~**-spirited** Gemeinsinn haben

publish *vt* veröffentlichen. ~**er** *n* Verleger(in) *m*(*f*); (*firm*) Verlag *m*. ~**ing** *n* Verlagswesen *nt*

pudding *n* Pudding *m*; (*course*) Nachtisch *m*

puddle *n* Pfütze *f*

puff *n* (*of wind*) Hauch *m*; (*of smoke*) Wölkchen *nt* ●*vt* blasen, pusten; ~ **out** ausstoßen. ●*vi* keuchen; ~ **at** paffen an (+ *dat*) <*pipe*>. ~**ed** *a* (*out of breath*) aus der Puste. ~ **pastry** *n* Blätterteig *m*

pull *n* Zug *m*; (*jerk*) Ruck *m*; ([!] *influence*) Einfluss *m* ●*vt* ziehen; ziehen an (+ *dat*) <*rope*>; ~ **a muscle** sich (*dat*) einen Muskel zerren; ~ **oneself together** sich zusammennehmen; ~ **one's weight** tüchtig mitarbeiten; ~ **s.o.'s leg** [!] jdn auf den Arm nehmen. ~ **down** *vt* herunterziehen; (*demolish*) abreißen. ~ **in** *vt* hereinziehen ●*vi* (*Auto*) einscheren. ~ **off** *vt* abziehen; [!] schaffen. ~ **out** *vt* herausziehen ●*vi* (*Auto*) ausscheren. ~ **through** *vt* durchziehen ●*vi* (*recover*) durchkommen. ~ **up** *vt* heraufziehen; ausziehen <*plant*> ●*vi* (*Auto*) anhalten

pullover *n* Pullover *m*

pulp *n* Brei *m*; (*of fruit*) [Frucht]fleisch *nt*
pulpit *n* Kanzel *f*
pulse *n* Puls *m*
pulses *npl* Hülsenfrüchte *pl*
pummel *vt* (*pt*/*pp* **pummelled**) mit den Fäusten bearbeiten
pump *n* Pumpe *f* ● *vt* pumpen; [!] aushorchen. ~ **up** *vt* (*inflate*) aufpumpen
pumpkin *n* Kürbis *m*
pun *n* Wortspiel *nt*
punch¹ *n* Faustschlag *m*; (*device*) Locher *m* ● *vt* boxen; lochen <*ticket*>; stanzen <*hole*>
punch² *n* (*drink*) Bowle *f*
punctual *a*, **-ly** *adv* pünktlich. ~**ity** *n* Pünktlichkeit *f*
punctuat|e *vt* mit Satzzeichen versehen. ~**ion** *n* Interpunktion *f*
puncture *n* Loch *nt*; (*tyre*) Reifenpanne *f* ● *vt* durchstechen
punish *vt* bestrafen. ~**able** *a* strafbar. ~**ment** *n* Strafe *f*
punt *n* (*boat*) Stechkahn *m*
puny *a* (**-ier, -iest**) mickerig
pup *n* = **puppy**
pupil *n* Schüler(in) *m*(*f*); (*of eye*) Pupille *f*
puppet *n* Puppe *f*; (*fig*) Marionette *f*
puppy *n* junger Hund *m*
purchase *n* Kauf *m*; (*leverage*) Hebelkraft *f* ● *vt* kaufen. ~**r** *n* Käufer *m*
pure *a* (**-r, -st,**) **-ly** *adv* rein
purge *n* (*Pol*) Säuberungsaktion *f* ● *vt* reinigen
puri|fication *n* Reinigung *f*. ~**fy** *vt* (*pt*/*pp* **-ied**) reinigen
puritanical *a* puritanisch
purity *n* Reinheit *f*
purple *a* [dunkel]lila
purpose *n* Zweck *m*; (*intention*) Absicht *f*; (*determination*) Entschlossenheit *f*; **on** ~ absichtlich. ~**ful** *a*, **-ly** *adv* entschlossen. ~**ly** *adv* absichtlich
purr *vi* schnurren
purse *n* Portemonnaie *nt*; (*Amer: handbag*) Handtasche *f*
pursue *vt* verfolgen; (*fig*) nachgehen (+ *dat*). ~**r** *n* Verfolger *m*
pursuit *n* Verfolgung *f*; Jagd *f*; (*pastime*) Beschäftigung *f*
pus *n* Eiter *m*
push *n* Stoß *m*; **get the** ~ [!] hinausfliegen ● *vt*/*i* schieben; (*press*) drücken; (*roughly*) stoßen. ~ **off** *vt* hinunterstoßen ● *vi* ([!] *leave*) abhauen. ~ **on** *vi* (*continue*) weitergehen/-fahren; (*with activity*) weitermachen. ~ **up** *vt* hochschieben; hochtreiben <*price*>
push: ~**-button** *n* Druckknopf *m*. ~**-chair** *n* [Kinder]sportwagen *m*
pushy *a* [!] aufdringlich
puss *n*, **pussy** *n* Mieze *f*
put *vt* (*pt*/*pp* **put**, *pres p* **putting**) tun; (*place*) setzen; (*upright*) stellen; (*flat*) legen; (*express*) ausdrücken; (*say*) sagen; (*estimate*) schätzen (**at** auf + *acc*); ~ **aside** *or* **by** beiseite legen ● *vi* ~ **to sea** auslaufen ● *a* **stay** ~ dableiben. ~ **away** *vt* wegräumen. ~ **back** *vt* wieder hinsetzen/-stellen/-legen; zurückstellen <*clock*>. ~ **down** *vt* hinsetzen/-stellen/-legen; (*suppress*) niederschlagen; (*kill*) töten; (*write*) niederschreiben; (*attribute*) zuschreiben (**to** *dat*). ~ **forward** *vt* vorbringen; vorstellen <*clock*>. ~ **in** *vt* hineinsetzen/-stellen/-legen; (*insert*) einstecken; (*submit*) einreichen ● *vi* ~ **in for** beantragen. ~ **off** *vt* ausmachen <*light*>; (*postpone*) verschieben; ~ **s.o. off** jdn abbestellen; (*disconcert*) jdn aus der Fassung bringen. ~ **on** *vt* anziehen <*clothes, brake*>; sich (*dat*) aufsetzen <*hat*>; (*Culin*) aufsetzen; anmachen <*light*>; aufführen <*play*>; annehmen

<*accent*>; ~ **on weight** zunehmen. ~ **out** *vt* hinaussetzen/-stellen/-legen; ausmachen <*fire, light*>; ausstrecken <*hand*>; (*disconcert*) aus der Fassung bringen; ~ **s.o./oneself out** jdm/sich Umstände machen. ~ **through** *vt* durchstecken; (*Teleph*) verbinden (**to** mit). ~ **up** *vt* errichten <*building*>; aufschlagen <*tent*>; aufspannen <*umbrella*>; anschlagen <*notice*>; erhöhen <*price*>; unterbringen <*guest*> ● *vi* (*at hotel*) absteigen in (+ *dat*); ~ **up with sth** sich (*dat*) etw bieten lassen

putrid *a* faulig

putty *n* Kitt *m*

puzzl|e *n* Rätsel *nt*; (*jigsaw*) Puzzlespiel *nt* ● *vt* **it ~es me** es ist mir rätselhaft. **~ing** *a* rätselhaft

pyjamas *npl* Schlafanzug *m*

pylon *n* Mast *m*

pyramid *n* Pyramide *f*

python *n* Pythonschlange *f*

Qq

quack *n* Quaken *nt*; (*doctor*) Quacksalber *m* ● *vi* quaken

quadrangle *n* Viereck *nt*; (*court*) Hof *m*

quadruped *n* Vierfüßer *m*

quadruple *a* vierfach ● *vt* vervierfachen ● *vi* sich vervierfachen

quaint *a* (**-er, -est**) malerisch; (*odd*) putzig

quake *n* [!] Erdbeben *nt* ● *vi* beben; (*with fear*) zittern

qualif|ication *n* Qualifikation *f*; (*reservation*) Einschränkung *f*. **~ied** *a* qualifiziert; (*trained*) ausgebildet; (*limited*) bedingt

qualify *v* (*pt/pp* **-ied**) ● *vt* qualifizieren; (*entitle*) berechtigen; (*limit*) einschränken ● *vi* sich qualifizieren

quality *n* Qualität *f*; (*characteristic*) Eigenschaft *f*

qualm *n* Bedenken *pl*

quantity *n* Quantität *f*, Menge *f*; **in ~** in großen Mengen

quarantine *n* Quarantäne *f*

quarrel *n* Streit *m* ● *vi* (*pt/pp* **quarrelled**) sich streiten. **~some** *a* streitsüchtig

quarry[1] *n* (*prey*) Beute *f*

quarry[2] *n* Steinbruch *m*

quart *n* Quart *nt*

quarter *n* Viertel *nt*; (*of year*) Vierteljahr *nt*; (*Amer*) 25-Cent-Stück *nt*; **~s** *pl* Quartier *nt*; **at [a] ~ to six** um Viertel vor sechs ● *vt* vierteln; (*Mil*) einquartieren (**on** bei). **~-final** *n* Viertelfinale *nt*

quarterly *a & adv* vierteljährlich

quartet *n* Quartett *nt*

quartz *n* Quarz *m*

quay *n* Kai *m*

queasy *a* **I feel ~** mir ist übel

queen *n* Königin *f*; (*Cards, Chess*) Dame *f*

queer *a* (**-er, -est**) eigenartig; (*dubious*) zweifelhaft; (*ill*) unwohl

quell *vt* unterdrücken

quench *vt* löschen

query *n* Frage *f*; (*question mark*) Fragezeichen *nt* ● *vt* (*pt/pp* **-ied**) infrage stellen; reklamieren <*bill*>

quest *n* Suche *f* (**for** nach)

question *n* Frage *f*; (*for discussion*) Thema *nt*; **out of the ~** ausgeschlossen; **the person in ~** die fragliche Person ● *vt* infrage stellen; ~ **s.o.** jdn ausfragen; <*police*:> jdn verhören. **~able** *a* zweifelhaft. **~mark** *n* Fragezeichen *nt*

questionnaire *n* Fragebogen *m*

queue *n* Schlange *f* ● *vi* **~ [up]** Schlange stehen, sich anstellen (**for** nach)

quibble *vi* Haarspalterei treiben

quick *a* (**-er, -est**), **-ly** *adv* schnell; **be ~!** mach schnell! ● *adv* schnell. **~en** *vt* beschleunigen ● *vi* sich beschleunigen

quick: ~sand *n* Treibsand *m*. **~-tempered** *a* aufbrausend

quid *n inv* [!] Pfund *nt*

quiet *a* (**-er, -est**), **-ly** *adv* still; (*calm*) ruhig; (*soft*) leise; **keep ~ about** [!] nichts sagen von ● *n* Stille *f*; Ruhe *f*

quiet|en *vt* beruhigen ● *vi* **~en down** ruhig werden. **~ness** *n* Stille *f*; Ruhe *f*

quilt *n* Steppdecke *f*. **~ed** *a* Stepp-

quintet *n* Quintett *nt*

quirk *n* Eigenart *f*

quit *v* (*pt/pp* **quitted** or **quit**) ● *vt* verlassen; (*give up*) aufgeben; **~ doing sth** aufhören, etw zu tun ● *vi* gehen

quite *adv* ganz; (*really*) wirklich; **~ [so]!** genau! **~ a few** ziemlich viele

quits *a* quitt

quiver *vi* zittern

quiz *n* Quiz *nt* ● *vt* (*pt/pp* **quizzed**) ausfragen. **~zical** *a*, **-ly** *adv* fragend

quota *n* Anteil *m*; (*Comm*) Kontingent *nt*

quotation *n* Zitat *nt*; (*price*) Kostenvoranschlag *m*; (*of shares*) Notierung *f*. **~ marks** *npl* Anführungszeichen *pl*

quote *n* [!] = **quotation; in ~s** in Anführungszeichen ● *vt/i* zitieren

Rr

rabbi *n* Rabbiner *m*; (*title*) Rabbi *m*

rabbit *n* Kaninchen *nt*

rabid *a* fanatisch; <*animal*> tollwütig

rabies *n* Tollwut *f*

race[1] *n* Rasse *f*

race[2] *n* Rennen *nt*; (*fig*) Wettlauf *m* ● *vi* [am Rennen] teilnehmen; <*athlete, horse:*> laufen; ([!] *rush*) rasen ● *vt* um die Wette laufen mit; an einem Rennen teilnehmen lassen <*horse*>

race: ~course *n* Rennbahn *f*. **~horse** *n* Rennpferd *nt*. **~-track** *n* Rennbahn *f*

racial *a*, **-ly** *adv* rassisch; <*discrimination*> Rassen-

racing *n* Rennsport *m*; (*horse-*) Pferderennen *nt*. **~ car** *n* Rennwagen *m*. **~ driver** *n* Rennfahrer *m*

racis|m *n* Rassismus *m*. **~t** *a* rassistisch ● *n* Rassist *m*

rack[1] *n* Ständer *m*; (*for plates*) Gestell *nt* ● *vt* **~ one's brains** sich (*dat*) den Kopf zerbrechen

rack[2] *n* **go to ~ and ruin** verfallen; (*fig*) herunterkommen

racket *n* (*Sport*) Schläger *m*; (*din*) Krach *m*; (*swindle*) Schwindelgeschäft *nt*

racy *a* (**-ier, -iest**) schwungvoll; (*risqué*) gewagt

radar *n* Radar *m*

radian|ce *n* Strahlen *nt*. **~t** *a*, **-ly** *adv* strahlend

radiat|e *vt* ausstrahlen ● *vi* <*heat:*> ausgestrahlt werden; <*roads:*> strahlenförmig ausgehen. **~ion** *n* Strahlung *f*

radiator *n* Heizkörper *m*; (*Auto*) Kühler *m*

radical *a*, **-ly** *adv* radikal ● *n* Radikale(r) *m*/*f*

radio *n* Radio *nt*; **by ~** über Funk ● *vt* funken <*message*>

radio|active *a* radioaktiv. **~activity** *n* Radioaktivität *f*

radish *n* Radieschen *nt*

radius *n* (*pl* **-dii**) Radius *m*, Halbmesser *m*

raffle *n* Tombola *f*

raft *n* Floß *nt*

rafter *n* Dachsparren *m*

rag *n* Lumpen *m*; (*pej: newspaper*) Käseblatt *nt*

rage *n* Wut *f*; **all the ~** [!] der letzte Schrei ● *vi* rasen

ragged *a* zerlumpt; <*edge*> ausgefranst

raid *n* Überfall *m*; (*Mil*) Angriff *m*; (*police*) Razzia *f* ● *vt* überfallen; (*Mil*) angreifen; <*police*> eine Razzia durchführen in (+ *dat*); (*break in*) eindringen in (+ *acc*). **~er** *n* Eindringling *m*; (*of bank*) Bankräuber *m*

rail *n* Schiene *f*; (*pole*) Stange *f*; (*hand~*) Handlauf *m*; (*Naut*) Reling *f*; **by ~** mit der Bahn

railings *npl* Geländer *nt*

railroad *n* (*Amer*) = **railway**

railway *n* [Eisen]bahn *f*. **~ station** *n* Bahnhof *m*

rain *n* Regen *m* ● *vi* regnen

rain: ~bow *n* Regenbogen *m*. **~coat** *n* Regenmantel *m*. **~fall** *n* Niederschlag *m*

rainy *a* (**-ier, -iest**) regnerisch

raise *n* (*Amer*) Lohnerhöhung *f* ● *vt* erheben; (*upright*) aufrichten; (*make higher*) erhöhen; (*lift*) [hoch]heben; aufziehen <*child, animal*>; aufwerfen <*question*>; aufbringen <*money*>

raisin *n* Rosine *f*

rake *n* Harke *f*, Rechen *m* ● *vt* harken, rechen

rally *n* Versammlung *f*; (*Auto*) Rallye *f*; (*Tennis*) Ballwechsel *m* ● *vt* sammeln

ram *n* Schafbock *m* ● *vt* (*pt*/*pp* **rammed**) rammen

rambl|e *n* Wanderung *f* ● *vi* wandern; (*in speech*) irrereden. **~er** *n* Wanderer *m*; (*rose*) Kletterrose *f*. **~ing** *a* weitschweifig; <*club*> Wander-

ramp *n* Rampe *f*; (*Aviat*) Gangway *f*

rampage[1] *n* **be/go on the ~** randalieren

rampage[2] *vi* randalieren

ramshackle *a* baufällig

ran *see* **run**

ranch *n* Ranch *f*

random *a* willkürlich; **a ~ sample** eine Stichprobe ● *n* **at ~** aufs Geratewohl; <*choose*> willkürlich

rang *see* **ring**[2]

range *n* Serie *f*, Reihe *f*; (*Comm*) Auswahl *f*, Angebot *nt* (**of** an + *dat*); (*of mountains*) Kette *f*; (*Mus*) Umfang *m*; (*distance*) Reichweite *f*; (*for shooting*) Schießplatz *m*; (*stove*) Kohlenherd *m* ● *vi* reichen; **~ from ... to** gehen von ... bis. **~r** *n* Aufseher *m*

rank *n* (*row*) Reihe *f*; (*Mil*) Rang *m*; (*social position*) Stand *m*; **the ~ and file** die breite Masse ● *vt*/*i* einstufen; **~ among** zählen zu

ransack *vt* durchwühlen; (*pillage*) plündern

ransom *n* Lösegeld *nt*; **hold s.o. to ~** Lösegeld für jdn fordern

rape *n* Vergewaltigung *f* ● *vt* vergewaltigen

rapid *a*, **-ly** *adv* schnell. **~ity** *n* Schnelligkeit *f*

rapist *n* Vergewaltiger *m*

raptur|e *n* Entzücken *nt*. **~ous** *a*, **-ly** *adv* begeistert

rare[1] *a* (**-r, -st**), **-ly** *adv* selten

rare[2] *a* (*Culin*) englisch gebraten

rarefied *a* dünn

rarity *n* Seltenheit *f*

rascal *n* Schlingel *m*

rash[1] *n* (*Med*) Ausschlag *m*

rash[2] *a* (**-er, -est**), **-ly** *adv* voreilig

rasher *n* Speckscheibe *f*

raspberry *n* Himbeere *f*

rat *n* Ratte *f*; ([!] *person*) Schuft *m*; **smell a ~** [!] Lunte riechen

rate *n* Rate *f*; (*speed*) Tempo *nt*; (*of payment*) Satz *m*; (*of exchange*) Kurs *m*; **~s** *pl* (*taxes*) ≈ Grundsteuer *f*; **at any ~** auf jeden Fall; **at this ~** auf diese Weise ● *vt* einschätzen; **~ among** zählen zu ● *vi* **~ as** gelten als

rather *adv* lieber; (*fairly*) ziemlich; **~!** und ob!

rating *n* Einschätzung *f*; (*class*) Klasse *f*; (*sailor*) [einfacher] Matrose *m*; **~s** *pl* (*Radio, TV*) ≈ Einschaltquote *f*

ratio *n* Verhältnis *nt*

ration *n* Ration *f* ● *vt* rationieren

rational *a*, **-ly** *adv* rational. **~ize** *vt/i* rationalisieren

rattle *n* Rasseln *nt*; (*of windows*) Klappern *nt*; (*toy*) Klapper *f* ● *vi* rasseln; klappern ● *vt* rasseln mit

raucous *a* rau

rave *vi* toben; **~ about** schwärmen von

raven *n* Rabe *m*

ravenous *a* heißhungrig

ravine *n* Schlucht *f*

raving *a* **~ mad** [!] total verrückt

ravishing *a* hinreißend

raw *a* (**-er, -est**) roh; (*not processed*) Roh-; <*skin*> wund; <*weather*> nasskalt; (*inexperienced*) unerfahren; **get a ~ deal** [!] schlecht wegkommen. **~ materials** *npl* Rohstoffe *pl*

ray *n* Strahl *m*

razor *n* Rasierapparat *m*. **~ blade** *n* Rasierklinge *f*

re *prep* betreffs (+ *gen*)

reach *n* Reichweite *f*; (*of river*) Strecke *f*; **within/out of ~** in/außer Reichweite ● *vt* erreichen; (*arrive at*) ankommen in (+ *dat*); (**~** *as far as*) reichen bis zu; kommen zu <*decision, conclusion*>; (*pass*) reichen ● *vi* reichen (**to** bis zu); **~ for** greifen nach

react *vi* reagieren (**to** auf + *acc*)

reaction *n* Reaktion *f*. **~ary** *a* reaktionär

reactor *n* Reaktor *m*

read *vt/i* (*pt/pp* **read**) lesen; (*aloud*) vorlesen (**to** *dat*); (*Univ*) studieren; ablesen <*meter*>. **~ out** *vt* vorlesen

readable *a* lesbar

reader *n* Leser(in) *m*(*f*); (*book*) Lesebuch *nt*

readily *adv* bereitwillig; (*easily*) leicht

reading *n* Lesen *nt*; (*Pol, Relig*) Lesung *f*

readjust *vt* neu einstellen ● *vi* sich umstellen (**to** auf + *acc*)

ready *a* (**-ier, -iest**) fertig; (*willing*) bereit; (*quick*) schnell; **get ~** sich fertig machen; (*prepare to*) sich bereitmachen

ready: ~-made *a* fertig. **~-to-wear** *a* Konfektions-

real *a* wirklich; (*genuine*) echt; (*actual*) eigentlich ● *adv* (*Amer* [!]) echt. **~ estate** *n* Immobilien *pl*

realis|m *n* Realismus *m*. **~t** *n* Realist *m*. **~tic** *a*, **-ally** *adv* realistisch

reality *n* Wirklichkeit *f*

realization *n* Erkenntnis *f*

realize *vt* einsehen; (*become aware*) gewahr werden; verwirklichen <*hopes, plans*>; einbringen <*price*>

really *adv* wirklich; (*actually*) eigentlich

realm *n* Reich *nt*

realtor *n* (*Amer*) Immobilienmakler *m*

reap *vt* ernten

reappear *vi* wiederkommen

rear[1] *a* Hinter-; (*Auto*) Heck- ● *n* **the ~** der hintere Teil; **from the ~** von hinten

rear[2] *vt* aufziehen ● *vi* **~ [up]** <*horse:*> sich aufbäumen

rearrange *vt* umstellen

reason *n* Grund *m*; (*good sense*) Vernunft *f*; (*ability to think*) Verstand *m*; **within ~** in vernünftigen Grenzen ● *vi* argumentieren; **~ with** vernünftig reden mit. **~able** *a* vernünftig; (*not expensive*) preiswert. **~ably** *adv* (*fairly*) ziemlich

reassur|ance *n* Beruhigung *f*; Versicherung *f*. **~e** *vt* beruhigen; **~e s.o. of sth** jdm etw (*gen*) versichern

rebel[1] *n* Rebell *m*

rebel[2] *vi* (*pt/pp* **rebelled**) rebellieren. **~lion** *n* Rebellion *f*. **~lious** *a* rebellisch

rebound[1] *vi* abprallen

rebound[2] *n* Rückprall *m*

rebuild *vt* (*pt/pp* **-built**) wieder aufbauen

rebuke *n* Tadel *m* ● *vt* tadeln

recall *n* Erinnerung *f* ● *vt* zurückrufen; abberufen <*diplomat*>; (*remember*) sich erinnern an (+ *acc*)

recant *vi* widerrufen

recap *vt/i* 🄸 = **recapitulate**

recapitulate *vt/i* zusammenfassen; rekapitulieren

recapture *vt* wieder gefangen nehmen <*person*>; wieder einfangen <*animal*>

reced|e *vi* zurückgehen. **~ing** *a* <*forehead, chin*> fliehend

receipt *n* Quittung *f*; (*receiving*) Empfang *m*; **~s** *pl* (*Comm*) Einnahmen *pl*

receive *vt* erhalten, bekommen; empfangen <*guests*>. **~r** *n* (*Teleph*) Hörer *m*; (*of stolen goods*) Hehler *m*

recent *a* kürzlich erfolgte(r,s). **~ly** *adv* vor kurzem

receptacle *n* Behälter *m*

reception *n* Empfang *m*; **~ [desk]** (*in hotel*) Rezeption *f*. **~ist** *n* Empfangsdame *f*

receptive *a* aufnahmefähig; **~ to** empfänglich für

recess *n* Nische *f*; (*holiday*) Ferien *pl*

recession *n* Rezession *f*

recharge *vt* [wieder] aufladen

recipe *n* Rezept *nt*

recipient *n* Empfänger *m*

recital *n* (*of poetry, songs*) Vortrag *m*; (*of instrumental music*) Konzert *nt*

recite *vt* aufsagen; (*before audience*) vortragen

reckless *a*, **-ly** *adv* leichtsinnig; (*careless*) rücksichtslos. **~ness** *n* Leichtsinn *m*; (*carelessness*) Rücksichtslosigkeit *f*

reckon *vt* rechnen; (*consider*) glauben ● *vi* **~ on/with** rechnen mit

reclaim *vt* zurückfordern; zurückgewinnen <*land*>

reclin|e *vi* liegen. **~ing seat** *n* Liegesitz *m*

recluse *n* Einsiedler(in) *m(f)*

recognition *n* Erkennen *nt*; (*acknowledgement*) Anerkennung *f*; **in ~** als Anerkennung (**of** *gen*)

recognize *vt* erkennen; (*know again*) wieder erkennen; (*acknowledge*) anerkennen

recoil *vi* zurückschnellen; (*in fear*) zurückschrecken

recollect *vt* sich erinnern an (+ *acc*). **~ion** *n* Erinnerung *f*

recommend *vt* empfehlen. **~ation** *n* Empfehlung *f*

recon|cile *vt* versöhnen; **~cile oneself to** sich abfinden mit. **~ciliation** *n* Versöhnung *f*

reconnaissance *n* (*Mil*) Aufklärung *f*

R

reconnoitre *vi* (*pres p* **-tring**) auf Erkundung ausgehen
reconsider *vt* sich (*dat*) noch einmal überlegen
reconstruct *vt* wieder aufbauen; rekonstruieren <*crime*>
record[1] *vt* aufzeichnen; (*register*) registrieren; (*on tape*) aufnehmen
record[2] *n* Aufzeichnung *f*; (*Jur*) Protokoll *nt*; (*Mus*) [Schall]platte *f*; (*Sport*) Rekord *m*; **~s** *pl* Unterlagen *pl*; **off the ~** inoffiziell; **have a [criminal] ~** vorbestraft sein
recorder *n* (*Mus*) Blockflöte *f*
recording *n* Aufnahme *f*
re-count[1] *vt* nachzählen
re-count[2] *n* (*Pol*) Nachzählung *f*
recover *vt* zurückbekommen ● *vi* sich erholen. **~y** *n* Wiedererlangung *f*; (*of health*) Erholung *f*
recreation *n* Erholung *f*; (*hobby*) Hobby *nt*. **~al** *a* Freizeit-; **be ~al** erholsam sein
recruit *n* (*Mil*) Rekrut *m*; **new ~** (*member*) neues Mitglied *nt*; (*worker*) neuer Mitarbeiter *m* ● *vt* rekrutieren; anwerben <*staff*>. **~ment** *n* Rekrutierung *f*; Anwerbung *f*
rectang|le *n* Rechteck *nt*. **~ular** *a* rechteckig
rectify *vt* (*pt/pp* **-ied**) berichtigen
rector *n* Pfarrer *m*; (*Univ*) Rektor *m*. **~y** *n* Pfarrhaus *nt*
recur *vi* (*pt/pp* **recurred**) sich wiederholen; <*illness:*> wiederkehren
recurren|ce *n* Wiederkehr *f*. **~t** *a* wiederkehrend
recycle *vt* wieder verwerten
red *a* (**redder, reddest**) rot ● *n* Rot *nt*
redd|en *vt* röten ● *vi* rot werden. **~ish** *a* rötlich
redecorate *vt* renovieren; (*paint*) neu streichen; (*wallpaper*) neu tapezieren
redeem *vt* einlösen; (*Relig*) erlösen
redemption *n* Erlösung *f*
red: ~-haired *a* rothaarig. **~-handed** *a* **catch s.o. ~-handed** jdn auf frischer Tat ertappen. **~ herring** *n* falsche Spur *f*. **~-hot** *a* glühend heiß. **~ light** *n* (*Auto*) rote Ampel *f*. **~ness** *n* Röte *f*
redo *vt* (*pt* **-did**, *pp* **-done**) noch einmal machen
redouble *vt* verdoppeln
red tape *n* [!] Bürokratie *f*
reduc|e *vt* verringern, vermindern; (*in size*) verkleinern; ermäßigen <*costs*>; herabsetzen <*price, goods*>; (*Culin*) einkochen lassen. **~tion** *n* Verringerung *f*; (*in price*) Ermäßigung *f*; (*in size*) Verkleinerung *f*
redundan|cy *n* Beschäftigungslosigkeit *f*. **~t** *a* überflüssig; **make ~t** entlassen; **be made ~t** beschäftigungslos werden
reed *n* [Schilf]rohr *nt*; **~s** *pl* Schilf *nt*
reef *n* Riff *nt*
reek *vi* riechen (**of** nach)
reel *n* Rolle *f*, Spule *f* ● *vi* (*stagger*) taumeln ● *vt* **~ off** (*fig*) herunterrasseln
refectory *n* Refektorium *nt*; (*Univ*) Mensa *f*
refer *v* (*pt/pp* **referred**) ● *vt* verweisen (**to** an + *acc*); übergeben, weiterleiten <*matter*> (**to** an + *acc*) ● *vi* **~ to** sich beziehen auf (+ *acc*); (*mention*) erwähnen; (*concern*) betreffen; (*consult*) sich wenden an (+ *acc*); nachschlagen in (+ *dat*) <*book*>; **are you ~ring to me**? meinen Sie mich?

referee *n* Schiedsrichter *m*; (*Boxing*) Ringrichter *m*; (*for job*) Referenz *f* ● *vt/i* (*pt/pp* **refereed**) Schiedsrichter/Ringrichter sein (bei)

reference *n* Erwähnung *f*; (*in book*) Verweis *m*; (*for job*) Referenz *f*; **with ~ to** in Bezug auf (+ *acc*); **make [a] ~ to** erwähnen. **~ book** *n* Nachschlagewerk *nt*

referendum *n* Volksabstimmung *f*

refill¹ *vt* nachfüllen

refill² *n* (*for pen*) Ersatzmine *f*

refine *vt* raffinieren. **~d** *a* fein, vornehm. **~ment** *n* Vornehmheit *f*; (*Techn*) Verfeinerung *f*. **~ry** *n* Raffinerie *f*

reflect *vt* reflektieren; <*mirror:*> [wider]spiegeln; **be ~ed in** sich spiegeln in (+ *dat*) ● *vi* nachdenken (**on** über + *acc*). **~ion** *n* Reflexion *f*; (*image*) Spiegelbild *nt*; **on ~ion** nach nochmaliger Überlegung. **~or** *n* Rückstrahler *m*

reflex *n* Reflex *m*

reflexive *a* reflexiv

reform *n* Reform *f* ● *vt* reformieren ● *vi* sich bessern

refrain¹ *n* Refrain *m*

refrain² *vi* **~ from doing sth** etw nicht tun

refresh *vt* erfrischen. **~ing** *a* erfrischend. **~ments** *npl* Erfrischungen *pl*

refrigerat|e *vt* kühlen. **~or** *n* Kühlschrank *m*

refuel *vt/i* (*pt/pp* **fuelled**) auftanken

refuge *n* Zuflucht *f*; **take ~** Zuflucht nehmen

refugee *n* Flüchtling *m*

refund¹ *n* **get a ~** sein Geld zurückbekommen

refund² *vt* zurückerstatten

refusal *n* (*see* **refuse¹**) Ablehnung *f*; Weigerung *f*

refuse¹ *vt* ablehnen; (*not grant*) verweigern; **~ to do sth** sich weigern, etw zu tun ● *vi* ablehnen; sich weigern

refuse² *n* Müll *m*

refute *vt* widerlegen

regain *vt* wiedergewinnen

regal *a*, **-ly** *adv* königlich

regard *n* (*heed*) Rücksicht *f*; (*respect*) Achtung *f*; **~s** *pl* Grüße *pl*; **with ~ to** in Bezug auf (+ *acc*) ● *vt* ansehen, betrachten (**as** als). **~ing** *prep* bezüglich (+ *gen*). **~less** *adv* ohne Rücksicht (**of** auf + *acc*)

regatta *n* Regatta *f*

regime *n* Regime *nt*

regiment *n* Regiment *nt*. **~al** *a* Regiments-

region *n* Region *f*; **in the ~ of** (*fig*) ungefähr. **~al** *a*, **-ly** *adv* regional

register *n* Register *nt*; (*Sch*) Anwesenheitsliste *f* ● *vt* registrieren; (*report*) anmelden; einschreiben <*letter*>; aufgeben <*luggage*> ● *vi* (*report*) sich anmelden

registrar *n* Standesbeamte(r) *m*

registration *n* Registrierung *f*; Anmeldung *f*. **~ number** *n* Autonummer *f*

registry office *n* Standesamt *nt*

regret *n* Bedauern *nt* ● *vt* (*pt/pp* **regretted**) bedauern. **~fully** *adv* mit Bedauern

regrettab|le *a* bedauerlich. **~ly** *adv* bedauerlicherweise

regular *a*, **-ly** *adv* regelmäßig; (*usual*) üblich ● *n* (*in pub*) Stammgast *m*; (*in shop*) Stammkunde *m*. **~ity** *n* Regelmäßigkeit *f*

regulat|e *vt* regulieren. **~ion** *n* (*rule*) Vorschrift *f*

rehears|al *n* (*Theat*) Probe *f*. **~e** *vt* proben

reign *n* Herrschaft *f* ● *vi* herrschen, regieren

rein *n* Zügel *m*

reindeer *n inv* Rentier *nt*
reinforce *vt* verstärken. **~ment** *n* Verstärkung *f*; **send ~ments** Verstärkung schicken
reiterate *vt* wiederholen
reject *vt* ablehnen. **~ion** *n* Ablehnung *f*
rejects *npl* (*Comm*) Ausschussware *f*
rejoic|e *vi* (*liter*) sich freuen. **~ing** *n* Freude *f*
rejoin *vt* sich wieder anschließen (+ *dat*); wieder beitreten (+ *dat*) <*club, party*>
rejuvenate *vt* verjüngen
relapse *n* Rückfall *m* ● *vi* einen Rückfall erleiden
relate *vt* (*tell*) erzählen; (*connect*) verbinden
relation *n* Beziehung *f*; (*person*) Verwandte(r) *m/f*. **~ship** *n* Beziehung *f*; (*link*) Verbindung *f*; (*blood tie*) Verwandtschaft *f*; (*affair*) Verhältnis *nt*
relative *n* Verwandte(r) *m/f* ● *a* relativ; (*Gram*) Relativ-. **~ly** *adv* relativ, verhältnismäßig
relax *vt* lockern, entspannen ● *vi* sich lockern, sich entspannen. **~ation** *n* Entspannung *f*. **~ing** *a* entspannend
relay¹ *vt* (*pt/pp* **-layed**) weitergeben; (*Radio, TV*) übertragen
relay² *n*. **~ [race]** *n* Staffel *f*
release *n* Freilassung *f*, Entlassung *f*; (*Techn*) Auslöser *m* ● *vt* freilassen; (*let go of*) loslassen; (*Techn*) auslösen; veröffentlichen <*information*>
relent *vi* nachgeben. **~less** *a*, **-ly** *adv* erbarmungslos; (*unceasing*) unaufhörlich
relevan|ce *n* Relevanz *f*. **~t** *a* relevant (**to** für)
reliab|ility *n* Zuverlässigkeit *f*. **~le** *a*, **-ly** *adv* zuverlässig
relian|ce *n* Abhängigkeit *f* (**on** von). **~t** *a* angewiesen (**on** auf + *acc*)
relic *n* Überbleibsel *nt*; (*Relig*) Reliquie *f*
relief *n* Erleichterung *f*; (*assistance*) Hilfe *f*; (*replacement*) Ablösung *f*; (*Art*) Relief *nt*
relieve *vt* erleichtern; (*take over from*) ablösen; **~ of** entlasten von
religion *n* Religion *f*
religious *a* religiös
relinquish *vt* loslassen; (*give up*) aufgeben
relish *n* Genuss *m*; (*Culin*) Würze *f* ● *vt* genießen
reluctan|ce *n* Widerstreben *nt*. **~t** *a* widerstrebend; **be ~t** zögern (**to** zu). **~tly** *adv* ungern, widerstrebend
rely *vi* (*pt/pp* **-ied**) **~ on** sich verlassen auf (+ *acc*); (*be dependent on*) angewiesen sein auf (+ *acc*)
remain *vi* bleiben; (*be left*) übrig bleiben. **~der** *n* Rest *m*. **~ing** *a* restlich. **~s** *npl* Reste *pl*; **[mortal] ~s** [sterbliche] Überreste *pl*
remand *n* **on ~** in Untersuchungshaft ● *vt* **~ in custody** in Untersuchungshaft schicken
remark *n* Bemerkung *f* ● *vt* bemerken. **~able** *a*, **-bly** *adv* bemerkenswert
remarry *vi* wieder heiraten
remedy *n* [Heil]mittel *nt* (**for** gegen); (*fig*) Abhilfe *f* ● *vt* (*pt/pp* **-ied**) abhelfen (+ *dat*); beheben <*fault*>
remember *vt* sich erinnern an (+ *acc*); **~ to do sth** daran denken, etw zu tun ● *vi* sich erinnern
remind *vt* erinnern (**of** an + *acc*). **~er** *n* Andenken *nt*; (*letter, warning*) Mahnung *f*
reminisce *vi* sich seinen Erinnerungen hingeben. **~nces**

npl Erinnerungen *pl*. **~nt** *a* **be ~nt of** erinnern an (+ *acc*)
remnant *n* Rest *m*
remorse *n* Reue *f*. **~ful** *a*, **-ly** *adv* reumütig. **~less** *a*, **-ly** *adv* unerbittlich
remote *a* fern; (*isolated*) abgelegen; (*slight*) gering. **~ control** *n* Fernsteuerung *f*; (*for TV*) Fernbedienung *f*
remotely *adv* entfernt; **not ~** nicht im Entferntesten
removable *a* abnehmbar
removal *n* Entfernung *f*; (*from house*) Umzug *m*. **~ van** *n* Möbelwagen *m*
remove *vt* entfernen; (*take off*) abnehmen; (*take out*) herausnehmen
render *vt* machen; erweisen <*service*>; (*translate*) wiedergeben; (*Mus*) vortragen
renegade *n* Abtrünnige(r) *m*/*f*
renew *vt* erneuern; verlängern <*contract*>. **~al** *n* Erneuerung *f*; Verlängerung *f*
renounce *vt* verzichten auf (+ *acc*)
renovat|e *vt* renovieren. **~ion** *n* Renovierung *f*
renown *n* Ruf *m*. **~ed** *a* berühmt
rent *n* Miete *f* ● *vt* mieten; (*hire*) leihen; **~ [out]** vermieten; verleihen. **~al** *n* Mietgebühr *f*; Leihgebühr *f*
renunciation *n* Verzicht *m*
reopen *vt*/*i* wieder aufmachen
reorganize *vt* reorganisieren
rep *n* [!] Vertreter *m*
repair *n* Reparatur *f*; **in good/bad ~** in gutem/schlechtem Zustand ● *vt* reparieren
repatriate *vt* repatriieren
repay *vt* (*pt*/*pp* **-paid**) zurückzahlen; **~ s.o. for sth** jdm etw zurückzahlen. **~ment** *n* Rückzahlung *f*
repeal *n* Aufhebung *f* ● *vt* aufheben
repeat *n* Wiederholung *f* ● *vt*/*i* wiederholen; **~ after me** sprechen Sie mir nach. **~ed** *a*, **-ly** *adv* wiederholt
repel *vt* (*pt*/*pp* **repelled**) abwehren; (*fig*) abstoßen. **~lent** *a* abstoßend
repent *vi* Reue zeigen. **~ance** *n* Reue *f*. **~ant** *a* reuig
repercussions *npl* Auswirkungen *pl*
repertoire, repertory *n* Repertoire *nt*
repetit|ion *n* Wiederholung *f*. **~ive** *a* eintönig
replace *vt* zurücktun; (*take the place of*) ersetzen; (*exchange*) austauschen. **~ment** *n* Ersatz *m*
replay *n* (*Sport*) Wiederholungsspiel *nt*; **[action] ~** Wiederholung *f*
replenish *vt* auffüllen <*stocks*>; (*refill*) nachfüllen
replica *n* Nachbildung *f*
reply *n* Antwort *f* (**to** auf + *acc*) ● *vt*/*i* (*pt*/*pp* **replied**) antworten
report *n* Bericht *m*; (*Sch*) Zeugnis *nt*; (*rumour*) Gerücht *nt*; (*of gun*) Knall *m* ● *vt* berichten; (*notify*) melden; **~ s.o. to the police** jdn anzeigen ● *vi* berichten (**on** über + *acc*); (*present oneself*) sich melden (**to** bei). **~er** *n* Reporter(in) *m*(*f*)
reprehensible *a* tadelnswert
represent *vt* darstellen; (*act for*) vertreten, repräsentieren. **~ation** *n* Darstellung *f*
representative *a* repräsentativ (**of** für) ● *n* Bevollmächtigte(r) *m*/(*f*); (*Comm*) Vertreter(in) *m*(*f*); (*Amer Pol*) Abgeordnete(r) *m*/*f*
repress *vt* unterdrücken. **~ion** *n* Unterdrückung *f*. **~ive** *a* repressiv
reprieve *n* Begnadigung *f*; (*fig*) Gnadenfrist *f* ● *vt* begnadigen
reprimand *n* Tadel *m* ● *vt* tadeln
reprint[1] *n* Nachdruck *m*

R

reprint² *vt* neu auflegen
reprisal *n* Vergeltungsmaßnahme *f*
reproach *n* Vorwurf *m* ● *vt* Vorwürfe *pl* machen (+ *dat*). **~ful** *a*, **-ly** *adv* vorwurfsvoll
reproduc|e *vt* wiedergeben, reproduzieren ● *vi* sich fortpflanzen. **~tion** *n* Reproduktion *f*; (*Biol*) Fortpflanzung *f*
reptile *n* Reptil *nt*
republic *n* Republik *f*. **~an** *a* republikanisch ● *n* Republikaner(in) *m(f)*
repugnan|ce *n* Widerwille *m*. **~t** *a* widerlich
repuls|ion *n* Widerwille *m*. **~ive** *a* abstoßend, widerlich
reputable *a* <*firm*> von gutem Ruf; (*respectable*) anständig
reputation *n* Ruf *m*
request *n* Bitte *f* ● *vt* bitten
require *vt* (*need*) brauchen; (*demand*) erfordern; **be ~d to do sth** etw tun müssen. **~ment** *n* Bedürfnis *nt*; (*condition*) Erfordernis *nt*
resale *n* Weiterverkauf *m*
rescue *n* Rettung *f* ● *vt* retten. **~r** *n* Retter *m*
research *n* Forschung *f* ● *vt* erforschen; (*Journ*) recherchieren. **~er** *n* Forscher *m*; (*Journ*) Rechercheur *m*
resem|blance *n* Ähnlichkeit *f*. **~ble** *vt* ähneln (+ *dat*)
resent *vt* übel nehmen; einen Groll hegen gegen <*person*>. **~ful** *a*, **-ly** *adv* verbittert. **~ment** *n* Groll *m*
reservation *n* Reservierung *f*; (*doubt*) Vorbehalt *m*; (*enclosure*) Reservat *nt*
reserve *n* Reserve *f*; (*for animals*) Reservat *nt*; (*Sport*) Reservespieler(in) *m(f)* ● *vt* reservieren; <*client:*> reservieren lassen; (*keep*) aufheben; sich (*dat*) vorbehalten <*right*>. **~d** *a* reserviert
reservoir *n* Reservoir *nt*
reshuffle *n* (*Pol*) Umbildung *f* ● *vt* (*Pol*) umbilden
residence *n* Wohnsitz *m*; (*official*) Residenz *f*; (*stay*) Aufenthalt *m*
resident *a* ansässig (**in** in + *dat*); <*housekeeper, nurse*> im Haus wohnend ● *n* Bewohner(in) *m(f)*; (*of street*) Anwohner *m*. **~ial** *a* Wohn-
residue *n* Rest *m*; (*Chem*) Rückstand *m*
resign *vt* **~ oneself to** sich abfinden mit ● *vi* kündigen; (*from public office*) zurücktreten. **~ation** *n* Resignation *f*; (*from job*) Kündigung *f*; Rücktritt *m*. **~ed** *a*, **-ly** *adv* resigniert
resilient *a* federnd; (*fig*) widerstandsfähig
resin *n* Harz *nt*
resist *vt/i* sich widersetzen (+ *dat*), (*fig*) widerstehen (+ *dat*). **~ance** *n* Widerstand *m*. **~ant** *a* widerstandsfähig
resolut|e *a*, **-ly** *adv* entschlossen. **~ion** *n* Entschlossenheit *f*; (*intention*) Vorsatz *m*; (*Pol*) Resolution *f*
resolve *n* Entschlossenheit *f*; (*decision*) Beschluss *m* ● *vt* beschließen; (*solve*) lösen
resort *n* (*place*) Urlaubsort *m*; **as a last ~** wenn alles andere fehlschlägt ● *vi* **~ to** (*fig*) greifen zu
resound *vi* widerhallen
resource *n* **~s** *pl* Ressourcen *pl*. **~ful** *a* findig
respect *n* Respekt *m*, Achtung *f* (**for** vor + *dat*); (*aspect*) Hinsicht *f*; **with ~ to** in Bezug auf (+ *acc*) ● *vt* respektieren, achten
respect|able *a*, **-bly** *adv* ehrbar; (*decent*) anständig; (*considerable*)

ansehnlich. **~ful** *a*, **-ly** *adv* respektvoll
respective *a* jeweilig. **~ly** *adv* beziehungsweise
respiration *n* Atmung *f*
respite *n* [Ruhe]pause *f*; (*delay*) Aufschub *m*
respond *vi* antworten; (*react*) reagieren (**to** auf + *acc*)
response *n* Antwort *f*; Reaktion *f*
responsibility *n* Verantwortung *f*; (*duty*) Verpflichtung *f*
responsib|le *a* verantwortlich; (*trustworthy*) verantwortungsvoll. **~ly** *adv* verantwortungsbewusst
rest[1] *n* Ruhe *f*; (*holiday*) Erholung *f*; (*interval & Mus*) Pause *f*; **have a ~** eine Pause machen; (*rest*) sich ausruhen ● *vt* ausruhen; (*lean*) lehnen (**on** an/auf + *acc*) ● *vi* ruhen; (*have a rest*) sich ausruhen
rest[2] *n* **the ~** der Rest; (*people*) die Übrigen *pl* ● *vi* **it ~s with you** es ist an Ihnen (**to** zu)
restaurant *n* Restaurant *nt*, Gaststätte *f*
restful *a* erholsam
restive *a* unruhig
restless *a*, **-ly** *adv* unruhig
restoration *n* (*of building*) Restaurierung *f*
restore *vt* wiederherstellen; restaurieren <*building*>
restrain *vt* zurückhalten; **~ oneself** sich beherrschen. **~ed** *a* zurückhaltend. **~t** *n* Zurückhaltung *f*
restrict *vt* einschränken; **~ to** beschränken auf (+ *acc*). **~ion** *n* Einschränkung *f*, Beschränkung *f*. **~ive** *a* einschränkend
rest room *n* (*Amer*) Toilette *f*
result *n* Ergebnis *nt*, Resultat *nt*; (*consequence*) Folge *f*; **as a ~** als Folge (**of** *gen*) ● *vi* sich ergeben (**from** aus); **~ in** enden in (+ *dat*); (*lead to*) führen zu
resume *vt* wieder aufnehmen ● *vi* wieder beginnen
résumé *n* Zusammenfassung *f*
resumption *n* Wiederaufnahme *f*
resurrect *vt* (*fig*) wieder beleben. **~ion** *n* **the R~ion** (*Relig*) die Auferstehung
resuscitat|e *vt* wieder beleben. **~ion** *n* Wiederbelebung *f*
retail *n* Einzelhandel *m* ● *a* Einzelhandels- ● *adv* im Einzelhandel ● *vt* im Einzelhandel verkaufen ● *vi* **~ at** im Einzelhandel kosten. **~er** *n* Einzelhändler *m*
retain *vt* behalten
retaliat|e *vi* zurückschlagen. **~ion** *n* Vergeltung *f*; **in ~ion** als Vergeltung
retarded *a* zurückgeblieben
reticen|ce *n* Zurückhaltung *f*. **~t** *a* zurückhaltend
retina *n* Netzhaut *f*
retinue *n* Gefolge *nt*
retire *vi* in den Ruhestand treten; (*withdraw*) sich zurückziehen. **~d** *a* im Ruhestand. **~ment** *n* Ruhestand *m*
retiring *a* zurückhaltend
retort *n* scharfe Erwiderung *f*; (*Chem*) Retorte *f* ● *vt* scharf erwidern
retrace *vt* **~ one's steps** denselben Weg zurückgehen
retrain *vt* umschulen ● *vi* umgeschult werden
retreat *n* Rückzug *m*; (*place*) Zufluchtsort *m* ● *vi* sich zurückziehen
retrial *n* Wiederaufnahmeverfahren *nt*
retrieve *vt* zurückholen; (*from wreckage*) bergen; (*Computing*) wieder auffinden
retrograde *a* rückschrittlich
retrospect *n* **in ~** rückblickend. **~ive** *a*, **-ly** *adv* rückwirkend; (*looking back*) rückblickend

R

return *n* Rückkehr *f*; (*giving back*) Rückgabe *f*; (*Comm*) Ertrag *m*; (*ticket*) Rückfahrkarte *f*; (*Aviat*) Rückflugschein *m*; **by ~ [of post]** postwendend; **in ~** dafür; **in ~ for** für; **many happy ~s!** herzlichen Glückwunsch zum Geburtstag! ●*vt* zurückgehen/-fahren; (*come back*) zurückkommen ●*vt* zurückgeben; (*put back*) zurückstellen/-legen; (*send back*) zurückschicken

return ticket *n* Rückfahrkarte *f*; (*Aviat*) Rückflugschein *m*

reunion *n* Wiedervereinigung *f*; (*social gathering*) Treffen *nt*

reunite *vt* wieder vereinigen

reuse *vt* wieder verwenden

rev *n* (*Auto* [!]) Umdrehung *f* ●*vt*/*i* **~ [up]** den Motor auf Touren bringen

reveal *vt* zum Vorschein bringen; (*fig*) enthüllen. **~ing** *a* (*fig*) aufschlussreich

revel *vi* (*pt*/*pp* **revelled**) **~ in sth** etw genießen

revelation *n* Offenbarung *f*, Enthüllung *f*

revenge *n* Rache *f*; (*fig & Sport*) Revanche *f* ●*vt* rächen

revenue *n* [Staats]einnahmen *pl*

revere *vt* verehren. **~nce** *n* Ehrfurcht *f*

Reverend *a* **the ~ X** Pfarrer X; (*Catholic*) Hochwürden X

reverent *a*, **-ly** *adv* ehrfürchtig

reversal *n* Umkehrung *f*

reverse *a* umgekehrt ●*n* Gegenteil *nt*; (*back*) Rückseite *f*; (*Auto*) Rückwärtsgang *m* ●*vt* umkehren; (*Auto*) zurücksetzen ●*vi* zurücksetzen

revert *vi* **~ to** zurückfallen an (+ *acc*)

review *n* Rückblick *m* (**of** auf + *acc*); (*re-examination*) Überprüfung *f*; (*Mil*) Truppenschau *f*; (*of book, play*) Kritik *f*, Rezension *f* ●*vt* zurückblicken auf (+ *acc*); überprüfen <*situation*>; rezensieren <*book, play*>. **~er** *n* Kritiker *m*, Rezensent *m*

revis|e *vt* revidieren; (*for exam*) wiederholen. **~ion** *n* Revision *f*; (*for exam*) Wiederholung *f*

revival *n* Wiederbelebung *f*

revive *vt* wieder beleben; (*fig*) wieder aufleben lassen ●*vi* wieder aufleben

revolt *n* Aufstand *m* ●*vi* rebellieren ●*vt* anwidern. **~ing** *a* widerlich, eklig

revolution *n* Revolution *f*; (*Auto*) Umdrehung *f*. **~ary** *a* revolutionär. **~ize** *vt* revolutionieren

revolve *vi* sich drehen; **~ around** kreisen um

revolv|er *n* Revolver *m*. **~ing** *a* Dreh-

revue *n* Revue *f*; (*satirical*) Kabarett *nt*

revulsion *n* Abscheu *m*

reward *n* Belohnung *f* ●*vt* belohnen. **~ing** *a* lohnend

rewrite *vt* (*pt* **rewrote**, *pp* **rewritten**) noch einmal [neu] schreiben; (*alter*) umschreiben

rhetoric *n* Rhetorik *f*. **~al** *a* rhetorisch

rheumatism *n* Rheumatismus *m*, Rheuma *nt*

Rhine *n* Rhein *m*

rhinoceros *n* Nashorn *nt*, Rhinozeros *nt*

rhubarb *n* Rhabarber *m*

rhyme *n* Reim *m* ●*vt* reimen ●*vi* sich reimen

rhythm *n* Rhythmus *m*. **~ic[al]** *a*, **-ally** *adv* rhythmisch

rib *n* Rippe *f*

ribbon *n* Band *nt*; (*for typewriter*) Farbband *nt*

rice *n* Reis *m*

rich *a* (**-er, -est**), **-ly** *adv* reich; <*food*> gehaltvoll; (*heavy*) schwer

● *n* **the ~** *pl* die Reichen; **~es** *pl* Reichtum *m*

ricochet *vi* abprallen

rid *vt* (*pt/pp* **rid**, *pres p* **ridding**) befreien (**of** von); **get ~ of** loswerden

riddance *n* **good ~!** auf Nimmerwiedersehen!

ridden *see* **ride**

riddle *n* Rätsel *nt*

riddled *a* **~ with** durchlöchert mit

ride *n* Ritt *m*; (*in vehicle*) Fahrt *f*; **take s.o. for a ~** [!] jdn reinlegen ● *v* (*pt* **rode**, *pp* **ridden**) ● *vt* reiten <*horse*>; fahren mit <*bicycle*> ● *vi* reiten; (*in vehicle*) fahren. **~r** *n* Reiter(in) *m(f)*; (*on bicycle*) Fahrer(in) *m(f)*

ridge *n* Erhebung *f*; (*on roof*) First *m*; (*of mountain*) Grat *m*, Kamm *m*

ridicule *n* Spott *m* ● *vt* verspotten, spotten über (+ *acc*)

ridiculous *a*, **-ly** *adv* lächerlich

riding *n* Reiten *nt* ● *attrib* Reit-

riff-raff *n* Gesindel *nt*

rifle *n* Gewehr *nt* ● *vt* plündern; **~ through** durchwühlen

rift *n* Spalt *m*; (*fig*) Riss *m*

rig *n* Ölbohrturm *m*; (*at sea*) Bohrinsel *f* ● *vt* (*pt/pp* **rigged**) **~ out** ausrüsten; **~ up** aufbauen

right *a* richtig; (*not left*) rechte(r,s); **be ~** <*person:*> Recht haben; <*clock:*> richtig gehen; **put ~** wieder in Ordnung bringen; (*fig*) richtig stellen; **that's ~!** das stimmt! ● *adv* richtig; (*directly*) direkt; (*completely*) ganz; (*not left*) rechts; <*go*> nach rechts; **~ away** sofort ● *n* Recht *nt*; (*not left*) rechte Seite *f*; **on the ~** rechts; **from/to the ~** von/nach rechts; **be in the ~** Recht haben; **by ~s** eigentlich; **the R~** (*Pol*) die Rechte. **~ angle** *n* rechter Winkel *m*

rightful *a*, **-ly** *adv* rechtmäßig

right-handed *a* rechtshändig

rightly *adv* mit Recht

right-wing *a* (*Pol*) rechte(r,s)

rigid *a* starr; (*strict*) streng. **~ity** *n* Starrheit *f*; Strenge *f*

rigorous *a*, **-ly** *adv* streng

rigour *n* Strenge *f*

rim *n* Rand *m*; (*of wheel*) Felge *f*

rind *n* (*on fruit*) Schale *f*, (*on cheese*) Rinde *f*; (*on bacon*) Schwarte *f*

ring¹ *n* Ring *m*; (*for circus*) Manege *f*; **stand in a ~** im Kreis stehen ● *vt* umringen

ring² *n* Klingeln *nt*; **give s.o. a ~** (*Teleph*) jdn anrufen ● *v* (*pt* **rang**, *pp* **rung**) ● *vt* läuten; **~ [up]** (*Teleph*) anrufen ● *vi* <*bells:*> läuten; <*telephone:*> klingeln. **~ back** *vt/i* (*Teleph*) zurückrufen

ring: ~leader *n* Rädelsführer *m*. **~ road** *n* Umgehungsstraße *f*

rink *n* Eisbahn *f*

rinse *n* Spülung *f*; (*hair colour*) Tönung *f* ● *vt* spülen

riot *n* Aufruhr *m*; **~s** *pl* Unruhen *pl*; **run ~** randalieren ● *vi* randalieren. **~er** *n* Randalierer *m*. **~ous** *a* aufrührerisch; (*boisterous*) wild

rip *n* Riss *m* ● *vt/i* (*pt/pp* **ripped**) zerreißen; **~ open** aufreißen. **~ off** *vt* [!] neppen

ripe *a* (**-r**, **-st**) reif

ripen *vi* reifen ● *vt* reifen lassen

ripeness *n* Reife *f*

rip-off *n* [!] Nepp *m*

ripple *n* kleine Welle *f*

rise *n* Anstieg *m*; (*fig*) Aufstieg *m*; (*increase*) Zunahme *f*; (*in wages*) Lohnerhöhung *f*; (*in salary*) Gehaltserhöhung *f*; **give ~ to** Anlass geben zu ● *vi* (*pt* **rose**, *pp* **risen**) steigen; <*ground:*> ansteigen; <*sun, dough:*> aufgehen; <*river:*> entspringen; (*get up*) aufstehen; (*fig*) aufsteigen (**to** zu). **~r** *n* **early ~r** Frühaufsteher *m*

rising *a* steigend; <*sun*> aufgehend

risk *n* Risiko *nt*; **at one's own ~** auf eigene Gefahr ● *vt* riskieren

risky *a* (**-ier, -iest**) riskant

rite *n* Ritus *m*

ritual *a* rituell ● *n* Ritual *nt*

rival *a* rivalisierend ● *n* Rivale *m*/Rivalin *f*. **~ry** *n* Rivalität *f*; (*Comm*) Konkurrenzkampf *m*

river *n* Fluss *m*

rivet *n* Niete *f* ● *vt* [ver]nieten; **~ed by** (*fig*) gefesselt von

road *n* Straße *f*; (*fig*) Weg *m*

road: ~-map *n* Straßenkarte *f*. **~ safety** *n* Verkehrssicherheit *f*. **~side** *n* Straßenrand *m*. **~way** *n* Fahrbahn *f*. **~-works** *npl* Straßenarbeiten *pl*. **~worthy** *a* verkehrssicher

roam *vi* wandern

roar *n* Gebrüll *nt*; **~s of laughter** schallendes Gelächter *nt* ● *vi* brüllen; (*with laughter*) schallend lachen. **~ing** *a* <*fire*> prasselnd; **do a ~ing trade** [!] ein Bombengeschäft machen

roast *a* gebraten, Brat-; **~ beef/pork** Rinder-/Schweinebraten *m* ● *n* Braten *m* ● *vt/i* braten; rösten <*coffee, chestnuts*>

rob *vt* (*pt/pp* **robbed**) berauben (**of** *gen*); ausrauben <*bank*>. **~ber** *n* Räuber *m*. **~bery** *n* Raub *m*

robe *n* Robe *f*; (*Amer: bathrobe*) Bademantel *m*

robin *n* Rotkehlchen *nt*

robot *n* Roboter *m*

robust *a* robust

rock¹ *n* Fels *m*; **on the ~s** <*ship*> aufgelaufen; <*marriage*> kaputt; <*drink*> mit Eis

rock² *vt/i* schaukeln

rock³ *n* (*Mus*) Rock *m*

rockery *n* Steingarten *m*

rocket *n* Rakete *f*

rocking: ~-chair *n* Schaukelstuhl *m*. **~-horse** *n* Schaukelpferd *nt*

rocky *a* (**-ier, -iest**) felsig; (*unsteady*) wackelig

rod *n* Stab *m*; (*stick*) Rute *f*; (*for fishing*) Angel[rute] *f*

rode *see* **ride**

rodent *n* Nagetier *nt*

rogue *n* Gauner *m*

role *n* Rolle *f*

roll *n* Rolle *f*; (*bread*) Brötchen *nt*; (*list*) Liste *f*; (*of drum*) Wirbel *m* ● *vi* rollen; **be ~ing in money** [!] Geld wie Heu haben ● *vt* rollen; walzen <*lawn*>; ausrollen <*pastry*>. **~ over** *vi* sich auf die andere Seite rollen. **~ up** *vt* aufrollen; hochkrempeln <*sleeves*> ● *vi* [!] auftauchen

roller *n* Rolle *f*; (*lawn, road*) Walze *f*; (*hair*) Lockenwickler *m*. **R~blades** (**P**) *npl* Rollerblades (P) *mpl*. **~ blind** *n* Rollo *nt*. **~-coaster** *n* Berg-und-Talbahn *f*. **~-skate** *n* Rollschuh *m*

rolling-pin *n* Teigrolle *f*

Roman *a* römisch ● *n* Römer(in) *m(f)*

romance *n* Romantik *f*; (*love-affair*) Romanze *f*; (*book*) Liebesgeschichte *f*

Romania *n* Rumänien *nt*. **~n** *a* rumänisch ● *n* Rumäne *m*/-nin *f*

romantic *a*, **-ally** *adv* romantisch. **~ism** *n* Romantik *f*

Rome *n* Rom *nt*

romp *vi* [herum]tollen

roof *n* Dach *nt*; (*of mouth*) Gaumen *m* ● *vt* **~ [over]** überdachen. **~-top** *n* Dach *nt*

rook *n* Saatkrähe *f*; (*Chess*) Turm *m*

room *n* Zimmer *nt*; (*for functions*) Saal *m*; (*space*) Platz *m*. **~y** *a* geräumig

roost *n* Hühnerstange *f*

root¹ *n* Wurzel *f*; **take ~** anwachsen ● *vi* Wurzeln schlagen. **~ out** *vt* (*fig*) ausrotten

root² *vi* **~ about** wühlen; **~ for s.o.** [!] für jdn sein

rope *n* Seil *nt*; **know the ~s** [!] sich auskennen. **~ in** *vt* [!] einspannen

rose¹ *n* Rose *f*; (*of watering-can*) Brause *f*

rose² *see* **rise**

rostrum *n* Podium *nt*

rosy *a* (**-ier, -iest**) rosig

rot *n* Fäulnis *f*; ([!] *nonsense*) Quatsch *m* ● *vi* (*pt/pp* **rotted**) [ver]faulen

rota *n* Dienstplan *m*

rotary *a* Dreh-; (*Techn*) Rotations-

rotat|e *vt* drehen ● *vi* sich drehen; (*Techn*) rotieren. **~ion** *n* Drehung *f*; **in ~ion** im Wechsel

rote *n* **by ~** auswendig

rotten *a* faul; [!] mies; <*person*> fies

rough *a* (**-er, -est**) rau; (*uneven*) uneben; (*coarse, not gentle*) grob; (*brutal*) roh; (*turbulent*) stürmisch; (*approximate*) ungefähr ● *adv* **sleep ~** im Freien übernachten ● *vt* **~ it** primitiv leben. **~ out** *vt* im Groben entwerfen

rough draft *n* grober Entwurf *m*

rough|ly *adv* (*see* **rough**) rau; grob; roh; ungefähr. **~ness** *n* Rauheit *f*

rough paper *n* Konzeptpapier *nt*

round *a* (**-er, -est**) rund ● *n* Runde *f*; (*slice*) Scheibe *f*; **do one's ~s** seine Runde machen ● *prep* um (+ *acc*); **~ the clock** rund um die Uhr ● *adv* **all ~** ringsherum; **ask s.o. ~** jdn einladen ● *vt* biegen um <*corner*>. **~ off** *vt* abrunden. **~ up** *vt* aufrunden, zusammentreiben <*animals*>; festnehmen <*criminals*>

roundabout *a* **~ route** Umweg *m* ● *n* Karussell *nt*; (*for traffic*) Kreisverkehr *m*

round trip *n* Rundreise *f*

rous|e *vt* wecken; (*fig*) erregen. **~ing** *a* mitreißend

route *n* Route *f*; (*of bus*) Linie *f*

routine *a*, **-ly** *adv* routinemäßig ● *n* Routine *f*; (*Theat*) Nummer *f*

row¹ *n* (*line*) Reihe *f*

row² *vt/i* rudern

row³ *n* [!] Krach *m* ● *vi* [!] sich streiten

rowdy *a* (**-ier, -iest**) laut

rowing boat *n* Ruderboot *nt*

royal *a*, **-ly** *adv* königlich

royalt|y *n* Königtum *nt*; (*persons*) Mitglieder *pl* der königlichen Familie; **-ies** *pl* (*payments*) Tantiemen *pl*

RSI *abbr* (**repetitive strain injury**) chronisches Überlastungssyndrom *nt*

rub *vt* (*pt/pp* **rubbed**) reiben; (*polish*) polieren; **don't ~ it in** [!] reib es mir nicht unter die Nase. **~ off** *vt* abreiben ● *vi* abgehen. **~ out** *vt* ausradieren

rubber *n* Gummi *m*; (*eraser*) Radiergummi *m*. **~ band** *n* Gummiband *nt*

rubbish *n* Abfall *m*, Müll *m*; ([!] *nonsense*) Quatsch *m*; ([!] *junk*) Plunder *m*. **~ bin** *n* Abfalleimer *m*. **~ dump** *n* Abfallhaufen *m*; (*official*) Müllhalde *f*

rubble *n* Trümmer *pl*

ruby *n* Rubin *m*

rudder *n* [Steuer]ruder *nt*

rude *a* (**-r, -st**), **-ly** *adv* unhöflich; (*improper*) unanständig

rudimentary *a* elementar; (*Biol*) rudimentär

ruffian *n* Rüpel *m*

ruffle *vt* zerzausen

rug *n* Vorleger *m*, [kleiner] Teppich *m*; (*blanket*) Decke *f*

rugged *a* <*coastline*> zerklüftet

ruin *n* Ruine *f*; (*fig*) Ruin *m* ● *vt* ruinieren

rule *n* Regel *f*; (*control*) Herrschaft *f*; (*government*) Regierung *f*; (*for measuring*) Lineal *nt*; **as a ~** in der Regel ● *vt* regieren, herrschen über (+ *acc*); (*fig*) beherrschen; (*decide*)

R

entscheiden; ziehen <*line*> ● *vi* regieren, herrschen. ~ **out** *vt* ausschließen
ruled *a* <*paper*> liniert
ruler *n* Herrscher(in) *m*(*f*); (*measure*) Lineal *nt*
ruling *a* herrschend; <*factor*> entscheidend; (*Pol*) regierend ● *n* Entscheidung *f*
rum *n* Rum *m*
rumble *n* Grollen *nt* ● *vi* grollen; <*stomach:*> knurren
rummage *vi* wühlen; ~ **through** durchwühlen
rumour *n* Gerücht *nt* ● *vt* **it is ~ed that** es geht das Gerücht, dass
rump *n* Hinterteil *nt*. ~ **steak** *n* Rumpsteak *nt*
run *n* Lauf *m*; (*journey*) Fahrt *f*; (*series*) Serie *f*, Reihe *f*; (*Theat*) Laufzeit *f*; (*Skiing*) Abfahrt *f*; (*enclosure*) Auslauf *m*; (*Amer: ladder*) Laufmasche *f*; ~ **of bad luck** Pechsträhne *f*; **be on the ~** flüchtig sein; **in the long ~** auf lange Sicht ● *v* (*pt* **ran**, *pp* **run**, *pres p* **running**) ● *vi* laufen; (*flow*) fließen; <*eyes:*> tränen; <*bus:*> verkehren; <*butter, ink:*> zerfließen; <*colours:*> [ab]färben; (*in election*) kandidieren ● *vt* laufen lassen; einlaufen lassen <*bath*>; (*manage*) führen, leiten; (*drive*) fahren; eingehen <*risk*>; (*Journ*) bringen <*article*>; ~ **one's hand over sth** mit der Hand über etw (*acc*) fahren. ~ **away** *vi* weglaufen. ~ **down** *vi* hinunter-/herunterlaufen; <*clockwork:*> ablaufen; <*stocks:*> sich verringern ● *vt* (*run over*) überfahren; (*reduce*) verringern; (🅵 *criticize*) heruntermachen. ~ **in** *vi* hinein-/hereinlaufen. ~ **off** *vi* weglaufen ● *vt* abziehen <*copies*>. ~ **out** *vi* hinaus-/herauslaufen; <*supplies, money:*> ausgehen; **I've ~ out of sugar** ich habe keinen Zucker mehr. ~ **over** *vt* überfahren. ~ **up** *vi* hinauf-/herauflaufen; (*towards*) hinlaufen ● *vt* machen <*debts*>; auflaufen lassen <*bill*>; (*sew*) schnell nähen
runaway *n* Ausreißer *m*
run-down *a* <*area*> verkommen
rung[1] *n* (*of ladder*) Sprosse *f*
rung[2] *see* **ring**[2]
runner *n* Läufer *m*; (*Bot*) Ausläufer *m*; (*on sledge*) Kufe *f*. ~ **bean** *n* Stangenbohne *f*. **~-up** *n* Zweite(r) *m*/*f*
running *a* laufend; <*water*> fließend; **four times ~** viermal nacheinander ● *n* Laufen *nt*; (*management*) Führung *f*, Leitung *f*; **be/not be in the ~** eine/keine Chance haben
runny *a* flüssig
run: ~-up *n* (*Sport*) Anlauf *m*; (*to election*) Zeit *f* vor der Wahl. **~way** *n* Start- und Landebahn *f*
rupture *n* Bruch *m* ● *vt*/*i* brechen
rural *a* ländlich
ruse *n* List *f*
rush[1] *n* (*Bot*) Binse *f*
rush[2] *n* Hetze *f*; **in a ~** in Eile ● *vi* sich hetzen; (*run*) rasen; <*water:*> rauschen ● *vt* hetzen, drängen. **~-hour** *n* Hauptverkehrszeit *f*, Stoßzeit *f*
Russia *n* Russland *nt*. **~n** *a* russisch ● *n* Russe *m*/Russin *f*; (*Lang*) Russisch *nt*
rust *n* Rost *m* ● *vi* rosten
rustle *vi* rascheln ● *vt* rascheln mit; (*Amer*) stehlen <*cattle*>. ~ **up** *vt* 🅵 improvisieren
rustproof *a* rostfrei
rusty *a* (**-ier, -iest**) rostig
rut *n* Furche *f*
ruthless *a*, **-ly** *adv* rücksichtslos. **~ness** *n* Rücksichtslosigkeit *f*
rye *n* Roggen *m*

sabbath *n* Sabbat *m*
sabotage *n* Sabotage *f* ● *vt* sabotieren
sachet *n* Beutel *m*; (*scented*) Kissen *nt*
sack *n* Sack *m*; **get the ~** [!] rausgeschmissen werden ● *vt* [!] rausschmeißen
sacred *a* heilig
sacrifice *n* Opfer *nt* ● *vt* opfern
sacrilege *n* Sakrileg *nt*
sad *a* (**sadder, saddest**) traurig; <*loss, death*> schmerzlich. **~den** *vt* traurig machen
saddle *n* Sattel *m* ● *vt* satteln; **~ s.o. with sth** [!] jdm etw aufhalsen
sadist *n* Sadist *m*. **~ic** *a*, **-ally** *adv* sadistisch
sad|ly *adv* traurig; (*unfortunately*) leider. **~ness** *n* Traurigkeit *f*
safe *a* (**-r, -st**) sicher; <*journey*> gut; (*not dangerous*) ungefährlich; **~ and sound** gesund und wohlbehalten ● *n* Safe *m*. **~guard** *n* Schutz *m* ● *vt* schützen. **~ly** *adv* sicher; <*arrive*> gut
safety *n* Sicherheit *f*. **~-belt** *n* Sicherheitsgurt *m*. **~-pin** *n* Sicherheitsnadel *f*. **~-valve** *n* [Sicherheits]ventil *nt*
sag *vi* (*pt/pp* **sagged**) durchhängen
saga *n* Saga *f*; (*fig*) Geschichte *f*
said *see* **say**
sail *n* Segel *nt*; (*trip*) Segelfahrt *f* ● *vi* segeln; (*on liner*) fahren; (*leave*) abfahren (**for** nach) ● *vt* segeln mit
sailing *n* Segelsport *m*. **~-boat** *n* Segelboot *nt*. **~-ship** *n* Segelschiff *nt*
sailor *n* Seemann *m*; (*in navy*) Matrose *m*
saint *n* Heilige(r) *m/f*. **~ly** *a* heilig
sake *n* **for the ~ of ...** um ... (*gen*) willen; **for my/your ~** um meinet-/deinetwillen
salad *n* Salat *m*. **~-dressing** *n* Salatsoße *f*
salary *n* Gehalt *nt*
sale *n* Verkauf *m*; (*event*) Basar *m*; (*at reduced prices*) Schlussverkauf *m*; **for ~** zu verkaufen
sales|man *n* Verkäufer *m*. **~woman** *n* Verkäuferin *f*
saliva *n* Speichel *m*
salmon *n* Lachs *m*
saloon *n* Salon *m*; (*Auto*) Limousine *f*; (*Amer: bar*) Wirtschaft *f*
salt *n* Salz *nt* ● *a* salzig; <*water, meat*> Salz- ● *vt* salzen; (*cure*) pökeln; streuen <*road*>. **~-cellar** *n* Salzfass *nt*. **~ water** *n* Salzwasser *nt*. **~y** *a* salzig
salute *n* (*Mil*) Gruß *m* ● *vt/i* (*Mil*) grüßen
salvage *n* (*Naut*) Bergung *f* ● *vt* bergen
salvation *n* Rettung *f*; (*Relig*) Heil *nt*
same *a & pron* **the ~** der/die/das gleiche; (*pl*) die gleichen; (*identical*) der-/die-/dasselbe; (*pl*) dieselben ● *adv* **the ~** gleich; **all the ~** trotzdem
sample *n* Probe *f*; (*Comm*) Muster *nt* ● *vt* probieren; kosten <*food*>
sanatorium *n* Sanatorium *nt*
sanction *n* Sanktion *f* ● *vt* sanktionieren
sanctuary *n* (*Relig*) Heiligtum *nt*; (*refuge*) Zuflucht *f*; (*for wildlife*) Tierschutzgebiet *nt*
sand *n* Sand *m* ● *vt* **~ [down]** [ab]schmirgeln
sandal *n* Sandale *f*

sand: ~bank *n* Sandbank *f*. **~paper** *n* Sandpapier *nt*. **~-pit** *n* Sandkasten *m*
sandwich *n*; Sandwich *m* ● *vt* **~ed between** eingeklemmt zwischen
sandy *a* (**-ier, -iest**) sandig; <*beach, soil*> Sand-; <*hair*> rotblond
sane *a* (**-r, -st**) geistig normal; (*sensible*) vernünftig
sang *see* **sing**
sanitary *a* hygienisch; <*system*> sanitär. **~ napkin** *n* (*Amer*), **~ towel** *n* [Damen]binde *f*
sanitation *n* Kanalisation und Abfallbeseitigung *pl*
sanity *n* [gesunder] Verstand *m*
sank *see* **sink**
sap *n* (*Bot*) Saft *m* ● *vt* (*pt/pp* **sapped**) schwächen
sarcas|m *n* Sarkasmus *m*. **~tic** *a*, **-ally** *adv* sarkastisch
sardine *n* Sardine *f*
sash *n* Schärpe *f*
sat *see* **sit**
satchel *n* Ranzen *m*
satellite *n* Satellit *m*. **~ television** *n* Satellitenfernsehen *nt*
satin *n* Satin *m*
satire *n* Satire *f*
satirical *a*, **-ly** *adv* satirisch
satir|ist *n* Satiriker(in) *m*(*f*)
satisfaction *n* Befriedigung *f*; **to my ~** zu meiner Zufriedenheit
satisfactory *a*, **-ily** *adv* zufrieden stellend
satisfy *vt* (*pp/pp* **-ied**) befriedigen; zufrieden stellen <*customer*>; (*convince*) überzeugen; **be ~ied** zufrieden sein. **~ing** *a* befriedigend; <*meal*> sättigend
saturate *vt* durchtränken; (*Chem & fig*) sättigen
Saturday *n* Samstag *m*
sauce *n* Soße *f*; (*cheek*) Frechheit *f*. **~pan** *n* Kochtopf *m*
saucer *n* Untertasse *f*
saucy *a* (**-ier, -iest**) frech
Saudi Arabia *n* Saudi-Arabien *n*
sauna *n* Sauna *f*
saunter *vi* schlendern
sausage *n* Wurst *f*
savage *a* wild; (*fierce*) scharf; (*brutal*) brutal ● *n* Wilde(r) *m/f*. **~ry** *n* Brutalität *f*
save *n* (*Sport*) Abwehr *f* ● *vt* retten (**from** vor + *dat*); (*keep*) aufheben; (*not waste*) sparen; (*collect*) sammeln; (*avoid*) ersparen; (*Sport*) verhindern <*goal*> ● *vi* **~ [up]** sparen
saver *n* Sparer *m*
saving *n* (*see* **save**) Rettung *f*; Sparen *nt*; Ersparnis *f*; **~s** *pl* (*money*) Ersparnisse *pl*
savour *n* Geschmack *m* ● *vt* auskosten. **~y** *a* würzig
saw[1] *see* **see**[1]
saw[2] *n* Säge *f* ● *vt/i* (*pt* **sawed**, *pp* **sawn** *or* **sawed**) sägen
saxophone *n* Saxophon *nt*
say *n* Mitspracherecht *nt*; **have one's ~** seine Meinung sagen ● *vt/i* (*pt/pp* **said**) sagen; sprechen <*prayer*>; **that is to ~** das heißt; **that goes without ~ing** das versteht sich von selbst. **~ing** *n* Redensart *f*
scab *n* Schorf *m*; (*pej*) Streikbrecher *m*
scaffolding *n* Gerüst *nt*
scald *vt* verbrühen
scale[1] *n* (*of fish*) Schuppe *f*
scale[2] *n* Skala *f*; (*Mus*) Tonleiter *f*; (*ratio*) Maßstab *m* ● *vt* (*climb*) erklettern. **~ down** *vt* verkleinern
scales *npl* (*for weighing*) Waage *f*
scalp *n* Kopfhaut *f*
scamper *vi* huschen
scan *n* (*Med*) Szintigramm *nt* ● *v* (*pt/pp* **scanned**) ● *vt* absuchen; (*quickly*) flüchtig ansehen; (*Med*) szintigraphisch untersuchen
scandal *n* Skandal *m*; (*gossip*) Skandalgeschichten *pl*. **~ize** *vt* schockieren. **~ous** *a* skandalös

Scandinavia *n* Skandinavien *nt*. **~n** *a* skandinavisch ● *n* Skandinavier(in) *m(f)*
scanner *n* Scanner *m*
scanty *a* (**-ier, -iest**), **-ily** *adv* spärlich; <*clothing*> knapp
scapegoat *n* Sündenbock *m*
scar *n* Narbe *f*
scarc|e *a* (**-r, -st**) knapp; **make oneself ~e** [!] sich aus dem Staub machen. **~ely** *adv* kaum. **~ity** *n* Knappheit *f*
scare *n* Schreck *m*; (*panic*) [allgemeine] Panik *f* ● *vt* Angst machen (+ *dat*); **be ~d** Angst haben (**of** vor + *dat*)
scarf *n* (*pl* **scarves**) Schal *m*; (*square*) Tuch *nt*
scarlet *a* scharlachrot
scary *a* unheimlich
scathing *a* bissig
scatter *vt* verstreuen; (*disperse*) zerstreuen ● *vi* sich zerstreuen. **~ed** *a* verstreut; <*showers*> vereinzelt
scatty *a* (**-ier, -iest**) [!] verrückt
scene *n* Szene *f*; (*sight*) Anblick *m*; (*place of event*) Schauplatz *m*; **behind the ~s** hinter den Kulissen
scenery *n* Landschaft *f*; (*Theat*) Szenerie *f*
scenic *a* landschaftlich schön
scent *n* Duft *m*; (*trail*) Fährte *f*; (*perfume*) Parfüm *nt*. **~ed** *a* parfümiert
sceptic|al *a*, **-ly** *adv* skeptisch. **~ism** *n* Skepsis *f*
schedule *n* Programm *nt*; (*of work*) Zeitplan *m*; (*timetable*) Fahrplan *m*; **behind ~** im Rückstand; **according to ~** planmäßig ● *vt* planen
scheme *n* Programm *nt*; (*plan*) Plan *m*; (*plot*) Komplott *nt* ● *vi* Ränke schmieden
schizophrenic *a* schizophren
scholar *n* Gelehrte(r) *m/f*. **~ly** *a* gelehrt. **~ship** *n* Gelehrtheit *f*; (*grant*) Stipendium *nt*
school *n* Schule *f*; (*Univ*) Fakultät *f* ● *vt* schulen
school: ~boy *n* Schüler *m*. **~girl** *n* Schülerin *f*. **~ing** *n* Schulbildung *f*. **~master** *n* Lehrer *m*. **~mistress** *n* Lehrerin *f*. **~-teacher** *n* Lehrer(in) *m(f)*
scien|ce *n* Wissenschaft *f*. **~tific** *a* wissenschaftlich. **~tist** *n* Wissenschaftler *m*
scissors *npl* Schere *f*; **a pair of ~** eine Schere
scoff[1] *vi* **~ at** spotten über (+ *acc*)
scoff[2] *vt* [!] verschlingen
scold *vt* ausschimpfen
scoop *n* Schaufel *f*; (*Culin*) Portionierer *m*; (*Journ*) Exklusivmeldung *f* ● *vt* **~ out** aushöhlen; (*remove*) auslöffeln
scooter *n* Roller *m*
scope *n* Bereich *m*; (*opportunity*) Möglichkeiten *pl*
scorch *vt* versengen. **~ing** *a* glühend heiß
score *n* [Spiel]stand *m*; (*individual*) Punktzahl *f*; (*Mus*) Partitur *f*; (*Cinema*) Filmmusik *f*; **on that ~** was das betrifft ● *vt* erzielen; schießen <*goal*>; (*cut*) einritzen ● *vi* Punkte erzielen; (*Sport*) ein Tor schießen; (*keep score*) Punkte zählen. **~r** *n* Punktezähler *m*; (*of goals*) Torschütze *m*
scorn *n* Verachtung *f* ● *vt* verachten. **~ful** *a*, **-ly** *adv* verächtlich
Scot *n* Schotte *m*/Schottin *f*
Scotch *a* schottisch ● *n* (*whisky*) Scotch *m*
Scot|land *n* Schottland *nt*. **~s, ~tish** *a* schottisch
scoundrel *n* Schurke *m*
scour *vt* (*search*) absuchen; (*clean*) scheuern

S

scout *n* (*Mil*) Kundschafter *m*; **[Boy] S~** Pfadfinder *m*

scowl *n* böser Gesichtsausdruck *m* ● *vi* ein böses Gesicht machen

scram *vi* [!] abhauen

scramble *n* Gerangel *nt* ● *vi* klettern; **~ for** sich drängen nach. **~d egg[s]** *n[pl]* Rührei *nt*

scrap[1] *n* ([!] *fight*) Rauferei *f* ● *vi* sich raufen

scrap[2] *n* Stückchen *nt*; (*metal*) Schrott *m*; **~s** *pl* Reste; **not a ~** kein bisschen ● *vt* (*pt/pp* **scrapped**) aufgeben

scrapbook *n* Sammelalbum *nt*

scrape *vt* schaben; (*clean*) abkratzen; (*damage*) [ver]schrammen. **~ through** *vi* gerade noch durchkommen. **~ together** *vt* zusammenkriegen

scrappy *a* lückenhaft

scrapyard *n* Schrottplatz *m*

scratch *n* Kratzer *m*; **start from ~** von vorne anfangen; **not be up to ~** zu wünschen übrig lassen ● *vt/i* kratzen; (*damage*) zerkratzen

scrawl *n* Gekrakel *nt* ● *vt/i* krakeln

scream *n* Schrei *m* ● *vt/i* schreien

screech *n* Kreischen *nt* ● *vt/i* kreischen

screen *n* Schirm *m*; (*Cinema*) Leinwand *f*; (*TV*) Bildschirm *m* ● *vt* schützen; (*conceal*) verdecken; vorführen <*film*>; (*examine*) überprüfen; (*Med*) untersuchen

screw *n* Schraube *f* ● *vt* schrauben. **~ up** *vt* festschrauben; (*crumple*) zusammenknüllen; zusammenkneifen <*eyes*>; ([✖] *bungle*) vermasseln

screwdriver *n* Schraubenzieher *m*

scribble *n* Gekritzel *nt* ● *vt/i* kritzeln

script *n* Schrift *f*; (*of speech, play*) Text *m*; (*Radio, TV*) Skript *nt*; (*of film*) Drehbuch *nt*

scroll *n* Rolle *f* ● *vt* **~ up/down** nach oben/unten rollen. **~ bar** *n* Rollbalken *m*

scrounge *vt/i* schnorren. **~r** *n* Schnorrer *m*

scrub *vt/i* (*pt/pp* **scrubbed**) schrubben

scruff *n* **by the ~ of the neck** beim Genick

scruffy *a* (**-ier, -iest**) vergammelt

scrum *n* Gedränge *nt*

scruple *n* Skrupel *m*

scrupulous *a*, **-ly** *adv* gewissenhaft

scuffle *n* Handgemenge *nt*

sculpt|or *n* Bildhauer(in) *m(f)*. **~ure** *n* Bildhauerei *f*; (*piece of work*) Skulptur *f*, Plastik *f*

scum *n* Schmutzschicht *f*; (*people*) Abschaum *m*

scurry *vi* (*pt/pp* **-ied**) huschen

scuttle[1] *vt* versenken <*ship*>

scuttle[2] *vi* schnell krabbeln

sea *n* Meer *nt*, See *f*; **at ~** auf See; **by ~** mit dem Schiff. **~food** *n* Meeresfrüchte *pl*. **~gull** *n* Möwe *f*

seal[1] *n* (*Zool*) Seehund *m*

seal[2] *n* Siegel *nt* ● *vt* versiegeln; (*fig*) besiegeln. **~ off** *vt* abriegeln

sea-level *n* Meeresspiegel *m*

seam *n* Naht *f*; (*of coal*) Flöz *nt*

seaman *n* Seemann *m*; (*sailor*) Matrose *m*

seance *n* spiritistische Sitzung *f*

search *n* Suche *f*; (*official*) Durchsuchung *f* ● *vt* durchsuchen; absuchen <*area*> ● *vi* suchen (**for** nach). **~ engine** *n* Suchmaschine *f*. **~ing** *a* prüfend, forschend **~light** *n* [Such]scheinwerfer *m*. **~-party** *n* Suchmannschaft *f*

sea: ~sick *a* seekrank. **~side** *n* **at/to the ~side** am/ans Meer

season *n* Jahreszeit *f*; (*social,*

tourist, sporting) Saison *f* ● *vt* (*flavour*) würzen. **~al** *a* Saison-. **~ing** *n* Gewürze *pl*

season ticket *n* Dauerkarte *f*

seat *n* Sitz *m*; (*place*) Sitzplatz *m*; (*bottom*) Hintern *m*; **take a ~** Platz nehmen ● *vt* setzen; (*have seats for*) Sitzplätze bieten (+ *dat*); **remain ~ed** sitzen bleiben. **~-belt** *n* Sicherheitsgurt *m*; **fasten one's ~-belt** sich anschnallen

sea: ~weed *n* [See]tang *m*. **~worthy** *a* seetüchtig

seclu|ded *a* abgelegen. **~sion** *n* Zurückgezogenheit *f*

second *a* zweite(r,s); **on ~ thoughts** nach weiterer Überlegung ● *n* Sekunde *f*; (*Sport*) Sekundant *m*; **~s** *pl* (*goods*) Waren zweiter Wahl ● *adv* (*in race*) an zweiter Stelle ● *vt* unterstützen <*proposal*>

secondary *a* zweitrangig; (*Phys*) Sekundär-. **~ school** *n* höhere Schule *f*

second: ~-best *a* zweitbeste(r,s). **~ class** *adv* <*travel, send*> zweiter Klasse. **~-class** *a* zweitklassig

second hand *n* (*on clock*) Sekundenzeiger *m*

second-hand *a* gebraucht ● *adv* aus zweiter Hand

secondly *adv* zweitens

second-rate *a* zweitklassig

secrecy *n* Heimlichkeit *f*

secret *a* geheim; <*agent, police*> Geheim-; <*drinker, lover*> heimlich ● *n* Geheimnis *nt*

secretarial *a* Sekretärinnen-; <*work, staff*> Sekretariats-

secretary *n* Sekretär(in) *m*(*f*)

secretive *a* geheimtuerisch

secretly *adv* heimlich

sect *n* Sekte *f*

section *n* Teil *m*; (*of text*) Abschnitt *m*; (*of firm*) Abteilung *f*; (*of organization*) Sektion *f*

sector *n* Sektor *m*

secular *a* weltlich

secure *a*, **-ly** *adv* sicher; (*firm*) fest; (*emotionally*) geborgen ● *vt* sichern; (*fasten*) festmachen; (*obtain*) sich (*dat*) sichern

securit|y *n* Sicherheit *f*; (*emotional*) Geborgenheit *f*; **~ies** *pl* Wertpapiere *pl*

sedan *n* (*Amer*) Limousine *f*

sedate *a*, **-ly** *adv* gesetzt

sedative *a* beruhigend ● *n* Beruhigungsmittel *nt*

sediment *n* [Boden]satz *m*

seduce *vt* verführen

seduct|ion *n* Verführung *f*. **~ive** *a*, **-ly** *adv* verführerisch

see *v* (*pt* **saw**, *pp* **seen**) ● *vt* sehen; (*understand*) einsehen; (*imagine*) sich (*dat*) vorstellen; (*escort*) begleiten; **go and ~** nachsehen; (*visit*) besuchen; **~ you later!** bis nachher! **~ing that** da ● *vi* sehen; (*check*) nachsehen; **~ about** sich kümmern um. **~ off** *vt* verabschieden; (*chase away*) vertreiben. **~ through** *vt* (*fig*) durchschauen <*person*>

seed *n* Samen *m*; (*of grape*) Kern *m*; (*fig*) Saat *f*; (*Tennis*) gesetzter Spieler *m*; **go to ~** Samen bilden; (*fig*) herunterkommen

seedy *a* (**-ier, -iest**) schäbig; <*area*> heruntergekommen

seek *vt* (*pt/pp* **sought**) suchen

seem *vi* scheinen

seen *see* **see**[1]

seep *vi* sickern

seethe *vi* **~ with anger** vor Wut schäumen

see-through *a* durchsichtig

segment *n* Teil *m*; (*of worm*) Segment *nt*; (*of orange*) Spalte *f*

segregat|e *vt* trennen. **~ion** *n* Trennung *f*

seize *vt* ergreifen; (*Jur*) beschlagnahmen; **~ s.o. by the arm** jdn am Arm packen. **~ up** *vi* (*Techn*) sich festfressen

seldom *adv* selten

S

select *a* ausgewählt; (*exclusive*) exklusiv ● *vt* auswählen; aufstellen <*team*>. **~ion** *n* Auswahl *f*

self *n* (*pl* **selves**) Ich *nt*

self: ~-assurance *n* Selbstsicherheit *f*. **~-assured** *a* selbstsicher. **~-catering** *n* Selbstversorgung *f*. **~-centred** *a* egozentrisch. **~-confidence** *n* Selbstbewusstsein *nt*, Selbstvertrauen *nt*. **~-confident** *a* selbstbewusst. **~-conscious** *a* befangen. **~-contained** *a* <*flat*> abgeschlossen. **~-control** *n* Selbstbeherrschung *f*. **~-defence** *n* Selbstverteidigung *f*; (*Jur*) Notwehr *f*. **~-employed** selbstständig. **~-esteem** *n* Selbstachtung *f*. **~-evident** *a* offensichtlich. **~-indulgent** *a* maßlos. **~-interest** *n* Eigennutz *m*

self|ish *a*, **-ly** *adv* egoistisch, selbstsüchtig. **~less** *a*, **-ly** *adv* selbstlos

self: ~-pity *n* Selbstmitleid *nt*. **~-portrait** *n* Selbstporträt *nt*. **~-respect** *n* Selbstachtung *f*. **~-righteous** *a* selbstgerecht. **~-sacrifice** *n* Selbstaufopferung *f*. **~-satisfied** *a* selbstgefällig. **~-service** *n* Selbstbedienung *f* ● *attrib* Selbstbedienungs-. **~-sufficient** *a* selbstständig

sell *v* (*pt/pp* **sold**) ● *vt* verkaufen; **be sold out** ausverkauft sein ● *vi* sich verkaufen. **~ off** *vt* verkaufen

seller *n* Verkäufer *m*

Sellotape (P), *n* ≈ Tesafilm (P) *m*

sell-out *n* **be a ~** ausverkauft sein; ([!] *betrayal*) Verrat sein

selves *see* **self**

semester *n* (*Amer*) Semester *nt*

semi|breve *n* (*Mus*) ganze Note *f*. **~circle** *n* Halbkreis *m*. **~circular** *a* halbkreisförmig. **~colon** *n* Semikolon *nt*. **~-detached** *a* & *n* **~-detached [house]** Doppelhaushälfte *f*. **~-final** *n* Halbfinale *nt*

seminar *n* Seminar *nt*

senat|e *n* Senat *m*. **~or** *n* Senator *m*

send *vt/i* (*pt/pp* **sent**) schicken; **~ for** kommen lassen <*person*>; sich (*dat*) schicken lassen <*thing*>. **~-er** *n* Absender *m*. **~-off** *n* Verabschiedung *f*

senile *a* senil

senior *a* älter; (*in rank*) höher ● *n* Ältere(r) *m/f*; (*in rank*) Vorgesetzte(r) *m/f*. **~ citizen** *n* Senior(in) *m(f)*

seniority *n* höheres Alter *nt*; (*in rank*) höherer Rang *m*

sensation *n* Sensation *f*; (*feeling*) Gefühl *nt*. **~al** *a*, **-ly** *adv* sensationell

sense *n* Sinn *m*; (*feeling*) Gefühl *nt*; (*common ~*) Verstand *m*; **make ~** Sinn ergeben ● *vt* spüren. **~less** *a*, **-ly** *adv* sinnlos; (*unconscious*) bewusstlos

sensible *a*, **-bly** *adv* vernünftig; <*suitable*> zweckmäßig

sensitiv|e *a*, **-ly** *adv* empfindlich; (*understanding*) einfühlsam. **~ity** *n* Empfindlichkeit *f*

sensual *a* sinnlich. **-ity** *n* Sinnlichkeit *f*

sensuous *a* sinnlich

sent *see* **send**

sentence *n* Satz *m*; (*Jur*) Urteil *nt*; (*punishment*) Strafe *f* ● *vt* verurteilen

sentiment *n* Gefühl *nt*; (*opinion*) Meinung *f*; (*sentimentality*) Sentimentalität *f* **~al** *a* sentimental. **~ality** *n* Sentimentalität *f*

sentry *n* Wache *f*

separable *a* trennbar

separate[1] *a*, **-ly** *adv* getrennt, separat

separat|e[2] *vt* trennen ● *vi* sich trennen. **~ion** *n* Trennung *f*

September *n* September *m*

septic *a* vereitert

sequel *n* Folge *f*; (*fig*) Nachspiel *nt*

sequence *n* Reihenfolge *f*

serenade *n* Ständchen *nt* ● *vt* **~ s.o.** jdm ein Ständchen bringen

seren|e *a*, **-ly** *adv* gelassen. **~ity** *n* Gelassenheit *f*

sergeant *n* (*Mil*) Feldwebel *m*; (*in police*) Polizeimeister *m*

serial *n* Fortsetzungsgeschichte *f*; (*Radio, TV*) Serie *f*. **~ize** *vt* in Fortsetzungen veröffentlichen/(*Radio, TV*) senden

series *n inv* Serie *f*

serious *a*, **-ly** *adv* ernst; <*illness, error*> schwer. **~ness** *n* Ernst *m*

sermon *n* Predigt *f*

servant *n* Diener(in) *m*(*f*)

serve *n* (*Tennis*) Aufschlag *m* ● *vt* dienen (+ *dat*); bedienen <*customer, guest*>; servieren <*food*>; verbüßen <*sentence*>. **it ~s you right!** das geschieht dir recht! ● *vi* dienen; (*Tennis*) aufschlagen

service *n* Dienst *m*; (*Relig*) Gottesdienst *m*; (*in shop, restaurant*) Bedienung *f*; (*transport*) Verbindung *f*; (*maintenance*) Wartung *f*; (*set of crockery*) Service *nt*; (*Tennis*) Aufschlag *m*; **~s** *pl* Dienstleistungen *pl*; (*on motorway*) Tankstelle und Raststätte *f*; **in the ~s** beim Militär; **out of/in ~** <*machine:*> außer/in Betrieb ● *vt* (*Techn*) warten

service: ~ area *n* Tankstelle und Raststätte *f*. **~ charge** *n* Bedienungszuschlag *m*. **~man** *n* Soldat *m*. **~ station** *n* Tankstelle *f*

serviette *n* Serviette *f*

servile *a* unterwürfig

session *n* Sitzung *f*

set *n* Satz *m*; (*of crockery*) Service *nt*; (*of cutlery*) Garnitur *f*; (*TV, Radio*) Apparat *m*; (*Math*) Menge *f*; (*Theat*) Bühnenbild *nt*; (*Cinema*) Szenenaufbau *m*; (*of people*) Kreis *m* ● *a* (*ready*) fertig, bereit; (*rigid*) fest; <*book*> vorgeschrieben; **be ~ on doing sth** entschlossen sein, etw zu tun ● *v* (*pt/pp* **set**, *pres p* **setting**) ● *vt* setzen; (*adjust*) einstellen; stellen <*task, alarm clock*>; festsetzen, festlegen <*date, limit*>; aufgeben <*homework*>; zusammenstellen <*questions*>; [ein]fassen <*gem*>; einrichten <*bone*>; legen <*hair*>; decken <*table*> ● *vi* <*sun:*> untergehen; (*become hard*) fest werden. **~ back** *vt* zurücksetzen; (*hold up*) aufhalten; (! *cost*) kosten. **~ off** *vi* losgehen; (*in vehicle*) losfahren ● *vt* auslösen <*alarm*>; explodieren lassen <*bomb*>. **~ out** *vi* losgehen; (*in vehicle*) losfahren ● *vt* auslegen; (*state*) darlegen. **~ up** *vt* aufbauen; (*fig*) gründen

settee *n* Sofa *nt*, Couch *f*

setting *n* Rahmen *m*; (*surroundings*) Umgebung *f*

settle *vt* (*decide*) entscheiden; (*agree*) regeln; (*fix*) festsetzen; (*calm*) beruhigen; (*pay*) bezahlen ● *vi* sich niederlassen; <*snow, dust:*> liegen bleiben; (*subside*) sich senken; <*sediment:*> sich absetzen. **~ down** *vi* sich beruhigen; (*permanently*) sesshaft werden. **~ up** *vi* abrechnen

settlement *n* (*see* **settle**) Entscheidung *f*; Regelung *f*; Bezahlung *f*; (*Jur*) Vergleich *m*; (*colony*) Siedlung *f*

settler *n* Siedler *m*

set-up *n* System *nt*

seven *a* sieben. **~teen** *a* siebzehn. **~teenth** *a* siebzehnte(r,s)

S

seventh *a* siebte(r,s)
seventieth *a* siebzigste(r,s)
seventy *a* siebzig
several *a & pron* mehrere, einige
sever|e *a* (**-r, -st,**) **-ly** *adv* streng; <*pain*> stark; <*illness*> schwer. **~ity** *n* Strenge *f*; Schwere *f*
sew *vt/i* (*pt* **sewed**, *pp* **sewn** *or* **sewed**) nähen
sewage *n* Abwasser *nt*
sewer *n* Abwasserkanal *m*
sewing *n* Nähen *nt*; (*work*) Näharbeit *f*. **~ machine** *n* Nähmaschine *f*
sewn *see* **sew**
sex *n* Geschlecht *nt*; (*sexuality, intercourse*) Sex *m*. **~ist** *a* sexistisch
sexual *a*, **-ly** *adv* sexuell. **~ intercourse** *n* Geschlechtsverkehr *m*
sexuality *n* Sexualität *f*
sexy *a* (**-ier, -iest**) sexy
shabby *a* (**-ier, -iest**), **-ily** *adv* schäbig
shack *n* Hütte *f*
shade *n* Schatten *m*; (*of colour*) [Farb]ton *m*; (*for lamp*) [Lampen]schirm *m*; (*Amer: window-blind*) Jalousie *f* ● *vt* beschatten
shadow *n* Schatten *m* ● *vt* (*follow*) beschatten
shady *a* (**-ier, -iest**) schattig; (! *disreputable*) zwielichtig
shaft *n* Schaft *m*; (*Techn*) Welle *f*; (*of light*) Strahl *m*; (*of lift*) Schacht *m*
shaggy *a* (**-ier, -iest**) zottig
shake *n* Schütteln *nt* ● *v* (*pt* **shook**, *pp* **shaken**) ● *vt* schütteln; (*shock*) erschüttern; **~ hands with s.o.** jdm die Hand geben ● *vi* wackeln; (*tremble*) zittern. **~ off** *vt* abschütteln
shaky *a* (**-ier, -iest**) wackelig; <*hand, voice*> zittrig
shall *v aux* **we ~ see** wir werden sehen; **what ~ I do?** was soll ich machen?
shallow *a* (**-er, -est**) seicht; <*dish*> flach; (*fig*) oberflächlich
sham *a* unecht ● *n* Heuchelei *f* ● *vt* (*pt/pp* **shammed**) vortäuschen
shambles *n* Durcheinander *nt*
shame *n* Scham *f*; (*disgrace*) Schande *f*; **be a ~** schade sein; **what a ~!** wie schade!
shame|ful *a*, **-ly** *adv* schändlich. **~less** *a*, **-ly** *adv* schamlos
shampoo *n* Shampoo *nt* ● *vt* schamponieren
shan't = **shall not**
shape *n* Form *f*; (*figure*) Gestalt *f* ● *vt* formen (**into** zu). **~less** *a* formlos; <*clothing*> unförmig
share *n* [An]teil *m*; (*Comm*) Aktie *f* ● *vt/i* teilen. **~holder** *n* Aktionär(in) *m*(*f*)
shark *n* Hai[fisch] *m*
sharp *a* (**-er, -est**), **-ly** *adv* scharf; (*pointed*) spitz; (*severe*) heftig; (*sudden*) steil; (*alert*) clever; (*unscrupulous*) gerissen ● *adv* scharf; (*Mus*) zu hoch; **at six o'clock ~** Punkt sechs Uhr ● *n* (*Mus*) Kreuz *nt*. **~en** *vt* schärfen; [an]spitzen <*pencil*>
shatter *vt* zertrümmern; (*fig*) zerstören; **~ed** <*person:*> erschüttert; (! *exhausted*) kaputt ● *vi* zersplittern
shave *n* Rasur *f*; **have a ~** sich rasieren ● *vt* rasieren ● *vi* sich rasieren. **~r** *n* Rasierapparat *m*
shawl *n* Schultertuch *nt*
she *pron* sie
shears *npl* [große] Schere *f*
shed[1] *n* Schuppen *m*
shed[2] *vt* (*pt/pp* **shed**, *pres p* **shedding**) verlieren; vergießen <*blood, tears*>; **~ light on** Licht bringen in (+ *acc*)
sheep *n inv* Schaf *nt*. **~-dog** *n* Hütehund *m*

sheepish *a*, **-ly** *adv* verlegen

sheer *a* rein; (*steep*) steil; (*transparent*) hauchdünn

sheet *n* Laken *nt*, Betttuch *nt*; (*of paper*) Blatt *nt*; (*of glass, metal*) Platte *f*

shelf *n* (*pl* **shelves**) Brett *nt*, Bord *nt*; (*set of shelves*) Regal *nt*

shell *n* Schale *f*; (*of snail*) Haus *nt*; (*of tortoise*) Panzer *m*; (*on beach*) Muschel *f*; (*Mil*) Granate *f* ● *vt* pellen; enthülsen <*peas*>; (*Mil*) [mit Granaten] beschießen. **~ out** *vi* [!] blechen

shellfish *n inv* Schalentiere *pl*; (*Culin*) Meeresfrüchte *pl*

shelter *n* Schutz *m*; (*air-raid* **~**) Luftschutzraum *m* ● *vt* schützen (**from** vor + *dat*) ● *vi* sich unterstellen. **~ed** *a* geschützt; <*life*> behütet

shelve *vt* auf Eis legen; (*abandon*) aufgeben

shelving *n* (*shelves*) Regale *pl*

shepherd *n* Schäfer *m* ● *vt* führen

sherry *n* Sherry *m*

shield *n* Schild *m*; (*for eyes*) Schirm *m*; (*Techn & fig*) Schutz *m* ● *vt* schützen (**from** vor + *dat*)

shift *n* Verschiebung *f*; (*at work*) Schicht *f* ● *vt* rücken; (*take away*) wegnehmen; (*rearrange*) umstellen; schieben <*blame*> (**on to** auf + *acc*) ● *vi* sich verschieben; ([!] *rush*) rasen

shifty *a* (**-ier, -iest**) (*pej*) verschlagen

shimmer *n* Schimmer *m* ● *vi* schimmern

shin *n* Schienbein *nt*

shine *n* Glanz *m* ● *v* (*pt/pp* **shone**) ● *vi* leuchten; (*reflect light*) glänzen; <*sun:*> scheinen ● *vt* **~ a light on** beleuchten

shingle *n* (*pebbles*) Kiesel *pl*

shiny *a* (**-ier, -iest**) glänzend

ship *n* Schiff *nt* ● *vt* (*pt/pp* **shipped**) verschiffen

ship: ~building *n* Schiffbau *m*. **~ment** *n* Sendung *f*. **~per** *n* Spediteur *m*. **~ping** *n* Versand *m*; (*traffic*) Schifffahrt *f*. **~shape** *a & adv* in Ordnung. **~wreck** *n* Schiffbruch *m*. **~wrecked** *a* schiffbrüchig. **~yard** *n* Werft *f*

shirt *n* [Ober]hemd *nt*; (*for woman*) Hemdbluse *f*

shit *n* (*vulg*) Scheiße *f* ● *vi* (*pt/pp* **shit**) (*vulg*) scheißen

shiver *n* Schauder *m* ● *vi* zittern

shoal *n* (*fish*) Schwarm *m*

shock *n* Schock *m*; (*Electr*) Schlag *m*; (*impact*) Erschütterung *f* ● *vt* einen Schock versetzen (+ *dat*); (*scandalize*) schockieren. **~ing** *a* schockierend; ([!] *bad*) fürchterlich

shoddy *a* (**-ier, -iest**) minderwertig

shoe *n* Schuh *m*; (*of horse*) Hufeisen *nt* ● *vt* (*pt/pp* **shod**, *pres p* **shoeing**) beschlagen <*horse*>

shoe: ~horn *n* Schuhanzieher *m*. **~-lace** *n* Schnürsenkel *m*. **~-string** *n* **on a ~-string** [!] mit ganz wenig Geld

shone *see* **shine**

shoo *vt* scheuchen ● *int* sch!

shook *see* **shake**

shoot *n* (*Bot*) Trieb *m*; (*hunt*) Jagd *f* ● *v* (*pt/pp* **shot**) ● *vt* schießen; (*kill*) erschießen; drehen <*film*> ● *vi* schießen. **~ down** *vt* abschießen. **~ out** *vi* (*rush*) herausschießen. **~ up** *vi* (*grow*) in die Höhe schießen/<*prices:*> schnellen

shop *n* Laden *m*, Geschäft *nt*; (*workshop*) Werkstatt *f*; **talk ~** [!] fachsimpeln ● *vi* (*pt/pp* **shopped**, *pres p* **shopping**) einkaufen; **go ~ping** einkaufen gehen

shop: ~ assistant *n* Verkäufer(in) *m(f)*. **~keeper** *n* Ladenbesitzer(in) *m(f)*. **~-lifter** *n* Ladendieb *m*. **~-lifting** *n* Ladendiebstahl *m*

shopping *n* Einkaufen *nt*; (*articles*) Einkäufe *pl*; **do the ~** einkaufen. **~ bag** *n* Einkaufstasche *f*. **~ centre** *n* Einkaufszentrum *nt*. **~ trolley** *n* Einkaufswagen *m*

shop-window *n* Schaufenster *nt*

shore *n* Strand *m*; (*of lake*) Ufer *nt*

short *a* **(-er, -est)** kurz; <*person*> klein; (*curt*) schroff; **a ~ time ago** vor kurzem; **be ~ of ...** zu wenig ... haben; **be in ~ supply** knapp sein ● *adv* kurz; (*abruptly*) plötzlich; (*curtly*) kurz angebunden; **in ~** kurzum; **~ of** (*except*) außer; **go ~** Mangel leiden

shortage *n* Mangel *m* (**of** an + *dat*); (*scarcity*) Knappheit *f*

short: ~bread *n* ≈ Mürbekekse *pl*. **~ circuit** *n* Kurzschluss *m*. **~coming** *n* Fehler *m*. **~ cut** *n* Abkürzung *f*

shorten *vt* [ab]kürzen; kürzer machen <*garment*>

short: ~hand *n* Kurzschrift *f*, Stenographie *f*. **~list** *n* engere Auswahl *f*

short|ly *adv* in Kürze; **~ly before/after** kurz vorher/danach. **~ness** *n* Kürze *f*; (*of person*) Kleinheit *f*

shorts *npl* Shorts *pl*

short: ~-sighted *a* kurzsichtig. **~-sleeved** *a* kurzärmelig. **~ story** *n* Kurzgeschichte *f*. **~-tempered** *a* aufbrausend. **~-term** *a* kurzfristig. **~ wave** *n* Kurzwelle *f*

shot *see* **shoot** ● *n* Schuss *m*; (*pellets*) Schrot *m*; (*person*) Schütze *m*; (*Phot*) Aufnahme *f*; (*injection*) Spritze *f*; ([!] *attempt*) Versuch *m*; **like a ~** [!] sofort. **~gun** *n* Schrotflinte *f*. **~-put** *n* (*Sport*) Kugelstoßen *nt*

should *v aux* **you ~ go** du solltest gehen; **I ~ have seen him** ich hätte ihn sehen sollen; **I ~ like** ich möchte; **this ~ be enough** das müsste eigentlich reichen; **if he ~ be there** falls er da sein sollte

shoulder *n* Schulter *f* ● *vt* schultern; (*fig*) auf sich (*acc*) nehmen. **~-blade** *n* Schulterblatt *nt*

shout *n* Schrei *m* ● *vt/i* schreien. **~ down** *vt* niederschreien

shouting *n* Geschrei *nt*

shove *n* Stoß *m* ● *vt* stoßen; ([!] *put*) tun ● *vi* drängeln. **~ off** *vi* [!] abhauen

shovel *n* Schaufel *f* ● *vt* (*pt/pp* **shovelled**) schaufeln

show *n* (*display*) Pracht *f*; (*exhibition*) Ausstellung *f*, Schau *f*; (*performance*) Vorstellung *f*; (*Theat, TV*) Show *f*; **on ~** ausgestellt ● *v* (*pt* **showed**, *pp* **shown**) ● *vt* zeigen; (*put on display*) ausstellen; vorführen <*film*> ● *vi* sichtbar sein; <*film:*> gezeigt werden. **~ in** *vt* hereinführen. **~ off** *vi* [!] angeben ● *vt* vorführen; (*flaunt*) angeben mit. **~ up** *vi* [deutlich] zu sehen sein; ([!] *arrive*) auftauchen ● *vt* deutlich zeigen; ([!] *embarrass*) blamieren

shower *n* Dusche *f*; (*of rain*) Schauer *m*; **have a ~** duschen ● *vt* **~ with** überschütten mit ● *vi* duschen

show-jumping *n* Springreiten *nt*

shown *see* **show**

show: ~-off *n* Angeber(in) *m*(*f*). **~room** *n* Ausstellungsraum *m*

showy *a* protzig

shrank *see* **shrink**

shred *n* Fetzen *m*; (*fig*) Spur *f* ● *vt* (*pt/pp* **shredded**) zerkleinern; (*Culin*) schnitzeln. **~der** *n* Reißwolf *m*; (*Culin*) Schnitzelwerk *nt*

shrewd *a* **(-er, -est)**, **-ly** *adv* klug. **~ness** *n* Klugheit *f*

shriek *n* Schrei *m* ● *vt/i* schreien

shrill *a*, **-y** *adv* schrill

shrimp *n* Garnele *f*, Krabbe *f*

shrink *vi* (*pt* **shrank**, *pp* **shrunk**) schrumpfen; <*garment:*> einlaufen; (*draw back*) zurückschrecken (**from** vor + *dat*)

shrivel *vi* (*pt*/*pp* **shrivelled**) verschrumpeln

Shrove *n* **~Tuesday** Fastnachtsdienstag *m*

shrub *n* Strauch *m*

shrug *n* Achselzucken *nt* ● *vt*/*i* (*pt*/*pp* **shrugged**) ~ **[one's shoulders]** die Achseln zucken

shrunk *see* **shrink**

shudder *n* Schauder *m* ● *vi* schaudern; (*tremble*) zittern

shuffle *vi* schlurfen ● *vt* mischen <*cards*>

shun *vt* (*pt*/*pp* **shunned**) meiden

shunt *vt* rangieren

shut *v* (*pt*/*pp* **shut**, *pres p* **shutting**) ● *vt* zumachen, schließen ● *vi* sich schließen; <*shop:*> schließen, zumachen. ~ **down** *vt* schließen; stilllegen <*factory*> ● *vi* schließen. ~ **up** *vt* abschließen; (*lock in*) einsperren ● *vi* [!] den Mund halten

shutter *n* [Fenster]laden *m*; (*Phot*) Verschluss *m*

shuttle *n* (*Tex*) Schiffchen *nt*

shuttle service *n* Pendelverkehr *m*

shy *a* (**-er, -est**), **-ly** *adv* schüchtern; (*timid*) scheu. **~ness** *n* Schüchternheit *f*

siblings *npl* Geschwister *pl*

Sicily *n* Sizilien *nt*

sick *a* krank; <*humour*> makaber; **be** ~ (*vomit*) sich übergeben; **be ~ of sth** [!] etw satt haben; **I feel ~** mir ist schlecht

sick|ly *a* (**-ier, -iest**) kränklich. **~ness** *n* Krankheit *f*; (*vomiting*) Erbrechen *nt*

side *n* Seite *f*; **on the ~** (*as sideline*) nebenbei; **~ by ~** nebeneinander; (*fig*) Seite an Seite; **take ~s** Partei ergreifen (**with** für) ● *attrib* Seiten- ● *vi* ~ **with** Partei ergreifen für

side: ~board *n* Anrichte *f*. **~-effect** *n* Nebenwirkung *f*. **~lights** *npl* Standlicht *nt*. **~line** *n* Nebenbeschäftigung *f*. **~-show** *n* Nebenattraktion *f*. **~-step** *vt* ausweichen (+ *dat*). **~walk** *n* (*Amer*) Bürgersteig *m*. **~ways** *adv* seitwärts

siding *n* Abstellgleis *nt*

siege *n* Belagerung *f*; (*by police*) Umstellung *f*

sieve *n* Sieb *nt* ● *vt* sieben

sift *vt* sieben; (*fig*) durchsehen

sigh *n* Seufzer *m* ● *vi* seufzen

sight *n* Sicht *f*; (*faculty*) Sehvermögen *nt*; (*spectacle*) Anblick *m*; (*on gun*) Visier *nt*; **~s** *pl* Sehenswürdigkeiten *pl*; **at first ~** auf den ersten Blick; **lose ~ of** aus dem Auge verlieren; **know by ~** vom Sehen kennen ● *vt* sichten

sightseeing *n* **go ~** die Sehenswürdigkeiten besichtigen

sign *n* Zeichen *nt*; (*notice*) Schild *nt* ● *vt*/*i* unterschreiben; <*author, artist:*> signieren. ~ **on** *vi* (*as unemployed*) sich arbeitslos melden; (*Mil*) sich verpflichten

signal *n* Signal *nt* ● *vt*/*i* (*pt*/*pp* **signalled**) signalisieren; ~ **to s.o.** jdm ein Signal geben

signature *n* Unterschrift *f*; (*of artist*) Signatur *f*

significan|ce *n* Bedeutung *f*. **~t** *a*, **-ly** *adv* (*important*) bedeutend

signify *vt* (*pt*/*pp* **-ied**) bedeuten

signpost *n* Wegweiser *m*

silence *n* Stille *f*; (*of person*) Schweigen *nt* ● *vt* zum Schweigen bringen. **~r** *n* (*on gun*) Schalldämpfer *m*; (*Auto*) Auspufftopf *m*

silent *a*, **-ly** *adv* still; (*without speaking*) schweigend; **remain ~** schweigen

silhouette *n* Silhouette *f*; (*picture*) Schattenriss *m* ● *vt* **be ~d** sich als Silhouette abheben
silicon *n* Silizium *nt*
silk *n* Seide *f* ● *attrib* Seiden-
silky *a* (**-ier, -iest**) seidig
sill *n* Sims *m & nt*
silly *a* (**-ier, -iest**) dumm, albern
silver *a* silbern; <*coin, paper*> Silber- ● *n* Silber *nt*
silver: ~-plated *a* versilbert. **~ware** *n* Silber *nt*
similar *a*, **-ly** *adv* ähnlich. **~ity** *n* Ähnlichkeit *f*
simmer *vi* leise kochen, ziehen ● *vt* ziehen lassen
simple *a* (**-r, -st**) einfach; <*person*> einfältig. **~-minded** *a* einfältig
simplicity *n* Einfachheit *f*
simpli|fication *n* Vereinfachung *f*. **~fy** *vt* (*pt/pp* **-ied**) vereinfachen
simply *adv* einfach
simulate *vt* vortäuschen; (*Techn*) simulieren
simultaneous *a*, **-ly** *adv* gleichzeitig
sin *n* Sünde *f* ● *vi* (*pt/pp* **sinned**) sündigen

since
● *preposition*
····➤ seit (+ *dat*). **he's been living here since 1991** er wohnt* seit 1991 hier. **I had been waiting since 8 o'clock** ich wartete* [schon] seit 8 Uhr. **since seeing you** seit ich dich gesehen habe.
● *adverb*
····➤ seitdem. **I haven't spoken to her since** seitdem habe ich mit ihr nicht gesprochen. **the house has been empty ever since** das Haus steht seitdem leer. **he has since remarried** er hat danach wieder geheiratet. **long since** vor langer Zeit
● *conjunction*
····➤ seit. **since she has been living in Germany** seit sie in Deutschland wohnt*. **since they had been in London** seit sie in London waren*. **how long is it since he left?** wie lange ist es her, dass er weggezogen ist? **it's a year since he left** es ist ein Jahr her, dass er weggezogen ist
····➤ (*because*) da. **since she was ill, I had to do it** da sie krank war, musste ich es tun

! *Note the different tenses in German

sincere *a* aufrichtig; (*heartfelt*) herzlich. **~ly** *adv* aufrichtig; **Yours ~ly** Mit freundlichen Grüßen
sincerity *n* Aufrichtigkeit *f*
sinful *a* sündhaft
sing *vt/i* (*pt* **sang**, *pp* **sung**) singen
singe *vt* (*pres p* **singeing**) versengen
singer *n* Sänger(in) *m(f)*
single *a* einzeln; (*one only*) einzig; (*unmarried*) ledig; <*ticket*> einfach; <*room, bed*> Einzel- ● *n* (*ticket*) einfache Fahrkarte *f*; (*record*) Single *f*; **~s** *pl* (*Tennis*) Einzel *nt* ● *vt* **~ out** auswählen
single: ~-handed *a & adv* allein. **~ parent** *n* Alleinerziehende(r) *m/f*
singly *adv* einzeln
singular *a* eigenartig; (*Gram*) im Singular ● *n* Singular *m*
sinister *a* finster
sink *n* Spülbecken *nt* ● *v* (*pt* **sank**, *pp* **sunk**) ● *vi* sinken ● *vt* versenken <*ship*>; senken <*shaft*>. **~ in** *vi* einsinken; (**!** *be understood*) kapiert werden
sinner *n* Sünder(in) *m(f)*
sip *n* Schlückchen *nt* ● *vt* (*pt/pp* **sipped**) in kleinen Schlucken trinken

siphon *n* (*bottle*) Siphon *m*. **~ off** *vt* mit einem Saugheber ablassen

sir *n* mein Herr; **S~** (*title*) Sir; **Dear S~s** Sehr geehrte Herren

siren *n* Sirene *f*

sister *n* Schwester *f*; (*nurse*) Oberschwester *f*. **~-in-law** *n* Schwägerin *f*

sit *v* (*pt/pp* **sat**, *pres p* **sitting**) ● *vi* sitzen; (*sit down*) sich setzen; <*committee:*> tagen ● *vt* setzen; machen <*exam*>. **~ back** *vi* sich zurücklehnen. **~ down** *vi* sich setzen. **~ up** *vi* [aufrecht] sitzen; (*rise*) sich aufsetzen; (*not slouch*) gerade sitzen

site *n* Gelände *nt*; (*for camping*) Platz *m*; (*Archaeol*) Stätte *f*

sitting *n* Sitzung *f*; (*for meals*) Schub *m*

situat|e *vt* legen; **be ~ed** liegen. **~ion** *n* Lage *f*; (*circumstances*) Situation *f*; (*job*) Stelle *f*

six *a* sechs. **~teen** *a* sechzehn. **~teenth** *a* sechzehnte(r,s)

sixth *a* sechste(r,s)

sixtieth *a* sechzigste(r,s)

sixty *a* sechzig

size *n* Größe *f*

sizzle *vi* brutzeln

skate *n* Schlittschuh *m* ● *vi* Schlittschuh laufen. **~board** *n* Skateboard *nt* ● *vi* Skateboard fahren. **~boarding** *n* Skateboardfahren *nt*. **~r** *n* Eisläufer(in) *m(f)*

skating *n* Eislaufen *nt*. **~-rink** *n* Eisbahn *f*

skeleton *n* Skelett *nt*. **~ key** *n* Dietrich *m*

sketch *n* Skizze *f*; (*Theat*) Sketch *m* ● *vt* skizzieren

sketchy *a* (**-ier**, **-iest**), **-ily** *adv* skizzenhaft

ski *n* Ski *m* ● *vi* (*pt/pp* **skied**, *pres p* **skiing**) Ski fahren *or* laufen

skid *n* Schleudern *nt* ● *vi* (*pt/pp* **skidded**) schleudern

skier *n* Skiläufer(in) *m(f)*

skiing *n* Skilaufen *nt*

skilful *a*, **-ly** *adv* geschickt

skill *n* Geschick *nt*. **~ed** *a* geschickt; (*trained*) ausgebildet

skim *vt* (*pt/pp* **skimmed**) entrahmen <*milk*>

skimp *vt* sparen an (+ *dat*)

skimpy *a* (**-ier**, **-iest**) knapp

skin *n* Haut *f*; (*on fruit*) Schale *f* ● *vt* (*pt/pp* **skinned**) häuten; schälen <*fruit*>

skin: ~-deep *a* oberflächlich. **~-diving** *n* Sporttauchen *nt*

skinny *a* (**-ier**, **-iest**) dünn

skip¹ *n* Container *m*

skip² *n* Hüpfer *m* ● *v* (*pt/pp* **skipped**) *vi* hüpfen; (*with rope*) seilspringen ● *vt* überspringen

skipper *n* Kapitän *m*

skipping-rope *n* Sprungseil *nt*

skirmish *n* Gefecht *nt*

skirt *n* Rock *m* ● *vt* herumgehen um

skittle *n* Kegel *m*

skive *vi* [!] blaumachen

skull *n* Schädel *m*

sky *n* Himmel *m*. **~light** *n* Dachluke *f*. **~scraper** *n* Wolkenkratzer *m*

slab *n* Platte *f*; (*slice*) Scheibe *f*; (*of chocolate*) Tafel *f*

slack *a* (**-er**, **-est**) schlaff, locker; <*person*> nachlässig; (*Comm*) flau ● *vi* bummeln

slacken *vi* sich lockern; (*diminish*) nachlassen ● *vt* lockern; (*diminish*) verringern

slain *see* **slay**

slam *v* (*pt/pp* **slammed**) ● *vt* zuschlagen; (*put*) knallen [!]; ([!] *criticize*) verreißen ● *vi* zuschlagen

slander *n* Verleumdung *f* ● *vt* verleumden

slang *n* Slang *m*. **~y** *a* salopp

slant *n* Schräge *f*; **on the ~** schräg ● *vt* abschrägen; (*fig*) färben <*report*> ● *vi* sich neigen

slap *n* Schlag *m* ● *vt* (*pt*/*pp* **slapped**) schlagen; (*put*) knallen [!] ● *adv* direkt

slapdash *a* [!] schludrig

slash *n* Schlitz *m* ● *vt* aufschlitzen; [drastisch] reduzieren <*prices*>

slat *n* Latte *f*

slate *n* Schiefer *m* ● *vt* [!] heruntermachen; verreißen <*performance*>

slaughter *n* Schlachten *nt*; (*massacre*) Gemetzel *nt* ● *vt* schlachten; abschlachten <*men*>

Slav *a* slawisch ● *n* Slawe *m*/ Slawin *f*

slave *n* Sklave *m*/ Sklavin *f* ● *vi* ~ **[away]** schuften

slavery *n* Sklaverei *f*

slay *vt* (*pt* **slew**, *pp* **slain**) ermorden

sledge *n* Schlitten *m*

sleek *a* (**-er, -est**) seidig; (*well-fed*) wohlgenährt

sleep *n* Schlaf *m*; **go to ~** einschlafen; **put to ~** einschläfern ● *v* (*pt*/*pp* **slept**) ● *vi* schlafen ● *vt* (*accommodate*) Unterkunft bieten für. **~er** *n* Schläfer(in) *m(f)*; (*Rail*) Schlafwagen *m*; (*on track*) Schwelle *f*

sleeping: ~-bag *n* Schlafsack *m*. **~-pill** *n* Schlaftablette *f*

sleep: ~less *a* schlaflos. **~-walking** *n* Schlafwandeln *nt*

sleepy *a* (**-ier, -iest**), **-ily** *adv* schläfrig

sleet *n* Schneeregen *m*

sleeve *n* Ärmel *m*; (*for record*) Hülle *f*. **~less** *a* ärmellos

sleigh *n* [Pferde]schlitten *m*

slender *a* schlank; (*fig*) gering

slept *see* **sleep**

slew *see* **slay**

slice *n* Scheibe *f* ● *vt* in Scheiben schneiden

slick *a* clever

slid|e *n* Rutschbahn *f*; (*for hair*) Spange *f*; (*Phot*) Dia *nt* ● *v* (*pt*/*pp* **slid**) ● *vi* rutschen ● *vt* schieben. **~ing** *a* gleitend; <*door, seat*> Schiebe-

slight *a* (**-er, -est**), **-ly** *adv* leicht; <*importance*> gering; <*acquaintance*> flüchtig; (*slender*) schlank; **not in the ~est** nicht im Geringsten; **~ly better** ein bisschen besser ● *vt* kränken, beleidigen ● *n* Beleidigung *f*

slim *a* (**slimmer, slimmest**) schlank; <*volume*> schmal; (*fig*) gering ● *vi* eine Schlankheitskur machen

slim|e *n* Schleim *m*. **~y** *a* schleimig

sling *n* (*Med*) Schlinge *f* ● *vt* (*pt*/*pp* **slung**) [!] schmeißen

slip *n* (*mistake*) Fehler *m*, [!] Patzer *m*; (*petticoat*) Unterrock *m*; (*paper*) Zettel *m*; **give s.o. the ~** [!] jdm entwischen; **~ of the tongue** Versprecher *m* ● *v* (*pt*/*pp* **slipped**) ● *vi* rutschen; (*fall*) ausrutschen; (*go quickly*) schlüpfen ● *vt* schieben; **~ s.o.'s mind** jdm entfallen. **~ away** *vi* sich fortschleichen. **~ up** *vi* [!] einen Schnitzer machen

slipper *n* Hausschuh *m*

slippery *a* glitschig; <*surface*> glatt

slipshod *a* schludrig

slip-up *n* [!] Schnitzer *m*

slit *n* Schlitz *m* ● *vt* (*pt*/*pp* **slit**) aufschlitzen

slither *vi* rutschen

slog *n* **[hard] ~** Schinderei *f* ● *vi* (*pt*/*pp* **slogged**) schuften

slogan *n* Schlagwort *nt*; (*advertising*) Werbespruch *m*

slop|e *n* Hang *m*; (*inclination*) Neigung *f* ● *vi* sich neigen. **~ing** *a* schräg

sloppy *a* (**-ier, -iest**) schludrig; (*sentimental*) sentimental

slosh *vi* [!] schwappen

slot *n* Schlitz *m*; (*TV*) Sendezeit *f* ● *v* (*pt*/*pp* **slotted**) ● *vt* einfügen ● *vi* sich einfügen (**in** in + *acc*)

slot-machine *n* Münzautomat *m*; (*for gambling*) Spielautomat *m*

slouch *vi* sich schlecht halten

slovenly *a* schlampig

slow *a* (**-er, -est**), **-ly** *adv* langsam; **be ~** <*clock:*> nachgehen; **in ~ motion** in Zeitlupe ● *adv* langsam ● *vt* verlangsamen ● *vi* **~ down, ~ up** langsamer werden. **~ness** *n* Langsamkeit *f*

sludge *n* Schlamm *m*

slug *n* Nacktschnecke *f*

sluggish *a*, **-ly** *adv* träge

sluice *n* Schleuse *f*

slum *n* Elendsviertel *nt*

slumber *n* Schlummer *m* ● *vi* schlummern

slump *n* Sturz *m* ● *vi* fallen; (*crumple*) zusammensacken; <*prices:*> stürzen; <*sales:*> zurückgehen

slung *see* **sling**

slur *vt* (*pt*/*pp* **slurred**) undeutlich sprechen

slurp *vt*/*i* schlürfen

slush *n* [Schnee]matsch *m*; (*fig*) Kitsch *m*

slut *n* Schlampe *f* [!]

sly *a* (**-er, -est**), **-ly** *adv* verschlagen ● *n* **on the ~** heimlich

smack *n* Schlag *m*, Klaps *m* ● *vt* schlagen ● *adv* [!] direkt

small *a* (**-er, -est**) klein ● *adv* **chop up ~** klein hacken ● *n* **~ of the back** Kreuz *nt*

small: ~ ads *npl* Kleinanzeigen *pl*. **~ change** *n* Kleingeld *nt*. **-pox** *n* Pocken *pl*. **~ talk** *n* leichte Konversation *f*

smart *a* (**-er, -est**), **-ly** *adv* schick; (*clever*) schlau, clever; (*brisk*) flott; (*Amer* [!]*: cheeky*) frech ● *vi* brennen

smarten *vt* **~ oneself up** mehr auf sein Äußeres achten

smash *n* Krach *m*; (*collision*) Zusammenstoß *m*; (*Tennis*) Schmetterball *m* ● *vt* zerschlagen; (*strike*) schlagen; (*Tennis*) schmettern ● *vi* zerschmettern; (*crash*) krachen (**into** gegen). **~ing** *a* [!] toll

smear *n* verschmierter Fleck *m*; (*Med*) Abstrich *m*; (*fig*) Verleumdung *f* ● *vt* schmieren; (*coat*) beschmieren (**with** mit); (*fig*) verleumden ● *vi* schmieren

smell *n* Geruch *m*; (*sense*) Geruchssinn *m* ● *v* (*pt*/*pp* **smelt** *or* **smelled**) ● *vt* riechen; (*sniff*) riechen an (+ *dat*) ● *vi* riechen (**of** nach)

smelly *a* (**-ier, -iest**) übel riechend

smelt *see* **smell**

smile *n* Lächeln *nt* ● *vi* lächeln; **~ at** anlächeln

smirk *vi* feixen

smith *n* Schmied *m*

smock *n* Kittel *m*

smog *n* Smog *m*

smoke *n* Rauch *m* ● *vt*/*i* rauchen; (*Culin*) räuchern. **~less** *a* rauchfrei; <*fuel*> rauchlos

smoker *n* Raucher *m*; (*Rail*) Raucherabteil *nt*

smoking *n* Rauchen *nt*; **'no ~'** 'Rauchen verboten'

smoky *a* (**-ier, -iest**) verraucht; <*taste*> rauchig

smooth *a* (**-er, -est**), **-ly** *adv* glatt ● *vt* glätten. **~ out** *vt* glatt streichen

smother *vt* ersticken; (*cover*) bedecken; (*suppress*) unterdrücken

smoulder *vi* schwelen

smudge *n* Fleck *m* ● *vt* verwischen ● *vi* schmieren

smug *a* (**smugger, smuggest**), **-ly** *adv* selbstgefällig

smuggl|e *vt* schmuggeln. **~er** *n* Schmuggler *m*. **~ing** *n* Schmuggel *m*

snack *n* Imbiss *m*. **~-bar** *n* Imbissstube *f*

snag *n* Schwierigkeit *f*, [!] Haken *m*

snail *n* Schnecke *f*; **at a ~'s pace** im Schneckentempo

snake *n* Schlange *f*

snap *n* Knacken *nt*; (*photo*) Schnappschuss *m* ● *attrib* <*decision*> plötzlich ● *v* (*pt/pp* **snapped**) ● *vi* [entzwei]brechen; **~ at** (*bite*) schnappen nach; (*speak sharply*) [scharf] anfahren ● *vt* zerbrechen; (*say*) fauchen; (*Phot*) knipsen. **~ up** *vt* wegschnappen

snappy *a* (**-ier, -iest**) (*smart*) flott; **make it ~!** ein bisschen schnell!

snapshot *n* Schnappschuss *m*

snare *n* Schlinge *f*

snarl *vi* [mit gefletschten Zähnen] knurren

snatch *n* (*fragment*) Fetzen *pl* ● *vt* schnappen; (*steal*) klauen; entführen <*child*>; **~ sth from s.o.** jdm etw entreißen

sneak *n* [!] Petze *f* ● *vi* schleichen; ([!] *tell tales*) petzen ● *vt* (*take*) mitgehen lassen ● *vi* **~ in/out** sich hinein-/hinausschleichen

sneakers *npl* (*Amer*) Turnschuhe *pl*

sneer *vi* höhnisch lächeln; (*mock*) spotten

sneeze *n* Niesen *nt* ● *vi* niesen

snide *a* [!] abfällig

sniff *vi* schnüffeln ● *vt* schnüffeln an (+ *dat*)

snigger *vi* [boshaft] kichern

snip *n* Schnitt *m* ● *vt/i* **~ [at]** schnippeln an (+ *dat*)

snippet *n* Schnipsel *m*; (*of information*) Bruchstück *nt*

snivel *vi* (*pt/pp* **snivelled**) flennen

snob *n* Snob *m*. **~bery** *n* Snobismus *m*. **~bish** *a* snobistisch

snoop *vi* [!] schnüffeln

snooty *a* [!] hochnäsig

snooze *n* Nickerchen *nt* ● *vi* dösen

snore *vi* schnarchen

snorkel *n* Schnorchel *m*

snort *vi* schnauben

snout *n* Schnauze *f*

snow *n* Schnee *m* ● *vi* schneien; **~ed under with** (*fig*) überhäuft mit

snow: ~ball *n* Schneeball *m*. **~-drift** *n* Schneewehe *f*. **~drop** *n* Schneeglöckchen *nt*. **~fall** *n* Schneefall *m*. **~flake** *n* Schneeflocke *f*. **~man** *n* Schneemann *m*. **~plough** *n* Schneepflug *m*

snub *n* Abfuhr *f* ● *vt* (*pt/pp* **snubbed**) brüskieren

snub-nosed *a* stupsnasig

snuffle *vi* schnüffeln

snug *a* (**snugger, snuggest**) behaglich, gemütlich

snuggle *vi* sich kuscheln (**up to** an + *acc*)

so *adv* so; **so am I** ich auch; **so I see** das sehe ich; **that is so** das stimmt; **so much the better** umso besser; **if so** wenn ja; **so as to** um zu; **so long!** [!] tschüs! ● *pron* **I hope so** hoffentlich; **I think so** ich glaube schon; **I'm afraid so** leider ja; **so saying/doing, he/she** ... indem er/sie das sagte/tat, ... ● *conj* (*therefore*) also; **so that** damit; **so what!** na und! **so you see** wie du siehst

soak *vt* nass machen; (*steep*) einweichen; ([!] *fleece*) schröpfen ● *vi* weichen; <*liquid:*> sickern. **~ up** *vt* aufsaugen

soaking *a & adv* **~ [wet]** patschnass [!]

soap *n* Seife *f*. **~ opera** *n* Seifenoper *f*. **~ powder** *n* Seifenpulver *nt*

soapy *a* (**-ier, -iest**) seifig

soar *vi* aufsteigen; <*prices:*> in die Höhe schnellen

sob *n* Schluchzer *m* ● *vi* (*pt/pp* **sobbed**) schluchzen

sober *a*, **-ly** *adv* nüchtern; (*serious*) ernst; <*colour*> gedeckt. **~ up** *vi* nüchtern werden

so-called *a* sogenannt

soccer *n* [!] Fußball *m*

sociable *a* gesellig

social *a* gesellschaftlich; (*Admin, Pol, Zool*) sozial

socialis|m *n* Sozialismus *m*. **~t** *a* sozialistisch ● *n* Sozialist *m*

socialize *vi* [gesellschaftlich] verkehren

socially *adv* gesellschaftlich; **know ~** privat kennen

social: ~ security *n* Sozialhilfe *f*. **~ worker** *n* Sozialarbeiter(in) *m(f)*

society *n* Gesellschaft *f*; (*club*) Verein *m*

sociolog|ist *n* Soziologe *m*. **~y** *n* Soziologie *f*

sock *n* Socke *f*; (*kneelength*) Kniestrumpf *m*

socket *n* (*of eye*) Augenhöhle *f*; (*of joint*) Gelenkpfanne *f*; (*wall plug*) Steckdose *f*

soda *n* Soda *nt*; (*Amer*) Limonade *f*. **~ water** *n* Sodawasser *nt*

sodden *a* durchnässt

sofa *n* Sofa *nt*. **~ bed** *n* Schlafcouch *f*

soft *a* (**-er, -est**), **-ly** *adv* weich; (*quiet*) leise; (*gentle*) sanft; ([!] *silly*) dumm. **~ drink** *n* alkoholfreies Getränk *nt*

soften *vt* weich machen; (*fig*) mildern ● *vi* weich werden

soft: ~ toy *n* Stofftier *nt*. **~ware** *n* Software *f*

soggy *a* (**-ier, -iest**) aufgeweicht

soil¹ *n* Erde *f*, Boden *m*

soil² *vt* verschmutzen

solar *a* Sonnen-

sold *see* **sell**

soldier *n* Soldat *m* ● *vi* **~ on** [unbeirrbar] weitermachen

sole¹ *n* Sohle *f*

sole² *n* (*fish*) Seezunge *f*

sole³ *a* einzig. **~ly** *adv* einzig und allein

solemn *a*, **-ly** *adv* feierlich; (*serious*) ernst

solicitor *n* Rechtsanwalt *m*/-anwältin *f*

solid *a* fest; (*sturdy*) stabil; (*not hollow, of same substance*) massiv; (*unanimous*) einstimmig; (*complete*) ganz

solidarity *n* Solidarität *f*

solidify *vi* (*pt/pp* **-ied**) fest werden

solitary *a* einsam; (*sole*) einzig

solitude *n* Einsamkeit *f*

solo *n* Solo *nt* ● *a* Solo-; <*flight*> Allein- ● *adv* solo. **~ist** *n* Solist(in) *m(f)*

solstice *n* Sonnenwende *f*

soluble *a* löslich

solution *n* Lösung *f*

solvable *a* lösbar

solve *vt* lösen

solvent *n* Lösungsmittel *nt*

sombre *a* dunkel; <*mood*> düster

some *a & pron* etwas; (*a little*) ein bisschen; (*with pl noun*) einige; (*a few*) ein paar; (*certain*) manche(r,s); (*one or the other*) [irgend]ein; **~ day** eines Tages; **I want ~** ich möchte etwas/ (*pl*) welche; **will you have ~ wine?** möchten Sie Wein? **do ~ shopping** einkaufen

some: ~body *pron & n* jemand; (*emphatic*) irgendjemand. **~how** *adv* irgendwie. **~one** *pron & n* = **somebody**

somersault *n* Purzelbaum *m* [!], (*Sport*) Salto *m*; **turn a ~** einen Purzelbaum schlagen/einen Salto springen

something *pron & adv* etwas; (*emphatic*) irgendetwas; **~ different** etwas anderes; **~ like this** so etwas [wie das]

some: ~time *adv* irgendwann ● *a* ehemalig. **~times** *adv* manchmal.

S

~what *adv* ziemlich. **~where** *adv* irgendwo; <*go*> irgendwohin

son *n* Sohn *m*

song *n* Lied *nt*. **~bird** *n* Singvogel *m*

son-in-law *n* (*pl* **~s-in-law**) Schwiegersohn *m*

soon *adv* (**-er, -est**) bald; (*quickly*) schnell; **too ~** zu früh; **as ~ as possible** so bald wie möglich; **~er or later** früher oder später; **no ~er had I arrived than ...** kaum war ich angekommen, da ...; **I would ~er stay** ich würde lieber bleiben

soot *n* Ruß *m*

sooth|e *vt* beruhigen; lindern <*pain*>. **~ing** *a*, **-ly** *adv* beruhigend; lindernd

sophisticated *a* weltgewandt; (*complex*) hoch entwickelt

sopping *a & adv* **~ [wet]** durchnässt

soppy *a* (**-ier, -iest**) [!] rührselig

soprano *n* Sopran *m*; (*woman*) Sopranistin *f*

sordid *a* schmutzig

sore *a* (**-r, -st**) wund; (*painful*) schmerzhaft; **have a ~ throat** Halsschmerzen haben ● *n* wunde Stelle *f*. **~ly** *adv* sehr

sorrow *n* Kummer *m*

sorry *a* (**-ier, -iest**) (*sad*) traurig; (*wretched*) erbärmlich; **I am ~** es tut mir Leid; **she is** *or* **feels ~ for him** er tut ihr Leid; **I am ~ to say** leider; **~!** Entschuldigung!

sort *n* Art *f*; (*brand*) Sorte *f*; **he's a good ~** [!] er ist in Ordnung ● *vt* sortieren. **~ out** *vt* sortieren; (*fig*) klären

sought *see* **seek**

soul *n* Seele *f*

sound[1] *a* (**-er, -est**) gesund; (*sensible*) vernünftig; (*secure*) solide; (*thorough*) gehörig ● *adv* **be ~ asleep** fest schlafen

sound[2] *n* (*strait*) Meerenge *f*

sound[3] *n* Laut *m*; (*noise*) Geräusch *nt*; (*Phys*) Schall *m*; (*Radio, TV*) Ton *m*; (*of bells, music*) Klang *m*; **I don't like the ~ of it** [!] das hört sich nicht gut an ● *vi* [er]tönen; (*seem*) sich anhören ● *vt* (*pronounce*) aussprechen; schlagen <*alarm*>; (*Med*) abhorchen <*chest*>

soundly *adv* solide; <*sleep*> fest; <*defeat*> vernichtend

soundproof *a* schalldicht

soup *n* Suppe *f*

sour *a* (**-er, -est**) sauer; (*bad-tempered*) griesgrämig, verdrießlich

source *n* Quelle *f*

south *n* Süden *m*; **to the ~ of** südlich von ● *a* Süd-, süd- ● *adv* nach Süden

south: S~ Africa *n* Südafrika *nt*. **S~ America** *n* Südamerika *nt*. **~-east** *n* Südosten *m*

southerly *a* südlich

southern *a* südlich

southward[s] *adv* nach Süden

souvenir *n* Andenken *nt*, Souvenir *nt*

Soviet *a* <*History*> sowjetisch; **~ Union** Sowjetunion *f*

sow[1] *n* Sau *f*

sow[2] *vt* (*pt* **sowed**, *pp* **sown** *or* **sowed**) säen

soya *n* **~ bean** Sojabohne *f*

spa *n* Heilbad *nt*

space *n* Raum *m*; (*gap*) Platz *m*; (*Astr*) Weltraum *m* ● *vt* **~ [out]** [in Abständen] verteilen

space: ~craft *n* Raumfahrzeug *nt*. **~ship** *n* Raumschiff *nt*

spacious *a* geräumig

spade *n* Spaten *m*; (*for child*) Schaufel *f*; **~s** *pl* (*Cards*) Pik *nt*

Spain *n* Spanien *nt*

span[1] *n* Spanne *f*; (*of arch*) Spannweite *f* ● *vt* (*pt/pp* **spanned**) überspannen; umspannen <*time*>

span[2] *see* **spick**

Span|iard *n* Spanier(in) *m*(*f*). **~ish** *a* spanisch ● *n* (*Lang*)

Spanisch *nt*; **the ~ish** *pl* die Spanier

spank *vt* verhauen

spanner *n* Schraubenschlüssel *m*

spare *a* (*surplus*) übrig; (*additional*) zusätzlich; <*seat, time*> frei; <*room*> Gäste-; <*bed, cup*> Extra- ● *n* (*part*) Ersatzteil *nt* ● *vt* ersparen; (*not hurt*) verschonen; (*do without*) entbehren; (*afford to give*) erübrigen. **~ wheel** *n* Reserverad *nt*

sparing *a*, **-ly** *adv* sparsam

spark *n* Funke *nt*. **~[ing]-plug** *n* (*Auto*) Zündkerze *f*

sparkl|e *n* Funkeln *nt* ● *vi* funkeln. **~ing** *a* funkelnd; <*wine*> Schaum-

sparrow *n* Spatz *m*

sparse *a* spärlich. **~ly** *adv* spärlich; <*populated*> dünn

spasm *n* Anfall *m*; (*cramp*) Krampf *m*. **~odic** *a*, **-ally** *adv* sporadisch

spat *see* spit[2]

spatter *vt* spritzen; **~ with** bespritzen mit

spawn *n* Laich *m* ● *vt* (*fig*) hervorbringen

speak *v* (*pt* **spoke**, *pp* **spoken**) ● *vi* sprechen (**to** mit) **~ing!** (*Teleph*) am Apparat! ● *vt* sprechen; sagen <*truth*>. **~ up** *vi* lauter sprechen; **~ up for oneself** seine Meinung äußern

speaker *n* Sprecher(in) *m(f)*; (*in public*) Redner(in) *m(f)*; (*loudspeaker*) Lautsprecher *m*

spear *n* Speer *m* ● *vt* aufspießen

spec *n* **on ~** [!] auf gut Glück

special *a* besondere(r,s), speziell. **~ist** *n* Spezialist *m*; (*Med*) Facharzt *m*/-ärztin *f*. **~ity** *n* Spezialität *f*

special|ize *vi* sich spezialisieren (**in** auf + *acc*). **~ly** *adv* speziell; (*particularly*) besonders

species *n* Art *f*

specific *a* bestimmt; (*precise*) genau; (*Phys*) spezifisch. **~ally** *adv* ausdrücklich

specification *n* & **~s** *pl* genaue Angaben *pl*

specify *vt* (*pt/pp* **-ied**) [genau] angeben

specimen *n* Exemplar *nt*; (*sample*) Probe *f*; (*of urine*) Urinprobe *f*

speck *n* Fleck *m*

speckled *a* gesprenkelt

spectacle *n* (*show*) Schauspiel *nt*; (*sight*) Anblick *m*. **~s** *npl* Brille *f*

spectacular *a* spektakulär

spectator *n* Zuschauer(in) *m(f)*

speculat|e *vi* spekulieren. **~ion** *n* Spekulation *f*. **~or** *n* Spekulant *m*

sped *see* **speed**

speech *n* Sprache *f*; (*address*) Rede *f*. **~less** *a* sprachlos

speed *n* Geschwindigkeit *f*; (*rapidity*) Schnelligkeit *f* ● *vi* (*pt/pp* **sped**) schnell fahren ● (*pt/pp* **speeded**) (*go too fast*) zu schnell fahren. **~ up** (*pt/pp* **speeded up**) ● *vt/i* beschleunigen

speed: ~boat *n* Rennboot *nt*. **~ camera** *n* Geschwindigkeitsüberwachungskamera *f*. **~ing** *n* Geschwindigkeitsüberschreitung *f*. **~ limit** *n* Geschwindigkeitsbeschränkung *f*

speedometer *n* Tachometer *m*

speedy *a* (**-ier, -iest**), **-ily** *adv* schnell

spell[1] *n* Weile *f*; (*of weather*) Periode *f*

spell[2] *v* (*pt/pp* **spelled** *or* **spelt**) ● *vt* schreiben; (*aloud*) buchstabieren; (*fig: mean*) bedeuten ● *vi* richtig schreiben; (*aloud*) buchstabieren. **~ out** *vt* buchstabieren; (*fig*) genau erklären

spell[3] *n* Zauber *m*; (*words*) Zauberspruch *m*. **~bound** *a* wie verzaubert

spell checker *n* Rechtschreibprogramm *nt*

spelling *n* (*of a word*) Schreibweise *f*; (*orthography*) Rechtschreibung *f*

spelt *see* **spell**[2]

spend *vt/i* (*pt/pp* **spent**) ausgeben; verbringen <*time*>

spent *see* **spend**

sperm *n* Samen *m*

sphere *n* Kugel *f*; (*fig*) Sphäre *f*

spice *n* Gewürz *nt*; (*fig*) Würze *f*

spicy *a* würzig, pikant

spider *n* Spinne *f*

spik|e *n* Spitze *f*; (*Bot, Zool*) Stachel *m*; (*on shoe*) Spike *m*. **~y** *a* stachelig

spill *v* (*pt/pp* **spilt** *or* **spilled**) ● *vt* verschütten ● *vi* überlaufen

spin *v* (*pt/pp* **spun**, *pres p* **spinning**) ● *vt* drehen; spinnen <*wool*>; schleudern <*washing*> ● *vi* sich drehen

spinach *n* Spinat *m*

spindl|e *n* Spindel *f*. **~y** *a* spindeldürr

spin-drier *n* Wäscheschleuder *f*

spine *n* Rückgrat *nt*; (*of book*) [Buch]rücken *m*; (*Bot, Zool*) Stachel *m*. **~less** *a* (*fig*) rückgratlos

spin-off *n* Nebenprodukt *nt*

spinster *n* ledige Frau *f*

spiral *a* spiralig ● *n* Spirale *f* ● *vi* (*pt/pp* **spiralled**) sich hochwinden. **~ staircase** *n* Wendeltreppe *f*

spire *n* Turmspitze *f*

spirit *n* Geist *m*; (*courage*) Mut *m*; **~s** *pl* (*alcohol*) Spirituosen *pl*; **in low ~s** niedergedrückt. **~ away** *vt* verschwinden lassen

spirited *a* lebhaft; (*courageous*) beherzt

spiritual *a* geistig; (*Relig*) geistlich

spit[1] *n* (*for meat*) [Brat]spieß *m*

spit[2] *n* Spucke *f* ● *vt/i* (*pt/pp* **spat**, *pres p* **spitting**) spucken; <*cat:*> fauchen; <*fat:*> spritzen; **it's ~ting with rain** es tröpfelt

spite *n* Boshaftigkeit *f*; **in ~ of** trotz (+ *gen*) ● *vt* ärgern. **~ful** *a*, **-ly** *adv* gehässig

splash *n* Platschen *nt*; ([!] *drop*) Schuss *m*; **~ of colour** Farbfleck *m* ● *vt* spritzen; **~ s.o. with sth** jdn mit etw bespritzen ● *vi* spritzen. **~ about** *vi* planschen

splendid *a* herrlich, großartig

splendour *n* Pracht *f*

splint *n* (*Med*) Schiene *f*

splinter *n* Splitter *m* ● *vi* zersplittern

split *n* Spaltung *f*; (*Pol*) Bruch *m*; (*tear*) Riss *m* ● *v* (*pt/pp* **split**, *pres p* **splitting**) ● *vt* spalten; (*share*) teilen; (*tear*) zerreißen ● *vi* sich spalten; (*tear*) zerreißen; **~ on s.o.** [!] jdn verpfeifen. **~ up** *vt* aufteilen ● *vi* <*couple:*> sich trennen

splutter *vi* prusten

spoil *n* **~s** *pl* Beute *f* ● *v* (*pt/pp* **spoilt** *or* **spoiled**) ● *vt* verderben; verwöhnen <*person*> ● *vi* verderben. **~sport** *n* Spielverderber *m*

spoke[1] *n* Speiche *f*

spoke[2], **spoken** *see* **speak**

spokesman *n* Sprecher *m*

sponge *n* Schwamm *m* ● *vt* abwaschen ● *vi* **~ on** schmarotzen bei. **~-cake** *n* Biskuitkuchen *m*

sponsor *n* Sponsor *m*; (*godparent*) Pate *m*/Patin *f* ● *vt* sponsern

spontaneous *a*, **-ly** *adv* spontan

spoof *n* [!] Parodie *f*

spooky *a* (**-ier, -iest**) [!] gespenstisch

spool *n* Spule *f*

spoon *n* Löffel *m* ● *vt* löffeln. **~ful** *n* Löffel *m*

sporadic *a*, **-ally** *adv* sporadisch

sport *n* Sport *m* ● *vt* [stolz] tragen. **~ing** *a* sportlich

sports: ~ car *n* Sportwagen *m*. **~ coat** *n*, **~ jacket** *n* Sakko *m*. **~man** *n* Sportler *m*. **~woman** *n* Sportlerin *f*

sporty *a* (**-ier, -iest**) sportlich

spot *n* Fleck *m*; (*place*) Stelle *f* (*dot*) Punkt *m*; (*drop*) Tropfen *m*; (*pimple*) Pickel *m*; **~s** *pl* (*rash*) Ausschlag *m*; **on the ~** auf der Stelle ● *vt* (*pt/pp* **spotted**) entdecken

spot: ~ check *n* Stichprobe *f*. **~less** *a* makellos; ([!] *very clean*) blitzsauber. **~light** *n* Scheinwerfer *m*; (*fig*) Rampenlicht *nt*

spotted *a* gepunktet

spouse *n* Gatte *m*/Gattin *f*

spout *n* Schnabel *m*, Tülle *f* ● *vi* schießen (**from** aus)

sprain *n* Verstauchung *f* ● *vt* verstauchen

sprang *see* **spring**[2]

sprawl *vi* sich ausstrecken

spray[1] *n* (*of flowers*) Strauß *m*

spray[2] *n* Sprühnebel *m*; (*from sea*) Gischt *m*; (*device*) Spritze *f*; (*container*) Sprühdose *f*; (*preparation*) Spray *nt* ● *vt* spritzen; (*with aerosol*) sprühen

spread *n* Verbreitung *f*; (*paste*) Aufstrich *m*; ([!] *feast*) Festessen *nt* ● *v* (*pt/pp* **spread**) ● *vt* ausbreiten; streichen <*butter, jam*>; bestreichen <*bread, surface*>; streuen <*sand, manure*>; verbreiten <*news, disease*>; verteilen <*payments*> ● *vi* sich ausbreiten. **~ out** *vt* ausbreiten; (*space out*) verteilen ● *vi* sich verteilen

spree *n* [!] **go on a shopping ~** groß einkaufen gehen

sprightly *a* (**-ier, -iest**) rüstig

spring[1] *n* Frühling *m* ● *attrib* Frühlings-

spring[2] *n* (*jump*) Sprung *m*; (*water*) Quelle *f*; (*device*) Feder *f*; (*elasticity*) Elastizität *f* ● *v* (*pt* **sprang**, *pp* **sprung**) ● *vi* springen; (*arise*) entspringen (**from** *dat*) ● *vt* **~ sth on s.o.** jdn mit etw überfallen

spring: ~-cleaning *n* Frühjahrsputz *m*. **~time** *n* Frühling *m*

sprinkl|e *vt* sprengen; (*scatter*) streuen; bestreuen <*surface*>. **~ing** *n* dünne Schicht *f*

sprint *n* Sprint *m* ● *vi* rennen; (*Sport*) sprinten. **~er** *n* Kurzstreckenläufer(in) *m*(*f*)

sprout *n* Trieb *m*; **[Brussels] ~s** *pl* Rosenkohl *m* ● *vi* sprießen

sprung *see* **spring**[2]

spud *n* [!] Kartoffel *f*

spun *see* **spin**

spur *n* Sporn *m*; (*stimulus*) Ansporn *m*; **on the ~ of the moment** ganz spontan ● *vt* (*pt/pp* **spurred**) **~ [on]** (*fig*) anspornen

spurn *vt* verschmähen

spurt *n* (*Sport*) Spurt *m*; **put on a ~** spurten ● *vi* spritzen

spy *n* Spion(in) *m*(*f*) ● *vi* spionieren; **~ on s.o.** jdm nachspionieren. ● *vt* ([!] *see*) sehen

spying *n* Spionage *f*

squabble *n* Zank *m* ● *vi* sich zanken

squad *n* Gruppe *f*; (*Sport*) Mannschaft *f*

squadron *n* (*Mil*) Geschwader *nt*

squalid *a*, **-ly** *adv* schmutzig

squall *n* Bö *f* ● *vi* brüllen

squalor *n* Schmutz *m*

squander *vt* vergeuden

square *a* quadratisch; <*metre, mile*> Quadrat-; <*meal*> anständig; **all ~** [!] quitt ● *n* Quadrat *nt*; (*area*) Platz *m*; (*on chessboard*) Feld *nt* ● *vt* (*settle*) klären; (*Math*) quadrieren

squash *n* Gedränge *nt*; (*drink*) Fruchtsaftgetränk *nt*; (*Sport*) Squash *nt* ● *vt* zerquetschen; (*suppress*) niederschlagen. **~y** *a* weich

squat *a* gedrungen ● *vi* (*pt/pp* **squatted**) hocken; **~ in a house** ein Haus besetzen. **~ter** *n* Hausbesetzer *m*

squawk *vi* krächzen

squeak *n* Quieken *nt*; (*of hinge, brakes*) Quietschen *nt* ● *vi* quieken; quietschen

squeal *n* Kreischen *nt* ● *vi* kreischen

squeamish *a* empfindlich

squeeze *n* Druck *m*; (*crush*) Gedränge *nt* ● *vt* drücken; (*to get juice*) ausdrücken; (*force*) zwängen

squiggle *n* Schnörkel *m*

squint *n* Schielen *nt* ● *vi* schielen

squirm *vi* sich winden

squirrel *n* Eichhörnchen *nt*

squirt *n* Spritzer *m* ● *vt/i* spritzen

St *abbr* (**Saint**) St.; (**Street**) Str.

stab *n* Stich *m*; ([!] *attempt*) Versuch *m* ● *vt* (*pt/pp* **stabbed**) stechen; (*to death*) erstechen

stability *n* Stabilität *f*

stable[1] *a* (**-r, -st**) stabil

stable[2] *n* Stall *m*; (*establishment*) Reitstall *m*

stack *n* Stapel *m*; (*of chimney*) Schornstein *m* ● *vt* stapeln

stadium *n* Stadion *nt*

staff *n* (*stick & Mil*) Stab *m* ● (*& pl*) (*employees*) Personal *nt*; (*Sch*) Lehrkräfte *pl* ● *vt* mit Personal besetzen. **~-room** *n* (*Sch*) Lehrerzimmer *nt*

stag *n* Hirsch *m*

stage *n* Bühne *f*; (*in journey*) Etappe *f*; (*in process*) Stadium *nt*; **by** *or* **in ~s** in Etappen ● *vt* aufführen; (*arrange*) veranstalten

stagger *vi* taumeln ● *vt* staffeln <*holidays*>; versetzt anordnen <*seats*>; **I was ~ed** es hat mir die Sprache verschlagen. **~ing** *a* unglaublich

stagnant *a* stehend; (*fig*) stagnierend

stagnate *vi* (*fig*) stagnieren

stain *n* Fleck *m*; (*for wood*) Beize *f* ● *vt* färben; beizen <*wood*>; **~ed glass** farbiges Glas *nt*. **~less** *a* <*steel*> rostfrei

stair *n* Stufe *f*; **~s** *pl* Treppe *f*. **~case** *n* Treppe *f*

stake *n* Pfahl *m*; (*wager*) Einsatz *m*; (*Comm*) Anteil *m*; **be at ~** auf dem Spiel stehen ● *vt* **~ a claim to sth** Anspruch auf etw (*acc*) erheben

stale *a* (**-r, -st**) alt; <*air*> verbraucht. **~mate** *n* Patt *nt*

stalk *n* Stiel *m*, Stängel *m*

stall *n* Stand *m*; **~s** *pl* (*Theat*) Parkett *nt* ● *vi* <*engine:*> stehen bleiben; (*fig*) ausweichen ● *vt* abwürgen <*engine*>

stalwart *a* treu ● *n* treuer Anhänger *m*

stamina *n* Ausdauer *f*

stammer *n* Stottern *nt* ● *vt/i* stottern

stamp *n* Stempel *m*; (*postage ~*) [Brief]marke *f* ● *vt* stempeln; (*impress*) prägen; (*put postage on*) frankieren ● *vi* stampfen. **~ out** *vt* [aus]stanzen; (*fig*) ausmerzen

stampede *n* wilde Flucht *f* ● *vi* in Panik fliehen

stance *n* Haltung *f*

stand *n* Stand *m*; (*rack*) Ständer *m*; (*pedestal*) Sockel *m*; (*Sport*) Tribüne *f*; (*fig*) Einstellung *f* ● *v* (*pt/pp* **stood**) ● *vi* stehen; (*rise*) aufstehen; (*be candidate*) kandidieren; (*stay valid*) gültig bleiben; **~ still** stillstehen; **~ firm** (*fig*) festbleiben; **~ to reason** logisch sein; **~ in for** vertreten; **~ for** (*mean*) bedeuten ● *vt* stellen; (*withstand*) standhalten (+ *dat*); (*endure*) ertragen; vertragen

<*climate*>; (*put up with*) aushalten; haben <*chance*>; **~ s.o. a beer** jdm ein Bier spendieren; **I can't ~ her** [!] ich kann sie nicht ausstehen. **~ by** *vi* daneben stehen; (*be ready*) sich bereithalten ● *vt* **~ by s.o.** (*fig*) zu jdm stehen. **~ down** *vi* (*retire*) zurücktreten. **~ out** *vi* hervorstehen; (*fig*) herausragen. **~ up** *vi* aufstehen; **~ up for** eintreten für; **~ up to** sich wehren gegen

standard *a* Normal- ● *n* Maßstab *m*; (*Techn*) Norm *f*; (*level*) Niveau *nt*; (*flag*) Standarte *f*; **~s** *pl* (*morals*) Prinzipien *pl*. **~ize** *vt* standardisieren; (*Techn*) normen

stand-in *n* Ersatz *m*

standing *a* (*erect*) stehend; (*permanent*) ständig ● *n* Rang *m*; (*duration*) Dauer *f*. **~-room** *n* Stehplätze *pl*

stand: ~-offish *a* distanziert. **~point** *n* Standpunkt *m*. **~still** *n* Stillstand *m*; **come to a ~still** zum Stillstand kommen

stank *see* **stink**

staple[1] *a* Grund-

staple[2] *n* Heftklammer *f* ● *vt* heften. **~r** *n* Heftmaschine *f*

star *n* Stern *m*; (*asterisk*) Sternchen *nt*; (*Theat, Sport*) Star *m* ● *vi* (*pt/pp* **starred**) die Hauptrolle spielen

starboard *n* Steuerbord *nt*

starch *n* Stärke *f* ● *vt* stärken. **~y** *a* stärkehaltig; (*fig*) steif

stare *n* Starren *nt* ● *vt* starren; **~ at** anstarren

stark *a* (**-er, -est**) scharf; <*contrast*> krass

starling *n* Star *m*

start *n* Anfang *m*, Beginn *m*; (*departure*) Aufbruch *m*; (*Sport*) Start *m*; **from the ~** von Anfang an; **for a ~** erstens ● *vi* anfangen, beginnen; (*set out*) aufbrechen; <*engine:*> anspringen; (*Auto, Sport*) starten; (*jump*) aufschrecken; **to ~ with** zuerst ● *vt* anfangen, beginnen; (*cause*) verursachen; (*found*) gründen; starten <*car, race*>; in Umlauf setzen <*rumour*>. **~er** *n* (*Culin*) Vorspeise *f*; (*Auto, Sport*) Starter *m*. **~ing-point** *n* Ausgangspunkt *m*

startle *vt* erschrecken

starvation *n* Verhungern *nt*

starve *vi* hungern; (*to death*) verhungern ● *vt* verhungern lassen

state *n* Zustand *m*; (*Pol*) Staat *m*; **~ of play** Spielstand *m*; **be in a ~** <*person:*> aufgeregt sein ● *attrib* Staats-, staatlich ● *vt* erklären; (*specify*) angeben

stately *a* (**-ier, -iest**) stattlich. **~ home** *n* Schloss *nt*

statement *n* Erklärung *f*; (*Jur*) Aussage *f*; (*Banking*) Auszug *m*

statesman *n* Staatsmann *m*

static *a* statisch; **remain ~** unverändert bleiben

station *n* Bahnhof *m*; (*police*) Wache *f*; (*radio*) Sender *m*; (*space, weather*) Station *f*; (*Mil*) Posten *m*; (*status*) Rang *m* ● *vt* stationieren; (*post*) postieren. **~ary** *a* stehend; **be ~ary** stehen

stationery *n* Briefpapier *nt*; (*writing materials*) Schreibwaren *pl*

station-wagon *n* (*Amer*) Kombi[wagen] *n*

statistic *n* statistische Tatsache *f*. **~al** *a*, **-ly** *adv* statistisch. **~s** *n* & *pl* Statistik *f*

statue *n* Statue *f*

stature *n* Statur *f*; (*fig*) Format *nt*

status *n* Status *m*, Rang *m*

statut|e *n* Statut *nt*. **~ory** *a* gesetzlich

staunch *a* (**-er, -est**), **-ly** *adv* treu

stave *vt* **~ off** abwenden

stay *n* Aufenthalt *m* ● *vi* bleiben; (*reside*) wohnen; **~ the night**

übernachten. ~ **behind** *vi* zurückbleiben. ~ **in** *vi* zu Hause bleiben; (*Sch*) nachsitzen. ~ **up** *vi* <*person:*> aufbleiben

steadily *adv* fest; (*continually*) stetig

steady *a* (**-ier, -iest**) fest; (*not wobbly*) stabil; <*hand*> ruhig; (*regular*) regelmäßig; (*dependable*) zuverlässig

steak *n* Steak *nt*

steal *vt/i* (*pt* **stole**, *pp* **stolen**) stehlen (**from** *dat*). ~ **in/out** *vi* sich hinein-/hinausstehlen

stealthy *a* heimlich

steam *n* Dampf *m* ● *vt* (*Culin*) dämpfen, dünsten ● *vi* dampfen. ~ **up** *vi* beschlagen

steam engine *n* Dampfmaschine *f*; (*Rail*) Dampflokomotive *f*

steamer *n* Dampfer *m*

steamy *a* dampfig

steel *n* Stahl *m*

steep *a*, **-ly** *adv* steil; ([!] *exorbitant*) gesalzen

steeple *n* Kirchturm *m*

steer *vt/i* (*Auto*) lenken; (*Naut*) steuern; ~ **clear of s.o./sth** jdm/etw aus dem Weg gehen. **~ing** *n* (*Auto*) Lenkung *f*. **~ing-wheel** *n* Lenkrad *nt*

stem¹ *n* Stiel *m*; (*of word*) Stamm *m*

stem² *vt* (*pt/pp* **stemmed**) eindämmen; stillen <*bleeding*>

stench *n* Gestank *m*

stencil *n* Schablone *f*

step *n* Schritt *m*; (*stair*) Stufe *f*; **~s** *pl* (*ladder*) Trittleiter *f*; **in ~** im Schritt; ~ **by** ~ Schritt für Schritt; **take ~s** (*fig*) Schritte unternehmen ● *vi* (*pt/pp* **stepped**) treten; ~ **in** (*fig*) eingreifen. ~ **up** *vt* (*increase*) erhöhen, steigen; verstärken <*efforts*>

step: ~brother *n* Stiefbruder *m*. **~child** *n* Stiefkind *nt*. **~daughter** *n* Stieftochter *f*. **~father** *n* Stiefvater *m*. **~-ladder** *n* Trittleiter *f*. **~mother** *n* Stiefmutter *f*. **~sister** *n* Stiefschwester *f*. **~son** *n* Stiefsohn *m*

stereo *n* Stereo *nt*; (*equipment*) Stereoanlage *f*. **~phonic** *a* stereophon

stereotype *n* stereotype Figur *f*

steril|e *a* steril. **~ize** *vt* sterilisieren

sterling *a* Sterling-; (*fig*) gediegen ● *n* Sterling *m*

stern¹ *a* (**-er, -est**), **-ly** *adv* streng

stern² *n* (*of boat*) Heck *nt*

stew *n* Eintopf *m*; **in a ~** [!] aufgeregt ● *vt/i* schmoren; **~ed fruit** Kompott *nt*

steward *n* Ordner *m*; (*on ship, aircraft*) Steward *m*. **~ess** *n* Stewardess *f*

stick¹ *n* Stock *m*; (*of chalk*) Stück *nt*; (*of rhubarb*) Stange *f*; (*Sport*) Schläger *m*

stick² *v* (*pt/pp* **stuck**) ● *vt* stecken; (*stab*) stechen; (*glue*) kleben; ([!] *put*) tun; ([!] *endure*) aushalten ● *vi* stecken; (*adhere*) kleben, haften (**to** an + *dat*); (*jam*) klemmen; ~ **at it** [!] dranbleiben; ~ **up for** [!] eintreten für; **be stuck** nicht weiterkönnen; <*vehicle:*> festsitzen, festgefahren sein; <*drawer:*> klemmen; **be stuck with sth** [!] etw am Hals haben. ~ **out** *vi* abstehen; (*project*) vorstehen ● *vt* hinausstrecken; herausstrecken <*tongue*>

sticker *n* Aufkleber *m*

sticking plaster *n* Heftpflaster *nt*

sticky *a* (**-ier, -iest**) klebrig; (*adhesive*) Klebe-

stiff *a* (**-er, -est**), **-ly** *adv* steif; <*brush*> hart; <*dough*> fest; (*difficult*) schwierig; <*penalty*> schwer; **be bored ~** [!] sich zu Tode langweilen. **~en** *vt* steif machen ● *vi* steif werden. **~ness** *n* Steifheit *f*

stifl|e *vt* ersticken; (*fig*) unterdrücken. **~ing** *a* **be ~ing** zum Ersticken sein
still *a* still; <*drink*> ohne Kohlensäure; **keep ~** stillhalten; **stand ~** stillstehen ● *adv* noch; (*emphatic*) immer noch; (*nevertheless*) trotzdem; **~ not** immer noch nicht
stillborn *a* tot geboren
still life *n* Stillleben *nt*
stilted *a* gestelzt, geschraubt
stimulant *n* Anregungsmittel *nt*
stimulat|e *vt* anregen. **~ion** *n* Anregung *f*
stimulus *n* (*pl* **-li**) Reiz *m*
sting *n* Stich *m*; (*from nettle, jellyfish*) Brennen *nt*; (*organ*) Stachel *m* ● *v* (*pt/pp* **stung**) ● *vt* stechen ● *vi* brennen; <*insect:*> stechen
stingy *a* (**-ier, -iest**) geizig, [!] knauserig
stink *n* Gestank *m* ● *vi* (*pt* **stank**, *pp* **stunk**) stinken (**of** nach)
stipulat|e *vt* vorschreiben. **~ion** *n* Bedingung *f*
stir *n* (*commotion*) Aufregung *f* ● *v* (*pt/pp* **stirred**) *vt* rühren ● *vi* sich rühren
stirrup *n* Steigbügel *m*
stitch *n* Stich *m*; (*Knitting*) Masche *f*; (*pain*) Seitenstechen *nt*; **be in ~es** [!] sich kaputtlachen ● *vt* nähen
stock *n* Vorrat *m* (**of** an + *dat*); (*in shop*) [Waren]bestand *m*; (*livestock*) Vieh *nt*; (*lineage*) Abstammung *f*; (*Finance*) Wertpapiere *pl*; (*Culin*) Brühe *f*; (*plant*) Levkoje *f*; **in/out of ~** vorrätig/nicht vorrätig; **take ~** (*fig*) Bilanz ziehen ● *a* Standard- ● *vt* <*shop:*> führen; auffüllen <*shelves*>. **~ up** *vi* sich eindecken (**with** mit)
stock: ~broker *n* Börsenmakler *m*. **S~ Exchange** *n* Börse *f*
stocking *n* Strumpf *m*
stock: ~market *n* Börse *f*. **~-taking** *n* (*Comm*) Inventur *f*
stocky *a* (**-ier, -iest**) untersetzt
stodgy *a* pappig [und schwer verdaulich]
stoke *vt* heizen
stole, stolen *see* **steal**
stomach *n* Magen *m*. **~-ache** *n* Magenschmerzen *pl*
stone *n* Stein *m*; (*weight*) 6,35kg ● *a* steinern; <*wall, Age*> Stein- ● *vt* mit Steinen bewerfen; entsteinen <*fruit*>. **~-cold** *a* eiskalt. **~-deaf** *n* [!] stocktaub
stony *a* steinig
stood *see* stand
stool *n* Hocker *m*
stoop *n* **walk with a ~** gebeugt gehen ● *vi* sich bücken
stop *n* Halt *m*; (*break*) Pause *f*; (*for bus*) Haltestelle *f*; (*for train*) Station *f*; (*Gram*) Punkt *m*; (*on organ*) Register *nt*; **come to a ~** stehen bleiben; **put a ~ to sth** etw unterbinden ● *v* (*pt/pp* **stopped**) ● *vt* anhalten, stoppen; (*switch off*) abstellen; (*plug, block*) zustopfen; (*prevent*) verhindern; **~ s.o. doing sth** jdn daran hindern, etw zu tun; **~ doing sth** aufhören, etw zu tun; **~ that!** hör auf damit! ● *vi* anhalten; (*cease*) aufhören; <*clock:*> stehen bleiben ● *int* halt!
stop: ~gap *n* Notlösung *f*. **~over** *n* (*Aviat*) Zwischenlandung *f*
stoppage *n* Unterbrechung *f*; (*strike*) Streik *m*
stopper *n* Stöpsel *m*
stop-watch *n* Stoppuhr *f*
storage *n* Aufbewahrung *f*; (*in warehouse*) Lagerung *f*; (*Computing*) Speicherung *f*
store *n* (*stock*) Vorrat *m*; (*shop*) Laden *m*; (*department ~*) Kaufhaus *nt*; (*depot*) Lager *nt*; **in ~** auf Lager; **be in ~ for s.o.** (*fig*) jdm bevorstehen ● *vt* aufbewahren; (*in warehouse*)

lagern; (*Computing*) speichern. **~-room** *n* Lagerraum *m*

storey *n* Stockwerk *nt*

stork *n* Storch *m*

storm *n* Sturm *m*; (*with thunder*) Gewitter *nt* ● *vt/i* stürmen. **~y** *a* stürmisch

story *n* Geschichte *f*; (*in newspaper*) Artikel *m*; ([!] *lie*) Märchen *nt*

stout *a* (**-er, -est**) beleibt; (*strong*) fest

stove *n* Ofen *m*; (*for cooking*) Herd *m*

stow *vt* verstauen. **~away** *n* blinder Passagier *m*

straggl|e *vi* hinterherhinken. **~er** *n* Nachzügler *m*. **~y** *a* strähnig

straight *a* (**-er, -est**) gerade; (*direct*) direkt; (*clear*) klar; <*hair*> glatt; <*drink*>; pur; **be ~** (*tidy*) in Ordnung sein ● *adv* gerade; (*directly*) direkt, geradewegs; (*clearly*) klar; **~ away** sofort; **~ on** *or* **ahead** geradeaus; **~ out** (*fig*) geradeheraus; **sit/stand up ~** gerade sitzen/stehen

straighten *vt* gerade machen; (*put straight*) gerade richten ● *vi* gerade werden; **~ [up]** <*person:*> sich aufrichten. **~ out** *vt* gerade biegen

straightforward *a* offen; (*simple*) einfach

strain *n* Belastung *f*; **~s** *pl* (*of music*) Klänge *pl* ● *vt* belasten; (*overexert*) überanstrengen; (*injure*) zerren <*muscle*>; (*Culin*) durchseihen; abgießen <*vegetables*>. **~ed** *a* <*relations*> gespannt. **~er** *n* Sieb *nt*

strait *n* Meerenge *f*; **in dire ~s** in großen Nöten

strand[1] *n* (*of thread*) Faden *m*; (*of hair*) Strähne *f*

strand[2] *vt* **be ~ed** festsitzen

strange *a* (**-r, -st**) fremd; (*odd*) seltsam, merkwürdig. **~ly** *adv* seltsam, merkwürdig; **~ enough** seltsamerweise. **~r** *n* Fremde(r) *m/f*

strangle *vt* erwürgen; (*fig*) unterdrücken

strap *n* Riemen *m*; (*for safety*) Gurt *m*; (*to grasp in vehicle*) Halteriemen *m*; (*of watch*) Armband *nt*; (*shoulder ~*) Träger *m* ● *vt* (*pt/pp* **strapped**) schnallen

strapping *a* stramm

strategic *a*, **-ally** *adv* strategisch

strategy *n* Strategie *f*

straw *n* Stroh *nt*; (*single piece, drinking*) Strohhalm *m*; **that's the last ~** jetzt reicht's aber

strawberry *n* Erdbeere *f*

stray *a* streunend ● *n* streunendes Tier *nt* ● *vi* sich verirren; (*deviate*) abweichen

streak *n* Streifen *m*; (*in hair*) Strähne *f*; (*fig: trait*) Zug *m*

stream *n* Bach *m*; (*flow*) Strom *m*; (*current*) Strömung *f*; (*Sch*) Parallelzug *m* ● *vi* strömen

streamline *vt* (*fig*) rationalisieren. **~d** *a* stromlinienförmig

street *n* Straße *f*. **~car** *n* (*Amer*) Straßenbahn *f*. **~lamp** *n* Straßenlaterne *f*

strength *n* Stärke *f*; (*power*) Kraft *f*; **on the ~ of** auf Grund (+ *gen*). **~en** *vt* stärken; (*reinforce*) verstärken

strenuous *a* anstrengend

stress *n* (*emphasis*) Betonung *f*; (*strain*) Belastung *f*; (*mental*) Stress *m* ● *vt* betonen; (*put a strain on*) belasten. **~ful** *a* stressig [!]

stretch *n* (*of road*) Strecke *f*; (*elasticity*) Elastizität *f*; **at a ~** ohne Unterbrechung; **have a ~** sich strecken ● *vt* strecken; (*widen*) dehnen; (*spread*) ausbreiten; fordern <*person*>; **~ one's legs** sich (*dat*) die Beine vertreten ● *vt* sich erstrecken; (*become wider*) sich dehnen;

<person:> sich strecken. **~er** *n* Tragbahre *f*

strict *a* (**-er, -est**), **-ly** *adv* streng; **~ly speaking** streng genommen

stride *n* [großer] Schritt *m*; **take sth in one's ~** mit etw gut fertig werden ● *vi* (*pt* **strode**, *pp* **stridden**) [mit großen Schritten] gehen

strident *a*, **-ly** *adv* schrill; *<colour>* grell

strife *n* Streit *m*

strike *n* Streik *m*; (*Mil*) Angriff *m*; **be on ~** streiken ● *v* (*pt/pp* **struck**) ● *vt* schlagen; (*knock against, collide with*) treffen; anzünden *<match>*; stoßen auf (+ *acc*) *<oil, gold>*; abbrechen *<camp>*; (*impress*) beeindrucken; (*occur to*) einfallen (+ *dat*); **~ s.o. a blow** jdm einen Schlag versetzen ● *vi* treffen; *<lightning:>* einschlagen; *<clock:>* schlagen; (*attack*) zuschlagen; *<workers:>* streiken

striker *n* Streikende(r) *m/f*

striking *a* auffallend

string *n* Schnur *f*; (*thin*) Bindfaden *m*; (*of musical instrument, racket*) Saite *f*; (*of bow*) Sehne *f*; (*of pearls*) Kette *f*; **the ~s** (*Mus*) die Streicher *pl*; **pull ~s** [!] seine Beziehungen spielen lassen ● *vt* (*pt/pp* **strung**) (*thread*) aufziehen *<beads>*

stringent *a* streng

strip *n* Streifen *m* ● *v* (*pt/pp* **stripped**) ● *vt* ablösen; ausziehen *<person, clothes>*; abziehen *<bed>*; abbeizen *<wood, furniture>*; auseinander nehmen *<machine>*; (*deprive*) berauben (*of gen*); **~ sth off sth** etw von etw entfernen ● *vi* (*undress*) sich ausziehen

stripe *n* Streifen *m*. **~d** *a* gestreift

stripper *n* Stripperin *f*; (*male*) Stripper *m*

strive *vi* (*pt* **strove**, *pp* **striven**) sich bemühen (**to** zu); **~ for** streben nach

strode *see* **stride**

stroke[1] *n* Schlag *m*; (*of pen*) Strich *m*; (*Swimming*) Zug *m*; (*style*) Stil *m*; (*Med*) Schlaganfall *m*; **~ of luck** Glücksfall *m*

stroke[2] ● *vt* streicheln

stroll *n* Bummel *m* [!] ● *vi* bummeln [!]. **~er** *n* (*Amer: pushchair*) [Kinder]sportwagen *m*

strong *a* (**-er, -est**), **-ly** *adv* stark; (*powerful, healthy*) kräftig; (*severe*) streng; (*sturdy*) stabil; (*convincing*) gut

strong: ~hold *n* Festung *f*; (*fig*) Hochburg *f*. **~-room** *n* Tresorraum *m*

strove *see* **strive**

struck *see* **strike**

structural *a*, **-ly** *adv* baulich

structure *n* Struktur *f*; (*building*) Bau *m*

struggle *n* Kampf *m*; **with a ~** mit Mühe ● *vt* kämpfen; **~ to do sth** sich abmühen, etw zutun

strum *v* (*pt/pp* **strummed**) ● *vt* klimpern auf (+ *dat*) ● *vi* klimpern

strung *see* **string**

strut[1] *n* Strebe *f*

strut[2] *vi* (*pt/pp* **strutted**) stolzieren

stub *n* Stummel *m*; (*counterfoil*) Abschnitt *m*. **~ out** *vt* (*pt/pp* **stubbed**) ausdrücken *<cigarette>*

stubble *n* Stoppeln *pl*

stubborn *a*, **-ly** *adv* starrsinnig; *<refusal>* hartnäckig

stubby *a*, (**-ier, -iest**) kurz und dick

stuck *see* **stick**[2]. **~-up** *a* [!] hochnäsig

stud *n* Nagel *m*; (*on clothes*) Niete *f*; (*for collar*) Kragenknopf *m*; (*for ear*) Ohrstecker *m*

student *n* Student(in) *m(f)*; (*Sch*) Schüler(in) *m(f)*

studio *n* Studio *nt*; (*for artist*) Atelier *nt*

studious *a* lerneifrig; (*earnest*) ernsthaft

stud|y *n* Studie *f*; (*room*) Arbeitszimmer *nt*; (*investigation*) Untersuchung *f*; **~ies** *pl* Studium *nt* ● *v* (*pt/pp* **studied**) ● *vt* studieren; (*examine*) untersuchen ● *vi* lernen; (*at university*) studieren

stuff *n* Stoff *m*; ([!] *things*) Zeug *nt* ● *vt* vollstopfen; (*with padding, Culin*) füllen; ausstopfen <*animal*>; (*cram*) [hinein]stopfen. **~ing** *n* Füllung *f*

stuffy *a* (**-ier, -iest**) stickig; (*old-fashioned*) spießig

stumbl|e *vi* stolpern; **~e across** zufällig stoßen auf (+ *acc*). **~ing-block** *n* Hindernis *nt*

stump *n* Stumpf *m* ● **~ up** *vt/i* [!] blechen. **~ed** *a* [!] überfragt

stun *vt* (*pt/pp* **stunned**) betäuben

stung *see* **sting**

stunk *see* **stink**

stunning *a* [!] toll

stunt *n* [!] Kunststück *nt*

stupendous *a*, **-ly** *adv* enorm

stupid *a* dumm. **~ity** *n* Dummheit *f*. **~ly** *adv* dumm; **~ly [enough]** dummerweise

sturdy *a* (**-ier, -iest**) stämmig; <*furniture*> stabil; <*shoes*> fest

stutter *n* Stottern *nt* ● *vt/i* stottern

sty *n* (*pl* **sties**) Schweinestall *m*

style *n* Stil *m*; (*fashion*) Mode *f*; (*sort*) Art *f*; (*hair~*) Frisur *f*; **in ~** in großem Stil

stylish *a*, -ly *adv* stilvoll

stylist *n* Friseur *m*/ Friseuse *f*. **~ic** *a*, **-ally** *adv* stilistisch

suave *a* (*pej*) gewandt

subconscious *a*, **-ly** *adv* unterbewusst ● *n* Unterbewusstsein *nt*

subdivi|de *vt* unterteilen. **~sion** *n* Unterteilung *f*

subdue *vt* unterwerfen. **~d** *a* gedämpft; <*person*> still

subject[1] *a* **be ~ to sth** etw (*dat*) unterworfen sein ● *n* Staatsbürger(in) *m(f)*; (*of ruler*) Untertan *m*; (*theme*) Thema *nt*; (*of investigation*) Gegenstand *m*; (*Sch*) Fach *nt*; (*Gram*) Subjekt *nt*

subject[2] *vt* unterwerfen (**to** *dat*); (*expose*) aussetzen (**to** *dat*)

subjective *a*, **-ly** *adv* subjektiv

subjunctive *n* Konjunktiv *m*

sublime *a*, **-ly** *adv* erhaben

submarine *n* Unterseeboot *nt*

submerge *vt* untertauchen; **be ~d** unter Wasser stehen ● *vi* tauchen

submission *n* Unterwerfung *f*

submit *v* (*pt/pp* **-mitted**, *pres p* **-mitting**) ● *vt* vorlegen (**to** *dat*); (*hand in*) einreichen ● *vi* sich unterwerfen (**to** *dat*)

subordinate[1] *a* untergeordnet ● *n* Untergebene(r) *m/f*

subordinate[2] *vt* unterordnen (**to** *dat*)

subscribe *vi* spenden; **~ to** (*fig*); abonnieren <*newspaper*>. **~r** *n* Spender *m*; Abonnent *m*

subscription *n* (*to club*) [Mitglieds]beitrag *m*; (*to newspaper*) Abonnement *nt*; **by ~** mit Spenden; <*buy*> im Abonnement

subsequent *a*, **-ly** *adv* folgend; (*later*) später

subside *vi* sinken; <*ground:*> sich senken; <*storm:*> nachlassen

subsidiary *a* untergeordnet ● *n* Tochtergesellschaft *f*

subsid|ize *vt* subventionieren. **~y** *n* Subvention *f*

substance *n* Substanz *f*

substandard *a* unzulänglich; <*goods*> minderwertig

substantial *a* solide; <*meal*> reichhaltig; (*considerable*) beträchtlich. **~ly** *adv* solide; (*essentially*) im Wesentlichen

substitut|e *n* Ersatz *m*; (*Sport*) Ersatzspieler(in) *m(f)* ● *vt* **~e A for B** B durch A ersetzen ● *vi* **~e for s.o.** jdn vertreten. **~ion** *n* Ersetzung *f*

subterranean *a* unterirdisch

subtitle *n* Untertitel *m*

subtle *a* (**-r, -st**), **-tly** *adv* fein; (*fig*) subtil

subtract *vt* abziehen, subtrahieren. **~ion** *n* Subtraktion *f*

suburb *n* Vorort *m*. **~an** *a* Vorort-. **~ia** *n* die Vororte *pl*

subway *n* Unterführung *f*; (*Amer: railway*) U-Bahn *f*

succeed *vi* Erfolg haben; <*plan:*> gelingen; (*follow*) nachfolgen (+ *dat*); **I ~ed** es ist mir gelungen; **he ~ed in escaping** es gelang ihm zu entkommen ● *vt* folgen (+ *dat*)

success *n* Erfolg *m*. **~ful** *a*,**-ly** *adv* erfolgreich

succession *n* Folge *f*, (*series*) Serie *f*; (*to title, office*) Nachfolge *f*; (*to throne*) Thronfolge *f*; **in ~** hintereinander

successive *a* aufeinander folgend

successor *n* Nachfolger(in) *m(f)*

succumb *vi* erliegen (**to** *dat*)

such

● *adjective*

····➤ (*of that kind*) solch. **such a book** ein solches Buch; so ein Buch [!]. **such a person** ein solcher Mensch, so ein Mensch [!]. **such people** solche Leute. **such a thing** so etwas. **no such example** kein solches Beispiel. **there is no such thing** so etwas gibt es nicht; das gibt es gar nicht. **there is no such person** eine solche Person gibt es nicht. **such writers as Goethe and Schiller** Schriftsteller wie Goethe und Schiller

····➤ (*so great*) solch; derartig. **I've got such a headache!** ich habe solche Kopfschmerzen! **it was such fun!** das machte solchen Spaß! **I got such a fright that ...** ich bekam einen derartigen *od* [!] so einen Schrecken, dass ...

····➤ (*with adjective*) so. **such a big house** ein so großes Haus. **he has such lovely blue eyes** er hat so schöne blaue Augen. **such a long time** so lange

● *pronoun*

····➤ **as such** als solcher/solche/solches. **the thing as such** die Sache als solche. (*strictly speaking*) **this is not a promotion as such** dies ist im Grunde genommen keine Beförderung

····➤ **such is**: **such is life** so ist das Leben. **such is not the case** das ist nicht der Fall

····➤ **such as** wie [zum Beispiel]

suchlike *pron* [!] dergleichen

suck *vt/i* saugen; lutschen <*sweet*>. **~ up** *vt* aufsaugen ● *vi* **~ up to s.o.** [!] sich bei jdm einschmeicheln

suction *n* Saugwirkung *f*

sudden *a*, **-ly** *adv* plötzlich; (*abrupt*) jäh ● *n* **all of a ~** auf einmal

sue *vt* (*pres p* **suing**) verklagen (**for** auf + *acc*) ● *vi* klagen

suede *n* Wildleder *nt*

suet *n* [Nieren]talg *m*

suffer *vi* leiden (**from an** + *dat*) ● *vt* erleiden; (*tolerate*) dulden

suffice *vi* genügen

sufficient *a*, **-ly** *adv* genug, genügend; **be ~** genügen

suffocat|e *vt/i* ersticken. **~ion** *n* Ersticken *nt*

sugar *n* Zucker *m* ● *vt* zuckern; (*fig*) versüßen. **~ basin, ~-bowl** *n* Zuckerschale *f*. **~y** *a* süß; (*fig*) süßlich

S

suggest *vt* vorschlagen; (*indicate, insinuate*) andeuten. **~ion** *n* Vorschlag *m*; Andeutung *f*; (*trace*) Spur *f*. **~ive** *a*, **-ly** *adv* anzüglich
suicidal *a* selbstmörderisch
suicide *n* Selbstmord *m*
suit *n* Anzug *m*; (*woman's*) Kostüm *nt*; (*Cards*) Farbe *f*; (*Jur*) Prozess *m* ● *vt* (*adapt*) anpassen (**to** *dat*); (*be convenient for*) passen (+ *dat*); (*go with*) passen zu; <*clothing:*> stehen (**s.o.** *jdm*); **be ~ed for** geeignet sein für; **~ yourself!** wie du willst!
suit|able *a* geeignet; (*convenient*) passend; (*appropriate*) angemessen; (*for weather, activity*) zweckmäßig. **~ably** *adv* angemessen; zweckmäßig
suitcase *n* Koffer *m*
suite *n* Suite *f*; (*of furniture*) Garnitur *f*
sulk *vi* schmollen. **~y** *a* schmollend
sullen *a*, **-ly** *adv* mürrisch
sultry *a* (**-ier, -iest**) <*weather*> schwül
sum *n* Summe *f*; (*Sch*) Rechenaufgabe *f* ● *vt/i* (*pt/pp* **summed**) **~ up** zusammenfassen; (*assess*) einschätzen
summar|ize *vt* zusammenfassen. **~y** *n* Zusammenfassung *f* ● *a*, **-ily** *adv* summarisch; <*dismissal*> fristlos
summer *n* Sommer *m*. **~time** *n* Sommer *m*
summery *a* sommerlich
summit *n* Gipfel *m*. **~ conference** *n* Gipfelkonferenz *f*
summon *vt* rufen; holen <*help*>; (*Jur*) vorladen
summons *n* (*Jur*) Vorladung *f* ● *vt* vorladen
sumptuous *a*, **-ly** *adv* prunkvoll; <*meal*> üppig
sun *n* Sonne *f* ● *vt* (*pt/pp* **sunned**) **~ oneself** sich sonnen
sun: ~bathe *vi* sich sonnen. **~-bed** *n* Sonnenbank *f*. **~burn** *n* Sonnenbrand *m*
Sunday *n* Sonntag *m*
sunflower *n* Sonnenblume *f*
sung *see* **sing**
sunglasses *npl* Sonnenbrille *f*
sunk *see* **sink**
sunny *a* (**-ier, -iest**) sonnig
sun: ~rise *n* Sonnenaufgang *m*. **~-roof** *n* (*Auto*) Schiebedach *nt*. **~set** *n* Sonnenuntergang *m*. **~shade** *n* Sonnenschirm *m*. **~shine** *n* Sonnenschein *m*. **~stroke** *n* Sonnenstich *m*. **~-tan** *n* [Sonnen]bräune *f*. **~-tanned** *a* braun [gebrannt]. **~-tan oil** *n* Sonnenöl *nt*
super *a* ⓘ prima, toll
superb *a* erstklassig
superficial a, -ly *adv* oberflächlich
superfluous *a* überflüssig
superintendent *n* (*of police*) Kommissar *m*
superior *a* überlegen; (*in rank*) höher ● *n* Vorgesetzte(r) *m/f*. **~ity** *n* Überlegenheit *f*
superlative *a* unübertrefflich ● *n* Superlativ *m*
supermarket *n* Supermarkt *m*
supernatural *a* übernatürlich
supersede *vt* ersetzen
superstiti|on *n* Aberglaube *m*. **~ous** *a*, **-ly** *adv* abergläubisch
supervis|e *vt* beaufsichtigen; überwachen <*work*>. **~ion** *n* Aufsicht *f*; Überwachung *f*. **~or** *n* Aufseher(in) *m(f)*
supper *n* Abendessen *nt*
supple *a* geschmeidig
supplement *n* Ergänzung *f*; (*addition*) Zusatz *m*; (*to fare*) Zuschlag *m*; (*book*) Ergänzungsband *m*; (*to newspaper*) Beilage *f* ● *vt* ergänzen. **~ary** a zusätzlich
supplier *n* Lieferant *m*

supply *n* Vorrat *m*; **supplies** *pl* (*Mil*) Nachschub *m* ● *vt* (*pt/pp* **-ied**) liefern; ~ **s.o. with sth** jdn mit etw versorgen

support *n* Stütze *f*; (*fig*) Unterstützung *f* ● *vt* stützen; (*bear weight of*) tragen; (*keep*) ernähren; (*give money to*) unterstützen; (*speak in favour of*) befürworten; (*Sport*) Fan sein von. **~er** *n* Anhänger(in) *m(f)*; (*Sport*) Fan *m*

suppose *vt* annehmen; (*presume*) vermuten; (*imagine*) sich (*dat*) vorstellen; **be ~d to do sth** etw tun sollen; **not be ~d to** 🅘 nicht dürfen; **I ~ so** vermutlich. **~dly** *adv* angeblich

supposition *n* Vermutung *f*

suppress *vt* unterdrücken. **~ion** *n* Unterdrückung *f*

supremacy *n* Vorherrschaft *f*

supreme *a* höchste(r,s); <*court*> oberste(r,s)

sure *a* (**-r**, **-st**) sicher; **make ~** sich vergewissern (**of** *gen*); (*check*) nachprüfen ● *adv* (*Amer* 🅘) klar; **~ enough** tatsächlich. **~ly** *adv* sicher; (*for emphasis*) doch; (*Amer: gladly*) gern

surf *n* Brandung *f* ● *vi* surfen

surface *n* Oberfläche *f* ● *vi* (*emerge*) auftauchen

surfboard *n* Surfbrett *nt*

surfing *n* Surfen *nt*

surge *n* (*of sea*) Branden *nt*; (*fig*) Welle *f* ● *vi* branden; **~ forward** nach vorn drängen

surgeon *n* Chirurg(in) *m(f)*

surgery *n* Chirurgie *f*; (*place*) Praxis *f*; (*room*) Sprechzimmer *nt*; (*hours*) Sprechstunde *f*; **have ~** operiert werden

surgical *a*, **-ly** *adv* chirurgisch

surly *a* (**-ier**, **-iest**) mürrisch

surname *n* Nachname *m*

surpass *vt* übertreffen

surplus *a* überschüssig ● *n* Überschuss *m* (**of** an + *dat*)

surpris|e *n* Überraschung *f* ● *vt* überraschen; **be ~ed** sich wundern (**at** über + *acc*). **~ing** *a*, **-ly** *adv* überraschend

surrender *n* Kapitulation *f* ● *vi* sich ergeben; (*Mil*) kapitulieren ● *vt* aufgeben

surround *vt* umgeben; (*encircle*) umzingeln; **~ed by** umgeben von. **~ing** *a* umliegend. **~ings** *npl* Umgebung *f*

surveillance *n* Überwachung *f*; **be under ~** überwacht werden

survey[1] *n* Überblick *m*; (*poll*) Umfrage *f*; (*investigation*) Untersuchung *f*; (*of land*) Vermessung *f*; (*of house*) Gutachten *nt*

survey[2] *vt* betrachten; vermessen <*land*>; begutachten <*building*>. **~or** *n* Landvermesser *m*; Gutachter *m*

survival *n* Überleben *nt*; (*of tradition*) Fortbestand *m*

surviv|e *vt* überleben ● *vi* überleben; <*tradition:*> erhalten bleiben. **~or** *n* Überlebende(r) *m/f*; **be a ~or** nicht unterzukriegen sein

susceptible *a* empfänglich/ (*Med*) anfällig (**to** für)

suspect[1] *vt* verdächtigen; (*assume*) vermuten; **he ~s nothing** er ahnt nichts

suspect[2] *a* verdächtig ● *n* Verdächtige(r) *m/f*

suspend *vt* aufhängen; (*stop*) [vorläufig] einstellen; (*from duty*) vorläufig beurlauben. **~ders** *npl* (*Amer: braces*) Hosenträger *pl*

suspense *n* Spannung *f*

suspension *n* (*Auto*) Federung *f*. **~ bridge** *n* Hängebrücke *f*

suspici|on *n* Verdacht *m*; (*mistrust*) Misstrauen *nt*; (*trace*) Spur *f*. **~ous** *a*, **-ly** *adv* misstrauisch; (*arousing suspicion*) verdächtig

S

sustain *vt* tragen; (*fig*) aufrechterhalten; erhalten <*life*>; erleiden <*injury*>

sustenance *n* Nahrung *f*

swagger *vi* stolzieren

swallow[1] *vt/i* schlucken. ~ **up** *vt* verschlucken; verschlingen <*resources*>

swallow[2] *n* (*bird*) Schwalbe *f*

swam *see* **swim**

swamp *n* Sumpf *m* ● *vt* überschwemmen

swan *n* Schwan *m*

swank *vi* [!] angeben

swap *n* [!] Tausch *m* ● *vt/i* (*pt/pp* **swapped**) [!] tauschen (**for** gegen)

swarm *n* Schwarm *m* ● *vi* schwärmen; **be ~ing with** wimmeln von

swat *vt* (*pt/pp* **swatted**) totschlagen

sway *vi* schwanken; (*gently*) sich wiegen ● *vt* (*influence*) beeinflussen

swear *v* (*pt* **swore**, *pp* **sworn**) ● *vt* schwören ● *vi* schwören (**by** auf + *acc*); (*curse*) fluchen. **~-word** *n* Kraftausdruck *m*

sweat *n* Schweiß *m* ● *vi* schwitzen

sweater *n* Pullover *m*

Swed|e *n* Schwede *m*/Schwedin *f*. **~en** *n* Schweden *nt*. **~ish** *a* schwedisch

sweep *n* Schornsteinfeger *m*; (*curve*) Bogen *m*; (*movement*) ausholende Bewegung *f* ● *v* (*pt/pp* **swept**) ● *vt* fegen, kehren ● *vi* (*go swiftly*) rauschen; <*wind:*> fegen

sweeping *a* ausholend; <*statement*> pauschal; <*changes*> weit reichend

sweet a (**-er**, **-est**) süß; **have a ~ tooth** gern Süßes mögen ● *n* Bonbon *m & nt*; (*dessert*) Nachtisch *m*

sweeten *vt* süßen

sweet: ~heart *n* Schatz *m*. **~ness** *n* Süße *f*. **~ pea** *n* Wicke *f*. **~-shop** *n* Süßwarenladen *m*

swell *n* Dünung *f* ● *v* (*pt* **swelled**, *pp* **swollen** *or* **swelled**) ● *vi* [an]schwellen; <*wood:*> aufquellen ● *vt* anschwellen lassen; (*increase*) vergrößern. **~ing** *n* Schwellung *f*

swelter *vi* schwitzen

swept *see* **sweep**

swerve *vi* einen Bogen machen

swift *a* (**-er**, **-est**), **-ly** *adv* schnell

swig *n* [!] Schluck *m*

swim *n* **have a ~** schwimmen ● *vi* (**pt swam**, *pp* **swum**) schwimmen; **my head is ~ming** mir dreht sich der Kopf. **~mer** *n* Schwimmer(in) *m(f)*

swimming *n* Schwimmen *nt*. **~-baths** *npl* Schwimmbad *nt*. **~-pool** *n* Schwimmbecken *nt*; (*private*) Swimmingpool *m*

swimsuit *n* Badeanzug *m*

swindle *n* Schwindel *m*, Betrug *m* ● *vt* betrügen. **~r** *n* Schwindler *m*

swine *n* (*pej*) Schwein *nt*

swing *n* Schwung *m*; (*shift*) Schwenk *m*; (*seat*) Schaukel *f*; **in full ~** in vollem Gange ● (*pt/pp* **swung**) ● *vi* schwingen; (*on swing*) schaukeln; (*dangle*) baumeln; (*turn*) schwenken ● *vt* schwingen; (*influence*) beeinflussen

swipe *n* [!] Schlag *m* ● *vt* [!] knallen; (*steal*) klauen

swirl *n* Wirbel *m* ● *vt/i* wirbeln

Swiss *a* Schweizer, schweizerisch ● *n* Schweizer(in) *m(f)*; **the ~** *pl* die Schweizer. **~ roll** *n* Biskuitrolle *f*

switch *n* Schalter *m*; (*change*) Wechsel *m*; (*Amer, Rail*) Weiche *f* ● *vt* wechseln; (*exchange*) tauschen ● *vi* wechseln; **~ to** umstellen auf (+ *acc*). **~ off** *vt* ausschalten; abschalten <*engine*>. ~ **on** *vt* einschalten

switchboard *n* [Telefon]zentrale *f*

Switzerland *n* die Schweiz

swivel *v* (*pt/pp* **swivelled**) ● *vt* drehen ● *vi* sich drehen

swollen *see* **swell**

swoop *n* (*by police*) Razzia *f* ● *vi* ~ **down** herabstoßen

sword *n* Schwert *nt*

swore *see* **swear**

sworn *see* **swear**

swot *n* [!] Streber *m* ● *vt* (*pt/pp* **swotted**) [!] büffeln

swum *see* **swim**

swung *see* **swing**

syllable *n* Silbe *f*

syllabus *n* Lehrplan *m*; (*for exam*) Studienplan *m*

symbol *n* Symbol *nt* (**of** für). ~**ic** *a*, **-ally** *adv* symbolisch ~**ism** *n* Symbolik *f*. ~**ize** *vt* symbolisieren

symmetr|ical *a*, **-ly** *adv* symmetrisch. ~**y** *n* Symmetrie *f*

sympathetic *a*, **-ally** *adv* mitfühlend; (*likeable*) sympathisch

sympathize *vi* mitfühlen

sympathy *n* Mitgefühl *nt*; (*condolences*) Beileid *nt*

symphony *n* Sinfonie *f*

symptom *n* Symptom *nt*

synagogue *n* Synagoge *f*

synchronize *vt* synchronisieren

synonym *n* Synonym *nt*. ~**ous** *a*, **-ly** *adv* synonym

synthesis *n* (*pl* **-ses**) Synthese *f*

synthetic *a* synthetisch

Syria *n* Syrien *nt*

syringe *n* Spritze *f*

syrup *n* Sirup *m*

system *n* System *nt*. ~**atic** *a*, **-ally** *adv* systematisch

Tt

tab *n* (*projecting*) Zunge *f*; (*with name*) Namensschild *nt*; (*loop*) Aufhänger *m*; **pick up the** ~ [!] bezahlen

table *n* Tisch *m*; (*list*) Tabelle *f*. **at [the]** ~ bei Tisch. ~**-cloth** *n* Tischdecke *f*. ~**spoon** *n* Servierlöffel *m*

tablet *n* Tablette *f*; (*of soap*) Stück *nt*

table tennis *n* Tischtennis *nt*

tabloid *n* kleinformatige Zeitung *f*; (*pej*) Boulevardzeitung *f*

taciturn *a* wortkarg

tack *n* (*nail*) Stift *m*; (*stitch*) Heftstich *m*; (*Naut & fig*) Kurs *m* ● *vt* festnageln; (*sew*) heften ● *vi* (*Naut*) kreuzen

tackle *n* Ausrüstung *f* ● *vt* angehen <*problem*>; (*Sport*) angreifen

tact *n* Takt *m*, Taktgefühl *nt*. ~**ful** *a*, **-ly** *adv* taktvoll

tactic|al *a*, **-ly** *adv* taktisch. ~**s** *npl* Taktik *f*

tactless *a*, **-ly** *adv* taktlos. ~**ness** *n* Taktlosigkeit *f*

tag *n* (*label*) Schild *nt* ● *vi* (*pt/pp* **tagged**) ~ **along** mitkommen

tail *n* Schwanz *m*; ~**s** *pl* (*tailcoat*) Frack *m*; **heads or** ~**s?** Kopf oder Zahl? ● *vt* ([!] *follow*) beschatten ● *vi* ~ **off** zurückgehen

tail: ~**back** *n* Rückstau *m*. ~ **light** *n* Rücklicht *nt*

tailor *n* Schneider *m*. ~**-made** *a* maßgeschneidert

taint *vt* verderben

take *v* (*pt* **took**, *pp* **taken**) ● *vt* nehmen; (*with one*) mitnehmen; (*take to a place*) bringen; (*steal*) stehlen; (*win*) gewinnen;

(*capture*) einnehmen; (*require*) brauchen; (*last*) dauern; (*teach*) geben; machen <*exam, subject, holiday, photograph*>; messen <*pulse, temperature*>; ~ **sth to the cleaner's** etw in die Reinigung bringen; **be ~n ill** krank werden; ~ **sth calmly** etw gelassen aufnehmen ● *vi* <*plant:*> angehen; ~ **after s.o.** jdm nachschlagen; (*in looks*) jdm ähnlich sehen; ~ **to** (*like*) mögen; (*as a habit*) sich (*dat*) angewöhnen. ~ **away** *vt* wegbringen; (*remove*) wegnehmen; (*subtract*) abziehen; **'to ~ away'** 'zum Mitnehmen'. ~ **back** *vt* zurücknehmen; (*return*) zurückbringen. ~ **down** *vt* herunternehmen; (*remove*) abnehmen; (*write down*) aufschreiben. ~ **in** *vt* hineinbringen; (*bring indoors*) hereinholen; (*to one's home*) aufnehmen; (*understand*) begreifen; (*deceive*) hereinlegen; (*make smaller*) enger machen. ~ **off** *vt* abnehmen; ablegen <*coat*>; sich (*dat*) ausziehen <*clothes*>; (*deduct*) abziehen; (*mimic*) nachmachen ● *vi* (*Aviat*) starten. ~ **on** *vt* annehmen; (*undertake*) übernehmen; (*engage*) einstellen; (*as opponent*) antreten gegen. ~ **out** *vt* hinausbringen; (*for pleasure*) ausgehen mit; ausführen <*dog*>; (*remove*) herausnehmen; (*withdraw*) abheben <*money*>; (*from library*) ausleihen; ~ **it out on s.o.** [!] seinen Ärger an jdm auslassen. ~ **over** *vt* hinüberbringen; übernehmen <*firm, control*> ● *vi* ~ **over from s.o.** jdn ablösen. ~ **up** *vt* hinaufbringen; annehmen <*offer*>; ergreifen <*profession*>; sich (*dat*) zulegen <*hobby*>; in Anspruch nehmen <*time*>; einnehmen <*space*>; aufreißen <*floorboards*>; ~ **sth up with s.o.** mit jdm über etw (*acc*) sprechen

take: ~-away *n* Essen *nt* zum Mitnehmen; (*restaurant*) Restaurant *nt* mit Straßenverkauf. **~-off** *n* (*Aviat*) Start *m*, Abflug *m*. **~-over** *n* Übernahme *f*

takings *npl* Einnahmen *pl*

talcum *n* ~ **[powder]** Körperpuder *m*

tale *n* Geschichte *f*

talent *n* Talent *nt*

talk *n* Gespräch *nt*; (*lecture*) Vortrag *m* ● *vi* reden, sprechen (**to/with** mit) ● *vt* reden; ~ **s.o. into sth** jdn zu etw überreden. ~ **over** *vt* besprechen

talkative *a* gesprächig

tall *a* (**-er, -est**) groß; <*building, tree*> hoch. ~ **story** *n* übertriebene Geschichte *f*

tally *vi* übereinstimmen

tame *a* (**-r, -st**), **-ly** *adv* zahm; (*dull*) lahm [!] ● *vt* zähmen. **~r** *n* Dompteur *m*

tamper *vi* ~ **with** sich (*dat*) zu schaffen machen an (+ *dat*)

tampon *n* Tampon *m*

tan *a* gelbbraun ● *n* Gelbbraun *nt*; (*from sun*) Bräune *f* ● *v* (*pt/pp* **tanned**) ● *vt* gerben <*hide*> ● *vi* braun werden

tang *n* herber Geschmack *m*; (*smell*) herber Geruch *m*

tangible *a* greifbar

tangle *n* Gewirr *nt*; (*in hair*) Verfilzung *f* ● *vt* ~ **[up]** verheddern ● *vi* sich verheddern

tank *n* Tank *m*; (*Mil*) Panzer *m*

tanker *n* Tanker *m*; (*lorry*) Tank[last]wagen *m*

tantrum *n* Wutanfall *m*

tap *n* Hahn *m*; (*knock*) Klopfen *nt*; **on ~** zur Verfügung ● *v* (*pt/pp* **tapped**) ● *vt* klopfen an (+ *acc*); anzapfen <*barrel, tree*>; erschließen <*resources*>; abhören <*telephone*> ● *vi* klopfen. **~-**

dance *n* Stepp[tanz] *m* ●*vi* Stepp tanzen, steppen

tape *n* Band *nt*; (*adhesive*) Klebstreifen *m*; (*for recording*) Tonband *nt* ●*vt* mit Klebstreifen zukleben; (*record*) auf Band aufnehmen

tape-measure *n* Bandmaß *nt*

taper *vi* sich verjüngen

tape recorder *n* Tonbandgerät *nt*

tar *n* Teer *m* ●*vt* (*pt/pp* **tarred**) teeren

target *n* Ziel *nt*; (*board*) [Ziel]scheibe *f*

tarnish *vi* anlaufen

tarpaulin *n* Plane *f*

tart[1] *a* (**-er, -est**) sauer

tart[2] *n* ≈ Obstkuchen *m*; (*individual*) Törtchen *nt*; (☒ *prostitute*) Nutte *f* ●*vt* ~ **oneself up** [!] sich auftakeln

tartan *n* Schottenmuster *nt*; (*cloth*) Schottenstoff *m*

task *n* Aufgabe *f*; **take s.o. to** ~ jdm Vorhaltungen machen. ~ **force** *n* Sonderkommando *nt*

tassel *n* Quaste *f*

taste *n* Geschmack *m*; (*sample*) Kostprobe *f* ●*vt* kosten, probieren; schmecken <*flavour*> ●*vi* schmecken (**of** nach). ~**ful** *a*, **-ly** *adv* (*fig*) geschmackvoll. ~**less** *a*, **-ly** *adv* geschmacklos

tasty *a* (**-ier, -iest**) lecker

tat *see* **tit**[2]

tatters *npl* **in** ~**s** in Fetzen

tattoo *n* Tätowierung *f* ●*vt* tätowieren

tatty *a* (**-ier, -iest**) schäbig; <*book*> zerfleddert

taught *see* **teach**

taunt *n* höhnische Bemerkung *f* ●*vt* verhöhnen

taut *a* straff

tawdry *a* (**-ier, -iest**) billig und geschmacklos

tax *n* Steuer *f* ●*vt* besteuern; (*fig*) strapazieren. ~**able** *a* steuerpflichtig. ~**ation** *n* Besteuerung *f*

taxi *n* Taxi *nt* ●*vi* (*pt/pp* **taxied**, *pres p* **taxiing**) <*aircraft:*> rollen. ~ **driver** *n* Taxifahrer *m*. ~ **rank** *n* Taxistand *m*

taxpayer *n* Steuerzahler *m*

tea *n* Tee *m*. ~**-bag** *n* Teebeutel *m*. ~**-break** *n* Teepause *f*

teach *vt/i* (*pt/pp* **taught**) unterrichten; ~ **s.o. sth** jdm etw beibringen. ~**er** *n* Lehrer(in) *m(f)*. ~**ing** *n* Unterrichten *nt*

tea: ~**-cloth** *n* (*for drying*) Geschirrtuch *nt*. ~**cup** *n* Teetasse *f*

teak *n* Teakholz *nt*

team *n* Mannschaft *f*; (*fig*) Team *nt*; (*of animals*) Gespann *nt*

teapot *n* Teekanne *f*

tear[1] *n* Riss *m* ●*v* (*pt* **tore**, *pp* **torn**) ●*vt* reißen; (*damage*) zerreißen; ~ **oneself away** sich losreißen ●*vi* [zer]reißen; (*run*) rasen. ~ **up** *vt* zerreißen

tear[2] *n* Träne *f*. ~**ful** *a* weinend. ~**fully** *adv* unter Tränen. ~**gas** *n* Tränengas *nt*

tease *vt* necken

tea: ~**-set** *n* Teeservice *nt*. ~ **shop** *n* Café *nt*. ~**spoon** *n* Teelöffel *m*

teat *n* Zitze *f*; (*on bottle*) Sauger *m*

tea-towel *n* Geschirrtuch *nt*

technical *a* technisch; (*specialized*) fachlich. ~**ity** *n* technisches Detail *nt*; (*Jur*) Formfehler *m*. ~**ly** *adv* technisch; (*strictly*) streng genommen. ~ **term** *n* Fachausdruck *m*

technician *n* Techniker *m*

technique *n* Technik *f*

technological *a*, **-ly** *adv* technologisch

technology *n* Technik *f*

teddy *n* ~ **[bear]** Teddybär *m*

tedious *a* langweilig

tedium *n* Langeweile *f*

T

teenage *a* Teenager-; **~ boy/girl** Junge *m*/Mädchen *nt* im Teenageralter. **~r** *n* Teenager *m*
teens *npl* **the ~** die Teenagerjahre *pl*
teeter *vi* schwanken
teeth *see* **tooth**
teeth|e *vi* zahnen. **~ing troubles** *npl* (*fig*) Anfangsschwierigkeiten *pl*
teetotal *a* abstinent. **~ler** *n* Abstinenzler *m*
telebanking *n* Telebanking *nt*
telecommunications *npl* Fernmeldewesen *nt*
telegram *n* Telegramm *nt*
telegraph pole *n* Telegrafenmast *m*
telephone *n* Telefon *nt*; **be on the ~** Telefon haben; (*be telephoning*) telefonieren ● *vt* anrufen ● *vi* telefonieren
telephone: ~ booth *n*, **~ box** *n* Telefonzelle *f*. **~ directory** *n* Telefonbuch *nt*. **~ number** *n* Telefonnummer *f*
telephoto *a* **~ lens** Teleobjektiv *nt*
telescop|e *n* Teleskop *nt*, Fernrohr *nt*. **~ic** *a* (*collapsible*) ausziehbar
televise *vt* im Fernsehen übertragen
television *n* Fernsehen *nt*; **watch ~** fernsehen; **~ [set]** Fernseher *m* [!]
teleworking *n* Telearbeit *f*
tell *vt/i* (*pt/pp* **told**) sagen (**s.o.** jdm); (*relate*) erzählen; (*know*) wissen; (*distinguish*) erkennen; **~ the time** die Uhr lesen; **time will ~** das wird man erst sehen; **his age is beginning to ~** sein Alter macht sich bemerkbar. **~ off** *vt* ausschimpfen
telly *n* [!] = **television**
temp *n* [!] Aushilfssekretärin *f*
temper *n* (*disposition*) Naturell *nt*; (*mood*) Laune *f*; (*anger*) Wut *f*; **lose one's ~** wütend werden ● *vt* (*fig*) mäßigen
temperament *n* Temperament *nt*. **~al** *a* temperamentvoll; (*moody*) launisch
temperate *a* gemäßigt
temperature *n* Temperatur *f*; **have** *or* **run a ~** Fieber haben
temple[1] *n* Tempel *m*
temple[2] *n* (*Anat*) Schläfe *f*
tempo *n* Tempo *nt*
temporary *a*, **-ily** *adv* vorübergehend; <*measure, building*> provisorisch
tempt *vt* verleiten; (*Relig*) versuchen; herausfordern <*fate*>; (*entice*) [ver]locken; **be ~ed** versucht sein (**to** zu). **~ation** *n* Versuchung *f*. **~ing** *a* verlockend
ten *a* zehn
tenaci|ous *a*, **-ly** *adv* hartnäckig. **~ty** *n* Hartnäckigkeit *f*
tenant *n* Mieter(in) *m(f)*; (*Comm*) Pächter(in) *m(f)*
tend *vi* **~ to do sth** dazu neigen, etw zu tun
tendency *n* Tendenz *f*; (*inclination*) Neigung *f*
tender *a* zart; (*loving*) zärtlich; (*painful*) empfindlich. **~ly** *adv* zärtlich. **~ness** *n* Zartheit *f*; Zärtlichkeit *f*
tendon *n* Sehne *f*
tenner *n* [!] Zehnpfundschein *m*
tennis *n* Tennis *nt*. **~-court** *n* Tennisplatz *m*
tenor *n* Tenor *m*
tense *a* (**-r, -st**) gespannt ● *vt* anspannen <*muscle*>
tension *n* Spannung *f*
tent *n* Zelt *nt*
tentative *a*, **-ly** *adv* vorläufig; (*hesitant*) zaghaft
tenterhooks *npl* **be on ~** wie auf glühenden Kohlen sitzen
tenth *a* zehnte(r,s) ● *n* Zehntel *nt*
tepid *a* lauwarm
term *n* Zeitraum *m*; (*Sch*) ≈ Halbjahr *nt*; (*Univ*) ≈ Semester

nt; (*expression*) Ausdruck *m*; **~s** *pl* (*conditions*) Bedingungen *pl*; **in the short/long ~** kurz-/langfristig; **be on good/bad ~s** gut/nicht gut miteinander auskommen

terminal *a* End-; (*Med*) unheilbar ●*n* (*Aviat*) Terminal *m*; (*of bus*) Endstation *f*; (*on battery*) Pol *m*; (*Computing*) Terminal *nt*

terminat|e *vt* beenden; lösen <*contract*>; unterbrechen <*pregnancy*> ●*vi* enden

terminology *n* Terminologie *f*

terminus *n* (*pl* **-ni**) Endstation *f*

terrace *n* Terrasse *f*; (*houses*) Häuserreihe *f*. **~d house** *n* Reihenhaus *nt*

terrain *n* Gelände *nt*

terrible *a*, **-bly** *adv* schrecklich

terrific *a* [!] (*excellent*) sagenhaft; (*huge*) riesig

terri|fy *vt* (*pt/pp* **-ied**) Angst machen (+ *dat*); **be ~fied** Angst haben. **~fying** *a* Furcht erregend

territorial *a* Territorial

territory *n* Gebiet *nt*

terror *n* [panische] Angst *f*; (*Pol*) Terror *m*. **~ism** *n* Terrorismus *m*. **~ist** *n* Terrorist *m*. **~ize** *vt* terrorisieren

terse *a*, **-ly** *adv* kurz, knapp

test *n* Test *m*; (*Sch*) Klassenarbeit *f*; **put to the ~** auf die Probe stellen ●*vt* prüfen; (*examine*) untersuchen (**for** auf + *acc*)

testament *n* Testament *nt*

testify *v* (*pt/pp* **-ied**) ●*vt* beweisen; **~ that** bezeugen, dass ●*vi* aussagen

testimonial *n* Zeugnis *nt*

testimony *n* Aussage *f*

test tube *n* Reagenzglas *nt*

tether *n* **be at the end of one's ~** am Ende seiner Kraft sein ●*vt* anbinden

text *n* Text *m* ● *vt/i* texten. **~book** *n* Lehrbuch *nt*

textile *a* Textil- ●*n* **~s** *pl* Textilien *pl*

text message *n* Textnachricht *f*

texture *n* Beschaffenheit *f*; (*Tex*) Struktur *f*

Thai *a* thailändisch. **~land** *n* Thailand *nt*

Thames *n* Themse *f*

than *conj* als

thank *vt* danken (+ *dat*); **~ you [very much]** danke [schön]. **~ful** *a*, **-ly** *adv* dankbar. **~less** *a* undankbar

thanks *npl* Dank *m*; **~!** [!] danke! **~ to** dank (+ *dat or gen*)

that

pl **those**

● *adjective*

····➤der (*m*), die (*f*), das (*nt*), die (*pl*); (*just seen or experienced*) dieser (*m*), diese (*f*), dieses (*nt*), diese (*pl*). **I'll never forget that day** den Tag werde ich nie vergessen. **I liked that house** dieses Haus hat mir gut gefallen

● *pronoun*

····➤der (*m*), die (*f*), das (*nt*), die (*pl*). **that is not true** das ist nicht wahr. **who is that in the garden?** wer ist das [da] im Garten? **I'll take that** ich nehme den/die/das. **I don't like those** die mag ich nicht. **is that you?** bist du es? **that is why** deshalb

····➤**like that** so. **don't be like that!** sei doch nicht so! **a man like that** ein solcher Mann; so ein Mann [!]

····➤(*after prepositions*) da .... **after that** danach. **with that** damit. **apart from that** außerdem

····➤(*relative pronoun*) der (*m*), die (*f*), das (*nt*), die (*pl*). **the book that I'm reading** das Buch, das ich lese. **the people that you got it from** die Leute, von denen du es bekommen hast. **everyone that I know** jeder, den ich kenne

● *adverb*

····➤so. **he's not that stupid** so blöd ist er [auch wieder] nicht. **it wasn't that bad** so schlecht war es auch nicht. **a nail about that long** ein etwa so langer Nagel

····➤(*relative adverb*) der (*m*), die (*f*), das (*nt*), die (*pl*). **the day that I first met her** der Tag, an dem ich sie zum ersten Mal sah. **at the speed that he was going** bei der Geschwindigkeit, die er hatte

● *conjunction*

····➤dass. **I don't think that he'll come** ich denke nicht, dass er kommt. **we know that you're right** wir wissen, dass du Recht hast. **I'm so tired that I can hardly walk** ich bin so müde, dass ich kaum gehen kann

····➤**so that** (*purpose*) damit; (*result*) sodass. **he came earlier so that they would have more time** er kam früher, damit sie mehr Zeit hatten. **it was late, so that I had to catch the bus** es war spät, sodass ich den Bus nehmen musste

thatch *n* Strohdach *nt*. **~ed** *a* strohgedeckt

thaw *n* Tauwetter *nt* ●*vt/i* auftauen; **it's ~ing** es taut

the *def art* der/die/das; (*pl*) die; **play ~ piano/violin** Klavier/Geige spielen ●*adv* **~ more ~ better** je mehr, desto besser; **all ~ better** umso besser

theatre *n* Theater *nt*; (*Med*) Operationssaal *m*

theatrical *a* Theater-; (*showy*) theatralisch

theft *n* Diebstahl *m*

their *a* ihr

theirs *poss pron* ihre(r), ihrs; **a friend of ~** ein Freund von ihnen; **those are ~** die gehören ihnen

them *pron* (*acc*) sie; (*dat*) ihnen

theme *n* Thema *nt*

themselves *pron* selbst; (*refl*) sich; **by ~** allein

then *adv* dann; (*at that time in past*) damals; **by ~** bis dahin; **since ~** seitdem; **before ~** vorher; **from ~ on** von da an; **now and ~** dann und wann; **there and ~** auf der Stelle ●*a* damalig

theology *n* Theologie *f*

theoretical *a*, **-ly** *adv* theoretisch

theory *n* Theorie *f*; **in ~** theoretisch

therap|ist *n* Therapeut(in) *m*(*f*). **~y** *n* Therapie *f*

there *adv* da; (*with movement*) dahin, dorthin; **down/up ~** da unten/oben; **~ is/are** da ist/sind; (*in existence*) es gibt ●*int* **~, ~!** nun, nun!

there: ~abouts *adv* da [in der Nähe]; **or ~abouts** (*roughly*) ungefähr. **~fore** *adv* deshalb, also

thermometer *n* Thermometer *nt*

Thermos (P) *n* **~ [flask]** Thermosflasche (P) *f*

thermostat *n* Thermostat *m*

these *see* **this**

thesis *n* (*pl* **-ses**) Dissertation *f*; (*proposition*) These *f*

they *pron* sie; **~ say** (*generalizing*) man sagt

thick *a* (**-er, -est**), **-ly** *adv* dick; (*dense*) dicht; <*liquid*> dickflüssig; (! *stupid*) dumm ●*adv* dick ●*n* **in the ~ of** mitten in (+ *dat*). **~en** *vt* dicker machen; eindicken <*sauce*> ●*vi* dicker werden; <*fog:*> dichter werden; <*plot:*> kompliziert werden. **~ness** *n* Dicke *f*; (*density*) Dichte *f*; (*of liquid*) Dickflüssigkeit *f*

thief *n* (*pl* **thieves**) Dieb(in) *m*(*f*)

thigh *n* Oberschenkel *m*

thimble *n* Fingerhut *m*

thin *a* (**thinner, thinnest**), **-ly** *adv* dünn ●*adv* dünn ●*v* (*pt/pp* **thinned**) ●*vt* verdünnen <*liquid*> ●*vi* sich lichten

thing *n* Ding *nt*; (*subject, affair*) Sache *f*; **~s** *pl* (*belongings*) Sachen *pl*; **for one ~** erstens; **just the ~!** genau das Richtige! **how are ~s?** wie geht's? **the latest ~** [!] der letzte Schrei
think *vt/i* (*pt/pp* **thought**) denken (**about/of** an + *acc*); (*believe*) meinen; (*consider*) nachdenken; (*regard as*) halten für; **I ~ so** ich glaube schon; **what do you ~ of it?** was halten Sie davon? **~ over** *vt* sich (*dat*) überlegen. **~ up** *vt* sich (*dat*) ausdenken
third *a* dritte(r,s) ● *n* Drittel *nt*. **~ly** *adv* drittens. **~-rate** *a* drittrangig
thirst *n* Durst *m*. **~y** *a*, **-ily** *adv* durstig; **be ~y** Durst haben
thirteen *a* dreizehn. **~th** *a* dreizehnte(r,s)
thirtieth *a* dreißigste(r,s)
thirty *a* dreißig
this *a* (*pl* **these**) diese(r,s); (*pl*) diese; **~ one** diese(r,s) da; **I'll take ~** ich nehme diesen/diese/dieses; **~ evening/morning** heute Abend/Morgen; **these days** heutzutage ● *pron* (*pl* **these**) das, dies[es]; (*pl*) die, diese; **~ and that** dies und das; **~ or that** dieses oder das da; **like ~** so; **~ is Peter** das ist Peter; (*Teleph*) hier [spricht] Peter; **who is ~?** wer ist das? (*Teleph, Amer*) wer ist am Apparat?
thistle *n* Distel *f*
thorn *n* Dorn *m*
thorough *a* gründlich
thoroughbred *n* reinrassiges Tier *nt*; (*horse*) Rassepferd *nt*
thorough|ly *adv* gründlich; (*completely*) völlig; (*extremely*) äußerst. **~ness** *n* Gründlichkeit *f*
those *see* **that**
though *conj* obgleich, obwohl; **as ~** als ob ● *adv* [!] doch
thought *see* **think** ● *n* Gedanke *m*; (*thinking*) Denken *nt*. **~ful** *a*, **-ly** *adv* nachdenklich; (*considerate*) rücksichtsvoll. **~less** *a*, **-ly** *adv* gedankenlos
thousand *a* **one/a ~** [ein]tausend ● *n* Tausend *nt*. **~th** *a* tausendste(r,s) ● *n* Tausendstel *nt*
thrash *vt* verprügeln; (*defeat*) [vernichtend] schlagen
thread *n* Faden *m*; (*of screw*) Gewinde *nt* ● *vt* einfädeln; auffädeln <*beads*>. **~bare** *a* fadenscheinig
threat *n* Drohung *f*; (*danger*) Bedrohung *f*
threaten *vt* drohen (+ *dat*); (*with weapon*) bedrohen; **~ s.o. with sth** jdm etw androhen ● *vi* drohen. **~ing** *a*, **-ly** *adv* drohend; (*ominous*) bedrohlich
three *a* drei. **~fold** *a & adv* dreifach
thresh *vt* dreschen
threshold *n* Schwelle *f*
threw *see* **throw**
thrift *n* Sparsamkeit *f*. **~y** *a* sparsam
thrill *n* Erregung *f*; [!] Nervenkitzel *m* ● *vt* (*excite*) erregen; **be ~ed with** sich sehr freuen über (+ *acc*). **~er** *n* Thriller *m*. **~ing** *a* erregend
thrive *vi* (*pt* **thrived** *or* **throve**, *pp* **thrived** *or* **thriven**) gedeihen (**on** bei); <*business:*> florieren
throat *n* Hals *m*; **cut s.o.'s ~** jdm die Kehle durchschneiden
throb *n* Pochen *nt* ● *vi* (*pt/pp* **throbbed**) pochen; (*vibrate*) vibrieren
throes *npl* **in the ~ of** (*fig*) mitten in (+ *dat*)
throne *n* Thron *m*
throttle *vt* erdrosseln
through *prep* durch (+ *acc*); (*during*) während (+ *gen*); (*Amer: up to & including*) bis einschließlich ● *adv* durch; **wet ~** durch und durch nass; **read sth ~**

etw durchlesen ● *a* <*train*> durchgehend; **be ~** (*finished*) fertig sein; (*Teleph*) durch sein

throughout *prep* **~ the country** im ganzen Land; **~ the night** die Nacht durch ● *adv* ganz; (*time*) die ganze Zeit

throve *see* **thrive**

throw *n* Wurf *m* ● *vt* (*pt* **threw**, *pp* **thrown**) werfen; schütten <*liquid*>; betätigen <*switch*>; abwerfen <*rider*>; ([!] *disconcert*) aus der Fassung bringen; [!] geben <*party*>; **~ sth to s.o.** jdm etw zuwerfen. **~ away** *vt* wegwerfen. **~ out** *vt* hinauswerfen; (**~** *away*) wegwerfen; verwerfen <*plan*>. **~ up** *vt* hochwerfen ● *vi* sich übergeben

throw-away *a* Wegwerf-

thrush *n* Drossel *f*

thrust *n* Stoß *m*; (*Phys*) Schub *m* ● *vt* (*pt/pp* **thrust**) stoßen; (*insert*) stecken

thud *n* dumpfer Schlag *m*

thug *n* Schläger *m*

thumb *n* Daumen *m* ● *vt* **~ a lift** [!] per Anhalter fahren. **~tack** *n* (*Amer*) Reißzwecke *f*

thump *n* Schlag *m*; (*noise*) dumpfer Schlag *m* ● *vt* schlagen ● *vi* hämmern; <*heart:*> pochen

thunder *n* Donner *m* ● *vi* donnern. **~clap** *n* Donnerschlag *m*. **~storm** *n* Gewitter *nt*. **~y** *a* gewittrig

Thursday *n* Donnerstag *m*

thus *adv* so

thwart *vt* vereiteln; **~ s.o.** jdm einen Strich durch die Rechnung machen

tick[1] *n* **on~** [!] auf Pump

tick[2] *n* (*sound*) Ticken *nt*; (*mark*) Häkchen *nt*; ([!] *instant*) Sekunde *f* ● *vi* ticken ● *vt* abhaken. **~ off** *vt* abhaken; [!] rüffeln

ticket *n* Karte *f*; (*for bus, train*) Fahrschein *m*; (*Aviat*) Flugschein *m*; (*for lottery*) Los *nt*; (*for article deposited*) Schein *m*; (*label*) Schild *nt*; (*for library*) Lesekarte *f*; (*fine*) Strafzettel *m*. **~ collector** *n* Fahrkartenkontrolleur *m*. **~ office** *n* Fahrkartenschalter *m*; (*for entry*) Kasse *f*

tick|le *n* Kitzeln *nt* ● *vt/i* kitzeln. **~lish** *a* kitzlig

tidal *a* **~ wave** Flutwelle *f*

tide *n* Gezeiten *pl*; (*of events*) Strom *m*; **the ~ is in/out** es ist Flut/Ebbe ● *vt* **~ s.o. over** jdm über die Runden helfen

tidiness *n* Ordentlichkeit *f*

tidy *a* (**-ier, -iest**), **-ily** *adv* ordentlich ● *vt* **~ [up]** aufräumen

tie *n* Krawatte *f*; Schlips *m*; (*cord*) Schnur *f*; (*fig: bond*) Band *nt*; (*restriction*) Bindung *f*; (*Sport*) Unentschieden *nt*; (*in competition*) Punktgleichheit *f* ● *v* (*pres p* **tying**) ● *vt* binden; machen <*knot*> ● *vi* (*Sport*) unentschieden spielen; (*have equal scores, votes*) punktgleich sein. **~ up** *vt* festbinden; verschnüren <*parcel*>; fesseln <*person*>; **be ~d up** (*busy*) beschäftigt sein

tier *n* Stufe *f*; (*of cake*) Etage *f*; (*in stadium*) Rang *m*

tiger *n* Tiger *m*

tight *a* (**-er, -est**), **-ly** *adv* fest; (*taut*) straff; <*clothes*> eng; <*control*> streng; ([!] *drunk*) blau ● *adv* fest

tighten *vt* fester ziehen; straffen <*rope*>; anziehen <*screw*>; verschärfen <*control*> ● *vi* sich spannen

tightrope *n* Hochseil *nt*

tights *npl* Strumpfhose *f*

tile *n* Fliese *f*; (*on wall*) Kachel *f*; (*on roof*) [Dach]ziegel *m* ● *vt* mit Fliesen auslegen; kacheln <*wall*>; decken <*roof*>

till[1] *prep & conj* = **until**

till[2] *n* Kasse *f*

tilt *n* Neigung *f* ● *vt* kippen; [zur Seite] neigen <*head*> ● *vi* sich neigen

timber *n* [Nutz]holz *nt*

time *n* Zeit *f*; (*occasion*) Mal *nt*; (*rhythm*) Takt *m*; **~s** (*Math*) mal; **at ~s** manchmal; **~ and again** immer wieder; **two at a ~** zwei auf einmal; **on ~** pünktlich; **in ~** rechtzeitig; (*eventually*) mit der Zeit; **in no ~** im Handumdrehen; **in a year's ~** in einem Jahr; **behind ~** verspätet; **behind the ~s** rückständig; **for the ~ being** vorläufig; **what is the ~?** wie spät ist es? wie viel Uhr ist es? **did you have a nice ~?** hat es dir gut gefallen? ● *vt* stoppen <*race*>; **be well ~d** gut abgepaßt sein

time: ~ bomb *n* Zeitbombe *f*. **~less** *a* zeitlos. **~ly** *a* rechtzeitig. **~-switch** *n* Zeitschalter *m*. **~-table** *n* Fahrplan *m*; (*Sch*) Stundenplan *m*

timid *a*, **-ly** *adv* scheu; (*hesitant*) zaghaft

timing *n* (*Sport, Techn*) Timing *nt*

tin *n* Zinn *nt*; (*container*) Dose *f* ● *vt* (*pt/pp* **tinned**) in Dosen konservieren. **~ foil** *n* Stanniol *nt*; (*Culin*) Alufolie *f*

tinge *n* Hauch *m*

tingle *vi* kribbeln

tinker *vi* herumbasteln (**with** an + *dat*)

tinkle *n* Klingeln *nt* ● *vi* klingeln

tinned *a* Dosen-

tin opener *n* Dosenöffner *m*

tinsel *n* Lametta *nt*

tint *n* Farbton *m* ● *vt* tönen

tiny *a* (**-ier, -iest**) winzig

tip¹ *n* Spitze *f*

tip² *n* (*money*) Trinkgeld *nt*; (*advice*) Rat *m*, [!] Tipp *m*; (*for rubbish*) Müllhalde *f* ● *v* (*pt/pp* **tipped**) ● *vt* (*tilt*) kippen; (*reward*) Trinkgeld geben (**s.o.** jdm) ● *vi* kippen. **~ out** *vt* auskippen. **~ over** *vt/i* umkippen

tipped *a* Filter-

tipsy *a* [!] beschwipst

tiptoe *n* **on ~** auf Zehenspitzen

tiptop *a* [!] erstklassig

tire *vt/i* ermüden. **~d** *a* müde; **be ~d of sth** etw satt haben; **~d out** [völlig] erschöpft. **~less** *a*, **-ly** *adv* unermüdlich. **~some** *a* lästig

tiring *a* ermüdend

tissue *n* Gewebe *nt*; (*handkerchief*) Papiertaschentuch *nt*

tit *n* (*bird*) Meise *f*

titbit *n* Leckerbissen *m*

title *n* Titel *m*

to

● *preposition*

····➤ (*destinations: most cases*) zu (+ *dat*). **go to work/the station** zur Arbeit/zum Bahnhof gehen. **from house to house** von Haus zu Haus. **go/come to s.o.** zu jdm gehen/kommen

····➤ (*with name of place or points of compass*) nach. **to Paris/Germany** nach Paris/Deutschland. **to Switzerland** in die Schweiz. **from East to West** von Osten nach Westen. **I've never been to Berlin** ich war noch nie in Berlin

····➤ (*to cinema, theatre, bed*) in (+ *acc*). **to bed with you!** ins Bett mit dir!

····➤ (*to wedding, party, university, the toilet*) auf (+ *acc*).

····➤ (*up to*) bis zu (+ *dat*). **to the end** bis zum Schluss. **to this day** bis heute. **5 to 6 pounds** 5 bis 6 Pfund

····➤ <*give, say, write*> + *dat*. **give/say sth to s.o.** jdm etw geben/sagen. **she wrote to him/the firm** sie hat ihm/an die Firma geschrieben

····➤ <*address, send, fasten*> an (+ *acc*). **she sent it to her brother** sie schickte es an ihren Bruder

····➤ (*in telling the time*) vor. **five to eight** fünf vor acht. **a quarter to ten** Viertel vor zehn

● *before infinitive*

····➤ (*after modal verb*) (*not translated*). **I want to go** ich will gehen. **he is learning to swim** er lernt schwimmen. **you have to** du musst [es tun]

····➤ (*after adjective*) zu. **it is easy to forget** es ist leicht zu vergessen

····➤ (*expressing purpose, result*) um ... zu. **he did it to annoy me** er tat es, um mich zu ärgern. **she was too tired to go** sie war zu müde um zu gehen

● *adverb*

····➤ **be to** <*door, window*> angelehnt sein. **pull a door to** eine Tür anlehnen

····➤ **to and fro** hin und her

toad *n* Kröte *f*

toast *n* Toast *m* ● *vt* toasten <*bread*>; (*drink a ~ to*) trinken auf (+ *acc*). **~er** *n* Toaster *m*

tobacco *n* Tabak *m*. **~nist's [shop]** *n* Tabakladen *m*

toboggan *n* Schlitten *m* ● *vi* Schlitten fahren

today *n & adv* heute; **~ week** heute in einer Woche

toddler *n* Kleinkind *nt*

toe *n* Zeh *m*; (*of footwear*) Spitze *f* ● *vt* **~ the line** spuren. **~nail** *n* Zehennagel *m*

toffee *n* Karamell *m & nt*

together *adv* zusammen; (*at the same time*) gleichzeitig

toilet *n* Toilette *f*. **~ bag** *n* Kulturbeutel *m*. **~ paper** *n* Toilettenpapier *nt*

toiletries *npl* Toilettenartikel *pl*

token *n* Zeichen *nt*; (*counter*) Marke *f*; (*voucher*) Gutschein *m* ● *attrib* symbolisch

told *see* **tell** ● *a* **all ~** insgesamt

tolerable *a*, **-bly** *adv* erträglich; (*not bad*) leidlich

toleran|ce *n* Toleranz *f*. **~t** *a*, **-ly** *adv* tolerant

tolerate *vt* dulden, tolerieren; (*bear*) ertragen

toll *n* Gebühr *f*; (*for road*) Maut *f* (*Aust*); **death ~** Zahl *f* der Todesopfer

tomato *n* (*pl* **-es**) Tomate *f*

tomb *n* Grabmal *nt*

tombstone *n* Grabstein *m*

tom-cat *n* Kater *m*

tomorrow *n & adv* morgen; **~ morning** morgen früh; **the day after ~** übermorgen; **see you ~!** bis morgen!

ton *n* Tonne *f*; **~s of** [!] jede Menge

tone *n* Ton *m*; (*colour*) Farbton *m* ● *vt* **~ down** dämpfen; (*fig*) mäßigen. **~ up** *vt* kräftigen; straffen <*muscles*>

tongs *npl* Zange *f*

tongue *n* Zunge *f*; **~ in cheek** [!] nicht ernst

tonic *n* Tonikum *nt*; (*for hair*) Haarwasser *nt*; (*fig*) Wohltat *f*; **~ [water]** Tonic *nt*

tonight *n & adv* heute Nacht; (*evening*) heute Abend

tonne *n* Tonne *f*

tonsil *n* (*Anat*) Mandel *f*. **~litis** *n* Mandelentzündung *f*

too *adv* zu; (*also*) auch; **~ much/little** zu viel/zu wenig

took *see* **take**

tool *n* Werkzeug *nt*; (*for gardening*) Gerät *nt*. **~bar** *n* Werkzeugleiste *f*

tooth *n* (*pl* **teeth**) Zahn *m*

tooth: ~ache *n* Zahnschmerzen *pl*. **~brush** *n* Zahnbürste *f*. **~less** *a* zahnlos. **~paste** *n* Zahnpasta *f*. **~pick** *n* Zahnstocher *m*

top[1] *n* (*toy*) Kreisel *m*

top[2] *n* oberer Teil *m*; (*apex*) Spitze *f*; (*summit*) Gipfel *m*; (*Sch*) Erste(r) *m/f*; (*top part or half*)

Oberteil *nt*; (*head*) Kopfende *nt*; (*of road*) oberes Ende *nt*; (*upper surface*) Oberfläche *f*; (*lid*) Deckel *m*; (*of bottle*) Verschluss *m*; (*garment*) Top *nt*; **at the/on ~** oben; **on ~ of** oben auf (+ *dat/acc*); **on ~ of that** (*besides*) obendrein; **from ~ to bottom** von oben bis unten ● *a* oberste(r,s); (*highest*) höchste(r,s); (*best*) beste(r,s) ● *vt* (*pt/pp* **topped**) an erster Stelle stehen auf (+ *dat*) <*list*>; (*exceed*) übersteigen; (*remove the ~ of*) die Spitze abschneiden von. **~ up** *vt* nachfüllen, auffüllen

top: ~ hat *n* Zylinder[hut] *m*. **~-heavy** *a* kopflastig

topic *n* Thema *nt*. **~al** *a* aktuell

topple *vt/i* umstürzen

torch *n* Taschenlampe *f*; (*flaming*) Fackel *f*

tore *see* **tear**[1]

torment[1] *n* Qual *f*

torment[2] *vt* quälen

torn *see* **tear**[1] ● *a* zerrissen

torpedo *n* (*pl* **-es**) Torpedo *m* ● *vt* torpedieren

torrent *n* reißender Strom *m*. **~ial** *a* <*rain*> wolkenbruchartig

tortoise *n* Schildkröte *f*. **~shell** *n* Schildpatt *nt*

tortuous *a* verschlungen; (*fig*) umständlich

torture *n* Folter *f*; (*fig*) Qual *f* ● *vt* foltern; (*fig*) quälen

toss *vt* werfen; (*into the air*) hochwerfen; (*shake*) schütteln; (*unseat*) abwerfen; mischen <*salad*>; wenden <*pancake*>; **~ a coin** mit einer Münze losen ● *vi* **~ and turn** (*in bed*) sich [schlaflos] im Bett wälzen

tot[1] *n* kleines Kind *nt*; (🄸 *of liquor*) Gläschen *nt*

tot[2] *vt* (*pt/pp* **totted**) **~ up** 🄸 zusammenzählen

total *a* gesamt; (*complete*) völlig, total ● *n* Gesamtzahl *f*; (*sum*) Gesamtsumme *f* ● *vt* (*pt/pp* **totalled**); (*amount to*) sich belaufen auf (+ *acc*)

totalitarian *a* totalitär

totally *adv* völlig, total

totter *vi* taumeln

touch *n* Berührung *f*; (*sense*) Tastsinn *m*; (*Mus*) Anschlag *m*; (*contact*) Kontakt *m*; (*trace*) Spur *f*; (*fig*) Anflug *m*; **get/be in ~** sich in Verbindung setzen/in Verbindung stehen (**with** mit) ● *vt* berühren; (*get hold of*) anfassen; (*lightly*) tippen auf/an (+ *acc*); (*brush against*) streifen [gegen]; (*fig: move*) rühren; anrühren <*food, subject*>; **don't ~ that!** fass das nicht an! ● *vi* sich berühren; **~ on** (*fig*) berühren. **~ down** *vi* (*Aviat*) landen. **~ up** *vt* ausbessern

touch|ing *a* rührend. **~y** *a* empfindlich

tough *a* (**-er, -est**) zäh; (*severe, harsh*) hart; (*difficult*) schwierig; (*durable*) strapazierfähig

toughen *vt* härten; **~ up** abhärten

tour *n* Reise *f*, Tour *f*; (*of building, town*) Besichtigung *f*; (*Theat, Sport*) Tournee *f*; (*of duty*) Dienstzeit *f* ● *vt* fahren durch ● *vi* herumreisen

touris|m *n* Tourismus *m*, Fremdenverkehr *m*. **~t** *n* Tourist(in) *m(f)* ● *attrib* Touristen-. **~t office** *n* Fremdenverkehrsbüro *nt*

tournament *n* Turnier *nt*

tour operator *n* Reiseveranstalter *m*

tousle *vt* zerzausen

tow *n* **give s.o./a car a ~** jdn/ein Auto abschleppen ● *vt* schleppen; ziehen <*trailer*>

toward[s] *prep* zu (+ *dat*); (*with time*) gegen (+ *acc*); (*with respect to*) gegenüber (+ *dat*)

towel *n* Handtuch *nt*. **~ling** *n* (*Tex*) Frottee *nt*

T

tower *n* Turm *m* ● *vi* ~ **above** überragen. ~ **block** *n* Hochhaus *nt*. ~**ing** *a* hoch aufragend

town *n* Stadt *f*. ~ **hall** *n* Rathaus *nt*

tow-rope *n* Abschleppseil *nt*

toxic *a* giftig

toy *n* Spielzeug *nt* ● *vi* ~ **with** spielen mit; stochern in (+ *dat*) <*food*>. ~**shop** *n* Spielwarengeschäft *nt*

trace *n* Spur *f* ● *vt* folgen (+ *dat*); (*find*) finden; (*draw*) zeichnen; (*with tracing-paper*) durchpausen

track *n* Spur *f*; (*path*) [unbefestigter] Weg *m*; (*Sport*) Bahn *f*; (*Rail*) Gleis *nt*; **keep ~ of** im Auge behalten ● *vt* verfolgen. ~ **down** *vt* aufspüren; (*find*) finden

tracksuit *n* Trainingsanzug *m*

tractor *n* Traktor *m*

trade *n* Handel *m*; (*line of business*) Gewerbe *nt*; (*business*) Geschäft *nt*; (*craft*) Handwerk *nt*; **by ~** von Beruf ● *vt* tauschen; ~ **in** (*give in part exchange*) in Zahlung geben ● *vi* handeln (**in** mit)

trade mark *n* Warenzeichen *nt*

trader *n* Händler *m*

trade: ~ union *n* Gewerkschaft *f*. ~ **unionist** *n* Gewerkschaftler(in) *m*(*f*)

trading *n* Handel *m*

tradition *n* Tradition *f*. ~**al** *a*, **-ly** *adv* traditionell

traffic *n* Verkehr *m*; (*trading*) Handel *m*

traffic: ~ circle *n* (*Amer*) Kreisverkehr *m*. ~ **jam** *n* [Verkehrs]stau *m*. ~ **lights** *npl* [Verkehrs]ampel *f*. ~ **warden** *n* ≈ Hilfspolizist *m*; (*woman*) Politesse *f*

tragedy *n* Tragödie *f*

tragic *a*, **-ally** *adv* tragisch

trail *n* Spur *f*; (*path*) Weg *m*, Pfad *m* ● *vi* schleifen; <*plant:*> sich ranken ● *vt* verfolgen, folgen (+ *dat*); (*drag*) schleifen

trailer *n* (*Auto*) Anhänger *m*; (*Amer: caravan*) Wohnwagen *m*; (*film*) Vorschau *f*

train *n* Zug *m*; (*of dress*) Schleppe *f* ● *vt* ausbilden; (*Sport*) trainieren; (*aim*) richten auf (+ *acc*); erziehen <*child*>; abrichten/(*to do tricks*) dressieren <*animal*>; ziehen <*plant*> ● *vi* eine Ausbildung machen; (*Sport*) trainieren. ~**ed** *a* ausgebildet

trainee *n* Auszubildende(r) *m/f*; (*Techn*) Praktikant(in) *m*(*f*)

train|er *n* (*Sport*) Trainer *m*; (*in circus*) Dompteur *m*; ~**ers** *pl* Trainingsschuhe *pl*. ~**ing** *n* Ausbildung *f*; (*Sport*) Training *nt*; (*of animals*) Dressur *f*

trait *n* Eigenschaft *f*

traitor *n* Verräter *m*

tram *n* Straßenbahn *f*

tramp *n* Landstreicher *m* ● *vi* stapfen; (*walk*) marschieren

trample *vt/i* trampeln

trance *n* Trance *f*

tranquil *a* ruhig. ~**lity** *n* Ruhe *f*

tranquillizer *n* Beruhigungsmittel *nt*

transaction *n* Transaktion *f*

transcend *vt* übersteigen

transfer[1] *n* (*see* **transfer[2]**) Übertragung *f*; Verlegung *f*; Versetzung *f*; Überweisung *f*; (*Sport*) Transfer *m*; (*design*) Abziehbild *nt*

transfer[2] *v* (*pt/pp* **transferred**) ● *vt* übertragen; verlegen <*firm, prisoners*>; versetzen <*employee*>; überweisen <*money*>; (*Sport*) transferieren ● *vi* [über]wechseln; (*when travelling*) umsteigen

transform *vt* verwandeln. ~**ation** *n* Verwandlung *f*. ~**er** *n* Transformator *m*

transfusion *n* Transfusion *f*

transistor *n* Transistor *m*
transit *n* Transit *m*; (*of goods*) Transport *m*; **in ~** <*goods*> auf dem Transport
transition *n* Übergang *m*. **~al** *a* Übergangs-
translat|e *vt* übersetzen. **~ion** *n* Übersetzung *f*. **~or** *n* Übersetzer(in) *m*(*f*)
transmission *n* Übertragung *f*
transmit *vt* (*pt/pp* **transmitted**) übertragen. **~ter** *n* Sender *m*
transparen|cy *n* (*Phot*) Dia *nt*. **~t** *a* durchsichtig
transplant¹ *n* Verpflanzung *f*, Transplantation *f*
transplant² *vt* umpflanzen; (*Med*) verpflanzen
transport¹ *n* Transport *m*
transport² *vt* transportieren. **~ation** *n* Transport *m*
transpose *vt* umstellen
trap *n* Falle *f*; ([!] *mouth*) Klappe *f*; **pony and ~** Einspänner *m* ● *vt* (*pt/pp* **trapped**) [mit einer Falle] fangen; (*jam*) einklemmen; **be ~ped** festsitzen; (*shut in*) eingeschlossen sein. **~door** *n* Falltür *f*
trash *n* Schund *m*; (*rubbish*) Abfall *m*; (*nonsense*) Quatsch *m*. **~can** *n* (*Amer*) Mülleimer *m*. **~y** *a* Schund-
trauma *n* Trauma *nt*. **~tic** *a* traumatisch
travel *n* Reisen *nt* ● *v* (*pt/pp* **travelled**) ● *vi* reisen; (*go in vehicle*) fahren; <*light, sound*> sich fortpflanzen; (*Techn*) sich bewegen ● *vt* bereisen; fahren <*distance*>. **~ agency** *n* Reisebüro *nt*. **~ agent** *n* Reisebürokaufmann *m*
traveller *n* Reisende(r) *m*/*f*; (*Comm*) Vertreter *m*; **~s** *pl* (*gypsies*) Zigeuner *pl*. **~'s cheque** *n* Reisescheck *m*
trawler *n* Fischdampfer *m*
tray *n* Tablett *nt*; (*for baking*) [Back]blech *nt*; (*for documents*) Ablagekorb *m*
treacher|ous *a* treulos; (*dangerous, deceptive*) tückisch. **~y** *n* Verrat *m*
tread *n* Schritt *m*; (*step*) Stufe *f*; (*of tyre*) Profil *nt* ● *v* (*pt* **trod**, *pp* **trodden**) ● *vi* (*walk*) gehen; **~ on/in** treten auf/ in (+ *acc*) ● *vt* treten
treason *n* Verrat *m*
treasure *n* Schatz *m* ● *vt* in Ehren halten. **~r** *n* Kassenwart *m*
treasury *n* Schatzkammer *f*; **the T~** das Finanzministerium
treat *n* [besonderes] Vergnügen *nt* ● *vt* behandeln; **~ s.o. to sth** jdm etw spendieren
treatment *n* Behandlung *f*
treaty *n* Vertrag *m*
treble *a* dreifach; **~ the amount** dreimal so viel ● *n* (*Mus*) Diskant *m*; (*voice*) Sopran *m* ● *vt* verdreifachen ● *vi* sich verdreifachen
tree *n* Baum *m*
trek *n* Marsch *m* ● *vi* (*pt/pp* **trekked**) latschen
trellis *n* Gitter *nt*
tremble *vi* zittern
tremendous *a*, **-ly** *adv* gewaltig; ([!] *excellent*) großartig
tremor *n* Zittern *nt*; **[earth] ~** Beben *nt*
trench *n* Graben *m*; (*Mil*) Schützengraben *m*
trend *n* Tendenz *f*; (*fashion*) Trend *m*. **~y** *a* (**-ier, -iest**) [!] modisch
trepidation *n* Beklommenheit *f*
trespass *vi* **~ on** unerlaubt betreten
trial *n* (*Jur*) [Gerichts]verfahren *nt*, Prozess *m*; (*test*) Probe *f*; (*ordeal*) Prüfung *f*; **be on ~** auf Probe sein; (*Jur*) angeklagt sein

T

(**for** wegen); **by ~ and error** durch Probieren
triang|le *n* Dreieck *nt*; (*Mus*) Triangel *m*. **~ular** *a* dreieckig
tribe *n* Stamm *m*
tribunal *n* Schiedsgericht *nt*
tributary *n* Nebenfluss *m*
tribute *n* Tribut *m*; **pay ~** Tribut zollen (**to** *dat*)
trick *n* Trick *m*; (*joke*) Streich *m*; (*Cards*) Stich *m*; (*feat of skill*) Kunststück *nt* ● *vt* täuschen, [!] hereinlegen
trickle *vi* rinnen
trick|ster *n* Schwindler *m*. **~y** *a* (**-ier, -iest**) *a* schwierig
tricycle *n* Dreirad *nt*
tried *see* **try**
trifl|e *n* Kleinigkeit *f*; (*Culin*) Trifle *nt*. **~ing** *a* unbedeutend
trigger *n* Abzug *m*; (*fig*) Auslöser *m* ● *vt* **~ [off]** auslösen
trim *a* (**trimmer, trimmest**) gepflegt ● *n* (*cut*) Nachschneiden *nt*; (*decoration*) Verzierung *f*; (*condition*) Zustand *m* ● *vt* schneiden; (*decorate*) besetzen. **~ming** *n* Besatz *m*; **~mings** *pl* (*accessories*) Zubehör *nt*; (*decorations*) Verzierungen *pl*
trio *n* Trio *nt*
trip *n* Reise *f*; (*excursion*) Ausflug *m* ● *v* (*pt/pp* **tripped**) ● *vt* **~ s.o. up** jdm ein Bein stellen ● *vi* stolpern (**on/over** über + *acc*)
tripe *n* Kaldaunen *pl*; (*nonsense*) Quatsch *m*
triple *a* dreifach ● *vt* verdreifachen ● *vi* sich verdreifachen
triplets *npl* Drillinge *pl*
triplicate *n* **in ~** in dreifacher Ausfertigung
tripod *n* Stativ *nt*
tripper *n* Ausflügler *m*
trite *a* banal
triumph *n* Triumph *m* ● *vi* triumphieren (**over** über + *acc*). **~ant** *a*, **-ly** *adv* triumphierend
trivial *a* belanglos. **~ity** *n* Belanglosigkeit *f*
trod, trodden *see* **tread**
trolley *n* (*for food*) Servierwagen *m*; (*for shopping*) Einkaufswagen *m*; (*for luggage*) Kofferkuli *m*; (*Amer: tram*) Straßenbahn *f*
trombone *n* Posaune *f*
troop *n* Schar *f*; **~s** *pl* Truppen *pl*
trophy *n* Trophäe *f*; (*in competition*) ≈ Pokal *m*
tropics *npl* Tropen *pl*. **~al** *a* tropisch; <*fruit*> Süd-
trot *n* Trab *m* ● *vi* (*pt/pp* **trotted**) traben
trouble *n* Ärger *m*; (*difficulties*) Schwierigkeiten *pl*; (*inconvenience*) Mühe *f*; (*conflict*) Unruhe *f*; (*Med*) Beschwerden *pl*; (*Techn*) Probleme *pl*; **get into ~** Ärger bekommen; **take ~** sich (*dat*) Mühe geben ● *vt* (*disturb*) stören; (*worry*) beunruhigen ● *vi* sich bemühen. **~-maker** *n* Unruhestifter *m*. **~some** *a* schwierig; <*flies, cough*> lästig
trough *n* Trog *m*
troupe *n* Truppe *f*
trousers *npl* Hose *f*
trousseau *n* Aussteuer *f*
trout *n inv* Forelle *f*
trowel *n* Kelle *f*
truant *n* **play ~** die Schule schwänzen
truce *n* Waffenstillstand *m*
truck *n* Last[kraft]wagen *m*; (*Rail*) Güterwagen *m*
trudge *vi* latschen
true *a* (**-r, -st**) wahr; (*loyal*) treu; (*genuine*) echt; **come ~** in Erfüllung gehen; **is that ~?** stimmt das?
truly *adv* wirklich; (*faithfully*) treu; **Yours ~** mit freundlichen Grüßen
trump *n* (*Cards*) Trumpf *m* ● *vt* übertrumpfen
trumpet *n* Trompete *f*. **~er** *n* Trompeter *m*

truncheon *n* Schlagstock *m*
trunk *n* [Baum]stamm *m*; (*body*) Rumpf *m*; (*of elephant*) Rüssel *m*; (*for travelling*) [Übersee]koffer *m*; (*Amer: of car*) Kofferraum *m*; **~s** *pl* Badehose *f*
trust *n* Vertrauen *nt*; (*group of companies*) Trust *m*; (*organization*) Treuhandgesellschaft *f*; (*charitable*) Stiftung *f* ● *vt* trauen (+ *dat*), vertrauen (+ *dat*); (*hope*) hoffen ● *vi* vertrauen (**in**/**to** auf + *acc*)
trustee *n* Treuhänder *m*
trust|ful *a*, **-ly** *adv*, **~ing** *a* vertrauensvoll. **~worthy** *a* vertrauenswürdig
truth *n* (*pl* **-s**) Wahrheit *f*. **~ful** *a*, **-ly** *adv* ehrlich
try *n* Versuch *m* ● *v* (*pt*/*pp* **tried**) ● *vt* versuchen; (*sample, taste*) probieren; (*be a strain on*) anstrengen; (*Jur*) vor Gericht stellen; verhandeln <*case*> ● *vi* versuchen; (*make an effort*) sich bemühen. **~ on** *vt* anprobieren; aufprobieren <*hat*>. **~ out** *vt* ausprobieren
trying *a* schwierig
T-shirt *n* T-Shirt *nt*
tub *n* Kübel *m*; (*carton*) Becher *m*; (*bath*) Wanne *f*
tuba *n* (*Mus*) Tuba *f*
tubby *a* (**-ier, -iest**) rundlich
tube *n* Röhre *f*; (*pipe*) Rohr *nt*; (*flexible*) Schlauch *m*; (*of toothpaste*) Tube *f*; (*Rail* [!]) U-Bahn *f*
tuberculosis *n* Tuberkulose *f*
tubular *a* röhrenförmig
tuck *n* Saum *m*; (*decorative*) Biese *f* ● *vt* (*put*) stecken. **~ in** *vt* hineinstecken; **~ s.o. in** *or* **up** jdn zudecken ● *vi* ([!] *eat*) zulangen
Tuesday *n* Dienstag *m*
tuft *n* Büschel *nt*
tug *n* Ruck *m*; (*Naut*) Schleppdampfer *m* ● *v* (*pt*/*pp* **tugged**) ● *vt* ziehen ● *vi* zerren (**at** an + *dat*)
tuition *n* Unterricht *m*
tulip *n* Tulpe *f*
tumble *n* Sturz *m* ● *vi* fallen. **~down** *a* verfallen. **~-drier** *n* Wäschetrockner *m*
tumbler *n* Glas *nt*
tummy *n* [!] Bauch *m*
tumour *n* Tumor *m*
tumult *n* Tumult *m*
tuna *n* Thunfisch *m*
tune *n* Melodie *f*; **out of ~** <*instrument*> verstimmt ● *vt* stimmen; (*Techn*) einstellen. **~ in** *vt* einstellen: ● *vi* **~ in to a station** einen Sender einstellen. **~ up** *vi* (*Mus*) stimmen
tuneful *a* melodisch
Tunisia *n* Tunesien *nt*
tunnel *n* Tunnel *m* ● *vi* (*pt*/*pp* **tunnelled**) einen Tunnel graben
turban *n* Turban *m*
turbine *n* Turbine *f*
turbulen|ce *n* Turbulenz *f*. **~t** *a* stürmisch
turf *n* Rasen *m*; (*segment*) Rasenstück *nt*
Turk *n* Türke *m*/Türkin *f*
turkey *n* Truthahn *m*
Turk|ey *n* die Türkei. **~ish** *a* türkisch; **the ~ish** die Türken
turmoil *n* Aufruhr *m*; (*confusion*) Durcheinander *nt*
turn *n* (*rotation*) Drehung *f*; (*bend*) Kurve *f*; (*change of direction*) Wende *f*; (*Theat*) Nummer *f*; ([!] *attack*) Anfall *m*; **do s.o. a good ~** jdm einen guten Dienst erweisen; **take ~s** sich abwechseln; **in ~** der Reihe nach; **out of ~** außer der Reihe; **it's your ~** du bist an der Reihe ● *vt* drehen; (**~** *over*) wenden; (*reverse*) umdrehen; (*Techn*) drechseln <*wood*>; **~ the page** umblättern; **~ the corner** um die Ecke biegen ● *vi* sich drehen; (**~** *round*) sich umdrehen; <*car:*>

wenden; <*leaves:*> sich färben: <*weather:*> umschlagen; (*become*) werden; ~ **right/left** nach rechts/links abbiegen; ~ **to s.o.** sich an jdn wenden. ~ **away** *vt* abweisen ● *vi* sich abwenden. ~ **down** *vt* herunterschlagen <*collar*>; herunterdrehen <*heat, gas*>; leiser stellen <*sound*>; (*reject*) ablehnen; abweisen <*person*>. ~ **in** *vt* einschlagen <*edges*> ● *vi* <*car:*> einbiegen; ([!] *go to bed*) ins Bett gehen. ~ **off** *vt* zudrehen <*tap*>; ausschalten <*light, radio*>; abstellen <*water, gas, engine, machine*> ● *vi* abbiegen. ~ **on** *vt* aufdrehen <*tap*>; einschalten <*light, radio*>; anstellen <*water, gas, engine, machine*>. ~ **out** *vt* (*expel*) vertreiben, [!] hinauswerfen; ausschalten <*light*>; abdrehen <*gas*>; (*produce*) produzieren; (*empty*) ausleeren; [gründlich] aufräumen <*room, cupboard*> ● *vi* (*go out*) hinausgehen; (*transpire*) sich herausstellen. ~ **over** *vt* umdrehen. ~ **up** *vt* hochschlagen <*collar*>; aufdrehen <*heat, gas*>; lauter stellen <*sound, radio*> ● *vi* auftauchen

turning *n* Abzweigung *f*. ~**-point** *n* Wendepunkt *m*

turnip *n* weiße Rübe *f*

turn: ~**-out** *n* (*of people*) Beteiligung *f*. ~**over** *n* (*Comm*) Umsatz *m*; (*of staff*) Personalwechsel *m*. ~**pike** *n* (*Amer*) gebührenpflichtige Autobahn *f*. ~**table** *n* Drehscheibe *f*; (*on record player*) Plattenteller *m*. ~**-up** *n* [Hosen]aufschlag *m*

turquoise *a* türkis[farben] ● *n* (*gem*) Türkis *m*

turret *n* Türmchen *nt*

turtle *n* Seeschildkröte *f*

tusk *n* Stoßzahn *m*

tutor *n* [Privat]lehrer *m*

tuxedo *n* (*Amer*) Smoking *m*

TV *abbr of* **television**

tweed *n* Tweed *m*

tweezers *npl* Pinzette *f*

twelfth *a* zwölfter(r,s)

twelve *a* zwölf

twentieth *a* zwanzigste(r,s)

twenty *a* zwanzig

twice *adv* zweimal

twig *n* Zweig *m*

twilight *n* Dämmerlicht *nt*

twin *n* Zwilling *m* ● *attrib* Zwillings-

twine *n* Bindfaden *m*

twinge *n* Stechen *nt*; ~ **of conscience** Gewissensbisse *pl*

twinkle *n* Funkeln *nt* ● *vi* funkeln

twin town *n* Partnerstadt *f*

twirl *vt/i* herumwirbeln

twist *n* Drehung *f*; (*curve*) Kurve *f*; (*unexpected occurrence*) überraschende Wendung *f* ● *vt* drehen; (*distort*) verdrehen; ([!] *swindle*) beschummeln; ~ **one's ankle** sich (*dat*) den Knöchel verrenken ● *vi* sich drehen; <*road:*> sich winden. ~**er** *n* [!] Schwindler *m*

twit *n* [!] Trottel *m*

twitch *n* Zucken *nt* ● *vi* zucken

twitter *n* Zwitschern *nt* ● *vi* zwitschern

two *a* zwei

two: ~**-faced** *a* falsch. ~**-piece** *a* zweiteilig. ~**-way** *a* ~**-way traffic** Gegenverkehr *m*

tycoon *n* Magnat *m*

tying *see* **tie**

type *n* Art *f*, Sorte *f*; (*person*) Typ *m*; (*printing*) Type *f* ● *vt* mit der Maschine schreiben, [!] tippen ● *vi* Maschine schreiben, [!] tippen. ~**writer** *n* Schreibmaschine *f*. ~**written** *a* maschinegeschrieben

typical *a*, **-ly** *adv* typisch (**of** für)

typify *vt* (*pt/pp* **-ied**) typisch sein für

typing *n* Maschineschreiben *nt*
typist *n* Schreibkraft *f*
tyrannical *a* tyrannisch
tyranny *n* Tyrannei *f*
tyrant *n* Tyrann *m*
tyre *n* Reifen *m*

Uu

ugl|iness *n* Hässlichkeit *f*. **~y** *a* (**-ier, -iest**) hässlich; (*nasty*) übel
UK *abbr see* **United Kingdom**
ulcer *n* Geschwür *nt*
ultimate *a* letzte(r,s); (*final*) endgültig; (*fundamental*) grundlegend, eigentlich. **~ly** *adv* schließlich
ultimatum *n* Ultimatum *nt*
ultraviolet *a* ultraviolett
umbrella *n* [Regen]schirm *m*
umpire *n* Schiedsrichter *m* ● *vt/i* Schiedsrichter sein (bei)
umpteen *a* [!] zig. **~th** *a* [!] zigste(r,s)
unable *a* **be ~ to do sth** etw nicht tun können
unabridged *a* ungekürzt
unaccompanied *a* ohne Begleitung; <*luggage*> unbegleitet
unaccountable *a* unerklärlich
unaccustomed *a* ungewohnt; **be ~ to sth** etw (*acc*) nicht gewohnt sein
unaided *a* ohne fremde Hilfe
unanimous *a*, **-ly** *adv* einmütig; <*vote, decision*> einstimmig
unarmed *a* unbewaffnet
unassuming *a* bescheiden
unattended *a* unbeaufsichtigt
unauthorized *a* unbefugt
unavoidable *a* unvermeidlich
unaware *a* **be ~ of sth** sich (*dat*) etw (*gen*) nicht bewusst sein. **~s** *adv* **catch s.o. ~s** jdn überraschen
unbearable *a*, **-bly** *adv* unerträglich
unbeat|able *a* unschlagbar. **~en** *a* ungeschlagen; <*record*> ungebrochen
unbelievable *a* unglaublich
unbiased *a* unvoreingenommen
unblock *vt* frei machen
unbolt *vt* aufriegeln
unbreakable *a* unzerbrechlich
unbutton *vt* aufknöpfen
uncalled-for *a* unangebracht
uncanny *a* unheimlich
unceasing *a* unaufhörlich
uncertain *a* (*doubtful*) ungewiss; <*origins*> unbestimmt; **be ~** nicht sicher sein. **~ty** *n* Ungewissheit *f*
unchanged *a* unverändert
uncharitable *a* lieblos
uncle *n* Onkel *m*
uncomfortable *a*, **-bly** *adv* unbequem; **feel ~** (*fig*) sich nicht wohl fühlen
uncommon *a* ungewöhnlich
uncompromising *a* kompromisslos
unconditional *a*, **~ly** *adv* bedingungslos
unconscious *a* bewusstlos; (*unintended*) unbewusst; **be ~ of sth** sich (*dat*) etw (*gen*) nicht bewusst sein. **~ly** *adv* unbewusst
unconventional *a* unkonventionell
uncooperative *a* nicht hilfsbereit
uncork *vt* entkorken
uncouth *a* ungehobelt
uncover *vt* aufdecken
undecided *a* unentschlossen; (*not settled*) nicht entschieden
undeniable *a*, **-bly** *adv* unbestreitbar
under *prep* unter (+ *dat/acc*); **~ it** darunter; **~ there** da drunter; **~ repair** in Reparatur; **~**

construction im Bau; **~ age** minderjährig ● *adv* darunter
undercarriage *n* (*Aviat*) Fahrwerk *nt*, Fahrgestell *nt*
underclothes *npl* Unterwäsche *f*
undercover *a* geheim
undercurrent *n* Unterströmung *f*; (*fig*) Unterton *m*
underdog *n* Unterlegene(r) *m*
underdone *a* nicht gar; (*rare*) nicht durchgebraten
underestimate *vt* unterschätzen
underfed *a* unterernährt
underfoot *adv* am Boden
undergo *vt* (*pt* **-went**, *pp* **-gone**) durchmachen; sich unterziehen (+ *dat*) <*operation, treatment*>
undergraduate *n* Student(in) *m*(*f*)
underground[1] *adv* unter der Erde; <*mining*> unter Tage
underground[2] *a* unterirdisch; (*secret*) Untergrund- ● *n* (*railway*) U-Bahn *f*. **~ car park** *n* Tiefgarage *f*
undergrowth *n* Unterholz *nt*
underhand *a* hinterhältig
underlie *vt* (*pt* **-lay**, *pp* **-lain**, *pres p* **-lying**) zugrunde liegen (+ *dat*)
underline *vt* unterstreichen
underlying *a* eigentlich
undermine *vt* (*fig*) unterminieren, untergraben
underneath *prep* unter (+ *dat*/*acc*) ● *adv* darunter
underpants *npl* Unterhose *f*
underpass *n* Unterführung *f*
underprivileged *a* unterprivilegiert
underrate *vt* unterschätzen
undershirt *n* (*Amer*) Unterhemd *nt*
understand *vt*/*i* (*pt*/*pp* **-stood**) verstehen; **I ~ that ...** (*have heard*) ich habe gehört, dass ... **~able** *a* verständlich. **~ably** *adv* verständlicherweise
understanding *a* verständnisvoll ● *n* Verständnis *nt*; (*agreement*) Vereinbarung *f*; **reach an ~** sich verständigen
understatement *n* Untertreibung *f*
undertake *vt* (*pt* **-took**, *pp* **-taken**) unternehmen; **~ to do sth** sich verpflichten, etw zu tun
undertaker *n* Leichenbestatter *m*; **[firm of] ~s** Bestattungsinstitut *n*
undertaking *n* Unternehmen *nt*; (*promise*) Versprechen *nt*
undertone *n* (*fig*) Unterton *m*; **in an ~** mit gedämpfter Stimme
undervalue *vt* unterbewerten
underwater[1] *a* Unterwasser-
underwater[2] *adv* unter Wasser
underwear *n* Unterwäsche *f*
underweight *a* untergewichtig; **be ~** Untergewicht haben
underworld *n* Unterwelt *f*
undesirable *a* unerwünscht
undignified *a* würdelos
undo *vt* (*pt* **-did**, *pp* **-done**) aufmachen; (*fig*) ungeschehen machen
undone *a* offen; (*not accomplished*) unerledigt
undoubted *a* unzweifelhaft. **~ly** *adv* zweifellos
undress *vt* ausziehen; **get ~ed** sich ausziehen ● *vi* sich ausziehen
undue *a* übermäßig
unduly *adv* übermäßig
unearth *vt* ausgraben; (*fig*) zutage bringen. **~ly** *a* unheimlich; **at an ~ly hour** [!] in aller Herrgottsfrühe
uneasy *a* unbehaglich
uneconomic *a*, **-ally** *adv* unwirtschaftlich
unemployed *a* arbeitslos ● *npl* **the ~** die Arbeitslosen
unemployment *n* Arbeitslosigkeit *f*
unending *a* endlos
unequal *a* unterschiedlich; <*struggle*> ungleich. **~ly** *adv* ungleichmäßig

unequivocal *a*, **-ly** *adv* eindeutig

unethical *a* unmoralisch; **be ~** gegen das Berufsethos verstoßen

uneven *a* uneben; (*unequal*) ungleich; (*not regular*) ungleichmäßig; <*number*> ungerade

unexpected *a*, **-ly** *adv* unerwartet

unfair *a*, **-ly** *adv* ungerecht, unfair. **~ness** *n* Ungerechtigkeit *f*

unfaithful *a* untreu

unfamiliar *a* ungewohnt; (*unknown*) unbekannt

unfasten *vt* aufmachen; (*detach*) losmachen

unfavourable *a* ungünstig

unfeeling *a* gefühllos

unfit *a* ungeeignet; (*incompetent*) unfähig; (*Sport*) nicht fit; **~ for work** arbeitsunfähig

unfold *vt* auseinander falten, entfalten; (*spread out*) ausbreiten ● *vi* sich entfalten

unforeseen *a* unvorhergesehen

unforgettable *a* unvergesslich

unforgivable *a* unverzeihlich

unfortunate *a* unglücklich; (*unfavourable*) ungünstig; (*regrettable*) bedauerlich; **be ~** <*person:*> Pech haben. **~ly** *adv* leider

unfounded *a* unbegründet

unfurl *vt* entrollen

unfurnished *a* unmöbliert

ungainly *a* unbeholfen

ungrateful *a*, **-ly** *adv* undankbar

unhappiness *n* Kummer *m*

unhappy *a* unglücklich; (*not content*) unzufrieden

unharmed *a* unverletzt

unhealthy *a* ungesund

unhurt *a* unverletzt

unification *n* Einigung *f*

uniform *a*, **-ly** *adv* einheitlich ● *n* Uniform *f*

unify *vt* (*pt/pp* **-ied**) einigen

unilateral *a*, **-ly** *adv* einseitig

unimaginable *a* unvorstellbar

unimportant *a* unwichtig

uninhabited *a* unbewohnt

unintentional *a*, **-ly** *adv* unabsichtlich

union *n* Vereinigung *f*; (*Pol*) Union *f*; (*trade ~*) Gewerkschaft *f*

unique *a* einzigartig. **~ly** *adv* einmalig

unison *n* **in ~** einstimmig

unit *n* Einheit *f*; (*Math*) Einer *m*; (*of furniture*) Teil *nt*, Element *nt*

unite *vt* vereinigen ● *vi* sich vereinigen

united *a* einig. **U~ Kingdom** *n* Vereinigtes Königreich *nt*. **U~ Nations** *n* Vereinte Nationen *pl*. **U~ States [of America]** *n* Vereinigte Staaten *pl* [von Amerika]

unity *n* Einheit *f*; (*harmony*) Einigkeit *f*

universal *a*, **-ly** *adv* allgemein

universe *n* [Welt]all *nt*, Universum *nt*

university *n* Universität *f* ● *attrib* Universitäts-

unjust *a*, **-ly** *adv* ungerecht

unkind *a*, **-ly** *adv* unfreundlich; (*harsh*) hässlich

unknown *a* unbekannt

unlawful *a*, **-ly** *adv* gesetzwidrig

unleaded *a* bleifrei

unleash *vt* (*fig*) entfesseln

unless *conj* wenn ... nicht; **~ I am mistaken** wenn ich mich nicht irre

unlike *prep* im Gegensatz zu (+ *dat*)

unlikely *a* unwahrscheinlich

unlimited *a* unbegrenzt

unload *vt* entladen; ausladen <*luggage*>

unlock *vt* aufschließen

unlucky *a* unglücklich; <*day, number*> Unglücks-; **be ~** Pech haben; <*thing:*> Unglück bringen

unmarried *a* unverheiratet. **~ mother** *n* ledige Mutter *f*

unmask *vt* (*fig*) entlarven
unmistakable *a*, **-bly** *adv* unverkennbar
unnatural *a*, **-ly** *adv* unnatürlich; (*not normal*) nicht normal
unnecessary *a*, **-ily** *adv* unnötig
unnoticed *a* unbemerkt
unobtainable *a* nicht erhältlich
unobtrusive *a*, **-ly** *adv* unaufdringlich; <*thing*> unauffällig
unofficial *a*, **-ly** *adv* inoffiziell
unpack *vt*/*i* auspacken
unpaid *a* unbezahlt
unpleasant *a*, **-ly** *adv* unangenehm
unplug *vt* (*pt*/*pp* **-plugged**) den Stecker herausziehen von
unpopular *a* unbeliebt
unprecedented *a* beispiellos
unpredictable *a* unberechenbar
unprepared *a* nicht vorbereitet
unpretentious *a* bescheiden
unprofitable *a* unrentabel
unqualified *a* unqualifiziert; (*fig: absolute*) uneingeschränkt
unquestionable *a* unbezweifelbar; <*right*> unbestreitbar
unravel *vt* (*pt*/*pp* **-ravelled**) entwirren; (*Knitting*) aufziehen
unreal *a* unwirklich
unreasonable *a* unvernünftig
unrelated *a* unzusammenhängend; **be ~** nicht verwandt sein; <*events:*> nicht miteinander zusammenhängen
unreliable *a* unzuverlässig
unrest *n* Unruhen *pl*
unrivalled *a* unübertroffen
unroll *vt* aufrollen ● *vi* sich aufrollen
unruly *a* ungebärdig
unsafe *a* nicht sicher
unsatisfactory *a* unbefriedigend
unsavoury *a* unangenehm; (*fig*) unerfreulich
unscathed *a* unversehrt
unscrew *vt* abschrauben
unscrupulous *a* skrupellos
unseemly *a* unschicklich
unselfish *a* selbstlos
unsettled *a* ungeklärt; <*weather*> unbeständig; <*bill*> unbezahlt
unshakeable *a* unerschütterlich
unshaven *a* unrasiert
unsightly *a* unansehnlich
unskilled *a* ungelernt; <*work*> unqualifiziert
unsociable *a* ungesellig
unsophisticated *a* einfach
unsound *a* krank, nicht gesund; <*building*> nicht sicher; <*advice*> unzuverlässig; <*reasoning*> nicht stichhaltig
unstable *a* nicht stabil; (*mentally*) labil
unsteady *a*, **-ily** *adv* unsicher; (*wobbly*) wackelig
unstuck *a* **come ~** sich lösen; ([!] *fail*) scheitern
unsuccessful *a*, **-ly** *adv* erfolglos; **be ~** keinen Erfolg haben
unsuitable *a* ungeeignet; (*inappropriate*) unpassend; (*for weather, activity*) unzweckmäßig
unthinkable *a* unvorstellbar
untidiness *n* Unordentlichkeit *f*
untidy *a*, **-ily** *adv* unordentlich
untie *vt* aufbinden; losbinden <*person, boat, horse*>
until *prep* bis (+ *acc*); **not ~** erst; **~ the evening** bis zum Abend ● *conj* bis; **not ~** erst wenn; (*in past*) erst als
untold *a* unermesslich
untrue *a* unwahr; **that's ~** das ist nicht wahr
unused[1] *a* unbenutzt; (*not utilized*) ungenutzt
unused[2] *a* **be ~ to sth** etw nicht gewohnt sein
unusual *a*, **-ly** *adv* ungewöhnlich
unveil *vt* enthüllen
unwanted *a* unerwünscht
unwelcome *a* unwillkommen

unwell *a* **be** *or* **feel ~** sich nicht wohl fühlen
unwieldy *a* sperrig
unwilling *a*, **-ly** *adv* widerwillig; **be ~ to do sth** etw nicht tun wollen
unwind *v* (*pt/pp* **unwound**) ● *vt* abwickeln ● *vi* sich abwickeln; (🅘 *relax*) sich entspannen
unwise *a*, **-ly** *adv* unklug
unworthy *a* unwürdig
unwrap *vt* (*pt/pp* **-wrapped**) auswickeln; auspacken <*present*>
unwritten *a* ungeschrieben
up *adv* oben; (*with movement*) nach oben; (*not in bed*) auf; <*road*> aufgerissen; <*price*> gestiegen; **be up for sale** zu verkaufen sein; **up there** da oben; **up to** (*as far as*) bis; **time's up** die Zeit ist um; **what's up?** 🅘 was ist los? **what's he up to?** 🅘 was hat er vor? **I don't feel up to it** ich fühle mich dem nicht gewachsen; **go up** hinaufgehen; **come up** heraufkommen ● *prep* **be up on sth** [oben] auf etw (*dat*) sein; **up the mountain** oben am Berg; (*movement*) den Berg hinauf; **be up the tree** oben im Baum sein; **up the road** die Straße entlang; **up the river** stromaufwärts; **go up the stairs** die Treppe hinaufgehen
upbringing *n* Erziehung *f*
update *vt* auf den neuesten Stand bringen
upgrade *vt* aufstufen
upheaval *n* Unruhe *f*; (*Pol*) Umbruch *m*
uphill *a* (*fig*) mühsam ● *adv* bergauf
uphold *vt* (*pt/pp* **upheld**) unterstützen; bestätigen <*verdict*>
upholster *vt* polstern. **~y** *n* Polsterung *f*
upkeep *n* Unterhalt *m*
upmarket *a* anspruchsvoll
upon *prep* auf (+ *dat*/*acc*)
upper *a* obere(r,s); <*deck, jaw, lip*> Ober-; **have the ~ hand** die Oberhand haben ● *n* (*of shoe*) Obermaterial *nt*
upper class *n* Oberschicht *f*
upright *a* aufrecht
uprising *n* Aufstand *m*
uproar *n* Aufruhr *m*
upset[1] *vt* (*pt/pp* **upset**, *pres p* **upsetting**) umstoßen; (*spill*) verschütten; durcheinander bringen <*plan*>; (*distress*) erschüttern; <*food*> nicht bekommen (+ *dat*); **get ~ about sth** sich über etw (*acc*) aufregen
upset[2] *n* Aufregung *f*; **have a stomach ~** einen verdorbenen Magen haben
upshot *n* Ergebnis *nt*
upside down *adv* verkehrt herum; **turn ~** umdrehen
upstairs[1] *adv* oben; <*go*> nach oben
upstairs[2] *a* im Obergeschoss
upstart *n* Emporkömmling *m*
upstream *adv* stromaufwärts
uptake *n* **slow on the ~** schwer von Begriff; **be quick on the ~** schnell begreifen
upturn *n* Aufschwung *m*
upward *a* nach oben; <*movement*> Aufwärts-; **~ slope** Steigung *f* ● *adv* **~[s]** aufwärts, nach oben
uranium *n* Uran *nt*
urban *a* städtisch
urge *n* Trieb *m*, Drang *m* ● *vt* drängen; **~ on** antreiben
urgen|cy *n* Dringlichkeit *f*. **~t** *a*, **-ly** *adv* dringend
urine *n* Urin *m*, Harn *m*
us *pron* uns; **it's us** wir sind es
US[A] *abbr* USA *pl*
usable *a* brauchbar
usage *n* Brauch *m*; (*of word*) [Sprach]gebrauch *m*
use[1] *n* (*see* **use**[2]) Benutzung *f*; Verwendung *f*; Gebrauch *m*; **be (of) no ~** nichts nützen; **it is no ~**

es hat keinen Zweck; **what's the ~?** wozu?

use² *vt* benutzen <*implement, room, lift*>; verwenden <*ingredient, method, book, money*>; gebrauchen <*words, force, brains*>; **~ [up]** aufbrauchen

used¹ *a* gebraucht; <*towel*> benutzt; <*car*> Gebraucht-

used² *pt* **be ~ to sth** an etw (*acc*) gewöhnt sein; **get ~ to** sich gewöhnen an (+ *acc*); **he ~ to say** er hat immer gesagt; **he ~ to live here** er hat früher hier gewohnt

useful *a* nützlich. **~ness** *n* Nützlichkeit *f*

useless *a* nutzlos; (*not usable*) unbrauchbar; (*pointless*) zwecklos

user *n* Benutzer(in) *m(f)*

usher *n* Platzanweiser *m*; (*in court*) Gerichtsdiener *m*

usherette *n* Platzanweiserin *f*

USSR *abbr* (*History*) UdSSR *f*

usual *a* üblich. **~ly** *adv* gewöhnlich

utensil *n* Gerät *nt*

utility *a* Gebrauchs-

utilize *vt* nutzen

utmost *a* äußerste(r,s), größte(r,s) ● *n* **do one's ~** sein Möglichstes tun

utter¹ *a*, **-ly** *adv* völlig

utter² *vt* von sich geben <*sigh, sound*>; sagen <*word*>

U-turn *n* (*fig*) Kehrtwendung *f*; **'no ~s'** (*Auto*) 'Wenden verboten'

Vv

vacan|cy *n* (*job*) freie Stelle *f*; (*room*) freies Zimmer *nt*; **'no ~cies'** 'belegt'. **~t** *a* frei; <*look*> [gedanken]leer

vacate *vt* räumen

vacation *n* (*Univ & Amer*) Ferien *pl*

vaccinat|e *vt* impfen. **~ion** *n* Impfung *f*

vaccine *n* Impfstoff *m*

vacuum *n* Vakuum *nt*, luftleerer Raum *m* ● *vt* saugen. **~ cleaner** *n* Staubsauger *m*

vagina *n* (*Anat*) Scheide *f*

vague *a* (**-r, -st**), **-ly** *adv* vage; <*outline*> verschwommen

vain *a* (**-er, -est**) eitel; <*hope, attempt*> vergeblich; **in ~** vergeblich. **~ly** *adv* vergeblich

valiant *a*, **-ly** *adv* tapfer

valid *a* gültig; <*claim*> berechtigt; <*argument*> stichhaltig; <*reason*> triftig. **~ity** *n* Gültigkeit *f*

valley *n* Tal *nt*

valour *n* Tapferkeit *f*

valuable *a* wertvoll. **~s** *npl* Wertsachen *pl*

valuation *n* Schätzung *f*

value *n* Wert *m*; (*usefulness*) Nutzen *m* ● *vt* schätzen. **~ added tax** *n* Mehrwertsteuer *f*

valve *n* Ventil *nt*; (*Anat*) Klappe *f*; (*Electr*) Röhre *f*

van *n* Lieferwagen *m*

vandal *n* Rowdy *m*. **~ism** *n* mutwillige Zerstörung *f*. **~ize** *vt* demolieren

vanilla *n* Vanille *f*

vanish *vi* verschwinden

vanity *n* Eitelkeit *f*

vapour *n* Dampf *m*

variable *a* unbeständig; (*Math*) variabel; (*adjustable*) regulierbar
variant *n* Variante *f*
variation *n* Variation *f*; (*difference*) Unterschied *m*
varied *a* vielseitig; <*diet*:> abwechslungsreich
variety *n* Abwechslung *f*; (*quantity*) Vielfalt *f*; (*Comm*) Auswahl *f*; (*type*) Art *f*; (*Bot*) Abart *f*; (*Theat*) Varieté *nt*
various *a* verschieden. **~ly** *adv* unterschiedlich
varnish *n* Lack *m* ● *vt* lackieren
vary *v* (*pt*/*pp* **-ied**) ● *vi* sich ändern; (*be different*) verschieden sein ● *vt* [ver]ändern; (*add variety to*) abwechslungsreicher gestalten
vase *n* Vase *f*
vast *a* riesig; <*expanse*> weit. **~ly** *adv* gewaltig
vat *n* Bottich *m*
VAT *abbr* (**value added tax**) Mehrwertsteuer *f*, MwSt.
vault[1] *n* (*roof*) Gewölbe *nt*; (*in bank*) Tresor *m*; (*tomb*) Gruft *f*
vault[2] *n* Sprung *m* ● *vt*/*i* ~ **[over]** springen über (+ *acc*)
VDU *abbr* (**visual display unit**) Bildschirmgerät *nt*
veal *n* Kalbfleisch *nt* ● *attrib* Kalbs-
veer *vi* sich drehen; (*Auto*) ausscheren
vegetable *n* Gemüse *nt*; **~s** *pl* Gemüse *nt* ● *attrib* Gemüse-; <*oil, fat*> Pflanzen-
vegetarian *a* vegetarisch ● *n* Vegetarier(in) *m*(*f*)
vegetation *n* Vegetation *f*
vehement *a*, **-ly** *adv* heftig
vehicle *n* Fahrzeug *nt*
veil *n* Schleier *m* ● *vt* verschleiern
vein *n* Ader *f*; (*mood*) Stimmung *f*; (*manner*) Art *f*
velocity *n* Geschwindigkeit *f*
velvet *n* Samt *m*
vending-machine *n* [Verkaufs]automat *m*
vendor *n* Verkäufer(in) *m*(*f*)
veneer *n* Furnier *nt*; (*fig*) Tünche *f*. **~ed** *a* furniert
venerable *a* ehrwürdig
Venetian *a* venezianisch. **v~ blind** *n* Jalousie *f*
vengeance *n* Rache *f*; **with a ~** gewaltig
Venice *n* Venedig *nt*
venison *n* (*Culin*) Reh(fleisch) *nt*
venom *n* Gift *nt*; (*fig*) Hass *m*. **~ous** *a* giftig
vent *n* Öffnung *f*
ventilat|e *vt* belüften. **~ion** *n* Belüftung *f*; (*installation*) Lüftung *f*. **~or** *n* Lüftungsvorrichtung *f*; (*Med*) Beatmungsgerät *nt*
ventriloquist *n* Bauchredner *m*
venture *n* Unternehmung *f* ● *vt* wagen ● *vi* sich wagen
venue *n* (*for event*) Veranstaltungsort *m*
veranda *n* Veranda *f*
verb *n* Verb *nt*. **~al** *a*, **-ly** *adv* mündlich; (*Gram*) verbal
verbose *a* weitschweifig
verdict *n* Urteil *nt*
verge *n* Rand *m* ● *vi* ~ **on** (*fig*) grenzen an (+ *acc*)
verify *vt* (*pt*/*pp* **-ied**) überprüfen; (*confirm*) bestätigen
vermin *n* Ungeziefer *nt*
vermouth *n* Wermut *m*
versatil|e *a* vielseitig. **~ity** *n* Vielseitigkeit *f*
verse *n* Strophe *f*; (*of Bible*) Vers *m*; (*poetry*) Lyrik *f*
version *n* Version *f*; (*translation*) Übersetzung *f*; (*model*) Modell *nt*
versus *prep* gegen (+ *acc*)
vertical *a*, **-ly** *adv* senkrecht ● *n* Senkrechte *f*
vertigo *n* (*Med*) Schwindel *m*
verve *n* Schwung *m*
very *adv* sehr; **~ much** sehr; (*quantity*) sehr viel; **~ probably** höchstwahrscheinlich; **at the ~**

V

most allerhöchstens ● *a* (*mere*) bloß; **the ~ first** der/die/das allererste; **at the ~ end/beginning** ganz am Ende/Anfang; **only a ~ little** nur ein ganz kleines bisschen

vessel *n* Schiff *nt*; (*receptacle & Anat*) Gefäß *nt*

vest *n* [Unter]hemd *nt*; (*Amer: waistcoat*) Weste *f*

vestige *n* Spur *f*

vestry *n* Sakristei *f*

vet *n* Tierarzt *m* /-ärztin *f* ● *vt* (*pt/pp* **vetted**) überprüfen

veteran *n* Veteran *m*

veterinary *a* tierärztlich. **~ surgeon** *n* Tierarzt *m* /-ärztin *f*

veto *n* (*pl* **-es**) Veto *nt*

VHF *abbr* (**very high frequency**) UKW

via *prep* über (+ *acc*)

viable *a* lebensfähig; (*fig*) realisierbar; <*firm*> rentabel

viaduct *n* Viadukt *nt*

vibrat|e *vi* vibrieren. **~ion** *n* Vibrieren *nt*

vicar *n* Pfarrer *m*. **~age** *n* Pfarrhaus *nt*

vice[1] *n* Laster *nt*

vice[2] *n* (*Techn*) Schraubstock *m*

vice[3] *a* Vize-; **~ chairman** stellvertretender Vorsitzender *m*

vice versa *adv* umgekehrt

vicinity *n* Umgebung *f*; **in the ~ of** in der Nähe von

vicious *a*, **-ly** *adv* boshaft; <*animal*> bösartig

victim *n* Opfer *nt*. **~ize** *vt* schikanieren

victor *n* Sieger *m*

victor|ious *a* siegreich. **~y** *n* Sieg *m*

video *n* Video *nt*; (*recorder*) Videorecorder *m* ● *attrib* Video-

video: ~ cassette *n* Videokassette *f*. **~ game** *n* Videospiel *nt*. **~phone** *n* Bildtelefon *nt*. **~ recorder** *n* Videorecorder *m*

Vienn|a *n* Wien *nt*. **~ese** *a* Wiener

view *n* Sicht *f*; (*scene*) Aussicht *f*, Blick *m*; (*picture, opinion*) Ansicht *f*; **in my ~** meiner Ansicht nach; **in ~ of** angesichts (+ *gen*); **be on ~** besichtigt werden können ● *vt* sich (*dat*) ansehen; besichtigen <*house*>; (*consider*) betrachten ● *vi* (*TV*) fernsehen. **~er** *n* (*TV*) Zuschauer(in) *m*(*f*)

view: ~finder *n* (*Phot*) Sucher *m*. **~point** *n* Standpunkt *m*

vigilan|ce *n* Wachsamkeit *f*. **~t** *a*, **-ly** *adv* wachsam

vigorous *a*, **-ly** *adv* kräftig; (*fig*) heftig

vigour *n* Kraft *f*; (*fig*) Heftigkeit *f*

vile *a* abscheulich

villa *n* (*for holidays*) Ferienhaus *nt*

village *n* Dorf *nt*. **~r** *n* Dorfbewohner(in) *m*(*f*)

villain *n* Schurke *m*; (*in story*) Bösewicht *m*

vindicat|e *vt* rechtfertigen. **~ion** *n* Rechtfertigung *f*

vindictive *a* nachtragend

vine *n* Weinrebe *f*

vinegar *n* Essig *m*

vineyard *n* Weinberg *m*

vintage *a* erlesen ● *n* (*year*) Jahrgang *m*. **~ car** *n* Oldtimer *m*

viola *n* (*Mus*) Bratsche *f*

violat|e *vt* verletzen; (*break*) brechen; (*disturb*) stören; (*defile*) schänden. **~ion** *n* Verletzung *f*; Schändung *f*

violen|ce *n* Gewalt *f*; (*fig*) Heftigkeit *f*. **~t** *a* gewalttätig; (*fig*) heftig. **~tly** *adv* brutal; (*fig*) heftig

violet *a* violett ● *n* (*flower*) Veilchen *nt*

violin *n* Geige *f*, Violine *f*. **~ist** *n* Geiger(in) *m*(*f*)

VIP *abbr* (**very important person**) Prominente(r) *m*/*f*

viper *n* Kreuzotter *f*

virgin *a* unberührt ● *n* Jungfrau *f*. **~ity** *n* Unschuld *f*

viril|e *a* männlich. **~ity** *n* Männlichkeit *f*

virtual *a* **a ~** ... praktisch ein ... **~ly** *adv* praktisch

virtu|e *n* Tugend *f*; (*advantage*) Vorteil *m*; **by** *or* **in ~e of** auf Grund (+ *gen*)

virtuoso *n* (*pl* **-si**) Virtuose *m*

virtuous *a* tugendhaft

virus *n* Virus *nt*

visa *n* Visum *nt*

visibility *n* Sichtbarkeit *f*; (*Meteorol*) Sichtweite *f*

visible *a*, **-bly** *adv* sichtbar

vision *n* Vision *f*; (*sight*) Sehkraft *f*; (*foresight*) Weitblick *m*

visit *n* Besuch *m* ● *vt* besuchen; besichtigen <*town, building*>. **~or** *n* Besucher(in) *m(f)*; (*in hotel*) Gast *m*; **have ~ors** Besuch haben

visor *n* Schirm *m*; (*Auto*) [Sonnen]blende *f*

vista *n* Aussicht *f*

visual *a*, **-ly** *adv* visuell. **~ display unit** *n* Bildschirmgerät *nt*

visualize *vt* sich (*dat*) vorstellen

vital *a* unbedingt notwendig; (*essential to life*) lebenswichtig. **~ity** *n* Vitalität *f*. **~ly** *adv* äußerst

vitamin *n* Vitamin *nt*

vivaci|ous *a*, **-ly** *adv* lebhaft. **~ty** *n* Lebhaftigkeit *f*

vivid *a*, **-ly** *adv* lebhaft; <*description*> lebendig

vocabulary *n* Wortschatz *m*; (*list*) Vokabelverzeichnis *nt*; **learn ~** Vokabeln lernen

vocal *a*, **-ly** *adv* stimmlich; (*vociferous*) lautstark

vocalist *n* Sänger(in) *m(f)*

vocation *n* Berufung *f*. **~al** *a* Berufs-

vociferous *a* lautstark

vodka *n* Wodka *m*

vogue *n* Mode *f*

voice *n* Stimme *f* ● *vt* zum Ausdruck bringen. **~ mail** *n* Voicemail *f*

void *a* leer; (*not valid*) ungültig; **~ of** ohne ● *n* Leere *f*

volatile *a* flüchtig; <*person*> sprunghaft

volcanic *a* vulkanisch

volcano *n* Vulkan *m*

volley *n* (*of gunfire*) Salve *f*; (*Tennis*) Volley *m*

volt *n* Volt *nt*. **~age** *n* (*Electr*) Spannung *f*

voluble *a*, **-bly** *adv* redselig; <*protest*> wortreich

volume *n* (*book*) Band *m*; (*Geom*) Rauminhalt *m*; (*amount*) Ausmaß *nt*; (*Radio, TV*) Lautstärke *f*

voluntary *a*, **-ily** *adv* freiwillig

volunteer *n* Freiwillige(r) *m/f* ● *vt* anbieten; geben <*information*> ● *vi* sich freiwillig melden

vomit *n* Erbrochene(s) *nt* ● *vt* erbrechen ● *vi* sich übergeben

voracious *a* gefräßig; <*appetite*> unbändig

vot|e *n* Stimme *f*; (*ballot*) Abstimmung *f*; (*right*) Wahlrecht *nt* ● *vi* abstimmen; (*in election*) wählen. **~er** *n* Wähler(in) *m(f)*

vouch *vi* **~ for** sich verbürgen für. **~er** *n* Gutschein *m*

vowel *n* Vokal *m*

voyage *n* Seereise *f*; (*in space*) Reise *f*, Flug *m*

vulgar *a* vulgär, ordinär. **~ity** *n* Vulgarität *f*

vulnerable *a* verwundbar

vulture *n* Geier *m*

Ww

wad *n* Bausch *m*; (*bundle*) Bündel *nt*. **~ding** *n* Wattierung *f*
waddle *vi* watscheln
wade *vi* waten
wafer *n* Waffel *f*
waffle[1] *vi* [!] schwafeln
waffle[2] *n* (*Culin*) Waffel *f*
waft *vt/i* wehen
wag *v* (*pt/pp* **wagged**) ● *vt* wedeln mit ● *vi* wedeln
wage *n*, & **~s** *pl* Lohn *m*
wager *n* Wette *f*
wagon *n* Wagen *m*; (*Rail*) Waggon *m*
wail *n* [klagender] Schrei *m* ● *vi* heulen; (*lament*) klagen
waist *n* Taille *f*. **~coat** *n* Weste *f*. **~line** *n* Taille *f*
wait *n* Wartezeit *f*; **lie in ~ for** auflauern (+ *dat*) ● *vi* warten (**for** auf + *acc*); (*at table*) servieren; **~ on** bedienen ● *vt* **~ one's turn** warten, bis man an der Reihe ist
waiter *n* Kellner *m*; **~!** Herr Ober!
waiting: ~-list *n* Warteliste *f*. **~-room** *n* Warteraum *m*; (*doctor's*) Wartezimmer *nt*
waitress *n* Kellnerin *f*
waive *vt* verzichten auf (+ *acc*)
wake[1] *n* Totenwache *f* ● *v* (*pt* **woke**, *pp* **woken**) **~ [up]** ● *vt* [auf]wecken ● *vi* aufwachen
wake[2] *n* (*Naut*) Kielwasser *nt*; **in the ~ of** im Gefolge (+ *gen*)
Wales *n* Wales *nt*
walk *n* Spaziergang *m*; (*gait*) Gang *m*; (*path*) Weg *m*; **go for a ~** spazieren gehen ● *vi* gehen; (*not ride*) laufen, zu Fuß gehen; (*ramble*) wandern; **learn to ~** laufen lernen ● *vt* ausführen <*dog*>. **~ out** *vi* hinausgehen; <*workers:*> in den Streik treten; **~ out on s.o.** jdn verlassen
walker *n* Spaziergänger(in) *m(f)*; (*rambler*) Wanderer *m*/Wanderin *f*
walking *n* Gehen *nt*; (*rambling*) Wandern *nt*. **~-stick** *n* Spazierstock *m*
wall *n* Wand *f*; (*external*) Mauer *f*; **drive s.o. up the ~** [!] jdn auf die Palme bringen ● *vt* **~ up** zumauern
wallet *n* Brieftasche *f*
wallflower *n* Goldlack *m*
wallop *vt* (*pt/pp* **walloped**) [!] schlagen
wallow *vi* sich wälzen; (*fig*) schwelgen
wallpaper *n* Tapete *f* ● *vt* tapezieren
walnut *n* Walnuss *f*
waltz *n* Walzer *m* ● *vi* Walzer tanzen
wander *vi* umherwandern, [!] bummeln; (*fig: digress*) abschweifen. **~ about** *vi* umherwandern
wangle *vt* [!] organisieren
want *n* Mangel *m* (**of** an + *dat*); (*hardship*) Not *f*; (*desire*) Bedürfnis *nt* ● *vt* wollen; (*need*) brauchen; **~ [to have] sth** etw haben wollen; **~ to do sth** etw tun wollen; **I ~ you to go** ich will, dass du gehst; **it ~s painting** es müsste gestrichen werden ● *vi* **he doesn't ~ for anything** ihm fehlt es an nichts. **~ed** *a* <*criminal*> gesucht
war *n* Krieg *m*; **be at ~** sich im Krieg befinden
ward *n* [Kranken]saal *m*; (*unit*) Station *f*; (*of town*) Wahlbezirk *m*; (*child*) Mündel *nt* ● *vt* **~ off** abwehren
warden *n* (*of hostel*) Heimleiter(in) *m(f)*; (*of youth*

hostel) Herbergsvater *m*; (*supervisor*) Aufseher(in) *m(f)*
warder *n* Wärter(in) *m(f)*
wardrobe *n* Kleiderschrank *m*; (*clothes*) Garderobe *f*
warehouse *n* Lager *nt*; (*building*) Lagerhaus *nt*
wares *npl* Waren *pl*
war: ~fare *n* Krieg *m*. **~like** *a* kriegerisch
warm *a* (**-er, -est**), **-ly** *adv* warm; <*welcome*> herzlich; **I am ~** mir ist warm ●*vt* wärmen. **~ up** *vt* aufwärmen ●*vi* warm werden; (*Sport*) sich aufwärmen. **~-hearted** *a* warmherzig
warmth *n* Wärme *f*
warn *vt* warnen (**of** vor + *dat*). **~ing** *n* Warnung *f*; (*advance notice*) Vorwarnung *f*; (*caution*) Verwarnung *f*
warp *vt* verbiegen ●*vi* sich verziehen
warrant *n* (*for arrest*) Haftbefehl *m*; (*for search*) Durchsuchungsbefehl *m* ●*vt* (*justify*) rechtfertigen; (*guarantee*) garantieren
warranty *n* Garantie *f*
warrior *n* Krieger *m*
warship *n* Kriegsschiff *nt*
wart *n* Warze *f*
wartime *n* Kriegszeit *f*
wary *a* (**-ier, -iest**), **-ily** *adv* vorsichtig; (*suspicious*) misstrauisch
was *see* **be**
wash *n* Wäsche *f*; (*Naut*) Wellen *pl*; **have a ~** sich waschen ●*vt* waschen; spülen <*dishes*>; aufwischen <*floor*>; **~ one's hands** sich (*dat*) die Hände waschen ●*vi* sich waschen. **~ out** *vt* auswaschen; ausspülen <*mouth*>. **~ up** *vt/i* abwaschen, spülen ●*vi* (*Amer*) sich waschen
washable *a* waschbar
wash-basin *n* Waschbecken *nt*
washer *n* (*Techn*) Dichtungsring *m*; (*machine*) Waschmaschine *f*
washing *n* Wäsche *f*. **~-machine** *n* Waschmaschine *f*. **~-powder** *n* Waschpulver *nt*. **~-up** *n* Abwasch *m*; **do the ~-up** abwaschen, spülen. **~-up liquid** *n* Spülmittel *nt*
wasp *n* Wespe *f*
waste *n* Verschwendung *f*; (*rubbish*) Abfall *m*; **~s** *pl* Öde *f* ●*a* <*product*> Abfall- ●*vt* verschwenden ●*vi* **~ away** immer mehr abmagern
waste: ~ful *a* verschwenderisch. **~ land** *n* Ödland *nt*. **~ paper** *n* Altpapier *nt*. **~-paper basket** *n* Papierkorb *m*
watch *n* Wache *f*; (*timepiece*) [Armband]uhr *f* ●*vt* beobachten; sich (*dat*) ansehen <*film, match*>; (*keep an eye on*) achten auf (+ *acc*); **~ television** fernsehen ●*vi* zusehen. **~ out** *vi* Ausschau halten (**for** nach); (*be careful*) aufpassen
watch: ~-dog *n* Wachhund *m*. **~ful** *a*, **-ly** *adv* wachsam. **~man** *n* Wachmann *m*
water *n* Wasser *nt*; **~s** *pl* Gewässer *nt* ●*vt* gießen <*garden, plant*>; (*dilute*) verdünnen ●*vi* <*eyes:*> tränen; **my mouth was ~ing** mir lief das Wasser im Munde zusammen. **~ down** *vt* verwässern
water: ~-colour *n* Wasserfarbe *f*; (*painting*) Aquarell *nt*. **~cress** *n* Brunnenkresse *f*. **~fall** *n* Wasserfall *m*
watering-can *n* Gießkanne *f*
water: ~-lily *n* Seerose *f*. **~logged** *a* **be ~logged** <*ground*> unter Wasser stehen. **~ polo** *n* Wasserball *m*. **~proof** *a* wasserdicht. **~-skiing** *n* Wasserskilaufen *nt*. **~tight** *a* wasserdicht. **~way** *n* Wasserstraße *f*

W

watery *a* wässrig

watt *n* Watt *nt*

wave *n* Welle *f*; (*gesture*) Handbewegung *f*; (*as greeting*) Winken *nt* ● *vt* winken mit; (*brandish*) schwingen; wellen <*hair*>; ~ **one's hand** winken ● *vi* winken (**to** *dat*); <*flag:*> wehen. **~length** *n* Wellenlänge *f*

waver *vi* schwanken

wavy *a* wellig

wax *n* Wachs *nt*; (*in ear*) Schmalz *nt* ● *vt* wachsen. **~works** *n* Wachsfigurenkabinett *nt*

way *n* Weg *m*; (*direction*) Richtung *f*; (*respect*) Hinsicht *f*; (*manner*) Art *f*; (*method*) Art und Weise *f*; **~s** *pl* Gewohnheiten *pl*; **on the ~** auf dem Weg (**to** nach/zu); (*under way*) unterwegs; **a little/long ~** ein kleines/ganzes Stück; **a long ~ off** weit weg; **this ~** hierher; (*like this*) so; **which ~** in welche Richtung; (*how*) wie; **by the ~** übrigens; **in some ~s** in gewisser Hinsicht; **either ~** so oder so; **in this ~** auf diese Weise; **in a ~** in gewisser Weise; **lead the ~** vorausgehen; **make ~** Platz machen (**for** *dat*); **'give ~'** (*Auto*) 'Vorfahrt beachten'; **get one's [own] ~** seinen Willen durchsetzen ● *adv* weit; **~ behind** weit zurück. **~ in** *n* Eingang *m*

way out *n* Ausgang *m*; (*fig*) Ausweg *m*

WC *abbr* WC *nt*

we *pron* wir

weak *a* (**-er, -est**), **-ly** *adv* schwach; <*liquid*> dünn. **~en** *vt* schwächen ● *vi* schwächer werden. **~ling** *n* Schwächling *m*. **~ness** *n* Schwäche *f*

wealth *n* Reichtum *m*; (*fig*) Fülle *f* (**of** an + *dat*). **~y** *a* (**-ier, -iest**) reich

weapon *n* Waffe *f*

wear *n* (*clothing*) Kleidung *f*; **~ and tear** Abnutzung *f*, Verschleiß *m* ● *v* (*pt* **wore**, *pp* **worn**) ● *vt* tragen; (*damage*) abnutzen; **what shall I ~?** was soll ich anziehen? ● *vi* sich abnutzen; (*last*) halten. **~ off** *vi* abgehen; <*effect:*> nachlassen. **~ out** *vt* abnutzen; (*exhaust*) erschöpfen ● *vi* sich abnutzen

weary *a* (**-ier, -iest**), **-ily** *adv* müde

weather *n* Wetter *nt*; **in this ~** bei diesem Wetter; **under the ~** [!] nicht ganz auf dem Posten ● *vt* abwettern <*storm*>; (*fig*) überstehen

weather: ~-beaten *a* verwittert; wettergegerbt <*face*>. **~ forecast** *n* Wettervorhersage *f*

weave[1] *vi* (*pt/pp* **weaved**) sich schlängeln (**through** durch)

weave[2] *n* (*Tex*) Bindung *f* ● *vt* (*pt* **wove**, *pp* **woven**) weben. **~r** *n* Weber *m*

web *n* Netz *nt*. **the W~** das Web; **~cam** *n* Webcam *f*, Webkamera *f*. **~master** *n* Webmaster *m*. **~ page** *n* Webseite *f*. **~site** *n* Website *f*

wed *vt/i* (*pt/pp* **wedded**) heiraten. **~ding** *n* Hochzeit *f*

wedding: ~ day *n* Hochzeitstag *m*. **~ dress** *n* Hochzeitskleid *nt*. **~-ring** *n* Ehering *m*, Trauring *m*

wedge *n* Keil *m* ● *vt* festklemmen

Wednesday *n* Mittwoch *m*

wee *a* [!] klein ● *vi* Pipi machen

weed *n* & **~s** *pl* Unkraut *nt* ● *vt/i* jäten. **~ out** *vt* (*fig*) aussieben

weedkiller *n* Unkrautvertilgungsmittel *nt*

weedy *a* [!] spillerig

week *n* Woche *f*. **~day** *n* Wochentag *m*. **~end** *n* Wochenende *nt*

weekly *a* & *adv* wöchentlich ● *n* Wochenzeitschrift *f*

weep *vi* (*pt/pp* **wept**) weinen

weigh *vt/i* wiegen. **~ down** *vt* (*fig*) niederdrücken. **~ up** *vt* (*fig*) abwägen

weight *n* Gewicht *nt*; **put on/lose ~** zunehmen/abnehmen
weight-lifting *n* Gewichtheben *nt*
weighty *a* (**-ier, -iest**) schwer; (*important*) gewichtig
weir *n* Wehr *nt*.
weird *a* (**-er, -est**) unheimlich; (*bizarre*) bizarr
welcome *a* willkommen; **you're ~!** nichts zu danken! **you're ~ to (have) it** das können Sie gerne haben ●*n* Willkommen *nt* ●*vt* begrüßen
weld *vt* schweißen. **~er** *n* Schweißer *m*
welfare *n* Wohl *nt*; (*Admin*) Fürsorge *f*. **W ~ State** *n* Wohlfahrtsstaat *m*
well[1] *n* Brunnen *m*; (*oil ~*) Quelle *f*
well[2] *adv* (**better, best**) gut; **as ~** auch; **as ~ as** (*in addition*) sowohl ... als auch; **~ done!** gut gemacht! ●*a* gesund; **he is not ~** es geht ihm nicht gut; **get ~ soon!** gute Besserung! ●*int* nun, na
well: ~-behaved *a* artig. **~-being** *n* Wohl *nt*
wellingtons *npl* Gummistiefel *pl*
well: ~-known *a* bekannt. **~-off** *a* wohlhabend; **be ~-off** gut dransein. **~-to-do** *a* wohlhabend
Welsh *a* walisisch ●*n* (*Lang*) Walisisch *nt*; **the ~** *pl* die Waliser. **~man** *n* Waliser *m*
went *see* **go**
wept *see* **weep**
were *see* **be**
west *n* Westen *m*; **to the ~ of** westlich von ●*a* West-, west- ●*adv* nach Westen. **~erly** *a* westlich. **~ern** *a* westlich ●*n* Western *m*
West: ~ Germany *n* Westdeutschland *nt*. **~ Indian** *a* westindisch ●*n* Westinder(in) *m(f)*. **~ Indies** *npl* Westindische Inseln *pl*
westward[s] *adv* nach Westen
wet *a* (**wetter, wettest**) nass; <[!] *person*> weichlich, lasch; **'~ paint'** 'frisch gestrichen' ●*vt* (*pt/pp* **wet** or **wetted**) nass machen
whack *vt* [!] schlagen. **~ed** *a* [!] kaputt
whale *n* Wal *m*
wharf *n* Kai *m*

what

● *pronoun*

····➤(*in questions*) was. **what is it?** was ist das? **what do you want?** was wollen Sie? **what is your name?** wie heißen Sie? **what?** ([!] *say that again*) wie?; was? **what is the time?** wie spät ist es? (*indirect*) **I didn't know what to do** ich wusste nicht, was ich machen sollte

> ! The equivalent of a preposition with **what** in English is a special word in German beginning with *wo-* (*wor-* before a vowel): **for what? what for?** = wofür? wozu? **from what?** wovon? **on what?** worauf? worüber? **under what?** worunter? **with what?** womit? etc. **what do you want the money for?** wozu willst du das Geld? **what is he talking about?** wovon redet er?

····➤(*relative pronoun*) was. **do what I tell you** tu, was ich dir sage. **give me what you can** gib mir, so viel du kannst. **what little I know** das bisschen, das ich weiß. **I don't agree with what you are saying** ich stimme dem nicht zu, was Sie sagen

····➤(*in phrases*) **what about me?** was ist mit mir? **what about a cup of coffee?** wie wäre es mit einer Tasse Kaffee? **what if she doesn't come?** was ist, wenn sie nicht kommt?

● *adjective*

····➤ (*asking for selection*) welcher (*m*), welche (*f*), welches (*nt*), welche (*pl*). **what book do you want?** welches Buch willst du haben? **what colour are the walls?** welche Farbe haben die Wände? **I asked him what train to take** ich habe ihn gefragt, welchen Zug ich nehmen soll

····➤ (*asking how much/many*) **what money does he have?** wie viel Geld hat er? **what time is it?** wie spät ist es? **what time does it start?** um wie viel Uhr fängt es an?

····➤ **what kind of ...?** was für [ein(e)]? **what kind of man is he?** was für ein Mensch ist er?

····➤ (*in exclamations*) was für (+ *nom*). **what a fool you are!** was für ein Dummkopf du doch bist! **what cheek/luck!** was für eine Frechheit/ein Glück! **what a huge house!** was für ein riesiges Haus! **what a lot of people!** was für viele Leute!

whatever *a* [egal] welche(r,s) ● *pron* was ... auch; **~ is it?** was ist das bloß? **~ he does** was er auch tut; **nothing ~** überhaupt nichts

whatsoever *pron & a* ≈ **whatever**

wheat *n* Weizen *m*

wheel *n* Rad *nt*; (*pottery*) Töpferscheibe *f*; (*steering ~*) Lenkrad *nt*; **at the ~** am Steuer ● *vt* (*push*) schieben ● *vi* kehrtmachen; (*circle*) kreisen

wheel: ~barrow *n* Schubkarre *f*. **~chair** *n* Rollstuhl *m*. **~-clamp** *n* Parkkralle *f*

when *adv* wann; **the day ~** der Tag, an dem ● *conj* wenn; (*in the past*) als; (*although*) wo ... doch; **~ swimming/reading** beim Schwimmen/Lesen

whenever *conj & adv* [immer] wenn; (*at whatever time*) wann immer; **~ did it happen?** wann ist das bloß passiert?

where *adv & conj* wo; **~ [to]** wohin; **~ [from]** woher

whereabouts¹ *adv* wo

whereabouts² *n* Verbleib *m*; (*of person*) Aufenthaltsort *m*

whereas *conj* während; (*in contrast*) wohingegen

whereupon *adv* worauf[hin]

wherever *conj & adv* wo immer; (*to whatever place*) wohin immer; (*from whatever place*) woher immer; (*everywhere*) überall wo; **~ possible** wenn irgend möglich

whether *conj* ob

which

● *adjective*

····➤ (*in questions*) welcher (*m*), welche (*f*), welches (*nt*), welche (*pl*). **which book do you need?** welches Buch brauchst du? **which one?** welcher/welche/welches? **which ones?** welche? **which one of you did it?** wer von euch hat es getan? **which way?** (*which direction*) welche Richtung?; (*where*) wohin?; (*how*) wie?

····➤ (*relative*) **he always comes at one, at which time I'm having lunch/by which time I've finished** er kommt immer um ein Uhr; dann esse ich gerade zu Mittag/bis dahin bin ich schon fertig

● *pronoun*

····➤ (*in questions*) welcher (*m*), welche (*f*), welches (*nt*), welche (*pl*). **which is which?** welcher/welche/welches ist welcher/welche/welches? **which of you?** wer von euch?

····➤ (*relative*) der (*m*), die (*f*), das (*nt*), die (*pl*); (*genitive*) dessen (*m, nt*), deren (*f, pl*); (*dative*)

dem (*m, nt*), der (*f*), denen (*pl*); (*referring to a clause*) was. **the book which I gave you** das Buch, das ich dir gab. **the trial, the result of which we are expecting** der Prozess, dessen Ergebnis wir erwarten. **the house of which I was speaking** das Haus, von dem *od* wovon ich redete. **after which** wonach; nach dem. **on which** worauf; auf dem. **the shop opposite which we parked** der Laden, gegenüber dem wir parkten. **everything which I tell you** alles, was ich dir sage

whichever *a & pron* [egal] welche(r,s); ~ **it is** was es auch ist

while *n* Weile *f*; **a long** ~ lange; **be worth** ~ sich lohnen; **it's worth my** ~ es lohnt sich für mich ●*conj* während; (*as long as*) solange; (*although*) obgleich ●*vt* ~ **away** sich (*dat*) vertreiben

whilst *conj* während

whim *n* Laune *f*

whimper *vi* wimmern; <*dog:*> winseln

whine *vi* winseln

whip *n* Peitsche *f*; (*Pol*) Einpeitscher *m* ●*vt* (*pt/pp* **whipped**) peitschen; (*Culin*) schlagen. ~**ped cream** *n* Schlagsahne *f*

whirl *vt/i* wirbeln. ~**pool** *n* Strudel *m*. ~**-wind** *n* Wirbelwind *m*

whirr *vi* surren

whisk *n* (*Culin*) Schneebesen *m* ●*vt* (*Culin*) schlagen

whisker *n* Schnurrhaar *nt*

whisky *n* Whisky *m*

whisper *n* Flüstern *nt* ●*vt/i* flüstern

whistle *n* Pfiff *m*; (*instrument*) Pfeife *f* ●*vt/i* pfeifen

white *a* (**-r, -st**) weiß ●*n* Weiß *nt*; (*of egg*) Eiweiß *nt*; (*person*) Weiße(r) *m/f*

white: ~ **coffee** *n* Kaffee *m* mit Milch. ~**-collar worker** *n* Angestellte(r) *m*. ~ **lie** *n* Notlüge *f*

whiten *vt* weiß machen ●*vi* weiß werden

whiteness *n* Weiß *nt*

Whitsun *n* Pfingsten *nt*

whiz[z] *vi* (*pt/pp* **whizzed**) zischen. ~**-kid** *n* [!] Senkrechtstarter *m*

who *pron* wer; (*acc*) wen; (*dat*) wem ●*rel pron* der/die/das, (*pl*) die

whoever *pron* wer [immer]; ~ **he is** wer er auch ist; ~ **is it?** wer ist das bloß?

whole *a* ganz; <*truth*> voll ●*n* Ganze(s) *nt*; **as a** ~ als Ganzes; **on the** ~ im Großen und Ganzen; **the** ~ **of Germany** ganz Deutschland

whole: ~**food** *n* Vollwertkost *f*. ~**-hearted** *a* rückhaltlos. ~**meal** *a* Vollkorn-

wholesale *a* Großhandels- ●*adv* en gros; (*fig*) in Bausch und Bogen. ~**r** *n* Großhändler *m*

wholly *adv* völlig

whom *pron* wen; **to** ~ wem ●*rel pron* den/die/das, (*pl*) die; (*dat*) dem/der/dem, (*pl*) denen

whopping *a* [!] Riesen-

whore *n* Hure *f*

whose *pron* wessen; ~ **is that?** wem gehört das? ●*rel pron* dessen/deren/dessen, (*pl*) deren

why *adv* warum; (*for what purpose*) wozu; **that's** ~ darum

wick *n* Docht *m*

wicked *a* böse; (*mischievous*) frech, boshaft

wicker *n* Korbgeflecht *nt* ●*attrib* Korb-

wide *a* (**-r, -st**) weit; (*broad*) breit; (*fig*) groß ●*adv* weit; (*off target*) daneben; ~ **awake** hellwach; **far**

W

and ~ weit und breit. **~ly** *adv* weit; <*known, accepted*> weithin; <*differ*> stark

widen *vt* verbreitern; (*fig*) erweitern ● *vi* sich verbreitern

widespread *a* weit verbreitet

widow *n* Witwe *f*. **~ed** *a* verwitwet. **~er** *n* Witwer *m*

width *n* Weite *f*; (*breadth*) Breite *f*

wield *vt* schwingen; ausüben <*power*>

wife *n* (*pl* **wives**) [Ehe]frau *f*

wig *n* Perücke *f*

wiggle *vi* wackeln ● *vt* wackeln mit

wild *a* (**-er, -est**), **-ly** *adv* wild; <*animal*> wild lebend; <*flower*> wild wachsend; (*furious*) wütend ● *adv* wild; **run ~** frei herumlaufen ● *n* **in the ~** wild; **the ~s** *pl* die Wildnis *f*

wilderness *n* Wildnis *f*; (*desert*) Wüste *f*

wildlife *n* Tierwelt *f*

---

will[1]

● *auxiliary verb*
past **would**

····➤ (*expressing the future*) werden. **she will arrive tomorrow** sie wird morgen ankommen. **he will be there by now** er wird jetzt schon da sein

····➤ (*expressing intention*) (*present tense*) **will you go?** gehst du? **I promise I won't do it again** ich verspreche, ich machs nicht noch mal

····➤ (*in requests*) **will/would you please tidy up?** würdest du bitte aufräumen? **will you be quiet!** willst du ruhig sein!

····➤ (*in invitations*) **will you have/would you like some wine?** wollen Sie/möchten Sie Wein?

····➤ (*negative: refuse to*) nicht wollen. **they won't help me** sie wollen mir nicht helfen. **the car won't start** das Auto will nicht anspringen

····➤ (*in tag questions*) nicht wahr. **you'll be back soon, won't you?** du kommst bald wieder, nicht wahr? **you will help her, won't you?** du hilfst ihr doch, nicht wahr?

····➤ (*in short answers*) **Will you be there? — Yes I will** Wirst du da sein? – Ja

---

will[2] *n* Wille *m*; (*document*) Testament *nt*

willing *a* willig; (*eager*) bereitwillig; **be ~** bereit sein. **~ly** *adv* bereitwillig; (*gladly*) gern. **~ness** *n* Bereitwilligkeit *f*

willow *n* Weide *f*

will-power *n* Willenskraft *f*

wilt *vi* welk werden, welken

wily *a* (**-ier, -iest**) listig

win *n* Sieg *m* ● *v* (*pt/pp* **won**; *pres p* **winning**) ● *vt* gewinnen; bekommen <*scholarship*> ● *vi* gewinnen; (*in battle*) siegen. **~ over** *vt* auf seine Seite bringen

wince *vi* zusammenzucken

winch *n* Winde *f* ● *vt* **~ up** hochwinden

wind[1] *n* Wind *m*; ([!] *flatulence*) Blähungen *pl* ● *vt* **~ s.o.** jdm den Atem nehmen

wind[2] *v* (*pt/pp* **wound**) ● *vt* (*wrap*) wickeln; (*move by turning*) kurbeln; aufziehen <*clock*> *vi* <*road:*> sich winden. **~ up** *vt* aufziehen <*clock*>; schließen <*proceedings*>

wind: ~ farm *n* Windpark *m*. **~ instrument** *n* Blasinstrument *nt*. **~mill** *n* Windmühle *f*

window *n* Fenster *nt*; (*of shop*) Schaufenster *nt*

window: ~-box *n* Blumenkasten *m*. **~-cleaner** *n* Fensterputzer *m*. **~-pane** *n* Fensterscheibe *f*. **~-shopping** *n* Schaufensterbummel *m*. **~-sill** *n* Fensterbrett *nt*

windpipe *n* Luftröhre *f*
windscreen *n*, (*Amer*) **windshield** *n* Windschutzscheibe *f*. **~-wiper** *n* Scheibenwischer *m*
wind surfing *n* Windsurfen *nt*
windy *a* (**-ier, -iest**) windig
wine *n* Wein *m*
wine: ~-bar *n* Weinstube *f*. **~ glass** *n* Weinglas *nt*. **~-list** *n* Weinkarte *f*
winery *n* (*Amer*) Weingut *nt*
wine-tasting *n* Weinprobe *f*
wing *n* Flügel *m*; (*Auto*) Kotflügel *m*; **~s** *pl* (*Theat*) Kulissen *pl*
wink *n* Zwinkern *nt*; **not sleep a ~** kein Auge zutun ● *vi* zwinkern; <*light:*> blinken
winner *n* Gewinner(in) *m(f)*; (*Sport*) Sieger(in) *m(f)*
winning *a* siegreich; <*smile*> gewinnend. **~-post** *n* Zielpfosten *m*. **~s** *npl* Gewinn *m*
wint|er *n* Winter *m*. **~ry** *a* winterlich
wipe *n* **give sth a ~** etw abwischen ● *vt* abwischen; aufwischen <*floor*>; (*dry*) abtrocknen. **~ out** *vt* (*cancel*) löschen; (*destroy*) ausrotten. **~ up** *vt* aufwischen
wire *n* Draht *m*
wiring *n* [elektrische] Leitungen *pl*
wisdom *n* Weisheit *f*; (*prudence*) Klugheit *f*. **~ tooth** *n* Weisheitszahn *m*
wise *a* (**-r, -st**), **-ly** *adv* weise; (*prudent*) klug
wish *n* Wunsch *m* ● *vt* wünschen; **~ s.o. well** jdm alles Gute wünschen; **I ~ you could stay** ich wünschte, du könntest hier bleiben ● *vi* sich (*dat*) etwas wünschen. **~ful** *a* **~ful thinking** Wunschdenken *nt*
wistful *a*, **-ly** *adv* wehmütig
wit *n* Geist *m*, Witz *m*; (*intelligence*) Verstand *m*; (*person*) geistreicher Mensch *m*; **be at one's ~s' end** sich (*dat*) keinen Rat mehr wissen
witch *n* Hexe *f*. **~craft** *n* Hexerei *f*
with *prep* mit (+ *dat*); **~ fear/cold** vor Angst/Kälte; **~ it** damit; **I'm going ~ you** ich gehe mit; **take it ~ you** nimm es mit; **I haven't got it ~ me** ich habe es nicht bei mir
withdraw *v* (*pt* **-drew**, *pp* **-drawn**) ● *vt* zurückziehen; abheben <*money*> ● *vi* sich zurückziehen. **~al** *n* Zurückziehen *nt*; (*of money*) Abhebung *f*; (*from drugs*) Entzug *m*
wither *vi* [ver]welken
withhold *vt* (*pt/pp* **-held**) vorenthalten (**from s.o.** jdm)
within *prep* innerhalb (+ *gen*) ● *adv* innen
without *prep* ohne (+ *acc*); **~ my noticing it** ohne dass ich es merkte
withstand *vt* (*pt/pp* **-stood**) standhalten (+ *dat*)
witness *n* Zeuge *m*/ Zeugin *f* ● *vt* Zeuge/Zeugin sein (+ *gen*); bestätigen <*signature*>
witticism *n* geistreicher Ausspruch *m*
witty *a* (**-ier, -iest**) witzig, geistreich
wives *see* **wife**
wizard *n* Zauberer *m*
wizened *a* verhutzelt
wobb|le *vi* wackeln. **~ly** *a* wackelig
woke, woken *see* **wake**[1]
wolf *n* (*pl* **wolves**) Wolf *m*
woman *n* (*pl* **women**) Frau *f*. **~izer** *n* Schürzenjäger *m*
womb *n* Gebärmutter *f*
women *npl see* **woman**
won *see* **win**
wonder *n* Wunder *nt*; (*surprise*) Staunen *nt* ● *vt/i* sich fragen; (*be surprised*) sich wundern; **I ~** da frage ich mich; **I ~ whether she is**

ill ob sie wohl krank ist? **~ful** *a*, **-ly** *adv* wunderbar

won't = **will not**

wood *n* Holz *nt*; (*forest*) Wald *m*; **touch ~!** unberufen!

wood: ~ed *a* bewaldet. **~en** *a* Holz-; (*fig*) hölzern. **~pecker** *n* Specht *m*. **~wind** *n* Holzbläser *pl*. **~work** *n* (*wooden parts*) Holzteile *pl*; (*craft*) Tischlerei *f*. **~worm** *n* Holzwurm *m*

wool *n* Wolle *f* ● *attrib* Woll-. **~len** *a* wollen

woolly *a* (**-ier, -iest**) wollig; (*fig*) unklar

word *n* Wort *nt*; (*news*) Nachricht *f*; **by ~ of mouth** mündlich; **have a ~ with** sprechen mit; **have ~s** einen Wortwechsel haben. **~ing** *n* Wortlaut *m*. **~ processor** *n* Textverarbeitungssystem *nt*

wore *see* **wear**

work *n* Arbeit *f*; (*Art, Literature*) Werk *nt*; **~s** *pl* (*factory, mechanism*) Werk *nt*; **at ~** bei der Arbeit; **out of ~** arbeitslos ● *vi* arbeiten; <*machine, system:*> funktionieren; (*have effect*) wirken; (*study*) lernen; **it won't ~** (*fig*) es klappt nicht ● *vt* arbeiten lassen; bedienen <*machine*>; betätigen <*lever*>. **~ off** *vt* abarbeiten. **~ out** *vt* ausrechnen; (*solve*) lösen ● *vi* gut gehen, [!] klappen. **~ up** *vt* aufbauen; sich (*dat*) holen <*appetite*>; **get ~ed up** sich aufregen

workable *a* (*feasible*) durchführbar

worker *n* Arbeiter(in) *m(f)*

working *a* berufstätig; <*day, clothes*> Arbeits-; **be in ~ order** funktionieren. **~ class** *n* Arbeiterklasse *f*

work: ~man *n* Arbeiter *m*; (*craftsman*) Handwerker *m*. **~manship** *n* Arbeit *f*. **~shop** *n* Werkstatt *f*

world *n* Welt *f*; **in the ~** auf der Welt; **think the ~ of s.o.** große Stücke auf jdn halten. **~ly** *a* weltlich; <*person*> weltlich gesinnt. **~-wide** *a & adv* weltweit

worm *n* Wurm *m*

worn *see* **wear** ● *a* abgetragen. **~-out** *a* abgetragen; <*carpet*> abgenutzt; <*person*> erschöpft

worried *a* besorgt

worry *n* Sorge *f* ● *v* (*pt/pp* **worried**) ● *vt* beunruhigen; (*bother*) stören ● *vi* sich beunruhigen, sich (*dat*) Sorgen machen. **~ing** *a* beunruhigend

worse *a & adv* schlechter; (*more serious*) schlimmer ● *n* Schlechtere(s) *nt*; Schlimmere(s) *nt*

worsen *vt* verschlechtern ● *vi* sich verschlechtern

worship *n* Anbetung *f*; (*service*) Gottesdienst *m* ● *vt* (*pt/pp* **-shipped**) anbeten

worst *a* schlechteste(r,s); (*most serious*) schlimmste(r,s) ● *adv* am schlechtesten; am schlimmsten ● *n* **the ~** das Schlimmste

worth *n* Wert *m*; **£10's ~ of petrol** Benzin für £10 ● *a* **be ~ £5** £5 wert sein; **be ~ it** (*fig*) sich lohnen. **~less** *a* wertlos. **~while** *a* lohnend

worthy *a* würdig

would *v aux* **I ~ do it** ich würde es tun, ich täte es; **~ you go?** würdest du gehen? **he said he ~n't** er sagte, er würde es nicht tun; **what ~ you like?** was möchten Sie?

wound[1] *n* Wunde *f* ● *vt* verwunden

wound[2] *see* **wind**[2]

wove, woven *see* **weave**[2]

wrangle *n* Streit *m*

wrap *n* Umhang *m* ● *vt* (*pt/pp* **wrapped**) **~ [up]** wickeln; einpacken <*present*> ● *vi* **~ up**

warmly sich warm einpacken. **~per** *n* Hülle *f*. **~ping** *n* Verpackung *f*

wrath *n* Zorn *m*

wreath *n* (*pl* **-s**) Kranz *m*

wreck *n* Wrack *nt* ●*vt* zerstören; zunichte machen <*plans*>; zerrütten <*marriage*>. **~age** *n* Wrackteile *pl*; (*fig*) Trümmer *pl*

wren *n* Zaunkönig *m*

wrench *n* Ruck *m*; (*tool*) Schraubenschlüssel *m*; **be a ~** (*fig*) weh tun ●*vt* reißen; **~ sth from s.o.** jdm etw entreißen

wrestl|e *vi* ringen. **~er** *n* Ringer *m*. **~ing** *n* Ringen *nt*

wretch *n* Kreatur *f*. **~ed** *a* elend; (*very bad*) erbärmlich

wriggle *n* Zappeln *nt* ●*vi* zappeln; (*move forward*) sich schlängeln; **~ out of sth** [!] sich vor etw (*dat*) drücken

wring *vt* (*pt/pp* **wrung**) wringen; (**~** *out*) auswringen; umdrehen <*neck*>; ringen <*hands*>

wrinkle *n* Falte *f*; (*on skin*) Runzel *f* ●*vt* kräuseln ●*vi* sich kräuseln, sich falten. **~d** *a* runzlig

wrist *n* Handgelenk *nt*. **~-watch** *n* Armbanduhr *f*

write *vt/i* (*pt* **wrote**, *pp* **written**, *pres p* **writing**) schreiben. **~ down** *vt* aufschreiben. **~ off** *vt* abschreiben; zu Schrott fahren <*car*>

write-off *n* ≈ Totalschaden *m*

writer *n* Schreiber(in) *m(f)*; (*author*) Schriftsteller(in) *m(f)*

writhe *vi* sich winden

writing *n* Schreiben *nt*; (*handwriting*) Schrift *f*; **in ~** schriftlich. **~-paper** *n* Schreibpapier *nt*

written *see* **write**

wrong *a*, **-ly** *adv* falsch; (*morally*) unrecht; (*not just*) ungerecht; **be ~** nicht stimmen; <*person*:> Unrecht haben; **what's ~?** was ist los? ●*adv* falsch; **go ~** <*person*:> etwas falsch machen; <*machine*:> kaputtgehen; <*plan*:> schief gehen ●*n* Unrecht *nt* ●*vt* Unrecht tun (+ *dat*). **~ful** *a* ungerechtfertigt. **~fully** *adv* <*accuse*> zu Unrecht

wrote *see* **write**

wrung *see* **wring**

wry *a* (**-er, -est**) ironisch; <*humour*> trocken

Xx

Xmas *n* [!] Weihnachten *nt*

X-ray *n* (*picture*) Röntgenaufnahme *f*; **~s** *pl* Röntgenstrahlen *pl* ●*vt* röntgen; durchleuchten <*luggage*>

Yy

yacht *n* Jacht *f*; (*for racing*) Segeljacht *f*. **~ing** *n* Segeln *nt*

yank *vt* [!] reißen

Yank *n* [!] Ami *m* [!]

yap *vi* (*pt/pp* **yapped**) <*dog*:> kläffen

yard[1] *n* Hof *m*; (*for storage*) Lager *nt*

yard[2] *n* Yard *nt* (= *0,91 m*)

yarn *n* Garn *nt*; ([!] *tale*) Geschichte *f*

yawn *n* Gähnen *nt* ●*vi* gähnen

year *n* Jahr *nt;* (*of wine*) Jahrgang *m;* **for ~s** jahrelang. **~ly** *a & adv* jährlich

yearn *vi* sich sehnen (**for** nach). **~ing** *n* Sehnsucht *f*

yeast *n* Hefe *f*

yell *n* Schrei *m* ● *vi* schreien

yellow *a* gelb ● *n* Gelb *nt*

yelp *vi* jaulen

yes *adv* ja; (*contradicting*) doch ● *n* Ja *nt*

yesterday *n & adv* gestern; **~'s paper** die gestrige Zeitung; **the day before ~** vorgestern

yet *adv* noch; (*in question*) schon; (*nevertheless*) doch; **as ~** bisher; **not ~** noch nicht; **the best ~** das bisher beste ● *conj* doch

Yiddish *n* Jiddisch *nt*

yield *n* Ertrag *m* ● *vt* bringen; abwerfen <*profit*> ● *vi* nachgeben; (*Amer, Auto*) die Vorfahrt beachten

yoga *n* Yoga *m*

yoghurt *n* Joghurt *m*

yoke *n* Joch *nt;* (*of garment*) Passe *f*

yolk *n* Dotter *m*, Eigelb *nt*

you *pron* du; (*acc*) dich; (*dat*) dir; (*pl*) ihr; (*acc, dat*) euch; (*formal*) (*nom & acc, sg & pl*) Sie; (*dat, sg & pl*) Ihnen; (*one*) man; (*acc*) einen; (*dat*) einem; **all of ~** ihr/Sie alle; **I know ~** ich kenne dich/euch/Sie; **I'll give ~ the money** ich gebe dir/euch/Ihnen das Geld; **it does ~ good** es tut einem gut; **it's bad for ~** es ist ungesund

young *a* (**-er, -est**) jung ● *npl* (*animals*) Junge *pl;* **the ~** die Jugend *f*. **~ster** *n* Jugendliche(r) *m/f;* (*child*) Kleine(r) *m/f*

your *a* dein; (*pl*) euer; (*formal*) Ihr

yours *poss pron* deine(r), deins; (*pl*) eure(r), euers; (*formal, sg & pl*) Ihre(r), Ihr[e]s; **a friend of ~** ein Freund von dir/Ihnen/euch; **that is ~** das gehört dir/Ihnen/euch

yourself *pron* (*pl* **-selves**) selbst; (*refl*) dich; (*dat*) dir; (*pl*) euch; (*formal*) sich; **by ~** allein

youth *n* (*pl* **-s**) Jugend *f;* (*boy*) Jugendliche(r) *m*. **~ful** *a* jugendlich. **~ hostel** *n* Jugendherberge *f*

Yugoslavia *n* Jugoslawien *nt*

Zz

zeal *n* Eifer *m*

zealous *a*, **-ly** *adv* eifrig

zebra *n* Zebra *nt*. **~ crossing** *n* Zebrastreifen *m*

zero *n* Null *f*

zest *n* Begeisterung *f*

zigzag *n* Zickzack *m* ● *vi* (*pt/pp* **-zagged**) im Zickzack laufen/ (*in vehicle*) fahren

zinc *n* Zink *nt*

zip *n* **~ [fastener]** Reißverschluss *m* ● *vt* **~ [up]** den Reißverschluss zuziehen an (+ *dat*)

zip code *n* (*Amer*) Postleitzahl *f*

zipper *n* Reißverschluss *m*

zodiac *n* Tierkreis *m*

zone *n* Zone *f*

zoo *n* Zoo *m*

zoological *a* zoologisch

zoolog|ist *n* Zoologe *m*/gin *f*. **~y** Zoologie *f*

zoom *vi* sausen. **~ lens** *n* Zoomobjektiv *nt*

Summary of German grammar

Regular verbs

Most German verbs are regular and add the same endings to their stem. You find the stem by taking away the **-en** (or sometimes just **-n**) from the end of the infinitive. The infinitive of the verb, for example **machen**, is the form you look up in the dictionary. The stem of **machen** is **mach-**. There are six endings for each tense, to go with the different pronouns:

ich = *I*	du = *you*	er/sie/es = *he/she/it*
wir = *we*	ihr = *you*	sie/Sie = *they/you* (*polite form*).

Present tense

For example, *I make, I am making,* or *I do make*:

infinitive	ich	du	er/sie/es	wir	ihr	sie/Sie
machen	mache	machst	macht	machen	macht	machen

Imperfect tense

For example, *I made, I was making,* or *I used to make*:

infinitive	ich	du	er/sie/es	wir	ihr	sie/Sie
machen	machte	machtest	machte	machten	machtet	machten

Future tense

For example, *I will make* or *I shall make*. This is formed by using the present tense of **werden**, which is the equivalent of *will* or *shall*, with the infinitive verb: **ich werde machen**.

infinitive	ich	du	er/sie/es	wir	ihr	sie/Sie
werden	werde	wirst	wird	werden	werdet	werden

Perfect tense

For example, *I made* or *I have made*. For most German verbs the perfect is formed by using the present tense of **haben**, which is the equivalent of *have*, with the past participle: **ich habe gemacht**. Some verbs take **sein** instead of **haben**, and these are all marked (***sein***) in the dictionary. They are mainly verbs expressing motion and involving a change of place:

he drove to Berlin today = er ist heute nach Berlin gefahren

Or they express a change of state, and this includes verbs meaning to happen (**geschehen**, **passieren**, **vorkommen**):

he woke up = er ist aufgewacht

infinitive	ich	du	er/sie/es	wir	ihr	sie/Sie
haben	habe	hast	hat	haben	habt	haben
sein	bin	bist	ist	sind	seid	sind

Irregular verbs and other forms

Some German verbs are irregular and change their stem or add different endings. All the irregular verbs that appear in the dictionary are given in the section *German irregular verbs* on pages 601–606.

The subjunctive

This is a form of the verb that is used to express speculation, doubt, or unlikelihood. It is rarely used in English (*if I were you* instead of *if I was you* is an exceptional example), but is still used in both written and spoken German.

Present tense

infinitive	ich	du	er/sie/es	wir	ihr	sie/Sie
machen	mache	machest	mache	machen	machet	machen
sein	sei	sei(e)st	sei	seien	seid	seien

Imperfect tense

For regular verbs this is the same as the normal imperfect forms, but irregular verbs vary.

infinitive	ich	du	er/sie/es	wir	ihr	sie/Sie
machen	machte	machtest	machte	machten	machtet	machten
werden	würde	würdest	würde	würden	würdet	würden
sein	wäre	wär(e)st	wäre	wären	wär(e)t	wären

The imperfect subjunctive of werden is used with an infinitive to form the conditional tense. This tense expresses what would happen if something else occurred.

he would go = er würde gehen
I wouldn't do that = das würde ich nicht machen

Reflexive verbs

The object of a reflexive verb is the same as its subject. In German, the object is a reflexive pronoun. This is usually in the accusative (I wash = **ich wasche mich**). The reflexive pronouns of some verbs are in the dative (I imagine = **ich stelle mir vor**), and these are marked in the English–German part of the dictionary with (*dat*).

infinitive	ich	du	er/sie/es	wir	ihr	sie/Sie
sich waschen	wasche mich	wäschst dich	wäscht sich	waschen uns	wascht euch	waschen sich
sich vorstellen	stelle mir vor	stellst dir vor	stellt sich vor	stellen uns vor	stellt euch vor	stellen sich vor

The passive

In the passive form, the subject of the verb experiences the action rather than performs it: he was asked = **er wurde gefragt**. In German, the passive is formed using parts of **werden** with the past participle:

PRESENT PASSIVE	*it is done*	es wird gemacht
IMPERFECT PASSIVE	*it was done*	es wurde gemacht
FUTURE PASSIVE	*it will be done*	es wird gemacht werden
PERFECT PASSIVE	*it has been done*	es ist gemacht worden

When forming the perfect passive, note that the past participle of **werden** becomes **worden** rather than **geworden**.

Separable verbs

Separable verbs are marked in the German–English part of the dictionary with the label *sep*. In the perfect tense, the **ge-** of the past participle comes between the prefix and the verb, for example **er/sie/es hat an**ge**fangen**.

Articles

There are two articles in English, the definite article *the* and the indefinite article *a/an*. The way these are translated into German depends on the gender, number, and case of the noun with which the article goes.

There are three genders of nouns in German: masculine (**der Mann** – the man), feminine (**die Frau** = the woman), and neuter (**das Buch** = the book). There are two forms of number: singular (**der Baum** = the tree) and plural (**die Bäume** = the trees). And there are four cases, which show the part a noun plays in a sentence: nominative, accusative, genitive, and dative.

Definite article

the = der/die/das, (*plural*) = die

	SINGULAR masculine	feminine	neuter	PLURAL all genders
NOMINATIVE	**der** Mann	**die** Frau	**das** Buch	**die** Bäume
ACCUSATIVE	**den** Mann	**die** Frau	**das** Buch	**die** Bäume
GENITIVE	**des** Mannes	**der** Frau	**des** Buches	**der** Bäume
DATIVE	**dem** Mann	**der** Frau	**dem** Buch	**den** Bäumen

Indefinite article

a/*an* = ein/eine/ein. This article can only be singular.

	masculine	feminine	neuter
NOMINATIVE	**ein** Mann	**eine** Frau	**ein** Buch
ACCUSATIVE	**einen** Mann	**eine** Frau	**ein** Buch
GENITIVE	**eines** Mannes	**einer** Frau	**eines** Buches
DATIVE	**einem** Mann	**einer** Frau	**einem** Buch

Nouns

In German, all nouns start with a capital letter: **das Buch** = the book.

Gender

There are three genders of nouns in German: masculine (**der Mann** = the man), feminine (**die Frau** = the woman), and neuter (**das Buch** = the book). These three examples are logical, with masculine for a male person, feminine for a female person, and neuter for an object. But it is not always like this with German nouns. Gender is sometimes determined by a noun's ending. For example, **das Mädchen** (= the girl) is neuter rather than feminine, simply because the ending **-chen** is always neuter.

The gender of German nouns is given in the dictionary. There are some general rules regarding the gender of groups of nouns, but individual genders must be checked by looking them up.

Masculine nouns

- male persons and animals: **der Arbeiter** = worker; **der Bär** = bear
- 'doers' and 'doing' instruments ending in **-er** in German: **der Gärtner** = gardener; **der Computer** = computer
- days, months, and seasons: (**der**) **Montag** = Monday

- words ending in **-ich**, **-ig**, and **-ling**: **der Honig** = honey; **der Lehrling** = apprentice
- words ending in **-ismus**, **-ist**, and **-ant**.

Feminine nouns

- female persons and animals: **die Schauspielerin** = actress; **die Henne** = hen; the feminine form of professions and animals is made by adding **-in** to the masculine (**der Schauspieler/die Schauspielerin** = actor/actress)
- nouns ending in **-ei**, **-ie**, **-ik**, **-in**, **-ion**, **-heit**, **-keit**, **-schaft**, **-tät**, **-ung**, **-ur**: **die Gärtnerei** = gardening; **die Energie** = energy
- most nouns ending in **-e**: **die Blume** = flower; note that there are many exceptions, including **der Name** = name, **der Käse** = cheese, **das Ende** = end.

Neuter nouns

- names of continents, most countries, and towns: (**das**) **Deutschland** = Germany; (**das**) **Köln** = Cologne
- nouns ending in **-chen** and **-lein** (indicating *small*): **das Mädchen**, **das Fräulein** = girl.
- most (but not all!) nouns beginning with **Ge-** or ending in **-nis**, **-tel**, or **-um**: **das Geheimnis** = secret; **das Zentrum** = centre
- infinitives of verbs used as nouns: **das Lachen** = laughter; **das Essen** = food.

Compound nouns

When two nouns are put together to make one compound noun, it takes the gender of the second noun:

der Brief + die Marke = die Briefmarke.

Plural

There are no absolutely definitive rules for the plural forms of German nouns. Plurals generally add an ending (**der Freund**, **die Freunde**), and change a vowel to an umlaut (**der Gast**, **die Gäste**; **das Haus**, **die Häuser**). Feminine words ending in **-heit**, **-keit**, and **-ung** add **-en** to make the plural (**die Abbildung**, **die Abbildungen**).

The plurals of all nouns are given in the German–English part of the dictionary.

Case

There are four cases, which show the part a noun plays in a sentence: nominative, accusative, genitive, and dative. The noun's article changes according to the case, and the ending of the noun changes in some cases:

	SINGULAR masculine	feminine	neuter
NOMINATIVE	der Mann	die Frau	das Buch
ACCUSATIVE	den Mann	die Frau	das Buch
GENITIVE	des **Mannes**	der Frau	des **Buches**
DATIVE	dem Mann	der Frau	dem Buch

	PLURAL masculine	feminine	neuter
NOMINATIVE	die Männer	die Frauen	die Bücher
ACCUSATIVE	die Männer	die Frauen	die Bücher
GENITIVE	der Männer	der Frauen	der Bücher
DATIVE	den **Männern**	den Frauen	den **Büchern**

The nominative is used for the subject of a sentence; in sentences with **sein** (to be) and **werden** (to become), the noun after the verb is in the nominative.

the dog barked = der Hund bellte
that is my car = das ist mein Wagen

The accusative is used for the direct object and after some prepositions (listed on page 597):

she has a son = sie hat einen Sohn

The genitive shows possession, and is also used after some prepositions (listed on page 597):

my husband's dog = der Hund meines Mannes

The dative is used for the indirect object. Some German verbs, such as **helfen**, take only the dative. The dative is also used after some prepositions (listed on page 596):

she gave the books to the children = sie gab den Kindern die Bücher

The following sentence combines all four cases:

der Mann gibt der Frau den Bleistift des Mädchens = *the man gives the woman the girl's pencil*
der Mann *is the subject* (*in the nominative*)
gibt *is the verb*
der Frau *is the indirect object* (*in the dative*)
den Bleistift *is the direct object* (*in the accusative*)
des Mädchens *is in the genitive* (*showing possession*).

Adjectives

An adjective is a word qualifying a noun. In German, an adjective in front of a noun adds endings that vary with the noun's gender, number, and case. Adjectives that come after a noun do not add endings.

With the definite article

Adjectives following **der/die/das** take these endings:

	SINGULAR masculine	feminine	neuter	PLURAL all genders
NOMINATIVE	der rote Hut	die rote Lampe	das rote Buch	die rot**en** Autos
ACCUSATIVE	den rot**en** Hut	die rote Lampe	das rote Buch	die rot**en** Autos
GENITIVE	des rot**en** Hutes	der rot**en** Lampe	des rot**en** Buches	der rot**en** Autos
DATIVE	dem rot**en** Hut	der rot**en** Lampe	dem rot**en** Buch	den rot**en** Autos

Some German adjectives follow the pattern of the definite article, and adjectives after them change their endings in the same way as after **der/die/das**. For example, **dieser/diese/dieses** (= this):

	SINGULAR masculine	feminine	neuter	PLURAL all genders
NOMINATIVE	dieser	diese	dieses	diese
ACCUSATIVE	diesen	diese	dieses	diese
GENITIVE	dieses	dieser	dieses	dieser
DATIVE	diesem	dieser	diesem	diesen

Other common examples are:

jeder/jede/jedes = *every, each*
jener/jene/jenes = *that*
mancher/manche/manches = *many a, some*
solcher/solche/solches = *such*
welcher/welche/welches = *which*

With the indefinite article

Adjectives following **ein/eine/ein** take these endings:

	SINGULAR masculine	feminine	neuter
NOMINATIVE	ein rot**er** Hut	eine rote Lampe	ein rot**es** Buch
ACCUSATIVE	einen rot**en** Hut	eine rote Lampe	ein rot**es** Buch
GENITIVE	eines rot**en** Hutes	einer rot**en** Lampe	eines rot**en** Buches
DATIVE	einem rot**en** Hut	einer rot**en** Lampe	einem rot**en** Buch

Some German adjectives follow the pattern of the indefinite article, and adjectives after them change their endings in the same way as after **ein/eine/ein**. They are:

dein = *your*	kein = *no*
euer = *your*	mein = *my*
Ihr = *your*	sein = *his/its*
ihr = *her/their*	unser = *our*

These adjectives can also go with plural nouns: no cars = **keine Autos**. All genders take the same endings in the plural:

	PLURAL all genders
NOMINATIVE	kein**e** roten Autos
ACCUSATIVE	kein**e** roten Autos
GENITIVE	kein**er** roten Autos
DATIVE	kein**en** roten Autos

Without an article

Adjectives in front of a noun on their own, without an article, take the following endings:

	SINGULAR masculine	feminine	neuter	PLURAL all genders
NOMINATIVE	gut**er** Wein	frisch**e** Milch	kalt**es** Bier	alt**e** Leute
ACCUSATIVE	gut**en** Wein	frisch**e** Milch	kalt**es** Bier	alt**e** Leute
GENITIVE	gut**en** Weins	frisch**er** Milch	kalt**en** Biers	alt**er** Leute
DATIVE	gut**em** Wein	frisch**er** Milch	kalt**em** Bier	alt**en** Leuten

Adjectives as nouns

In German, adjectives can be used as nouns, spelt with a capital letter: **alt** = old, **ein Alter** = an old man, **eine Alte** = an old woman.

With the definite article (**der/die/das**), these nouns take the following endings:

	SINGULAR masculine	feminine	PLURAL both genders
NOMINATIVE	der Fremde	die Fremde	die Fremden
ACCUSATIVE	den Fremden	die Fremde	die Fremden
GENITIVE	des Fremden	der Fremden	der Fremden
DATIVE	dem Fremden	der Fremden	den Fremden

The feminine noun refers to a female stranger or foreigner.

With the indefinite article (**ein/eine/ein**), these nouns take the following endings:

	SINGULAR masculine	feminine	PLURAL both genders without an article
NOMINATIVE	ein Fremder	eine Fremde	Fremde
ACCUSATIVE	einen Fremden	eine Fremde	Fremde
GENITIVE	eines Fremden	einer Fremden	Fremder
DATIVE	einem Fremden	einer Fremden	Fremden

Comparative and superlative

In English, the comparative of the adjective *small* is *smaller*, and of *difficult* is *more difficult*. The superlatives are *smallest* and *most difficult*. In German, there is just one way to form the comparative and superlative: by adding the endings **-er** and -(**e**)**st**:

small, smaller, smallest = klein, kleiner, der/die/das kleinste

Many adjectives change their vowel to an umlaut in the comparative and superlative:

cold, colder, coldest = kalt, kälter, der/die/das kälteste

Some important adjectives are irregular:

big, bigger, biggest = groß, größer, der/die/das größte
good, better, best = gut, besser, der/die/das beste
high, higher, highest = hoch, höher, der/die/das höchste
much, more, most = viel, mehr, der/die/das meiste
near, nearer, nearest = nah, näher, der/die/das nächste

Comparative and superlative adjectives take the same endings as basic adjectives:

a smaller child = ein kleineres Kind
the coldest month = der kälteste Monat

Adverbs

In German almost all adjectives can also be used as adverbs, describing a verb, an adjective, or another adverb.

she sings beautifully = sie singt schön

Some words, such as **auch** (= also), **fast** (= almost), **immer** (= always), and **leider** (= unfortunately) are used only as adverbs:

she is very clever = sie ist sehr klug

Comparative and superlative

The comparative is formed by adding **-er** to the basic adverb, and the superlative by putting **am** in front of the basic adverb and adding the ending **-(e)sten**:

clearly, more clearly, most clearly	= klar, klarer, am klarsten

Some important adverbs are irregular:

soon, earlier, at the earliest	= bald, früher, am frühesten
well, better, best	= gut, besser, am besten
willingly, more willingly, most willingly	= gern, lieber, am liebsten

Pronouns

Pronouns are words—such as *he*, *which*, and *mine* in English—that stand instead of a noun.

Personal pronouns

These pronouns, such as he/she/it = **er/sie/es**, refer to people or things.

	I	you	he/it	she/it	it	we	you	they	you
NOMINATIVE	ich	du	er	sie	es	wir	ihr	sie	Sie
ACCUSATIVE	mich	dich	ihn	sie	es	uns	euch	sie	Sie
DATIVE	mir	dir	ihm	ihr	ihm	uns	euch	ihnen	Ihnen
	me	*you*	*him/it*	*her/it*	*it*	*us*	*you*	*them*	*you*

The genitive form is not given, because it is so rarely used.

In German there are two forms for you, **du** and **Sie**. **Du** is less formal and is used when speaking to someone you know well, a child, or a family member. When speaking to a person or a group of people you do not know very well, use the polite form, **Sie**.

German pronouns agree in gender with the noun they refer to. In the nominative case, *it* might be translated by **er** or **sie**, as well as **es**:

it (*the pencil*) *is red* = er (der Bleistift) ist rot
it (*the rose*) *is beautiful* = sie (die Rose) ist schön
it (*the car*) *is expensive* = es (das Auto) ist teuer

Possessive pronouns

The possessive pronouns are:

mine = meiner/meine/mein(e)s
yours (*informal singular*) = deiner/deine/dein(e)s
his = seiner/seine/sein(e)s
hers = ihrer/ihre/ihr(e)s
its = seiner/seine/sein(e)s
ours = unserer/unsere/unser(e)s
yours (*informal plural*) = eurer/eure/eures
theirs = ihrer/ihre/ihr(e)s
yours (*polite*) = Ihrer, Ihre, Ihr(e)s

They all take endings like **meiner/meine/mein(e)s**, as follows:

	SINGULAR masculine	feminine	neuter	PLURAL all genders
NOMINATIVE	meiner	meine	mein(e)s	meine
ACCUSATIVE	meinen	meine	mein(e)s	meine
GENITIVE	meines	meiner	meines	meiner
DATIVE	meinem	meiner	meinem	meinen

As can be seen in the table, in the neuter form an **-e-** can be added (making **meines**). This applies to all the possessive pronouns, but the extra **-e-** is rare.

Relative pronouns

These pronouns are used to introduce and link a new clause. In English they are *who*, *which*, *that*, and *what*. In German they are **der**, **die**, or **das**, depending on the noun referred to:

	SINGULAR masculine	feminine	neuter	PLURAL all genders
NOMINATIVE	der	die	das	die
ACCUSATIVE	den	die	das	die
GENITIVE	dessen	deren	dessen	deren
DATIVE	dem	der	dem	denen

Relative pronouns can be left out in English, but never in German:

the book (that) I'm reading = das Buch, das ich lese

They agree in gender and number with the noun they refer back to:

the man who visited us = der Mann, der uns besucht hat (**der** is masculine singular)

But the case of the pronoun depends on its function in the clause it introduces:

the pencil I bought yesterday = der Bleistift, den ich gestern gekauft habe

(**den** is masculine singular, but accusative because it is the object of the clause it introduces)

Interrogative pronouns

These pronouns are used to ask questions:

who? = wer?
what? = was?
which? = welcher/welche/welches?

Wer changes as follows:

NOMINATIVE	wer?
ACCUSATIVE	wen?
GENITIVE	wessen?
DATIVE	wem?

Reflexive pronouns

The object of a reflexive verb is the same as its subject. In German, the object is a reflexive pronoun. This is usually in the accusative (I wash = **ich wasche** mich). The reflexive pronouns of some verbs are in the dative (I imagine = **ich stelle** mir **vor**).

Indefinite pronouns

These pronouns do not refer to identifiable people or objects. In German, many indefinite pronouns, such as **etwas** (= something) and **nichts** (= nothing), never change. But some do take endings:

	someone	no one
NOMINATIVE	jemand	niemand
ACCUSATIVE	jemanden	niemanden
DATIVE	jemandem	niemandem

The genitive case is rarely used.

Prepositions

Prepositions are small words like *in*, that stand in front of a noun or pronoun. In German, the noun following a preposition always has to be in one of three cases—dative, accusative, or genitive.

Prepositions can be prefixes and form separable verbs:

to walk along the street = die Straße entlanggehen
he is walking along the street = er geht die Straße entlang

In the dictionary, the case governed by a preposition is given:

mit (+ *dat*) *means* mit *always takes the dative case.*

The most common case used after prepositions is the dative. The following prepositions always take the dative:

aus	mit	von
außer	nach	zu
bei	seit	

Some prepositions always take the accusative:

bis	entlang	gegen	um
durch	für	ohne	

Some prepositions always take the genitive:

anstatt	während
trotz	wegen

There is a group of prepositions that can take the dative or the accusative, depending on the sentence. They are:

an	in	unter
auf	neben	vor
hinter	über	zwischen

If the phrase containing one of these prepositions describes position—where something is happening—the dative case is used:

she sat in the kitchen = sie saß in der Küche

But if the phrase containing the preposition describes movement—motion towards something—the accusative follows:

she went into the kitchen = sie ging in die Küche

Some forms of the definite article are usually shortened when used with prepositions:

am (an dem); **ans** (an das); **aufs** (auf das); **beim** (bei dem); **durchs** (durch das); **fürs** (für das); **im** (in dem); **ins** (in das); **ums** (um das); **vom** (von dem); **zum** (zu dem); **zur** (zu der).

Conjunctions

Conjunctions are small words, such as *and* = **und**, which join clauses together in a sentence.

These common conjunctions link clauses together:

aber = *but*
denn = *for*
oder = *or*
sondern = *but* (*on the contrary*)
und = *and*

These conjunctions do not change normal word order in the two clauses:

ich gehe, und er kommt auch = *I am going, and he is coming too*

But there are many other conjunctions that send the verb to the end of the subordinate clause:

als = *when*, = *as*	dass = *that*	weil = *because*
bevor = *before*	ob = *whether*	
bis = *until*	während = *while*	
da = *since*	wenn = *when*, = *if*	

er konnte nicht in die Schule gehen, *weil* er krank *war* = *he couldn't go to school, because he was ill*

Word order

The basic rule for German word order is that the verb comes second in a sentence. The subject of the sentence usually comes before the verb:

meine Mutter fährt am Freitag nach Köln = *my mother is going to Cologne on Friday*

When the verb is made up of two parts, such as in the perfect and the future tenses, the auxiliary verb comes second in the sentence, while the past participle (in the perfect) or infinitive (in the future tense) goes to the end:

wir haben sehr lang gewartet = *we waited a very long time*
sie wird sicher bald kommen = *she is sure to turn up soon*

Past participles and infinitives go to the end in other sentences too:

ich kann dieses Lied nicht leiden = *I can't stand this song*
du musst hier bleiben = *you must stay here*

When a sentence starts with a subordinate clause, the verb stays in second place:

da ich kein Geld hatte, blieb ich zu Hause = *since I had no money, I stayed at home*

In the clause itself, the verb goes to the end:

er konnte nicht in die Schule gehen, weil er krank war

The relative pronouns **der**, **die**, and **das**, as well as a number of conjunctions, send the verb to the end of the clause:

der Junge, der hier wohnt = *the boy who lives here*

When separable verbs separate, the prefix goes to the end:

der Film fängt um acht Uhr an = *the film starts at 8 o'clock*

In questions and commands, the verb is usually first in the sentence:

kommst du heute Abend? = *are you coming this evening?*
komm schnell rein! = *come in quickly!*

When there are a number of phrases in a sentence, the usual order for the different elements is 1 time, 2 manner, 3 place:

wir fahren heute mit dem Auto nach München = *we are driving to Munich today* (*time* = heute; *manner* = mit dem Auto; *place* = nach München)

German irregular verbs

1st, 2nd, and 3rd person present are given after the infinitive, and past subjunctive after the past indicative, where there is a change of vowel or any other irregularity.

Compound verbs are only given if they do not take the same forms as the corresponding simple verb, e.g. *befehlen*, or if there is no corresponding simple verb, e.g. *bewegen*.

An asterisk (*) indicates a verb which is also conjugated regularly.

Infinitive	Past tense	Past participle
abwägen	wog (wöge) ab	abgewogen
ausbedingen	bedang (bedänge) aus	ausbedungen
backen (du bäckst, er bäckt)	buk (büke)	gebacken
befehlen (du befiehlst, er befiehlt)	befahl (beföhle, befähle)	befohlen
beginnen	begann (begänne)	begonnen
beißen (du/er beißt)	biss (bisse)	gebissen
bergen (du birgst, er birgt)	barg (bärge)	geborgen
bewegen[2]	bewog (bewöge)	bewogen
biegen	bog (böge)	gebogen
bieten	bot (böte)	geboten
binden	band (bände)	gebunden
bitten	bat (bäte)	gebeten
blasen (du/er bläst)	blies	geblasen
bleiben	blieb	geblieben
bleichen*	blich	geblichen
braten (du brätst, er brät)	briet	gebraten
brechen (du brichst, er bricht)	brach (bräche)	gebrochen
brennen	brannte (brennte)	gebrannt
bringen	brachte (brächte)	gebracht
denken	dachte (dächte)	gedacht
dreschen (du drischst, er drischt)	drosch (drösche)	gedroschen
dringen	drang (dränge)	gedrungen

Infinitive	Past tense	Past participle
dürfen (ich/er darf, du darfst)	durfte (dürfte)	gedurft
empfehlen (du empfiehlst, er empfiehlt)	empfahl (empföhle)	empfohlen
erlöschen (du erlischst, er erlischt)	erlosch (erlösche)	erloschen
erschrecken (du erschrickst, er erschrickt)	erschrak (erschräke)	erschrocken
erwägen	erwog (erwöge)	erwogen
essen (du/er isst)	aß (äße)	gegessen
fahren (du fährst, er fährt)	fuhr (führe)	gefahren
fallen (du fällst, er fällt)	fiel	gefallen
fangen (du fängst, er fängt)	fing	gefangen
fechten (du fichtst, er ficht)	focht (föchte)	gefochten
finden	fand (fände)	gefunden
flechten (du flichtst, er flicht)	flocht (flöchte)	geflochten
fliegen	flog (flöge)	geflogen
fliehen	floh (flöhe)	geflohen
fließen (du/er fließt)	floss (flösse)	geflossen
fressen (du/er frisst)	fraß (fräße)	gefressen
frieren	fror (fröre)	gefroren
gären*	gor (göre)	gegoren
gebären (du gebierst, sie gebiert)	gebar (gebäre)	geboren
geben (du gibst, er gibt)	gab (gäbe)	gegeben
gedeihen	gedieh	gediehen
gehen	ging	gegangen
gelingen	gelang (gelänge)	gelungen
gelten (du giltst, er gilt)	galt (gölte, gälte)	gegolten
genesen (du/er genest)	genas (genäse)	genesen
genießen (du/er genießt)	genoss (genösse)	genossen
geschehen (es geschieht)	geschah (geschähe)	geschehen
gewinnen	gewann (gewönne, gewänne)	gewonnen
gießen (du/er gießt)	goss (gösse)	gegossen
gleichen	glich	geglichen
gleiten	glitt	geglitten
glimmen	glomm (glömme)	geglommen
graben (du gräbst, er gräbt)	grub (grübe)	gegraben
greifen	griff	gegriffen

Infinitive	Past tense	Past participle
haben (du hast, er hat)	hatte (hätte)	gehabt
halten (du hältst, er hält)	hielt	gehalten
hängen[2]	hing	gehangen
hauen	haute	gehauen
heben	hob (höbe)	gehoben
heißen (du/er heißt)	hieß	geheißen
helfen (du hilfst, er hilft)	half (hülfe)	geholfen
kennen	kannte (kennte)	gekannt
klingen	klang (klänge)	geklungen
kneifen	kniff	gekniffen
kommen	kam (käme)	gekommen
können (ich/er kann, du kannst)	konnte (könnte)	gekonnt
kriechen	kroch (kröche)	gekrochen
laden (du lädst, er lädt)	lud (lüde)	geladen
lassen (du/er lässt)	ließ	gelassen
laufen (du läufst, er läuft)	lief	gelaufen
leiden	litt	gelitten
leihen	lieh	geliehen
lesen (du/er liest)	las (läse)	gelesen
liegen	lag (läge)	gelegen
lügen	log (löge)	gelogen
mahlen	mahlte	gemahlen
meiden	mied	gemieden
melken	molk (mölke)	gemolken
messen (du/er misst)	maß (mäße)	gemessen
misslingen	misslang (misslänge)	misslungen
mögen (ich/er mag, du magst)	mochte (möchte)	gemocht
müssen (ich/er muss, du musst	musste (müsste)	gemusst
nehmen (du nimmst, er nimmt)	nahm (nähme)	genommen
nennen	nannte (nennte)	genannt
pfeifen	pfiff	gepfiffen
preisen (du/er preist)	pries	gepriesen
raten (du rätst, er rät)	riet	geraten
reiben	rieb	gerieben
reißen (du/er reißt)	riss	gerissen
reiten	ritt	geritten
rennen	rannte (rennte)	gerannt
riechen	roch (röche)	gerochen
ringen	rang (ränge)	gerungen
rinnen	rann (ränne)	geronnen

Infinitive	Past tense	Past participle
rufen	rief	gerufen
salzen* (du/er salzt)	salzte	gesalzen
saufen (du säufst, er säuft)	soff (söffe)	gesoffen
saugen*	sog (söge)	gesogen
schaffen[1]	schuf (schüfe)	geschaffen
scheiden	schied	geschieden
scheinen	schien	geschienen
scheißen (du/er scheißt)	schiss	geschissen
schelten (du schiltst, er schilt)	schalt (schölte)	gescholten
scheren[1]	schor (schöre)	geschoren
schieben	schob (schöbe)	geschoben
schießen (du/er schießt)	schoss (schösse)	geschossen
schlafen (du schläfst, er schläft)	schlief	geschlafen
schlagen (du schlägst, er schlägt)	schlug (schlüge)	geschlagen
schleichen	schlich	geschlichen
schleifen[2]	schliff	geschliffen
schließen (du/er schließt)	schloss (schlösse)	geschlossen
schlingen	schlang (schlänge)	geschlungen
schmeißen (du/er schmeißt)	schmiss (schmisse)	geschmissen
schmelzen (du/er schmilzt)	schmolz (schmölze)	geschmolzen
schneiden	schnitt	geschnitten
schrecken* (du schrickst, er schrickt)	schrak (schräke)	geschreckt
schreiben	schrieb	geschrieben
schreien	schrie	geschrie[e]n
schreiten	schritt	geschritten
schweigen	schwieg	geschwiegen
schwellen (du schwillst, er schwillt)	schwoll (schwölle)	geschwollen
schwimmen	schwamm (schwömme)	geschwommen
schwinden	schwand (schwände)	geschwunden
schwingen	schwang (schwänge)	geschwungen
schwören	schwor (schwüre)	geschworen
sehen (du siehst, er sieht)	sah (sähe)	gesehen
sein (ich bin, du bist, er ist,wir sind, ihr seid, sie sind)	war (wäre)	gewesen

Infinitive	Past tense	Past participle
senden[1]	sandte (sendete)	gesandt
sieden	sott (sötte)	gesotten
singen	sang (sänge)	gesungen
sinken	sank (sänke)	gesunken
sitzen (du/er sitzt)	saß (säße)	gesessen
sollen (ich/er soll, du sollst)	sollte	gesollt
spalten*	spaltete	gespalten
spinnen	spann (spönne, spänne)	gesponnen
sprechen (du sprichst, er spricht)	sprach (spräche)	gesprochen
sprießen (du/er sprießt)	spross (sprösse)	gesprossen
springen	sprang (spränge)	gesprungen
stechen (du stichst, er sticht)	stach (stäche)	gestochen
stehen	stand (stünde, stände)	gestanden
stehlen (du stiehlst, er stiehlt)	stahl (stähle)	gestohlen
steigen	stieg	gestiegen
sterben (du stirbst, er stirbt)	starb (stürbe)	gestorben
stinken	stank (stänke)	gestunken
stoßen (du/er stößt)	stieß	gestoßen
streichen	strich	gestrichen
streiten	stritt	gestritten
tragen (du trägst, er trägt)	trug (trüge)	getragen
treffen (du triffst, er trifft)	traf (träfe)	getroffen
treiben	trieb	getrieben
treten (du trittst, er tritt)	trat (träte)	getreten
triefen*	troff (tröffe)	getroffen
trinken	trank (tränke)	getrunken
trügen	trog (tröge)	getrogen
tun (du tust, er tut)	tat (täte)	getan
verderben (du verdirbst, er verdirbt)	verdarb (verdürbe)	verdorben
vergessen (du/er vergisst)	vergaß (vergäße)	vergessen
verlieren	verlor (verlöre)	verloren
verzeihen	verzieh	verziehen
wachsen[1] (du/er wächst)	wuchs (wüchse)	gewachsen
waschen (du wäschst, er wäscht)	wusch (wüsche)	gewaschen
wenden[2]*	wandte (wendete)	gewandt
werben (du wirbst, er wirbt)	warb (würbe)	geworben

Infinitive	Past tense	Past participle
werden (du wirst, er wird)	wurde (würde)	geworden
werfen (du wirfst, er wirft)	warf (würfe)	geworfen
wiegen[1]	wog (wöge)	gewogen
winden	wand (wände)	gewunden
wissen (ich/er weiß, du weißt)	wusste (wüsste)	gewusst
wollen (ich/er will, du willst)	wollte	gewollt
wringen	wrang (wränge)	gewrungen
ziehen	zog (zöge)	gezogen
zwingen	zwang (zwänge)	gezwungen